D0323198

NO LONGER THE
PROPERTY OF
ELON UNIVERSITY LIBRARY

# Biographical Dictionary of Social Welfare in America

# BIOGRAPHICAL DICTIONARY OF SOCIAL WELFARE IN AMERICA

---

**Walter I. Trattner, EDITOR**

**Greenwood Press**
New York • Westport, Connecticut • London

870625

**Library of Congress Cataloging in Publication Data**

Main entry under title:

Biographical dictionary of social welfare in America.

    Bibliography: P.
    Includes index.
    1. Social workers—United States—Biography—
Dictionaries.   I.Trattner, Walter I.
HV27.B57   1986      361'.922 [B]      85–9831
ISBN 0–313–23001–3 (lib. bdg. : alk. paper)

Copyright © 1986 by Walter I. Trattner

All rights reserved. No portion of this book may be
reproduced, by any process or technique, without the
express written consent of the publisher.

Library of Congress Catalog Card Number: 85–9831
ISBN: 0–313–23001–3

First published in 1986

Greenwood Press, Inc.
88 Post Road West
Westport, Connecticut 06881

Printed in the United States of America

The paper used in this book complies with the
Permanent Paper Standard issued by the National
Information Standards Organization (Z39.48–1984).

10  9  8  7  6  5  4  3  2  1

To those people—some of whom appear in this book
and others who do not—who devoted their lives
to helping others and to the quest for
social justice in America

History is the essence of innumerable Biographies
—Thomas Carlyle, ''Biography,'' 1832


There is properly no History, only Biography
—Ralph Waldo Emerson, ''History,'' 1841

# Contents

# Advisory Board

Robert H. Bremner, Ohio State University

Clarke A. Chambers, University of Minnesota

Allen F. Davis, Temple University

Gerald N. Grob, Rutgers University

Roy Lubove, University of Pittsburgh

Kathryn Kish Sklar, University of California, Los Angeles

Louise Wade, University of Oregon

# Preface

The *Biographical Dictionary of Social Welfare in America* was compiled to provide a convenient source of information on some of the people who have been important in American social welfare from colonial times to the recent period. It is predicated on the belief that history is the collective action of innumerable individuals—and that it loses much of its significance when it is divorced from those men and women who made it, as so often is the case. In a small way, then, this work attempts to rectify that situation, at least in the area of social welfare.

Unfortunately, however, the term "social welfare" never has been precisely defined—and, in fact, may very well defy an exact definition. It certainly has been used—and continues to be used—to mean different things to different people at different times. One of the first tasks in compiling this work, therefore, was to establish a specific and reasonably manageable definition of the term, however arbitrary it might be. Thus, for the purpose of this volume, social welfare was defined to mean

preventive and ameliorative efforts by private individuals (who either acted alone or with others through voluntary organizations) and paid personnel, including educators and paid public officials at the local, state, and national levels, to improve communities or promote the financial, physical, and emotional well-being of individuals or groups that needed such assistance.

Even so defined, an almost endless number of people could have fallen under the term social welfare. The next, and perhaps most difficult, task, then, was to select the figures to be included in the work, which, because of limitations imposed by the publisher, had to be confined to approximately 300 in number. I decided, therefore, to exclude (1) all living people; (2) all people who were known primarily for their work as elected public officials; (3) all philanthropists (as opposed to those who might be referred to as social reformers); and (4) all those who were primarily abolitionists, feminists, labor union leaders, and "intellectuals" (theorists, writers, educators), as opposed to activists—with the exception of some who were exceedingly important in the history of social work education. The emphasis, then, rightly or wrongly, was on including people who were doers (or thinkers and doers), not solely thinkers, however important their ideas (and writings) may have been, and not mainly givers, however important their financial contributions may have been.

Having established such criteria, I then put together a lengthy list of people who, in my opinion, were worthy of consideration for inclusion in the work. Next, I circulated that list, and several successive shortened and revised versions of it, to numerous scholars—including seven who agreed to serve on an Advisory Board for the purpose of selection—and to the heads of a number of important organizations in the field, including the National Conference on Social Welfare, the Council on Social Work Education, and the National Association of Social Workers. On each occasion, I asked them to go over the list and delete the names of those whom they thought should be excluded and add the names of others whom they thought should be included but were missing from the list. In that way, a list of some 325 names was arrived at, which, it should be noted, was further amended (on a number of occasions) when it proved impossible to find material on some of those included, when it was discovered (in three or four instances) that some of the people on the list still were alive, and when some of the contributors to the volume subsequently brought to my attention the names of people who previously had been overlooked.

Before leaving the subject, let me add a few more words about the final list of entries. In compiling it, every effort was made to include members of minority groups—racial, religious, and ethnic—or those who worked with them. Similarly, I tried to cover as many of the areas of social welfare as was feasible, including child welfare, public health, mental hygiene, social insurance, and so on. In addition, however much help I received in putting the list together, I am responsible for the final decision on all the entries. And finally, as with all such lists of "leaders" or "representative" figures, there no doubt will be disagreement over those who were included—and perhaps even more over those who were excluded. That, of course, is inevitable. However, faced with many limitations and having established certain criteria, I did the best job I could. Admittedly, however, what follows is by no means a perfect or a comprehensive work; rather, it is a sampling of the subject and, it is hoped, a well reasoned and a good one.

Contributors were secured in the traditional manner. I wrote to scholars in the field asking for their assistance; some responded favorably, others did not. Various people I contacted suggested others, to whom I then wrote. Others who heard about the project in one way or another—including word of mouth or through advertisements placed in selected professional journals and newsletters—simply wrote, or called, and volunteered their services. All-in-all, the response was heartening.

All contributors were sent directions that carefully indicated that the *BDSWA* was to be a reference work designed to provide a concise and accurate summary of each subject's life. Through a blend of "factual" material and analytical comments, it was to enable the reader to obtain a brief but comprehensive overview of the biographee's life, career, and significance for American social welfare history. Each article was to be a fresh, original, and scholarly treatment based upon the best possible sources, written in good literary form and style. In addition, through a bibliographic essay at the end of each entry, the reader was to be apprised of the major accessible sources on the subject should he or she wish to check some point or do additional research on the person.

I wish I could say that every entry conformed fully to the above; that, however, is not the case. As in any such work—especially one that includes more than 300 articles written by close to 200 authors—there is variation in their quality. Some are excellent, some are not. All, however, are more than adequate. It should be said, though, that whereas responsibility for the choice of entries and all the other technical aspects of the book rests with the editor, responsibility for the substance of the articles—including their interpretation and emphasis— rests with their authors.

Perhaps it also should be mentioned that while the more important figures were allotted more space at the outset, the lengths of the final sketches do not necessarily reflect that; sometimes their length may be a reflection of the number of schools the subjects attended, the positions they held, the books they authored, or the abundance or paucity of available information, rather than being a reflection of their significance.

Entries are arranged alphabetically and contain asterisks to cross-reference people mentioned who have their own entry elsewhere in the volume. I hope that all of them, however long or short, perfect or imperfect they may be, will prove useful, whether it be to beginning students in the area, to advanced scholars, or to those somewhere in between.

As already suggested, this work could not have been completed without the generous assistance of a great many people. It might be appropriate to indicate at the outset, however, that it was conceived, quite a while ago, by Marilyn Brownstein, Acquisitions Editor at Greenwood Press. More recently, I have received splendid cooperation from Cynthia Harris, Reference Book Editor, and Neil Kraner, production editor at Greenwood Press. To them, and to others at the Press who have helped, I express my thanks.

I also wish to thank publicly the seven kind souls who, at my request, graciously agreed to serve as members of an Advisory Board for this project, and who thus assisted me in deciding on the list of entries, in identifying and locating contributors, and in some cases authoring sketches as well—Robert Bremner, Clarke Chambers, Allen Davis, Gerald Grob, Roy Lubove, Kathryn Kish Sklar, and Louise Wade. I, of course, also wish to express my gratitude to all the authors, especially those who met their various deadlines and, in some cases, contributed several articles; they are too numerous to mention individually, but they know who they are—and how much I appreciate their efforts. My special thanks, however, go to Stanley Mallach and William Bremer, who prepared seven and six entries, respectively, considerably more than others—and who did them exceedingly well, I should add.

In addition, I wish to extend my thanks to those people who offered to write sketches but who, for one reason or another, never did so. I owe a special debt to Don Fixico, Reginald Horsman, and especially Paul Prucha for their assistance in helping me to select appropriate Native Americans or those who worked with them for inclusion in the work, and to Marie Meyer for her secretarial and typing assistance. Finally, but by no means least important, I wish to thank the members of my family, especially my wife, Joan, and my daughter, Anne, for all the help they provided, especially during the more tedious early stages of the project when, on several occasions, we sat around the kitchen table and collated material and stuffed envelopes for hours at a time. To use the old but nonetheless true cliché, without the kind help of all these people this work never would have been completed.

WALTER I. TRATTNER

# Biographical Dictionary of Social Welfare in America

# A

**Abbott, Edith** (September 26, 1876–July 28, 1957), social work researcher, educator, administrator, and reformer, was born in Grand Island, Nebraska, to Elizabeth (Griffin) Abbott and Othman Ali Abbott, the older of two daughters and the second of four children.

Elizabeth Griffin was a graduate of Rockford Female Seminary and prior to her marriage was a respected high school principal. Othman Abbott served in the Civil War, settled in Nebraska, where he established a law practice, and became Nebraska's first lieutenant-governor. He was a vigorous man and supported his daughters' ambitions. From his shared experiences in law and politics, Edith and her sister Grace Abbott* learned reasoned and orderly thinking. From their mother the Abbott sisters acquired concern for the oppressed, pacifist beliefs, interest in progressive reform, and commitment to equal rights for women.

At age twelve Edith Abbott entered Brownell Hall, a girls' boarding school in Omaha. She graduated in 1893 and hoped to enter college. Severe economic times prohibited this, and she began teaching high school in Grand Island. Combining correspondence courses, summer sessions, and full-time study, she received the A.B. degree from the University of Nebraska in 1901.

During a 1902 summer session at the University of Chicago, Abbott's potential was recognized by economists Thorstein Veblen and James L. Laughlin. She was offered a small fellowship which, combined with her own modest savings, enabled her to enter the University of Chicago for full-time study. She received the Ph.D. in economics in 1905.

Her first postdoctoral employment was as the secretary of the Women's Trade Union League in Boston, combined with a research assignment for the Carnegie Institute. In 1906 she went to England and studied at the University of London's University College and London School of Economics and Political Science. There, she was strongly influenced by Beatrice and Sidney Webb and their convictions about the need to abolish punitive poor laws and replace them with modern public welfare systems. During part of her stay in London she lived and worked at St. Hilda's settlement house in Bethnal Green, where she began to learn more personally about poor people and their struggles. Her year in England was highly significant in shaping the direction and focus of Edith Abbott's life work.

In the fall of 1907 Abbott joined the faculty of Wellesley College as an instructor in economics. She was committed to coeducational education, however, and attracted to Chicago's vigorous environment. Sophonisba Breckinridge* and Julia Lathrop* offered Abbott the opportunity to live at Hull-House and work as assistant director of social research at the Chicago School of Civics and Philanthropy. By the fall of 1908 Edith Abbott had joined her sister Grace in Chicago. Together they lived most of the time at Hull-House until 1920 and became closely associated with the remarkable women and men whom Jane Addams* attracted to her mission.

At Hull-House the Abbott sisters began to develop the far-ranging and effective partnership which was at the heart of their work thereafter. Together they were advocates for woman suffrage, the admission of women to trade unions, a ten-hour law to protect working women, restrictions on child labor, the rights of immigrants, and the improvement of tenement housing. Edith Abbott's primary role in their common endeavors was social investigation. Her intent was to establish the facts to guide rational solutions to social problems. To documentary evidence she added her own insightful introductions and interpretations. The result was more than 100 books and articles that provided a sound historical, legal, and philosophical base for social policy formulation and brought her the title of "passionate statistician" in the pages of the *Nation*. Abbott made lasting contributions to social work education, particularly after 1920, when she and Breckinridge (her longtime close friend and professional collaborator) were influential in the transfer of the School of Civics and Philanthropy to the University of Chicago, the first instance of a graduate school of social work within a large coeducational university. She became dean of the school—the School of Social Service Administration, as it then was called—in 1924.

Abbott wanted social work students to have access to advanced social science courses and research facilities, with faculty teaching and research subject to rigorous standards of university scholarship. With Breckinridge she developed a curriculum that included political science, economics, law, medicine, studies of immigration, labor problems, and governmental processes. Students were expected to go into the community and apply disciplined methods of social investigation as a means of documenting needed changes in public policy.

In 1927 Abbott and Breckinridge established the *Social Service Review*, which became an influential professional journal. They also launched a Chicago Social Services Series of books and monographs, some of which became classics, such as Abbott's *Immigration: Select Documents and Case Records* (1924) and *Historical Aspects of the Immigration Problem: Select Documents* (1926). Her expertise as a scholar of immigration was reflected in her appointment as chair of the Committee on Crime and the Foreign Born of the Wickersham National Commission on Law Observance and Enforcement (1923–1931).

Persuasively outspoken about the outworn concept of local responsibility for public assistance, Abbott voiced vigorous objection to the evils of patronage in public welfare programs and pointed out the effect tax subsidies to private agencies had in delaying the development of a network of professional public social services. In the Great Depression Abbott deplored the disclaimer of a national emergency by the Hoover administration and called for leadership in relief programs for individual citizens caught by the deepening economic crisis of the 1930s. At the same time she spoke convincingly about the danger of make-work programs and the need for establishing comprehensive social insurance measures. Her views were published in professional journals, government bulletins, proceedings of the National Conference of Social Work, and in the *Nation* and the *New Republic*, as well as in her classic book, *Public Assistance* (1941).

An attractive woman, Edith Abbott was tall and slender, with fine features and bright brown eyes. During all her adult life she worked tremendously hard. As she grew older she tended to dress somewhat severely. As did her sister, Edith had a keen sense of humor, but hers often had a biting edge. With the loss of her beloved sister in 1939, Edith Abbott grew more brusque and uncompromising. Students remembered the heavy demands she made upon them for achievement and adherence to her goals. They remembered as well her intellectualism, her integrity, her commitment to social justice, and, among the more perceptive students, the sensitivity and caring beneath her austerity.

Abbott retired as dean of the School of Social Service Administration in 1942 but continued her writing, teaching, and editorship of the *Social Service Review*. She was the recipient of honorary degrees and other forms of recognition; her final professional triumph was her acceptance speech when she was given the Survey Award at the 1951 National Conference of Social Work. The bronze plaque noted her "imaginative and constructive contributions to social work." The conference had been largely devoid of calls for social action, and the slight, frail seventy-five-year-old woman who came to the podium startled and delighted the large general session audience by her strong-voiced demand that something be done to abolish the means test and to establish children's allowances. In 1954 she retired and returned to Grand Island. She lived in the old family home, now converted into three apartments, along with her brothers Othman Jr. and Arthur. She grew increasingly infirm and died there at the age of eighty.

The primary source is the Grace and Edith Abbott Collection in the Regenstein Library, University of Chicago. Other relevant materials are found in the Social Welfare History Archives, University of Minnesota (the Survey Associates Papers and the Paul U. Kellogg Papers), the Nebraska State Historical Society, the Sophonisba P. Breckinridge Manuscripts in the Regenstein Library, and the Jane Addams Memorial Collection, University of Illinois at Chicago.

A complete list of Edith Abbott's publications is included in Lela B. Costin, *Two Sisters for Social Justice: A Biography of Grace and Edith Abbott* (1983).

The only full-length biography of the Abbott sisters is *Two Sisters* (cited above). Three accounts and evaluations of Edith Abbott's career are found in the *Social Service Review*: Helen Wright, "Three Against Time: Edith and Grace Abbott and Sophonisba P. Breckinridge" (March, 1954), 41–53; Elizabeth Wisner, "Edith Abbott's Contributions to Social Work Education" (March, 1958), 1–10; and Stephen J. Diner, "Scholarship in the Quest for Social Welfare: A Fifty-Year History of the *Social Service Review*" (March, 1977), 1–66. Other sources of biographical information include *National Cyclopedia of American Biography* (1930), 517; *Current Biography* (1941), pp. 3–4; and *Notable American Women* (1980), 1–3.

LELA B. COSTON

**Abbott, Grace** (November 17, 1878–June 19, 1939), public administrator, social reformer, and chief of the U.S. Children's Bureau, was born in Grand Island, Nebraska, to Elizabeth (Griffin) Abbott and Othman Ali Abbott, the youngest of two daughters and the third of four children.

A graduate of Rockford Female Seminary (1868) and a respected high school principal at the time of her marriage, Elizabeth Griffin, from a Quaker family of the Genesee valley of New York, believed deeply in pacifism, women's rights, and the worth of formal learning. Othman A. Abbott served bravely in the Civil War, then migrated from Illinois to Nebraska and established a law practice. He demonstrated for his daughters vigor, a love of new experiences, and fearlessness in the face of challenge. A supporter of woman suffrage, he encouraged his daughters to pursue their individual ambitions.

Grace Abbott graduated from Grand Island High School and earned a bachelor's degree from Grand Island College in 1898. She obtained a teaching position in the Broken Bow high school, which she gave up after six months when she contracted a serious case of typhoid fever. After a spring and summer of convalescence, she taught for eight years at Grand Island High School. In 1907, motivated by lack of opportunity in her small town and an awareness of her own unmet potential, she entered the University of Chicago. She earned a master's degree in political science with a thesis that analyzed the legal position of married women in the United States.

In 1908 Sophonisba Breckinridge* arranged Grace Abbott's appointment as director of the newly formed Chicago Immigrants' Protective League (IPL), a post she held (except for brief leaves of absence) for more than a decade. Abbott held a liberal position in relation to the "immigrant problem." She showed an uncommon ability not only in fact-finding and analysis but in successful use of her findings to garner influential support for a creative style of work on behalf of immigrants. She wrote for various publications about the abuse of immigrants, lobbied in the state capital for legislative reform, and testified before Congress against the literacy test. To enlarge her understanding of the origins and expectations of immigrants who poured into Chicago, she spent four months in 1911 in Eastern Europe and by means of interviews and observations studied the cultures and life styles of the peasant villages from which so many immigrants had come to Chicago.

During her work with the IPL Grace and her sister Edith Abbott* lived at Hull-House together. Grace Abbott quickly gained the trust of Jane Addams* and became a close associate in common endeavors, including the Chicago garment workers strike of 1910, the Progressive Party Presidential candidacy of Theodore Roosevelt in 1912, the fight for woman suffrage in Illinois (achieved in 1913), and attendance in 1915 at the International Congress of Women to protest against war.

The Abbott sisters' years at Hull-House provided them the opportunity to establish a partnership of coinciding interests, values, and goals, although with different personality traits and particular competencies. The result was an unusually effective division of labor—in brief, Edith as the scholar, Grace as the translator of knowledge into action.

From her post as chief of the U.S. Children's Bureau, Julia Lathrop* persuaded Grace Abbott to join her staff in 1917 to administer new federal child labor legislation. In this assignment Abbott demonstrated an innovative form of collaboration in federal–state relations and secured the cooperation of states in the enforcement of a statute that ran counter to the traditions and special interests of large sections of the country.

When the U.S. Supreme Court ruled that the federal legislation was unconstitutional, Grace Abbott acted as consultant to the War Policies Board and played a major role in the government's decision to require child labor provisions in all wartime procurement contracts. She worked tirelessly in the 1920s to secure a child labor amendment to the Constitution. Throughout her life, Abbott continued to provide leadership in the long struggle for child labor protection. She was credited by Frances Perkins* with having been responsible in a major way for the last-minute insertion of child labor provisions in the Fair Labor Standards Act of 1938.

During her tenure on Lathrop's staff, Abbott represented the Department of Labor on the official planning committee for the International Labor Organization, and she served as organizer of the 1919 Children's Year Conference on Child Welfare Standards. These assignments, combined with her child labor administrative experience and her earlier work with industrial problems of immigrants, gave her a breadth of knowledge about national and international labor problems, particularly in relation to children and women.

When her role as administrator of the federal child labor law ended in 1919, Grace Abbott returned to Chicago. She was appointed by Governor Frank O. Lowden to head a new Illinois Immigration Commission with broad investigative powers. She had completed two significant social investigations and was rapidly developing a sound public welfare agency when she was asked by a new administration to supply a roster of her staff by political party and precinct. When she refused, Governor Len Small abolished the Commission by vetoing its annual appropriation. With the sanction of the Immigrants' Protective League board, Abbott renewed the work of this voluntary organization.

When Julia Lathrop retired in 1921 as chief of the Children's Bureau, Grace Abbott succeeded her. Her first major challenge was to administer the new maternal and infancy protection legislation (the Sheppard-Towner Act), an unprecedented venture into social welfare under federal auspices. The ultimate goal was to reduce the shocking incidence of infant and maternal mortality. In her work with the separate states to enable them to take advantage of the federal matching grants which the legislation offered, Abbott took a liberal stance with respect to differences among the states. She wanted each program to grow out of a state's particular conditions. She supplied factual data, consultation on technical matters, and innovative ideas, and demonstrated an uncommonly effective federal–state administrative partnership. She also reached out to women's groups all over the country to urge them to work at the state and local level in proposing programs and to lobby in the state capital so that the region could utilize the benefits of the new legislation. By the time the act came to an end (allowed by Congress to lapse in 1929), only three states had not accepted matching grants and established prenatal and child health programs.

Throughout the life of the Sheppard-Towner Act, Grace Abbott came under heavy attack by forces representing special interests: states' rights, a conservative fiscal policy, opposition to woman suffrage, the domain of the medical profession, and "patriotic" organizations who abhorred what they considered to be leftist ideologies. A proposal by the Hoover administration to transfer major functions of the Children's Bureau to the Public Health Service was forcefully opposed by Abbott as well as by her constituencies of women, whose resentment over the expiration of the Sheppard-Towner Act continued strong. Abbott's successful opposition to the transfer rested on her philosophy of the whole child, and her preference for a unified, social, economic, and industrial approach that would embrace all the interests of childhood.

During the demanding years of the 1920s and early 1930s, Abbott continued the Bureau's research function with widespread dissemination of findings. In addition she provided effective representation of the United States on the League of Nations' Advisory Committee on Traffic in Women and Children, to which she was appointed by the Secretary of State in late 1922, a post she held until 1934.

With the advent of the Great Depression, Grace Abbott became a nationally recognized advocate for the old and new poor. Counter to the philosophy of the Hoover administration, she spoke of the imperative need to get children out of the breadlines. Through studies of "transient boys" and of children in coal-mining counties, and in monthly statistical reports of relief, she showed the failure of an outmoded system of poor relief to meet modern social and industrial conditions and the inability of voluntary agencies to shoulder the burden of relief to hungry families.

In 1930 Abbott emerged in a spontaneous movement as a candidate for appointment as Secretary of Labor. Thousands of signatures and letters were collected and forwarded to President Hoover, with support not only from women's organizations but from university faculties, the Urban League, and the influential men who had supported Abbott since her days with the Chicago Immigrants' Protective League. Abbott realized that Hoover knew her record of independence and did not expect to be appointed. She took satisfaction, however, in having helped to pave the way for Frances Perkins' appointment a few years later. Abbott and Perkins established an impressive degree of trust between them, and given Abbott's intimate knowledge of the Department of Labor, Perkins sought her advice on problems of departmental organization and policy that went beyond matters affecting the Children's Bureau. Grace Abbott retired from the Children's Bureau in 1934, telling friends that she knew the Bureau was safe with Perkins there to defend it against those who wanted to weaken or destroy it.

In the fall of 1934 Abbott joined her sister's faculty at the University of Chicago's School of Social Service Administration. To students with conservative backgrounds, Abbott appeared as a vigorous liberal; their exposure to her in the classroom had a tonic effect on their social outlook. She continued to receive more requests than she could meet for public service on a national and international level. She served as chair of the U.S. delegation to the seventh Pan-American Child Congress in Mexico in 1935; as government delegate at the meeting of the International Labor Organization in 1935 and in 1937, the latter time as head delegate; and as a member of the Textile Industry Committee of the Wage and Hours Division of the Department of Labor. She served as well on the Advisory Committee on Economic Security under President Roosevelt's appointment and, in an impressive demonstration of collegial collaboration with Katharine Lenroot* and Martha Eliot*, gave leadership in the proposal and passage of the children's provisions of the Social Security Act.

Grace Abbott was a problem-solver with a forceful intellect. As a child she displayed self-confidence and a zest for new experiences. In manner she was forthright, sometimes abrupt, and was perceived by some who did not know her well as formidable. She believed deeply in free speech, even for extremists, and was singularly free of resentment about personal criticism. In international meetings she was courteous but unimpressed by the aura of authority in such an environment. She had a quick sense of humor which tended to clear the air, cut through any person's self-assumed importance, and bring about a more relaxed perspective to the question at hand, even as she bore in with a reminder of the data and a proposed line of action.

Amidst her heavy schedule of work, Abbott experienced a series of health problems, including two periods of enforced bedrest for tuberculosis. She died in Chicago at age sixty of multiple myeloma.

Grace Abbott's personal papers are in the Regenstein Library of the University of Chicago. Other relevant materials are in the Children's Bureau Papers, National Archives; the Survey Associates Papers and the Paul U. Kellogg Papers, the Social Welfare History Archives, Universty of Minnesota; the Nebraska State Historical Society; the Jane Addams Memorial Collection, University of Illinois at Chicago; the papers of Clara Beyer, Martha Eliot, M.D., Alice Hamilton, M.D., and Mary Dewson, Schlesinger Library, Radcliffe College; the Felix Frankfurter Papers, Library of Congress; the Immigrants' Protective League Papers, University of Illinois at Chicago; and the Katharine Lenroot Papers, Columbia University.

A complete list of Grace Abbott's publications is found in Lela B. Costin, *Two Sisters for Social Justice: A Biography of Grace and Edith Abbott* (1983). Notable among these are *The Child and the State*, vols. 1 and 2 (1938); *The Immigrant and the Community* (1917); and *From Relief to Social Security*, ed. Edith Abbott (1941).

The only full-length biography of the Abbott sisters is Costin's *Two Sisters*, cited above. Other accounts of Grace Abbott's life are found in Edith Abbott, "A Sister's Memories," *Social Service Review* (September, 1939), 351–408, and "Grace Abbott and Hull-House, 1908–1921," ibid. (September and December, 1950), 374–394, 493–518; Helen Wright, "Three Against Time: Edith and Grace Abbott and Sophonisba P. Breckinridge," ibid. (March, 1954), 41–53; Stephen J. Diner, "Scholarship in a Quest for Social Welfare: A Fifty-Year History of the *Social Service Review*," ibid. (March, 1977), 1–66. Other sources include *Dictionary of American Women, National Cyclopedia of American Biography* (1941), and *Notable American Women* (1971).

LELA B. COSTIN

**Abrams, Charles** (September 20, 1901–February 22, 1970), lawyer, public housing advocate, and urban critic, was born in Vilna, Poland (then part of the Russian Empire), the youngest of four children of Abraham and Freda (Rabinowitz) Abrams. His father, an Orthodox Jew, was a tradesman who took the family to the United States in 1904, settling in Williamsburg, Brooklyn, a crowded immigrant quarter, where he peddled food from an outdoor stand. Charles attended the public schools and worked at odd jobs, which included lamplighter with the gas company and office boy with Western Union. He went to Brooklyn Law School at night, clerking in law offices, and passed the bar examination in 1923. He gravitated to real estate law and made a tidy fortune investing in Greenwich Village brownstones. He moved into a Tenth Street house with his wife, the painter Ruth Davidson, and his two daughters, and found in the West Village a neighborhood vitality and urban cosmopolitanism that would sustain him for a lifetime.

In the late 1920s Abrams joined the anti-Tammany campaigns of a Village acquaintance and production-for-use visionary, Langdon W. Post, who ran for Manhattan borough president on Fiorello H. La Guardia's Fusion ticket. Post lost, but he brought Abrams into a succession of housing reform struggles, including the work of the Slum Clearance Committee, which promoted the idea of a municipal housing authority. Abrams joined a team of attorneys, headed by state housing official Louis H. Pink,* whose draft bill ultimately established the New York City Housing Authority in 1934. Post became the Authority's chairman and named Abrams chief counsel, where he wrestled with the new agency's uncertain powers. Up to this time, the ability of municipalities to eradicate the slums rested on their narrow ''police'' power to get rid of unsafe, unsanitary structures. The kind of broad-scale eminent domain that many housing advocates believed was needed to build truly low-rent projects remained untested in the courts, as judges particularly questioned the condemnation of private property for the benefit of a single ''class,'' that is, to build low-rent housing for the poor. While colleagues urged caution, Abrams chose to forge ahead. He handled the ticklish negotiations with the Astor estate, which condemned property for the Housing Authority's first project, wrote the landmark brief, and argued the successful lower court battles. These preliminaries set the precedent for the New York State Court of Appeals decision, *New York City Housing Authority v. Muller* (1936), which sanctioned the first grant of eminent domain to a municipal housing authority.

Having established this great extension of social welfare power, Abrams spent the next years worrying about its side effects. Caught in the middle of a personality clash between Langdon Post and Mayor La Guardia, Abrams left the Authority in 1937, but not before he began to question wholesale slum clearance that failed to provide new housing for displaced tenants. As a consultant to the United States Housing Authority, he consistently urged new public housing construction on vacant outer borough sites, where land was cheap and the destructive impact of tenement clearance could be minimized. In a devastating critique of slum clearance as tenant displacement, he warned that unless housing authorities concentrated on building new housing, their policies would end up ravaging the homes and inflating the rents of the poor. These concerns led to his involvement on the eve of World War II, along with Algernon D. Black of the Ethical Culture Society, in the City-Wide Citizens Committee on Harlem, the first sustained attempt by white liberals to come to grips with black ghetto squalor. Abrams drafted its 1942 report on housing, which called for Harlem rent control, stricter building code enforcement, and phased integration of Blacks into new housing in the outer boroughs. A year later, when the New York State urban redevelopment law gave Metropolitan Life Insurance Company the power of eminent domain to create Stuyvesant Town for white tenants only, Abrams led the attack on the Jim Crow plan and the ''vicious'' policy which allowed a private company to raze low-income housing without providing for replacement shelter.

At the height of the war, Abrams articulated the themes that would dominate his writings for his remaining years: government's great power—and duty—to delegate authority to private institutions for decent public purposes; the legal manipulation of land to promote bigotry; and the ambiguous role of private power in the rejuvenation of cities. Over the next ten years he contributed to numerous liberal journals, urging a federal commitment to a national housing program; at the same time, his scathing exposés of restrictive covenants and Jim

Crow rentals made uncomfortable reading in the *Nation* and *Commentary*. But his strenuous arguments within *Commentary*'s parent body, the American Jewish Committee, laid the basis for much of the modern "fair housing" movement. With friends on the City-Wide Citizens Committee and with the help of the Ethical Culture Society, he launched the New York State Committee Against Discrimination (SCAD) and helped make it an effective clearing house for a national war on race and religious restrictions in housing, the details of which Abrams distilled in his classic *Forbidden Neighbors* (1955). In the early 1950s Abrams and SCAD attacked Robert Moses' Title I redevelopments for the relocation burdens they thrust upon New York's Blacks and Hispanics. Along with Algernon Black and Jane Jacobs, Abrams became the most influential critic of the Moses bulldozer. By the 1960s his writings, his worldwide portrayal of urban dislocations as a result of his United Nations-sponsored consultancies, and his teaching at the Massachusetts Institute of Technology and Columbia University gave his urban criticism a wide following among a new generation of urban specialists. His *The City Is the Frontier* (1965) was well received as a manifesto for an urban renewal that had coherence and an ethical responsibility toward the displaced, but above all that respected the city for its complex of neighborhoods, each with an integrity and vitality worth preserving. Abrams resided at his brownstone house on New York City's West Tenth Street until his death there from cancer on February 22, 1970.

The Charles Abrams Papers are at Cornell University. His fascinating "Reminiscences" are in the Oral History Collection at Columbia University. These can be supplemented with the New York City Housing Authority Papers at Fiorello H. La Guardia Community College, Long Island City, New York; the files of the Citizens' Housing and Planning Council, New York City; and the Algernon D. Black Papers, Columbia University.

Abrams was a prolific writer; his books include *Revolution in Land* (1939); *The Future of Housing* (1948); *Man's Struggle for Shelter in an Urbanizing World* (1964); and *The Language of Cities* (1971). His "Slum Clearance or Vacant Land Development?" *Shelter* (February, 1939), remains a telling critique of large-scale clearance. Virtually the housing columnist for the *Nation* in the late 1940s, his muckraking articles against discrimination include "The Walls of Stuyvesant Town" (March 24, 1945); his attack on the Truman administration's failure to push for a real housing program, "Homeless America" (December 21 and 28, 1946); and the memorable review, "Race Bias in Housing" (July 19, August 2, and August 16, 1947); to which must be added his "Homes for Aryans Only," *Commentary* (May, 1947). His weekly housing columns in the *New York Post*, from 1947 to 1950, reveal his knack for practical problem-solving, his impatience with the indignities heaped on his fellow New Yorkers, and his hearty good humor.

Abrams' obituary appeared in the *New York Times*, February 23, 1970.

JOEL SCHWARTZ

**Addams, Jane** (September 6, 1860–May 21, 1935), social reformer, settlement house director, peace activist, and author, was born in Cedarville, Illinois, the daughter of John Huy Addams and Sarah (Weber) Addams, the former an entrepreneur—sawmill and gristmill owner, land and railroad investor, and president of a life insurance company—and the latter a very busy housewife.

Addams' mother died shortly after giving birth to her ninth child three years after Jane's birth. Nurses and hired girls helped Mary Addams, an older sister, raise Jane until John Addams remarried. John Addams was a dominant influence on Jane's life and thought. He was a Hicksite Quaker who believed in hard work and civic duty, the latter fulfilled in part by his participation in the founding of the Republican Party in 1854 and his service in the Illinois State Senate from that date to 1870.

Jane Addams suffered from ill health as a child, and her illness continued into adult life. Her major ailment was tuberculosis of the spine, which permanently damaged her back and affected the carriage of her head. Although her early life was sheltered, she aspired to become educated and wanted to attend Smith College. Her father did not encourage this ambition and instead urged her to matriculate at Rockford Seminary. She did so and graduated in 1881, still hoping to obtain a degree from Smith.

That summer she was physically ill and emotionally depressed, a condition aggravated by the sudden and unexpected death of her father. Giving up her dream of attending Smith, she enrolled at the Woman's Medical College in Philadelphia in the fall of 1881. After a six-month stint, she became ill again and dropped out. Following an operation on her back and a year at Cedarville attending to personal and business affairs, she embarked on a tour of Europe with her stepmother and college friends. The tour was both cultural and educative, advancing Addams' interest in art.

Following her return to the United States, she still had not found a suitable career. She found both the career and a friend to help initiate it on her next tour of Europe in 1887. The career was to be a settlement house director. She became interested in mission work in general and settlement house work in particular through her acquaintance with Toynbee Hall, a pioneer effort in London's East End designed to introduce young ministers to the lives of the urban poor. The friend was Ellen Gates Starr,* who had traveled to Europe with Jane and had nursed her back to health after another siege of illness there.

On September 18, 1889, Jane Addams and Ellen Starr moved into an old mansion formerly owned by Charles J. Hull located in a blighted area on South Halsted Street in Chicago. Their purpose at the start was to introduce young, middle-class American women, who had been satiated with too much study, to life itself. Both these women and the poor they met would benefit by mutual acquaintance and help.

Although Addams and Starr began with few specific ideas of what should be done next, they soon found opportunities to move ahead. At its largest extension, Hull-House had thirteen buildings and a staff of sixty-five persons, most of whom were college-educated. Among the activities and facilities at Hull-House were plays, concerts, and lectures, an art studio, a music school, the Hull-House Players (a drama group), a book bindery, a boarding club for working women, a boys' club, a gymnasium, a community kitchen, a women's club, a day nursery, and a labor museum.

Hull-House earned a deserved reputation as a training ground for social workers, many of whom became famous in their own right. Included in this category were Edith* and Grace Abbott,* Alice Hamilton,* Florence Kelly,* and Julia Lathrop.* Hull-House, because of its programs and personnel, became a recognized leader in the settlement house movement.

As the fame of Hull-House grew, so did the fame of Jane Addams. She became involved in politics as a municipal reformer. Her year as inspector of streets and alleys in the Hull-House ward won her national attention in 1895, but she had served on the mediation commission for the Pullman strike a year earlier. Later she served on the Chicago School Board and became involved in the building trades strike in 1900, the national anthracite strike of 1902, the Chicago Stockyards strike of 1904, and the textile strike of 1910.

But labor relations and municipal reform were not her only interests. Her visit to Tolstoy in 1896 and the coming of the Spanish-American War stimulated her interest in peace movements, and she included this topic as a subject in her increasing numbers of lectures to a variety of interested groups. Her lectures on social ethics at the University of Chicago in 1899 became her first book, *Democracy and Social Ethics* (1902). In it Addams called for each person to identify with the common humanity. Her lectures at the University of Wisconsin were published in 1907 as *Newer Ideals of Peace*. The book combined a call for municipal reform with a plea for Tolstoyian pacifism. Her third book of revised lectures covered the topic of juvenile delinquency and appeared in 1909 under the title of *The Spirit of Youth and City Streets*. Her most famous book, *Twenty Years at Hull-House*, came out in 1910 and achieved much acclaim and added to her popularity. She followed this work with a more controversial one, *A New Conscience and an Ancient Evil*, the following year. The book concerned vice and prostitution and was based on the records of the Juvenile Protective Association, a group she helped found in 1909.

That year she was elected the first woman to head the National Conference of Charities and Correction. By 1912 she probably was at the pinnacle of her fame as she campaigned for Theodore Roosevelt as the Progressive Party candidate for president. Roosevelt and segments of the American public were soon to turn against her, however, with the coming of World War I. Active in the Woman's Peace Party, which she chaired in 1915, she attended the International Congress of Women at The Hague that year. Her calls for peace and her connection with Henry Ford's ill-fated Peace Ship brought much criticism from interventionists. Even her service as part of Herbert Hoover's Department of Food Administration during and after the war did not allay these criticisms. Following the war, her critics attacked her as being both a communist and pro-German. The Daughters of the American Revolution revoked her membership. She, however, continued her activities with the Women's International League for Peace and Freedom, which required much overseas travel, and defended her position in her first book in ten years, *Peace and Bread in Time of War* (1922). She spent less time with Hull-House, in part because of her travels overseas and in part because of increasing health problems.

In 1930 *The Second Twenty Years at Hull-House* appeared as a sequel to *Twenty Years at Hull-House*. While a less successful book than its predecessor, it helped to restore some of her popularity, and honors began to accumulate. The most notable was the Nobel Peace Prize—an award her friends had sought to have bestowed upon her for a decade—shared with Nicholas Murray Butler in 1931. In 1932 she put together a selection of funeral remarks and memorial talks in a book, *The Excellent Becomes the Permanent*, possibly in anticipation of her own demise. She did not live to finish her biography of Julia Lathrop, *My Friend, Julia Lathrop* (1935), completed by Alice Hamilton, as she died May 21, 1935, in Chicago.

The major collection of the Jane Addams papers and correspondence is in the Swarthmore Peace Collection at Swarthmore College, but other libraries also have special collections of their own which are of value. Among the latter are the Jane Addams Memorial Collection at the University of Illinois at Chicago; the University of Kansas Library at Lawrence; the Lilly Library at the University of Indiana; and the Stephenson County Historical Museum at Freeport, Illinois.

In addition to the works cited above, there are two useful collections of Addams' work. One is Jane Addams, *A Centennial Reader* (1960), and the other is Christopher Lasch, ed., *The Social Thought of Jane Addams* (1965).

There are several biographies of Jane Addams in addition to her autobiographical works. The most recent is Allen F. Davis' *American Heroine: The Life and Legend of Jane Addams* (1973), which is a balanced, critical view of Addams' life and some of the myths surrounding it. John C. Farrell's *Belovd Lady: A History of Jane Addams' Ideas on Reform and Peace* (1967) is less critical and is, instead, an intellectual biography. Daniel Levine's *Jane Addams and the Liberal Tradition* (1971) attempts to place Addams in the framework of her times. The most complete biography of Addams is an older book, James Weber Linn's *Jane Addams: A Biography* (1935), which has not been superseded. Cornelia Lynd Meigs' *Jane Addams: Pioneer for Social Justice* (1970) is a popular work intended for general audiences.

DWIGHT W. HOOVER

**Alexander, Will W.** (July 15, 1884–January 13, 1956), minister, educator, race relations expert, and promoter of human welfare, was born in Morrisville, Missouri, the only child of William Alexander, a farmer, and Arabella (Winton) Alexander, who taught school until Will's birth. Also in the family were two children by a previous marriage of the father's, John and George. The family had little income but enjoyed the security associated with rural self-sufficiency and a life style that did not make large financial demands. However, the father was not robust, and the family's economic condition deteriorated as his health failed in later life.

As a child, Will's deep respect for the land and love for people were strongly influenced by his father, but it was his mother who seemed to exert the strongest influence on his learning and early career. His education was devoted to preparing for the ministry. As an undergraduate Alexander attended Scarritt-Morrisville College in Missouri. Graduate work was undertaken at Vanderbilt University, where he received a degree in divinity.

Following his graduation from Vanderbilt, Alexander became pastor of a Methodist church in Nashville, Tennessee. This four-year tenure proved to be very important in his life. It was during this period that he met and married Mabelle A. Kinkead. This marriage subsequently produced three sons: Edgar K., John W., and William M. It was also during this period that Alexander became impressed with two problems in the South that were to later dictate much of his life's work. These were race relations and poverty. As he began addressing these two problems a profound paradox, perhaps incubating since childhood, began taking form. Although Alexander appreciated the need for broad-based programs and objective facts, he felt that energies devoted to these two areas frequently mitigated efforts to help people; that the institutions could become self-elaborating and too intricate; and that research frequently emphasized gathering data to the exclusion of doing something with the data. This apparent difficulty in reconciling structure and information-elaborating activities with his personal commitment to improving social and economic conditions seems to have exerted a strong influence on Alexander's style, for he did not leave a legacy of numerous research projects, publications, and edifices. He did, however, initiate and contribute to a remarkable number of projects and programs that provided immediate help to individuals and had a significant impact on the major social problems of his day.

Largely because he could not impact social problems significantly through the church, Alexander accepted a position with the National War Work Council in 1917. Although not a part of his assigned duties with the Council, he took a special interest in the black soldier. The special knowledge that he gained of black soldiers and their families made him attractive to groups addressing race relations after World War I. A number of such groups came into existence following the war. Some aborted. Some were ineffectual. One, however, enjoyed notable success. Formed in 1919, when several interested persons met in Atlanta, this group adopted the name the Interracial Committee. Will Alexander served as director of this organization throughout its twenty-five-year existence.

This group did much to improve race relations and conditions for the Negro through encouraging university courses and research, arranging for legal defense, and improving educational opportunities and public relations. It had another, indirect effect on Alexander's career, as it brought him to the attention of several of the large national philanthropies. Thus, in 1930, after demonstrating the efficacy of a fellowship program in developing intelligent leaders in the South, he was elected to the board of directors of the Julius Rosenwald Fund. He served in this capacity until 1948, when the foundation was closed. During this time (as his biographers point out), he, Edwin Embree, and Charles S. Johnson became known as the "triumvirate that directed the liberal South."

Efforts also were directed at improving the advanced education available to Blacks and the economic conditions of tenant farmers. In the former area, Alexander was instrumental in bringing several marginal institutions in Atlanta under the administrative control of Atlanta University as well as the merger of two small Negro colleges in New Orleans to create Dillard University. He became acting president of Dillard University when it opened in 1935. In the area of tenant farming, the triumvirate originated the idea of the President's Committee on Farm Tenancy and formed the Committee on Negroes in the Economic Reconstruction in 1934. With funds from both the Rosenwald and Rockefeller foundations studies were arranged on the results of the government's farm program. This ultimately led to the publication of *The Collapse of Cotton Tenancy* (1935), the only book that Alexander either authored or coauthored.

In addressing rural poverty Alexander worked closely with the presidential advisors of the New Deal programs and, after a stint with the Resettlement Administration, initially as assistant director, then as director, he joined their ranks as a "dollar-a-year" man in 1940. As such he provided many services, including coordinating youth programs for the National Defense Commission, reducing problems of employment discrimination of minorities in war industries, heading a department on minority problems for the National Defense Advisory Commission (later called the Office of Production Management), and assisting in defusing rumors through the Office of War Information.

Alexander's work with the Rosenwald Fund during this time was directed primarily to reducing segregation, in which interest he founded the American Council on Race Relations and chaired a church group that authored the "declaration of emancipation for the Protestant institutions."

In 1948 he entered a form of "retirement," moving to a farm he purchased near Chapel Hill, North Carolina. Actually, he remained quite active until nearly the time of his death. Serving as executive director of the Edgar Stern Family Fund, devoted primarily to the development of community leadership, Alexander explored the dynamics of politics and power and the channels through which these forces might be directed for the public good. Many people continued to seek his counsel throughout this period of retirement. Among them were representatives of the National Planning Association, the Civil Rights Commission appointed by President Truman, philanthropic organizations, the National Social Science Research Council, and a number of colleges and universities. Alexander passed away in Chapel Hill on January 13, 1956.

The largest collection of primary materials on the life and career of Alexander is housed at Dillard University in New Orleans; the collection contains many of his personal papers, letters, and short discourses written in longhand. Other manuscript sources can be found in the files of the Commission on Interracial Cooperation at Atlanta University, the Farm Security Administration records in the National Archives in Washington, D.C., and the files of the Rosenwald Fund at Fisk University in Nashville, Tennessee. Also useful are Alexander's reminiscences in the Columbia University Oral History Project and his two publications, *The Collapse of Cotton Tenancy* (1935) and "Our Conflicting Racial Policies," *Harper's Magazine* (January, 1945), 172–179. The best secondary account of Alexander's life is Wilma Sykeman and James Stokely, *Seeds of Southern Change: The Life of Will Alexander* (1962).

ROBERT A. PERKINS

**Alger, George William** (November 12, 1872–April 19, 1967), lawyer and social reformer, was born in Burlington, Vermont, of Yankee stock, to Charles Jonathan Alger, a lawyer, school superintendent, and editor, and Harriett (Murdoch) Alger, a teacher and former headmistress of the Rochester, New York, Free Academy. George Alger grew up in Burlington strongly influenced by his father's political independence, respect for education, and concern for the less fortunate. The Vermont environment shaped his personality; community values such as living within one's means, respect for individual eccentricities, and economy of speech were absorbed early. Educated at a private school, Alger read widely in his father's library and attended a Sunday school taught by John Dewey. He was graduated from the University of Vermont in 1892 and attributed his sense of literature, morality, and philosophy to its classical curriculum.

Determined to seek his fortune outside Vermont, he taught school in Yonkers, New York, attended the Chicago World's Fair of 1893, and then moved to New York City. After considering a career as a professor of literature, he attended New York University Law School, receiving his LL.B in 1895. Observing the results of industrial accidents in his early clients, and angered by the courts' extension of laissez-faire principles to include an employee's freedom to risk working in an unsafe shop, Alger was drawn into the growing movement for social justice. He was a founding member of the New York Child Labor Committee in 1902, remaining with the group until it disbanded in 1941 and serving as its chairman during the years 1920–1932. Alger drafted many of the forty child labor laws the Committee helped to enact in New York State. Active in other groups such as the Henry Street Settlement and the People's Institute, Alger drew up the New York Employers Liability Act of 1902 and served as associate counsel to the Wainwright Commission, which drafted New York's pioneering Workmen's Compensation Law of 1910. His circle of associates included Florence Kelley,* Lillian D. Wald,* Mary K. Simkhovitch,* Charles C. Burlingham, Felix Warburg, Alfred E. Smith, Morris Hillquit, Norman Hapgood, Franklin H. Giddings, and Ray Stannard Baker. Concentrating his reform efforts on specific cases where pragmatic justice could be obtained by changes in the law, Alger later credited Lillian Wald with the greatest influence on his career as a reformer.

Writing came easily to him; with the collaboration of his wife, Grace E. Drew, a journalist and former actress whom he married in 1903, he authored forty-seven articles on social politics and the law, most of which were published in the *Atlantic Monthly*. Two articles, on sensational journalism and the law and on equivocal rights of labor, attracted the favorable attention of President Theodore Roosevelt and resulted in an offer of a federal judgeship. Alger turned it down because the salary was too low, but he remained a lifelong admirer of Roosevelt and helped with the Taft campaign in 1908, although he worked unofficially and ran for office himself only once. In 1932 he was persuaded by the New York Bar Association to make a symbolic protest run for the New York Supreme Court against two major party candidates whom the Association considered unfit, but he was defeated.

Alger became one of the most skillful corporation lawyers in the country. Rarely appearing in court, he founded his career on his relationship with Loton Horton, who, with Alger's help, created the Sheffield Farms dairy enterprise out of the chaotic New York Milk Shed. Later Alger would help to reorganize RKO Pictures. He was a power in the New York bar, closely associated with Louis Brandeis, Charles Evans Hughes, Charles C. Burlingham, Learned Hand, John W. Davis, Benjamin Cardozo, and Harold Medina.

Alger's work in the field of employer liability and child labor led to his appointment in 1919 as legal counsel for a state commission investigating prison conditions; in 1926, through the influence of Adolph Lewisohn and the City Club, he was appointed by Governor Alfred E. Smith as Moreland Act Commissioner to conduct a full study of the operation and management of New York's prisons and Board of Parole. He prepared a widely hailed report, but nothing was done until the 1929–1930 prison riots at Auburn and Dannemora. Governor Franklin D. Roosevelt then appointed Alger to a new committee which secured a new parole law.

Between 1931 and 1935 Alger virtually administered New York's cloak and suit industry, serving as the state-appointed impartial chairman to prevent sweating and racketeering, and then as National Recovery Administration (NRA) Chairman of the Cloak and Suit Authority. In 1933 he was again appointed as Moreland Commissioner to investigate a $2 billion default in the guaranteed mortgage business. A number of company officials were indicted as a result of his 1934 report. Alger's final public service came during 1947–1952, when he was appointed to President Harry S. Truman's Loyalty Review Board. In this post he exercised moderation, although he was pleased when the Supreme Court sustained the Smith Act in 1951. He believed that the United States could best defeat communism by engaging in fewer witch hunts and concentrating instead on projecting a more positive world image. George Alger was a vintage progressive. A small-town New Englander who won legal fame in New York City, he served corporate clients and social reform causes with equal enthusiasm. An admirer of Elihu Root, Theodore Roosevelt, Louis Brandeis, and Herbert H. Lehman, he believed passionately in limited reform through the application of legislative remedies to specific, clearly defined problems. His most significant reform contributions were his drafting of legislation in the areas of child labor and prison reform and his work for the Henry Street Settlement.

Alger died in New York City on April 19, 1967.

The George W. Alger Papers at the University of Vermont (four boxes) contain copies of some of his published articles, copies of some of his official reports to the state of New York, one box of his Loyalty Review Board files, and assorted minor correspondence. A copy of his Columbia University oral history memoir (Oral History Collection of Columbia University, 538 pp., 1952) is also in the Vermont papers.

Some of Alger's writings have been reprinted in G. W. Alger, *Moral Overstrain* (1906) and G. W. Alger, *The Old Law and the New Order* (1913). His Sheffield Scientific School (Yale) lecture on "production" is printed in *Morals in Modern Business* (1909).

Alger's work on the New York Child Labor Committee is discussed in Jeremy P. Felt, *Hostages of Fortune: Child Labor Reform in New York State* (1965). An accurate obituary notice is in the *New York Times*, April 20, 1967, 43.

JEREMY P. FELT

**Alinsky, Saul David** (January 30, 1909–June 12, 1972), community organizer, was born in a Chicago slum to Sarah (Tannenbaum) Alinsky and Benjamin Alinsky, a tailor. His parents were Russian Jewish immigrants who divorced when he was thirteen. His father moved to Los Angeles, his mother remained in Chicago, and Saul moved back and forth between them. After graduating in 1926 from Hollywood High School in California, he enrolled in the University of Chicago, graduating with a bachelor's degree in archeology in 1930. He then reentered the University of Chicago (1930–1932) on a graduate fellowship to study criminology. At the time, University of Chicago sociologists were emphasizing individual and group self-interest, conflict, and its resolution. Criminologists were exploring the concept of the delinquent subculture and the role of social organization in controlling deviant behavior. Alinsky worked first for the Illinois State Division of Criminology and then, in 1933, for the State Prison Classification Board. Meanwhile, he was becoming more involved in radical left politics. He helped raise money for southern sharecroppers, the Spanish International Brigade, and the Newspaper Guild, and also worked as an organizer for the Congress of Industrial Organizations (CIO). He soon came to the conclusion that poverty and discrimination were the root causes of crime. That belief led him to move from criminology to community organizing to achieve social change.

Alinsky's first major experience with community organizing began in 1938.

He joined Joseph Meegan, and the two put together the Back of the Yards Council in the homogeneous, working-class, Catholic neighborhood near Chicago's stockyards. Meegan became executive secretary of the Council, and Alinsky was its chief publicist. Their goal was to give the neighborhood people power to effect change by helping them create a truly representative organization that the neighborhood people themselves would control. Alinsky saw his role as that of a facilitator or teacher of methods, *not* a policy-maker. He deliberately sought out and relied on indigenous leaders. To attract people who ordinarily avoided formal organizations, Alinsky emphasized group self-interest. He personalized social problems, focused anger on a scapegoat or "villain," created conflict situations in which he pitted his group against others, and utilized direct action tactics. The rewards his group sought were concrete and attainable changes. When these changes were won, previously apathetic people discovered power through organization. Alinsky, having taught his methods, then withdrew to let his "people's organization" function totally on its own. In this way, the Back of the Yards Council became a permanent, flourishing group.

In 1939 Alinsky became executive director of the Industrial Areas Foundation, whose purpose was to organize and foster the growth of people's organizations. Alinsky trained organizers and acted as a consultant and organizer around the United States. Alinsky scholar Joan Lancourt puts the number of organizations he created, or regularly consulted for, at fourteen, although he spoke to or consulted on a one-time basis with many more. After the Back of the Yards Council, his next people's organization was in Kansas City (1940), followed by one in St. Paul (1941).

Alinsky was a superb publicist of his methods. Most of his writing was aimed at the general public rather than the academic community. While jailed in Kansas City in 1945, he wrote his masterpiece, *Reveille for Radicals* (1946), in which he preached a hard-nosed realism in goal-getting combined with innovative, direct action tactics in order to achieve grassroots-based social change. He became known for his sharp, abrasive style, and his comments in private conversation could be even sharper than what he wrote. He was also witty and charming.

His personal life was marred by tragedy. In 1947 his first wife, Helene Simon Alinsky, whom he had married in 1932 and by whom he had two children, Kathryn and Lee David, drowned while trying to save a child. His second marriage, to Jean Graham, who contracted multiple sclerosis, ended in divorce in 1970. In May, 1971, he married Irene McGinnis.

Following *Reveille for Radicals*, Alinsky began organizing Mexican Americans in California barrios and worked with the Community Service Organization in Los Angeles (1947). His success with Mexican Americans attracted the attention of New York Senator Herbert Lehman, who suggested to the New York Foundation that it hire Alinsky to organize Puerto Ricans. However, Alinsky's methods were controversial. Critics charged that he was more authoritarian than democratic, that he lacked an ideology, that he simply provided a vehicle for allowing people to vent their anger rather than achieve fundamental solutions to their problems, and that he compulsively attacked established agencies. Because many of the local social workers were anti-Alinsky, the New York Foundation sought a local agency to sponsor his effort there, and Hudson Guild agreed. Hudson Guild subsequently became an Alinsky target. In an effort to restore harmony to the Guild's neighborhood, the Chelsea Community Organization, created in 1956, formally disbanded in 1960. Meanwhile, Alinsky worked with groups in Lackawanna, New York (1957), Butte, Montana (1959), and the Hyde Park/Kenwood neighborhood of Chicago (1959). The only group to achieve much permanence, however, was the original Back of the Yards Council.

Before the 1960s, Alinsky was little more than an underground hero to radical social workers, but then he and his ideas came into vogue. In 1961 he met charges of racism in his organizations with the successful creation of TWO (The Woodlawn Organization) in the black slum immediately south of Chicago's Hyde Park neighborhood. TWO survived, but his Northwest Community Organization, also in Chicago (1963), failed to develop indigenous leadership. Meanwhile, the War on Poverty was seeking new approaches and gave Alinsky's ideas widespread support. His Rochester organization, FIGHT (1965), pressured Eastman Kodak to hire more Blacks. He also promoted people's organizations in Syracuse (1965), Kansas City, Missouri (1966), Buffalo (1967), and Chicago (1971). These organizations were widely imitated; Alinsky was a much sought after speaker (even with a lecture fee of $2,000), and his ideas became a standard part of community organization courses in schools of social work across America.

Toward the end of the 1960s, Alinsky turned to organizing among the white middle class. He died in Carmel, California, on June 12, 1972.

Saul Alinsky's papers and the Industrial Areas Foundation records are at the University of Illinois at Chicago. Some items relating to Alinsky organizations that touched specific settlement houses may be found in the National Federation of Settlements Records and United Neighborhood Houses Records at the Social Welfare History Archives, University of Minnesota, and, to a lesser extent, in the Chicago Commons Records at the Chicago Historical Society.

Of the published writings by Alinsky, only "Community Analysis and Organization," *American Journal of Sociology* (May, 1941), 797, is aimed specifically at an academic audience. Other articles are "The War on Poverty: Political Pornography," *Journal of Social Issues* (January, 1965), 41–47, and "The I.A.F.—Why Is It Controversial?," *Church in Metropolis* (Summer, 1965), 13–15. Marion K. Sanders edited her Alinsky interviews to produce *The Professional Radical* (1970). *John L. Lewis: An Unauthorized Biography* (1949) and *Rules for Radicals* (1971) were other books by Alinsky.

Material written about Alinsky can be found in books on community organization, especially David Finks, *Radical Vision of Saul Alinsky* (1984), Joan E. Lancourt, *Confront or Concede* (1979), and Robert Fisher, *Let the People Decide: Neighborhood Organizing in America* (1984). Unpublished sources include Michael P. Connolly, "An Historical Study of Change in Saul D. Alinsky's Community Organization Practice and Theory, 1939–1972," Ph.D. dissertation, University of Minnesota, 1976, and Bruce K. Irvine, "Saul Alinsky in Chelsea: A History of the Chelsea Community Council, 1956–1960," Master's thesis, Columbia University, n.d. Articles about Alinsky include Farnsworth Fowle, "Saul Alinsky, 63, Poverty Fighter and Social Organizer, Is Dead," *New York Times*, June 13, 1972, 46; Stephen C. Rose, "Saul Alinsky and His Critics," *Christianity and Crisis* (July, 1964), 142–152; and Judith Ann Trolander, "Social Change: Settlement Houses and Saul Alinsky, 1939–1965," *Social Service Review* (September, 1982), 346–365.

JUDITH ANN TROLANDER

**Allen, Nathan** (April 25, 1813–January 1, 1889), physician, writer, and public servant, was born in Princeton, Massachusetts, to Mehitable (Oliver) and Moses Allen, a farmer. Allen graduated from Amherst College in 1836 and in 1841 received his M.D. from Pennsylvania Medical College. While in medical school he served for a brief period as editor of the *American Phrenological Journal and Miscellany* and was an active contributor to the publication. Upon graduation he returned to Lowell, Massachusetts, where he practiced medicine for the rest of his life.

Allen had three intertwined careers as physician, writer, and public servant. He practiced medicine in Lowell for forty-eight years and was a member of the American Medical Association, the American Academy of Medicine, the American Public Health Association, and the Massachusetts Medical Society. He served on the Lowell Board of Health and also as an examining surgeon for pensions. His medical training led to an interest in physical culture, population physiology, insanity, and heredity, and he published a number of articles and books on these and other subjects. Allen's views on social welfare and on insanity guided his activities in appointive state offices, most notably as a member of the Massachusetts Board of State Charities.

Allen wrote extensively about the declining birthrate of native New England women. While his main focus was on the so-called laws of population, his work was often cited in discussions of race suicide and of the need to control the foreign-born population. Allen attributed the declining birthrate of New England women to the overdevelopment of their brains at the expense of their physical stamina, in essence blaming civilization and high living for slowing the native birth rate while having no effect on the fertility of the foreign-born. He articulated in his various articles the growing perception that fecund foreigners were changing the character of New England life, a view that ultimately would help lead to restrictions on immigration and other outpourings of nativism.

A prolific writer whose interests included the opium trade in China and India, physical culture, education, and the laws of marriage, Allen spoke to a number of different audiences. He addressed the social welfare and medical communities as well as the general public. Among the groups he spoke to were the American

Social Science Association, the National Conference of Charities and Correction, the American Association for the Protection of the Insane, and the American Academy of Medicine. His articles were published in journals ranging from the *North American Review* to *Popular Science Monthly* to the *Boston Medical and Surgical Journal*. Many of his most significant pieces can be found in the collection *Physical Development, or the Laws Governing the Human System* (1888).

Allen held a number of appointive offices. In 1856 the Massachusetts state legislature appointed Allen a trustee of his alma mater, Amherst College. He played an active role in establishing a department of physical culture at the college and in 1873 was given an honorary LL.D. by Amherst for his public service and his research.

The governor of Massachusetts appointed Allen to the newly established Board of State Charities in 1864. He was successively reappointed to the Board on several occasions, serving throughout the fifteen years of its existence, including several periods as its chairman. Among the duties assigned to the Board were investigating, reporting, and recommending changes to promote efficiency and economy in public charitable and correctional institutions. The creation of the Board was the result of the growing perception that state social welfare policies and state institutions required leadership from a more rationalized and centralized body than had previously been the case. In performing this task the Board, under the leadership of Franklin B. Sanborn* and Samuel Gridley Howe,* proved to be an influential body, inspiring the creation of similar organizations in other states. Allen contributed to the annual reports of the Board, and his own thinking appears to have been influenced by Howe's ideas regarding the relationship between heredity and social disorder.

In 1872 Allen was an American delegate to the International Congress on Prison Reform which met in London. The Congress enabled penologists from Europe and the United States to share information and ideas about running penitentiaries and reformatories and to discuss topics such as administration, discipline, labor, sanitary conditions, and the causes of crime.

Appointed Massachusetts State Commissioner of Lunacy in 1874 along with Wendell Phillips, Allen investigated the laws relating to the mentally ill and the state lunatic asylums. When Phillips was unable to perform his duties, Allen alone reported to the state legislature in 1875. He discussed the number of mentally ill persons in state care and their treatment, recommending the building of several small institutions in place of large congregate asylums and suggesting a system of classification be initiated to separate the chronically insane from those experiencing acute episodes of illness. He also suggested that a permanent, independent body be established to oversee the care of the mentally ill and the administration of the state hospitals. His recommendation reflected the attitude of the Board of State Charities, which had favored the reorganization of congregate asylums into smaller institutions which would allow for the greater classification of inmates. In 1879 the Massachusetts State Board of Health and the Massachusetts

Board of State Charities were abolished and a new State Board of Health, Lunacy, and Charity was created in its place. Allen served for a year on the new Board, and his report appears to have been partially responsible for its development.

While fulfilling his obligations as public servant, Allen continued his medical practice in Lowell. In 1841 he married Sarah H. Spaulding of Wakefield, Massachusetts. She died in 1856. In 1857 he married Annie A. Waters of Salem, Massachusetts, by whom he had four children. Allen died in Lowell, Massachusetts, in 1889.

There are no manuscript materials for Nathan Allen listed in the *National Union Catalog of Manuscript Collections*. Allen wrote many articles and several books, most of which are listed in the *Index Catalog of the Surgeon-General's Office, United States Army*, First Series, vol. 1 (1880), 197–198; Second Series, vol. 1 (1896), 264; and Third Series, vol. 1 (1918), 298. Among his publications were *An Essay on the Connection of Mental Philosophy with Medicine* (1841); *An Essay on the Opium Trade* (1850); *Physical Culture in Amherst College* (1869); *The Physiological Laws of Human Increase* (1870); *Report of the Commissioners of Lunacy, to the Commonwealth of Massachusetts* (1875); *Physical Development; Or, The Laws Governing the Human System* (1888).

For biographies of Allen, see William B. Atkinson, ed., *A Biographical Dictionary of Contemporary American Physicians and Surgeons*, 2nd ed. (1880), 49–50; *New England Medical Monthly* (February, 1884), 215–219; Howard A. Kelly and Walter L. Burrage, eds., *A Dictionary of American Medical Biography* (1928), 18–19; Allen Johnson, ed., *Dictionary of American Biography*, vol. 1 (1928), 201–202; R. French Stone, ed., *Biographies of Eminent American Physicians and Surgeons* (1894), 11–12. For obituaries of Allen, see *Boston Evening Transcript*, January 2, 1889, 3; *Boston Medical and Surgical Journal* (January, 1889), 52.

JANET GOLDEN

**Altmeyer, Arthur Joseph** (May 8, 1891–October 17, 1972), Social Security administrator and influential policy-maker, was born in De Pere, Wisconsin, the son of Carrie (Smith) and John G. Altmeyer. After earning a Phi Beta Kappa key and receiving his B.A. from the University of Wisconsin in Madison in 1914, Altmeyer taught high school, served as a school principal, and (in July, 1916) married Ethel M. Thomas. In 1918 he left the field of education to become a statistician for the Wisconsin Tax Commission. Between 1920 and 1933 Altmeyer served as chief statistician and then executive secretary of the Wisconsin Industrial Commission. During this period he also managed to earn an M.A. and a Ph.D. from his alma mater and to write two books dealing with labor law administation and insurance matters at the state level.

Franklin D. Roosevelt summoned Altmeyer to Washington in 1933 to direct the compliance division of the National Recovery Administration. A year later he became second assistant secretary of labor. In this capacity, he chaired the technical board that assisted the Committee on Economic Security in drafting the original Social Security bill. Altmeyer was named in 1935 to a three-member Social Security Board, which was charged with overseeing operations for the nation's new social insurance program and for devising ways to improve the system. Shortly after becoming chairman of the Social Security Board in 1937, Altmeyer wrote, "Social legislation requires the development of new [governmental] techniques, calling for resourcefulness and imagination of a high order. Its success lies entirely in its administration."

Altmeyer's career demonstrates that even a concept as unfamiliar as social insurance could become an accepted and acceptable feature of American life if administrators knew how to use their power and serve the public. Altmeyer deserves much credit for developing orderly procedures and recruiting a loyal and efficient staff to operate Social Security. The omnibus legislation provided relief for the elderly poor, the blind, and families with dependent children, collected money from those soon entitled to old-age retirement benefits, coordinated a federal–state unemployment system, and played a role in developing public health services. A shrewd tactician, Altmeyer was instrumental in securing the enactment of the 1939 Social Security amendments. During the war he advocated extending coverage to farmers and other workers, the adoption of a disability program, and other benefit increases. While Congress did not act on these recommendations, Altmeyer nonetheless had indicated Social Security's future direction.

In 1946 Altmeyer became the first Commissioner of Social Security when his growing bureaucracy was transferred to the Federal Security Agency. For the next seven years he successfully fought off conservative assaults on the program. He was the chief architect of the 1950 amendments, which provided a 77 percent increase in old-age insurance benefits. He also actively engaged in international affairs: between 1942 and 1952 he served as chairman of the Inter-American Committee on Social Security, and he was the U.S. representative on a United Nations commission while he headed the Social Security Administration.

Altmeyer described his experiences in shaping the nation's social insurance program in *The Formative Years of Social Security* (1968). This volume remains an invaluable source for reconstructing the early administrative and legislative history of Social Security. It also provides a revealing portrait of an insider's views of the constraints and challenges that federal bureaucrats faced in the 1940s and 1950s.

After stepping down from his government position in 1953, Altmeyer was elected president of the National Conference of Social Work. He also continued to participate in a variety of international commissions dealing with the advancement of Social Security and with social welfare problems in Pakistan, Iran, Peru, and Colombia. He also served as an advisor to several foreign governments and on a variety of civic boards until his death in Madison, Wisconsin, on October 17, 1972.

The most useful bibliographic sources are the accounts in *Who Was Who in America*, vol. 5 (1973), 12; *Current Biography* (1946), 14; and his obituary in the *New York Times*, October 18, 1972, 50. His role in Social Security receives considerable attention in his book, *The Formative Years of Social Security* (1968), as well as in two more recent histories, Martha Derthick, *Policymaking for Social Security* (1979), and Carolyn L. Weaver, *The Real Crisis in Social Security* (1982).

W. ANDREW ACHENBAUM

**Amidon, Beulah Elizabeth** (August 19, 1894–September 24, 1958), journalist and editor, was born in Fargo, North Dakota, the first child of Charles Fremont Amidon and Beulah (McHenry) Amidon, whose shared engagement in social reform filled their home with talk of national issues.

Charles Amidon had come to the Dakota Territory as a teacher; he soon turned to law, and in 1896 became judge in the federal district court in Fargo. He was prominent in the American Bar Association and the Republican Party, and his judicial decisions reflected a liberal philosophy that tied him to other progressives and to insurgent midwestern farm politics. Mrs. Amidon worked with her husband in local temperance and suffrage societies and played a major role in extending the women's club movement throughout North Dakota.

Encouraged to be independent, Beulah E. Amidon left Fargo after one year of study at North Dakota State University and entered Barnard College in New York City, where she combined studies in history and economics with dramatics, creative writing, and participation in a suffrage club. In 1915 she completed her A.B. and went to Los Angeles to study law, sharing her father's confidence that legal and political institutions could improve the world. However, poor health, which would periodically interrupt her work, caused her to leave her studies and to consider journalism as an alternate means of livelihood and social purpose.

In 1917 Amidon joined the Press Department of the National Woman's Party (NWP) in Washington, D.C., interpreting its actions for the general press and writing spirited material for the party's paper, the *Suffragist*. On occasion she lobbied North Dakota legislators regarding suffrage via her father's connections with the Non-Partisan League (NPL), and in 1918 she returned to the state to write political copy for the League's network of papers. A younger brother also had worked for the League, portraying—as she did—farmers' struggles against the monied interests as a people's crusade. Her job ended in 1919 with marriage to Paul G. Ratliff, a flyer recently returned from Europe with whom she had two children, and Beulah assumed that her wage-earning career was over.

However, during the next half dozen years the Ratliffs lived first in Mississippi, then in California, where raising a daughter and a son was combined with volunteer work and writing. Her articles were published in national magazines, and by 1925 she was turning out fiction to balance the family budget. At the tenth reunion of her graduating class, friends who had both children and careers strengthened Beulah's decision to leave her husband and move east with the children. One classmate knew of an opening at the *Survey* in New York, the nation's leading magazine dealing with social welfare, edited by Paul Kellogg.*

Kellogg and the *Survey* staff welcomed her writing as well as her familiarity with the country and the contacts she brought from her own and her parents' activities. In October, 1925, she was hired to assist the editors of the Education and Industrial Department. Six months later she was promoted to associate editor and by 1930 was in charge of both areas. Meanwhile, her husband had died in an accident shortly after she left California. As a widow, she once more called herself Beulah Amidon, and it was that by-line that appeared in the *Survey* from 1926 to 1952 and occasionally in other magazines as well.

Amidon was one of the first journalists who identified discrepancies in the touted affluence of the 1920s when her research, in 1928, revealed technological unemployment, thus signaling hard times ahead. Her description of local efforts to fight unemployment came to be supplemented by accounts of programs started in Washington, D.C., during the Great Depression. Indeed, readers came to know and understand the New Deal's intervention in industry and the transitions occurring in the work force through her many insightful articles, including ones on the controversy over Section 7–A of the National Industrial Recovery Act (NIRA; in 1934), the ineffectiveness of the NIRA codes (in 1935), the politics of the burgeoning Congress of Industrial Organizations (in 1936), and the Supreme Court hearings on the Wagner National Labor Relations Act (in 1937). Then when mobilization began for World War II, she examined old injustices as well as new opportunities coming to female and black workers.

While the public came to know her field research in Washington or at labor conflicts on industrial sites through her widely read articles, much of her work on the *Survey* (which from the 1920s through the 1940s actually was published as two separate journals, the *Survey Graphic*, for a broad, general audience, and the *Survey Midmonthly*, for professional social workers) was hidden. As associate editor she was responsible for others' contributions, especially for soliciting and editing their work. With the death of managing editor Arthur Kellogg* in 1934, preparation of the *Survey Graphic* for monthly publication fell to her. She often had to juggle the needs of her children with the needs of the *Graphic*, always doing both well, however.

Amidon's work ensured that readers got a factually accurate and broad-based analysis of industrial events and policy development. While distrusting big money, power, communism, and at times even feminism, she consistently sought out innovative programs in industry and education as possible answers to the nation's problems in uncertain times.

She firmly believed that in a democracy people must have access to the facts, and as fascism spread in Europe she edited a book, *Democracy's Challenge to Education* (1940). Amidon's concern for public education, an interest shared by her siblings, led to activity with the Public Affairs Project initiated by the Twentieth Century Fund. The Public Affairs Committee began publishing pamphlets in 1935 to make economic research and social policy available to the public in a readable, inexpensive format. Amidon compiled a few of its bulletins and in 1941 joined the editorial board; in 1943 she became board treasurer and continued in that capacity until her death.

Meanwhile, however, Amidon tendered her resignation to the *Survey*, declaring that although the magazine had become her life, "new blood" was essential for its survival. She did not cut all ties with the journal, however, as she continued to steer it in new directions until it ceased operation in 1952. She continued to live in New York City, doing freelance writing and editing as she coped with deteriorating health until her death there in 1958.

Biographic information on Beulah E. Amidon is slight; however, correspondence related to her position at the *Survey*, 1925–1952, can be found in the Paul U. Kellogg Collection and the Survey Associates Collection in the Social Welfare History Archives at the University of Minnesota in Minneapolis. Yearbooks and the Alumnae Register in the Wollman Library Archives at Barnard College in New York City offer brief descriptions of her activities in college and at intervals thereafter. Irwin Kenneth Smemo's "Progressive Judge: The Public Career of Charles Fremont Amidon," Ph.D. dissertation, University of Minnesota, 1967, provides an analysis of Judge Amidon's career with limited mention of his family.

Beulah Amidon's early journalism can be found in the NWP's *Suffragist*, available on microfilm from the Library of Congress for 1913–1921, and the Non-Partisan League's paper, the *National Leader* or *Non-Partisan Leader*, 1915–1923, also on microfilm. After 1926 most of her articles appeared in the *Survey*.

Information on the integration of Beulah Amidon's career with the *Survey* appears in Clarke A. Chambers' *Paul U. Kellogg and the Survey, Voices for Social Welfare and Social Justice* (1971). Brief mention of her involvement with the National Woman's Party is included in Inez Haynes Irwin's *The Story of Alice Paul and the National Woman's Party* (1964, 1977). Frank Luther Mott, in *A History of American Magazines*, vol. 4 (1957), includes Amidon in a larger discussion about the *Survey*. Dorothy Woolf interviewed her for a column, "Projections," *Barnard College Alumnae Monthly* (November, 1934), 11–12; here Amidon sketches and interprets her experiences between graduation and 1934. An obituary notice in the *New York Times* (September 25, 1958, 33:2), contains errors about her responsibilities at the *Survey* and on the Public Affairs board.

BEVERLY A. STADUM

**Anderson, Mary** (August 27, 1872–January 29, 1964), social and labor reformer and government official, was the youngest of seven children born to Matilda and Magnus Anderson, a farmer in Linkoping, Sweden. Economic hardship led the family to migrate to the United States in 1889. With minimal education at a Swedish Lutheran school and no knowledge of English, Anderson found a series of menial domestic jobs in the lumbering areas of Michigan and then factory work in Chicago.

She was employed in a Chicago shoe factory when she joined the International Boot and Shoe Workers Union in 1899. Soon after the turn of the century, she also became a member of the Chicago branch of the Women's Trade Union League (WTUL), founded in 1903 to promote union organizing among female factory workers through cross-class cooperation between working- and middle-class women. Attention to the working conditions of women in industry and close ties with the WTUL and other women's reform organizations were the dominant marks of Anderson's long public career.

After the Chicago WTUL helped striking women garment workers gain union recognition and an agreement with Hart, Schaffner & Marx, Anderson assumed a full-time position with the League. She helped organize women, teach the principles of trade unionism, and enforce arbitration arrangements between labor and management in the men's clothing industry.

United States entry into World War I brought new federal government involvement in issues concerning female employment—and a new job for Mary Anderson. From 1905 academic activists and reform-minded women had urged the creation of a federal agency that would study and report on the conditions of working women on a national scale. This campaign by social feminists for a women's bureau within the Department of Labor made no headway in Congress and gained little support from the trade unionists affiliated with the American Federation of Labor (AFL). Not until the wartime emergency did Congress establish an independent Woman-in-Industry Service headed by Mary Van Kleeck,* with Mary Anderson as her assistant.

The Service floundered once the war ended, but in 1920 congressional action sanctioned a permanent Women's Bureau. From the agency's creation until her retirement in 1944, Anderson served as its head. Throughout her tenure the Bureau employed a small but dedicated group of women of outstanding educational background who were committed to ameliorating the condition of wage-earning women. But the agency was continually understaffed and operated on minimal appropriations. Mary Anderson commanded the loyalty of workers, many of whom worked for the Bureau as long as she did, but in terms of concrete contributions to improving the welfare of working women, results fell short of intentions.

In part, the limitations of the Women's Bureau were rooted in the marginal position of women generally. Established to create a climate favorable to raising wages, reducing hours, and improving the work environment of working women, the Bureau met with indifference bordering on hostility from the business community. Speaking for women who were largely excluded from trade unions based on skill and craft, and more committed to protective legislation for women than to union membership, the agency was ignored by organized labor. Comparatively small and underfunded in the federal bureaucracy, the Women's Bureau and its chief found few friendly proponents in government circles. Only among the women's organizations that had worked hard for its creation and that continued to support Anderson's position on issues related to women in industry did the Bureau find a constituency.

Close relationships with the social feminists of the League of Women Voters, the National Consumers' League, and the Women's Trade Union League highlighted many of the ideological contradictions shared by these associations and the Bureau. Committed to equal opportunities in the labor market as well as equal pay for equal work, Anderson shared with her staff and her allies conventional views toward women's physical nature and prescribed social roles. The published bulletins that marked the investigations of her staff into employment conditions bore the apparent neutrality of statistical evidence and interviewees' testimony. But conclusions betrayed belief that female employment was an unfortunate necessity and that women workers needed special legislation that limited hours, prohibited night work, banned women from certain occupations, and set limits on what they could perform in others.

Anderson's firm stance on behalf of protective legislation for women placed her in direct opposition to the feminists who proposed an equal rights amendment to the Constitution. Even when the Fair Labor Standards Act of 1938 survived its Supreme Court challenge and institutionalized work standards for men and women alike, Anderson's position remained unchanged, and her opposition to amendment backers became personally bitter as well as ideologically intractable. Her stance toward protective legislation even overshadowed her commitment to trade unionism. When the thrust of industrial unionization encompassed thousands of women within the ranks of unions for the first time during the late 1930s and World War II, insistence on special treatment for women at work operated at cross-purposes with women's position within union structures.

While the shortcomings of Anderson's tenure were largely structural and ideological, she bore some personal responsibility as well. Her working-class background and lack of education did not preclude political acumen or intellectual curiosity, but she was significantly lacking in both. She was an effective speaker with firm convictions as to what practices would promote the welfare of women workers, yet in the end she preached most often to the converted and lacked the ability to promote concrete policy. With the great influx of women into the labor force during World War II, her inability to establish a close working relationship with Secretary of Labor Frances Perkins* during the 1930s was further magnified. While the watchdog role of the Women's Bureau grew, Anderson could not enlarge her staff or her budget. She resigned her post in mid-1944, leaving behind the numerous Bureau publications that are a storehouse of information for labor historians and testimony to faith in the investigatory and educational processes as instruments to promote worker well-being.

She continued to live in Washington after leaving the Bureau, keeping in close touch with former staff investigators and friends from the WTUL and promoting protective legislation for women workers. She died in Washington, D.C., in 1964 at the age of ninety-two.

Mary Anderson's papers are housed at the Schlesinger Library and microfilmed as part of the WTUL Collection. Her official correspondence is part of the Women's Bureau records at the National Archives. Her autobiography, *Women at Work* (1951), was written with the help of Bureau worker and WTUL colleague Mary Winslow. Edward T. James wrote her biographical entry in *Notable American Women: The Modern Period* (1980). Judith Sealander's *As Minority Becomes Majority: Federal Reaction to the Phenomenon of Women in the Work Force 1920–1963* (1983) is an informative, critical history of the Women's Bureau that extends beyond Anderson's tenure.

                                                                               LOIS SCHARF

**Andrews, John Bertram** (August 2, 1880–January 4, 1983), promoter of sound labor legislation and social insurance, was born in the town of South Wayne, in rural Wisconsin, to Philo Edmund and Sarah Jane Andrews. Young John grew up in comfortable surroundings, and when it was time to go to college it seemed natural to send him to the state university at Madison, then in the process of acquiring a national reputation for innovative education.

Andrews received his B.A. in 1904. During the next year he studied economics and taught elementary courses on the subject at Dartmouth, from which he received a master's degree in 1905. Then he made what turned out to be a significant decision to return to the University of Wisconsin to study for the doctorate. Between 1905 and 1908 he studied economics and economic history at Wisconsin, serving as a teaching assistant to and working closely with John R. Commons.* Commons interested Andrews in the study of labor legislation, and Andrews, in turn, became the student whom many would regard as Commons' most prominent. From Commons, Andrews learned to apply economic theory to the solution of practical problems.

After receiving his doctorate in 1908, Andrews assisted Commons with one of his many outside interests, the American Association for Labor Legislation (AALL). By 1909 Andrews had become the executive secretary of that organization, a post that he was to hold until his death. Under Andrews' leadership, the AALL moved from being a purely academic organization designed to study labor conditions to being an advocate of what the Association termed "desirable" legislation. When the Association moved to New York in 1910, Andrews came out from under Commons' shadow. He transformed the organization into a strong advocate for such Progressive Era reforms as minimum wages for women and, most important of all, the passage of state workers' compensation laws.

Although the Association maintained a small staff and had such luminaries as economist Richard Ely as president, Andrews ran the Association. His career was largely defined by the Association. On August 8, 1910, he married the other full-time staff member, Irene Osgood, who also had studied institutional economics at Wisconsin. John and Irene Osgood Andrews often collaborated on articles that described the progress of labor legislation in the various states.

Between 1910 and 1942 Andrews edited the *American Labor Legislation*

*Review.* Although the Association had only 3,000 members in 1919, the *Review* enjoyed a relatively wide circulation. Along with Paul Kellogg's* *Survey*, the *Review* represented an important source of information about labor legislation and the passage of social welfare laws. Each year, for example, Andrews printed a map of the United States indicating the states that had failed to pass workers' compensation legislation. The *Review* also contained such material as model bills on unemployment and health insurance.

The AALL represented an important influence over the passage of state and, beginning in 1935, national social welfare legislation. In addition to model bills, the Association often presented testimony on such topics as occupational diseases. The Association only rarely resorted to pressure tactics. Instead, it relied on the Progressive Era faith that the facts would in themselves stir up enough outrage to provoke political action. After the passage of the Social Security Act in 1935, private organizations like the Association (and others, such a the National Consumers' League, which contained an extensive overlap in membership with the Association) became less important political actors. The formation of the Social Security Board in 1935 created a new source for research and analysis in the federal government that superseded such organizations as the AALL.

The Progressive Era and the twenties represented the apex of the influence of the American Association for Labor Legislation and, by extension, of John B. Andrews. During these years the Association gave a national voice to what has been called the Wisconsin Idea in labor legislation.

Perhaps the most dramatic triumph came early in Andrews' career. In 1909 Andrews, assisted by the United States Bureau of Labor, studied the use of poisonous phosphorous in the manufacture of matches. The results were published in *Bulletin 88* of the U.S. Bureau of Labor. These results revealed the existence of an occupational disease known as "phossy jaw." Andrews and the Association worked to introduce a bill in Congress that placed a high tax on the use of phosphorous and encouraged the use of a harmless and less expensive substitute. The bill passed Congress, and on January 28, 1911, the Diamond Match Company allowed its patent on the substitute process to be cancelled by President Taft. Here, then, was a plan of research that led to legislative action. It exemplified how Andrews and the AALL worked.

Andrews and the AALL did not limit themselves to the passage of labor laws. They devoted more of their efforts to the improvement of such laws. In 1915, for example, the AALL launched an investigation of the operation of the New Jersey state workers' compensation law. The study revealed the need to end court administration of the law and to create an industrial commission. Andrews was in the forefront of the national drive to create such industrial commissions.

Andrews worked on nearly every important area of labor legislation during the course of his career. In 1916 he helped to write a model health insurance bill for which he received requests for 8,000 copies. In 1922 he carried on an active campaign to induce mine operators to rock dust their mines and to secure legislation requiring such action. In 1934 he helped to draft the Wagner-Lewis bill that paved the way for the passage of unemployment compensation in 1935.

In unemployment compensation, as in other labor legislation matters, Andrews clung to the methods he learned in Wisconsin. This predilection caused him to favor state laws that placed pressure on individual companies to act in a socially responsible manner. In the field of unemployment compensation, for example, the Wisconsin approach favored the creation of employer reserves. This approach became the one favored by Andrews.

Andrews served on many committees and commissions that reported on labor legislation. In 1913 and 1914 he was a member of the (New York) Mayor's Commission on Unemployment; in 1921 he participated in the President's Unemployment Conference; in 1919 he had served as a government delegate to the International Labor Conference in Geneva, and throughout his life he played an active role in the International Labor Organization.

Andrews also remained an active teacher and scholar throughout his life. He often lectured on labor legislation at Columbia University, and he collaborated with Commons and others to produce important books and articles on labor legislation. He helped to write Commons' seminal *History of Labor in the United States* (1918), covering the period from 1860 to 1877. His *Principles of Labor Legislation*, written with Commons and published in 1936, became the standard source on the subject. He wrote numerous other books that described labor laws and their implementation, including *Administrative Labor Legislation* (1936).

The *American Labor Legislation Review* ceased publication in 1942, and Andrews died soon thereafter, in the Post Graduate Hospital in New York City.

John B. Andrews' personal papers and the more important papers of the American Association for Labor Legislation are housed at the New York State School of Industrial and Labor Relations at Cornell University. A good obituary appeared on page 20 of the *New York Times*, January 5, 1943. In addition to Andrews' extensive writings, Clarke Chambers' *Seedtime of Reform* (1963) and the privately printed proceedings of the John B. Andrews Memorial Symposium held in November, 1949 (and sent to a number of major research libraries), provide a good background.

EDWARD D. BERKOWITZ

**Armstrong, Barbara Nachtrieb** (August 4, 1890–January 18, 1976), author and leader in the social insurance movement, was born in San Francisco, California, to Anna (Day) and John Jacob Nachtrieb. She received all of her education in the Bay area, first in local public schools and then at the University of California, where she majored in economics, receiving a bachelor's degree in 1913 and a Ph.D. in 1921 as well as a law degree (J.D.) in 1915. Admitted to the bar in 1915, Armstrong served for four years as executive secretary of the California Institutions Commission. She then returned to Berkeley, joining the faculty at Boalt Hall. The nation's first female law professor, she taught law and economics there for thirty-eight years. Meanwhile, however, in 1926 she married Ian Armstrong, an importer, with whom she had one child, a daughter, Patricia.

In 1932 Armstrong published *Insuring the Essentials*, a thorough historical and cross-national review of the evolution of social insurance and minimum wage laws. In 565 pages of analysis and another 150 pages of technical appendices, Armstrong demonstrated that while minimum wages and social insurance were complementary features of a "living wage program," these two institutions had quite independent histories. She detected no trend that explained why and when different nations adopted family allowances and established minimum wage provisions. Similarly, there was a surge of interest in social insurance after World War I, but no clear pattern of interest internationally had emerged by the Great Depression. Nearly all countries provided insurance against industrial injuries, and most European nations underwrote sickness insurance. Old-age and invalidity insurance protection existed, but there were marked variations in financing, coverage, and benefits. Only a half-dozen countries, however, followed England's lead in establishing unemployment insurance. Armstrong excoriated America for doing so little: "Except in the field of industrial accident provision, the United States is in the position of being the most backward of all the nations of commercial importance in insuring the essentials to its workers. Nor is there available the excuse that superior conditions in the United States render preventive measures unnecessary. . . . Relief expenditures from public treasuries are constant reminders of the shortcomings of American economic organization," she lamented.

Largely because of the acclaim *Insuring the Essentials* received, Armstrong was invited to Washington in 1934 to serve as director of studies for the old-age security staff of President Franklin Roosevelt's Committee on Economic Security. Her sharp tongue and inability to suffer fools and bureaucrats gladly did not serve her well. Fortunately, however, she greatly respected her colleague J. Douglas Brown, a Princeton economist; together, they drafted the key provisions of Title I (old-age assistance) and Title II (old-age insurance) of the 1935 Social Security Act.

Besides her work on social insurance, Armstrong wrote on macro-economic matters for legal journals and published *The Health Insurance Doctor—His Role in Great Britain, Denmark and France* (1939). Barbara Armstrong died in Berkeley, California, on January 18, 1976, at the age of eighty-five.

The best biographical information on Armstrong appears in her obituary in the *New York Times*, January 21, 1976, 40. For other biographical details, see *Who Was Who in America*, vol. 6 (1976), 11. For more on her role in shaping the 1935 Social Security Act, see J. Douglas Brown, *The Genesis of Social Security* (1969); and Edwin E. Witte, *Development of the Social Security Act* (1963), 30, 122. See also the oral histories done by Barbara N. Armstrong and J. Douglas Brown in Columbia University's Oral History Collection.

W. ANDREW ACHENBAUM

**Armstrong, Samuel Chapman** (January 30, 1839–May 11, 1893), educator of Afro-Americans and American Indians, was born on the island of Maui in the Hawaiian Islands, the sixth of eight children of Richard Armstrong and Clarissa (Chapman) Armstrong, transplanted Yankees. Having gone to the islands as missionaries of the Congregational Church, the Armstrongs became increasingly convinced of the need of the Hawaiian peoples for education, one that included industrial elements which would teach the Protestant ethic and Yankee work habits. Toward that end, Richard Armstrong added public service to his pastoral duties, including in 1847 the position of Minister of Public Education for the King. Growing up in a setting that he would always remember as idyllic, Samuel Chapman Armstrong developed a zest for outdoor life, comfort in living with a diverse population, and, at the same time, solid scholastic talents. Together with other missionary youth and the children of the Hawaiian royalty, he attended the Royal School at Punahou and its successor, Oahu College, finishing two years of study there.

In 1860 Samuel Armstrong left the islands to finish his education in New England. His mother insisted that the accidental death of her husband in September of that year not deter Samuel from fulfilling their plans that he attend Williams College, his father's alma mater. There he earned a record of strong scholarship and leadership as well as the esteem of Mark Hopkins, the school's renowned president. Service in the Union army followed his graduation from Williams and led to his first involvement on behalf of social reform when he became an officer of U.S. Colored Troops. Rising to the rank of general and commander of the Ninth Regiment, U.S.C.T., Armstrong decided, as he wrote to his mother, that it was "a grand thing to be identified with this Negro movement." After the war he became the Freedmen's Bureau subcommissioner for the Virginia peninsula. In 1868 he persuaded the American Missionary Association (AMA) to establish a school for the freedmen at Hampton, Virginia, close to the large population of refugees from slavery that had gathered in the Fortress Monroe area during the Civil War. Named Hampton Institute, this school emerged as the leading example of the industrial model of education for the ex-slaves. It served as the focus of Armstrong's considerable energies for the remainder of his life and as a vehicle by which he influenced his northern contemporaries as well as black and white southerners with his vision of the necessities of freedom, first for the freedmen, and subsequently for American Indians. Armstrong married Emma Dean Walker in 1869 and twelve years after her death married Mary Alice Ford in 1890. The Armstrong family remained an important force at Hampton, most notably through the general's son-in-law, Arthur Howe, who was its president from 1930 to 1940.

General Armstrong offered an alternative to the more classics-oriented high schools and colleges being established elsewhere in the South for the freedmen. While Mark Hopkins had instilled in him the ideal of education for the whole man as a prerequisite for leadership, Armstrong's reflections upon his father's work as a missionary educator in Hawaii, his receptivity to the racialistic thinking of his time, and his experience as an officer of black troops persuaded him that a special model was necessary for "the despised races." They needed to learn the discipline and develop the character that came from productive labor. Thus the Hampton approach was not primarily the teaching of skills, but was an "education for life": an effort to inculcate in the students the work ethic of mid-nineteenth century genteel Americans. Its graduates, of which Booker T. Washington* was the ideal type, would be missionaries of civilization to their communities. After a decade of work with black students, Armstrong persuaded Secretary of the Interior Carl Schurz to extend the model to American Indians as part of a new effort to replace warfare with a policy of assimilation. As the first eastern boarding school for Indians, it became the model for Indian schooling of the era.

The force of his personality and the strength of his convictions, together with his recognition of the value of cultivating prominent public officials, placed Armstrong and his school in the national limelight. Central to the attention which he gained for the school, however, was Armstrong's harmony with postbellum trends of ameliorative activity. He appealed to private charity to support his work and offered a paternalistic solution to the plight of freedmen and American Indians. Their circumstances would improve only as they assimilated and internalized the ethic of hard work and acquisitiveness. His approach was comforting to northern elites who worried about the injustices visited upon these peoples but opposed excessive federal interference and were anxious for socioeconomic stability in the wake of the Civil War. Gifts to Hampton Institute would help the masses lift themselves up by their bootstraps and remove issues of race and class from the political agenda. Moreover, Armstrong's gospel of self-help included a message of racial solidarity that promised to set aside issues of social equality.

To this comforting message, Armstrong added innovations in fund-raising that earned Hampton Institute a large share of the funds for black education. An inspiring and tireless speaker to church groups and prospective donors, Armstrong recognized that charisma was not enough. By establishing independence from the AMA while retaining its representatives on the board of trustees, he maintained regular support from the churches even as he began to reach the new industrial philanthropists by strategic appointments to his board. Especially effective was his marshalling of evidence concerning the success of the school's alumni in spreading the message of accommodation and hard work even as they achieved economic progress. The *Southern Workman*, a monthly magazine edited by the Hampton staff and printed by the students, was as important for reaching and retaining benefactors for the school as it was in reinforcing the school's gospel to its alumni. While dependent upon private donors, Armstrong developed public sources, most notably a share of the Virginia land-grant allotment and, with the arrival of Indian students, a per capita allotment to pay their expenses from the Office of Indian Affairs. He was one of the earliest advocates for national aid for education in the South, supporting legislation to that end throughout the

1880s. His switch to opposition to such aid, while couched in laissez-faire terms, came only when it seemed hopeless and after he had developed ties with large private donors which promised solvency for Hampton Institute.

Armstrong's vision of Hampton brought controversy as well as endowment. His effort to secure support from southern white conservatives for black education bore fruit in almost direct proportion to the discomfort of white and black advocates of collegiate education. His call for an education of "the head, the hand and the heart" and for the preparation of common school teachers unversed in the classics did not require the abandonment of black colleges. Yet his descriptions of Hampton's role for the masses often included phrases suggesting the dangers of too much education and undermined the fund-raising of the colleges. His advocacy of self-help and expressions of confidence in the freedmen's future sparked the hopes of some Blacks as well as Whites. Booker T. Washington was only the most famous of the alumni and supporters who appreciated Armstrong's support for their aspirations as educators and businessmen. Others found his emphasis on the accommodation of the masses to their circumstances to require a surrender of gains and aspirations bought dearly during the Civil War and Reconstruction. His criticism of political activity and courting of southern white support led some critics, such as African Methodist Episcopal Bishop Henry McNeal Turner, to regret the prominence which Hampton was achieving. On the other hand, congressmen from the South and West, especially Democrats, regularly challenged subsidies to Hampton because of its integration of red and black students and its advocacy of the interests of those groups.

As General Armstrong developed the Hampton idea, he contributed to three spheres of reform activity. His speeches and the publications about Hampton Institute strengthened the interest in industrial and vocational education. As a regular participant in the annual Lake Mohonk Conferences on the Indian Question and the Indian Rights Association, he shaped Indian policy reform to make education a corollary to land allotment. In his reliance upon the support of the "best [white] men," South and North, he was a prime mover in the road to reunion of these sections and, unintentionally, in the continued subordination of black southerners.

Samuel Chapman Armstrong left Hampton Institute on sound financial footing and with a loyal alumni spread throughout the South and among more than thirty tribes in the West. However, while advocates of genteel reform celebrated his accomplishments and those of his students, the resistance to equal opportunity deeply embedded in American society caused him some private concern in his last years; within a decade of his death at Hampton on May 11, 1893, it called forth more basic criticism of his legacy.

The Samuel C. Armstrong Papers, Hampton Institute Archives, Hampton, Virginia, and the Armstrong Family Papers, Williams College Archives, Williamstown, Massachusetts, provide rich documentation of the general's life. His published expressions are found most completely in the *Southern Workman*

(1872–1892), especially the editorials. *Samuel Chapman Armstrong: A Biography*, (1904), by his daughter, Edith Talbot, is the only full-length biography, but see also the study written to celebrate Hampton's fiftieth anniversary by the prominent social welfare educator and trustee of Hampton, Francis Greenwood Peabody, *Education for Life: The Story of Hampton Institute* (1919). Robert F. Engs, *Freedom's First Generation: Black Hampton, Virginia, 1861–1890* (1979), chap. 8, and Louis R. Harlan, *Booker T. Washington: The Making of a Black Leader, 1856–1901* (1972), chap. 3, offer careful assessments of Armstrong's work. James D. Anderson, "The Hampton Model of Normal School Industrial Education, 1868–1900," in *New Perspectives on Black Educational History*, ed. V. P. Franklin and J. D. Anderson (1978), 61–96, sees more to regret in Armstrong's contribution.

WILBERT H. AHERN

**Augustus, John** (?, 1784–June 21, 1859), shoemaker and pioneer probation officer, was born in Woburn, Massachusetts, some time in 1784. There is no record of his parents or their occupations. He moved to Lexington, Massachusetts, in 1805, however, and prospered there as a shoemaker. In 1819 he donated about nine acres of land for the establishment of Lexington Academy, but in 1827 he moved his shoe- and bootmaking business to Boston.

In 1841 he began his second career, that of a probation officer, by posting bail for a man accused of drunkenness. He began to do this regularly, at first accepting only men but within a year doing the same for women as well. Later he added youthful offenders to the list of those he aided. His method was to post bail for the offender and then to provide friendship and assistance for the person (finding a job and the like) between arraignment and trial. At the trial he would detail progress made toward rehabilitation and often win a favorable sentence from the judge. He was careful to take only those clients whom he believed had a chance of reforming, thus anticipating the investigative function of modern probation officers. In the period between the first court appearance and sentencing, Augustus provided the kind of assistance and supervision of offenders that also is central to the modern concept of probation.

In 1852 Augustus published *A Report of the Labors of John Augustus for the Last Ten Years* (1852), in which he described his methods and defended his approach. He also functioned as a general social worker of sorts, placing out homeless children and unfortunate young women. He was a critic of the criminal justice system and advocated something akin to the modern public defender. By 1858 he had "bailed out" 1,152 men and 794 women. He originally tried to continue his shoemaking business while engaged in his efforts to help those who had gone afoul of the law, but found that he had to devote full time to his probation activities, which he funded with his own money.

Augustus died in Boston in 1859.

The major primary source on Augustus is his own *A Report of the Labors of John Augustus for the Last Ten Years* (1852), reprinted in 1972 (under a slightly different title) with an introduction by Sheldon Glueck. Unfortunately, however, biographical details in this work are quite sketchy. Also see Augustus' *Letter Concerning the Labors of Mr. John Augustus* (1858) and a sensational journalistic treatment of Augustus by Ball Fenner, *Raising the Veil* (1856).

Major secondary sources include an obituary in the *Boston Herald* (June 22, 1859) and sketches in the *Dictionary of American Biography* (1928), the *National Cyclopoedia of American Biography* (1929), *Appleton's Cyclopedia of American Biography* (1887), and *Who Was Who* (1963). Also see Joseph M. Hawes, *Children in Urban Society* (1971), and Robert S. Mennel, *Thorns and Thistles* (1974).

JOSEPH M. HAWES

**Ayres, Philip Wheelock** (May 26, 1861–November 3, 1945), pioneer social work administrator and educator and forestry conservationist, was born in Winterset, Iowa, son of Elias Jeffrey Ayres, a horticulturist, and Sarah Ardelia (Wheelock) Ayres. When he was sixteen, he began teaching school to earn money for his college education, which occurred at Cornell University, from which he graduated in 1884 with a Ph.B. degree. In 1885 he entered graduate study at Johns Hopkins University, obtaining a Ph.D. in history and economics in 1888. He was a contemporary of Amos Warner,* who at that time was general agent of the Baltimore Charity Organization Society (COS) and with whom Ayres is said to have done field work as a friendly visitor. Ayres thus entered the charity organization movement, of which the Baltimore society was the intellectual pacesetter in the United States.

After two years at the Brooklyn Bureau of Charities, 1888–1890, Ayres became general secretary to the Cincinnati Associated Charities. The hard times associated with the Panic of 1893 and the depression that followed severely tested doctrinaire COS ideas about relief, and Ayres became a spokesman for carefully planned work relief projects which would maintain the conditions of life for poor victims of the collapsed economy. In 1896 he became secretary of the Bureau of Charities in Chicago. He also was chairman of a committee of COS leaders, including Mary Richmond,* to revise and refine the pioneering national statistical report forms for charity organization societies which had been developed ten years earlier under the leadership of Amos Warner. The committee's work was reported by Ayres in "The Study of the Causes of Distress," published in *Charities Review* for December, 1898.

In 1898 he became assistant secretary of the Charity Organization Society of New York. One of his major responsibilities was setting up and conducting the first organized training program for social workers in America—the Summer School in Philanthropic Work—established by the Society that year. Ayres, Mary Richmond, and others had conducted in-service training classes for the volunteer and paid workers of their agencies, but this was the first time that students, volunteers, and paid workers from a variety of organizations had been brought together for a formal (six-week) program of lectures, field visits, and field instruction. Ayres thus helped establish the pattern of combined academic classroom instruction and extensive practical instruction in the field that became the hallmark of social work education. From the start, the school aspired to provide graduate education for persons planning to enter the field, although agencies were permitted to send promising staff members who did not have college degrees.

From the start, too, there was a difference of opinion in the field over the relative weighting of the academic and the experiential, sometimes almost apprentice-like, parts of the program. Ayres leaned toward an agency-orientedemphasis on the field component, while his superior, Edward T. Devine,* general secretary of the New York COS, was an outspoken advocate of coordinate university affiliation. Perhaps this philosophical difference, when combined with health problems, was what led Ayres to resign as assistant secretary of the COS in 1900, although he continued as director of the Summer School until 1904, when a nine-month school program was initiated with Devine as director.

In 1900, one year after he married one of his students, Alice Stanley Taylor (with whom he would have two children), Ayres picked up his father's horticultural interests and returned to Cornell for a year's study of forestry. He then entered a long career with the Society for the Protection of New Hampshire Forests, from which he retired in 1936. His first tasks were to protect the forests of the White Mountains and the Dartmouth College Grant in extreme northern New Hampshire, which were being stripped, with resulting soil erosion. Under his direction, the Society succeeded in establishing a state forestry department, the White Mountain National Forest, and the Lost River Reservation. It also secured preservation of Crawford Notch and Franconia Notch, including the Old Man of the Mountains and the Flume. He received numerous awards for his forestry work, including an honorary doctorate from the University of New Hampshire in 1926.

Ayres died in Riverdale, New York, in 1945.

Information on Ayres' early family background and his employment record can be found in the Cornell University archives. There is very little written about him, however. Perhaps the best general account of his life, one marred, though, by some inaccurate dates, is his obituary in the *New York Times* (November 5, 1945). See also Ayres' own writings, most of which were published in the *Proceedings* of the National Conference of Charities and Correction, especially between the years 1895 and 1900. Also, for accounts of the COS Summer School in Philanthropy, and Ayres' role in it, see the *Charities Review* (May, 1898), and Elizabeth G. Meier, *A History of the New York School of Social Work* (1954).

RALPH E. PUMPHREY

# B

Baker, Sara Josephine (November 15, 1873–February 22, 1945), physician, public health administrator, and child health specialist, was born in Poughkeepsie, New York, to Orlando Daniel Mosher Baker, a successful lawyer, and Jenny (Brown) Baker, a member of the first class to enter Vassar College. Her maternal grandmother, Arvilla Danforth Brown, was a descendant of Samuel Danforth, one of the committee that voted the funds to found Harvard College. Her maternal grandfather, Merritt H. Brown, migrated to New York State from New England.

Josephine Baker enjoyed a comfortable middle-class life while growing up in Poughkeepsie, where she attended the Misses Thomas' School. When she was sixteen, both her brother and her father died, the latter of typhoid fever. When it was revealed that the family was in financial difficulty, she gave up plans to attend Vassar and decided instead to pursue a career in medicine, a decision made in spite of the objections of her mother and several friends. She found out that the New York Infirmary for Women and Children had a medical college and decided to apply for admittance. On learning that she needed a certificate from the New York Board of Regents, she determined to pursue a course of study that would enable her to pass the exam. Her determination paid off, and she passed the Regents' exam, graduated from the medical school in 1898, and became an intern at the New England Hospital for Women and Children in Boston. She had been used to spending summers with the family at her grandmother's home in Dansville, New York, and while working there at a local sanitarium she became acquainted with William Dean Howells and Louisa M. Alcott, who were there as "guests."

Her first year's earnings in New York City, after interning in Boston, totaled $185. Nevertheless, she perservered and then took an examination for a job as medical inspector in the New York City Department of Health. Her initial wages were $30 a month in that position, but in a short time she moved up to a job which paid $100 a month for checking on sick babies in "Hell's Kitchen" on New York's West Side. Working first as an assistant to a local physician, she later became assistant to the Commissioner of Health.

Shocked by the high infant mortality rate in the Hell's Kitchen area—as many as 1,500 infant deaths weekly during the hot summer months—she designed some unique programs to combat the problem. Her first effort was to send into the neighborhood a team of thirty nurses who concentrated on a preselected area, teaching breast feeding, ventilation, bathing, and the importance of proper clothing. Her area showed a significant drop in infant deaths, in contrast to the others, proving this approach to be at least one method of attacking the problem.

Her autobiography describes the problems encountered when she was detailed to track down the source of an outbreak of typhoid fever. The strongest suspect was one Mary Mallon, later known as "Typhoid Mary," who used several stratagems to avoid Dr. Baker, but who was finally taken into custody, examined, and found to be the cause of the outbreak. "Typhoid Mary" had to be incarcerated for community health reasons after she persisted in seeking out restaurant employment; she died in 1938 at Riverside Hospital on North Brother Island, where she had been a "prisoner" of the city since 1908.

A newly created Division of Child Hygiene—the first of its kind in America and one that would be emulated throughout the nation—was placed under Baker's jurisdiction from 1908 until she retired in 1923. As head of this new municipal agency, she pioneered in public health education. Child hygiene information was distributed by means of simply printed instructions. Midwives were registered, encouraged to attend classes, and licensed when they met the proper requirements. She also helped design a package that allowed midwives to put a drop of 1 percent silver nitrate in the infant's eye after birth to prevent gonorrheal infection. School tests for infectious diseases were implemented, and "Baby Health Stations" were set up to emphasize pure milk. Since there already were other organizations at work in the area, such as the Nathan Strauss milk stations and a diet kitchen supervised by Mrs. Henry Villard, Baker saw the need for coordinated effort. Thus the Children's Welfare Federation of New York City was formed as a clearing house for those organizations dealing with child welfare. She served as president of that organization and later was the chair of its executive committee.

Shocked at the high death rate of infants in the city's foundling hospitals, she worked hard to get those children placed out in foster homes; the result was a predictable downturn in mortality. She also designed some simple and lightweight infant clothing that was copied and distributed nationally. After reading John Spargo's *Bitter Cry of the Children*, she got the idea for the formation of Little Mothers' Leagues. Reasoning that children were going to be used as baby sitters in any case, her theory was that they should be given instructions on how to properly care for young children, including brothers and sisters.

Earlier (1910), she had been one of the founders of the American Association for the Study and Prevention of Infant Mortality. When she admitted to the mayor of Boston that they had trouble raising funds for the organization, he suggested a name change since no one was going to write such a long title on a check. Hence, the name was changed to the American Child Hygiene Association.

In 1923, when Herbert Hoover became president of the organization, the name again was changed, this time to the Child Health Organization of America.

Beginning in 1916, she lectured annually for fifteen years, both at Columbia University and at New York University-Bellevue Hospital Medical School. She accepted the lecture invitation from the latter institution on the condition that she be permitted to enroll in its new doctoral program in public health. In 1917 she was awarded a Doctor of Public Health degree from the Bellevue Hospital Medical College, the first one awarded to a woman, after writing a dissertation that dealt with children's repiratory diseases and classroom ventilation.

She promised herself that she would retire when all forty-eight states had a bureau of child hygiene, and when this happened in 1923 she stepped down from the New York City Health Department and pursued her lectures at Columbia and New York University and also served as a consultant to the U.S. Children's Bureau and the U.S. Public Health Service. The government would not allow her to go to France during World War I to work with refugee and homeless children, as she wished, but she was made Assistant Surgeon General and awarded the rank of major. Her comment was that it was six times safer to be a soldier in France than to be born a baby in the United States caused some public reaction.

Meanwhile, in 1914, she had read a paper before the Philadelphia College of Physicians, the first woman to do so. The Daughters of the American Revolution (DAR) put her on their blacklist, possibly because she belonged to Heterodoxy, a women's club in New York City that championed some unpopular causes. An original member of the College Women's Suffrage League, she marched and lectured to promote the cause. When President Wilson met a group of women at the White House in 1919 and gave his support to the suffrage cause, she was among them.

From 1922 to 1924 she represented the United States on the Health Committee of the League of Nations and also served as president of the American Medical Women's Association. Although encountering male prejudice, both on and off the job, she continued as a dedicated professional in her field. In 1929 the Congress of Women of the World's Fair bestowed on her recognition for her achievements in the field of public health, naming her one of the outstanding fifty women in the country. The General Federation of Women's Clubs made use of her talents, and she was invited to speak in Europe in her field of expertise.

She adopted a no-nonsense approach to most of the problems she faced. In fact, she confessed that she preferred to work with Tammany politicians rather than with reformers because the latter usually did too much talking and too little acting. Clearly, the New York City infant mortality rate—and the rate elsewhere in America as well—was lowered significantly due to her efforts.

Her final years were spent at her home, Trevenna Farm, in Bellemead, New Jersey. She died of cancer in New York Hospital on February 22, 1945.

Baker was the author of *Healthy Mothers, Healthy Babies,* and *Healthy Children,* all in 1920; *The Growing Child* (1923); and *Child Hygiene* (1925). Her autobiography, *Fighting for Life,* was published in 1939. She authored numerous articles in both popular periodicals and professional journals. An obituary is in the *Journal of the American Medical Association* (March 17, 1945). A good source of information is an article by Leona Baumgartner in *Notable American Women 1607–1950* (1971), 85–86.

                                                                        JAMES E. JOHNSON


**Balch, Emily Greene** (January 8, 1867–January 9, 1961), social worker, economist, and peace advocate, was born in Jamaica Plain, Massachusetts, daughter of Francis V. Balch, a distinguished Boston attorney, and Ellen Maria (Noyes) Balch. Both parents descended from early settlers in the Bay Colony, and she was, by birthright, a member of the Yankee, Unitarian Boston establishment with its traditions of social consciousness and public service.

Educated in private schools in Boston, especially the famous Miss Ireland's School, Balch attended Bryn Mawr College in Philadelphia, graduating in 1889 in the Quaker school's first commencement. She undertook further study in Paris, concentrating on economics and sociology. In 1892, at a summer institute sponsored by the Ethical Culture Society, she met Jane Addams,* and the founder of Chicago's Hull-House became her idol and role model for her subsequent career. Later in 1892 she helped to establish Denison House, a Boston settlement, and served briefly as the institution's head worker. This experience brought her into contact with militant organizers in the labor movement and deepened her interest in economics as a reform discipline.

Between 1892 and 1896 Balch studied economics at Radcliffe, the University of Chicago, and the University of Berlin, and at the latter institution she absorbed the reformist perspectives of her mentors, the historical economists Adolf Wagner and Gustav Schmoller. Returning to the United States, she accepted a position in economics at Wellesley College, a post which she held until 1918. At Wellesley she developed pioneering courses in economic history, immigration, and social pathology, courses in which she utilized field trips to introduce her students, the sheltered offspring of privileged families, to the realities of immigrant neighborhoods, sweatshops, and union halls. She described her interest in economics as practical and ethical, and, reflective of her concern with the practical, she served on a Massachusetts commission which, in 1913, drafted the first successful American minimum wage legislation.

In the years 1904–1906 Balch conducted an elaborate study of Slavic immigration, the result of which was a substantial and still useful volume, *Our Slavic Fellow Citizens* (1910). This book, her only scholarly work, was a sympathetic account of both the European backgrounds and American experiences of the disparate Slavic peoples, then little-known but often maligned components of the American population. In its preparation she spent a year of intense research in the Slavic areas in Europe, a year made noteworthy by the close friendship she established with the Czech humanitarian and patriot Thomas G. Masaryk. She concluded her research with a year of residence in settlement houses and immigrant homes in the United States. The product of her labors became an immigration classic.

Emily Balch's priorities and occupation underwent a drastic change in the context of World War I. She embraced the cause of peace and in 1915 served as an American delegate to an international conference of women opposed to the war which assembled in The Hague. The outgrowth of this meeting, formalized by a 1919 conference in Zurich, was the creation of the Women's International League for Peace and Freedom, commonly known as WIL. To this organization and to the cause of peace Balch devoted the remainder of her active life. In the United States she became an ardent opponent of Woodrow Wilson's preparedness program and of American belligerency, and she played a prominent role in such pacifist groups as the Woman's Peace Party, the People's Council of America, and the American Union Against Militarism. These activities provoked Wellesley College to terminate her position in 1918, effectively ending her academic career.

The turning point in Balch's life was the Zurich conference of 1919 and the formal creation of WIL. She became the organization's first international secretary-treasurer and editor of its official publication, *Pax et Libertas*, serving in these capacities from 1919 to 1922 and again in 1934–1935. Consistent with her convictions, in 1921 she affiliated with the Society of Friends. Throughout most of the 1920s and 1930s she led a peripatetic existence, traveling widely and organizing for WIL in the United States, North Africa, the Balkans, and the Middle East. But home, after 1925, was a small apartment in a house in Wellesley, Massachusetts, which she affectionately called *domichek*, or "little house." Her diverse activities in these decades included the organization of international summer schools and the periodic conferences of WIL, and efforts to apprise League of Nations officials of the women's position on international issues. Honors came to her in due course—president of the United States Section of WIL, honorary international president of the organization, and finally, at the age of seventy-nine, a share of the 1946 Nobel Peace Prize. Her writings were as varied as her activities, ranging from an official tract on the WIL, *A Venture in Internationalism* (1938), to a volume of poetry, *The Miracle of Living* (1941).

Emily Balch often remarked that her objective in life was to be useful. Not surprisingly, she eschewed philosophical consistency and devoted her energies to specific problems and concrete solutions. Always a shy, reticent person, her talents lay in organization and execution rather than in leadership. Her special genius was the preparation of proposals, position papers which, under the aegis of WIL, were pressed upon international leaders. The range of her proposals was astonishing and included, as early as the mid-1930s, the peaceful use of the world's airspace and waterways and the internationalization of the polar regions. Her admirers described her as a citizen of the world, and in the 1930s she began to espouse the concept of a planetary civilization.

Yet she was more than a citizen of the world. She was also Miss Balch, one of the prominent members of the remarkable first generation of American professional women, most of whom rejected marriage and traditional women's roles in favor of lifelong commitments to humanitarian causes. In addition, she possessed a measure of Yankee eclecticism. In the 1940s, at considerable risk to her reputation, she supported American involvement in World War II, though she devoted the war years to efforts to guarantee humane treatment for conscientious objectors and Japanese Americans. It is ironic that she received the Nobel Peace Prize in the aftermath of the only war to which she gave a grudging approval, but the prize itself was a fitting end to a long career. Increasing frailty forced her to establish residence in a Cambridge, Massachusetts, nursing home in 1956, and she died in that facility on January 9, 1961, a day after her ninety-fourth birthday.

Emily Balch accumulated voluminous material pertinent to her interests and activities. Hence the Emily Greene Balch Papers (1893–1948), domiciled in the Peace Collection, Friends Historical Library, Swarthmore College, comprise a substantial collection. The same repository contains the papers of the United States Section, Women's International League for Peace and Freedom (1915–       ) and of the American Union Against Militarism (1915–1922). The Women's Archives, Radcliffe College Library, house the records of Denison House (1892–1960).

Balch's writings are fundamental to an understanding of her life and work. The most important are *Our Slavic Fellow Citizens* (1910; repr. 1969); *Women at The Hague*, with Jane Addams and Alice Hamilton (1915); *Approaches to the Great Settlement* (1918); and *A Venture in Internationalism* (1938). Mercedes M. Randall edited an anthology of Balch's shorter writings, *Beyond Nationalism: The Social Thought of Emily Greene Balch* (1972).

Olga Opfell, *The Lady Laureates* (1978), contains a brief survey of Balch's contributions. Also useful is a pamphlet by John H. Randall, Jr., *Emily Greene Balch of New England, Citizen of the World* (1946). The only full treatment of Balch's career is Mercedes M. Randall, *Improper Bostonian: Emily Greene Balch* (1964), an elegantly written but eulogistic biography. An obituary and portrait appear in the *New York Times*, January 11, 1961.

                                                                    KAREL D. BICHA

**Baldwin, Roger Nash** (January 21, 1884–August 26, 1981), civil libertarian, social worker, teacher, and political organizer, was born in Wellesley, Massachusetts, to Frank Fenno Baldwin, a shoe manufacturer, and Lucy Cushing (Nash) Baldwin. Both parents were Mayflower descendants and Unitarians. Baldwin had three sisters and two brothers. His paternal grandfather was friend to such notables as Henry Wadsworth Longfellow, Henry David Thoreau, Oliver Wendell Holmes, Ralph Waldo Emerson, and Phillips Brooks, all of whom young Baldwin met. Another neighbor of his boyhood days was Bradford Torrey, the editor of Thoreau's journals.

The family home was the site of discussions about social problems, as well as an interracial and interethnic gathering place for young friends of Baldwin's public school days. Thus Baldwin was exposed to the great New England tradition which blended culture, individualism, and social reform.

Baldwin as a matter of course entered Harvard, where he acquired a B.A. in three years and an M.A. in anthropology a year later, in 1905. Deciding to leave Boston to secure independence from his large and influential family, Baldwin accepted an offer to inaugurate a course in sociology at Washington University in St. Louis and to head a settlement house in the city's tough Kerry Patch district. While continuing to teach, from 1906 to 1909, Baldwin in 1907 was appointed chief probation officer of the municipal juvenile court and subsequently was elected secretary of the National Probation Association.

Between 1910 and 1917 Baldwin served as executive secretary of the St. Louis Civic League, a private organization monitoring civic corruption. During this period, by his own account, he experienced his first concern for civil liberties when the police denied Margaret Sanger* the right to advocate birth control at a privately sponsored meeting. In 1909 Baldwin attended a lecture by the anarchist Emma Goldman, which stimulated him to read Tolstoy, Kropotkin, and others advocating individual freedom and mutual aid through cooperatives. His belief in the individual as opposed to state power was stimulated further.

When World War I began, opponents of America's involvement in the conflict formed the American Union Against Militarism. In 1917 Baldwin was invited to assume its directorship. Concerned about the mounting threat to civil liberties in wartime America, Baldwin established a subsidiary, the National Civil Liberties Bureau, which soon assumed independent status and to which Baldwin devoted full time. Under his determined leadership it became the foremost defender of wartime civil liberties. In 1920 this organization became the American Civil Liberties Union (ACLU), which Baldwin headed until 1950. In 1918 Baldwin served nine months of a one-year sentence for refusing to register for military service.

Following his release, Baldwin married Madeline Z. Doty, a lawyer, feminist, and prison reformer. The marriage ended on friendly terms after fifteen childless years. In 1936 Baldwin married Evelyn Preston, also a feminist and a union organizer. A daughter of this union predeceased Baldwin, as did both his wives.

Following Baldwin's release from prison, he joined the Industrial Workers of the World (''Wobblies'') and for four months toured the West as an itinerant laborer. After this ''proletarian experiment'' he returned to the ACLU. Now that the war was over and pacifism was a moot issue, a broader organization was needed to defend the rights of labor organizers, radicals, aliens, novelists, and other unpopular minorities. Many of the pacifists dropped out, to be replaced by a membership ranging from the chairman of the Communist Party to a Harvard law professor, later a Supreme Court justice.

In its early years the ACLU defended many free-speech and assembly cases of labor or left-wing origin. The Union helped abolish the notorious Pennsylvania Coal and Iron Police; participated in the Sacco-Vanzetti case; was instrumental in lifting the barriers to James Joyce's *Ulysses*; achieved free press rights for

Jehovah's Witnesses (a religious sect) and the right of their children to not salute the American flag; and defended free speech for Henry Ford, the Ku Klux Klan, the German-American Bund, and members of the San Francisco Chamber of Commerce.

The Union's most celebrated and publicized case was the 1925 "Monkey Trial" in Dayton, Tennessee. The Union advertised that it would defend any teacher who would test the state's ban on teaching Darwin's theory of evolution. Clarence Darrow represented the Union. The case, of course, was lost, but the cause was won.

Up to the time of the New Deal and the subsequent development of strong labor organizations, one of the ACLU's main efforts involved the defense of labor's rights. Baldwin fought antilabor court injunctions, contested local authorities' denial of peacable assembly rights, raised bail for strike leaders, and obtained lawyers to defend them on a variety of charges. During the 1924 silk-workers strike in Paterson, New Jersey, Baldwin was arrested and given a six-month sentence for unlawful assembly. The subsequent reversal of the conviction invalidated a repressive statute dating from 1796.

During the 1920s and 1930s, though belonging to no political party, Baldwin was active in the American left through participation in "united front" committees. He believed that the Soviet system would provide an economic justice for workers lacking under capitalism. His growing disillusionment with the Soviets climaxed with the 1940 Nazi-Soviet nonaggression pact. The ACLU adopted Baldwin's proposal barring from its board or staff anyone espousing a totalitarian doctrine. One unanticipated consequence was the pattern it set for government loyalty oaths in the 1950s, which the ACLU fought in court.

At the onset of World War II the Union unsuccessfully protested the relocation without hearings of some 115,000 Japanese Americans, most of them U.S.-born citizens. Baldwin deemed this the worst single violation of civil rights in U.S. history. It also was a low point for the ACLU, as suppression of the Bill of Rights came not from mobs or local jurisdictions but from the federal government itself.

In 1947, at General Douglas MacArthur's invitation, Baldwin visited Japan to evaluate civil liberities under the American occupation. His recommendations led to the establishment of a Japanese Civil Liberties Union in 1948. That year he performed the same function in the American zone of occupied Germany, but without similar results. In 1950 Baldwin retired fron the ACLU. The civil liberties movement, launched as an activity practiced part-time by lawyers, social workers, educators, and clergymen, had, under Baldwin's thirty-year leadership, matured into a full-time professional enterprise of national scope.

Following retirement Baldwin assumed the new post of chairman of the ACLU National Advisory Committee (1950–1955). At sixty-nine he chaired the International League for the Rights of Man, which coordinated civil liberties groups in eighteen countries and, through the United Nations, secured passage of an International Bill of Rights. Baldwin also served twenty-five years on the governing committee of the National Urban League. In later years he lectured at the New School of Social Research and for several years taught civil liberties law at the University of Puerto Rico. At eighty-four he undertook a canoe trip on the Missouri River, reflecting his lifelong interest in nature. His twenty-year membership in the Audubon Society included service as a vice president. He was an acknowledged expert on bird identification as well as a superb cook. He reversed Thoreau, who had made nature his vocation and civil liberties his hobby.

For Baldwin people had rights as human beings rather than as members of any political, racial, or religious group. For him civil liberties were indivisible, however inconvenient to the majority or the socially powerful their realization might be. He died in Ridgewood, New Jersey, in his ninety-eighth year.

The American Civil Liberties Union, 132 W. 43 St., New York, New York 10036, has available copies of its annual reports and of three pieces by Baldwin: "Biographical Notes on Roger N. Baldwin as of June 1969"; "The Roger Baldwin Story, a Prejudiced Account by Himself" (June, 1969); "Memorandum on the Origins of the ACLU" (November 8, 1973).

Baldwin also wrote *Human Rights, World Declaration and American Practice*, Public Affairs Pamphlet No. 167 (1950, and, with Clarence B. Randall, *Civil Liberties and Industrial Conflict* (1938). Bernard Flexner and Baldwin wrote *Juvenile Courts and Probation* (1914). Baldwin also edited *Kropotkin's Revolutionary Pamphlets* (1927) and *A New Slavery; Forced Labor: The Communist Betrayal of Human Rights* (1953).

Studies of Baldwin and his work include Dwight MacDonald's two-part series in the *New Yorker*, "Profiles: The Defense of Everybody" (July 11–18, 1953), and Peggy Lamson's biography, *Roger Baldwin* (1976). The *New York Times* published a lengthy obituary on August 27, 1981.

ARTHUR K. BERLINER

**Ballard, Russell Ward** (November 25, 1893–June 4, 1980), teacher, social worker, superintendent of the Illinois State Training School for Delinquent Boys, and director of Hull-House, was born in the rural village of Donnellson, Illinois, to Mary S. (Lee) Ballard, the daughter of a prosperous farmer, and Elbert Suveyor Ballard, the son of a poor farmer who also was unsuccessful, first at farming and then at selling insurance. In an effort to make a living, the senior Ballard moved his family to the Oklahoma Territory in 1906. Until his death twelve years later, Ballard's father traveled constantly, returning home only for periodic visits. Ballard was the youngest of four children. His only sister, who was next in age, was eight years older. Thus Ballard's mother became the primary influence in his formative years, and from her he developed a sense of tolerance and a devotion to Methodism, but this was not sufficient to offset the feelings of insecurity engendered both by poverty, with its dearth of cultural amenities, and the awareness of his parents' incompatibility.

Self-supporting from the age of twelve, Ballard worked at odd jobs usually obtained through influential friends. He entered Oklahoma Methodist University in 1911. While attending college, Ballard tried to aid his alcoholic brother and thus could not be a full-time student. In 1915 he was appointed deputy revenue collector in Oklahoma City. Inspired by William Jennings Bryan, during 1916 he studied public speaking at OMU and began lecturing to educational and prison groups. Through volunteering in a private agency, he also became aware of organized social work. When the United States entered World War I, he enlisted for army officer's training, eventually becoming a captain in the infantry. Ballard credited his wartime experience for a reassessment of values which resulted in his youthful desire for position and place giving way to a determination to be of service to the disadvantaged.

Discharged from the army and still undecided about a career, in 1920 Ballard attended the National Conference of Social Work in New Orleans, where he learned that there was opportunity for a man in the field. Graham Taylor,* of Chicago Commons, told Ballard of the new school of social work beginning at the University of Chicago in the autumn. Thus, on borrowed money supplemented by part-time work, Ballard became a member of the first class of the University of Chicago School of Social Service Administration, where he developed a close relationship with his teachers, especially Edith Abbott* and Sophonisba Breckinridge.* On September 1, 1921, he married Ethel Horn, whom he had met at OMU in 1911. The union produced two children, John Horn and William Lee Ballard. After his marriage Ballard took a job as a physical education instructor at the Riley School in Indiana Harbor, Indiana, commuting from there to the University of Chicago, where he received his Ph.D. degree in 1922.

Riley was a poor school with twenty-seven nationalities represented in the student body. Ballard taught the children to appreciate their cultural heritage, and, as a result, was placed in charge of immigrant education for the entire school system, as well as being made supervisor for visual education. He also was offered the newly created position of director of community recreation, which he used to develop community consciousness through holiday observances and special events. Ballard became the principal of Riley School in 1925 and proceeded to make it a child-centered institution. Bringing his interest in social work to the educational field, Ballard introduced a child guidance service to treat delinquency. He remained at Riley for eleven years, attending the Graduate School of Education at the University of Chicago for ten summers to qualify for a principal's license. He also ran evening classes for adults in the Division of Immigrant Education in East Chicago, Indiana. With his facility for public speaking, he became a well-known figure in the area and in public welfare circles.

Ballard accepted the appointment as director of the newly created Lake County Department of Public Welfare in 1936. As director he invited staff participation and delegated authority, thus encouraging a democratic type of administration. He desegregated the department, inaugurated a merit system with standards defined by training and experience, required applicants for social work positions to take examinations, and encouraged older employees to avail themselves of opportunities for professional study.

University of Chicago contacts urged Ballard to apply for the superintendency of the Illinois State Training School in 1941. The school, located at St. Charles, was a home for delinquent boys ranging in age from nine to twenty who were committed there in lieu of the penitentiary because of their age. Long criticized by the newspapers for incompetence of staff, harsh treatment of inmates, and inadequate security, the institution was to be reorganized and its administration freed from political influence. Ballard was intrigued by the challenge. Six weeks after he arrived at St. Charles, the United States entered World War II. Many of his efforts at improvement were stymied when good employees were lured away by the higher salaries paid by war industries, and older personnel, unsympathetic to his new approach, sabotaged some of his programs. Nevertheless, Ballard, who believed the school should be a treatment center to rehabilitate inmates rather than just hide them away, created a more open institution by establishing democratic practices such as desegregation, serving the boys the same quality food as the staff, and abolishing corporal punishment, silence at meals, and verbal abuse by employees.

In the summer of 1943 Ballard was approached, again through a University of Chicago connection, to consider becoming director of Hull-House. He accepted the position after being assured that the reforms he had instituted at St. Charles would be continued. Ballard arrived at a practically moribund Hull-House, almost devoid of programs, suffering from budgetary problems and the difficulty of finding professional staff during wartime. Jane Addams* had died eight years earlier, and Ballard's immediate predecessor, Charlotte Carr,* had left because of a rift with the trustees. Louise deKoven Bowen,* the financial angel of the institution and president of the board, did not initially want a man to occupy Jane Addams' position, although she reluctantly accepted Ballard and came to respect him. Within a year the aging Bowen stepped down and Ballard succeeded in establishing his authority.

In his nearly twenty-year tenure, Ballard restored the reputation of the settlement, making it once again a vital force in the community, a showplace of democracy, and a center for ethnic groups and new arrivals adjusting to life in Chicago. He sought Afro-American and Mexican American social workers to better reach those populations. With the welfare of children and youth as his major objective, he introduced new activities and programs and selected capable, professional staff, delegated responsibilty, and rewarded achievement.

In part because of his belief that delinquency was a product of poor housing, Hull-House became a catalyst for neighborhood renewal. A group of young men came to Ballard, in 1947, to enlist the aid of the settlement in organizing a community effort to improve the Harrison-Halsted area. Supported by Hull-House funds and residents, the Near West Side Planning Board was established and people were encouraged to develop their own plan for the area. Despite friction between ethnic groups and interference from ward politicians, over a thirteen-year period the grass-roots organization succeeded in some land clearance and planned to construct individual houses. Both the Planning Board and the Hull-House trustees, who were projecting a capital funds campaign for extensive rehabilitation, were caught by surprise when in 1960 the Land Clearance Area, the settlement, and some adjacent property were offered by Mayor Daley as a possible site for a branch of the University of Illinois in Chicago. Communication between area residents, trustees, and city decision-makers quickly broke down.

Although he recognized that it was futile, in an effort to keep faith with the neighbors who looked to Hull-House for leadership, Ballard appeared before the City Council Committee on Housing and Planning to protest the change in land usage as a betrayal of the people. The Committee voted without discussion to approve the site for the university, a move that Ballard thought reflected orders from the mayor. Ballard remained a year beyond his planned retirement to demonstrate his support of area residents in their effort to prevent the city from breaking its promise to rehabilitate the neighborhood. The battle eventually was lost after two years in the courts. Jane Addams' old home would be preserved and the university's School of Social Work would be built around it, but the Hull-House settlement would have to relocate.

Ballard resigned as director of Hull-House on January 31, 1962, at age sixty-eight, whereupon he became a part-time teacher at Roosevelt University, a consultant to Midway Technical Institute in Chicago, and the recipient of many awards. He died at age eighty-seven in Maywood, Illinois.

Russell Ward Ballard's papers, including drafts of speeches, copies of published articles, and an unedited transcript of his autobiographical memoirs, are deposited in the Manuscript Collection of the University of Illinois at Chicago.

His published writings include "Social Work: City Streets," *Public Welfare in Indiana* (November, 1940), 13; "State Training School, Local Services for Children Planned as Part of Delinquency Prevention Program with Extension to Every County," *Welfare Bulletin* (April, 1942), 8–10; "Juvenile Delinquency—Prevention and Treatment," *Bulletin of Illinois Congress of Parents and Teachers* (October, 1942), 14–15.

The best secondary source on Ballard is Allen F. Davis and Mary Lynn McCree, eds., *Eighty Years at Hull House* (1969), which discusses his tenure at Hull-House and reprints one of his articles, "An Evening at Hull House," and his testimony before the Committee on Housing and Planning of the Chicago City Council, April 12, 1961. His obituary appears in the *Chicago Tribune*, June 5, 1980.

PAULA F. PFEFFER

**Bane, Frank** (April 7, 1893–January 3, 1983), leader in public welfare administration during its period of expansion and elaboration from 1920 to 1960, was born in Smithfield, Virginia, to Carrie Howard (Buckner) and Charles Lee Bane, a farm boy from West Virginia who kept country schools and later joined the Methodist ministry, for which he prepared at Randolph-Macon College. While Frank's boyhood is obscure, he too attended Randolph-Macon, graduating in 1914. Tall, athletic, amiable, and an outstanding student, he then became principal of Nansemond High School and in 1916, at age twenty-three, superintendent of schools in that rural Virginia county. He wanted to be a lawyer and took classes at Columbia University while he was teaching. There he impressed professors George Kirchwey and Edward T. Devine,* well-known authorities on welfare administration. After World War I, in which he was a pilot trainee, the Virginia State Board of Charities was expanding its activities, and an influential Board member, a vice president of Randolph-Macon, thought that Bane's association with experts at Columbia qualified him to become the Board's secretary; he thus was offered the job, beginning a long and distinguished career in public welfare.

The principal influence on his early career was Louis Brownlow, an acquaintance in Virginia and a leading practitioner of "pubic administration" who had moved to Knoxville, Tennessee. In 1923 Brownlow brought Bane to Knoxville to take charge of welfare services in a major reorganization of municipal government; there, Bane learned from his mentor that government is a service, and that although elected officials properly lay down policy, administration is properly the business of experts, and citizens get what they pay for. These notions had deep roots in the battle against the spoils system and for a career civil service; they were enthusiasms of the businessman-turned-progressive and were a guide for Governor Harry F. Byrd's reorganization of Virginia's state government (1926–1927), which brought Bane back to that state.

From 1926 to 1932 Bane served as the first executive of the Virginia State Department of Social Welfare in Byrd's reorganized state government, which gained national attention. During these years he also was prominent in the National Conference of Social Work, and in 1931 he helped form the American Public Welfare Association, which called him to be its first executive (1932). He served on President Hoover's Emergency Committee for Employment (1930) and the President's Organization on Unemployment Relief (1931–1932). The Social Security Board, appointed to implement the Social Security Act of 1935, chose him as its executive, and he thus oversaw the founding of the Social Security Administration. In 1938 he resigned to become director of the Council of State Governments at a time when it merged, in effect, with the National Governors' Conference, and until his retirement in 1958 he stood at the center of the transformation of state governments in the era of "cooperative federalism," when directives and grants-in-aid from Washington helped states cope with the exuberant growth of the affluent society—and, incidentally, its complex problems of welfare administration. Meanwhile, he had occasional ties with the academic world, as professor of sociology at the University of Virginia (1926–1928); consultant to the Brookings Institution in many influential surveys of administration (1931–1935); lecturer at the University of Chicago School of Social Service

Administration for many years; and Regent's Professor at the University of California, Berkeley (1965).

Bane had no special academic preparation for administration; he learned about the services on the job by conscientiously visiting and consulting people who ran successful agencies. As executive of the American Public Welfare Association and the Council of State Governments, he built well on the range and quality of these personal acquaintances. He was famous for tact, humor, and appreciation of both technical and political issues, and for his genuine respect for the people who presented them. As the executive of the Social Security Administration, his work was largely outside the office, with federal and state officials. (When he resigned, he assured anxious observers that he was not forced out by politics; he was getting better pay for a very challenging job.) Preparation, experience, or teaching did not lead him to theorize about social welfare services or public administration beyond commenting on obvious trends in government—it was getting bigger and more involved in expert service, state officials were playing larger roles, and so forth.

Bane's career suggests that the relation between "social administration"(a specialty of professional social work) and "public administration" was likely to be tenuous; he clearly found his inspiration and identification in the latter. He began by inspecting prisons and orphanages and ended by worrying about intergovernmental relations and qualified personnel in the whole range of state services.

Bane died in the Washington House Retirement Home, Alexandria, Virginia, on January 3, 1983.

Bane's publications were by-products of his official interests and duties. Two articles at the time of his retirement, in *State Government* (April, 1958), 4–8, 184–189, summarize his testament, and there is much personal information in an oral history, "Public Administration and Public Welfare" (typed transcript of tape-recorded interviews conducted by James Leiby in 1965 for the Regional Oral History Office, Bancroft Library, University of California, Berkeley). Two books by Arthur Wilson James present information about circumstances and developments during Bane's years in Virginia: *Virginia's Social Awakening* (1940), with a preface by Bane; and *The State Becomes a Social Worker: An Administrative Interpretation* (1942). Louis Brownlow's ideas and influence appear in his autobiography, especially volume 2, *A Passion for Anonymity* (1958). Bane's work for the Social Security Administration is recounted in *Launching Social Security: A Capture and Record Account*, by Charles McKinley and Robert W. Frase (1970). Bane's comments about his resignation in 1938 appear in *Survey* (November, 1938), 344.

JAMES LEIBY

**Barnard, Kate** (May 23, 1875?–February 23, 1930), political and labor organizer, state welfare administrator, and social reformer, was born in Geneva, Nebraska, to John P. and Rachel (Shell) Barnard. Her father was a lawyer and civil engineer who is reputed to have been the primary influence behind Kate's political and social philosophy, especially since her mother died when she was eighteen months old. Kate and her father lived in Nebraska, Kansas, and finally Oklahoma, where her father purchased a 160–acre farm outside Oklahoma City when she was twelve years old. She first attended a public school and then finished her education at St. Joseph's Academy, a Catholic secondary school. Her first job was as a teacher in an Oklahoma City public school, but she was drawn to the plight of the immigrant poor and quickly became involved in improving the quality of their lives.

Barnard resurrected the moribund United Provident Association and very quickly became recognized as an activist in getting citizens to volunteer their goods and services to help the poor. At one point she organized a clothing drive that generated over 10,000 garments that were distributed to the poor immigrants who were flooding the new state. With the help of the publisher of the *Daily Oklahoman* newspaper, she became the matron of the United Provident Association and was encouraged to broaden her social work efforts.

Guided by her philosophy that the elimination of poverty and suffering could come only from the unionization of labor, higher wages, and the consumption and use of union-made products, Barnard busied herself in the early 1900s with organizing activities. She formed the Women's International Union Label League in 1905, which served as an educational group urging people to buy union products. She also founded the Federal Union of unskilled laborers in 1907 and formed a partnership with the Territorial Federation of Labor. All of this activity occurred prior to Oklahoma statehood in 1907 and clearly illustrated her skills as a political organizer and her commitment as a staunch supporter of the downtrodden. She gained recognition by the poor and working classes as a fighter for their welfare, and they encouraged and supported her political efforts on their behalf.

Although slender, petite, and graceful in appearance, with pretty dark hair and flashing eyes, Barnard was a dynamo of energy and had an eloquent rapid-fire method of articulating the issues and verbally painting the horrible conditions of the poor. Her ability to convince audiences of the need for reform, coupled with her extensive skills at organizing political and labor groups, made her a favorite and trusted leader of the poor farmers and labor union men. Because of this skill and her political constituency, she was a powerful leader of these groups at the first constitutional convention, where she controlled a majority of the delegates. She was instrumental in the drafting of the progressive resolutions that became part of the state's constitution, earning Oklahoma the early reputation of having the most radical constitution in the nation. Her efforts resulted in the successful inclusion of child labor protections, compulsory education, prisoners' rights, and other welfare items in the constitution and earned her a national reputation as an effective leader in social welfare reform.

After she was elected as Oklahoma's first Commissioner of Charities and Corrections in 1907 (a constitutional office created for her), collecting more votes than any other official, including the Governor, and becoming the first woman in the nation to be elected by the people to a state office, she became a regular speaker at regional and national conferences dealing with charities and corrections and other social welfare issues. She contacted and secured assistance from other national leaders, including Alexander Johnson* and Hastings H. Hart* because of her interest in protective legislation for children, Samuel J. Barrows* for prison reform matters, and Judge Benjamin Lindsey* for juvenile court reform. Her reform activities as Commissioner included an investigation of charges of brutality and corruption at the Kansas state penitentiary, where Oklahoma convicts were incarcerated on contract, and she almost single-handedly orchestrated that scandal into a successful prodding of the Oklahoma legislature to establish its own prison system. By 1909 she had won legislative support for a juvenile court. She won the gratitude of Indian orphans and the political ire of many legislators and lawyers throughout the state when she combined the power of her office and the authority of the child welfare laws to investigate illegalities in estate administration and successfully returned more than $2 million to the orphans.

Physcially exhausted and in ill health, Kate Barnard retired from her elected office and did not seek reelection in 1915. She accepted a position as a juvenile court case worker from her longtime friend Judge Ben Lindsey in Denver, Colorado. She became ill in 1922 and retired from her position. She died in Denver in 1930.

To date no collection of Kate Barnard's personal or professional papers has been located. The Julee A. Short Collection, Oklahoma Department of Libraries, Division of Archives and Records, includes primary and secondary historical materials that concentrate on Kate Barnard's life. Scholars should check Judge Ben Lindsey's collection housed in the Library of Congress. Because Barnard constantly sought assistance from national leaders of social welfare and social justice reform movements, the manuscript collections of these individuals may include correspondence from and to her. Much of her official activity in Oklahoma is detailed in the annual reports of the Commissioner of Charities and Corrections from 1908 to 1915. These reports are full of descriptions of social conditions, recommendations for lergislation, and position statements from Barnard on social issues.

Her writings were limited to personal correspondence to other reform leaders and a small number of articles by and about her in popular magazines such as the *Survey* from 1909 to 1912. There is a personal view of her life in *Good Housekeeping* (November, 1912) and a statement about working for the poor in the *Independent* (November, 1907). In addition, she was a regular speaker at national meetings of professional associations from 1907 to about 1912. She spoke often at the National Conferences of Charities and Correction.

In addition to descriptive articles in the *Survey*, there are a few scholarly treatments of Barnard's role in social reform. For an interesting but uncritical biography see Julia A. Short, *Kate Barnard: Liberated Woman*, Master's thesis,

1970, University of Oklahoma. Her active role on penal reform is clearly demonstrated in John A. Conley, *A History of the Oklahoma Penal System 1907–1967*, Ph.D. dissertation, Michigan State University, 1977, and "Revising Conceptions About the Origin of Prisons: The Importance of Economic Considerations," *Social Science Quarterly* (1981). See also Harvey R. Hougen, "Kate Barnard and the Kansas Penitentiary Scandal, 1908–09," *Journal of the West* (1978). See Keith L. Bryant's three articles: "Juvenile Court Movement: Oklahoma as a Case Study," *Social Science Quarterly* (1968), for her important role in establishing a juvenile court in the state; "Kate Barnard, Organized Labor, and Social Justice in Oklahoma During the Progressive Era," *Journal of Southern History* (1969); and "Labor in Politics: The Oklahoma State Federation of Labor During the Age of Reform," *Labor History* (1970), for her ability to organize and lead political groups to support social welfare reforms.

JOHN A. CONLEY

**Barnum, Gertrude** (September 29, 1866–June 17, 1948), social worker and labor reformer, was born in Chester, Illinois, the second daughter and second child of William Henry and Clara Letitia (Hyde) Barnum. Her father, a prominent attorney and federal judge, moved the family to Chicago, where Gertrude spent most of her childhood. In 1883 she planned to study both literature and languages at Evanston Township High School. Although there is no record of her graduation, in 1891 she continued her education by enrolling in an English course at the University of Wisconsin. She found her academic work unfulfilling, however, and chose to leave the university after only one year. Increasingly troubled by the upper-class life style of her parents when she returned home, Barnum refused to have a formal debut in Chicago society.

Like other young college-educated women at the turn of the century who decided to leave behind their traditional roles, Barnum channeled her energies into settlement work by joining Jane Addams'* Hull-House. She quickly proved her abilities for social reform, and from 1902 to 1903 she served as head organizer of Henry Booth House, another Chicago settlement. As a settlement worker, Barnum gained firsthand experience and exposure to the poor living conditions of working women and their families. At the same time, however, she became discouraged with the settlement's approach of ameliorating the economic problems confronted by the urban poor rather than offering real solutions. Barnum believed that settlement work avoided the fundamental issues of improving wages or shortening hours of unskilled female workers. Her growing disenchantment with settlement work prompted her to direct her reform activities toward the cause of the labor movement.

Early in 1904 Barnum helped establish both the Chicago and New York Women's Trade Union Leagues, which were local branches of a larger organization, the National Women's Trade Union League of America (NWTUL). Founded in 1903 by a small group of social reformers and settlement house residents, the NWTUL was significantly different from other progressive reform groups because of its strong commitment to trade unionism. Joining forces with women of the New York League, including Leonora O'Reilly,* Margaret Dreier Robins,* and Rose Schneiderman,* Barnum readily supported the early strategy of the WTUL, which concentrated on assisting female workers in forming their own unions. Since there were few women's trade unions at the beginning of the twentieth century, and because the established labor unions provided little support for organizing women wage earners, the WTUL represented a crucial advance for women in the labor movement. The League was also a distinctive progressive organization because it successfully mobilized the combined support of working women and their middle-class allies.

Barnum represented in many ways the typical League ally: she was single, well-educated, and financially independent. Like other middle-class women who became active members of the WTUL, she had gained most of her reform experience as an industrial investigator for the settlements. In 1905 Barnum played an important leadership role when she was appointed full-time executive secretary and the first national organizer for the WTUL. In this capacity, she supervised the strike activities of the female textile workers in Fall River, Massachusetts, laundry workers in Troy, New York, and corset workers in Aurora, Illinois. By 1906 Barnum was part of a core of capable organizers, strike leaders, speakers, and negotiators in the League.

Many of Barnum's reform efforts also revolved around educating both the female workers and the public at large about the necessity of trade unions. As a way to gain public support, Barnum often published accounts of strike activities which stressed the difficult working conditions confronted by most female factory workers. Trade journals which appealed to a readership of working women, like the *Ladies Garment Worker* and the *Weekly Bulletin of the Clothing Trades*, also regularly carried Barnum's short stories. In these stories Barnum featured heroic young women who learned the importance of economic autonomy, self-improvement, and the advantages of unions. Barnum's writings reflected the pervasive concern of most members of the WTUL that training women as unionists also required challenging traditional female roles. Barnum also supported the cause of woman suffrage, and in 1909, with Florence Kelley* and Leonora O'Reilly, she served as an executive board member of Harriet Stanton Blatch's Equality League of Self-Supporting Women. Throughout her career Barnum viewed the issues of suffrage and other equal rights for women as being inseparable from her activities as a labor reformer.

In 1913, two years after the disastrous Triangle Shirtwaist Company fire of 1911, Barnum was recruited as a special agent of the International Ladies' Garment Workers' Union. Hired to educate as well as to organize women workers, she successfully directed the strike activities of the New York wrapper and kimono workers and effectively organized the union of the children's dressmakers. Besides coordinating the labor union activities of the female garment workers, Barnum also gained significant outside support from non-unionist sources. Barnum adroitly staged a major publicity event by convincing Theodore Roosevelt and several newspaper reporters to meet the garment worker strikers, which effectively aroused public sympathy for the concerns of the workers.

In 1914 Barnum chose to leave her position as a union organizer and accepted an appointment as special agent for President Wilson's newly established United States Commission on Industrial Relations. She continued to work for the government when she received another position as the assistant director of the investigation service of the federal Department of Labor from 1918 to 1919. Barnum retired from her labor work in 1919 and died in 1948 in Los Angeles, California, at the age of eighty-one.

Personal and professional correspondence by Barnum can be found in the National Women's Trade Union League of America Papers, Library of Congress, and in the Leonora O'Reilly Papers at Radcliffe College.

Barnum contributed the following articles and stories to both popular and trade journals: "The Story of a Fall River Mill Girl," *Independent* (1905), 241–243; "Fall River Mill Girls in Domestic Service," *Charities* (1905), 550–551; "The Pittsburgh Convention and Women Unionists," *Charities and the Commons* (1906), 441–442; "Women Workers," *Weekly Bulletin of the Clothing Trades* (1906), 8; "A Story with a Moral," ibid. (1908), 6; "At the Shirtwaist Factory: A Story," *Ladies Garment Worker* (1910), 8; "The Modern Society Woman," ibid. (1911), 8; "Button, Button, Who's Got the Button?" *Survey*(1911), 253–255; "The Pig-Headed Girl," *Ladies Garment Worker* (1912), 26–27; "How Industrial Peace Has Been Brought About in the Clothing Trade," *Independent* (1912), 777–781; "Women in the American Labor Movement," *American Federationist* (1915), 731–733.

Information on Barnum's life and professional career can be found in the following sources: Hyman Berman, "Era of the Protocol: A Chapter in the History of the International Ladies' Garment Workers' Union, 1910–1916," Ph.D. dissertation, Columbia University, 1956; Melvin Dubofsky, "Barnum, Gertrude," *Notable American Women 1607–1950* (1971); Nancy Schrom Dye, "The Women's Trade Union League of New York, 1903–1920," Ph.D. dissertation, University of Wisconsin, 1974, and *As Equals and As Sisters: Feminism, the Labor Movement, and the Women's Trade Union League of New York* (1980); Alice Henry, *Women and the Labor Movement* (1923); *Hull-House Bulletin* (January, 1896–April-May, 1899); Louis Levine, *The Women's Garment Workers: A History of the International Ladies' Garment Union* (1924); and Robert A. Woods and Albert J. Kennedy, *Handbook of Settlements* (1911).

                                                                NANCY G. ISENBERG

**Barrett, Katherine (Kate) Waller** (January 24, 1857–February 23, 1925), protector of unmarried women with children, antiprostitution crusader, and advocate of improved women's health, was born in Falmouth, Virginia, to plantation owner Withers Waller and Ann Eliza (Stribbling) Waller. Kate Waller was educated at home and attended Arlington Institute for Girls in Alexandria for two years. She graduated from the Women's Medical College of Georgia in 1892, and in 1894 completed a postgraduate course in nursing at St. Thomas Hospital, London. She married Episcopal minister Robert Barrett on July 19, 1876, and they had six children.

Kate Waller Barrett began her activities in the social welfare field as part of her responsibilities as a minister's wife in Atlanta, Georgia. She was instrumental in the establishment of that city's first rescue home for former prostitutes, and during the project she became associated with the National Florence Crittenton Mission. The Mission, founded in 1883 by wealthy New York druggist and evangelist Charles Nelson Crittenton, was dedicated to providing homes for fallen women, and by 1906 included a chain of seventy-three homes located throughout the United States.

Following Robert Barrett's untimely death in 1896, Kate Waller Barrett devoted full time to Crittenton Mission work, first as the national superintendent and then, upon Crittenton's death in 1909, as the national president. Barrett's dedication, medical training, and organizational skills allowed her to lead the Mission to national prominence and influence in the conduct of institutions for dependent women and children, especially unmarried mothers and their offspring. Through her writings and personal visits, Barrett's philosophy provided the framework for Florence Crittenton development. In *Fourteen Years' Work with Erring Girls* (1903) and "Maternity Work—Motherhood a Means of Regeneration" (1904), Barrett outlined procedures for rescue work. She emphasized the importance of a home-like environment and often referred to the refining, elevating, and redeeming attributes of home life. In addition, Barrett stressed discipline and training that would prepare charges for employment and self-support, probably in domestic service or nursing. Kate Waller Barrett's most significant contribution to Crittenton policy was the requirement that mothers and children not be separated for at least six months. This represented a radical departure from traditional methods of dealing with illegitimate children, but Barrett was convinced that the rule improved infant health and prevented mothers from returning to lives of sin.

Through the National Florence Crittenton Mission Training School for Christian workers, national conventions begun in 1897, and the Florence Crittenton magazine, *Girls*, established in 1898, Kate Waller Barrett's views on the operation of institutions for women and children reached ever wider audiences. Barrett amazed other social welfare workers at the first White House Conference on Dependent Children in 1909 by advocating government inspection and licensing of institutions for children. She was convinced that public scrutiny would reveal the superiority of Crittenton methods.

Kate Waller Barrett and the National Florence Crittenton Mission were at the forefront of progressive efforts to end prostitution and the white slave trade. Barrett was an active campaigner on behalf of the Mann Act, and Florence Crittenton Homes provided shelter for Mann Act witnesses. Barrett was particularly concerned with immigrant women and their susceptibility to the white slave conspiracy. As a special agent of the U.S. Department of Labor, she investigated conditions for women passengers on ships and visited Europe to gather information on the plight of immigrant women at departure points. She was an outspoken critic of many U.S. deportation policies regarding these women. The antiprostitution crusade peaked during America's mobilization for World War I, and Barrett's cooperation with the Commission on Training Camp Activities led Florence Crittenton Homes near army bases to devote their efforts exclusively to war work.

One of Kate Waller Barrett's pet projects was Ivakota Farms, a 400–acre tract near Washington, D.C. The farm provided residential treatment for female juvenile delinquents and allowed Crittenton workers to send charges to a rural location away from the influences of city life. Black women, excluded from segregated Crittenton Homes in the South, became Ivakota residents. Women and children suffering from venereal disease were sent from local homes that did not have adequate facilities for treating them.

Kate Waller Barrett and other Crittenton workers were in the vanguard of efforts to obtain adequate health care for women, especially in the area of obstetrics and gynecology. In many locations Crittenton organizations established their own hospital facilities for use both by Crittenton inmates and women from the community. They employed women physicians whenever possible. Crittenton people believed that women physicians were more sympathetic to the plight of unmarried mothers than were their male counterparts. The workers also appreciated the difficulties many women doctors encountered in attempting to practice in public hospitals. Some Crittenton facilities refused to allow access to male physicians. The most up-to-date maternity care available, coupled with an environment that catered to women's needs and preferences, was an important characteristic of Florence Crittenton hospitals.

Her involvement with unmarried mothers led Kate Waller Barrett to deal with a variety of social problems. Aid to poor, homeless, and destitute women and children became a significant facet of Crittenton activities. This stemmed from the workers' belief that poverty threatened families because poor economic conditions led to the bad home environment that sometimes resulted in immorality and delinquency. Many poor and working-class families had a fragile nature about them. An emergency could easily upset the delicate balance and result in the family's disintegration. The absence of the mother due to illness or childbirth, temporary unemployment, domestic squabbles, and numerous other problems could place families in crisis situations. Crittenton activities attempted to avert these catastrophes through short-term aid, providing shelter and assisting in job location.

Local Crittenton groups established some of the earliest day nurseries. The nurseries enabled working mothers to obtain good quality day care at little or no cost. Crittenton Homes were early havens for women victims of abuse and desertion. Women who had no place to go were certain to find shelter and protection there. In some localities these cases accounted for more than half of the Crittenton work. Crittenton officials championed the rights of illegitimate children and provided legal assistance for women seeking to gain support from the fathers.

Kate Waller Barrett's numerous accomplishments made her a sought-after speaker, and by 1920 she was delivering over sixty major addresses a year. In addition to the Florence Crittenton presidency, she served as national president of the American Legion Auxiliary and of the National Federation of Women, and was active in the Needlework Guild of America, the National Prison Association, and the National Congress of Mothers. She died in Alexandria, Virginia.

Manuscript sources dealing with Kate Waller Barrett and the Florence Crittenton Mission are scattered. The most significant and accessible are Minneapolis: University of Minnesota, Social Welfare History Archives, the National Florence Crittenton Mission Papers; Washington, D.C.: Library of Congress, the Kate Waller Barrett Papers; Chicago: University of Illinois, Chicago Circle Campus Library, the Florence Crittenton Anchorage Collection; Detroit: Detroit Public Library, Burton Collection, Florence Crittenton Home E & M File; and Detroit: Wayne State University, Archives of Labor and Urban History, United Community Services Collection.

Several works by Florence Crittenton workers shed light on Barrett's career. These include Charlton Edholm, *Traffic in Girls and the Florence Crittenton Mission* (1893), and Otto Wilson, *Fifty Years' Work with Girls 1883–1933: A Story of the Florence Crittenton Homes* (1933). Aside from Barrett's works cited above, the most important source available is the National Florence Crittenton Mission magazine, *Girls*.

For a survey of Kate Weller Barrett's activities and the history of the National Florence Crittenton Mission, see Katherine G. Aiken, "The National Florence Crittenton Mission, 1883–1925: A Case Study in Progressive Reform," Ph.D. dissertation, Washington State University, 1980.

KATHERINE AIKEN

**Barrows, Isabel Hayes Chapin** (April 17, 1845–October 15, 1913), physician, journalist, and social reformer, was born in Irasburg, Vermont, the daughter of Henry and Anna (Gibb) Hayes, emigrants from Scotland. Her father was a physician and her mother was a school teacher. Isabel Hayes, a Unitarian, was educated at home and later in private schools. She graduated from Adams Academy in Derry, New Hampshire, in 1862. She was exposed early to the professions she would study in later years. During her childhood years, she spent time with her physician father on his visits to patients. At age nine, she used her sister's Webster's shorthand book to learn the alphabet.

On September 26, 1863, Isabel Hayes married William W. Chapin. In January 1864 they sailed to India to do missionary work, but ten months after beginning their work William Chapin died of diphtheria at the age of twenty-eight. Isabel

Hayes Chapin, a widow at nineteen, stayed on for six months teaching Hindu girls and studying medicine. She then decided to return home and study medicine in order to prepare for a career as a medical missionary.

Chapin went to Dansville, New York, to study at a sanatorium where her brother was acting superintendent. Under the supervision of Dr. James C. Jackson, she studied water cure treatment. While there, she met Samuel June Barrows,* who was there as a patient and as a stenographer to Dr. Jackson.

On June 28, 1867, Isabel Hayes Chapin and Samuel Barrows were married in New York. Isabel Barrows continued her medical studies and began seriously studying stenography, while Samuel Barrows found work on several newspapers. She helped him rewrite articles and even wrote some of his assignments. This marked the beginning of their joint writing efforts, which lasted the remainder of their lives together.

Isabel and Samuel Barrows moved to Washington, D.C., when, in October, 1867, William Seward, Secretary of State, offered Samuel Barrows a position as his private secretary. In the summer of 1868 Samuel Barrows became ill, and Isabel Barrows temporarily took his place as stenographer to the Secretary of State, thus becoming the first woman stenographer at the State Department. After a while Isabel Barrows returned to New York to continue her medical studies at the Woman's Medical College.

Their marriage was based on mutual understanding and individual satisfaction. In 1869 Samuel encouraged his wife to attend the University of Vienna for advanced medical studies. She and her friend Mary Stafford were the first women admitted to that institution. After a year of study there, Isabel Barrows returned to Washington, D.C., and established a practice in ophthalmology, foregoing a career as a medical missionary. She was in charge of the eye department at Freedman's Hospital and lectured at Howard University Medical College. Never idle for a moment, she also resumed her work as a stenographer and became the first woman stenographer for U.S. congressional commitees.

In 1873 her daughter, Mabel, was born. In 1885 she adopted her brother's son, William Burnet Barrows, whose mother had died in childbirth.

Versatile in her interests and accustomed to change in her life, Isabel Barrows took on the responsibilities of a minister's wife in Dorcester, Massachusetts, from 1876 to 1880. After her husband became the editor of the *Christian Register* in 1880, she became the newspaper's associate editor. This mutually agreed upon arrangement at the *Register* lasted for sixteen years. The editorial office became a frequent meeting place for reformers, including Zilpha D. Smith* and Alice Stone Blackwell.

Isabel Barrows' various interests got her involved in movements on behalf of the prisoner, the Indian, the Negro, international peace, and justice. She made trips abroad in the name of peace. For nearly twenty years (until 1904), she was the editor and official reporter of the National Conference of Charities and Correction. The Association of Superintendents of Institutions for the Feeble Minded also made use of her stenographic services. She was reporter and assistant secretary of the National Prison Association for over fifteen years, and secretary and editor for over seventeen years of the Lake Mohonk Conference on the Indian Question and the Lake Mohonk Conference on the Negro Question. She was a frequent attender of the New York State Conference of Charities and Correction, not merely as secretary or a reporter.

Thus, at the 1891 National Conference of Charities and Correction, Isabel Barrows was listed as a delegate representing the friendly visitors of the Associated Charities of Massachusetts. At the conference, she became involved in the discussion of institutional care of the feebleminded and described the excellent care feebleminded children were receiving in an Elwyn, Pennsylvania, school. At the 1892 conference she cited the importance of the trained friendly visitor. In 1894 she made a formal address on training the feebleminded in conjunction with an exhibit of work produced by institutionalized feebleminded persons. And so on.

At times Isabel and Samuel Barrows' humanitarian interests overlapped. In 1899, when Samuel Barrows was appointed corresponding secretary for the Prison Association of New York, the family moved to Manhattan. Isabel Barrows accompanied her husband on his frequent trips to inspect prisons in the United States and abroad. A member of the Women's Committee to Inspect Women's Institutions, she wrote about one of her and her husband's experiences in an article entitled "The Pacific Coast." Isabel Barrows also was contributing editor of the *Survey* and wrote frequent articles about crime and prisons.

A devoted humanitarian, Isabel Barrows opened both her heart and her home to others. Living for others was the philosophy that guided her activities in the various causes with which she was associated. She died at her daughter's home at Croton-on-Hudson, New York, on October 15, 1913.

Isabel Barrows was a prolific writer of articles and books on numerous subjects. Some of her views on the feebleminded and the prison systems can be found, respectively, in "Manual Training for the Feeble-Minded," *Proceedings of the National Conference of Charities and Correction* (1894), 179–187, and in "The Pacific Coast," *Charities and the Commons* (November, 1908), 305–307.

For her interests in international peace and justice, see "Alice Stone Blackwell (1857–1950): A Symposium," *Armenian Affairs* (Spring, 1950), 139–142; and Isabel Barrows' biography of her husband, *A Sunny Life* (1913), 238. *A Sunny Life* also offers insight to the interrelatedness of Isabel and Samuel Barrows' work as well as their personal relationship.

The most extensive information about her life is in Madeline B. Stern, *We the Women* (1974). Biographical information is also in *Christian Register* (November 13, 1913), 1098; *Howard University Medical Department: A Historical, Biographical and Statistical Souvenir* (1900), 117; *Revolution* (January 5, 1871), 3; and *Student Journal* (July, 1891), 15–16. She is also listed in *Who Was Who in America, 1897–1942*, vol. 1 (1943), and *Woman's Who's Who of America 1914–1915* (1916/1976). Two items in the *Survey* (November 1, 1913), 107,

140, marked her death, and a letter from a Russian penologist in the *Survey* (January 10, 1914), 453, illustrates the international influence she had in her lifetime.

MINDY R. WERTHEIMER

**Barrows, Samuel June** (May 26, 1845–April 21, 1909), Unitarian clergyman, editor, reformer, and United States Representative from Massachusetts, was born on the Lower East Side of New York City, one of five children born to Richard and June (Weekes) Barrows. His father, an employee in the printing-press establishment of his uncle, Richard Hoe, died when Samuel was three years old. The family was left poverty-striken, and young Barrows participated in the family shoe-blacking business until, at the age of nine, he joined the Hoe printing establishment as an errand boy. Although he had only three years of formal primary education, he was an indefatigable learner, attending—after his eleven hours of daily work—the company night school and, later, the newly created night school at Cooper Union. At age twelve he taught himself telegraphy and shorthand, and operated the first private telegraph line in New York. A professional stenographer by age eighteen, he joined the *New York Tribune* as a reporter in 1866. He was aided in his reporting work for the *Tribune* and the *World* by his fiancée, Isabel Hayes Chapin (Barrows*), who rewrote many of his stories and assumed some of his assignments. They were married on June 28, 1867, by Henry Ward Beecher. Very accomplished, Isabel C. Barrows was a medical student and missionary who found time to work closely with her husband throughout his career, accompanying him on numerous prison tours abroad and writing scholarly papers on the women's reformatory movement. They had a daughter, Mabel Hay, and adopted a son, William Burnet.

In 1868 Barrows accepted an invitation to become private secretary to William H. Seward, Secretary of State. At about this time he abandoned the Baptist Church for Unitarianism, a decision that was made with some professional sacrifice, including the loss of his position as recording secretary of the YMCA, an organization whose active members were limited to those belonging to some evangelical church. In the fall of 1871 he entered Harvard Divinity School. He supported himself during his student years as correspondent for the *Tribune*, going on distant expeditions to cover railroad surveys conducted in the West by Major-General D. S. Stanley and Indian wars with his close friend, General George A. Custer. He was ordained and installed as a Unitarian minister in Dorchester, Massachusetts, in 1876.

In 1880 Barrows became editor of the *Christian Register*. He held this position with the Unitarian periodical for sixteen years, during which time his interest in social welfare flowered. With his wife acting unofficially as assistant editor, he traveled widely. He covered the meetings of the National Prison Congress and the National Conference of Charities and Correction, and was an active member in the International Prison Congresses in Europe and the Society for International Law. He also belonged to the Academy of Political Science, for which he contributed publications. His editorship of the *Register* ended in 1896, when he accepted the Republican nomination for Congress and won a seat representing the Boston area. Serving only one term, he was a member of the Committee on Indian Affairs and was an advocate of international peace, serving as the first delegate from the United States to the International Arbitration Conference. He also was a strong opponent of the Spanish-American War. His greatest impact, however, was in the area of criminal justice reform. He was the nation's leading advocate of probation and the indeterminate sentence. He supported parole for federal prisoners and drafted a bill providing for a United States probation law applicable to minors. He was nominated for a second term but was defeated for reelection.

Continuing his interest in criminal justice reform, Barrows was instrumental in helping organize the Massachusetts Prison Association and in securing legislation for probation there. In 1899 he began his nearly decade-long tenure as corresponding secretary of the Prison Association of New York and in that capacity drafted New York's first probation law, passed in 1901. In addition to the extension and improvement of probation, other social reforms he championed included the abolition of the system of paying sheriffs by fees determined by the number of prisoners cared for; enlarging the scope and function of children's courts; the categorization of prisoners to provide special care for first offenders and the mentally incompetent; the provision of useful prison work with adequate compensation; jails for detention only; the application of the indeterminate sentence to both felons and misdemeanants, with a grading and marking system; unpartisan boards of parole, with medical and judicial representatives; the extensive use of probation for misdemeanants; the improvement of physical conditions in prisons as well as the recruitment of better guards; and parole for all prisoners, with record expungement for those with five years' success. By correspondence and travel he reached forty states and over twenty nations. From 1895 to 1904 he was Commissioner for the United States on the International Prison Commission, and the congressional reports that he edited and introduced as Commissioner rank among the more important works in American penological literature. Additionally, he was a member of the first New York State Probation Commission, 1905–1906, and was elected president of the International Prison Congress in 1905. In short, Barrows was one of the nation's great advocates of enlightened treatment for the criminal and delinquent. He was also a tireless promoter of the general social welfare, working on behalf of total abstinence, woman's suffrage, and Indian and Negro education. He was a friend of Booker T. Washington* and the Tuskegee Institute, and wrote on racial issues for the *Atlantic Monthly* and the *Christian Register*. He also participated in Russian famine relief and promoted international peace as the first American to join the Interparliamentary Union for Arbitration.

While extremely dedicated to his many activities, to his continued education, and to his writing and public speaking, Barrows was very amiable and found time to help personally many needy persons, including hundreds of probationers, and he opened his home to orphans of all races and creeds. His numerous public addresses were said to be energetic, forceful, and witty, and were informed by his insatiable curiosity for cross-cultural investigation. He was fluent in a dozen languages and studied Latin, Greek, history, art, and philosophy at Columbia, Leipzig, and the Sorbonne. In addition, he was an amateur organist and flautist, and a worker in metals. He died in New York City.

Barrows wrote five books, two of which were short theological works, *The Doom of the Majority of Mankind* (1891) and *A Baptist Meeting House* (1890). Another book, written jointly with Mrs. Barrows, was about life at their Lake Memphremagog camp, *The Shaybacks in Camp* (1887). His fourth monograph, *New Legislation as to Crimes, Misdemeanors, and Penalties*, was published in 1897. *The Isles and Shrines of Greece* (1898) was about his travels. He was editor of a half-dozen periodicals, and he wrote numerous magazine articles on peace, reform, religion, foreign travel, crime, and temperance. Most of his religious writings appear in the *Christian Register*, and his detailed reports on the scores of prison regimes examined during his travels to fourteen nations appear in the various annual reports to the legislature for the Prison Association of New York, especially those for the years 1902–1907. Perhaps most valuable were the reports he prepared for the International Prison Commission, including "The Criminal Insane in the United States and in Foreign Countries," *Senate Document No. 273*, 55 Cong., 2 Sess.; "The Reformatory System in the United States," *House Document No. 459*, 56 Cong., 1 Sess.; "Prison Systems of the United States," *House Document No. 566*, 56 Cong., 1 Sess.; and "Children's Courts in the United States: Their Origin, Development, and Results," *House Document No. 701*, 58 Cong., 2 Sess.

The principal source is *A Sunny Life* (1913), a biography written by his wife, Isabel C. Barrows. See also Guillaume Louis, *Dr. Samuel J. Barrows, Ancien Président de la Commission Pénitentiare Internationale* (1909); *Dictionary of American Biography* (1929); *Unitarian Year Book* (1909); *Biographical Congressional Dictionary* (1903); *Christian Register* (April 21, 29, May 6, 13, 20, 27, 1909); *Survey* (May 29, 1909); *New York Evening Post* (April 22, 1909).

ROBERT P. WEISS

**Barton, Clara (Clarissa Harlowe)** (December 21, 1821–June 13, 1912), founder of the American Red Cross, was born on a farm in North Oxford (between Worcester and Webster), Massachusetts. Her father, Stephen Barton, Jr., was a farmer and horse breeder. Her mother, Sarah (Stone) Barton, was a housewife.

Clara Barton was raised in a prosperous and influential family. Her father served as moderator of town meetings and was a selectman and member of the state legislature. Barton was the youngest of five children, and her parents and siblings provided much of her education and training. Her parents strongly influenced her to become a teacher. At age eighteen Clara Barton entered a career which would eventually span twenty years. Her only formal education beyond high school was at the Liberal Institute in Clinton, New York, which she attended in 1850 after a decade as a teacher.

Clara Barton never married. She said repeatedly that she felt more useful to the world outside of marriage. In 1854 she became a clerk in the Patent Office in Washington, D.C., one of the first women to receive such an appointment. Eventually she became confidential clerk to the Superitendent of Patents, a position she held until the outbreak of the Civil War in 1861.

Clara Barton's first service to the military came in 1861 when wounded soldiers were billeted in government buildings. She read to homesick soldiers and established a pantry of food and supplies to help them, a practice which she continued throughout the next few years. This early exposure to the effects of war on soldiers deepened her conviction that the greatest need lay in helping the wounded on the battlefield.

Although allowing volunteers, especially women, to attend soldiers on the battlefield was unheard of, Clara Barton was successful in her efforts to provide this assistance. In the four years that followed, she was present at most of the major battles of the Civil War: the battle of the Wilderness, Fredericksburg, the second battle of Bull Run, and Antietam. She fed and dressed the wounded, assisted surgeons in operations, and performed most of the services associated with the nursing profession. In June, 1864, she was appointed Superintendent of the Department of Nurses for the Army of the James, a position which placed her in charge of the hospitals for an entire army corps. By this time she had earned two sobriquets which were to remain with her for the rest of her life. She was alternately referred to as ''Angel of the Battlefield'' and as the ''Florence Nightingale of America.''

As the war drew to a close, Clara Barton devoted her efforts to locating thousands of missing Union soldiers. She convinced President Abraham Lincoln to take steps to locate or account for these soldiers and to place her in charge of this endeavor.

In 1866 she began to lecture on the Civil War. She continued this activity until a nervous breakdown forced her to stop. In 1869, on the advice of doctors, she went to Europe for a rest. There she met representatives of the International Red Cross and was asked to assist them at the outbreak of the Franco-Prussian War. She worked in Switzerland, Germany, and France during this period and established hospitals for the wounded. At the close of the war she received honors from several countries, including the Iron Cross from the Emperor and Empress of Germany. Unfortunately, the illness which brought her to Europe still affected her. She collapsed and for a period of time was almost blind. In 1873 she returned to the United States and spent the next three years in a sanitarium attempting to overcome the debilitating malady with which she was afflicted.

In 1878 Clara Barton began a public campaign to have the Red Cross recognized in this country. Four years later, on March 1, 1882, the American Red Cross (ARC) received presidential approval; by this time Barton had already been named president of the fledgling organization upon nomination by President Garfield. Unlike European Red Cross organizations, the ARC was organized to meet any great public need, not just war. In the years following, the Red Cross went into action in forest fires, floods, famines, tornados, earthquakes, hurricanes, typhoid epidemics, and the Spanish-American War. Barton never accepted pay for her services and personally oversaw most of the Red Cross activities in the twenty calamities which occurred between 1881 and 1904.

In the ensuing twenty years the growth of the Red Cross brought a variety of problems with which Clara Barton was not equipped to cope. After several years of internal turmoil in the organization, she resigned in 1904, severing all connection with the ARC. She spent the last few years of her life working to train citizens in the use of first aid, a goal which was later adopted by the Red Cross.

Clara Barton provided America with both a philosophy and means for delivering help to those in need. Her efforts to deliver medical services close to the battlefield presaged mobile army surgical hospitals and military medics. Her interest in the welfare of soldiers missing in action was similarly continued by others in subsequent years. In the American Red Cross she founded a voluntary disaster response organization which to this day provides major assistance in this area and many others. She believed that the help given by the ARC should not pauperize those receiving it, and she stressed self-reliance. During her life she probably received more honors than any other woman of the time. Her contemporaries and friends included Susan B. Anthony, Julia Ward Howe, Florence Nightingale, and Dorothea Dix.*

The character and temperament of Clara Barton can be seen as both strengths and limitations. That we have such a good reservoir of materials to judge her contributions is due to her habit of saving every scrap of paper and to her prodigious writing. At her death she left no fewer than thirty-seven diaries as well as a veritable trove of records, letters, and documentation regarding her life and the American Red Cross. Throughout her life she was given to self-accusation while at the same time being overly sensitive to criticism. She was modest and self-reliant in her relations with others. Her habit of relying on herself and her intense dislike of committees became part of her undoing in the years preceding her resignation from the ARC. She chose to act without consulting her board of directors and attempted to maintain a personal grip on affairs of the Red Cross as she had on her efforts during the Civil War. The needs of a modern organization overtook her ability to adjust, and she was unable to graciously retire. Her recalcitrance caused harm to the organization she had worked so hard to create, and it was only when she saw no other option that she elected to step aside.

In 1899 Clara Barton completed *The Red Cross*, a history of that organization. She died at her home in Glen Echo, Maryland, in her ninety-first year.

Clara Barton's papers, including correspondence, lecture notes, photographs, newspaper clippings, reports, and thirty-seven diaries, are available at the Library of Congress. Additional material on Barton is available in the library of the

National Headquarters of the American Red Cross in Washington, D.C. In addition, Barton authored *The Red Cross* (1899). See also William Barton, *The Life of Clara Barton*, vols. 1 and 2 (1969); Fairfax Downey, *Disaster Fighters* (1938); Ishbel Ross, *Angel of the Battlefield* (1956); and Martin Gumpert, *Dunant: The Story of the Red Cross* (1938).

                                                                                        GRAFTON HULL, JR.

**Bauer, Catherine Krouse** (May 11, 1905–November 22, 1964), housing expert, city planner, and social reformer, was born in Elizabeth, New Jersey, to Jacob Louis and Alberta Louise (Krouse) Bauer. She was the eldest of the couple's three children. Her father was a prominent highway engineer who, while in the employ of the state of New Jersey, is credited with the development of such innovations as the cloverleaf interchange. Bauer's early interest in design was influenced by her father's professional activities, while her later concern with conservation was stimulated by her mother's encouragement of outdoor activities. Bauer was temperamentally inclined to challenge authority and tradition, and as a consequence was often at odds with her mother's conservative middle-class values.

After attending the Vail-Deane School in Elizabeth, she enrolled in Vassar College, where she graduated in 1926 after having spent a year studying architecture at Cornell University. Upon graduation, Bauer became part of the expatriot generation, pursuing her architectural and literary interests in the bohemian artistic milieu of Paris. During this time she became interested in housing developments in Europe and wrote a series of articles on the topic.

Upon returning to America, she found a job at Harcourt Brace Publishers in their advertising department. In 1929 she met Lewis Mumford, who at the time had a book in press with the publishing house. Their mutual interest in architecture brought them together, and they were to become lovers and confidants. This relationship had a profound effect on Bauer, helping to transform her from an aesthete into a social reformer.

Under Mumford's tutelage she began her career as a reformer. In 1931 she assumed the position of executive director of an organization that Mumford had founded several years earlier, the Regional Planning Association of America. Others associated with the organization included Tracey Augur, Russell Black, Robert Bruere, Joseph Hart, and Edith Elmer Wood.* The Association was not a formal organization, being basically a loose circle of friends and acquaintances who shared similar views on the desirability of social planning. Mumford also encouraged Bauer to enter an essay competition sponsored by *Fortune* magazine. She submitted an article on contemporary housing trends in Germany and was awarded first prize.

During the early 1930s she published a number of articles on housing in both art publications and in such periodicals as the *New Republic*. This intellectual output culminated in the publication of *Modern Housing* (1934), an event that quickly led to her being acclaimed as a housing expert. This book signified a turn toward analyzing housing problems in sociopolitical context, and it led to a proposal for the establishment of a housing movement in the United States. Bauer argued that, in contrast to the European scene, America had not yet developed a genuine political movement. She was highly critical of what she perceived to be a cult of expertise which sought to portray the housing dilemma solely in technical and administrative terms. In contrast to this "disinterested" approach, Bauer called for the creation of a political coalition that would bring intellectuals, social workers, and religious leaders together with consumers and organized labor. She also argued against piecemeal incrementalism, contending that the time was ripe for bold actions. She advanced the development of new communities, urged that rental housing be removed from the dictates of market forces (being pegged instead to the consumer's ability to pay), and endorsed the view that decent housing ought to be seen as a fundamental right of citizens.

Bauer had a keen appreciation of the nature and scope of the opposition to housing reform posed by such groups as the National Association of Real Estate Boards, the National Association of Home Builders, and the American Savings and Loan League, who profited from a situation devoid of state intervention in housing markets. To challenge these political forces, she joined with others in 1934, under the auspices of the National Association of Housing Officials, to begin the process of formulating housing legislation. She also served as the executive director of the Labor Housing Conference, helping to establish American Federation of Labor (AFL) committees in seventy-five cities and speaking tirelessly on behalf of the public housing movement in general and the Wagner-Steagall bill in particular.

After its passage as the U.S. Housing Act of 1937 and the establishment of the United States Housing Authority to administer the public housing program, Bauer was appointed to the directorship of the agency's research office. Though a fervent advocate of applied social research, she did not find employment in the federal bureaucracy conducive to her temperament, and thus in 1940 she resigned to begin an academic career at the University of California, Berkeley.

While there she met a prominent local architect, William W. Wurster, and they were married on August 13, 1940. Three years later the couple moved to Cambridge, Massachusetts, where Wurster would serve as the dean of the School of Architecture and Planning at the Massachusetts Institute of Technology. Their only child, Sarah Louise, was born in 1945. During the decade spent on the East Coast, Bauer was actively involved in current debates concerning legislative proposals for an urban renewal program. She returned to the faculty at Berkeley in 1950, where she would remain until her death.

Bauer functioned during the last fourteen years of her life, in her roles as academician, consultant, and government advisor, as a sympathetic yet persistent critic of the very programs that she had helped to design. During this period she served as vice president of the National Housing Conference and as a member of the advisory committee of the Housing and Home Finance Agency's Division of Slum Clearance and Urban Redevelopment. She did not want to be, in her own words, a prophet "crying in the wilderness forever," and therefore sought to test her ideas in a constant dialogue with the planning profession.

In a widely discussed article on the "dreary deadlock" of public housing, Bauer suggested that the limbo-like state of the program was due only in part to the crippling tactics of the opposition. She contended that it was also necessary to recognize various internal weaknesses which were reflections of a movement produced by the crisis of the 1930s, but which in the relative prosperity of the postwar era had lost much of its earlier vigor. She criticized the Corbusier-inspired "technocratic mania" that produced high-density, high-rise housing projects which were isolated islands essentially unattached to the rest of the city. In addition, she was concerned about the welfare stigma that was attached to public housing. Nevertheless, she did not call for the abandonment of subsidized housing because she continued to believe that the private market was incapable of providing for the housing needs of low-income families.

In a similar vein, Bauer assessed urban renewal and regional planning initiatives. Highly skeptical of monolithic planning, she advocated the development of balanced residential areas which contained representative cross-sections of the population, and she did not want to see decisions concerning the revitalization of commercial districts left solely in the hands of the business community. She sought to chart a course for planners between the Scylla of technocratic homogenization and the Charybdis of romantic naturalism which she saw, for example, in the work of Jane Jacobs.

A number of themes recur in her work during these later years. First, Bauer voiced her concern that the Cold War diverted both public attention and needed resources from domestic to foreign policy. Secondly, she sought to assist the planning community in developing mechanisms for translating the choices they saw confronting the nation to the public in a clear and explicit fashion. Finally, during this time she linked the issue of race to the issue of planning, seeing well-designed legislative policies as the key to this American dilemma. Bauer's active involvement in the issues that consumed her professional life for over three decades continued until her untimely death, which resulted from a hiking accident on California's Mount Tamalpais.

The Bancroft Library at the University of California, Berkeley, houses Catherine Bauer's papers written between 1940 and 1964. For the pre-1940 period, the library at the Department of Housing and Urban Development in Washington, D.C., contains useful information on the legislative history of the U.S. Housing Act of 1937, and the State Historical Society of Wisconsin contains the records of the Labor Housing Coalition.

Important books written by Bauer include *Modern Housing* (1934), *Labor and the Housing Program* (1938), *A Citizen's Guide to Public Housing* (1940), and *Social Questions in Housing and Town Planning* (1952). Among her most influential articles on housing issues are "Now, at Last: Housing," *New Republic* (September 8, 1937); "Housing: Paper Plans, or a Worker's Movement," in

*America Can't Have Housing*, ed. Carol Aronovici (1934); and "The Dreary Deadlock of Public Housing," *Architectural Forum* (May, 1957). Articles of particular note devoted to urban redevelopment include "Cities in Flux," *American Scholar* (Winter, 1943–1944); "Social Questions in Housing and Community Planning," *Journal of Social Issues* (1950); "Redevelopment: A Misfit in the Fifties," in *The Future of Cities and Urban Development*, ed. Coleman Woodbury (1953); "Framework for an Urban Society," in *Goals for America*, ed. Stuart Chase (1940); and "The Form and Structure of the Future Urban Complex," in *Cities and Space: The Future Use of Urban Land*, ed. Lowdon Wingo (1963).

A treatment of Bauer's role in the passage of the Housing Act of 1937 is found in Mary Sue Cole's "Catherine Bauer and the Public Housing Movement: 1926–1937," Ph.D. dissertation, George Washington University, 1975. Bauer wrote a brief autobiographical piece in the November, 1944, issue of the *Journal of Housing* ("We Present Catherine Bauer in Her Own Words"). Lewis Mumford describes his relationship with Bauer in *My Works and Days: A Personal Chronicle* (1979). An obituary appeared in the *New York Times* on November 24, 1964.

PETER KIVISTO

**Beers, Clifford Whittingham** (March 30, 1876–July 9, 1943), mental patient, author of a famous autobiography describing his hospital experiences, and founder of the modern mental health movement, was born in New Haven, Connecticut, the fifth of six living sons of Robert Anthony Beers and Ida (Cook) Beers. His father, originally of New York State, was in the produce business; his mother was a native of Savannah, Georgia. As far as Clifford Beers knew, his was the first generation of his family to experience mental eccentricity. Little is known about his childhood. His father was a gregarious, optimistic, gentle soul, his mother a worrier and somewhat withdrawn emotionally. Clifford was raised in part by an aunt, who with her two sisters and a brother lived in the Beers household for many years. After attending local public schools, Clifford enrolled in 1894 in Yale University's Sheffield Scientific School. That year his next oldest brother experienced what was believed to be an attack of epilepsy that eventually proved fatal. A morbid fear of a similar fate haunted Clifford, who helped to take care of his brother, but he managed to graduate from Yale in 1897 with a Ph.B. degree and then went to New York City to pursue a career in business.

In 1900, while working for an interior designer, he broke down mentally and attempted suicide; he suffered from hallucinations and delusions and then manic-depressive episodes. From August, 1900, to September, 1903, he went from one to another of three Connecticut mental institutions—Stamford Hall, the Hartford Retreat (later renamed the Institute of Living), and the Connecticut State Hospital at Middletown—before being discharged from the last as improved but with the physicians' expectation that he would experience subsequent incidences of manic depression.

The violence and indignities that Beers himself suffered and observed inflicted upon other patients at the hands of attendants and physicians spurred him to devise an extensive program to reform mental hospitals. But his family persuaded him to establish himself first in the business world, and he returned to work in New York City. He soon became excited and late in 1904 had to return to the Hartford Retreat for a month. Upon his release he began to write *A Mind That Found Itself*, a fast-paced, vivid depiction of his illness and his experiences in mental hospitals and an exposition of his plans to convert such hospitals from places of mistreatment into humane institutions with a therapeutic orientation. Published in 1908 with the help of William James and other prominent men, the book caused a sensation. It was reviewed enthusiastically in hundreds of newspapers and scientific journals in the United States and abroad and also brought letters to Beers from many readers who described the book's profound effect upon them. *A Mind That Found Itself* quickly attained the status of a classic in its genre; it was issued in several editions and numerous printings and translated into several foreign languages.

For Beers the success of his book was gratifying but not enough to effect reform. In his view a national organization was needed. Always a good organizer and persuader, he won to his cause Dr. Adolf Meyer,* then the leading psychiatrist in the United States; Dr. William Welch of Johns Hopkins University Medical School, the dean of American medicine; as well as William James and other important men and women. Beers first founded the Connecticut Society for Mental Hygiene in 1908 as a demonstration that prevention of mental disorders and improvement in the care of the mentally ill were realizable goals. A number of other groups on the Connecticut model were afterwards organized throughout the United States and Canada. In February, 1909, Beers founded the National Committee for Mental Hygiene, headquartered in New York City, to initiate and coordinate reform and education on a nationwide basis. On June 27, 1912, Beers married Clara Louise Jepson of New Haven, who gave him unstinting support in his work. They would have no children, a decision they made out of fear that the mental illness that had struck Beers and (in 1912) a younger brother might be transmitted to any offspring. That brother died in a mental hospital, and later the two remaining Beers brothers succumbed to mental depression and were committed to mental hospitals, where they each committed suicide.

Despite his family troubles Beers carried on his work. An effective salesman, intense, clever, talkative, and witty, he was able to convince wealthy people to contibute many hundreds of thousands of dollars to the National Committee and his other organizations, which he usually served officially as secretary. Eventually millions of dollars in foundation grants were obtained as well. By the 1920s and into the 1940s the National Committee achieved leadership in almost every area involving mental health in the United States, including treatment, research, popular and professional education in psychiatry, and child care. Its work prefigured the programs sponsored by the federal government after World War II and served as the basis for the activities of mental health associations to the present.

Beers' compulsion to dominate his environment led to difficulties, especially with the physicians in the leadership of his organizations. As a result he eventually turned to international work. In 1919 he had originated the idea of an international mental hygiene movement, an effort he began to pursue seriously in 1922. Later in the decade he proposed and raised the funds for the First International Congress for Mental Hygiene, which met in Washington, D.C., in May, 1930, attended by more than 3,500 representatives from fifty-three nations. Beers considered the congress, which resulted in the formation of the International Committee for Mental Hygiene and attracted the leading psychiatrists, psychologists, and social workers from around the world, the high point of his career. He subsequently received, both in the United States and on numerous trips abroad, recognition and honor as the founder and leader of the modern mental health movement.

Throughout, Beers retained his position as secretary of the National Committee for Mental Hygiene, but the onset of glaucoma arteriosclerosis forced him by 1934 to moderate his activity. For the first time he took up a hobby, oil painting, into which he threw himself with characteristic enthusiasm. When financial stringency, caused largely by the Great Depression, led the National Committee to curtail its programs, Beers sought to save the ship by resuming fund-raising, including a trip around the United States. He felt inadequate, however, to the strenuous work. He lost self-confidence, became depressed and suspicious, and finally, in June, 1939, committed himself to Butler Hospital, Providence, Rhode Island, a private mental institution, where he remained for the rest of his life.

Beers had modeled himself upon the industrial tycoons he so greatly admired, and with something like their success, albeit in a much different and more difficult field of endeavor. He is best compared with Dorothea Dix,* his famous predecessor in reform of the care of the mentally ill. Unlike Dix, he could collaborate with others in spite of his individualism and his propensity to control. His accomplishments were broader in scope than hers; his was an age of large enterprises. He was able to enlist many of the most gifted men and women of his time in a movement that was national and international in scale and that survives to this day. His book is still read and in print, the latest edition appearing in 1980; it remains one of the best personal accounts of mental illness ever published. Beers, however, died of bronchial pneumonia (after a cerebral thrombosis) at Butler Hospital in Providence in 1943.

The major manuscript source about Beers and the movement he founded is the Clifford W. Beers Collection in the Archives of Psychiatry of the New York Hospital–Cornell University Medical Center, New York City. This collection includes several drafts of Beers' autobiography, copies of articles, drafts of speeches and other writings, scrapbooks, notebooks, letters received, and copies of almost every letter written by Beers from 1902 to his death; there are also numerous documents and other material relating to the affairs of the organizations Beers founded. The Archives of Psychiatry also contain Beers' personal and family papers and other collections useful to a study of Clifford Beers. Early drafts of the autobiography are at the Beinecke Library, Yale University, and the Beers Collection in the Menninger Foundation Archives, Topeka, Kansas, includes Beers' personal correspondence. Further unpublished sources are discussed and cited in Norman Dain, *Clifford W. Beers, Advocate for the Insane* (1980). Important published primary sources are the various editions and printings of *A Mind That Found Itself*, which contain a running account of the mental hygiene movement; copies of them are in the Beers Collection in New York Hospital. Another such source is a collection of tributes to Beers and memoirs of the movement, *Twenty-Five Years After: Sidelights on the Mental Hygiene Movement and Its Founder*, ed. Wilbur L. Cross (1934).

Important secondary works are Norman Dain's biography, *Clifford W. Beers, Advocate for the Insane*, which contains extensive biographic notes, and several histories of mental illness and mental hygiene: Albert Deutsch, *The Mentally Ill In America*, 2d ed., rev. (1949); Barbara Sicherman, *The Quest for Mental Health in America, 1880–1917* (1979); Gerald N. Grob, *Mental Illness and American Society, 1875–1940* (1983). Short biographies of Beers are in *Dictionary of American Biography*, Suppl. 3 (1973), 40–52; and *National Cyclopedia of American Biography*, vol. 34 (1948), 140–141. Memorial articles and obituaries include those in *Mental Hygiene* (April, 1944); *American Journal of Psychiatry* (April, 1944); the *New York Times* and the *New York Herald Tribune* (July 10, 1943); see also Robin McKown, *Pioneers in Mental Health* (1961).

NORMAN DAIN

**Bell, Alexander Graham** (March 3, 1847–August 2, 1922), educator of the deaf, inventor of the telephone, social reformer, and eugenicist, was born in Edinburgh, Scotland, the second son of Alexander Melville Bell and Eliza Grace (Symonds) Bell, both teachers. He had very little formal schooling, although he graduated, at age fourteen, from the Royal High School in Edinburgh. His brief stay at that institution, however, had little influence on his subsequent career. Much more important was the private tutoring he received from his father and grandfather in elocution, and the former's encouragement of dabbling in "scientific" projects. (Thus, when still adolescents, Bell and his brother tried to build a talking machine and attempted to use their father's speech-teaching methods to teach a dog to speak English.) In 1870 he and his parents immigrated to Ontario, Canada. Later, Bell made the United States his home. There he married Mabel Hubbard (on July 11, 1877) and became wealthy and famous for his invention of the telephone.

Bell was responsible for significant changes in the American approach to the education of deaf persons. Before the late nineteenth century, nearly all deaf Americans who received education did so in state-supported residential schools, wherein all instruction was in sign language, and little attention was given to developing students' abilities to speak or to read speech from the lips. Bell devoted much of his life and fortune to reversing this situation, to convincing government bodies, parents of deaf children, and professionals working with deaf individuals that every deaf person must be taught to speak and to speechread.

Bell's interest in deaf people and speech developed from several factors. His mother was hard of hearing, requiring her to use an ear trumpet. His father and paternal grandfather were both skilled elocutionists and teachers of speech. The former also invented a system, called Visible Speech, for rendering with symbols all speech sounds. When Bell first came to the United States, in 1871, he taught Visible Speech to instructors at the Boston School for the Deaf, one of the first American schools to employ speech and speechreading exclusively. The financial backers of Bell's telephone experiments, Thomas Sanders and Gardiner Green Hubbard, each had a deaf child. Bell tutored George Sanders, the deaf son of the former, and married the deaf daughter of the latter.

Bell believed that deaf persons could be educated with sign language, but he thought that doing so had three negative effects: it discouraged deaf people from learning English; it tended to drive a wedge between deaf signers and hearing English speakers, creating a deviant group; and it led deaf people to intermarry and produce more deaf children.

Bell's concern about the growth of a deaf minority group was first expressed publicly in 1883 when he addressed a meeting of the National Academy of Sciences with a paper entitled "Memoir upon the Formation of a Deaf Variety of the Human Race." Bell concluded that deaf parents were many times more likely to have deaf children than were hearing parents and that the intermarriage of deaf adults would produce a defective (deaf) strain of humanity. He suggested, therefore, that American society take steps to prevent deaf people from marrying each other.

Bell did not recommend laws against deaf intermarriage but proposed removing the social conditions that encouraged it. He wished to make deaf people figuratively less deaf, more comfortable with hearing people, and thus more willing to take hearing spouses. This entailed the curtailment of the nascent deaf community, with its churches, clubs, reunions, teachers, periodicals, and sign language.

Bell pursued his goal of assimilating the deaf community in several ways. He helped establish the American Association to Promote the Teaching of Speech to the Deaf, the Volta Bureau, and the *Association Review*, all committed to the proposition that deaf people should be taught without sign language. Bell testified to the Wisconsin legislature in support of a bill integrating the state's deaf and hearing students. Before Congress, he argued against an attempt by Gallaudet College, a liberal arts institution for deaf students, to establish a normal school that he believed would train deaf people to be teachers. He established a small experimental school that mixed deaf and hearing students. Bell also wrote voluminously for educational and scientific magazines and spoke before professional groups.

The efforts of Bell and his many allies were successful in changing the communication methods used to teach deaf children and in raising expectations that deaf individuals could be integrated fully into American society. Between

1880 and 1925 the number of deaf students taught by means of sign language dwindled to a small minority. The number of deaf teachers declined similarly. Bell converted influential groups: the National Education Association, the American Medical Association, and the Convention of American Instructors of the Deaf all came to endorse speech and speechreading so that deaf children would become assimilated, normal citizens.

Though Bell's main reform efforts were directed toward deaf people, he proposed other eugenic measures to homogenize and improve American society. A member of the Committee on Eugenics of the American Breeders Association, Bell supported a literacy test for immigrants, believing that illiterates carried undesirable genetic tendencies, and he wished to encourage immigration from supposedly genetically superior Northern European populations. Bell's propensity for genetic determinism led him to argue that longevity, resistance to disease, idiocy, blindness, and deafness were inherited. The major hope for human improvement, he argued, lay in better breeding.

Bell exhorted the government to encourage scientifically valid and healthy marriages to improve America's genetic stock. In 1910 he suggested that government certificates of fitness be issued to men between twenty and forty years of age who could pass an examination by an approved physician. These able-bodied young men, Bell reasoned, would then become especially attractive to women looking for marriage partners.

Bell's attempts to improve America by encouraging selective marriage patterns, immigration restrictions, and shrinkage of the deaf community were not unpopular with most influential people during the Progressive Era, but they were loathed by many deaf people. Although Bell believed that deaf individuals who had a good command of spoken and written English were more likely to shun the company of other deaf persons and to seek a normal life among hearing people, the facts belie this assumption. Ironically, the individuals who led the struggle for the use of sign language and for the creation of a strong, viable, and permanent deaf community in the United States most often had excellent English skills and deaf spouses.

Like most of his peers, Bell never understood cultural diversity. Though married to a deaf woman and committed to the amelioration of deaf people's problems, and though an immigrant himself, Bell failed to see that his attempts to make everyone alike were bound to alienate those whom he labeled defective. Bell died on August 2, 1922, in Nova Scotia.

The Bell Papers are in the Manuscript Division of the Library of Congress in Washington, D.C. The Volta Bureau, also in Washington, holds a valuable collection of the papers of the American Association to Promote the Teaching of Speech to the Deaf, the *Association Review*, and the Volta Bureau.

Bell did not write any true monographs, but he published articles, most between 1890 and 1920, in periodicals such as the *National Geographic*, the *Educator*, the *Journal of Heredity*, and, most imporant, the *Association Review* (now the *Volta Review*) and the *American Annals of the Deaf*.

The most thorough monographic study of Bell is Robert B. Bruce, *Bell: Alexander Graham Bell and the Conquest of Solitude* (1973). A more focused and analytic study is Richard M. Winefield, "Bell, Gallaudet, and the Sign Language Debate: An Historical Analysis of the Communication Controversy in Education of the Deaf," D.Ed. dissertation, Harvard University, 1981. The most useful early work is Catherine MacKenzie, *Alexander Graham Bell: The Man Who Contracted Space* (1928).

JOHN V. VAN CLEVE

**Bellows, Henry Whitney** (June 11, 1814–January 30, 1882), clergyman, United States Sanitary Commission founder, and civil service reformer, was born in Boston to Betsy (Eames) and John Bellows, a prominent merchant. First he attended the progressive Round Hill School, which was run by the well-known historian George Bancroft, then he attended Harvard University, where he was an outstanding student. After graduation he taught at his brother's girls' school in Cooperstown, New York, and then became a tutor on a Louisiana plantation.

Deeply religious and convinced that his talents were being wasted, Bellows returned to Cambridge in 1835 and entered Harvard Divinity School. There he developed his oratorical abilities and gained a reputation as a persuasive and dynamic speaker. Graduating in 1837, Bellows accepted a pastorate in Mobile, Alabama, but left because of his distaste for slavery. His next call was from the prestigious First Congregational (Unitarian) Church in New York City. Although only twenty-five years old when he went to New York City, he already was recognized as one of the outstanding young ministers in the Unitarian Church and was instantly successful in his new ministry. He also married at this time Eliza Nevins Townsend of New York. When she died some thirty years later, he married Anna Huidekoper of Boston.

The First Congregational Church proved to be ideal for Bellows' talents and ambitions, and it provided him access to the educated and wealthy elites of New York. In education, social background, and ideals Bellows had much in common with the church membership.

Although a firm believer in the basic tenets of Unitarian theology, he disagreed with other church leaders on questions concerning its organization. Determining that loose and ineffective Unitarian Church organization caused its lack of growth in the 1830s and 1840s, Bellows came to distain what he called "disintegrating individualism" and stressed instead the value of institutions and the dependence of society on organization.

The change in Bellows' attitude toward the church was also manifested by a similar change in his attitude toward reform. Originally having little sympathy for the poor and the working classes, by the 1850s Bellows argued that the clergy had a duty to participate in movements of social protest and reform. When a severe recession hit New York City in 1854, Bellows also altered his views on poverty. As a traditionalist before the recession, he viewed poverty as a "spiritual disease" and warned against too much charity. By the late 1850s, however, he maintained that the only effective solution to the problem was protective legislation, social rights, and popular education. This new outlook similarly influenced his views on crime. Bellows gradually adopted the belief that the only remedy was the material improvement of the condition of the poor.

The outbreak of the Civil War in April, 1861, provided Bellows an opportunity to combine his new social consciousness with his belief in organization and institutions. Bellows became involved in the organization of a medical aid and relief society, for which he requested official recognition from the government. This medical organization, known as the United States Sanitary Commission, became the most active and successful philanthropic society during the war. It spent more than $4.5 million and was primarily repsonsible for the organization of the North's medical and hospital services.

Bellows' eloquent appeals to communities and individuals for funds, as well as his leadership, gave authority to the work of the United States Sanitary Commission, whose activities reflected Bellows' belief that medical problems, like poverty, should be eradicated. The primary goal of the Commission was scientific and preventative, while the secondary objective was the relief of suffering and want. Among its preventative policies the Commission stressed the elimination of waste, incompetence, and inefficiency and the regulation of medical facilities through the collection of statistics. Reports of the Commission's achievements affected developments abroad as well as at home, most notably in the operations of the International Red Cross and the creation of state and municipal boards of health.

In February, 1863, Bellows also helped to organize the Union League Club. This association of prominent New Yorkers became active in raising a regiment of Negro troops and supporting a Loyal Publication Society. Later, it opposed legislation which attempted to segregate Blacks on the elevated railroads of New York.

Because of his activities in the Union League Club and the United States Sanitary Commission, Bellows was nationally recognized as a leading reformer by the end of the war. The successes which greeted Bellows' efforts during the war inspired him to turn his attention to the problem of Unitarian Church reform. Thus, in January, 1865, believing the Civil War was almost over, Bellows called for a special convention to reorganize the Unitarian Church.

The convention, which met in April, formed the National Conference of Unitarian Churches. Bellows was elected its president, an office he retained almost continuously until September, 1879, when he resigned. His work in the Conference cannot be overestimated; he was its leading exponent of liberal Christianity.

To counteract a loss of national standards and ideals, which Bellows believed had been corrupted by war, he joined the growing crusade for civil service reform, and in 1877 became president of the New York Association. Yet another movement which attracted Bellows in the 1870s was a crusade to improve the tenements. Although convinced that social problems were products of environmental influences, Bellows did not see the solution for tenement problems in laws regulating housing; instead, he pushed for the construction of elevated railways, which he believed would minimize the pressure on the city's limited housing.

Bellows was not a scholar, but he was a man of wide reading and quick insight who possessed great organizational abilities. He published numerous books, sermons, and articles; the best known are *The Treatment of Social Diseases* (1857), *Restatements of Christian Doctrine* (1860), and *Twenty-Four Sermons* (1886). His visit to Europe in 1867–1868 resulted in his two-volume *The Old World in Its New Face* (1868). While often conservative and aristocratic in bearing, he was liberal in thought and action. He did his most effective work as an inspirer of others and posssessed an exceptional talent for public action and religious organization.

Bellows died at his home in Boston on January 30, 1882.

Manuscript sources relating to Bellows' religious work, his interest in Antioch College, and his work on the United States Sanitary Commission are located in the Massachusetts Historical Library in Boston. The papers pertaining to the United States Sanitary Commission are available in the library of Boston University.

Helpful sources for Bellows include John W. Chadwick, *Henry W. Bellows: His Life and Character* (1882); Clifford E. Clark, Jr., "Religious Beliefs and Social Reforms in the Gilded Age: The Case of Henry Whitney Bellows," *New England Quarterly* (March, 1970), 59–78; *Dictionary of American Biography*, vol. 1, part 2 (1929), 169; and *National Cyclopedia of American Biography*, vol. 3 (1893), 261. Bellows' obituary appeared in the *New York Times*, January 31, 1882, 2. Charles J. Stille, *History of the United States Sanitary Commission* (1868), documents Bellows' work during the Civil War.

LARRY D. GIVENS

**Bernstein, Charles** (December 21, 1872–June 13, 1942), institutional administrator and reformer (in the field of mental retardation), was born in Carlisle, New York, to Abraham Bernstein, a country store owner, and Eva Anne (Young) Bernstein, a homemaker. His father died when he was four years old; his mother, when he was nine. After the death of his parents, his maternal uncle, Madison Young, a school teacher, raised Bernstein.

In 1894 Bernstein graduated from the Albany Medical College and in the same year interned at the Albany Hospital. In 1895 he assumed a second internship at the Rome State Custodial Asylum for Unteachable Idiots (later the Rome State School for Mental Defectives). Converted from a state hospital for the mentally ill in 1893, the asylum had been established by the New York State legislature for the permanent institutional care of mentally retarded persons. Upon completion of his internship, Bernstein was appointed assistant physician at Rome, a duty he maintained until 1902. With the resignation of the asylum's first superintendent,

Bernstein was appointed acting superintendent, and in 1904 he became superintendent, a position he held until his death in 1942.

Bernstein was a member of the American Medical Association and the American Psychiatric Association. He was also an active member of the American Association for the Study of the Feebleminded (later the American Association on Mental Deficiency), whose presidency he held in 1907–1908 and 1915–1916. Bernstein was married in 1904 to Lillian Stebbins of Warsaw, New York, who died in 1935. They had no children.

Bernstein's forty-eight-year career in the field of mental deficiency was at one location—the Rome State School for Mental Defectives, situated about seventy miles from his birthplace. Set in rural New York, the Rome facility was typical of such institutions of the time—bucolic, spacious, and isolated. Like most such institutions, too, its purpose was the permanent and total custody of "the unteachable feebleminded." As a newly appointed superintendent in 1904, Bernstein expressed concern with both the setting and the purpose of the Rome facility. This concern began what was to become a career-long effort to challenge many of the shibboleths in the field of mental deficiency. This effort would eventually give Bernstein national exposure and would spread his ideas beyond the provincial confines of upstate New York.

What were these ideas? Quite simply, Bernstein held that custodial institutions segregated retarded people from ordinary communities, from ordinary people, and from ordinary life experiences. He also insisted that, given the rapidly growing demands made by community officials to house mentally retarded individuals, custodial institutions would soon be too costly for the state to maintain. On moral and economic grounds, then, Bernstein waged a campaign for a deemphasis of institutions as custodial facilities and for a rediscovery of institutions as places for training handicapped people for community placement. Through much of his career, he would wage this campaign nearly alone. Only in the 1920s and 1930s would other institutional officials join Bernstein and begin to question the efficacy of permanent custodial institutions.

To provide an alternative to custodial institutions, Bernstein, in 1903, in his first annual report as acting superintendent, advocated what he called the "colony plan." By the time of his death in 1942, Bernstein had founded sixty-two colonies for mentally retarded people. While he cannot be credited with establishing the first such colony (under Walter E. Fernald's* direction, for example, Massachusetts purchased land for a colony in 1899), Bernstein must be given credit for aggressively advocating their expansion and for experimenting with alternative forms for extra-institutional care.

For Bernstein, the colony functioned as a half-way point between the institution and the community. Operated under the administrative structure of the institution, the colony was located in a large house, usually on a farm but occasionally in a town. In these settings clients were trained in agricultural and industrial trades. If the training in the colony over the course of a few years proved to be successful, clients were "paroled" to the community. There social workers provided aftercare services.

In 1914 Bernstein expanded his colony efforts by opening the first colony in the United States for women. While others influenced by the eugenics movement expressed fear about allowing retarded women to go unattended into "the world," Bernstein was convinced that with training these women would become productive and law abiding citizens.

Bernstein's willingness to break with prevailing views of the time was extended to other areas as well. As early as 1917, when others in the field were full of praise for the newly developed Binet-Simon tests, Bernstein expressed doubts. Unlike most of his fellow physician-superintendents, Bernstein maintained a distrust of the efficacy of sterilization. Early in his career he supported the integration of sexes in institutions. He opposed marriage restriction laws for mentally retarded people. He was unconvinced that "bad stock led to more bad stock," just as he was unconvinced that immigrants were responsible for mental degeneracy. Within his own institution, he prohibited corporal punishment. Instead he emphasized training, recreational activities, contact with the public, and kindly interaction between staff and clients. In 1905 he began a training program for his attendants. This program eventually expanded to a summer school for the training of public school teachers and other professionals in subjects related to mental retardation. By 1935 over 1,000 students had attended this summer school.

Bernstein was known as a bombastic speaker and a highly opinionated discussant. He liked a good argument, and, given his controversial positions, he often got one. He was not without views that today are unexpected. For example, he opposed the teaching of reading and writing skills to clients. He could not be called a skilled scientist. He never fully grasped, for example, the methodological nuances and the theoretical implications of psychometrics.

Bernstein's contribution to the field of mental deficiency, then, was a contribution made by an advocate, not by a scientist. As an advocate, Bernstein introduced a method of treatment, the colony plan, which became the precursor of the deinstitutionalization and normalization movements of the 1970s and 1980s. As an advocate also, Bernstein remained one of the few figures in the first quarter of the twentieth century to speak out consistently on behalf of the rights and potentiality of mentally retarded citizens. He died in Rome, New York, on June 13, 1942.

Bernstein wrote articles which described his efforts in institutional reform and colony development. The majority of these articles appeared between 1905 and 1935 in the *Journal of Psycho-Asthenics*, the official publication of the American Association for the Study of the Feebleminded. This journal also contains minutes and discussions from the annual meetings of this association. Bernstein's remarks are recorded in nearly every edition of the *JPA* between 1905 and 1935.

The only biography of Bernstein is James G. Riggs' *Hello Doctor: A Brief*

*Biography of Charles Bernstein* (1936). Although hagiographic, this work provides interesting information about Bernstein and the Rome State School. Other biographical information may be found in Ward W. Millias, "Charles Bernstein, 1872–1942," *American Journal of Mental Deficiency* (1942–1943), 17–19; and in an obituary in the *New York Times* (May 14, 1942), 46.

JAMES W. TRENT

**Bethune, Mary McLeod** (July 10, 1875–May 17, 1955), humanitarian, civil rights activist, educator, and organizer, was born in a three-room log cabin on a rice and cotton farm about five miles from Mayesville, South Carolina, the fifteenth of seventeen children of Samuel McLeod and Patsy (McIntosh) McLeod, slaves freed after the Civil War. One day at age nine McLeod went with her mother (who did special work for a white family) while she did her chores. McLeod went into a play house with some white girls; when she picked up one of their books, one of the white girls said, "You can't read that—put that down. I will show you some pictures over here." This was the first hurt that came into her childhood.

This little incident touched off a determination and drive that would span more than seven decades. She was eleven before she saw her first classroom. She entered the Northern Presbyterian Mission school in Mayesville, and upon completion of course requirements, in 1887 entered the Scotia Seminary (now Barber-Scotia College), located in Concord, North Carolina. When her work was completed at Scotia, she accepted a scholarship to attend the Moody Bible Institute in Chicago, Illinois (1894–1896). After completing her work at Moody Institute, she applied to the Presbyterian Mission Board in New York for a chance to go to Africa. They informed her that no openings were available where they could place Negro missionaries, so they sent her to Augusta, Georgia, to instruct at Haines Institute. McLeod remained at Haines one year (1896–1897), after which she went to Sumter, South Carolina, to work at Kindle Institute (1897–1898).

She never tired, working with people in jails, with the underprivileged, and with the choir of her church. While at Kindle she met a young man, Albertus Bethune, a student at Avery Institute, Charleston, South Carolina, with whom she became well acquainted and then married in May, 1898. Albertus found business employment in Savannah, Georgia, where they moved and had their son, Albert. During this period she took a year off from "active" work. Mr. Bethune, who lacked one year from completing his course work at Avery Institute, was not interested in educational work, but put no barriers in his wife's way. He died before seeing the fruits of her labor.

In 1899, Bethune began a parochial school in connection with the Presbyterian Church in Palatka, Florida. She stayed there for five years. With a little money saved up from selling insurance for the Afro-American Insurance Company and from her school work, she ventured to Daytona Beach. There she found hundreds of Negroes who had gathered for railroad construction work, dense ignorance, and meager educational facilites. She studied the situation and saw the importance of someone doing something about it.

When she arrived at Daytona she had $1.50 in cash. Nevertheless, she rented a little house for $11, and after months of begging and borrowing, she opened its doors to five girls and her son; that little house became the Daytona Educational Institute and Training School. From 1911 to 1930 the Institute also housed the McLeod Hospital and Training School for Nurses, the only such facility along a 200–mile stretch of the Atlantic coast.

In 1923 her school merged with a Methodist men's college, Cookman Institute, in Jacksonville, Florida, to become the Daytona Collegiate Institute. In 1928 the school was renamed Bethune-Cookman College, and Bethune served as its president until 1942. She resumed the presidency in 1946, serving one more year before stepping down and becoming a trustee of the college.

Beginning in 1934, however, Bethune, a longtime friend of (Anna) Eleanor Roosevelt's,* also served the federal government as a member of the National Advisory Committee to the National Youth Administration (NYA). Two years later, in 1936, President Franklin Roosevelt appointed her director of the NYA's Division of Negro Affairs, an agency that brought many tangible benefits to Negro young people. It worked vigorously to erase race differentials in the National Youth Administration and to extend training and educational opportunities to black Americans. In fact, no federal agency did more to stimulate higher education among young Negroes than did the NYA under her forceful administration. At the same time she worked with other federal agencies to provide adult education opportunities and facilities for the parents of those youngsters. In 1944, however, Bethune ended her work with the federal government when the NYA ceased operations.

During her tenure, though, her relationship with President Roosevelt was outstanding. Probably no Negro in American history has been as close a confidante and advisor to a U.S. president as was Mary McLeod Bethune. She was called on regularly to come to the White House to confer with and advise FDR, whose customary greeting to her was, "I'm always glad to see you, Mrs. Bethune, for you always come asking help for others, never for yourself."

Bethune was active in a variety of other organizations and good causes. Thus, among other things, in 1935 she organized the National Council of Negro Women (in Washington, D.C.) and then served as its president until 1949. She also served as vice president of the National Urban League and as an active member of the National Association for the Advancement of Colored People, and she played a prominent role in the Southern Conference for Human Welfare from 1938 to 1948. In 1951 President Harry Truman apppointed her to the Committee of Twelve for National Defense.

In March, 1953, Bethune organized the Mary McLeod Bethune Foundation for research, interracial activity, and the sponsorship of wider educational opportunities for black Americans. Some twenty years later, in the summer of 1974, the Bethune Memorial would be unveiled in Washington, D.C., and in the summer of 1976 her portrait was placed on display in the South Carolina Statehouse—in both instances marking the first time an Afro-American was so honored. In the meantime, however, Mary McLeod Bethune, truly a woman of heroic stature, had died on May 17, 1955, in Daytona Beach, Florida.

The Mary McLeod Bethune Foundation, located in Daytona Beach, Florida, has a large collection of Bethune's papers, as does the Special Collections Section of the library at Bethune-Cookman College. In addition, readers should consult the weekly columns Bethune wrote for several black newspapers, especially the *Pittsburgh Courier* and the *Chicago Defender*. She also wrote some important articles for *Ebony Magazine*, including "My Secret Talks with F.D.R." (April 1949), which discusses her relationship with the President and their mutual respect for each other, and "My Last Will and Testament" (August, 1955), which was written several months before her death and reveals the many things she felt strongly about at that time.

Sadie Iola Daniel's *Women Builders* (1931; rev. 1970) has a fairly good sketch of Bethune's life, as does De Witt S. Dykes' entry on her in John A. Garraty's *Encyclopedia of American Biography* (1977). Another brief, fact-laden sketch is in *Who's Who in Colored America* (1937). Two very favorable biographies which together capture the essense of Bethune's many achievements are Catherine Owens Peare's *Mary McLeod Bethune* (1931) and Emma Gelders Sterne's work by the same name, published in 1957. The best piece on her, despite its brevity, is Elaine Smith's sketch of Bethune in *Notable American Women: The Modern Period* (1980); all readers should consult it and the lengthy bibliographic essay at its conclusion.

PHILIP BOOKER, JR.

**Biggs, Hermann Michael** (September 29, 1859–June 28, 1923), physician and public health administrator and reformer, was born in Trumansburg, Tompkins County, New York, the son of Joseph Hunt and Melissa I. (Pratt) Biggs. Following the death of his father in 1876, he interrupted his education in local schools to work in his family's dry goods store. He entered Cornell University in 1879. Working at an accelerated pace, he completed the A.B. degree in 1882. In the meantime, however, Biggs had entered Bellevue Medical College in New York City (in 1881), from which he received the M.D. degree in 1883. Following an internship at Bellevue Hospital, he studied for six months (in 1884–1885) at the universities of Berlin and Graifswald in Germany.

During Biggs' forty years of professional life, he was simultaneously a pathologist, a medical educator, a public health official, and a private practitioner of medicine. Although one or several of these roles predominated at different times in his life, Biggs' historical importance is a result of the variety and interrelatedness of his many activities. As a medical student he was deeply influenced by outstanding physician-educators who were distinguished in each of these roles, some in several of them. Throughout his career Biggs retained close contact with these mentors.

Biggs was active in academic medicine throughout his career. When he returned from Europe, in 1885, he became director of the Carnegie Laboratory at Bellevue. From 1885 to 1889 he was pathologist to Bellevue Hospital, and from 1886 to 1899 to City Hospital. He served as professor of pathological anatomy at Bellevue Hospital Medical College from 1885 to 1894. During the remainder of his life he was professor of therapeutics and of clinical medicine (1894–1907), associate professor (1907–1914), and professor of medicine (1914–1923) at the merged New York University and Bellevue Medical Schools. He published numerous scientific papers—most of them in the years before and just after the turn of the century—lectured regularly to medical students, and participated actively in clinical teaching.

He was deeply committed to the private practice of medicine. His thriving practice, conducted from his various homes, included many notable New Yorkers. One of his patients, Charles Murphy, leader of Tammany Hall, was of considerable assistance to Biggs in his work with the New York City Health Department.

In large measure as a result of Biggs' leadership, the New York City Health Department achieved worldwide fame for its innovations in public policy. The achievements with which Biggs was associated included the "Report on the Prevention of Pulmonary Tuberculosis" prepared by Biggs and two other pathologists in 1889; the establishment of the first municipal public health laboratory in the world in 1892; the production and distribution of antidiphtheria toxin by New York City in 1893; free bacteriological examination of sputum in 1894; and compulsory notification of the Health Department by physicians of cases of tuberculosis in 1897. By the turn of the century, eminent international figures in medicine, Robert Koch and Joseph Lister to name just two, considered the New York City Health Department to be the most effective in the world and assigned most of the credit for this distinction to Biggs.

Biggs held several positions in the New York City Health Department, but he refused repeated offers to become the commissioner because of the competing demands of his academic and patient care responsibilities. In 1887 he was appointed consulting pathologist to the Department. Five years later he became pathologist and director of the Bacteriological Laboratories of the City of New York. In 1901 he became general medical officer of the Health Department, a position from which he resigned in January, 1914.

Between 1914 and 1923 Biggs served as New York State Commissioner of Health, implementing a reorganization he had helped to design a year earlier as chairman of a commission to revise the state's public health law. Biggs was a part-time commissioner. He continued his practice and teaching, and served abroad as consultant on tuberculosis to the Rockefeller Foundation in 1917 and 1918 and as an official of the League of Red Cross Societies for long periods in 1919–1921. Nevertheless, he made significant contributions to public health policy in New York State, culminating in a law of 1923 providing subsidies to counties to construct health facilities. This law was part of a comprehensive plan, developed by Biggs several years earlier, to create a hierarchy of health institutions in rural regions.

Biggs was a major international figure in health affairs for three decades. His speeches and papers were widely distributed. His advice was sought by colleagues in Europe and the United States and by the Rockefeller Foundation—which served, in these years, as the only analogue in the United States to ministries of health abroad. His creativity in developing and implementing public policy was admired. An epigram he wrote was for a generation the most frequently quoted statement in health affairs: "Public Health is Purchasable. Within Natural Limitations any Community can Determine its own Death-Rate."

Biggs married Frances Richardson of Hornellsville, New York, on August 18, 1898. They had two children, a boy and a girl. He died in New York City after a brief illness on June 28, 1923.

Most of Biggs' papers seem to have been lost. A great many important letters and memoranda are, however, extensively quoted in Winslow's biography (see below). A seven-page typescript biography with corrections in Biggs' hand is in the Rare Book Room of the New York Academy of Medicine, which also has a few of Biggs' letters and a radio-talk memoir of him by James Alexander Miller. The Library of the New York Academy has a processed *Report of the Lectures on Materia Medica and Therapeutics Delivered at the Bellevue Hospital Medical College by Professor Hermann M. Biggs from 1894–95*. Some unpublished material relating to Biggs' career is in the Mayors' Papers and the Health Department files of the New York City Municipal Archives and Records Center. Some material is in the papers of C.-E.A. Winslow at the Yale Historical Medical Library.

Biggs published ninety-two items between 1885 and 1923; a full list is Appendix 7 of Winslow's biography. The publication discuss aspects of particular diseases (notably tuberculosis, diphtheria, cholera, and venereal disease) and health administration. Much of what he wrote was printed or reprinted abroad. In addition, Biggs wrote much of the annual reports of the New York City Department of Health between 1889 and 1914.

Charles-Edward Amory Winslow, *The Life of Hermann M. Biggs: Physician and Statesman of the Public Health* (1929), is an outstanding biography by a colleague and friend. More recent secondary sources include John Duffy, *History of Public Health in New York City, 1866–1966* (1974); Daniel M. Fox, "Social Policy and City Politics: Tuberculosis Reporting in New York, 1889–1900," *Bulletin of the History of Medicine* (1975), 169–195; and Milton Terris, "Hermann Biggs' Contribution to the Modern Concept of the Health Center," *Bulletin of the History of Medicine* (1946), 387–412.

DANIEL M. FOX

**Billikopf, Jacob** (June 1, 1883–December 31, 1950), social work administrator, leader in Jewish philanthropy, and labor–management relations expert, was born in Vilna, Russia, the son of Louis Billikopf and Glika (Katzenelenbogen) Billikopf. When he was thirteen, the family came to the United States to settle in Richmond, Virginia. The youthful immigrant, unable to speak English, was required to enroll in the first grade of public school despite his age and previous schooling in Russia. Three years later, however, Billikopf was granted a high school diploma and entered Richmond College. After supporting himself through three years at Richmond, an article for the college *Messenger* won him a fellowship to study at the University of Chicago. Billikopf graduated from Chicago in 1903 (with a Ph.B.) and then pursued graduate study there and at the New York School of Philanthropy (1905). He married Ruth Marshall on February 23, 1920, and had two children, Florence and David. After his first wife's death in 1936, he married Esther B. Freeman on January 8, 1942.

Throughout his career as a social welfare leader and labor arbitrator, Billikopf also was involved in numerous charitable boards and institutions. Soon after his first job in New York with the Industrial Removal Office, Billikopf became active in Jewish social service agencies in several midwestern cities. He was appointed superintendent of the Jewish Settlement in Cincinnati in 1904, then transferred to Milwaukee to serve as superintendent of the United Jewish Charities there during 1905 and 1906. With his move to Kansas City in 1907, where he continued to work in a similar capacity, he gained prominence as a community leader. Billikopf, a young superintendent of United Jewish Charities, turned his attention to the plight of the city's needy. His efforts in Kansas City helped promote a remedial loan agency, municipal baths, and public night schools. In addition, under his guidance the nation witnessed the establishment of its first tax-supported mothers' assistance fund, a free legal aid bureau, and an unprecedented municipal farm for first offenders. To coordinate these new enterprises in community service, Billikopf joined with other civic leaders to organize and participate in the pioneering Kansas City Board of Public Welfare. During his term in Kansas City, he was also president of the Missouri State Conference on Charities (1911–1912), vice president of the Kansas City Board of Pardons and Paroles, and secretary of the Municipal Recreation Commission. In other aspects of his career, Billikopf was lecturer of sociology at the University of Missouri, director of the Jewish Educational Institute of Kansas City, and president of the National Conference of Jewish Social Workers.

After distinguishing himself in social welfare circles in the Midwest, Billikopf moved to New York City in 1918. In New York, where he met his first wife, Billikopf successfully directed a national campaign to raise $25 million for Jewish war victims. This commitment to aiding refugees, in the aftermath of World War I, also was evident in Billikopf's work toward coordinating relief efforts during World War II. In these undertakings, as in other communal projects to which he contributed his energies, Billikopf's talents in mobilizing and consolidating diverse groups were admired and valued.

Meanwhile, in 1919 Billikopf had settled in Philadelphia to become executive director of the Federation of Jewish Charities, a post he held until 1935. In addition to his work on behalf of Jewish philanthropy, which continued even after his tenure at the Federation, the city also provided a base for numerous achievements in the labor field. Billikopf served as mediator of labor–management disputes in the women's garment industry in Philadelphia, where he also was director of labor relations for local department stores. During this same period, from 1924 to 1934, he was an impartial arbitrator for the New York City men's clothing industry and board chairman of its unemployment insurance fund. In conjunction with this concern for aid to the jobless, Billikopf was chairman of the Philadelphia Committee of One Hundred on Unemployment Relief from 1930 to 1931. In addition, he was a member of the Pennsylvania State Welfare Commission. Furthermore, he championed the cause of unemployment insurance on a federal level, urging national solutions for the problems of the unemployed in his writings and in appearances before various Senate committees. One result of his accomplishments in these arenas was his appointment as chairman of the government's Labor Relations Board for the Philadelphia region during the New Deal years, from 1935 to 1936. Later, beginning in 1938, Billikopf was director of the Labor Standards Association. In this phase of his multifaceted career, Billikopf merged skills in reconciling differences for the purpose of collaboration with a vision of what society's obligation to its less fortunate members should be.

Billikopf's foresight about the aims of social welfare prompted his activism on behalf of various other untried causes. In the realm of the elderly, for example, he was vice president of the American Association for Old Age Security. Another concern was reflected in his leadership role in a special military clemency board during World War II. Before and during World War II, alert to the approaching danger of the Hitler regime, he turned his attention to assisting emigrants from Europe. In addition to the aforementioned nationwide relief efforts which he coordinated, Billikopf actively supported the New School for Social Research and its "University in Exile." The school's agenda for new standards of higher education matched his long-standing commitment to narrowing the gap between seemingly disparate groups. This hope of overcoming barriers to cooperation, in educational as well as in other settings, motivated him to serve on the boards of the New School and Howard University as well.

The ideals upon which Billikopf based his activity—the notion that social welfare, public and private, was a social duty—were formulated in numerous acticles, many of which were published in the *Nation* and *Survey* magazines, both of which he served as a trustee. Billikopf died in Philadelphia on December 31, 1950.

For items relating to Billikopf's career, including correspondence and news clippings, see the Jacob Billikopf Papers at the American Jewish Archives in Cincinnati, Ohio. Many of Billikopf's ideas appeared in the publications of the

Jewish social service organizations. Some of his pieces in those publications were reprinted in an anthology edited by Robert Morris and Michael Freund, *Trends and Issues in Jewish Social Welfare in the United States, 1899–1952* (1966). In addition, the following articles are typical of Billikopf's writing in areas of his specialty: "Advanced Settlement Work," *Jewish Charities* (February, 1915), 161–165; with Maurice B. Hexter, "The Jewish Situation in Eastern Europe Including Russia and the Work of the Joint Distribution Committee," paper delivered at the National Conference of the United Jewish Campaign and the Joint Distribution Committee, October 9–10, 1926; "The Social Duty to the Unemployed," *Annals of the American Academy of Political and Social Science* (March, 1931), 65–72; and "A Message from the President of the National Conference of Jewish Social Service," *Jewish Social Service Quarterly* (December, 1933), 143–144.

Short sketches of Billikopf's life can be found in the *Biographical Encyclopedia of American Jews* (1935), the *Dictionary of American Biography* (1974), the *Encyclopedia Judaica* (1971), and *Who Was Who in America* (1966). Obituaries appeared in the *Philadelphia Inquirer* (January 1, 1951), the *New York Times* (January 1, 1951), and the *Philadelphia Jewish Exponent* (January 5, 1951). Also see Paul Kellogg's tribute, "Jacob Billikopf," *Survey* (February, 1951), 50.

HANNAH KLIGER

**Billings, John Shaw** (April 12, 1838–March 11, 1913), physician, librarian, educator, and sanitarian, was born in Cotton Township, Switzerland County, Indiana, the first surviving child of Abby (Shaw) and James Billings. At age five he moved with his parents to a farm on Narragansett Bay, Rhode Island, then back to Indiana some five years later. They settled in Allensville, where his father was a storekeeper.

As a youth Billings was an incessant reader and managed to learn both Latin and Greek. He aspired to college and in 1852 passed the entrance examination for the subfreshman class of Miami University in Oxford, Ohio. Graduating as a salutatorian in 1857, he worked for a year and then entered the Medical College of Ohio. In spite of his poverty (Billings earned his keep by residing in the hospital and tending the dissecting rooms, at one point subsisting on seventy-five cents a week), he was an independent and intellectually aggressive student, preferring library books to his professors' repetitive lectures. He learned, however, in preparing his dissertation on the surgical treatment of epilepsy, that medical volumes were often poorly indexed and that collections were scattered, making research difficult. This was a problem he would later confront and largely solve.

First he fought a war. Billings cut short a career in academic medicine to serve the Union and was appointed first lieutenant and surgeon on April 16, 1862. Shortly thereafter, on September 3, 1862, he married Katherine Mary Stevens, daughter of former Michigan Congressman Hester Stevens. They had five surviving children: Mary Clare; Kate Sherman and Jessie Ingram (twins); John Sedgwick; and Margaret Janeway.

During the war Billings was in charge of several hospitals and also saw action as a field surgeon: "I am covered with blood and am tired out almost completely," he wrote to his wife, from Gettysburg. "I have been operating all day long and have got the chief part of the butchering done in a satisfactory manner." Eventually the strain became too much, and in 1864 he was transferred to the Surgeon-General's Office. He remained attached to that office until 1895, when he retired from the military as lieutenant colonel and deputy surgeon-general.

The Civil War toughened Billings, as it did so many of his generation. It tested and confirmed his key traits—self-discipline, organization, and leadership. Contemporaries described the mature Billings as an absolutely serious and reliable man, imperious yet inspiring. He gave completely of himself and expected others to do likewise; he did not suffer fools gladly.

Billings' postbellum interests and projects were unusually broad. He inspected and reorganized government hospitals, was an officer of several scientific and sanitary organizations, presided over the Army Medical Museum, investigated Texas fever and yellow fever, and assisted the Census Office in the compilation of vital statistics. His reputation, however, rests on three unique achievements: his assembly of the Surgeon-General's Library and its indices; his design of the Johns Hopkins Hospital; and his creation of the New York Public Library. Any one of these would suffice to establish him as a major figure.

When Billings was assigned to the Surgeon-General's Office he assumed responsibility for its library, then containing only 2,250 volumes. For the next three decades he worked assiduously to create a comprehensive medical research library. By 1880 he had assembled 50,000 volumes and 60,000 pamphlets. Billings created two indices, the *Index-Catalogue of the Library of the Surgeon-General's Office* and *Index Medicus*. The former was intended to cover all books, pamphlets, and journal articles in the Surgeon-General's Library; the latter was designed as a monthly publication to allow access to current medical literature in a more timely manner than was possible through the *Index-Catalogue*. These bibliographic efforts were the precursors of the National Library of Medicine's on-line database, Medlars.

Billings had a long association with Johns Hopkins Medical School. In 1876 he was asked to become an advisor to the Johns Hopkins trustees and to submit a plan for a teaching hospital. He drew on his experience in military hospital administration; his plans were accepted over those of four others. As medical advisor to Johns Hopkins president Daniel C. Gilman, Billings not only assisted in the building design but in faculty recruitment and curriculum development as well. Doctors William Welch and William Osler were both recommended by Billings for their key positions at Johns Hopkins. Billings also urged a baccalaureate degree as a prerequisite for entrance into medical school, and that the course of instruction for an M.D. degree should consist of two years in the basic sciences and two years of clinical experience in a teaching hospital. These ideas, revolutionary at the time, eventually became part of the national standard.

In 1895 Billings left the Surgeon-General's Office to become professor of hygiene at the University of Pennsylvania. He remained in this position only one year, accepting the directorship of the New York Public Library in 1896. That institution was created when the Astor, Lenox, and Tilden Libraries and associated foundations agreed to consolidate their assets and construct a research library on land donated by the city of New York. Billings developed the original design and administered the recataloguing of the three collections. The New York Public Library and its forty-two branches held well over 2 million items at the time of Billings' death (while recovering from surgery) in New York City on March 11, 1913.

The letters and papers of John Shaw Billings are located primarily at the National Library of Medicine, Bethesda, Maryland, and at the New York Public Library. Billings' major contributions to the literature of medicine and librarianship are available in Frank Bradway Rogers, ed., *Selected Papers of John Shaw Billings* (1965).

Fielding H. Garrison's *John Shaw Billings: A Memoir* (1915) remains the fullest biography and contains extensive passages from Billings' own works. Harry Miller Lydenberg, *John Shaw Billings* (1924), is a slender volume that nevertheless contains some interesting anecdotal material. Rogers, Garrison, and Lydenberg all have bibliographies of Billings' writings. Researchers may also use the National Library of Medicine databases Histline and Catline to generate additional bibliographic citations about Billings and his work. Walter F. Willcox has a chapter on Billings in his book, *Studies in American Demography* (1940), 480–490; he also wrote the entry on Billings in the *Dictionary of American Biography*, vol. 2 (1929), 266–268.

Recognition of Billings' achievements continues. Florence E. Oblensky provides a brief review and summary in "John Shaw Billings—12 April 1838–11 March, 1913: On the One Hundred and Twenty-Ninth Anniversary of His Birth," *Military Medicine* (April, 1967), 286–291. The foresight of Billings in the promotion of national standards for public hygiene is the focus of George Rosen's "John Shaw Billings and the Plan for a Sanitary Survey of the United States," *American Journal of Public Health* (May, 1976), 492–495. Finally, the year 1979 was the 100th anniversary of the first publication of *Index Medicus*. This anniversary was the subject of Jeffrey Kunz, "Index Medicus: A Century of Citation," *Journal of the American Medical Association* (January 26, 1979), 387–390, and Martin M. Cummings, "Index Medicus, 1879–1979, Editorial," *Military Medicine* (December, 1979), 829–830.

DAVID T. COURTWRIGHT and RALPH D. ARCARI

**Birtwell, Charles** (November 23, 1860–May 18, 1932), child welfare leader and promoter of sex education, was born in Lawrence, Massachusetts, the son of Tempest and Sarah (Pickels) Birtwell. After attending local schools, Birtwell enrolled at Harvard University in 1881, where he took Dr. Francis Peabody's famous philosophy class on the ethics of social reform. This educational experience proved to be inspirational to Birtwell, as it would for so many other social welfare leaders who were taught by Peabody. Thus, immediately after graduating from Harvard in 1885, Birtwell began employment with the Children's Aid Society of Boston.

Birtwell's leadership, as general secretary of the Boston Children's Aid Society, had a profound impact on social welfare in New England and elsewhere. As a professional in the community, he was a pioneer in encouraging young college-educated men to enter the field of child and social welfare, and his agency served as a site for training such workers, especially after Francis Peabody invited Birtwell to be an evening speaker in his series on social reform at Harvard. Birtwell became an especially close friend and stimulating influence to fellow Harvard graduate Homer Folks.* Birtwell encouraged Folks to accept a position with the Pennsylvania Children's Aid Society upon Folks' graduation, and in 1893, when Birtwell was involved with the Chicago Columbian Exposition's special conference on child saving, he invited Folks to be a speaker at that historic affair, thus launching the latter's national reputation.

In 1894 Birtwell coedited, with Anna Garlin Spencer, *The Care of Dependent, Neglected and Wayward Children*, one of the first works of its kind. In the same year he participated, as secretary of the section on dependent children, in the International Congress of Charities, Correction and Philanthropy, held in Chicago; began a ten-year term as director of the Social Service Committee of Harvard University; and (on October 16) married Helen Dow, with whom he had one child, a son, Roger.

In 1895, at the National Conference of Charities and Correction, Birtwell reported on the work of the child saving section, which he chaired. He served as an associate editor of *Charities Review* from 1897 to 1903, and in 1902 he was a delegate to the Conference on Charity and Correction in Cuba. And also that year, in Detroit, Michigan, Birtwell chaired the National Conference's committee on destitute and neglected children. In 1908, joining with other prominent child welfare advocates, including Homer Folks, Edward Devine,* John Glenn,* Hastings Hart,* Julian Mack,* Thomas Mulry,* and James West, Birtwell wrote a letter to President Theodore Roosevelt requesting the calling of a federal conference on dependent children, which resulted in the historic 1909 White House Conference on the Care of Dependent Children.

Birtwell was prominent in children's work at the turn of the century due to his position at the Children's Aid Society and because of his views on social work with dependent children. He was an early advocate of placing children with foster care families rather than placing them in long-term care institutions. He also championed the sound administration of out-of-home placements. Under his leadership, the Boston Children's Aid Society developed systematic means of studying and selecting foster care homes for neglected and dependent children—methods that were emulated throughgout the nation. He stressed the importance of knowing the potential foster home. While stressing the need to learn from experience, he stated that home studies should be made free from assumptions and/or preconceptions so that foster homes would be studied from a fresh, individualized point of view. His emphasis not only on the careful investigation but supervision of child-caring homes was a pioneering effort to systematize and introduce quality administration to the work of child care. These ideas were communicated to students, colleagues, and the wider community through Birtwell's conference and other professional involvements.

Charles Birtwell left the Children's Aid Society in 1911. He then became the general secretary of the American Federation for Sex Hygiene for one year. In 1912 he joined the Massachusetts Society for Sex Education. That year he also was the chairman of the National Conference on Charities and Correction's committee on sex hygiene. In this position, he urged that a new and harmless nomenclature be developed to be used in teaching sexual matters to school children. To his work at the Society for Sex Education he brought the optimism and energy which he had evidenced in his child-care work. He urged and believed that knowledge would overcome superstition and ignorance concerning sexual (as other) matters. In 1913 Birtwell served as a member of the Massachusetts Commission to Investigate the White Slave Traffic. He left the Society for Sex Education in 1916 and became involved in efforts to bring an end to World War I and maintain world peace. Thus, he served the General Committee of the League of Free Nations Association of Massachusetts, the League to Enforce Peace, and in 1918 the World Peace Foundation.

Between 1919 and his death some thirteen years later, Birtwell held numerous positions, especially with financial and charitable institutions of one kind or another. His primary contribution to social welfare, however, already had been made through his earlier leadership of the Boston Children's Aid Society, particularly with regard to the placing-out of needy youngsters and the development of sound administrative techniques to safeguard their welfare.

Charles Birtwell died in Brooklyn, New York, on May 18, 1932.

There are no biographies or major collections of works of Charles Birtwell. Nor apparently are there any obituaries. Two major sources of information on Birtwell, however, are the *Proceedings* of the National Conference of Charities and Correction (later Social Work) and Frank Bruno's *Trends in Social Work, 1874–1956* (1957). In addition, see the following secondary works: Nathan Huggins, *Protestants Against Poverty* (1971); James Leiby, *A History of Social Welfare and Social Work in the United States* (1978); Robert Bremner, ed., *Children and Youth in America: A Documentary History*, vol. 2 (1971); and Walter I. Trattner, *Homer Folks: Pioneer in Social Welfare* (1968).

GARY R. ANDERSON

**Blackwell, Elizabeth** (February 3, 1821–May 31, 1910), the first woman to acquire a medical degree, public health enthusiast, and medical educator, was born near Bristol, England, the third of the twelve children of Samuel and Hannah (Lane) Blackwell, well-to-do parents with a history of fighting for liberal causes;

in the best English middle-class tradition, both had a keen social awareness. Her father, a successful sugar refiner, was an ardent advocate of the abolition of slavery, temperance, women's rights, and other social reforms, and he imbued his children with progressive ideas. Since dissenters in England were barred from schools, the Blackwell children, girls, as well as boys, were educated by private tutors. Although small, barely over five feet, Elizabeth very early demonstrated qualities of determination and leadership.

The loss of his sugar refinery by fire in 1832, when Elizabeth was eleven, led Samuel Blackwell to leave England for New York City. Since slavery was associated with cane sugar, Blackwell tried unsuccessfully to refine beet sugar. The resultant losses, combined with the depression of 1837, weakened his financial position, and in 1838 he sought to recuperate by moving his family to Cincinnati, only to die shortly after his arrival. Samuel's death left his large family in dire straits, forcing Elizabeth, her sisters, and her mother into the teaching profession.

In 1844, while teaching in Asheville, North Carolina, Elizabeth determined to study medicine; her decision resulted in part from the medical problems of a woman friend and in part, as she wrote in her autobiography, to place a "strong barrier" between herself and matrimony. She was fortunate to find encouragement in the person of John Dickson, an Asheville physician who tutored and encouraged her to work toward a medical degree. In 1847 she moved to Charleston to study with Dickson's brother, Samuel, a professor at the Charleston Medical College. Meanwhile, she began seeking admission to a medical school, but despite strong support from several leading physicians, her efforts failed. After many rejections, she turned to the smaller medical colleges and was finally accepted by Geneva Medical School. Ironically, she was admitted because the faculty and students thought her application had been submitted by a rival medical college as a practical joke.

Greeted at first by a mixture of amusement and derision by students and faculty, and ostracized by the townspeople, she endured slights and insults with such quiet dignity that she soon won respect and a measure of admiration from all she encountered. Realizing the need for further training after receiving her medical degree in January, 1849, she returned to England, where family connections enabled her to spend several months working with some leading physicians in various hospitals. From there she journeyed to Paris, only to discover that the only way to gain experience was to register as a student midwife in La Maternité. On her return to England in 1850, her family connections again proved useful, and she was admitted to St. Bartholomew's Hospital. At the same time she entered an influential intellectual circle in London which included such luminaries as Florence Nightingale and Michael Faraday.

Feeling well qualified in medicine, in 1851 she returned to New York to practice. Her first experiences were bitterly disappointing. Patients were skeptical of a woman physician, the medical profession was suspicious, and she was barred from practicing in dispensaries or hospitals. Fortunately, her father's antislavery sentiments had brought him in contact with a number of leading

ELON COLLEGE LIBRARY

social reformers, among whom were several well-to-do Quakers. With their help Blackwell, in 1854, established a small part-time dispensary in a slum section of New York to treat poor women. In 1856 she was joined by her sister, Emily, who had followed her into medicine. The addition of a third female physician, Dr. Marie E. Zakrewska, and a growing circle of patrons enabled Elizabeth to establish the New York Infirmary for Women and Children in 1857.

The following year Blackwell returned to England to promote the cause of women in medicine. Influenced by Florence Nightingale, in 1859 she came back to New York determined to establish a nursing school and a medical college for women. The outbreak of the Civil War disrupted her plans, and she quickly became involved in war work. She played an active role in organizing the Women's Central Association of Relief, one of the agencies responsible for establishing the United States Sanitary Commission in June, 1861. This civilian body forced a major overhaul of the Army Medical Corps, improved the sanitary condition of army camps, and immeasurably contributed to the welfare of sick and wounded soldiers. Elizabeth and Emily also began a program for recruiting and training nurses. Elizabeth was the logical choice to head the Union army's female nurses, but the army, which was reluctant to accept women in any capacity, could not be expected to give recognition to a female physician. Hence the position of superintendent of female nurses was given to Dorothea Dix,* a reformer of national reputation. Her appointment led to a public outcry against exposing delicate females to the horrors of war, one quickly dispelled, however, by the remarkable work of female nurses on both sides.

The outstanding contributions of the Blackwell sisters and other women during the war demonstrated the value of women in the health professions and stimulated the opening of nursing schools and female medical colleges. In 1868 Blackwell was instrumental in organizing the Woman's Medical College of New York, an institution whose requirements generally exceeded those of most medical schools in the United States. Recognizing that if women expected to make major inroads into the medical profession, they would need far better qualifications than male physicians, she set her medical school standards at a level well beyond those of the average medical school. Significantly, she assumed the chair of hygiene, one of the first such chairs in the country.

With the medical school and infirmary firmly established, she returned to England in 1869 to make it her permanent home. As with most reformers, Blackwell always had been aware of the deplorable conditions of the poor. In her first medical paper on an 1849 typhus epidemic she emphasized the need for personal hygiene and sanitation in combatting the disease, and she constantly stressed in her lectures the value of exercise, personal cleanliness, and social hygiene.

In her later years she had the courage to write on sexual behavior and to attack the "double standard." She was always a major advocate of preventive medicine and public health, and toward the end of her life she espoused the cause of

Christian socialism and its belief in a more equitable distribution of income. She died peacefully at her longtime home in Hastings, England, at the age of eighty-nine.

The major manuscript sources are the Blackwell Family Papers in the Library of Congress and the Schlesinger Library, Radcliffe College, and the letters of Elizabeth Blackwell to Barbara L.S. Bidichon in the Columbia University Library. Basic to any understanding of Elizabeth Blackwell are her autobiography, *Pioneer Work in Opening the Medical Profession to Women* (1885), and her *Essays in Medical Sociology*, 2 vols. (1902). The standard biography is Isabel Ross, *Child of Destiny* (1944), but Elinor Rice Hays, *Those Extraordinary Blackwells* (1967), is a useful supplement. Among the obituaries and better short works are: *The Times* (London) (June 2, 1910); *Woman's Journal* (June 12, 1909, June 4, 1910); New York Academy of Medicine, *In Memory of Dr. Elizabeth and Dr. Emily Blackwell* (1911); Victor Robinson, "Elizabeth Blackwell," *Medical Life* (July, 1928); and Laurence G. Roth, "Elizabeth Blackwell—1821–1910," *Yale Journal of Biology and Medicine* (October, 1947). The best brief account of her life is the sketch by Elizabeth H. Thompson in *Notable American Women*, vol. 1 (1971).

JOHN DUFFY

**Boardman, Mabel Thorp** (October 12, 1860–March 17, 1946), Red Cross leader, was born in Cleveland, Ohio, the eldest of six children of Florence (Sheffield) and William Jarvis Boardman. Young Mabel boasted a distinguished family heritage. Her father, a successful lawyer, was descended from William Bradford, first governor of the Plymouth Colony, and from Senator Elijah Boardman of Connecticut, whose large land holdings drew Mabel's grandfather to Ohio. Her mother was a daughter of Joseph Earl Sheffield, a New Haven merchant and benefactor of the Sheffield Scientific School at Yale University.

Following her education in private schools in Cleveland, New York, and Europe, which stimulated her interest in international affairs, she became part of a socially elite circle of well-known women in Washington, D.C., involved in humanitarian efforts, especially the American Red Cross when, in 1900, a congressional charter gave that struggling association new life and hope. Miss Boardman's name was placed on the list of incorporators, apparently without her knowledge, or so she always insisted. Nevertheless, she lost little time in becoming actively involved in the organization, which was plagued by controversy.

Clara Barton* maintained a nearly autocratic rule of the organization she had founded in 1881 but came under heavy criticism for the Red Cross' perfunctory efforts during the Spanish-American War. Boardman attacked Barton not only for the paltry showing of the organization during the war but for her poor management skills as well, which convinced her that Barton would have to be replaced before the Red Cross could succeed. The acrimonious feelings between the two quickly developed into a feud. A climax was reached in December,

1902, when Boardman proposed increasing the governing body. Barton defeated the proposal and, in fact, had new laws passed making herself president for life.

Mabel Boardman now looked to her political connections for help in ousting Barton. These connections included Anna Roosevelt Cowles, sister of President Theodore Roosevelt, and Secretary of War William Howard Taft. The White House severed ties with the Red Cross until a congressional investigation into financial malfeasance and general mismanagement could be made. Boardman and her followers were then suspended by the Barton faction. Ultimately, however, Barton and the Red Cross were cleared of all charges following a promise that she would resign as president—and Mabel Boardman was elected to succeed her in 1904.

With the power she had been seeking, Boardman now set out to redirect the future course of the Red Cross. She drafted a revised congressional charter that gave the President of the United States the power to appoint the chief officer and allowed Red Cross accounts to be audited by the War Department. This gave the organization the political affiliation and the legitimacy she had been looking for in expanding the scope of the Red Cross.

She reconstructed the Red Cross into an institution engaged in several programs, using large numbers of volunteers, in preparing for various national emergencies. Gaining the support of influential people, she established an endowment fund of nearly $2 million. She raised over $800,000, with matching federal funds, for a headquarters, which also was to serve as a monument to the women of the Civil War, although it disparagingly came to be called the "Marble Palace." Always looking for ways to raise money, she accepted the idea of Emily Perkins Bissell that Christmas Seals be sold to garner funds.

Prior to and during the early stages of World War I, Mabel Boardman was in charge of the Red Cross. As Ernest P. Bicknell, staff director of the Red Cross, put it, "Miss Boardman was the chief, make no mistake about that." Early in the conflict, Boardman was full of vitality, sending supplies to both sides, but as American public opinion mounted in favor of an Allied victory, her position began to crumble. Unable to withstand the barrage and to manage the vast effort, her control of the organization collapsed, and others took over. She was relegated to trivial matters, such as the design of uniforms.

After the war, however, following a brief stint on the Board of Commissioners of the District of Columbia, she resumed an active, although reduced, role with the Red Cross. One question that plagued the organization at that time was whether or not it should take on a permanent full-time welfare responsibility. Boardman believed that it should not do so, and played a prominent role in persuading its leaders to follow the traditional Red Cross policy of concentrating on emergency relief.

Meanwhile, Boardman was gaining acclaim as head of the Red Cross' Volunteer Special Services. She built a choice group of carefully selected, well-trained volunteers to serve as nurse's aides, as members of the Motor Corps and Home Services agencies, and the famous Gray Ladies. Although often criticized for being too selective in the choice of volunteers, as acceptance came to depend on social standing, her work nevertheless attracted many people and strengthened what otherwise might have become a weak Red Cross during the Great Depression.

Mabel Boardman retired from the Red Cross in the early 1940s, while in her eighties. The woman who had spent so much of her life working to restructure and stabilize an unsteady Red Cross received much tribute. Indeed, thanks in large part to her efforts, the organization went from a small, floundering effort in 1900 to a giant, flourishing establishment by midcentury. Boardman died at her home in Washington, D.C., on March 17, 1946.

Mabel Thorp Boardman's papers are in the Manuscript Division of the Library of Congress in Washington, D.C., and in the Archives of the American Red Cross, also in the nation's capital. Boardman's book, *Under the Red Cross Flag at Home and Abroad* (1919), is a good source for understanding her thinking about the early Red Cross.

Some of the better secondary accounts on Boardman, and the Red Cross, are Foster Rhea Dulles, *The American Red Cross: A History* (1950); Ernest P. Bicknell, *Pioneering with the Red Cross* (1935), and *In War's Wake* (1936); and the entry on her in *Notable American Women 1607–1950* (1971). Also see the sketch in *Current Biography: 1941* and Charlotte Goldwaite's *Boardman Genealogy, 1525–1895* (1895), on her family background.

WILLIAM H. HARDIN

**Bond, Thomas** (May 2, 1713–March 26, 1784), physician and pioneer public health reformer, was born in Calvert County, Maryland, the son of Richard and Elizabeth (Benson) Bond. Aspiring to a medical career, he migrated to Philadelphia about 1730. During 1738 and 1739 he studied in London and Paris as one of the first half-dozen American medical students in Europe, although he did not receive a degree. After returning to Philadelphia, he developed one of the largest medical practices in the city. In 1735 Bond married Susannah Roberts, who died childless before he left for Europe. From his second marriage to Sarah Venables he fathered seven children, including Thomas, Jr., also a noted physician.

Bond inspired the establishment in 1751 of the Pennsylvania Hospital for the Sick Poor. From 1751 to 1752 he served as one of the original managers of the hospital, and practiced on its medical staff from 1752 until shortly before his death. The oldest and largest such institution in the colonies, the hospital averaged over 100 resident patients in the decade before the Revolution, about 90 percent of whom were charity cases. The establishment and success of the hospital were the outgrowth of several developments in eighteenth century Philadelphia, in all of which Bond participated actively.

The thrust of the hospital was partly humanitarian, encouraged by religious benevolence. The number of sick poor in Philadelphia mounted by midcentury, which Bond was aware of from his professional involvement with public health. He had a deep interest in epidemiology and had been appointed port inspector for contagious diseases in 1741. The Society of Friends, which had a strong presence in colonial Philadelphia, encouraged humanitarian measures to meet such problems (a majority of managers of the hospital before the Revolution were Quakers). Bond was raised as a Quaker and absorbed their ethics, although he was disowned in 1742 for "disunity" (presumably for marrying Venables, an Anglican). Religion continued to be important to Bond, as he served on the vestry of Christ Church (Anglican) from 1747 to 1748. The humanitarian aspect of the hospital was reinforced by the policy of its medical staff, including Bond, of serving without pay.

A related, more secular impulse behind the hospital was the practical spirit of doing good, encouraged by Benjamin Franklin.* Franklin secured the public and private financing necessary to establish the hospital. Bond, a friend of Franklin's, had assisted him previously in establishing several civic enterprises, including the American Philosophical Society in 1743 and the Academy of Philadelphia (subsequently the University of Pennsylvania) in 1749. Bond was also a member of the St. John's Masonic Lodge, the Hand-in-Hand Fire Company, and the Library Company of Philadelphia, other prominent voluntary associations designed to advance the public good. As the largest and richest city in the colonies, Philadelphia could afford to identify problems for such agencies to alleviate.

The hospital also was an outgrowth of fears about potential social and economic upheavals resulting from the increasing numbers of poor persons in colonial Philadelphia. Inspired by the establishment in England of a voluntary hospital, St. George's, at Hyde Park in 1733, rich Philadelphians tried to reduce their poor rates and enlarge the pool of laborers to choose from by rehabilitating the sick poor. Hence the hospital admitted only the "deserving" poor, those with recommendations from a prominent citizen attesting to their morality and industriousness. Social harmony would increase as a result of the patients' gratitude to the hospital. Bond was wealthy (among the top 5 percent of tax assessments on the 1775 return) and no doubt generally shared the social values of his strata. Furthermore, if he did not see English voluntary hospitals when he was studying abroad, he probably learned about them from his brother Phineas, also a physician, who studied at London and Edinburgh before returning to Philadelphia in 1743.

The establishment of the hospital also was a method of professional advancement for Philadelphia physicians, including Bond. As in England, serving on the staff of such a hospital provided experience and professional recognition not available elsewhere. (Bond took a salary, for example, as physician to the less prestigious almshouse, reorganized in 1767 to assist the nonsick poor for reasons similar to the hospital's). The hospital also offered a site for medical education, another interest of Bond's. In 1766 he initiated at the hospital the colonies' first clinical course in medicine.

Bond remained active until near the end of his life. He supported the American Revolution, treating military personnel at the hospital. He was president of the Humane Society, which was founded in 1780 to assist in the rescue of drowning persons. Throughout his career, Bond involved himself closely in the life of eighteenth century Philadelphia and reflected the multiple attitudes toward social welfare which existed in that city. He died there in 1784 at age seventy.

Manuscript ledgers and letters by Bond are at the library of the College of Physicians in Philadelphia. Bond published several articles on medical subjects, such as "An Account of a Worm Bred in the Liver," *Medical Enquiries and Observations* (1757).

Bond's obituary appeared in the *Pennsylvania Gazette*, April 3, 1784. Unpublished family history materials are at the Genealogical Society of Pennsylvania, Philadelphia. The best account of his life is Elizabeth H. Thomson, "Thomas Bond, 1713–1784," *Journal of Medical Education* (1958); 614–624. The sketch in the *Dictionary of American Biography*, vol. 2 (1929), 433–434, is not reliable. The most recent history of the hospital, William H. Williams, *America's First Hospital: The Pennsylvania Hospital, 1751–1841* (1976), emphasizes "social control" as motivation for Bond's work, a theme applied generally to social welfare in colonial Philadelphia by Gary B. Nash in *The Urban Crucible: Social Change, Political Consciousness, and the Origins of the American Revolution* (1980). The emphasis is on disinterested benevolence in Francis R. Packard, *Some Account of the Pennsylvania Hospital from 1751 to 1938* (1938).

ROBERT J. GOUGH

**Bookman, Clarence Monroe** (February 17, 1882–July 2, 1963), social worker and activist, was born in Lancaster, Ohio, the son of Fred and Katherine (Fuhr) Bookman. Very little is known about his early life although he apparently came from a rather affluent family. He attended Otterbein College during the early twentieth century and received a B.A. degree from that institution in 1904. Thereafter he decided to pursue graduate studies, and in 1906 was conferred an M.A. degree from Otterbein. At Otterbein College Bookman met and dated Ethel Metz. Their relationship matured, and in 1907 they were married. His wife ultimately bore him four children: Elizabeth Ann, Helen Fuhr, Barbara, and John Frederick Bookman.

Bookman studied mathematics at Otterbein, and in 1908 he was hired at Central High School in Columbus, Ohio, to teach the subject. Eventually he became the chairman of the mathematics department and served in that post between 1909 and 1913. In 1913, however, he decided to abandon his teaching career and subsequently was hired by the American Book Company as an editor and writer. While employed there, Bookman published a book entitled *Business Arithmetic* (1913). He remained in that post until 1914, when he entered the social service field in ernest.

Bookman became involved in social work during the second decade of the twentieth century and in 1914 was named the associate director of the Council of Social Agencies in Cincinnati, Ohio. He showed great skill in this post. In fact, the collections of the Council of Social Agencies grew nearly 20 percent in the first year of his associate directorship. Bookman, because of his success, was subsequently named the director of the Council in 1916. One of his trademarks was frugality, and he carried this trait into the operation of the Council of Social Agencies. In 1917 he resigned his post as director and thereupon became the executive director of the Community Chest of Cincinnati and the remainder of Hamilton County. An ardent supporter of its development, Bookman would remain associated with the Community Chest throughout the rest of his life.

Meanwhile, during the early 1920s, Clarence Bookman began to make his mark on the larger social work field. As a member of the National Conference of Social Work he wrote numerous articles and essays on social work as a viable profession. Beginning in 1921, he issued a series of articles calling for the professionalization of social work in America. While he agreed that private funding was essential to the development of social work, he also began to press for a larger role for the government in the provision of social services.

In 1922 he addressed the National Conference of Social Work and outlined his vision of government provision of social services. The poverty problem in America seemed to him to require a more direct role by the federal government. Bookman, however, also believed that social workers should continue to promote and expand community chests in the United States. In essence, Bookman called upon his social work colleagues to make social services a mainstream concern to all American communities. While little heed was paid initially to Bookman's rhetoric, and American apathy toward social services continued, the community chest movement gained steam during the 1920s, thanks in large part to Bookman's efforts.

During the 1920s he traveled the breadth of the country, urging the public, and especially social workers, to pay closer attention to the poverty-stricken in the United States. In 1923, at the annual meeting of the National Conference of Social Work, he made a rousing speech calling upon social workers to become advocates of social reform in their communities. He made note of the fact that social workers could influence public opinion and thereby enhance social services in most American communities. His speech was greeted with much applause and subsequently was published in the *Proceedings* of the conference.

Because of his increased stature, he was elected president of the Association of Community Chests and Councils, a post he held between 1927 and 1928. Bookman's heyday as a social work reformer and activist, however, came during the 1930s. As it did most Americans, the Great Crash of 1929 took Bookman by surprise. He became one of the first, though, to call for direct government intervention to meet the needs of those suffering from the economic collapse. He wrote essays for both the *Survey* and *Survey Graphic* throughout the 1930s calling for more public as well as private action to assist the poor of the United States.

In 1931 Bookman had been elected president of the National Conference of Social Work. As president of that organization, he called upon the government and private interests to redouble their efforts in relieving the suffering caused by the Depression. In his 1932 speech to the National Conference, Bookman noted that between 1931 and 1932 the unemployed had lost nearly $22 billion in lost wages, whereas relief agencies, such as they were, could only make up 2 percent of this loss. Bookman saw the Depression as an opportunity to increase the status and role of the social work profession. To end poverty in America, Bookman advocated a plan of economic reorganization. He subsequently called upon the President to establish a special commission to analyze relief efforts and the massive unemployment problem. Bookman also offered his own plan to relieve the unemployed in America. His plan embodied three basic principles: (1) unemployment reserve funds, (2) public works projects, and (3) work relief.

In 1933 Franklin D. Roosevelt took office and immediately embarked on a massive program to restore the American economy—and provide federal assistance to the needy. One of his first measures was the establishment of the Federal Emergency Relief Administration (FERA), which embodied many of the precepts Bookman made public in 1932. Bookman subsequently became an assistant administrator in the FERA. Throughout, however, he continued to press for the establishment of a national commission to review the relief efforts of the New Deal, and in 1939 FDR named Bookman to the Relief Study National Resources Planning Board, a position he remained in until 1941 and the outbreak of World War II. Even after World War II commenced, however, Bookman continued to push for further government involvement in social services.

With the outbreak of World War II, Bookman was appointed to the War Chest of Cincinnati and Hamilton County, a position he held until 1946, when he ceased to be actively involved in social welfare matters, although he continued to attend annual meetings of the National Conference of Social Work.

Clarence Bookman, who deeply believed that mankind had an obligation to the poverty-stricken in its midst, was an innovator in the field of social welfare. His contributions to social work are both apparent and subtle. During the early1920s he was a prime mover in the development of the community chest movement. But as an officer of various social service agencies and organizations, he also helped to define the mission of modern social work and to professionalize it. Bookman's significance, however, went far beyond these contributions. As an activist, he had an important influence on the social welfare policies undertaken in the 1930s, many of which remain crucial features in today's social welfare programs. His actions, coupled with those of others, also assisted in giving the social work profession an activist rather than merely a reactive tradition to fall back on in today's world.

Bookman died in Cincinnati, Ohio, on July 2, 1963.

Manuscript sources on Bookman are rather scant and dispersed. The records of the *Survey* and *Survey Graphic*, in which Bookman published many articles, contain a number of documents pertaining to his life and career. Readers should consult the Social Welfare History Archives Center at the University of Minnesota in Minneapolis for the Survey Associates records.

Works by Bookman are too numerous to list here. He was a prodigious writer, and his work spanned nearly thirty years. Some of his more important pieces are "Unemployment: Cost and Care," *Survey* (June 15, 1932), 267; "Social Work and the Public Temper," *Survey* (November, 1935), 326–328; and "Federal Emergency Relief Administration: Its Problems and Significance," *Proceedings of the National Conference of Social Work* (1934), 13–31.

A number of monographs have brief references to Bookman and his influence on the social work field. Among the best are Clarke A. Chambers, *Seedtime of Reform: American Social Service and Social Action, 1918–1933* (1963); Donald S. Howard, *The WPA and Federal Relief Policy* (1973); Paul A. Kurzman, *Harry Hopkins and the New Deal* (1974); and Roy Lubove, *The Professional Altruist: The Emergence of Social Work as a Career, 1880–1930* (1969). For his career and obituary, see *Who's Who in America*, vol. 18 (1934), and the *Cincinnati Inquirer*, July 2, 1963.

JOHN S. LEIBY

**Bowditch, Henry Ingersoll** (August 9, 1808–January 14, 1892), physician, abolitionist, educator, and public health leader, was born in Salem, Massachusetts, the third son of Nathaniel Bowditch, the famous mathematician, and Mary (Ingersoll) Bowditch. He attended Salem Private Grammar School until 1823, when his father accepted a position as actuary of the Massachusetts Hospital Life Insurance Company in Boston. Henry, a dutiful son in a privileged and closely knit family, followed his father's plans for his education and attended the Boston Public Latin School and Harvard College, class of 1828. Without great enthusiasm for business, the law, or the ministry, he decided to go to Harvard Medical School. There his studies with Dr. James Jackson inflamed his devotion to his profession as a noble and challenging opportunity to serve humanity. After receiving his medical degree from Harvard, he went to Paris in 1832, where he continued his medical studies for the next two years. His work in Paris with the famous clinician Pierre Charles Alexandre Louis emphasized careful clinical observation and postmortem studies. He developed skill in auscultation, the relatively new use of listening through the stethoscope to diagnose lung problems, and became a convert to Louis' use of statistical analysis as a medical research tool. Young Dr. Bowditch's respect for Louis and his work bordered on reverence and lasted throughout his life.

In Paris, and in his visits to London, his father's reputation gave him entrance to the most famous scientific circles. While he was abroad, he met Olivia Yardley, an English girl who was studying in Paris, and later married her in New York, in 1838; they had four children.

The five years after his return from Europe were significant in his career development. He opened an office for medical practice on busy Washington Street in Boston, was made admitting physician at Massachusetts General Hospital, became a worker at the Warren Street Chapel, and became an active, fiery abolitionist. The Warren Street Chapel had been founded to aid the children of poor parents, and Bowditch spent every Sunday counseling, caring for, and teaching the children. His decision to become a forceful voice for abolition came suddenly in 1835, when he encountered an angry mob intent on punishing William Lloyd Garrison because he had held a meeting for abolitionists. His sense of justice, commitment to free speech, and moral outrage at the existence of slavery prompted him to join the abolitionist cause with religious zeal. His belief in treating all human beings with justice led to his resignation from the Warren Street Chapel in 1842, because black children were denied admission and because his antislavery talks were disapproved of by some of his associates there. The previous year he had resigned as admitting physician at Massachusetts General Hospital when the trustees enacted a rule excluding black people, partly in response to complaints that Bowditch had been admitting too many. His resignation prompted the trustees to reconsider the order. His association with Massachusetts General Hospital lasted throughout the rest of his life; he was visiting physician (1846–1863) and consulting physician there from 1863 until his death.

Much of Bowditch's time and energy during the 1840s and 1850s were consumed with his abolitionist activities. He attempted to prevent the rendition of fugitive slaves and was instrumental in gaining passage of a law in Massachusetts forbidding the retention of runaway slaves in town or state jails.

His unflagging interest in the study of medical problems, especially lung diseases, and his skill and success in auscultation and percussion led to his writing *The Young Stethoscopist* (1846). The book was adopted by medical schools and helped to establish his reputation as an expert in the field of lung diseases. That year he also founded the Boston Society for Medical Observation for the purpose of discussing medical papers presented at the group meetings twice a month by its members.

He brought his enthusiasm and ability to the promotion of the technique of paracentesis thoracis, the use of the aspirating trocar or hollow needle and suction pump to tap the lungs of victims of pleurisy and other lung diseases. In conjunction with Dr. Morrill Wyman, a surgeon who devised and used the technique, Bowditch insisted that the method was far safer for the patient than surgical incision. Bowditch gave lectures, wrote papers, and traveled to Europe in 1859 to publicize the method, and made thereby a significant contribution to clinical medicine. When he returned from Europe, he began his duties as Jackson Professor of Clinical Medicine at Harvard Medical School, a position he held until 1867, when pressure of other duties led to his resignation.

The advent of the Civil War was for him the moral crusade to expunge the evil of slavery. His eldest son, Nathaniel, a medical student at Harvard, enlisted, and his father volunteered to give medical aid to the wounded. In his service in Virginia, Bowditch was appalled at the lack of care for the wounded and the absence of an ambulance system. Determined that an enlisted corps of trained ambulance attendants be established, he vigorously lobbied for the passage of a bill in Congress. Within days after the bill was defeated in the Senate, his son

Nathaniel was wounded and lay for hours alone and forgotten on the field of battle; he died the following day. His grief-stricken father added an appendix to a plan he had prepared, addressed to the public, for an ambulance system. The result was a dramatic surge of support for the passage of a bill for a trained ambulance corps for the army. The goal was accomplished when Congress passed such a bill.

His landmark report on consumption in Massachusetts was published in 1864. This was the result of almost ten years of statistical study of responses to questions sent by Bowditch to physicians throughout the state and of his own observations. He concluded that residence on damp soil was a causative factor in tuberculosis. He also believed that consumption might be contagious. The impact of his reputation and the evidence he put forward helped to promote the idea that dry soil, sunshine, and fresh air could alleviate some cases of the disease. He continued to study tuberculosis and published his conclusions on the devastating "white plague" until he died. His published observations and the techniques of auscultation and aspiration were powerful weapons in the battle against premature death from tuberculosis.

When in 1869 the Massachusetts legislature, prodded by the persistent pressure of Dr. Bowditch and other advocates, created the first modern State Board of Health, Bowditch was appointed to the Board. He was named chairman and would serve in that position for ten years. A staunch proponent of the idea he called "State Medicine," that is, the obligation of the state authorities to promote and protect the public health by trying to prevent disease and the spread of disease, Bowditch was a forceful champion of the modern public health movement. The Board was active; its annual reports attained international recognition during his tenure.

His interest in improving the wretched living conditions of the poor led him to inspect the work of Octavia Hill and others in London. He returned to Boston convinced that decent housing at moderate rentals could work here. He and some associates formed the Boston Co-operative Building Company in 1871; he was its director until 1880. The company had greater success in providing small homes for the poor than it did in rehabilitating overcrowded, unsanitary tenement houses.

His interest in medical research and his belief in ease of access to sources prompted him and five of the members of the Boston Observation Society to found the Boston Medical Library in 1874. The holdings of the Library soon made this one of the nation's leading depositories of medical literature.

In 1876 the address he gave to the International Medical Congress in Philadelphia was widely hailed. He spent a year gathering data and preparing the address, which was published the following year. He surveyed the progress of preventive medicine in the United States. His advocacy of the concept of state preventive medicine was significant in publicizing and popularizing the belief that the state and local governments had an obligation to study the prevention of disease and to preserve the public health. His work had a profound impact at a crucial time in the development of the modern public health movement, for it revealed a woeful lack of planning in the nation and offered an optimistic challenge for change.

Partly as a result of the impact of the Centennial Address, he was chosen president of the American Medical Association in 1877. Ten years before, at its convention in Ohio, he had been hissed when he spoke in favor of a motion to accept women as members. Undaunted, characterizing the oft-expressed argument that women were physiologically too weak for the rigors of a medical education as "twaddle," he lobbied for their admission. It did not come until 1915, long after his death. He had greater success in his campaign to have women physicians accepted to membership in the Massachusetts Medical Society. The Society, in which he had served as secretary, 1849–1854, responded to his persistent campaign and admitted women as members in 1884. His vigorous efforts to persuade Harvard Medical School to allow coeducation failed. To Bowditch the issue of equal rights for women, as well as men, to choose a medical education and membership in professional societies was an essential part of human liberty.

The popularizing of the ideas of the public health movement and preventive medicine, in which his work was instrumental, led to the establishment by Congress in 1879 of the National Board of Health. Dr. Bowditch was a member from its inception until 1881, when poor health required him to resign. During his tenure, however, a severe yellow fever epidemic, which had been ravaging the South, was confined to one large southern city, Memphis, through the application of the ideas of preventive medicine and new public health investigations.

An enthusiastic advocate for society's underprivileged and for the highest professional standards in medicine and public health reform, Henry Bowditch was warmly regarded by his associates. A gentle, kind, and optimistic person, he could express himself with explosive speech and gestures against injustice. Deeply religious, he was not a parishioner of any church, for he had been so distressed at the failure of ministers to use their pulpits to oppose the moral evil of slavery that he resolved to imitate Christ and live according to his teachings without any formal affiliation. He, more than any other individual, by his tireless efforts, writings, and speeches engendered public support for the concept of public responsibility for ameliorating conditions which led to premature death and disease. His support of innovative techniques in treating lung diseases and his observations on tuberculosis causation and incidence led to longer lives and hope for countless victims. The experiments he supported in providing decent housing for the poor focused attention on tenement house evils and sparked imitation. The trained ambulance corps for the army was largely the result of his persistent public effort. His life, so enthusiastically devoted to the causes he believed in, ended on January 14, 1892, in the home he loved in Boston.

The papers of Dr. Henry I. Bowditch, which include his journals, casebooks, and letterbooks, are in the Francis A. Countway Library of Medicine, Holmes Hall, at the Harvard University Medical School in Boston, Massachusetts. The most significant of Bowditch's studies of consumption are *Consumptionin New England: or, Locality One of Its Chief Causes. An Address Delivered Before the Massachusetts Medical Society* (1862) and *Is Consumption Ever Contagious?* (1864). Also see his *A Brief Plea for an Ambulance System for the Army of the United States, As Drawn from the Extra Sufferings of the Late Nathaniel Bowditch and a Wounded Comrade* (1863) and *Public Hygiene in America: Being the Centennial Discourse Delivered Before the International Medical Congress, Philadelphia, September, 1876* (1877).

Careful synopses of the work of the Boston Co-operative Building Company to provide decent housing for the poor during Bowditch's years as director can be found in the *Annual Reports of the Boston Co-operative Building Company* (1872–1880), while the *Annual Reports of the State Board of Health of Massachusetts* (1870–1880), carefully prepared by Bowditch during his tenure as chairman, reveal his multifaceted activity in public health research and continuing analysis of tuberculosis incidence and causation.

The most important work on Bowditch is the biography by his son, Vincent Y. Bowditch, *Life and Correspondence of Henry Ingersoll Bowditch by His Son in Two Volumes* (1902). Also see the sketch of him in *Dictionary of American Biography*, vol. 2 (1929), 492–494. The most recently published study of the Massachusetts State Board of Health is Barbara Rosenkrantz's *Public Health and the State: Changing Views in Massachusetts, 1842–1936* (1972). For a history of the work of public health reformers, including Bowditch, in Boston, see Dorothy T. Scanlon, "Public Health Movement in Boston, 1870–1910" Ph.D. dissertation, Boston University, 1956.

DOROTHY T. SCANLON

**Bowen, Louise deKoven** (February 26, 1859–November 9, 1953), philanthropist, suffragist, and social reformer, was born in Chicago, the only child of John and Helen (Hadduck) deKoven. Her father was a Chicago banker, and her mother, the third white child born within the Fort Dearborn stockade, was the daughter of a pioneer Chicagoan who amassed a great fortune during the city's early years, a fortune which Bowen would inherit. Louise's energy and intelligence were evident from childhood as she explored and reacted to the rough and adventurous life in the fast-growing western town of Chicago. Her education at a locally fashionable girl's school, the Dearborn Seminary, seemed a waste of time to her because she learned nothing practical.

In spite of her father's attempt to mold her into a typical young woman of the period with interests limited to family and church, Louise became a citizen reformer and social welfare worker. Her first steps into the cauldron of industrial, immigrant Chicago were appropriately through church work, still a bit unusual for a young woman in the mid-1870s. She started a Bible class at St. James Episcopal Church for older boys, who came to the city for work but also found loneliness. She also established and paid for a clubhouse for the boys on Huron Street, her first large public philanthropy. Typical of her entire career as an unpaid social welfare worker, Louise did not merely start a program; she joined in the lives of club members, visiting their homes and helping in varied ways. This taught her firsthand about the conditions of working people's lives. Her next effort was also within the traditional woman's role in the 1880s. With Eleanor Ryerson she established a Kitchen Garden Association to help poor girls learn housekeeping. Later this work was put into the school curriculum. Bowen recognized that the weakness of such a program was that the girls had little possibility of ever keeping house in a way that measured up to the idealistic standards taught them.

In 1886 Louise deKoven married Joseph T. Bowen, with whom she had four children. For the next ten years she divided her time between her children and her hospital activities. During the decade 1886–1896, she was president of the Board of Children's Memorial Hospital, president of the Women's Board of Passavant Hospital, and vice president of the Woman's Board of St. Luke's Hospital. In 1893 Bowen met Jane Addams* and started her long association with Hull-House and Addams, who became her most intimate friend. Then in 1903 Bowen became a trustee, and in 1907 treasurer, of Hull-House. From this time forward her energies, devotion, and funds predominantly went toward its many and varied activities. As president of the Hull-House Woman's Club she gave the hall which served not only the Club but many of the general social and educational activities at Hull-House. She also built a five-story structure to house the activities of men and boys. After her husband died in 1911, she built a summer camp for Hull-House at Waukegan, Illinois—the Joseph Tilton Bowen Country Club. Men, women, and children from Hull-House enjoyed outings for many years at this beautiful site; Bowen herself spent many days vacationing there in her own cottage, participating with the campers.

Bowen and other women associated with Hull-House were influential in establishing in 1899 the Chicago Juvenile Court, the first such court in the United States. The women then organized a Juvenile Court Committee to assist the court in its operation and to make sure that the intent behind its establishment became the reality. Julia Lathrop,* a resident of Hull-House and later the first chief of the U.S. Children's Bureau, became president of the body. The following year Bowen succeeded her, and for seven years led the Committee in securing salaries for the probation officers, for whom no public funds were allocated; interviewing candidates; and advising the probation staff. The Committee continually worked at legislation to upgrade court services and the court's budget. The Committee also established and financially supported a detention home. Bowen and others saw firsthand the conditions they believed responsible for juvenile delinquency. The Juvenile Court Committee, with Bowen at its head, developed a Juvenile Protective Association to deal with environmental causes of delinquency, including family conditions and neighborhood temptations. This pioneer effort was copied by many communities. The Association investigated about 6,000 complaints a year. Bowen investigated places of recreation to determine their "wholesomeness." She worked to develop standards for dance halls, recognizing the need for such young people's activities but deploring bad influences and practices. The Association in 1907 also established the first juvenile psychiatric institute in the world. Many of the pamphlets published by the Juvenile Protective Association about children in the city were written by Bowen and were the basis of her first book, *Safeguards for City Children at Work and Play*, published in 1914. The philosophy which guided Bowen in her social welfare work was the idea that the Association should work for the release of virtue rather than merely the suppression of vice. Although today the weaknesses of the kind of moral reform which Bowen and the Association practiced are evident, in 1900 the approach was rather modern.

From 1907 to 1917 Bowen also helped establish the Visiting Nurses Association in Chicago, worked on the Committee for School Nurses, and supported dozens of other charities while trying to reform society so that charity would be replaced by social justice. From 1917 to 1919 she served as the only woman on the Illinois State Council of Defense, and headed the Woman's Committee, which had 692,229 women registered to work for national defense with 7,700 chairwomen in villages and towns throughout Illinois. In April, 1922, she was an official delegate to the Pan-American Congress of Women held in Baltimore.

Bowen also worked long and hard for woman's suffrage and was on the executive board of the National American Woman's Suffrage Association for two years. She wrote and spoke, encouraging women to participate in politics with the same dedication and energy she gave to her earlier social work. In 1914 she was a founding member of Woman's City Club of Chicago, an organization devoted to the education of women and action by them in all arenas of civic reform, and served as president of the body for fifteen years. She helped found and was president of the Woman's Roosevelt Republican Club, which supported reform candidates locally and statewide. In the 1920s, under her leadership, this club sponsored a Woman's World Fair in Chicago, a showplace for female accomplishments, which was held for four consecutive years. For these and her many other activities, Bowen received an honorary Doctor of Humane Letters degree from Tufts University in 1926.

Though less active in the 1930s, Bowen served as vice president of the United Charities of Chicago during the early years of the Great Depression. She also continued to visit Hull-House every day and served as its treasurer until 1952. Each year she spent the summer at Bowen Country Club in her cottage, enjoying the contacts with the children and protesting the lack of adequate social services in Waukegan, especially garbage removal.

In 1948 the historian Mary Beard wrote that Bowen, more than any other public figure, had combined the qualities of mind and heart to achieve so much. (Incidentally, shortly before her death Bowen said that modern social work should have less theory and more heart.) The exemplification of the best qualities of volunteerism in American social welfare work, the "First Lady of Illinois," as some referred to her, or "Chicago's Conscience," as others called her, continued to be consulted by politicians and officials seeking solutions to Chicago's social ills until her death there in 1953, at the age of ninety-four.

One of the best sources for information on Louise deKoven Bowen is her scrapbooks at the Chicago Historical Society. The collection includes pictures, newspaper clippings, Hull-House publications, and pamphlets written by Bowen and published by the Juvenile Protective Agency. Also at the Chicago Historical Society are minutes of the Woman's City Club of Chicago and the United Charities of Chicago. Another good source of manuscript material is the University of Illinois at Chicago, where the Jane Addams Memorial Collection and the Papers of the Juvenile Protective Agency are housed. In addition, three books by Bowen and a published collection of her letters and speeches are indispensable: *Safeguards for City Youth at Work and Play* (1914); *Growing Up with a City* (1926); *Open Windows: People and Places* (1946); and *Speeches, Addresses, and Letters of Louise deKoven Bowen, Reflecting Social Movements in Chicago*, 2 vols., ed. M. E. Humphries (1937).

In addition, two general works are very helpful: Kathleen McCarthy's *Noblesse Oblige: Charity and Cultural Philanthropy in Chicago, 1849–1929* (1982), and Anthony Platt's *The Child Savers* (1969), a critique from a modern point of view of the late nineteenth and early twentieth century reforms and reformers which includes remarks about Bowen and the Juvenile Protective Agency.

MARILYN A. DOMER

**Brace, Charles Loring** (June 19, 1826–August 11, 1890), child welfare worker, was born in Litchfield, Connecticut, to John Pierce and Lucy (Porter) Brace, who were both from old New England families. When Charles was born, John Brace was principal of Litchfield Academy, but in 1832 he took charge of a female seminary in Hartford. Later he became editor of the *Hartford Courant*. Charles was educated at home by his father. His mother died in 1840, when he was fourteen. In 1842 he entered Yale and graduated with honors in 1846. He taught school for a year, entered Yale Divinity School, and later transferred to Union Theological Seminary in New York City. He enjoyed the diversity of the city, but he made few friends and realized how cut off he was from his family. He also began to have doubts about a career in the ministry. In 1850–1851, when he toured Europe with two old friends from Connecticut, John and Frederick Olmsted, Brace became interested in English and German philanthropic and correctional institutions. He also met his future wife, Letitia Neill, whom he returned to marry in Belfast, Ireland, on August 21, 1854.

After the European tour, Brace came back to New York City to work with the Reverend Lewis M. Pease, a Methodist city missionary, at the Five Points Mission in one of the most impoverished sections of the city. Here Brace became troubled by the thousands of boys and girls who wandered the streets, homeless and unemployed. In 1849 the city's chief of police complained of the same problem, and several clergymen, including Brace, responded by establishing special religious meetings for vagrant boys. Himself a stranger to the city, Brace sympathized with the boys' loneliness and rootlessness, and he also admired their independence and toughness. Yet the boys' meetings were not entirely successful, for the youngsters fought over benches, threw rocks, and hissed at the speakers. In 1853 the ministers tried a new tactic and formed the Children's Aid Society with the twenty-seven-year-old Brace as its chief officer. He had now found both a career and a secure niche in the big city.

Within a year, Brace had begun a multifaceted program to assist New York's indigent young. In December 1853, his Children's Aid Society opened a vocational or industrial school in a neighborhood where young vagrant girls often became prostitutes. Brace recruited middle-class women to teach the girls decorum and sewing. Despite a rough beginning, pupils and teachers soon settled into an acceptable routine. In March, 1854, Brace opened the agency's first lodging house. He observed that many children were enterprising and hard working, admirable traits, but were without adequate housing and food. Brace expected the News Boys' Lodging House to ameliorate these problems and to encourage self-help and cleanliness by requiring the boys to pay six cents a night for lodging and four cents for supper, and to bathe before bed. In 1862 the Children's Aid Society established a Girls' Lodging House to encourage the same virtues in young girls. By 1892 Brace's agency operated twenty-seven industrial schools and six lodging houses in the city. Brace's program was unique because it was voluntary and preventive. Instead of trying to educate and reform children after they broke the law (as did juvenile reformatories), he tried to prevent lawbreaking and poverty by teaching the children skills and encouraging hard work, honesty, punctuality, and order.

However, the most controversial of Brace's programs was neither his schools nor his lodging houses but his plan to place city children in farm families in the West. In 1854 he sent the first party of forty-six children to Michigan with an agent, who took them before the assembled townspeople in the local church and explained the children's need for homes. Within a week, farm families claimed all the children. Later Brace improved the system by sending some agents into the city to discover needy children, and others to the West to arrange homes for them. After placement, the child could write to the agency and perhaps visit with its agent once a year. By 1862 Brace had sent 60,000 children west.

Placing out needy children in farm families, where their labor was in demand, had long been accepted practice for almshouses, orphanages, houses of refuge, and reformatories. Brace was innovative because he placed out youngsters without an indenture contract and did not institutionalize children before placement. He believed that indenture contracts were too binding on child and master. Without them both would be free—the child to leave a bad home, the master to dismiss a lazy or disrespectful youngster. As for institutionalization, Brace argued that it was too costly and that it stifled children's independent spirit. Eventually, he came to feel that asylums built on the cottage plan were better than congregate institutions, but he always believed that the family home was best for a child.

Although Brace's placing-out program was popular with New York's newspapers and its wealthy citizens, who provided it generous financial support, the program garnered critics as well. Westerners charged that Brace sent out young criminals, who filled western reform schools. Juvenile asylum officials maintained that vagrant city children needed to be disciplined in an institution before placement. Catholics objected to putting Catholic youth in Protestant homes, and social workers argued that Brace's agency did not properly supervise children in their new homes. Brace vigorously defended his program in speeches and in print, but by the 1880s began to stress his urban programs over out-of-city placement, which was eventually terminated in 1929, well after his death. Still, the Children's Aid Society was widely imitated, and Brace's successors modified his program into foster care, still the most acceptable method for dealing with homeless, needy children.

Brace was exceptional for his day in that he admired and accepted both the city and the vagrant child. He felt that cities offered the young opportunities to start over, to escape the impoverished homes into which they were born. His industrial schools and lodging houses were designed to facilitate this escape. And while Brace believed that vagrant children as a group were a threat to society (he called them the ''dangerous classes'' in a book of the same name), he admired individual street urchins for their enterprise and free spirit. His western placement program was intended to give each child more scope in which to exercise these virtues.

Charles Loring Brace died in Campfer, Switzerland, on August 11, 1890, at the age of sixty-four.

Some of Brace's correspondence can be found in: Washington, D.C., Library of Congress, Papers of Frederick Law Olmstead; and in Cambridge, Massachusetts, Harvard University, Houghton Library, Papers of Charles Greeley Loring.

The most important of Brace's own publications are *The Best Method of Disposing of Our Pauper and Vagrant Children* (1859); *Short Sermons to News Boys, with a History of the Formation of the News Boys' Lodging House* (1866); *Address on Industrial Schools, Delivered to the Teachers of the Schools, Nov. 13, 1868* (1868); *The Dangerous Classes of New York and Twenty Years' Work Among Them* (1872); ''The Placing Out Program for Homeless and Vagrant Children,'' *National Conference of Charities and Corrections, Proceedings* (1876), 135–144; ''Child Helping in New York,'' *Journal of Social Science* (May, 1884), 289–305.

Almost every text on nineteenth century reform mentions Brace. The most useful are Thomas Bender, *Toward an Urban Vision: Ideas and Institutions in Nineteenth Century America* (1975); Paul Boyer, *Urban Masses and Moral Order in America, 1820–1920* (1978); Emma Brace, *Life of Charles Loring Brace; Chiefly Told in His Own Letters* (1894); Homer Folks, *The Care of Destitute,*

*Neglected, and Delinquent Children* (1902); Joseph M. Hawes, *Children in Urban Society: Juvenile Delinquency in Nineteenth Century America* (1971); Miriam Z. Langsam, *Children West: A History of the Placing-Out System of the New York Children's Aid Society, 1853–1890* (1964); R. Richard Wohl, "The 'Country Boy' Myth and Its Place in American Urban Culture: The Nineteenth Century Contribution," *Perspectives in American History* (1969), 77–156.

PRISCILLA FERGUSON CLEMENT

**Brackett, Jeffrey Richardson** (October 20, 1860–December 4, 1949), welfare administrator and social work educator, was born in Quincy, Massachusetts, son of Jeffrey Richardson Brackett, a merchant, and Sarah Cordelia Brackett. He descended from a long line of prosperous New England bankers and merchants. Orphaned at age sixteen (his parents died within six months of each other), Brackett was raised in the home of a young friend. In spite of the loss of his parents, Brackett's inheritance provided him with the comforts of the leisure class both as a youth and in later life. He graduated from Adams Academy in Quincy in 1879 and, four years later, received an A.B. degree from Harvard College. After a year of study and travel in Europe, Brackett entered graduate school in history and political science at the Johns Hopkins University in Baltimore. There he studied with the foremost exemplar of the "scientific" history of his day, Professor Herbert Baxter Adams. At Johns Hopkins, Brackett wrote the first in what would become a long line of Ph.D. dissertations on black slavery completed at that institution. He received his Ph.D. in 1889, the same year that his *The Negro in Maryland: A Study of the Institution of Slavery* appeared in the Johns Hopkins University Studies in Historical and Political Science. Brackett's *Progress of the Colored People of Maryland* appeared in the same series in 1890. He married Susan Katharine Jones on June 16, 1886. She died in 1931. On June 22, 1935, Brackett married Louisa de Berniere Bacot.

Upon receiving his doctorate, Brackett joined the Johns Hopkins faculty as an instructor in history and government. He and other members of the Johns Hopkins community committed themselves to volunteer work with the city's poor. In 1881 Johns Hopkins president Daniel Coit Gilman had founded the Charity Organization Society (COS) of Baltimore. Gilman, Adams, Brackett, and other scholars at Johns Hopkins viewed the COS as a social laboratory to observe social problems firsthand. They championed the idea that theoretical and applied social science deserved as much attention from researchers as the physical sciences. They prided themselves in accumulating "scientific" data about the disadvantaged by employing the casework technique. The COS opposed direct relief to the impoverished. Instead, it celebrated the virtues of hard work, helped the indigent to help themselves, and worked to make them self-sufficient. In 1895 Brackett questioned the value of large-scale relief and public aid. Local churches and "small bands of workers," he said, best represented the charity organization movement. Even so, Brackett found little fault with relief except for its inadequacy. He expressed less concern with the form of aid than with eradicating the causes of poverty itself. Brackett condemned the excesses of industrial capitalism, inadequate vocational training, social barriers, and public apathy.

Brackett played an active role in the COS, and his work with this agency served as an apprenticeship for his distinguished career in the field of social welfare. Writing in 1903, he underscored the importance of cure and prevention in charity work over mere alleviation or short-term care. His efforts, for instance, in the area of personal contact with clients led to the establishment of Baltimore's Wayfarer's Inn, an innovative concept in its day for the housing of transients. According to Brackett, social service work should be aimed less at protecting society by restraints on the poor and more at protection of needy individuals by societal reform. He condemned the fee system of payment of policemen, jails that bred new crime and disease, and the lethargy of officials in implementing sanitation laws. In 1897 Brackett chaired a municipal committee that recommended reforms in the care of public dependents. This resulted in the creation of Baltimore's Board of Supervisors of City Charities. In 1900 Brackett became chairman of this board as well as head of the city's Department of Charities and Corrections, with a seat on the city council. He held both posts until 1904. In that year Brackett also chaired the City Relief Committee to assist victims of Baltimore's devastating fire of 1904. As a measure of his rapid rise in stature, in 1903–1904 Brackett was elected president of the National Conference of Charities and Correction.

But Brackett's importance lies in his role as a pioneer in the history of social work education. From 1899 to 1904 he lectured on public aid, charity, and correction at Johns Hopkins. Through the years he remained dedicated to the systematic training of professional social workers. Brackett insisted that social workers receive instruction not only in the methodology of charity, but broadly based academic preparation as well. He, alone among early social work educators, differentiated between classes in social service theory and apprenticeships. In 1904 he left Baltimore to organize the Boston School for Social Workers (later the Boston School of Social Work) under the cosponsorship of Harvard University and Simmons College. This school was the first institution affiliated with a college or university to provide full-time social work training both in academic and field settings. Brackett served as director of the school until his retirement in 1920. An innovator in social work curriculum, he integrated the school's course offerings both with Boston's welfare agencies and Massachusetts General Hospital's social service department. In doing so Brackett led the way in the training of medical social workers. He also insisted that research become a fundamental component of social work education. His philosophy of training soon became the norm in schools of social work throughout America.

While in Massachusetts Brackett left a broad imprint on his native state's social welfare programs. From 1906 to 1919, for instance, he served on the Massachusetts State Board of Charity, and in 1913 he chaired the Boston Associated Charities. Later (1920–1934) he sat on the advisory board of the Massachusetts

Board of Public Welfare. In these roles Brackett worked to update and improve various forms of public assistance to the needy, especially the state's programs for foster children and the aged and infirm. He championed two notable bills, the Mothers' Aid Law (1912) and the Old Age Assistance Law (1931). He achieved less success, though, as an advocate of decentralized, localized welfare offices. Determined in his efforts to aid the needy, Brackett dedicated himself to combatting poverty and suffering. He left behind important legacies, both in the training of social workers and by his tireless and unselfish service to the betterment of his fellow man.

Jeffrey Brackett died of an intestinal disorder in Charleston, South Carolina, on December 4, 1949.

Brackett's papers are deposited in the Simmons College Archives in Boston. For glimpses into his views regarding social welfare and social work education, see the following works by Brackett: *The Charity Organization Movement: Its Tendency and Its Duty* (1895); *Supervision and Education in Charity* (1903); *Social Service Through the Parish* (1923); *The Transportation Problem in American Social Work* (1936). For analyses of Brackett's early historical writings on slavery, see John David Smith, *An Old Creed for the New South: Black Slavery as Metaphor and History, 1865–1918* (forthcoming). And for useful insights into Brackett's work with the Charity Organization Society of Baltimore, see William Gibson, "A History of Family and Child Welfare Agencies in Baltimore, 1849–1943," Ph.D. dissertation, Ohio State University, 1969. The most useful biographical source, though uncritical and eulogistic in tone, is Katharine D. Hardwick, Rose Weston Bull, and Louisa deB. Bacot Brackett, *Jeffrey Richardson Brackett: "Everyday Puritan"* (1956).

JOHN DAVID SMITH

**Bradford, Cornelia Foster** (December 4, 1847–January 15, 1935), settlement house founder and longtime head resident, was born in Granby, New York, in the Finger Lakes region of the state, the second of three children of Benjamin Franklin Bradford and Mary Amory (Howe) Bradford. Her father, originally from Rhode Island, and a descendant of Governor William Bradford of the Plymouth Colony, served as a minister in a succession of churches, first Methodist and then Congregational. Her mother was a New Englander too, hailing from Massachusetts. Both Bradfords participated in a number of antebellum reform causes, including temperance, abolition, and woman's rights, the latter of which might have inspired the two Bradford girls to attain an education. Cornelia "Nellie" Bradford graduated from Houghton Seminary in Clinton, New York, and then attended Olivet College in Michigan.

Her mid-twenties found Cornelia Bradford living with her father and sister in Chester, New Jersey. She and her sister taught Sunday school in her father's church, while her brother was himself a minister in nearby Montclair. Cornelia Bradford's activities from then through her thirties and early forties are largely unknown. She probably traveled and studied, however, since she occasionally lectured on travel, history, and literature.

Bradford's forty-fifth year was her turning point. In 1892 she was in London studying the settlement house movement, which had been born there in 1884 with the establishment of Toynbee Hall. Bradford visited Toynbee Hall and lived for a while in an East London settlement house, Mansfield House. Returning to America, she was drawn to Jane Addams'* Hull-House in Chicago, where she resided for several months. Then, in December, 1893, she set off to found her own settlement.

Why Bradford chose to settle in Jersey City, New Jersey, is unknown, although it certainly deserved a reformer's efforts. Across from New York City, Jersey City's waterfront was home in the 1890s to Irish, Italian, and an increasing contingent of Eastern European immigrants. Some lived on filled-in marshland with basements and privies that flooded at high tide; others lived a few blocks inland, squeezed three families to a house in a once handsome neighborhood. The view of the New York skyline was obscured by fences, railroad yards, factories, warehouses, and tenements. In this neighborhood, operating at first from a furnished room in the large, public "People's Palace," Bradford drew local people into a variety of clubs and sports activities. Soon, with her brother's financial help, she bought one of the few fine mansions left in the area. Sponsors among Jersey City's upper-class women and local businessmen helped her furnish the building comfortably. This genteel haven in the midst of waterfront squalor attracted young, educated middle-class women and a few men, all, like Bradford, interested in working and living with like-minded individuals and helping their poorer neighbors.

Bradford named her settlement Whittier House and adopted lines from the poet John Greenleaf Whittier for its motto: "He serves Thee best who loveth most / His brothers and Thy own." Bradford hoped through personal bonds and social uplift to heal what she perceived as widening rifts between classes, experienced largely as ethnic differences in heterogeneous New Jersey. Bradford hoped that personal relations with the poor could transcend class or ethnic divisions. She hoped that she and her residents would, by example, inculcate in their neighbors middle-class values and aspirations. Thus, the art, literature, and dance classes at Whittier, the free flower distribution, even the very ambience of mahogany furniture, doilies, and potted palms, were not frivolous or self-indulgent but, on one hand, an expression of Bradford's desire to share her privileges with her poor neighbors, and on the other, a demonstration of the rewards of hard work and study.

More practically, Whittier House did offer varied opportunities for study in both academic and vocational topics. It sponsored a series of health clinics, culminating in the early 1920s with the opening of a Babies' Hospital, for mothers and babies, and a Diet Kitchen, to prepare formulas for underweight children and babies. Other activities included the usual variety of clubs, classes, and programs offered by a settlement house.

Bradford also belonged to organizations besides Whittier House. For instance, the New Jersey Consumers' League was formed at Whittier House in 1898. As part of the National Consumers' League, it was a women's organization concerned with the working conditions of women and children. Bradford served as vice president and lobbyist, and personally investigated child labor in New Jersey's glass industry for the organization.

A housing investigation, performed by Whittier resident Mary Sayles, sparked the formation of the Tenement House Protective League in 1903. It met regularly at Whittier, and Bradford was a member. When New Jersey's governor appointed a Tenement House Commission, housing inspectors were invited to live at the settlement. Bradford herself was appointed to both the State Board of Charities, Aids, and Corrections and to the State Board of Children's Guardians.

Bradford also was active in other private organizations, most notably the New Jersey Neighborhood Workers' Association, which she helped to organize. She served as president of the Association and, for years, as chair of its Legislation Committee. In 1920 Bradford also was president of the New Jersey Conference for Social Welfare.

Thus, Bradford and many of her residents as well were embedded in a dense network of social reform organizations. Contained within this network was a community of middle- and upper-class women, connected to one another through their reform work. Perhaps this explains why Bradford considered herself an "ardent feminist." She spoke to the New Jersey Woman's Suffrage Association, a moderate group, on "The Value of the Vote in Social Service Work," and petitioned the Governor for the Congressional Union, a militant group, forerunner of the National Woman's Party.

Like other feminists, Bradford also was active in the peace movement, joining the Women's International League for Peace and Freedom and the Woman's Peace Party. But like so many others, she abandoned her opposition to war with America's entry into World War I, and during that conflict she turned Whittier House into a home for uprooted soldiers. Her attitudes toward her neighbors had changed, too. In fact, as early as 1912, alienated perhaps by the increasing numbers of Eastern European immigrants in her neighborhood, Bradford had begun to complain of her neighbors' "clannishness" and of their apathy. Disenchantment led her to fervent participation in the Americanization movement of World War I. She even offered to spy secretly on her Polish neighbors for the nativist North American Civic League for Immigrants.

Bradford mourned for the Whittier House of old after the war. Financial difficulties compounded the lack of direction in the settlement movement in general and in Whittier House specifically. Contributing to the waning of her sense of mission at Whittier was Bradford's incredible success in getting Jersey City's government to fund and administer programs she and her residents had initiated. By 1917 Jersey City provided kindergartens, playgrounds, legal aid, industrial, educational, and art classes, public libraries, public baths, district nursing, a milk dispensary, and a medical dispensary, all started at Whittier

House. A huge medical center built in the 1920s displaced the Babies' Hospital. Contributing as well to Bradford's sense of loss was the dispersal of the community of women reformers she had helped form. With suffrage and greater job opportunities, women were not sustaining the Progressive Era's women's institutions. Rather, they were moving into the traditional political parties or into new professions, such as social work. Bradford personally was criticized by a later head worker as unprofessional, and her generation was seen as too sentimental and romantic.

Bradford retired in 1925, living nine more years in Montclair with her brother before her death there on January 15, 1935.

The major primary source for information on Cornelia Foster Bradford is in the Whittier House Papers, New Jersey Historical Society, Newark, New Jersey. Additional Whittier House Annual Reports are available at the Social Welfare Archive Center, University of Minnesota, Minneapolis, and at the Jersey City Public Library. Some information is available in the New Jersey Consumers' League Records, Special Collections, Rutgers University, New Brunswick, New Jersey.

Besides her lengthy annual reports, Cornelia Bradford wrote several articles: "For Jersey City's Social Uplift: Life at Whittier House," *Commons* (February, 1905), 101–106; "Schools and Civic Co-operation in Organized Charity," *Proceedings* of the Seventh Annual Meeting of the New Jersey State Conference of Charities and Correction (February, 1908), 270–276; "The Settlement Movement in New Jersey," *New Jersey Review of Charities and Corrections*(April, 1912), 23–28.

The most recent and detailed account of Cornelia Bradford's life is in Ella Handen, "In Liberty's Shadow: Cornelia Bradford and Whittier House," *New Jersey History* (Fall/Winter, 1982), 49–69. Roy Lubove, "Cornelia Foster Bradford," in *Notable American Women*, vol. 1 (1971), 218–219, is equally useful. Both include information unavailable elsewhere, although they also disagree on minor points. For a placement of Bradford and Whittier House in Jersey City's political terrain, see Eugene M. Tobin, "The Progressive as Humanitarian: Jersey City's Search for Social Justice, 1890–1917," *New Jersey History* (Autumn/ Winter, 1975), 77–98, and his "Mark Fagen and the Politics of Urban Reform: Jersey City, 1900–1917," Ph.D. dissertation, Brandeis University, 1972.

CLAUDIA CLARK

**Branch, Anna Hempstead** (March 18, 1875–September 8, 1937), settlement house resident, philanthropist, and poet, was born at Hempstead House in New London, Connecticut, to John Locke Branch and Mary Lydia (Bolles) Branch. Hempstead House, which her mother's family had lived in since 1640, is among the oldest historic homes in the United States. Anna and her older brother John Bolles, who died at the age of thirteen, were the tenth generation of Hempsteads.

Anna traced her American ancestry to Elder Brewster and other Mayflower passengers. Her mother later founded the Connecticut Mayflower Society.

Both sides of the family were active in politics, law, and literature. Her grandfather, John Rogers Bolles, moreover, was involved in the antislavery cause before it became a widespread movement.

Most of her youth was spent in Brooklyn, New York, and in New York City, where her father practiced law. Her mother was an author and illustrator of children's stories. Anna was brought up as an Episcopalian and maintained a lifetime affiliation with that church. She attended Froebel and Adelphi academies in Brooklyn, and in 1897 she graduated from Smith College, where she had been editor-in-chief of the college literary monthly. After graduation she studied at the American Academy of Dramatic Arts in New York City and received a degree in dramaturgy in 1900. She never married.

Anna Hempstead Branch is mainly known as a writer of poetry. She published many volumes of poetry and still is highly regarded among the minor poets in the United States. However, she also invested significant parts of thirty-five years of her life in volunteer social services activities in New York City and in New London.

In 1897 Branch served with Josiah Strong and others on the first board of directors of Christodora House, a newly established social settlement in New York City. This social settlement was mainly built and financed by Mrs. Arthur Curtiss James, a classmate and friend of Branch's at Smith College. Christodora, or "gift of Christ," was somewhat atypical of social settlements in that it identified itself as a Christian social institution. Its target population, however, was a predominantly Jewish neighborhood on the Lower East Side.

Though Branch had a lifetime tie with Christodora House, her twenty-five years of volunteer service were intermittent. Between 1905 and 1912, for instance, winter months were spent bringing poetry to the settlement's audience, especially youth. Her dedication to bringing literature, especially poetry, to all people never diminished. She also gave years of service to advising young poets and artists.

At Christodora House she played the major part in the establishment of the Poets' Guild in 1920. Anna Branch's considerable organizational skills, coupled with her vision and dynamism, motivated others to join her in this and in her other projects. Among the literary figures recruited for the Poets' Guild were Edwin Arlington Robinson, Percy MacKaye, and Margaret Widdemer. These members and others contributed poetry readings and classes, organizational and technical writing skills, as well as modest financial donations—and they recruited friends who participated in other Guild programs, such as acting, dancing, writing, diction, and handicrafts.

The Guild published several books and used the profits to further its cultural activities. It paid for a printing press that was set up in a shed behind Hempstead House. Anna Branch used this equipment to create and edit different anthologies. Her *Unbound Anthology* was a looseleaf collection of English and American verse. The poems were sold cheaply by the sheaf to enable Lower East Siders to gradually build collections. Branch regarded the poems as a way to share core values. She publicized this work of the Guild as a valuable form of Americanization for immigrants in speeches to organizations such as the Daughters of the American Revolution.

Branch was so convinced that poetry was a vehicle for promoting brotherhood among nations that she initiated several international anthologies—the Consuls and the Ambassadors Series. She enlisted the support of consulates in New York City and legations and embassies in Washington, D.C., in these projects. New York City consulates, for example, contributed sixty-three poems to the series.

In her international anthologies as well as in her vision of a Children's City, a kind of Children's Commonwealth of the World, Anna Branch expressed her strong feelings for international brotherhood. She did not embrace any economic or social theory about society, but was concerned with exerting moral influence for peace. Her life style was so permeated with spiritual matters that her close friends compared her to St. Theresa. Her methodology, however, was pragmatic in that she tried to build cooperation among diverse groups by working together in common projects. Her career in social service showed the capacity to formulate many inspired plans for combining social work and art; however, she was not always capable of, or did not have the means of carrying them out. Some schemes were impractical, and funding usually was a problem.

In addition to her social service work with Christodora House, Branch was instrumental in starting the playground movement in New London, Connecticut. She was active in that project from 1900 to 1910. She also recruited Connecticut College students to work in that community in a prototype of a social settlement, Charter House. In addition, she was a major benefactor of Connecticut College.

After a debilitating struggle with cancer, she died at Hempstead House on September 9, 1937.

The collected papers of Anna Hempstead Branch are at the Smith College Library. The bulk of her papers, however, is in an uncatalogued collection at Connecticut College.

Anna Hempstead Branch wrote about "The Poets' Guild" in the *Smith Alumnae Quarterly* (November, 1920), 57–59. Some of her later poetry is in *Christodora House Papers* (n.d.). Some useful sources about her life include Julian T. Baird, Jr., "Anna Hempstead Branch," in *Notable American Women*, vol. 1 (1971), 226–228; Stanley J. Kunitz and Howard Haycroft, eds., *Twentieth Century Authors* (1942); and Margaret Widdemer, *Golden Friends I Had* (1964). Her obituary appeared in the *New York Times*, September 9, 1937, 23.

JOHN J. CAREY

**Brandt, Lilian** (May 15, 1873–June 4, 1951), social welfare researcher and writer, was born in Indianapolis, Indiana, one of three children of the Rev. Dr. John B. and Emily Brandt. Dr. Brandt was an "organizer of churches" and served several in St. Louis during his daughter's school years (Brandt Memorial Presbyterian Church in St. Louis is named for him).

Lilian Brandt graduated from Wellesley College in 1895. Before obtaining her M.A. in economics at Wellesley in 1901, she taught history and classical languages at Lindenwood College, St. Charles, Missouri, and at Bradford Academy, Bradford, Massachusetts. During that time, she also spent a year in Europe studying and traveling. Influenced by the work of W. E. B. Du Bois,* her master's thesis was entitled "The Negroes of St. Louis." She taught history and economics at National Park Seminary, Forest Glen, Maryland, in 1901–1902, before attending the New York Charity Organization Society's Summer School in Philanthropy in 1902. This, the forerunner of the New York School of Social Work, now the Columbia University School of Social Work, was at the time directed by Philip W. Ayres* and was the only professional education available for social workers.

Edward T. Devine,* the general secretary of the New York COS, immediately selected Brandt to be statistician of the Society's Committee on the Prevention of Tuberculosis. In 1904, when the School of Philanthropy became a full-year program with Devine as its director, Brandt was made secretary of the Committee on Social Research for both the COS and the school. At this time she published pioneering studies on tuberculosis and was associated with Devine and Paul Kellogg* (a classmate at the Summer School of Philanthropy in 1902) in the development of the preventive aspects of the new antituberculosis campaign. She also taught at the school and worked with Devine on a variety of other projects. Thus she participated in disaster relief activities in connection with the San Francisco earthquake in 1906 and the Dayton, Ohio, flood in 1913. She remained with the COS until 1931, when she joined the staff of the Welfare Council of New York. After 1940 she engaged in a variety of special assignments, most notably with the Community Service Society of New York and the Russell Sage Foundation.

While Lilian Brandt contributed to the study and development of social work in many ways, because she had a particular ability to interpret the significance of the factual material that she assembled, perhaps her greatest contributions to the field were her many publications. Among her early writings were "Social Aspects of Tuberculosis," in the *Annals* of the American Academy of Political and Social Science (1903), and two publications for the COS, *A Directory of Institutions and Societies Dealing with Tuberculosis* (1905) and *Five Hundred and Seventy-four Deserters and Their Families* (1905). In 1918 she assisted Devine in preparing a monograph for the Carnegie Endowment for International Peace on the ways in which the then warring countries, including Germany and Austria, were caring for their casualties. This was published in 1919 as *Disabled Soldiers and Sailors Pensions and Training* and served as a stimulus to rehabilitation programs in the United States. During the 1930s the Welfare Council published three of her studies: *An Impressionistic View of the Winter of 1930–31 in New York City* (1932), *Glimpses of New York in Previous Depressions* (1933), and *History of the Relief of the Unemployed in New York City, 1929–37* (1940). Later she wrote histories of the Community Service Society of New

York (formed by the merger of the COS and the Association for Improving the Condition of the Poor) and the New York School of Social Work (which by then was affiliated with Columbia University). She also was coauthor of *Russell Sage Foundation, 1907–1946*, a two-volume study published by the Foundation in 1947.

Lilian Brandt died in New York City on June 4, 1951.

Information regarding Lilian Brandt's early family background can be found in the archives of Wellesley College and the Tyler Place Presbyterian Church in St. Louis, Missouri. Very little has been written about her, however. The only other major sources for an understanding of her ideas and contributions are her own works, the chief of which have been cited above. The most extensive readily available account of her life is the obituary in the *New York Times*, June 6, 1951.

MURIEL W. PUMPHREY

**Breckinridge, Sophonisba** (April 1, 1866–July 30, 1948), social worker, political activist, and educator who pioneered in both university social science education and the professionalization of social work in America, was born in Lexington, Kentucky, to William and Issa (Desha) Breckinridge. An ambitious, ferociously energetic woman, Sophonisba Breckinridge was a member of the prominent Kentucky Breckinridge family. She was a great-granddaughter of United States Senator John Breckinridge, a cousin of John C. Breckinridge, Abraham Lincoln's opponent in the presidential campaign of 1860. Her father, William Breckinridge, a former Confederate colonel and a lawyer, served in the United States Congress.

Encouraged by her family, Sophonisba Breckinridge graduated from Wellesley College in 1888, taught briefly as a mathematics tutor, then returned to Kentucky to study law with her father. In 1894 Breckinridge became the first woman to pass the Kentucky bar examination. Her future, however, was not to lie with the practice of law. Deeply unhappy in Kentucky, Breckinridge, the same year she passed the bar, made a decision which dramatically changed her life. She moved to Chicago and applied to earn a doctorate at the University of Chicago. In the late nineteenth and early twentieth centuries the University of Chicago provided a uniquely encouraging environment to bright women graduate students. At a time when other major universities banned women, the University of Chicago offered them scholarships. Of the women in attendance at the twenty major American graduate schools in 1905–1906, for instance, 45 percent were either at the University of Chicago or Columbia University. Breckinridge, who won a fellowship in the Political Science Department, began a lifelong professional association with the University of Chicago. She also began lifelong friendships with other women graduate students. Frances Kellor,* Katharine Bement Davis,* and, most important, Edith Abbott,* were to be co-workers and collaborators for decades, decades during which Sophonisba Breckinridge would continually seek to merge scholarship and social action.

Breckinridge stayed in Chicago once she received, in 1901, the first Ph.D. in political science awarded to an American woman. She remained as a faculty member at the University of Chicago, creating new courses, departments, even schools, pioneering the teaching of social science and social work, not retiring from her professorship until 1942, at age seventy-six. Teaching and scholarly publication were to be her most important professional contributions. In 1904 Breckinridge began to teach courses on family law and family economics in the university's new Department of Household Administration. By 1907 she combined her University of Chicago duties with teaching at the Chicago School of Civics and Philanthropy, a private training school for social workers founded in 1903 by sociologist Graham Taylor,* an associate of Jane Addams* at Hull-House. By 1920 Breckinridge and Edith Abbott, whom Breckinridge had recruited as a fellow teacher, had wrested control of the School of Civics and Philanthropy from Taylor and had convinced the University of Chicago to absorb it as its new Graduate School of Social Service Administration. Both Abbott, as dean, and Breckinridge, as Deutsch Professor of Public Welfare Administration, remained associated with the School of Social Service Administration until their retirement. The two women, whose careers as colleagues and coauthors so closely intertwined that each almost became the other's *doppelganger*, shaped the School of Social Service Administration to be a bridge between academe and community as well as a model professional school for the new field of social work. Detailed and difficult course work and practical experience both received emphasis. By Breckinridge's death in 1948, the school had become large and prestigious, its students scattered in jobs throughout the country.

Breckinridge combined scholarly writing and editing with teaching. In 1927 she and Abbott founded the *Social Service Review*, still an influential journal. From the twenties through the forties, the two edited a series of books on social service published by the University of Chicago Press. Alone or with Abbott, Breckinridge wrote many books and scholarly articles, among them analyses of immigration—*New Homes for Old* (1921); women's social and work roles—*Women in the Twentieth Century* (1931); and juvenile delinquency—*Truancy and Non Attendance in Chicago Schools* (1917).

Breckinridge set herself apart from other progressive race theorists, opposed restrictive immigration legislation, and identified discrimination and lack of education, rather than heredity, as causes for many immigrants' problems. She passionately defended women's right to assume many different social and economic roles and denounced those who would limit the activities of women. Breckinridge argued that truancy and juvenile crime were often signs of family neglect. Rather than being inherently prone to wrongdoing, delinquent children were usually victims of poverty and adult abuse. Society, and not just their immediate families, had an obligation to try to reclaim these children.

A woman with a dual career, Breckinridge was not just a prominent educator and scholar, she was also a practicing social worker herself and a key figure in transforming social work into a professional career. Drawn into Jane Addams' circle of social reforms, Breckinridge was an enthusiastic supporter of Hull-House. In fact, she occasionally lived at the settlement house until 1920. Breckinridge, as social worker, fought for a progressive agenda of reforms. Key to that agenda was advocacy of greater state involvement in social issues. Breckinridge, in roles as a Chicago city health inspector, a probation officer for the Chicago Juvenile Court, a member of the executive committee of the Consumers' League, a member of the National Association for the Advancement of Colored People, and as secretary of the Immigrants' Protective League, demanded government intervention under the aegis of laws and agencies. She worked hard for civil rights and compulsory education laws, the minimum wage, the abolition of child labor, the eight-hour day, the establishment of a federal Children's Bureau, and the state's right to remove children from abusive parents.

Breckinridge was ahead of most of her contemporaries when in the 1910s and 1920s she urged federal as well as state and local government intervention to help solve social welfare problems such as illiteracy, unemployment, child labor, excessive work hours, and poverty. She argued that suffering had to be a national and not solely a local concern. With the New Deal, her views found greater acceptance. Many of her students became federal and state administrators in programs like the Civilian Conservation Corps (CCC) and the Works Progress Administration (WPA). Interestingly, Breckinridge herself neither sought nor held any government office during the New Deal. Already in her sixties by the time of Franklin Roosevelt's inauguration, she preferred the roles of academic consultant and scholarly researcher. In 1934, in recognition of her leadership, members of the American Association of Schools of Social Work elected her president.

Sophonisba Breckinridge never married, and never, after her arrival at the University of Chicago in 1894, lived anywhere else other than in the city of Chicago. Many of the women whose friendships she had won during her first years in Chicago as student and then professor remained intimates for forty years. Students recalled the familiar sight of Edith Abbott and Sophonisba Breckinridge sweeping through campus, wearing old-fashioned clothing, large straw hats, and long Victorian dresses. Sophonisba Breckinridge officially retired in 1942 but still swept through the University of Chicago campus almost daily, still writing and editing for scholarly journals until a few months before her death in Chicago in 1948 of a perforated ulcer at age eighty-two.

Important manuscript sources for Sophonisba Breckinridge include the meticulously detailed Sophonisba Breckinridge Papers at the Library of Congress, Washington, D.C., and the unpublished "Sophonisba Breckinridge Autobiography," University of Chicago Department of Special Collections, Chicago, Illinois. Sophonisba Breckinridge was a truly prolific writer. Among her significant books not mentioned above are *Legal Tender: A Study in English and American Monetary History* (1903); ed., *The Child in the City* (1912); and ed., *Marriage and the Civic Rights of Women* (1934). Sophonisba Breckinridge also wrote dozens of scholarly articles, alone or as a coauthor with Edith Abbott. Among scholarly works which evaluate the life and career of Sophonisba Breckinridge are Lela Costin, *Two Sisters for Social Justice: A Biography of Grace and Edith Abbott* (1983); Ellen Fitzpatrick, "Academics and Activists: Women Social Scientists and the Impulse for Reform, 1892–1920," Ph.D. dissertation, Brandeis University, 1981; Werner Harder, *The Emergence of a Profession: Social Work Education in Chicago, 1903–1920* (1976); *Notable American Women* (1971); Rebecca Sherrick, "Private Visions, Public Lives: The Hull-House Women in the Progressive Era," Ph.D. dissertation, Northwestern University, 1980; Anthony Travis, "Sophonisba Breckinridge, Militant Feminist," *Mid-America* (1976), 111–118.

JUDITH SEALANDER

**Bremer, Edith Terry** (October 9, 1885–September 12, 1964), promoter of immigrant social welfare and founder of the International Institute movement, was born in Hamilton, New York, to Benjamin Stites Terry, a Baptist minister and history professor (first at Colgate University and later at the University of Chicago), and Mary (Baldwin) Terry, the daughter of a Baptist clergyman. Edith spent most of her childhood in Chicago. She attended the University of Chicago, receiving the A.B. degree in 1907. Influenced by the ferment of social reform in Progressive Era Chicago, she went on to do graduate work at the Chicago School of Civics and Philanthropy (1907–1908), where her training included field research on women workers for the Chicago Women's Trade Union League. In 1908, under the direction of Julia Lathrop,* she served as a field investigator for the Chicago Juvenile Court. During the following two years, she worked as a special agent for the United States Immigration Commission and as a settlement house resident, first at the University of Chicago Settlement and later at the Union Settlement in New York City. In 1910 she became a national field secretary for the National Board of the Young Women's Christian Association (YWCA) in New York. Her special charge was to initiate YWCA work with immigrant girls and women. In 1912 she married Harry M. Bremer, a social worker at New York's Greenwich House settlement and later an investigator for the National Child Labor Committee. They had no children.

Edith Terry Bremer's chief contribution to the field of immigrant social welfare lay in the establishment of the International Institute movement, an outgrowth of her YWCA work. In her work with immigrant girls, she organized in 1910 an educational and social service center in New York's Greenwich Village. This initial experiment, named the International Institute, successfully provided English classes, recreational activities, and aid in solving employment, housing, naturalization, and other problems faced by immigrant and second-generation girls. Bremer envisioned the New York International Institute as a service and adjustment center much like the Immigrants' Protective League of Chicago, organized by Chicago social workers in 1908. Drawing on her Chicago experience, and with the strong support of the National YWCA, Bremer promoted the idea of Institute work with immigrant women in other cities. By the mid-1920s some fifty-five International Institutes had been established by local YWCAs, mostly in northeastern and midwestern cities with large immigrant populations.

Many different agencies were engaged in social service work with immigrants during this period, but the International Institutes were unique in several ways. Bremer emphasized the importance of approaching the ethnic communities on their own terms and in their own languages. Thus, Institute case workers generally were immigrant or second-generation women, trained in social work and knowledgeable about the immigrant communities and their traditions. These nationality workers, as they were called, carried out the International Institute mission at each individual agency. Increasingly, in their case work and group work activities, Institute nationality workers dealt with families and even entire communities rather than with the problems of women and girls. Their ethnic backgrounds and language skills made them especially valuable social workers.

The International Institutes were unique in another way: they promoted ethnic pluralism at a time when most other agencies sought the rapid assimilation of immigrants. Although she began as an assimilationist in her Chicago and early YWCA work, Edith Bremer had always opposed the heavy-handed Americanization programs which typified work with immigrants in the early twentieth century. She was especially disturbed by the nativism of the World War I era and the intolerance of the postwar red scare. Reacting to the xenophobia of those years, Bremer led the International Institutes in the 1920s to a new emphasis on the importance of ethnic cultures and traditions in easing the adjustment process. Influenced by her own experience, as well as by such writers as Horace M. Kallen, Bremer gradually became an advocate of cultural pluralism.

Under Bremer's leadership the International Institutes increasingly developed programs not only to facilitate immigrant adjustment but also to preserve the ethnic heritage and transmit the old culture to the second generation in America. Bremer believed that immigrant heritages should be kept alive in America. She was especially concerned about the maintenance of old-country languages, and in 1930 she directed every Institute to initiate mother-tongue classes for the children of the immigrants. Cultural pluralism, Bremer believed, was an ideology which conformed to the best principles of Americanism. A truly democratic society was one which tolerated and accepted those who were different, which respected individuality and ethnic diversity, and which accorded dignity to all. These were remarkable goals and programs during the years of war, intolerance, and depression.

Although each International Institute was essentially independent, the ideals set forth by Edith Terry Bremer supplied a directing influence. Indeed, Bremer's social work philosophy was put into practice by a remarkable group of Institute directors, women with long tenure in their positions who had a strong loyalty to Edith Terry Bremer and the Institute movement generally. During the 1920s and early 1930s, Bremer guided the Institute movement as head of the YWCA's Department of Immigration and Foreign Communities. A creative and energetic woman, Bremer made field visits to the Institutes to advise on programs, helped to organize new Institutes, sponsored annual meetings of Institute workers, lobbied in Congress for more flexible and humane immigration legislation, wrote dozens of articles publicizing the immigrant cause, and coordinated Institute activities through a constant stream of newsletters and policy statements from the national office. These communications alerted Institute workers to new developments in immigration law, urged sympathetic and sensitive dealings with the ethnic communities, and generally adhered to the ideals of cultural pluralism.

In 1933, with YWCA approval, Bremer founded the National Institute of Immigrant Welfare (renamed the American Federation of International Institutes in 1944). This new national agency became the umbrella organization for the individual International Institutes, most of which separated from their local YWCAs. As executive director of the new organization from 1933 until her retirement in 1954, Edith Bremer continued to direct and inspire the work of the local Institutes. During the thirties and forties, she promoted the reform of the immigration laws and sought fair treatment for immigrants and aliens. When wartime tensions stimulated ethnic conflict, the International Institutes developed programs for cooperation and interethnic understanding. In the postwar years the Institutes aided in the resettlement of European refugees, displaced persons, and Japanese Americans who had been incarcerated during the war. The pluralism which motivated Institute workers was tempered in postwar years, as assistance in employment, housing, and technical immigration matters became predominant concerns. It is a tribute to Edith Terry Bremer that some two dozen of the International Institutes continue to function in the 1980s, although now under a new national umbrella organization, the American Council for Nationalities Service. Edith Terry Bremer died of cancer in 1964 at her home in Port Washington, New York.

Manuscript collections which contain material about Edith Terry Bremer and the International Institute movement include the YWCA Archives, New York City; the YWCA Papers, Sophia Smith Collection, Smith College; the Edward Corsi Papers, George Arents Research Library, Syracuse University; and the Papers of the American Council for Nationalities Service, Immigration History Research Center, University of Minnesota. The records of many individual International Institutes contain Bremer correspondence as well. An essential guide to this material is Nicholas V. Montalto, *The International Institute Movement: A Guide to Records of Immigrant Service Agencies in the United States* (1978). Bremer's voluminous writings include *The International Institutes in Foreign Community Work: Their Program and Philosophy* (1923), an important statement of her ideas about immigrant social work. Among her important articles are "Foreign Community and Immigration Work of the National Young Women's Christian Association," *Immigrants in America Review* (January, 1916); "The Foreign Language Worker in the Fusion Process," National Conference on Social Work, *Proceedings* (1919); "Immigrants and Foreign Communities," *Social*

*Work Yearbook, 1929* (1930); "Development of Private Social Work with the Foreign Born," American Academy of Political and Social Sciences, *Annals* (March, 1949); and about two dozen articles in the YWCA magazine, *Association Monthly* (renamed *Womans Press* in 1922), between 1913 and 1934. Secondary sources which deal with Bremer and the Institute movement include Julia Talbot Bird, "Immigrant Women and the International Institutes of the Young Women's Christian Association," Master's thesis, Yale University, 1932; Raymond A. Mohl, "The American Federation of International Institutes," in Peter Romanofsky, ed., *Greenwood Encyclopedia of American Institutions: Social Service Organizations* (1978); Raymond A. Mohl, "The International Institute Movement and Ethnic Pluralism," *Social Science* (Winter, 1981); and Raymond A. Mohl, "Cultural Pluralism in Immigrant Education: The International Institutes of Boston, Philadelphia, and San Francisco, 1920–1940," *Journal of American Ethnic History* (Spring, 1982).

RAYMOND A. MOHL

**Brigham, Amariah** (December 26, 1798–September 8, 1849), asylum superintendent and founder of the *American Journal of Insanity*, was born in New Marlboro, Massachusetts, to Phoebe (Clark) and John Brigham, a farmer. Apparently, Brigham had little formal medical schooling, at least at the outset of his career. According to some accounts, he spent one term at the College of Physicians in New York. He, however, apprenticed briefly with his uncle, Dr. Origin Brigham, and for three years with Dr. Edmund C. Peet. He began his medical practice in 1820 with Dr. Ovid Plumb. Thereafter he practiced on his own in Enfield and Greenfield, Massachusetts, becoming a noted surgeon. In 1828 he gave up his practice to study for a year at several European medical centers. Upon returning, he resumed his practice and then, in 1831, moved to Hartford, Connecticut. In 1833 he married Susan C. Root, by whom he had four children. Brigham spent 1837 in New York, teaching anatomy at the College of Physicians and Surgeons, and returned to Hartford the following year.

In Hartford Brigham began his career as a writer and psychiatrist. In 1832 he published *Remarks on the Influence of Mental Cultivation upon Health*, the most popular American work on psychosomatic medicine in the early nineteenth century. Brigham believed that insanity was caused by overstimulation of the mind, and protested the tendency to stimulate children's minds at too early an age. In 1833 he published an appendix to J. G. Spurzheim's *Observations on the Deranged Manifestations of the Mind, or Insanity*. Spurzheim was one of the founders of phrenology, and Brigham adopted his view that insanity had nonintellectual causes. Like many of his contemporaries, Brigham believed in moral insanity, defined as the belief that deranged emotions as well as a deranged mind could result in illness. Equally important, he believed that the social environment contained causes of insanity. In 1835 he published his most disputed work, *Observations on the Influence of Religion upon the Health and Welfare of Mankind*, arguing that religious customs, including revival meetings, could lead to mental illness.

Despite his interest in mental diseases, Brigham spent only nine years as a psychiatrist. In 1840 he assumed the superintendency of the Hartford Retreat, one of three private asylums founded in the early nineteenth century. The Retreat had developed a prominent reputation under its first superintendent, Dr. Eli Todd, Brigham's friend and mentor. Although Brigham's appointment was controversial, in light of his denunciation of revival meetings and his Jacksonian politics, he proved an able leader, upholding the institution's commitment to kind treatment of the mentally ill.

In 1843 Brigham became the first superintendent of the New York State Asylum for the Insane at Utica. There he attempted to institute the moral treatment typically found in private hospitals. Inspired by Philippe Pinel and William Tuke, he emphasized moral rather than medical treatment of patients. Under his directions, patients were given opportunities to engage in occupational therapy, such as working in shops or in agriculture; to participate in various amusements, including sports and theatrical events; and to stimulate their intellect by attending school, joining the debating society, or visiting the museum at the asylum. Brigham understood that the asylum had two purposes: to provide an environment in which the curable would be restored to health, and to offer humane treatment to the incurable, who would otherwise languish in jails or almshouses. The role of asylum superintendent was likewise twofold: Brigham felt that he had to exert his moral influence on the curable while using his administrative talents to insure the well-being of all others. In this regard he stressed the minimal use of mechanical restraints and forbade attendants to use violence, while commanding them to treat all patients with respect.

Brigham was interested in both the causes of insanity and the treatment of the mentally ill. The *Annual Reports* from the Utica Asylum included the first tables of statistics on the causes of mental illness as well as other statistical tables which set the standard for reporting on mental diseases. In 1844 he founded and edited the *American Journal of Insanity* (*AJI*) (today the *American Journal of Psychiatry*), the first English-language journal devoted to the subject of mental illness. The journal was published at Brigham's expense and printed with the help of asylum patients. In addition to incorporating reports from the Utica Asylum, the *AJI* included articles by leading asylum superintendents. The journal was both a vehicle for transmitting research and a means of articulating theories of treatment. Much of the research it reported was poorly conducted and often incorrect in its conclusions, providing, for example, an overly optimistic picture of the possibility of curing insanity. Nevertheless, the research helped to justify the treatment of the mentally ill in asylums (rather than jails) and to promote the professionalization of psychiatry.

Brigham was one of the thirteen founding members of the Association of Medical Superintendents of American Institutions for the Insane (now the American Psychiatric Association). In 1844 the organization met to establish guidelines for the care and treatment of the mentally ill. Brigham served on several key committees established by the organization, published notices of the meetings in the *AJI*, and was elected vice president of the group in 1848.

Although he was wrong about the causes of insanity, overly optimistic about the potential for curing the sick, and unable to insure that asylums would not become overcrowded and underfunded, Brigham's humanitarian concern, organizational zeal, and intellectual leadership were important legacies, ultimately helping to improve the care of the mentally ill. Brigham died in Utica, New York, in 1849.

Manuscript materials on Brigham include a journal from his European tour which is located at the Osler Library, McGill University, Montreal, Canada, and letters in various collections including the Pliny Earle Papers, American Antiquarian Society, Worcester, Massachusetts (thirty-one letters); the Thomas Story Kirkbride Papers, Archive of the Institute of Pennsylvania Hospital, Philadelphia, Pennsylvania (eight letters); and the Dorthea Lynde Dix Papers, Harvard University, Cambridge, Massachusetts (two letters).

Brigham wrote several books and over fifty articles, the majority of which were published in the *American Journal of Insanity*. For a complete bibliography and outstanding biographical essay see Eric T. Carlson, "Amariah Brigham: I. Life and Works," *American Journal of Psychiatry* (April, 1956), 831–836, and "Amariah Brigham: II. Psychiatric Thought and Practice," ibid. (April, 1957), 911–916. Other useful sources include *American Journal of Insanity* (October, 1849), 185–191; Richard H. Hutchings, "The First Four Editors," *American Journal of Psychiatry* (April, 1944), 29–33; *Boston Medical and Surgical Journal* (October 31, 1849), 250–255; *Buffalo Medical Journal* (December, 1849), 397–403; John Curwen, *The Original Thirteen Members of the Association of Medical Superintendents of American Institutions for the Insane* (1885), 27–28; *Dictionary of American Biography*, vol. 3 (1929), 42–43; Howard A. Kelly and Walter L. Burrage, eds., *American Medical Biographies* (1920), 144–145; Samuel D. Gross, *Lives of Eminent American Physicians and Surgeons of the Nineteenth Century* (1861), 520–544; *One Hundred Years of American Psychiatry* (1944), 56–58; and *Transactions of the American Medical Association*, vol. 3 (1850), 434–436.

JANET GOLDEN

**Brockway, Zebulon Reed** (April 28, 1827–October 21, 1920), progressive penologist and originator of the indeterminate sentence and the parole system, was born at Brockway's Ferry in Lyme, Connecticut, to Zebulon and Caroline Brockway. His father was a successful merchant and a prominent local leader who served as a magistrate, county commissioner, state railroad commissioner, and state prison inspector, and also was a member of the state house of representatives and the state senate in the 1850s. His mother assumed a traditional maternal-domestic role, providing Zebulon and his three brothers (Wesley, Wilbur, and Hugh) and three sisters (Semantha, Fannie, and Mary) with mental and moral instruction. In 1836 the family moved to Hadlyme, Connecticut, where Zebulon's father had opened a shipyard. Zebulon resided with his parents until he moved to Austinburg, Ohio, in the mid-1840s, where he worked in a cheese shipping firm for two years. Ill health then caused him to move to Guilford, Connecticut, where he remained until 1848.

Zebulon Reed Brockway's career was redirected when he accepted a position as a clerk at the Wethersfield Prison in Connecticut in 1848. His clerical duties included keeping records and accounts, purchasing supplies, and attending to other managerial details. Under the direction of Superintendent Elisha Johnson, and later Superintendent Leonard Willis, he was introduced to the Auburn, or "silent," system of penal reform. In 1851, at the age of twenty-four, he was appointed assistant superintendent of the Albany County Penitentiary in Albany, New York. This position was particularly profitable as the institution's superintendent, Amos Pilsbury, was one of the country's foremost penologists. Pilsbury introduced his young assistant superintendent to the finer details of prison administration, particularly the application of the Auburn system in a correctional institution for misdemeanants and minor felons. In 1853 Brockway became the superintendent of the Municipal and County Almshouse in Albany, New York. The stewardship of 1,000 men, women, and children who were committed for indigency, insanity, and/or physical illness was an exceptionally difficult but enlightening assignment. The year was personally eventful in other ways. On April 13, 1853, he married Jane Woodhouse, who later would bear two daughters, Caroline and Emma. Brockway also contracted a life-threatening case of cholera in 1853. He left his arduous assignment to become the first superintendent of the Monroe County Penitentiary in Rochester, New York, in the autumn of 1854. He was particularly proud of the financial success of the institution under his seven-year tenure. This period was also crucial, for he and his entire family found new religious fervor as they converted to the Congregational Church.

Brockway's fifth penal assignment—the first superintendent of the Detroit House of Correction in April, 1861—was particularly significant. His contributions at this institution, especially the drafting of an indeterminate sentencing law which passed the Michigan legislature in 1869, established his position as one of the nation's leading penologists. Brockway's status was enhanced by his selection at the 1870 meeting of the National Prison Association to author, with other prominent penologists, the Association's acclaimed "Declaration of Principles." A paper presented at this conference entitled "The Ideal of a True Prison System for a State" also received considerable recognition. In 1872, however, Brockway resigned as superintendent of the Detroit House of Correction. Michigan court decisions limiting the use of the indeterminate sentencing law which he had championed, disputes with the mayor of Detroit and the city council, and several critical investigations of the institution, as well as the illness of his daughter Emma, created an insufferable climate. Brockway interrupted nearly twenty-five continuous years of penal service in December, 1872, by accepting an offer from his friends, James McMillan and John S. Newberry, to become vice president of the Michigan Car Company. A downturn in the economy prompted him to resign this position in August, 1874. He then became a partner in a furniture business, Marcus Stevens and Company, which unfortunately went bankrupt. Although Brockway was able to recoup part of his investment, his losses were considerable, and he was on the verge of bankruptcy. In April, 1876, he was forced to vacate his house, put his furniture in storage, and send his wife and two daughters to stay with relatives while he moved in with his friend, James McMillan. Brockway's business ventures, in short, were complete failures.

Brockway was saved from the depths of despair in May, 1876, when Louis Pilsbury, the son of his mentor at the Albany County Penitentiary and the superintendent of state prisons in New York, offered him the superintendency of the newly constructed Elmira Reformatory in Elmira, New York. On May 12, 1876, Brockway was sworn in as superintendent of the nation's first correctional institution for male felons between the ages of sixteen and thirty. He was immediately granted complete freedom in shaping the inchoate organizational structure of the institution, which at the time of his appointment had not yet received an inmate. Brockway relished the assignment. The regimen of reform which he developed—the Elmira system—transformed American corrections by putting innovations espoused in the 1870 "Declaration of Principles" into practice. Specifically, inmates were committed to the Elmira Reformatory on indeterminate sentences. Under Brockway's "mark system," inmates earned merits for good behavior and demerits for misbehavior; the accumulation of merits was rewarded by promotion to higher classes and increased privileges within the institution. The accumulation of a fixed number of merits ultimately was rewarded with release. In essence, then, an inmate's future was determined by his own behavior. As important, inmates were conditionally released; hence, Brockway has been credited with introducing parole into the American correctional system. The rehabilitative impact of the institutions was, in theory, enhanced by innovative academic and vocational instruction, religious ministration, and later an innovative military organization. By the 1880s the Elmira Reformatory was heralded as a model institution. New reformatories for young adults were constructed across the country; aspects of Brockway's Elmira system also were incorporated into adult prisons and juvenile reformatories. Accordingly, Zebulon Brockway was hailed as one of the world's leading penologists.

Brockway's tenure at Elmira was not, however, immune from criticism. Investigations of the institution in 1882 by the Joint Legislative Committee on State Prisons, in 1886 by the Prison Labor Reform Commission, and most significantly, in 1893–1894 by the State Board of Charities and Correction, raised questions about inconsistencies between the theory and practice of the institution. In particular, severe corporal punishments administered by Brockway were examined. Although Brockway successfully negated the impact of these inquiries, they caused severe emotional strain. Interference by the state legislature with the institution's labor plan, the influx of more hardened inmates, and severe overcrowding also mitigated Brockway's reformatory zeal. The appointment of a new and critical board of managers in May, 1899, resulted in an irreconcilable rift with the superintendent. Apparently, they were not impressed with his selection as president of the National Prison Association for 1897–1898. In July, 1900, Zebulon Brockway submitted his resignation just as the Elmira system and the "New Penology" were gaining national acclaim.

Zebulon Brockway's retirement years were spent in Elmira, where he resided with his widowed daughter, Emma Blossom, her children, and his own wife. He remained active in penal reform, giving lectures, presenting papers at conferences, and serving as a prison inspector for the Prison Association of New York. In 1905, to even his own surprise, he was selected as a nonpartisan, fusion candidate as mayor of Elmira and served until 1907. In 1910 he served as honorary president of the International Prison Congress in Washington, D.C. Brockway continued his efforts at penal reform until his death in Elmira, New York, on October 21, 1920.

The records of the Elmira Reformatory are now in the New York State Archives in Albany, New York. This collection is extensive and provides important insights into the operation of the institution.

Zebulon Brockway's *Fifty Years of Prison Service: An Autobiography*(1912; repr. 1969) reviews his career from birth to 1912. Brockway's "The Ideal of a True Prison System for a State" is in the appendix of his autobiography, pp. 389–408. Other important works by Brockway include "Needed Reforms in Prison Management," *North American Review* 137 (1883), 40–48; "Felons and Misdemeanants, Best Treatment," *American Journal of Social Science* (1901), 196–216; "An Absolute Indeterminate Sentence," in Prison Association of New York, *Annual Report, 1907* 72–77; "Prison Reform," American Prison Association, *Proceedings, 1910*, 162–187; and "American Reformatory by Prison System," *American Journal of Sociology* 15 (1910), 454–477.

The reports of Brockway's achievements by his contemporaries are exonerative. Alexander Winter's *The New York State Reformatory in Elmira* (1891) is extensive. Shorter descriptions are provided by C. D. Warner, "A Study of Prison Management," *North American Review* (1885), 291–308; C. Collin, "Moral Education in Prisons," in *Papers in Penology* (1886), 47–73; and P. Dorado, "The Elmira Reformatory as Viewed Through Spanish Eyes," in *Papers in Penology* (1898), 1–60. Surprisingly, there is no extensive recent history of Brockway or of the Elmira Reformatory, though contemporary correctional historians invariably include a cursory discussion of his contributions. Torsten Eriksson's *The Reformers: An Historical Survey of Pioneer Experiments in the Treatment of Criminals* (1976), 98–106, provides a brief overview of Elmira. Alexander W. Pisciotta's "Scientific Reform: The 'New Penology' at Elmira, 1876–1900," *Crime and Delinquency* 29 (1983), 613–630, offers a critical revisionist interpretation of Brockway and the Elmira system.

ALEXANDER W. PISCIOTTA

**Bronner, Augusta Fox** (July 22, 1881–December 11, 1966), clinical psychologist, criminologist, pioneer in mental testing, and co-innovator of the team concept in mental health clinics, was born in Louisville, Kentucky, to Gustave Bronner, a wholesale milliner, and Hannah (Fox) Bronner. Of German ancestry, the Bronner family, prosperous and cultured, was prominent in the Louisville Jewish community. Augusta, the middle child of three in a close-knit family, was not taught domestic skills. Her mother and maternal grandmother, wife of the founder of Louisville's Reform Jewish Temple, encouraged her, instead, to pursue a career.

An early childhood ambition to teach prompted Bronner to enter the Louisville Normal School. Eye problems interrupted her education, and she spent a *Wanderjahre* in Europe with an aunt. Returning, she finished school in 1901, and in her first job demonstrated her skill with youngsters by bringing under control an unruly class of fourth graders. Bronner continued her education at Columbia University's Teachers College, earning the B.S. in 1906 and the M.A. in 1909. While there, she worked grading papers for the noted educational psychologist Edward L. Thorndike.

After teaching from 1906 to 1911 at the Louisville high school from which she had graduated, she returned to Teachers College for doctoral study, again serving as Thorndike's assistant. Her dissertation, studying groups of girls, tested the prevailing belief that retardation was a significant cause of delinquency. Published in 1914, Bronner's results showed that no correlation existed between delinquency and intelligence. Her findings forever changed the climate of opinion concerning the causes of delinquency.

In 1913 Bronner attended a Harvard University summer school course on the motivations of juvenile offenders, taught by William Healy,* a pioneer in the individual treatment of delinquents. Impressed with Bronner's ability, Healy hired her as a psychologist for the Chicago Juvenile Psychopathic Institute, which he headed. Their work was limited to research. This frustrated their mutual interest in follow-up treatment. Thus when Bonner told Healy of the interest of some Boston philanthropists in his work, Healy decided to move. The Judge Baker Foundation (later Guidance Center), with Healy as director and Bronner as assistant director, opened in Boston in 1917. The Center became the model for child guidance clinics in the United States and abroad.

Bronner at first concentrated on psychological testing; she also interviewed many adolescent and younger children. As the Center grew, Bronner's duties expanded to include administration and supervision of the psychologists and social workers. In 1930 Bronner became Center codirector. During this period Healy's wife died, and in 1932 he and Bronner married. Their professional collaboration now extended to weekends and evenings.

In 1916 and 1917 Bronner published works of long-term significance. A widely cited paper, "Attitude as It Affects Performances of Tests," stressed the importance of affective factors in influencing test results. *The Psychology of Special Abilities and Disabilities*, reprinted in several editions, emphasized the limitations of mental testing and promoted, perhaps even initiated, the development of vocational testing. Increasingly, Bronner collaborated with Healy in publishing their work.

Their joint labors exerted a profound influence in both clinical psychology and criminology. *A Manual of Individual Mental Tests and Testing*, appearing in 1927, served as a major guide to the nascent mental testing movement. Subsequent to about 1930, diagnosis and treatment were regularly provided each Center client and a precedent was established for systematic case follow-up. This led to the publication of *Treatment and What Happened Afterward* (1940).

Bronner achieved success as an administrator and supervisor of psychologists and social workers. She scheduled the Center's case conferences. Her equality of status with the physician led the way to Bronner and Healy's development of the team concept—bringing social worker, psychologist, and representatives of other disciplines into case planning with the physician. Their prototype became the standard in clinical psychiatric settings.

Bronner's professional commitments encompassed other activities. She was associate director of the Yale Research Institute on Human Relations during 1929–1932, and from time to time lectured to the public, and to students at the Boston University School of Education; she served as lecturer in mental hygiene at Simmons College from 1942 to 1949. With Healy, she taught a special course to Federal Bureau of Investigation (FBI) agents in training. Bronner became a fellow of the American Academy of Arts and Sciences and held memberships in the American Psychological Association, the Association of Clinical Criminologists, and the American Orthopsychiatric Association, which she served as president in 1932. She also belonged to the National Conference of Social Work and the Ethical Culture Society.

Bronner's work had both theoretical and practical import. Her efforts enriched the fields of mental testing, delinquency, and mental health. Numbers of deviant children and adolescents benefited from her concerned counsel. In 1946 Bronner became director emeritus of the Judge Baker Guidance Center, and in 1950 she and Healy moved to Florida. In December, 1966, three years after her husband's death, Bronner died at her home in Clearwater.

Most of Bronner's papers were destroyed when she retired. However, some are available in the Judge Baker Guidance Center Archives in the Francis A. Countway Library of Medicine in Boston. Some of Bronner's letters also are filed among the Ethel Sturges Dummer Papers in the Radcliffe College Schlesinger Library.

Indicative of the range of Bronner's interests is the following partial list of her publications: *A Comparative Study of the Intelligence of Delinquent Girls* (1914); "A Research on the Proportion of Mental Defectives Among Delinquents," *Journal of Criminal Law and Criminology* 5 (1914), 561–568; "Effect of Adolescent Instability on Conduct," *Psychological Clinic* 8 (1915), 249–265; with W. Healy, "An Outline for Institutional Education and Treatment of Young Offenders," *Journal of Educational Psychology* 6 (1915), 301–316; "What Do

Psychiatrists Mean?'' *Journal of Nervous and Mental Disorders* 44 (1916), 30–33; with W. Healy, ''Youthful Offenders: A Comparative Study of Two Groups, Each of 1,000 Young Recidivists,'' *American Journal of Sociology* 22 (1916), 38–52; ''Attitude as It Affects Performance of Tests,'' *Psychological Review* 23 (1916), 303–331; *The Psychology of Special Abilities and Disabilities* (1917); ''Individual Variations in Mental Equipment,'' *Mental Hygiene* 4 (1920), 521–536; ''The Apperceptive Abilities of Delinquents,'' *Juvenile Delinquency* 7 (1922), 43–54; with W. Healy, *Case Studies*, vol. 1 (1923); with W. Healy, *Delinquents and Criminals, Their Making and Unmaking: Studies in Two American Cities* (1926); with W. Healy, G. M. Lowe, and M. E. Shimberg, *A Manual of Individual Mental Tests and Testing* (1927); with W. Healy, E. M. H. Baylor, and J. P. Murphy, *Reconstructing Behavior in Youth: A Study of Problem Children in Foster Families* (1929); with W. Healy and A. M. Bowers, *The Structure and Meaning of Psychoanalysis* (1930); ''Psychiatric Concepts of the Early Greek Philosophers,'' 2 (1932), 103–113; and with William Healy, ''The Child Guidance Clinic: Birth and Growth of an Idea,'' in Lawson G. Lowrey and Victoria Sloane, eds., *Orthopsychiatry, 1923–1948: Retrospect and Prospect* (1948), which, in addition to being autobiographical, contains a useful bibliography.

Oral history interviews with Healy and Bronner were conducted by John C. Burnham in 1960 and 1961. Copies of the typescript repose in the Judge Baker Guidance Center and at Harvard University's Houghton Library. An obituary was published in the *Boston Globe*, December 12, 1966.

                                                                    ARTHUR K. BERLINER

**Brooks, John Graham** (July 19, 1846–February 2, 1938), minister, lecturer, social scientist, and reformer, was born in Acworth, New Hampshire, the son of Chapin Kidder Brooks, a local merchant, and Parmelia (Graham) Brooks.

John Graham Brooks came from an old New England family which traced its roots back to an ancestor who migrated to Massachusetts in 1631. Although underage, he tried to enlist in the Civil War but was rejected. He went to Oberlin for two years (1869 to 1871) and then to Harvard Divinity School, where he earned an S.T.B. in 1875. He then served as a Unitarian minister at the First Religious Society of Roxbury, Massachusetts, a position he left in 1882.

In 1880 he married Helen Lawrence (Appleton) Washburn, a daughter of a prominent Boston family who shared his interest in improving American society. In 1882 the Brookses went to Germany, where John studied social theory and observed contemporary German society at the universities of Jena, Berlin, and Freiburg. He was in Germany during the passage of the famous social insurance program in 1884, which gave him an issue to discuss for much of his life. Brooks returned to the United States in 1885 to become minister of the Unitarian church in Brockton, Massachusetts. He also began to lecture to a variety of groups on economic and social issues of the day. He became part of a group of young reformers of similar background and theological training, among them Minot J. Savage, Charles G. Ames, and Philip Moxom. Brooks was for labor unions and women's rights and opposed the predatory capitalism of the day. Yet he was not the dangerous radical his more conservative contemporaries thought him to be, as he rejected doctrinaire socialism and supported antitrust measures and civil service reform. He was one of the first generation of professional social scientists who wished to apply the methods of that discipline to society.

He became a member of the American Social Science Association in 1887 when he presented a paper supportive of trade unions at its meeting. In 1890 he became acting secretary of the group in the temporary absence of Franklin Sanborn.* Meanwhile, he was teaching a course in the Harvard Economics Department reputed to be the first advocating reform economics at that institution, beginning in 1889. In 1891 he abandoned the pulpit for good and moved to Cambridge. For the remainder of his life he was a lecturer, freelance expert, and writer. In 1893, at the behest of Carroll D. Wright, he undertook a study of German social insurance for the United States Bureau of Labor. His report, which he said fell on deaf ears, detailed the reasons why the Germans developed the concept and why the United States would delay such development another ten years. The Germans had the advantages of rapid industrial growth, an ideology of state intervention promoted by thinkers such as Johann Gottlieb Fichte and economists such as Adolf Wagner and Albert Schaeffle, and a strong labor movement. American disadvantages were a federal system of government with divided sovereignty and a spoils system rather than an efficient civil service. Instead of compulsory insurance, he advocated compulsory savings. His position was best expressed in his "Insurance of the Unemployed," published in the *Quarterly Journal of Economics* in April, 1896.

Brooks continued to lecture and write; he also participated widely in the public life of Cambridge and the United States. He helped reorganize the Associated Charities of Cambridge in 1899; he became active in the National Consumers' League, of which he was president in 1915. He was friends with William James and Theodore Roosevelt. In 1901 he replaced Frank Sanborn as a lecturer on social economy at Harvard.

The following year he published his first book, *The Social Unrest*, an analysis of America's labor–capital problem and a plea for cooperation. The same year he was appointed to a special committee on social insurance of the National Conference of Charities and Correction. The committee reported in 1905. Meanwhile, in 1904, Brooks had been elected president of the American Social Science Association, the next-to-last president of that dying organization, and had spoken on the German system of social insurance at the 1904 St. Louis World's Fair. His report in 1905 echoed his earlier recommendations against transferring the German model to this country, saying that the Germans had an efficient civil service and that the scale of German pensions was too low for American needs.

Brooks continued to lecture and write during the Progressive period. He was the mainstay of the League for Political Education (Town Hall, New York); his 1911 lectures at the University of California appeared as *American Syndicalism*

(1913). Here he argued that the energies of the Industrial Workers of the World (IWW) should be harnessed for a better, more cooperative society. Brooks became less active after 1920 because of health problems. He lived another eighteen years, however, dying at home in Cambridge, Massachusetts, on February 2, 1938.

The papers of John Graham Brooks are in private hands, last held by Judge Lawrence Brooks of Medford, Massachusetts.

In addition to the books noted in the text, Brooks wrote three others: *An American Citizen* (1910), *As Others See Us* (1908), and *Labor's Challenge to the Social Order* (1920). These, like his other works, are discursive, combining personal experience and views with the issues of the day. His earlier views can be found in these representative articles: "A New Hope for Charity," *Lend a Hand* (January, 1894), 6–13; "The Future Problem of Charity," *Annals* of the American Academy of Political and Social Science (July, 1894), 1–27; and "The Tragedy of Industry," *Journal of Social Science* (December, 1902), 12–18.

There is but one biography of Brooks, and that is privately printed. It is James E. Mooney's *John Graham Brooks, Prophet of Social Justice: A Career Story* (1968).

DWIGHT W. HOOVER

**Brown, Josephine Chapin** (October 20, 1887–October 25, 1976), rural social worker and public relief administrator, was born in Ogdensburg, New York, to Silas Edgar Brown (or Browne), a surgeon, and Mary Chapin Bacon. Brown received her early schooling at the Ogdensburg Free Academy and the Balliol School in Utica, New York. She attended Bryn Mawr College from 1906 to 1908 and then again from 1911 to 1913, graduating with an A.B. degree in physics and biology. During her college years, Brown's family moved to St. Paul, Minnesota. In 1908 Brown was forced to leave college for two years due to financial difficulties; during this time she successfully taught Latin and mathematics at the Oak Hall School for Girls in St. Paul. Helped by the efforts of M. Carey Thomas, President of Bryn Mawr, who held her in high esteem, Brown secured scholarship gifts which enabled her to finish her college education.

After her graduation Brown took a position as teacher of Greek and social problems at the Misses Shipley's School in Bryn Mawr, Pennsylvania. With the characteristic restlessness of the social reformer, Brown soon became dissatisfied with her teaching activities in that exclusive girls' school and decided to return to Minnesota. In 1915 she took a position at the Home School for Girls at Sauk Center, a farm school for delinquent girls, where she worked as substitute officer, house mother, and teacher until 1916. At Sauk Center Brown was introduced to farm work and wrote about her role guiding the girls in their work in the fields as well as in their chores in the house and in their school work.

Brown sympathized with the ideals of the Country Life movement, which had blossomed following Theodore Roosevelt's Country Life Commission and aimed at obtaining recognition for the contributions of the farmer to national life, preventing the desertion of farms and villages, enhancing the quality of life in the countryside, and attracting would-be ruralites back to the land. As a "countrylifer," Brown and a friend who also lived in St. Paul joined forces in two successive farming efforts. Before embarking upon a career in farming, Brown took a short agricultural extension course at the University of Wisconsin that would serve her well in later years and would familiarize her with the Extension Service. Brown's first farming venture was a fairly large and apparently diversified farm in Idaho which proved to be too much for the two young "back-to-the-landers" and ended within a year. Her second venture, a chicken farm near Marine, Minnesota, lasted until 1920, and must have proven more rewarding. Years later, Brown would take great pride in these experiences and relied on the direct understanding of village life and of farm people she had gained as a farmer. Brown also would speak sympathetically of the stresses and demands of farm life and interpret for social workers some of the reasons for the apparent lack of cooperation that farmers exhibited toward the well-intended efforts set forth for their betterment.

In 1920 Brown formally entered the field of social work, taking a position with the United Charities of St. Paul, an agency that was, at the time, responsible not only for casework services but for the administration of some direct relief. Between 1921 and 1923 Brown served as executive secretary of the Dakota County Welfare Association, also in Minnesota. It was during those years that Brown began to forge her thoughts on rural social service delivery. Having distinguished herself at Mary Richmond's* Social Casework Institute in 1922, Brown began to publish her ideas on meaningful social casework for rural areas. Brown stressed the salience of environmental factors in rural casework, the importance of education and prevention and not just remediation, and the central role of volunteers in service delivery in the hinterland. "In the town," Brown told the National Conference of Social Work in 1922, "the volunteer is on trial. In the country, it is the social worker who is in that equivocal position." Brown was convinced that the country social worker required many personal attributes not essential to her city counterpart. Humility, good sense, and tact in abundance were part of Brown's prescription for successful rural work.

Toward the end of 1923, Brown moved east to assume the position of associate field director in charge of eight southeastern states for the Family Welfare Association of America (FWAA). Brown was based in Louisville, Kentucky, but traveled through Indiana, Kentucky, Tennessee, Arkansas, Louisiana, Mississippi, Alabama, Georgia, Florida, and South Carolina providing consultation to member agencies. Between 1929 and 1930 Brown took a leave of absence from FWAA to act as secretary of the Sub-Committee on Rural Social Work of the Committee on Social and Economic Research in Agriculture of the Social Science Research Council (SSRC), a prestigious organization based in New York City. At the Council, Brown worked with many of the prominent rural sociologists of the time and developed an understanding of and a familiarity with the system of agricultural colleges. Her close association with many agricultural college leaders at the SSRC would eventually make her the target of criticism. Years later, Brown suggested that the training of rural relief workers needed to capitalize on the agricultural college system, a proposition perceived by some social work educators as second best, or a sort of "normal school training" for social work.

At the SSRC Brown also assisted in the production of *Research in Rural Social Work Scope and Method*, a volume which, among other things, criticized the imposition of urban social service organizations on rural communities, called for the study of local conditions in the planning of social work services in the hinterland, and called on social workers to make better use of local people in the provision of those services. Many of these principles were further developed by Brown in *The Rural Community Social Casework* (1933), in which she advanced the idea of training "undifferentiated" (generalist) social workers to serve people in the remote counties of the nation.

On April 9, 1934, Brown was appointed administrative assistant in the Federal Emergency Relief Administration (FERA), where she worked under Harry Hopkins* and Aubrey Williams.* Although Brown performed various functions at the FERA, one of her major tasks was the planning and implementation of training for FERA relief workers. FERA made available substantial amounts of money for the training of relief workers in various states. Brown played a key role attempting to insure that workers from the most remote counties, where the need was greatest, were also sent to the institutes and short courses, and to the schools of social work that had been approved to offer FERA courses. Although the FERA training courses stirred some controversy among schools of social work—not all the existing schools had been included in the approved list—the FERA program reached unprecedented numbers of people and introduced professional social workers to public relief. Toward the end of the federal relief program, as the country moved into Social Security and Brown went to work for the Works Progress Administration (WPA), she became concerned about the transitional period. She used the platform of the National Conference of Social Work to urge social workers to help the states as they took over relief functions. Between 1937 and 1939 Brown took on the monumental task of documenting the history of relief efforts through the Depression decade. Her second book, *Public Relief 1929–1939*, published in 1940, was dedicated to the regional social workers of the FERA/WPA and traced the history of relief from its voluntary, local origins to the Social Security Act.

In 1939 Brown left the WPA and was appointed instructor at the School of Social Work of Catholic University of America. Brown, originally a Presbyterian, had converted to Catholicism sometime in the thirties. She was concerned with reconciling Catholic charitable teachings with the provision of professional services, and she often spoke on the subject. At Catholic University she was in charge of the public welfare sequence and devoted much time to its development. During the years of World War II, Brown's teaching interests broadened to encompass other important issues. She was often a spokesperson on matters of child care. She was opposed to the war-related employment of mothers with young children and believed that it was the role of social workers to discourage those mothers from seeking war-related positions. However, Brown pragmatically recognized that if mothers accepted employment anyway, provisions for appropriate day care for their children needed to be made by social workers.

It was also during World War II that Brown became concerned about and publicly criticized the American economic system—a system that she felt "subordinated workers' interests to the interests of trade." "As a result of this system," she wrote in the Catholic University *Bulletin* in 1942, "the worker's employment and economic advancement are not relative to the real value of his services but to the extent to which his employer can profit by his enterprise."

During her years at Catholic University, Brown discovered that her eyesight was rapidly failing her due to cataracts and glaucoma. In July, 1952, she resigned from her position as associate professor and retired to Princeton, New Jersey. Those who knew Brown reported that she always had been a quiet and independent person. She apparently remained that way until her death but for the need to rely on others to read to her once she no longer could see. She devoted the final years of her life primarily to religious activities, retaining few if any connections with the professional world, except with her longtime friend, Katharine Lenroot.* She died in Princeton, New Jersey, four days after her eighty-ninth birthday.

Materials by or about Josephine Chapin Brown can be found at the National Social Welfare Assembly, the Council on Social Work Education (American Association of Schools of Social Work Files), and the Family Service Association of St. Paul collections, all at the Social Welfare History Archives of the University of Minnesota Libraries. Information about her college years and early career can also be found in the Alumni Files and in the M. Carey Thomas Collection at the Bryn Mawr College Archives. Information on Brown's work at the Minnesota Home School for Girls can be found in the Archives of the Minnesota Historical Society in St. Paul. Personnel records for Brown's career as a civilian employee of the FERA/WPA are located at the National Personnel Records Center in St. Louis, Missouri. Descriptive material on her work with the FERA/WPA can be examined in the National Archives (FERA Old and New Series Files) at the Library of Congress. Personal correspondence and some papers by Brown are available in the Katharine Lenroot Collection at the Rare Books and Manuscript Library of Columbia University. Information about Brown's academic work and professional activities after 1939 can be found in the Archives of the School of Social Work, Catholic University of America. Information on Brown's retirement and death was obtained from the personal files of Mrs. Marjorie Cuyler of Princeton, New Jersey. Interviews with Dr. Dorothy Mohler of the Catholic University of America and with Mrs. Marjorie Cuyler were used in this work to supplement the written record.

There are four entries for Josephine Chapin Brown in the *National Union*

*Catalog, Pre-1956 Imprints*. Two relate to a monograph, *Field Work with Public Welfare Agencies*, produced by the American Public Welfare Association (1936). Two refer to her well-circulated books, *The Rural Community and Social Casework* (1933) and *Public Relief 1929–1939* (1940). Many single news items about Brown can be found in the pages of the *Survey* (primarily between 1924 and 1940). Brown wrote the entry on "Rural Social Work" in the *1936 Social Work Yearbook*. She delivered papers at many meetings of the National Conference of Social Work. Most are printed in the *Proceedings* (1922, 1935, 1936). Brown was the author of several articles which appeared in various professional journals. Notable examples are "A City Case Worker in the Country" *The Family* (1922); "Rural Families on Relief" *The Annals of the American Academy of Political and Social Science* (1922); "Government and Social Work," *Survey* (1936) and *Catholic Charities Review* (1936); "In Service Training for Public Welfare I and II," *Survey* (1938); "Rural Public Assistance and National Defense," *Rural Sociology* (1942); "Public Social Services and Private Charity," *Catholic University Bulletin* (1942). No published obituaries could be located.

EMILIA E. MARTINEZ-BRAWLEY

**Bruere, Henry** (January 15, 1882–February 17, 1958), social welfare administrator, municipal reformer, public official, business and financial executive, and presidential advisor, was born in St. Charles, Missouri, to Cornelia (Schoenich) and John E. Bruere, a medical doctor. Little is known about him until his college education. He attended Cornell University for two years and graduated in 1901 with a bachelor of philosophy degree from the University of Chicago, where he studied under Thorstein Veblen. He then studied at two law schools, Harvard and New York University. In addition, he did graduate work in political science at Columbia. He married Jane Munroe in 1904. The couple had four children: Richard, Geoffrey, Honora, and Alison.

Henry Bruere's career fused several different talents and interests, one of which was social welfare. While at Harvard he became involved in boys' club work at College Settlement. In 1902 he became a resident at University Settlement in New York City. Robert Hunter,* author of the influential study *Poverty* (1904), counted among his early social work friends. But Bruere's choice of a career twisted in one direction, then another. For two years, 1903–1905, he directed the personnel department of International Harvester Company's McCormick Works and probably developed some of the innovative welfare methods being used by its management in labor relations. Then he returned to New York to found and direct the Bureau of Municipal Research. The Bureau investigated corruption and waste in city government and conducted a training program in administrative efficiency. By exposing abusive practices and introducing economies in programs such as pension planning, Bruere built his reputation as a civic reformer.

When John Purroy Mitchel took office as mayor in 1914, thirty-one-year-old Henry Bruere became city chamberlain, the equivalent of a treasurer. He used his position to implement budget reforms and reorganize municipal departments.

Mitchel's administration championed the conservative fiscal and structural reforms associated with the good government movement, but Bruere, who led some conservative changes, was also a key figure in liberal actions involving poverty and social welfare. He served on the Mayor's Committee on Unemployment, which prepared a city plan to fight a recession in 1914–1915, headed the Mayor's Pension Committee, and was president of the city's Board of Child Welfare. These duties enabled him to work with a group of social workers, including Harry Hopkins* and Jane Hoey,* who would join forces with Franklin D. Roosevelt during the era of the Great Depression. After Mayor Mitchel left office in 1918, Bruere was a director of the state division of the United States Employment Service.

His work in city government established Bruere's fiscal expertise. During the war years, he was financial advisor to the government of Mexico. Soon thereafter he entered private business, where he remained for the rest of his career. He became a vice president of the Metropolitan Life Insurance Company. In 1927 he joined the Bowery Savings Bank as vice president and treasurer. Bowery was the world's largest savings institution, and Bruere became its president in 1931, holding that position until 1949 and concluding his career in 1952 as chairman of the board and chief executive officer. Yet, during the last thirty years of his life, he frequently crossed the bridge between business and public service, serving, for example, as director of the 1939 New York World's Fair and on the World War II Savings Bond Commission.

Even though his commitments shifted to business and finance, Bruere never abandoned social welfare. During the 1920s and early 1930s, he was a member of the executive committee and board of directors of the Welfare Council of New York City, which led a drive for public unemployment relief after 1929. In 1930 state Industrial Commissioner Frances Perkins* appointed him chairman of the Committee on Stabilization of Industry, which advised Governor Franklin Roosevelt and issued a report that called for joint business and government action in combatting the economic dislocations of a depression. The report prefigured many activities of the National Recovery Administration of 1933. Bruere also counseled Governor Roosevelt on the funding of the Temporary Emergency Relief Administration, the first state agency to assist the unemployed, and on old-age and unemployment insurance. After FDR became President, Bruere advised him on the fiscal policies of the Home Owners Loan Corporation and Farm Credit Administration. He was also a state advisor to the Reconstruction Finance Corporation until 1939.

Bruere's four books, all published between 1912 and 1930, summed up his ideas about government, business, and social welfare during the active middle years of his changing career: *The New City Government*; *New York City's Administrative Progress, 1914–1916*; *Applied Budgeting* (with Arthur Lazarus); and *Profitable Personnel Practice* (with Grace Pugh). Though never a social worker by profession, Henry Bruere nevertheless worked at the cutting edge of the profession's concerns. He died in Winter Park, Florida, in 1958.

Because of his mixture of interests and occupations, Bruere's life is potentially rich for scholars who wish to analyze the relationships among municipal reform, progressive business practices, and social welfare policies from the Progressive period into the New Deal era. Yet Bruere seems to have left no collection of personal papers, and documents bearing upon his ideas and actions are scarce. The Oral History Collection at Columbia University (New York City) has a transcript of an interview that is detailed and informative. The Archives of the City of New York hold materials pertinent to the Mitchel mayoral years, and the Franklin D. Roosevelt Papers at the Franklin D. Roosevelt Library (Hyde Park, New York) contain letters and notes of conversations between the two men. But Bruere's work is not well represented in any single collection. His published writings, though hardly numerous, offer a useful start for a possibly extensive study.

Books and articles about municipal reform in New York, the Mitchel mayoral years, and the Roosevelt gubernatorial years mention Bruere and sometimes discuss his work, especially his service as chairman of the Committee on Stabilization of Industry, but his contribution to government and social reform between 1900 and 1940 has not been fully examined. Students of social welfare history would be most interested in that period of time. Bruere's public service, however, extended beyond 1940 and included many more significant actions taken on behalf of his city and country.

WILLIAM W. BREMER

**Buell, Bradley** (January 29, 1893–March 22, 1976), health and welfare planner, social survey researcher, and founder of the American Association of Social Workers, was born in Chicago, Illinois, to Viola Nancy and Lincoln E. Buell. Young Bradley, however, grew up in Ann Arbor, Michigan, where his father served as state secretary of the Young Men's Christian Association (YMCA). In 1915 he received a bachelor's degree from Oberlin College, and in 1916 he entered the New York School of Philanthropy (now the Columbia University School of Social Work). In 1917 Buell married Alice Standish, an artist who served on the board of the Art Students League. Returning to graduate school in 1917, he obtained a master's degree from Columbia University. Subsequently, he did graduate work at Brown University and the New School for Social Research.

Buell entered the New York School of Philanthropy during a period of considerable social reform and a growing urge to achieve professionalism in the field of social service. Associated with the social reform of that day was the early movement toward emancipation of women. This movement provided part of the incentive to establish the Intercollegiate Bureau of Occupations, which was to have a strong influence on Buell's career. Initially this organization was created to assist the increasing numbers of women graduating from college who were interested in following careers. A special social work division was formed in the organization under the active guidance of Mary Van Kleeck* of the Russell Sage Foundation. Eventually this special division split off and became known as the National Social Workers' Exchange. It was financed through membership fees, fees for finding persons employment, and significant contributions from the Russell Sage Foundation.

As a graduate student, Buell became associated with this organization. Initially the association was somewhat marginal and came about when Van Kleeck, who as a board member continued to take an active part in the organization, engaged him to complete a study for the Russell Sage Foundation on working conditions in the cigar-making industry. His association with the Exchange was temporarily interrupted, first by service in the U.S. Army in World War I, then by being reengaged by the Russell Sage Foundation to participate in a study of the United States Employment Service.

His role in this study was to identify the factors involved in organizing the labor market. In this role he traveled extensively around the country interviewing private employers, representatives of organized labor, operators of private employment agencies, and community leaders. These efforts led to two important conclusions. The first was that, contrary to the concept of Sir William Beveridge, people cannot be moved about like pins on a map. The second was that, for an employment exchange to endure, it must be part of an organization with a larger objective to command a broad basis of support.

Thus, when he was approached in 1919 to help in revitalizing the National Social Workers' Exchange, Buell recommended the organizing of a professional association that would operate the Exchange as a basic service. He was appointed organizing secretary of the Exchange and became one of the leaders in the efforts that led to the formation of the American Association of Social Workers at the 1921 meeting of the National Conference of Charities and Correction. Until 1923 he was active in the new organization, first as secretary and later as associate director.

It is not unusual, when the structure of an existing organization is dramatically modified to form a new organization, for animosities to be generated and for these animosities to endure over time. Such was the case in the formation of the American Association of Social Workers, and largely because of this condition Buell left the Association in 1923 to become secretary of the New York City Council on Immigrant Education. In 1925 he left this position to become the associate director of the Community Chest and Council of New Orleans, where he remained until 1930. In that year he became field director of the National Community Chests and Councils, Inc. In this capacity he was involved in the Community Chests and Councils' efforts to respond to the overwhelming demand for services produced by the Depression. Among his contributions was the carrying out of over 100 surveys of community services as communities and agencies were gearing up for the escalating demand for services.

In 1943 Buell was made executive editor of *Survey Midmonthly*, a publication of Survey Associates, Inc. As editor of this journal, he wrote prolifically on the problems and methodology of community planning.

Community Research Associates, Inc., was founded by Buell in 1947. He remained associated with this organization, first as executive director, then as chief consultant, until his retirement in 1972. While active with Community Research Associates Buell set up and carried out six operations research projects and provided survey and consultant services to cities, counties, states and the federal government in 156 communities in the United States. In 1952 he authored *Community Planning for Human Services*, published by Columbia University Press. This book analyzed the work of 108 public and private health, welfare, and recreation agencies in St. Paul, Minnesota. One of the most notable findings of this study was that a comparatively small group of multiproblem families absorbed over 50 percent of the health and welfare services delivered in St. Paul. This finding has subsequently been confirmed in other communities and has contributed importantly to health and welfare service planning.

Buell's first wife died in 1960. In 1962 he married Alice L. Voiland, a social caseworker and researcher. Ten years later he retired to Sanibel Island, Florida, and on March 22, 1976, he died in a hospital in Fort Myers, Florida.

At this time no comprehensive biography exists on the life of Bradley Buell. There is a short biographical entry in the *Encyclopedia of Social Work* (1977), and an unpublished manuscript, entitled "Taped Recollections of Steps Leading to Organization of the American Association of Social Workers," prepared in 1966, is available at the Social Welfare History Archives Center of the University of Minnesota. His professional papers and manuscripts are also available at this location. There are a number of published works authored or edited by Buell, including "Is Prevention Possible?" in *Community Organization*(1959); "A Philosophy of Community Action," *American Journal of Orthopsychiatry* (July, 1954); *Community Planning for Human Services* (1952); and *Solving Community Problems* (1973).

ROBERT A. PERKINS

**Burns, Allen Tibbals** (August 29, 1876–March 9, 1953), social worker, was born in Haverhill, Massachusetts, the second oldest of three boys and a girl born to William Treat and Ella Louise (Marsh) Burns. His maternal grandfather, a Baptist minister, taught mathematics at Denison University in Ohio. His father also became a Baptist minister, but died at age forty-one. Burns, then thirteen years old, moved with the family from a New York parish, where it had settled, to a maternal uncle's household in Chicago.

Burns entered the first class at the University of Chicago, majoring in Greek and Latin. He received his A.B. on October 1, 1897. After a year teaching Latin, he returned to the University of Chicago for graduate studies (1899–1903). Appointed a divinity fellow, he taught biblical theology, and in the summers, as a licensed minister, he preached in a St. Louis Baptist church.

He entered industrial social work in the Chicago branch of the Young Men's Christian Association (1903–1907). As a resident in workingmen's boarding houses run by the YMCA, he was struck by the benumbing, machine-bound monotony of the lives of the workingmen in the stockyards and railroad districts; he saw their troubles—poverty, unemployment, and accidental injury—as "the problems of a class, not an individual." The riddle he posed in 1904 was, How shall the wage earners not merely exist, but live a human life, a life worthy, a life the right of every man within whom is the spark of the divine?

In Chicago he moved into the orbit of settlement leaders Graham Taylor and Julia Lathrop.* With Charles Henderson's* sponsorship, he became associate director of the Chicago School of Civics and Philanthropy (1907–1909). With Lathrop he studied juvenile proceedings and concluded that the courts' harsh treatment missed the essential nature of delinquent acts. "Lathrop, Burns, and I," wrote William Healy,* went "to a small conference at Hull-House in 1908 to discuss what should be or could be done." The outcome, with Ethel Dummer's* help, was the Juvenile Psychopathic Institute for the scientific study of the bases of delinquent behavior in children.

Frances Perkins,* who met Burns in the Chicago period, remembered him as a vigorous, active person who exerted an impact on the direction of her life. She wrote, "His fresh . . . approach to what was then thought to be merely 'doing good to the poor' was illuminating, stimulating, and unforgettable for me. Dinner table conversations in which he laid down the principles as he saw them—often in debate with Dr. Graham Taylor . . . —opened up to me avenues of service and usefulness that had never even crossed my mind."

Burns applied the lessons of Chicago in Pittsburgh, where he attempted to build on the high hopes for reform raised by the Pittsburgh Survey. The vehicle, the Pittsburgh Civic Improvement Commission, of which he was secretary (1909–1914), challenged corrupt political control of city and school government by obtaining a new city charter and instituting tax, budgetary, and regulatory reforms in civic governance. During this period he also got married (on July 20, 1911), to Jessie G. Wadsworth, with whom he had two children. In 1937, after her death, he would marry Florence Seder.

Meanwhile, Burns' conceptualization of his experience marked him as a leader in the new community organization field. "Our future social programs," he told social workers in 1916, "must be based on a general social knowledge for all, a common understanding of a few present pressing needs, instead of the more comprehensive programs understood and vouched for by a few with the highest social intelligence. We must be willing to start with the crowd and go only so far as the crowd can be led." The tools he advocated, public education (in the Deweyan sense of teaching critical thinking about institutions) and the fact-finding survey were joined by other means forged in Pittsburgh, political campaigning, and administrative consolidation of gains through lay advisory group support.

During World War I, Burns was director (1914–1918) of the Cleveland Foundation. Using the "surplus" wealth Clevelanders designated for social service through the community trust, Burns perfected the carefully orchestrated survey as a technique for ascertaining social service needs while eliciting broad-based community support for programs to meet them.

Burns, and a few men experimenting with a new form of federated fund-raising developed first in Cleveland, founded the American Association for Community Organization (AACO) in 1918. When he became executive director of the war chests' charity-endorsement agency, the National Information Bureau (NIB, 1922–1925), the NIB was designated AACO's secretariat. Then, sponsored by community chest leaders from Ohio, Burns became executive director of an independent AACO, renamed the Association of Community Chests and Councils (ACCC, 1926–1942).

While moving toward his major contribution to social welfare through the ACCC, Burns directed the Carnegie Corporation's Study of Methods of Americanization (1918–1921) and served as arbiter on the Labor Adjustment Board of the Rochester Clothing Industry (1921–1922). Interest in immigration and labor relations weave like minor themes through his life, visible in Chicago as the secularization of his religious impulse, continued in the Foreign Language Information Service later, and becoming dominant in the 1940s. He helped bring organized labor into the community chest movement and played a behind-the-scenes role in securing the passage of the Displaced Persons Act of 1948.

Paul Kellogg* thought of Burns in 1919 as a man of ideas, with the gifts to execute them. It was to the task of national agency "interrelation" that Burns turned. In a presidential address to the National Conference of Social Work (1921), he set forth an agenda for the next two decades "to bring order, organization, and system" into the social welfare enterprise. The national agencies, however, resisted NIB overtures to "coordinate and correlate" their work, in effect, to serve as their secretariat. Instead, they reacted with suspicion and distrust to NIB's studies of national agencies, regarded Burns as "a protagonist of the Chests," and withheld from AACO membership in the National Social Work Council throughout the 1920s.

In the ACCC, Burns effectively cultivated the support of leading businessmen and industrialists (the "lay" leaders of the community chest movement), fought for changes in the federal tax code to make corporate contributions deductible (the 5 percent rule), and executed the Relief and Welfare Mobilization campaigns of the Depression years in their names.

Corporate support formed the stable bedrock of local community chest budgets in the 1930s, as individual giving dropped. When it became evident to Burns that the voluntary sector could not bear the brunt of relief needs, he worked with Walter West* and others for the assumption of federal responsibility, enabling private social work agencies to survive the Depression.

Burns built on a spontaneously erupting, locally based movement, trying to temper zeal with knowledge, promoting institution building for the long run. He attracted competent executive men and women into the movement, and devoted resources to university training programs, conferences, institutes, field work, and surveys. Burns died in Ft. Myers, Florida, in 1953.

The United Way of America, Alexandria, Virginia, retains the Minute Books of Community Chests and Councils, Inc., and its predecessor organizations beginning in 1918.

The National Social Welfare Assembly Papers, Supplement No. 1, illuminate the origins of the National Information Bureau and the attitudes of the moving spirits in the National Social Work Council toward Burns and the AACO. The Survey Associates, Inc., Papers and Paul U. Kellogg Papers contain correspondence with Burns. These collections are found in the Social Welfare History Archives, University of Minnesota Libraries, Minneapolis. On Burns' active role in the affairs of the Foreign Language Information Service, see the American Council for Nationalities Services Papers at the Immigration History Research Center, also at the University of Minnesota.

The U.S. National Archives and Records Service contains scattered references to Burns' contacts with the American Red Cross (Record Group 200), with the President's Organization on Unemployment Relief (Record Group 73), and with the 1932 Mobilization campaign (Record Group 40). Burns' role in lobbying for federal responsibility for relief can be traced in the National Association of Social Workers Papers in the Social Welfare History Archives at Minnesota. The Presidential Papers of Theodore Roosevelt and Calvin Coolidge at the Library of Congress show Coolidge's use of the NIB as a "detective agency" and Roosevelt's lack of involvement in the Americanization Studies while on its Advisory Council. The *New York Times* contains editorials, letters to the editor, and articles by or about Burns.

Burns' journal articles are numerous, appearing in the *Commons, Charities and the Commons*, the *Survey, American City, School and Society, Annals of the American Academy of Political and Social Science*, the YMCA *Association Men* and *Association Seminar*, and in the proceedings of the National Conference of Social Work. The ACCC *Bulletin*, later *Community*,is also useful.

Obituaries appeared in the *New York Times, Social Service Review*, and *Community*. A privately printed volume, with contributions by Bradley Buell, C. M. Bookman, David Holbrook, Frances Perkins (excerpts from a letter), and staff is informative: *In Memoriam: Allen T. Burns, 1876–1953* (1954), held at the United Way Information Center in Alexandria.

On Burns' leadership of the community chest movement, see Morrell Heald, *The Social Responsibility of Business: Company and Community, 1900–1960* (1970). For the pre-chest period see William Healy and Augusta F. Bronner, "The Child Guidance Clinic: Birth and Growth of an Idea," in *Orthopsychiatry, 1923–1948*, ed. Lawson G. Lowrey and Victoria Sloane (1948), and Clarke A. Chambers, *Paul U. Kellogg and the Survey: Voices for Social Welfare and Social Justice* (1971).

JACQUELINE K. PARKER

**Burritt, Bailey Barton** (May 31, 1878–June 18, 1954), social worker and administrator, public health reformer, and "father" of family health maintenance, was born in Monroe County, New York, to Miranda H. (Horton) and Melville C. Burritt. He received a B.A. in 1902 from the University of Rochester and an M.A. from Columbia University the following year. He married Ruth Dennis, herself a graduate of the University of Rochester, in May, 1909, and the couple had six children, four girls and two boys.

Burritt became a social worker, as he once observed, "quite by accident." He had, through his youth, planned on a career as an educator. But he had been teaching only a few years when the head of the New York State Charities Aid Association asked him in 1908 to undertake a survey of hospital conditions in New York City. So well did he carry out this task that he was hired as assistant secretary of the State Charities Aid Association. In 1910 he also became executive secretary of the Committee on Criminal Courts of the New York Charity Organization Society.

As assistant secretary of the State Charities Aid Association, Burritt studied the treatment of public drunkenness, and his report led to legislation authorizing New York, and all first- and second-class cities in the state, to establish institutions to deal with the problem of public intoxication. The purpose of the legislation was to substitute remedial and medical supervision of drunkards—in particular habitual drunkards—for judicial and penal regulation of such persons. In Burritt's reasoned view, a good deal more in the way of reformation could be hoped for by sending an inebriate to a hospital or "farm colony" than by confining him or her to an unwholesome workhouse or a crowded prison cell.

In his capacity as executive secretary of the Committee on Criminal Courts, Burritt was able to secure important changes in the inferior courts of New York City. Thus, improvements were made in the quantity and quality of probation work; reforms were instituted in the children's court; the records of the courts were systematized; and changes of method were brought about in the work of the Night Court for Women and the Domestic Relations Court.

Burritt's next move came in 1913 when he was engaged as director of the Department of Social Welfare of the New York Association for Improving the Condition of the Poor (AICP). Here, among other things, he showed particular interest in the movement to improve and extend the public baths.

Burritt's rapid rise in the social work field continued when, in 1914, he was appointed general director of the AICP, succeeding John A. Kingsbury.* He remained with the Association until 1939, when it merged with the New York Charity Organization Society to form the Community Service Society of New York. Meanwhile, he had a significant impact on the Association during his tenure as general director.

Struck by the close connection between poverty and ill health, Burritt focused the activities of the AICP on the field of public health. On the one hand, the poor were more likely than the well-to-do to become sick. Especially convincing to Burritt in this regard was the high incidence of tuberculosis in the poorer districts of the city. (He was, as he once put it, "a firm believer" in "good incomes as essential allies" in the public health field.) On the other hand, when the breadwinner of an economically marginal family was badly injured or became seriously ill, that family usually found itself in financial difficulty. (Not surprisingly, Burritt was a staunch supporter of workmen's compensation.)

Under Buritt, the AICP adopted an innovative strategy to deal with this large and challenging social problem. The AICP, of course, provided relief to families in economic difficulty. In 1924, for example, more than a third of the material relief distributed by the Association was used for families where tuberculosis was a major factor. But Burritt was eager to move into the area of preventive medicine. And so, in 1918, the Association opened the Mulberry Health Center in a congested part of the city. Here attention was given to such programs as prenatal educational care for mothers, educational nursing and follow-up services for youngsters of preschool age, and dental care for children. The center also provided an educational nutrition service (sound nutrition being an area of much interest and concern to Burritt).

In 1918 the Association also set up the Columbus Hill Health Center, and in later years the AICP established other clinics in the city. Moreover, Burritt's plan for medical, and then dental, care for low-income families rapidly spread.

Burritt's efforts in the field of social services suffered no diminution when the AICP and the Charity Organization Society joined forces in 1939 to form the Community Service Society. He was appointed chairman of the executive council of the new society, a post he held until 1944. Retiring that year, he was honored at a dinner. It is suggestive of the reputation he had achieved that on that occasion President Franklin D. Roosevelt sent a message to the gathering commending Burritt for contributing "greatly" to "rooting out" those conditions which underlay poverty and illness.

Though he had retired from the Community Service Society, Burritt, in his own view, retained a "store of energy" which he believed could best be used to continue his work. Thus, he served as president of the New York Tuberculosis and Health Association. And as executive director of the National Health Council, between 1947 and 1948, Burritt's sound guidance and seasoned judgment were credited with boosting the Council to a leading position among national health organizations.

In the meantime, following seven years of planning under Burritt's direction, the Community Service Society, Montefiore Hospital, and the College of Physicians and Surgeons of Columbia University began in 1951 a "keep well" medical project. Known as the Family Health Maintenance Demonstration, the project had as its purpose to keep people well rather than to wait until illness struck. The project was designed to maintain the health of the family group, through the combined activities of clinical medicine, social work, psychology, psychiatry, and education.

Fittingly, in 1953 Burritt received the William Freeman Snow Medal for distinguished service to humanity from the American Social Hygiene Association. He died the following year at his home in Yonkers, New York.

The following articles are illustrative of Burritt's thinking on various social welfare issues: "The Habitual Drunkard," *Survey* (October 1, 1910), 24–41; "Raising the Standards of Living in the Anti-Tuberculosis Campaign," *Proceedings of the National Conference of Social Work* (1919), 181–185; "The

Place of the Nutrition Worker in the Health Program,'' *Journal of Home Economics* (December, 1921), 579–586; ''Disease as a Factor in Poverty,'' *Proceedings of the National Conference of Social Work* (1923), 80–88; ''Workmen's Compensation and the Family,'' ibid. (1928), 293–301; ''Social Work in a Troubled World,'' remarks by Bailey B. Burritt at the closing session of the Annual Meeting of New Jersey Welfare Council, December 6, 1940 (Reproduced from typewritten copy, 1940); ''Life, Death and Tuberculosis as Affected by Standard of Living,'' published by the State Committee on Tuberculosis and Public Health, State Charities Aid Association, New York (1946).

For biographical information, see *Survey* (June 14, 1913), 378; *New York Times*, October 21, 1944, 30, and June 19, 1954, 15.

RICHARD HARMOND and THOMAS J. CURRAN

# C

**Cabot, Richard Clarke** (May 21, 1868–May 7, 1939), physician and founder of medical social work, was born in Brookline, Massachusetts, the fifth of seven sons of Elizabeth (Dwight) and James Elliot Cabot. The family was wealthy by inheritance and intimately connected with other Brahmin families, among them the Jacksons, Lowells, Lees, and Dudleys. This elite presumed cultural and political influence but also valued social and intellectual achievement. James Cabot wrote a biography of Ralph Waldo Emerson and edited the first collection of his works. Cousin Joseph Lee* devoted his life to social work, while Frederick P. Cabot, another cousin, gained recognition as judge of the Boston Juvenile Court.

Richard Cabot flourished in this milieu. He attended Harvard, where he sang in Hasty Pudding and took final honors in philosophy, graduating summa cum laude in 1889. After three years at Harvard Medical School, he received his M.D. degree. In 1894 Richard Cabot married Ella Lyman of Waltham, Massachusetts (d. 1934), in a Swedenborgian ceremony, reflecting the couple's belief in direct communion between the material world and the spiritual realm. Ella Lyman Cabot, a cousin of Harvard president Charles Eliot, wrote and lectured on ethics and campaigned for public school reform in Boston. The marriage was childless by mutual choice and, according to all sources, characterized by deep devotion.

Richard Cabot pursued both medical and social interests throughout his career, but medical research dominated his earlier years. His initial studies were *A Guide to the Clinical Examination of the Blood* (1897) and *Serum Diagnosis of Disease* (1899). The latter, based upon his experience as a medical officer in the Spanish-American War, showed how to differentiate typhoid fever from malaria. His research culminated in a classic paper, "The Four Common Types of Heart Disease" (1914), emphasizing etiological diagnosis instead of structural examination, which then was the standard method in cardiology. Cabot received appointments at Massachusetts General Hospital (1898) and Harvard Medical School (1899), where he introduced several innovative and popular practices, most notably the clinicopathological conference and postgraduate summer courses for practitioners.

Cabot's research and teaching abilities were widely praised, but his blunt personality and strong convictions made him something of an outsider in local professional circles. The Massachusetts Medical Society considered expelling him for his contention that most physicians' diagnoses, including his own, were based on guesswork. He aroused further opposition for advocating, with his younger brother, Dr. Hugh Cabot, prepaid group practice over the prevailing fee-for-service system. Also, at a time when the somatic approach to mental illness was dominant, he supported Reverend Elwood Worcester's Emmanuel movement, which sought to unite the clerical and medical professions in plans of patient treatment.

Richard Cabot's conviction that medicine was both art and science led to his principal accomplishment, the inauguration of medical social service. As a director of the Boston Children's Aid Society, he had been impressed by the staff's careful compilation of case histories. By contrast, physicians' diagnoses at Massachusetts General Hospital, especially in the out-patient department (which he headed) seemed hurried and uninterested in considering the influence of personal and social problems on illness and injury. In order to "make treatment effective," Cabot established in 1905 a social service unit that was initially funded by his friends and Boston "cousins." He selected Ida M. Cannon,* sister of the physiologist Dr. Walter B. Cannon, to head the new venture. She proved an excellent choice, not only because of her experience as a public health nurse but also because of her personal warmth and diplomatic ability, which won over suspicious doctors on the hospital staff.

Cabot vigorously supported Cannon's work and promoted the cause in various ways. His official reports and other writings created the literature on the subject: *Social Service and the Art of Healing* (1909); *Social Work: Essays on the Meeting Ground of Doctor and Social Worker* (1919); and a volume of papers edited by Cabot, *The Goal of Social Work* (1927). His *What Men Live By* (1914), focusing on the powerful and interrelated motivations of work, play, love, and worship, became a core text in the emerging schools of social work.

Regarded by early social workers as a patriarch of the profession, Cabot was in 1931 elected president of the National Conference of Social Work. He received honorary degrees from the University of Rochester, Syracuse University, and Colby College. Such acclaim never turned his head. He constantly reminded the social work profession of the need to submit its most cherished programs to critical evaluation, praising, for example, Sheldon and Eleanor Glueck's *One Thousand Delinquents* (1934), which cast doubt on the treatment at Boston's prestigious Judge Baker Guidance Center. A bequest from his estate funded the famous Cambridge-Somerville youth study (1951), which reached a similarly bleak conclusion regarding the value of therapy.

Richard Cabot expressed deep philosophical and religious interests throughout his life. He and his wife regularly attended Josiah Royce's ethics seminar at

Harvard, and in 1902–1903 he lectured in the course. Cabot applied Royce's idealist philosophy in two publications, *Psychotherapy and Its Relations to Religion* (1913) and *The Christian Approach to Social Morality* (1920). Also in 1920, he received his second Harvard appointment, the chair of social ethics, which he occupied until 1934. During that period he taught courses on human relations, using the case method and lecturing with characteristic vigor "to make men better themselves." His writings on the subject included *Adventures on the Borderlands of Ethics* (1926), *The Meaning of Right and Wrong* (1933), *Christianity and Sex* (1937), and *Honesty* (1938). Like the Puritans, from whom he was descended, Cabot believed that human development required ascetic discipline but also respect for individual liberty. Thus, he saw no contradiction in serving both as president of the Anti-Saloon League of Massachusetts and as advisor to the American Civil Liberties Union.

Richard Cabot maintained this spirit to the end. Slowly dying from heart disease, he insisted that his physicians be as candid with him as he had been with his own patients. From his bed, he gave his final class—a seminar at Andover-Newton Theological School on ministering to the sick. He died at his home in Cambridge, Massachusetts, two weeks before his seventy-fifth birthday.

The principal sources on Cabot's life are his books, most of which have been noted above, and his papers at the Harvard University Archives. The papers of Ella Lyman Cabot, housed at the Schlesinger Library, Radcliffe College are also informative. The following works include discussion of the various phases of Cabot's career: Ray Stannard Baker, *New Ideals in Healing* (1909); Ida M. Cannon, *On the Social Frontier of Medicine* (1952); Thomas A. Dodds, "Opening the Windows: Richard Cabot and the Care of the Patient During America's Progressive Era, 1890–1920," Honors thesis, Harvard University, 1980; and David Potts, "Social Ethics at Harvard, 1881–1931," in Paul Buck, ed., *Social Sciences at Harvard, 1860–1920* (1965), 91–128. For family information see L. Vernon Briggs, *History and Genealogy of the Cabot Family*, 2 vols. (1927). Among numerous obituaries see the *New York Times*, May 9, 1939, and the *Harvard University Gazette*, October 7, 1939. See also *Dictionary of American Biography*, Supp. 2 (1958), 83–85.

ROBERT M. MENNEL

**Campbell, Helen Stuart** (July 4, 1839–July 22, 1918), writer, home economist, and reformer, was born in Lockport, New York, to Homer and Jane (Campbell) Stuart, both of Scottish descent. Helen moved at an early age from central New York State to New York City, where her father entered a long and successful career as an attorney. Educated in New York public schools, the Gamell School of Warren, Rhode Island, and Mrs. Cook's Seminary in Bloomfield, New Jersey, she was married about 1860 to Grenville M. Weeks, a medical student. He served as a surgeon in the Civil War and as an Indian agent in the West, not returning until 1871; thereafter the couple separated, eventually divorcing.

In the 1860s Campbell successfully supported herself as a writer of children's stories, under the name of Mrs. Weeks. She also wrote adult novels under the name she soon permanently adopted, Helen Stuart Campbell, and wrote shorter fiction for popular magazines, such as *Harper's*, *Lippincott's*, and the *New England Magazine*.

In the late 1870s she launched a new career by joining the emerging home economics movement, teaching in 1878 in the Raleigh Cooking School in North Carolina, and in 1881 publishing a household textbook. In 1880 she and Mrs. Anna Lowell Woodbury founded a mission cooking school and diet kitchen in Washington, D.C.

In 1882 Campbell began yet another career as a social scientist and reformer with the publication of *The Problem of the Poor*. Based on her experience with a city mission on the New York waterfront run by a reformed criminal, Campbell's book was an important indicator of changes in attitudes toward poverty; it rejected the Social Darwinist view of the poor as unfit, and the evangelical Christian view of the poor as needing conversion. Instead, Campbell emphasized the problem of low wages. Sounding a theme that grew stronger in the decades ahead, Campbell especially stressed the evil effects of low wages on working women. In 1886 she earned popular acclaim with a novel that explored that theme, *Mrs. Herndon's Income*. Extending her readership even further, in 1887 she accepted a commission from the *New York Tribune* to study the lives of New York's wage-earning women. After appearing serially in the Sunday edition of the *Tribune*, her report was published in 1887 as *Prisoners of Poverty: Women Wage Earners, Their Trades and Their Lives*. Writing in an ethnographic vein, Campbell provided minute details about the persons she interviewed and the households within which they lived. Lengthy quotations from their conversations gave the book the air of fiction, but its stories of human disaster, misery, and greed were only too real.

This book brought her to the attention of the younger group of reformers then emerging within the first generation of college-educated women, who were born about twenty years later than Campbell, especially Florence Kelley,* who became a close friend. In December, 1887, when Campbell was preparing for a tour of Britain and Europe to investigate poverty among wage-earning women, Kelley wrote Friedrich Engels to expect a visit from her friend when she was in London. The results of her trip were published in 1889 as *Prisoners of Poverty Abroad*. That year she also published "Child Labor and Some of Its Results," in the *Chautauquan*, reflecting the active interest of women reformers in New York City in this topic.

In the 1890s Campbell's writings achieved a new maturity, and she was accepted by many of her scholarly contemporaries as a social scientist. Her 1893 book, *Women Wage Earners: Their Past, Their Present, and Their Future*, won an award from the American Economic Association and included an introduction by Richard T. Ely, liberal economist at the University of Wisconsin, who praised her valuable contributions to the literature of social science. Emphasizing legislative solutions for many of the problems facing wage-earning women, Campbell's book highlighted the work of the New York Consumers' League, founded by Josephine Shaw Lowell* in 1890, together with its predecessor, the Working Women's Society of New York. In an appendix she provided the cumulative text of New York's factory inspection law, 1886–1892.

Living a peripatetic existence in the 1890s, Helen Campbell began the decade in Boston, where she joined the First Nationalist Club of Boston. In 1894–1895 she joined Charlotte Perkins Gilman (author of *Women and Economics*, 1898) in San Francisco, where the two edited a weekly newspaper, *Impress*, the official journal of the Woman's Press Association. That spring she gave two series of lectures at the University of Wisconsin, "Household Science" and "Social Science," although a hoped-for academic appointment did not occur. Campbell and Gilman moved to Chicago in 1895–1896, where they headed Unity settlement, not far from Hull-House. Campbell's last major publication was her popular text in 1897, *Household Economics*, which she dedicated to Gilman. There Campbell defined her subject as a connecting link between the economics of the individual and the social economics of the state.

Helen Campbell helped shape changing attitudes toward poverty in the 1880s and 1890s and helped popularize, among professionals and lay people alike, the importance of the household unit as a category of social analysis. After 1900 she lived a more retired life with Charlotte Perkins Gilman in New York in what both described as a mother-daughter relationship, until 1912, when she moved to Boston, dying in her Dedham home when she was seventy-nine.

Helen Campbell's letters survive in scattered manuscript collections, but they have not been gathered into a central repository. Contemporary mention of her can be found in Frances E. Willard and Mary A. Livermore, eds., *A Woman of the Century* (1893); the *National Cyclopaedia of American Biography*, vol. 9 (1907); *Who's Who in America*, vols. 1–9 (1899–1916); and an obituary in the *Boston Transcript*, July 23, 1918. Her relationship with Gilman can be traced in Gilman's *The Living of Charlotte Perkins Gilman, An Autobiography* (1935; repr. 1975). The most complete biographical account is Ross E. Paulson, "Helen Stuart Campbell," in *Notable American Women* (1971). The best analysis of her place in the home economics movement is in Dolores Hayden, *The Grand Domestic Revolution: A History of Feminist Designs for American Homes, Neighborhoods, and Cities* (1981).

KATHRYN KISH SKLAR

**Cannon, Ida Maud** (June 28, 1877–July 8, 1960), founder of medical social work, was born in Milwaukee, Wisconsin, the second child of Colbert Hanchett Cannon and Wilma (Demio) Cannon. The Cannon family, however, moved to St. Paul, Minnesota, when Ida was a young child. When Ida was four, her mother died. Although her father held a stable position with the Great Northern Railroad, he steadily nurtured an ambition to be a doctor throughout his children's formative years. His passion for medical knowledge was evident in his large library of medical books, an expense which put considerable strain on the family's resources.

Her father's passion for medicine played a significant role in her professional life, and in that of her older brother as well: Walter Bradford Cannon, the only male of the four children, went on to Harvard College and Harvard Medical School and became a widely respected physiologist. Ida Cannon graduated from the Saint Paul City and County Hospital Training School for Nursing in 1898, and from the School for Social Workers in Boston (later known as Simmons College) in 1907.

Upon completion of her education, Cannon went to work in the Outpatient Department of Massachusetts General Hospital, becoming part of the first group of hospital social workers in the United States. In concert with Dr. Richard Cabot,* she expanded the domain of social work practice at Massachusetts General Hospital. In 1914 Cannon was appointed chief of social service, a position she held for the next thirty-one years.

Cannon's particular contribution to the field was to develop, implement, and disseminate the principles of medical social work, first in her own hospital, but ultimately to other hospitals, schools, and aspiring professionals throughout the United States and Europe. This is a remarkable achievement in itself. What makes it all the more notable, however, is that she accomplished this when the profession itself was in its infancy, resting upon an underdeveloped knowledge base and an uncertain practice domain.

According to Ida Cannon, the central purpose of medical social work was to treat the social complications of physical disease using the medical diagnosis, the social situation of the patient, and the well-grounded principles of sociology. She emphasized the interdependence of medicine and social work in the firm belief that (1) medical and social interests were closely interrelated, and (2) the quality of the medical and social work treatments were highly dependent upon each other, with each having the ability to vitiate the treatment in the other's domain.

It is interesting to note that Cannon implicitly recognized that the focus of social work's effort should be upon a confluence of interacting factors in the client and his or her environment as early as 1913, when she wrote *Social Work in Hospitals*. This recognition predates by four years similar ideas set forth in *Social Diagnosis*, Mary Richmond's* landmark book, which first organized a theory and methodology for social work.

The notion that patient treatment could be neither complete nor of high quality without interdisciplinary collaboration also is remarkable for its early appearance in Cannon's writings. As she was one of the first social workers in a hospital setting in this country, there were no models of interdisciplinary collaboration that could be pursued. It was from her own practice and observation, then, that team treatment evolved, a practice that prevails to this day.

It is important to note that, even before 1919, the year in which the Social

Service Department at Massachusetts General Hospital became fully integrated into the hospital's functions, medical social work was on its way to widespread acceptance in the United States and Europe. Both Cannon and Dr. Cabot traveled extensively, interpreting developments in the new field of social service at conferences and medical meetings. In addition, interested professionals throughout the United States came to Massachusetts General Hospital to meet with her and Cabot about the burgeoning field.

Ida Cannon contributed to the firm entrenchment of medical social work along a number of other channels. In 1912 she collaborated with Simmons College in offering a course in medical social work and in supervising field instruction at area hospitals. She continued this activity until 1925. In addition, in 1918 she was a prime mover in the formation of the American Association of Hospital Social Workers (later the American Association of Medical Social Workers): she was one of nine original signers of its articles of incorporation as well as its first vice president. In 1920 she became its president.

Cannon held other positions within the organization as well, using its auspices and resources effectively to move the profession to new frontiers. In 1929 she became the chairperson of a new committee on medical education, observing the state of the art and authoring reports on teaching medical students the social implications of disease. Through trial and error, Cannon came to believe in the case teaching approach as the most effective for hospital residents. By her persistence and her common sense, and in cooperation with physicians, she and the other social workers were able to offer educational training in the social aspects of the cases under study.

In October, 1945, Ida Cannon retired from the Social Service Department at Massachusetts General Hospital. She left in her wake thirty-one social workers serving 8,000 patients annually. Her service to the profession and the community had earned her many well-deserved accolades.

She died in Boston, Massachusetts, on July 8, 1960.

The Archives of the Social Service Department at Massachusetts General Hospital are the major repository of material by and on Ida Cannon, including biographical material, correspondence to and from her, diary inscriptions, and the like. Also useful are the *Annual Reports* of the Social Service Department at the Massachusetts General Hospital, and some correspondence between Cannon and Dr. Richard Cabot which can be found in the Cabot Papers in the Harvard University Archives. Cannon's own writings, particularly *Social Work in Hospitals* (1913) and *On the Social Frontier of Medicine: Pioneering in Medical Social Service* (1952), provide insights into her thinking about the profession at those points in time.

The most informative secondary accounts on her life and career are Harriet Bartlett's "Ida M. Cannon: Pioneer in Medical Social Work," *Social Service Review* (June, 1975), 208–229; and the sketch of Cannon in *Notable American Women: The Modern Period* (1980). Also see Roy Lubove's *The Professional*

*Altruist: The Emergence of Social Work as a Career* (1965) for a good account of the emergence and early development of medical social work.

ALICE A. LIEBERMAN

**Cannon, Mary Antoinette** (March 22, 1884–March 17, 1962), medical social worker and educator, was born in Deposit, New York, to Robert M. Cannon and his wife, who died when Mary was a young girl and whose name cannot be ascertained. After preparation at Miss Florence Baldwin's School in Bryn Mawr, Pennsylvania, she entered Bryn Mawr College, from which she graduated in 1907 intent on a career in biological research. Instead, Dr. Richard Cabot* convinced her to work with neurasthenics—those who were feebleminded, or had epilepsy, hysterical paralyses, or borderline psychoses—as a social work assistant on Dr. James Putnam's Neurological Service at Massachusetts General Hospital. In 1909 Cannon worked in Boston Consumptive Hospital's Department of Social Service. From 1913 to 1915 she taught in the high school of the town in which she was born. In 1916 she received an M.A. degree from Columbia University, and on graduation became an agent for dependent children for the New York State Charities Aid Association.

From 1916 until 1921 Cannon was director of social work for the University Hospital of Philadelphia (now known as the Hospital of the University of Pennsylvania). There, in her teaching and practice, she stressed the importance of community and of using psychological understanding to help address social problems. In 1918, dividing her time between the hospital and her professional association, Cannon became the first secretary of the American Association of Hospital Social Workers. When a prestigious advisory group to the American Hospital Association suggested that a Committee on Training for Hospital Social Work be appointed, Cannon was designated executive secretary. The work of this committee, which was funded by the Russell Sage Foundation, influenced the formulation of standards for the education and practice of medical social work.

In 1921 Cannon moved to New York to join the faculty of the New York School of Social Work (now the Columbia University School of Social Work), where she remained until her retirement in 1945. During that time, she helped many schools of social work across the country to develop courses in medical and psychiatric social work. Also during that period, she published many papers and two books. With Philip Klein, Cannon edited *Social Casework: An Outline for Teaching* (1933), and in 1944 she published *Outline for a Course in Planned Parenthood* (1944).

Cannon's speeches and writings reflected her interest in a wide range of practice issues. For example, in "Medical Social Work and the Influenza Epidemic," published in the *Hospital Social Service Quarterly* (1919), Cannon wrote, "If this country needed to be shown what a medical-social problem was, we had our demonstration in the epidemic of . . . 1918." Next, in a 1920 issue of the *Hospital Social Service Quarterly* on "Health Problems of the Foreign Born from the Point of View of the Hospital Social Worker,'' Cannon called for public measures to provide sanitary living quarters and individual instruction and casework on a basis of knowledge of underlying causes. In a talk on ''Trends in Intensive Medical Social Practice'' delivered to the National Conference of Social Work in 1932, she said, ''The idea of a free personal relationship as a force in treatment has unquestionably been gaining ground in the social casework field. . . . Medical social work, too, has something to give in the deliberate leaving of responsibility to the patient.'' In ''The Uses of Medical Social Work,'' published in the *Bulletin of the American Association of Medical Social Workers*, she recommended sheltered workshops for the handicapped that could compete in the economy and sell successfully in the open market: ''Especially now with unemployment so widespread it is hard for a person with any known health hazard to find work . . . . A sheltered shop . . . must sell successfully in the open market while protecting the health of its workers. . . . If all handicapped could be given such an opportunity, disability would much decrease, for the demands would be within the capacities.''

In 1933 her paper on ''Recent Changes in the Philosophy of Social Workers'' was awarded the Pugsley Prize, given annually by the National Conference of Social Work for the paper that made the most important contribution to the subject matter of social work. One theme in that paper was echoed again and again in her work—''the movement of society itself toward what we may call social self consciousness,'' and ''the desirability, the possibility, the meaning of conscious control of society by itself.''

In the Great Depression Cannon was an advisor to the Social Service Division of the Texas Relief Commission. In addition, she was a founder and member of the executive committee of the Social Service Employees' Union. From 1941 to 1942 she directed the social work program at the University of Puerto Rico. After her retirement from the Columbia University School of Social Work, Cannon remained very active in professional affairs. She was a consultant to the Department of Labor of the Commonwealth of Puerto Rico and directed the Social Service Section of the New York office. During that period, she worked with the New York City Department of Public Welfare in order to improve the conditions of Puerto Ricans living in the city. With a group of social workers from New York City, she conducted the first Social Workers Workshop in Puerto Rico in 1953. Later, Cannon was volunteer director of the James Weldon Johnson Community Center in Harlem.

Antoinette Cannon was described as a woman of kindly humor and great tolerance. Friends and colleagues felt that the William James quotation which she kept on her desk spoke to her view of life: ''Keep the faculty of effort alive by a little gratuitous exercise every day.'' Throughout her life, she vacationed in the old family house in Deposit, New York, where she died on March 17, 1962, at age seventy-seven.

There are a number of primary materials on the life and career of Cannon. The archives of the Social Work Department at the University of Pennsylvania Hospital include *Annual Reports* between 1916 and 1921 written and signed by

Cannon. The Dead Alumnae Files in the archives of Bryn Mawr College contain newspaper and college magazine writings by and about Cannon, including obituaries. The Faculty Files in Columbia University's Butler Library contain copies of Cannon's published works and obituaries as well. The Alumnae Records at the Baldwin School also contain material on Cannon, including the report cards she received during her residence there.

Also see Alice Hawkins, "Mary Antoinette Cannon," *Bryn Mawr Alumnae Bulletin* (1962), which offers a brief discussion of her life at the college and her contribution to medical social work. Ida M. Cannon's *On the Social Frontier of Medicine* (1952) describes the beginnings of medical social work at Massachusetts General Hospital and Cannon's work there, and Mary A. Stites' *History of the American Association of Medical Social Workers* includes a description of Cannon's positions in and activities for that body.

                                                                                        TOBA SCHWABER KERSON


**Carey, Mathew** (January 28, 1760—September 16, 1839), social reformer, was born in Dublin, Ireland, to Christopher Carey, a baker and contractor to the army, and a woman whose name cannot be ascertained. Mathew was largely self-educated. As a teenager, he wanted to be a printer and bookseller and apprenticed himself to one. Carey published his first essay at the age of seventeen, and in 1783 he was the proprietor of a newspaper, the *Volunteer's Journal*, which defended Ireland against English encroachments. Such defense resulted in Carey's arrest and imprisonment and his decision to flee to America. He sailed to Philadelphia on September 7, 1784, and, with the help of friends, there began a new publishing career. In 1791 he married Bridget Flahavan of Philadelphia, and they had nine children, three of whom died young.

Carey's commitment to Ireland and to Catholicism led to his first charitable activities. In the 1790s he helped form the Hibernian Society of Philadelphia, an association of Irishmen who met all ships coming from Ireland and assisted needy passengers, and he also joined the interdenominational Sunday School Society to educate indigent children. In 1808–1809 he was president of the Roman Catholic Society of St. Joseph, which built Philadelphia's first orphanage.

However, it was not until after 1824, when Carey turned his printing business over to his sons, that he became especially active as a social reformer. In the 1820s Philadelphia and other American cities experienced a welfare crisis occasioned by the resumption of immigration and the depression that followed the War of 1812. Thousands applied for and received public and private relief. Relief applicants were criticized, for most Americans assumed that, no matter how troubled the economy, if a person wanted work he or she could find a job and earn an adequate income. In Philadelphia Carey spearheaded the attack on public welfare when in July, 1827, writing in the newspapers under the pseudonym "Howard," he charged that Philadelphia spent too much money on the poor (73 cents per person per year), especially on mothers with illegitimate children. He called for an end to public relief to the poor in their own homes (most of which went to women and children) and the requirement that all poor seeking public aid enter the almshouse. On July 25, 1827, Carey convened a public meeting in Philadelphia and served on a committee it appointed to draft a proposal for a change in the poor laws to reduce the cost of public welfare. This report eventuated in a new 1828 poor law which eliminated outdoor cash relief in Philadelphia once a new and larger almshouse was built.

After evaluating public welfare, Carey went on to assess private charities in Philadelphia in a series of essays in the newspapers. He theorized that private aid, like public aid, encouraged idleness, but soon discovered that charities alleviated genuine distress. He visited with poor persons and became one of the first Americans to graphically catalogue their economic and physical disabilities. In pamphlets published and circulated at his own expense, Carey described the low wages paid to men who labored in cities and on canals and turnpikes. He even formulated budgets for working-class families of various sizes and concluded that a day laborer with a wife and one child could probably just get by, but that men who headed larger families or who were unemployed for more than eight weeks a year because of sickness, bad weather, or economic depression could not survive on the income typically earned by a laborer.

However, Carey's greatest concern became female laborers, for whom the only "respectable" work available was making shirts and pantaloons. On a weekly basis, seamstresses earned $1.25 compared to the $4.50 take-home pay of unskilled male laborers. Carey formulated a budget for a seamstress and found that she could get by if she supported only herself. Yet most women who became seamstresses were single mothers with young children who had to work at home and frequently made up for their shortfall in earnings by begging, seeking charity, or becoming prostitutes. Carey deplored this situation and urged higher wages for seamstresses, job training to permit them to enter better paying occupations (as shopkeepers or cooks), more contributions to charities for them, and, ironically, a resumption of public outdoor relief payments to them. By 1835 Carey recognized his error in pressing for reduction in public assistance to women and children and petitioned the state legislature to reinstate outdoor aid in Philadelphia, which it did in 1839. In 1838 Carey was also instrumental in founding a charity which sought to improve the job skills of poor women.

Mathew Carey's major contribution to social welfare reform was to eschew moral judgment of the poor as a group in favor of honest, realistic assessment of the plight of individual male and female laborers. He died on September 16, 1839, in Philadelphia.

Carey's papers and voluminous correspondence can be found in Philadelphia, Pennsylvania, Historical Society of Pennsylvania, Edward Carey Gardiner and Simon Gratz Collections; at the University of Pennsylvania, Rare Book Room, Carey's Diary, 1822–1826; and at the American Philosophical Society, Miscellaneous Letters, Pamphlets, 1820s. Additional material can be found in Worcester, Massachusetts, American Antiquarian Society, Mathew Carey Papers, 1788–1857.

Carey's own writings on poverty and welfare include "Pauperism, No. II," *Poulson's American Daily Advertiser* (Philadelphia), July 18, 1827; "Pauperism, III," *Poulson's*, July 21, 1827; "Essays on the Public Charities of Philadelphia, Nos. 1 to 7," *United States Gazette*, January 6, 9, 15, 20, 28, February 5, 14, 1829; *Appeal to the Wealthy of the Land . . .* (1833); *Female Wages and Female Oppression* (1835); *Letters on the Condition of the Poor . . .* (1836); *A Solemn Address to the Mothers, Wives, Sisters and Daughters of the Citizens of Philadelphia . . .* (1837); *Constitution and Report of the Board of Managers of the Society for Improving the Condition and Elevating the Character of Industrious Females* (1838); *The Case of the Out-Door Poor Once More* (1838); *From the National Gazette, To the Editor* (1839).

The best source on Carey's life is his "Autobiography," *New England Magazine* (July, 1833–December, 1834; repr. 1942). On Carey's social concerns see Priscilla Ferguson Clement, "The Philadelphia Welfare Crisis of the 1820s," *Pennsylvania Magazine of History and Biography* (April, 1981), 150–165, and *Welfare and the Poor in the Nineteenth Century City: Philadelphia, 1800 to 1854* (1985).

                                                    PRISCILLA FERGUSON CLEMENT

**Carr, Charlotte Elizabeth** (May 3, 1890–July 12, 1956), social worker and public welfare administrator, was born in Dayton, Ohio, to Joseph Henry Carr, a successful businessman, and Edith (Carver) Carr.

As a young girl Carr observed, through the work of her father's collection agency, the effects of hard times on the poor. Always strong-willed, she ran away from home to convince her parents to send her to Vassar, from which she graduated with a B.A. in 1915. After college, Carr worked as a matron in an orphan asylum in Columbus, Ohio. She then worked with delinquent children for the New York State Charities Aid Association and the New York Probation and Protective Association. Carr also served during World War I as a New York City policewoman, patrolling at night under the Brooklyn Bridge.

From 1921 to 1923 Carr was a personnel manager in private industry, where she learned about industrial employment conditions. She returned to welfare work in 1923 as assistant director to Francis Perkins* at the New York State Labor Department's Bureau of Women in Industry. Two years later, she established a similar bureau in Pennsylvania, which she ran until she was fired in 1927 for refusing to contribute to a campaign fund. She returned to Pennsylvania in 1931, when she was named by Governor Gifford Pinchot as Deputy Secretary of Labor and Industry; she was appointed Pennsylvania's first woman Secretary of Labor in 1933.

After Pinchot's term expired, Carr returned to New York, where Mayor Fiorello La Guardia named her director of the Emergency Relief Bureau in 1935. With a staff of 18,000, a budget of $9 million a month, and nearly 1 million clients, Carr gained a reputation as a tough, scrappy welfare administrator, and in the process earned the nickname "Scarlet." As bureau director, Carr argued for the importance of work relief over home relief. Her efforts at transferring cases to federal works programs reduced New York's relief rolls by some 100,000. She also maintained that relief administration should be less concerned with "humane" treatment of individuals and more focused on the larger causes of poverty. An example of this controversial viewpoint was her policy of deducting the earnings of children from a family's relief allotment. While some argued that children whose wages were turned over to their families might run away from home, Carr responded that unless the children's wages were deducted from the relief allotment, parents might keep their children in the work force and stay home themselves, thus contributing to child labor, adult unemployment, and swelling relief rolls.

Carr left the New York bureau in 1937 to succeed Jane Addams* as head of Hull-House, the pioneering social settlement in Chicago. There she promoted efforts in adult education and the organization of labor, and also worked to eliminate racial and ethnic prejudice. At Hull-House, Carr deemphasized the traditional projects in arts and crafts, while initiating investigations into such issues as city planning and public health. She brought with her a modern conception of settlement work, stressing decentralized community centers because, she said, slums were the problem of a whole community, not just isolated neighborhoods. Carr maintained throughout her tenure there that the people of the neighborhood should have a major voice in the affairs of the settlement, an idea not always well received by the settlement's trustees. In 1942 Carr resigned from her post at Hull-House, reacting to tensions caused by her avid support of the reelection of President Franklin Delano Roosevelt as well as her work for other political candidates.

Carr then served as assistant to the vice chairman of the War Manpower Commission until 1945, when she was named director of the Citizens' Committee on Children of New York City. She headed the Committee until her retirement in 1953. During her term the Committee established day care, kindergartens, and health stations in public housing, a foster home program in the welfare department, and improved police services for juveniles.

Charlotte Carr was large and imposing and often described herself as a "fat Irishwoman." Forceful and aggressive, with heavily browed eyes, she was once called the female counterpart of John L. Lewis, the leader of the United Mine Workers. She was also described as genial, witty, and politically astute. Her contemporaries lauded her skills as an administrator, as well as her policies and programs for the betterment of living and industrial conditions for men and women and for the abolition of child labor.

As a frequent contributor to social work journals and as a participant at conventions and conferences, Carr was a visible and respected member of her profession. She was also a director of the National Child Labor Committee and a member of the Women's Trade Union League. At the time of her death in New York City, Carr was working on housing rehabilitation projects as a consultant to the city welfare commissioner.

Manuscript material, including newspaper clippings, on Carr's work at Hull-House can be found in the Jane Addams Memorial Collection, the Hull-House Associates Papers, and the West Side Historical Collection, all at the University of Illinois at Chicago. Carr's Hull-House years also are covered in Allen Davis and Mary Lynn McCree, *Eighty Years at Hull House* (1969).

Biographical accounts can be found in George Britt, "Charlotte Carr at Hull House," *Survey Graphic* (February, 1938); *Dictionary of American Biography* (1980); Milton S. Mayer, "Charlotte Carr—Settlement Lady," *Atlantic Monthly* (December 1938); and *Who Was Who in America*, vol. 3 (1966). An obituary notice which is especially useful for information on Carr's relief work appears in the *New York Times*, July 13, 1956.

LYNN Y. WEINER

**Carstens, Christian Carl** (April 2, 1865–July 4, 1939), child welfare advocate, was born in Bredstedt, Schleswig-Holstein, Germany, the son of Broder and Christina Maria (Ibsen) Carstens. The family immigrated to the United States when Carstens was a young boy and made its home in Iowa.

Carstens completed high school in Davenport, Iowa, and earned his undergraduate degree from Iowa College (now Grinnell College), Grinnell, Iowa, in 1891. Between 1891 and 1899 Carstens taught or was principal in school districts in Ames, Creston, and Marshalltown, Iowa. He then returned to graduate school, attending the Summer School of Philanthropy in New York City and earning a master's degree from the University of Pennsylvania in 1900. Between 1900 and 1903 Carstens worked at the Philadelphia Society for Organizing Charity with Mary Richmond.* At the same time, he pursued his Ph.D. at the University of Pennsylvania and wrote a dissertation entitled "Some Worn Out American Charitable Endowments."

Following completion of his doctoral work in 1903, Carstens and his wife— the former Blanche McMeans, an Iowa College classmate—moved their family of three children to New York City. There he served as assistant secretary of the New York Charity Organization Society from 1903 to 1907. Carstens then accepted the director's post at the Massachusetts Society for the Prevention of Cruelty to Children. In addition, however, Carstens made substantial contributions to the four White House Conferences on children and youth between 1909 and 1940; represented the United States at the 1922 and 1927 Pan-American Child Welfare Congresses; served as president of the American Association of Social Workers between 1921 and 1923; and was active in the Non-Sectarian Committee for German Refugee Children.

Although Carstens is remembered as a staunch advocate of all measures that improved the care of abused, neglected, or orphaned children, his chief contribution to social welfare came during his tenure as director of the Child Welfare League of America from 1921 until his death in 1939. League historians trace its origin to the 1915 National Conference of Charities and Correction. At that meeting, Carstens, as chairman of the conference's Committee on Children, urged social workers to develop a national plan for child welfare work. Such a plan should draw upon the experiences of both private and public child-caring agencies, Carstens recommended. The shared information, he predicted, would benefit workers seeking to create or reshape child welfare agencies.

The evening before Carstens delivered the children's committee report, "A Community Plan in Children's Work," eighteen persons representing fourteen different child-caring institutions agreed that some type of national agency concerned with child welfare should be created. Information exchange and service to the variety of children's agencies would be the new agency's primary responsibilities. Thus, the Bureau for Exchange of Information among Child Helping Agencies was born. Carstens, a member of the Bureau's executive committee, was named the full-time director when the Bureau was reorganized as the Child Welfare League of America (CWLA) in September, 1920; he assumed office January 2, 1921.

Carstens' early reports of League activities indicate that he was a tireless worker. During the League's first six months, he visited more than forty child welfare agencies from the East Coast to the Midwest, and by 1939 he had visited children's agencies in every state and U.S. territory except Alaska and Nevada. As a result of these visitations and the numerous surveys of children's services the League conducted, Carstens became an extremely knowledgeable source on the state of child welfare in the United States. Indeed, Emma Lundberg, in *Unto the Least of These* (1947), named Carstens as the person with the most intimate knowledge of child-caring institutions and agencies throughout the country.

The Child Welfare League of America had realized as early as 1917 that setting standards for child welfare was an important task, and under Carstens' direction it soon became the leader in that arena. Carstens and the League also came to recognize that children's agencies had a responsibility greater than simply finding homes for children. Family counseling, foster care, housekeeping services, and other types of social services also had to be considered, in his opinion, and he and the League worked tirelessly to implement such services. Carsten died in New York City in July, 1939.

Carstens was a prolific writer and a frequent speaker; his writings and speeches make up the bulk of the sources available to study his life. The Social Welfare History Archives at the University of Minnesota hold a C. C. Carstens Collection, which consists entirely of typescript copies of Carstens' writings and speeches. The Social Welfare History Archives are also home to the records of the Child Welfare League of America, in which some biographical material, in addition to reports and minutes dating from the League's early years, is available.

Additionally, researchers may also wish to consult some of Carstens' published writings, including *Public Pensions to Widows with Children: A Study of Their Administration* (1913); "Public Pensions to Widows with Children," *Survey* (January 4, 1913), 459; "The Next Steps in the Work of Child Protection," *Proceedings of the National Conference of Social Work* (1924), 124; "Child

Welfare Work Since the White House Conference," *Proceedings of the National Conference of Social Work* (1927), 122; and "Dependent and Neglected Children," *Social Work Yearbook, 1929* (1930), 128.

For a brief account of Carstens' life, see the *Encyclopedia of Social Work*, 17th ed. (1977), 94; and the November, 1939, edition of the CWLA's *Bulletin*, which is a memorial issue devoted to Carstens. An account of the Child Welfare League of America's past is in *Social Service Organizations*, ed. Peter Romanofsky and Clarke Chambers (1978), 225.

SUSAN D. STEINWALL

**Chapin, Charles Value** (January 17, 1856–January 31, 1941), epidemiologist and public health reformer, was born in Providence, Rhode Island, to Joshua Bicknell Chapin, a physician forced by deafness into a photographic career, and Jane Catherine Louise (Value) Chapin, a talented painter. After graduating from the English and Classical High School for Boys in Providence, he followed the usual pattern of local upper-class children by attending Brown University, graduating from there in 1876. Having decided to follow his father's original profession of medicine, he began his studies with a one-year preceptorship under Dr. George D. Wilcox, a leading homeopathic practitioner. Skeptical of homeopathy, the following year he elected to enroll in a first-class orthodox medical school, the College of Physicians and Surgeons in New York City. After one year, in 1878, he transferred to Bellevue Hospital Medical College, a school of comparably high standing but one which offered the clinical advantages of Bellevue Hospital and Charity Hospital on Blackwell's Island. He received an M.D. degree from Bellevue in 1879, served a one-year internship in Bellevue Hospital, and then entered private practice.

To augment his limited income as a practitioner, in 1880 he accepted a position as attending physician to the Providence Dispensary and two years later took three other part-time jobs: pathologist and librarian to the Rhode Island Hospital, lecturer in the Rhode Island Training School for Nurses, and instructor in physiology at Brown University. A blunt, forthright individual, Chapin was not temperamentally suited for the role of private practitioner, and he happily gave up his practice on receiving a full-time appointment as superintendent of health for the city of Providence in 1884. The $2,000 annual salary which went with the post also enabled him to resign from his appointments with the Providence Dispensary and Rhode Island Hospital, but he retained his connection with Brown University until 1895.

In a day when full-time health officers were rare and few of them had a sound medical background, Chapin was exceptionally well prepared. His medical training had not only brought him in contact with a number of leading physicians, many of whom were active in public health, but it also had educated him in the newly developing field of bacteriology. Whereas public health work had been based upon the filth theory, that is, disease was spontaneously generated in dirt and putrefying matter, Chapin was prepared to improve the traditional sanitary methods by applying the new knowledge about pathogenic organisms.

As a well-to-do American, Chapin firmly believed in private initiative and had serious qualms about the authority of the state to enforce sanitary measures if it involved interfering with private rights. The success of the British public health movement in drastically reducing death rates, however, convinced him that the growing health problems of Providence required firm municipal action. He was aware that any demand for government action on the social front would raise the cry of socialism, but Providence was a rapidly growing industrial city with all the concomitant health problems. As Chapin later wrote, an individual living by himself can do as he pleases, but those who crowd together in cities must necessarily surrender certain liberties. Municipal sanitation was a community necessity that went beyond the capacity of private initiative. He proposed a broad public health program that must have shocked the conservative elite of Providence. In addition to fighting communicable diseases, removing nuisances and garbage, and inspecting water and milk supplies, he advocated the registration and analysis of vital statistics; scientific research on sanitary matters; a program of public health education; and strict supervision of factories, trades, schools, and public institutions.

His success as a public health leader came in part from his ability to convince the conservative Republican leaders of Providence of the need for reform. He dressed conservatively, avoided the appearance of radicalism, martialed his facts and evidence, and by his easy manner avoided antagonizing his opponents. These qualities were all the more important in his career since Providence never gave its health officer the broad authority granted to health departments in New York and certain other cities. In consequence, even on routine sanitary matters he was constantly fighting administrative obstacles and pressure groups.

One of his major accomplishments was to help lay the basis for safe municipal water supplies. In the post–Civil War years Providence established a new municipal water system with a consequent sharp reduction in the typhoid fever rate. In the succeeding years the new water supply became polluted, leading to a typhoid epidemic in 1888. Chapin traced the source of the epidemic, and then, determined to use bacteriological techniques to test water-filtering devices, he established a municipal bacteriological laboratory in 1888, the first of its kind in the United States. Its work on water purification helped establish a national reputation for Chapin and his health department.

Chapin's greatest contribution to public health, however, was his insistence that dirt *per se* did not cause disease. In the nineteenth century, public health and sanitation were virtually synonymous, and it was assumed that particles of diseases were spread by fomites, or articles coming in contact with the sick. By the end of the century elaborate methods had developed for fumigating the homes and possessions of the sick. In 1906 Chapin shocked the sanitary world by arguing that these methods of "terminal disinfection" were useless. The main factor in spreading disease, he asserted, was direct contact, and the chief reliance should be placed upon personal cleanliness. Four years earlier Chapin equally outraged many traditional sanitationists by suggesting that garbage collection and routine sanitary work did not belong in a health department. Chapin summarized these views in his book, *The Sources and Modes of Infection*, published in 1910. This work, which became a classic, virtually put an end to the filth and fomite theories of disease transmission and initiated the idea of specific measures for dealing with specific diseases.

Despite his support for private medicine, Chapin recognized that medical care and preventive medicine could not be separated, and in 1913 he embarked on a program of providing medical care for the sick poor in their homes. Although he doubted that the American public would vote for health insurance, he believed that health centers which would provide both preventive and curative health services were the wave of the future. He retired from his position as health officer in October, 1931, having served for forty-eight years, and died at his home in Providence on January 31, 1941.

The most valuable collection of Chapin papers is to be found in the Rhode Island Medical Society Library, but the John Hay Library of Brown University and the Rhode Island Historical Society also hold some correspondence and other material. In addition to *The Sources and Modes of Infection* (1910), Chapin's writings include *Municipal Sanitation in the United States* (1901); *Report on State Public Health Work* (1916); *How to Avoid Infection* (1917); and *Papers of Charles V. Chapin, M.D.* (1934). The standard biography is James H. Cassedy, *Charles V. Chapin and the Public Health Movement* (1962). Other useful works are John E. Donely, "Charles Value Chapin—The Man and His Work," *Rhode Island Medical Journal* (1954), 311–316; Haven Emerson, "Foreword," and Clarence L. Scamman, "Charles V. Chapin," both in *Papers of Charles V. Chapin, M.D.* (1934); and Metropolitan Life Insurance Company, *Charles Value Chapin* (1944).

JOHN DUFFY

**Chapin, Francis Stuart** (February 3, 1888–July 7, 1974), sociologist, social work educator, and administrator, was born in Brooklyn, New York, the son of Florence (Johnson) and Charles Brookes Chapin, a Presbyterian minister. His grandfather, Henry Barton Chapin, was for many years principal of the Chapin Collegiate School in New York City. Born to a family of ministers and professional men, Chapin was influenced by an uncle, New York pediatrician Henry Dwight Chapin.* He majored in science at the University of Rochester and Columbia University, where he received the Bachelor of Arts degree in 1909. A year later he received a Master of Arts degree in sociology, and in 1911 the Ph.D. from Columbia. He then married Nellie Estelle Peck, who bore him three children— Edward Barton, Francis Stuart, Jr., and Florence Estelle—and he taught economics at Wellesley College for a year. In 1912 Chapin accepted a sociology position at Smith College, in Northhampton, Massachusetts, where he was to remain for ten years, advancing from the rank of instructor to full professor and chairman of the department.

While at Smith, Chapin was a member of the board of the Hampshire County Society for the Prevention of Cruelty to Children, and chairman of the Hampshire County Red Cross. With the coming of World War I, he became a member of the National Red Cross committee to develop "home service" work, on which he served with such important social workers of the day as Frank Bruno, Porter Lee,* and W. Frank Persons. In 1918 Chapin became director of the Smith College School for Social Work, where, together with Associate Director Mary C. Jarrett,* he created the block placement, necessary at Smith because Northampton lacked sufficient agencies for student field placements. He also recommended that social work be a permanent part of the Smith College program, not an emergency wartime measure. Chapin served as director of the school until 1921, when he resigned due to illness, and was succeeded by Professor Everett Kimball, a historian.

A year later, Chapin accepted an appointment as professor and chairman of the Department of Sociology and director of the Training Course for Social Work at the University of Minnesota, succeeding Frank Bruno, a social worker who had served as interim chairman of the program. Under Chapin's leadership, that program emerged into a school of social work, and Chapin served as director of the school until 1949 as well as chairman of the Department of Sociology until 1952, during which time he developed a reputation as one of the foremost research methodologists in the field.

Meanwhile, Chapin's first wife died, and on February 19, 1927, he married Eula Elizabeth Pickard. That same year he was elected president of the Minnesota Conference of Social Work. Between 1929 and 1931 he was on leave from the University of Minnesota to serve as editor of *Social Science Abstracts*, an early attempt to develop an interdisciplinary abstracting service. Upon failure of that venture, attributed to the Great Depression and the ambitious scope of the project, Chapin returned to Minnesota. During the 1930s he engaged in research on housing and on the effects of work relief on welfare clients. He also served as vice president of the board of the Minnesota Council of Social Agencies and was instrumental in establishing a bureau of social research in that organization. He was elected president of the American Sociological Association in 1936, the year it established the *American Sociological Review* as its official journal.

Throughout the 1930s social workers urged that the Minnesota School of Social Work be increased in size. Chapin and the associate director of the social work program at Minnesota, Gertrude Vaile,* who had been appointed to her position in 1930 while Chapin was on leave, succeeded in acquiring graduate status for the discipline, including approval for a doctoral program. By 1941, 51 percent of the graduate students in the social sciences at the University of Minnesota were in sociology and social work. Thus, it was no surprise when, one year later, the School of Social Work was established at the university, with Chapin as its director.

Earlier, in the 1920s and 1930s, Chapin had become the major advocate for what then was known as field research in sociology. He coauthored, with Stuart A. Queen, an influential monograph, *Research Memorandum on Social Work in the Depression*, published by the Social Science Research Council in 1937. He was also the author of many articles, numerous monographs, and two major textbooks, *Field Work and Social Research* (1920) and *Experimental Designs in Sociological Research* (1947, revised in 1955). As an author and as an academic administrator, Chapin fostered an empirical, quantitative approach to research in social work and sociology.

Upon his retirement in 1953, Chapin moved to Asheville, North Carolina, where for many years he continued to be active as a writer and editor. He died there on July 7, 1974.

The F. Stuart Chapin Papers at the University of Minnesota Archives are a rich source of information. While most of the collection is concerned with *Social Science Abstracts*, it contains transcripts of interviews with Chapin and many of his associates conducted by Ronald Althouse in the 1960s. Much material on Chapin exists in the records of the Department of Sociology and the records of the School of Social Work in the University of Minnesota Archives. He is mentioned in many of the collections in the Social Welfare History Archives at the University of Minnesota, in particular the papers of Mildred Dennett Mudgett, a social worker who was a member of the Minnesota faculty in the 1920s. The only biography of Chapin is a dissertation completed at the University of Minnesota by Ronald Althouse, "The Intellectual Career of F. Stuart Chapin: An Examination of the Development and Contribution of a Pluralistic Behaviorist," Ph.D. dissertation, University of Minnesota, 1964. Chapin is also discussed extensively in Don Martindale, *The Romance of a Profession: A Case in the Sociology of Sociology* (1976), a history of the Department of Sociology at Minnesota. Martindale's obituary of Chapin, which appeared in *ASA Footnotes* (October 1974), is reprinted on pp. 79–83 of *The Romance of a Profession*.

PAUL STUART

**Chapin, Henry Dwight** (February 4, 1857–June 28, 1942), pediatrician and social reformer, was born in Steubenville, Ohio, to Henry Barton Chapin, a minister, and Harriet Ann (Smith) Chapin. Chapin's family moved several times before settling in New York City, where his father became principal of the Collegiate School for Boys, later known as the Chapin Collegiate School. After attending the Collegiate School, Chapin went to Princeton University, graduating in 1877. He received an M.D. in 1881 from the College of Physicians and Surgeons. He is said to have held internships at Bellevue Hospital and at the leper colony on Ward's Island.

Chapin began his medical practice in 1884 and in 1885 became affiliated with the New York Post-Graduate Hospital, where he served as professor of diseases of children, director of pediatrics, and in various other positions for the remainder of his professional career. He held attending or consulting positions at a number of other hospitals including the Willard Parker Hospital, Riverside Hospital, Randall's Island Hospital, St. Agnes Hospital, and the Hackensack (New Jersey) Hospital.

Pediatrics was a new and largely unrecognized field of medical practice when Chapin began to specialize in diseases of children, and he contributed a great deal to its development through his teaching, research, and professional activities. He was one of the founders of the American Pediatric Society, becoming president in 1910. In 1912 he was chair of the pediatric section of the American Medical Association and in 1913 was chair of the pediatric section of the New York Academy of Medicine. Chapin published numerous scientific and popular articles and five books. In addition to two medical textbooks, he wrote *Vital Questions* (1905), which discussed community social problems and the role of the physician; *Health First: The Fine Art of Living* (1917); and *Heredity and Child Culture* (1922), in which he expressed his philosophy of medicine and child development.

Acutely conscious of the social responsibilities of medicine, Chapin helped to link pediatrics to the infant and child welfare movements and other social reforms of the period. Pediatrics was, to him, the prevention of illness and the treatment of social needs as well as the care of sick children. Believing that children required individual attention and family care, he sought to break down the barriers between home and hospital. He instituted a weekly visiting period for the parents of hospitalized children at a time when hospital wards were closed to outsiders. More important, he organized a hospital social service program in 1890 to provide follow-up visits to patients discharged from the Babies Ward of the Post-Graduate Hospital. The "Sunbeam Committee" of lady visitors called at the homes of former patients to offer instruction in health and hygiene. As the work expanded it was taken over by a trained nurse who made a formal assessment of the home, offered instruction in child care, and, when necessary, helped the family to secure relief.

One of Chapin's most notable and laudable efforts on behalf of child welfare was the founding, in 1902, of the Speedwell Society. Chapin vigorously opposed the institutional care of sick or dependent children, and yet he recognized that many children discharged from the hospital could not be returned home without further risk to their health. Under the Speedwell system, convalescent babies were boarded with families living in rural areas surrounding New York City. The plan had the dual advantage of a lower mortality rate than institutional care and a lower cost. Between 1902 and 1940 the Speedwell Society successfully placed over 20,000 children. Each Speedwell community had a local board of women managers who visited the foster family to inspect the homes and offer advice, and a local physician and nurse to provide constant medical oversight. Foster families were well supervised and well paid, including an incentive bonus for weight gained by the infant boarders. Chapin described the Speedwell program in his books and articles, suggesting that it could be instituted on a wider basis, thereby eliminating many of the health problems associated with institutional care.

Chapin married Alice Delafield in 1907. The Chapins, in 1910, took in an abandoned baby girl, cared for her until she was in good health, and oversaw her adoption. A year later they established the Alice Chapin Adoption Nursery. By 1942 the Nursery had overseen 1,700 adoptions and the placement of 2,000 other children. Following the death of Dr. Chapin the Nursery merged with the Spence Alumni Association to become the Spence-Chapin Adoption Service.

Chapin was active in a number of social welfare organizations and charities, and involved in a variety of ways in promoting child health. He served on the Advisory Council of the Public Education Association of New York in 1895. He was president from 1909 to 1920 of the Working Woman's Protective Union, an organization providing legal protection for self-supporting women. He was affiliated as well with the Havens Relief Fund Society, the Life Saving Benevolent Association, the Hospital Service Association of New York, and the Children's Welfare Federation, of which he was president in 1924.

Through his professional work Chapin helped to establish pediatrics as a medical specialty and to gain acceptance for the idea that children were profoundly different from adults in terms of their medical needs. Through his philanthropic and organizational efforts he joined pediatric medicine to the efforts of child welfare advocates, expanding the social role of medicine. Chapin retired from medical practice in 1926. He died at his home in Bronxville, New York, in 1942.

There are no manuscript materials for Chapin or the Speedwell Society. Chapin, however, wrote several books and many articles on pediatrics and on child health and welfare. Among the publications discussing his beliefs and activities regarding social welfare are "Child Study in the Hospital—A Record of Six Hundred Cases," *Forum* (March, 1894), 125–128; "The Function of Public Education," *North American Review* (January, 1896), 122–125; "The Proper Management of Foundlings and Neglected Infants," *Medical Record* (February, 1911), 283–288, 323–325; "Are Institutions for Infants Necessary?," *Journal of the American Medical Association* (January, 1915), 1–3; "Hospital Social Service for Children," *Medical Record* (March, 1917), 353–355; "Family vs. Institution," *Survey* (January, 1926), 485–488; *Hereditary and Child Culture* (1922); "Babies Wanted," *American Review of Reviews* (August, 1928), 183–185; "Homes or Institutions?" *Review of Reviews* (July, 1929), 49–51.

For biographies of Chapin, see *American Men of Science* 6th ed. (1938), 240–241; *National Cyclopedia of American Biography*, vol. 31 (1944), 439–441; *Who Was Who in America*, vol. 2 (1950), 110; *Dictionary of American Biography*, Supplement 3 (1973), 159–160. For obituaries of Chapin, consult *American Journal of Diseases of Children* (September, 1942), 535–538; *Journal of Pediatrics* (March, 1955), 348–357; *New York Times*, June 28, 1942, 33; and the obituary of Alice (Delafield) Chapin, *New York Times*, February, 21, 1964,

27. Other useful sources include the annual reports of the Speedwell Society, the annual reports of the New York Post-Graduate Hospital and Babies Ward, and "Dr. and Mrs. Chapin," *American Review of Reviews* (August, 1928), 182–183; "Henry Dwight Chapin (1857–1942): Pediatric Social Service Pioneer," *Medical Press* (February, 1957), 119; Isaac A. Abt, ed., *Abt-Garrison History of Pediatrics* (1965); Harold Kniest Faber and Rustin McIntosh, *History of the American Pediatric Society 1887–1965* (1966); and Peter Romanofsky, "Infant Mortality, Dr. Henry Dwight Chapin, and the Speedwell Society 1890–1920," *Journal of the Medical Society of New Jersey* (January, 1976), 33–38.

JANET GOLDEN

**Christman, Elisabeth** (September 2, 1881–April 26, 1975), labor organizer and child and working woman's welfare activist, was born in Germany to Henry Christman, a Bavarian-born musician and union cabinetmaker, and to Barbara (Guth) Christman, of Donaveschingen in Baden; they immigrated to America while Elisabeth was still a child. She was reared with her two brothers and three sisters. There was a strong Lutheran influence in her home as well as in the German Lutheran schools she attended until age thirteen. At age thirteen, Elisabeth began work at the Eisendrath glove factory in Chicago. While still in her teens, she organized, along with Agnes Nestor,* the Operators Local 1 of the International Glove Workers Union (IGWU) from an operatives' strike in her place of employ. For Christman, this marked the beginning of numerous activities on behalf of labor reform.

She served as the Local's chairman of shop stewards and treasurer, 1905–1911, and as president from 1912 to 1917. In 1916 she was a delegate from the IGWU to the American Federation of Labor convention. For fifteen years (1916–1931), Christman acted as secretary-treasurer of the IGWU and assumed the responsibilities of the vice presidency of that organization from 1931 until it affiliated with the Amalgamated Clothing Workers of America in 1937.

Overlapping these duties, Christman served for nineteen years on the regional executive board of the Chicago branch of the Women's Trade Union League (WTUL), from 1910 to 1929, and was elected to the executive board at the 1919 convention. In years to come she served as a finance committee chairperson, secretary-treasurer (1921–1950, full-time), and in 1923 and 1928 as a WTUL international delegate, first in Vienna, Austria, next in Honolulu. A third international stint sent her to Geneva in 1931.

Demonstrative of her commitment to labor reform are her efforts on behalf of the WTUL's school for working women, 1914–1926. The Training School for Women Organizers was an innovative leader in the education of workers; Christman also supported other labor education schools. Christman was, in short, a tireless fundraiser and a vital part of the administrative backbone of the WTUL.

Simultaneous with her numerous labor-related efforts, Christman assumed a number of national social welfare appointments. Oftentimes, in fact, the nature of her appointments bridged the concerns of both labor and social welfare. During

World War I she served as chief of women field representatives for the National War Labor Board (NWLB). Her task was to aid women in presenting their complaints to the NWLB; her work accomplished some of its goals, securing equal pay for equal work, although the Board fell short of implementing this for women workers in lower grades of work. Her 1918–1919 NWLB appointment was followed in 1921 with her selection, by President Warren G. Harding, to his Unemployment Conference. Charged with outlining measures that might offer relief, this body made its observations and recommendations to relieve unemployment. In 1933 Christman served on a similar committee instituted for the same purpose by President Herbert Hoover, the Organization on Unemployment Relief.

In 1929 Christman assumed a second Hoover appointment, this time one whose focus was primarily social welfare. As one member of a group of 1,200 experts, her work on the vocational guidance and child labor subcommittee of the White House Conference on Child Health and Protection surveyed American child health and welfare problems over one year. Ever mindful of the social interplay between labor reform and human welfare, in 1934 Christman became the first woman appointed to a National Recovery Administration code authority; she represented labor for the leather and woolen knit glove industry.

Reflecting her steadfast belief in improving children's and working women's welfare through education, Christman was appointed, in 1936, to President Franklin D. Roosevelt's Commission on Vocational Guidance (which was renamed the Advisory Committee on Education). A task force that produced nineteen studies, the group addressed itself to the relationship between the federal government and education. In 1937 Christman expanded her involvement in social welfare by serving on a national committee that studied the problems of older workers.

Once more recruited for her expertise and tireless efforts on behalf of children's welfare, Christman was appointed to the National Conference Committee on Children in a Democracy in 1938 by Secretary of Labor Frances Perkins.* These efforts were complemented by work in 1939 on the Follow-Up Committee on Children in a Democracy.

In 1940, at the request of Mary Anderson,* director of the United States Women's Bureau (and a familiar colleague from WTUL campaigns), Christman headed the Bureau's effort to address problems emanating from women's increased employment in war industries: specifically, equal pay and the securing of trade union support for these women workers. Still acting as secretary-treasurer for the WTUL, Christman was granted a leave of absence (April, 1942–March, 1943) from those duties so that she might devote herself full-time to the problems at hand. Observers agree that her tact and skill yielded considerable results.

Even after the WTUL ceased to operate (1950) and she retired (1952), Christman continued her efforts on behalf of labor reform, working for the Amalgamated Clothing Workers of America a short while as their legislative representative. Simultaneously, she sustained her interest in working women's issues.

Christman served as editor of *Life and Labor Bulletin*, the publication of the WTUL, and also penned articles in labor publications. She sought to institute and strengthen protective legislation for women workers through the passage of labor law, which, she firmly believed, would improve their quality of life.

Christman was a top-notch administrative organizer and a fund-raiser of significant skill. Despite colleaguial encouragement, she chose to decline primary leadership in the WTUL, although her commitment to that body is underscored by her return to it despite offers to remain at the Women's Bureau. A lifelong Democrat, Christman never married (although she was engaged once) and considered strong influences on her life to be women in social welfare and labor reform, and her church, which taught her the importance of service to one's fellow man, a creed to which her productive and well-regarded efforts serve as testimonial. Christman died in Delphi, Indiana, at age ninety-three.

Manuscript collections that have extensive holdings on Christman are housed at the Schlesinger Library of Radcliffe College in the WTUL Papers and the Mary Anderson Papers. Further manuscript sources are the WTUL Collection at the Library of Congress, and the Margaret Dreier Robins Papers at the University of Florida.

Books to be consulted include Mary Anderson, *Women at Work* (1951); Gladys Boone, *The Women's Trade Union Leagues in Great Britain and the United States of America* (1942); Mary E. Dreier, *Margaret Dreier Robins: Her Life, Letters, and Work* (1950); and Agnes Nestor, *Woman's Labor Leader* (1954). Relevant articles include Alice Henry, "Service Is Their Watchword," *Life and Labor* (July, 1921), 205–207; Eleanor Ellis Perkins, "Elisabeth Christman: 'Co-Worker,' " *Christian Science Monitor Magazine* (January 19, 1946), 6; "The National Women's Trade Union League," *Life and Labor* (October 1913), 320; "Trade Union Women Serving Uncle Sam," *Life and Labor* (October, 1918), 213–215; "Who's Who—National League Officers," *Life and Labor Bulletin* (October, 1926), 2–4.

Also informative for their chronological rendering of her social welfare and labor reform activities are *Biographical Dictionary of American Labor Leaders* (1974), 58–59; *Current Biography* (1947), 104–106; Robin Miller Jacoby, "Elisabeth Christman," in *Notable American Women* (1980), 148–150, a particularly revealing essay on Christman's gender consciousness, WTUL activism, and personality; and *Who's Who in Labor* (1946). Also see Christman's obituary in the *Washington Post*, April 29, 1975.

SUSAN E. CAYLEFF

**Clopper, Edward Nicholas** (January 1, 1879–November 30, 1953), social worker and child labor reformer, was born in Cincinnati, Ohio, the son of Mary Caroline (McClintock) and Edward Nicholas Clopper, Sr. Clopper, an Episcopalian, was educated at the public schools in Cincinnati, at Bethany College in West Virginia, where he received a B.S. in 1897, and at the University of Cincinnati, where he received his Ph.D. in 1912 after writing a dissertation on child labor in the so-called street trades. Two years later he married Grace Moser, with whom he had three children—Rhoda, Josephine, and Cornelius Jansen.

Clopper began his career earlier, in the field of education in Puerto Rico. With his Spanish-speaking ability, he maintained several positions within the Puerto Rican school system, including superintendent of schools for the District of San Juan and general superintendent of schools for the island. In 1908, however, he left Puerto Rico to become Ohio Valley secretary for the National Child Labor Committee (NCLC), a position he held until 1912, when his doctoral dissertation, which has become a classic, was published as *Child Labor in City Streets*.

Clopper became a trustee for the Cincinnati Experimental Study of Children in 1910, a position he held until 1926. While serving as a trustee, he also held several other important honorary positions in the field of child welfare. More important, however, in 1912 he became superintendent of the Cincinnati House of Refuge for Children, and a year later, in 1913, Clopper again joined the National Child Labor Committee as a field secretary. He remained with the NCLC until 1921.

It was during this time that Clopper did his most important work for child welfare. He traveled throughout the United States conducting studies of various child labor problems and prepared, edited, and published numerous reports and pamphlets for both the NCLC and many of its state affiliates, including "The Majesty of the Law in Mississippi" (1914); *Child Labor in the Sugar-Beet Fields of Colorado* (1916); *Farmwork and Schools in Kentucky* (1917); *Child Welfare in Alabama* (1918); *Child Welfare in Oklahoma* (1918); *Child Welfare in Kentucky* (1919); "State Programs for Legislation" (1919); and *Child Welfare in Tennessee* (1920).

While working for the NCLC, Clopper's title changed from field seccretary to assistant secretary to director of field work. His responsibilities increased, but his duties remained in the area of field investigations. He directed local and state research, edited state and national reports, and represented the NCLC at numerous meetings. One of his most important such functions came in 1916 when he attended the first Pan American Child Welfare Congress in Buenos Aires, Argentina. Because of his ability to speak Spanish, Clopper was able to interpret the problems of child labor in the United States to the conference delegates. He was appointed as the Conference's representative for the United States and was authorized to develop a Committee on Arrangements for the next International Conference, which was held in Montevideo, Uruguay, in 1918.

Throughout his employment with the NCLC, Clopper maintained his home in Cincinnati. Because of his leadership in field investigations, his Cincinnati office became a prominent branch of the NCLC, which had its headquarters in New York City. Most of the legislative work, lobbying, publishing of studies, and issuing of legal information came from Cincinnati. The focus was on both state and federal legislation. States were developing children's codes in the 1910s, and the federal government was struggling with attempts to regulate child labor;

Clopper spearheaded NCLC involvement in both of these matters. One of his greatest concerns was the failure of the Owen-Keating statute, the first federal child labor law, although he never lost sight of the need for state regulation.

Meanwhile, however, jurisdictional and philosophical differences arose between the NCLC general secretary, Owen R. Lovejoy,* and Clopper. By the end of 1921 these differences were too great to be reconciled, and Clopper resigned from the NCLC. Clopper had questioned what he felt was an infringement on his authority by Lovejoy and the investment of a good deal of time in legislative proposals he thought useless. Primarily, by that time he had become convinced of the need for a national children's code and/or a federal amendment to the Constitution as the only viable means of addressing the problem.

Clopper, however, continued his child welfare work after he left the NCLC. His first task, in 1921–1922, was to prepare the New York State legislative measures on child welfare. After that, he returned to the Ohio Valley, where he spent the rest of his life in various social welfare agencies or in teaching. He served as secretary for the Council of Social Agencies in Cincinnati, Ohio, from 1922 to 1925, and as executive secretary of the Pittsburgh Federation of Social Agencies from 1925 to 1933. For the next five years, Clopper was a sociology professor at the University of Cincinnati, in charge of graduate training in public welfare administration. From 1951 until his death, he was the associate editor of the quarterly published by the Ohio Historical and Philosophical Society.

Edward Clopper died in Cincinnati on November 30, 1953.

Clopper's best-known work in child welfare and child labor came while he was employed by the National Child Labor Committee. That work is documented in several places. The publications of various state studies for which he was responsible are listed in ''The Long Road,'' the Fortieth Anniversary Report of the NCLC, located in the Ephemera Collection at the Social Welfare History Archives Center, University of Minnesota, Minneapolis, Minnesota. Clopper's actual work is documented in the National Child Labor Committee Papers in the Manuscript Division of the Library of Congress in Washington, D.C., especially the board's *Minute Books*, 1920–1922. Also see various secondary accounts of child labor and the attempts to regulate it in America, especially Walter Trattner's *Crusade for the Children: A History of the National Child Labor Committee and Child Labor Reform in America* (1970).

JOANNE CATHERINE NEHER

**Cohn, Fannia Mary** (April 5, 1885?–December 24, 1962), labor leader, educator, and reformer, was born in Kletzk, Minsk, Russia, the fourth of five children of Hyman and Anna (Rosofsky) Cohn. Not much is known about Fannia Cohn's early life, including the year of her birth, over which there is some discrepancy. However, her father was manager of a family-owned flour mill. Privately educated, she was groomed for a professional career. But she was drawn into radical politics, joining the outlawed Socialist Revolutionary Party. In 1904 she immigrated to New York City. Deciding to devote her life to labor organizational work, she took a job in a garment factory as a sleevemaker in 1905. Four years later she was elected to the executive board of the newly organized Wrapper, Kimono, and House Dress Makers' Local 41 of the International Ladies' Garment Workers' Union (ILGWU). In 1914 she moved to Chicago to attend the National Women's Trade Union League's Training School for Women Organizers. Although dropping out after a few months, she stayed on in Chicago as an ILGWU organizer and in August, 1915, led the first successful strike by that city's dress and white goods workers.

After her return to New York the following year, Cohn became the first woman elected to a vice presidency of the ILGWU. In late 1918 she was named executive secretary of its Educational Department. She proceeded to build the ILGWU's program into the largest such undertaking in the country. So-called Unity Centers located in neighborhood public school buildings offered courses and lectures; a Workers' University provided more systematic instruction in labor problems, government, history, and literature; an Extension Division sent speakers and discussion leaders out into the field. Along with this educational program, the Department promoted a wide range of social and recreational activities, whose capstone was the summer vacation resort of Unity House in Pennsylvania's Pocono Mountains. A tireless evangelist for workers' education, Cohn did not limit her involvement to the ILGWU. In 1921 she played a leading role in the establishment of the Workers' Education Bureau of America as a coordinating body for union educational efforts, in the founding of the Brookwood Labor College as the first residential college for workers in the United States, and in the formation of the Labor Publication Society. In 1924 she helped launch the experimental Manumit School for Workers' Children and the Pioneer Youth of America, a recreational program for working-class children.

Cohn saw workers' education as serving a larger purpose than simply enriching the lives of individual workers, or even training future union leaders. Her ambition was an independent labor party along the lines of the British Labour Party; her long-range goal was "to change economic and social conditions so that those who produce shall own the product of their labor." Reflecting her hostility to the narrow focus of pure and simple trade unionism upon "the temporary every day needs of the workers," she sympathized with Brookwood's director, Abraham J. Muste,* in his battle with the leadership of the American Federation of Labor. The climax of the struggle over the direction of workers' education came in 1929 when the Workers' Education Bureau—over Cohn's protest—expelled Brookwood because of its alleged radicalism. But she herself had become sufficiently disillusioned with Muste's leftward tilt to refuse to join his new Conference for Progressive Labor Action. After Muste was forced out of Brookwood in 1933, Cohn strove to keep the institution going as a nonpolitical training school for union organizers. Lack of union financial support, however, led to Brookwood's closing its doors four years later.

By that time Cohn had been largely shunted aside even within the ILGWU.

During the twenties she remained neutral in the struggle over the communist bid to control the union on the ground that workers' education should not be associated with any factional ideology. Partly because she was caught in the resulting crossfire, and partly because of her lack of a power base in the locals, in 1925 she was defeated for reelection to a fifth term as vice president. Although she remained executive secretary of the Educational Department, the union's desperate plight meant that no money was available for educational programs. She herself went without salary and was forced to rely upon relatives for financial support. Under the New Deal, the ILGWU succeeded in making impressive membership gains. But its pragmatically minded president, David Dubinsky, thought Cohn out of touch with the interests of the new younger, American-born members whose loyalty he wished to cement. While she retained her official title, effective control over the educational program was placed in the hands of Mark Starr after he was named educational director in 1935.

Cohn's position as a woman in a largely male-dominated union hierarchy contributed to her difficulties. She repeatedly lamented the labor movement's "not realizing the importance of placing the interests of women on the same basis as of men." The accompanying frictions were aggravated by her domineering, even authoritarian, personality. Perhaps most important, the objective of workers' education had shifted away from an attempt to establish a new social order to a concern with the more practical needs of the union movement. By contrast, Cohn continued to adhere to the now outdated concept of workers' education as an instrument for promoting "a new vision of a future society based on cooperative effort." In August, 1962, she was pushed into retirement. Four months later, she died of a stroke in New York City.

The Fannia Cohn Papers are in the Manuscript Division of the New York Public Library. A complete listing of her articles on and in behalf of workers' education can be found in Richard E. Dwyer, *Labor Education in the U.S.: An Annotated Bibliography* (1977).

The fullest biographical account is Ricki Carole Myers Cohen, "Fannia Cohn and the International Ladies' Garment Workers' Union," Ph.D. dissertation, University of Southern California, 1976; a briefer sketch by Susan Stone Wong is in *Notable American Women: The Modern Period* (1980), 154–155. Additional information can be found in Louis Levine, *The Women's Garment Workers: A History of the International Ladies' Garment Workers' Union* (1924); Benjamin Stolberg, *Tailor's Progress: The Story of a Famous Union and the Men Who Made It* (1954); Alice Kessler-Harris, "Organizing the Unorganizable: Three Jewish Women and Their Union," *Labor History* (Winter, 1976), 5–23; James O. Morris, *Conflict Within the AFL: A Study of Craft Versus Industrial Unionism, 1901–1938* (1958); and Jo Ann Ooiman Robinson, *Abraham Went Out: A Biography of A. J. Muste* (1981).

JOHN BRAEMAN

**Coit, Stanton** (August 11, 1857–February 15, 1944), founder of the settlement house movement in America and Ethical Culture leader, was born to Harvey and Elizabeth (Greer) Coit in Columbus, Ohio. He was the seventh generation descended from John Coit, who emigrated from England to the Massachusetts Bay Colony about 1630. Coit's father was a prosperous merchant who raised his son in the Episcopal Church. His religious life, however, was more influenced by the fervent spiritualism of his mother. Coit early showed a philosophical bent of mind and discovered the writings of Ralph Waldo Emerson at fifteen. He was an eclectic thinker who worked out his own synthesis.

Coit received his B.A. from Amherst College in 1879. He was elected to Phi Beta Kappa. Though he severed ties to formal religious bodies during his college years, Coit had a reputation for piety. Ministers even tried to hire him to tutor problem sons. He spent his first year out of Amherst tutoring a student in his parents' home. For the next two years he was an English instructor at Amherst.

In 1881, at the suggestion of a friend, Coit traveled to New York City to listen to a lecture by Felix Adler, founder of the Ethical Culture Society. Right away he decided to become a lecturer in the new society and volunteered his services to Adler. He prepared for his new career by attending Columbia University in 1882–1883. But for Adler, a graduate degree from a German university was a kind of informal requirement for participation in Ethical Culture. Adler was a major influence in Coit's life. He financed Coit's trip to Europe and two years of study at the University of Berlin. In Europe Coit experienced a cultural shock in that he was sensitized to the differences in cultural arrangements among societies. From his experience in Germany, he borrowed the concept of the positive state—a state using its power to promote the general welfare.

Coit received the Ph.D. from the University of Berlin in December, 1885. He spent the next few months at Toynbee Hall, home of the social settlement. Coit criticized this version of the social settlement because of its disconnected social betterment activities and lack of a broad social goal.

Coit returned to New York City in 1886 to become an assistant to Adler in the Ethical Culture Society. His parallel plan to do social settlement work, moreover, was congruent with Ethical Culture's stress on the expression of personal virtue through social service. Coit first experimented by taking the city poor at his own expense to outings on Staten Island. In August, 1886, he rented rooms in a tenement on the Lower East Side. Neighborhood youngsters were organized into six clubs with the expectation that parents would follow. In February, 1887, Charles Stover,* recreation reformer, joined Coit as a co-worker. They established the tradition in the United States—but not always followed in social settlements—of unpaid service and even made personal financial contributions to the enterprise. This financial arrangement meant that settlement residents had a certain degree of independence of action.

In 1891 Coit published *Neighborhood Guilds*, which discussed the social settlement scheme and his version of the good society. The target population was the lower middle class. The guild was to teach the working class—normal, but culturally deprived people—organizational skills and cooperation through recruitment into age-graded clubs. It planned to use the family ethos in tenement districts to promote a greater sense of social solidarity. The New York City Neighborhood Guild, for instance, tried to teach mutual aid by using 25 percent of club dues to help the poor and the sick. Coit believed that on-the-spot involvement of outsiders like himself was only temporary, because of his overly optimistic view that guilds would be financially self-supporting and self-propagating as well. *Neighborhood Guilds* also supported unions, the eight-hour day, and gradual reform on the way to a cooperative or socialistic society.

Coit's pilot tenement project helped generate a national social settlement movement in the United States. His model identified many of the main lines of settlement work. Coit, however, was an idea man with limited but creative front-line social work experience. He devoted only a scattered series of months to the new form of social work. Ethical Culture was his main commitment. In 1887 he proselytized in England and was invited to return to South Place Religious Society as its first lecturer in Ethical Culture in July, 1888. Coit did not return to New York City until after the Neighborhood Guild was reorganized as University Settlement Society. Between 1892 and 1894 he held dual positions as settlement director and Ethical Culture leader. In the sixteen months that he spent as settlement director, his innovations included neighborhood social reform groups and an experiment with a dairy cooperative.

The onset of a depression in the winter of 1893–1894 caused terrible hardships in Coit's tenement neighborhood. Coit became embroiled in a controversy with the trustees of University Settlement because of newspaper reports that he had told unemployed workers to pressure political leaders to provide jobs through public works projects. Coit denied being an agitator, but defended his public works proposal in an article published in the *Forum*. He resigned as director and spent the rest of his life in England. In infrequent trips to the United States he delivered lectures on social issues, some of which were published. In *The Soul of America*, which was published in 1914, he reaffirmed his faith in human brotherhood. Coit died in Birling Gap (Sussex), England, in 1944.

The University Settlement Society of New York Papers, which are located at the State Historical Society of Wisconsin, have internal reports made by Coit as director in the early 1890s.

Coit's conception of the social settlement is contained in *Neighborhood Guilds: An Instrument of Social Reform* (1891), and in *University Settlement Society, Annual Report*, 1892–1893. His rationale for a public works program is in "Necessity of State Aid to the Unemployed," *Forum* (May, 1894), 276–286. His views about the United States as a nation are in *The Soul of America* (1914).

*Stanton Coit, 1857–1944: Selections from His Writings with a Prefatory Memoir* (1944), ed. Harold J. Blackham, has the most comprehensive biographical information about Coit. Its focus, however, is mainly on his Ethical Culture career.

JOHN J. CAREY

**Colcord, Joanna Carver** (March 18, 1882–April 8, 1960), social work administrator, researcher, and writer, was born at sea in the South Pacific— delivered by her captain father midpoint in a commercial trade voyage—to Jane (Sweetser) Colcord and Lincoln Alden Colcord. Both of her parents came from generations of Maine seafarers accustomed to family separations; however, a captain's prerogative to bring his family aboard meant that Joanna and a younger brother, Lincoln, spent many years at sea and in foreign ports. Later Colcord reflected on the lessons those experiences had taught: the necessity of carrying out tasks quickly and honestly and of respecting individual differences. Composing letters to relatives while on board ship also taught her writing skills, which, along with her mother's tutoring, enabled Joanna to earn her high school diploma by correspondence and to enter the University of Maine in 1902.

By 1909 her interest in natural sciences had led to an undergraduate and a master's degree in biological chemistry. Employment at a Boston chemical factory and nutritional research at the Maine State Agricultural Experimental Station were interjected with the course work, but Colcord's satisfaction with such inquiries waned. Encouraged by a favorite teacher, she entered the New York School of Philanthropy and studied under Mary Richmond* for a year before becoming a district supervisor for the New York Charity Organization Society (COS) in 1911.

Colcord's bold common sense, her appetite for hard work, and her clarity about the integration of professional knowledge with human needs led to greater responsibilities at the COS central office. At various times she worked there with Edward Devine,* Frank Bruno, and Karl de Schweinitz,* helping to direct the agency's modernization, its responses to the unemployment crisis of 1914– 1915, and its renowned program to train Red Cross volunteers for World War I service.

Joanna Colcord was always a forceful advocate of social work as a profession with a vital and developing role in humanizing society. Such a view was evident in her first book, *Broken Homes: A Study of Family Desertion and Its Social Treatment* (1919), a volume in the casework series initiated by Mary Richmond as director of the Charity Organization Department of the Russell Sage Foundation. In the work, Colcord analyzed not only family dynamics but workers' changing attitudes over time, and outlined new methods for the prevention of family breakdown as well as for treatment.

In the next years she chaired the Family Division of the National Conference of Social Work and various committees of the American Association for Organizing Family Social Work. Her articles on family life and casework appeared in the *Survey*, the *Family*, and other journals. Joanna Colcord, however, was not content to limit her energy to this field. Seeking new challenges, she took a one-year sabbatical from the COS in 1920 to travel to the Virgin Islands with a Red Cross expedition. There she dealt with both the occupying U.S. Navy and rural peasants, supervising the introduction of health and education programs; in the 1930s she would serve on a federal committee to advise the Islands' government.

Colcord moved again in 1925, having successfully competed against male applicants for the executive position Frank Bruno vacated at the Minneapolis Associated Charities in Minnesota, later called Minneapolis Family and Children's Service. She quickly moved into leadership roles in city and state social welfare activities, even as she continued sitting on national committees and speaking to social work groups around the country. In 1928 her old friend, Mary Richmond, died, and the Russell Sage Foundation asked Colcord to fill the opening thus created; the next year she returned to New York City.

Collaborating with Ruth Mann, Colcord's first project at the Foundation was to interpret her predecessor's contribution to social work in *The Long View: Papers and Addresses by Mary E. Richmond* (1930). This book, which traced developments and conflicts in the profession through Mary Richmond's work, coincided with the end of an era. The Great Depression shifted social workers' concerns from casework in private agencies to local public relief and then to state and federal employment and welfare programs.

In Minneapolis, as early as 1927, Colcord and her agency had coped with increasing unemployment and demands for financial relief. When bad times looked permanent in 1930, she called a national Conference on the Coming Winter so that agency heads could discuss strategies for dealing with these problems. In a *Survey* article at the same time, "Facing the Coming Winter" (November 15, 1930, 206), she suggested how agencies might work out a satisfactory compromise between professional standards, inadequate funding levels, and good service. She evaluated local relief initiatives to enable communities to learn from others' experiences in *Community Planning in Unemployment Emergencies* (1930), *Setting Up a Program of Work Relief* (1931), and (with Mary Johnston) *Community Programs for Subsistence Gardens* (1933), all published by the Russell Sage Foundation.

As New Dealers began discussing remedies for unemployment, Colcord joined a small group from the American Association of Social Workers who organized an *ad hoc* Conference on Federal Action on Unemployment. This body welcomed federal intervention and sought to offer to decision-makers social workers' knowledge about communities and "helping." Colcord chaired committees, wrote, and spoke, reiterating the position that local, state, and federal governments each had roles, and that work programs should be nonpartisan and administered apart from relief. She was successful on two fronts: convincing other social workers to see that taking positions on federal policy was professionally appropriate behavior, and finding officials who were receptive to professional social workers' views. In 1933 she was asked to advise the federal Civil Works Administration, and at succeeding national conferences she interpreted public relief programs to social workers. This use of herself and Russell Sage Foundation books and bulletins to establish a flow of information between the profession, local communities, and the federal government was novel. From 1932 to 1935 the *Survey* formally tapped into this "network" by paying her and her assistant,

Russell Kurtz, to write a department called "Unemployment and Community Action."

Trained as a scientist, Colcord always rejected hearsay and looked for facts, documenting the results of cash versus in-kind relief programs, and supervising research on various work relief programs and food stamp proposals. An early advocate of federal action, by 1936 she was critical of the categorical approach to Social Security and impatient with the welfare gaps perpetuating worker insecurity. Examining security on a local level became the topic of *Your Community, Its Provisions for Health, Education, Safety, and Welfare* (1939), which outlined a research approach eagerly adopted by scores of citizens' groups and officials around the country.

Colcord's concerns ranged from the local to the international, and she often represented the United States in activities of the International Conference of Social Work. When another war in Europe brought mobilization, she became a government consultant on how industrial and military displacement affected communities. However, old age and ill health began to reduce her involvements, and in 1945 she retired from the Russell Sage Foundation to live with her brother's family in Searsport, Maine.

Never having felt far from the sea, Colcord published a book on the life of a sailor in 1945, but her public career was over. When, in 1950, her good friend of almost forty years, Frank Bruno, became a widower, the two were married; the ideals of family life and devotion about which she had once written became real in the couple's infirmity. And the service that commemorated Bruno's death in 1955 also acknowledged Colcord's role in shaping professional social work and implementing it as a civilizing agent in the breadth of social relations. Joanna Colcord died in Lebanon, Indiana, on April 8, 1960.

Materials related to Joanna Colcord's professional career and family can be found in papers of the Community Service Society of New York; Minneapolis Family and Children's Service; Paul U. Kellogg; National Association of Social Workers; Survey Associates; Louis Towley; and Benjamin Youngdahl, all in collections at the Social Welfare History Archives, University of Minnesota, Minneapolis, Minnesota.

In addition to the publications mentioned already, Colcord wrote *Cash Relief* (1936), and with William C. Koplovitz and Russell H. Kurtz compiled *Emergency Work Relief as Carried out in Twenty-Six American Communities, 1930–1931* (1932). Her books about the sea include *Roll and Go, Songs of American Sailormen* (1924), republished as *Songs of American Sailormen* (1938), and *Sea Language Comes Ashore* (1945).

Articles by her appeared in the *Family*, 1920–1935, and the *Survey*, 1929–1943. Her addresses at the National Conference of Social Work are transcribed in its *Proceedings*, 1919–1943.

An interpretive essay on Colcord has been written by Clarke A. Chambers in *Notable American Women, the Modern Period: A Biographical Dictionary* (1980).

Briefer biographical information is provided in the *Encyclopedia of Social Work*, issue 15, vol. 1 (1965), and repeated in succeeding issues; here Colcord's birth date is listed incorrectly. Her career from 1929 to 1945 is covered by John W. Glenn, Lilian Brandt, and F. Emerson Andrews in *The Russell Sage Foundation* (1947). She is included in *Who Was Who in America*, vol. 7 (1981).

Two features emphasizing her youth are by J. M. Stenbuck, "The World Was Their Backyard," *Coronet* (February, 1946), 38–41, and "Childhood at Sea an Early Education in the Realities of Life," *Portland* (Maine) *Sunday Telegram*, July 12, 1936, 1. The "Editorial" in the *Family* (March, 1929), 16, has essentially the same information as that found in "The Log of Joanna Colcord," *Survey* (March 15, 1929), 822–823. See also "Joanna C. Colcord Retires," *Survey Midmonthly* (October, 1945), 273.

Brief obituaries appeared in the *New York Times* (April 9, 1960), 23:3, and the *Social Service Review* (June, 1960), 233. A number of sources exist about Lincoln Colcord, Joanna Colcord's brother, who was a journalist and author.

BEVERLY A. STADUM

**Collier, John** (May 4, 1884–May 8, 1968), urban community center worker and community organizer, Indian rights advocate, United States Commissioner of Indian Affairs, educator, and author, was born in Atlanta, Georgia, the middle of seven children of Charles Allen Collier, lawyer, banker, and local civic leader, and Susie (Rawson) Collier. The family was prominent and affluent, and Collier's early childhood was privileged and secure. His teenage years, however, were unsettled and marked by tragedy, first by his mother's death in 1897 following a long period of declining physical and emotional health, then, four years later, by his father's death of a self-inflicted gunshot wound that Collier never believed was accidental. These events broke up the family and plunged Collier into despondency, from which he extricated himself by absorption in the literature of nineteenth century romanticism and nature mysticism and by long sojourns in the southern Appalachian wilds, where he had mystical experiences and admired the sequestered communal life and spiritual strength of the Indian and ethnic mountain people.

Collier was educated in Atlanta public schools and, for a period following his mother's death, at a rural Georgia convent, where he was briefly converted to Catholicism. Following his graduation from high school, Collier attended Columbia University in New York from 1902 to 1904. There he studied literature, philosophy, sociology, and biology, observed the vivid community life of the city's ethnic enclaves and read widely in contemporary social criticism, further confirming his belief in the importance of the spiritual and communal dimensions of life, the creative human will, and the intuition. From the end of 1904 to the summer of 1906, Collier lived in the South again, working first as a promoter of an ill-fated scheme to revitalize the South with large infusions of immigrants from northern cities, then as the director of the Associated Charities of Atlanta, and finally as a reporter and acting city editor of the Macon, Georgia, *Telegraph*.

In 1906 and 1907 Collier traveled in Europe, studied abnormal psychology under Pierre Janet at the College de France in Paris, and became better acquainted with the Celtic renaissance and the practice of European labor, cooperative, and socialist movements.

Collier returned to New York City late in 1907, and, early in 1908, went to work as civic secretary for the People's Institute, an organization that sponsored lectures, recreational and cultural programs, and civic organization among the immigrants of the Lower East Side. A talented publicist, lobbyist, and political organizer, and a prolific writer and speaker, Collier soon developed extensive connections in city politics and government and among the intellectual and literary left of the city. He became a moving force in many new enterprises dedicated to protecting and organizing the immigrant neighborhoods of New York, including the city's flourishing school community center system, the New York Training School for Community Workers, the Child Health Organization, and the city's elaborate wartime community council system. At the same time, Collier emerged as a leader in the burgeoning national community center movement. He helped to organize the National Conference of Community Centers in 1916 and afterward edited its periodical, the *Community Center*, and served as the president of the organization. During this period of rapid growth and increasing philanthropic and municipal support and control of the community center movement, Collier was a leader of a decentralist faction that espoused cultural pluralism as an alternative to the prevailing assimilationist goals of the movement; widespread citizen participation in public affairs through independent, self-supporting, and locally controlled neighborhood and community organizations; and the delivery of municipal and social services through local community clearing houses.

After the war Collier lost his position in the New York community center movement. In 1919 he moved to California, working first as director of the state's community organization and education program and then teaching social science at San Francisco State Teachers' College. Fascinated by the strong, independent culture of the Indians of the Southwest, especially the Pueblos, Collier soon began to take a leading role as organizer, publicist, and lobbyist for civic groups attempting to protect the natural resources, civil rights, and welfare of these Indians. In 1923 Collier became the executive secretary of the newly formed American Indian Defense Association. From this position, through the remainder of the 1920s and into the early 1930s, he led an assault on existing federal Indian policy, which since the Dawes Act of 1887 had attempted to force the rapid assimilation of Indians into the dominant culture. Collier believed that this was wrong in principle and a failure in fact; and he was joined by many others who deplored the miserable economic and social conditions on the reservations and the infringement of Indian civil and property rights by outside interests.

By the late 1920s, this critique had begun to effect changes in federal policy, a process vastly accelerated in 1933, when Collier was appointed United States

Commissioner of Indian Affairs, a position which he continued to hold until he resigned in 1945. As the head of the Bureau of Indian Affairs during the Roosevelt years, Collier was the architect of the Indian New Deal, a profound change in federal Indian policy, the principal purposes of which were to restore Indian political autonomy, develop Indian economic resources, and revive Indian pride, social organization, culture, and religion. To achieve these ends, Collier's administration sought to organize and empower tribal governments; terminate the dispersal of reservation land to individual ownership; develop community economic planning and natural resource management on the reservations; increase federal assistance; and reduce the presence of bureaucrats, politicians, missionaries, boarding schools, and other outside influences in reservation life. The Indian New Deal went into decline after 1940, as congressional support for Collier's policies eroded and the onset of war diverted federal money and interest and drained able Indians from the reservations.

During World War II and in the postwar years, Collier extended his interest in the protection of ethnic and native cultures to encompass the world. He served as a director of the National Indian Institute and the Inter-American Indian Institute, as an advisor to the United States delegation to the United Nations on trusteeship matters, and as the president of the Institute of Ethnic Affairs in Washington, D.C. He was professor of sociology and anthropology at City College in New York from 1947 to 1954 and a visiting professor of anthropology at Knox College in Galesburg, Illinois, in 1955–1956. He continued to write widely for the popular and scholarly press. After leaving the federal service, he became a forceful critic of postwar federal Indian and foreign policy, which he regarded as the systematic and unremitting exploitation and subjugation of native peoples around the world.

Collier was a small, slightly built man of enormous will and energy, whose strong opinions and forceful ways some found abrasive. He was a tenacious and gifted publicist, a formidable lobbyist, and an agile political and bureaucratic manipulator for causes in which he believed. He was also drawn to nature and contemplation, and periodically throughout his life, after exhausting himself in his multiple causes, he would withdraw to wild places to recuperate, read, and write, only to rebound into public affairs with renewed determination. For more than fifty years, beginning in the Progressive period, Collier was an unrelenting proponent of his radical vision of cultural pluralism and community and small group empowerment, which he attempted to apply, against all odds and with mixed success, to the ethnic neighborhoods of New York, rural California towns, Indian reservations, and the nations of the Third World. In the process, Collier became a pioneer in the theory and practice of group work, community organization, community development, and public administration, as well as a recognized authority on ethnic and native cultures. The recession of his ideals in the community movement and in federal Indian and foreign policy saddened and embittered him. While some attributed these reversals to his willful and impractical objectives, Collier himself blamed the corrosive materialism, individualism, rationalism, and growing concentration of power in Western civilization. His concern to preserve alternative cultures became more intense as his suspicion grew that Western society lacked the capacity to ever reform itself sufficiently to satisfy the inner spiritual cravings and social needs of mankind.

Collier was thrice married, first to Lucy Wood from 1906 to 1943, then to Laura Thompson from 1943 to 1955, and last to Grace Volk in 1957. The first two marriages ended in divorce. From the first marriage, Collier had three sons: Charles Wood, Donald, and John.

Collier retired in the mid-1950s to Ranchos de Taos, New Mexico, where he continued to reflect and write about the matters that concerned him until his death there at age eighty-four.

The papers and other publications of the People's Institute in the New York Public Library are important sources for Collier's work in New York City. The best manuscript sources for Collier's Indian work are in the National Archives at Washington, D.C., and the Collier Papers at Yale University.

A representative sample of Collier's voluminous writing includes: "Social Centers," *National Municipal Review* (July, 1913); *The City Where Crime Is Play*, with Edward Barrows (1914); "The Organized Laity and the Social Expert: The Meaning of Public Community Centers," National Conference of Social Work *Proceedings* (1917); "Community Councils—Democracy Every Day," *Survey* (August 31, September 21, September 28, 1918); "Community Councils—What They Have Done and What Is Their Future," National Conference of Social Work *Proceedings* (1919); "The Red Atlantis," *Survey* (October 1, 1922); "The Pueblos' Last Stand," *Sunset* (February, 1923); *America's Colonial Record* (1947); *Indians of the Americas* (1947); *On the Gleaming Way* (1962); and *From Every Zenith: A Memoir and Some Essays on Life and Thought* (1963). The various periodicals that Collier founded or edited are important sources of his writings: the *Civic Journal*, the *Community Center*, *American Indian Life*, *Indians at Work*, and the *Newsletter* of the Institute of Ethnic Affairs.

Recent monographs critically reassessing Collier's work, concentrating mostly on the Indian period, include: Lawrence C. Kelly, *The Assault on Assimilation: John Collier and the Origins of Indian Policy Reform* (1983), the first of a projected two-volume study; Lawrence M. Hauptman, *The Iroquois and the New Deal* (1981); Donald L. Parman, *The Navajos and the New Deal* (1976); Kenneth R. Philp, *John Collier's Crusade for Indian Reform, 1920–1954* (1977); and Graham D. Taylor, *The New Deal and American Indian Tribalism: The Administration of the Indian Reorganization Act, 1934–1945* (1980).

THOMAS MARSHALL TODD

**Coman, Katharine** (November 23, 1857–January 11, 1915), educator, social reformer, and economic historian, was born in Newark, Ohio, the fourth of seven children and the first daughter of Martha (Seymour) Coman and Levi Parsons Coman. Her father, an ardent abolitionist and free soiler who graduated from

Hamilton College, was a teacher and lawyer. Returning from the Civil War in impaired health, he moved the family to a farm near Hanover, Ohio, where Katharine spent an "ideal" childhood. Under her father's supervision, and with the firm support of her mother, who had graduated from an Ohio seminary, Coman studied Latin and mathematics with her brothers. She began study at Steubenville Female Seminary in 1873, but transferred to the high school of the University of Michigan when the seminary's male principal refused to provide her with advanced work because of her sex. Coman entered the University of Michigan in the fall of 1874. After two years there, she taught in Ottawa, Illinois, for two years, then returned to the university for her junior and senior years, graduating in 1880 with a Ph.B. degree.

Following her college friend Alice Freeman to Wellesley College, Coman joined the faculty as an instructor in rhetoric. She was appointed instructor in history in 1881; professor of history and political economy in 1883; and professor of political economy and sociology in 1900, when she also became chair of the department of economics.

Much loved by her students, Coman was a creative teacher known for her tolerance of different opinions and her encouragement of original thinking. She was part of an unusual all-female faculty community at Wellesley. Her most intimate friend was Katharine Lee Bates, professor of English, with whom she lived for many years. Coman made her headquarters in a sunny room known as "Bohemia" in the "Scarab," as the last home she shared with Miss Bates came to be called.

Coman coauthored three textbooks on English history with Elizabeth Kendall, as well as *English History Told by English Poets*, written with Katharine Lee Bates. More significant were two books in economic history, *The Industrial History of the United States* (1905), reprinted seventeen times, and the two-volume *Economic Beginnings of the Far West* (1912), which critics found more interesting by virtue of its vivid style and wealth of primary source material, collected by Coman as she traveled through the United States. Coman's "History of Contract Labor in the Hawaiian Islands" (1903), and "The Negro as a Peasant Farmer" (1905), published by the American Economic Association and the American Statistical Association, also relied on firsthand observation. Her "Some Unsettled Problems of Irrigation" appeared as the first article in the first issue of the *American Economic Review*.

Coman was deeply involved in social reform efforts to improve the conditions of workers, particularly women. In 1890 she founded the Thursday Evening Club, an organization of women tailors in Boston, and became its first president. A few years later, with her friend Cornelia Warren, she started an experimental, cooperative tailor shop, which, however, failed after several months. Coman was involved in formulating plans for the College Settlement Association (CSA), founded in 1890 to establish settlements and encourage women graduates to undertake settlement house residence. She served as president of the electoral board and as chairman of the Association's standing committee from 1900 to

1907, establishing its first fellowship program. From 1911 to 1914 she served as associate elector of the CSA.

Coman chaired the committee which opened Denison House in Boston's South End in December, 1892, the third CSA settlement. Though she never became a resident, she worked closely with its staff, serving successively as secretary, chairman, and member of its executive committee. Coman's colleagues believed that her instinct for organization and attention to the smallest details of administration helped guarantee the settlement's success. Her advocacy of the interests of working people stimulated Denison House to become a center for labor organizing.

Coman was a charter member of the National Consumers' League, strongly endorsing its strategy of aiding working women by bringing consumer pressure to bear on manufacturers. She served on the executive committee of the Massachusetts branch, and was honorary vice president of the League until her death. In 1910, while visiting Chicago, Coman came to the aid of the striking United Garment Workers, writing articles to explain the causes of the strike and serving as chairman of the Grievance Committee of the Women's Trade Union League.

In 1913, after several years of ill health, Coman retired from Wellesley, though she had actually stopped teaching in 1910. She volunteered her services to the National Progressive Service, organized to implement the social justice planks of the Progressive Party platform. In 1913–1914, at the suggestion of Jane Addams* that she undertake a study of social insurance in Europe, Coman toured England, Spain, Denmark, and Sweden with her former student, Olga Halsey, a trip that culminated in the publication of nine articles on social insurance for *Survey* magazine; a posthumous book, *Unemployment Insurance: A Summary of European Systems* (1915); and the drafting of tentative social insurance legislation adapted to American conditions.

A deeply spiritual woman, Coman, through her moral vision and organizational skills, helped launch and guide the settlement movement. Never a detached scholar, she cherished direct contacts with working women and was influential in directing a younger generation of college graduates into settlement work. Coman's scholarly, scientific approach to social problems, always coupled with a focus on the "warm and human," as Jane Addams observed, made her an exemplar of progressive women's work in social reform.

Coman died of cancer at her home in Wellesley, Massachusetts, in 1915.

The best summary of Coman's life is provided in Allen F. Davis' biographical portrait in *Notable American Women*, vol. 1 (1971). The Wellesley College Archives hold various papers of Katharine Coman and some biographical material. Papers of Denison House, the College Settlement Association, the Women's Trade Union League, and the National Consumers' League are at Schlesinger Library. The Jane Addams Papers in the Swarthmore College Peace Collection contain some letters from Coman.

Also see Dorothy Burgess, *Dream and Deed: The Story of Katharine Lee Bates* (1952); *Memories of Martha Seymour Coman* (1915), ed. Katharine Coman; Florence Converse, *Wellesley College* (1939); Jean Glassock, ed., *Wellesley College 1875–1975: A Century of Women* (1975); Alice B. Hackett, *Wellesley, Part of the American Story* (1949); an obituary article on Coman by Olga Halsey in *Survey* (January 23, 1915); Patricia Ann Palmieri, "In 'Adamless Eden': A Social Portrait of the Academic at Wellesley College," Ph.D. dissertation, Harvard University, 1981; Vida Scudder, *On Journey* (1937); and the entry on Coman in *Who's Who in America*, vol. 1 (1942). Biographical material and assessments by Coman's associates are provided in a special edition of the *Wellesley College News*, "In Memorium: Katharine Coman" (April, 1915). Sonnets written by Katharine Lee Bates in memory of Katharine Coman may be found in *Yellow Clover* (1922).

JOYCE ANTLER

**Commons, John Rogers** (October 13, 1862–May 11, 1945), economist, labor historian, educator, and reformer, was born in Hollandsburg, Ohio, the eldest surviving child of John and Clarissa (Rogers) Commons. His father, who edited small-town newspapers, and his mother, a school teacher and Oberlin College graduate, shared abolitionist views and strong religious and philosophical beliefs. Illness delayed his bachelor's degree at Oberlin until 1888, whereupon he studied economics with Richard T. Ely for two years at Johns Hopkins University. He never completed his doctorate, but taught successively until 1899 at Wesleyan University (Middletown, Connecticut), Oberlin, Indiana University, and Syracuse University. His extensive publication of scholarly and popular books and articles, beginning in 1892, and his classroom teaching gave him an unfair reputation for radicalism in the tense America of the 1890s and cut short his teaching appointments. For the next five years Commons abandoned teaching in favor of staff work, including work for the United States Industrial Commission and the National Civic Federation.

At the invitation of Ely, Commons joined the department of political economy (which then meant economics, anthropology, and sociology) at the University of Wisconsin in 1904. Despite lacking the Ph.D., Commons made himself in the next twenty-eight years at the university one of the best known and most distinguished of the large cluster of University of Wisconsin social scientists who changed the character of their disciplines and fashioned a new role in service to the state. Never a brilliant lecturer, Commons nevertheless stimulated student thought and discussion and particularly attracted graduate students; his correspondence reveals continuing contact with and influence over his students, who came to assume important academic, governmental, and institutional roles.

Commons had rejected classical economics and its theories very early in his studies and had adopted instead the obligation for thorough research of economic activity, both historical and contemporary. He became a prominent teacher of institutional economics, that is, the what and the how of the elements composing the economic system and not the theories that logic was said to impose on the system. He came to believe strongly in a pragmatic approach to public affairs, in the testing of theory through practice, in the efficacy of compromise, and in the possibility of useful reform. Philosophically a democrat and a gradualist, he moved away from the ideology of class conflict and revolution espoused by many contemporary thinkers.

A major focus for Commons was labor economics and labor history. He and his students completed an Ely editorial project, *A Documentary History of American Industrial Society* (ten volumes, 1910–1911); and he assembled student writings into a *History of Labor in the United States* (two volumes, each, 1918 and 1935). The latter emphasized trade unionism of the Gompers variety and ameliorative labor legislation as the most appropriate American responses to Marxism. With his student and colleague at Wisconsin, Selig Perlman, he enunciated the conservative approach of the "Wisconsin School" to the history of American labor, a dominant viewpoint during his lifetime.

Commons' influence, however, extended beyond the classroom and his students. His arrival on the Madison campus coincided with the reelection of Governor Robert M. La Follette (1910–1916) to a third term and the climax of his reform governorship. Commons' assistance to La Follette and his successors in the drafting of reform legislation, such as civil service legislation (1905), a public utilities law (1907), and the formation of the Industrial Commission (1911), exemplified what came to be known as the "Wisconsin Idea," that is, the informal participation of University of Wisconsin faculty in progressive reforms. Commons believed in the usefulness of empirical studies by academic experts in shaping legislation; in the efficacy of state legislation in dealing with the new problems of an industrial and urban society; and in the value of administrative boards and commissions to augment the traditional three branches of government. With Charles McCarthy* of the Legislative Reference Library and his faculty colleagues in the social sciences—Paul Reinsch, Thomas S. Adams, Balthasar Meyer, and about forty others at one time or another—Commons transformed the state's legislative process, especially in his drafting of a workmen's compensation bill in 1911 and his two years of service thereafter on the Industrial Commission.

His progressive faith in the investigation of social problems as a prelude to their solution led Commons into the pioneer "Pittsburgh Survey" of the Russell Sage Foundation, and service on the staff of *Survey Magazine*; and during 1911–1912 he supervised a similar effort, a Bureau of Economy and Efficiency, for Socialist Mayor Emil Seidel and Congressman Victor Berger of Milwaukee.

Commons was similarly committed to an active role in national reform. With Ely and others he founded the American Association for Labor Legislation in 1906, long led by his student John B. Andrews.* He was a member of the United States Commission on Industrial Relations in the Wilson era, a longtime president of the National Consumers' League (1923–1935), an organizer of the

National Safety Council, and active in other state and national organizations. He was president of the American Economic Association in 1918.

Traditional patriotism led Commons to support the United States in World War I, even to a break with Robert La Follette, then a U.S. Senator, and to support the Americanization movement which emerged in Milwaukee and Wisconsin. During the 1920s his personal involvement in reform diminished, but his influence persisted through his students, who influenced state and federal insurance programs.

Commons married his Oberlin classmate Ella Brown Downey in 1890. Only two of their five children survived infancy, and further family tragedies marred the years surrounding Commons' retirement from teaching in 1932. He later moved from Madison to Ft. Lauderdale, Florida, and died of myocarditis while on a visit to Raleigh, North Carolina.

Commons' personal papers, those of his colleagues and associates, and materials he gathered for his writing and editing on labor and socialism are in the State Historical Society of Wisconsin and the University of Wisconsin Archives (both in Madison). *Myself* (1934, 1963) is a frank and self-conscious autobiography, while *Legal Foundations of Capitalism* (1924) and *Institutional Economics* (1934) set forth his governing ideas. Lafayette G. Harter, Jr., *John R. Commons: His Assault on Laissez-Faire* (1962), combines biography with analysis of Commons' thinking. *Dictionary of American Biography*, Supp. 3 (1973), and *Dictionary of Wisconsin Biography* (1960) contain shorter sketches.

FREDERICK I. OLSON

**Cooley, Harris Reed** (October 18, 1857–October 24, 1936), "minister" to the needs of the poor, sick, and aged, and director of charities and corrections in Cleveland, Ohio (1901–1910, 1912–1916), was born in Royalton Township, Cuyahoga County, Ohio, to Laura and Lathrop Cooley. A prominent minister of the Disciple Church, Lathrop Cooley provided his son with opportunities for travel abroad as well as an excellent formal education. His father's effort to minister to the poor of Cleveland, and his own study of new methods of treating social pathology in England had a profound influence on Harris Cooley's religious and social philosophy. After receiving the B.A. degree from Hiram College in 1877, Cooley attended Oberlin, receiving the M.A. degree in 1880, while serving on occasion as minister of Disciple churches in Brunswick and Aurora, Ohio.

In 1880 Cooley came to Cleveland as minister to the Erie Street Christian Mission, founded by his father. In 1883 the mission moved to Cedar Avenue. Cooley continued as minister of the Cedar Avenue Christian Church until 1901. An exponent of the Social Gospel and greatly influenced by the Progressive movement in politics, Cooley preached and counseled that an unequitable and inhumane environment, not a sinful human nature, was the cause of human suffering and social delinquency. In January, 1900, he married Cora Clark, a professor of languages at Hiram College, who proved to be a lifelong supporter of his efforts to minister to the needs of the poor, sick, and aged.

In 1901 Cooley resigned as minister of the Cedar Avenue church and accepted the position of director of charities and corrections in Tom L. Johnson's administration of Cleveland. A member of Cooley's church, Johnson, when questioned about the wisdom of appointing a minister to so important an office, asserted that he had never experienced or heard of service rendered to a municipality of so high an order as that given by Cooley to Cleveland.

From 1901 to the end of 1915, when he retired from public service, Cooley inspired and directed a major reformation of the charitable, public health, and correctional system of Cleveland. Although he was out of office from 1910 to 1912, Cooley's projects were generally carried forward by the Republican administration. The city government underwent several changes from 1901 to 1915, but Cooley's responsibilities remained essentially the same, except that in 1909–1910 he was in charge of the fire and police departments. Cooley's primary duties involved oversight of the infirmary, the workhouse, hospital facilities, and young delinquents.

Upon taking office, Cooley put into practice a philosophy of reform based on simple but deeply held beliefs. He was convinced that society—especially the economic system of industrialized, capitalistic urban America—was responsible for poverty, and that poverty bred vice, crime, and disease. A normal, healthy environment, however, would produce a normal, healthy life. To combat the effects of slum environments, Cooley proposed the establishment of a farm, or cottage, colony in the country near the city. There, living in a cooperative, family-style setting where they might work on the land, the aged, ill and delinquent would have the best opportunity to realize self-worth and positive social adjustment.

In 1901 Cooley instituted a more lenient parole system for the City Workhouse, and in 1903 helped begin a night school for the inmates. In 1902 Cooley established a training home for truant and wayward boys on a 285–acre site at Hudson, Ohio. By 1906 the Hudson Boys' Home consisted of eight cottages with room for 120 boys, a school, and two teachers. From 1903 to 1906, 285 boys, staying an average of six months to a year, participated in life at the home, which included schooling, vocational training, work with the famous diary cattle, construction of buildings, and gardening. Living under an honor system that allowed them much personal freedom, the boys, by 1914, had helped to build a power plant, a sewage disposal plant, and a greenhouse. The incidence of recidivism significantly declined among the boys sent to the home. In 1914 Cooley oversaw the establishment of a Girls' Home, patterned after the Hudson Boys' Home. The school at the Girls' Home opened in 1915.

From 1903 until the close of his public service, Cooley successfully pressed for the construction of a new municipal hospital. His great work, however, was the development of a farm colony complex for the care of the city's aged, sick, and delinquent. By 1905 the city had purchased 1,500 acres adjoining the municipal cemetery at Warrensville. That year the infirmary was moved to the Warrensville site. In 1906 the city began construction of a cottage home and dining facility for aged women, and planned cottage facilities for aged men and couples. By 1907 the complex comprised the Colony Farm for infirmary inmates, Overlook Farm, site of a projected tuberculosis sanitarium (in operation by 1913), Correction Farm for former workhouse inmates, and Highland Park Farm, the municipal cemetery.

In 1907 the city council gave the name Cooley Farms to the entire Warrensville establishment. By 1909 about 1,000 people were living at Cooley Farms. Before he retired, Cooley's farm colony, as well as his other reform projects, had become models for welfare reform nationally and internationally. Following retirement, Cooley remained active until the last few years of his life, lecturing and preaching on the subject of Cooley Farms and the principles that had guided him in its creation. He died in Cleveland, Ohio, in 1936.

For a short introduction to Cooley's reform philosophy, see Harris Reed Cooley, "The Outdoor Treatment of Crime," *Outlook* (February, 1911), 402–408.

The *Annual Reports of the Departments of Government of the City of Cleveland* (yearly reports, 1902–1915), provide a chronological view of Cooley's career in the administrations of Tom L. Johnson and Newton Baker. Jean A. Herring, "Harris Reed Cooley," Master's thesis, Ohio State University, 1949, deals largely with the development of Cooley Farms. A highly laudatory account of Cooley's contributions to the Cleveland reform movement is in Tom L. Johnson, *My Story*, ed. Elizabeth J. Hauser (1913). Henry K. Shaw, *Buckeye Disciples: A History of the Disciples of Christ in Ohio* (1952), offers some insight into the ministries of Cooley and his father. An accurate, if eulogistic, obituary of Cooley is in the *Cleveland Plain Dealer*, October 25, 1936, 4A.

PAUL C. BOWERS, JR.

**Coyle, Grace Longwood** (March 22, 1892–March 8, 1962), educator, pioneer group worker, and author, was born in North Adams, Massachusetts, the daughter of Mary Allerton (Cushman) and John Patterson Coyle, a minister in the Congregational Church. She received her A.B. from Wellesley College in 1914, where she was elected to Phi Beta Kappa. In 1915 she earned a certificate from the New York School of Philanthropy (now Columbia University School of Social Work). From 1915 until 1918 she was a settlement worker, and from 1918 to 1926 she was on the staff of the Industrial Woman's Department of the Young Women's Christian Association (YWCA). Coyle earned a master's degree in economics from Columbia University in 1928 and a doctorate in sociology from Columbia in 1931, a year after she rejoined the YWCA staff as director of the Laboratory Division of the National Board. She remained in this position until 1934, when she joined the faculty of Case Western Reserve University, a position she held until her death in 1962.

Grace Coyle's first book, *Social Process in Organized Groups*, published in

1931 and based on her dissertation, marked the beginning of her efforts to develop a social science framework for work with individuals and groups. The impact of Coyle's book on group work has been compared to that of Mary Richmond's* *Social Diagnosis* on casework practice. Of particular importance was her examination of the conditions of group cohesion, morale, and the role of ritual and symbols in modern societies. Her interest in social science theory continued throughout her professional life, and she published numerous articles on the subject as well as the monographs *Social Science in the Professional Education of Social Worker* (1958) and *Social Process, Community and Group* (1958).

Prior to the 1930s, work with groups was done primarily by individuals in leisure-time, education, recreation, or character-building agencies, such as the scouts, the Ys, the settlements, and the Jewish Centers. Group workers tended to deal with fairly well-adjusted individuals and were concerned with social reform, education, and the enhancement of life. Caseworkers, on the other hand, dealt more with those who needed treatment before they were ready to take part in normal social activities. There was concern by many leading groups that if group work were to become a part of social work, it would lose its special identity and its commitment to social action.

Coyle felt that casework and group work had a common philosophy and that both would be enriched by their integration. She argued that the uniting of the two would result in better-quality service for the client. She argued that group workers needed to become more aware of personality issues and family relationships, while at the same time caseworkers needed to be more knowledgeable of group dynamics and the use of leisure activities. It was also her belief that a better acquaintance with casework by group workers would reveal the therapeutic possibilities of the group experience.

In 1935 Coyle, along with a number of other group workers, was invited to present a paper on group work at the National Conference of Social Work in Montreal. Her paper, "Group Work and Social Change," was given the Pugsley Award, presented by the National Conference to the author of the paper that made the most important contribution to the subject matter of social work at that year's conference. Coyle's presentation, in addition to the other group work presentations, served as a turning point in group work's assimilation into social work.

Coyle's vision of group work as a part of the social work profession was articulated in the *Social Work Year Book 1937*, where she delineated group work from education, recreation, character-building, and the group life of the community. She wrote that because group work, as a method, was consciously directed toward social ends, it could more properly be called *social* group work. The aim of this method of helping was the development of persons through the interplay of personalities in group situations, and the creation of such group situations provided for integrated, cooperative group action for common ends.

From her experience in the settlement movement and in the YWCA, Coyle learned firsthand the needs of new immigrants, factory workers, the poor, and other oppressed men and women. In addition, she was sensitive to the problems that are a part of urbanization. It was her belief that one of social work's unique contributions was that of changing the environment so as to make life more satisfactory. She was fearful that social workers, as they became more professional, would lose their historical commitment to social action.

Group work, according to Coyle, rested on two pillars of conviction. The first was the emphasis on creative experience as preferable to formalized, imitative, or passive programs. The second was the emphasis on participation and the experience of democratic control by the members. The hoped for results of membership in a group led by a group worker were individuals who developed their powers to the fullest and who were able to devote those powers to the social good by full participation in the society in which they live.

Group workers were encouraged by Coyle to be sensitive to both the group's dynamics, that is, decision-making, leadership, bonding, and so on, and to the interpersonal relationships within the group. This was best articulated in her book, *Group Work with American Youth* (1948), in which she presented concrete and detailed examples of leadership and program skills. Through the use of case examples Coyle described ways in which the worker could examine the creative forces that brought the group into existence, its social structure, personal relationships, leadership and authority issues, the use of program activities, and the sense of esprit de corps within the group. Coyle felt that it was important that the group's development and the worker's activities not be left to chance but occur through the conscious use of self by the worker.

Long before it was fashionable, Coyle emphasized the interrelatedness of mind, body, and emotions. Workers were to view group members as "whole" persons rather than separate out and focus on the social, physical, or psychological aspects of the person's life. Behaviors, such as aggressiveness and shyness, according to Coyle, were only symptomatic, and the sensitive worker needed to go beneath the surface and determine the meaning of these behaviors for the person.

In addition to her practical experience and her teaching and writing, Grace Coyle was instrumental in shaping the profession of social work practice, knowledge, and education through her leadership in various professional associations. Most important, she served as president of the National Conference of Social Work (1940), the American Association of Social Workers (1942–1944), and the Council on Social Work Education (1958–1960).

Grace Coyle died in Cleveland, Ohio, on March 8, 1962.

By the time of her death, Coyle had published more than twenty-six articles and six books and monographs on a wide range of subjects including social change, democracy, social science theory, professional education, casework, family interaction, and group work.

A collection of her manuscripts, course outlines, and correspondence is located in the Archives of Case Western Reserve University, Cleveland, Ohio.

Coyle's thoughts and ideas on the relationship of group work and social work are most evident in such writings as "Case Work and Group Work: Where the Two Areas Meet and Contribute to Each Other," *Survey* (April, 1937); "Social Group Work: As Aspect of Social Work Practice," *Journal of Social Issues* (1939); and "Concepts Relevant to Helping the Family as a Group," *Social Casework* (July, 1962). The reader is also encouraged to review Coyle's articles in the 1935, 1937, and 1954 editions of *Social Work Year Book* in which she examines group work's identity as it relates to social work, recreation, and other fields of service.

The themes of social action and democratic values, while apparent in much of her writing, are best articulated in "Group Work and Social Change," *Proceedings of the National Conference of Social Work* (1935), and "The Limitations of Social Work in Relation to Social Reorganization," *Social Forces* (October, 1935). They are also explored in depth in her books and monographs: *Group Experiences and Democratic Values* (1947); *Group Work with American Youth* (1948); and *Social Process in the Organized Groups*, with Margaret E. Hartford (1958).

Tributes in memory of Grace Coyle are included in *Social Casework* (July, 1962), 376, and in *American Sociological Review* (January, 1963).

KENNETH E. REID

**Cutting, Robert Fulton** (June 24, 1852–September 21, 1934), financier, philanthropist, civic leader, and reformer, was born in New York City; he was a descendant of Robert Fulton and the son of Fulton Cutting and Justine (Bayard) Cutting. He received a B.A. from Columbia University in 1871 and an M.A. in 1875 from the same institution. Subsequently, he was trained as a private banker in companies controlled by the family. His first wife was Nathalie C.P. Schenck, who died in 1875, leaving a son. Eight years later, Cutting married Helen Suydam, by whom he had six children.

Though now largely a forgotten figure, Cutting had a considerable impact on his native city. His interests were wide and his achievements many and varied. Beginning in 1893, Cutting served nineteen years as president of the New York Association for Improving the Condition of the Poor (AICP). During his tenure, the Association expanded its budget from $60,000 to over $500,000 and broadened its range of activities with the establishment of a number of institutions.

Among these was the Cooper Union Labor Bureau. This agency, which opened its door in 1895, was a free labor exchange, bringing together the unemployed and prospective employers. Careful of its reputation with both sides, the Bureau sedulously checked the references of jobless candidates, while also insisting that the employer pay the going wage. (Another Bureau policy was to avoid supplying workingmen in case of strikes.)

As there existed at the time a certain ideological tension between charity organizations like the AICP and the settlement house movement, a more daring addition to the Association's institutions was the Hartley House Settlement, established in 1897. A major objective of Hartley House was to help the laboring class. Thus, it provided instruction in the buying and preparing of food, supplied work (such as sewing) to destitute women, maintained a free library, kindergarten, and playground, and retained a resident, full-time nurse.

The Labor Bureau and Hartley House are illustrative of the variety of agencies established by the AICP during Cutting's incumbency. Others founded while Cutting headed the Association included the Milbank Memorial Bath, Sea Breeze Hospital, Caroline Rest House and Caroline Country Club, and the Home Hospital.

Well before he had taken on the job as president of the AICP, Cutting had been interested in tenement house reform. But nothing he had previously done in this area approached the size and scope of the City and Suburban Homes Company. Incorporated in 1896, City and Suburban Homes was a limited-dividend company with an initial capital stock of $1 million. The company was pledged to build decent, sanitary housing for working people. Over the next generation the company met its pledge, erecting both rental housing and privately owned homes (in Brooklyn).

City and Suburban Homes attracted the support of a number of prominent individuals, including Alfred T. White,* Isaac N. Seligman, and Elgin R.L. Gould.* As for Cutting, he was not only one of the founders of the company, but also served at one time or another as president and as chairman of the board of directors (a post he held at the time of his death).

Along with his responsibilities at the AICP and the City and Suburban Homes Company, Cutting accepted the headship of several other institutions. He was for many years the president of Cooper Union, where he took an active part in its enterprises. Again, beginning in 1899 he assumed the presidency of the New York Trade School, which had been founded in 1881 to train young men for practical and mechanical trades. And he was the president and later chairman of the board of the Metropolitan Opera and Real Estate Company.

Given Cutting's involvement in so many areas of New York City life, as well as his personal convictions, it was perhaps inevitable that he would, at some point, turn his attention to politics and reform. Though originally a Democrat, he grew increasingly critical of Tammany Hall and the "corrupting" influence of the prevailing spoils system. And so in 1897 he helped to found the nonpartisan Citizens' Union, and was its first chairman. He became interested in the career of Seth Low, former mayor of Brooklyn, and largely through Cutting's efforts the latter was elected mayor of New York City in 1901 on a Republican-Fusion ticket. But two years later, much to Cutting's surprise, Low lost his bid for reelection.

Still, Cutting remained committed to the goals of reform and improved city government. He was, for instance, one of the founders of the Bureau of City Betterment, which in 1907 was renamed the Bureau of Municipal Research. The purpose of this organization was to investigate municipal misgovernment and to propose constructive measures to rectify abuses and increase efficiency. The Bureau, bringing advances in accounting techniques to bear on New York City's government, became a force for responsible fiscal administration in New York as well as a model for similar bureaus in other cities, both at home and abroad.

As Cutting was generous with his time and energy, so was he liberal with his personal fortune. As early as 1878, for example, he gave $70,000 to the debt-ridden church of St. Ann's on the Heights—upon the condition that the church discard the pew system and become free to all. Over the years he gave liberally to the YMCA and in 1927 provided a gift of $250,000 to the American Society for the Control of Cancer.

Cutting was a prominent churchman and a senior warden of St. George's Protestant Episcopal Church. The role of the church in modern society was, in fact, a matter of much concern to him, and in his book, *The Church and Society* (1912), he expressed his views on the subject. He recognized that society was passing from an age of individualism to an era where the state was steadily enlarging the scope of its social activities and assuming the initiative in wrestling with the problems growing out of the "disabilities" of the multitude. Cutting, nonetheless, insisted that the church had an important place, namely, to take a more active part in vitalizing the administrative functions of the state. Thus, he urged the church to cooperate actively with school boards and teachers, health officers, superintendents of the poor, and the police.

Such advice typified Cutting's own public career. For over four decades he gave practical, forceful, disinterested, and unofficial service to the people—and in particular the laboring people—of New York City. He was primarily concerned with better homes and improved conditions for the working poor, with practical education, and with the abolition of public waste and graft. Once known as "the first citizen of New York," he died at his summer home in Tuxedo Park, New York, on September 21, 1934.

An illuminating sample of Cutting's writings would include the following: "Public Ownership and the Social Conscience," *Municipal Affairs* (March, 1900), 3–12; "Objects, Aims and Scope of the Greatest Organization Pledged to Civic Reform in America as Told by R. Fulton Cutting, President of the Citizens' Union at a Dinner Given in His Honor," in Milo T. Bogard, ed., *The Redemption of New York* (1902), 49–56; "The Closed Shop," *Survey* (January 29, 1910), 587–588; "The Major Beneficence," *North American Review* (July–December, 1911), 377–382.

Biographical information on Cutting can be found in *Banquet to R. Fulton Cutting and Elgin R.L. Gould, Given by Their Friends* (1902); and the obituaries in the *New Herald Tribune* and the *New York Times*, September 22, 1934. For data relating to the City and Suburban Homes Company, see Roy Lubove, *The Progressive and the Slums: Tenement House Reform in New York City, 1890–1917* (1962), 100–113.

RICHARD HARMOND

# D

**Davis, Katharine Bement** (January 15, 1860–December 10, 1935), sociologist, penologist, social worker, social hygienist, and feminist, was born in Buffalo, New York, the daughter of Frances F. (Bement) and Oscar Bill Davis; she was the oldest of five children, three girls and two boys. Her family came from Wales, England, and France; their history in America dated back to the 1630s. Her ancestors included Ethan Allen and an abolitionist-feminist grandmother, Rhoda Denison Bement, who attended the first woman's rights convention in Seneca Falls, New York (1848). The Davis family moved to Dunkirk, New York, when Katharine was three years old, and to Rochester in 1877, where she attended the Free Academy and developed a lifelong passion for science. After her graduation in 1879, her family could not afford to further her education. She taught science at Dunkirk High School, saved her salary, studied at night, and entered Vassar College as a junior in 1890, graduating with honors in 1892. Her commencement address, "The Missing Term in the Food Problem," and the first five years of her postgraduate career reflected her interest in the application of science to the problems of households and families in urban industrial settings.

Davis did graduate work in food chemistry at Columbia University, while teaching science at the Brooklyn Heights Seminary (1892–1893). Her studies led to a position as director of a model workingman's home, an exhibit at the World's Columbian Exposition in Chicago (1893). A visitor to the exhibit, impressed with her work, offered her a job as head resident of St. Mary's College Settlement in Philadelphia. Her activities there brought her into contact with Russian Jewish immigrants whose political sophistication and intense conversations fascinated her. She left the settlement in 1897 for graduate study in political economy and sociology at the University of Chicago.

At the university she entered a community where faculty and students had strong reform interests. In the social science departments, soon to become internationally prominent, students learned to observe, survey, and analyze urban social conditions with an eye for amelioration. Davis worked with the iconoclastic Thorstein Veblen, whose radical views she found to her liking. In 1898 a European

Fellowship from the New England Women's Educational Association took her to the universities of Berlin and Vienna. Her dissertation, "Causes Affecting the Standard of Living and Wages" (1900), compared the socioeconomic status of Bohemians in Europe to those in Chicago.

Davis belonged to a coterie of outstanding female graduate students nurtured by Chicago's redoubtable dean of women, Marion Talbot, and by such off-campus leaders as Jane Addams.* This women's network, in particular Talbot's friendship with Josephine Shaw Lowell,* helped Davis secure appointment as the first superintendent of the model women's reformatory at Bedford Hills, New York. Davis and other women intellectuals of her generation often remained in reform work after completing their degrees, partly because their training stressed both the theory and practice of reform, and partly because of women's difficulties in making academic careers.

Davis took the job at Bedford Hills after stipulating that she must be allowed to run the reformatory as an educational institution. Bedford Hills was, in fact, intended for young first offenders with a maximum sentence of three years, including time on parole. Most of the inmates had been convicted of prostitution and virtually all had led what Davis called "sexually irregular" lives, outside the bounds of Victorian morality. Her penology combined hereditarian and environmentalist ideas with a strong belief in scientific mental testing. Through this testing she hoped to classify inmates and apply the correct treatment to each group—permanent custodial care for the congenitally "feeble-minded" or "degenerate"; educatiton, training, and extended time on parole for "mentally normal" but "fallen" women, who would then return to society. At Bedford Hills she put the prisoners to work farming, building furniture, even pouring concrete, and attending classes of all kinds. She organized their living arrangements on the "cottage plan." She refused to segregate black and white prisoners, a common practice, or to denounce, as others did, close friendships and sexual relationships between inmates. She invited women psychologists to the institution to begin the testing and classifying so important to her theories. Despite severe overcrowding and lack of funds, Bedford Hills became well known as a successful experiment. In 1912 John D. Rockerfeller, Jr., read about Davis' theories, and offered a five-year contract for a Laboratory of Social Hygiene at Bedford Hills to aid in the classification work.

Davis left the reformatory in 1914 to become Commissioner of Corrections in New York City under the reform administration of Mayor John P. Mitchel—the first woman to head a city department. She quickly became controversial as she shut down prison drug traffic and corruption, tightened regulations, tried to provide prisoners with meaningful work, planned a women's detention center, replaced the traditional striped prison garb with plain work clothes, and dealt with prisoners as "errant children." A riot at Blackwell's Island, led by Industrial Workers of the World leader and future Columbia University history professor Frank Tannenbaum, was easily quelled, but led to complaints that the Davis regime was too harsh and repressive. A 1915 investigation by the State Prisons

Commission upheld the charges, but the Prison Association of New York, the Mayor, and other reformers defended her, claiming that she had modernized the prison system. In the end most people thought well of her administration. Davis had lobbied successfully for legislation permitting indeterminate sentences and paroles, and left the Department of Corrections in 1916 to chair the city's first parole commission.

When Mitchel's ticket was defeated for reelection, she became general secretary of the Rockefeller-funded Bureau of Social Hygiene, a position she held from 1918 until her retirement in 1928. Under her direction the Bureau, founded to help eradicate prostitution, broadened its scope, funding and publishing studies of the international white slave trade, public health, and sex education. Davis' major work, *Factors in the Sex Life of 2200 Women* (1929), discussed "normal" middle-class women.

Davis' high-powered career did not keep her from participating in other reform activities such as suffrage, the Progressive Party, and relief work following a 1908 Italian earthquake.

During and after World War I, Davis concentrated on social hygiene causes— eliminating prostitution, preventing the spread of venereal disease, and providing sex education for women. This work, emphasizing control of prostitutes and sometimes violating their civil liberties to do so, caused conflict with European and American feminists who stressed persuasion and rehabilitation of sex offenders rather than regulation and imprisonment. After retirement she consulted with the American Social Hygiene Assocation to promote sex education programs in women's clubs.

Katharine Davis' achievements were honored during her lifetime. Rockefeller called her "the cleverest woman I ever met," and Carrie Chapman Catt referred to her as one of the "superwomen of the United States." The League of Women Voters named her one of the twelve greatest living Americans, and she held honorary degrees from several colleges and universities. The guest list at her retirement dinner at the Waldorf Astoria on February 2, 1928, read like a social welfare reform roll of honor.

Part of the first generation of college and professional women, Davis joined intellectual, scientific, and research interests with social activism during her career. Like other progressives, she believed that science could uncover the causes of social problems and that professionals could then use that knowledge to uplift and improve society. She combined in her work a liberal spirit of compassion and outreach with more conservative beliefs in efficiency, order, and social control.

Davis moved to California in 1930 to live with her sisters, and died (of cerebral arteriosclerosis) five years later.

Katharine Davis left behind few personal papers or documents. At one time she planned to write "An Autobiographical Biography," but ill health and death intervened. Some biographical material may be found in the Special Collections of the Vassar College Library and at the Alumnae House in Poughkeepsie, New York. Data on her career as prison reformer and penologist may be found in the *Superintendent's Reports*, 1901–1914, New York State Reformatory for Women, Bedford Hills, New York, and the Minutes of the Board of Managers, New York State Reformatory for Women at Bedford, 1902–1911, New York State Executive Department Papers, New York State Library, Albany, New York. Her activities as Commissioner of Corrections (1914–1915) and chair of the New York City Parole Commission (1916–1917) are documented in the New York City newspapers for that period; in the Mayors' Papers, New York City Municipal Archives; and in the annual reports of the Department of Corrections, New York City Municipal Reference and Research Center. Davis' work at the Bureau of Social Hygiene may be followed in the Bureau's records at the Rockefeller Archive Center, North Tarrytown, New York. More Davis material may be found at the Archive Center in the Office of the Messrs. Rockefeller Collection, Rockefeller Family Archive 1895–1960, especially for the 1920s.

Useful biographical articles on Davis can be found in *Notable American Women*, vol. 1 (1971), 439–441; *The Dictionary of American Biography*, vol. 21, suppl. 1 (1944), 227–228; *The National Cyclopaedia of American Biography*, Current Vol. A (1930), 262–263; and Mabel Ward Cameron, ed., *Biographical Cyclopaedia of American Women* (1924), 117–120. See also both editions of Rebecca Deming Moor, *When They Were Girls* (1923 and 1937). Information on her work at the St. Mary's College Settlement can be found in the *Buffalo Courier*, August 26, 1894; on her rescue work in Italy, see the *New York Evening Post*, March 16, 1909. Her superintendency at Bedford Hills is discussed in Eugenia C. Lekkerkerker, *Reformatories for Women in the United States* (1931), and more briefly in Black McKelvey, *American Prisons* (1977). For her term as Commissioner of Corrections, see *Prison Progress in 1916* (1917), the seventy-second annual report of the Prison Association of New York; Mary B. Harris, *I Knew Them in Prison* (1936); and Jean Henry Lare, "A Man's Job," *University of Chicago Magazine* (January, 1934), 105–108. Her suffrage ideas and feminist philosophy can be found in Ida Husted Harper, ed., *The History of Woman Suffrage*, vol. 6, 1900–1920 (1922), 425, 459–468, 496–500. Davis' obituaries in the *New York Times* and the *New York Herald Tribune* (both December 11, 1935) also contain helpful information.

Katharine Davis's place in history, the role of her generation as reformers and social scientists, and her life as a professional woman are assesed in Ellen F. Fitzpatrick, "Academics and Activists: Women Social Scientists and the Impulse for Reform, 1892–1920," Ph.D. dissertation, Brandeis University, 1981; and Estelle B. Freedman, *Their Sisters' Keepers: Women's Prison Reform in America, 1830–1930* (1981).

I am indebted to Ellen F. Fitzpatrick for sharing her unpublished work on Davis and for suggesting several citations for this article.

LYNN D. GORDON

**Davis, Michael Marks, Jr.** (November 19, 1879–August 19, 1971), advocate of quality medical care for all Americans and leader in the health care field, was born in New York City to Miriam (Peixotto) and Michael Marks Davis, a merchant who had settled in New York after the Civil War. His mother, a daughter of Dr. Daniel Peixotto, an early president of the New York Medical Society, was descended from early Jewish immigrants to the American colonies.

As a youth, Davis was greatly influenced by cousins from San Francisco, Dr. Jessica Peixotto, founder of the University of California School of Social Work, and her brother, Sidney Peixotto, active in the settlement house movement. After graduating from Columbia University in 1900 with a major in chemistry, he undertook graduate studies in political economy, receiving his Ph.D. in 1906. His first professional job, 1905–1909, was at the People's Institute in New York, an informal educational institution akin to settlement houses. As a graduate student, Davis was close to the intellectual center of the Progressive movement. Among other stimulating faculty, his "prime mentor and guide" was E. R. A. Seligman. Two particularly influential student contemporaries were Paul Kellogg* and Frank Mussey, afterwards editors of the *Survey* and the *Nation*, respectively. A lifelong association among the three developed around the Unitarian minister's family into which Mussey and Davis himself married, when he wedded Janet Hayes on June 5, 1907. (After her death in March, 1950, he married Alice L. Taylor.) Although Davis thus drifted away from Judaism as a religion, he never rejected his Jewish heritage.

Davis' activism interfered with with his career at the People's Institute—and in 1910 also prevented an administrative appointment under the New York City Recreation Commission.

Reluctantly he accepted an appointment as director of the century-old, professionally traditional Boston Dispensary. However, backed by a reform-minded board president, he quickly developed a showcase of medical administration. Encouraged by Dr. Richard Cabot,* pioneer of hospital social work, he created a strong research-oriented social work staff responsible directly to him rather than to the physicians. Members of the American Medical Association (AMA) were unprepared for the sophisticated statistical analysis of dispensary research which he presented in 1912.

Administrative procedures were adjusted to support the physicians better, and pay clinics were invented to meet the needs of "middle-class" working poor who could not afford ordinary physicians' fees. A small in-patient children's service demonstrated advantages in integrating out- and in-patient services. Repeatedly, novel ideas which he advanced in one convention of the American Hospital Association (AHA) were presented by others the following year as accepted truth. His 1916 analysis of European experience with sickness insurance pointed to fee-for-service payments as a universal drawback, one which the United States should avoid, thus foreshadowing future proposals for prepaid group practice. He sponsored a sickness insurance bill in 1917 in Massachusetts. He spent increasing amounts of time away from the Boston Dispensary on research and consultation. He was involved in the establishment of both the American Association of Hospital Social Workers (1918) and the American Association of Social Workers (1920).

In 1920 the Rockefeller Foundation selected Davis to head the Committee on Dispensary Development's seven-year research/demonstration project. Under it, the Cornell Clinic demonstrated successful operation of pay services for low-income persons by a medical school. Another project reached a pioneering citywide agreement on standards for clinics. These led to national standards adopted by the AHA.

In 1928 Davis became director of medical services for the Julius Rosenwald Fund, commissioned to work for better medical care for all Americans. Blue Cross hospital insurance, the beginnings of prepaid medical care, and improved training for physicians and nurses, especially among Blacks in the South, were fostered. Major attention was devoted to the work of the Committee on the Costs of Medical Care (CCMC), which Davis had helped organize in 1927. CCME studies provided a base on which most subsequent research in medical economics was built. In 1932 the Committee's report contained two key recommendations: group practice of medicine and experimentation in ways to distribute costs through insurance. Both reflected positions long held by Davis, and both were rejected violently by the AMA, precipitating political and professional conflict over several decades.

Davis was active in unsuccessful efforts to include health insurance in the Social Security Act of 1935, but helped persons sympathetic to his ideas to secure key research positions on the Social Security Board. He aided them in planning a National Health Survey and other research projects used by staff and legislative leaders to develop national health proposals in 1939 and later. In 1944 President Franklin Roosevelt revived the political push for a national health program. Davis provided information and consultation at all levels, including helping to shape President Harry Truman's November, 1945, message to Congress.

In 1936 the trustees of the Julius Rosenwald Fund provided Davis with a major grant for the support of the Committee for Research in Medical Economics (CRME), which he had established. Through this committee, Davis stimulated numerous studies relating to medical economics and public health. He also edited a scientific journal, *Medical Care*, from 1941–1944. His offices both at the Julius Rosewald Fund and the CRME were focal points for international exchange of information in such areas as medical and nursing education, the medical aspects of public welfare, prepaid medical practice, and the organization of medical care in countries around the world.

Davis' efforts became more frankly political in 1945 when he organized the Committee on the Nation's Health to support the Truman proposals. Never well financed to compete with the AMA and other groups, politically the CCMC proved to be a lost cause. Wealthy supporters began to withdraw in 1950, but with labor support, CCMC struggled on until 1955, when the unions shifted to collective bargaining. Davis retired, but continued writing and advising.

A brilliant man with a vibrant personality, Davis dedicated himself to achieving quality medical care for all Americans. An early colleague recalled that "he wanted to go too fast!" However, as a sought-after speaker, a prolific writer, and an overpowering debater, he exercised a great influence. Many of his ideas, once rejected as too radical, have become commonplace in American medicine. Davis died in Sherburne, Quebec, on August 19, 1971.

Little has been written about Davis. See the biographical sketch in *Who Was Who in America*, vol. 5 (1973), 173. His thinking can be traced in four major books: *Dispensaries*, with A. R. Warner (1917); *Clinics, Hositals, and Health Centers* (1927); *America Organizes Medicine* (1941); and *Medical Care for Tomorrow* (1954). Two articles about his early career by Ralph E. Pumphrey are "Michael M. Davis and the Development of the Health Care Movement, 1900–1928," *Societas*, vol. 2, no. 1 (1972), 27–41; and "Michael M. Davis and the Transformation of the Boston Dispensary," *Bulletin of the History of Medicine*, vol. 49, no. 4 (1975), 451–65. Records of Davis' professional life include a large amount of research material and correspondence, mostly from after 1935.

RALPH E. PUMPHREY

**Day, Dorothy May** (November 8, 1897–November 29, 1980), Catholic social reformer, journalist, and lecturer, was born in Brooklyn, New York, to John I. Day and Grace (Satterlee) Day. She was the third in a family of five children, three of whom became notable in their own right: Sam Day, as editor of the New York *Journal American*; Donald Day, the strongly anti-Soviet Eastern European correspondent for the Chicago *Tribune* during the years just prior to World War II; and Donald Day, journalist and editor. A sister, Della, until her death in May, 1980, was Dorothy's close friend and companion.

In 1903 John I. Day, a newspaper horse-racing editor, moved the family to San Francisco and then to Chicago after the destruction of his newspaper's plant by the earthquake of 1906. In Chicago the family lived precariously until the elder Day got a job as racing editor for the Chicago *Inter Ocean*. Dorothy's girlhood was given over to the performance of household chores and to reading. She was always very sociable, possessing a considerable amount of what her mother called "presence." But her inclination toward sociability took second place to her delight in reading.

In 1914 Dorothy won a citywide academic competition sponsored by the Hearst press that enabled her to attend the University of Illinois for two years. At the university she indulged her reading, did some writing, and gave a theoretical structure to her strongly emerging social consciousness in the cause of socialism. By her second year she had learned to smoke and to say "damn" and "hell," and had become an atheist. Her university years had one center of warmth and graciousness—her friendship with Rayna Prohme. A few years later Prohme would become active in the international ramifications of the Russian Revolution.

She died in Moscow in 1927 and has been memorialized in Vincent Sheean's *Personal History*.

In 1915 the Day family moved to New York, and there Dorothy began her journalistic career as a reporter for the socialist *Call*. In the decades following, her politics were of a socialist-anarchist disposition and her life was that of an observer and sometimes participant in the bohemianism of Greenwich Village, where, in the winter of 1918, she was for a brief period the close friend and companion of Eugene O'Neill. But she always stoutly denied having a Village viewpoint, saying that her true home was among the East Side Jews and that it was from them that she had gotten the essential ideas and values, her religion in particular, that shaped her life and work. Later, during World War II, her voice as a Catholic was one of the clearest and most persistent in calling for succor for the Jews of Europe. "The Jews are a priestly people," she would say.

In 1919 she began living with a flamboyant journalist, Lionel Moise, who even then was something of a legend for his accomplishments as a barroom brawler and fascinator of women. The affair ended with Day's having an abortion, a circumstance that was virtually forced upon her and which filled her with such bitterness that she was brought to the brink of suicide.

In 1923, after a year in Europe, a brief, unhappy marriage, and two desolate years in Chicago, where she tried to reestablish a life with Moise, she went to New Orleans, where she got a job as a journalist and taxi-dancer, the latter to serve as a vehicle for a series of columnar revelations. Fortunately, she was spared a lengthy dedication to this work by the sale of a novel, *The Eleventh Virgin*. However questionable the merits of this work, it, by its title alone, brought her $2,500. Possessing what she considered to be an inexhaustible fortune, she returned to New York to take up life again with her literary and radical friends.

In the spring of 1924 she bought a small cottage on the western end of Staten Island and there, with the waters of Raritan Bay just off her small porch, she continued writing and took as her common-law husband a marine biologist named Forster Batterham. This was a tranquil and happy time in her life, her happiness brought to ecstatic heights by the birth of her daughter, Tamar Therese, in March, 1926. It was the beauty of nature and her role in the creation of life that brought about her conversion to God. In December, 1927, she was baptized into the Catholic Church, not because of any extensive study of the Church but because of its antiquity. This action brought about a rupture with Batterham and placed her in the role of breadwinner for herself and her daughter.

For the next five years she lived by doing small writing jobs, in lower New York City, briefly in California, for a year in Mexico, and then again in New York City in the spring of 1932. During this period she persevered with rare dedication in the matter of understanding and practicing her faith. But there was one problem that remained unsolved: how to relate her faith to her social concern, especially as this concern was intensified by the travail which so many were undergoing as a consequence of the depression. In December, 1932, she went to Washington to witness the hunger marches, and the experience produced in her an emotional and spiritual crisis. The two concerns of her being—her faith and her awareness of human suffering—seemed two different aspects of her life. Anguished, she went to Washington's Shrine of the Immaculate Conception to pray and, as she wrote on a number of occasions thereafter, when she returned to New York, "I found Peter Maurin."

Peter Maurin was the kind of person about whom epic novels are composed. Throughout the latter years of her life Day referred to him as "a saint and a genius"—a saint in his poverty, in his utter humility, and in the way his life was totally dedicated to study and thought, and a genius in his analysis of the question of what it meant to be human and of the kind of social order that would give life to his vision of an angelic human destiny. Seizing upon Day as the student worthy of his special mission, he spent the remainder of his years teaching her what she called a "correlation of the material with the spiritual."

Essentially, what Maurin taught was a personalist revolt, moved by spiritual conviction, against the contemporary process of history, which in his view was accelerating toward an objectivized social complexity. In the end, the necessities of this complexity would reduce the person to slavery. Here it can be observed that Maurin's thought along this line, in its apprehension of the nullification of personality through the loss of creative work and of community, is somewhat similar to Peter Kropotkin's and to that of the French religious thinker Simone Weil.

As a consequence of this position, it followed that the attempt to solve the increasing social pathology in contemporary society through an extension of the public social apparatus, whether in the form of the state or through highly institutionalized private forms, would in the end be dehumanizing. The answer to the social problem, then, was the rebuilding of a human community through personal action, extending into wide areas of social interaction through the principle of voluntary cooperation.

Peter, as Day always called him, was so persuasive in his logic and so selfless in his person that she was immediately convinced and remained so through the rest of her years. Thus it was that on May Day, 1933, the first issue of the *Catholic Worker*, selling for a penny a copy, was hawked by Dorothy Day and a few friends in New York's Union Square. This was the journal in which Day for the remainder of her life wrote of the plight of the world's dispossessed and advocated their relief through personalist action. In the years just before World War II the paper's circulation rose to over 100,000 each month.

The paper was first published from Day's tenement apartment on Fifteenth Street, three rooms and a small back yard. Small though it was, at Maurin's urging it was turned into a house of hospitality for street people. From this beginning the house of hospitality principle of the Catholic Worker movement, as it came to be called, grew to include several hundred persons and a food line that at times went to over 1,000.

Dorothy Day had a remarkable personality, one which, whatever the situation, commanded attention. In its early years her Worker movement attracted the enthusiasm and dedication of many young people, some of whom went to New York to staff the Worker house there, but many of whom initiated Worker houses of their own throughout the country. On the eve of World War II there were nearly forty houses of hospitality. Communal farms were operated in conjunction with many of these houses. The farms were expressions of Maurin's idea of a communal nucleus for social reconstruction, but they also were inspired by a Catholic land use idea formulated by Monsignor Luigi Ligutti.

Almost without exception, the support for the houses of hospitality and the farms came from contributions sent in by readers of the *Catholic Worker*. They were small contributions, frequently less than a dollar, but somehow they always kept fed the lines of men and women.

Dorothy Day's passion, however, was not organizational efficiency or organizational effectiveness. Her passion was God, and she rejected the proposition that any part of creation, humankind or nature itself, was beyond reclamation: "All are saved," she would say in her latter years. Her religious quest never ceased. She was truly a pilgrim of the Absolute.

Her religious seeking, however, did not preclude or in any way diminish her social concern. At the beginning of World War II she announced in the *Worker* that she would not support the war, nor would she make invidious judgments about the combatants. For the remainder of her life her great social concern was to end war, a concern that manifested itself by an implacable pacifism.

Ill with a failing heart, Day spent the last two years of her life in her room at Maryhouse, the Catholic Worker house for women on New York's Third Street. On her eightieth birthday Cardinal Terence Cooke visited her in her room to give her birthday greetings from Pope Paul. Three weeks later, on November 29, 1980, she died there while chatting with her daughter Tamar.

The entire body of *Catholic Worker* papers, including all of Dorothy Day's personal papers, has been collected and deposited in the Marquette University Memorial Library Archives in Milwaukee, Wisconsin. Day was an indefatigable writer, and there is no complete list of her publications. The most comprehensive published source for her life and thought can be found in her "On Pilgrimage" column, which was a monthly feature of the *Catholic Worker* for nearly forty years. Day wrote six books, all of which were autobiographical. The most useful of these is *The Long Loneliness*, first published in 1952. Her *House of Hospitality* (1936) describes life in a Worker house.

Two secondary accounts of Day's life and thought were written by William Miller: *A Harsh and Dreadful Love* (1972) and *Dorothy Day, a Biography* (1982).

WILLIAM D. MILLER

**Deardorff, Neva Ruth** (February 11, 1887–August 21, 1958), social welfare statistician and reformer, was born in Hagerstown, Indiana to Daniel W. and Sarah Elizabeth (Teetor) Deardorff. Little information is available about Deardorff's childhood or adolescent years. She enrolled at the University of

Michigan in September, 1904, where she completed an A.B. degree in 1908. Her major subjects were economics, sociology, and history. In 1908, after deciding to do doctoral work, she entered the University of Pennsylvania, where she was a Moore Fellow (1908–1909) and a Joseph Bennett Fellow (1909–1911). While formally a student of history, she continued to pursue studies in economics and sociology. She received her Ph.D. from the University of Pennsylvania in 1911. Between 1911 and 1912 Deardorff traveled in Europe collecting data for her doctoral dissertation, *English Trade in the Baltic During the Reign of Elizabeth*, subsequently published as part of a collection on the history of commerce by the University of Pennsylvania (1912).

Between 1912 and 1914 Deardorff was on the staff of the Philadelphia Bureau of Municipal Research. In 1914 she became chief of the Department of Vital Statistics of the Philadelphia Municipal Bureau of Health. Indications are that during her tenure with the city of Philadelphia, Deardorff developed an interest in the application of social statistics to the resolution of welfare problems. Between May 1918 and 1920 Deardorff was assistant to the director general of civilian relief of the American Red Cross, and between 1920 and 1921 she served as assistant to the Red Cross general manager. At the Red Cross, Deardorff documented that it was in the period immediately following the discharge of a man from service that the greatest number of family problems occurred. Deardorff envisioned and worked for a unified Red Cross Service that would encompass the Health Service, the Home Service, and the Nursing and Junior Services, one that would serve local communities.

During the latter part of her tenure at the Red Cross, in November, 1919, she was appointed nonresident lecturer in the Department of Social Economy at Bryn Mawr College in Pennsylvania. At Bryn Mawr she held seminars on the family as a social institution and on social economy as applied to social relief and social guardianship, apparently Deardorff's areas of recognized expertise. Deardorff continued as nonresident lecturer until March, 1921, when she was appointed, for a period of one year, director of the (Emma) Carola Woerishoffer* Department of Social Economy and Social Research. In 1922 Deardorff was promoted to associate professor at Bryn Mawr, but on April 24, 1924, she submitted her reignation from the school following her appointment by Governor Gifford Pinchot as executive secretary of the Pennsylvania Children's Commission.

The Pennsylvania Commission to Study All Laws Relating to Child Welfare and to Review and Revise All Statutes, as the Children's Commission was formally known, brought Deardorff in contact with many prominent national figures, for it led her to visit Washington, D.C., in an attempt to enlist the Department of Labor's aid in reforming anachronisms in the Pennsylvania statutes that allowed children to be bound out as apprentices as late as 1924. The Pennsylvania Children's Commission accomplished many reforms and disseminated its findings in a 1926 publication by Deardorff. Additionally, based on her work on the Commission, Deardorff authored *The Extent of Child Dependency and Delinquency in Seven Pennsylvania Counties* (1927). Deardorff was one of the first social reformers to make extensive use of statistical data in documenting and defending policy stances.

Between 1919 and 1924 Deardorff served as associate editor of the *Survey* and contributed many items to the journal. In a 1924 issue of the *Survey*, Deardorff was reported to have a "weather eye out for the little tragedies and comedies of children which flash across the vision of most social workers but which are too infrequently caught and recorded." In later years, Gertrude Springer* of the *Survey* would refer to Deardorff as one of the most distinguished social workers of her time. Deardorff's *Survey* relationships would last for many years and would result in a number of collaborative endeavors. For example, in 1928 she and Paul Kellogg,* the *Survey*'s editor, presented a paper at the International Conference on Social Work in Paris. With characteristic enthusiasm for the merits of scientific analysis, Kellogg and Deardorff advocated the use of the inductive methods of the social sciences as tools for social engineering. Their Paris paper described a successful attack on tuberculosis, beginning with research, moving on to education, care, and prevention, and culminating with proposals for the control of the disease.

Between 1927 and 1946 Deardorff held many responsible positions in the Research Bureau of the Welfare Council of Greater New York. The Bureau's objectives were to encourage the use of facts as a basis for community planning and to promote team work among social agencies; to improve social work standards; and to develop greater public support for social work. Deardorff's work was particularly responsive to the Research Bureau's objectives. Deardorff sought to integrate sociological research methods into the practice of social work and to meaningfully present those methods to practitioners. She made frequent presentations at the National Conference of Social Work emphasizing the importance of fact-finding. Although she advised that "propagandists" might color the facts with "overzealous aspirations for program making," she was convinced that fact-finding and program development in social work needed to be integrated. She often expressed concern that much sociological information of value failed to influence social workers because it was presented in language too technical for practitioners, was overlaid with unfriendly criticism, and evidenced a patronizing attitude. On the improvement of communication and work among social agencies, Deardorff advocated systematic, coordinated geographic decentralization of the various city social service offices. In many ways, her ideas were a precursor of the "single door" approach; she advocated locating various social services in a single building within a neighborhood or a community. "The boundaries of the districts," she wrote, referring to New York City, "are so divergent that one wonders whether there is something repugnant in the idea of having common boundaries for any two services, however closely related they may be or ought to be."

Deardorff was well acquainted with many of the most notable and progressive thinkers of her age, including Edith Abbott,* Beulah Amidon,* Helen Hall,* Gertrude Springer, and others. In a 1942 letter written to Hall in Australia,

Deardorff revealed many of the central themes that occupied her mind. "The old but ever new concept of need keeps me awake . . . nights," she commented. She also stressed the importance of the labor movement's contributions to fundraising for social welfare. In letters to Hall, Deardorff also revealed a little about the leisure-time activities she enjoyed, such as the remodeling of a small apartment building in the New Jersey suburbs.

Deardorff was one of the planners and initiators of the Health Insurance Plan of Greater New York (HIP) in 1947. The HIP was a close antecedent of modern health maintenance organizations. Its primary objective was to enable families of moderate income to budget virtually the total cost of medical care through prepayment. Deardorff worked as director of research of the plan from 1947 almost until her death in 1958. Although she announced her retirement from the HIP in 1954, her plans never materialized. She was still working in 1957, in spite of failing health, while her friends continued to urge her not to overdo it.

During her career, Deardorff was active in many professional and voluntary organizations. Of special interest was her role in the Philadelphia Women's Trade Union League. Especially active in the 1920s, the League exemplified the involvement of middle-class social reformers in assisting industrial women employees through the development of trade unions and in securing protective legislation for women workers.

Deardorff died at Southampton Hospital in New York City after a heart attack.

Materials by and about Neva Ruth Deardorff can be found in the Survey Associates Collection, the United Neighborhood Houses Supplement Collection, the Helen Hall and the Henry Street Settlement Collection, and the Child Welfare League of America (Board Minutes, 1915–1933) Collection, all at the Social Welfare History Archives of the University of Minnesota Libraries. Biographical material and some correspondence between Neva Ruth Deardorff and Bryn Mawr president M. Cary Thomas can be found at the Bryn Mawr College Archives. News articles and other biographical notes can be found in the Alumni Records files of the University of Michigan. Biographical sketches of Neva Ruth Deardorff were published in *Indiana Authors and Their Books, 1917–1966* (1974) and in *Who Was Who in America, 1951–1960* (1966). *Obituaries on File*, vol. 1, lists two obituaries for Neva R. Deardorff, one published by the *New York Times*, (August 23, 1958), and another by the *Social Service Review* (December, 1958).

A full listing of books and pamphlets authored or edited by Neva Ruth Deardorff can be found in the *National Union Catalog Pre-1956 Imprints*. Deardorff was found to be a frequent contributor to *Social Forces*, the *Annals of the American Academy of Political and Social Sciences*, and the *Proceedings of the National Conference of Social Work*. Most articles by Deardorff published in those sources appeared between 1919 and 1947. In addition to those cited above, worth special mention are: "The School's Responsibility for the Leisure Time of the Child in Relation to the Services of the School" (1922); "Philadelphia as a Provider for Dependent Children" (1925); "Fact Finding and Research as a Basis of Program Making in Social Work" (1928); "Sociological Research Studies: What Are the Values for the Social Worker of the More Recent Sociological Type of Community Study" (1930), all published in the *Proceedings of the National Conference of Social Work*; "The Relation of Applied Sociology to Social Work," *Social Forces* (1932); and "The Health Insurance Plan of Greater New York Begins Service," *Social Service Review* (1947).

                                                    EMILIA E. MARTINEZ-BRAWLEY

**De Forest, Robert Weeks** (April 25, 1848–May 6, 1931), social reformer, was born in New York City, one of four children of Henry G. de Forest, a lawyer, and Julia Weeks de Forest. Wealth and distinguished ancestry tracing back to seventeenth century New York were de Forest's at birth. Later, his marriage to Emily Johnston (with whom he had four children: Johnston, Henry Lockwood, Ethel, and Frances Emily), the daughter of a railroad president and a founder of the Metropolitan Museum of Art, reinforced his social position and improved his finances. Throughout his adult life he used his wealth and social contacts to assist an enormous number of causes and organizations.

De Forest received his education at Williston Academy; Yale College, from which he received a B.A. in 1870 and an M.A. in 1873; the University of Bonn; and Columbia University Law School, from which he received an LL.D. in 1872. Professionally, he practiced law from 1872 until his death, first with his father's firm and then with the firm De Forest Brothers, which he helped establish in 1893. He also sat on the governing board of numerous corporations. Throughout his life, de Forest earned handsome sums of money from his legal and business interests. Around the age of fifty he began leaving much of the work in them to associates as he started devoting most of his time to social welfare activities.

Beginning in the 1880s, de Forest was affiliated with a staggering number of social welfare, conservation, and art organizations and projects. In many of them he was an active founder, or officer, or financial supporter, or all three. Among the organizations he served were the National Conference of Charities and Correction, the National Housing Association, the Prison Association of New York, the Welfare Council of New York City, the New York State Charities Aid Association, the National Child Labor Committee, the Presbyterian Hospital of New York, the National Association for the Study and Prevention of Tuberculosis, the National Employment Exchange, the American National Red Cross, the Adirondack Mountain Reserve, the movement to create a state park at Niagara Falls, the Municipal Art Commission, the American Federation of Arts, and the Metropolitan Museum of Art in New York City.

De Forest's most important specific contributions to social welfare and social reform were the result of his long affiliation with two organizations: the Charity Organization Society of New York and the Russell Sage Foundation. Through them he sought to help the "deserving poor" achieve self-respect, a measure of economic security, and a healthier, fuller life. He also hoped that these organizations would help end poverty through research and education, demonstration projects, changes in economic and social conditions, and coordination of the activities of social welfare organizations. De Forest acted primarily out of a patrician sense of noblesse oblige. Another motive, however, was his desire to preserve the health, safety, and social and economic position of the middle and upper classes.

Under the influence of Josephine Shaw Lowell,* de Forest joined the New York Charity Organization Society in 1883. In 1888 he became president and retained that post until his death. Aside from his general duties he initiated or was active in a number of influential Society projects. One of his early notable achievements, in 1894, was his leadership in the founding of the Provident Loan Society to provide low-interest loans to the poor. He persuaded wealthy friends like J. P. Morgan and Seth Low to contribute money for the bank's capital, and he served the institution as president for many years.

De Forest was especially proud of his significant role in advancing the education and professionalization of social workers. As chairman of the Charity Organization Society's Committee on Philanthropic Education, in 1898 he helped found what became the New York School of Philanthropy, the first institution in America to train social workers. He actively served on the school's governing board until 1926 and helped support the institution financially.

Also as chairman of the Charity Organization Society's Committee on Publications, de Forest contributed money and leadership, in 1891, to launch the *Charities Review*, one of America's first social work journals. He then was actively involved in transforming that journal, in several stages, into the *Survey*, a national magazine that covered all aspects of social welfare for a broad range of professional social workers and reformers. He also served as president of Survey Associates from 1912 until his death.

De Forest also was a vital force in housing reform, where he enjoyed his major achievements as a social reformer. In 1898 he was instrumental in bringing the Charity Organization Society into the sporadic movement to improve tenement housing in New York City. A housing exhibition prepared for the Society by Lawrence Veiller* induced Governor Theodore Roosevelt to create a state Tenement House Commission in 1900. He appointed de Forest chairman. The Commission's work resulted in 1901 in a widely influential law that regulated sanitary, lighting, and ventilation standards in tenement housing. Also in 1901, Mayor Seth Low appointed de Forest head of New York City's Tenement House Department to enforce the new law.

Many of de Forest's other major achievements were the result of his association with the Russell Sage Foundation, which was established in 1907. In a sense he was the creator of the essential character of the Foundation. As Margaret Olivia Sage's lawyer, he counseled her and prepared some of the key documents that provided the organization with enormous flexibility to fund or carry out itself an astonishing variety of large-scale projects throughout the nation. De Forest was the principal officer of the Foundation from 1907 until his death.

His main work was as an administrator, counselor, and, most important, a major voice in decisions on what projects and organizations would be funded.

From the beginning, the Foundation provided support for a number of organizations in which de Forest was involved. For example, it gave money to the New York School of Philanthropy, Survey Associates, and the American Federation of Arts, and it assumed support of the Pittsburgh Survey from the Charity Organization Society in order to permit an extension of the scope and duration of the project. De Forest also was active in several projects the Foundation funded or conducted itself: the creation in 1912 of the Chattel Loan Society of New York; the building during the second decade of the twentieth century of a planned suburban community in Forest Hills, New York; and the carrying out of the most important city planning study of the 1920s, the *Regional Plan of New York and Its Environs*.

Throughout his career in social welfare, de Forest's blueblooded background, wealth, and law practice put him in contact with powerful people who could provide money or smooth the way for projects and organizations that interested him. Though instinctively conservative in his thinking, he possessed a mind remarkably open to new ideas, and he also had the vision to recognize important projects and the ability to recruit and work with talented social workers and reformers who were more liberal than he was. His use of these attributes in numerous organizations and projects enabled him to become one of the most effective and influential social welfare activists of his time. He died in New York City in 1931.

Robert de Forest left no collection of private papers. Some of his publications provide insight into his thinking and activities. On the charity organization movement, "What is Charity Organization," *Charities Review* (November, 1891), 1–5, and "The Broadening Sphere of Organized Charity: Why It Increasingly Emphasizes Preventive and Constructive Social Service," *Charities*(December 31, 1904), 316–320, are instructive. Robert W. de Forest and Lawrence Veiller, eds., *The Tenement House Problem*..., 2 vols. (1903), is a classic in the literature of housing reform. For his views on the Russell Sage Foundation, see "Initial Activities of the Russell Sage Foundation," *Survey* (April 3, 1909), 68–75; and on Forest Hills, see "Forest Hills Gardens," *Survey* (Januaryy 7, 1911), 568–569.

James A. Hijiya, "Four Ways of Looking at a Philanthropist: A Study of Robert Weeks de Forest," *Proceedings of the American Philosophical Society* (December, 1980), 408–418, is the fullest available study of de Forest. The most complete histories of the Charity Organization Society are two works by Lilian Brandt: *The Charity Organization Society of the City of New York, 1882–1907*, which was part of the Society's twenty-fifth annual report in 1907, and *Growth and Development of the AICP and COS (A Preliminary and Exploratory Review)* (1942). The archives of the Community Service Society in New York City contain the records of the Charity Organization Society of New York. In John M. Glenn et al., *Russell Sage Foundation, 1907–1946*, 2 vols. (1947), some of de Forest's associates clearly show his importance in the organization's work.

On the 1901 tenement house law, Roy Lubove, *The Progressives and the*

*Slums: Tenement House Reform in New York City, 1890–1917* (1962), and Anthony Jackson, *A Place Called Home: A History of Low-Cost Housing in Manhattan* (1976), are standard works. Clarke A. Chambers, *Paul U. Kellogg and the Survey* (1971), discusses de Forest's role in the creation of the *Survey* and its predecessors and the launching of the Pittsburgh Survey. Elizabeth G. Meier, *A History of the New York School of Social Work* (1954), and *The Provident Loan Society of New York, 1894–1944: Fifty Years of Remedial Lending* (1944), discuss de Forest's work with these organizations. Paul T. Ringenbach, *Tramps and Reformers, 1873–1916: The Discovery of Unemployment in New York* (1973), shows aspects of de Forest's conservatism.

STANLEY MALLACH

**De Schweinitz, Karl** (November 26, 1887–April 20, 1975), social welfare administrator, social work educator, and author, was born in Northfield, Minnesota, to Paul and Mary Catherine (Daniel) de Schweinitz. The son of a Moravian minister, he was the first de Schweinitz male to decide not to make the ministry his life work. Religion, however, was a major influence in his life and contributed to his interest in serving others.

He graduated from Moravian College, in Bethlehem, Pennsylvania, in 1906 with an undergraduate degree in humanities. He decided to pursue a second baccalaureate degree at the University of Pennsylvania and graduated in 1907 from that institution. In 1932 he was awarded an honorary doctorate of letters by Moravian College.

He was first married, on October 14, 1914, to Jessie Logan Dickson, and they had two children, Mary and Karl, Jr. This marriage was to end in divorce. On August 29, 1937, he married Elizabeth McCord, a social worker. Together they pursued vigorous careers in the social work field, both as authors and educators.

While at the University of Pennsylvania, he cultivated his childhood journalistic interests, and upon graduation became a reporter for the *Philadelphia Public Ledger*. After approximately four years in this job, he accepted the position of executive secretary of the Pennsylvania Tuberculosis Society in 1911. Two years later he was to move to New York and join the staff of the Charity Organization Society (COS) of New York. This decision to move more directly into the social work arena, although it allowed him to focus on his journalistic interest, apparently was a result of his experiences at the 1912 National Conference of Charities and Correction. It was at this meeting that he was introduced to the call for social change and the growing field of social work as a discipline attempting to respond to that call. For the next five years, he was to come to know the emerging leaders in social welfare, particularly Mary E. Richmond* and Porter R. Lee.* From 1918 to 1930 de Schweinitz continued to be associated with the COS movement as the general secretary for the Family Service Society of Philadelphia.

In 1930 Karl de Schweinitz was to shift his responsibilities from the direct administration of relief to social welfare coordination. This was accomplished by accepting the post of executive director of the Community Council of

Philadelphia, a position he remained in until 1936. While in this position, he also served on the Committee of 100 on Unemployment. At this group's urging, legislation was passed which created the State Emergency Relief Board to secure public funds to financially aid the unemployed. This activity was to redirect de Schweinitz's career interest to the public welfare sector, resulting in his appointment as the first Secretary of Public Assistance for Pennsylvania in July, 1937. He held this post for one year and left after a period of controversy about the workings of the agency.

By 1938 de Schweinitz had also established himself as a social work educator, serving as the director of the Pennsylvania School of Social Work from 1933 to 1936. He also held a dual appointment at the University of Pennsylvania during this period, a fact which aided him in negotiating a formal affiliation of the School of Social Work with the university in 1936. After his service to the Pennsylvania Department of Public Assistance, he was to return to the school as its director from 1938 to 1942. He left the school to become a training consultant for the federal Social Security Board in Washington, D.C., where he focused on the development of training materials and procedures for the administration of Social Security. This led to a position, during the period of 1944 to 1949, as the director of the Committee for Education and Social Security of the American Council on Education.

Beginning in 1950 and continuing to his retirement in 1958, de Schweinitz was associated with the School of Social Welfare at the University of California at Los Angeles. Whereas much of his early teaching emphasis had been on the administration of social welfare, this period of his career was characterized by an emphasis on social welfare history and its contributions to understanding and acting upon contemporary social welfare issues. In addition to being known as a social welfare historian—he was in fact a primary force in the creation of the Social Welfare History Group and served as its first chair—he continued to be sought after as a consultant on Social Security issues. In 1956–1957 he was a Senior Fulbright Scholar at the London School of Economics.

Throughout his professional career and even in his retirement, de Schweinitz maintained his interest in writing. He authored several articles, pamphlets, and books over the years. While associated with the American Red Cross, he wrote *Home Service* (1917) and *This Side of the Trenches with the American Red Cross* (1918). He was always interested in the family, and a book that has endured over the years has been *Growing Up* (1928), one of the earliest efforts to introduce young children to the process of reproduction, birth, and growth. Within the field of social work, he is probably most remembered for two significant works: *The Art of Helping People out of Trouble* (1924) and *England's Road to Social Security* (1943). These books reflect the breadth of his professional interests in the development of social casework principles for those not trained in social work, as well as his belief that history was a key source of knowledge for contemporary decision-making. He was unable to complete the professional text that was to be the capstone of his writing career. During his teaching days at

UCLA he had begun a history of poor relief and social insurance to be titled *The Dilemma of Need*; however, he was later to make extensive revisions in this work and retitle it *They Spoke for the Poor and for the Common Weal*. Unfortunately, this project was not completed at the time of his death. He also published numerous articles in the *Survey* and the *Family*, a journal he personally helped create and on whose first editorial board he served. He also coauthored, with his wife, Elizabeth, *Interviewing in Social Security*. This book was to become a classic training tool in the field of public assistance. In 1962 he and his wife were corecipients of the Florena Lesker Award for their contributions to the field of social work.

Karl de Schweinitz died on April 20, 1975, in Hightstown, New Jersey.

Major sources of unpublished material regarding de Schweinitz may be found in the collection of Karl and Elizabeth de Schweinitz Papers housed in the Social Welfare History Archives at the University of Minnesota. His contributions to the field of social work may also be found in a Ph.D. dissertation by Steven Maier, "Karl de Schweinitz, 1887–1975: Social Worker and Social Statesman," Bryn Mawr, 1982. His obituary appeared in the *New York Times* on April 21, 1975.

He authored *People and Process in Social Security* and *Social Security for Egypt*, as well as the following articles, illustrative of his interests: "Philadelphia No Longer Corrupt and Unashamed," *Survey* (January 18, 1913); "Need of a Code of Ethics for Private Charity," *Survey* (November 29, 1914); "Are the Poor Really Poor?" *Survey* (January 15, 1928); "Where There's a Will—What's the Way?" *Family* (May, 1920); "The Cultivation of Family Life," *Family* (December, 1924); "Tomorrow in Family Social Work," *Family* (December, 1933); "The Function of the Liberal Arts College: In Preparation for Life and Work with Special Reference to Social Work," *Compass* (April, 1945); "The Development of Government Responsibility for Human Welfare," *Public Welfare* (August, 1949); "Social Work in the Public Social Services," *Social Work Journal* (July, 1955); and "Social Values and Social Action—The Intellectual Base as Illustrated in the Study of History," *Social Service Review* (June, 1956).

BARRY L. LOCKE

**Deutsch, Albert** (October 23, 1905–June 18, 1961), author and promoter of better care for the mentally ill, was the fourth of nine children born on the Lower East Side of New York to Barnett and Kate (Knopke) Deutsch. Brought up in severe poverty, he obtained his education in New York City public schools, never attending college. In fact, he left home even before completing high school in search of various odd jobs throughout the country—as a longshoreman in New Orleans, a farmhand in Georgia, a shipyard worker in California, a bit actor with various West Coast theater groups, and a researcher and writer for encyclopedias. Deutsch began his career in social welfare in 1934 when, in desperate need of money, he accepted a work relief position with the New York

State Department of Welfare surveying old documents for a projected history of the department. Deutsch thus conducted extensive research for David Schneider's *The History of Public Welfare in New York State, 1609–1866* (Chicago, 1938); three years later he coauthored with Schneider the second volume of that work, *The History of Public Welfare in New York State, 1867–1940* (Chicago, 1941).

In the meantime, while undertaking research for these volumes, Deutsch had become interested in the care and treatment of the mentally ill. With encouragement from Clifford W. Beers* and a modest grant from the American Foundation for Mental Hygiene, he studied the subject and, in 1937, published his classic study, *The Mentally Ill in America: A History of Their Care and Treatment from Colonial Times* (1937). This volume, in which Deutsch claimed that care for the mentally ill historically had been inadequate because society had not provided the financial resources needed to provide proper care—a view that would be challenged by "revisionists" in the 1960s who would argue that mental illness was a mere abstraction used by professionals and others to rationalize the confinement of people who displayed economically unproductive behavior—helped to establish Deutsch's reputation as an accurate and solid reporter and writer, and in 1941 he was hired by the New York City newspaper *PM* to write daily health and welfare columns.

In addition to his regular chores, throughout the 1940s Deutsch wrote numerous investigative articles and columns on state mental hospitals, Veterans Administration (VA) hospitals, and institutions for juvenile delinquents. In 1944 he began a survey of VA hospitals which led to an extended series of articles in *PM* which described poor conditions within these facilities. In 1946 he investigated about twenty state mental hospitals and published a newspaper series on his findings the following year. At the end of 1947, he began a survey of institutions for juvenile delinquents and later published his findings in two articles in *Women's Home Companion* and two series of newspaper columns. Two of these research projects culminated in the publication of monographs: *The Shame of the States*, which covered conditions in state mental hospitals and was published in 1948, and *Our Rejected Children*, about institutions for juvenile delinquents, which appeared in 1950.

Deutsch used the same strategy for these three research projects. He visited institutions near major urban centers in states with prosperous economies to avoid, as he claimed, charges that he concentrated his research on unrepresentative facilities in isolated, poverty-stricken areas. For each project, Deutsch inspected a dozen or more institutions, interviewed local administrators, and studied reports and documents. He then published a series of articles or newspaper columns which were written for the general public and which highlighted abuses and poor medical care and treatment within these institutions.

As a result of his investigative efforts, Deutsch appeared before congressional committees on several occasions. In 1945 he was summoned to testify before the House Veterans Committee. When Deutsch refused to tell Committee members the names of several VA officials who had given him information for his series of articles on VA hospitals, the Committee cited him for contempt. Amidst widespread criticism of the action against Deutsch, the Committee rescinded the charge a few days later, and Deutsch completed his testimony. Within several months, General Omar Bradley was appointed head of the Veterans Administration and implemented several reforms, including establishing ties with teaching hospitals, improving salary schedules for physicians and nurses, and constructing new hospitals near urban centers and not in isolated areas, as had occurred in the past. While Deutsch had urged and now applauded these developments, he was neither the only advocate nor solely responsible for these changes. Several journalists had written critical articles about the Veterans Administration. Medical associations and consultants within the VA had recommended these reforms over a year earlier, and a Senate committee had issued a report outlining the cricitisms made against the VA.

Deutsch also testified in the Senate on behalf of the National Mental Health Act which became law in 1947. This legislation authorized the establishment of the National Institute of Mental Health and provided funds to support community mental health clinics and psychiatric research and training programs.

While Deutsch criticized conditions within state mental hospitals, VA hospitals, and institutions for juvenile delinquents, he remained optimistic that these facilities could be improved. He felt that an informed public was essential both to curb the abuses he identified and to raise the necessary funds to improve care within public institutions. Deutsch gained the support of many members of the medical and psychiatric profession because they often sought the same changes he was advocating and agreed with many of his criticisms.

In 1948 Deutsch joined the staff of the *New York Evening Post* and in 1950 became a freelance writer. During the 1940s and 1950s he received several awards, including the Newspaper Guild's Heywood Broun citation (1945, 1946) and the Adolf Meyer* Memorial Award in Mental Health (1953). At the time of his death in 1961, Deutsch was examining the status of psychiatric research in the United States. He was engaged to be married to Pearl Simburg, a psychiatric social worker; an earlier marriage had ended in divorce. On June 18, 1961, Deutsch died of a heart attack in Horsham, England, where he had been attending a meeting of the World Federation of Health.

Relatively little information about Albert Deutsch is readily available. Correspondence by Deutsch is included in the records of Big Brothers of America at the University of Minnesota Library of Social Welfare History. The best published sources are introductions and prefaces to Deutsch's books, including *The Mentally Ill in America: A History of Their Care and Treatment from Colonial Times* (1937, 1949), *Our Rejected Children* (1950), and *The Shame of the States* (1948), and an article by Jeanne L. Brand, "Albert Deutsch: The Historian as Social Reformer," *Journal of the History of Medicine and Allied Sciences*, vol. 18 (1963), 150–157. Obituary notices appeared in the *New York Times*, June 19, 1961; *Publishers Weekly*, July 3, 1961; and *Time Magazine*,

June 30, 1961. An entry about Deutsch is included in *Who Was Who in America*, vol. 4 (1968).

CATHERINE J. WHITAKER

**Devine, Edward Thomas** (May 6, 1867–February 27, 1948), educator, social services administrator, and writer, was born and raised on a farm near Union, Iowa. His father, John Devine, emmigrated from Ireland, and his mother, Laura (Hall) Devine, came from New England. He attended country schools until enrolling at Cornell College in Mt. Vernon, Iowa. He earned bachelor and master of arts degrees there (1887, 1890) while interfusing his education with jobs as teacher and school principal in three Iowa communities—Albion, Marshalltown, and Mt. Vernon. Edward studied for a year at the University of Halle in Germany and was awarded the doctor of philosophy degree by the University of Pennsylvania in 1893. His academic specialty was economics. He married another Iowan, Hattie Evelyn Scovell, in 1889. The couple had two children, Thomas and Ruth.

Edward T. Devine was tremendously productive during the first fifty years of his life. Between 1896 and 1917 he held faculty positions simultaneously at a university and a professional school (often directing the program of the latter), administered activities of the nation's largest local charity, edited a professional journal, and published ten books. His career emphasized actions and deeds rather than theoretical contemplation, yet his influence, including that of his teaching and writing, hastened the development of modern conceptions of science and professionalism in social work.

Devine spent much time in schools and classrooms. He served as a lecturer in economcs for the American Society for the Extension of University Teaching from 1891 to 1896. During the summer sessions between 1892 and 1896, he taught abroad at Oxford and Edinburgh universities. He was director of the New York School of Philanthropy (1904–1907, 1912–1917) and worked on its faculty in addition to holding the appointment of professor of social economy at Columbia University from 1905 to 1919. In 1926 he became dean of the Graduate School and professor of social economics at American University in Washington, D.C., from which he resigned in 1928. But teaching was not his primary occupation.

During the 1920s New Yorkers called Edward T. Devine the dean of social welfare because he had devoted his career to helping troubled people. Indeed, he built up institutions of private philanthropy and then aided the transfer of their services to the public sector. In 1896 he had joined the New York Charity Organization Society (COS) as general secretary. He directed the COS for the next twenty-one years. Acting under its auspices, Devine displayed extraordinary creativity, becoming a founder of several important social welfare institutions. In 1897 he started and edited *Charities*, a COS publication that became *Charities and the Commons*, and then, in 1909, the professional journal *Survey*, which he served as first editor. (He was associate editor from 1912 to 1921 under Paul U. Kellogg.*) In 1898 Devine helped create what became the New York School of Philanthrophy, the first professional school of its kind in the United States.

It later became the New York School of Social Work (1919) and eventually became affiliated with Columbia University. In 1904 he was an organizer of the National Child Labor Committee and of the National Association for the Study and Prevention of Tuberculosis. He first led the campaign—highlighted by the dramatic photographs of Lewis Hine*—for child labor laws. Devine also founded the Wayfarers Lodge in New York City, which became the Municipal Lodging House; the National Employment Exchange, an experimental job placement service; and the Tenement House Committee, which led the drive for housing regulation and reform. During 1906–1907, when the precepts of social and economic environmentalism were displacing poor law thinking in many cities, Devine was elected to the presidency of the National Conference of Charities and Correction. His innovations had made him a standard-bearer.

Edward Devine also became an expert in ameliorating human disasters. He completed three special missions for the American Red Cross, and his humanitarianism reached one-third of the way around the globe. In 1906 he took charge of relief following the great earthquake in San Francisco. In 1913 he directed storm and flood relief in stricken Dayton, Ohio. During 1917 and 1918 he was American Commission chief with the Bureau of Refugees and Relief in France and brought succor to homeless Europeans displaced by war.

Up to 1917 few social welfare administrators had met such a demanding schedule and exerted such influence on social work. Devine moved his emerging profession away from its nineteenth century focus on charity and into its years of progressive social action. Yet he returned from France and the Great War to find his career in limbo. Perhaps his thinking had grown stale or the new currents of change that carried social work toward psychology and psychiatric casework during the prosperous 1920s bypassed his steadfast emphasis on the economics of social injustice. After a brief stint during 1922–1923 as a member of the U.S. Coal Commission, Devine channeled his social service energies into New York City projects.

During the prewar reform administration of Mayor John Purroy Mitchel, Devine had been on the Mayor's Committee on Unemployment, which drafted an aborted city plan for emergency relief. Years later, he helped implement part of it during the Great Depression. In the meantime, he was chairman of the recreation, education, and neighborhood activities division of the Welfare Council of New York City. In 1929–1930 he directed a medical services program known as the Bellevue-Yorkville Health Demonstration. He was vice chairman under Alfred E. Smith of the 1931 New York Committee of 100, which raised donations for unemployment relief. At the time, he headed the Housing Association of New York, and during 1931–1932 he presided over a settlement organization, the United Neighborhood Houses. Devine ended his career as executive director of the Emergency Work Bureau and Emergency Relief Bureau of Nassau County, New York. Thus, he participated in administering the first state program of public unemployment relief under New York's Temporary Emergency Relief

Administration and the first national program under the New Deal's Federal
Emergency Relief Administration.

Between 1898 and 1939 Edward T. Devine wrote fourteen books and numerous
additional reports. His many publications track the evolution of social thought
from moralism to environmentalism. Social work schools and agencies used *The
Principles of Relief* (1904) as an early textbook on pauperism. *Misery and Its
Causes* (1909) gave a revealing account of the economic and social reasons for
poverty and suggested remedies through government action. *Progressive Social
Action* (1933) stressed public welfare programs at the dawn of the New Deal
era. Devine's ideas created a bridge spanning prewar progressivism and the
reforms of the 1930s. Probably more than his writings, however, his institutional
innovations at the turn of the century affected the careers of New York social
workers such as Frances Perkins,* Harry L. Hopkins,* and W. Frank Parsons,
who led national changes in welfare policies under President Franklin D. Roosevelt.
Devine's final book was the autobiographical *When Social Work Was Young*
(1939), in which he summed up the new spirit of social action in public welfare
that had inspired a metamorphosis of private charity.

At the point of his retirement in 1934–1935, Devine joined Paul U. Kellogg,
Helen Hall,* and other social workers who moved to the left of the New Deal
and became dissenters. He helped draft statements that criticized the
administration's Social Security and relief programs. In 1944 the farmer's son
from Iowa left his adopted home, New York City, and moved back to Oak Park,
Illinois, where he died in 1948.

Devine's work can be traced through the Charity Organization Society Papers,
which include a file of his correspondence, at the Archives of the Community
Service Society (New York City). He is also well represented in the Survey
Papers at the Social Welfare History Archives (Minneapolis, Minnesota). But
he left no personal collection of papers, and neither of the collections noted
above covers the entirety of his career. Documents relevant to his life are held
in numerous collections at the New York Public Library (New York City), the
Columbia University School of Social Work and the Manuscript Division of
Columbia University Library (New York City), and the Social Welfare History
Archives.

In addition to his many books and published reports, most of which are listed
in *Who Was Who in America*, vol. 2 (1950), 154, Devine wrote numerous articles
and papers that appeared in publications such as the *Proceedings* of the National
Conference of Social Work and the *Proceedings* of the National Conference on
Charities and Correction. For *Charities*, *Charities and the Commons*, and *Survey*,
he wrote editorials, reports, and articles that gave insight into his changing ideas.
No complete listing of his publications, however, has been compiled.

Most books pertaining to social welfare history mention Edward T. Devine,
and some discuss one or more of his projects in detail. Examples of the latter
include Paul T. Ringenbach, *Tramps and Reformers, 1873–1916: The Discovery*

*of Unemployment in New York* (1973); Clarke A. Chambers, *Paul U. Kellogg and the Survey: Voices for Social Welfare and Social Justice* (1971); and Walter I. Trattner, *Crusade for the Children: A History of the National Child Labor Committee and Child Labor Reform in America* (1970). No biography of Devine has been published, and his work has not been given thorough treatment.

WILLIAM W. BREMER

**Dewson, Mary (Molly) Williams** (February 18, 1876–October 21, 1962), social worker, reformer, suffragist, and Democratic Party official, was born in Quincy, Massachusetts, the youngest of four sons and two daughters of Edward Henry and Elizabeth Weld (Williams) Dewson. Molly Dewson's father suffered from poor health, so the family never prospered, but from him Dewson acquired an interest in history and government. Her mother, the backbone of the family, provided a happy, secure home. Molly Dewson was influenced by a number of female relatives including her aunt, Elizabeth Cabot Putnam, a leader in prison reform. As a child, Molly played with her brothers and boy cousins. She emerged as a leader both at home and at school, where she played on the boys' baseball team and became an excellent tennis player.

Dewson attended Miss French's School in Quincy from 1880 until 1889, Miss Ireland's School in Boston for two years, and Dana Hall School in Wellesley for two more. She entered Wellesley College in 1893, where she was inspired by professors such as Katherine Coman* and Emily Greene Balch,* who related economics, history, and sociolgy to the problems of industrial America.

Upon graduation from Wellesley in 1897, Dewson became secretary of the Domestic Reform Committee of the Women's Educational and Industrial Union, the most influential women's social and reform club in Boston. The task of the Committee was to professionalize housework, thereby providing working women with an attractive alternative to factory work and freeing middle-class women to pursue activities outside of the home. Dewson conducted statistical studies of the home, reorganized the Union's employment office for domestics, formed social clubs for them, and taught at a school of housekeeping organized by Ellen Richards. She published her *Twentieth Century Expense Book* (1899) as an aid to women in budgeting.

In 1900 Dewson became superintendent of the parole department of the Massachusetts State Industrial School for Girls. The department began to keep records of all offenders in order to develop an understanding of female delinquency and crime and to aid in rehabilitation. Dewson applied to penal reform many of the evolving techniques of modern social work. She wrote several articles on her work and presented a paper, "The Delinquent Girl on Parole," at the National Conference of Charities and Correction in 1911.

By 1911 Molly Dewson had become involved in the minimum wage movement under the leadership of Florence Kelley* and the National Consumers' League (NCL). Dewson became executive secretary of the Massachusetts minimum wage investigating commission, in charge of planning and carrying out a statistical study of wages of women and children in the state. The commission's report became the basis for the minimum wage act passed in 1912, the first in modern industrial America. The report brought Dewson national recognition among reformers as the preeminent authority on minimum wage legislation.

Dewson, like many social feminists, believed that woman suffrage would promote welfare legislation. She became chairman of the Worcester County suffrage organization and a member of the Massachusetts state association's executive board. During World War I, from 1917 to 1919, she was in France with the American Red Cross's Bureau of Refugees. After the war, Dewson became Florence Kelley's chief assistant in the National Consumers' League drive for state minimum wage laws for women and children.

In 1924, discouraged over adverse court decisions and public apathy, Dewson resigned her position in the NCL and focused her reform energies in New York State. As president of the New York Consumers' League from 1925 to 1931, Molly Dewson became the leader of the lobbying effort of the Women's Joint Legislative Conference, a coalition organization. She played an important role in the passage of a 1930 New York law limiting working women to a forty-eight-hour week.

Molly Dewson believed that she could most effectively advance social justice legislation by strengthening women's activities within the Democratic Party. She organized women for the presidential campaigns of Alfred E. Smith in 1928 and Franklin D. Roosevelt in 1932. When Roosevelt became president, Dewson and (Anna) Eleanor Roosevelt* worked closely together to increase the influence of women and promote social welfare issues in the New Deal. Dewson became head of the Women's Division of the Democratic National Committee, where she was able to bring women party workers into state government. She was also influential in securing the appointment of Frances Perkins* as Secretary of Labor. With Eleanor Roosevelt's support, she secured high-level appointments for many women in New Deal agencies, especially the Social Security Administration and the National Recovery Administration.

Dewson was a reformer more than a feminist. She promoted women in politics because she believed that they had a special sensitivity to human welfare that was badly needed in public life. Throughout the 1930s she tried to extend the influence of women in party activities and was a decisive force in increasing their political leverage within the party.

Dewson was also a member of the President's Committee on Economic Security, which did much to shape the Social Security Act of 1935. She was nominated to the Social Security Board in 1937, where she encouraged effective federal–state cooperation in the administration of unemployemnt and old-age assistance programs. Dewson resigned from the Social Security Board in 1938 because of ill health. In her retirement she shared a home in Castine, Maine, with Mary Porter. She acted as elder stateswoman to the Women's Division of the Democratic

National Committee and became vice president of the state's Democratic Advisory Committee in 1954. Molly Dewson died in Castine of bronchopneumonia following a stroke in 1962.

The Mary W. Dewson Papers at the Schlesinger Library, Radcliffe College, contain two volumes of autobiography covering the years 1928–1940. The Elizabeth Glendower Evans and Sue Shelton White Papers, also at the Schlesinger Library, have additional information. The basic sources for her Democratic Party activities are in the Franklin D. Roosevelt Library, Hyde Park, New York, especially the Mary W. Dewson Papers, including the Dewson letterbooks; the papers of the Women's Division of the Democratic National Committee, which contain many valuable Dewson letters; the Eleanor Roosevelt Papers; the Louis M. Howe Papers; and President Roosevelt's official and personal files. Books by people who knew her well are Eleanor Roosevelt and Lorena Hickok, *Ladies of Courage* (1954), and Bess Furman, *Washington By-Line* (1949). The New York State Democratic Party's Women's Division publication, *Women's Democratic News*, May, 1925–December 1930, reports on the work of Dewson and other women party members in New York. The *Democratic Digest*, November 1933–December 1940, documents the development of the Dewson program for the Women's Division of the Democratic National Committee.

Secondary information about Dewson's work in industrial relations can be found in James T. Patterson, "Mary Dewson and the American Minimum Wage Movement," *Labor History* (Spring 1964), 134–152; and Clarke A. Chambers, *Seedtime of Reform* (1963). Susan Ware, *Beyond Suffrage: Women in the New Deal* (1981), covers Dewson career in the 1930s. Secondary sources which discuss her political career are Arthur M. Schlesinger, Jr., *The Politics of Upheaval* (1960); Joseph P. Lash, *Eleanor and Franklin* (1971); and George Martin, *Madame Secretary: Frances Perkins* (1976). An obituary appeared in the *New York Times*, October 25, 1962. See also the excellent biographical essay by Paul C. Taylor in *Notable American Women: The Modern Period* (1980).

WINIFRED D. WANDERSEE

**Dinwiddie, Courtenay** (October 9, 1892–September 13, 1943), social worker and child labor reformer, was born in Alexandria, Virginia, the son of William and Emily (Albertine) Dinwiddie. He was educated at the Greenwood (Virginia) School for Boys, Southwestern University, where he received a B.A. in 1901, and the University of Virginia, where he did postgraduate work from 1901 to 1903. On May 8, 1907, he married Susan Anderson Ellis of Clarksville, Tennesse, with whom he had four children—Courtenay Lee, Hope, Jean, and Donald.

After a brief stint as manager of a fruit farm, Dinwiddie began his career in the field of social welfare in 1905 as secretary to the board of the Bellevue and Allied Hospitals in New York City. For the next several years he held various executive positions in social welfare agencies, including the New York City

Visiting Committee of the New York State Charities Aid Association (1906–1910), The Duluth City Board of Public Welfare (1910–1912), and the Associated Charities of Duluth (1912–1913). In 1913 he became superintendent of the Cincinnati Anti-Tuberculosis League, where he met Edward N. Clopper,* who then was active in the National Child Labor Committee. From 1917 to 1920 Dinwiddie was an organizer for the Cincinnati Public Health Federation and an active member of the Cincinnati Social Unit Experiment. For one year, 1921–1922, he was an instructor in community organization at Johns Hopkins University.

Dinwiddie began his important work in the areas of child health and child labor in 1920 when he became executive secretary of the National Child Health Council. When he was appointed director of the American Child Health Association (ACHA) in 1922, he also began to direct demonstration projects for the Commonwealth Fund. He was instrumental in leading the Fund into a concentrated focus on child health and welfare matters in the 1920s. When he left the ACHA in 1926, he became full-time director of child health demonstrations for the Commonwealth Fund. Successful projects he directed in Rutherford County, Tennessee, and Marion County, Oregon, formed the core for health departments in those counties, and in Fargo, North Dakota, and Athens, Georgia, the projects he led were incorporated into exisitng local health departments.

In 1930 Dinwiddie left the Commonwealth Fund to become general secretary of the National Child Labor Committee (NCLC), which he directed for the next thirteen years. He took over leadership of the NCLC during the early years of the Great Depression, when child labor was only one facet of a larger employment problem. As the new NCLC delegate to the National Social Welfare Council, in November, 1930, Dinwiddie summed up the child labor situation in many states at that time. He stressed the lack of adequate regulatory bodies, the poor reporting systems, and the willingness of employers to hire children rather than unemployed adults. These themes formed the basis of Dinwiddie's—and the NCLC's—work throughout the 1930s.

For the first few years of his administration at the NCLC, Dinwiddie worked to keep children out of the labor market by supporting other state and federal organizations in their efforts. He formed a coalition with organizations such as the American Farm Bureau Federation, the U.S. Children's Bureau, and the American Association for Labor Legislation. He proposed new state regulations and directed organizational efforts toward passage of the unsuccessful federal child labor amendment to the Constitution.

In 1935 Guy Helvering, Commissioner of the Internal Revenue Service, ruled that the NCLC was not entitled to tax exemption status because it was engaged in promoting legislation, including the child labor amendment. As a result, many contributors withdrew their support for the organization because their gifts no longer were tax deductible, thus creating a crisis for Dinwiddie and the NCLC. Yet, thanks to Dinwiddie's skills as a fund-raiser, he managed to secure enough financial support to keep the organization afloat and active.

In 1937 Dinwiddie and the NCLC worked on behalf of both the child labor amendment and the federal Fair Labor Standards bill. While the amendment was never ratified, the Fair Labor Standards measure, which included child labor regulations for which the NCLC had worked since the early 1920s, was enacted. Dinwiddie was credited with playing a crucial role in its passage.

Dinwiddie was a forward-looking man who planned well for future NCLC work, in particular its strenuous support of resettlement and rehabilitation efforts for mining families, especially those who labored in Missouri tiff mines. During World War II he became chairman of the Emergency Committee for Food Production. Once again, his organizational and fund-raising skills were utilized, as he lobbied for expansion of the Farm Security Administration in order to improve food production and to foster effective prevention of migratory child labor. Dinwiddie, a tireless, committed worker on behalf of the nation's children and the policies affecting them, was still involved in those efforts when he died in New York City on September 13, 1943.

The National Child Labor Committee Minute Books, which are located in the Manuscript Division of the Library of Congress, Washington, D.C., provide a detailed account of Dinwiddie's activities both before and during his tenure as NCLC general secretary. There is much stress placed on Dinwiddie's brilliant administrative abilities as well as his successful fund-raising. The minutes contain discussions, speeches, and correspondence in which Dinwiddie was involved in guiding the NCLC through the Great Depression and into the World War II era. Some of the earlier minutes in the 1920s make reference to Dinwiddie's work through the Commonwealth Fund. Papers from the NCLC not at the Library of Congress can be found in the Ephemera Collection at the Social Welfare History Archives Center, University of Minnesota, Minneapolis. These include documents, pamphlets, and a few publications from the late 1930s.

The work of the NCLC has been detailed in several volumes. Two of the best are Walter Trattner's *Crusade for the Children* (1970), and Peter Romanofsky, ed., *Social Service Organizations* (1978). Trattner's book describes the work of patrician reformers who fought for child labor legislation, including the federal amendment, to which, as general secretary of the NCLC, Dinwiddie was deeply committed. *Social Service Organizations* gives a brief overview of the NCLC as a reform organization involved in the shaping of social policy in the United States.

As a vehicle for social reform, *Survey* editorials provided much information about reform activities in the 1920s and 1930s. In the Survey Collection at the Social Welfare History Archives Center can be found more documentation of Dinwiddie's organizational and fund-raising skills. His lobbying efforts are detailed from 1921 to 1941, including his work on behalf of the federal child labor amendment and the federal Fair Labor Standards Act.

JOANNE CATHERINE NEHER

**Dinwiddie, Emily Wayland** (August 14, 1879–March 11, 1949), social worker and housing reformer, was born in Greenwood, Virginia, the seventh of eight children of William and Emily Albertine (Bledsoe) Dinwiddie. Of the Dinwiddie's two daughters, she was the only one to survive infancy. Her father, who had two daughters by a previous marriage, was a Presbyterian evangelical minister. Her mother was a daughter of Albert Taylor Bledsoe, Assistant Secretary of War in the Confederacy. Emily Dinwiddie's brother, Albert Bledsoe Dinwiddie, served as president of Tulane University from 1918 to 1935; her younger brother Courtenay Dinwiddie* had a long and varied career as a social worker who achieved distinction as an outstanding community organizer and child labor reformer.

Having grown up on her father's farm in Greenwood, Virginia, Dinwiddie developed an enthusiasm for such out-of-door activities as botany, camping, hiking, and swimming. She received her B.A. degree at Peace Collegiate Institute in Raleigh, North Carolina, where she remained afterwards for two years teaching Latin. It is believed that Dinwiddie's interest in social work was influenced by her aunt, Sophia (Bledsoe) Herrich, who lived in New Jersey and was a member of the editorial staff of the *Century* magazine. Dinwiddie's first experience in social work began in 1901 when she became an investigator for the New Jersey State Board of Children's Guardians. In the summer of 1902, she enrolled in a course offered by the New York School of Philanthropy and joined the staff of the New York Charity Organization Society (COS). She served as the New York COS investigation bureau visitor, assistant district agent, and acting agent (1901–1902), and as editor of the *Charities Directory* (1903). Emily Dinwiddie's first contact with housing problems resulted from her experience in 1903 as an inspector for the New York City Tenement House Department. Later in 1903 she accepted an assignment which took her to Philadelphia until 1904; there she worked as special investigator of housing conditions for the Octavia Hill Association. During this time she took graduate courses in sociology and economics at the University of Pennyslvania. She returned to the New York COS in 1904 as assistant secretary (1904–1905) and then as secretary (1905–1909) of its tenement house committee. During 1907–1908 she studied the housing situation in Pittsburgh under the auspices of the Pittsburgh Survey and the supervision of Lawrence Veiller,* a nationally known housing reformer.

Dinwiddie served as supervisor of dwellings for New York's Trinity Church from 1910 to 1918. This position served as a benchmark for her distinctive contribution to the betterment of housing on the Lower West Side of New York City. Trinity Church was one of the largest owners of low-income housing in New York City and had been the target of damaging criticism by the New York State Tenement House Commission as well as the press. The criticism focused on the alleged faulty structural and sanitary conditions of the dwellings, as well as uses of the properties for saloons, gambling, and prostitution. Oftentimes the criticism did not differentiate between those houses owned by Trinity and those leased on a long-term basis over which the church had no control. During the heyday of the muckracking era, the Trinity vestry board authorized an investigation by the tenement house committee of the Charity Organization Society. Emily Dinwiddie was in charge of that investigation. Her report revealed that the majority of the 334 dwellings owned by Trinity provided a satisfactory home environment for the families occupying them. In view of Dinwiddie's objectivity and skillful execution of the investigation, Trinity employed her to manage all the properties, to promulgate policies regarding their maintenance, and to ensure the welfare of the tenants.

Emily Dinwiddie was a person of tact, patience, and quiet charm. Though dignified in manner, she possessed a fine sense of humor. These characteristics, in tandem with her experience as a caseworker, housing investigator, and administrator, served her well in her new position at Trinity. She patterned her housing program, in part, on the work of Ellen Collins in New York and that of the Octavia Hill Association of Philadelphia. Under her management, Trinity Church became a model landlord. The church systematically acquired houses as leases expired; it renovated houses upon repossession or tore them down if structurally unsound; it eliminated rear tenements and forbade the use of its property for immoral purposes as well as for rag or junk shops and home manufacturing. In addition to encouraging the church to keep rent low and giving preference to tenants with large families, Dinwiddie encouraged the tenants to match the church's efforts in maintaining a sanitary environment and to beautify their homes and the neighborhood by planting flowers and vegetable gardens in the yards.

In early 1918 Dinwiddie left Trinity Church to join the American Red Cross. She served a year in wartine France as director of the social service exchange, giving aid to refugees. She returned to the United States in 1919 and settled in Washington, D.C., as associate director of the Red Cross Information Service, advancing to director in 1921 and to assistant executive secretary of the Red Cross in 1922. In 1923 she left the Red Cross to become a social work consultant to St. Elizabeth Hospital (1923–1927) in Washington, D.C. (where she also took courses in psychiatry), and lectured in social casework at George Washington University (1924–1927). She assumed the position of director of the Children's Bureau of the Virginia Department of Public Welfare in 1927. As director of the Bureau, she devoted a great deal of time to the task of coordinating the Bureau's work with that of the state's public and private welfare agencies. In addition, she prepared a detailed report on Virginia's mental hospitals.

In 1934 Dinwiddie left Virginia to become state case supervisor of the Kansas Emergency Relief Committee, and then assistant state superintendent of relief. From 1936 until her retirement in 1938, she served as state superintendent of the child welfare program. As head of the Committee's children's program, she supervised the use of federal funds to improve county and rural children's services through training local workers and coordinating local welfare activities.

Emily Dinwiddie was a remarkable woman who devoted her life to social work. Her versatile career spanned thirty-seven years. Her most outstanding achievement during those years was the transformation of Trinity Church's reputation from one of corporate irresponsibility into that of a responsible, social-minded landlord. Dinwiddie's significance for American social welfare also can be found in the competent, innovative manner in which she administered and applied the principles inherent in the charity organization, housing, and child welfare movements. Her administrative talents were also supplemented by her penchant for objective investigation and field research. Emily Dinwiddie died in Waynesboro, Virginia, at the age of sixty-nine.

Dinwiddie's writings include the following reports on housing surveys: *Housing Conditions in Philadelphia* (1904); "Housing Conditions in Philadelphia," *Charities* (April 1, 1905); "Pittsburgh's Housing Laws," *Charities and the Commons* (February 6, 1909). Some of Dinwiddie's ideas on the subject of housing management are found in "The Tenant's Responsibility," National Housing Association, *Process* 1 (1911), 52–60; and "Tenant House Supervision," *Journal of Home Economics* (February, 1912). Her scholarly research on Virginia's state mental institutions appears in *Virginia State Hospitals for Mental Patients—Report on Receiving System and Hospitalization Needs* (1934).

Biographical data on Emily Dinwiddie are found in Lilian Brandt, *The Charity Organization Society of the City of New York, 1882–1907* (1907), 236–237; Durward Howes, ed., *American Women* (1939–1940); *Notable American Women: A Biographical Dictionary*, vol. 1 (1971); and the obituary in the *New York Times*, March 13, 1949.

SAYDE L. LOGAN

**Divine, Father** (?–September 10, 1965), Afro-American religious figure and social reformer, was born about 1880, somewhere between Virginia and Georgia. Father Divine cloaked his birth and early life in mystery, never responding directly to questions about his parents, his given name, or his date and place of birth, lest he undermine a cult religion that believed in his divine origins. Scholarly opinion can add only that he seemed to have firsthand knowledge of sharecropping, that he had little or no formal education, and that he almost certainly spent his youth suffering from poverty, dislocation, and racial discrimination. Frustrated by southern injustice, he migrated to Baltimore, where in 1899 he was living as George Baker—landscape laborer, Baptist Sunday school teacher, and evangelist-activist. Dissatisfied with orthodox religion and distraught over the advance of Jim Crow, he returned to the deep South. He later recalled that he was arrested thirty-two times for trying to bring the power of love and earth-centered religion to bear on the forces of evil. However uncertain these claims, Father Divine's biographers agree that he served time on a Georgia chain gang before he returned to Baltimore, sometime before 1906.

After 1906 the story takes on greater substance and reliability, as George Baker evolved steadily toward his new identity as Father Divine. For six years he worked under the influence of two black evangelists, who incorporated Baker into a holy triumvirate with "Father Jehovia" at the center, flanked by Baker and his counterpart as demigod "Messengers." Baker increasingly challenged Father Jehovia's monopoly on godliness, and in 1912 the Baltimore triumvirate fell apart. Baker returned to the South, on higher authority, to appeal once again for spiritual rebirth and social change. In 1914, at Valdosta, Georgia, not far from a place designated by H. L. Mencken as the "crossroads of hell," Baker was arrested as a public nuisance and placed in jail. By this time he had begun to deify himself, signing his arrest papers as "John Doe, alias God," an act which probably made it easier for the authorities to dismiss him as another crazy cultist to be expelled from the state. Deciding that he had paid his dues in Babylonia, he preached his way north, unconsciously participating in one of the major events of modern social history—the Great Migration of southern Blacks to northern cities. This exodus would later provide him an urban base of the poor and oppressed for the launching of his combined career as deity and social worker.

He kept a low profile, however, as he settled into New York City during 1915. Known once again as the Messenger, he gathered a new spiritual flock and began a quiet communal existence in Brooklyn. The commune served as something of a settlement house and an employment bureau, especially for black domestics working in white suburban homes. In 1919 he assumed the title of Father Divine, but he withdrew even further from the urban masses by acquiring an elegant residence in Sayville, Long Island, where his followers continued their discreet, puritanical life style. At this time he also acquired "Mother Divine," a valuable disciple known otherwise only as Pinninnah.

Sayville offered Father Divine a comfortable interlude. Serene and beatific, he trimmed the hedge of his estate and preached a mild-mannered utopianism. He continued to find suburban employment for black women, who made up 75 percent of his following, and he increasingly recruited a more prosperous black servant class from the fancy hotels and wealthy homes of Suffolk and Nassau counties. As "live ins," they required no room and board at the commune, yet they pooled their wages with the lesser folk, enabling Father Divine to retire his debts and enlarge his Sayville quarters into a conspicuous house of worship, soon renowned for its weekly banquets set before the poor.

In 1926 the first Whites joined the commune, an unsettling event for surrounding Sayville, whose residents became thoroughly alarmed when the Great Depression struck and the Sunday throngs descended on the village to feast with Father Divine. In 1931 these fears led to Father Divine's arrest and conviction for disturbing the peace. The presiding judge deplored the interracial character of the movement and sentenced Father Divine to the maximum one year in prison. Three days later the judge died, prompting Father Divine to utter his most famous words, "I hated to do it."

Sensational publicity, desparate times, and charismatic leadership transformed Father Divine's ministry into one of the significant social movments of the 1930s. Robert Weisbrot, the most thorough and thoughtful biographer of Father Divine, places the movement in the context of other popular appeals of that period, like those of Huey Long and Father Coughlin, who combined the call of social justice with the cult of personality.

In the case of Father Divine, the institutional basis for such a comparison was established in 1933 when he moved from Sayville to Harlem and began organizing his celebrated network of cooperatives known as the Peace Mission. Peace was indeed a serious ideological matter for Father Divine, as were temperance, chastity, and the ascetic life. But for the history of social welfare, the significance of the Peace Mission rests not in its spiritual ideals but in its secular behavior.

Business enterprise, based on communal labor and the pooling of profits, formed the heart of the Peace Mission activity. In urban areas the Peace Mission operated restaurants, hotels, grocery stores, and barber shops, among other businesses, providing employment, food, and shelter for the otherwise poor and homeless. By 1935 the Peace Mission movement had 50,000 members and was the largest owner of real estate in Harlem. In addition, it began a program of rural cooperatives—the Promised Land—in Ulster County and elsewhere in New York, eventually numbering over 700 holdings, including an estate across the Hudson River from President Roosevelt's home at Hyde Park. The cooperative farms anticipated some of the most radical ideas of the New Deal in their resettlement and employment of the poor. Father Divine took immense pride in the success of these ventures and the lessons in thrift and industry they taught. Aside from the Sunday feasts, Father Divine frowned on direct welfare without productive labor. Public welfare, in fact, was forbidden among his followers, and it has been estimated that his self-help programs saved the state of New York more than $2 million in welfare costs during the Depression.

Father Divine also commanded his disciples to seek formal education. In 1935, according to Weisbrot, 20 percent of all students enrolled in New York City's public night schools were Divinites. In addition, the Peace Mission created its own education department and opened several private schools in northern cities. As part of his political activities, Father Divine lobbied the New York Commissioner of Education on the rights of handicapped children, and he protested the admission policies of colleges and universities that discriminated against minorities.

If Father Divine functioned as an opiate or as an instrument of social control, it was despite his agenda for reform. Since God was already on earth, there was little need to look to the other world; thus, all righteous political causes became his causes, including the Scottsboro boys, Angelo Herndon, and the federal antilynching bill. In 1936 he helped organize Harlem's All People's Party, a radical coalition demanding full employment and electoral support for Vito Marcantonio, the radical New York City congressman. For a time Father Divine openly cooperated with the Communist Party, furnishing thousands of Peace Mission marchers for joint rallies against racial discrimination, war, and fascism. Also, in 1936, he staged a three-day convention at the Rockland Palace in Harlem, where 6,000 Peace Mission delegates ratified a Righteous Government

Platform calling for economic cooperation, the nationalization of banking, sweeping civil rights legislation, a minimum wage law, free required universal education, and the aboliton of capital punishment.

The Righteous Government Platform marked the high point of Father Divine's activism. He never forgave Franklin Roosevelt for failing to support an antilynching bill, and he counseled a boycott of presidential politics. He grew disillusioned with communism, yet the socialists shunned him because of his communist affiliation, and labor unions were mutual antagonists of the Peace Mission. In a historic pattern of American reform, pieces of his platform were absorbed by the center, and an improving economy, along with the urgency of foreign affairs, left him an increasingly forgotten figure. In 1942 he moved his headquarters to Philadelphia, where he and the second Mother Divine ruled over the remains of his empire. After a long period of failing health, Father Divine died in Philadelphia on September 10, 1965.

Although there is no manuscript collection for Father Divine, much of what he wrote, including correspondence, was printed in the two official organs of the Peace Mission: the *Spoken Word* (October 20, 1934–July 31, 1937) and the *New Day* (May 21, 1936). For the critical 1930s, the other good primary source is the *New York Amsterdam News*.

The best and most recent secondary source on Father Divine is Robert Weisbrot, *Father Divine and the Struggle for Racial Equality* (1983). The interested student should consult Weisbrot's bibliography, which includes both an essay on sources and a list of relevant works.

WALTER B. WEARE

**Dix, Dorothea Lynde** (February 11, 1802–July 17, 1887), teacher and crusader for humane treatment of the mentally ill, was born in Hampden, Maine, the daughter of Joseph and Mary (Bigelow) Dix.

Dorothea Dix's childhood was influenced by a number of unfortunate circumstances. Her paternal grandfather, Elijah Dix, was a wealthy physician and land speculator. The marriage of his son to a woman much older than he displeased him greatly. Not only was Mary Bigelow beneath their class, he believed, but the marriage meant that his son could not complete his Harvard degree since Harvard refused to allow married men to matriculate.

Nevertheless, Elijah Dix made Joseph land agent for his Maine holdings, and the couple moved to Hampden, Maine. Life was fraught with hardships there: they lived in a one-room shack, and winters were long and cold. It was into this environment that their daughter Dorothea was born.

A theological background obtained while he was a student at Harvard laid the groundwork for Joseph Dix's "conversion" to the Methodist faith. He subsequently abandoned his job for the life of an itinerant preacher and rarely saw his family. Dorothea's mother became depressed and discouraged, and was unable to give her the love and attention children need.

Dorothea Dix's grandparents exerted great influence upon her childhood. Both loved her very much, but her grandfather died when Dorothea was only seven. At the age of twelve, she left her parents to live with her grandmother in Boston.

In reflecting upon these years as an adult, Dix stated that she "never knew" childhood. The literature about her childhood alludes to draconian punishments meted out to her by both her parents and her grandmother, much of it in the name of instilling discipline, neatness, and respect.

Little is known of Dorothea Dix's early education. She either learned to read and write from her parents or attended the Hampden Academy while she lived there. Her first vocation, however, was teaching, which she began in 1816 at the age of fourteen, in Worcester, Massachusetts. Five years later, she opened her first school in Orange Court, at her grandmother's home.

For the next fifteen years, Dorothea Dix ran the school and published a number of books, mostly small literary works with religious overtones. Many of the works written about her life indicate that it was the hectic pace of her activities, combined with her poor constitution, which set the stage for her well-documented physical and emotional collapse in 1836.

In 1837 Dorothea Dix journeyed to England for a period of rest and recovery which lasted eighteen months. It was during this time that she learned about York Retreat, an asylum for the mentally ill which operated on a scientific model of treatment.

By 1841 her grandmother had died. She left a portion of her estate to Dorothea, and this, combined with her own savings from teaching, meant that Dorothea had enough to live on for the rest of her life. She decided to volunteer her time and energies, and in the spirit of Christian giving accepted an offer to teach a Sunday school class to the women incarcerated in the East Cambridge jail.

Her first visit to the jail marked the beginning of a new chapter in Dorothea Dix's life. She walked through the jail and spoke with the prisoners. Along with the criminals, she found poor women who had been imprisoned for no reason other than mental illness. The quarters reserved for the mentally ill were bare and cold. In response to her query as to why there was no heat in their quarters, the jailer informed Dix that "lunatics" were impervious to the cold.

Dorothea Dix was deeply angered and sickened by the conditions in which the mentally ill women were existing at Cambridge, and she knew that the indigent mentally ill probably were treated no better elsewhere. No doubt cognizant of the fact that this might have been her lot had she been poor at the time of her emotional collapse, Dorothea Dix resolved to make the humanization of treatment for the indigent mentally ill her life's work.

She began in her own backyard—the state of Massachusetts—by first conducting an extensive survey of all the facilities in the state housing mentally ill people. Much of what she saw was actually worse than what she had witnessed at the Cambridge jail, and, with the help of Dr. Samuel Gridley Howe,* she wrote a memorial to the Massachusetts legislature which documented what she saw and requested that the state legislature mandate funds for hospital treatment of the indigent mentally ill. Although this memorial failed to gain sufficient support in the legislature the first time it was introduced, it did pass in 1843, the second time around.

Dorothea Dix next turned her attention to the neighboring states of New York, Rhode Island, and Connecticut. In her spare time, she read as much as possible on the nature and treatment of mental illness. Reform work in New Jersey and Pennsylvania soon followed. Bringing change to the state of New Jersey was particularly difficult because there were virtually no provisions at all for the mentally ill until Dix began her efforts there. The establishment of the State Hospital in Trenton is considered her first major victory. In state after state, she followed the same modus operandi: survey and document the conditions of the state, prepare a reform bill, and lobby for its passage. The formula was extremely successful. Over the next decade or so, thirty-two state hospitals were established in ten states, an achievement that is testimony to her superb organizational skills.

In 1848 Dorothea Dix went to Washington D.C. She believed that the time had come for the federal government to participate in the care and treatment of its less fortunate citizens. Working with several key congressmen, she got a bill introduced which was to provide land grants to the states for mental hospitals. In 1854, after six years of setbacks and intense lobbying, the bill passed both houses of Congress. Unfortunately, President Franklin Pierce vetoed the bill on both constitutional and economic grounds.

The defeat of the bill deeply disappointed her, and she sailed for Europe shortly thereafter. Upon her return, she went to work again for the states to secure legislative mandates for additional hospitals.

In 1861 the Civil War broke out, and on June 10 she was granted a commission as Superintendent of United States Army Nurses. Her task was to recruit nurses for the Union Army, but she also worked to improve the quality of conditions in army hospitals.

It must be noted that, while she continued to be selfless in her devotion to this cause, her rigidity and intransigence won her few friends. She remained as Superintendent of Army Nurses for the duration of the war, but in 1863 her authority was diminished by a directive of the Surgeon General, who, from that point on, reserved authority to appoint nurses. As disappointed as she was by this turn of events, she resolved to stay on until no longer needed. In 1866 she finally left Washington, D.C., to continue her work on behalf of the mentally ill.

In the remaining years of her life, Dix was forced to contend with the fact that her health was deteriorating. She nevertheless continued her crusade for the mentally ill, but in October, 1881, she returned to the Trenton Hospital which she had been so instrumental in creating, and stayed there until her death on July 17, 1887.

The most important collection of Dix's papers is in the Houghton Library at Harvard University in Cambridge, Massachusetts. The most informative biography of Dix, one for which the author used extensive primary materials, is

Helen E. Marshall, *Dorothea Dix: The Forgotten Samaritan* (1937). Marshall also wrote the excellent short sketch of Dix for *Notable American Women* (1971). Another useful work for those interested in a cursory view of Dix's life and career, is Seth Curtis Beach, *Daughters of the Puritans: A Group of Brief Biographies* (1967).

Most studies of Dix allude, in varying degrees, to a relationship between her and President Millard Filmore. For those wishing more information on that subject, Charles M. Snyder, *The Lady and the President: The Letters of Dorothea Dix and Millard Fillmore* (1975), is an excellent source. Finally, Norman Dain's *Concepts of Insanity in the United States, 1789–1865* (1964) provides good contextual material for understanding both attitudes and the state of the art in thinking about mental illness at the time Dix was fighting for reform.

JOSEPH D. KREISLER and ALICE A. LIEBERMAN

**Dodge, Grace Hoadley** (May 21, 1856–December 27, 1914), social worker and educator, was born in New York City to William Earl Dodge, Jr., a prosperous businessman in the metals trade with evangelical and humanitarian interests, and Sarah (Hoadley) Dodge. Her family had a long tradition of social activism; David Low Dodge, her paternal great-grandfather, had founded the New York Peace Society.

After an education consisting primarily of private tutoring, Grace Dodge at the age of eighteen began to teach Sunday school. By the age of twenty she determined to devote her life to social service, and her father directed her to Louisa Lee Schuyler,* head of the New York State Charities Aid Association. There Dodge became involved in tenement house reform and served as chairman of the Committee on the Elevation of the Poor in their Homes.

Dodge viewed her welfare work as a regular, disciplined occupation, with limited vacations and long hours. Her interests eventually coalesced around movements for the betterment of working women and for the improvement of education in the public schools.

Her concern with the status of young working women occurred at a time when ''working girls'' were a fast-growing segment of the American labor force. As more occupations opened to women and wage work became increasingly acceptable as a female pursuit, reformers like Dodge sought to remedy the worst abuses of housing, recreation, and working conditions by casting a net of domestic influences around young women living or working away from home.

Leisure-time activity was one area of concern for working women. Dodge led efforts to establish recreation clubs for working girls. In 1884 she founded the Working Girls Association of Clubs, a group with the goal of elevating the character and lightening the burdens of working women through club work, classes, and moral instruction. By 1890 the Association comprised seventy-five clubs with over 2,000 members. Dodge served as president of this organization until 1905.

That same year, Dodge mediated the merger of two rival Young Women's

Christian Association groups into the united YWCA of the United States. She brought together the International Board, an eastern, liberal group, with the American Committee, a midwestern evangelical group. In 1906 she was named president of the national board of the YWCA, an office which engaged much of her energy for the rest of her life.

Dodge contributed to other welfare movements as well. She fostered the merger of various organizations into the American Social Hygiene Association in 1912, maintaining that it should pursue educational, legislative, and law enforcement activities. Similarly, she engineered the unification of the travelers' aid movement. Travelers' aid had become by the 1890s a network of mostly church-supported matrons who patrolled railroad and ship depots to watch out especially for the welfare of women traveling alone. In 1907 Dodge consolidated many of these travelers' aid groups into the New York Travelers' Aid Society. In 1912 she led effots to organize the National Travelers' Aid Society and contributed to the international travelers' aid movement as well.

Dodge's second major interest was education. She was a strong advocate for the introduction of domestic, manual, and industrial training into the public schools. In 1880 she helped found the Kitchen Garden Association, which she reorganized into the Industrial Education Association in 1884. Recognizing that teachers of these subjects needed proper training, Dodge contributed to the reorganization of the Industrial Education Association into the New York College for the Training of Teachers, which became Teachers College of Columbia University in 1892. Dodge, who had been one of the first two women appointed to the New York City Board of Education in 1886, was further recognized for her educational work by being named treasurer of the Teachers College board of trustees in 1892.

Dodge's varied interests were united by her deep concern with improving the conditions of life for working-class women and children. Her work was characterized by her energentic and successful efforts at bringing like-minded welfare groups to form more powerful, consolidated associations. In addition to devoting a lifetime to social service, Dodge bequeathed about $1.5 million to her philanthropies. She died in New York City at the age of fifty-eight.

Manuscript material on Dodge's life and work is scattered among the Presidential Papers, Teachers College Library, Columbia University; the National Travelers' Aid Association Papers, Social Welfare History Archives, University of Minnesota; and the Archives of the National Board of the Young Women's Christian Association, New York.

Dodge's principle publications include *A Bundle of Letters to Busy Girls on Practical Matters* (1887), *A Brief Sketch of the Early History of Teachers College* (1899), and *What Women Can Earn* (1899).

For a recent discussion of the various movements to aid the "working girl" of Dodge's era, see Lynn W. Weiner, *From Working Girl to Working Mother: The Female Labor Force in the United States, 1820–1980* (1985). Interpretive accounts of Dodge's career can be found in Abbie Graham, *Grace H. Dodge: Merchant of Dreams* (1926); Esther Katz, "Grace Hoadley Dodge: Women and the Emerging Metropolis, 1856–1914," Ph.D. dissertation, New York University, 1980; Ellen Condliffe Lagemann, *A Generation of Women: Education in the Lives of Progressive Reformers* (1979); and Marion O. Robinson, *Eight Women of the YWCA* (1966). A volume of the YWCA *Association Monthly* (March, 1915) contains memorials to Dodge.

There are also biographical entries for Dodge in *Dictionary of American Biography*, supp. 3 (1959); *National Cyclopaedia of American Biography* (1922); *Notable American Women* (1971); and Francis Willard and Mary Livermore, *A Woman of the Century* (1893). Obituaries were published in the *New York Times* and the *New York Tribune*, December 28, 1914.

LYNN Y. WEINER

**Dodge, Josephine Marshall Jewell** (February 11, 1855–March 6, 1928), pioneer in the U.S. day nursery movement, was the eldest of two daughters born in Hartford, Connecticut, to Marshall Jewell and Esther (Dickenson) Jewell. Josephine was reared in a wealthy and powerful family. Her father was a successful manufacturer as well as a three-term governor of Connecticut, minister to Russia, and postmaster general in the Grant administration. Josephine was educated at Vassar College. She married Arthur Murray Dodge, son of New York philanthropist William Dodge and manager of his family's timber business, on October 6, 1875. She bore six sons and was widowed in 1896.

The Dodge family tradition of social service influenced Josephine's later career; her husband was a founder of the Charity Organization Society in New York, while his niece, Grace Hoadley Dodge,\* was active in various welfare movements for women.

Josephine Dodge found her niche in the day nursery movement. Day nurseries were established as early as the 1820s in the United States, sponsored by private groups for the benefit of poor working women and widows. But these nurseries were few and far between—only six were recorded by 1880. The children of poor working mothers were more often institutionalized in orphanages and asylums, or their mothers were supported at home by private charity.

Dodge began her day nursery efforts with her involvement in the Virginia Day Nursery, founded in 1878 on New York's East Side. Under her leadership, the day nursery movement gradually changed its direction. Rather than merely providing a day care service for working mothers, the day nursery, as conceived by Dodge, would provide a superior "second home" for the children of working-class mothers and would provide a middle-class environment with middle-class ideals. The children of immigrants and poor women would be "morally improved" while physically tended. At the same time, mothers would be protected from the evil of dependency on the state, because by being able to work for wages they could provide for their own families.

Dodge founded the Jewell Day Nursery in New York City in 1888 to practice her ideals, and organized the first conference on day nurseries in 1892. In 1893 she established the model day nursery at the World's Columbian Exposition in Chicago to popularize her movement, and some 10,000 children of visitors to the fair were cared for at the exhibit. Dodge founded the Association of Day Nurseries of New York City in 1895, and three years later organized the National Federation of Day Nurseries. By 1912 over 500 day nurseries had been set up in the United States; by 1928 the National Federation of Day Nurseries had some 700 affiliates.

Day nurseries never did reach the majority of working mothers—they were still too few and understaffed. In a Philadelphia day nursery in 1891, for example, up to fifty children at a time were cared for by one matron, a nurse, cook, and housemaid. Still, the didactic and philanthropic function of the nurseries, as formulated by Dodge and her followers, shaped the idea of day care which would persist well into the twentieth century.

While many of the women reformers of Dodge's era became avid supporters of woman suffrage, she took a contrary position. By 1899 she had taken a public stand as an ardent antisuffragist, and in 1911 she became president of the National Association Opposed to Woman Suffrage, a post she held until 1917. In her later years she continued to work for the promotion of the day nursery movement, and often lived in Europe, where her son Geoffrey was in business. She died in 1928 in Cannes, France.

Although there is no principal source for her papers, some manuscript material on Dodge's work with the National Association of Day Nurseries can be found in the records of the Child Welfare League of America, at the Social Welfare History Archives, University of Minnesota.

For an example of Dodge's perspective on the day nursery movement, see her article, "Neighborhood Work and Day Nurseries," in the *Proceedings of the National Conference of Charities and Correction* (1912). A good overview of the history of day nurseries is presented in Margaret O'Brien Steinfels, *Who's Minding the Children? The History and Politics of Day Car in America* (1973).

For biographical data, see summaries on Dodge in *Notable American Women* (1971); *Who Was Who in America*, vol. 1 (1943); and the *Woman's Who's Who of America, 1914–1915* (1915/1976). Obituaries appeared in the *New York Times*, March 7, 1928, and the Hartford, Connecticut, *Daily Courant*, March 8, 1928.

LYNN Y. WEINER

**Douglass, William** (1691–October 22, 1752), physician, philanthropist, and pioneer charity administrator, was born in Gifford, Scotland, some time in 1691. His father, George Douglass, worked as a portioner; his mother's name is not known. There is little information on his early life; he was educated at several universities, including Edinburgh, and earned his medical degree at Leyden under the renowned Herman Boerhaave.

Although more eminent for his medical practice and his acerbic pen, Dr.

William Douglass devoted considerable effort to helping the poor and can be termed a pioneer in early American social welfare. He brought new ideas for charity to colonial Boston and applied them to one organization, the Scots Charitable Society. It was founded in Boston in 1657 by mariners, artisans, and former Scottish prisoners of war transported to New England by Oliver Cromwell. These men banded together to form a mutual aid society for Scottish immigrants, and it served as the focal point for their social activities, hospitality, and charity. Indeed, as the first charity organization in the colonies, it served as the model for future associations in America's annals.

Douglass joined the Society in 1716, several months after his arrival in Boston, but then departed for the West Indies. He returned to New England in 1718 and "resolved to fix here, and ramble no more." Within several years he emerged as the leader of the medical profession in Boston and devoted part of his practice to the poor, of whom he said, "I advise and visit without my expectation of fees." In 1721 the Society's members elected him vice-president, and for the next three decades he changed its approach to charity.

The Society, prior to the arrival of Douglass, had limited its aid to immigrants and mariners, who tended to be transient people in colonial society. Under the tenure of Dr. Douglass, the Society extended assistance to residents of the Scottish community within Boston. For the first time, it gave aid to Scottish veterans of the colonial wars and then gradually provided pensions to old members or to their widows. By 1725 the pension system guaranteed each recipient £4 a year, which, as an early form of social insurance, granted them a small supplement to their meager incomes. From 1721 to 1736 Douglass served as the Society's vice president and in that time significantly broadened the scope of the organization's charity. For the first time in the Society's annals, the elderly, the widowed, and the orphaned received regular assistance. Douglass also added a measure of compassion when he personally authorized charity funds for special cases, such as an unwed mother and a Scotsman in jail.

When he was elected the Society's president in 1736, Douglass inherited an organization with serious financial problems. He resolved the difficulties when he quietly removed the treasurer, initiated a system of annual audits, broadened the Society's investments, and retained an attorney for recalcitrant bond holders. His management assured the Society of financial stability at a time when new problems affected the poor. Economic difficulties throughout New England created new hardships and created a new transiency among the poor. Boston officials complained about the influx of "Poor Persons who are crept in amongst Us," and tended to restrict public poor relief from them. In contrast, Douglass expanded the Society's charity to include the new indigents. For the next decade his orders for immediate charity were familiar notations in the Society's ledgers as he condoned their transience with a deep humanitarian spirit. Douglass, in his compassionate response, overruled the Society's regulations and led the Scots to an important shift in their benevolence. By 1742 the Society voted to allow immediate charity funds to the poor as a new formal policy. In the meantime,

Douglass continued the Society's aid to the local poor, whether it was to a "fatherless and motherless" child, to a "Poor Scots man lame [and] dismissed from ye Army," or to a man destitute and in "Lo Surcomstance." When a serious smallpox epidemic struck Boston in 1752, Douglass quickly authorized extra funds for the "feverd poor."

Meanwhile, Douglass had devised grand plans for charity in New England. He wrote that he intended "doing charities in my life by donations" and advocated "frugality in every thing excepting charities." He suggested that each county build an orphanage and an almshouse, proposed a chair of medicine for Harvard College, and donated £500 to the town of New Sherburn. While his philanthropic ideas and gifts influenced people throughout New England, his foremost legacy was to the poor of the Scottish community in Boston.

To the Scots he was a compassionate man devoted to their poor; he had no family of his own, and his spirit of giving was directed to his people in Boston. Through his work the Scots Charitable Society developed into a strong benevolent organization (it still operates today) with excellent management, stable finances, and a humanitarian approach to the needs of the poor. He brought the ideas of the Scottish Enlightenment to Boston and changed the benevolent association that would be the model for future immigrant aid organizations. It is no wonder that the Society members deeply mourned the loss of the man who had been wise and generous in "his Charity and benevolence to the poor" when Douglass died suddenly in Boston on October 22, 1752.

Most of the William Douglass papers were destroyed shortly after his death, and his surviving letters were published by Jared Sparks, ed., "Letters of Dr. William Douglass to Cadwallader Colden of New York," Massachusetts Historical Society, *Collections*, Fourth Series, 2 (1854), 164–189.

Biographical information on Douglass can be found in several older sources, but a full-length study of his life should be undertaken with the benefit of the most recent scholarship: W. L. Burrage, "Dr. William Douglass," in *American Medical Biographies*, ed. H. A. Kelly and W. L. Burrage (1920); John F. Fulton "William Douglass," in *The Dictionary of American Biography* vol. 3 (1930), 407–408; Brooke Hindle, *The Pursuit of Science in Revolutionary America, 1735–1789* (1956); Raymond Muse, "William Douglass, Man of the American Enlightenment, 1691–1752," Ph.D. dissertation, Stanford University, 1948; and George H. Weaver, "Life and Writings of William Douglass, M.D.," Society of Medical History of Chicago, *Bulletin* 11 (1921), 229–259.

For his ideas on social welfare in early America," see "Letter from Dr. William Douglass," *Boston Medical and Surgical Journal*, 104 (1881), 537–538, and his colonial survey, *A Summary, Historical and Political . . . of the British Settlements in North America*, 2 vols. (1749–1751).

The main source for new information on Douglass and the Scots is the Scots Charitable Society Manuscripts in the New England Historical Genealogical Society (Boston, Massachusetts). For the story of that remarkable charity organization, see Charles E. Banks, "Scotch Prisoners Deported to New England by Cromwell, 1651–52," Massachusetts Historical Society, *Proceedings*, vol. 61 (1928), 4–29; E. N. Hartley, *Ironworks on the Saugus* (1957); Scots Charitable Society, *Constitution and By-Laws* (1896); and Peter R. Virgadamo, "Colonial Charity and the American Character: Boston, 1630–1775," Ph.D. dissertation, University of Southern California, 1982.

PETER R. VIRGADAMO

**Du Bois, William Edward Burghardt** (February 23, 1868–August 27, 1963), teacher, author, Pan-Africanist, and inspirer of much black protest thought, was born in Great Barrington, Massachusetts, to Alfred and Mary Silvinia (Burghardt) Du Bois. His father deserted the family when William was a small child, and thus he had no influence upon the family except to leave it virtually penniless.

Du Bois was left without resources when his mother died in 1884. He worked at odd jobs, continued his education, and graduated from Great Barrington High School later in the same year. With the aid of a scholarship, he enrolled at Fisk University, Nashville, Tennessee, in the fall of 1885, graduating with a B.A. degree in 1888. He then entered the junior class at Harvard, again with financial assistance, and graduated cum laude in 1890. The next year he was awarded an M.A. by Harvard. He then spent the next two years at the University of Berlin, returning to the United States to complete his Ph.D. at Harvard in 1895—the first black American to be awarded a Harvard doctoral degree.

On May 12, 1896, Du Bois married Nina Gomer. They had two children, Burghardt Gomer, who died as a small child, and Nina Yolande, who was born in 1900 and lived to maturity. Nina Gomer Du Bois died on July 1, 1950. On February 14, 1951, Du Bois married Shirley Graham, who survived him. They had no children.

Du Bois' academic career began in 1895 at Wilberforce University, where he taught Latin, Greek, German, and English for two years. In 1897 he moved to the original Atlanta University, where he taught economics and history until 1910. By the time his career began, Du Bois had grasped the true dimensions of the race problem. Never having experienced discrimination in Great Barrington, he learned his lesson at Fisk and came away with a hatred of white people which he maintained and which drove him for the rest of his life. Also, while he was a student he had vowed to spend his life working hard to make a name for himself and to achieve equality for his race.

During his tenure at Atlanta University, Du Bois wrote extensively, editing fourteen major publications on the life and culture of the American Negro. He also served as secretary of the Pan-African Conference of 1900 in London, founded the Niagara movement in 1905 in opposition to the conservative policies of Booker T. Washington,* and founded two periodocals, *Moon* in 1906 and *Horizon* in 1907. In 1909–1910 Du Bois was a founder of the National Association for the Advancement of Colored People (NAACP). He became its director of publicity and research and a member of its board of directors, and served as editor of its publication, the *Crisis*, from 1910 until 1934.

In 1910 Du Bois left the academic world to work full time for the NAACP. While serving as editor of the *Crisis*, he also attended the First Universal Race Congress in England in 1911, investigated the discriminatory treatment of Negro troops in Europe in 1919, and founded and edited the *Brownies' Book* in 1920. In 1923 he was a special representative of the United States government to the inauguration of the President of Liberia. In the years following World War I he was chief organizer of four Pan-African Congresses: Paris (1919); London, Brussels, and Paris (1921); London and Lisbon (1923); and New York City (1923). The main theme of all the Pan-African Congresses was freedom and self-governemnt for black colonies throughout the world.

Du Bois resigned from the *Crisis* in 1934 to become chairman of the Sociology Department of the new Atlanta University. He returned to the NAACP in 1944 as director of research and remained there for four years. During that time he represented the NAACP at the 1945 United Nations Conference in San Francisco and presided at the fifth Pan-African Congress in Manchester, England, in the same year. From 1948 to 1951 Du Bois was co-chairman of the Council on African Affairs. During that period he also was involved with the organization of the Cultural and Scientific Conference for World Peace in 1949, and in 1950 he ran unsuccessfully for the United States Senate on the Progressive Party ticket.

Meanwhile, during the first decades of the twentieth century and after, Du Bois, Booker T. Washington, and Marcus Garvey,* were the most important leaders in the movement for the equality of black Americans. Du Bois differed strongly with the philosophies of the other two, however. He believed that Washington's approach, which required that black Americans seek justice on the white man's terms, was not only conservative but that it led to disfranchisement, the decline of black education, and the firmer establishment of the color line throughout the nation. In spite of these harsh criticisms, however, Du Bois never questioned Washington's commitment or his intellectual prowess. On the other hand he regarded Marcus Garvey as little more than a lunatic and had no sympathy whatsoever for Garvey's desire to Africanize the American Negro. Du Bois' own position varied little throughout his life. He demanded the immediate recognition of the political, social, and economic rights of all black citizens, and he vowed that he never would rest until his goal was achieved.

Despairing of the possibility of ending racism and exploitation in America, in 1961, at the age of ninety-three, Du Bois joined the Communist Party and became a resident of Ghana. Two years later he took Ghanian citizenship, intending to live out the remainder of his life in the African nation. He died there on August 27, 1963 and was buried in Accra.

Du Bois was a prolific author. His major works include *The Souls of Black Folk* (1903), a balanced critique of Booker T. Washington; *The Suppression of the African Slave Trade to the United States of America, 1638–1870* (1896), his

DUDLEY, HELENA STUART

dissertation; *John Brown* (1909), a passionate defense of the radical abolitionist; *The Gift of Black Folk: Negroes in the Making of America* (1924), an exaggerated account of the contributions made by Negroes to civilation; *Black Reconstruction in America: An Essay Toward a History of the Part Which Black Folk Played in the Attempt to Reconstruct America, 1860–1880* (1935), a Marxist interpretation; *Dusk of Dawn: An Essay Toward an Autobiography of the Race Concept* (1940), his first autobiography; *Color and Democracy: Colonies and Peace* (1945); and *The Autobiography of W. E. B. Du Bois: A Soliloquy on Viewing My Life from the Last Decade of Its First Century*, ed. Herbert Aptheker (1968). Du Bois also wrote several novels, including *Quest of the Silver Fleece* (1911); *Dark Prince: A Romance* (1928); and *The Black Flame Trilogy*.

The Du Bois Papers are in the Archives of the University of Massachusetts at Amherst. Other major sources include Herbert Aptheker, *Annotated Bibliography of the Published Writings of W. E. B. Du Bois* (1973); Francis L. Broderick, *W. E. B. Du Bois: Negro Leader in a Time of Crisis* (1959); Shirley D. Du Bois, *His Day Is Marching On: Memories of W. E. B. Du Bois* (1971); *The Correspondence of W. E. B. Du Bois*, ed. Herbert Aptheker, 3 vols. (1973–1978); Philip Foner, ed., *W. E. B. Du Bois Speaks*, 2 vols. (1970); Hugh Hawkins, *Booker T. Washington and His Critics*, 2nd ed. (1974); Robert M. McDonnell, ed., *Papers of W. E. B. Du Bois, 1803 (1877–1963)* (1981); Jack B. Moore, *W. E. B. Du Bois* (1981); Paul Partington, *W. E. B. Du Bois: A Bibliography of His Published Writings* (1979); Arnold Rampersad, *The Art and Imagination of W. E. B. Du Bois* (1976); Elliot M. Rudwick, *W. E. B. Du Bois: Propagandist of the Negro Protest*, 2nd ed. (1968); Emma G. Sterne, *His Was the Voice: The Life of W. E. B. Du Bois* (1971).

KENNETH E. HENDRICKSON, JR.

**Dudley, Helena Stuart** (August 31, 1858–September 29, 1932), settlement worker and pacifist, was born in (Florence?) Nebraska, the only child of Judson H. and Caroline (Bates) Dudley. Her father, the son of a Baptist clergyman, came from Canandaigua, New York, and was at the time of her birth residing in Florence, Nebraska, serving as a representative of the Emigrant Aid Society of New York. In 1858, he left for Colorado to join the mining boom, and as one of the original settlers of Denver, subsequently prospered in silver mining and real estate enterprises. He is said to have made and spent several fortunes in mining ventures in Colorado, Idaho, Montana, and South Dakota.

Despite her grandfather's religious affiliations, Helena Dudley was an Episcopalian and throughout her life maintained a strong religious faith. Her early life, although sparsely documented, may have been unsettled due to her father's business travels and the death of her mother in 1877. After working at various jobs, Helena went to Boston in 1884 to study science at the Massachusetts Institute of Technology. Transferring to Bryn Mawr after one year at MIT, in 1889 she became a member of the first class to graduate from that institution. As a biology major, she worked as a laboratory assistant to defray college expenses, and after graduation taught biology at Pratt Institute in Brooklyn. The following year, she was employed in the same capacity at Packer Institute, also in Brooklyn.

Helena Dudley's interest in social service began at Bryn Mawr, where she and her classmate Emily Greene Balch* both heard visitors from the new settlement house movement describe plans to "settle" college women in a house on Rivington Street, New York City. Dudley subsequently was a Bryn Mawr representative at the founding of the College Settlement Association, and a member of the Association's electoral board. The secretary of the board, Vida Scudder,* was to become her close friend and associate in settlement work.

By 1892 Helena Dudley had abandoned her teaching career and moved from Brooklyn to become head worker at the College Settlement House in Philadelphia. The following year, she replaced Emily Greene Balch as head resident of Denison House, the Association's new settlement in Boston's South End, the organization with which her name is primarily associated. Arriving at the height of the Panic of 1893, Dudley immediately undertook assistance and relief work. Settlements normally had not provided relief for their constituencies, but the Denison House sewing rooms she started soon kept 300 unemployed women busy.

Cooperating with nearby South End Settlement House, Denison residents sponsored an art exhibition and an investigation of housing, and mounted a campaign for public baths and gymnasiums. The Denison House gymnasium, opened in 1900, was taken over by the city a year later. Other activities at Denison House, such as clubs, lectures, and educational programs, were similar to programs at other settlement houses of the time.

Dudley herself was well known in the settlement movement primarily because of her influence on others and her prominence as head of one of the first settlements. Her ideas on settlement work usually appeared only in Denison House and College Settlements Association annual reports; she wrote little for wider publication.

From the outset, Helena Dudley spent much of her time at Denison House in activities aimed at helping workers secure a living wage. She opened Denison House to labor union meetings and joined Federal Labor Union 5915, American Federation of Labor, which was composed of workers in unorganized trades. In 1894 Denison House workers succeeded in organizing the women garment workers of Boston through the union. With Vida Scudder, who continued as her close associate in Denison House work, Dudley served as a union delegate to the Boston Central Labor Union, and in 1903 she joined William English Walling,* Emily Greene Balch, Mary Morton Kehew,* Mary Kenney O'Sullivan, and others in organizing the National Women's Trade Union League (NWTUL). She also served the NWTUL as vice president of the Boston branch.

Helena Dudley opposed labor violence, but she did sympathize with the militance of the Industrial Workers of the World (IWW) and was particularly supportive of their cause during the 1912 textile workers' strike in Lawrence, Massachusetts. It was her views on the strike, and on other radical causes, that led directly to her abandonment of settlement work. Believing that her views were alienating potential supporters of the settlement, Dudley resigned her post as head resident of Denison House in 1912.

Most of Helena Dudley's work after 1912 went into the cause of world peace. She was a board member of the Massachusetts branch of the Women's International League for Peace and Freedom, and after World War I she helped promote the League of Nations. She made several trips to Europe, and in the 1920s, growing disillusioned with the lack of progress made by the peace movement, became a member of the Socialist Party. Continuing to reside in Massachusetts, in the late 1920s she moved into the Wellesley home of Vida Scudder, who shared her political and religious views.

Helena Stuart Dudley died at the age of seventy-four in Geneva, Switzerland, after attending a meeting of the Women's International League in Grenoble, France.

Some material by and about Dudley is in the Denison House Records, 1891– 1961, located in the Schlesinger Library, Radcliffe College. Except for reports of Denison House and articles in the annual reports of the College Settlements Association, Dudley wrote little for publication. There are two published articles: "Relief Work Carried on in the Wells Memorial Inst.," American Academy of Political and Social Science *Annals* (November, 1894), and "Women's Work in Boston Settlements," *Municipal Affairs* (September, 1898).

The most comprehensive assessment of Helena Dudley is the article by Allen F. Davis in *Notable American Women: A Biographical Dictionary*, vol. 1 (1971), 526–527; there is an older sketch in *Woman's Who's Who of America, 1914– 15* (1915/1976). An obituary appears in the *Bryn Mawr Alumnae Bulletin* (November, 1932), 23–24. Unlike some of her associates, Dudley never wrote an autobiography. Writings by colleagues contain some information; see Vida Scudder's *On Journey* (1937) and a pamphlet titled *A Heart That Held the World: An Appraisal of the Life of Helena Stuart Dudley* (1939), in the Schlesinger Library. Mercedes M. Randall's *Improper Bostonian: Emily Greene Balch* (1964) provides additional information. Material on the life of Judson H. Dudley is in a biographical sketch in the Denver publication *Trail* (October, 1911), 15–17.

JANE A. ROSENBERG

**Dummer, Ethel Sturges** (October 23, 1866–February 25, 1954), philanthropist and social reformer, was born in Chicago, the third of nine children and the first of six girls of George and Mary (Delafield) Sturges. Family life was characterized by spirited debate on public issues. George Sturges, a bank president, took an active role in community affairs by supporting David Swing, a Presbyterian minister who was defrocked for refusing to preach infant damnation. In 1885 Ethel Sturges finished her formal education at the private Kirkland School. Her teachers, including Ellen Gates Starr,* cofounder of Hull-House, stressed the social obligations of wealthy women, and through the Kirkland Alumnae Association Ethel Sturges became aware of the problems of working women.

In 1888 Ethel Sturges married William Francis Dummer, a banker and a descendant of the distinguished Massachusetts Dummer family. Frank Dummer, like George Sturges, was civic-minded, joining actively in the Chicago Playground Association founded by Graham R. Taylor.* The Dummers had five children, four girls and a last-born boy whose death in infancy (1902) cast a tragic shadow upon their lives. Ethel and Frank Dummer believed in the value of education through planned activity, and they raised their daughters accordingly. Mr. Dummer blamed the "mediocrity of mankind" on parents and teachers who failed to help children coordinate muscles and senses; by using phonetic exercises which he had observed at the Illinois State School for the Deaf, he taught his daughters to speak by their first birthday. Ethel Dummer aided the family tutors in teaching the girls through handicrafts, dramatics, and anagrammatic play with foreign languages. At their Chicago townhouse and at vacation homes in Lake Geneva, Wisconsin, and Coronado, California, the family became the center of the Sturges and Dummer clans.

Ethel Dummer later wrote that this leisured life had given her "no conception of the other 98 percent of humanity." Her friends included reformers such as Mary E. McDowell* of the University of Chicago Settlement and Allen B. Pond, humanitarian and architect of Hull-House, but she remained relatively inactive until 1905, when child labor articles appearing in the *Outlook* led her to join the National Child Labor Committee and the Chicago Juvenile Protective Association. "From a trim and orderly garden," she recalled, "I slipped into a jungle."

Dummer's philanthropy was initially guided by her concern with the problems of urban life, especially as these affected children. In 1908 she became a founding trustee of the Chicago School of Civics and Philanthropy and, soon thereafter, underwrote two University of Chicago lecture series on social problems as well as Mary McDowell's survey of sanitation policies in European cities. In 1909 she provided funds to establish the (Chicago) Juvenile Psychopathic Institute, where William Healy* began *The Individual Delinquent* (1915), the first major psychological study of juvenile offenders. Healy's case studies related persistent misbehavior to incorrect nurture, thus taking issue with the prevailing hereditarian viewpoint. The Institute's teamwork approach, utilizing psychiatrists, psychologists, and social workers, became the model for the guidance clinic movement in the 1920s.

In the World War I era, Ethel Dummer studied prostitution and unwed motherhood. As a member of protective committees working near military camps, she rejected the conventional belief that prostitutes were inferior and unchangeable types. She also opposed forced marriages and legal penalties for prostitution, believing that the girls had suffered shell shock like trench warfare combatants. Envisioning sympathetic institutional treatment as the best therapy, Dummer aided the founding of special detention homes like Miriam Van Waters'* El Retiro in Los Angeles. After studying European laws and programs affecting unwed mothers, such as Norway's Castberg Law, Ethel Dummer campaigned for the repeal of state laws discriminating against these women and their children.

Throughout her career, Ethel Dummer drew upon the pedagogy of English writer Mary Everest Boole, wife of the logician George Boole. Mrs. Boole sought to integrate progressive educational values into a philosophy synthesizing Darwinian biology and religion. Thus, organized play encouraged the development of the conscious mind which, as God's special gift to mankind, was both the means through which the unconscious found expression and the basis for social activity. Conversely, antisocial behavior indicated the continuance in adult life of the child's animal or instinctual mind and reflected a person's neglected or prematurely abstract education.

Boolean ideas not only confirmed Ethel Dummer's familial educational practices but also guided her support for men and women in the new social science professions. She assisted Miriam Van Waters' 1922 *Survey Graphic* study of schools for delinquent girls and also aided her during the writing of *Youth in Conflict* (1925). When University of Chicago sociologist William I. Thomas lost his job for philandering, she provided him with research and living expenses and later assisted him and his second wife, Dorothy Swaine Thomas, in the preparation of their essay on child study programs, *The Child in America* (1928).

Ethel Dummer's primary interest remained the promotion of educational programs seeking to coordinate the development of children's minds and bodies. In Chicago she underwrote Florence Beaman's class for retarded, truant, and delinquent boys at the Montefiore School. In 1932 Neva Boyd of Hull-House used the Dummers' living room to instruct elementary school teachers on the development of exercise programs. "If I could live to see every seat in the first grade rooms removed," said Ethel Dummer, "I should feel that I had not lived in vain." Her activities in later years were consistent with this view. She helped her daughter, Ethel D. Mintzer, director of San Diego's Francis W. Parker School, promote Boole blocks, which were designed to teach algebraic formulae and fractional parts. In the 1940s she sponsored Northwestern University child development courses which introduced the work of Jean Piaget.

Although she avoided publicity, Ethel Dummer received many awards, most notably an honorary doctorate from Northwestern (1940). Unpretentious in dress and manner, she always was eager to discuss new ideas. To the end, she retained mystical faith that humanity would continue to improve. Confronted by Hitler, she paraphrased William Blake: "God has given a body to evil that he may cast it out."

Ethel Dummer's life was devoted to encouraging the creation of new knowledge and helping to establish connections between creative people. She spent her last years at the home of her daughter, Katherine D. Fisher, in Winnetka, Illinois, where she died on February 25, 1954, following a stroke.

The main biographical sources are Ethel Dummer's autobiography *Why I Think So—The Autobiography of an Hypothesis* (1937), and the Ethel Struges Dummer Collection, Schlesinger Library, Radcliffe College. Her papers are particularly informative as a portrait of genteel family life and as a deposit for her remarkable and diverse professional correspondence. Some of her essays appear as prefaces or introductions in the following studies: William I. Thomas, *The Unadjusted Girl* (1923); *The Unconscious: A Symposium* (1928); and *The Collected Works of Mary Everest Boole* (1931). Her other writing includes *The Evolution of a Biological Faith* (1943); *What Is Thought?* (1945); and *Mary E. Boole: A Pioneer Student of the Unconscious* (1945). For family information see Ebenezer Buckingham, comp., *Solomon Sturges and His Descendants* (1907). Obituaries appeared in the *New York Times*, February 27, 1954; *Proceedings* of the Institute of Medicine in Chicago (1954), 201–202; and *American Journal of Orthopsychiatry* (July, 1954), 646–647.

ROBERT M. MENNEL

**Dunham, Arthur** (August 3, 1893–September 1, 1980), social worker and professor of community organization and development, was the only child born to William Armstrong and Lottie Mae (Rickart) Dunham. Raised in St. Louis in a modest, middle-class, devoutly Presbyterian home, he described himself as having been very close to a great aunt who exposed him, at the age of nine, to life in Missouri almshouses. His interest in social work, however, developed much later. He initially thought of a career in law.

He attended Washington University in St. Louis, largely because he lacked funds to study elsewhere. The professors who impressed him most taught history and English; he found his courses in sociology (which exposed him to Amos Warner's* *American Charities*) dreadful. Meanwhile, his studies in philosophy and his experience with the social mission of the "institutional" church led him away from evangelical Christianity to a more "liberal" Christianity. After completing work for his bachelor's degree in 1914, he obtained a scholarship to study for a master's degree in political science at the University of Illinois. He hoped to use that degree to obtain a teaching position, save money, and then study law at Harvard University. After completing a year of studies, he was forced to leave due to lack of funds, working to support himself and doing research to complete his master's thesis, which was finally accepted in 1917.

The work that he found, almost by accident, marked the beginning of his career in social work. In 1915 he was employed by an "institutional" church in St. Louis, which gave him experience in helping single men in a "skid row" area, and in providing recreation for the children of very low income families. He also was exposed to the operations of police courts, which horrified him, and to the possibilities of a council of social agencies, which he found inspiring. For a brief period, in 1917–1918, he practiced family social work for the St. Louis Provident Association, where he worked with black refugees of the East St. Louis race riots, among others.

Dunham met Esther Francis Schneider at this time and they were engaged in September, 1917. Schneider was a religious pacifist, and their discussions influenced him profoundly. He thus refused service when drafted into the army in July, 1918. Court-martialed on November 12, 1918, Dunham was found guilty, and sentenced to twenty-five years of hard labor, and incarcerated at Fort Leavenworth until his sentence was overturned on January 27, 1919. After being released from Leavenworth, Dunham joined his fiancée in Philadelphia, where she had been working as a social worker, and they were married on May 31, 1919. Later they would adopt two chldren, Ruth and Richard.

In Philadelphia Dunham was employed, through his wife's connections and with her encouragement, as executive secretary of the Social Service Exchange. In 1923 he moved to Newton, Massachusetts, where he became secretary of that city's Council of Social Agencies. There he organized studies of public health, recreation, and school social work in the area, and worked with a citizens' group on organizing a community chest.

Two years later he went back to Philadelphia as secretary of that city's Public Charities Commission's family and child welfare division, a position he held until 1935. Among the issues he worked on were problems of mothers' assistance, legislative campaigns to increase appropriations, marriage law reform, and a ten-year plan for child welfare in Pennsylvania. When the Depression hit, however, his services frequently were lent to other agencies, including the state's emergency relief agency and the Family Service Association of America in New York City, where he studied the impact of public relief on families.

In 1930 Dunham had been offered a teaching position at the New York School of Social Work, which he declined because of other commitments. But in the summers of 1931 and 1933 he taught six-week sessions at the Chicago School of Social Service Administration. In 1935 he was invited to join the faculty at what became the University of Michigan's School of Social Work, a position he accepted partly to get away from the constant travel required by his work in Philadelphia. His appointment at the University of Michigan would end twenty-eight years later, in 1963.

In his years at the University of Michigan, where he served as acting director of the school from 1949 to 1951, he taught courses in community organization, social welfare administration, and community development, a subject in which he developed an intense interest, one which continued for the rest of his life. He also held visiting appointments at many other universities and accepted a number of special assignments outside the university, including service as a member of the research staff for the Michigan Welfare Relief Study Commission (1936–1937) and as a member (1931–1960) and chairman (1954–1960) of the Advisory Committee to the Social Work Yearbook. Although he retired from the University of Michigan in 1963, he continued to write and teach as a visiting professor in a number of other institutions at home and abroad.

Arthur Dunham's principal contributions to social welfare were in the areas of community organization and community development practice, which were inextricably linked with his religious convictions, his exposure to the institutional church, and especially his relationship with his wife. He felt strongly that settling conflict by violent means produced more negative consequences than positive ones. He was interested in building a sense of community and felt that this could best be done through open and unfettered discussions among all parties. He believed that social change could best be achieved by bringing together the people experiencing problems, the professionals, and those who held influence so that all could take appropriate actions. He will also be remembered as a man with an intense interest in the people with whom he worked, particularly foreign students and their families. Arthur Dunham died in Ann Arbor, Michigan, in 1980.

A biographical sketch of Arthur Dunham can be found in *Who's Who in America*, vol. 27 (1952). An oral history prepared by Vida S. Grayson as part of the National Association of Social Workers Oral History Project, entitled *An Oral Memoir of Arthur Dunham, 1893–1980*, can be found in the Bentley Historical Library of the University of Michigan, Ann Arbor, which also contains an extensive collection of Dunham's papers, including an unpublished manuscript describing his experiences as a conscientious objector during World War I.

Among his most significant publications are *Community Welfare Organization: Principles and Practice* (1958); *Community Organization in Action: Basic Literature and Critical Comments*, with Ernest B. Harper (1959); and *Trends in Community Organization*, with Monna Heath (1963). He continued to write after his retirement in 1963. This work included *The New Community Organization* (1970); and "Community Development in North America," which appeared in a United Nations publication entitled *Popular Participation in Development* (1971). With Lee J. Carry, he edited *Community Development: A Select Bibliography* (1973), and with Charlotte Nusberg and Sujata Basu Sengupta he wrote *Toward Planning for the Aging in Local Communities: An International Perspective* (1978).

                                                                FRED M. COX

**Dunn, Loula Friend** (May 2, 1896–June 27, 1977), public welfare official and American Public Welfare Association director, was born in Grove Hill, Alabama, to William Dickson and Minnie Savage (Dickinson) Dunn. Her father and both grandfathers were members of the Alabama legislature. After completing local schools, Dunn became a teacher in 1916 in the Alabama public schools. Experiences in teaching low-income, illiterate, and rural adults left a mark on her. She often recalled that the gratitude expressed to her by one man, after she had taught him to write his name, convinced her that she should enter a field of social service broader than that of teaching. She enrolled in social work courses at the Alabama Polytechnic Institute in 1917. She continued to teach, but after attending the University of North Carolina in 1923, she left teaching to become a caseworker in the Foster Home Division of the Alabama Child Welfare Department. During the next decade she rose from caseworker to field representative to assistant director of that agency. When federal funds became available under the New Deal in 1933, she became the director of social services for the Alabama Relief Commission. In 1934 Harry L. Hopkins* named her regional social worker and director of employment for the Federal Emergency Relief Administration,a position she retained under the Works Progress Administration. Headquartered in New Orleans, she gained a national reputation both for the candid reports she wrote on the relief work under way in the six states under her jurisdiction and because of her success in establishing sound federal–state relationships. During that time she and Frank Bane,* then director of the American Public Welfare Association (APWA), worked together to assist southern states in creating departments of public welfare.

At the request of Alabama Governor Bibb Graves, Dunn resigned the WPA post in 1937 to become Commissioner of the State Department of Public Welfare. Her stature within professional circles increased as colleagues recognized her competence, ability, and the soundness of her administration, particularly in the establishment of statewide child welfare services. She expressed concern in professional journals and before congressional committees about the effects upon children of the deprivations of depression and the dislocations of World War II. She was an effective advocate for children through a number of committee and supervisory posts. Included among them were the chairmanship of the children's committee of the APWA, the vice presidency of the Child Welfare League of America (1940–1950), membership on the Advisory Committee on Community Child Welfare Services of the U.S. Children's Bureau, and membership on the boards of the Alabama Boys Industrial School and the State Training School for Girls. During the war she was a member of the Children's Bureau Commission on Children in Wartime, and she toured the British Isles in 1945 as a representative of the Office of War Information. In the 1960s she was a member of the United States Committee of the International Conference of Social Work.

Dunn was a leader of the major national organizations in the field of social welfare and administration. Following yeoman service on various committees and boards, she became the vice president of the American Association of Social Workers (1935–1936), and both vice president (1940–1942) and president (1944–1946) of the APWA. She was vice president of the American Society of Public Administrators (1946–1947) and of the Southern Sociological Society (1946). She was on the executive committees of the National Council on Social Work Education (1949), the National Council of State Public Welfare Administrators (1944–1945), and the National Conference of Social Work (1940–1945). She also was prominent in Alabama organizations, heading the Alabama Conference of Social Work in 1938–1939. She was called upon to work in a number of nonwelfare-related areas, particularly during World War II, when her first work with Oveta Culp Hobby was as an advisor to the War Department in determining criteria for Women's Army Corps officers.

Dunn could have returned to a federal post in 1939, when she declined an appointment as a regional Director of Social Security. In 1949, however, she did leave Alabama to become the director of the American Public Welfare Association. She was the first woman director in the twenty years of the

Association's existence. When she assumed her duties at the national office in Chicago, the APWA suffered severe financial difficulties, which she alleviated by going personally to the Rockefeller Brothers Fund and other funding sources. While the Association had been important in the development of national social policy and programs, participation by individuals, agencies, and state officials of public welfare was not extensive. Within a short time, through her structure of state membership committees and national recruitment campaigns, the Association boasted 5,000 individual and 900 agency memberships. Dunn knew hundreds of people on a first-name basis. Hence, she was effective in promoting participation by lay workers in APWA conferences and in developing staff expertise in medical care, aging, child welfare, and professional training. Throughout the 1950s and 1960s she involved state and local welfare leaders directly in the drafting of major social legislation. Often she brought state welfare directors to Washington, where she joined them to meet with congressional leaders and Department of Health, Education and Welfare officials. When crucial legislation lay before Congress she was quick to mobilize the states. Associates attributed much of the expansion of the public assistance, survivor's benefits, and health care provisions of Social Security to her political astuteness and timing. She herself was proudest of her work as a member of the Consultants Group on Social Security in 1953, the Advisory Council on Public Assistance in 1959, and the important Advisory Council on Social Security Financing in 1964–1965.

"Miss Loula," as she was addressed by most associates, had personal attributes which added to her effectiveness. While she was tenacious and aggressive, she was also extremely charming and attractive. Her soothing southern accent, gentle manner, and gracious gestures were great assets in her work. She was the recipient of many honors, including the APWA's W. S. Terry Award, given her in 1965, the year after she retired as director. The commendation cited the "exceptional energies, talents, wisdom, and skills" which she had devoted to public welfare throughout the major portion of her life. After retirement she lived in Washington, D.C., until her death there at the age of eighty-one.

There is a small collection of Loula Dunn Papers in the Social Welfare History Archives, University of Minnesota; her work as APWA director is better reflected in the APWA Papers in the Archives. There is Dunn correspondence in the Frank Bane Papers at the University of Virginia, and very fine insights of her influence and style are in the Columbia Oral History Collection interviews of Maurine Mulliner, Charles I. Schottland, and Dunn herself. Biographical sketches may be found in *Current Biography* (1951) and *Who's Who in America* (1950–1951). Representative of her views are her "Public Welfare Services to Children in Alabama," Child Welfare League *Bulletin* (March, 1942), and "Potentialities for State and Local Public Welfare," *Social Welfare Forum 1957* (1957). Her successive reports as APWA director are to be found in various issues of *Public*

*Welfare* during her tenure. Obituaries are in the *Washington Post* (June 30, 1977) and the *Washington Report* (APWA newsletter, August, 1977). See also ''Loula Dunn Honored at Washington Reception,'' *Washington Report* (August, 1976).

MARTHA H. SWAIN

# E

Eastman (Ohiyesa), Charles Alexander (February 19, 1858–January 8, 1939), physician and minister to Indians and author and lecturer on Indian Affairs, was born the grandson of Captain Seth Eastman and the son of Mary Nancy Eastman and Many Lightnings (Ite Wakanhdi: Ota). Born biologically three-fourths Sioux and raised wholly Indian until the Minnesota Sioux War of 1862 forced his exile in Canada, Eastman returned to join his family at Flandreau in Dakota Territory to enter a process of acculturation. Many Lightnings had been scheduled to hang for his participation in the war but was spared the gallows at Mankato, and for this act of mercy he had accepted Christianization along with cultural adaptation. He transmitted his new posture to an older son, John, who became a prominent Presbyterian minister; and to Charles, whom he sent away for formal education. After attending Alfred Riggs' Congregational Santee Normal Training School in Nebraska, and Stephen Riggs' academic residence at Beloit in Wisconsin, he moved on to Knox College in Illinois, to Dartmouth College in New Hampshire, and finally to the School of Medicine at Boston University.

Equipped with education in liberal arts as well as in health care delivery, Dr. Eastman moved into a diverse and visible public career. He served as government physician at Pine Ridge (during the Wounded Knee Affair), where he met and married the Superintendent of Education for western Sioux, Elaine Goodale. For his bicultural understanding, he was chosen to investigate the claims of his own Santee tribe against the government for its losses due to the Minnesota War. He worked as an "outing agent" for Carlisle Indian School Superintendent Richard Henry Pratt,* monitoring progress in acculturation among students assigned to live with white Christian foster families. Again he served as a physician, at Crow Creek Reserve, then helped straighten out surnames on Santee tribal rolls. Finally, he turned to a career as lecturer and author, from which evolved a series of important volumes produced with the assistance of his distinguished wife.

Eastman's books bespoke the significance of his life beyond the particular tasks he performed. All of them focused on the dynamics of culture: they recorded ancient Indian values, they eulogized eminent Indian leaders, and with autobiographical narratives they addressed the necessity for Indians to accept a multicultural posture. They also heralded the value of learning as the principal means of adjustment to a changing world. And (as a chronicle of Eastman's personal saga couched in literature that conformed to the standards of excellence set by non-Indian academicians) they honored their principal author as a model in the process of inevitable change.

Pointing the way for fellow Sioux (and members of other tribes) toward acculturation, he was not entirely alone. Sharing this responsibility with such other Sioux models as educational leader Chancey Yellow Robe, Episcopal clergyman Philip J. Deloria, and writer Luther Standing Bear. But none was more celebrated than Eastman. Across both the United States and Western Europe, serving various organizations such as the Society of American Indians, he was heard and recognized often. Among other honors, he received a place among the modern Indian elite by Indian Council Fire the year of the Chicago World's Fair. This and other honors acknowledged his having served both Indians and Whites through cultural exchange and mutual accommodation, which he personified and preached as social gospel through most of his life.

Charles Eastman died in Detroit, Michigan, on January 8, 1939.

Eastman left few personal papers. Two biographical studies, condense most of the important information about his life: David R. Miller's "Charles Alexander Eastman: One Man's Journey in Two Worlds," Master's thesis, University of North Dakota, 1975; and Raymond Wilson's *Ohiyesa: Charles Eastman, Santee Sioux* (1983). Among Eastman's writings, *Indian Boyhood* (1902), *The Soul of the Indian* (1911), and *From the Deep Woods to Civilization*(1916) are the most useful, and the most readily available in reprint editions. Readers also may wish to consult Herbert T. Hoover's *The Sioux: A Critical Bibliography*(1979) for additional titles.

HERBERT T. HOOVER

**Eastman, Crystal** (June 25, 1881–July 27, 1928), lawyer, social invesigator, author, publisher, peace worker, and feminist, was born in Marlborough, Massachusetts, to Samuel Elijah and Annis Bertha (Ford) Eastman, both ordained Congregational ministers. The third of four children and the only daughter, Crystal grew up in a family in which the mother was the most notable parent. Annis, an outspoken feminist who emphasized the equality of men and women to her children, was listed in *Who's Who in America* (first entry 1903–1905 volume). In the entry she was described as an independent minister, which reflected the fact that her religious questioning caused her to lead her congregation into a Unitarian stance.

The Eastman family was financially secure enough to insure that the three children who survived to adulthood all received college educations. Crystal graduated from Vassar in 1903 and moved to New York City, where she took an M.A. in sociology at Columbia University in 1904. She then entered the Law

School of New York University and supported herself by running a recreation center on weekday nights. In this period, she shared an apartment with a social worker and was a worker at the Greenwich Settlement House. Eastman obtained her LL.D. and was admitted to the New York bar in 1907. That fall she moved to Pittsburgh to become a member of the staff of the Pittsburgh Survey. Between late 1907 and 1909 she investigated and analyzed over 1,000 industrial accidents in Allegheny County and published articles on aspects of her study in *Charities and the Commons* (March 7, 1908; January 2 and March 6, 1909). The final results, the first major inductive investigation of work accidents and the economic burden they produced, appeared in May, 1910, as *Work-Accidents and the Law*, the second volume published in the Pittsburgh Survey series. Eastman found the actions of employers or their agents the prime cause of 30 percent of the accidents she investigated. Employee negligence was, she said, the major cause of 28 percent of the accidents and contributed to another 16 percent of the accidents. She held that the other 26 percent of the accidents had to be blamed not on individuals, but on the hazardous nature of the work performed. While finding that work accidents stemmed from a variety of causes, Eastman emphasized that in most cases the burden of the financial loss caused by accident or death in the workplace fell on the worker or the worker's family. Maintaining that employers were not "wicked," but like workers often "held closely in the grip of economic motives," she argued for the creation of laws that would provide uniform and guaranteed compensation to the victims of industrial accidents. Henry R. Seager, who reviewed the work in the *Survey* (August 6, 1910), correctly predicted that *Work-Accidents* would have great influence because what Eastman described was happening in all of the nation's manufacturing centers. Writing in 1919, Paul Kellogg,* director of the Pittsburgh Survey, asserted that Eastman's work had been instrumental in helping to produce the successful campaign for workers' compensation in America.

Eastman's pioneering efforts in the field of investigating work accidents and creating workers' compenstion led to her appointment in 1909 as secretary and treasurer of the New York branch of the American Association for Labor Legislation. In that same year, Governor Charles Evans Hughes of New York appointed her to the state's Commission on Employers' Liability and Causes of Industrial Accidents, Unemployment and Lack of Farm Labor. Eastman, the only woman on the fourteen-member Commission, served as its salaried secretary. She was the principal author of the Commission's report, which led to New York obtaining what in time became a model workers' compensation law. While serving on the Commission, she delivered a paper at the 1910 National Conference of Charities and Correction (NCCC), "Work-Accidents and Employers' Liability," and also helped to arrange the following year's conference. She continued her social welfare reform work in 1911 by speaking to the American Academy of Political and Social Science on how to create the ideal factory department to minimize work accidents. Not surprisingly, she stressed that such efforts must begin with a careful analysis of statistics on accidents in the work area. In 1913 she served on the NCCC's Committee on Standards of Living and Labor, and it was primarily her work as a social welfare investigator and social welfare reformer that led to her inclusion in *Who's Who in America* at this time. But by 1914 she already was shifting her focus from social welfare issues to other reform causes.

Eastman, who possessed great physical beauty as well as charisma, was a dedicated worker for equal rights for women. She used her husband's name after she married Wallace J. Benedict, an insurance agent from Milwaukee, in May, 1911. But when she divorced him in 1916, she once again wrote under her maiden name and refused all alimony, noting that no self-respecting feminist would depend on an ex-husband for support. She continued to write as Crystal Eastman after she married Walter Fuller (d. 1927), an English pacifist who arranged folk music concerts, in 1916. While living in Milwaukee, she served as campaign manager of the Wisconsin suffragist organization, the Political Equality League (1911–1912). From 1912 through 1914 she was active in organizing and speaking at the national conventions of the National American Woman Suffrage Association. In 1913 she was one of the founding officers of the Congressional Union for Woman Suffrage (later the National Woman's Party). Eastman's commitment to equality between the sexes led her to take a generally unpopular reform stance on a vital social welfare issue: she opposed laws designed to protect and favor women because she believed that equality had to mean fully equal treatment for both sexes. She continued to work actively as a suffragist until the vote was won, after which she continued to champion the ideal of equal rights for women. Meanwhile, when World War I commenced, Eastman, who had firmly embraced socialism, increasingly devoted her energies to the cause of pacifism. She was the driving force behind the American Union Against Militarism, an active member of the Woman's Peace Party, and the primary founder and leading spokesperson of the Women's Peace Party of New York (1914–1919). In 1918 she and her brother Max, who were principal owners and coeditors, began publication of the *Liberator* (successor to the *Masses*). Her management role with the magazine ended in February, 1921. Between 1922 and 1927, her place of residence was England, where she helped create a branch of the National Woman's Party. She returned to the United States in the summer of 1927, planning extensive work on what was to be her new area of reform work: education and child care.

Although Crystal Eastman's major work in the field of social welfare reform was in the short period between 1907 and 1913, where she was, as Paul Kellogg observed, an important pioneer, especially in workers' compensation, she was throughout her life, as her brother Max incisively put it in his 1948 publication *Enjoyment of Living*, "always and incorrigibly a reformer." Eastman died in Erie, Pennsylvania, on July 27, 1928.

Eastman manuscript sources can be found in the Social Welfare History Archives Center of the University of Minnesota; the Swarthmore Peace Collection; and the Schlesinger Library of Radcliffe College. Special permission must be obtained to use the items in the Max Eastman Papers housed at Lilly Library (Indiana University). Important manuscript items, such as Eastman's college journal, are in the private possession of Max Eastman's widow (Yvette Eastman) or of Crystal's daugher (Annis Young). The FBI has a Crystal Eastman file.

Many of Eastman's published essays have been brought together in Blanche W. Cook, ed., *Crystal Eastman on Women and Revolution* (1978).

The fullest and best biography of Eastman is that provided by Cook in her edition of the Eastman essays. Especially important obituaries appeared in the *Nation* (August 8, 1928), the *Survey* (August 15, 1928), and the *New York Times*, (July 29, 1928). A useful entry on Eastman appears in *Notable American Women, 1607–1950: A Biographical Dictionary*, 3 vols. (1971).

JOHN K. ALEXANDER

**Eddy, Thomas** (September 5, 1758–September 16, 1827), merchant, philanthropist, and social reformer, was born in Philadelphia, Pennsylvania, to Mary (Darragh) and James Eddy, a Quaker merchant who died in 1766. Mary Eddy, also a Quaker although she came from Presbyterian stock, continued the business after her husband's death. In 1771 Thomas was apprenticed to a tanner but remained at that post for only two years. Of Tory persuasion, in 1780 he moved to New York City and became a merchant supplying goods to the British occupying forces, for which he was persecuted after the war. Later he became an insurance broker and was one of the early backers of the Erie Canal. He married Hannah Hartshorne on March 20, 1782.

Early in his career, however, Eddy became interested in social reform, especially as it concerned prisons, and was active in the design of the municipal ("Newgate") prison of New York, which opened in 1796. He then served as its director and agent. Actually, Eddy was the principal advocate of the solitary confinement idea which dominated American penal thinking in the early nineteenth century. He was one of the primary founders of the American penitentiary system and (along with John Griscom*) the New York House of Refuge, which began the tradition of separate institutions for youthful offenders. His advocacy of the penitentiary idea led to the founding of the New York State Prison at Auburn, which used a modified version of the solitary confinement approach, and the Pennsylvania Prison at Cherry Hill, which relied on complete solitary confinement.

He did not confine his efforts to prison reform, however. During the early nineteenth century he was active in a number of other social welfare and reform causes. His memberships included the New York Manumission Society, the Free School Society, the American Bible Society, and the Society for the Reformation of Juvenile Delinquents. Among his other causes were the New York Hospital, efforts to make the treatment of the mentally ill more humane, missionary efforts to the New York Indians, and the establishment of savings banks for the poor. He said of himself in his autobiogrphy: "From early life, all improvements of a pubic nature, that tended to benefit the country or in any shape promote the happiness and welfare of mankind, were considered by me as highly important and claimed my attention.''

Eddy died in New York City on September 16, 1827.

Eddy's major works include *Observations on Canal Navigation* (1810); *Hints for Introducing an Improved Mode of Treating the Insane in the Asylum* (1815); and *An Account of the State Prison or Penitentiary House in the City of New York* (1801).

Major secondary accounts include Samuel L. Knapp, *The Life of Thomas Eddy* (1834; repr. 1976); his obituary in the *New York Mirror*, March 8, 1834; and sketches in the *Dictionary of American Biography* (1931), the *National Cyclopaedia of American Biography* (1893), *Appleton's Cyclopedia of American Biography* (1888), and *Who Was Who in America* (1962). Also see Raymond A. Mohl, *Poverty in New York, 1783–1825* (1971); Robert S. Pickett, *The New York House of Refuge* (1968); Robert S. Mennel, *Thorns and Thistles* (1974); and Joseph M. Hawes, *Children in Urban Societ* (1971).

JOSEPH M. HAWES

**Eliot, Martha May** (April 7, 1891–February 19, 1978), public health advocate, longtime member of the U.S. Children's Bureau and its chief from 1951 to 1956, was born in Dorchester, Massachusetts, to Christopher Rhodes and Mary Jackson (May) Eliot. Her father was a Unitarian clergyman, while T. S. Eliot, the poet, was her first cousin. She attended Winsor High School in the Back Bay section of Boston from 1904 to 1909. A member of Phi Betta Kappa, she received her Bachelor of Arts degree from Radcliffe in 1913. After receiving an M.D. degree from Johns Hopkins University in 1918, she became house officer at Peter Bent Brigham Hospital in Boston. From 1919 to 1920 she was an intern and assistant resident in pediatrics at St. Louis Children's Hospital. She was appointed as an assistant in the Children's Clinic in the Massachusetts General Hospital in Boston from 1920 to 1921.

In 1921 Dr. Edwards A. Park urged her to pursue what he believed to be her real interest, group work, as resident in pediatrics at the New Haven Hospital (Connecticut), where she stayed until 1923. Joining the Yale University School of Medicine in 1923, she advanced from instructor to associate professor in pediatrics. In 1934 she was appointed assistant chief of the U.S. Children's Bureau and devoted her talents to that organization until 1956.

In New Haven, in conjunction with Dr. Park, she made a community investigation of rickets and later conducted the same kind of research in Puerto Rico. Both studies, sponsored by the U.S. Children's Bureau, revealed that sunlight and cod liver oil were the elements that helped to ameliorate rickets in children.

In 1924 Grace Abbott,* chief of the U.S. Children's Bureau, asked Eliot to join its staff as director of the Division of Child and Maternal Health. She accepted the offer and commuted between New Haven and Washington until 1934, when she accepted the position as assistant chief.

When Grace Abbott retired as chief of the Children's Bureau in 1934, Martha Eliot and Katharine Lenroot* were the persons viewed most likely to be her successor. Eliot had the backing of the American Pediatric Society and Josephine* and Pauline Goldmark,* along with that of the National Consumers' League. She probably was viewed as a good choice because she might have been able to resolve some of the difficulties between the Children's Bureau and the Public Health Service. Most of her backers saw her as more of a fighter than Lenroot. Frances Perkins* chose to recommend Katharine Lenroot to President Roosevelt, however, but the Lenroot-Eliot-Abbott friendship remained strong in spite of the tensions. Grace and Edith Abbott* wanted Dr. Eliot to be with Grace whenever possible during her recurring illnesses. She accompanied Grace to the Mayo Clinic in Rochester, Minnesota, in 1932 when she underwent surgery, and was with her in Chicago during her last illness. For years after Grace Abbott died, her sister Edith sent flowers or a telegram to Eliot on Grace's birthday.

When the Social Security Act was still in the embryo stage, Eliot, along with Katharine Lenroot and Grace Abbott, served as a resource person for the Committee on Economic Security. Children were covered by the act primarily because of the efforts of these three. Eliot was obviously concerned about the ways in which the act covered such matters as maternal and child health. When the Social Security Act was passed in 1935, she was given responsibility for administering federal grants-in-aid to the states for developing health services for children and mothers. She also had responsibility for updating the *Infant Care* pamphlet, the most popular of all Children's Bureau publications.

Dr. Eliot became associate chief of the Children's Bureau in 1941 and in the same year was the only woman appointed to a civilian defense committee by President Franklin D. Roosevelt. At the same time, she traveled to England to observe British methods of evacuating children from areas likely to be bombed. In 1942 she voiced a concern for the wives of servicemen who lacked medical care during pregnancy. Congress responded in 1943 with the Emergency Maternal and Infant Care program (EMIC). The wives of servicemen in the lower grades were the ones eligible, and the Children's Bureau was the agency designated to administer the program. A total of more than $125 million was spent, and about 1.5 million women and children were helped before the program ended in 1947. Congress responded to the need primarily to raise morale in the armed forces, but surely Eliot viewed it as a step forward in a broad program of child welfare. Eliot urged that the program be continued after the war, but it was allowed to lapse in 1947.

Like her colleague in the Children's Bureau, Katharine Lenroot, she was interested in the needs of child welfare outside of the United States. In 1935 she attended meetings in Geneva, Switzerland, and of the Child Welfare Committee of the League of Nations Advisory Commission for the Protection and Welfare of Children and Young People. The following year she was appointed by the

Health Organization of the League of Nations to serve with a group to study the problem of nutrition for infants. After World War II, she was vice chairperson of the United States delegation to the International Health Conference of the United Nations. Then, in 1947, she acted as chief medical consultant to the United Nations International Children's Emergency Fund. She traveled to several European countries to study the problem, and the result was the goal of providing at least one good meal a day for 20 million children.

Her involvement in social welfare was enhanced by her expertise in matters involving health. A fellow of the American Medical Association, she also belonged to the American Academy of Pediatrics, the American Pediatric Society, the American Institute of Nutrition, the National Organization for Public Health Nursing, the Society for Research in Child Development, and the National Committee for Mental Hygiene. In 1947 she was elected president of the American Public Health Association at its annual conference in Atlantic City, the first woman to hold that position. The same group honored her in 1964 by establishing an annual award in her name to recognize achievement in maternal and child health. In addition, she was the recipient of the *Parents' Magazine* Medal in 1948 for outstanding service to children and in the same year was given the Lasker Award for her work in organizing the EMIC program during World War II. The *Parents' Magazine* Medal paid tribute to her work in safeguarding the lives of mothers and babies, her contribution to the lives of crippled children, and her suprvision of the program for medical and hospital care for the wives and infants of servicemen.

Dr. Eliot had a great deal to do with the use of social workers in public health programs. She continued to call attention to the problem of juvenile delinquency in the 1950s, as did her predecessor, Katharine Lenroot. She was ever ready to point out the high prenatal and infant mortality rates in the United States, and often compared America's record unfavorably to that of other countries that were doing a better job.

President Harry Truman appointed Eliot as chief of the Children's Bureau in September, 1951. She retired in 1956 to become professor of maternal and child health at Harvard University and held that post until she retired in 1960. She then served as the director of the Massachusetts Committee for Children and Youth until 1971. She died in Cambridge, Massachusetts, on February 19, 1978, and was eulogized at a memorial service held at Harvard University in mid-March.

The Eliot Papers are located at the Schlesinger Library, Radcliffe College, including twenty hours of taped interviews recounting her experiences and accomplishments in the Children's Bureau. Other Papers are in the Children's Bureau holdings of the National Archives. Some of her early publications were *The Control of Rickets: Preliminary Discussion of the Demonstration in New Haven* (1925); with Edwards A. Parks, *The Diseases of Childhood* (1933); and *The Effect of Tropical Sunlight on the Development of Bones of Children in*

*Puerto Rico: A Roentgenograhic and Clinical Study of Infants and Young Children with Special Reference to Rickets and Related Factors.* Her *The Social Security Act and Crippled Children* (1936) further reflects her interests. Katharine F. Lenroot and Martha M. Eliot, "Security for Children," in U.S. Committee on Economic Security, *Social Security in America* (1937), details the Children's Bureau recommendations for including children in the Social Security Act. She was responsible for several revisions of the Children's Bureau publication *Infant Care* (1929, 1932, and 1935). *Current Biography, Who's News and Why* (1948) has an informative article, and obituaries can be found in the *New York Times* (February 23, 1978) and the *Washington Post* (February 19, 1978)

JAMES E. JOHNSON

**Elliott, John Lovejoy** (December 2, 1868–April 12, 1942), Neighborhood Guild organizer, teacher, and leader of the Ethical Culture Society, was born in Princeton, Illinois, the son of a Civil War colonel, Isaac Elliott, and Elizabeth (Denham) Lovejoy, stepdaughter of the antislavery movement martyr Owen Lovejoy. Elliott's parents provided him with strong ideals. They belonged to no religious organizations; rather, their devotion was to the institutions of America—the traditions of freedom and democracy and the ideals of Abraham Lincoln. Their close family friend was Robert Ingersoll, orator and salesman of Darwin, Huxley, Emerson, Susan Anthony, Henry George, Edward Bellamy, and the reform novelists of the nineteenth century. Young Elliott was strongly influenced by the entreaty to do, and to think more broadly than traditional Christianity would allow. Although his youth was rich in ideas and education, provided mostly by his mother, whom he adored and to whom he remained devoted all of her life, his family's farm had little material prosperity. Still, Elliott and his three brothers had the freedom to explore the Illinois countryside on horseback and to dream the dreams of youth.

Somehow, he managed to go to college—at Cornell University in Ithaca, New York. He rose to leadership in his election as class president. More essential to his future, however, was his attendance at Dr. Felix Adler's speech in 1889. It marked his life. Adler's message was that one's religious creed was not what mattered; it was the deeds a person performed and the ethical integrity which motivated them that produced the worthy life. Ethical Culture became Elliott's spiritual home, and Adler, the founder of the Ethical Culture Society, became a lifelong senior partner of Elliott's. Under the auspices of the Society, he was sent to the University of Halle in Germany, where he completed the Ph.D.

Upon his return to New York, Elliott began the career that defined his life: teacher of ethics in the Ethical Culture School, founder and head of the Hudson Guild in New York's Chelsea district, and finally, leader of the Ethical Culture Society after the death of Adler. His myriad activities—committees, chairmanships, commissions, and speaking engagements—grew out of his ethical commitment to "express the sense of the ultimate sacredness in daily living and in the work of the world," as he put it. His close friends among social reformers were Jane Addams,* Paul Kellogg,* Lillian Wald,* Helen Hall,* and Mary Simkhovitch,* and the Fabians Beatrice and Sidney Webb in England. Among the Americans were the leaders of the organizations they founded for social reform and social justice. Elliott was president of the National Federation of Settlements from 1919 to 1923. He never lost his enormous energy to tackle seemingly insurmountable problems or his ability to laugh heartily, especially at himself, as he lived out his seventy-three years in New York's tenement district of Chelsea. His love for children, especially the less gifted and the recalcitrant, was noteworthy. So was his deep appreciation for devoted motherhood evidenced by the long-suffering women of Chelsea and his own mother. Yet he never married, devoting his love and great capacity for friendship to his neighbors from all over the world and all conditions of life.

The Hudson Guild (incorporated in 1896) followed many of the patterns now familiar to students of the social settlement as the social reform mode of the Progressive Era, but which were rather novel when Elliott put them into effect. He provided clubhouse space for boys of all ages, places for recreation and gymnastic activity, the opportunity for mothers to come together to learn better ways of raising their families in the city's environment, and whatever else provided the opportunity for increased community organization and neighborliness. He helped people organize to help themselves in countless public projects. The Cellar Players developed a notable off-Broadway reputation.

Two long-term accomplishments of the Hudson Guild were unique. One was the establishment, in 1912, of a printing school under the tutelage of Arthur Blue. Its apprentice program won the cooperative support of the tightly organized printers' union and the printing houses: unions made two nights a week in class obligatory for apprentices, and the printing houses gave the boys one afternoon a week for training without reducing their wages. Classes covered not only the craft and the history of union organization, but grammar, literature, and economics—the gaps in the boys' educations. When Blue died in 1924, it was the largest printing school in America and a symbol of practical results through education.

The second long-term accomplishment was one which Elliott was destined never to see: it was the building of appropriate housing for the Chelsea neighborhood. At his death, during World War II, new building materials were unavailable, so the Guild sat surrounded by the rubble of demolished tenements. But when the housing was finally completed, it was named in honor of Elliott, its most persistent advocate.

For many years Elliott taught at the innovative Ethical Culture School, founded to provide learning opportunities for the city's less fortunate children, but so rich in its educational theory and practice that the children of the well-to-do were attracted as well. Elliott had a gift for storytelling, centering his tales on pioneer life, American traditions, and Lincoln. His goal was to help young people discover their own ethical ideals and goals for living.

World War I brought a personal test of ideals. Elliott chose to argue in print against militarism, advocating that university presidents from America's most prestigious institutions should disassociate themselves from the government's military summer training camps for college students and work instead for the active teaching of the methods to create a lasting peace. Furthermore, with Roger Baldwin,* L. Hollingsworth Wood, Norman Thomas, Helen Phelps Stokes, and others, he met weekly to develop the work of the Civil Liberties Bureau in defense of conscientious objectors and civil liberties. After the war it became the American Civil Liberties Union.

As a man of seventy, he put himself on the line against another form of oppression: Nazism. Hearing of the arrest of the two leaders of the Ethical Culture movement in Vienna, he secured the appropriate papers and went personally to Berlin to meet with German authorities to negotiate their release. The two leaders and their wives became part of the growing crowd of refugees in New York. Characteristically, Elliott became involved in efforts to ameliorate the many problems the refugees faced. As an attempt to draw together the many, often competing, refugee organizations into an organized effort, he built the Good Neighbor Committee. Active support for his efforts came from (Anna) Eleanor Roosevelt,* who sponsored its conference at Hyde Park.

Elliott remained active, and honored by all of New York, until complications from a cold forced his hospitalization. His last words, uttered on April 12, 1942, while he lay on a New York City hospital bed, proved to be a fitting epitaph for his life: "The only things I have found worth living for, and working for, and dying for," he said, "are love and friendship." He died shortly thereafter at the age of seventy-three.

I know of no manuscript sources for John Lovejoy Elliott. The central way into his ideas and beliefs is through his own words. His essay "University Presidents and the Spirit of Militarism in the United States" is printed in two places: Association for International Conciliation: American Branch, Special Bulletin, New York (August, 1911); and the Standard (May, 1914–May, 1915), 98–191. Three essays expressing the core of his thinking about ethics and social reform are included in studies of the Ethical Culture movement: The Faith of John Lovejoy Elliott: Selections from Addresses and Writings, foreword by Algernon D. Black (1948); "The Relation of the Ethical Ideal to Social Reform," Aspects of Ethical Religion: Essays in Honor of Felix Adler, ed. Horace J. Bridges (1926; repr. 1968); and "Spiritual Discoveries," in The Fiftieth Anniversary of the Ethical Movement: 1876–1926 (1926).

The basic biography is Tay Hohoff, A Ministry to Man: The Life of John Lovejoy Elliott (1959). It is an interpretation of personality and presence, with the facts of Elliott's life and his accomplishments relegated to a secondary position. More focused on the way in which Elliott's life connected with the Ethical Culture movement is Henry Neumann, Spokesmen for Ethical Religion (1951).

MARY ELLEN SCHMIDER

**Epstein, Abraham** (April 20, 1892–May 2, 1942), author and pioneer in the social insurance movement, was born in Luban, Russia (near Pinsk), to Bessie (Levovitz) and Leon Epstein, a poor innkeeper. In poverty and with few opportunities open to Jews in Russia, he immigrated to America in 1910, at age eighteen, and became a citizen in 1917, the same year in which he received a B.S. from the University of Pittsburgh's School of Business Administration. After spending a year in graduate school at the University of Pittsburgh, he became research director of the Pennsylvania Commission on Old Age Pensions. Chief architect of an old-age assistance bill introduced to the Pennsylvania legislature in 1921, he was instrumental in securing passage of a statewide measure two years later. This work made him one of the nation's leading experts on the econmic and social problems people faced in later years. "Poverty in old age can no longer be made impervious by mere hard work, frugality and good habits," he argued in *Facing Old Age* (1922). "Our fortune has become dependent on altogether too many forces beyond our control," he added—a theme he would elaborate in subsequent books, including *The Problem of Old Age Pensions in Industry* (1926) and *The Challenge of the Aged* (1928), as well as in numerous articles he published in the decade's leading periodicals.

Meanwhile, in February, 1925, Epstein married Henrietta Costen, with whom he had one son, Pierre Leon. Two hears later, he founded the American Association for Old Age Security. He changed the name of this organization to the American Association for Social Security (AASS) six years later, in an effort to broaden his crusade for unemployment insurance and aid to the sick. In 1933 he published his best-known work, *Insecurity: A Challenge to America*, which underscored the extent to which workers were threatened by sickness, disability, unemployment, and old-age penury. The book described experiences in other countries. Despite his expertise and tireless lobbying in Washington, Epstein played a relatively minor role in shaping the original Social Security bill. He was ill part of the time; when he did serve as a consultant or expert witness, his style and pungent criticisms won him few supporters among pivotal executive and legislative policy-makers.

Although many officials had been inclined to view Epstein as a crank in 1935, they listened more closely to his advice after Social Security became law. Townsendites and conservative extremists sought to abolish the fledgling system with their radical panaceas. Economists asserted that the recession of 1937 was partly due to the fact that workers were required to pay Federal Insurance Contribution Act (FICA) taxes without getting any immediate benefits from Social Security. "The situation cries for a bold national policy," Epstein warned in "Killing Social Security with Kindness," an article published in the July, 1937, issue of *Harper's Magazine*. "The chief aim of federal aid is to provide more adequately for the *dependent* aged and to establish national standards," he consistently maintained as editor of *Social Security*, the official organ of AASS, and as an activist fighting to ensure the growth of federal programs to benefit workers and their families. Many of his ideas were grafted onto the landmark 1939 amendments, which fundamentally changed the direction and scope of Social Security before the first retirement check was ever distributed. Abraham Epstein died in New York City in May, 1942.

Biographical details on Epstein's life appear in his obituary in the *New York Times*, May 3, 1942, 53; and in W. Andrew Achenbaum, *Old Age in the New Land* (1978), 122. As of 1984, Epstein's widow still had many of his private papers. For good assessments of Epstein's ideas, see Roy Lubove, *The Struggle for Social Security* (1968); and Louis Lenotta, "Abraham Epstein and the Movement for Old Age Security," *Labor History* (Summer, 1975), 364–382. For Epstein's role in shaping the Social Security Act of 1935, see Edwin Witte, *The Development of the Social Security Act* (1963), 82–83; see also the oral histories by J. Douglas Brown and Barbara N. Armstrong in the Columbia University Oral History Collection.

W. ANDREW ACHENBAUM

**Evans, Elizabeth Glendower** (February 28, 1856–December 12, 1937), social reformer whose commitment to social justice encompassed active support of the labor movement, prison reform, woman's suffrage, and the international peace movement, was born in New Rochelle, New York, to Edward and Sophia (Mifflin) Gardiner, both from aristocratic families. A Philadelphia architect, Elizabeth's father moved the family to Texas during the depression of the late 1850s. With his death in 1859, the family moved to Boston, where Elizabeth and four siblings grew up under the shadow of her wealthy paternal grandfather.

Living in a privileged environment, but being a "poor relation" herself, she became sensitized to economic and social differences. By age five, she had developed an affinity for the downtrodden. Privately educated, she was an intellectually curious and physically active youth. From age twelve, she was absorbed with religion, anticipating a career as a missionary until the summer of 1877, when she met Glendower Evans, a Harvard law student who became her husband in 1882. Evans, a religious skeptic, had great impact on Elizabeth's intellectual growth. He shared with her the worlds of philosophy and politics and an awareness of the persistent existence of broad social injustices. After his death in 1886, she gradually ceased involvement with organized religion, assumed the name Elizabeth Glendower Evans, and dedicated herself to the pursuit of social justice.

During her marriage, Mrs. Evans developed intimate friendships with William James and Louis Brandeis, each of whom played a vital role in encouraging her toward reform efforts. Following her husband's death, she became a trustee of the Massachusetts State Reform Schools, where she worked closely with Elizabeth Cabot Putnam. She contributed significantly to a more progressive juvenile penal system during her twenty-eight years of service. It was through these efforts that she came to understand the relationship between delinquency and socioeconomic conditions. Her understanding would later benefit the thinking of Dr. Richard

C. Cabot,* founder of medical social work. In 1891 she was appointed to a committee to inspect Boston's correctional institutions, where her efforts resulted in major institutional reforms.

In 1905 she raised funds for strikers in Haverhill, Massachusetts, beginning her long association with the labor movement. Two years later, she became involved in child labor legislation. Her commitment led her to Georgia and Alabama, where she investigated thirteen cotton mills with the expectation of recruiting support among northern stockholders for protective legislation. She traveled to England in 1908 to study the labor movement and the degree of government responsibility for public welfare. While there, she solidified her socialist ideology and developed lasting friendships with reformers such as Ramsay MacDonald. Returning to America, she attended the Women's Trade Union League convention in Chicago with her friend Florence Kelley,* beginning her involvement in the League. This same year she assumed an active role in supporting the weavers' strike in Roxbury, Massachusetts.

A late supporter of woman's suffrage, she was brought to the movement by her concern for the rights of working-class women and eventually lectured for the National American Woman Suffrage Association. She campaigned with Belle LaFollette in Wisconsin in 1912 and two years later embarked on a four-state tour, speaking sixty-four consecutive days. With the outbreak of war, she combined her interest in woman's suffrage with the cause of world peace. She became a U.S. delegate in 1915 to the International Congress of Women in The Hague, which she attended with her friend, Jane Addams.*

Evans' involvement in women's suffrage became closely tied to her concern for laborers' working conditions. In 1911 the governor of Massachusetts appointed her the only woman to the Minimum Wage Commission. As a strong workers' advocate, she used her appointment to successfully organize a campaign supporting a minimum wage law for women which the state legislature passed in 1912. She also secured the appointment of Mary W. Dewson* as executive secretary to the Commission. Meanwhile, she was attending labor meetings, supporting strikers in the 1912 Lawrence textile strike, and authoring numerous articles. A trip to the Panama Canal in 1914 offered her material for an extensive article on labor conditions there, published in the *Socialist Review*.

Evans' reputation in the labor movement was enhanced through her involvement in the second Lawrence strike (1919), which lasted seventeen weeks. As a Boston socialite, she exerted major influence on the strike's outcome by joining workers on the picket line. Her growing awareness of the need for organized advocacy to protect people's democratic rights spurred her interest in the American Civil Liberties Union; she served as a national director from 1920 to 1937.

Evans played a major part in the lives of Nicola Sacco and Bartolomeo Vanzetti during their incarceration and trial from 1920 to 1927. Her involvement was intimate and consistent, and demonstrated unflinching faith in their innocence and the injustice of the American legal system. She was faithfully in the courtroom each day. She put up Liberty Bonds for their bail, wrote articles of protest proclaiming their innocence, and recruited other supporters, including Felix Frankfurter, H. L. Mencken, and William C. Thompson. Her participation in the Sacco and Vanzetti Defense League helped raise funds for their legal fees. Her belief in them never faltered, and one year after their executions, she spoke at a memorial where she acknowledged that knowing them was one of the great privileges of her life. Deeply disappointed with the American criminal justice system, she nevertheless remained committed to legal and penal reforms.

Evans was a dynamic writer of events appealing to the public's sense of justice and their belief in democratic ideals. She was a prolific author of pamphlets, essays, and editorials; her writings ranged from political, historical, and economic analyses to sketches of such notables as Ramsay MacDonald, Alice Hamilton,* Jessie Hodder,* and Florence Kelley. Her works were published in many newspapers and a variety of magazines, including the *Atlantic Monthly*, *Catholic World*, the *New Republic*, and the *Socialist Review*. She was contributing editor for *LaFollette's Weekly* for twenty-four years.

In 1933 Elizabeth Glendower Evans was awarded the Ford Hall Forum Medal for distinguished service to human welfare. She lived her remaining years in semi-retirement. Throughout her life, she poured her time, energy, and personal inheritance into advocacy for the poor, the underprivileged, and the incarcerated. She died in 1937 at the age of eighty-one in Brookline, Massachusetts.

Elizabeth Glendower (Gardiner) Evans (1856–1937) Papers, Schlesinger Library, Radcliffe College, available on microfilm, are the major source of information. The papers include correspondence, diaries, writings, and speaking notes concerning Evans as well as articles and speeches about her.

In addition to numerous articles (1909–1935) in *LaFollette's Weekly* (later the *Progressive*), Evans' principal writings incude "The Roxbury Carpet Factory Strike," *Survey* (May 24, 1910), 337–338; "The Parable of Panama," *Socialist Review* (July-September, 1914); "Woman's Party—Right or Wrong?: The Woman's Party Is Wrong," *New Republic* (September 26, 1923), 123–124; "Sacco and Vanzetti," *Survey* (June 15, 1926), 364–365; "William James and His Wife," *Atlantic Monthly* (September, 1929), 374–387; "Ramsay MacDonald," *Atlantic Monthly* (October, 1929), 536–544; and "Mr. Justice Brandeis," *Survey* (November 1, 1931), 138–141.

Brief biographical essays of Evans appear in *Biographical Encyclopedia of American Women*, the *New York Times* (obituary), Dec. 13, 1937, *Notable American Women* (1971), and *Who Was Who in America* (1968). No book-length treatment of Evans is available. However, the following books have useful information: Ida Cannon, *On the Social Frontier of Medicine* (1952), about her contribution to the social aspects of delinquency; Marion D. Frankfurter, *The Letters of Sacco and Vanzetti* (1928), with letters written to and from Evans; Josephine Goldmark, *Impatient Crusader* (1953), on the life of Florence Kelley, with Evans' involvement in the Women's Trade Union League and the Minimum

Wage Commission; Louis Joughlin, *The Legacy of Sacco and Vanzetti* (1948), on her relationship to the case; and Alfred Lief, *Brandeis* (1936), about their friendship and her board appointments.

PAMELA A. BROWN

# F

**Falconer, Martha Platt** (March 17, 1862–November 26, 1941), social worker and pioneer in the area of juvenile corrections and rehabilitation for girls, was born in Delaware, Ohio, the last of seven children born to Cyrus Platt, an optician and a jeweler, and Helen (Hulme) Platt, a housewife who died in 1877, when Martha was fifteen years of age. Martha, who had Quaker roots, then lived with an older sister in Philadelphia, where she attended a Quaker school. She later moved to Topeka, Kansas, to live with another sister, and it was there, on March 21, 1885, that she married Cyrus Falconer, an employee of the Santa Fe Railroad. A daughter, Helen, was born in Topeka.

In 1888 the family moved to Oak Park, Illinois, a suburb of Chicago, where two sons subsequently were born—Douglas Platt and Cyrus. While in Chicago, Martha Falconer began what was to be a long and distinguished career in the emerging field of social work. Impelled by her religious convictions, and dressed in plain Quaker garb, she first volunteered her time as a teacher at Chicago Commons, the settlement house in Chicago's Seventeenth Ward, an area populated by people of European and Scandinvian origins and characterized by its poor housing, sanitation, and schools. While working under the expert leadership of the settlement's founder, Graham Taylor,* Falconer's awareness of deep human needs, the stifling social conditions, and her strategies for helping began to coalesce.

In 1898, after separating from her husband and needing gainful employment, Falconer worked with Dr. Hastings Hart* of the Illinois Children's Home and Aid Society. In this progressive child welfare agency she learned about and became involved in the area of juvenile corrections as a field worker, with child placement and probation cases. She later was appointed assistant superintendent and gained executive and administrative experience in that role.

Meanwhile, she had become an active member of the Chicago Woman's Club, a philanthropic organization of long standing known for its work in improving conditions in local jails, police stations, and the Cook County Poorhouse. As early as 1892, this group of civic-minded women became concerned about children being incarcerated with hardened adult criminals, and began working for the creation of a separate system to deal with juvenile delinquents. They were instrumental, along with others, especially those involved with Chicago's settlement houses, in establishing in 1899 the Cook County Juvenile Court—the nation's first, one which provided a special judge, separate hearings, and probation. Under the auspices of the Chicago Woman's Club, Falconer served under Judge Julian Mack* as one of the court's first probation officers. Here her involvement and interest in juvenile delinquency reform, especially for girls, intensified, and she also became acquainted with such prominent social reformers as Jane Addams,* Florence Kelley,* and Julia Lathrop.*

In January, 1906, Falconer began a new and important phase of her life and work. Having been recommended by Dr. Hart and Judge Mack, she moved to Philadelphia to assume the directorship of the Girls' Department of the Philadelphia House of Refuge, a penal institution for girls. This private corporation, founded in 1828, was funded jointly by private and public funds. It was there that she began the impressive efforts at reform in juvenile correction facilities that led the way for other programs across the country. Seeing the offenses for which the girls were committed as being the result of physical and moral neglect, lack of schooling, and inadequate mothering rather than personal shortcomings, Falconer transformed the Philadelphia House of Refuge from a punitive, custodial penal institution into a model rehabilitation program providing more humane treatment, home-like atmosphere, education, and training for productive living. A staunch advocate of prevention, she supported measures which would safeguard the home and thus, it was hoped, make commitment unnecessary.

She was strongly influenced in her philosophy and practice by her attendance at the Conference for the Care of Dependent Children, (the first White House Conference on Dependent Children, held in January, 1909); many of the conclusions reached by the group of 200 pioneers in the child welfare field inspired her subsequent thinking and endeavors. Among the themes that emerged from the conference were the need for prevention of dependency and delinquency; a commitment to care for children in their own homes whenever possible; advocacy for the cottage system rather than large custodial arrangements in residential institutions; the establishment of rudimentary standards in these institutions; and the need for accurate and complete keeping of case records.

Under her able leadership the Girls' Department was moved in 1910 to the suburb of Darling, Pennsylvania, a country setting already occupied by the boys' division. The dual facility was officially named Glen Mills School, but the girls' facility became known informally as Sleighton Farm. It was physically arranged around the main farmhouse building, utilizing the then-modern "cottage plan." In an extensive research study published in 1929, Sleighton Farm was frequently cited for its progressive program. One of the precedents established by Falconer was the hiring of young female college graduates as matrons and staff members to work with the girls, instead of the common practice of hiring older women experienced in custodial and punitive approaches. Falconer felt that younger women would better be able to relate to the girls and that they also would provide them with role models in functional living. This practice served as an example for other girls' facilities and also served to inspire many of these young graduates to enter the field of social work.

During her twelve years as superintendent, Sleighton Farm provided a program of rehabilitation including academics, medical care, recreation, and skills and training for daily living, as well as cultural, social, moral, and religious education. Another of her forward-thinking innovations, one which spread to other institutions, was the establishment of a student government system wherein the girls carried much of the responsiblity for the daily discipline and management of their cottage. Due to Martha Falconer's earnest commitment to incorporate the best of the then-known theories of juvenile rehabilitation, Sleighton Farm became one of the most advanced training schools for girls in the country.

Active on other levels as well, Falconer was known for her advocacy of careful case study before commitment, and for the separation of the "feebleminded" from the delinquent population. She helped in the establishment of the Philadelphia Training School of Social Work and in 1915 served as the chairperson of the Committee on Social Hygiene of the National Conference of Charities and Correction. During World War I she took a leave of absence from Sleighton Farm to head the federal Commission on Training Camp Activities, which administered a large fund to develop plans for the care of delinquent girls and women who found their way to the military camps as prostitutes.

In 1919 she began the next phase in her career by becoming the director of the Department of Protective Social Measures of the American Social Hygiene Association in New York. In this role she addressed international conferences in Europe and toured institutions in Europe and England. In 1924 she accepted the position of executive secretary of the Federation Caring for the Protestant Children in New York City (later known as the New York Federation of Protestant Welfare Agencies). She retired in 1927 at the age of sixty-five, but continued to serve as a consultant to institutions and agencies dealing with delinquent girls and women, and in 1928 was the New York delegate to the International Conference of Social Work in Paris.

In the 1930s, Falconer—whose career followed a distinguished path from volunteer to international figure as a leader and innovator in the field of corrections, especially for young girls and women—lived with her daughter in Buffalo, New York; and in 1938 she began living with her son in East Aurora, New York, where she died on November 26, 1941, of a heart attack.

More detailed biographical information may be found in Emma O. Lundberg's *Unto the Least of These: Social Services for Childre* (1947), 255–258, where Falconer is highlighted as one of the leading reformers of "The Middle Period." Also see information from twenty-two years of personal association, a two-day interview, and information from relatives and acquaintances, reported by Mary Dewees in *Notable American Women*, (1971), 594–596.

Obituary articles in *Social Services Review* (March, 1942) and from *Survey Midmonthly* (December, 1941) succinctly note her major accomplishments and contributions.

Although Falconer is not mentioned directly, her involvement can be safely inferred from background information about the development of the Chicago Juvenile Court and the role of the Chicago Woman's Club found in the chapter entitled "The Background of the Juvenile Court in Illinois" by Julia Lathrop in *The Child, the Clinic, and the Court* (1925), ed. J. Addams, C. J. Herrick, A. L. Jacoby, *et al.*, 290–297.

The recommendations to the President of the United States from the delegates of the first White House Conference on Child Welfare can be found in the *Proceedings of the Conference on the Care of Dependent Children, 1909* (1909) 192–197. These proceedings can also be found in *Children and Youth in America: A Documentary History. Vol. 2, 1866–1932, Parts 1–6*, ed. Robert H. Bremmer (1971), 364–369. Also, the significance of this conference is highlighted in Dorothy Zietz, *Child Welfare: Services and Perspectives*, 2nd ed. (1969).

An extensive research study done by Margaret Reeves, sponsored by the Russell Sage Foundation in 1925 and published in 1929, is entitled *Training Schools for Delinquent Girls*. Sleighton Farm was one of fifty-two such institutions studied in detail. Falconer's innovative programs instituted earlier are noted, and the results in general cite Sleighton Farm to be one of the most progressive.

BETTY G. DAWSON

**Farrand, Livingston** (June 14, 1867–November 8, 1939), anthropologist, public health administrator, and university president, was born in Newark, New Jersey, the third of four sons of Samuel Ashbel and Louise (Wilson) Farrand. Descended from a Huguenot forebear who had come to this country in the mid-seventeenth century, Farrand attended the Newark Academy, where his father was headmaster. He received his undergraduate degree from Princeton University in 1888 and his M.D. from Columbia University's College of Physicians and Surgeons three years later. Unattracted by the practice of medicine, he went on to study physiological psychology at Cambridge, England, and Berlin. He was appointed instructor in psychology at Columbia in 1893, was promoted to adjunct professor in 1901, and served as secretary of the American Psychological Association from 1895 to 1903. From the start, however, he was strongly interested in anthropology. After doing field work with Franz Boas studying the Indians of the Pacific Northwest, he was named professor of anthropology in 1903. The following year, he contributed the volume on the Indians—*Basis of American History, 1500–1900*—to the American Nation series.

Although Farrand continued to teach anthropology at Columbia until 1914, the major focus of his interests shifted to the field of public health. In January, 1905, he became executive secretary of the National Association for the Study and Prevention of Tuberculosis. The Association had been founded the preceding year by a group of socially minded physicians and laymen in the conviction that the spread of public knowledge about the disease—then the leading cause of death throughout the world—was the key to its ultimate control. During Farrand's nine years as executive secretary, the Association provided the catalyst for the formation of affiliated groups across the country, for organized campaigns at the state and local levels pushing for the adoption of preventive measures and mandatory reporting requirements, and for expansion of treatment facilities. The result was dramatic reductions in the incidence of the disease along with improved survival rates for those afflicted. In the process, the Association became the model for similar voluntary organizations dedicated to the eradication of a growing list of diseases.

Active in the work of the American Public Health Association, Farrand served as its treasurer and as editor of the *American Journal of Public Health* from 1912 to 1914. In 1914 he accepted the presidency of the University of Colorado. His major achievement was winning legislative approval of a new tax levy that would make possible substantial expansion of the university's physical plant. In 1917, however, Farrand took a leave of absence to chair the special commission sent to France by the International Health Board of the Rockefeller Foundation to counter the wartime spread of tuberculosis. In his antituberculosis work, Farrand had forged close ties with the American Red Cross, and in 1919 he resigned from Colorado to become its executive head (chairman of the central committee). Before its mushroom growth during the war, the Red Cross had existed largely as a skeletal organization for the provision of relief in emergencies. Under Farrand's leadership, the Red Cross continued the foreign civilian relief efforts begun before his appointment. More important, he laid the basis for its assuming a new and larger domestic peacetime role. He pushed forward its transformation from an organization relying primarily upon volunteers to one manned by a paid, full-time professional staff; he broadened the scope of its concerns beyond disaster aid to include promotion of public health and social welfare; an expanded nursing program; establishment of community health centers; rural hygiene efforts; campaigns against tuberculosis, venereal diseases, and mental illness; and institution of family welfare services. And he was instrumental in the formation of the National Health Council, serving as its first president.

In 1921 Farrand resigned his Red Cross position to assume the presidency of Cornell University. But he continued to be involved in the public health area. As a member of the technical board of the Milbank Memorial Fund, he was influential in planning the Fund's New York health demonstration projects to promote the establishment of district health centers. In 1930 Governor Franklin D. Roosevelt appointed him chairman of a special public health commission; from 1932 until his death he was a member of the state's Public Health Council. As president of Cornell, his major accomplishment was the joining of Cornell Medical College with New York Hospital to form a major new medical center. Otherwise, his tenure there was a disappointment. In part, Cornell's relative decline in stature was due to financial difficulties resulting from the Great

Depression, which hit Cornell harder than most major private universities. In part, however, Farrand himself lacked—or at least was unable to implement effectively—any clear-cut sense of educational purpose and direction. He retired in 1937 and died two years later in New York City.

The Livingston Farrand Papers are located in the Collection of Regional History, Cornell University Library. The major source of biographical information is the entry written by Paul W. Gates in the *Dictionary of American Biography,* Supplement 2 (1958), 176–178. Additional sources of information include, re Farrand's Columbia years: Sally Falk Moore, ''The Department of Anthropology,'' in R. Gordon Hoxie et al., *A History of the Faculty of Political Science, Columbia University* (1955); the Tuberculosis Association: Richard H. Shryock, *National Tuberculosis Association, 1904–1954* (1957); the Red Cross: Foster R. Dulles, *The American Red Cross: A History* (1950); the Milbank Memorial Fund: John Duffy, *A History of Public Health in New York City, 1866–1966* (1974); University of Colorado: Frederick S. Allen et al., *The University of Colorado, 1876–1976* (1976); and Cornell: Morris Bishop, *A History of Cornell* (1962).

JOHN BRAEMAN

**Fernald, Walter Elmore** (February 11, 1859–November 27, 1924), physician, social scientist, diagnostician, educator, and creator of programs for the feebleminded, was born in Kittery, Maine, the son of Margaret F. and William Fernald, a bridge builder for the Boston and Maine Railroad. Both parents were of old New England lineage. Walter Fernald attended public shool in Maine and then preparatory school in New Hampshire—the New Hampden Literary Institution. He then attended the Medical School of Maine, where he received his M.D. in 1881.

Fernald began his career as the assistant phsycian at the State Insane Hospital in Mendota, Wisconsin (1882–1887), where he gained experience working with the mentally handicapped. In 1887, the year he married Kate M. Nolan of Janesville, Wisconsin, with whom he had two children (Helen Fernald and Thomas), he moved to Massachusetts to become the first resident superintendent at the State School for the Feeble-Minded in its new facility in Waverley, Massachusetts (now Waltham). He remained there for forty-two years, until 1929. As part of his new role, Fernald directed the farm school at Templeton, Massachusetts, an enterprise which later was to become part of a larger program of colonies in which older retarded people were trained to have employable skills and be partially self-sufficient. Fernald also built a large library on the mentally defective. The physical plant, (whose actual building he supervised), the programs he instigated, and the library he built resulted in the school becoming an international model to which many interested in mental retardation flocked.

Like many of his contemporaries, Fernald embraced social science as a means by which to correctly diagnose and treat the socially dependent, especially the mentally deficient. He applied new scientific postulates to his own research and devised a method to diagnose, treat, and educate the feebleminded according to the seeming capacity of each. As part of this educational program, he standardized manual labor according to individual capacity.

Fernald's discomfort with the use of Henry H. Goddard's* adaptation of the Binet-Simon psychological test as the sole evaluative measure for diagnosis led to his devising a more comprehensive evaluation: "The Ten Fields of Inquiry," intended to draw a more comprehensive picture of the patient. In addition to his scientific research, Fernald was a prolific writer and published more than twenty articles dealing with the treatment of the feebleminded. Two of his most famous articles were "Standardized Fields of Inquiry for Clinical Studies of Borderline Defectives" (1919) and, with colleagues E. E. Southard and Annie Taft, "The Waverly Researches." All of his articles voiced his belief that scientific reasoning could result in appropriate treatment for the feebleminded.

Fernald also was actively involved in the diagnosis and treatment of the delinquent. He visited Massachusetts reform schools to test delinquents and suggest appropriate care for those he relabeled defective delinquents. He had many of these transferred to the Massachusetts School for the Feeble-Minded. Along with Judge Harvey Baker, the first judge of the Massachusetts Juvenile Court, he wrote a fostering and saving code to be enacted in a separate juvenile court. Subsequently, he worked on a legislative committee to determine correct treatment for adult offenders.

Fernald extended his work to the public schools, where he set up clinics to try to detect retarded children. He then worked with their parents and teachers in an effort to develop a comprehensive way to help them. He also was involved in developing teacher training programs for those working with these children. In recognition of his work with practitioners and students, Fernald was invited to teach at both Tufts University Medical School and the Harvard Graduate School of Education, where he was granted an honorary M.A.

Fernald held prominent positions in a multitude of social scientific organizations. He was nominated president of the Massachusetts School of Psychiatry, the National Society of Mental Health, the Boston School for Occupational Therapy, the American Association for the Study of the Feeble-Minded (twice), and the New England School of Psychiatry. He also was vice president of the Massachusetts Eugenics Society.

Although a leader in the eugenics movement, he opposed sterilization, advocated by many of his colleagues, and supported full supervised custody instead. Later he helped develop laws which created provisions for the registration and care of the feebleminded. These laws also allowed some of the feebleminded to live independently of an institution, but under carefully supervised probation.

Although the eugenics movement has been debunked, much of Fernald's work is still regaraded as a significant contribution to the care of the retarded. Soon after his death, the Massachusetts School for the Feeble-Minded was renamed the Walter E. Fernald State School in his honor. It is still in operation. He died at the school, in Waverly, Massachusetts, on November 27, 1929, at age seventy-five.

Fernald's unpublished correspondence is housed at the Walter E. Fernald State School. The school library also houses Fernald's public lectures, handwritten case records, and annotated photographs of inmates. There are also teaching books of teachers at the school, and scrapbooks containing important news clippings, especially on the eugenics movement. Published documents of superintendents' reports are also in the school library.

Most of the important writings of Fernald are contained in a memorial volume of the *Bulletin of the Massachusetts Department of Mental Diseases*, April, 1930. The bibliography is very extensive, but references to his work can be obtained, arranged by years, in the *Bulletin of the Massachusetts Department of Mental Diseases*, pp. 246–258.

Secondary sources include the following: Robert C. Bannister, *Social Darwinism: Science and Myth in Anglo-American Social Thought* (1979); Barbara M. Brenzel, *Daughters of the State: A Social Portrait of the First Reform School for Girls in North America 1856–1905* (1983); Allan Chase, *The Legacy of Malthus: The Social Costs of the New Scientific Racism* (1975); Mark H. Haller, *Eugenics: Hereditarian Attitudes in American Thought* (1963); and Walter I. Trattner, *From Poor Law to Welfare State: A History of Social Welfare in America* (1974).

Fernald's literary biography can be found in the *Bulletin of the Massachusetts Department of Mental Diseases* (1930)

BARBARA M. BRENZEL

**Finley, John Huston** (October 19, 1863–March 7, 1940), welfare administrator, editor, and educator, was born in Grand Ridge, Illinois, in the north central part of the state, to James Gibson Finley and the former Lydia Margaret McCombs. He attended Knox College in Galesburg, Illinois, from which he received his A.B. degree in 1887. Two years of private study at Johns Hopkins University followed. On June 29, 1892, Finley married Martha Ford Boyden, who bore him four children, Ellen Boyden, Margaret Boyden, Robert Lawrence, and John Huston.

John Finley was a man of many careers, all of them successful. His significance to the history of social welfare in America came early, however, during the two or three years immediately after college which he spent as secretary of the New York State Charities Aid Association (NYSCAA) and, for a while, as editor of the newly created *Charities Review*, the official publication of the New York Charity Organization Society. During this period (1889–1892), brief as it was, Finley displayed great energy and leadership in the emerging field of social work, especially child welfare.

Under his dynamic leadership, extolled as "brilliant" by Frank J. Bruno, the

NYSCAA, founded in 1872 by the redoubtable Louisa Lee Schuyler,* was reinvigorated. During his first year with the Association, Finley not only visited numerous county poorhouses, insane asylums, children's homes, and other public welfare institutions, but also found time to establish and edit a monthly publication (the *Record*), a level of activity he apparently maintained throughout the remainder of his tenure with that organization. Furthermore, his annual reports were models of their kind. They represented a genuine concern for the helpless and a scorn for those he believed to be shirking their proper responsbilities, private citizens and public officials alike.

Finley quickly moved into national prominence, as was evidenced by his invitation to address the National Conference of Charities and Correction in 1890, at which time he called for the development of a volunteer service to join the struggle against need—a precursor to the social work profession. Finley's major address at the 1891 conference, however, was to have much greater significance. There, he spoke on "The Child Problem in the Cities," a subject which, judging from his annual reports to the Association, was of increasing concern to him and his organization. He was alarmed by the practice of confining child offenders in prisons with adult criminals. He also was troubled by faulty urban conditions which, unless remedied, he warned, would produce even greater numbers of delinquents and serious threats to society. Aware of the efforts of Charles Loring Brace* to deal with these problems by removing destitute and delinquent children from the city and its penal institutions, Finley believed that more along those lines had to be done. Thus he called for the "boarding out," or, in effect, carefully planned foster home placement, of needy children, a device which he claimed had been very successful wherever it had been tried.

One of the places where it had been successfully utilized was in Philadelphia, where, under the leadership of Homer Folks,* the Children's Aid Society of Pennsylvania had been engaged in that practice for some time. Accordingly, Finley had invited Folks to speak to the National Conference about his experiences in placing out both destitute and delinquent youngsters. Thus was launched one of social welfare's most illustrious careers, especially when a year later Finley left New York and charities work for a career as an educator and editor and was succeeded at the State Charities Aid Association by Folks.

In 1892, at age twenty-nine, Finley became president of his alma mater, Knox College. In 1899 he became editor of *Harper's Weekly*, and then in 1903 assumed the presidency of the City College of New York. From 1913 to 1921 he would be Commissioner of Education for New York State, and from 1921 to 1938 editor of the *New York Times*. His eminence in these and related fields was indicated by the bestowal upon him of no less than thirty-two honorary degrees by colleges and universities throughout America. He was also called upon by governments and private agencies throughout the world to lead many inquiries and to organize programs of education and relief, for which he received numerous additional awards and decorations.

When Finley died in New York City on March 7, 1940, the mourning was for that of a major statesman; Mayor Fiorello La Guardia ordered flags flown at half mast, the *New York Times* published a full-page obituary with a black-bordered photograph, and for months tributes poured in extolling his many accomplishments in a wide variety of fields.

Finley's publications fill three pages in the *National Union Catalog*. In addition to his writings on social welfare which appeared in the publications of the New York State Charities Aid Association and the *Proceedings* of the National Conference of Charities and Correction, his most significant books were: with Richard T. Ely, *Taxation in American Cities and States* (1889); with John F. Sanderson, *The American Executive and Excutive Methods* (1908); *The French in the Heart of America* (1915); *A Pilgrim in Palestine* (1919); and *The Mystery of the Mind's Desire* (1936).

Other useful sources of information on Finley are the many tributes to him published in the *New York Times* in the months following his death (as well as the obituary that appeared at the time he passed away). The best single sketch of his life, however, is by Harry J. Carman in the second supplement to the *Dictionary of American Biography* (1958). For other references to Finley, especially his contributions to social welfare, see Frank J. Bruno, *Trends in Social Work, 1874–1956* (1957); Walter I. Trattner, *Homer Folks: Pioneer in Social Welfare* (1968); and Savel Zimand, ed., *Public Health and Welfare* (1958).

MILTON D. SPEIZMAN

**Fitch, John Andrews** (April 20, 1881–June 15, 1959), editor, writer, teacher, labor economist, and labor relations theorist, was born in Cumberland, Wisconsin, the son of Edwin P. Fitch and Elizabeth (Powers) Fitch. He was graduated from Yankton College (South Dakota) in 1904 with a B.A. degree and taught for two years as an instructor of history and civics at Weeping Water Academy (Nebraska) before beginning graduate study at the University of Wisconsin. As a student of John R. Commons,* Fitch joined the staff of the Pittsburgh Survey in 1907. He spent most of a year studying working conditions in western Pennsylvania steel mills in preparation for *The Steel Workers* (1910).

This book was the beginning of a lifelong search for a theoretical yet practical solution to the "labor problem," that ongoing confrontation between capital and labor that had threatened the national tranquility since the 1877 railroad strike. One solution, Fitch believed, was to convince the public that the average steelworker was no boorish brute but a thoughtful, intelligent person whose voice has been silenced by company repression and dispersed along with the Amalgamated Association of Iron and Steel Workers. One function of the Pittsburgh Survey, Fitch believed, was to speak for the workers when they could not speak for themselves.

Fitch's second Progressive Era solution to the labor problem derived from a theory of power that may well have been rooted in a Protestant conception of sin. As Fitch understood economic history, the rapid industrialization of the late nineteenth century had created two great blocs of power—capital and labor—each easily and inevitably corrupted. As a result of the Homestead strike (1892) and economic concentration (1901), the steel industry was left with only one such bloc, and the temptation to corruption was that much greater. Thus Fitch analyzed the twelve-hour day, the speed-up, the stunted home life of the working class, and the atmosphere of censorhip and suspicion that permeated the mill as the product of management's desire for absolute control of every facet of mill operations. Recent scholars have been especially receptive to Fitch's argument that automation and promotion systems were designed less to make the steel mills more efficient than to reduce the power and increase control of the workers.

While some theorists of the labor problem argued the need for government intervention or advocated big labor as a counterpoise to big business, Fitch did neither. Though he acknowledged the existence of an inherent conflict of interest between capital and labor, Fitch believed that the basis for industrial harmony existed in the shared desire of capital and labor for increased productivity and overall prosperity. It was, he insisted, possible to decrease labor costs, raise wages, and increase production—simultaneously.

His work with the Pittsburgh Survey completed, Fitch took a position with the New York State Department of Labor (1909–1910) and, on September 1, 1909, married Florence Lee. They had two daughters, Faith Lee Fitch and Jean Andrews Fitch. From 1911 through 1919 Fitch was editor of and regular contributor to the Industrial Department of Paul U. Kellogg's* *Survey* magazine, an organ of middle-class social reform.

Fitch's seminal contribution to social welfare history was to publicize the issue of the twelve-hour day. He had first revealed the problem for the Pittsburgh Survey. In 1911 and 1912 Fitch found himself allied with Kellogg and U.S Steel stockholder Charles M. Cabot in an attempt to eliminate the twelve-hour day in that firm's operations through an appeal to other stockholders. In a report written for Cabot and based on field work in the steel communities, Fitch claimed that the twelve-hour day was more harmful socially than physically. Its most important result was a worker who lacked the time and the inclination to participate meaningfully in the church, the family, politics, and the ideology of social mobility. During the steel strike of 1919, Fitch again took to the field to study the hours issue for the *Survey*. In spite of his efforts, the twelve-hour day was not eliminated industry-wide until 1923.

Fitch joined the faculty of the New York School of Social Work in 1917 and taught labor problems and social legislation until his retirement in 1946. As a teacher, he was known for allegiance to facts and intellectual integrity.

Much earlier, however—by the mid-1920s—Fitch no longer was convinced that working conditions were a primary cause of the labor problem. In *The Causes of Industrial Unrest* (1924), he focused on the decline of the craft system and the implications of that decline for the spiritual and emotional life of the worker. Fitch joined liberal employers such as Boston department store owner Edward A. Filene in advocating a more participatory work environment, in which employees would help make decisions involving production and labor relations. Fitch also became increasingly interested in personnel administration and especially vocational guidance, a field he idealized as a form of social work that served the needs of the corporate world without sacrificing individualism. In 1931 Fitch helped form the People's Lobby, an *ad hoc* reform coalition chaired by John Dewey that called for direct federal relief, public works, and unemployment insurance.

Although Fitch believed that unions could serve as one source of the participatory environment he envisioned, he never felt completly comfortable with the union idea. He believed that unions, no less than employers, were subject to the corrupting influence of power, and his writings reveal a concern with union excesses. His last book, published in 1957, was critical of organized labor for its failure to live up to its social responsibilities. Fitch served as the public's representative on many labor arbitration boards. He died in New York City on June 15, 1959.

There is no collection of Fitch manuscripts. Fitch correspondence may be found in the Paul Underwood Kellogg Papers and in the Survey Associates Records, both in the Social Welfare History Archives of the University of Minnesota, Minneapolis. Additional material may be found in the United States Steel Corporation Library, New York City.

In addition to his many articles in the *Survey*, *American Magazine*, and other journals, Fitch authored five books and several pamphlets. The books include *Social Responsbilities of Organized Labor* (1957) and *Vocational Guidance in Action* (1935).

A brief biography can be found in *Who Was Who in America*, vol. 3 (1966), 285; An obituary appeared in the *New York Times*, June 17, 1959, 35. Secondary works that treat Fitch include Gerald G. Eggert, *Steelmasters and Labor Reform, 1886–1923* (1981); Katherine Stone, "The Origins of Job Structures in the Steel Industry," *Review of Radical Political Economics* (Summer, 1974), 113–173; Charles Hill, "Fighting the Twelve-Hour Day in the American Steel Industry," *Labor History* (Winter, 1974), 19–3; and Steven Roy Cohen, "Reconciling Industrial Conflict and Democracy: The 'Pittsburgh Survey' and the Growth of Social Research in the United States," Ph.D. dissertation, Columbia University, 1981.

WILLIAM GRAEBNER

**Fletcher, Alice Cunningham** (March 15, 1838–April 6, 1923), Indian welfare activist and anthropologist, was born in Havana, Cuba, where her parents, Lucia Adeline (Jenks) and Thomas Gilman Fletcher, an attorney, had journeyed from their New York City home seeking to improve her father's health. He died before Fletcher was two years old. Her mother returned to New York, where Fletcher was educated. She supported herself as an adult by teaching and public lecturing. Concerned with women's issues, she joined Sorosis, helped found the Association for the Advancement of Women in 1873, and was active in temperance and antitobacco efforts.

Fletcher's anthropological interests began with avocational archeology during the 1870s, working with Frederic Ward Putnam of the Harvard Peabody Museum. In 1880 she met Thomas Tibbles, an Indian rights activist, and Susette La Flesche, an educated Omaha woman he married. The meeting turned Fletcher's attention to ethnology. In 1881 she traveled to the Omaha Reservation in Nebraska and then set out on a strenuous camping trip with the Tibbles to the Rosebud Sioux Reservation in South Dakota. She was appalled by reservation living conditions and saw Indian Bureau paternalism as an assault on human dignity.

Returning to the Omaha, she found the tribe fearful that they might lose their land. Determined to help, Fletcher settled on a policy already promoted by many Whites concerned about Indians. She helped to design and then lobbied for the Omaha Allotment Act of 1882 and for the General Indian Allotment Act of 1887. Allotment provided 160 acres to family heads and smaller plots for individuals. After allotments were made, remaining reservation land was opened to public sale, the proceeds being used to start the Indians out as farmers. Allotments were to be tax free and inalienable for twenty-five years, after which the owners would be granted fee patents and citizenship. The legislation was soon amended to reduce the time for "competent" Indians, empowering them to sell their land.

Fletcher's Omaha work led to her employment by the Indian Bureau. In 1883 she was appointed allotting agent to the Omaha, assisted by Francis La Flesche, who became her associate in subsequent ethnological research and, in effect, her adopted son. In 1884 Fletcher was in charge of the Indian Bureau exhibit at the New Orleans Exposition. She completed a massive government report, "Indian Education and Civilization," in 1885, and the next year was sent on a tour of Indian communities, including the Eskimo and Aleut in Alaska.

Fletcher served as allotting agent to the Nebraska Winnebago, 1887–1888, and to the Nez Perce in Idaho, 1889–1892. She personally examined each allotment to be sure that the Indians got the best reservation land, a hard task in the rugged Nez Perce country, where the Indian people, unlike the Omaha and Winnebago, were hostile to allotment. Fletcher was a small woman, by then in her fifties and lamed by rheumatism, but she possessed enormous energy and iron conviction that allotment would benefit Indians. Lauded by such fervid reformist groups as the Annual Conference of Friends of the Indian at Lake Mohonk, New York, and the Indian Rights Association of Philadelphia, Fletcher ignored the anthropologically perceptive counsel of her friend Putnam, who questioned forcing civilization on the Indians. She confined communications with Putnam to apologies that she could not afford to pursue ethnology on a full-time basis.

The allotment policy soon proved disastrous and remains the underlying reason for the poverty on many reservations. Its failure can be traced to faulty assumptions. First, it relied simplistically on Lewis Henry Morgan's theory that societies evolve unilineally from savagery through barbarism to civilization; allotment was believed to hasten and smooth the Indians' way to the inevitable by providing private property. (Morgan himself opposed allotment, recognizing that unscrupulous Whites could manipulate it to the Indians' detriment.) Second, it was based on idealization of the small, diversified family farm, which already was being threatened in the 1880s by the trend to large, specialized agricultural enterprises as a response to growing urban markets, railroad expansion to carry produce, and the mechanization of farming itself. Most serious was the miscalculation of Indian demography. Tribal ranks had thinned alarmingly during the nineteenth century, and survivors were expected to vanish into the general population, but by 1900 the Indian population stabilized and increased steadily thereafter.

The Indians could not augment their land base, and their allotments were subject to American laws of inheritance, resulting in more and more heirs owing ever smaller parcels of land. The Indian Bureau's solution was to lease acreage to Whites for large-scale operations and distribute rent proceeds to the Indians. With the issuing of fee patents, Indians were subject to outrageous trickery to sell their land. Economic development on the reservations is impeded by the now fragmented resource base.

After the Nez Perce assignment, Fletcher could turn her full attention to anthropology, thanks to an endowment established for her by Mary Copley Thaw, a Philadelphia philanthropist. She made enduring contributions in her publications on the Omaha and other tribes, pioneered the study of Indian music, and was active in anthropological organizations. In her last years she resumed archeological interests. She died at her Washington, D.C., home, tended in her final illness by Francis La Flesche.

Major manuscript sources are Fletcher's personal papers and those of Francis La Flesche in the National Anthropological Archives, Smithsonian Institution; the F. W. Putnam Papers, containing Fletcher correspondence, in the Peabody Museum Papers, Harvard University Archives; and the records of the Bureau of Indian Affairs, National Archives, Washington, D.C.

Fletcher published extensively on ethnology, archeology, and Indian problems in scholarly and popular periodicals as well as in the publications of Indian rights organizations, but her best-known works are two monographs written with Indian associates: with James Murie, "The Hako: A Pawnee Ceremony," *Annual Reports*, vol. 22, Bureau of American Ethnology, Smithsonian Institution, Washington, D.C. (1904); and with Francis La Fleche, "The Omaha Tribe," ibid., vol. 27 (1911).

A full-length biography of Fletcher remains to be written, but there are a number of reliable, if brief, accounts of her life and work; the first noted below includes an almost complete bibliography of Fletcher's publications: Walter Hough, "Alice Cunningham Fletcher" (obituary), *American Anthropologist* 25 (1923), 254–258; Frederick Hoxie and Joan Mark, eds., *With the Nez Perce: Alice Fletcher in the Field, 1889–1892* (1981); Nancy Oestreich Lurie, "Women in Early Anthropology,'' in *Pioneers of American Anthropology*, ed. June Helm (1966), 31–81, esp. 43–54; Joan T. Mark, *Four American Anthropologists* (1980), 62–87; and Thurman Wilkins' sketch of Fletcher in *Notable American Women, 1607–1950* vol. 1 (1971), 630–633.

NANCY OESTREICH LURIE

**Flower, Lucy Louisa** (May 10, 1837–April 27, 1921), child welfare advocate, educational reformer, and pioneer promoter of the juvenile court system, was the adopted daughter of Samuel Elliott Coues (pronounced "Cows") and his second wife, Charlotte Haven Ladd. She probably was born in Boston, but no official records exist. Both parents had deep family roots in New England, and her father, a prosperous Portsmouth, New Hampshire, merchant, espoused many of the reform causes of antebellum America and served in 1841 as president of the American Peace Society. Lucy attended the Portsmouth public schools until the family moved to Washington, D.C., in 1953. Her formal education ended with a year's study at the Packer Collegiate Institute in Brooklyn. Subsequent employment in the U.S. Patent Office proved unfulfilling, and the young woman looked for greater challenges when she went to Madison, Wisconsin, in 1859.

In Madison, Lucy Coues was the only female instructor in the preparatory department of the state university. The resoluteness that characterized her later work evidenced itself here. When discontinued funds caused the department to close, Flower acquired the use of the building and conducted her own private institution. She maintained this work until 1863, the year of her marriage to James Monroe Flower, who would become a wealthy Chicago attorney and an influential participant in Republican Party politics in the Windy City. Three children—Elliott, Harriet Dean, and Louis Bertram—were born to the couple before the Flowers moved to Chicago in 1873.

Like many women active in social work, Flower began her activities in Chicago through her church affiliation. As chairman of the charity committee of the St. James Episcopal Church, she interested herself in the plight of city waifs and orphans. Those efforts involved her in an expanding network of institutions, including the Half-Orphan Asylum, the Home for the Friendless, and the Lake Geneva Fresh Air Association, a program to provide summer recreation for slum children. But her work also convinced Flower that effective benevolence required more than good will. Much of her career can be understood as an effort to impose professional standards and administrative efficiency on charity and social welfare work. And Flower did not hesitate to challenge the political interests that hindered those efforts. Appalled by the fact that many nurses at Cook County Hospital owed their appointments to politics, Flower joined with other women in 1880 to found the Illinois Training School for Nurses, to prepare workers with professional competence. She also served the institution for ten years as president. Flower became a leader, too, in the charity organization drive, a movement in which Chicago lagged behind eastern cities. Thus, calling for a clearing house for the city's many church, societal, and individual humanitarian undertakings, she helped to establish the Chicago Board of Charities in 1894.

Meanwhile, in 1891, Flower had been appointed to the Chicago Board of Education, where she sought to reform what she considered the antiquated curricula of the city's public schools. Flower embraced the increasingly popular educational theories of European thinkers—Johann Heinrich Pestalozzi, Friedrich Froebel, and Johann Friedrich Herbart—and stressed the need for attention to the individual child and the imperative of shifting from a passive to an active role for the child in the learning process. To this end she urged a manual training program for the school system. Against the defenders of the old curriculum and the ideal of education as mental discipline, Flower made her own pedagogical defense for enhancing manual and sensory skills. In addition, she linked educational reform to social reform, maintaining that the existing school programs effectively served only those who anticipated college education—a very small number. In fact, she demonstrated that only 5 percent of Chicago's primary and grammar students went on even to high school, while some 20,000 others avoided the schools altogether and learned only from the streets. Manual education, she insisted, would address the needs of many of these youngsters, primarily poorer children whose main interest was practical education. Her efforts prevailed when the Chicago Board of Education approved such programs in 1891, including sewing classes for girls.

Children were always the major focus of Flower's social work, but the situation of young lawbreakers pained her most; she especially decried their imprisonment with seasoned criminals. On this issue, too, she stressed the necessity of manual training, and when the city built a new school for that purpose next to the county prison, Flower and others were able to raise money for a dormitory in the school to house the younger inmates. By 1905, after six years of operation, the John Worthy Manual Training School had graduated more than 4,000 boys.

In the meantime, her sensitivity to the special needs of young offenders, and her belief that they should not be treated as adult criminals, also had motivated Flower to work for the establishment of a juvenile court in Cook County. Flower rallied the city's social welfare leaders, prominent lawyers and judges, and politicians to her cause. With its creation in July, 1899, the Cook County Juvenile Court became the first of its kind in the world. It used special judges to hear juvenile cases and assigned convicted youngsters to manual traning schools. To assist the new program, Flower founded a women's Juvenile Court Committee, headed by Julia Lathrop,* to raise money for salaries of probation officers. Flower herself was a frequent consultant to the bench of the new court.

Flower's career does not fit easily into any precise pattern. A petite woman with curly hair and light-rimmed glasses, she was amazingly energetic, usually uncompromising, and often vitriolic in criticism of opponents. On the one hand, she clearly belonged to a pattern of Gilded Age reform in which wealthy urban women, through social and cultural clubs, benevolent organizations, and individual sponsporships, became visibly active in combatting the physical and human blight of America's cities. Flower used her husband's political and professional connections to assist her causes, and, more important, she used her leadership in the influential Chicago Woman's Club, which she also served at one time as president, to chart her programs and carry them out. In other ways, however, Flower was somewhat exceptional. Many affluent women of her time defined their roles in benevolence as patronesses and stewardesses of humanitarian causes. They were less likely than the earlier volunteer women to confront firsthand the realities of poverty and slums. Flower's work, by contrast, always was empirical in character, and her reports were acutely matter-of-fact. But neither did Flower conform to the phenomenon of the "new woman" of her later period, whose venture outside the home embraced various female causes, especially suffrage. Indeed, Flower criticized proposals for universal woman suffrage, arguing that the registration lists already were too weighty with the uneducated and the illiterate. She insisted that a woman's first responsibility was to her family, and she did not undertake extensive social work until her children were grown. Also, unlike the rising generation of Progressive Era women reformers, Flower never joined her social work to larger schemes of economic or political reform.

Flower remained active in Chicago into the early twentieth century, but her husband's illness led to their move to Coronado, California, in 1902. As a tribute to her work, nine years later the Chicago Board of Education dedicated the Lucy Flower Vocational High School, which still stands. She died in Coronado in 1921.

The Lucy Flower "Scrapbooks," three volumes housed in the Archives of the Chicago Historical Society, contain newspaper clippings, apparently gathered by Flower, that describe her many activities in the city. Most of these are unmarked with respect to source and date, but they are very helpful in illuminating some of the controversies in which she was embroiled.

A brief biography of Lucy Flower, *Lucy Louisa Flower, 1837–1920 [sic]: Her Contribution to Education and Child Welfare in Chicago* (1924), is not wholly reliable. Flower herself contributed little to the literature of social reform, but see her "Adaption of Our School System to the Future Needs of the Republic," *New Cycle* 8 (1895), 781–793; "Women in Public Life," *Outlook* 56 (1894), 403–404; "The Illinois Training School for Nurses," *Reporter of Organized Charity* (November, 1877), 54.

For suggestive contextual information on Lucy Flower, see Kathleen D. McCarthy, *Noblesse Oblige: Charity and Cultural Philanthropy in Chicago, 1849–1929* (1982); Ellen Ryerson, *The Best-Laid Plans: America's Juvenile Court Experiment* (1978); and Anthony M. Platt, *The Child Savers: The Invention of Delinquency* (1969).

J. DAVID HOEVELER, JR.

**Folks, Homer** (February 18, 1867–February 13, 1963), child welfare and public health reformer and pioneer in social welfare, was born at Hanover, Michigan, the fourth of seven children, to James Folks, a farmer, and his second wife, Esther (Woodliffe) Folks, both of whom were of English birth and possessed by a sense of social responsibility. Folks grew up in Hanover, where he attended a one-room ungraded country school until he was twelve. He then entered Hanover High School, where he had a good record and earned high praise. Like Amos Warner,* Folks spent his childhood and youth in a small rural setting, with little to enlarge his horizons outside his immediate family, but managing, nonetheless, to find issues with which to wrestle. In 1883, when he graduated from high school, his father gave him the choice of a farm or a college education, the same choice he had given his other sons. Folks elected the college education and entered Albion College (originally Albion Wesleyan Seminary) in 1885, earning his B.A. degree in 1889. He was considered an outstanding student and was an active participant in college affairs. He brought to his college life the social consciousness instilled in his childhood. With the encouragement of a friendly member of the Albion faculty, he then enrolled at Harvard College, receiving a second B.A. in 1890.

Meanwhile, due to his demonstrated social concerns and to the high opinion held of him by an influential faculty member, he was recommended for, and secured, the position of general superintendent of the Children's Aid Society of Pennsylvania. This agency, founded in 1882 on the premise that children whose families could not care for them did not belong in institutions but in foster homes, was one of 109 children's agencies operating in Philadelphia, then the third largest city in America. The agency had neither an institutional nor an almsgiving program. Thus, the twenty-three-year-old Folks took on a new and pioneering approach to child care—home placement, even of delinquent youngsters. He embraced the challenge it offered, and succeeded so well that in 1891 he was asked to discuss his agency's foster home program for dependent, neglected, and delinquent children at the National Conference of Charities and Correction, which gave him national experience and exposure. In this same year he married Maude Beard, his high school sweetheart, by whom he was to have three daughters.

Folks found a task waiting for him, greater than the Children's Aid Society of Pennsylvania with its statewide constituency, but in line with its principles. That was the advancement of a social campaign to remove children from alms-houses and other institutions all over the United States. The 1880 census had revealed 6,000 children countrywide dragging out an existence in these "dumping grounds," along with the ill, the aged, the mentally deranged, and the criminal. Here Folks demonstrated awareness and skill in recognizing the importance of political pressure to secure legislation which would make such placements illegal, a tedious process in that by 1900 only one-fourth of the states had such legislation. His approach to the necessity of public pressure for improved legislation would have delighted Edith* and Grace Abbott,* who were, not so many years later, to make the concept of social engineering their life's work.

In 1893 Folks was again recognized as a leader in the art of child care, and was on the program of a special conference to consider problems of child saving, where he contributed considerably to the growth of the idea that foster family placement under the supervision of trained social workers should replace institutions, that government involvement and responsibility were vital, but that there was an important role for volunteers in both the planning and the delivery of such services.

In the same year Folks, who was having difficulty in establishing an acceptable role for himself as a policy-maker in the Pennsylvania agency, resigned to become the secretary of the State Charities Aid Association of New York, a position he was to hold until his retirement in February, 1947, and one which offered him an even more widespread and influential platform for his ideas. His whole future career would demonstrate what could be done by an individual secure in the base of operations from which he functioned, namely, an influential agency willing to give him a free hand in attacking any problem relevant to his and the agency's goals.

The scope of his activities was widened dramatically. In 1894 he was involved in New York's Constituitonal Convention as a welfare expert. In 1897 he served a term on New York City's Board of Aldermen. In 1899, after the Spanish-American War, he was sent to Cuba to establish there the equivalent of a state board of charities. In 1902 and 1903 he served a term as Commissioner of Public Charities for New York City. In that time he halved the child population of New York's children's institutions through placement with relatives and paid foster homes under the supervision of trained social workers. At this time he also published *The Care of Destitute, Neglected and Delinquent Children* (1904), a comprehensive and highly regarded review of problems and services available to, or needed by, children with a wide variety of problems.

He also helped found the National Child Labor Committee in 1904 and was intimately involved with preparations for the first White House Conference on Dependent Children in 1909 and with the formation of the U.S. Children's Bureau three years later. In addition, he went on to become president of the American Association for the Study and Prevention of Infant Mortality. His activities were not limited to children, however, for he gave considerable leadership to public health planning, especially by bringing the social aspects of public health services into national view, and he set out to break down the separation between services for the ill and disabled and those who simply were destitute and thus poorly cared for, making an especially outstanding contribution to the development of services for the tubercular.

In the final stages of World War I, the American Red Cross "borrowed" him to serve as director of its Department of Civil Affairs in France. Twice he was elected president of the National Conference of Charities and Correction (the National Conference of Social Work after 1917), the only person in the long history of the organization to be so honored.

The following years saw him active on a variety of public welfare issues at the state level, while the Great Depression of the 1930s again brought him into the field of national policy, serving as an advisor to President Franklin D. Roosevelt on many welfare matters. In 1940 he received the Medal of Honor awarded by the Roosevelt Memorial Association.

When he finally retired in February, 1947, at the age of eighty, Folks had left his mark as a compassionate individual who, as much as any other person in American history, had advanced the cause of social welfare. He died sixteen years later in his daughter's home in Riverdale, New York.

The best source of information on Folks is the Homer Folks Collection of papers at the Columbia University School of Social Work in New York City. Other very useful primary sources are the *Annual Reports*, *Minutes* of the board meetings, and the *News* of the New York State Charities Aid Association in New York City and the papers of the many stae and national organizations on which Folks served, including the National Child Labor Committee, the National Tuberculosis Association, and so on. See the extensive bibliography in the Trattner book cited below.

The best secondary accounts of Folks' life and career are an eighteen-page sketch by his son-in-law, Savel Zimand, in the introduction to Homer Folks' *Public Health and Welfare—The Citizens' Responsibility* (1958), and Walter Trattner's lengthy biography, *Homer Folks: Pioneer in Social Welfare* (1968). Biographies of other social welfare leaders at the time also are helpful; thus see Jane Addams, *My Friend Julia Lathrop* (1935) and *The Second Twenty Years at Hull-House* (1930); Josephine Goldmark, *Impatient Crusader: Florence Kelley's Life Story* (1953); C. E. A. Winslow, *The Life of Hermann Biggs* (1929); Ben Lindsey, *The Dangerous Life* (1931); and Emma Lunberg, *Unto the Least of These* (1947).

Because of a newspaper strike at the time of Folks' death, none of the New York City newspapers ran an obituary. Hundreds of other newspapers throughout the country, however, had lengthy ones and, in many cases, even articles. See, for example, the Yonkers (New York) *Herald Statesman*, February 14, 15, 1963.

KATHLEEN M. JACKSON

**Follett, Mary Parker** (September 3, 1868–December 18, 1933), political philosopher, theorist in group behavior and industrial management, was born in Quincy, Massachusetts, to parents from long-established New England families of British descent. Her father, Henry Allen Follett, was a factory machinist; her mother, Elizabeth Curtis Baxter, was a daughter of a well-to-do banker. At age fifteen, Follett graduated from Thayer Academy, Braintree, Massachusetts, where a gifted teacher had stimulated her interest in philosophy and politics. From 1888 to 1890 she attended the Society for the Collegiate Instruction of Women of Harvard (afterwards Radcliffe College). During 1890–1891 she studied philosophy under Henry Stidwick at Newnham College, Cambridge, England. A paper delivered there was expanded into her first book, *The Speaker of the House of Representatives* (1896). After interruptions to care for her invalid mother and younger brother, George, she resumed studies at Radcliffe under historian Albert Bushnell Hart and graduated A.B., summa cum laude, in 1898.

After another period of study in France and England, where she also observed the operations of youth and neighborhood organizations, she returned to Boston and began work at Roxbury Neighborhood House, in an underprivileged area. In 1900 she organized the Roxbury Debating Club for Boys, followed by other social and athletic organizations for young men. One, the Roxbury League, successfully demonstrated that public schools could be utilized for leisure activities at night. Follett took leadership in efforts to develop similar night-time social centers in schools throughout the city. During this period she was encouraged and assisted by Isabel Briggs, an Englishwoman interested in philanthropic activities. They lived together until 1926.

As Follett worked with various clubs, she was eager to share her own interests in music, art, and nature. She was on the boards of leading Boston social agencies interested in wage reforms, improved health facilities, more efficient city government, and vocational guidance. Observing political action, she began theorizing on the effective use of democratic institutions and friendly social interaction to improve living conditions. Her speculation on the relationship of individuals to the groups of which they were parts, including citizens to the state, gradually led to the idea that the two were reciprocal and that persons in groups can find solutions to social problems that no single member could conceive. She maintained that the individual should be the focus of all group activity, and from small groups of individuals power to improve conditions of life would be generated. Neighborhood groups could then join together at higher levels of political organization.

Follett was intent on practical applications of her political theories in collective enterprises of many kinds—capital and labor; civic reform; education. Her carefully worked out formulations were explained in *The New State: Group Organization and the Solution of Popular Government* (1918). It is regarded as the germinal stimulus for later social group work theory. She exchanged ideas with early promoters of social work, notably Eduard C. Lindeman* and Dr. Richard C. Cabot.* She extended her ideas concerning the importance of group discussion to the problems experienced in establishing the League of Nations, which she visited numerous times.

In *Creative Experience* (1924) she utilized psychological insights to emphasize the importance of considering the personal growth of individuals within group activities. She proposed organizational principles and means of resolving conflicts. As a member of the Massachusetts Minimum Wage Board she had seen how opposing viewpoints had to be recognized and resolved before positive change could occur. This led to an interest in problems of industrial management. She became much sought after as a lecturer to businessmen and was probably best known as an expert in management problem resolution, in England as well as in America. In her later published articles, she advanced the notion that principles of management organization were the same, whether in small neighborhoods, clubs, political parties, or large business corporations. From 1928 she lived in England at the home of Dame Katherine Furse, a prominent leader in the Red Cross and Girl Guides, lecturing at the London School of Economics. Her articles on management are cited in social work and public welfare publications dealing with adminsitrative problems and methods. She returned in 1933 to Boston, where she died.

Henry C. Metcalf and L. Urwick, eds., *Dynamic Administration* (1941), is a collection of Mary Follett's papers with a biographical introduction and a bibliography. For a contemporary summary and evaluation of her writings, see Arthur Evans Wood, "The Social Philosophy of Mary P. Follett," *Journal of Social Forces* 4 (1926), 759–769. See also Richard C. Cabot, "Mary Parker Follett: An Appreciation," *Radcliffe Quarterly* (April, 1924); and Dawn C. Crawford, "Mary Parker Follett," *Notable American Women* vol. 1 (1971), 639–641, in which Follett's personal characteristics and the organizations in which she worked are described.

MURIEL W. PUMPHREY

**Frankel, Lee Kaufman** (August 13, 1867–July 25, 1931), social service administrator, insurance executive, and author, was born in Philadelphia, the son of Louis and Aurelia (Lobenburg) Frankel. After attending public schools, he received a B.S. degree in 1887 and a Ph.D. in chemistry in 1891 from the University of Pennsylvania. Between 1888 and 1893 he served as an instructor in chemistry at the University of Pennsylvania. For the next six years he worked as a consulting chemist in Philadelphia. Between 1895 and 1898 he was vice president and then president of the chemical section of the Franklin Institute of Philadelphia. In 1898 he married Alice Reizenstein of Philadelphia; they had one son and one daughter.

Frankel became interested in philanthropy and social service in the Jewish community in the early 1890s. In an autobiographical sketch published in 1930, Frankel recalled that the large Jewish immigration from Russia stimulated his interest in social service. His acquaintances in the field of social welfare in Philadelphia included Mary E. Richmond* who, he later wrote, urged him to leave the field of chemistry when, in 1899, he was asked to become manager of the United Hebrew Charities of New York. According to one biographer, Frankel's appointment in New York initiated professional social service in Jewish organizations in the United States.

During his nine years at United Hebrew Charities, Frankel became prominent in the field of social service. He routinized methods for investigating and paying destitute clients, advocated the use of relief to preserve families, and initiated programs of home care for convalescent patients, particularly those suffering from tuberculosis. He also served as a member of the Ellis Island Commission appointed by President Theodore Roosevelt, as a commissioner of the New York State Board of Charities, and as an instructor at what then was the New York School of Philanthropy.

From 1908 until his death, Frankel's career was identified with insurance. In 1908 he was a special invesitgator for the Russell Sage Foundation, conducting a study, published in 1911, of social insurance in Europe. A year later Frankel became manager of the Industrial Department of the Metropolitan Life Insurance Company. In 1910 he was named assistant secretary in charge of the company's Welfare Department. He was promoted to vice president in 1912 and rose in subsequent years to the rank of second vice president.

Frankel organized landmark programs of public education and health research during twenty-two years at Metropolitan Life. His first project was a series of health tracts which were directed at women in working-class families and at school children. Over the years, the company distributed millions of pamphlets on the prevention and treatment of disease. Frankel also organized a model nursing home and visiting nurse service under the company's supervision. Notable projects of research and demonstration sponsored by Metropolitan Life included the Framingham (Massachusetts) Demonstration for the Control of Tuberculosis, begun in 1916, and a child health program at the Thetford Mines in southern Quebec, begun in 1921. He also initiated a program to collect and analyze statistical data about health status. These data provided a baseline for much health research over the next generation. Frankel also represented the insurance industry in major national organizations in health affairs, including the American Public Health Association, the National Health Council, the Life Extension Institute, and the National Conference of Social Work. Most of his publications, including several books on industrial hygiene and the prevention of illness, were derived from his work at the Metropolitan.

Frankel's commitment to the insurance industry influenced his opinions about public policy. He advocated compulsory social insurance in a book (written with Miles M. Dawson and Louis Dublin) which grew out of his European trip of 1908. In 1916, however, he argued that sickness and disability insurance should be both voluntary and universal. In the last year of his life, Frankel endorsed voluntary health insurance under which payments would be made to salaried physicians practicing in groups which were attached to hospitals.

Frankel was active in Jewish affairs throughout his career. He was a longtime member of the Free Synagogue of New York and the first chairman of the board of the Jewish Institute of Religion, and organized a pension plan for rabbis. In 1912 he was president of the National Conference of Jewish Charities. In the 1920s he made several contributions to international Jewish affairs. He led a commision that made a survey of Palestine under the auspices of the Jewish Agency in 1927. In 1928 and 1929, in collaboration with Louis D. Brandeis and Felix Warburg, among others, Frankel sought to unite Zionists and non-Zionists in the work of establishing a Jewish National Home in Palestine. In 1929 he was vice chairman of the executive committee of a community survey which led to the creation of the New York Federation for the Support of Jewish Philanthropic Societies.

Frankel died suddenly in Paris, France, on July 25, 1931, while visiting Europe to study social insurance for Metropolitan Life and to attend a meeting of the World Zionist Organization.

Considerable correspondence between Frankel and notable contemporaries has been preserved in the archives of the Metropolitan Life Insurance Company.

Frankel wrote voluminously, mainly articles and pamphlets. He is also listed as a coauthor of many of the sickness surveys of United States and Canadian cities conducted by Metropolitan Life. Many of his articles and pamphlets were catalogued as reprints by the New York Academy of Medicine, *Author Catalogue of the Library* (1969). Frankel's only scholarly book was written with Miles M. Dawson and Louis Dublin, *Workingmen's Insurance in Europe* (1911). Other books include *Health of the Worker: How to Safeguard it* (1924) and, with Donald B. Armstrong, *A Popular Encyclopedia of Health* (1926).

Biographical information about Frankel is available in several sources. He wrote an autobiographical sketch, "In the Early Days of the Charities," reprinted from the *Jewish Social Service Quarterly* (1930), in the collection of the New York Academy of Medicine. His obituary in the *New York Times* (July 26, 1931, 18:1), is the best source for his involvement in Zionism. An anonymous article, "Lee K. Frankel: A Leader in Public Health," reprinted from the *Statistical Bulletin* of Metropolitan Life (in the New York Academy of Medicine) describes his career in insurance. Louis Dublin, who worked with Frankel for many years, wrote about him in two books: *A Family of Thirty Million: The Story of the Metropolitan Life Insurance Company* (1943), and *After Eighty Years: The Impact of Life Insurance on the Public Health* (1966). Marquis James, *The Metropolitan: A Study in Business Growth* (1947), is a major source for Frankel's career in insurance.

DANIEL M. FOX

**Franklin, Benjamin** (January 17, 1707–April 17, 1790), printer, scientist, inventor, author, statesman, and philanthropist, was born in Boston, Massachusetts, the youngest son of Josiah Franklin and his second wife, Abiah (Folger) Franklin. Franklin could not remember a time when he was unable to read. At ten years of age, after only two years of formal schooling, he went to work in his father's candlemaking shop. Two years later he was apprenticed to his brother, James, a printer. During the five years Franklin served as apprentice he mastered the printing trade and furthered his education through reading, writing, and self-criticism.

In 1723 Franklin left Boston and made his way to Philadelphia where he found work as a printer. Before reaching the age of twenty he had spent two years in London practicing his trade and learning the ways of the world. On returning to Philadelphia in 1726 he again worked as a printer and in 1730 at age twenty-four, became sole owner of a printing house that published the *Pennsylvania Gazette*. His energy and aptitude for business were quickly recognized. He did most of the public printing for the colony of Pennsylvania and under his ownership the *Gazette* became the most widely read newspaper in America. The homely wisdom and robust wit of *Poor Richard's Almanac*, which he edited and published for twenty-five years starting in 1732, added to his reputation and influence throughout the colonies.

In 1730, the same year Franklin went into business for himself, he married Deborah Read, by whom he had a son who died in early childhood and a daughter, Sarah (Mrs. Richard Bache, 1743–1808), who directed soldiers' aid activities during the Revolutionary War. His son William (1730–1813), to whom he addressed the first part of his *Autobiography*, was the last royal governor of New Jersey and a loyalist during the American Revolution.

Franklin's success as a printer and publisher enabled him to retire from business in 1748. Even before retirement, however, he put into practice his maxim that leisure is time for being useful. In 1727 he organized the Junto, a voluntary association whose members debated issues and promoted mutual and civic improvement. Franklin took the lead in movements leading to the establishment of a circulating library, an academy (later the University of Pennsylvania), a hospital, expanded and improved municipal services, and the American Philosophical Society, the nation's first learned society.

Franklin devoted much of the decade after his retirement from business to scientific study and experimentation, most notably to the study of electricity, which gained him international fame as a scientist. Applying his scientific learning and ingenuity in practical directions, and without seeking profit for himself, he invented numerous useful devices including the Franklin stove, bifocal lenses, and lightning rods.

Public affairs dominated the latter half of Franklin's life. He was a member of the Pennsylvania Assenbly, 1751–1764, deputy postmaster-general of the colonies, 1753–1774, and agent of Pennsylvania and other colonies in England during the decade before the Revolution. He took part in the Second Continental Congress, signed the Declaration of Independence, represented the United States in France, 1776–1785, and played an important role in the peace negotiations ending the Revolutionary War. Despite advanced age and ill health, he attended meetings of the Constitutional Convention in 1787, and supported ratification of the Constitution.

On several occasions Franklin attributed his career as a useful citizen to the influence of Cotton Mather's *Essays to Do Good* (1710), which he read as a youth. Franklin shifted the emphasis of Mather's do-good gospel from pious works and personal charity to organized efforts to improve and enrich the community. His significance to the history of American social welfare derives both from his writing and from his advocacy and practice of volunarism. The former, particularly the *Autobiography* and *The Way to Wealth*, have nourished the popular conviction that individualism and self-help are the only effective means of improving human affairs; through his use of voluntary associations he demonstrated that the principle of self-help could be applied to social as well as individual goals. Following Franklin's example Americans have utilized voluntary associations to meet needs not provided by government or available on the market. Some of these services have subsequently been accepted as the respnsibility of government. As in Franklin's day, one of the continuing functions of voluntary organizations is to influence public policy in directions favored by their members.

Franklin criticized the English poor law on the grounds that availability of public relief encouraged dependency, and he opposed efforts by the British government to assist the laboring poor by prohibiting exports of grain. He was well-disposed toward charity for the deserving poor but was more interested in the prevention of poverty than in its relief. The best way to help the poor, in his opinion, was to widen opportunities for self-help and work for the establishment of conditions that would enable people to take care of themselves.

In an attempt to continue his usefulness beyond his own lifetime, Franklin provided in his will for two accumulating funds, one in Boston and one in Philadelphia, to be used to make interest-bearing loans to young tradesmen. Part of the funds matured in 1891; the remainder will become available for distribution in 1991. Neither reached the monetary size or degree of usefulness Franklin had anticipated, a circumstance a later philanthropist, Julius Rosenwald, cited in criticizing "the dead hand in philanthropy."

Franklin's importance as a philanthropist is more as a doer than as a donor. He obtained support for countless civic amenities and in his encouragement of voluntary association offered a method of improving social conditions that suited both the needs and inclinations of his countrymen.

Franklin died in Philadelphia on April 17, 1790.

The *Papers of Benjamin Franklin*, ed. Leonard W. Labaree and Whitefield J. Bell, Jr. (24) vols. to date, 1959–     ), is the definitive edition of Franklin's correspondence and writings. The most authoritative of many editions of Franklin's memoirs is *The Autobiography of Benjamin Franklin*, ed. Leonard W. Labaree et al. (1964). "Poor Richard Improved" (1758), often reprinted under the title, *The Way to Wealth*, is in *The Papers of Benjamin Franklin* 7 (1963), 326–350; for other statements by Franklin on poverty and the poor laws see *Papers* 4 (1961), 477–483; 13 (1969), 510–516; and 15 (1972), 103–107.

The best brief biography of Franklin is the sketch Carl Becker prepared for volume six (1931) of the *Dictionary of American Biography*; it is reprinted in *The American Plutarch*, ed. Eduard T. James (1964), 1–25. "Benjamin Franklin and Philadelphia" in *History of Philadelphia, 1609–1884*, ed. J. Thomas Scharf and Thomas Westcott (3 vols. 1884), 1, 218–243, is a perceptive and entertaining essay written about a century after Franklin's death. It can be read in conjunction with Harold A. Larrabee, "Poor Richard in an Age of Plenty," *Harper's Magazine* (June, 1956), 64–68, an article assaying Franklin's significance on the two-hundred-and-fiftieth anniversary of his birth.

Legislation for the relief of the poor in Philadelphia during Franklin's lifetime is examined by Hannah Benner Roach, "Philadelphia's Colonial Poor Laws," *The Pennsylvania Genealogical Magazine* 22 (1962), 159–185. John K. Alexander, *Render Them Submissive: Responses to Poverty in Philadelphia, 1760–1800* (1980), gives some attention to Franklin's activities. Robert H. Bremner,

*American Philanthropy* (1960), and Walter Trattner, *From Poor Law to Welfare State, A History of Social Welfare in America* (1974), comment on Franklin's significance in the history of philanthropy and social welfare. Franklin's bequests to Boston and Philadelphia are discussed in F. Emerson Andrews, *Philanthropic Foundations* (1956), 93–94 and Julius Rosenwald, "Principles of Public Giving," in *America's Voluntary Spirit*, ed. Brian O'Connell (1983), 121–122.

ROBERT H. BREMNER

# G

**Gallaudet, Edward Miner** (February 5, 1837–September 26, 1917), educator of the deaf, was born in Hartford, Connecticut, the youngest son of Thomas Hopkins Gallaudet,* the founder and first principal of the American School for the Deaf in Hartford, and Sophia (Fowler) Gallaudet, who was born deaf and who had been a pupil of Thomas Hopkins Gallaudet at the American School. This environment served to foster a deep appreciation and concern for the education of the deaf, which became his lifelong work.

When twenty years old and having just completed his education at Trinity College in Hartford, Gallaudet was hired as superintendent of a newly established school in Washington, D.C., the Columbia Institution for the Deaf and Dumb. The school had been established through the philanthropy of Amos Kendall, a former member of Andrew Jackson's cabinet.

Gallaudet began his duties as superintendent on June 13, 1857, with only five students. He soon increased this number by contracting for students with the state of Maryland, which had no school at that time. In 1865 he transferred the blind students to a Maryland facility with the belief that no institution should serve such a dual purpose.

Throughout the course of the Civil War, Gallaudet worked toward the fulfillment of a dream he had cultivated since he was seventeen years old, the establishment of a college for the deaf. Due to the original act of Congress which had established the institution, there was no age limit to which students could remain at the school. Gallaudet was at liberty to allow students to remain there until they had completed a collegiate course of instruction. He was not, however, able to award degrees for coursework completed by students. With this in mind, he submitted a bill to Congress which would enable the institution to grant such degrees. This bill passed both the House and the Senate, and on April 8, 1864, became law by the signature of Abraham Lincoln. On June 28, 1864, the National Deaf-Mute College (now known as Gallaudet College) celebrated its inauguration and publicized its readiness to receive pupils.

Three years later, in reaction to the growing popularity of the oral methodology which disallowed the use of sign language, Gallaudet traveled to Europe to study the methods of teaching the deaf used in the schools on the continent. Upon his return Gallaudet offered specific ideas to improve upon educational methods in use at schools for the deaf in the United States. Gallaudet supported the use of oral instruction as an additional method of educating the deaf. However, he strongly believed that manual communication was equally important and should be used in a "combined method." At a conference which he convened at the college, Gallaudet presented this proposal for a combined method which he hoped would act as a national approach to educating deaf students.

Gallaudet premised such a change on the fact that the schools had failed to teach their students to express themselves in adequate written English. He was convinced that the chief aim of education of the deaf was to provide students with this basic, essential skill.

He later reiterated these concerns at subsequent conventions of American instructors of the deaf. Although he considered sign language his mother tongue, he believed that a combined method would overcome the greatest obstacle prohibiting deaf students from acquiring acceptable written English skills. Many schools agreed to implement this philosophy, and it soon became a national method for educating deaf students.

Gallaudet also spent much of his time and energy on acquiring monies from Congress for the continued support of his institution. With this money the institution was allowed to add staff and faculty as well as construct additional buildings. He was, for example, able to acquire the services of the now famous landscape designer, Frederick Law Olmsted, to design the campus.

His success at acquiring continued congressional support is due in some measure to his involvement with social clubs and organizations in Washington, D.C. He was a founding member of the prestigious Cosmos Club and helped to establish the city's YMCA. He was a member of the Sons of the American Revolution and served as its historian general. He also was heavily involved with the Washington Literary Society, whose members included Alexander Graham Bell,* John Nicolay, and Joseph Henry. Undoubtedly, Gallaudet used these contacts to the advantage of the institution. If he could lure individuals to visit the institution, he felt that most would be convinced to support his work with deaf students. In addition, he was a charismatic, well-groomed, well-mannered person who believed in making personal visits to present his invitations or discuss matters of importance.

His talents also extended beyond the areas of administration and lobbying. He was fluent in both French and German. He received honorary degress from Trinity College and George Washington University for his work and publications in the area of education. Yale University awarded him an LL.D. in 1895 for his books and articles on international law. He always carried a full course load at the college as well, teaching courses on ethics, jurisprudence, and moral philosophy.

In 1886 Gallaudet allowed deaf women to enter the college program. In 1891 he acquired funds from Congress to establish a graduate program in education of the death at the college. Young men and women who had all their faculties were trained to be teachers of the deaf in what was the first program of its kind in the United States.

As Gallaudet neared his last years as president of the college, he busied himself with civic-related activities, such as getting the streets of Washington paved and working to establish a vocational school for black children. In February, 1910, he resigned as president at the age of seventy-three, and he died in Hartford, Connecticut, on September 26, 1917.

In addition to his own writings, principal sources of information concerning Edward Miner Gallaudet are Lloyd A. Ambrosen, "Contributions of Edward Miner Gallaudet to the Convention of American Instructors of the Deaf," Master's thesis, Gallaudet College, 1942; Maxine T. Boatner, *Voice of the Deaf: A Biography of Edward Miner Gallaudet* (1959); Richard M. Winefield, "Bell, Gallaudet, and the Sign Language Debate: An Historical Analysis of the Communication Controversy in Educatiton of the Deaf," Ed. D. Dissertation, Harvard University, 1981; the Edward Miner Gallaudet Papers, Manuscript Division, Library of Congress, Washington, D.C.; and the Edward Miner Gallaudet Papers, Gallaudet College Archives, Washington, D.C.

DAVID L. DE LORENZO

**Gallaudet, Thomas Hopkins** (December 10, 1787–September 10, 1851), educator and founder of deaf education in the United States, was born in Philadelphia, the first child of Peter Wallace Gallaudet, a merchant and the grandson of a French Huguenot minister who settled in New York, and Jane (Hopkins) Gallaudet, a descendant of Thomas Hooker, the first minister and a founder of Hartford, Connecticut. Religion and education were values central to the Gallaudet family and certainly to Thomas H. Gallaudet. Though of frail health throughout his life, he quickly proved a brilliant and devoted student. Growing up in Connecticut, he attended the Hartford Grammar School and at the age of fourteen entered Yale College, where he frequently debated at literary society meetings. He graduated in 1805 with the honor of delivering a commencement address, "On the Increase of Luxury in Connecticut, and Its Destructive Consequences."

Over the next nine years the young man struggled physically with ill health and mentally with doubts about his commitment as a Christian and the proper path for his career. During this period he served a brief apprenticeship with a law firm, returned to Yale to tutor and to earn an M.A. degree (1810), and then found work as a traveling sales agent to the rural lands of Ohio and Kentucky, hoping that the journey and fresh air would improve his health. By the end of this stint as a salesman Gallaudet had resolved his doubts about faith and returned to enroll at Andover to acquire a divinity degree and the license to preach.

During the summer of 1814, while on vacation from Andover, Gallaudet became acquainted with nine-year-old Alice Cogswell, deaf daughter of his neighbor, Mason F. Cogswell, a prominent Hartford physician. At their first meeting Gallaudet succeeded in teaching the previously uneducable Alice the word "hat." He continued to instruct her informally as time permitted.

Pleased by Gallaudet's success with his daughter, Cogswell wanted to continue her education but was thwarted by the lack of any school for the deaf in the United States. Cogswell organized a committee to sponsor a visit by Gallaudet to Europe for the purpose of learning methods used there to teach deaf people. The plan was for Gallaudet to set up a school in America upon his return. From some itinerant preaching in Connecticut, he had personally appraised the need for deaf education in America, and an 1812 ministers' census had counted eighty-four deaf citizens in Connecticut, which figure could be extrapolated to 400 in New England and to over 1,000 in the United States.

The American vision of a public school for the deaf contrasted with what Gallaudet observed during his visit to Europe in 1815–1816: privately run schools which served only paying students, or meagerly supported charitable institutions. In Britain he found the Braidwood family reluctant to share the teaching methods employed in their private oral schools, nor was he impressed by the results of the instruction he was allowed to observe. In Edinburgh he met the Scottish philosopher Dugald Stewart, whose theories of sensory perception and language acquisition helped further convince Gallaudet that a purely oral approach was not an expedient means of teaching deaf children. He then went to France, where he learned sign language and the manual method of instructing the deaf from the Abbé Sicard and his staff at the Royal Institution in Paris.

Returning to America in August, 1816, Gallaudet brought with him one of Sicard's prize pupils, Laurent Clerc, who had also been a leading teacher at the Paris school. Clerc and Gallaudet traveled throughout the Northeast, giving lecture-demonstrations to raise funds for an American school and to educate the public about deafness. Clerc's presence in the United States helped convince any skeptics that deaf education could succeed, and he also had the expertise to train future American teachers of the deaf. In April, 1817, Gallaudet was at last able to write in his diary that after two years of organizing, fund-raising, training teachers, locating students, writing press releases, and delivering public addresses, the Hartford Asylum (later called the American School for the Deaf) had opened to a class of seven pupils. Some $17,000 had been collected to fund the school, including $5,000 from the Connecticut General Assembly—the first appropriation of public money for a benevolent institution in the United States.

By the fall of 1818 the school had fifty to sixty pupils and an $8,000 debt and had begun to take on a national character. President Monroe had already visited the institution, and its students now came from ten different states. A federal land grant was sought and approved with the help of Henry Clay, then Speaker of the House. As principal, Gallaudet found it part of his regular duties to deliver speeches and conduct demonstrations in all of the major cities of the Northeast and to advocate the rights of deaf people before state legislatures and the Congress of the United States. He won respect for his oratorical prowess both in the pulpit and on the platform.

He continued as principal of the asylum until his retirement, due largely to failing health, in 1830. By then he had played a major role in promoting publicly supported deaf education in the United States and had guided the establishment of several state schools for the deaf. Even after his retirement Gallaudet remained a vital influence on the movement for deaf education, writing articles and delivering speeches that helped preserve the existence of American public education for the deaf while permanently shaping its theory of instruction. His interest in deafness affected his personal life as well, for in 1821 he married a deaf woman, Sophia Fowler, one of the first graduates of the Hartford school. Two of their children continued the Gallaudet involvement in deafness: Thomas Gallaudet, the eldest, became minister to a deaf congregation at St. Ann's Church in New York City, and Edward Miner Gallaudet,* the youngest, became the founding president of Gallaudet College, a liberal arts college for the deaf named after his father.

Gallaudet's retirement from the Hartford school afforded him the time to broaden his literary and rhetorical pursuits. For the American Tract Society he wrote a number of children's books on religion, among them the highly popular *Child's Book of the Soul*, first published in 1836. In addition, he promoted an original method for teaching reading, conducted a vigorous campaign for the establishment of teacher training programs, and took an active interest in the lyceum movement, particularly the Goodrich Association, which organized the first course of popular lectures delivered in Hartford. He maintained an interest in preaching as well, serving as part-time chaplain of the Hartford Retreat for the Insane. He also spent a year traveling through the central states as a spokesman for "Look Upward, Pass Onward," an organization dedicated to maintaining the Protestant faith in the new states.

Gallaudet was a man who employed language in written, oral, and manually signed form to influence the thought and conduct of his fellow citizens. Deeply religious, he saw a Christian education as a means to spiritual salvation as well as the cure for social life. Though small in stature and of quiet temperament, he was an energetic and vocal reformer who was not only the founder of deaf education in the United States but a major impetus behind the establishment of teacher education (or normal schools) in this country. He died in Hartford, Connecticut, in 1851.

Gallaudet's papers can be found in the Manuscript Division of the Library of Congress, Washington, D.C. The Library of the American School for the Deaf, West Hartford, Connecticut, also contains some of Gallaudet's correspondence and records relating to his tenure as principal of the school.

Though his publications are too numerous to list here, his most important writings about sign language and deaf education include "Expediency of Teaching the Deaf and Dumb to Articulate," *Christian Observer* (August, 1818); "On

Teaching the Deaf and Dumb," *Christian Observer* (October and December 1819; January, 1820); "On Oral Language and the Language of Signs," *Christian Observer* (August and September, 1826); "The Language of Signs, Auxiliary to the Christian Missionary," *Christian Observer* (October, 1826); "The Value and Uses of the Natural Language of Signs," *American Annals of the Deaf and Dumb* (October, 1847; January, 1848); and "Reminiscences of Deaf-Mute Instruction," *American Annals of the Deaf and Dumb* (January, 1849). His most fully developed address in behalf of deaf education was the sermon "On the Duty and Advantages of Affording Education to the Deaf and Dumb," first published in 1824 and reprinted in the biography by Barnard cited below.

The most complete accounts of Gallaudet's life and works are three nineteenth century biographies: Herman Humphrey, *The Life and Labors of the Rev. T. H. Gallaudet, LL.D.* (1857); Henry Barnard, *Tribute to Gallaudet* (1859); and Edward Miner Gallaudet, *The Life of Thomas Hopkins Gallaudet* (1888). More recent scrutinies of Gallaudet's accomplishments can be found in James J. Fernandes, "The Gate to Heaven: T. H. Gallaudet and the Rhetoric of the Deaf Education Movement," Ph.D dissertation, University of Michigan, 1980; Paul H. Mattingly, "Why NYU Chose Gallaudet," *New York University Education Quarterly* (Fall, 1981); James J. Fernandes, "Thomas Hopkins Gallaudet on Language and Communication," *American Annals of the Deaf* (August, 1983); and James J. Fernandes, "Thomas Hopkins Gallaudet," *Gallaudet Encyclopedia on Deafness* (1985).

JAMES J. FERNANDES

**Garvey, Malcus (Marcus) Mosiah, Jr.** (August 17, 1887–June 10, 1940), reformer, organizer, and president general of the Universal Negro Improvement Association, was born in St. Ann's Bay, Jamaica, West Indies, to Sarah Jane (Richards) Garvey and Malcus Mosiah Garvey, Sr. His mother, Sarah Jane was a farm laborer, and his father, Malcus, Sr., was a bricksman. The family also operated a small farm. Malcus, Sr., owned a home library, and Marcus read extensively as a child. Beginning in 1895, he was educated at the Church of England School at St. Ann's Bay. He also received some private tutoring and at age fourteen began serving a printer's apprenticeship with Alfred E. Burrowes and Company. At age sixteen he left school to become a full-time company employee. Active as a printer and union member, he edited several newsletters and pamphlets prior to leaving Jamaica in 1910 for Central America. In 1912 Garvey attended Birkbeck College in London. Between 1913 and 1914 he traveled in France, Scotland, and other parts of Europe. These life experiences combined with a Carribean philosophy of social justice to spearhead one of the most massive black social reform movements in history.

On July 20, 1914, Garvey returned to Jamaica from London and founded the Universal Negro Improvement (and Conservation) Association and African Communities League (UNIA and ACL). Originally, these were two organizations with separate objectives, but combined under one name. The ACL held a political goal of nation-building among African peoples of the world, while in its early development the UNIA was a benevolent self-help association with a nonpolitical focus. Much like the Horatio Alger or self-help philosophy of the latter nineteenth century, thrift and industry were viewed by Garvey as the keys to success. His attempts to unify oppressed Blacks, however, were reflected in the UNIA motto: "One God! One Aim! One Destiny!" By 1918 there would be a political fusion between the UNIA and the ACL.

Meanwhile, in June, 1916, Garvey had come to America on a thirty-eight-state public lecture tour, and in May, 1917, the New York branch of the UNIA was formed. In November, 1922, UNIA membership was reported at 3 million, 1 million of whom lived in the United States. By 1926 there were 996 branches of the UNIA in various parts of the world. In the United States, there were 725 branches in thirty-eight states, from coast to coast, north and south alike. Specific social welfare functions of the UNIA included a number of services important to grass-roots Blacks. Death benefits were provided for Blacks not insurable by regular insurance companies. Educational opportunities were provided through correspondence courses, adult clases, lectures, debates, and organized training centers. The industrial and agricultural education stressed by Booker T. Washington also was part of the UNIA manifesto. Local units were organized to respond to community needs. In some communities, dinner was provided to several hundred poor people on holidays, or flowers were distributed to poorhouse inmates and hospital patients. Aid to criminals was also part of general organizational objectives. Through the business activities of the UNIA, laundries, restaurants, and similar enterprises were established.

Garvey's political ideology of racial separation and black self-improvement was influenced by the Irish nationalistic revolt during the second decade of the twentieth century. Historian Robert Hill has noted the similarity between the Irish slogan, "The Irish Race at Home and Abroad," and Garvey's slogan, "Africa for the Africans at Home and Abroad." Also, the works of Sir Thomas More and Anglo-Saxon ideals helped form Garvey's utopian dreams of a separate land where Blacks could make noteworthy contributions to civilization. The Garvey movement was able to mobilize grass-roots Blacks excluded from other black organizations, and its leader was known to his followers as the Black Moses. A skillful orator, Garvey attracted large numbers of Blacks to public speaking events. On August 17, 1918, *Negro World*, the official newspaper of the UNIA, was first published. This newspaper helped in the widespread dissemination of Garvey's message of black unity.

The perceptions by black integrationists and other citizens that Garvey was a radical agitator caused suspicions of his aims and fears of racial disturbances. From 1918 on, Garvey was under investigation by the Federal Bureau of Investigation. In the midst of this turmoil, Garvey married twice—in 1919 to Amy Ashwood, co-founder of the UNIA, and in 1922 to Amy Jacques. On January 12, 1922, Garvey was arrested for using the mail to sell shares in the

Black Starline Steamship Company. Convicted in 1923 of violating postal laws, he was imprisoned for mail fraud in 1925.

After 1925 the UNIA lost its momentum. Garvey was deported from the United States in December, 1927. He attended his last UNIA convention in Canada in 1938, but still was committed to the movement at the time of his death in London in June, 1940. The strength of his ideas was not recognized until the resurgence of black nationalism at the grass roots during the sixties.

Marcus Garvey's correspondence and addresses, along with the Universal Negro Improvement Association Papers through 1920, can be found in Robert A. Hill, ed., *The Marcus Garvey and Universal Negro Improvement Association Papers* (1983), vols. 1 and 2; documents, a biographical sketch, and an analysis of Garvey's development are also included. Modified versions of Garvey's speeches and writings through 1922 are in Amy Jacques-Garvey, ed., *Philosophy and Opinions of Marcus Garvey* (1923). Universal Negro Improvement Association ideology and organizational struggles are discussed in Tony Martin, *Race First* (1976). The *New York Times* from 1921 to 1927 provides accounts of Garvey's criminal indictment, imprisonment, and deportation. The best secondary works on Garvey are E. David Cronon, *Black Moses: The Story of Marcus Garvey and the Universal Negro Improvement Association* (1955), and Elton C. Fax, *Garvey: The Story of a Pioneer Black Nationalist* (1972)

WILMA PEEBLES-WILKENS

**Gavit, John Palmer** (July 1, 1868–October 27, 1954), social worker, writer, and editor, was born in Albany, New York, the eldest son of Joseph and Fannie (Breese) Palmer. There is little information concerning his early life. In 1885 he became a cub reporter for the *Albany Evening Journal*. Gavit relocated to Connecticut in 1890 for a three-year period. During that time he married Lucy Lamont, reporter for the *Hartford Courant*, and earned a degree from the Hartford Theological Seminary. For the next nine years, he put the newspaper business aside and was a resident at settlement houses in Hartford, Chicago, and Pittsburgh. While in Chicago, he published the city's first social settlements directory, was appointed general executive for the first citywide recreation program, and completed graduate studies at Chicago Theological Seminary. Gavit revived his journalism career in 1902 with a series of assignments for the Associated Press. During the next ten years he served as the AP's Albany correspondent, then as the Washington, D.C., bureau chief, and finally, in Chicago, as superintendent of the Central American Division. He was named editor of the *New York Evening Post* from 1912 to 1918. This led to an association with the Americanization study being developed by the Carnegie Institute.

In 1918 Gavit became involved with a five-year study of resources utilized by various social service agencies to assimilate immigrants into the American mainstream. Using data from government studies, oral histories, and statistical reports, the editors published a series of ten books for the Carnegie Institute.

The enterprise created a sympathetic depiction of immigrants' difficulties in adapting to the new culture. Each work dealt with a unique topic and offered social workers appropriate guidelines and outlined responses to many of the common concerns in aiding the immigrants. Because of his background in social work and his proven verbal and editorial skills, Gavit was chosen to author the Carnegie work on naturalization. Gavit's book, *Americans by Choice*, published in 1920, exploded the entrenched stereotypes of the recent immigrants from Slavic, Baltic, and Southern European countries, portrayed in the media as inferior people unwilling to become involved in American civic life. Gavit's field team researched material from twenty-eight courts handling immigrant affairs and found that these groups had applied for citizenship status more quickly and in larger numbers than did earlier groups of immigrants. To support his contention, Gavit presented factual, but favorable, descriptions of typical immigrant families.

To him, they were young married couples, poor, frightened, and attuned to a different rhythm of life. They scrambled for the few available jobs. Theirs was a gradual and painful absorption of American language and traditions. Only after finding a degree of economic and social stability would they become interested in citizenship. Having become families with a stake in America they achieved citizenship at a high rate. The reason for this rapid assimilation was not any inherent racial or ethnic quality. These groups were refugees. They had fled from autocratic governments or poor economic opportunities to a society which offered, if nothing else, hope. They took citizenship very seriously. To demonstrate this point, Gavit introduced conclusions arrived at from studying immigrant voting patterns from three midwestern cities. The immigrants did not vote blindly in ethnic blocs; they were concerned with issues. He was able to draw two generalizations: the women were pragmatists, voting for their "pocketbook"; the men tended to be idealists, following candidates who promised honest government. As a result, this democratic process produced involved citizens unlikely to join the socialist groups attempting to organize in immigrant communities.

The interpretation of the new immigrant's decent character won Gavit favorable press. The book, according to critics, offered a sympathetic and balanced discussion of the particular problems and pressures placed on these people. His work done, Gavit returned to the *Post* in 1920, resuming his editorial responsibilities and publishing a controversial book on American college life. When the *Post* changed ownership in 1924, he was asked to leave. Two years later he released his study of the early twentieth century opium trade, the first of its kind, and then published a second work on immigrants, *Americans from Abroad*, which became a research tool for those who wished to understand the new immigrant problems by reading from primary materials. Drawing from autobiographies and novels, this short pamphlet outlined and critiqued the best works from Slavic and Italian-American authors. In 1927 he began an association with the *Survey*, a journal of social inquiry and reform edited by Paul Kellogg,* one that would continue for twenty-seven years. He started as a contributing editor, writing a monthly column.

Thirteen years later he was appointed business manager, and in 1946 he became vice president of Survey Publications, Inc., the publishing company. He served in that capacity until his death in Winter Park, Florida, on October 27, 1954.

Available material on John P. Gavit is scattered and fragmented. The best account of the essential facts of his life is his obituary in the *New York Times*, October 28, 1954. His own writings, however, provide the reader with the clearest picture of his personality and his ''mission.'' The works by Gavit cited above were written by a man intent on eradicating unflattering contemporary opinions on immigrants, especially the so-called new immigrant. Two later works, *Opium* (1926) and *College* (1925), present Gavit as a literate, sensitive, practical man with a highly defined sense of propriety and morality.

For Gavit's impact on further immigrant and naturalization studies, see the following: Peter A. Speek, *A Stake in the Land* (1921); Charles E. Merriam and Harold Gosnell, *Non-voting: Causes and Methods of Control* (1924); Annie Marion Machean, *Modern Immigration* (1925); Francis J. Brown and Joseph Slabey, *Our Racial and National Minorities* (1937); and *One American* (1946); Edward G. Hartman, *The Movement to Americanize the Immigrants* (1948); and John Higham, *Strangers in the Land* (1955).

EDWARD B. ROWE

**Gerry, Elbridge Thomas** (December 25, 1837–February 18, 1927), lawyer and founder of the Societies for the Prevention of Cruelty to Children, was born in New York City, the son of Thomas R. and Hannah G. (Goelet) Gerry. Elbridge Gerry was named after his famous grandfather, who had signed the Declaration of Independence, and served as vice president of the United States under James Madison, and whose creative districting while Governor of Massachusetts inspired the term ''gerrymandering.'' Gerry, then, was a member of a prominent political family in the Northeast. In 1857, at the age of twenty, he graduated from Columbia College in New York and immediately began study of the law; three years later he was admitted to the New York Bar Association.

Gerry was early recognized as a successful attorney and in 1867 was elected a member of the New York State Constitutional Convention. In 1870 he became legal counsel for the American Society for the Prevention of Cruelty to Animals (ASPCA), located in New York City and founded in 1866 by philanthropist Henry Bergh.

Gerry's involvement in social welfare reform began most prominently with his legal work for that agency, especially in the landmark child protection case of ''Mary Ellen.'' Mary Ellen was an eight-year-old abandoned girl who lived with guardians in New York City. A visitor to the tenement building in which she lived discovered that the girl was harshly mistreated by her guardians. (Mary Ellen later testified that she had been beaten daily with a rawhide whip and attacked with scissors.) The visitor contacted numerous child-caring agencies to ask for intervention on behalf of the young girl. When none responded, claiming that such protective services were not provided by their agencies, the woman, in desperation, called Henry Bergh. Bergh then contacted the police and the court and got the ASPCA to hire Gerry and an associate, Ambrose Monell, to institute legal proceedings designed to remove the girls from her guardians and place her under the custody of kinder people. The famous case, in the spring of 1874, came to an end when, after twenty minutes of deliberation, the jury returned a verdict of guilty; Mary Ellen's guardian-mother was sentenced to a year in prison, and the girl was sent to a children's institution. Gerry was so impressed by the case and the abuses of children that came to light during the trial that he devoted the rest of his life to the cause of child protection.

The Mary Ellen case illustrated the need for an agency to prevent and respond to child abuse and neglect. Gerry proposed beginning an organized society for the prevention of such cruelty to children. Although his friends were sympathetic, they were not sufficiently moved to join with him in organizing such a society. He continued to promote the idea, however, and eventually met John D. Wright, who shared his concern and commitment to act. The two men issued invitations to friends and interested citizens to attend an introductory organizational meeting. Thus, on December 29, 1874, approximately eight months after Gerry tried the Mary Ellen case, the first meeting of the fledgling New York Society for the Prevention of Cruelty to Children was convened by Gerry and Wright, with the support of Henry Bergh.

This meeting was chaired by Wright who, along with Gerry, gave speeches on the subject. The work of child-care agencies was commended, but they stressed the need for someone to seek out and rescue children from city slums, where many youngsters were abused by brutish guardians. Reflecting Gerry's civic-mindedness, the new Society was pledged to work with existing agencies and remain free from religious or political influence. On April 27, 1885, the Society for the Prevention of Cruelty to Children (SPCC) was incorporated as a social agency to enforce laws enacted to prevent the abuse of children. Gerry's vision, persistence, founding, and continuing interest and leadership in this agency resulted in its being called the "Gerry Society."

The Society was internally structured to have a paid secretary and volunteer officers. It was overseen by its members and their president. Gerry served as president from 1879 to 1901, although his active involvement not only preceded but succeeded his presidency. Thus, Gerry's role in child welfare went far beyond creating and supporting the New York Society; his concern for children extended throughout the state and the nation, and his "missionary" activity contributed to the establishment of hundreds of Society chapters all across the country. Gerry first articulated his philosophy of the Society in a speech entitled "The Relation of Societies for the Prevention of Cruelty to Children to Child Saving Work" at the National Conference of Charities and Correction in 1882. He then addressed numerous conferences, at home and abroad, on the subject, and through his travels, his speeches, and his organizing efforts, Society chapters dedicated to child protection and supporting legislation became international in scope.

In addition to promoting the Society's proliferation at home and abroad, Gerry's efforts included defending the agency mission and operation. This defense brought him into conflict with social welfare colleagues and reformers on several occasions. Thus Homer Folks criticized the Society's emphasis on children's institutions rather than on home placement, and in 1898 the Society legally challenged the New York State Board of Charities' newly gained supervisory authority over child-caring agencies, contending that the SPCC was not subject to the Board's oversight. The Court of Appeals narrowly ruled in favor of the Society on the grounds that it was not a charitable, correctional, or reformatory institution. The Society's concern for independence from state supervision, its fear of losing authority, and its defense of children's institutions at a time when home placement was growing kept it at odds with many reformers. The Society also opposed creation of the New York Child Labor Committee in 1902 and the U.S. Children's Bureau in 1912. The latter, Gerry and its members argued, was an expensive and unnecessary centralization of power that would dictate child welfare policy to the states. Such comments provoked replies by social welfare advocates, including Lillian Wald,* who charged Gerry not only with protecting the Society's interests but with opposing progressive child welfare measures.

As a prominent New York citizen and lawyer, Gerry served in a variety of other capacities. In 1878 he began thirty-four years as governor of New York Hospital. He also served on a state commission on capital punishment. In addition, he was a trustee of the General Theological Seminary (1877–1913) and the American Museum of Natural History (1895–1902). He traveled widely, maintained a villa in Newport, Rhode Island, owned New York City real estate, collected art, acquired a 30,000–volume law library, and was actively interested in politics, although he did not seek elective office himself. Despite these and other involvements, child protection was his primary occupation, one that continued throughout his life. Whatever his personal feelings and his stand on state supervision and federal involvement in social welfare may have been, Gerry was responsible for the creation throughout the world of more than 500 Societies for the Prevention of Cruelty to Children—a monumental contribution to social welfare.

At the age of ninety, Gerry fell and broke his hip. He was cared for at his New York City home, where he was confined to bed. Two weeks after the fall, he died peacefully in his sleep due to heart failure.

There is no collection of Gerry's papers, nor is there any full-length study of his life or of the Society for the Prevention of Cruelty to Children. A significant obituary is in the *New York Times*, February 19, 1927. Additional references can be found in Robert Bremner's *Children and Youth in America: A Documentary History* vol. 2 (1970–1974), and Walter Trattner's *Homer Folks: Pioneer in Social Welfare* (1968).

GARY R. ANDERSON

**Girard, Stephen** (May 20, 1750–December 26, 1831), social reformer and philanthropist, was born in Chartrous (near Bordeaux), France, to Pierre and Ann Marie (Lafarque) Girard. His first years were similar to those of other privileged French children of the time, but at the age of eight he lost his right eye in an accident and his formal schooling ended, a condition that preoccupied him for the rest of his life. In any event, as the result of a family quarrel, he left home at age fourteen and went to sea, never again returning to live with his family. Demonstrating an aptitude for the nautical life, he won a captain's commission by the time he was twenty-three, two years before it technically was allowed under French law. The following year, however, he took up residence in America, moving in 1776 to Philadelphia, where he remained until his death.

A shrewd businessman, Girard quickly amassed a substantial fortune, much of which he used to help support charitable institutions that provided for widows, orphans, the deaf and dumb, and the sick. In addition to these financial contributions, however, Girard became known for his personal services during the yellow fever epidemics which periodically ravaged the residents of Philadelphia. He distrusted American physicians, considering them incompetents, and particularly disapproved of the favorite treatments of his fellow Philadelphian, the celebrated patriot-physician Benjamin Rush,* signer of the Declaration of Independence.

In the great epidemic of 1793, after President Washington and Governor Mifflin had fled the city, Girard and Rush stayed behind to take leading and opposing positions in tending the afflicted. Girard and his friends acquired Bush Hill, a large, old mansion in which they installed a French physician who had dealt with yellow fever in the Caribbean, using methods generally rejected by Rush. Girard used his superb organizing abilities to turn a chaotic collecting house of the dead and dying into an efficient system for helping the sick. His services proved valuable in several epidemics that followed.

Girard remained doggedly loyal to his adopted country, resisting entreaties to return to France. During the War of 1812, he intervened when less than 50 percent of a needed government loan was subscribed. Through his personal efforts, he made it possible for the government to raise the money it required to pursue the war. Later, it was his assurance of support that made it possible to open the second Bank of the United States.

Despite his many actions, during his lifetime Girard was thought by some to be a tight-fisted tyrant. Thus, his place in the history of social welfare may not have been secured but for a creative and unusual portion of his will, one which was not actually implemented until more than a decade after his death, but which survives today.

When he died, Girard was a widower without children, and possibly the wealthiest man in America, with a fortune of about $7 million. Leaving less than $150,000 to surviving relatives, he designated a major portion of his money for bequests to the Pennsylvania Hospital; for improvement of Philadelphia streets; for development of canals in Pennsylvania; and for various agents of assorted philanthropies.

The residue of his estate, however, valued at about $6 million, was left for the establishment of a charitable foundation to erect and manage a "college for poor white male orphans." It was the largest single charitable foundation created in the United States before the Civil War.

The action was characteristic of Girard for several reasons. First, he made the will a complex instrument of his desires which was designed to withstand the assaults that he seemed to anticipate would be hurled against it. Daniel Webster himself led the final charge, and lost. Second, Girard took an uncommonly comprehensive view of the needs of his beneficiaries, making provision for their housing, clothing, education, books, food, physical care and comfort, and protection from what he considered unfit influences on the developing mind. To this end, he charged not only that the orphans should receive excellent physical care but that "no ecclesiastic, missionary, or minister of any sect whatsoever, shall ever hold or exercise any station or duty whatever in the said College; nor . . . be admitted for any purpose, or as a visitor, within the premises." It was a daring provision to make in a time when eleemosynary work was heavily influenced by religious motivations and agencies.

Finally, Girard's gigantic bequest directly challenged the prevailing prohibition against such foundations in the early republic. Many English laws specifically forbade charitable trusts, and they had been discouraged in the new nation after the Revolution, on two grounds. There were considered to be dangerous vehicles for religious interference and power; and they were held to withdraw resources which should be recirculated by each generation in a free economy, a position which seemed affirmed in an 1819 U.S. Supreme Court decision—*Philadelphia Baptist Association vs. Hart's Executors*—written by John Marshall. However, twenty-five years later, in the case of *Vidal vs. Girard's Executors* (1844), the Court decided in favor of the provisions of Girard's will, creating a new, permissive stance toward the establishment of large philanthropic trusts. Thus, Stephen Girard, through his remarkable will, developed a new approach to American social welfare philanthropy which became the model for many of the major foundations created thereafter—and still being created today.

Girard died at his home in Philadelphia from complications resulting from influenza and pneumonia on December 26, 1831.

Girard was enormously influential in his lifetime, and there is no shortage of bibliographic material about him, including full-dress biographies, the first of which appeared less than a year after his death. The Stephen Girard Collection of his letters and other papers is kept at Girard College, but microfilm copies are available at the American Philosophical Society Library, also in Philadelphia. The 1832 *Biography of Stephen Girard* by Stephen Simpson, son of a Girard cashier, was sharply attacked in *The Life and Character of Stephen Girard* by Henry Ingram (1892), one example of the controversies which have persisted about Girard. The most carefully examined aspects of his life have been his business practices and his philanthropic activities, but they have not been considered together. Thus, Donald Adams called Girard "the first of the great investment bankers" in his extensive study of Girard's business operations, *Finance and Free Enterprise in Early America* (1978), but did not make even a casual reference to his many charities. Conversely, in *Some American Pioneers of Social Welfare* (1937), Edith Abbott devotes a chapter to Girard's humanitarian activities alone. Unfortunately, neither of these common lines of inquiry gives attention to the extraordinary legal impact of Girard's remarkable will. That must be sought in studies and monographs on the origins of the American charity system and attendant laws. One excellent source is the slim volume *The Legal Foundations of American Philanthropy: 1776–1844* (1961). In it, Howard Miller discusses the "restrictive interlude" respecting charitable foundations, beginning with the Supreme Court's *Hart* decision in 1819 and continuing until the same Court ruled unanimously in favor of a more permissive legal stance in *Vidal vs. Girard's Executors* in 1844. Even though full implementation of the *Girard* decision took some years, the legal basis for all subsequent development of charitable trusts had been laid through the vision and foresight of Stephen Girard.

CHARLES GUZZETTA

**Glenn, John Mark** (October 28, 1858–April 20, 1950), social work administrator and foundation director, was born in Baltimore, Maryland, the eldest child of William Wilkins Glenn, a well-known lawyer, newspaper publisher, and businessman, and Ellen Mark (Smith) Glenn. He was raised in one of Baltimore's wealthiest and most socially prominent families whose male members usually distinguished themselves in areas such as law, finance, and industrial development. His uncle, John Glenn, was one of the major founders of the charity organization society movement of the late nineteenth century. After attending a small Episcopal school near his home on the outskirts of Baltimore, Glenn enrolled at Washington and Lee University, where he received a B.A. and an M.A. in 1878 and 1879, respectively; he then earned a law degree from the University of Maryland in 1882. He was a devout Episcopalian and was active in the charitable endeavors of that faith through his lifetime. On May 2, 1902, he married Mary Wilcox Brown (Mary Wilcox Glenn*), then general secretary of the Baltimore Charity Organization Society (COS) and later a distinguished figure in numerous national charitable and social service organizations and societies; they had no children.

At the age of twenty-nine, after several years of successfully expanding the Glenn family business and real estate holdings, he began his involvement in the charitable endeavors of Baltimore. He would play an important role in both the private and public assistance programs of that city for the next twenty years. His legal training and business acumen prepared him well for administrative positions in these activities, and he quickly became chairman of the executive committee of the Baltimore Charity Organization Society. Less ideological than may COS leaders, Glenn also was involved in the administration of Baltimore's rudimentary public assistance programs as president of the Board of Supervisors for city charities. He received his first significant national exposure as president of the National Conference of Charities and Correction, an influential organization composed of leaders from both the private and public charitable relief organizations and correctional institutions.

In 1907 Glenn was appointed the first director of the newly formed Russell Sage Foundation, requiring him to move from Baltimore to New York City, where he lived until his death in 1950. In 1906 Russell Sage, an immensely wealthy railroad financier, died and left his widow approximately $65 million. In memory of her husband, Mrs. Sage decided to set up a foundation to better social and living conditions in the United States, and one of the consultants she engaged concerning this prospective foundation was John Glenn. In the initial planning, it was decided that the foundation would be established with an endowment of $10 million, which would provide a yearly income of approximately $450,000. Foundations were a relative novelty then, and the Russell Sage Foundation was the ninth one established in the United States. None of the others had improvement of social conditions as a primary goal, nor did any of them have the wide latitude of inquiry and action that was invested in the Russell Sage Foundation. During the planning process it became apparent that Glenn would be a logical choice for the Foundation's first director because of his previous experience in both public and private charities and his national contacts gained through the National Conference of Charities and Correction.

Under Glenn's leadership the Foundation quickly became a major social welfare resource on a national scale with its three components of research, demonstration, and consultation. Glenn's famous quote, that the "first function of the foundation should be investigation, the second education," summed up the philosophy he provided for the Foundation during its first twenty-four years. He was one of the first prominent social workers to emphasize the need for research, and that effective social change and efficient social policies must be based on data obtained through research methods. He also was an influential figure in guiding the profession to the realization that successful social work practice must be based on empirical research. Glenn hired a permanent staff of highly qualified social workers to carry on the activities of the Foundation and organized its working operations into a number of divisions. Some of the specific divisions focused on child welfare, private charity, children's recreation, and working and housing conditions for the poor. Each of these divisions was assisted by separate departments of statistics and publications. Grants were made to outside sources as well, if the project appeared to be a worthwhile endeavor that would be completed quickly or subsequently would be supported through other funding.

Under Glenn's leadership, a number of important projects were conducted or funded by the Foundation. Among these were five-year grants to the four early schools of social work (New York, Chicago, Boston, and St. Louis) to enhance planning and curriculum development. A major grant was given to complete the Pittsburgh Survey, a pioneering effort in examining the social and economic conditions of the working poor. The five-volume work that emerged from that survey provided much ammunition for social reformers attempting to improve the working and living conditions of the poor in industrial cities throughout America. As one of his division heads, he hired Mary Richmond,* and in 1917 the Foundation published her classic book, *Social Diagnosis*. In all, eighty-four books and hundreds of pamphlets on social conditions, social work practice, child welfare, children's recreation, health conditions and services, education, and related topics were produced during the years Glenn was director of the Foundation. During his tenure he also oversaw the development of the Foundation's library, which soon became the largest and most comprehensive social work library in the country.

Glenn retired as director of the Foundation in 1931 but played an active part as a member of the board of trustees until 1948. In 1947, along with Lilian Brandt* and F. Emerson Andrews, he wrote a detailed two-volume history of the Foundation entitled *Russell Sage Foundation, 1907–1946*.

The legacy of John Glenn is closely interwoven with the foundation with which he was associated for many years. His concern for the less fortunate in society and his convictions that effective social changes and social work practice could be based only on reliable data and competent research were reflected in the activities and publications of the Russell Sage Foundation. Under his leadership, this foundation and its endeavors did much to change the conditions of the poor and greatly influenced the nature of social policies, social work education, and social services that were offered in this country. John Glenn died in New York City on April 20, 1950.

There are several good sources providing information concerning Glenn's life and professional accomplishments, even though a comprehensive biographical treatment of his life does not exist. A concise summary of his life is provided in his obituary in the *New York Times*, April 21, 1950, 24. Two short biographical sketches are contained in *Dictionary of American Biography*, Supplement 4 (1974), 332–334; and the *Encylcopedia of Social Work*, 17th issue, vol. 1 (1977), 507–508. Two books which discuss Glenn's work are Frank J. Bruno, *Trends in Social Work* (1948), and Roy Lubove, *The Professional Altruist* (1971). A final source that may be helpful is a tribute written by one of Glenn's closest associates: Shelby M. Harrison, "John Mark Glenn," *Survey* (June 1950), 308.

GARY MOOERS

**Glenn, Mary Wilcox** (December 14, 1869–November 3, 1940), private welfare organization leader, social casework advocate, and promoter of the professionalization of social work, was born in Baltimore, Maryland, the eldest daughter of John Wilcox Brown, a prominent banker and former colonel in the Confederate army, and Ellen Turner (Macfarland) Brown. She was raised in an affluent and achievement-oriented family of thirteen children. Several of her siblings also went on to noteworthy careers, including a sister, Elenor Brown

Merrill, who served for many years as executive director of the National Society for the Prevention of Blindness. As was common for young girls of her social status, she was educated at home and at a private women's college, Miss Hall's School in Baltimore. A devout Episcopalian, her deep religious convictions strongly influenced her lifelong activities in charitable and social welfare organizations and causes. On May 2, 1902, she married John Mark Glenn,* at the time a wealthy Baltimore attorney and volunteer leader in social welfare development and reform; they had no children.

She began her social work career after spending three years as an English teacher. In 1897 she took the position as general secretary of the Henry Watson Children's Aid Society of Baltimore. In 1900 she became general secretary of the Baltimore Charity Organization Society, replacing Mary Richmond.* This early relationship with Richmond matured and grew stronger as the two collaborated on many causes and projects until Richmond's death in 1928. Her marriage in 1902 to John Glenn marked the end of her paid employment in the social welfare field and began her long career as an organizer, advisor, and board member of many influential organizations involved with social reform and social service provision. For the next thirty-five years she would exert great influence in the developing social work profession in her various volunteer roles.

In 1907 John M. Glenn was chosen as the first executive head of the newly formed Russell Sage Foundation, a position he held until 1931. This position necessitated a move to New York City, where Mrs. Glenn resided for the rest of her life, and enabled her to shift the focus of her volunteer activities from the local charities in Baltimore to the more sophisticated organizations in New York. This rapidly led to leadership positions in both national and international organizations.

Mary Wilcox Glenn helped to organize and served on boards and committees of a multitude of religious, philanthropic, and professional organizations. Some of her more important contributions were made to the very influential Charity Organization Society of New York, where she served as a central council member from 1908 to 1939. She also was an active participant in the National Conference of Charities and Correction (which later evolved into the National Conference on Social Welfare), serving as the president of this organization in 1915. In addition, she was instrumental in founding, in 1919, and, as president, in administering the National Council of the Church Mission of Help (later the Episcopal Service for Youth), a national church-based organization to assist female delinquents. She served this organization in that capacity until 1937. Meanwhile, in 1924, she also became a charter member and an important figure in the American Committee of the International Migration Services, an international social work organization which assisted political exiles and displaced persons around the world. This interest led naturally to her helping to create and administer an organization called Hospites, which helped assimilate refugee social workers from various totalitarian countries in Europe during the 1930s. She also was a major figure in the Red Cross, both on a local and national level.

Perhaps her most important volunteer contribution, however, was with the Family Welfare Association of America, which she helped establish in 1911 and then served as either president or chairman of the board from 1920 to 1937. This was a most important organization which, under her leadership, stressed the need for professional training for social workers and the efficacy of the social casework method of treatment. In her leadership capacity in this organization, Glenn visited most of the major cities of the United States on a regular basis, lecturing at the early schools of social work and consulting with local private social work agencies. This role as the advocate of professional training and the social casework method is perhaps her most important legacy. She was, along with Mary Richmond, an early and major leader in the development of high standards of social work practice based on professional training. She was a regular lecturer at the early schools of social work, particularly the New York and Chicago schools, and offered much support and authority to their pioneering efforts. Her support of the social casework method and her expertise in this area also led her to represent the United States in two international social work conferences, in Paris in 1928 and in Frankfort in 1932.

Glenn's accomplishments were based not on extraordinary speaking abilities or remarkable writing skills, although she was capable at both. Her contributions came through her ability to organize, administer, and inspire others to work together toward common goals. Her obvious sincerity, her religious ideals, and her willingness to let others receive major credit for what was accomplished made her a much respected figure in the social work profession. Her long years of devoted volunteer service greatly influenced the development of professional social work training, the standards of casework practice, and the nature of social service provision in the United States from the turn of the century until the outbreak of World War II. Mary Wilcox Glenn died in New York City on November 3, 1940.

There has been no comprehensive biographical treatment of Glenn's life, but two helpful biographical sketches are included in *Notable American Women 1607–1950*, vol. 2 (1971), 52–53; and *Enclyclopedia of Social Work* 17th issue, vol. 1 (1977), 507–508. A useful summary of Glenn's life is provided in her obituary in the *New York Times*, November 5, 1940. Two other sources that may be of interest are tributes to Glenn that appeared in the December, 1940, editions of both the *Social Service Review* and the *Family*.

GARY MOOERS

**Goddard, Henry Herbert** (August 14, 1866–June 19, 1957), psychologist, teacher, and author, was born in Vassalboro, Maine, the son of Henry Clay Goddard and Sarah (Winslow) Goddard, both Quakers. His father was a modestly successful farmer who died in 1875. His mother was a traveling minister. The Society of Friends augmented her earnings, thus enabling young Henry to attend the Moses Brown School, Providence, Rhode Island, and then Haverford College, where he earned his B.A. in 1887. The next year Goddard taught botany, mathematics, and Latin at the University of Southern California. He returned to Haverford, finished his M.A. in 1889, and, on August 7, 1889, married Emma Florence Robbins. This was a happy marriage, albeit disappointingly childless. Goddard was a secondary school principal until 1896, when he entered Clark University to study with G. Stanley Hall. He received his Ph.D. in 1899; until 1906, he was a professor of psychology at the Pennsylvania State Normal School in West Chester. In March, 1900, Goddard visited the New Jersey Association for the Study of Children and Youth, where by chance he met Edward R. Johnstone, the dynamic superintendent of the New Jersey Training School for Feeble-Minded Girls and Boys, in Vineland. Johnstone converted Goddard to the study of feeblemindedness, thus setting the direction for Goddard's career as an applied psychologist who did research for social work. Soon Goddard advised Johnstone on scientific matters. In 1906 Johnstone appointed Goddard the first director of psychological research at Vineland.

Goddard remained at Vineland until 1918, becoming internationally renowned in his field. While in Europe in 1908 he discovered the scaled mental test of French psychologists Alfred Binet and Theodore Simon; he quickly saw its potential applicability for distinguishing among levels of mental retardation. In 1911, after much adaptation and standardization, he pronounced his version of the Binet test (the first American one) as capable of measuring fundamental mental processes. In 1909 he began a lengthy correspondence with Charles B. Davenport, the leader of American eugenics, which converted him to that cause. Goddard was convinced that low innate intelligence caused immoral or antisocial behavior. His best known work, *The Kallikak Family: A Study in the Heredity of Feeble-Mindedness* (1912), argued this position, as did, less certainly, *The Criminal Imbecile* (1915). Yet Goddard was simply applying to his special area the fundamental assumption of contemporary natural science, that psychobiological structure determines mental and cultural function. He believed that he was merely testing a hypothesis, not pronouncing an inflexible natural law. Even in *Feeble-Mindedness: Its Causes and Consequences* (1914), a survey of the Vineland inmates, he readily conceded that environment caused mental retardation in 20 percent of all cases. It was his lurid, melodramatic popular writing, in which he implied that mental defects caused antisocial conduct, which gave him an exaggerated reputation as a die-hard hereditarian.

Mindful that society never would support institutionalization of all retarded persons, in his last six years at Vineland he busied himself with working out practical means of training the so-called morons, the high-grade mental unfortunates between eight and twelve mental years, to live in a civilized society. As a consultant to the U.S. Children's Bureau, the Immigration Bureau, and the New York schools, among other institutions, he began to question some of his former assumptions. By 1918 he had decided that the real measure of a person's social worth was the ability to be a constructive citizen, not an intelligence quotient; indeed, he criticized that instrument, arguing for a full, interdisciplinary evaluation of the individual, thus anticipating modern clinical psychology. Although he participated in the preparation of the Army mental tests, he soon dissociated himself from the racial testing movement of the 1920s on scientific and humanitarian grounds.

In 1918 Goddard became the second director of the Ohio Bureau of Juvenile Research, in Columbus, an institution which he as a progressive Democrat had suggested to the reform governor James B. Cox in 1913. The Bureau was supposed to examine all minor offenders and recommend placement at appropriate state and county institutions. In working with a different research population, he came to understand that juvenile delinquency was caused by emotional conflicts, not low intelligence, as he explained in *Juvenile Delinquency* (1921), a book he wrote in part to save the Bureau and the new State Board of Control it represented. Goddard was no politician; the Bureau barely survived the 1921 legislative session, and in 1922 Goddard accepted a professorship of abnormal psychology at Ohio State University, where he became a legendary figure in classroom, office, and laboratory. In 1938 he reluctantly retired, and moved to Santa Barbara, California.

Goddard was one of the most important applied or child psychologists of his day. His work mirrored almost perfectly larger conceptual and therapeutic shifts in applied psychology and social work from structural descriptions to functional therapies; he marched at or near the head of the social workers' parade between 1900 and 1925. Because he was näive at politics and indifferent to public relations, after he left the Ohio Bureau of Juvenile Research he lost the great national recognition he enjoyed earlier. In actuality he was an uncomplicated, humane man who only wished to use science to aid others.

Goddard died in Santa Barbara in 1957.

Goddard's voluminous papers are located at the Archives of the History of American Psychology, University of Akron. Since he was a prolific correspondent, many of his outgoing letters can be found in other collections, for example, the Charles B. Davenport Papers, American Philosophical Society, in Philadelphia, Pennsylvania. Edgar A. Doll, ed., *Twenty-Fifth Anniversary: Vineland Laboratory, 1906–1931* (1932), is a guide to Goddard's publications, as is his entry in Carl Murchison, ed., *The Psychological Register* (1933). His other major works are *School Training of Defective Children* (1915); *The Psychology of the Normal and Subnormal* (1919); *Human Efficiency and Levels of Intelligence* (1920), which should be contrasted with "The Problem of the Psychopathic Child," *American Journal of Insanity* 77 (1920), 511–516; "Feeble-Mindedness and Delinquency," *Journal of Psycho-Asthenics* 25 (1920), 168–176; "The Sub-Normal Mind Versus the Abnormal," *Journal of Abnormal Psychology* 16 (1921), 47–54. See also Florence Mateer, "The Future of Clinical Psychology," *Journal of Delinquency* 6 (1921), 283–293. Obituaries appeared in the *New York Times* (June 22, 1957), *Newsweek* (July 1, 1957), and *American Journal of Psychology* (December, 1957).

Other accounts of Goddard may be found in Mark H. Haller, *Eugenics: Hereditarian Attitudes in American Thought, 1870–1930* (1963, 1984); and Hamilton Cravens, *The Triumph of Evolution: American Scientists and the Hereditary-Environment Controversy 1900–1941* (1978). A reasonably accurate guide to the ideas of Goddard's coprofessionals is Stanley Powell Davies, *Social Control of the Mentally Deficient* (1930); an example of retrospective methodological criticism by a contemporary scientist is Stephen Jay Gould, *The Mismeasure of Man* (1981), a work of chiefly polemical value.

HAMILTON CRAVENS

**Goldmark, Josephine Clara** (October 13, 1877–December 15, 1950), social investigator and reformer, was born in Brooklyn, New York, the youngest of ten children of Joseph and Regina (Wehle) Goldmark. Joseph Goldmark was born in Poland and educated in Austria. A graduate of the University of Vienna medical school and a physician, he also was a member of the Austrian parliament and a leader of the unsuccessful 1848 Revolution, after which his life was in danger. He thus fled, first to Switzerland and then to the United States, arriving in 1850 and quickly establishing himself as a doctor and a research chemist. He also helped to organize the Republican Party and secured several patents, including one for a compound used in percussion caps by Union soldiers during the Civil War. His wife, Regina, was a member of a wealthy Jewish family which had emigrated from Prague to the United States in 1849, settling in Indiana.

Following Dr. Goldmark's death in 1881, leadership in the family, which remained financially secure, was exercised in part by Josephine's eldest sister, Helen, and her husband, Felix Adler, founder of the Ethical Culture movement. Another sister, Alice, married Louis D. Brandeis, the well-known Boston lawyer and later U.S. Supreme Court justice. Her older brother, Henry, was an internationally known civil engineer.

Josephine Goldmark attended the Brackett School in New York City and then Bryn Mawr College, where she majored in English and received her B.A. in 1898. She then took a year of graduate work, in education, at Barnard College, where she served as a tutor from 1903 to 1905. Meanwhile, through her sister Pauline,* who was assistant secretary of the New York Consumers' League, she met Florence Kelley,* head of the National Consumers' League (NCL), for whom she served as a volunteer assistant at the organization's New York headquarters. In 1903, however, she was appointed publications secretary for the National Consumers' League, a position she held for the next five years. In that capacity, she compiled the League's annual handbooks, which summarized child labor legislation and led to the publication, in 1907, of her *Child Labor Legislation Handbook*.

In 1908 the NCL's Committee on Legislation and Legal Defense of Labor Laws was created and Josephine Goldmark became its chairman. That same year, she, her sister Pauline, and Florence Kelley persuaded Louis Brandeis to represent the state of Oregon before the U.S. Supreme Court in its effort to uphold the legality of a recently enacted statute which limited women to a maximum of ten hours' employment per day. That, in turn, led to the preparation of the famous "Brandeis brief" in the historic *Muller v. Oregon* case (1908), in which the Court unanimously ruled that, in the name of public welfare, the state had the right to regulate the number of hours women may work in industry. That brief, which rested on a massive amount of medical, economic, and social data quickly collected for Brandeis by the trio—data that clearly showed the ill effects that prolonged labor had on working women—marked the admission, for the first time, of such material as evidence in Supreme Court cases and, in the process, established the efficacy of social research as an instrument in social change.

Thereafter, Goldmark and Brandeis collaborated on a number of other successful legislative and legal battles on behalf of oppressed women and children—in Illinois, Virginia, Michigan, Louisiana, and elsewhere. In addition, with the help of U.S. Senator Robert La Follette of Wisconsin, Josephine Goldmark and Florence Kelley were instrumental in the passage of a law to protect working women in the nation's capital. Then, along with her sister Pauline, she also contributed significantly to the work of the New York State factory commission investigating the famous Triangle Shirtwaist Company fire in 1911, helping to prepare its recommendations for further legislation to safeguard workers' welfare. At the same time, in 1912, she published her monumental and best-known work, *Fatigue and Efficiency*, which established the scientific validity of fatigue as an adverse industrial phenomenon—one that not only harmed workers but decreased their efficiency and productivity—and proved to be a powerful weapon in the long struggle for shorter working hours.

When America entered World War I, Josephine Goldmark was summoned to national duty; as a member of the Committee on Industrial Fatigue of the Council of National Defense, she, along with Mary Hopkins, researched the effects on workers of ten-hour and eight-hour work shifts in wartime factories. She then completed what has been called a "brilliant health and hospital survey" of Cleveland, Ohio, which, in 1919, led to an invitation by Charles-Edward Amory Winslow* to serve as secretary to the Rockefeller Foundation's Committee for the Study of Nursing Education, which he chaired. That committee subsequently published *Nursing and Nursing Education in the United States* (1923), or the so-called Winslow-Goldmark report, which contained Goldmark's exhaustive study of more than seventy nursing schools and agencies across the country and was profoundly influential in the development of improved nurses' training. Her interest in public health and welfare also found an outlet in her service as a director of the New York Visiting Nurse Service for twenty years and in the National Consumers' League's campaign in the 1920s to secure legal safeguards for workers subject to poisoning from radium used in the production of luminous instrument dials.

In her last years, Josephine Goldmark, who believed that "human problems are not insoluble to educated intelligence" and who spent her long, productive life informing the public of social and economic injustice and waging war against it, lived with her sister Pauline in Hartsdale, New York; together they avidly pursued their lifelong avocation as amateur naturalists, until Josephine died of a heart condition in White Plains, New York, on December 15, 1950, at age seventy-three.

The Josephine Goldmark Papers are at the Women's Archives at Radcliffe College in Cambridge, Massachusetts, while the National Consumers' League Papers, which also contain mainy items by and about Josephine Goldmark, are in the Manuscript Division of the Library of Congress in Washington, D.C.

Some of Goldmark's more important publications not cited above are *Women in Industry: Muller v. Oregon* (1908); *The Case for the Shorter Work Day: Bunting v. the State of Oregon* (1916); *Studies in Industrial Psychology: Fatigue in Relation to Working Capacity* (1920); and *Impatient Crusader: Florence Kelley's Life Story* (1953), published posthumously.

Also see Carl Wittke's *Refugees of Revolution* (1952), which includes comments on Joseph Goldmark's contributions to America, and Mary M. Roberts' *American Nursing: History and Interpretation* (1959), which summarizes Goldmark's contributions to the nursing profession.

Also useful are Robert Bremner's entry on Josephine Goldmark in *Notable American Women* (1971), and brief sketches of her in the *Encyclopedia of Social Work* (1971), and *Social Service Review* (March, 1951). Finally, see also Robert Bremner's *Fromthe Depths: The Discovery of Poverty in the United States* (1956) and Louis Athey, ''The Consumers' Leagues and Social Reform, 1890–1923,'' Ph.D. dissertation, University of Delaware, 1965. An obituary appeared in the *New York Times*, December 15, 1950.

IRL E. CARTER

**Goldmark, Pauline Dorothea** (February 21, 1874–October 18, 1962), social reformer and author, was born in Brooklyn, New York, the ninth of ten children of Joseph and Regina (Wehle) Goldmark. Joseph Goldmark, a Vienna-trained physician and member of the Austrian parliament, fled to the United States (via Switzerland) following the unsuccessful 1848 Revolution, in which he participated. After settling in New York, he became a successful physician, research chemist, and inventor. His wife Regina was a member of a wealthy family which had migrated from Prague to Indiana. One of Pauline's sisters married Felix Adler, founder of the Ethical Culture movement, and another married Louis Brandeis, the renowned lawyer and later U.S. Supreme Court justice, while a brother, Harry, was an internationally known civil engineer.

Pauline attended the Brackett School in New York City and then Bryn Mawr College, from which she graduated in 1896 with a major in biology. She then took two years of graduate work at Columbia University and Barnard College (1896–1898) in botany, zoology, and sociology. From 1899 to 1905 she served as assistant secretary of the New York Consumers' League; in 1905 she was appointed the organization's executive head, a post she held until 1909. In addition, from 1908 to 1911 she chaired the League's legislative and investigative committee, and in 1909 began forty years of service on its governing board.

Throughout her career, her major concern was the welfare of women and children in industry. Thus, in 1902 she helped to organize the New York Child Labor Committee, and for many years thereafter assisted in drafting pioneering protective legislation. When, as the result of the Triangle Shirtwaist Company fire in 1911, in which 146 women workers perished behind locked doors, the New York State legislature created a factory investigation commission, Pauline Goldmark, already a recognized expert on the subject, was appointed to the body (along with such prestigious political and social figures as Robert Wagner, Alfred E. Smith, Frances Perkins,* and others) and authored two of its reports, one on sanitation in factories and the other on the employment of women in retail stores.

Meanwhile, she had joined the faculty of the New York School of Philanthropy as a lecturer, and, from 1910 to 1912, as supervisor of its Bureau of Social Research. In that capacity, she oversaw the research and writing of a number of other important studies, one on neighborhoods in New York City that was published in 1914 as *West Side Studies*, and another on working conditions on the docks that was published in 1915 as *The Longshoremen*. She also was a member of the Industrial Board of the New York State Labor Deparment from 1913 to 1915, and research secretary of the New York Consumers' League from 1915 to 1918.

In 1917, when America entered World War I, Goldmark accepted a number of important national and state appointments—among them secretary of the State Committee on Women in Industry of the Council of National Defense, and chairman of the Women in Industry Committee of the State Defense Council. Later she became national manager of the Women's Services Section of the U.S. Railroad Administration's Division of Labor (1918–1920); one of the most important positions held by a woman during the conflict, it required that she supervise more than 100,000 women employees in the railroad industry.

Following the war, Goldmark conducted a study of labor conditions in the telephone industry for the New York Consumers' League and in 1921 became a consultant on working conditions of women employees for the American Telegraph and Telephone Company in New York City. Two years later, she joined AT&T full time, first conducting time and motion studies and inquiries into the causes of fatigue among the company's workers, and then as a member of its benefits and medical department. When she finally retired in 1939, Pauline Goldmark not only was one of the nation's leading social reformers but her work had become a model for the kinds of activities that could be performed by social workers in industry.

In her final years, Pauline Goldmark and her sister Josephine* shared a home in Hartsdale, New York, until the latter's death in 1950; Pauline then lived alone at the Hartsdale home until her own death there on October 18, 1962, at the age of eighty-eight.

The Pauline Goldmark Papers are at the Women's Archives at Radcliffe College in Cambridge, Massachusetts, while the New York Consumers' League Papers, which also contain many items by and about Pauline Goldmark, are in the Labor Management Documentation Center at the Library of the New York School of Industrial and Labor Relations, Cornell University, Ithaca, New York.

Besides the works mentioned above, readers might wish to see Josephine Goldmark's "Adirondack Friendship," *Atlantic Monthly* (September-October, 1934), letters from William James to Pauline Goldmark that portray a fifteen-year friendship between the two that came to an end only with James' death. In addition, see the *Encyclopedia of Social Work* (1971); *Who Was Who in America* vol. 4 (1968); Robert H. Bremner, *From the Depths: The Discovery of Poverty in the United States* (1956); and Louis Athey, "The Consumers' Leagues and Social Reform 1890–1923," Ph.D. dissertation, University of Delaware, 1965.

IRL E. CARTER

**Gould, Elgin Ralston Lovell** (August 14, 1860–August 18, 1915), political economist, urban reformer, and philanthropic housing manager, was born in Oshawa, Ontario, the eldest son of Emily A. and John T. Gould, well-to-do Anglican gentry. He graduated from Victoria College of the University of Ontario in 1881 and then studied history and political science at Johns Hopkins University, one of the pioneer doctoral students in the rigorous seminars of Herbert Baxter Adams and Richard T. Ely. After receiving his Ph.D. in 1886 (with a dissertation on the origins of Pennsylvania local government), Gould taught in Washington, D.C., and joined the staff of Carroll D. Wright, the new U.S. Commissioner of Labor, who was embarking on his wide-ranging inquiries into the social conditions of America's laboring classes. Sent overseas in 1888 to investigate the comparative costs and productivity of European industrial workers, Gould returned with a volume filled with statistical tables on wages and living costs and voluminous translations from primary sources, along with a firm conviction that the superior moral and material conditions of American workers would enable them to resist pauperization. He also surveyed the Scandinavian liquor traffic and found that Sweden's state-licensed corporations provided an effective, if authoritarian, means to limit alcohol consumption. Gould clinched his reputation, however, with *The Housing of the Working People* (1895), a massive investigation of working-class housing conditions in Europe and America with the most comprehensive survey to date of the ameliorative forces at work, including an exhaustive compilation of model tenements and philanthropic trust housing. Although he emphasized the benefits of sanitary and police restrictions in upgrading the private sector's provision of housing for the working class, he was enthusiastic about the philanthropic movement in Europe and America, which seemed to have put the construction of model tenements for the working classes on a solid, paying basis.

Returning to a professorial career, Gould found that his views on housing reform were in demand in social reform circles. While teaching economics at the University of Chicago in 1896, he was invited to give the keynote address at a housing reform conference sponsored by the New York Association for Improving the Condition of the Poor (AICP), and then asked by Robert Fulton Cutting* and Alfred T. White* to organize the City and Suburban Homes Company with nearly $1 million taken up by AICP investors. For two decades, Gould remained City and Suburban's chief officer, shaping the fledgling company into a philanthropic giant which sheltered 13,000 people in new and remodeled tenements across the city and never failed to pay back 4 percent to investors. Gould built this venture in doing good on solid bedrock: careful screening of the "worthy poor" to obtain a reliable, industrious class of rent payers; importation of England's Octavia Hill system of female visitors, who each week made their rounds collecting rent and looking after the moral health of their residents; and the steady expansion of facilities to include uptown tenements with more amenities and higher rents, the Junior League House for single women, and the Homewood, Brooklyn, bungalows for purchase by working men. Homewood revealed Gould's penchant for cultivating steady economic habits among the responsible working class, with installment payments that included insurance protection for the workers' equity.

From the late 1890s, Gould remained at the center of New York's housing movement and other reform causes. A charter member of the Charity Organization Society's Tenement House Committee, he worked with Jacob Riis,* Felix Adler, and Homer Folks* in the struggle to end the city's laissez-faire approach to tenement house construction that reached fruition in the restrictive Tenement House Law of 1901. Gould and Cutting drafted the original call to service for the Citizens' Union, and he served as the campaign treasurer in the mayorality campaigns of reformer Seth Low in 1899 and 1901 (the latter resulted in Gould's appointment as city chamberlain in Low's administration). Gould remained prominent in the struggle for city charter reform, serving on a charter inquiry appointed in 1907 by Governor Charles Evans Hughes.

An able administrator in a field dominated by languid patricians, Gould took the model tenement idea as far as possible. Resting the philanthropic structure on an efficient management, disciplined tenant relations, and careful selection of the poor, Gould established City and Suburban as a convincing case for the practical rehousing of the poor on a mass basis. Gould himself was candid enough to admit that his philanthropy was not aimed at the less industrious or so-called unworthy poor. Just the same, the impression held that it was designed for all the needy, and subsequent proponents of publicly built housing, such as Edith Elmer Wood* and Mary K. Simkhovitch,* struggled for years to discredit Gould's claims for the possibilities of private housing philanthropy. They finally succeeded, only to find that the entrenched practices of the model tenements meant that they too had to run public housing on the basis of steady rent payments by the "worthy" poor. At the height of his influence in philanthropic reform circles,

Gould died (on August 18, 1915) on a train outisde Winnipeg, Manitoba, while heading back to New York City after a horseback-riding accident that occurred a few days earlier at Cartier, North Bay, in the Canadian Rockies.

Besides his massive social inquiries for the U.S. Commissioner of Labor, Gould published pamphlets and occasional papers that reflected his continued interest in the industrious classes: *The Social Condition of Labor* (1893); *The Gothenburg System of Liquor Traffic* (1893); and *Popular Control of the Liquor Traffic* (1895). An address before the Commercial Club of Chicago reflects his faith in philanthropy that paid a reasonable return: *The Meeting Ground of Business and Philanthropy* (1913).

Gould's insistence that restrictive legislation could upgrade private sector housing provided for the working classes is found in "The Economics of Improved Housing," *Yale Review* (May, 1896); while "The Only Cure for Slums," *Forum* (June, 1895), contains his strictures against municipally built housing. Gould discussed the economic and social factors that impinged on the housing of the worthy poor in several popular versions of his Commissioner of Labor research: "The Housing Problem," *Municipal Affairs* (March, 1899); and "The Housing Problem in Great Cities," *Quarterly Journal of Economics* (May, 1900). The City and Suburban Homes Company annual reports remain the best source for Gould's philanthropic achievement.

Gould's obituary appeared in the *New York Times*, August 19, 1915. Roy Lubove, *The Progressives and the Slums* (1962), and Eugenie Ladner Birch and Deborah S. Gardner, "The Seven-Percent Solution: A Review of Philanthropic Housing, 1810–1910," *Journal of Urban History* (August, 1981), contain perceptive appraisals of Gould's place in American housing reform.

JOEL SCHWARTZ

**Granger, Lester Blackwell** (September 16, 1896–January 9, 1976), social worker, longtime head of the National Urban League, and race relations expert, was born in Newport News, Virginia, the son of Dr. William Randolph Granger, a Barbados-born physician, and Mary L. (Turpin) Granger, a teacher. He was one of six sons and the the only sibling who did not become a physician or dentist. Granger grew up in Newark, New Jersey, where he attended local schools. He was graduated from Dartmouth College in 1917 and served in the 92nd Division of the United States Army in France. During the 1920s and early 1930s he taught in North Carolina and New Jersey.

He worked in 1919 for the Newark, New Jersey, Urban League, and later attended the New School for Social Research in New York City. In 1930 he organized the Los Angeles Urban League, worked for the League's *Opportunity* magazine, and headed the organization's Workers' Councils, which promoted trade unionism among Blacks. In 1941 he became the third executive director of the National Urban League, a position he would hold for the next twenty years.

During Granger's years as head of the League, it grew from thirty-seven to sixty-six affiliates; from 216 salaried employees to 504; and from an annual budget for the national and local chapters from $650,000 to $3 million. He developed the Pilot Placement Project to gain employment for Blacks in numerous professional, technical, and skilled occupations which previously were beyond their reach. He started the Commerce and Industry and Trade Union Advisory Councils to involve white businessmen and labor leaders in opening job opportunities for Blacks.

Granger also moved the League into greater involvement in the burgeoning civil rights movement despite a 1913 agreement with the NAACP to steer away from such activism since it would infringe upon the latter's field of work. Ignoring this pact strained relations between Granger and the NAACP's Walter White* and his successor, Roy Wilkins. Granger challenged the federal government to wipe out employment and housing discrimination. Despite disagreements with Presidents Roosevelt, Truman, and Eisenhower, he cooperated with some presidential initiatives. Granger, for example, served as a special assistant to the Secretary of the Navy, and he traveled widely during World War II to improve race relations within the armed forces and defense industries. A staunch Republican, he took great pleasure in the presence of Eisenhower in the White House, although the former general disappointed Granger with his lack of enthusiasm for civil rights.

Granger's preference for Republicans when most Blacks had become Democrats, and his difficulty in keeping up with more militant Blacks both inside the League and outside the organization, made his mandatory retirement in 1961 at age sixty-five welcome news to some. He then became president of the International Conference of Social Work, and with foundation backing, took time to travel and write about social work and race relations. He died on January 9, 1976, in Alexandria, Louisiana.

The principal primary sources on Granger are the Records of the National Urban League in the Library of Congress in Washington, D.C., and the General Education Board Records at the Rockefeller Archive Center in North Tarrytown, New York. *Opportunity*, the organ of the National Urban League, contains numerous articles about Granger and his career in the organization. The major secondary sources on Granger are the following: obituary notice, *New York Times*, January 10, 1976; Guichard Parris and Lester Brooks, *Blacks in the City: A History of the National Urban League* (1971); and Jesse T. Moore, Jr., *A Search for Equality: The National Urban League, 1910–1961* (1981).

DENNIS C. DICKERSON

**Griscom, John** (September 27, 1774–February 25, 1852), chemist, college professor, philanthropist, and social reformer, was born in Hancock's Bridge, New Jersey, to Rachel and William Griscom, a saddle and harness maker. As a child, Griscom spent a great deal of time in his father's shop and in the local school, which had a variety of itinerant teachers, one of whom taught the young Griscom Latin. In 1790 Griscom himself began to teach at the local school, thus starting his lifelong association with schools and educational institutions. In 1793 he went to Philadelphia to attend the Friends Academy but was forced to return home by the outbreak of a yellow fever epidemic. He married Abigail Hoskins in 1800 and in 1807 moved to New York, where he taught chemistry. Before his wife died in 1816, they had nine children, including a son, John Hoskins Griscom, who became a physician well known for his writings on public health, most notably *The Sanitary Condition of the Laboring Class of New York, with Suggestions for Its Improvement* (1845/rep. 1970).

Meanwhile, in 1814, Griscom had become professor of chemistry at Columbia College and a member of the Literary and Philosophical Society. In 1817 he offered a course in natural philosophy exclusively for women, and he drew large crowds to his lectures. In 1818 he toured Europe visiting eleemosynary institutions and well-known philanthropists and social theorists. His two-volume diary of the trip was published as *A Year in Europe*. Among those he visited were Elizabeth Fry, Hannah Moore, and Joseph Lancaster, all prominent reformers. He devoted much of his time to public affairs and became a member of the Society for the Prevention of Pauperism in 1817. He quickly played a major role in that organization's affairs and, in 1823, along with Thomas Eddy,* helped to transform it into the New York Society for the Reformation of Juvenile Delinquents; the Society later succeeded in erecting the New York House of Refuge, the first institution solely for juvenile delinquents established in the United States, thus initiating the practice of separating juvenile offenders from adult criminals, one, of course, still accepted today.

Griscom was active in a number of other social improvement organizations in New York, including the New York Mechanics' Association and the New York Bible Society, until he moved to Burlington, New Jersey, in 1840, where he served as the superintendent of schools. Three years later he married Rachel Dern.

While Griscom probably is best known as the first chemistry teacher in the United States, or as one of the early founders of the United States' educational system, his philanthropic and social welfare activities and reforms are equally important, especially his work with juvenile offenders. Griscom died in Burlington, New Jersey, on February 25, 1852.

The best work on Griscom is his son's account, John H. Griscom, *Memoir of John Griscom, Ll.D* (1859). Also see his own works, *A Year in Europe*, 2 vols. (1823), and *Monitorial Instruction* (1823), and the obituary of him in the *New York Times*, February 28, 1852.

The best secondary treatments of Griscom are Edgar F. Smith, *John Griscom, 1774–1852, Chemist* (1925), and the sketches of him in the *Dictionary of American Biography* (1932), the *National Cyclopedia of American Biography* (1909), *Appleton's Cyclopedia of American Biography* (1888), and *Who Was Who in*

*America* (1963). Also see Raymond A. Mohl, *Poverty in New York, 1783–1825* (1971); Robert Pickett, *The New York House of Refuge* (1968); Robert S. Mennel, *Thorns and Thistles* (1974); and Joseph M. Hawes, *Children in Urban Society* (1971).

JOSEPH M. HAWES

**Gruenberg, Sidonie Matzner** (June 10, 1881–March 11, 1974), director of the Child Study Association of America and author, was born near Vienna, Austria, the oldest of the four daughters and two sons of Idore and Augusta (Basseches) Matzner. Her mother was the daughter of a wealthy German Jewish grain importer. Her father, the son of an Austrian town mayor, was educated at the University of Kracow. In 1895 Idore Matzner took his family to live in New York; two years later he suffered a paralyzing stroke that left Augusta Matzner alone to manage with her six children.

As a child, Sidonie Matzner was tutored at the family home near Vienna and briefly attended the Hohere Tochterschule in Hamburg. Shortly after arriving in the United States, she was enrolled in Felix Adler's Ethical Culture School, then called the Workingman's School. Along with her parents, Sidonie came to share Adler's belief in science and reform and his Social Gospel philosophy of "deed before creed." Sidonie graduated in 1897, and to offset the hardships caused by her father's illness (and subsequent death in 1902), she went to work as a bilingual secretary at the age of sixteen.

In 1903 Sidonie married Benjamin Charles Gruenberg (1875–1965) in an Ethical Culture ceremony. He, too, came from an educated Jewish background and was attracted by Adler's reformist and egalitarian ideas. Gruenberg was a biologist, educator, and author with whom Sidonie coauthored three books and frequently collaborated as a consultant and lecturer over the course of their careers. They had four children: Herbert, Richard, Hilda, and Ernest.

Meanwhile, after studying at the Ethical Culture schools, Sidonie had taken child development courses at Teachers College, Columbia University, which sparked her interest in the study of children. Additionally motivated by the birth of her first child in 1907, she found herself strongly attracted to the work of the Federation of Child Study. The Federation began as a group of Ethical Culture mothers in 1888, encouraged by Felix Adler to study new ideas in child development. Largely due to Adler's influence, the early founders engaged in the work with missionary zeal. By 1907, however, the Federation had loosened its ties to Ethical Culture and had grown substantially, administering several study groups, work with other child-related agencies, and internally initiated research.

In 1923 the Federation was chosen by the Laura Spelman Rockefeller Memorial (LSRM) as a primary social welfare agency to help coordinate a national parent education movement. Under the direction of Lawrence Frank, the LSRM's intention was to launch a comprehensive national program for the benefit of mothers and children. The plan included funding research centers, dissemination of information, and direct parent education. The Federation also was designated by the LSRM as coordinating agency for all child welfare organizations and research institutions funded by the LSRM.

With its own LSRM grant, the Federation incorporated, becoming the Child Study Association of America (CSAA). The next year the CSAA cosponsored a conference with the LSRM on modern parenthood, bringing together for the first time current experts in the field of child development. With the formation of the CSAA, Gruenberg was named director, a post she held until her retirement in 1950. Between 1928 and 1936 she taught parent education at Teachers College and New York University.

Gruenberg was an active promoter of parent education from her earliest association with child study. She had a particular talent for understanding scientific material and translating it into language parents could understand and apply. It was this talent that made her a popular public speaker and writer. During her career, she published several books and scores of articles on child rearing for parents. As chief executive, she brought the CSAA to national prominence by promoting parent education throughout the country and abroad as an information exchange between professional researchers and families, and for teaching the study group technique to parents. Until Benjamin Spock's *Baby and Child Care* appeared in 1946, Gruenberg's name was synonymous with parent education and child-rearing advice.

The CSAA and Gruenberg represent a transitional period in the history of social welfare. In its beginning, the women were inspired by the nineteenth century Social Gospel obligation to make a contribution to society. By the next generation, the loftier ideal was replaced by dedication to the work for its inherent intellectual satisfaction. As one of the first child-related agencies, under Gruenberg the CSAA filled numerous social welfare and educational functions. It sponsored summer programs for underprivileged children, produced the *Child Study* magazine, held conferences, and ran 160 parent study groups. After 1930, however, child study splintered into numerous fields identified by specialized credentials, academic disciplines, and agenices. As these separate fields became institutionalized, they left behind the pioneers and generalists, like Gruenberg, who preferred an eclectic approach to popularizing a wide range of new medical and psychological research. By 1950 the CSAA was neither a lay nor a professional organization, peripheral to the segregated, more narrowly defined research and service disciplines.

After her retirement from the CSAA, Gruenberg became a special consultant to Doubleday for education and children's literature. Her most successful books, *The Wonderful Story of How You Were Born* (1952) and *The Encyclopedia of Child Care and Guidance* (1954), were written during this period. She also coauthored *The Many Lives of Modern Women* (1952) with her daughter Hilda Krech. Gruenberg died of cancer in her home in New York City at the age of ninety-two.

The Benjamin and Sidonie Gruenberg Collection at the Library of Congress contains extensive family and general correspondence from 1892 to 1970. The Social Welfare History Archives at the University of Minnesota has the CSAA papers, containing Gruenberg's professional collection. A full biography is in progress by Roberta Wollons. For general information, see *Current Biography* (1940); *Who's Who of American Women* (1974–1975); obituary, *New York Times*, March 13, 1974; *Notable American Women, The Modern Period* (1980); *American Women Writers*, vol. 2 (1980).

ROBERTA WOLLONS

# H

Hale, Edward Everett (April 3, 1822–June 10, 1909), clergyman, author, humanitarian, and social reformer, was born in Boston, Massachusetts, the son of Nathan Hale, a successful businessman and newspaper editor and nephew of the Revolutionary War hero of the same name, and Sarah Preston (Everett) Hale, sister of Edward Everett. His long life appears to have been happy, rewarding, and fruitful. He had a happy and secure childhood, being surrounded by a loving and gifted family, and being exposed to and influenced by many of society's elite in literature, business, politics, and the clergy. He entered Harvard at thirteen and graduated, Phi Beta Kappa, at seventeen, class poet and ranked second scholastically in his class. In 1852 he married Emily Perkins, granddaughter of Lyman Beecher. The couple had five children, four sons and one daughter.

Hale was a man who did many things well and with apparent ease. He was outstanding in at least three fields: the ministry, literature, and social reform. For over sixty years he advocated liberal causes from the pulpit, through literary journals, and through personal action. From his ordination as minister of the Church of Unity at Worcester on April 29, 1846, Hale felt that the church was a force to be used to bring about needed social change. As a result of his impressive manner, effective voice, and touching sermons he gained respect and recognition as a clergyman. He served as minister of the prestigious South Congregational Church in Boston from 1856 until 1899. In 1865 he was an active delegate at the first National Conference of Liberal Protestant Churchmen. This conference led to the founding of the Unitarian Church of America. In 1866 he was the leader of the second national conference. He was unanimously elected Chaplain of the United States Senate in 1903, a post he held until his death in 1909. He was a most impressive figure in the pulpit. Regardless of where he preached, he filled the church with throngs of people enthralled with his delivery and with his message.

Hale was a prolific writer who wrote about many subjects in many forms. Perhaps best known for his short stories, he also wrote novels, biographies, poems, magazine articles, sermons, and lectures. He became a contributor to the *Atlantic Monthly* in 1858, and in 1863 he wrote his most famous work, "The Man Without a Country," which had an immediate impact on the 1864 presidential election and which has become one of the most profound patriotic pieces in American literature. In 1869 he founded a magazine, *Old and New*, of which he was editor. All in all, he produced a total of more than 200 publications, including about 70 books, 30 edited works, and well over 100 printed addresses, sermons, and other pamphlets. He also wrote scores of magazine and journal articles. His most substantial piece of nonfiction was *Franklin in France*, which he wrote in collaboration with his son, Edward Everett Hale, Jr., in 1887.

Hale's influence as a humanitarian and social reformer was extensive. His motto, "Look forward and not backward—look out and not in," reveals much of his character and philosophy of life. He was a realist who was willing to confront the unpleasant conditions of life, but an optimist who had the deep conviction that people could, and should, do whatever was necessary to improve those conditions. He saw his age as "a time of protest against untruth." He led this protest very effectively in many different ways. As early as 1854 he spoke and wrote in behalf of the Emigrant Aid Society. Up to and during the Civil War he consistently took a strong antislavery position. In the war years Hale turned his efforts and energies to such organizations as the U.S. Sanitary Commission and the U.S. Freedmen's Bureau. In 1866 he became a member of the Harvard Board of Overseers and a trustee of Antioch College in Ohio. In 1869 he founded the "Lend a Hand Movement," one of numerous societies he organized to work for the good of others. In 1880 he led a fight to combat anti-Catholicism by supporting parochial schools. During this time he contributed to the development of associated charities and neighborhood settlement houses. In 1896 he participated in the Washington Arbitration Conferences for the Preservation of Peace. In his "New Civilization" he advocated progressive causes which would later be used by Presidents Franklin D. Roosevelt and John F. Kennedy as major parts in their programs for social justice, including adherence to the Four Freedoms and a plea to place country above self. He also wrote of the seriousness of urban slum conditions, the need for rapid transit, and the injustice of racial bigotry and discrimination. He implored the nation to raise the standard of living, support public education, and conserve natural resources through a system of national parks. He favored the public ownership of utilities, government regulation of monopolies, and profit sharing in industry.

Hale's personal literary friends included Henry Wadsworth Longfellow, James Russell Lowell, and William Dean Howells. He associated as confidant with senators, congressmen, and presidents, from Daniel Webster to Theodore Roosevelt. He aged with grace, and his national reputation and esteem grew with time. He became a truly venerated old man whose resonant voice and writing style continued to demand the respect of others, leaders and common men and women alike, until his death in Boston on June 10, 1909. A statue erected in his honor bore the inscription "1822–1909. Man of Letters. Preacher of the Gospel. Prophet of Peace. Patriot."

Among Hale's other more popular writings were "Ten Times One Is Ten"; "In His Name"; "His Level Best"; "Phillip Nolan's Friends"; *Kansas and Nebraska*; *The Story of Massachusetts*; and *A New England Boyhood: An Autobiographical Work*.

A leading biography of Edward Everett Hale is Jean Holloway's *Edward Everett Hale, A Biography*, a scholarly, well-documented, and well-written book which provides a vivid picture of the man and the times in which he lived. John R. Adams' *Edward Everett Hale* (1977) also is readable and informative. Reference books which have significant material on Hale include: Nathan Haskell Dole, Forrest Morgan, and Caroline Tickner, *The Bibliophile Library of Literature, Art and Rare Manuscripts* (1904); Thomas William Herringshaw, *Herringshaw's Encyclopedia of American Biography of the Nineteenth Century* (1904); Stanley J. Kunitz and Howard Haycroft, eds., *American Authors, 1600–1900: A Biographical Dictionary of American Literature* (1938); and Dumas Malone, ed., *Dictionary of American Biography*, vol. 8 (1932).

                                                                    MARTIN HOPE


**Hall, Helen** (January 5, 1892–August 31, 1982), settlement house leader, was born in Kansas City, Missouri, the daughter of Beatrice (Dakin), an artist, and Wilford Hall, a manufacturer. Helen, however, was raised in Port Chester, New York, where her father established a surgical instruments manufacturing plant, Wilford Hall Laboratories.

After attending public schools in Port Chester, Helen Hall studied art at Columbia University (between 1912 and 1913), intending to become a sculptor. However, as she explained in her autobiography, *Unfinished Business* (1971), she left her study of the arts because she was concerned with the welfare of poor people. She finished a year of study of social work at the New York School of Philanthropy in 1915 and then organized a small settlement house in Westchester County, Eastchester Neighborhood House. She also was a caseworker for the Westchester County Department of Child Welfare before joining the American Red Cross during World War I. The Red Cross sent Hall to Chateaureux and Solesmes, France, where she administered recreational units in American Expeditionary Force base hospitals.

Following the Armistice, Hall organized a girls' club for the YWCA in Mulhouse, Alsace. Between 1920 and 1922 she worked for the United States Army in China and in the Philippines, supervising women's relations and organizing recreational services for enlisted men. Upon returning to the United States, Hall elected to again turn her attention to settlement house work. Between 1922 and 1933 she directed the University Settlement in Philadelphia, and in August, 1933, she succeeded Lillian D. Wald* as head resident of the Henry Street Settlement on New York City's Lower East Side, a post she held until her retirement in 1967 at the age of seventy-five. She took one leave of absence from Henry Street in 1942–1943 to rejoin the American Red Cross and organize service clubs and rest homes for enlisted personnel in Australia and the South Pacific.

Meanwhile, on February 26, 1935, Hall married Paul U. Kellogg,* editor of the *Survey*. She continued to use her maiden name in her professional life; the couple had no children.

Although Hall was a member of the second generation of settlement house workers, she was a staunch advocate of the settlement philosophy. Committed to social action and justice, Hall continually emphasized changing public policy to secure a decent urban environment for her "neighbors."

Among Hall's earliest achievements was her work for the Unemployment Committee of the National Federation of Settlements. Appointed by Albert J. Kennedy* as committee chair in 1928, Hall directed the Committee's nationwide investigation of the toll that unemployment took on workers and their families. The Committee's work was significant for a number of reasons, including the National Federation of Settlements' early recognition of the coming depression. The Committee's work resulted in two publications: *Some Folks Won't Work*, by Clinch Calkins (1930); and *Case Studies of Unemployment*, by Helen Hall. Hall's work for the Unemployment Committee also gave her national recognition as she testified before Congress and served as an advisor on unemployment to Pennsylvania's Governor Gifford Pinchot. During the summer of 1932, Hall visited England and made comparative studies of British unemployment and methods of relief. Her findings were published in the *Atlantic Monthly*, *Survey Graphic*, and the *New Republic*.

In 1934 President Franklin Roosevelt appointed Hall to an Advisory Council to the Committee on Economic Security, which drafted the Social Security Act.

Hall also is remembered for her work on behalf of consumers. She helped organize and served as chair of the Consumers National Federation, 1936–1941, and joined the board of the Consumers Union in 1952. She also served as the consumers' representative to the New York State Milk Advisory Committee and on the consumer advisory committee to the United States Office of Price Administration.

In 1949–1950 Hall chaired a conference group formed by the National Social Welfare Assembly to investigate the living conditions of families whose annual incomes were less than $2,000. The committee, using an investigative technique similar to that used in the National Federation of Settlements' unemployment studies, accumulated data on many families living near the poverty line which were presented to a joint congressional Subcommittee on Low-Income Families and ultimately issued as a congressional report, *Making Ends Meet on Less Than $2,000 a Year*.

Juvenile delinquency and neighborhood revitalization were other issues on Hall's agenda in the years following World War II. In 1955 she helped found a neighborhood community group, the Lower Eastside Neighborhoods Association, and in 1957 she played a role in the planning of the famed Mobilization for Youth, the pioneer delinquency control project on New York's Lower East Side, funded in part by the federal government. She also was active in promoting the development of new housing projects and in attempting to place community services within them. Henry Street, for example, operated a day care center, a senior citizens' center, and home repair workshops in public housing projects.

While Helen Hall was thought of as a tough, hard-working, and shrewd advocate of the poor, she also is remembered as a kind woman with a quick wit and love of beauty and nature. Hall never was without several cats as companions and once remarked that cats made "splendid" settlement residents because of their ability to deal with people. Hall and Paul Kellogg bought an old farmhouse near Cornwall on the Hudson River, and it was there that they relaxed and channeled their energies into gardening and restoring old buildings.

After Hall retired in 1967, she maintained many of her board memberships and was an observer to the United Nations for the National Federation of Settlements and the International Federation of Settlements. In addition, she completed her memoirs, *Unfinished Business*, in 1971. She died in her Manhattan apartment in August, 1982, following a lengthy illness.

In addition to her published writings, scholars should also consult Helen Hall's personal papers at the Social Welfare History Archives, University of Minnesota Libraries. Related collections at the Social Welfare History Archives include the records of the Henry Street Settlement, the National Federation of Settlements, and the United Neighborhood Houses of New York, as well as the papers of Paul U. Kellogg.

Additionally, a set of sixty-five mimeographed documents is available. Most of these studies were distributed under the title "Henry Street Settlement Studies," although a published bibliography to the set is entitled "The Helen Hall Settlement Papers." An obituary of Hall appeared in the *New York Times*, September 2, 1982.

For a brief history of the Henry Street Settlement, see *Social Service Organizations*, ed. Peter Romanofsky and Clarke A. Chambers (1978), 345. Secondary readings regarding the settlement and reform movements during the period in which Hall was active include Judith Ann Trolander, *Settlement Houses and the Great Depression* (1975), and Clarke A. Chambers, *Seedtime of Reform* (1963).

SUSAN D. STEINWALL

**Hamilton, Alice** (February 27, 1869–September 22, 1970), physician specializing in industrial medicine and social activist, was born in New York City to Montgomery and Gertrude (Pond) Hamilton. However, she moved with her parents and older sister, Edith, to her paternal grandmother's home in Fort Wayne, Indiana, when she was an infant. Her father, who had immigrated to America when he was a young man, became an influential banker in Fort Wayne; her mother was from an established New York City family but had a spirit of adventure and strong convictions about social justice which she imbued in her five children. Alice's older sister, Edith, became an international scholar on Greek and Roman civilizations; another sister and her brother also had successful careers in the arts and education.

From a young age, Alice Hamilton had a desire to serve the poor as a medical missionary. In 1891 she entered the Medical School of the University of Michigan, where she was an outstanding student, and decided to specialize in pathology. She did her internship at the New England Hospital for Women and Children from 1893 to 1894 and welcomed the opportunity to serve medically needy families in the Roxbury slums, not far from the hospital. She spent the next two years doing graduate work in pathology in Germany and at Johns Hopkins University. Shortly before her trip to Germany in 1895 she had heard Jane Addams* make a presentation on the work at Hull-House and immediately determined that one day she wanted to live and work with Addams at America's most famous settlement house. That opportunity came when Dr. Alice Hamilton was offered her first paid appointment in 1897—teaching pathology at Woman's Medical College of Northwestern University.

Through her volunteer work at Hull-House and the well-baby clinic she established there, Hamilton learned about the dangers which the parents of many of the children she treated were exposed to in their occupations. "Phossy jaw," a disease contracted by workers in match factories who breathed in fumes from phosphorus which then invaded defective teeth and destroyed tissues in teeth and jawbones, was the first industrial disease with which Hamilton became familiar. Her first active involvement in researching and combatting industrial disease, however, began in 1909 when Governor Deneen of Illinois appointed her director and chief medical examiner of a nine-member state commission to survey industrial diseases in Illinois. The commission had only one year to plan, implement, and evaluate its findings and make recommendations to the state legislature. Given this limited time frame, Hamilton decided to emphasize poisonous trades and occupations; she herself directed a group of young physicians who examined lead factories in Illinois. In the course of her investigation she examined scores of workers with lead poisoning, interviewed the foremen and employers, listened to family members of lead workers, and laboriously accumulated and systematized data which demonstrated that industrial processes which utilized lead were endangering the lives of workers who were needlessly exposed to lead poisoning and its harmful physical and mental consequences. This arduous investigative effort convinced Hamilton that dangerous trades could be made safer by regulating them through law and by developing a system of cash benefits paid to sick workers who were needlessly harmed by their dangerous occupations.

As a result of her investigative work on lead poisoning in Illinois, in 1910 the U.S. Commissioner of Labor asked Hamilton to conduct a nationwide survey of the lead industry. As medical consultant of the United States Department of Labor, she was to systematically examine the dangerous trades in the lead industries and report her findings and recommendations to the U.S. Commissioner of Labor.

In the course of diligently, patiently, and systematically executing these assignments, Alice Hamilton became America's pioneer physician in the field of industrial toxicology.

While living at Hull-House, Hamilton sometimes served as Jane Addams' personal physician and sometimes joined her in working for international peace and social justice; for example, she was among the small group of American women who accompanied Jane Addams to the International Congress of Women at The Hague in 1915 in an effort to find a nonviolent resolution of World War I. Having failed in that mission, Hamilton was called to Washington again, this time to investigate the dangerous conditions in the proliferating munitions factories in America. At the war's end she was asked by the Department of Labor to investigate the dangers in copper mining and was asked by Jane Addams to help investigate starvation in Germany. In 1919 Hamilton was appointed assistant professor of industrial medicine at Harvard University, and for the next fifteen years she divided her time between those teaching responsibilities, her investigative work for the government, and her involvement in various social causes (for example, in opposition to capital punishment, as U.S. representative to the League of Nations' Health Committee, and as defender of civil liberties). For many years after her retirement she remained active in promoting industrial safety and social justice.

Dr. Alice Hamilton died at the age of 101 in her home in Hadlyme, Connecticut, on September 22, 1970.

Further information on Alice Hamilton can be found in the Arthur and Elizabeth Schlesinger Library of Women in America at Radcliffe College; the Sophia Smith Collection at Smith College; and the Swarthmore College Peace Foundation.

Important published works by Hamilton include *Exploring the Dangerous Trades* (1943) and "A Woman of Ninety Looks at Her World," *The Atlantic* (March, 1965).

A well-written biography of the subject is *Alice Hamilton: Pioneer Doctor in Industrial Medicine* (1967), by Madeleine P. Grant.

ROBERT M. HENDRICKSON

**Hamilton, Amy Gordon** (December 26, 1892–March 10, 1967), social work educator, relief administrator, and editor, known throughout her life simply as Gordon Hamilton, was born in Tenafly, New Jersey, to Bertha (Torrance) Hamilton and George Hamilton, a wealthy importer and an aristocratic Scottish immigrant. Bertha Torrance had immigrated to the United States from Canada in the 1870s with her family and became a Christian Scientist and an associate of Mary Baker Eddy. While Gordon never became a Christian Scientist, she did accede to her mother's wishes by never marrying.

All of the Hamilton children were educated at home. The two daughters, in particular (there were also two sons), were not encouraged to pursue academic preparation. This, coupled with chronic respiratory ailments which plagued Gordon throughout her life, posed a significant barrier to her attending college. She eventually obtained her parents' approval to further her education, and she entered Bryn Mawr College in 1911. There she majored in Greek and English, graduating in 1914 with an eye toward a career in journalism. Upon her return from a brief sojourn to Great Britain as the guest of the American ambassador, she began working for the American Red Cross in 1914. As a result of her poor health, she moved to Colorado, where she lived until 1920. While engaged in continuing Red Cross work there, she became acquainted with Mary Richmond,* whose encouragement and recommendation led to Hamilton's starting work as a caseworker for the New York Charity Organization Society (COS) in 1920. The stress of the work proved too much for her fragile health, however, so in 1921 she left casework to become research secretary for the COS. In 1923 Hamilton left the COS for a faculty appointment at the New York School of Social Work (later the Columbia University School of Social Work), where she remained until 1957.

Throughout her academic career she coupled practice-related activities with her teaching responsibilities. As a result, her writings show a constant evolution of thought. From 1925 to 1932 Hamilton was associate director of social service and later advisor on research at Presbyterian Hospital in New York. One outcome of this period was her first book, *Medical Social Terminology* (1927). With the onset of the Great Depression, Hamilton was involved with relief efforts both nationally, with her work for the Federal Emergency Relief Administration, and locally, as social services director for the New York State Temporary Emergency Relief Administration. For the latter position, she took a leave of absence from the NYSSW faculty from 1935 to 1936. After World War II, she became involved in international social welfare through work with the Church World Service and the United Nations Relief and Rehabilitation Administration from 1944 until 1952. She also worked as a research consultant at the Jewish Board of Guardians from 1947 until 1950.

She is best remembered, however, as a teacher and a writer. She was an inspirational teacher who could draw upon a classical education as well as a rich practice background to stimulate her students' thinking. She had a facility for language and a sharp wit which she used well in discussion and debate. She had strong beliefs about the quality and direction of social work education and was involved in the development of the doctoral program in social work at the Columbia University School of Social Work.

As for her writing, she was a prolific contributor to the social work literature and had a writing style of exceptional clarity. Her most important book was *The Theory and Practice of Social Case Work*, the first edition of which was published in 1940. The book represented the first full effort since Mary Richmond's *Social Diagnosis* (1917) to define and exhaustively examine the process of social casework. In this first edition, she followed Richmond by presenting casework as a process focusing on the delivery of hard services. She was suspicious of psychoanalytic thought, which had become increasingly influential in social work throughout the 1930s. This book and its later edition remained basic texts in social work for many years.

As an outgrowth of her work with the Jewish Board of Guardians, she published *Psychotherapy in Child Guidance* (1947). This book, being more sympathetic to psychoanalytic theory, reflected a shift in her thinking, although she made a strong distinction between psychoanalysis, which she saw as being outside the field of social work, and psychotherapy. In 1951 she published the revised edition of *The Theory and Practice of Social Case Work*. This edition clearly integrated psychoanalytic theory, although it retained its foundation in a more traditional, concrete services approach to casework.

After serving as associate dean at the NYSSW between 1952 and 1955, she retired from the faculty entirely in 1957 as a result of her continuing poor health. At that time she became the first editor of the journal of the new National Association of Social Workers, *Social Work*. From that position, she wrote quarterly editorials signed simply "G. H." Her most famous editorial appeared in 1962, when she proposed that social work rid itself of the "albatross of relief" by turning over to technicians the job of eligibility determination in public welfare. This position stood in striking contrast to her rather detailed and sympathetic approach to eligibility determination issues in *Theory and Practice*.

Hamilton retired from *Social Work* in 1962. She then moved to British Columbia and died there on March 10, 1967.

Gordon Hamilton published extensively throughout her career. Besides the works mentioned above, she published two other books, *Social Case Recording* (1936) and *Principles of Social Case Recording* (1946). Many of her articles appeared in the *Journal of Social Casework* (formerly called the *Family*) and the yearly *Proceedings* of the National Conference of Social Work. Her books were extensively reviewed, most consistently in the *Survey* and the *Journal of Social Casework*. Biographical material can be found in *Notable American Women* (1980) and *The Encyclopedia of Social Work* (1977). Brief tributes to her can be found in *Social Work* in 1962 and 1967 and in the Columbia University School of Social Work *Newsletter* (Spring, 1962). Her obituary appeared in the *New York Times*, March 11, 1967. Her close friend Anna Kempshall's "Gordon Hamilton, Some Intimate Glimpses" appeared in the NYSSW *Newsletter* (June, 1957). There is apparently some archival material on her, including dictated notes on her professional life, in the Columbia University Library. These were evidently moved recently from the School of Social Work Library to the main library archives, and this author was unable to locate them.

MERLE T. EDWARDS-ORR

**Harris, Elisha** (March 5, 1824–January 31, 1884), physician, sanitary reformer, and statistician, was born in Westminster, Vermont, the son of a farmer, James Harris, and his wife Eunice (Foster) Harris. After finishing his early education in the area common schools, Harris became the student of Dr. S. B. Woolworth.

In the decade between 1839 and 1849 he studied medicine while teaching and assisting his father on the farm. He obtained his M.D. degree in 1849 from the College of Physicians and Surgeons in New York City. In that same year, he married Eliza, the only daughter of Reverend Joseph B. Andrews. The Harrises had no children, and Harris never remarried after Eliza's death in 1867. Harris was described as a prematurely gray, suave, and dignified man with impressive organizational abilities and unusual powers of endurance.

Early in his career Harris relinquished private practice to devote himself to public service work at the local, state, and national level. He was among a group of reform-minded New York City physicians, including John Griscom,* Joseph M. Smith, and Stephen Smith,* who worked diligently to arouse interest in municipal sanitary problems. In the 1860s and 1870s these physicians organized commissions and health boards and lobbied for legislative power to carry out their plans. Elisha Harris was the secretary, editor, compiler, and statistician for the group. His efforts are reflected in his writings, which consist largely of various commission reports.

Harris' first public service appointment was as superintendent and physician-in-chief of the Quarantine Hospital on Staten Island in 1855. During his tenure Harris supervised the construction of New York's floating quarantine hospital in 1859 and served at the National Quarantine and Sanitary Convention in 1860 as a member of the Committee on Quarantine Regulations, which drafted the ''code of marine hygiene'' that was used to define quarantine practice for New York City.

At the outbreak of the Civil War, his experience in quarantine and disinfection led to his appointment to the all-volunteer United States Sanitary Commission, organized in 1861 by Reverend Henry W. Bellows* to advise and assist the Medical Department of the army. Harris was the only Commission member with practical sanitary experience. After the battle of Bull Run, Harris and Frederick Law Olmsted, the chief executive officer of the Commission, made sanitary inspections of the troop encampments near Washington. Harris devised the system for recording deaths and burials of soldiers which the army put into general use. The special hospital railway ambulance cars, designed by Harris, carried an estimated 225,000 wounded soldiers during the Civil War and were used by the Prussian army in the Franco-Prussian War. The ambulance gained international recognition with a bronze medal at the Exposition Universal in Paris in 1867 and the silver medal of the Société des Secours aux Blessés. Harris also was an editor of the Commission's *Sanitary Memoirs of the War of the Rebellion* (2 vols., 1867–1869).

Harris made his major contribution to the sanitary reform movement with his able use of statistics to correlate the incidence of disease with crowded, filthy living conditions, which showed that high death rates were preventable. While secretary of the Council of Hygiene and Public Health of the Citizens' Association of New York, he aided in the establishment of the Metropolitan Board of Health in 1866, which he served as registrar of records. His *Report of the Registrar of*

*Vital Statistics* (1867) shows that within two years he had instituted detailed procedures to collect and analyze data on births, deaths, and disease, and had brought order to the previously chaotic and unreliable records of the city. Harris forced the Board to address tenement reform. At his urging, after an inspection of more than 20,000 tenement buildings in New York and Brooklyn, over 50,000 windows were installed to improve light and ventilation. In 1869 Harris prodded the Board of Education to determine the extent of smallpox vaccination among school children. When the survey revealed that less than 4 percent were protected, Harris organized a major free public vaccination campaign. In 1870 Harris was forced out of office by the Tweed charter, only to be reappointed as registrar of vital statistics three years later after a change in administration. However, a reorganization of the Board of Health in 1876 placed vital statistics under the jurisdiction of the Sanitary Bureau and abolished his job. The reorganization may have been prompted, in part, by his conscientious use of vital statistics to point out health problems needing attention, which undoubtedly made him an annoyance to city politicians.

Harris sought to apply the environmental and statistical methods of sanitary science to the related problems of crime and pauperism. On behalf of the Prison Association of New York, of which he was corresponding secretary from 1872 to 1880, Harris wrote the foreword endorsing Robert L. Dugdale's controversial *"The Jukes," A Study of Crime, Pauperism, Disease and Heredity* (1877). While serving as state agent for discharged convicts in 1880, Harris also organized the philanthropic work of that office. His memberships included the New York Association for Improving the Condition of the Poor.

When the American Public Health Association was founded in 1872, Harris was among the originators, acting as secretary for the first four years and as president in 1877. In a report entitled "General Health Laws and Local Ordinances" to the Association in 1873, Harris articulated a plan for centralizing sanitary information and authority. The Association successfully urged Congress to form the National Board of Health in 1879, and Harris was appointed one of its eight seaport quarantine inspectors. The opportunity for him to be able to establish his sanitary policies came in 1880, when he was appointed one of three commissioners of the newly organized New York State Board of Health. He moved to Albany to accept the offices of secretary and state superintendent of vital statistics, the positions he held at the time of his death there in 1884.

Harris' writings consist primarily of the reports of the boards and commissions which he served as secretary. Among his more representative works are the *Annual Report of the Physician-in-Chief of the Marine Hospital at Quarantine* (1857); *Hints for the Control and Prevention of Infectious Diseases, in Camps, Transports, and Hospitals* (1863); "The Sanitary Commission," *North American Review* 98 (1864), 153–194, 370–419; *The Vital Statistics and Sanitary Condition of the Hospitals and Other Institutions in Which Medical Care Is Systematically Provided, in the Metropolitan Sanitary District* (1868); "A Report on Laws,

Provisions, and Methods for Securing General Vaccination Throughout the Country," in *Public Health Papers and Reports of the American Public Health Association* 3 (1876); "The Educational, and Correctional Treatment of Juvenile Delinquents, and of Depraved, Neglected, Abandoned, and Other Children in Danger of Falling into a Criminal Career," in *Transactions of the National Prison Association* (1877); and *Cleanliness and Disinfection*(1879).

Obituaries of Harris can be found in the *Journal of the American Medical Association* 2 (1884), 194–195; the *Medical Record* 25 (1884), 166–167; the *New York Herald*, February 1, 1884, 6; the *New York Times*, February 1, 1884, 8; and the *Public Health Papers and Reports of the American Public Health Association* 10 (1885), 509–510. Other biographical accounts of Harris' life can be found in the *Dictionary of American Biography* (1932); Howard A. Kelly and Walter L. Burrage, eds., *American Medical Biographies* (1920); and the *National Cyclopaedia of American Biography* (1907).

Also see John Duffy, *A History of Public Health in New York City*, 2 vols. (1968–1974); Stephen Smith, "Historical Sketch of the American Public Health Association," in *Public Health Papers and Reports of the American Public Health Association* 5 (1879), vii–liv; and Charles J. Stille, *History of the United States Sanitary Commission* (1866).

                                                                                      PATRICIA PECK GOSSEL

**Harrison, Shelby Millard** (February 15, 1881–August 27, 1970), social worker, director of the Russell Sage Foundation, and author, was born in Leaf River, Illinois, the son of Mary Ellen (Helman) and James Franklin Harrison, a school teacher. Young Harrison's high school education was interrupted by bank work for three years, providing him with professional and administrative experience that would prove useful in his later career. Working his way through college, he received his B.A. degree from Northwestern University in 1906, and then pursued graduate work at Boston University and Harvard University until 1909. In 1910 he married another Northwestern graduate, Patti Rodgers, of Charleroi, Pennsylvania. They had two sons, James Shelby and Rodger Scott.

Harrison's first position came in 1908 when he joined the staff of the Pittsburgh Survey, which was being funded by the newly established Russell Sage Foundation. Created in 1907 by Margaret Olivia Sage with money bequeathed to her by her husband Russell, the Foundation was designed to finance projects aimed at permanently improving social conditions. The Pittsburgh Survey, directed by Paul Kellogg,* was designed to study the living conditions in an industrial city as exhaustively and as carefully as possible. Harrison's findings showed that those who were least able to pay were being taxed most heavily, while some of the wealthiest members of the community, including large real estate holders, were being taxed only slightly. These findings by Harrison led to a reassessment of tax structures, in Pittsburgh and elsewhere, and a growing awareness of living conditions in other industrial cities.

Following his work in Pittsburgh, Harrison took a position on the editorial staff of *Survey* magazine, where he was in charge of the Department of Civics and Community Development. This experience, coupled with his work in Pittsburgh, led to his appointment in 1912 as director of the Russell Sage Foundation's Department of Surveys and Exhibits. The office was to be a clearing house for advice, information, and field assistance in organizing social surveys and exhibits.

The department, under Harrison's direction, conducted several "pathfinder," or preliminary, inquiries from 1913 to 1915 to determine whether conditions for other large surveys were favorable. It then focused on Springfield, Illinois—a medium-size city with a largely native-born, white population that was a trade center for an agricultural region as well as a coal mining district—as a typical, or representative, example of an American city.

For this study, another of the early comprehensive urban surveys made in America, Harrison delineated nine main lines of inquiry: public schools, recreation, housing, industrial conditions, public health, mental health, charities, correctional facilities, and city and county administration. Following the survey an exhibit was set up to show certain inadequacies and how to deal with them. A popular feature, and one that would have considerable impact later, was the use of short plays to illustrate some of the faulty social conditions and ways to improve them.

The Springfield survey clearly demonstrated the feasibility of survey techniques in fact-finding and in making those facts dynamic, or useful. It brought about a new way of thinking regarding the use of social surveys in amelioration of urban social problems—and it also established Shelby Harrison as a leader in their use to promote the social welfare.

Harrison also enlightened students as to the practicability of conducting social surveys by teaching classes at Columbia University, at Teachers College (of Columbia University), and at the New York School of Social Work. He told his students that social work was "the modern implementation of faith in humanity, the modern agency for transmitting this faith into works, and a discipline that seeks to serve all those in need."

Harrison attempted to serve those in need throughout his career. In 1924 he became vice general director of the Russell Sage Foundation. In 1925 he became a member of the Social Science Research Council, acting as chairman of its executive committee for twelve years, from 1933 to 1945. In 1929 he was appointed to the President's Research Committee on Social Trends, a committee to study trends on human welfare, serving as its secretary-treasurer. He became general director of the Russell Sage Foundation in 1931, remaining in that position until his retirement in 1947, completing thirty-five years of service with that useful organization.

His tenure as general director of the Foundation spanned two major episodes of American history, the Great Depression and World War II. It was a period of turbulence and experimentation in the Foundation's history, caused by financial instability. To Harrison's credit, he was able to guide the Foundation through this period with its financial basis intact, although declining income made it necessary to curtail some of its activities. Desired renewal of activities in such fields as social and community surveys could not be undertaken, to Harrison's dismay.

As World War II began Shelby Harrison was serving as president of the National Conference of Social Work, a well-deserved honor bestowed upon him by his colleagues in the field. From this position he explained that social work was responding to the world crisis along three main fronts: the immediate war program, the maintenance of its normal duties, and postwar reconstruction. Harrison led the Russell Sage Foundation in responding to the war along these three fronts, working closely with the United Nations Relief and Rehabilitation Administration throughout the war.

Following his retirement in 1947, Harrison served as executive director of the Babe Ruth Foundation and as a committee member of the Mid-Century White House Conference on Children and Youth. He also was actively involved with the National Council of the Churches of Christ. Throughout his life, Harrison was devoted to the betterment of humanity, largely through improving the communities in which people lived—and to him, such improvement could best be achieved through the scientific use of sociological surveys.

Shelby Harrison died at his New York City home on August 27, 1970, at age eighty-nine.

For the best account of Harrison's work with the Russell Sage Foundation, see John M. Glenn, Lilian Brandt, and F. Emerson Andrews, *The Russell Sage Foundation, 1907–1946*, 2 vols. (1947); and Maxine Black, ed., *Current Biography* (1943).

Harrison's works include *The Disproportion of Taxation in Pittsburgh* (1914); *Social Conditions in an American City* (1920); *Welfare Problems in New York City* (1926), with Allen Eaton; *A Bibliography of Social Surveys* (1930), with Allen Eaton; and *American Foundations for Social Welfare* (1946), with F. Emerson Andrews.

WILLIAM H. HARDIN

**Hart, Hastings Hornell** (December 14, 1851–May 9, 1932), clergyman, penologist, and child-saver, was born in Brookfield, Ohio, to Albert G. Hart, Civil War veteran and physician, and Mary (Hornell) Hart. Hart attended the Cleveland Institute, graduating in 1867, and received his A.B. (1875) and A.M. (1885) from Oberlin. His first wife was Mary A. Prosser, whom he married in 1880 and who died in 1881; his second, Laura E. Love, whom he married in 1886 and who died in 1900; and his third, Josephine M. Newton, whom he married in 1902 and who survived him. Hart fathered one child by Mary Prosser, four children by Laura Love, and two children by Josephine Newton.

Hart took a number of years to find his vocation. He first worked as a clerk in the U.S. Indian Service at the Sisseton Agency in South Dakota (1875–1877), resigning to study for the ministry. He graduated from Andover Theological

Seminary in 1880 and received a pastorate in Worthington, Minnesota. Hart was ordained a Congregational minister in 1881, but found a new calling two years later, becoming the secretary of the Minnesota State Board of Charities and Corrections. He remained in the field of social welfare for the rest of his life, becoming the superintendent of the Illinois Children's Home and Aid Society in 1898, the director of the child-helping department of the Russell Sage Foundation in 1909, and a consultant on delinquency and penology to the Russell Sage Foundation from 1924 until his death in 1932.

Hart's first interest was in prison reform. While secretary of the Minnesota State Board of Charities and Corrections, he drafted a law reorganizing the state prison system, and he designed a model jail. During his career, Hart investigated many state prison systems, including those of Florida, Alabama, Mississippi, Virginia, West Virginia, and South Carolina. His investigations led him to become a severe critic of the convict leasing system, used extensively in the South, in which private contractors leased the convicts' labor from the state. Hart also prepared a report for the Regional Plan of New York and Its Environs in 1929 in which he condemned the New York City jails, especially The Tombs, as overcrowded and unsanitary firetraps. At Hart's instigation, the U.S. House of Representatives held hearings on the treatment of federal prisoners, and bills passed in December, 1929, established two new federal prisons, provided for a federal parole board, and reorganized the administration of federal prisons. Hart's interest in penology led him to become the president of the American Prison Association (APA) in 1921–1922 and to serve two five-year terms as American vice president of the International Prison Congress in 1925 and 1930. He also served as chairman of the APA's committee on jails.

Hart championed defendants' rights as well. He condemned the use of the "third degree" in extorting confessions from prisoners. In a report to the American Prison Association, coauthored by B. Ogden Chisolm, Hart called for the establishment of a public defender who would be present when prisoners were interrogated and who could advise them of their rights. The report went on to propose the prohibition of threats of force or promises of leniency to secure confessions, and it called for publicly paid attorneys for indigent defendants.

Hart's other enduring interest was in child-saving. While working in Minnesota, he studied the children placed in the state by Charles Loring Brace's* New York Children's Aid Society. He found few examples of the depraved children critics thought were being dumped in the West, and too many examples of depraved adults who took children for venal motives. Hart's chief criticism of the Children's Aid Society was that it provided inadequate supervision. Children were placed in families without an investigation of the home, and the local committees of clergymen and luminaries who were to oversee placed children rarely performed their duties adequately. Despite the shortcomings of Brace's policies, Hart remained a firm believer in the idea of home placement. He used his position as president (1893) and secretary (1894–1901) of the National Conference of

Charities and Correction to advocate child placement and the noninstitutional treatment of children.

Hart lobbied for the construction of cottage or family-style reformatories. These institutions were a reaction against the massive congregate reformatories that characterized the first era of institution building. The family-style reformatory placed children in a setting that strove to be home-like, with cottage "parents" supervising a gentle regimen for the children. By contrast, the congregate reformatory was associated with large numbers of children kept orderly by military discipline. Neither reformatory proved in practice to be what advocates claimed in theory. Nonetheless, the family-style institution, together with child placement, represented a significant shift in thinking about child welfare. Families, rather than institutions, formed the paradigm of the age, and Hart was an important architect in its construction.

The juvenile court was another major Progressive Era contribution to child-saving, and Hastings Hart played a role in its establishment. As secretary of the Illinois Children's Home and Aid Society, Hart was part of the coalition of women's clubs and social welfare agencies that lobbied for a juvenile court in Chicago. Hart helped draft the legislation creating the court in 1899. He defended the court as a nonadversarial institution designed to secure the child's best interest. Incarceration was to be meted out as training, not punishment. However, probation lay at the philosophical center of the court since it permitted an informal and noninstitutional handling of a delinquent's case, kept the family intact, and still gave the court leverage over the family. Hart's philosophy of child welfare and his beliefs on the role of the court, placement, and the cottage reformatory are all discussed in his *Preventive Treatment of Neglected Children* (1910).

In 1909 Hart became the head of the child-helping department of the Russell Sage Foundation. Most of his major works, including *Cottage and Congregate Institutions* (1910), *Child Welfare in the District of Columbia* (1924), and his many pamphlets on prisons, county jails, and child welfare were written and published under the auspices of the Foundation. *Preventive Treatment of Neglected Children*, Hart's first report, served as a handbook for social work students and practitioners. He also established a bureau of exchange to coordinate child-saving efforts, and this evolved into the Child Welfare League of America. Hart died at his home in White Plains, New York, on May 9, 1932.

Apparently there is no collection of Hastings Hart papers. The most accessible sources of Hart's thought on social welfare, in addition to the works listed above, are to be found in the annual reports of the Minnesota State Board of Charities and Corrections and those of the Illinois Children's Home and Aid Society, as well as in the published proceedings of the American Prison Association and the National Conference of Charities and Correction. One might also consult the papers of the Survey Associates (University of Minnesota, Social Welfare History Archives).

There are good summaries of Hart's life in *The Dictionary of American Bi-*

*ography*, Supplement 1 (1944), 377–378; and *The National Cyclopedia of American Biography*, vol. 23 (1933), 170–171. For his obituary, see the *New York Times*, May 10, 1932. There are brief references to Hart in most standard works on child-saving, penology, and juvenile delinquency, but they are more useful for context than for any biographical information.

ERIC C. SCHNEIDER

**Hartley, Robert Milham** (February 17, 1796–March 3, 1881), social reformer and founder and longtime head of the New York Association for Improving the Condition of the Poor (AICP), was born in Cockersmouth, County of Cumberland, England, to Isaach and Isabella (Johnson) Hartley, a well-known English family. His father manufactured machinery used in the woolens trade and had many ties with American merchants, and his father's cousin, David Hartley, was a member of Parliament who had signed the Treaty of Paris (1783) which ended the United States War of Independence; his mother was the daughter of a prominent local family.

When Hartley was three years of age, his family immigrated to the United States, settling in New England, where Hartley studied the woolen industry by working in a woolen mill. Later, however, he began to prepare for the ministry when, at age twenty-four, he entered Fairfield Academy in Herkimer County, New York. Illness, though, forced him to leave, and he went to New York City, where he established himself as a dry goods merchant.

He remained a deeply religious young man, however. Thus, he became a lay reader in a nearby church and also was active in local Bible and tract societies. In 1829, with a group of others, he helped to organize the New York City Temperance Society and then served that organization as secretary.

Unlike many other businessmen, Hartley became a full-time social reformer and a part-time man of business. As secretary of the Temperance Society, Hartley visited all of the local distilleries and tried to address the owners directly and show them the alleged evils caused by their products. On these visits, he discovered the squalid sheds where cows were fed the distillery refuse. Hartley studied the matter carefully, and also discovered that those cows' milk was sold to some 25,000 tenement-dwelling infants. He was convinced that there was a direct correlation between the consumption of this milk and the rise of infant mortality among those same tenement children. In 1842 he wrote *An Historical, Scientific, and Practical Essay on Milk*, and eight years later expanded the study and called it *The Cow and the Dairy: A Treatise on Milk*.

In 1833 Hartley joined the New York City Mission Society. There he met a group of wealthy Christian businessmen who were concerned about what they perceived to be a decline in morality in the city. Poverty, in their view, was a manifestation of this immorality, especially intemperance and other individual moral defects. Yet the good Christian was obliged to provide the corporal works of mercy, as well as to attempt to uplift the character of the poor. The results of the Panic of 1837 gave them the opportunity to do so.

The financial collapse severely hit the economy of New York City. Distress was everywhere, overwhelming the city's charitable agencies and organizations. Hartley and his friends thus established a new citywide nonsectarian agency in 1843, the New York Association for Improving the Condition of the Poor. Hartley was named general agent of the new organization which, throughout its annual reports, authored by Hartley, dealt with defining the causes of poverty, always making a distinction between the so-called worthy and unworthy poor—those who wanted to work but because of age, injury, or illness were unable to do so, and those who presumably preferred to live off alms, begging, or stealing.

The major cause of poverty, according to Hartley and the AICP, was intemperance, followed by improvidence and extravagance (somewhat ironical, since the poor had little with which to be extravagant). Hartley and the AICP divided the city into twenty-two districts, which then were divided into 278 smaller sections. Each district had an advisory committee, and each section a visitor. These visitors—paternal guardians, as they were known—were recruited from wealthy middle- and upper-class churchgoers who volunteered their services and visited each family that sought assistance. In addition to providing physical help, they would try to uplift the character of the supplicants, which, of course, was assumed to be deficient.

Yet Hartley was aware that environmental factors did not make it easy for the poor. Thus the AICP set up medical dispensaries, condemned the high death rates in the slums, castigated the blue distillery milk, and worked with the city's Board of Health to require landlords to improve the sanitary conditions in their buildings. While the AICP, under Hartley's direction, pushed for tenement legislation, state officials ignored the agency's requests until the 1870s.

Hartley also believed, as he wrote to a friend, that "one of the primal and principle causes of poverty . . . is the want of early mental and moral culture." He thus had his visitors deliver pamphlets and tracts to the poor and press them to attend public and private elementary and secondary schools. Hartley pushed, too, for legislation to end truancy so as to curb "the vast amount of street begging and vagrancy." He saw education as a necessary form of social discipline, and the AICP helped push a truancy law through the New York State legislature in 1853. It was rarely enforced, however.

Hartley then encouraged the New York State legislature to emulate Massachusetts and pass a compulsory school attendance law. He denied relief to any families that did not send their children to school. Visitors were told that teachers would have to sign a form indicating that the child of a relief applicant had attended school. Hartley and the AICP got a good compulsory school attendance act passed in 1874. Again, however, enforcement continued to be a problem.

Hartley also pressed the AICP to establish an institution which would remove children from "dangerous and corrupting associations" and place them in a setting where they could become both industrious and virtuous. In 1851 the organization thus established the New York Juvenile Asylum when the city of

New York provided $50,000 per year for the purpose and when a similar sum was raised through private means. It was the first time the AICP accepted public monies. When the Panic of 1873 devastated the AICP's resources, however, it then sought and accepted public funding for many of its projects.

Meanwhile, Hartley's interest in eliminating unwholesome distillery milk from the city continued. He constantly called for the passage of an act to regulate the dairy industry, and in 1862 the state legislature passed such an act, but its enforcement was so lax that Hartley kept up the campaign.

Hartley also saw the need for "model tenements" where the poor could live. And as early as 1851 he recommended creation of an independent Board of Health. The cholera epidemic that struck Europe in 1865 prompted the state legislature to act, and in 1866 the Metropolitan Board of Health of New York City was established. The AICP visitors quickly informed the Board of any and all unsanitary conditions with which they came into contact; it was an effective partnership.

Hartley also became a passionate advocate for the establishment of a Society for the Relief of the Ruptured and Crippled. The Society, set up by Hartley in 1863, became in effect a hospital where artificial arms and legs and surgical attention were provided free to the poor. Hartley served as the organization's executive secretary from 1863 to 1876.

Hartley also subscribed to the fresh air campaigns begun by the *New York Times* and others. Rather than sponsor a fresh air campaign that would disrupt family life, Hartley suggested that the excursion to the countryside be a family affair. The AICP began its fresh air program with short excursions to Coney Island and the Rockaways.

When Hartley reached his eightieth birthday in 1876, he decided that it was time to retire. After his retirement, the AICP decentralized its functions, and its volunteer visitors became paid professionals. With that—the professionalization of social work—"amateur" directors of large-scale nonsectarian charitable organizations virtually disappeared; Hartley was among the last of his breed. In many ways, then, his career bridged the gap between the private charity of the nineteenth century and the public welfare of the twentieth.

Robert Hartley, referred to by one expert as "the most important single figure in American charity in the middle third of the nineteenth century," died of pneumonia in New York City on March 3, 1881.

The Robert Hartley Papers are in the offices of the Community Service Society Archives in New York City, as are the published annual reports of the AICP, written by Hartley; the reader can follow Hartley's thoughts on the pertinent social issues through these sources. Additional biographical information on Hartley can be found in his son's (Isaac C. Hartley) edited work, *Memorial of Robert Milham Hartley* (1882). For Hartley's English background and ancestry, see George Herbert Guttridge, *David Hartley, M.P., An Advocate of Conciliation, 1774–1783* (1926).

One of Hartley's successors at the AICP, William H. Allen, wrote a critical assessment of Hartley's years with the agency. See his *Efficient Democracy* (1907), especially pages 142–152, in which he argues that Hartley's reliance on volunteers was inefficient. Also see Roy Lubove's article, "The New York Association for Improving the Condition of the Poor: The Formative Years," *New York Historical Society Quarterly* 42 (1959), 307–327, in which he emphasizes the moral uplift, as opposed to the "charitable," character of the agency. A more extensive review of the AICP and Hartley's role in it can be found in Lilian Brandt, *The Growth and Development of the AICP and COS: A Preliminary and Exploratory Review* (1942). Additional sources are Maria Kleinburd, "Robert Hartley and the AICP: Urban Reform and Reformers in the Nineteenth Century," Ph.D. dissertation, Brown University, 1971; Dorothy Becker, "Visitors to the New York City Poor, 1843–1920," Ph.D. dissertation, Columbia University School of Social Work, 1949, some material of which was extracted for an article by that name that appeared in the *Social Service Review* 35 (1961), 382–396; Robert Padernacht, "The Contributions of the New York Association for Improving the Condition of the Poor to Child Welfare," Ph.D. dissertation, St. John's University, 1976; and Paul Boyer, *Urban Masses and Moral Order in America, 1820–1920* (1978).

THOMAS J. CURRAN

**Hathway, Marion** (July 31, 1895–November 18, 1955), social work educator and social activist, was born in North Tonawanda, New York, the second of three children of William W. and Alice R. (Shelley) Hathway. The family moved from New England to Denver, where she graduated from Denver High School East Side in 1911. She returned to the East to attend Radcliffe College from 1912 to 1916, where she majored in social ethics and economics. During her undergraduate days she volunteered in two settlement houses and worked for a woman suffrage group.

Over the next five years she was a teacher of mathematics in Miss Seabury's Preparatory School, a War Department statistician, and a field representative for the National Board of the YWCA; she also studied vocational guidance work at Columbia University for one summer. In 1921 she became assistant director for the Bureau of Child Welfare in the Denver public school system. During this time she decided to attend the University of Chicago School of Social Service Administration, where she received a master's degree in 1927. Her master's thesis was entitled "The Young Cripple and His Job."

Her first academic appointment was at the University of Washington, where she taught casework, child welfare, and community organization, and supervised field students. She initiated many research projects, including ones on homeless men, on the cost and volume of social service delivery, and on poor relief in Washington, later published as *Public Relief in Washington, 1853–1933*. At the same time, as executive secretary of the Washington State Conference of Social

Work, she developed district and regional social work conferences which carried out year-round programs.

Since her years at Chicago, she had maintained an active correspondence with Sophonisba Breckinridge,* who encouraged her to complete a doctorate in social work. For three summers she attended the University of Chicago and finally completed her degree by writing up a study carried out in Washington, entitled *The Migratory Worker and Family Life*. At that time she accepted a teaching position on the faculty at the University of Pittsburgh, where she remained from 1932 to 1951 (except for the period from 1938 to 1941, when she was on leave to work as the executive secretary of the American Association of Schools of Social Work).

On June 6, 1936, she was married to Colonel Theodore R. Parker, who was a history professor at the University of Pittsburgh. Throughout their nineteen years of marriage, Hathway retained her maiden name for professional reasons. There were no children from this marriage. Hathway was a visiting professor at American University in Washington (1936–1937), the University of Hawaii (summer, 1941) and the University of Puerto Rico (summer, 1944). After some dissatisfaction with the University of Pittsburgh, Hathway was appointed as the director of the Department of Social Economy at Bryn Mawr College, where she was particularly interested in strengthening its doctoral program. She remained there until her death.

Throughout her academic career, Hathway was actively involved in organizations that contributed to the professionalization of social work. As the first full-time secretary of the American Association of Schools of Social Work (AASSW), she received a grant from the Rockefeller Foundation for an analysis of personnel needs for the public social services. She was also a member of the National Conference of Social Work's executive committee (1947–1950) and the American Association of Social Workers' national board (1942–1945).

Hathway believed that social action and involvement were important parts of professional practice. She attacked discrimination against Negroes in national defense industries in a 1941 speech at the National Conference of Social Work. She called for adequate programs of social services and assurance of economic justice for all citizens. She was an active supporter of the labor movement and published an article entitled "Trade Unions for Social Workers" in *Social Work Today* in 1939.

In the Pittsburg community she was active in the Urban League, the Pittsburgh Council of American-Soviet Friendship, Inc., the Russian War Relief Committee, and the Federation of Social Agencies of Allegheny County, as well as numerous other agencies. On several occasions she spoke out in favor of peace and admonished social workers to stand firmly against the country's leaders who were moving the country toward war. She felt that faculty members in schools of social work might not necessarily be active in social action movements but that they should at least have strong convictions on the ethical issues of the times. In an article written in 1948, "Preparation for Social Responsibility," she challenged the social work profession to clarify its ethical values as a group. Applying her commitment to research and her interest in social economics, she suggested that social work students be taught to analyze and to make independent judgments about social problems in relation to the social-economic structure in which social work is practiced.

As a leader in the Progressive Party and an advocate for international peace and friendship, Hathway was frequently criticized in the late 1940s and 1950s for these and other activities. In 1950 a state judge denounced her "leftist" activities and demanded that state aid be cut off to the University of Pittsburgh, where Hathway taught. No action against the university was ever taken, but Hathway did resign from the Progressive Party even though she remained active in progressive issues.

As a social work scholar, she wrote numerous monographs and articles concerned with social work education and training, social change, and social action. In 1948 she became editor of a social service series for the Houghton Mifflin Company and guided the development of four texts: *American Social Security Systems*, by Evelyn Burns (1949), *Social Group Work*, by Gertrude Wilson and Gladys Ryland (1949), *Community Organization Practice*, by Campbell Murphy (1954), and *Casework Services for Children*, by Henrietta Gordon (1956). Hathway died in Bryn Mawr, Pennsylvania, in 1955 at age sixty while working on an introductory social work text for the series.

The Marion Hathway Papers, 1911–1955, are located in the Social Welfare History Archives, University of Minnesota, Minneapolis, Minnesota. The collection is quite extensive and covers her years at the University of Pittsburgh and at Bryn Mawr. Her obituary appeared in *Social Service Review* (March, 1956), and in *Who Was Who in America* (1966). In 1961 the Council on Social Work Education published a series of Marion Hathway Memorial Lectures entitled *Human Values and Social Responsibility* which included a short biography of Hathway.

Marion Hathway wrote many articles about social action, values, and social work education; prominent among these articles were "Education and Practice," *The Survey* (June, 1939); and "Twenty-Five Years of Professional Education for Social Work—and a Look Ahead," *Compass* (June, 1946).

JEAN K. QUAM

**Haynes, George Edmund** (May 11, 1880–January 8, 1960), social worker, educator, and cofounder and first executive director of the National Urban League, was born in Pine Bluff, Arkansas, to Louis Haynes, a laborer, and Mattie Sloan Haynes, a domestic. Haynes resided in Pine Bluff, where he attended elementary school, until his family moved to Hot Springs, Arkansas, in quest of better secondary schools. Later he enrolled at the Agricultural and Mechanical College in Normal, Alabama, but left after one year to attend Fisk University in Nashville,

Tennessee, where he earned a B.A. degree. In 1904 he received an M.A. from Yale University.

While studying at the University of Chicago during the summers of 1906 and 1907, Haynes became interested in social problems affecting black migrants from the South. This interest led him to the New York School of Philanthropy, from which he graduated in 1910. Two years later he received a Ph.D. from Columbia University. Columbia University Press published his doctoral dissertation, *The Negro at Work in New York City*, for which he gathered most of the information (about in-migration and working problems of Blacks in New York City) while studying on a fellowship granted him in 1908 by the New York Charity Organization Society's Bureau of Social Research. Within this period, he also involved himself in the activities of the American Association for the Protection of Colored Women, the Committee for Improving the Industrial Conditions of Negroes in New York, and the Committee on Urban Conditions Among Negroes. He then was instrumental in merging these groups into one organization, named the National League on Urban Conditions Among Negroes (NLUCAN), now known as the National Urban League. He served as its executive director from 1911 to 1918, during which time he argued that black people would be integrated into American society once educational and employment barriers were removed.

Earlier, while still a graduate student, he had been secretary of the Colored Men's Department of the International Committee of the YMCA, during which time he visited black colleges and encouraged students to achieve scholastic excellence and to help black colleges set high academic standards. With this latter goal in mind, he established the Association of Negro Colleges and Secondary Schools and served that organization as secretary from 1910 to 1918. He also helped the New York School of Philanthropy and NLUCAN in collaborative planning that led to the establishment of the first social work training center for black graduate students at Fisk, and he directed that center for the next eight years (1910–1918).

Meanwhile, in 1910, he had married Elizabeth Ross, who bore him one child, a son, George Edmund, Jr. In 1955, two years after his first wife died, he married Olyve L. Jeter. Marriage and fatherhood, however, did not slow Haynes down. Within those years, he supervised field placements of League fellows at the New York School and was professor of economics and sociology at Fisk. On leave from Fisk from 1918 to 1921, he served as Director of Negro Economics in the United States Department of Labor. As a special assistant to the Secretary of Labor, he was heavily involved in matters of racial conflict in employment, housing, and recreation. All during this time, he continued his earlier studies of exclusion of black workers from certain trade unions, interracial conditions in the workplace, and child labor—studies which resulted in numerous scholarly works. One of the most significant of these was *The Negro at Work During the World War and During Reconstruction*, published by the Government Printing Office in 1921. The work's widespread and profound impact resulted in his appointment as a member of the President's Unemployment Conference in 1921. When the position was not funded the following year, he continued his social welfare career in the church, an institution which he believed should be committed to social equality and justice, as the first executive secretary of the Department of Race Relations of the Federal Council of Churches of Christ. In that capacity, he initiated Race Relations Sunday and organized interracial clinics to handle racial tensions. In 1930 he took a leave of absence from that position to make a survey of the work of the YMCA in South Africa, and in 1947 he conducted a similar study of the organization's activities in other African nations. These efforts resulted in his being chosen as a consultant on Africa by the World Committee of YMCAs. His book *Trend of the Races* (1922) reflected his belief in the union of all peoples. For the last nine years of his life he taught at the City College of New York and served as an officer of the American Committee on Africa. Haynes died in New York City.

Extensive biographical information on Haynes can be found in *The Dictionary of American Negro Biography*, ed. Rayford Logan and Michael Winston (1982), and *Current Biography, 1946 (1947)*, ed. Anna Rothe. *Blacks in the City: A History of the National Urban League*, by Guichard Parris and Lester Brooks (1971), includes a thoroughly documented account of Haynes' role in founding the National Urban League and his work in developing the training center for social workers at Fisk University. Also see Nancy Weiss' *The National Urban League, 1910–1940* (1974). John Hope Franklin's *From Slavery to Freedom: A History of Negro Americans* (1974) emphasizes Haynes' research into minority employment as well as his social work activities. The *New York Times* obituary of Haynes (January 16, 1960) highlights the teaching career of his later years. "A Tribute to George E. Haynes" in the letters to the editor column of the *New York Times* (January 6, 1960) is an addendum to the obituary which describes Haynes' participation in the American Committee on Africa and mentions his book, *Africa: Continent of the Future* (1950). Articles by Haynes were published in the 1935 and 1939 volumes of the *Social Work Yearbook*.

MARJORIE HENTON MAYO

**Healy, William** (January 20, 1869–March 15, 1963), psychiatrist, pioneer in the scientific study of juvenile delinquency, and author, was born near Beaconsfield in Buckinghamshire County in central England, the son of poor tenant farmers, William and Charlotte (Hearne) Healy. In 1878, when William was nine years old, the Healy family immigrated to the United States, first to Rochester and then to Chicago. Healy's long career as psychiatrist-director, first of the Juvenile Psychopathic Institute in Chicago, then of the Judge Baker Guidance Center in Boston, spanned the years during which American child welfare advocates turned to psychological explanations of dependency and deviancy. Through his studies of juvenile delinquency Healy contributed to the development of the specialty of child psychiatry and to the creation of a child welfare system which emphasized family dynamics and the emotional well-being of the individual child. He was also instrumental in creating the institutional setting and procedural format for diagnosing and treating children with emotional and behavioral problems.

Healy described his youth as a rags-to-riches success story. He started life in the poverty that engulfed many immigrants in Chicago; left school at the age of thirteen to contribute to the family by working in a bank, where fellow employees educated him in music and literature; and made his way, through the aid of friends at the Ethical Culture Society, to Harvard University. His climb to professional distinction began with a degree from Harvard (earned in 1896 and granted in 1899), followed by three years at Harvard Medical School. Healy did not, however, receive his M.D. from Harvard. Instead, he finished his medical education at Rush Medical University in Chicago, hoping that the local degree would help him gain entry into practice in his home city. Following graduation in 1900, Healy spent one year as the physician to the Women's Division of the Mendota State Hospital in Wisconsin, married Mary Sylvia Tenney, fathered a son (Kent Tenney Healy), and set up a general private practice in Chicago. It was also during these first five years as a physician that Healy's attention turned to the treatment of nervous and mental diseases, the area in which he would practice for the next four decades.

Healy called his occupation "scientific medicine," although by science he meant the application of "common sense" to the study of psychological problems, and his theories of delinquency were derived from clinical observations. To acquire the credentials of a medical scientist, he, along with many other American physicians of that era, made the obligatory pilgrimage to European laboratories for a year's postgraduate training. Returning to Chicago in 1907, Healy resumed a teaching position at the Chicago Polyclinic and established a private practice in neurology. It was Julia Lathrop* of Hull-House and the sponsors of the Chicago juvenile court who turned Healy's career to the scientific study of juvenile delinquency.

Prodded by the political lobbying of female activists, in 1899 the Illinois legislators passed a juvenile court act which designated separate, age-segregated trial proceedings for youthful offenders as well as dependent and neglected children. During the next decade these same women perceived the need for a study of the causes of delinquency to assist juvenile court judges in making assignments among the variety of alternative placements available for young offenders. Aware of Healy's classroom discussions of the psychopathology of crime, they requested him to undertake a five-year research project into the causes of juvenile criminal recidivism. With a grant from Ethel Sturges Dummer* (a wealthy Chicago philanthropist and a member of the Hull-House circle), Healy established in 1909 the Juvenile Psychopathic Institute to serve as a diagnostic center for the Chicago juvenile court. By examining cases referred by the court's judge, Healy planned to analyze the mental and emotional problems of juvenile recidivists. When funding from Dummer ended in 1914, the institute was taken over by Cook County (and later by the state of Illinois) and renamed the Institute for Juvenile Research. Healy continued to work at this institution until 1917, when he moved to Boston as director of a new court-affiliated clinic, the Judge Baker Foundation (renamed in 1933 the Judge Baker Guidance Center), a position he held for thirty years.

Healy was a prolific scholar, writing or coauthoring thirteen books and numerous articles concerning the use of psychological concepts to explain delinquent behavior, the effectiveness of treatment programs, and the problem of repeat offenders. In addition, he edited two volumes of case studies and published two manuals of psychological tests to be used with delinquents. His most influential work was *The Individual Delinquent* (1915), a volume which served as an important source book for juvenile court judges and child guidance workers throughout the 1920s. Indeed, the categories of childhood emotional problems outlined in this book formed the basis for later child psychiatry classifications.

Basing his theories on case histories from the Juvenile Psychopathic Institute, Healy rejected the view that delinquency could be explained solely in environmental or genetic terms (the two competing contemporary ideological perspectives). Moreover, he recognized that the clinic had been misnamed; few of the youngsters could be classified as psychopathological personalities. Instead, Healy found that the causes of delinquency were exceedingly complex and unique to each individual child. Hence any program to rehabilitate the youths had to take individual differences into account. Three elements were crucial to Healy's analysis of delinquency. First, he attempted to uncover all of the facts relevant to the child's behavior. Second, he stressed the importance of the child's mental life, rather than the nature of the crime committed. Finally, he listened to the child's "own story," a technique Healy regarded as his unique contribution to delinquency studies and to child psychiatry. *The Individual Delinquent*, with its cataloguing of delinquency by motive rather than by criminal behavior, and its stress on the individual, was clearly a model of the progressives' approach to social problems.

Although Healy was interested in the "mental life" of the child, *The Individual Delinquent* was not simply a derivative of the ideas of Sigmund Freud. Rather, it reflected an American concept of psychiatry, identified with the "psychobiology" of Johns Hopkins psychiatrist Adolf Meyer.* Subsequently Healy became more sympathetic to Freudian concepts, and his interest turned increasingly to psychodynamic interpretations of delinquent behavior. With Augusta Bronner* (the Judge Baker Foundation psychologist who became his second wife in 1932), Healy created a primer of Freudian principles entitled *The Structure and Meaning of Psychoanalysis* (1930). The practical application of psychoanalysis to the rehabilitation of convicted criminals was undertaken in collaboration with analyst Franz Alexander. Although published in 1935 as *The Roots of Crime*, the results of this attempt to use psychoanalytic techniques with delinquents were inconclusive. In spite of his evident interest in Freudian concepts, Healy's approach to criminal behavior remained largely eclectic.

This eclecticism led Healy to incorporate the perspectives of other disciplines into the diagnosis of each individual case. At the Juvenile Psychopathic Institute

Healy instituted a child guidance "team" of psychiatrist, psychologist, and social worker. This group of experts assessed the social, psychological, medical, and emotional background of each child, and, at a staff conference, developed a character sketch and plan of treatment for the individual delinquent. The team became an integral part of child guidance work in the 1920s, and training in child psychiatry was always characterized by the collaboration of various professional specialties.

The psychologist's report played a significant part in the team's review of a delinquent's potential for rehabilitation. At the Juvenile Psychopathic Institute Healy pioneered in the use of psychological and intelligence tests to determine the mental capabilities of each child. More important than the tests he personally devised, however, was his condemnation of the belief that delinquency was due to mental retardation. Indeed, it was his faith in the fundamental "normality" of most delinquents that allowed him to supply an optimistic prognosis for many of his patients and helped to ensure the continued connection between psychiatry and rehabilitation programs.

The idea of a court-affiliated clinic, made operational by Healy's work at the Juvenile Psychopathic Institute, caught the interest of Progressive Era child welfare workers. In 1921 the National Committee for Mental Hygiene, directed by Dr. Thomas W. Salmon,* sponsored a conference to ascertain the need for additional court clinics. Healy represented the Judge Baker Foundation at this meeting, which recommended the establishment of seven demonstration guidance clinics to be financed by the Commonwealth Fund. Healy's dedication to spreading clinic services also resulted in a publication for the Children's Bureau designed to persuade other communities of the scientific need for comprehensive examinations of delinquents by a clinic team.

Child guidance clinics achieved a broad measure of public acceptance during the 1920s, and Healy, at the Judge Baker Foundation, was an acknowledged leader in both child psychiatry research and the training of clinic personnel. During the 1920s he negotiated with Smith College to provide practical training for their social work students. Healy's efforts to study the effectiveness of delinquency programs led in the 1930s to the cooperation of the Judge Baker Guidance Center in the Cambridge-Somerville Youth Study of delinquency prevention through personal counseling.

Although the child guidance movement continued to claim public support, clinics in general and the Judge Baker Center in particular were carefully scrutinized by other professionals during the Depression decade. Sheldon Glueck and Eleanor T. Glueck, in their follow-up study, *One Thousand Juvenile Delinquents* (1935), condemned the Boston clinic and court for failure to reduce significantly the amount of delinquent recidivism. Healy's last major work, written for the American Law Institute, attempted to answer his critics. In *Criminal Youth and the Borstal System* (1941), Healy and coauthor Benedict Alper challenged the effectiveness of the rehabilitative efforts at juvenile reformatories and praised the individualized program of the British borstal system for handling youthful offenders.

Nevertheless, Healy's emphasis on the individual and his rejection of any unidimensional theory of delinquency were beginning to lose credibility among a younger generation of social scientists with an affinity for cultural and environmental explanations of adolescent criminal behavior. In retrospect it is often difficult to differentiate these competing etiologies of delinquency. While Healy's catalogue of the causes of juvenile crime did take into account the social environment of the delinquent, his solutions, or treatment, more often stressed the child's "ideations" and interpersonal relationships. This approach proved unpopular with researchers and policy planners who emphasized "the social," in a Durkheimian sense, and sought to prevent delinquency through mass cultural regeneration.

Although Healy had begun his career by providing diagnoses for juvenile courts, he worked actively to extend clinic services to reach troublesome youths who were not legally "delinquent." An incentive for his move from Chicago to Boston was the promise of greater interaction with local child welfare agencies and the possibility of providing treatment at the clinic. Formal treatment programs were not created until 1930; in the intervening years both Healy and Bronner promoted the services offered by the clinic to public and private welfare agencies, schools, and individual families. Healy regarded *Honesty* (1915), his one effort to popularize delinquency research for a general audience, as an insignificant part of his work. Yet because of his efforts to publicize the work of the Judge Baker Foundation, the child guidance movement began to incorporate not only children who reached the courts but also those whose behavior disrupted any social group.

Healy's interest in the use of psychiatric tools to solve vexing social problems led him to participate in the creation of the American Orthopsychiatric Association. He served as the group's first president in 1925, an indication of his stature among his colleagues. In addition, Healy was requested by defense lawyer Clarence Darrow to participate in the psychiatric examinations of two notorious adolescents, Nathan Leopold and Richard Loeb, accused of brutally murdering young Bobby Franks in 1924. Yet, for all of his apparent influence, Healy remained in the shadow of psychiatrists with a larger national audience, preferring to pursue his studies with individual delinquents at the Boston clinic. In 1947 Healy retired from the Judge Baker Guidance Center. He spent the remainder of his life in Clearwater, Florida, where he died on March 15, 1963, at the age of ninety-four.

No manuscript collection exists for William Healy, although uncatalogued materials can be found in the George Gardner Papers at the Francis A. Countway Library of Medicine, Boston, Massachusetts. Information concerning the creation of the Juvenile Psychopathic Institute is contained in the Ethel Sturges Dummer Papers at the Arthur and Elizabeth Schlesinger Library, Radcliffe College, Cambridge, Massachusetts. See also the Adolf Meyer Papers located at the Alan Mason Chesney Medical Archives of the Johns Hopkins Medical Institutions, Baltimore, Maryland. The transcript of a lengthy interview with William Healy and Augusta Bronner, made by historian John Burnham in 1960, can be found at Houghton Library, Harvard University, Cambridge, Massachusetts.

Healy's most important work was *The Individual Delinquent: A Textbook of Diagnosis and Prognosis for All Concerned in Understanding Offenders*(1915). His sole popular work was *Honesty: A Study of the Causes and Treatment of Dishonesty among Children* (1915). Other studies include *Mental Conflict and Misconduct* (1917); with Augusta Bronner: *Delinquents and Criminals: Their Making and Unmaking* (1926), *The Structure and Meaning of Psychoanalysis as Related to Personality and Behavior* (1930), *New Light on Delinquency and Its Treatment* (1936), and *Treatment and What Happened After* (1939); with Franz Alexander: *Roots of Crime: Psychoanalytic Studies* (1935); with Benedict Alper: *Criminal Youth and the Borstal System* (1941).

The only extensive biographical study of William Healy is that by Grant Hulse Wagner, "William Healy, M.D., Father of the American Child Guidance Movement," Master's thesis, University of Maryland, 1981. See also H. Meltzer, "Contributions to the History of Psychology: VI. Dr. William Healy—1869–1963—The Man in His Time," *Psychological Reports* 20 (1967), 1028–1030; and Jon Snodgrass, "William Healy (1869–1963): Pioneer Child Psychiatrist and Criminologist," *Journal of the History of the Behavioral Sciences* 20 (1984), 331–339. Healy's work at the Judge Baker Foundation is discussed by Peter Holloran, "Boston's Wayward Children: Social Services for Homeless Children, 1800–1930," Ph.D. dissertation, Boston University, 1982; and Robert M. Mennel, *Thorns and Thistles: Juvenile Delinquents in the United States, 1825–1940* (1973).

Obituary notices appeared in the *Boston Herald* (March 16, 1963) and the *Boston Traveler* (March 15, 1963). See also Sheldon Glueck, "Remarks in Honor of William Healy, M.D.," *Mental Hygiene* 48 (1964), 318–322; and George Gardner, "William Healy, 1869–1963," *Journal of the American Academy of Child Psychiatry* 11 (1972), 1–29.

KATHLEEN W. JONES

**Heller, Florence Grunsfeld** (March 2, 1897–January 5, 1966), philanthropist and community and national organization leader, was born in Albuquerque, New Mexico, the daughter of Ivan Grunsfeld, a wholesale merchant, and Hannah (Nusbaum) Grunsfeld. Her paternal grandparents, Albert and Hildegarde (David) Grunsfeld, were among the first settlers in the New Mexico Territory. The family's religious affiliation was with the Jewish faith. After completing her primary education at the public schools of Albuquerque, Florence attended Bradford Academy in Boston, Massachusetts, and the Faulkner School for Girls in Chicago, Illinois. Settling permanently in Chicago in 1917, she was married to Walter E. Heller, a business executive from that city, on February 22, 1917. She eventually bore three sons: John Andrew, Peter Eugene, and Paul Walter.

Principal beneficiaries of Florence G. Heller's continuous and devoted philanthropic and organizational efforts were the Jewish Community Centers of Chicago, the National Jewish Welfare Board and its community centers, the United Service Organizations (USO), Brandeis University and its Florence Heller Graduate School, and the Weiss Memorial Hospital in Chicago. She began her philanthropic and charitable pursuits, however, during World War I, when she worked as a relief worker (in Chicago) for the American Red Cross. In the 1920s she was a volunteer worker at the United Jewish Charities Center in the Windy City, interviewing applicants for relief. This early work led her to volunteer with children at the Jewish People's Institute, from which developed the Jewish Community Centers of Chicago. The purpose of the Institute was to provide educational, recreational, and social programs for children of immigrants. After seventeen years (1923–1941) as president of the Institute's women's auxiliary, she served sixteen years (1948–1964) as vice president of the National Jewish Welfare Board and became its first woman president in 1964. She was an honorary director for life of the Jewish Community Centers of Chicago.

When the National Jewish Welfare Board joined with other organizations to establish the USO in 1941, Florence G. Heller was instrumental in both the formation and implementation of the activities of that new organization. She worked enthusiastically to develop the off-base clubs, lounges, and centers both in the United States and overseas for armed forces personnel for which the organization became known. At the time of her death, Heller was a member of the National Board of Governors of the USO.

In 1959 Florence Heller founded and endowed the Florence Heller Graduate School for Advanced Studies in Social Welfare at Brandeis University. The nationally respected Heller School currently offers a doctoral program in social policy planning, administration and research, and a master's degree in the management of human services. Florence Heller was a major contributor to Brandeis University and served as a trustee from 1961 until her death. She also founded and endowed the Florence Heller Isotope Laboratory and the Florence G. Heller Blood Bank at the Louis A. Weiss Memorial Hospital in Chicago.

Florence Heller also served as vice chairwoman of the National Women's Division of the Jewish Appeal from 1946 to 1947 and as chairwoman of the Management Committee of the Central USO Club of Chicago from 1942 to 1947. She also represented the National Jewish Welfare Board as chair of its Sixth Service Command and Armed Forces Committee from 1949 to 1956, served on the Board's Youth Services Committee, and served as representative for the Board on the Conference Group of the Non-Governmental Organizations of the United Nations. In addition, she served as a board member of the World Federation of Young Men's Hebrew Associations (YMHAs) and as a director of the Jewish Federation of Metropolitan Chicago. She also made generous personal contributions to the building fund of the YMHA building in Jerusalem, Israel.

Throughout her long years of service to health and welfare organizations, Florence Heller worked with dedication to improve the standards of social welfare agencies. While serving as president of the National Jewish Welfare Board, she made plans for recruiting trained social workers and expanding the scholarship program and made funds available to establish the Board's research center. In her position as director of the Jewish Federation of Metropolitan Chicago, she established a research fund to benefit its social welfare programs. It was these interests in enhancing the training of social workers and in promoting social welfare research that led her to work with Brandeis University to develop the Florence Heller Graduate School. Her unrelenting effort to elevate the quality of social welfare service was the paramount contribution of Florence Heller to the history of American social welfare.

In acknowledgment of her extended and generous efforts on behalf of social welfare, several honors and awards were conferred upon Heller. In 1953 she was the recipient of the Frank L. Weil award of the National Jewish Welfare Board; the annual award of the Institute for Group Work in Jewish Agencies was presented to her in 1960; the annual award of the National Conference on Social Welfare was granted to her in 1963; and she was cited by the Hebrew School Society of Philadelphia in 1964.

Florence G. Heller died in Chicago on January 5, 1966.

There is no collection of Florence G. Heller papers. Some biographical information on her, however, can be gleaned from the *National Cyclopedia of American Biography*, vol. 51 (1969); *Who Was Who in America*, vol. 5 (1973); *Who's Who of American Women*, 5th ed. (n.d.); and an obituary that appeared in the *New York Times* on January 6, 1966.

Other useful sources are historical accounts of the Jewish welfare movement during the years Florence Heller was actively involved in it. Among the better ones are "Jewish Social Services," *Encyclopedia of Social Work*, 15th ed. (1965); H. L. Lurie, *A Heritage Affirmed: The Jewish Federation Movement in America* (1961); and H. D. Stein, "Jewish Social Work in the United States (1654–1954)," *American Jewish Yearbook* (1956).

ELIZABETH D. HUTCHISON

**Henderson, Charles Richmond** (December 17, 1848–March 29, 1915), minister, professor, sociologist, and reformer, was born in Covington, Indiana, the son of Albert and Loranna (Richmond) Henderson. He was first educated at the old University of Chicago, graduating in 1870. In 1873 he received a Bachelor of Divinity degree at the Baptist Union Theological Seminary, married Ella Levering of Lafayette, Indiana, and was ordained as a Baptist minister. His first pastorate had been a small church near Chicago's stockyards where he ministered while a divinity student. In 1873, however, after graduation and ordination, he became the minister of the First Baptist Church of Terre Haute, Indiana, where he also served as the first president of that city's charity organization society.

In 1882 Henderson moved to the Woodward Avenue Baptist Church in Detroit, Michigan, where he again played a leadership role in the city's charity organization society and also gained labor relations experience as a successful arbitrator during a strike against the Detroit Street Car Company. Also during his Detroit pastorate, he studied prisons and their management, an interest that continued throughout his life. Meanwhile, these reform studies and activities brought attention to Henderson, who was offered a position in the newly created Department of Sociology at the University of Chicago. Thus in 1892 Charles Henderson became chaplain, assistant professor of ecclesiastical sociology, and recorder at the University of Chicago; twelve years later he would become chairman of the Department of Sociology, replacing Albion Small, the man who had hired him.

In the same year that Henderson began to teach at Chicago, Graham Taylor* came to teach at Chicago Theological Seminary. In October, 1903, Henderson joined Taylor in a new venture—teaching a twelve-week evening class on "Dependency and Preventive Agencies" to a dozen students involved in social work in Chicago. This successful course was the forerunner of the Chicago School of Civics and Philanthropy (1908), the second school in America to train social workers. Henderson's pioneering spirit in academia also was illustrated by his teaching the first course in rural sociology (at the University of Chicago in 1894–1895) and his contributions to the "Chicago School" of sociology through the use of the local survey method.

Like a number of other reformers in educational settings, Henderson facilitated an association between the university and social agencies in the community. He encouraged students to work in local settlement houses and charity organization societies. He frequently visited Hull-House himself, participating in that settlement's lecture and discussion series, and he worked with Graham Taylor at his settlement, Chicago Commons, to investigate and expose vice in Chicago.

In addition to his teaching and community involvement, Henderson was continually involved in numerous conferences and commissions—local, state, and national—which proliferated around the turn of the century. As a Christian sociologist, Henderson attended Reverend Josiah Strong's 1893 Chicago Conference and World Parliament of Religions, as did Jane Addams,* John Commons,* George Herron, Robert Woods,* and other notable reformers. In 1902 he was elected president of the American Prison Association, and in 1909 he was a representative to the International Prison Congress; a year later he was chosen president of the Congress. In 1910 Henderson (along with Dr. Alice Hamilton*) was appointed to the Illinois Occupational Disease Commission, and in 1913 he served as president of the United Charities of Chicago.

In addition, Henderson was a frequent speaker at the National Conference of Charities and Correction, which he served as president in 1898–1899. His first speech before that body, "Cooperation by the Churches" (1884), was based on his early charity organization experiences. In "Arguments Against Public Outdoor Relief," delivered at the 1891 National Conference, he argued that private charity was sufficient to provide for the needy and that tax-supported relief was stigmatizing, corrupting, and expensive, and that it tended to diminish the philanthropic spirit. In 1894 he was made chairman of the Conference's Commission on Public Relief. In his 1895 Conference speech on "The German Inner Mission," he evidenced his first interest in European activity and comparative social service delivery systems. Later speeches addressed the merit versus the spoils system in personnel practices in charitable and penal institutions (1896, 1898), overviews of charities and poor laws (1896, 1897), neglected children and juvenile courts (1901, 1904, 1907), and increasingly, the question of social insurance (1902 and after).

In response to his 1902 comments on German social insurance, Henderson was asked to chair a commission on workingmen's insurance and old-age pensions, concerns that would be of major interest to him the rest of his life. Henderson's interest in working people had its roots in his ministry in industrial cities, his exposure to the Chicago stockyards, and the impact the German social insurance movement had on him. Now, as chairman of the National Conference's Commission on Social Insurance in 1903, he studied the subject, but vacillated on the matter. Henderson's hesitancy to endorse the concept may have reflected the caution he earlier had expressed about public outdoor relief. Still, when the American Association for Labor Legislation (AALL) was founded in 1906, Henderson joined the organization and played an active role in it, especially with regard to utilizing his knowledge of research to gather material for that body. Before long, he became convinced of the need for such measures and strenuously endorsed old-age pensions, illness insurance, aid for widows and orphans, and, especially, unemployment insurance. Early in 1915 he optimistically wrote to the leader of the AALL that the public was getting ready to accept unemployment insurance, a prediction, of course, that was off the mark by about twenty years.

Charles Henderson was a deeply religious man whose life was characterized by extensive work for the major social causes of his day. In addition to his ministerial work, his teaching, his community efforts, and his national activities, he was a prolific writer. At the University of Chicago he published sixteen books, beginning with *Introduction to the Study of the Dependent, Defective, and Delinquent Classes* in 1893 and including *The Social Spirit of America* (1896), *Modern Methods of Charity* (1904), *Social Duties from the Christian Point of View* (1909), and *Citizens in Industry* (1915); wrote more than 100 articles; and held editorial positions on journals of theology, sociology, and criminal justice. Although in 1914 his doctors warned him against overwork, Henderson continued his many activities; he fell ill in March, 1915, and went to Charleston, South Carolina, for a two-week trip with his wife, hoping to recover his health. Unfortunately, he died there at the age of sixty-six.

There is no collection of Henderson's papers, nor is there any full-length study of his life. The best sources of information are his numerous writings, including his major speeches (many of which are reprinted in the *Proceedings* of the National Conference of Charities and Correction), and many books. Other sources include Frank Bruno, *Trends in Social Work, 1874–1956* (1957); George Lundberg, Read Bain, and Nels Anderson, *Trends in American Sociology* (1929); and Daniel Nelson, *Unemployment Insurance: The American Experience, 1915–1935* (1969).

GARY R. ANDERSON

**Hine, Lewis Wickes** (September 26, 1874–November 4, 1940), social photographer and child labor reformer, was born in Oshkosh, Wisconsin, one of three children of Douglas Hull Hine, the operator of a coffee shop and restaurant, and Sarah (Hayes) Hine.

Between 1892, the year of his father's accidental death and his graduation from high school, and 1900, Hine worked at a series of low-wage jobs and became friendly with Sara Ann Rich, a student at the Oshkosh Normal School whom he would marry in 1904 (and with whom he would have one child, a son, Corydon). Probably through her, he met Frank A. Manny, a teacher of education and psychology at the normal school. With Manny's encouragement he entered the University of Chicago in 1900 to earn a degree in education. After his graduation in 1901, he joined the faculty of the progressive Ethical Culture School in New York City at the invitation of Manny, who was the school's new superintendent. While teaching, he continued his own education, receiving a Pd.M. from New York University in 1905 and doing some graduate work in sociology at Columbia University in 1907.

In 1903 and 1904 Hine's life started to move in new directions. He met Paul* and Arthur Kellogg,* Florence Kelley,* John Spargo, and others who stimulated or reinforced his interest in social problems and reform. Meanwhile, at Manny's suggestion, Hine took up photography. He rapidly became extremely skillful with a camera. His photographs of immigrants at Ellis Island were his best images of this period. They displayed his developing talent for portraying sympathetically and truthfully the faces and lives of people who were completely outside America's middle-class culture.

By 1906 Hine had decided to make photography his vocation. Probably through the influence of friends like Kelley and the Kelloggs, he received some freelance work from the National Child Labor Committee. In 1907 he did some work for the National Consumers' League and for the Pittsburgh Survey. In 1908 he left the Ethical Culture School to work almost exclusively for the National Child Labor Committee. During the next ten years Hine traveled tens of thousands of miles for the Committee to investigate and photograph child labor conditions in America's factories, fields, and mines.

The most enduring product of his travels was his photographs. The best of them were direct and poignant pictures of children who were working long hours in unsafe and unhealthy environments, who were living in overcrowded and unsanitary housing, and who were being deprived of play and an adequate education. The Committee used Hine's photographs to illustrate books, articles, news releases, pamphlets, and lectures by Hine and others, and the images appeared in widely circulated exhibitions prepared by Hine and other child labor reformers. The purposes of the photographs were both to convey information about child labor conditions and to arouse people's sympathy for the children.

It is possible that no reform organization before the National Child Labor Committee had ever mounted such an extensive, persistent, and innovative publicity campaign. Certainly none had ever used such a plenitude of photographs in so many ways in the work of changing society. The widespread circulation of Hine's photographs in Committee publicity made him the best-known social photographer of his time. How well his photographs helped persuade people that child labor was an iniquitous waste of human resources cannot be measured.

In 1918 Hine left the Committee and joined the American Red Cross as an assistant to Homer Folks.* His major work was photographing the misery World War I and its aftermath inflicted on civilians in central, eastern, and southern Europe. Folks used some of Hine's photographs to illustrate his book, *The Human Costs of the War* (1920). After his return from Europe in 1919, Hine worked for the national headquarters of the Red Cross in New York City preparing exhibitions and taking photographs for some of the organization's domestic projects.

When he left the Red Cross in 1920, he was on his own. Never again would he have long-term patronage for his work. At the same time, his choice of subjects and photographic style changed. He began photographing assembly-line workers and craftsmen, not in the straightforward, informational style of his child labor photographs, but in a more formal, symbolic style. His images were a celebration of labor and laborers. Their theme was Hine's belief that men and women, not machines, produced the nation's wealth.

These photographs never attracted a significant following, so the 1920s were lean years for Hine. Paul Kellogg, the editor of *Survey*, helped him as much as possible with assignments and purchases of his work. He did a project on rural agriculture and education for the National Child Labor Committee in 1921, and during the rest of the decade worked briefly for the Milbank Memorial Fund, the National Consumers' League, the Amalgamated Clothing Workers of America, Western Electric, Tung-Sol Lamps, and Sloan's Liniment.

In 1930 Hine photographed construction of the Empire State Building. These images are among the most revealing and exciting pictures ever produced of people at work. They rank with some of Hine's child labor photographs as masterpieces of social photography. In 1932 he published *Men at Work*, a picture book for adolescents, and in 1933, *Through the Loom*, a portfolio of photographs of textile mill workers. During the rest of the decade he did some work for the Tennessee Valley Authority, the Rural Electrification Administration, the National Research Project, *Fortune* magazine, and a few other organizations. A retrospective exhibition of his work in New York City in 1939 gave a brief boost to his reputation, especially as a child labor photographer, and through his association with the Photo League of New York City he was able to pass on his experiences in social photography to the coming generation of social photographers.

Hine was probably the first American to make a career of social photography. His child labor photographs were an important part of a significant progressive reform movement. The influence of his photographs on the crusade against child labor and on social photography during his lifetime and after is unclear. What remain as an indelible part of the history of social welfare in America are his photographs. Hine died a very poor man in 1940 in Dobbs Ferry, New York.

Lewis Hine left no collection of private papers. However, important unpublished Hine materials appear in the National Child Labor Committee Papers, Library of Congress, Manuscript Division; and in the Elizabeth McCausland Papers, Smithsonian Institution, Archives of American Art, reels 1256 and D384G. Large collections of prints or negatives or both of Hine's work are at the Library of Congress, Prints and Photographs Division; the Library of the University of Maryland, Baltimore County; and the International Museum of Photography, George Eastman House, Rochester, New York. A microfiche publication, Jonathan L. Doherty, ed., *Lewis Wickes Hine's Interpretive Photography: The Six Early Projects* (1978), includes a large selection of Hine's child labor, Ellis Island, and Red Cross photographs.

*America and Lewis Hine: Photographs, 1904–1940*, comp. by Walter Rosenblum, Naomi Rosenblum, Alan Trachtenberg, and Marvin Israel (1977) contains a definitive chronology of Hine's life, a comprehensive list of his publications and publications in which his photographs appeared, a useful essay on his career, and a large selection of photographs. Verna Posever Curtis and Stanley Mallach, *Photography and Reform: Lewis Hine and the National Child Labor Committee* (1984), places Hine's child labor photography in a firm historical and photographic context. Judith Mara Gutman, *Lewis W. Hine, 1874–1940: Two Perspectives* (1974), and her article "Lewis Hine's Last Legacy," *New York Times Magazine* (April 17, 1983), 50–53, offer interpretations of Hine's work. The reprint of Lewis W. Hine, *Men at Work: Photographic Studies of Modern Men and Machines* (1977), contains Hine's selection of Empire State Building photographs that appeared in the 1932 edition of the book as well as additional photographs of the same subject.

STANLEY MALLACH

**Hodder, Jessie Donaldson** (March 30, 1867–November 19, 1931), social worker and prison reformer best known for the bold ideas and practices she brought to female corrections in the early decades of the twentieth century, was born in Cincinnati, Ohio, to William and Mary (Hall) Donaldson. Hodder was raised by her grandmother after her mother died and her father remarried. In 1890 Jessie Donaldson became the common-law wife of Alfred LeRoy Hodder of New York City, a doctoral student of William James. The Hodders were in Florence, Italy, in 1893 when their daughter, Olive, was born. The family then returned to the United States, where Alfred became an instructor at Bryn Mawr. Another child, J. Alan Hodder, was born in 1897. In 1898 Hodder sent his wife and children to Switzerland but did not follow. Instead he married a colleague, Mary Gwinn, in 1904. Shortly following this shock came the death of Olive. Overcome by grief, Jessie Hodder spoke of suicide but was encouraged by Mrs. James to return to the United States.

Upon her arrival in Boston in 1906, Hodder launched into a career in social work, translating some of her personal experiences into active programs. Mrs. James had arranged for Hodder to meet Elizabeth Glendower Evans,* a member of the board of trustees of the Massachusetts reformatories. Through Evans, Hodder gained a position as a housemother at the Industrial School for Girls in Lancaster, Massachusetts. Evans also arranged for a paternity suit to be brought against Alfred Hodder, but he died in 1907 before the case was heard.

As part of her work at the Lancaster school, Hodder began working with the Social Services Department of Massachusetts General Hospital counseling unwed mothers as well as syphilis patients and alcoholics. The social services program at Massachusetts General was inaugurated by the physician, medical reformer, and social worker Richard Clarke Cabot.* Cabot believed that social and psychological factors should also be evaluated in treating patients. Hodder integrated these aspects into her work with female delinquents.

In 1910 Hodder was appointed superintendent of the Massachusetts Prison Reformatory for Women at Framingham, Massachusetts. A former superintendent, Ellen Cheney Johnson, had begun the rehabilitative aspects of the reformatory, but Hodder enhanced the program. To emphasize her rehabilitative goals, Hodder had the word "prison" removed from the institution's name. In 1911 the facility became the Framingham Reformatory for Women. Hodder sought to reduce the prison atmosphere by removing barred windows and generally brightening the institution. She insisted on a professional, medical, scientific, and individual evaluation of each inmate, a process which included intelligence and psychiatric classifications. Treatment programs were individualized according to need. And she advocated using the full length of indeterminate sentences in order to guarantee adequate time to effect rehabilitation.

Hodder expanded rehabilitation programs in order to prepare the inmates for a useful return to society. She established a school within the facility and arranged for business school and university extension courses. She opposed the state's emphasis on prison industries, believing that these allowed too little time for education. Thus she insisted that industry be made as educational as possible. Her concern for the inmates' wage-earning capacity upon release led to a program of sending inmates to work by day in a local hospital. She justified this action under an old state indenture law of 1879 and as a temporary, emergency measure during the influenza epidemic of 1918. In Massachusetts men were paid for prison industries while women were not, and under Hodder's influence the practice of "day-work" for pay was continued. In 1947, when the day-work program was seriously threatened, Hodder's son, then a state representative from Framingham, introduced a bill to save it, but without success.

In addition to the medical, social, and educational rehabilitative programs, Hodder also stressed protection of maternal roles within the institution. As a social worker, Hodder had encouraged unwed mothers to keep their children, and as a superintendent she advocated that women be allowed to care for their children, until the age of two, at the reformatory. As many as fifty children resided at the institution at one time. Hodder developed programs that would not only improve the mother's ability to care for the child but also urged paternity suits so that the woman would not bear sole responsibility for the child. Hodder sought continually, although unsuccessfully, to develop a cottage system for mothers with children. Miriam Van Waters,* Hodder's successor, continued the maternal program and was able to secure a cottage system for women and their children.

Sheldon and Eleanor Glueck, in their study of Framingham, *Five Hundred Delinquent Women* (1934), stated that under Hodder, Framingham had become the leading women's institution in the country. Hodder, who more than anyone else integrated individualized social, psychiatric, and medical services into female corrections programs and developed positive, supportive methods for helping unwed mothers, enjoyed the support of leading reformers such as Dr. Richard C. Cabot, Dr. William Healy,* and Sanford Bates, Massachusetts' Commissioner of Correction, and her reputation as an enlightened, scientific, and dedicated reformer made her a sought-after expert not only in the United States but in Europe as well. In 1921 she toured European prisons (Framingham had served as an example for Prison de La Forêt in Belgium); in 1925 she was the sole United States representative to the International Prison Congress in London; in 1927 she served on the National Crime Commission appointed by President Calvin Coolidge. She would have represented the United States at the International Prison Conference in Prague, but illness prevented her from attending. She died at the reformatory in 1931.

The Jessie Hodder Papers are held at the Schlesinger Library, Radcliffe College, as are the related papers of Elizabeth Glendower Evans and Miriam Van Waters. The Massachusetts State Library, Boston, has the records of the reformatory as well as those of the Department of Correction.

Among Hodder's publications are "Indenture of Prisoners: An Experiment," *Journal of the American Institute of Criminal Law and Criminology* (May 1920); "The Next Step in the Correctional Treatment of Girl and Women Offenders," National Conference of Social Work, *Proceedings* (1918), 117–121; and "Disciplinary Measures in the Management of the Psychotic Delinquent Woman," ibid. (1920), 389–396.

Contemporary studies of Hodder's work are Sheldon Glueck and Eleanor T. Glueck, *Five Hundred Delinquent Women* (1934); and Eugenia C. Lekkerkerker, *Reformatories for Women in the U.S.* (1931). There is also information on

Hodder's work in Blake McKelvey, *American Prisons: A Study in American Social History Prior to 1915* (1936). For further information on the program at Framingham under Hodder, see Estelle B. Freedman, *Their Sisters' Keepers: Women's Prison Reform in America, 1830–1930* (1981). There is a biographical sketch of Hodder in *Notable American Women: 1607–1950*, vol. 2 (1971), 197–199.

Obituaries appeared in the (Springfield, Massachusetts) *Sunday Republican* (November 22, 1931); *Christian Century* (December 2, 1931); *Social Service Review* (December, 1931); and the *Boston Transcript* (November 19, 1931).

BARBARA EGGERS

**Hodson, William** (April 25, 1891–January 14, 1943), child welfare expert, social services administrator, and government official, was born in Minneapolis, Minnesota, to William and Anna (Redding) Hodson. His father died during his childhood, but little else, except that he was Episcopalian, is known about his family and early life. In 1913 he graduated Phi Beta Kappa from the University of Minnesota and enrolled at Harvard Law School, from which he received his bachelor of laws degree in 1916. He married Gertrude Prindle in 1918. The couple had three children: Judith, William, and Jeremy.

Hodson's involvement with social welfare began during his years as a law student, when he alternated between summer work for the Associated Charities of Minneapolis and service with the legal aid bureau of Harvard University and the Boston Associated Charities. In 1916 he joined the Minneapolis Legal Aid Society as chief counsel. The next year, he was appointed secretary and legal investigator of the Minnesota Child Welfare Commission. Hodson researched, codified, and later administered thirty-nine new laws of 1917 that constituted a children's code and made his state a leader in child welfare. From 1918 to 1922 he was a director of the Children's Bureau under Minnesota's State Board of Control.

A dozen years later, during the Great Depression, William Hodson would become Mayor Fiorello La Guardia's Commissioner of Public Welfare of New York City. He moved from Minneapolis to New York in 1922. The Russell Sage Foundation had hired him as director of its Division of Child Welfare Legislation, and two years later, in 1924, appointed him director of its Division of Social Legislation. Hodson's commitment to action through government legislation altered slightly in 1925, when he accepted the position of executive director of the newly founded Welfare Council of New York City. The Welfare Council was to be a vehicle for expressing the judgments of social workers on welfare issues, public and private, but its first task was to organize and coordinate the services of 1,200 private charities, settlement houses, and other welfare agencies. Aided by the Council's assistant director, Jane Hoey,* and by social work leaders such as Lillian Wald* and Homer Folks,* Hodson spent the next four years bringing nearly 700 agencies into the Council. In the meantime, he was an early president (1924–1926) of the American Association of Social Workers (AASW).

Hodson was also secretary of the Welfare Council's Coordinating Committee on Unemployment, which spearheaded a drive for government action after the economic reversals of 1929. Private philanthropy's inability to carry the burden of unemployment led to social work demonstrations during the winter of 1931. The Coordinating Committee pressured municipal and state officials to revise city charters to allow public aid for the jobless. The assembly and Governor Franklin D. Roosevelt approved, and Hodson led social work representatives in negotiations with city officials to establish New York's first public unemployment and work relief programs. He also pushed for the September, 1931, extraordinary session of the legislature that produced the first state program of assistance. In October, 1931, Hodson published an open letter to President Herbert Hoover suggesting that federal relief was needed. He was already associated with an AASW steering committee that would appear in Washington to testify at the end of December; there, Hodson documented the failure of charity and state and local public relief to offset the impact of the Great Depression. For the next eighteen months, he and three other former Minnesotans turned New Yorkers—David Holbrook,* Linton Swift,* and Walter West*—worked tirelessly for legislation that eventually emerged as the Federal Emergency Relief Act of 1933.

Hodson's leadership in changing relief programs secured his 1933 election as president of the National Conference of Social Work. He was closely associated with New York's Harry L. Hopkins* and Frances Perkins,* who were joining former governor Roosevelt in Washington, and he immediately became a spokesman for the New Deal. In 1934, after La Guardia's mayoral election, Hodson moved from private to public social work himself when he became Commissioner of Public Welfare. He was also chairman and executive director (1934–1935) of the city's Emergency Relief Bureau. Governor Herbert H. Lehman appointed him to the state's Temporary Emergency Relief Administration. Hodson's stature as a leading public welfare official was recognized when he served a term (1940–1941) as president of the American Public Welfare Association (APWA).

Those two markers in his career—president of the AASW and of the APWA—helped bridge the formerly separate worlds of professionalism in private social work and politics in public welfare administration. When negotiating for the Welfare Council with city officials early in the 1930s, Hodson had brought professional standards to bear on welfare department staffing and procedures. He always advocated responsible government engagement with the problems of poverty, unemployment, and dependency. His nine years as Commissioner enabled him to bring welfare personnel into the civil service and to spend $1.3 billion on public services. New York City also served as a social laboratory for the implementation of Harry Hopkins' federal work relief programs, two of which—the Federal Emergency Relief Administration and the Civil Works Administration—Hodson helped to formulate and then administered.

In 1943 Herbert Lehman, who had become wartime director of the Office of Foreign Relief and Rehabilitation, designated Hodson as head of a mission in

North Africa. Granted a leave of absence from his New York duties, William Hodson flew toward his new responsibilities and died in a plane crash at sea off the coast of Dutch Guiana.

William Hodson did not leave a collection of personal papers, but his work can be studied in other bodies of manuscript materials. For example, the Herbert H. Lehman Collection at Columbia University Library, New York City, holds much correspondence, and the Henry Street Settlement Papers at the same location have several folders of Welfare Council of New York City materials. The Special Collections Department of the New York Public Library houses complete sets of Welfare Council publications as well as some original reports. Many papers of New Yorkers and New York organizations with which Hodson was associated are held by the Social Welfare History Archives, Minneapolis, Minnesota, and shed light on Hodson's career. The Survey Papers and the National Social Work Council Papers are especially helpful. The Franklin D. Roosevelt Papers and the Harry L. Hopkins Papers at the Franklin D. Roosevelt Library, Hyde Park, New York, are also helpful.

Hodson published no books and was not a prolific writer. Some articles and speeches appeared during the 1920s and 1930s in *Survey*, *Survey Graphic*, *Social Service Review*, the *Proceedings* of the National Conference of Social Work, and *Vital Speeches of the Day*. Two important statements appeared in the 1929 volume of the *Proceedings* of the National Conference of Social Work (1930): "Community Planning for Social Welfare" and "The Social Worker and Politics." Hodson's activities before and after becoming Commissioner of Public Welfare can be traced through the Index of the *New York Times*.

No biography of William Hodson has been written, and he is infrequently mentioned in historical works, including studies of La Guardia's mayoral years. Clarke A. Chambers, "William Hodson," *Dictionary of American Biography*, Supplement 3 (1977), 361–362, is the best brief assessment.

WILLIAM W. BREMER

**Hoehler, Fred Kenneth** (June 6, 1893–January 18, 1969), public welfare administrator, was born in Shenandoah, Pennsylvania, to George Henry and Nina (Kimmel) Hoehler. After graduating from Philadelphia's Central High School in 1911, Hoehler enrolled in Pennsylvania State College, where he was awarded a B.S. in forestry in 1915. He then pursued graduate work at the University of Cincinnati.

Although Hoehler held a forestry degree, he actually devoted little of his career to conservation. In June, 1915, he was employed as the welfare and employment director of a lumber camp. But by the next fall, Hoehler was attending graduate school and working as the general secretary of the University of Cincinnati's YMCA. Hoehler married Dorothy Scovill Stevens on October 17, 1917, and then served in the U.S. Army between 1917 and 1919.

Following his military service, Hoehler returned to Cincinnati, where he resumed his graduate studies and assumed his old job at the YMCA. Hoehler's next position was as assistant director of the Berry Schools in Rome, Georgia. Accounts differ as to how long Hoehler remained in that post. One vita among his personal papers suggests that he stayed in Georgia between 1921 and 1925. However, a Cincinnati newspaper account of Hoehler's career, circa 1933, states that he stayed in Georgia only two years and then returned to the YMCA in Cincinnati.

Nonetheless, by 1926 Hoehler had assumed the directorship of the Cincinnati (and, as of 1929, Hamilton County) Department of Public Welfare. It was in this position that he was to make his first mark on the national social welfare scene. (By the end of his career, Hoehler was to have served as president of the National Conference on Social Welfare and as chair of the U.S. Committee of the International Conference on Social Welfare.) Hoehler's administration of the public welfare department during the Great Depression brought him praise for effective and efficient management. His administration also earned him a reputation as an expert in the developing field of public welfare administration. In 1933 Hoehler was appointed safety director for the city of Cincinnati. While he was responsible for the fire and police departments, his administration also technically included the welfare department. In a 1933 letter to the staff of the *Survey*, Hoehler confessed that he had been pressured into accepting the safety director's job.

Hoehler helped organize the American Public Welfare Association (APWA) in 1930. He served as president of that association between 1933 and 1935 and then became the Association's second executive director in 1936, when Frank Bane* stepped down. As APWA director, 1936–1943, Hoehler sought to bring public welfare administrators and social workers closer together. Noting that he suspected public welfare workers to be skeptical of social workers, he tried to close that perceived gap through the Association's biennial round table meetings. In an effort to give social workers a better picture of public welfare administration work, Hoehler put Gertrude Springer* of the *Survey* on the APWA field staff, giving her an opportunity to create a "Miss Bailey" series on public welfare agencies.

After leaving the APWA, Hoehler directed Office of Foreign Relief and Rehabilitation operations in North Africa and London and then directed the Division of Displaced Persons for the United Nations Relief and Rehabilitation Administration. By 1946 Hoehler had settled in Illinois, where he was to spend the remainder of his life. He directed the Community Fund of Chicago between 1946 and 1949. Illinois Governor Adlai Stevenson appointed Hoehler director of the state Department of Public Welfare in 1949, a position he was to hold until 1953.

While Hoehler had always been a rather political creature—at least his work for the city of Cincinnati suggests a certain political expertise—his Illinois years can well be considered his political years. An ally of Adlai Stevenson, Hoehler was also an early supporter of Mayor Richard Daley of Chicago. During Stevenson's presidential run in 1952, Hoehler was mentioned as a possible Illinois gubernatorial candidate. While supporting Stevenson's 1952 and 1956 presidential campaigns, Hoehler headed an anticrime group, Citizens of Greater Chicago, and then served as a consultant to the New World Foundation, a philanthropy established with a bequest from Mrs. Anita McCormick Blaine, daughter of reaper inventor Cyrus H. McCormick.

From 1955 until his retirement in 1964 due to poor health, Hoehler was employed by Mayor Daley of Chicago. He performed a number of different tasks for the city: superintendent of the city's House of Corrections between 1958 and 1960, consultant to the city's Civil Service Commission, and executive director of the city's Commission on Senior Citizens. Once again, newspapers did not fail to notice his political stature, mentioning him as a possible candidate for police chief (citing his experience as Cincinnati's public safety director) or deputy mayor. Hoehler died in Palatine, Illinois, in 1969.

In addition to publications prepared for the American Public Welfare Association and articles written for such journals as the *Survey*, Hoehler is the author of *Europe's Homeless Millions* (1946).

The Social Welfare History Archives at the University of Minnesota hold a collection of Fred Hoehler's personal papers in addition to the records of the American Public Welfare Association. Unfortunately, the latter collection contains little documentation from the period when Hoehler served as executive director. The Social Welfare History Archives also hold the records of the U.S. Committee of the International Conference on Social Welfare.

An obituary appeared in the *New York Times*, January 19, 1961, 1:73.

SUSAN D. STEINWALL

**Hoey, Jane M.** (January 15, 1892–October 6, 1968), social worker, welfare administrator, and government official, was born in Greeley County, Nebraska, the youngest of nine children of John and Catherine Mullen, Irish Catholic immigrants. The Hoeys had gone west to try their hand at ranching, but returned to New York City when Jane still was a young girl. John became a contractor and apparently provided well for his children, one of whom, James J., served two terms in the state assembly. Jane attended Hunter College for two years and received a bachelor's of arts degree from Trinity College (Washington, D.C.) in 1914. She then returned to New York, where she earned a master's degree in political science from Columbia University and a diploma from the New York School of Philanthropy, both in 1916. She never married.

For nearly two decades, Jane Hoey counted among a handful of powerful women in federal government. Her career began in local government in 1916, when she was appointed assistant secretary of the Board of Child Welfare of New York City during the mayoral years of John Purroy Mitchel. Her superior was Harry Hopkins,* and the two spent much of the next fourteen years working together in duties that paralleled one another. From 1917 to 1921 Hoey was director of field service for the Atlanta division of the American Red Cross. In 1923 she became secretary of the Bronx committee of the New York Tuberculosis and Health Association. In 1926 she was appointed assistant director of the

Welfare Council of New York City, an organization which, like the first two, Hopkins served as well. Hoey remained with the Welfare Council for a decade, assisting its first director, William Hodson,* until he became Mayor La Guardia's Commissioner of Public Welfare in 1934. The Welfare Council represented the city's private philanthropies and was an important force in directing a drive for public unemployment relief and other Depression Era services after 1929.

In the meantime, Jane Hoey devoted herself to advancing her profession. She was a well-known local figure and speaker who forged strong attachments with the settlement house movement and its leaders, including Lillian Wald.* Her Welfare Council was itself a watchdog for professional standards and brought greater unity to social work within the city. In 1925 Hoey was chairman of the New York chapter of the American Association of Social Workers. In 1928 she served as president of the State Conference of Social Work. She was also an executive officer of both national organizations (and president of the National Conference of Social Work in 1940–1941). In addition, her service in New York included five years as a member of the State Crime Commission and ten years on the Commission on Education of Inmates of Correctional Institutes.

By 1935 Harry Hopkins and many of Hoey's other close associates in New York had departed for Washington and jobs in Franklin Roosevelt's New Deal administration. As a spearhead in his drive for unemployment compensation, old-age pensions, and other welfare services, the President created the Committee on Economic Security (COES) in 1934. In addition to Hopkins, another New Yorker, Frances Perkins,* served on the COES, and she supervised appointments to a number of advisory bodies that helped formulate the Social Security Act. Jane Hoey joined the COES's Committee on Child Welfare, and, after the law's enactment in 1935, became a director of the Bureau of Public Assistance within the Social Security Administration.

The end of the Federal Emergency Relief Administration (FERA) in 1935 terminated the federal government's direct participation in the general relief programs of the states and localities. Even though an FERA principle of matching proportionately the funds of a state with federal dollars remained intact, the new Social Security program no longer guaranteed federal authority to set rules, standards, and personnel requirements for state programs. Thus, Hoey took charge of federal aid for the indigent elderly, the blind, and dependent children, but had no explicit power to impose professional guidelines on the states. Her goals, and those of the social work profession—to have benefits distributed in the form of cash rather than as relief in kind, to ensure efficient expenditure of funds, and to utilize the expertise of social work professionals—had to be sought through persuasion. Even though the 1939 amendments to the Social Security Act and reforms implemented by the Social Security Board strengthened standards, Hoey spent most of her nearly twenty years as a federal official trying to persuade governors and state officials to comply voluntarily with federal expectations. Within the Bureau of Public Assistance, she strengthened her own hand by requiring a statistical reporting system of the way in which federal funds were spent and by setting up a special unit to assist the states in getting professional staffs. Indeed, Hoey's personal effort brought professionalism to the administration of public welfare in most states.

Hoey's position was not protected by civil service regulations, and she was dismissed when Dwight D. Eisenhower and the Republicans took control of the executive branch in 1953. The decision created a great controversy. An outspoken Democrat who had served two Democratic Presidents, Hoey challenged the Republicans' action as political, and her social work supporters protested because they feared the removal from office of their champion of federal standards. After the protest failed, New York mayor Robert Wagner offered Hoey the position of Commissioner of Public Welfare, but she declined, choosing instead to become director of social research for the National Tuberculosis Association. Jane Hoey died in New York City in 1968.

Jane Hoey apparently did not leave a collection of personal papers, but materials bearing upon her life and work can be examined at several New York City locations. The city archives hold documents pertinent to her service with the Board of Child Welfare during the Mitchel mayoral years. The Oral History Collection at Columbia University has "The Reminiscences of Jane Hoey" (1965), and the Manuscript Division of Columbia University Libraries holds a useful set of Welfare Council of New York City materials in its Henry Street Settlement Papers. The Special Collections Department of the New York Public Library houses complete sets of Welfare Council publications and some original reports. Hoey's work with the Social Security Administration can be traced in the records of the Bureau of Public Assistance, Social Security Administration, Record Group 47, Washington National Records Center (Suitland, Maryland). The archives of Trinity College (Washington, D.C.) have articles by Hoey and clippings about her.

Hoey was an occasional author whose writings appeared in publications such as the *Proceedings* of the National Conference of Social Work, *Social Service Review*, and *Social Security Bulletin*. She wrote no books herself but did contribute to *Study of National Social Agencies in Fourteen American Communities*, with Porter Lee and Walter Pettit (1926); and *Democracy: Should It Survive?* (1943).

Jane Hoey is often mentioned in books that examine the Social Security Act and its administration, but she has not been the subject of a biography, nor has her work with the Social Security Administration been analyzed fully. The best short biography is Blanche D. Coll, "Jane Margueretta Hoey," in *Notable American Women*, vol. 4 (1980), 341–343.

WILLIAM W. BREMER

**Hoffer, Joe Ralph** (March 22, 1907–September 28, 1978), social work administrator and author, was born in New York City, the son of Andrew and Mary (Lottie) Hoffer. In 1932 he received a Bachelor of Science degree from Ohio State University, and in 1942 he was awarded the Ph.D. in Social

Administration from the same institution. Meanwhile, on November 28, 1936, he had married Mary B. Rusnak; the couple had no children.

Hoffer's early professional career began with a series of increasingly important administrative positions. He was first employed as director of an Ohio orphans' home and then became director of community organization for the National Youth Administration for the state of Ohio. Leaving Ohio, he served for five years as the secretary of the Community Division of the Philadelphia Council of Social Agencies. He then spent a year as the executive officer of the U.S. Joint Commission on Evacuation in Washington, D.C. These early positions provided Hoffer with sound administrative experience and a broad knowledge of the social welfare needs and resources in this country.

Following active duty with the U.S. Navy in World War II, Hoffer accepted a position with the United Nations Relief and Rehabilitation Administration in Nanking, China. This was a significant experience in Hoffer's career for three main reasons. First, it convinced him that social problems and the attendant social welfare efforts which attempted to alleviate these problems transcended national boundaries. Second, it led him to the conclusion that international relief assistance programs could be effective only when they were based on a sound knowledge of, and respect for, the cultural heritage and customs of the respective country. And finally, it also reinforced his belief that effective social welfare provisions depended on a systematic and knowledge-based planning process.

Following this year in China, Hoffer accepted a job as executive director of the Social Work Bureau of New York City and also served as a consultant to the American Association of Social Workers. He served in this dual capacity for two years, and this experience gave him visibility and recognition as one of the rising young social work administrators of the time.

In 1948 Hoffer assumed the position of executive director of the National Conference on Social Welfare while simultaneously being named the secretary general of the International Conference of Social Welfare. It was in these two organizations that he made his greatest impact. He served in the latter organization as secretary general until 1966, when the demands of the two positions became too great and necessitated that he give up one of them; he retained his position with the National Conference on Social Welfare until 1972. In both of these organizations Hoffer proved to be a progressive and able administrator who presided over organizations which had significant impacts on social policy and social service provision on both a national and international scale.

From this perspective as chief executive officer of the National Conference on Social Welfare and of the International Conference of Social Welfare, Hoffer had an excellent vantage point from which to view the unmet needs and gaps in service which inhibited the success of social welfare systems. He was a frequent contributor to the professional literature, advocating changes that he felt would ultimately result in more effective and knowledgeable social service delivery systems. Hoffer viewed the social work profession as having a mandate to both advance knowledge and impart this knowledge to others as well as gaining knowledge from other disciplines and professions. Most of his writing concerned overcoming barriers and obstacles to disseminating relevant information and suggesting innovations that would make this process easier and more efficient.

He was one of the first social workers to recognize the potential of computers and wrote extensively of their utility in advancing both social work practice and research methods. Hoffer emphasized that social workers needed to become proficient in using this emerging technology so that computer usage could be geared to the needs of the social work practitioner, administrator, and educator. As part of this concern about the flow of information, Hoffer also advocated the establishment of a national network of cooperating information centers. He envisioned centers which would utilize the latest technological advances in information storage and retrieval and would serve the needs of regional agencies and institutions by distributing the latest advances in knowledge to interested parties.

Perhaps Hoffer's most important contribution to the dissemination of knowledge and the opening up of social work literature and documents to individual researchers was his development of the KWIC (Key Word in Context) Index of National Conference on Social Welfare Publications. Hoffer was aware that social work scholars were handicapped in using original documents and articles because of the complexity of social service delivery and the changing terminology of the profession. Accordingly, he devised a number of related subject bibliographies which were arranged together because of key words in either the title or the text of various publications of the National Conference on Social Welfare. This was a pioneering effort in the social welfare arena that led to more sophisticated ones in the future.

The contributions of Joe Hoffer are closely connected with the two organizations that he headed for many years. His long tenure as the chief executive officer of both of those organizations attests to his abilities as a capable and far-sighted administrator. Under his leadership, both organizations were influential in effecting positive changes in social policy development and social service provision. His dual role gave him a national and international perspective that was truly unique. His leadership abilities, his dedication to the free exchange of knowledge, and his early recognition of the potential that information science technology could have on the social welfare field enabled him to be one of the most influential figures in the social work profession for over thirty years. He died in Columbus, Ohio, on September 28, 1978.

Hoffer had a number of articles published through the National Conference of Social Work. Perhaps the most notable is "East Meets West," in *Proceedings of the National Conference of Social Work* (1948). Two other important articles by Hoffer are "The Relationship of Natural and Social Sciences to Social Problems and the Contributions of the Information Scientist to Their Solutions," *American Documentation* (October, 1967); and "Information Science in Social Work Education: The NCSW Approach," *Journal of Education for Social Work*

(Spring, 1975). Very little biographical information is available concerning Hoffer. Brief biographical entries can be found in the following sources: *Who's Who in America*, vol. 1 (1976–1977); and *American Men and Women of Science: The Social and Behavioral Sciences*, vol. 1 (1973).

GARY MOOERS

**Holbrook, David Helm** (February 9, 1879–August 27, 1962), social worker, social work counselor, and administrator, was born in Lake Geneva, Wisconsin, the second child of David Leverett Holbrook and Sarah (Helm) Holbrook. David L. Holbrook, in addition to his responsibilities as a Congregational minister, actively involved himself in community affairs and pursued a wide range of avocational interests, developing considerable ability as a scientist, artist, and mechanic. Sarah Holbrook, a deeply religious woman, was an accomplished musician. The Holbrook family, which eventually included seven children, seems to have been particularly close-knit, bonded by a shared religious commitment and through a yearly cycle of family celebrations, customs, and observances.

Following high school, David Holbrook began study at Ripon College in nearby Ripon, Wisconsin, graduating in 1901 with a major in the social sciences. In college Holbrook met Gertrude Brewer, and the two married in 1902. They had one child, David Brewer Holbrook.

Between the years 1901 and 1914 Holbrook taught civics, history, and economics in the public school system, first in Fond du Lac, Wisconsin, and later in Minneapolis. While teaching in Fond du Lac Holbrook conceived of and helped install a system of visiting school teachers, a program that adumbrated Holbrook's later interest in social work, particularly in its relationship to the objectives of the school system. Beginning in 1914 Holbrook spent four years as Director of Attendance and Vocational Guidance in the Minneapolis School System, a position that moved him closer to the concerns of social work.

Moving directly into the realm of social work, Holbrook joined the Northern Division of the American Red Cross, Minneapolis, where he worked from 1918–1920, serving as assistant manager, and then, director of civilian relief. During this period Holbrook became familiar with the difficulties related to the adjustment, retraining, and placement of veterans returning to civilian life. This experience confirmed Holbrook's belief, formed during his years in the public schools, that educational work, of whatever kind, should not be separated from the family life and larger environment in which individuals live. Thus he maintained that social caseworkers could provide a useful service relating the special circumstances of individuals to more general educational goals. In his article "The Teacher Who Came Back" (1921), Holbrook described the ideal visiting teacher as a former public school teacher with casework experience, a person who, in Holbrook's estimation, could ably bridge the gap between home and classroom and could consider each student in terms of individual needs, background, and home environment.

Holbrook moved to New York in 1920, assuming the position of executive secretary of the American Association for Organizing Family Social Work. There he came under the influence of Francis H. McLean,* a former executive of the AAOFSW whom Holbrook greatly admired.

In early 1925 Holbrook accepted appointment as executive secretary of the National Social Work Council, an organization officially formed in 1923 as a roundtable where national social work agencies could discuss aspects of common concern, especially the issue of how to coordinate their efforts in more cooperative directions. It was as executive of the NSWC that Holbrook made his largest contribution to the social work profession. Holbrook gave effective guidance to the Council for over twenty years and also made an impact on the Council's successor organization, the National Social Welfare Assembly, serving as the Assembly's assistant director from its inception in 1945 until his retirement in 1949.

A firm believer in the economy of cooperative effort and convinced that group thinking achieved more creative results than individual effort, David Holbrook was primarily responsible for building the Council into an organization where divergent social work agencies could find basis for transcending their individual differences. Holbrook consistently urged member organizations not to be overly concerned with questions of technique and practice, but to focus on the larger purpose and meaning of social work—not method, but people. Consistent with this philosophy and his background as a teacher, Holbrook envisioned the Council less as an administrative body than as an educational one in which communication and learning might lead to better understanding, integration, and administration among and between existing social work agencies.

With a firm but patient hand, Holbrook pushed his colleagues on the Council to develop a clearer sense of purpose and direction, and to communicate the essential values of social work to the public. Holbrook criticized the obsession with money-raising and business efficiency that characterized some social work administrators, holding that financial support of social work should be considered a social investment, not a business investment but an investment in people. Through his keen insight into human relationships and his skill as an interpreter and mediator Holbrook facilitated the joint consideration of broad issues relating to social betterment, and helped make greater integration between national organizations and community-level agencies in the field of social work possible.

At his retirement in May, 1949, Holbrook's colleagues remembered him as a clear social analyst, a broad thinker, an effective and wise teacher, and a good friend. The next decade Holbrook spent largely removed from public activity, living with relatives and friends in California and Massachusetts. He died in San Diego, California, August 27, 1962.

Primary materials dealing with David Holbrook's life and professional career can be found in Papers of the American Association of Social Workers and the National Social Welfare Assembly (supplement 1), both of which are in the manuscript collections of the Social Welfare History Archives, University of Minnesota, Minneapolis, Minnesota.

Among Holbrook's published writings are "The Twilight Zone Between Vocational Re-Education and Social Service," *Proceedings of the National Conference of Social Work* (1919); "Social Work an Investment: But It Should Be an Investment of Personality Rather Than of Dollars," *The Woman's Press* (1927); "The Responsibility of the Social Worker in Assisting the School to Develop a Social Attitude Toward the Child," *The Family* (February, 1921); "The Teacher Who Came Back," *The Family* (1921); "The Leadership that Underlies Control of Social Programs," *Public Health Nursing* (1931); and "National Associations in Social Work," *Social Work Year Book* (1941, 1943).

An obituary notice in the *New York Times* (August 29, 1962, III:38, 203) incorrectly stated that Holbrook became Executive Secretary of the National Social Work Council in 1922.

RICHARD M. CHAPMAN

**Holmes, John Haynes** (November 29, 1879–April 3, 1964), religious leader and social reformer, was born in Philadelphia, Pennsylvania, to Marcus Morton and Alice (Haynes) Holmes, who had just moved to the City of Brotherly Love from Boston. Although raised in humble surroundings, young Holmes possessed a distinguished family ancestry. The Holmes family came from England to Plymouth in 1620, and in 1635, the Haynes family arrived in Boston, the city to which John and his parents returned in 1894, when his father took a job selling furniture.

Young John Haynes Holmes was educated in the public schools in Malden, a suburb of Boston. Teachers at Malden High School persuaded him to switch from commercial courses to college preparatory work and to enter Harvard University after graduation. With financial aid from his grandfather, he graduated from Harvard College, summa cum laude, in 1902, and then from Harvard Divinity School in 1904. In the same year he married Madeleine Hosmer Baker of Brooklyn, New York, with whom he had two children, Roger Wellington and Frances Adria.

Following graduation, Holmes took a position as minister in the Third Religious Society (Unitarian) in Dorchester, Massachusetts, in 1904, serving in that position for three years. Holmes then accepted a position at the Church of the Messiah in New York City in 1907, transforming it from a sectarian, Unitarian church into an intercreedal, intercultural, nondenominational church, encompassing a wide range of religious beliefs. Following a fire that destroyed the church in 1919, he led the congregation in rebuilding the structure and reshaping the concepts of the church. He withdrew from the Unitarian ministry and renamed the church the Community Church of New York.

Holmes was a leading spokesman for the Social Gospel of the early part of the twentieth century, using this as a basis for his concern for social justice. He subscribed to no formal creed and thus stood apart from evangelical Protestant Christianity. He did not call Jesus "the divine," "Son of God," or "the Christ," nor did he believe in Jesus as the Messiah. When he referred to Jesus, it was as a unique figure in religious history, to be honored as a heroic servant of humanity and an example for contemporary social relationships.

This philosophy led him into active participation in many movements for social justice. He was a founder of the National Association for the Advancement of Colored People (NAACP) in 1909. Speaking at the Women's Alliance of the Church of the Messiah on the centenary observance of Abraham Lincoln's birth, he described injustices that were being suffered by Blacks. He composed a proclamation, "The Call," for a conference to map strategy to oppose the wrongdoings. Working with Jane Addams,* W. E. B. Du Bois,* John Dewey, and Lincoln Steffens, he helped to found the NAACP to fight unfair treatment of Blacks. Holmes remained close to the organization, delivering many messages to and about the group, serving as its vice president, and regularly participating in its board meetings.

Holmes also was a dynamic force in the creation of the American Civil Liberties Union (ACLU) in 1918. Holmes and others feared that freedom of speech was being suppressed during World War I and the aftermath of the Bolshevik Revolution. The ACLU emerged from the Committee Against Militarism and the Committee Against Preparedness, both of which Holmes— who now embraced pacifism, another unpopular cause at the time—helped to create. Suppression of unorthodox and unconventional opinions, both economic and political, in the form of arrests and deportation of aliens, prompted Holmes, along with Harry F. Ward, Roger Baldwin,* and his close friend Rabbi Stephen Wise,* to organize the American Civil Liberties Union. Holmes served as vice chairman of the ACLU and was active in its struggles throughout his life.

The *New York Times* opined, however, that perhaps Holmes' greatest achievement was his role in the ouster from office of New York mayor James J. Walker. As chairman of the City Affairs Committee of New York from 1929 to 1938, Holmes, along with Rabbi Wise, launched an unrelenting assault upon the corruption and scandal surrounding Walker and Tammany Hall. The accusations of Holmes' committee led to the famous Seabury investigations and the eventual resignation of Walker in 1932.

Known for his pacifism through the two world wars and the interwar period, Holmes often was criticized for being antipatriotic. Drawing upon his belief in the perfectability of mankind, his pacifist views took shape in his book *New Wars for Old* (1916). These views were popularized in a play, *If This Be Treason*, that appeared on Broadway in 1935. He argued that the solving of conflicts could not be settled by violence, but rather by nonviolence.

His belief in nonviolence dovetailed with the views of a contemporary whom he greatly admired, Mohandas K. Gandhi. In 1921 Holmes said, "When I think of Mahatma Gandhi, I think of Jesus Christ." He considered Gandhi the "greatest man in the world," because of his nonviolent rebellion against British imperialism and Western industrialism. Holmes met Gandhi in London in 1931 and again in 1947, when he lectured in India after a Watamull Foundation invitation. The two became close friends, and Holmes can be given some credit for introducing and interpreting Gandhi to American audiences.

With the assassination of Gandhi in 1948 and the death of his close friend Stephen Wise in 1949, John Haynes Holmes lost two of the paramount sources of his inspiration. He resigned as minister of the Community Church on his seventieth birthday, November 29, 1949. He continued to preach on a part-time basis as minister emeritus, and he continued to write as well. He wrote over twenty books in his lifetime as well as numerous articles, and he served as editor for several religious publications. The uncompromising idealist, who was one of the twentieth century's greatest champions of social justice for all, died at his home in New York City on April 3, 1964, at age eighty-four.

The John Haynes Holmes Papers are in the Manuscript Division of the Library of Congress in Washington, D.C. See also his principal books, which include *The Revolutionary of the Modern Church* (1912); *New Wars for Old* (1916); *New Churches for Old* (1922); *Palestine Today and Tomorrow* (1929); *Rethinking Religion* (1938); *Out of Darkness* (1942); *The Second Christmas and Other Stories* (1943); *My Gandhi* (1953); and his autobiography, *I Speak for Myself* (1959).

Some good secondary works on Holmes are the following: Carl H. Voss, *Rabbi and Minister: The Friendship of Stephen S. Wise and John Haynes Holmes* (1964); E. D. Jones, *American Preachers of Today* (1971); and Mark Lieberman, *The Pacifists: Soldiers Without Guns* (1972). See also "John Haynes Holmes: Discoverer of Gandhi," *Christian Century* (May, 1964); Stanley J. Kunitz, ed., *Twentieth Century Authors* (1942); and the sketch in *Current Biography: 1941*.

WILLIAM H. HARDIN

**Holt, Luther Emmett** (March 4, 1855–January 24, 1924), physician/pediatrician, medical educator, and public health reformer, was born at Webster, New York (a small agricultural community near Rochester), to Horace and Sabrah (Curtice) Holt. Although not a wealthy family, the Holts were by no means impoverished farmers; their third child, Emmett, was educated at local schools and in 1875 graduated from the small Baptist University of Rochester. After graduation, Holt taught grammar school for one year, then altered his career plans and entered the University of Buffalo Medical College in 1876.

Although choosing medicine, Holt never repudiated teaching, and it was as an educator that he achieved his greatest fame. From his position as director of a New York City infants' hospital he guided the transition of pediatrics from art to science at the end of the nineteenth century and helped to create a powerful social role for the pediatrician as mothers' advisor. Moreover, he played a significant advisory role in public health campaigns to lower infant mortality rates by supplying city residents with uncontaminated milk.

Holt spent only one year at the University of Buffalo, then read medicine with a Rochester physician. Such education gave Holt sufficient credentials to practice in the world of nineteenth century medicine; however, ambition drew him out of Rochester to New York City. In 1878 Holt accepted a student intern position at the Hospital of the Society for the Relief of the Ruptured and Crippled; at the same time he registered for courses at the College of Physicians and Surgeons.

After receiving his medical degree in 1880, Holt chose an internship in the surgical service at Bellevue Hospital. This experience led him to reject a surgical career, but it introduced him to the world of scientific medical research. At Bellevue Holt worked in the bacteriology laboratory of William H. Welch, soon to become director of Johns Hopkins Medical School. Welch was one of a group of New York City physicians influenced by medical discoveries emanating from European laboratories. Holt thus early identified with scientific medicine and with those American physicians who placed their faith in laboratory research.

During the years in which Holt was establishing a general private practice, he was also pursuing a specialized interest in the diseases of children. Specialization was new to the American medical profession, and its legitimacy was the subject of debate among late nineteenth century physicians. Unlike Abraham Jacobi,* Holt's contemporary in the field of pediatrics, Holt actively sought to confine his interest and his practice to children. Not until 1891, however, was he able to restrict his new patients to youths.

Although his private patients were of all ages, Holt sought institutional affiliations which gave him specialized experience with the medical problems of children. He accepted posts at the Northwestern Dispensary, the New York Foundling Hospital, and the New York Infant Asylum. His work at the Babies' Hospital of the City of New York (now part of Columbia-Presbyterian Medical Center), however, made Holt the nation's preeminent specialist in childhood diseases. Founded in 1887, the Babies' Hospital was the first institution of its kind in the United States—a separate hospital for the care of infants to age three. Holt assumed the directorship in 1889 and continued in that capacity until his death in 1924, turning a small medical charity into a modern hospital and research center.

Hospital administration absorbed a good part of Holt's energy in the 1890s. He was soon recognized as an authority on the construction and hygienic operation of pediatric institutions. His presidential address to the American Pediatric Society in 1896 dealt with the medical management of hospitals for infants. Such hospitals, Holt advised, should be primarily teaching and research institutions. Since most childhood illnesses would not be treated in hospitals, physicians would discover from the small number of hospital cases how to treat successfully the vast majority of their patients. At the same time, these hospitals rendered medical charity to that class of patients unable to pay for the services of a private physician.

Holt used the Babies' Hospital for both teaching and research, although his interest in laboratory experiments was always secondary to his role as educator of both physicians and the public. He was, he said, a "middleman" of science, the connecting link between research and practical application. In 1890 Holt became professor of the diseases of children at the New York Polyclinic, a position he held until 1901, when, with the resignation of Abraham Jacobi, Holt was appointed professor of pediatrics at the College of Physicians and Surgeons. In addition, Holt held Saturday morning clinics at the Babies' Hospital for practicing New York physicians, to expose them to current pediatric knowledge. Students remembered his thoroughness as a clinician and his emphasis, in both teaching and text, on the common childhood illnesses—those the general practitioner and parent would generally encounter.

Interest in teaching led Holt to publish in 1897 his textbook of pediatrics, *The Diseases of Infancy and Childhood*. During his lifetime it was reissued in eleven editions (including several translations), becoming the standard American pediatric reference work. "Holt" lacked the flourish and style of many texts written by contemporaries; it was, instead, concise, informative, and infused with a statistical predilection gleaned from the practical experiences of the author.

While Holt's text helped to establish his reputation within the medical community, it was his guide to scientific child rearing that made his name a household word. In the half century before Dr. Spock, parents raised "Holt babies," infants reared according to regular, inflexible schedules and precise feeding instructions. Holt's child-rearing methods, primarily concerned with the physical care of children, were published in 1894 as *The Care and Feeding of Children*. The "catechism" for mothers evolved from a question and answer text designed for hospital nursery maids. Local mothers encouraged Holt to publish the rules for wider distribution, and the booklet went through seventy-five printings before it was superseded by Spock's *Baby and Child Care*.

In *The Care and Feeding of Children* Holt combined his role as an educator with his concern for prevention of childhood illnesses and the lowering of the high infant mortality rate in New York City. Using knowledge gathered at Babies' Hospital from his treatment of children of the poor, Holt offered more financially secure parents a scientifically sanctioned approach to infant feeding and care. Although children in these families were less likely to suffer from diseases caused by malnutrition or contaminated milk, Holt's advice on artificial feeding, culled from chemical comparisons of the composition of cow's milk and breast milk, appealed to a class of women who wished to turn mothering into a scientific profession. For children from the tenements Holt initiated a visiting physicians' program at Babies' Hospital in 1903 to offer scientific child-care suggestions. Holt's concern was reeducation of the individual mother; only at the end of his life would he pursue publicly sponsored, pediatrician-influenced preventive medicine programs.

Holt's primary contribution lay in helping to establish the connection between specialized clinical pediatrics and organized child welfare work. Initially, Holt sought a restricted social role for the American Pediatric Society. By the time of his second election as president, however, he had reversed this position, charging the younger generation of pediatricians to become active leaders in all fields relating to the development of children.

The 1923 presidential address, "American Pediatrics: A Retrospect and a Forecast," reflected the social interests that filled the last years of Holt's life, particularly the campaign for a sterile milk supply. Like other late nineteenth century physicians, Holt saw a connection between high rates of infant mortality due to diarrheal diseases, and nutrition, especially the quality of the milk fed to babies. Originally he believed that only raw, or unpasteurized, milk should be given to infants. After 1903, however, Holt revised his views and urged that infants be given pasteurized milk. While he continued to encourage the instruction of individual mothers, Holt was also drawn into governmental and private campaigns to supply the city with uncontaminated milk.

Holt served as a medical advisor at the Henry Street Settlement, directed by Lillian Wald.* He was also an active participant in the American Association for the Study and Prevention of Infant Mortality. This organization, founded in 1909, coordinated governmental, philanthropic, and medical efforts to lower the number of deaths in infancy and childhood. In 1919 Holt was a delegate to an international Red Cross conference which sought to unite Red Cross organizations of all countries into the human welfare department of the new League of Nations. The conference adopted Holt's plans for child welfare as the organization's official program.

The Red Cross invitation rested in part on Holt's stature in the medical profession. But it also reflected his appointment in 1918 as director of the Child Health Organization, an association growing out of wartime concern for the health of the nation's potential soldiers. Holt oversaw the organization's efforts to devise school programs to educate the child (and through the child the parents) in principles of public health and personal hygiene. In 1923 the Child Health Organization merged with the American Child Hygiene Association (formerly the Association for the Study and Prevention of Infant Mortality) to form the American Child Health Association with Herbert Hoover as president and Holt as vice president.

In addition to his public health and child welfare interests, Holt played an important role in the formation of the Rockefeller Institute for Medical Research in 1901 and served on the board of directors of that institute until his death. Although many of the first grants were awarded for laboratory research, the directors also allotted part of the first year's budget for a two-year study of the New York City milk supply. The report, presented by Holt, offered a scientific evaluation of the effectiveness of pasteurized milk stations in lowering infant mortality in city tenements.

In 1910 Holt received a Rockefeller Institute grant to study metabolism and nutrition of infants—his only venture into laboratory medicine. The results of his studies of caloric intake and mineral absorption provided useful norms, yet the work was of marginal significance. It was as an educator, not a scientist, that Holt excelled. He held the chair of pediatrics at the College of Physicians and Surgeons until 1921. In August, 1923, Holt sailed for China to assume yet another teaching position, at the Peking Union Medical College, founded by the Rockefeller Foundation. The Foundation sent well-known physicians to Peking to offer a few months of intense instruction in their specialties. Holt was asked to help organize pediatric services at the hospital, but the task was not completed. He died in Peking on January 24, 1924.

No manuscript collection for L. Emmett Holt is available. Correspondence relating to his role at the Rockefeller Institute for Medical Research can be found at the Rockefeller University Archives, New York, New York. See also the Rockefeller Foundation Archives and the Rockefeller Family Archives at the Rockefeller Archive Center, North Tarrytown, New York. Materials on the Child Health Organization are contained in the Laura Spelman Rockefeller Memorial Archives, also at the Rockefeller Archive Center.

Holt's published works can be found in the principal pediatrics journals of the period: *Archives of Pediatrics*; American Pediatric Society, *Transactions*; and, after 1911, the *American Journal of the Diseases of Children*, of which Holt was an editor. His three major publications were *The Care and Feeding of Children* (1894); *The Diseases of Infancy and Childhood* (1897); and *Food, Health and Growth* (1922).

Entries appear in the standard biographical dictionaries covering the period of Holt's life. More inclusive sources for Holt's life and career include Robert L. Duffus and L. Emmett Holt, Jr., *L. Emmett Holt: Pioneer of a Children's Century* (1940); Kathleen W. Jones, "Sentiment and Science: The Late Nineteenth Century Pediatrician as Mother's Advisor," *Journal of Social History* (Fall, 1983), 79–96; and Edwards A. Park and Howard H. Mason, "Pediatric Profiles: L. Emmett Holt," *Journal of Pediatrics* (September, 1956), 342–369. Holt's role at the Rockefeller Institute is discussed in George W. Corner, *A History of the Rockefeller Institute, 1901–1953: Origins and Growth* (1964).

Obituary notices appeared in *American Journal of the Diseases of Children* (March, 1924), 195–196; *Archives of Pediatrics* (January, 1924), 1–4; and *Journal of the American Medical Association* (January 26, 1924), 320.

KATHLEEN W. JONES

**Hope, Lugenia Burns** (1881–August 14, 1947), child welfare advocate, public health enthusiast, and community developer and organizer, was born in St. Louis, Missouri. The precise date of her birth and her parents' names and occupations, however, are unknown. After the death of her father, Lugenia, her deaf mother, and four younger brothers and sisters migrated to Chicago, Illinois, where she spent her childhood. She did not have much formal schooling, however, for she quickly assumed responsibility as the family breadwinner. A variety of work experiences influenced her greatly, especially her position as secretary to the Board of Directors of King's Daughters, a Chicago charity organization society. She also worked with young girls attending a training school operated by that organization, which was staffed primarily by University of Chicago students. In recognition of her outstanding contributions to the agency, she was appointed to the Cook County Board of King's Daughters, the first and only black person so honored. These early occupational experiences, her family's economic difficulties, and her mother's hearing disability all contributed to her altruistic nature.

During the summer of 1893, she met John Hope, whom she married in 1897 and with whom she had two children, Edward Swain and John, Jr. Lugenia Burns Hope then successfully combined the roles of wife, mother, and volunteer social worker, primarily helping to uplift the disadvantaged in Atlanta, Georgia, where her husband served as president, first of Morehouse College, and then of the Atlanta University system, which he helped to organize (by bringing together six competing black denominational colleges in Atlanta).

As a result of her work experiences in Chicago, especially with charity organization societies providing services to the poor, she initiated similar activities in the poor sections of the black community in Atlanta. Armed with the high status of the wife of a university president, a commitment to progressive social change, and concerned friends with resources, she began her community work. Her diligence resulted in the establishment of the Gate City Free Kindergarten in 1904, which ultimately led to the development of a chain of kindergartens for underprivileged children throughout Atlanta.

Struck by the vice, venality, poor housing and unsanitary conditions, and lack of child care and recreational facilities in the ghetto, she also set out to improve these conditions. Her immediate concern was for the care of children, particularly those of working mothers. She organized women associated with Spelman and Morehouse colleges, who assisted her in finding a place and starting activities for children of working mothers. Morehouse College agreed to permit use of a section of the college campus for a playground, and these women then became playground supervisors and untrained social workers. They also served as volunteer instructors, offering classes in sewing, cooking, home nursing, and handicrafts in their homes to area residents.

Lugenia Burns Hope did not stop there; she persisted in her pursuit of social and educational advancement for black people—as an ardent community organizer and as the founder of the Neighborhood Union. She organized the Neighborhood Union in 1908 and then acted as director and in a variety of other roles for over thirty years. "Love Thy Neighbor As Thyself" was the theme that provided the framework for the goals of the organization, which were to provide playgrounds, clubs, and neighborhood centers for the physical, moral, and intellectual development of community residents; to develop a spirit of helpfulness among neighbors; to set up lecture courses for the purpose of encouraging habits of cleanliness; to promote child welfare; to impart cultural heritage; to abolish slums; and to cooperate with juvenile courts and city officials in combatting criminal activity.

In pursuing these goals, Lugenia Hope divided the city into neighborhood districts and appointed a presiding officer and a group of women to be responsible for each one. Field workers conducted surveys and used case finding methods to determine the needs and problems of the districts' residents. In response to the identified problems, social services were provided by the Neighborhood Union. By 1911 the Neighborhood Union was incorporated and was viewed as a successful community social service agency. Black women in other southern states began to adopt the Neighborhood Union concept and utilized strategies formulated by Hope to ameliorate poor living conditions of black people in their respective states.

In 1915, under Hope's directorship, the Neighborhood Union established a health center which provided medical and dental services to children and adults. Moreover, women from the Neighborhood Union aggressively worked in antituberculosis drives and Red Cross campaigns which resulted in access to additional health services for black families.

She also planned and initiated a Social Service Institute at Morehouse College in 1918, and then organized its series of lectures on prenatal and infant care, juvenile delinquency, malnutrition, and the value of social services. She also taught "community organization" at the Institute, which was the cornerstone for the establishment of the Atlanta University School of Social Work, where she later served on the faculty. In 1922, under her leadership, the Neighborhood Union purchased a building which allowed for the centralization of its numerous activities. This building also served as a residence for social work students from Atlanta University. Like Hull-House in Chicago, Neighborhood Union became the locus of activity for social reform efforts and community services in Atlanta.

During the decade of the 1930s, she began to look not only at the dire individual needs of the poor but at the systematic constraints affecting black people in general. She accepted the ethos of the progressive period and viewed voting as a vehicle for effecting social change for black citizens. Subsequently, while holding the position of first vice president of the National Association for the Advancement of Colored People, she founded a Citizenship School in 1933. The school was organized to inform and acquaint the black citizens of Atlanta with their rights as citizens, to give them an introduction to the democratic process and the operations of government, and to encourage them to vote. Additionally, Hope conceived the idea of low-cost housing, and with the help of her husband, she implemented another important project—the University Homes Project for slum clearance. This development replaced one of the most deplorable slums in the city of Atlanta, Beaver Slide, with the construction of the first low-rent housing project in the United States. On September 29, 1934, Secretary of the Interior Harold Ickes approved the appropriation of funds for this development.

Lugenia Hope's social welfare activities extended beyond the environs of Atlanta. In 1915 she was invited to serve as chairwoman of the Drive for French War Babies by the Colored American Society for the Relief of French War Orphans. And later on, government officials on the national level recognized her contributions and sought her advice on various issues. Thus she was appointed by Secretary of Commerce Herbert Hoover a member of the Colored Advisory Commission, which, under the auspices of the National Red Cross, investigated the health and welfare status of black victims of the Mississippi River flood in 1927.

The advent of World War II directed Hope's attention to work with black servicemen and their families. The National War Work Council of the Young Women's Christian Association set up hostess houses around the country to respond to the needs of black servicemen and their families. Because of prior experience in war work at Camp Gordon, in Atlanta, Hope was asked to help with the delivery of services at Camp Upton, New York. She served as a social worker to the bereaved, she supervised other workers, and she trained hostesses for war work in other areas of the country.

In response to her outstanding contributions to social welfare and social work, she received numerous awards and certificates. Most notable among these, however, was a medal presented to her by the French government in recognition of her work for the benefit of children orphaned during the war.

Lugenia Hope did not accept the notions of social justice of her day; rather, she challenged the status quo. In so doing, she not only provided the impetus for improving living conditions resulting from poverty but is credited with the auspicious beginning of organized social work among black people in Atlanta, Georgia. Her accomplishments, extraordinary in themselves, are all the more outstanding when measured against the pressures of the times. Lugenia Burns Hope died in Nashville, Tennessee, on August 14, 1947.

The most extensive source of information on the life and work of Lugenia Burns Hope is the Neighborhood Union Collection at Atlanta University Center, Woodruff Library, Atlanta, Georgia, which includes biographical materials, correspondence, valuable reports, and photographs. Useful secondary sources are Louie D. Shivery, "History of Organized Social Work Among Negroes in Atlanta 1890–1935," Master's thesis, Atlanta University, 1936; Annie R. Beard, "Mrs. John Hope, Black Community Builders in Atlanta Georgia, 1900–1936," Master's thesis, Atlanta University, 1975; Edyth L. Ross, ed., *Black Heritage in Social Welfare, 1860–1930* (1978); and Ridgely Torrence, *The Story of John Hope* (1948). Additionally, the following articles also provide a comprehensive view of her achievements: Walter K. Chivers, "Neighborhood Union: An Effort of Community Organization," *Opportunity* (June, 1925); Gerda Lerner, "Early Community Work of Black Club Women," *Journal of Negro History* (April, 1974); *Morehouse Alumnus* (November 1947; March-April, 1948); and "First Ladies of Colored America—No. 12," *Crisis* (September 1943).

Lugenia Burns Hope's obituary appeared in the *Pittsburgh Courier* (August 30, 1947), and the *Chicago Defender*, National Edition (August 30, 1947).

                                                              ROBENIA B. GARY

**Hopkins, Harry Lloyd** (August 17, 1890–January 29, 1946), welfare worker and administrator, government official, and presidential advisor, was born in Sioux City, Iowa, one of five surviving children of David and Anna (Picket) Hopkins. His father, a harness maker who ventured into other trades, moved his family frequently and resided in Nebraska and Illinois before settling in Grinnell, Iowa, when Harry was eleven. A store that sold candy, tobacco products, and magazines, as well as harnesses, afforded the family a secure livelihood. Harry's mother, a native Canadian, was a gospel teacher and president of the Methodist Home Missionary Society of Iowa. Hopkins attended Grinnell College. He studied social sciences and graduated with Phi Beta Kappa honors in 1912. He married three times. He and Ethel Gross Hopkins divorced in 1930 after seventeen years of marriage. His second wife, Barbara Duncan Hopkins, died in 1937, and he married Louise Gill Macy in 1942. Three children, David, Robert, and Stephen, came from the first marriage, and one, Diana, from the second.

The man whom friends nicknamed the bishop of relief during the 1930s entered social work during the Progressive Era through the settlement house movement. Hopkins worked in a summer camp program and became a resident of Christodora House in New York City in 1912. In 1913 the Association for Improving the Condition of the Poor (AICP) hired him as an agent in its Bureau of Family Rehabilitation and Relief. Two AICP directors, John A. Kingsbury* and William H. Matthews, bolstered his early career. When Kingsbury became Commissioner of Public Charities in 1914, after the reform administration of Mayor John Purroy Mitchel took office, Matthews was appointed chairman of the city's Board of Child Welfare, which implemented the state's 1915 Widow's Pension Law, and Hopkins became executive secretary. He worked on the board with Jane Hoey* and Henry Bruere,* two among numerous New York colleagues, including Mary (Molly) Dewson* and Frances Perkins,* who would later serve Franklin D. Roosevelt. During 1914 Hopkins and Matthews also initiated an AICP experiment in work relief, developing park projects, and Kingsbury called on Hopkins to improve the city's Municipal Lodging Program. Mayor Mitchel's administration emphasized cost-cutting and efficiency, yet its initiatives in welfare anticipated reforms after 1929 and gave private philanthropy's social workers requisite experience in public welfare.

During wartime, Hopkins served with the Red Cross. In 1917 he became manager of the Southern Division and worked in New Orleans and Atlanta. Five years later, he returned to New York and the AICP, assuming the duties of assistant director until 1924. John Kingsbury had become director of the Milbank Fund, which supported medical and health services and funded a major project for the New York Tuberculosis Association soon after Hopkins became its director in 1924. Philanthropists and social workers founded the Welfare Council of New York City in 1925, forging a federation of settlement house, charity, and welfare action agencies to coordinate the services of private philanthropies throughout the metropolis. Hopkins helped organize its health division and later served as a member of the Council's executive committee and board of directors. William Hodson* was the Council's executive director; in 1931 he would decline appointment to New York State's Temporary Emergency Relief Administration (TERA), thus leaving the door open for Hopkins. In the meantime, Hopkins was building his organization into the New York Tuberculosis and Health Association, a conglomerate of health services. He was also a member of the New York chapter of the National Consumers' League, of which Molly Dewson was president, and represented White Door Settlement on the board of the United Neighborhood Houses. In 1928 two settlement leaders, Lillian Wald* of Henry Street and John Elliott* of Hudson Guild, renounced political nonpartisanship and endorsed the presidential candidacy of Al Smith. During the campaign, Harry Hopkins manned the social work desk at Democratic Party headquarters in New York.

In 1931 New York became the first state to provide public relief for the unemployed, and Hopkins secured appointment as executive director of the new TERA, which he later headed as chairman. Using a system of matching grants to stimulate local funding and to aid the jobless directly, the TERA encouraged counties and municipalities to develop work relief projects in addition to expanding home relief programs. The TERA also brought social workers into public welfare by adopting standards for administration that forced local welfare departments to hire professionals. Because of the TERA, Governor Franklin Roosevelt gained a reputation as a leader in creating innovative programs to combat the Great Depression. Another social worker, Frances Perkins, headed his state's Industrial Commission and was developing expertise in unemployment compensation and old-age pensions. Eventually, she and Harry Hopkins (as U.S. Secretary of Labor and chief federal relief administrator, respectively) would merge conceptions of social insurance and work relief when they served together as members of President Roosevelt's Committee on Economic Security during 1934–1935 and spearheaded the Social Security Act and Works Progress Administration Act of 1935.

Hopkins went to Washington during May, 1933, to become administrator of the Federal Emergency Relief Administration (FERA), a copy of New York's TERA. For the next two years, he used his experience to supplement state and local relief programs with federal funding and to infuse professional social work personnel, standards, and practices into public welfare. He insisted that the able-bodied unemployed had a right to work. During the winter of 1933–1934, he implemented the most daring work program of the 1930s, the Civil Works Administration (CWA), which employed 4 million job applicants and put them to work at employment standards that rivaled those of private industry. In 1935 Roosevelt's New Deal returned to relief rolls, means tests, and restrictions on workers' incomes under the federalized programs of the Works Progress Administration (WPA). The WPA (1935–1943) spent nearly $11 billion on work relief and employed more than 8.5 million different Americans.

As Hopkins often repeated proudly, 85 percent of WPA funds were spent for wages. The efficiency of work relief programs, their humanitarian commitment to meeting material needs, and their effect in maintaining the morale of the unemployed made them and their chief administrator popular. Critics charged the programs with waste, political manipulation, and socialism, yet FDR made Hopkins an intimate advisor and began grooming him as a possible successor.

Hopkins was Secretary of Commerce from 1938 to 1940, but poor health diminished his presidential prospects. Roosevelt sought a third term in 1940 and, following his reelection, Hopkins was named a special assistant to the President. He devoted the rest of his career to wartime policies. He coordinated efforts to meet Great Britain's need for supplies, headed the Lend-Lease Program, served as envoy to the British and Soviet governments, attended the Yalta Conference, and negotiated the format of the Potsdam Conference. After FDR's death and his own resignation from official duties, he was awarded the Distinguished Service Medal by President Harry S. Truman in September, 1945. Hopkins died in New York City four months later.

The Harry L. Hopkins Papers at the Franklin D. Roosevelt Library (Hyde Park, New York) constitute the most significant collection of Hopkins materials. Personal letters and other documents are located in numerous additional collections, such as the Franklin D. Roosevelt Papers and the Anna Eleanor Roosevelt Papers at the FDRL, and the Survey Papers and Paul U. Kellogg Papers at the Social Welfare History Archives (Minneapolis, Minnesota). The Federal Emergency Relief Administration Papers and the Works Progress Administration Papers at the National Archives (Washington, D.C.) offer much information about Hopkins as well as the agencies he administered.

Hopkins' name appears as author of about twenty articles, pamphlets, and books. His more important articles include ''The Developing National Program of Relief,'' *Proceedings* of the National Conference of Social Work (1933), 65–71; ''The War on Distress,'' *Today* (December 16, 1933), 8–9, 23; ''They'd Rather Work,'' *Collier's* (November 16, 1935), 7–9, 41; and ''The WPA Looks Forward,'' *Survey Midmonthly* (June, 1938), 195–198. *Spending to Save: The Complete Story of Relief* (1936) was his only book and his fullest statement about the origins and development of relief policies. It should be supplemented by two Hopkins pamphlets, *The Realities of Unemployment* (1937) and *What Is the "American Way"?* (1938). He was frequently cited in *Congressional Digest* and *Vital Speeches of the Day*. Harry L. Hopkins, *Principal Speeches of Harry L. Hopkins* (1938), is useful.

Nearly every book about Franklin D. Roosevelt and the New Deal discusses Hopkins and his work. He has been the subject of four biographies. Three of the biographies focus on his years as administrator of federal relief: Henry H. Adams, *Harry Hopkins* (1977); Searle F. Charles, *Minister of Relief: Harry Hopkins and the Depression* (1963); and Paul A. Kurzman, *Harry Hopkins and the New Deal* (1974). The fourth emphasizes his service during World War II: Robert E. Sherwood, *Roosevelt and Hopkins: An Intimate History*, rev. ed. (1950).

WILLIAM W. BREMER

**Howard, Oliver Otis** (November 8, 1830–October 29, 1909), officer in the United States Army and head of the U.S. Freedmen's Bureau, was born in Leeds, Maine, the oldest of three children, all sons, of Rowland Bailey Howard and Elizabeth (Otis) Howard. The family shared the farm and homestead of

Oliver's grandfather, Captain Seth Howard, who was part of the family until the untimely death of Oliver's father in 1840. Two years later, Oliver's mother married a widower with three sons, Colonel John Gilmore, and moved her family into the Gilmore home.

The Howards could trace their lineage to John Howard, who came from England soon after the *Mayflower* and who served as an aide to Miles Standish. Oliver's grandparents served in the Revolutionary War, and in his childhood he heard many stories of their adventures. As the oldest child, Oliver was first to leave home to attend Monmouth Academy, preparatory to his enrollment at Bowdoin College. He graduated in 1850, and at the recommendation of his mother's brother, attorney John Otis, he entered West Point Academy. He graduated fourth in his class in 1854.

Oliver had not planned a military career for himself. Early on he wanted to be a lawyer, like his uncle, and later was drawn to prepare himself for the ministry, but the opportunity to attend West Point and the outbreak of the Civil War prepared him firmly for his military profession.

Religious fervor was a constant ingredient of Oliver's daily existence, instilled early by his mother and encouraged later by his wife, Lizzie Waite, whom he married on February 14, 1855, after an eight-year courtship. Oliver practiced his religion by daily prayers and services in the form of conducting Bible classes, prayer meetings, lecturing, and writing wherever he was stationed. He became widely known as a Christian soldier, sometimes irritatingly so to other military personnel because of his tendency toward self-righteousness. Linked with his piety was his acceptance of the black man as a worthy person, capable of achievements equal to those of the white man.

Howard was a strong family man, a loving, considerate husband, and a devoted father to his seven children: Guy, Grace, James, Chauncey, John, Harry, and Bessie. Oliver also was close to both his brothers, Rowland and Charles, who also chose a military career and served as an aide to Oliver during the early days of the Freedmen's Bureau.

Howard was always a prolific reader interested in education as a path to self-development, especially for the freed slaves. While at college, he worked as a school teacher. After graduation from West Point, he returned as a teacher of mathematics for several years. As Commissioner of the Freedmen's Bureau, he would place high priority on establishing schools and colleges.

When the Freedmen's Bureau was mandated by law on March 15, 1865, it was placed in the War Department and was to use military officers and personnel. Its activities were limited to the former Confederate states and to Kentucky, Maryland, and the District of Columbia. In addition, it had no special appropriation; its head was to draw on existing military supplies, buildings, and equipment. The expectation was that there would be funds forthcoming from the sale or lease of abandoned lands; this was greatly reduced, however, when President Andrew Johnson quickly took steps to pardon the former rebels and return their lands to them.

In any event, Major Howard, who had served well in battle and was highly regarded as a loyal, humane, and competent administrator, seemed to be the best military officer for the assignment—one he eagerly accepted. The ambiguity of the Bureau's language left much to the discretion of its head, who was charged with controlling all subjects relating to the freedmen. Howard interpreted his authority broadly, and under his direction the Bureau undertook a wide variety of services and activities to be administered in an integrated, family-focused fashion. Among other things, the Bureau provided food rations to relieve hunger and destitution; set up hospitals and clinics to care for the sick and disabled; established institutions to care for the aged and for orphaned youngsters; created numerous schools and colleges; set up an employment bureau which not only found jobs for the unemployed but helped to negotiate labor contracts and transport former slaves to work and new homesteads; sought to locate and reunite missing family members; protected the legal rights of freedmen in existing courts and established new ones where needed; helped in the registration of voters; and performed numerous other valuable services.

The Bureau was most active during the first two years of its existence; throughout, it faced many obstacles, including a heavy turnover in personnel (as officers clamored to be discharged from such duty), a lack of finances, and the hostility of local white people and others who resisted the Bureau as an agency that was pauperizing and encouraging malingering among the freedmen. Then there was pressure from President Andrew Johnson, who sought to terminate the agency and vetoed legislation that sought to extend its life on the grounds that the needs of the freedmen were local responsibilities and that the activities of the Bureau therefore should be turned over to the states as soon as each one was readmitted to the Union. It thus was an uphill struggle all the way. Yet, despite such obstacles, which rendered many of the Bureau's programs inoperative by 1868, Howard persisted and did an amazingly good job until 1872, when the Bureau was officially closed. Its chief legacy was its impact on education, especially the establishment of numerous schools and colleges—sixty-one of the former and eleven of the latter, including Howard University in Washington, D.C., which still receives federal funds and which General Howard served as president from 1869 to 1874.

Howard was an extremely skillful administrator who not only managed to do a lot with very limited federal funds but also to establish close ties with many northern freedmen's aid societies, church groups, and other private agencies who supplied funds and other forms of assistance to help the freedmen. In 1893 he was given the Congressional Medal of Honor, one of numerous awards and honors he won over the years. He died on October 29, 1909, at his home in Burlington, Vermont.

General Howard wrote voluminously—letters, articles, reports, speeches, books, and so on. Collections of his papers are available at the institutions with which he was connected, especially Howard University in Washington, D.C., but also

Bowdoin College in Brunswick, Maine, and Lincoln Memorial University in
Harrogate, Tennessee. Of Howard's many books, his *Autobiography*, begun in
1896 and completed in two volumes in 1907, is most important. The official
documents and records of the Freedmen's Bureau are at the National Archives
in Washington, D.C.

The point of view of an army officer who served as one of the Bureau's local
administrators is given by John De Forest in *A Union Officer in the Reconstruction*, ed. James Croushore and David Potter (1948). The plight of the freedmen
at the hands of the Bureau is vividly and favorably described by W.E.B. Du
Bois in *Black Reconstruction* (1935).

Other important sources are Victoria Olds, "The Freedmen's Bureau as a
Social Agency," Ph.D. dissertation, Columbia University, 1966, and "The
Freedmen's Bureau as a Social Agency," *Social Casework* (May, 1963), 247–
254; George R. Bentley, *A History of the Freedmen's Bureau* (1955); John A.
Carpenter, *Sword and Olive Branch: Oliver Otis Howard* (1964); and William
S. McFeeley, *Yankee Stepfather: General O. O. Howard and the Freedmen*
(1968).

VICTORIA OLDS

**Howe, Samuel Gridley** (November 10, 1801–January 9, 1876), social worker
and abolitionist, was born in Boston, Massachusetts. He was one of the six
children of Joseph Neals and Patty (Gridley) Howe. Both parents were descended
from English and New England stock. Howe's father owned a rope and cordage
manufacture which prospered until the War of 1812, when the federal government
failed to pay for supplies it had ordered. Following graduation from Boston Latin
School, Howe attended Brown University (1817–1821) and received an M.D.
from Harvard (1824).

Slender and graceful in appearance, Howe combined a romantic impulsiveness
and idealism with seemingly contradictory traits of practicality and patience. His
agile mind did not express itself in scholarship or intellectual subtlety, but in
the ability to grasp and resolve a practical challenge swiftly. Nothing better
testified to the romantic element in Howe's personality than his decision in 1824
to sail for Greece to assist in the war of independence against the Turks (launched
in 1821). He participated in guerilla combat and served as a surgeon in the fleet,
returning to the United States in 1827–1828 to raise funds for the cause. Howe
personally managed the distribution of the funds in Greece; significantly, he
favored not charitable handouts but payments in return for labor on the public
works projects which he organized. Stricken with malaria in 1830 (a lifelong
source of disability), Howe toured Europe for a year, including medical studies
in Paris, and returned to the United States in 1831.

Certain only that he did not want to settle into a routine medical practice,
Howe could not decide upon a career. This period of aimless drifting ended
abruptly, however, when he accepted an offer from Dr. John T. Fisher to manage
the Massachusetts School for the Blind (incorporated in 1829 but not yet in

operation). Howe promptly returned to Europe to study methods of educating the blind, influenced mainly by the work of Valentin Haüy. While abroad, he was persuaded by Lafayette and others to transmit relief funds to Polish refugees in Prussia. Howe aroused the suspicion of the Prussian government and was arbitrarily imprisoned for several weeks in the winter of 1832.

Returning to the United States in the summer of 1832, Howe launched the Massachusetts School at his Boston home. Within a few months the state legislature, favorably impressed with Howe's achievements, voted to provide $6,000 annually, and the school was transferred to the mansion of Colonel Thomas H. Perkins on Pearl Street. It would move to larger facilities in South Boston in 1839, remaining there until 1912.

Howe's national leadership in the education of the blind was partly rooted in his technical innovations. He developed an improved form of raised-letter printing, devised textbooks superior to any in existence, and established a printing press in connection with the school. Howe's international renown was assured as a result of his success with Laura Bridgman, a blind deaf-mute brought to the institution in 1839 at the age of seven. Charles Dickens' account of Howe's success in educating the child, published in his *American Notes* (1842), preceded Howe's year-long tour of Europe in 1843–1844. This was ostensibly a honeymoon excursion with his bride, Julia Ward, but Howe found ample opportunity to visit every variety of European institution for the dependent or handicapped. The couple would have six children, four daughters and two sons (the last child, and second son, died at the age of four). Howe took great joy in his children, and his family provided his only respite from a life otherwise dedicated to philanthropy and reform.

Along with his technical accomplishments, Howe brought to the education of the blind a complex of beliefs about human nature and society which, in turn, influenced his treatment methods. Howe was the embodiment of the romantic and Christian idealism which permeated antebellum reform movements. In Howe, the romantic ideals of perfectibility and progress meshed with the Christian ideals of the fatherhood of God and the brotherhood of man (as exemplified in New England Unitarianism). He saw it as a Christian imperative to serve the handicapped, meaning the perfection of their minds and senses to the greatest extent possible. Howe detested a caretaker concept of treatment, favoring educational methods which would permit the handicapped maximum self-sufficiency. Eventually, Howe came to abhor large congregate institutions, favoring instead the diffusion of the handicapped within normal society whenever possible. Contact with the normal (especially the family unit) was the most effective form of education and growth, not only for the handicapped, but for all who were dependent.

These principles applied to the mentally retarded as well as the blind. Having taught several blind idiots after 1839, Howe instigated the appointment of a Massachusetts commission to study the subject in 1846. He served as chairman, and prepared the final report of 1848. Thanks to Howe's persuasive arguments, the legislature authorized an experimental grant for three years. Howe's success in improving the lot of the mentally retarded encouraged the legislature to establish the program on a permanent basis in 1850 with the creation of the Massachusetts School for Idiotic and Feeble-Minded Youth (subsequently the Walter E. Fernald* School).

Howe's interest in education as an instrument of human perfectibility and progress extended to normal children. This commitment was stimulated by Howe's close friendship with Horace Mann. Howe fiercely defended Mann's efforts in the 1840s to upgrade the Boston public schools and develop normal schools for teacher training. During the same decade, Howe participated in Dorothea Dix's* crusade to expand and improve state facilities for the insane; launched a movement in cooperation with Mann to encourage use of the articulation method of training for deaf mutes; and attempted to promote the Philadelphia system of solitary confinement for criminals. Howe also held his only two elective offices in the mid-forties: one term on the Boston School Board and a term in the state legislature.

After 1846 Howe's philanthropic energies would center increasingly on free soil and abolition (significantly, Howe's closest friends, along with Mann, were Charles Sumner and Theodore Parker). He plunged into protest movements against the abduction of free Negroes from the streets of Boston, became deeply involved in aid to Kansas emigrants in the 1850s, and provided John Brown with considerable financial assistance (claiming innocence, however, of Brown's intentions at Harper's Ferry). After the war started, he undertook a sanitary survey of Massachusetts troops at the request of Governor Andrews and accepted an appointment to the U.S. Sanitary Commission later in 1861. In 1863 he served as one of three commissioners appointed to the Freedman's Inquiry Commission by Secretary of War Stanton. Like his friend Sumner, Howe believed in full citizenship for the freedman and in his ability to achieve equality if given a fair chance to compete.

Despite his preoccupation with war-related activities, Howe was instrumental in persuading the Governor of Massachusetts to establish the first state board of charities in 1863. Appointed to the agency the following year, he served as chairman from 1865 to 1874. His reports summarized his philosophy of social work and public welfare, particularly his commitment to the diffusion rather than the concentration of the handicapped and delinquent. This was essential to prevent contamination and to expose such groups to the educational and moral influences of normal society.

A lifelong partisan of the Greek Revolution, Howe responded to the revolt of Crete in 1866 against continued Turkish rule. He sailed to the region in 1867 to manage the relief funds and supplies he had raised. His activities included the establishment of an industrial school for Cretan refugees in Athens. A final foreign expedition occurred in 1871, when President Grant appointed Howe one of three commissioners to study the prospect of annexing Santo Domingo. Although favored by Howe, Congress failed to approve the dubious undertaking.

Life and constructive philanthropy were synonymous for Samuel G. Howe.

Life's real purpose for a romantic and Christian idealist inhered in the liberation of the handicapped, the retarded, slaves, Greeks and, indeed, all those who could not achieve their potential because of ignorance or oppression. For Howe and his generation, Laura Bridgman, a child of seven—deprived of virtually all senses—demonstrated conclusively that a divine spark resided in all humanity, however obscured by circumstances. Howe died at his home in Boston at age seventy-four.

The major collection of Howe Papers is housed at the Houghton Library of Harvard University. Other papers are located in the Massachusetts Historical Society. An indispensable compilation of letters, journal extracts, and commentary is the two-volume set edited by one of Howe's daughters: Laura E. Richards, ed., *Letters and Journals of Samuel Gridley Howe: The Greek Revolution* (1909), and vol. 2: *The Servant of Humanity* (1909). More condensed is Laura E. Richards, *Samuel Gridley Howe* (1935). F. B. Sanborn, *Dr. S. G. Howe, the Philanthropist* (1891), is pietistic but contains substantial extracts from letters and other unpublished materials. Equally pietistic are Julia Ward Howe, *Memoir of Dr. Samuel Gridley Howe* (1876), and *Reminiscences, 1819–1899* (1899).

Howe's approach to social work and public welfare can be traced in his public documents: *Annual Report of the Perkins Institution and Massachusetts Asylum for the Blind* (1833–1875); *Reports of the Massachusetts Board of State Charities* (1865–1874); *Report Made to the Legislature of Massachusetts Upon Idiocy* (1848).

The only recent critical biography of Howe is Harold Schwartz, *Samuel Gridley Howe, Social Reformer, 1801–1876* (1956).

ROY LUBOVE

**Hoyt, Charles S.** (June 8, 1822–December 13, 1898), longtime secretary to the New York State Board of Charities, Superintendent of State and Alien Poor, and pioneer social statistician, was born on a farm in Ridgefield, Connecticut. Hoyt's early life could stand as an archetype of the antebellum American professional career. He moved during his childhood with his parents to western New York, where his father tried his luck in different towns before settling in Yates County in 1834. From the time he was fourteen years old until he was twenty-one, Hoyt alternated teaching school, working on the family farm, and attending Rushville Academy, where he preferred mathematics to classical subjects. When he was twenty-one, Hoyt began to study medicine with Dr. W. Webb of Rushville, although even then he continued to teach part-time to support himself. Not long afterwards, he entered Geneva Medical College, from which he graduated in 1847. He began to practice in Potter Center, Yates County, where, for five years, he was the town's superintendent of schools. Although Hoyt was elected to the state assembly as a radical Democrat in 1851, when the South seceded from the Union, he shifted his allegiance and helped form the Union Party in his county. Working hard to muster recruits for the Union army,

Hoyt joined it himself in 1862 and was appointed assistant surgeon for the 126th Regiment, New York Volunteers. Captured at Harper's Ferry, Hoyt was present at every major battle in which his regiment participated (although he missed a couple of skirmishes when he had been sent home sick with typhoid fever). In 1864 he was promoted to the field hospital, which he directed until the end of the war. By all accounts, Hoyt's war record was distinguished not only for bravery and medical skill but, equally, for administrative efficiency and competence.

In 1866 Hoyt married Dora Barnum, with whom he had three children, a son and two daughters. Meanwhile, he put his medical knowledge and experience as a health administrator to work when he returned to the state assembly in 1867 and served on the Committee on Public Health and Medical Colleges and Societies and the Committee on State Charitable Institutions. As chairman of the latter, he drafted the legislation that created the Board of Commissioners of Public Charities (later named the State Board of Charities). Subsequently becoming its secretary, Hoyt served until 1895, when he was named Superintendent of State and Alien Poor, a post created by the newly revised state constitution. In the latter position, he continued to perform essentially the same duties as before, relieved only of some administrative responsibilities.

As one of his longtime colleagues observed, Hoyt's first work as secretary of the Board "was to systematize." He immediately began to collect, tabulate, and report the statistics that he believed the Board needed in order to reach informed decisions. His passion for gathering accurate information continued throughout his career. Indeed, not long before his death he devised a system for the monthly reporting of data on children in state institutions.

The first institutions Hoyt visited after his appointment were the state's almshouses, which he found in shocking condition, and much of his subsequent career was spent advocating changes in them. He was instrumental not only in the improvement of their physical facilities and internal management but in the passage of the 1875 act that removed children from almshouses and in the creation of special institutions for the feebleminded, the insane, and epileptics.

Hoyt's duties included the administration of three very important laws. The first, the State Pauper Act of 1873, concerned paupers who had not resided in any county of the state for sixty days within one year prior to their application for relief. The second, the Alien Poor Act of 1880, authorized the return to their countries of origin of any crippled, blind, lunatic, or otherwise infirm aliens. The third, the Indian Poor Law of 1894, provided for the care of Indians in designated almshouses. The administration of the latter law was one of Hoyt's principal concerns at the time of his death.

In the twenty years between 1873 and 1893, 36,964 persons were cared for as state paupers in almshouses. Hoyt managed to send 24,402 of these out of the state or to friends or relatives willing to care for them. In the eighteen years between the passage of the Alien Poor Act and his death, he returned 3,350 immigrants to Europe. Through these means, it was estimated, Hoyt saved the state of New York over $40 million.

In May, 1873, the New York legislature ordered the State Board of Charities to make an exhaustive study of the causes of pauperism. Hoyt carried out the work. His report, published as an appendix to the tenth *Annual Report* of the Board in 1878, was the major empirical analysis of pauperism in nineteenth century America. It was taken as definitive, and its conclusions were widely quoted. For his study, Hoyt devised a schedule with sixty questions that attempted to elicit information about the habits, history, and family background of every inmate of every almshouse in the state. He supervised the administration of the questionnaire to 12,614 inmates.

Hoyt argued that his statistics showed that most pauperism was the result of intemperance and an unwillingness to work. Both of these, he claimed, usually had been inherited. Influenced especially by Robert Dugdale's work on the Jukes, Hoyt argued that very few paupers had reached almshouses because of causes outside of their own control. However, reanalysis of Hoyt's methods and data does not support his conclusions. First, he predetermined his results in a variety of ways, including the exclusion of the short-term inmates who made up the bulk of almshouse populations (and did not fit the image of long-term, feeble, permanent dependents that he claimed to show); his definition of anyone who drank at all as intemperate; and his indiscriminate inclusion of inmates in very different types of institutions within the same tablulations. Reanalysis of the data shows very few inmates with parents, children, or siblings dependent on public relief. The data, in fact, indicate that most of the inmates surveyed were elderly people who lacked a spouse or children to care for them. Hoyt's analysis is especially remarkable because it ignored the effects of the intense depression of the mid–1870s that was in its most severe stage during his survey.

Through his professional activities as well as his written reports, Hoyt's influence spread far beyond New York. He was one of the founders of the National Conference of Charities and Correction in 1874 and its president in 1888. His presidential address showed his essentially unchanged views about the causes of dependence and added a fear of the effects of the new immigration from Southern and Eastern Europe. Russia, Bohemia, Italy, and Poland, he believed, were especially important sources of degenerate aliens. By stopping the immigration of defective people at its source, Hoyt argued, America could reduce the burden of pauperism. Even more important, however, was redeeming the children of paupers. Despite their heredity, pauper children could be saved if they were separated early enough from their parents. This, Hoyt felt, should be a primary goal of public society.

More than any single person, Hoyt shaped the administration of public welfare in New York during its formative years. At the same time, through his investigations, reports, and professional activities, he influenced the interpretation of dependence throughout America. Hoyt's significance, however, rests not only on his administrative activities and contributions to ideas about dependence, but also on his role as an early advocate of statistically informed policy, accurate and complete records, and empirical research. Ironically, he demonstrated nothing so much as the potential abuses of social science and the power of preconceived ideas to shape social research.

Hoyt died "in harness" in Canandaigua, New York, as a result of pneumonia caught when he left an overheated train for the bitter cold of a late December day in upstate New York.

Hoyt left no manuscript collection. His professional correspondence can be found with the State Board of Charities Collection in the New York State Archives in Albany. Although he did not write books or journal articles, his ideas can be traced through his reports as secretary of the Board and, for a few years, as Superintendent of State and Alien Poor. The tenth report contains his famous paper on the causes of pauperism. Other sources in which to trace his ideas are the proceedings of the National Conference of Charities and Correction, at which he gave occasional papers and often made comments. See, especially, his presidential address, *Proceedings of the National Conference of Charities and Correction* (1888). Hoyt also spoke frequently at meetings of the County Superintendents of the Poor, and his comments can be found in their proceedings.

Hoyt and the State Board of Charities are discussed throughout David M. Schneider and Albert Deutsch, *The History of Public Welfare in New York State, 1867–1940* (1941). Hoyt's survey of the causes of pauperism is reanalyzed in Michael B. Katz, *Poverty and Policy in American History* (1983), 90–133. Biographical comments on Hoyt are found in S. R. Harlow and H. H. Boone, *Life Sketches of the State Officers, Senators, and Members of the Assembly of the State of New York in 1867* (1867), 274–276; William R. Stewart, "The Late Dr. Charles S. Hoyt," *New-York Tribune*, January 9, 1899, 5; "Dr. Charles S. Hoyt, Superintendent of State and Alien Poor," *Charities* (December 11, 1898), 3; and Julia S. Hoag, "Memorial to Dr. Charles S. Hoyt . . . ," *Thirty-Second Annual Report of the State Board of Charities*, Senate No. 19 (January 16, 1899), 165–184.

MICHAEL B. KATZ

**Hoyt, Franklin Chase** (September 7, 1876–November 13, 1937), lawyer, child welfare promoter, and juvenile court justice, was born in Pelham, New York, to Janet Ralston (Chase) and William Sprague Hoyt, who could trace his lineage in America to Simon Hoyt, who settled in Massachusetts in 1629. Young Franklin Hoyt's maternal grandfather was Salmon Portland Chase, Chief Justice of the United States Supreme Court from 1864 to 1873 who, prior to that, had been Secretary of the Treasury in Abraham Lincoln's administration. In addition, his paternal grandmother, Susan Sprague, was the daughter of William Sprague, the Governor of Rhode Island from 1860 to 1861. An Episcopalian, Hoyt thus grew up in a family of patrician standing, which was further reflected in his schooling; he graduated from St. Paul's School in Concord, New Hampshire,

Columbia University in New York City, and the New York School of Law. On June 8, 1918, he married Maud Rives Borland of Wappingers Falls, New York, with whom he had two daughters, Constance Maud and Beatrix Chase Hoyt.

Meanwhile, Hoyt was admitted to the New York State bar in 1897 and then began a legal career in private practice. Soon, however, he found himself appointed the assistant corporation counsel for the city of New York. As part of these responsibilities, he was the legal advisor to George B. McClellan, then mayor of New York. In 1908 he was appointed to the Court of Special Sessions of the city of New York—at age thirty-one the youngest person ever appointed to the post—and was assigned to the Children's Branch of the court.

Seven years after his appointment to the Court of Special Sessions, Hoyt was instrumental in the creation of a special court which would hear only cases involving children; it would be an independent branch of the courts of the city of New York. After its creation, Judge Hoyt served as presiding jurist of the "juvenile court" for eighteen years. Meanwhile, he worked for the extension of the children's court throughout New York State, participating in the drafting of a model juvenile court act for the purpose.

Judge Hoyt was known for his innovative approaches to handling the cases which came before him. Along with Merritt Willis Pinckney* in Chicago, he was instrumental in instituting the use of diagnostic procedures to evaluate children brought before him. Another important contribution of this learned and caring man was the inauguration of probation services. These and other activities on the court led him to be active in civic causes as well.

He served as the president of the Big Brother movement from 1911 to 1925. He was honorary president of the New York Council of Boy Scouts in 1918. He was president of the New York Conference of Charities and Correction in 1919, and from 1922 to 1934 he was chairman of the National Probation Association.

Judge Hoyt's appearance on the bench was described as grim-jawed with a skeptical gaze. Coupled with his rather forbidding presence, however, was an optimistic and mild demeanor. As the author of *Quicksands of Youth* (1921) and numerous articles on social problems affecting children, Judge Hoyt displayed an understanding of the need for the qualities of justice and fairness in dealing with the young people brought before him. Thus, many of the children who came before him and believed they would not be treated fairly by a person who represented the "establishment"—a belief that was the product of prior experiences with city officials—were pleasantly surprised by the treatment they received in Hoyt's courtroom. (Some of Hoyt's writings that depict his encounters with such children, and their parents, can be found in *Scribner's Magazine*.)

Hoyt stepped down from the bench in 1933 and two years later, in 1935, was named director of the Federal Alcohol Administration by President Franklin D. Roosevelt. Ironically, he was named to that position after having won a contest for the best proposed workable reform of the prohibition legislation, for which he received $25,000 from William R. Hearst. In any event, he held the position for only a few months, retiring as a result of ill health. Hoyt died in New York City on November 13, 1937.

There is very little written about Franklin Chase Hoyt, the man and the juvenile court judge. The best source of information is his own writings, including *Quicksands of Youth* (1921) and a series of articles he published in *Scribner's Magazine* from 1919 to 1921 dealing with circumstances he encountered while serving on the bench. A number of articles in *Time* and *Business Week* deal with his appointment as administrator of the Federal Alcohol Administration.

Most books and articles dealing with the origin and early development of the juvenile court in America have information on Hoyt; some of the better ones are Thomas D. Eliot, *The Juvenile Court and the Community* (1914); Bernard Flexner and Roger Baldwin, *Juvenile Courts and Probation* (1914); Herbert H. Lou, *Juvenile Courts in the United States* (1927); Robert M. Mennel, "Origins of the Juvenile Court," *Crime and Delinquency* 18 (1972), 68–78; Graham Parker, "The Juvenile Court: The Illinois Experience," *University of Toronto Law Journal* 26 (1976), 253–306; Anthony M. Platt, *The Child Savers: The Invention of Delinquency* (1977); and Ellen Ryerson, *The Best-Laid Plans: America's Juvenile Court Experiment* (1978). Also see *Who Was Who in America*, vol. 1 (1943).

GAYLE V. STRICKLER, JR.

**Hunter, Robert** (April 10, 1874–May 15, 1942), social worker, author, and socialist, was born Wiles Robert Hunter in Terre Haute, Indiana, to William Robert and Caroline (Fouts) Hunter. He dropped his first name and was known simply as Robert Hunter throughout his adult life. As his father was a successful carriage maker, Hunter lived comfortably, even fashionably, within the upper class. He was educated both in public schools and by private tutors in Terre Haute and graduated from Indiana University in 1896 with a B.A. degree.

His introduction to human suffering on a large scale appears to have occurred during the Panic of 1893, which led him to decide to enter social work upon graduation from college. Between 1896 and 1902 Hunter worked in the settlement house movement in Chicago, residing at Jane Addams'* Hull-House between 1899 and 1902. At the same time, he held a number of other positions, including organizing secretary of the Chicago Board of Charities, founder and superintendent of the Municipal Housing Lodge for Vagrants, and director of Chicago's first free children's dental clinic. In 1901 he served as chair of the Investigating Committee for the City Homes Association, and in that capacity published his first book, *Tenement Conditions in Chicago* (1901), a classic example of settlement house research, in which conditions in selected neighborhoods were meticulously examined. Such items as bathtubs and garbage boxes were counted and reported as measures of quality of life among the poor.

In 1902 Hunter moved to New York to become head worker at the University

Settlement on Rivington Street, on the Lower East Side of the city, the last paid full-time position of his career. While head worker there he chaired the New York Child Labor Committee and led its successful effort to pass New York State's progressive child labor law in 1903. In that same year he married Caroline Margaretha Phelps Stokes, a member of the wealthy and civically active New York family, thus cementing his ties both to the social elite and to New York's philanthropic community. This marriage produced four children, Robert, Phelps Stokes, Caroline Phelps, and Helene Louisa. Finally, in that same year he resigned as head worker at University Settlement and devoted himself full-time to research and social and political activism.

The first fruit of this move from settlement house work to social research and political activism proved to be his magnum opus, *Poverty*, published for the first time in 1904 and reprinted on numerous occasions thereafter. To the modern reader, *Poverty* is a curious mixture of careful statistical analysis and gross nativist stereotyping, but it represented, to a great extent, the methodology and assumptions of mainline sociology in its day. The book began with a carefully reasoned presentation, supported by statistics from a variety of sources, on the prevalence of poverty in the United States, which Hunter calculated to be at around 10 million, or one out of every eight Americans, a startling revelation. And while he showed no sympathy for the "pauper" or "vagrant" who had given up hope and lived only on charity, he noted that many, if not most, of the poor were in such a condition not by their own doing but as a result of sickness, unemployment, or old age. The book's contributions, then, were several. First, it was the most careful and objective study of its kind. Second, it documented the argument that poverty usually was caused by social factors and therefore required social solutions. And third, it was widely read, receiving extremely favorable comment from such luminaries as Florence Kelley* and H. G. Wells and, as a result, made a real impact on public discussion of the subject of poverty—and the need for environmental reform.

Meanwhile, Hunter's career underwent some curious changes. In 1903 and again in 1906–1907 he engaged in extended visits to Europe. During these visits he met with such leaders of European socialism and labor as Keir Hardie, Peter Kropotkin, and Vladimir Lenin. He also made a "pilgrimage" to see Tolstoy at his country estate. In the light of these European contacts and the directions in which his work and research in America had taken him, it is not surprising that in 1905 Hunter joined the American Socialist Party—the moderate wing of the American socialist movement as opposed to the revolutionary Socialist Labor Party and the Industrial Workers of the World (the "Wobblies"). Hunter rose rapidly in that organization, representing the United States at the Third International at Stuttgart in 1907, standing as a socialist candidate to the New York State Assembly in 1908, and serving on the party's central committee from 1909 until 1912. During this period he published *Socialists at Work* (New York, 1908), which described his observations of European socialism. In 1910 he stood as the socialist candidate for Governor of Connecticut, having moved to that state.

In that same year he attended another international socialist meeting at Copenhagen, and in 1914 he published his polemical study *Violence and the Labor Movement*, which featured scathing personal attacks on Mikhail Bakunin and other more revolutionary socialists, syndicalists, and anarchists.

The outbreak of World War I in 1914 marked the end of this phase of Hunter's career. The inability of the European socialist parties to prevent the outbreak of war soured Hunter on the entire socialist movement. (He later commented that the German socialists "got what they deserved" under Hitler). In poor health, in 1915 he moved to California, where he continued to write but where his interests and politics shifted continuously to the right, as was evidenced in 1919, when he published *Why We Fail as Christians*. He did not forsake reform entirely, however, serving on the Berkeley Board of Charity for several years and serving as its chairman in 1921 while he taught English and economics at the University of California.

With the coming of Franklin Roosevelt and the New Deal in the 1930s, Hunter became increasingly active in right-wing causes. As a member of the National Economic League, in 1934 he published an anti–New Deal pamphlet, "Inflation and Revolution." The publication, six years later, of *Revolution: Why, How, When* represented a full about-face from his days as a socialist. In this book he argued that poverty and despair did not cause revolution. Revolution, he stated, came out of economic and political instability and coalitions between the military and the middle class, an idea which, in light of the events in Germany and Spain, was not without some foundation. It was surprising, however, that the author of *Poverty* would assert some thirty-six years later that American capitalism had effectively eliminated poverty and the class conflict.

The latter stages of his career notwithstanding, Hunter's impact on American social welfare history was considerable, primarily, however, through the writing and publication of *Poverty* and his achievements as a settlement house resident and reformer in Chicago and New York. Hunter died on May 15, 1942, in Montecito, California, of angina pectoris.

Apparently, there is no collection of Hunter papers anywhere in existence. He, however, was a sufficiently major character in American socialism that references to him appear in many general histories on the topic, among them David A. Shannon, *The Socialist Party of America* (1955), and Ira A. Kipnis, *The American Socialist Movement, 1897–1912* (1952). *Poverty* receives a somewhat subdued footnote in Werner Sombart's *Why There Is No Socialism in America* (1976). Full biographical sketches appear in the *Dictionary of American Biography*, vol. 10 (1943), 372–374; *National Cyclopedia of American Biography*, vol. 14, 353–354, and vol. 31, 16. A good deal of biographical material appears in Peder d'A. Jones' introduction to the 1965 reprint of *Poverty*. Hunter's obituary appeared in the *New York Times* (May 17, 1942), and an editorial about him appeared two days later (May 19). In addition to the works mentioned above, Hunter also published *Labor in Politics* (1915).

MERLE T. EDWARDS-ORR

# J

**Jacobi, Abraham** (May 6, 1830–July 10, 1919), physician-reformer and "father of American pediatrics," was born at Hartum-in-Minden, Westphalia, Germany, the son of Eliezer and Julia (Abel) Jacobi, Jewish parents whose financial circumstances seemed to preclude an advanced education for their son. Only family sacrifice, particularly by Jacobi's mother, enabled him to enroll in the local gymnasium. After graduation in 1847, Jacobi began university studies which culminated in a medical degree from the University of Bonn in 1851.

The new physician spent the next two years in a German prison, having been arrested for participation in the revolutionary movement that swept through Germany in 1848. In 1853 Jacobi escaped, fleeing first to England and then, as did many other revolutionaries, to the United States. After a brief stay in Boston, Jacobi settled in New York City's expanding German community, opened a private medical practice, and began his career as physician-advocate of reforms to protect the health and well-being of women and children.

In medical circles Jacobi is known as the "father of American pediatrics," because, through teaching and professional activities, he succeeded in drawing the attention of the profession to the unique health problems of infants and children. Physicians, he asserted, had to be taught to appreciate the physiological differences between children and adults, and the ineffectiveness of treating childhood illnesses with proportionately smaller doses of medicines designed for adults. Jacobi's medical views coincided with the increasingly popular belief in the innocence of childhood and the need to segregate children in age-specific institutions. By combining a knowledge of pediatrics learned in Germany with the cultural milieu of his new home, Jacobi initiated the new medical specialty of pediatrics.

For forty-one years Jacobi taught pediatrics in New York medical schools. His appointment in 1860 to teach the diseases of children at the New York Medical College was the first separate pediatrics professorship in the United States. Prior to this appointment pediatric medicine, if taught at all, was part of the obstetrics and gynecology curriculum. Following the closing of the New

York Medical College in 1864, Jacobi accepted the chair of diseases of children in the medical department of the University of the City of New York and in 1870 assumed the clinical professorship of pediatrics at the College of Physicians and Surgeons, a post he held until 1901, when he was replaced by Luther Emmett Holt.*

Unlike many of his contemporaries, Jacobi emphasized practical or applied aspects of pediatric medicine, rather than scientific research. For example, Jacobi espoused the use of Joseph O'Dwyer's successful intubation procedure to treat diphtheria when others in the profession denounced it. Although at first doubting that the cause of diphtheria was bacteriological, once convinced that it was, Jacobi championed the widespread use of the newly developed diphtheria antitoxin.

To ensure that his students received clinical training, Jacobi initiated in the 1860s the practice of "bedside teaching" in pediatrics. In conjunction with the New York Medical College, he established a free pediatrics clinic at the New York Infirmary for Women and Children founded in 1853 by Elizabeth Blackwell.* In this institutional setting, Jacobi exhibited actual cases of common illnesses to supplement lecture and textbook learning. Such institutions proved to be important sources of cases for medical research and teaching, leading Jacobi to create charity clinics at each of his succeeding positions, clinics that were mutually beneficial to doctor and patient.

In addition to teaching, Jacobi helped to build the organizational network supporting the new specialty of pediatrics. He was responsible for the creation in 1880 of the pediatrics section of the American Medical Association, and served as first president of the American Pediatric Society in 1888. Yet, in spite of his stature in the profession, it was not until 1911 that Jacobi became president of the American Medical Association, due possibly to his earlier efforts to gain recognition for physicians who practiced homeopathy.

Jacobi was a prolific writer and frequent contributor to medical journals. During the more than sixty years of his medical career he wrote extensively on childhood ailments, including diphtheria, dentition, and intestinal diseases, considered three of the major causes of infant mortality in nineteenth century New York City. His views were brought together in a medical textbook, *Therapeutics of Infancy and Childhood* (1895).

Jacobi served as attending physician or consultant to many New York City hospitals for the poor. However, his tenure in these positions was not always tranquil. One such institution inviting Jacobi's services was the Nursery and Child's Hospital. Begun in 1854 as a "Nursery for the Children of Poor Women," the facility expanded rapidly to include a children's hospital, a lying-in hospital, and a foundling home for illegitimate infants. Power in the hospital was exercised by a Board of Lady Managers, thirty-five wealthy women with leisure and inclination to engage in voluntary charitable activities. Jacobi, the trained physician, came into conflict with the directors when he tried to impose medical ideas about proper diet, the admission of night air into the rooms, and the distribution of candy in the wards. Jacobi's outspokenness caused the hospital's medical board in 1870 to sever the institution's connections with New York City's recognized authority on the diseases of children.

Although discharged from his position, Jacobi continued his campaign to improve the treatment of children in hospitals and institutions. His 1872 address to the New York County Medical Society used mortality statistics from the Nursery and Child's Hospital to question the practice of raising foundlings in institutions. With hospital death rates as high as 50 percent yearly, Jacobi alleged that infants in working-class tenements had a better chance of surviving childhood than did those reared in charitable institutions. His solution, contrary to the institution-building mania that appealed to nineteenth century benevolent organizations, was to place infants in foster homes, in the country, with private families supervised by the state. Thus Jacobi challenged two major assumptions of nineteenth century child welfare reformers, believing that children could not be safely reared in large institutions and that voluntary charities could not effectively supervise the care of these young ones.

Jacobi's concern for the physical well-being of infants and children led him to popularize medical ideas about care and feeding, a move that helped to establish the pediatric profession's responsibility for maternal education and well-baby programs. In 1870 he drew up, at the request of the New York Public Health Association, infant feeding guidelines for distribution to mothers in New York tenements. Special emphasis was placed on the safe handling of milk during the summer months, when many infants died from digestive disorders caused by contaminated milk. Four years later, Jacobi's wife, Dr. Mary Putnam Jacobi, revised the rules and published them as *Infant Diet* (1874), the mothers' manual which would serve as the authoritative guide to scientific infant feeding until publication of L. Emmett Holt's *The Care and Feeding of Children* (1894).

Publication of Jacobi's popular guide also signified the medical profession's growing interest in infant feeding problems and in the purity of milk available to city residents. Jacobi advised that maternal nursing was the safest method, yet he knew that for working women breast feeding was nearly impossible. Consequently, he advocated laws requiring employers to give working mothers the opportunity to nurse. The only adequate substitute for mother's milk was cow's milk, and this, Jacobi warned, should be boiled before being offered to infants. "Boil until you see the bubbles" was his advice, a dictum he based on practical experience rather than Louis Pasteur's fermentation experiments.

Not all physicians agreed with Jacobi that boiling made the milk safe and nutritious. The scientific feeding issue fueled pediatric debates in the late nineteenth century, with Jacobi consistently recommending boiled rather than raw milk. Indicative of his concern was Jacobi's defense of philanthropist Nathan Straus' pasteurized milk depots. With Jacobi's advice, Straus established pasteurization plants to provide pure milk to infants of the city's poor. When Straus' efforts were attacked, Jacobi was instrumental in keeping the stations open until in 1911 the New York City Department of Health began to operate municipally financed pasteurized milk stations.

Although known as the founder of a separate medical discipline, Jacobi denied that his interest in childhood diseases categorized him among the growing number of medical specialists. He objected vociferously to medical specialization, and his private practice was never restricted to infants and children. However, as a physician, Jacobi played an early and significant role in New York City public health and child welfare campaigns to lower infant mortality by applying ''scientific'' expertise to the problems of caring for children in institutions and feeding them at home.

During a public career that spanned nearly seven decades, Jacobi became involved in a broad variety of social issues, often far removed from customary medical or pediatric concerns. Having found that medical problems frequently originated in social and economic conditions, Jacobi challenged his colleagues to rectify these injustices. It was, he felt, the duty of professional physicians to engage in political activities to create a responsible government.

Jacobi lent his support to child labor legislation and to the birth control movement. He participated in the National Association for the Study and Prevention of Tuberculosis and was actively involved in the American Clinical and Climatological Association, which sought to combat TB by moving patients to climates that seemed to aid in recovery. However, as a physician, Jacobi could not condone prohibition, and argued that medical science was on the side of alcohol.

Jacobi believed that government policies should be guided by the scientific acumen of physicians and other professionals. He helped to form the New York Civil Service Reform Association and remained active in this area until his death. To ensure professional representation in the government Jacobi advocated the creation of a cabinet-level national department of health. Interest in reform of the political system, however, did not extend fully to all areas. His wife was an unqualified suffragist, but Jacobi's support for woman suffrage was limited to approval in principle; it was the protection of working women rather than the expansion of the democratic process that aroused Jacobi's concern.

Although an octogenarian when World War I began, Jacobi once again linked his name to a popular crusade, lending support to Andrew Carnegie's ill-fated peace efforts. While he lived to see the war's end, he did not witness its impact on liberal reform in the 1920s. Jacobi was accustomed to spend summers away from New York City at a cottage on Lake George, and it was there that he died, in 1919, at age eighty-nine.

Abraham Jacobi's personal papers and the first chapters of an autobiography were burned in a fire at his Lake George home in 1918. Letters and notes by Jacobi, and letters to him, are contained in the manuscript collections of the New York Academy of Medicine, New York, New York, and in the Autograph Collection of the History of Medicine Division, National Library of Medicine, Bethesda, Maryland.

Jacobi's writings were collected by William J. Robinson, ed., *Collectanae*

*Jacobi*, 8 vols. (1909). Volumes 1–5 contain material on pediatrics; volumes 6–8 refer to more general subjects. Important among his many published medical monographs were *Dentition and Its Derangements* (1862); *A Treatise on Diphtheria* (1880); and *The Intestinal Diseases of Infancy and Childhood* (1887). His textbook was published as *Therapeutics of Infancy and Childhood* (1896). Jacobi's venture into popular medical literature was *Infant Diet*, revised and enlarged by Mary Putnam Jacobi (1874).

Entries appear in standard biographical dictionaries covering the period of Jacobi's life. See also Lytt I. Gardner, "Abraham Jacobi: Pediatric Pioneer," *Pediatrics* (August, 1959), 282–287; Jerome S. Leopold, "Abraham Jacobi," in Borden S. Veeder, ed., *Pediatric Profiles* (1957), 12–19; Eugene P. Link, "Abraham and Mary P. Jacobi, Humanitarian Physicians," *Journal of the History of Medicine and Allied Sciences* (Autumn, 1949), 382–392; Louis Pelner, "Abraham Jacobi, M.D., 1830–1919," *New York State Journal of Medicine* (September 1, 1970), 2237–2241; Victor Robinson, "The Life of A. Jacobi," *Medical Life* (May-June, 1928), 212–306; and Rhoda Truax, *The Doctors Jacobi* (1952), a popular biography.

Obituary notices include Fielding H. Garrison, "Dr. Abraham Jacobi (1830–1919)," *Science* (August 1, 1919), 102–104; Lillian D. Wald, "Abraham Jacobi, 1830–1919," *Survey* (July 19, 1919), 595; and the *New York Times*, July 12, 1919, 9.

KATHLEEN W. JONES

**Jarrett, Mary Cromwell** (June 21, 1877–August 4, 1961), founder of psychiatric social work and researcher in the area of chronic illness, was born in Baltimore, Maryland, the only child of Frank and Caroline (Cromwell) Jarrett. Her father, a bookkeeper, a partner in a tailoring business, and later a reporter, died when Mary was fifteen years of age.

Graduating from Woman's (later Goucher) College of Baltimore, she majored in English and taught school her first two years after graduation. The direction of her career, however, was permanently altered by her experience as a volunteer friendly visitor for the Baltimore Charity Organization Society, where Mary Richmond* also had begun her social work career.

In 1903 Mary Jarrett went to Boston, where she began work as a caseworker in the Boston Children's Aid Society under the direction of Charles Birtwell,* one of the first to apply the newly emerging scientific individualizing practice of social casework to child welfare. Her talents were quickly recognized, and she moved up in the agency to become the head of the casework department.

In the course of her work with troubled children, she consulted, on occasion, with social psychiatrist E. E. Southard, who was impressed with her unusual ability. In 1913 Southard asked her to join him at Boston Psychopathic Hospital, where he was director, to develop and lead a social service department. Social workers had been used in aftercare programs in New York and Massachusetts, but no one, to date, had envisioned as extensive a use of social casework as a part of the treatment of mental patients as did Southard and Jarrett.

It soon became apparent that special training was required to ready caseworkers for this specialized field, which Jarrett named "psychiatric social work," and in 1914 she and Southard initiated a training course at Boston Psychopathic for this purpose. In 1917, anticipating the need for trained staff in increasing numbers to work with returning soldiers suffering from war-related psychiatric difficulties, Boston Psychopathic, in association with the National Committee for Mental Hygiene, established an emergency summer training program at Smith College under Jarrett's direction. The goal of the program, as described by the director, was to train social workers who could secure social history essential to medical diagnosis; assist the physician in psychotherapy by such means as encouragement, reeducation, and explanation; and promote the social adjustment of patients upon discharge.

The success of this first effort led to the founding, the following year, of the Smith College Training School for Psychiatric Social Work with Mary Jarrett as associate director. Southard continued to work closely with Jarrett in developing curriculum and seeking out distinguished lecturers to enrich the program.

Also in 1919, Southard, a brilliant, creative, and highly controversial figure, left Boston Psychopathic and entered the new field of industrial psychiatry. Jarrett also resigned from the hospital and worked with Southard on a research project which explored the relationship of mental disorder to employees' functioning on the job and the practical application of mental hygiene to industry. The results of this work were published in *Kingdom of Evils* (1922). This volume was directed at social workers and offered an alternative conceptualization to Richmond's *Social Diagnosis* (1917). Southard and Jarrett presented their philosophy of social psychiatry and their view of social work's potential role in alleviating the effects of the evils that caused social dysfunction: illness, ignorance, vice, crime, and poverty.

Jarrett's vitally important relationship with Southard was abruptly ended by his sudden and untimely death in 1920. She completed and published *Kingdom of Evils* after his death and continued to provide leadership in the development and conceptualization of psychiatric social work. She founded, in 1920, the organization which was to become the American Association of Psychiatric Social Workers and presented major papers which spelled out the development of her thinking at the National Conference of Social Work yearly until 1922. In 1923 Jarrett was eased out of her position at Smith. Her subsequent abandonment of the field of practice she had done so much to fashion attests to the bitterness she felt.

In a short decade, Jarrett and Southard did much to change forever the character of social casework. First, they named and defined the new social work specialization of psychiatric social work and translated their thinking into a curriculum which was adopted throughout the country as other schools began to include psychiatry in their programs. Second, they defined the role of the social worker in the treatment of mental illness and specified the knowledge and skills required to practice this role. Finally, they established an educational institution which continues to the present day to train social workers with a strong psychiatric base.

But perhaps most important was Jarrett's influence, not on psychiatric social work, but on all social work. In her classic and influential paper, "The Psychiatric Thread Running Through All Social Case Work," delivered at the National Conference of Social Work in 1919, Jarrett stated that psychiatry not only provided a thread but was the warp of the fabric of all social casework. She criticized Mary Richmond's *Social Diagnosis* on the basis that in over 50 percent of the cases the clients were clearly psychopathic. From her study of case records from many social work settings, she felt that a large proportion of all people seen in social agencies had severe mental problems. Although agreeing with Richmond that the long-range goal of social casework was to bring the person into the best possible relationship with the environment, she heralded the shift from outer to inner focus by stating that it is primarily mental factors that determine the nature of the person–environment relation.

In 1923, at the age of forty-six, Mary Jarrett started a new career as researcher and program and policy analyst in the field of chronic illness. After four years with the U.S. Public Health Service and the Veterans Administration in Boston, she and Katrine Collins, with whom she shared a home, moved to New York. There she found a permanent professional base with the Welfare Council of New York City (later the Community Council of Greater New York). She began her work in New York by discovering that Manhattan had the highest infant mortality rate of the five boroughs. She then completed a health inventory of New York City, which was followed by an extensive study of chronic illness in New York. The latter study resulted in a major publication, *Chronic Illness in New York City* (1933). Revealing the lack of services available to the chronically ill, her work stimulated the development of the Committee on Chronic Illness, of which she was secretary, and eventually the construction of a hospital for chronic disease on Welfare Island (later Goldwater Memorial Hospital). Her findings also had an impact on the development of the programs for the chronically ill in the Social Security Act of 1935.

From 1935 to 1940 she directed a Works Progress Administration project demonstrating the use of home care for the chronically ill, anticipating by many decades the move toward deinstitutionalization. Jarrett retired from full-time employment in 1943 but consulted in many cities on planning long-term health care facilities until her own failing health made this impossible. She died in New York City in 1961.

Mary Jarrett's papers and correspondence are in the Sophia Smith Collection at Smith College in Northampton, Massachusetts. The development of Jarrett's thinking about psychiatric social work, however, can be found in her published papers, especially those in the *Proceedings* of the National Conference of Social

Work, 1919–1922, and in the book she coauthored with E. E. Southard, *The Kingdom of Evils* (1922). Her later work is exemplified in *Chronic Illness in New York City* (1933) and *Housekeeping Service for Home Care of Chronic Patients* (1938). The more important secondary accounts are Frederick P. Gay, *The Open Mind: Elmer Ernest Southard* (1938); the sketch of Jarrett by Vida S. Grayson in *Notable American Women* (1980); and Howard Parad, "The Smith College School for Social Work in Perspective," *Smith College Studies in Social Work* (February, 1960), 175–186. Her obituary appeared in the *New York Times*, August 5, 1961.

ANN HARTMAN

**Johnson, Alexander** (January 2, 1847–May 17, 1941), social worker and expert on the care of the feebleminded, was born in Ashton-under-Lyne, Lancashire, England, the youngest of four children, to John Johnson, a devout Baptist and a prosperous merchant tailor, and Amelia (Hill) Johnson. He was educated at private schools and at Owens (later Victoria) College in Manchester. He was exposed to social work, however, not through his education but in his home. His parents provided food and money to the families of striking textile workers in the 1850s and to victims of the "cotton famine" in the 1860s. Partly to escape these conditions, he immigrated to Canada in 1869 and settled in Hamilton, where he worked in a tailoring factory. He lived with his employer, William Johnston, and on June 6, 1872, married Johnston's daughter, Eliza Ann. They had seven children.

Shortly after his marriage, Johnson moved to Chicago, and then to Cincinnati, where he worked in the manufacture of clothing. In 1882 he volunteered as a "friendly visitor" to the poor for the Cincinnati Associated Charities, and two years later was offered the position of general secretary. In 1886 he was called to a similar position with the Chicago Charity Organization Society.

He thus was closely identified with "scientific" charity. He believed that indiscriminate almsgiving made people dependent. He advocated cooperation among agencies and a central registry to avoid duplication of services; investigation of the facts before providing a remedy; a work test to assess the character of the poor; and different methods for helping the worthy and unworthy. When relief was warranted, however, he thought that it should be adequate. He also thought that much poverty was due to social causes, such as lack of employment and low wages.

Opposition from the well-established Chicago Relief and Aid Society and an opportunity offered him in 1889 by his friend Oscar C. McCulloch* led Johnson to move to Indiana to become secretary of the newly created State Board of Charities, whose function was to oversee the state's welfare institutions. His skill in dealing with people of varied temperament, abilities, and political loyalties, and with administrators, politicians, and newspaper reporters, as well as his gentle tact and uncompromising integrity, resulted in wide acclaim. When in 1893 the governor needed someone to administer the state's school for the feebleminded, Johnson, with some trepidation, accepted the appointment as superintendent. There, he promoted humane permanent institutional care, prevention of reproduction through segregation of the sexes, and training in useful occupations. A master of economical administration, he believed that the feebleminded could be well cared for at little cost to the taxpayer by utilizing their labor, especially in caring for one another, in helping to construct their facilities, and in growing food. However, he resigned the superintendency in 1903 in the belief that his way of handling the problem was not favored by the new governor and the institution's board of trustees.

In 1904 Johnson became associate director of the New York School of Philanthropy and paid secretary of the National Conference of Charities and Correction (NCCC), whose meetings he had first attended in 1884 while employed by Cincinnati's Associated Charities (and which he had served as unpaid secretary for several years and as president in 1897). His increasing duties with the National Conference led him to resign his post with the New York School in 1906, although he continued to lecture there and at other schools of social work as well. Meanwhile, his work with the NCCC brought that organization wider participation and added financial strength and helped to make it a forum for social reform as well as improved administration of services. The Conference, which earlier had been dominated by the secretaries of the state boards of charities, was reorganized under his impetus to include those engaged in reform as well as those mainly providing services. He also believed that the records of the meetings were repositories of important information about social work administration and reform, and thus he carefully edited their *Proceedings* and prepared an index of the first thirty-three conferences as well as an annotated bibliography of the works cited in them.

In 1911 Johnson's wife died. Also, feeling that he had achieved a great deal in his work with the Conference, he sought a change, which he found with his brother, whom he had brought to Indiana years earlier to organize an educational program for his feebleminded charges. In 1912 his brother, who then was principal of the Vineland (New Jersey) Training School, invited Johnson to establish an extension program for his institution in order to spread its occupational training efforts to other such schools throughout the nation. When, in 1915, the "extension department" was moved to Philadelphia, Johnson became its field secretary, where he succeeded in promoting progressive legislation and programs for the improved treatment and training of the retarded in more than thirty states throughout America.

Having gone about as far as he could along those lines, in 1918 Johnson went to work for the American Red Cross, first in the Home Service division, where he assisted soldiers and their families, and later as a lecturer for the Red Cross in its southern division. He retired in 1922 but continued writing, consulting, and working with the National Conference.

Known to his many professional friends across the country as "Uncle Alec," Johnson was extremely capable, energetic, and devoted to his work, driving himself to the point of nervous exhaustion several times during his career. Yet he was humorous and an entertaining as well as an informative speaker, with a friendly and optimistic disposition. He died at the age of ninety-four in Aurora, Illinois.

The basic sources on Johnson's life are a piece on him by Hace Tishler in *Dictionary of American Biography*, 3rd supplement (1973); and Johnson's autobiography, *Adventures in Social Welfare* (1923). His book, *The Almshouse* (1911), and his addresses and articles in the *Proceedings* of the NCCC and in *Survey* magazine are also of interest. Other sources of interest are published at the end of Tishler's biographical sketch, referred to above.

He compiled the *Cumulative Index of the Proceedings of the National Conference of Charities and Correction, vols. 1–33* (1907), and *A Guide to the Study of Charities and Correction by Means of the Proceedings of the National Conference of Charities and Correction Using Thirty-Four Volumes, 1874–1907* (1908). He wrote *On Being a Director: An Open Letter to One of the Board of a Society for Organizing Charity* (1910) and *The Menace of the Mentally Defective*, with Margaret Johnson Lane (1916).

FRED M. COX

# K

Kahn, Dorothy (August 15, 1893–August 26, 1955), welfare administrator, community organizer, program planner, and policy developer in the areas of child and family services, immigration, relief administration, and international social work, was born in Seattle, Washington, to Julius and Viola (Cohen) Kahn. Her mother was the daughter of a famous rabbi (George Cohen). Her father, an innovative and successful businessman, was president of a large mail order house, and later, as an executive of a nationwide drug firm, originated the one-cent sale. Dorothy was the eldest of three children in the economically secure family, which moved to Chicago when she was a young girl. After attending high school in Chicago, she enrolled in Wellesley College, from which she graduated in 1915.

Kahn was a gifted musician, and her family hoped that she would pursue that as a career after graduating from college. Although music remained a great pleasure all her life, Kahn's interest in social work had been stimulated by her friend and neighbor Frances Taussig, executive head of the Jewish family agency in Chicago, and she returned to the Windy City to join its staff as a caseworker. This was the period of Grace* and Edith Abbott's* and Sophonisba Breckinridge's* pioneering work in social welfare in Chicago, and Kahn was influenced by these women.

Her unusual abilities were quickly recognized, and in 1919, at the age of twenty-six, she went to Baltimore to become superintendent of the Hebrew Benevolent Association, a traditional charity organization society operating in the spirit of "noblesse oblige." The new superintendent, who became imbued with the reformist views of the Chicago social work world, quickly challenged the agency's philosophy. She believed that social service, like education, should be universal and publicly supported, pointing out that the vast subsidization of colleges and other educational institutions did not undermine students or create a "dependency neurosis." She looked forward to the day when "a widow receiving a state pension may be the chief social case worker in her community and the erstwhile president of a family society may be the client of his staff member."

In 1929 Kahn assumed leadership of the Jewish Welfare Society of Philadelphia where, according to Rosa Wessel, case supervisor, she immediately initiated a study of the agency's philosophy of relief giving, questioning right down to the core its casualness, its sentimentality, and its control of the client. This was at a time when relief was to be used as a "tool in treatment" and when a major function of the family agency was the case distribution of financial assistance, associated with advice and counsel.

When the Great Depression brought the transfer of the relief function to the public sector, Kahn was appointed the first executive director of the Philadelphia County Relief Board. In this position, and as president of the American Association of Social Workers in 1934–1935, she fought for democratic principles in the development and administration of programs for public assistance. She attacked the commonly heard statement that because of the Depression, people were poor "through no fault of their own" on the grounds that such a statement was an expression of the popular belief that under other conditions, people were in need through some fault of their own, a view which she felt unfortunately shaped relief administration in the United States. She believed that the association of casework with relief giving grew out of this assumption and out of culturally determined sanctions connected with financial dependency.

She saw financial security as a right of all citizens and the administration of relief on a case-by-case basis as one halting step on the path to universal income maintenance. In 1935 she convened and keynoted the American Association of Social Workers' Delegate Conference called to study financial assistance. The proceedings of this conference, *The Business of Relief*, were widely read and highly influential. That same year she reported on relief practices in this country to the International Conference of Social Work. Her report was later published as *Unemployment and Its Treatment in the United States* (1937). During her years in Philadelphia, she was closely associated with the Pennsylvania School of Social Work, where she taught and also developed continuing education programs to prepare people to work in public welfare. Her influence was extended through her students, many of whom went on to occupy positions of leadership.

Dorothy Kahn's name was catapulted into the headlines in September, 1938, when, amidst controversy, she was fired without a hearing from her position as director of the Philadelphia Relief Board. City politicians had decided that control of public relief was an important political asset, and Dorothy Kahn was not to be controlled. Although a temporary victory for political party control of relief distribution, the firing of Dorothy Kahn gave great impetus to the growing movement to develop civil service standards and protection for public welfare employees.

Kahn left Philadelphia to become associate executive director of the American Association of Social Workers, where she worked on the development of training and standards for public welfare workers, on strengthening public welfare's relationship with professional social work, and on stimulating and establishing guidelines for the Association and its members to participate in social action.

During World War II she served as director of family service at the National Refugee Service, and as chairman of the Subcommittee on Unemployment Relief of the President's Committee on Social Security. Following the war, she became executive director of the Health and Welfare Council of New York City, focusing attention on groups suffering from unmet needs, such as the aged and newly immigrating Puerto Ricans.

As the boundaries of Dorothy Kahn's interest and concern continually enlarged, her last and perhaps most challenging position was as chief of the Social Welfare Section of the Department of Social Affairs of the United Nations from 1950 to 1955. In this position, she worked on such basic problems as nutrition for children throughout the world and the planning of education and welfare activities of governments in behalf of their children and youth. She advised Israel on the organization of that nation's Ministry of Social Welfare, represented the United Nations in conferences on child welfare in Madras and Bombay, and conducted a United Nations seminar on the training of auxiliary and community workers in Gandigram, India.

Dorothy Kahn involved herself with depth and intensity in everything she did, yet, despite the increasing responsibility and demands the years brought, she managed to return most weekends to the Bucks County farmhouse she shared with her friend Helen Wallerstein. There, at Hickory Farm, she involved herself with equal intensity in music, cooking, and gardening. She was a memorable hostess and loved to entertain. Upon her retirement from the United Nations, she returned to Hickory Farm, anticipating the free time to devote to her friend and to her many interests. A few months following her retirement, hurricane "Diana" swept through the area, bringing floods and desolation. Dorothy Kahn responded to the disaster with her accustomed dedication and spent herself in organizing emergency relief for her Bucks County neighbors. She died in New Hope, Pennsylvania, a few days later, on August 26, 1955.

Dorothy Kahn's life was expressed primarily in action rather than in words; consequently, there are few written sources on her life or work. However, her thinking can be traced through a series of published works appearing over the years, from "The Future of Family Social Work," in *The Family* 9 (1928), 185–188, to "The Challenge of World Wide Need," *Journal of Social Work Process* 6 (1955), 1–14. Also, several of her papers appeared in the *Proceedings* of the National Conference of Social Work, especially between 1933 and 1940. Obituaries appeared in the *New York Times*, August 27, 1955, and the *Journal of Social Work Process* 6 (1955), v-viii.

ANN HARTMAN

**Kander, Elizabeth (Lizzie) Black** (May 28, 1858–July 25, 1940), settlement worker, was born in Milwaukee, Wisconsin, one of six children of John Black, a prosperous dry goods merchant, and Mary (Pereles) Black. In 1881, several years after graduating from a local high school and deciding not to attend college, she married Simon Kander; the couple had no children.

Kander's reasons for becoming a social welfare activist were personal, social, and intellectual. She believed that upper-middle-class women should not live a life of idleness. Instead, they should use their characteristically feminine interests and talents for social improvement. Throughout her life she concentrated on improving the lives of women and children and strengthening families, all of which were considered distinctively female concerns. She devoted much of her time to working among her Jewish coreligionists because of her belief in Jewish traditions of charity, her fear that the poverty and behavior of Eastern European immigrants might stimulate anti-semitism, and her presumable adherence to Reform Judaism's ethical emphasis on creating social conditions that would allow people to fulfill their potential. Her knowledge of the ideas and activities of the Americanization, charity organization, and settlement house movements expanded the Jewish roots of her thought and provided her with guides for action. As she put her ideas into action in numerous organizations and committees, she became Milwaukee's best-known social welfare activist between around 1900 and the 1920s.

Kander was an early member of the Ladies Relief Sewing Society, a kind of almsgiving group founded in 1879 to provide warm clothing for the children of the poor. In the misery caused by the depression of the 1890s and the swell in Milwaukee's immigrant population, her work began to broaden, probably in response to the emergence of environmentalism in American social thought and the spread of new kinds of social welfare activities. In 1895 she led a group of educated, upper-middle-class Jewish women in founding the Keep Clean Mission. The Mission, which was housed in Kander's predominantly German Jewish Reform synagogue, was intended to impress upon Eastern European immigrant children the women's version of the American way of life through association with the volunteers and weekly meetings with sermons on cleanliness and regular school attendance. The children did not respond well to this program, so in 1896 Kander organized the Milwaukee Jewish Mission. This organization reduced sermonizing and added cooking and sewing classes, industrial education, and instruction in crafts. Educating the children of the poor for skilled jobs, Kander now believed, would reduce poverty in the long run, and the cooking and sewing classes would teach girls skills they would need to be effective housewives and mothers.

In 1900 Kander led the effort that brought together the Milwaukee Jewish Mission and the Sisterhood of Personal Service, which operated night classes for immigrants, to create The Settlement. This was one of the major achievements of Kander's life. At various times in its history, The Settlement provided night classes, a savings bank, clubs, social activities, a branch of the Milwaukee

Public Library, baths, recreational facilities for children, and a food business that provided jobs for unemployed women and mothers who wanted part-time work. As she worked among the poor, Kander discovered that some of their problems required political action. She used her influence to put pressure on the city government to enforce its housing laws and to clean the streets and alleys in the ghetto. She spread the influence of The Settlement by working with established public and private organizations on demonstration projects that these organizations adopted and carried on. For example, she joined with the public school system to create in the ghetto the first adequately equipped playground in the city and to introduce new aspects of industrial education into the schools, and she worked with the Milwaukee Normal School to start pre-kindergarten classes.

In 1912 The Settlement's name was changed to Abraham Lincoln House; Kander served as its president until 1918. In 1931 she was instrumental in spreading many of the educational and recreational activities of the Abraham Lincoln House from the ghetto to the entire Jewish community with the founding of the Jewish Center.

Some of the money to start the Jewish Center, as well as much of the money that supported The Settlement and the Abraham Lincoln House, came from the most innovative and best-known project with which Lizzie Kander was associated, the publication of *The Settlement Cook Book*. The first edition, published in 1901, was entitled *The Way to a Man's Heart*. One purpose of the book was to provide written recipes for women who could not attend cooking classes or who needed reinforcement for what they learned in the classes. Another was to offer advice on the American style of cooking and the preparation of inexpensive, nutritious meals. The book was an immediate success and became (and remains) one of the best-selling cookbooks of the twentieth century.

Kander's well-publicized interest in the problems of children and her work on their behalf led to her election to the Board of School Directors in 1907. She served until 1919. Her major achievement as a board member was leading the fight for the creation of the Girls' Trades and Technical High School, which opened in 1909.

Lizzie Kander's social welfare activities and reputation were primarily local. Though a significant portion of her work and thought had a Jewish cast, her activities themselves were little different in kind from those of thousands of other nonprofessional female social welfare activists in cities throughout the nation during the first two decades of the twentieth century. Kander died in 1940 in Milwaukee.

Sources for studying the life of Lizzie Kander are scarce and fragmentary. The principal ones are a small collection of papers at the Milwaukee County Historical Society and a larger and richer one available at both the State Historical Society of Wisconsin and the University of Wisconsin-Milwaukee Library Area Research Center. Also at the State Historical Society of Wisconsin are two other sources that contain Kander material: an oral history by Rae Ruscha and the staff reports of the Wisconsin Jewish Archives.

Ann Shirley Waligorski, "Social Action and Women: The Experience of Lizzie Black Kander," Master's thesis, University of Wisconsin-Madison, 1969, is an intelligent biographical study. Louis J. Swichkow and Lloyd P. Gartner, *The History of the Jews of Milwaukee* (1963), is the only comprehensive history of Milwaukee Jewry, but it must be used with caution. David Paul Thelen, *The New Citizenship: Origins of Progressivism in Wisconsin, 1885–1900* (1972), is an outstanding study that deals in part with urban problems and reforms and places Kander in a firm historical context. Useful for comparing Kander's settlement house with others across the nation are Robert A. Woods and Albert J. Kennedy, eds., *Handbook of Settlements* (1911), and Allen F. Davis, *Spearheads for Reform: The Social Settlements and the Progressive Movement, 1890–1914* (1967).

STANLEY MALLACH

**Kaplan, Mordecai Menachem** (June 11, 1881–November 8, 1983), rabbi, professor, Jewish communal leader, and founder of Jewish Reconstructionism, was born in Svencionys, Lithuania, to Rabbi Israel and Anna Kaplan. At age nine Kaplan migrated to the United States with his parents, who reared him in an atmosphere of traditional Judaism. Kaplan was enrolled, at age twelve, in the high school preparatory department of the Jewish Theological Seminary of America, beginning an association with JTS that was to last throughout most of his lifetime. While attending JTS, where he was ordained rabbi in 1902, Kaplan also matriculated at the City College of New York (B.A., 1900) and Columbia University (M.A., 1902).

During these years Kaplan studied and was influenced by the works of Emile Durkheim, Matthew Arnold, John Dewey, and George Herbert Mead. Their writings, along with those of the ancient rabbis and the contemporary cultural Zionist Ahad Haam, constituted the major sources for his own formulation of Jewish Reconstructionism. In a modern American society where the political autonomy of the Jewish people did not exist and where the belief in a supernatural, personal God who enjoyed a special relationship with the Jewish people was, in Kaplan's view, untenable, it was the Reconstructionist conception of Judaism, and the course of action that flowed from it, which Kaplan regarded as essential for the preservation of Judaism and the Jewish people.

Kaplan's Reconstructionism focused on the proposition that Judaism was the creation of the Jewish people and, as such, existed for the people's sake. This fostered, in Kaplan's phrase, a "Copernican Revolution" in Jewish thought, for it placed the people of Israel, not its God, at the center of Jewish religious reflection. Kaplan thus viewed Judaism as an "evolving religious civilization," and his classic work detailing his philosophy of Jewish Reconstructionism, published in 1934, was therefore entitled *Judaism as a Civilization*. In this, as well as in his other writings, Kaplan contended that the Jewish people, as the authors of their own religious forms, had engaged throughout history in a process of definition and redefinition of these forms, thereby allowing them to sustain the people. While theology and abstract ideas had a place in Judaism, that place was a pragmatic one, designed to enhance both the life of the group and the individuals who comprised it. The meaning attached to the various rites of Judaism, as well as the concepts of God and Torah, could thus be understood and evaluated only in relation to the reality of a living Jewish people. Judaism, to survive the exigencies of a modern, voluntaristic America, had to find a contemporary expression of the Jewish religion which would foster the establishment of an "organic community" where all the elements that constitute a civilization could play a role in the life of the Jew.

This expression, in Kaplan's view, was Reconstructionism, and he viewed the institution of the synagogue as central to this process of community-building. The synagogue now had to function as more than a house of prayer and study, and Kaplan set out to "reconstruct" that institution to meet the challenge of the day. He therefore proposed that the synagogue be converted into an all-embracing center of Jewish cultural and social activity. The synagogue building would become a "Jewish center," complete with pool, gym, library, and other facilities, the primary purpose of which no longer would be worship, but "social togetherness."

Kaplan's teachings attracted an audience early in his career, and the Orthodox Jewish Center of Manhattan, which partially viewed itself in Kaplanian terms, invited Kaplan to serve as its rabbi in 1915. He accepted the call and occupied this pulpit until 1921. His heterodox religious views ultimately clashed with a significant percentage of the membership, however, and in 1922, after leaving the Jewish Center, he established the Society for the Advancement of Judaism in New York, an organization he envisaged as fulfilling the cultural, spiritual, and social needs of its members. The large number of contemporary synagogues which follow this pattern, either wholly or in part, provides ample testimony to the influence of Kaplan's ideals on the American Jewish landscape.

Kaplan's ability to spread his teachings and transform his dream of an "organic Jewish community" into something of a reality occurred, in part, because of the key positions he held throughout his lifetime. In 1909 he became dean of the Teachers Institute at the Jewish Theological Seminary, and in 1910 he began teaching in the seminary's Rabbinical School, continuing in this role until 1963. Generations of Conservative rabbis and educators thus came under his direct tutelage. In addition, Kaplan's publications allowed him to disseminate his program among Reform rabbis, and he achieved a significant following among them. His philosophy of Reconstructionism and his plans for an organic community were also transmitted directly to the world of Jewish communal service, for besides his other posts, Kaplan taught at the Graduate School for Jewish Social Work in New York from 1925 to 1937. There he gave courses on such topics as "The Organization of Jewish Life" and "The Problems of Jewish Self-Adjustment." The popularity of Kaplan's philosophy of Jewish peoplehood among so many

Jewish social workers, and its embodiment in the Jewish Community Center movement, reflects the impact he had on many Jewish social work students during these years. His program of Jewish Reconstructionism transcended denominational affiliations, and though Kaplan had more than his share of theological critics, there is no doubt that his death in New York City at the age of 102 brought to a close the life of one of the seminal figures in American Jewish history.

Students of Kaplan can discover correspondence by and about him, and other archival sources concerning him, in the libraries of the American Jewish Archives, located on the campus of Hebrew Union College-Jewish Institute of Religion, in Cincinnati, Ohio, and the American Jewish Historical Society, in Waltham, Massachusetts, at Brandeis University. In addition, a major collection of Kaplan's papers and correspondence can be found in the Kaplan Archives at the Reconstructionist Rabbinical College in Wyncote, Pennsylvania. A catalogue of this correspondence has been published by Richard Libowitz in Ronald Brauner, ed., *Jewish Civilization: Essays and Studies*, vol. 2 (1981).

Kaplan's major works, besides *Judaism as a Civilization*, include *Questions Jews Ask* (1956), *Judaism Without Supernaturalism* (1958), *The Greater Judaism in the Making* (1960), *The Meaning and Purpose of Jewish Existence* (1964), and *The Religion of Ethical Nationhood* (1970).

Secondary works on Kaplan's life and thought have been voluminous, and numerous issues of two journals, *Judaism* and the *Reconstructionist*, have devoted countless essays and studies to Kaplan. Two secondary assessments of major importance are Ira Eisenstein and Eugene Kohn, eds., *Mordecai M. Kaplan: An Evaluation* (1952), and Charles Liebman, "Reconstructionism in American Jewish Life," *American Jewish Year Book*, vol. 71 (1970).

DAVID ELLENSON

**Kehew, Mary Morton Kimball** (September 8, 1859–February 13, 1918), social reformer and champion of working women, was born in Boston, Massachusetts, the daughter of Moses Day Kimball, a merchant and banker, and Susan (Tillinghast) Morton. Her family was a noted one in New England, dating back to the seventeenth century. Her maternal grandfather, Marcus Morton, had been governor of Massachusetts in 1825, 1840–1841, and 1843–1844. Her family was well-to-do and provided her with an education in American, French, German, and Italian private schools, where she developed an early interest in the social sciences.

On January 8, 1880, she married William B. Kehew of Boston. They had no children. Her husband was a successful merchant who, while not active in social reform, is thought to have encouraged his wife to participate in social causes.

Mary Kehew's earliest and most noted work was with the Women's Educational and Industrial Union. This organization was formed in 1877 to meet the social and economic needs of young working women in Boston. Like many similar organizations which were springing up throughout the country at this time, such as the YWCAs, the New York Women's Hotel, and the Boston Home for Working Women, it had been founded by female philanthropists to provide temporary shelter and employment information for working women. The Boston Women's Educational and Industrial Union provided, in addition, reading rooms, parlors for socializing, and low-cost meals. The Boston Union has been cited for its relative sensitivity to the then widespread problem of patronizing young women. In this regard, it has been considered a forerunner of the settlement house ethic.

Mary Kehew joined the Women's Educational and Industrial Union in 1886, and her work was soon well known. She became director of the Union in 1890 and served as its third president from 1892 to 1913. She returned to the presidency from 1914 to 1918 and served as chairman of the Board of Governors until her last years.

Through her involvement in the Union, Mary Kehew met and encouraged leading trade union organizers such as Mary Kenney, a former Hull-House worker, and John F. O'Sullivan. These two American Federation of Labor (AFL) leaders, later to be married to each other, are credited with establishing more than forty unions of women workers. Mary Kehew promoted the Women's Educational and Industrial Union as a base of activities for their work. Working with Mary Kenney, for example, she helped establish the Union for Industrial Progress, organizing bookbinders, laundry workers, tobacco workers, and women in the garment trades.

Kehew also was instrumental in establishing a research unit at the Women's Educational and Industrial Union (1905) to provide systematic data on industrial conditions and abuses—a forerunner of the Massachusetts Department of Labor and Industry. The body of data gathered by that unit, as well as its unique methods, came to be used in universities and colleges as illustrations of industrial data-gathering techniques. Under Kehew's guidance, the Union also took on an educational direction. In addition, schools of dressmaking, housekeeping, and salesmanship were started. Eventually, the Union began to include college women in its program and assisted them through its Appointment Bureau, begun in 1910.

Mary Kehew's other outstanding role was her assumption, in 1903, of the first presidency of the Women's Trade Union League. This organization was a natural outgrowth of the labor organizing that had gone on in the previous quarter century. The League was modeled on the British Women's Protective and Provident League, founded in 1874 by Emma Patterson and renamed in 1890 the Women's Trade Union League. Its goal was the formation and coalition of women's trade union organizations. The American philanthropist and settlement worker William English Walling* had visited the English organization and had been impressed by its mission. He went to Boston to enlist the cooperation of Mary Kenney O'Sullivan and the AFL, then meeting in Boston. The National Women's Trade Union League was officially organized in Faneuil Hall in Boston on November 14, 1903.

The new organization sought to link together in a national network all women who were members of unions or sympathetic to the trade union cause. When a slate of officers was chosen, Mary Kehew, with her national reputation in women's causes, was offered the first presidency, a move designed to promote broad public acceptance of the organization. Kehew served with Jane Addams* of Chicago's Hull-House, who was named first vice president, Mary Kenney O'Sullivan, who was secretary, and Mary Donovan of the Boot and Shoe Workers Union, who was treasurer. Serving on the first board were Lillian Wald* of New York's Henry Street Settlement, Mary McDowell* of the University Settlement of Chicago, and Leonora O'Reilly,* another New York settlement organizer and labor leader. The Women's Trade Union League ultimately was to become a major platform for progressive causes in labor and settlement work.

Kehew also was active in many other progressive social welfare activities. She assisted in the founding of the Massachusetts branch of the American Association for Labor Legislation and was one of the founders of Denison House, a settlement organization in Boston. She also was one of the founders of Woolson House, a settlement for blind women. Kehew's extensive efforts on behalf of the blind also included the development of the Massachusetts Association for Promoting the Interest of the Adult Blind, the founding of a Loan and Aid Association for the Blind, and the creation of a magazine entitled *The Outlook for the Blind*. She also was an active board member of the Public School Association, the Massachusetts State Commission for Industrial Education, the Massachusetts Child Labor Committee, the Massachusetts Factory Inspection Commission, and the Massachusetts Minimum Wage Commission. Mary Kehew also served as president of the General Federation of Women's Clubs and was a trustee of Simmons College.

Mary Kehew, the "socialite reformer," is remembered for her energy and dedication to so many progressive social causes. She was described by Wellesley economics professor and settlement worker Emily Balch* as "the greatest social statesman I have ever known." Her extensive ties with the leading social reformers of her era placed her in the mainstream of progressive social welfare. She died in Boston at the age of fifty-eight.

Papers of the Boston Women's Educational and Industrial Union are available through its Boston Office. Its study series, The Economic Relations of Women, prepared by its Department of Research, was published by Longman's, Green and Co., New York; a few volumes were published in-house. Some materials on the Women's Educational and Industrial Union are available at the Arthur and Elizabeth Schlesinger Library, Radcliffe College, Boston. See S. Agnes Donham, "History of the Women's Educational and Industrial Union," (1955). Simmons College has papers of the collaborative research conducted by the two organizations.

Papers of the Women's Trade Union League have been collected at the Library of Congress and the Arthur and Elizabeth Schlesinger Library, Radcliffe College. The two collections are available on microfilm and are indexed in *Papers of the*

*Women's Trade Union League and Its Principal Leaders, Guide to the Microfilm Edition* (1981). An annotated bibliography is included.

Secondary sources on the two organizations include Gladys Boone, *The Women's Trade Union League in Great Britain and the United States* (1942); Allen Davis, "The Women's Trade Union League: Origins and Organization," *Labor History* (Winter, 1964), 3–17; Eleanor Flexner, *Century of Struggle* (1974); Philip S. Foner, *Women and the American Labor Movement* (1979); Robin Jacoby, "The Women's Trade Union League and American Feminism," *Feminist Studies* (Fall, 1975); James J. Kenneally, *Women and American Trade Unions* (1981).

For biographical data on Kehew's family, see Leonard Allison Morrison and Stephen Paschall Sharples, *History of the Kimball Family in America from 1634 to 1897*, 2 vols. (1897). Obituary columns are in the *Boston Transcript* (February 13, 1918) and the *Boston Herald and Journal* (February 14, 1918). Kehew is also cited in *Dictionary of American Biography* (1961); *Notable American Women 1607–1950* (1971); and *The International Dictionary of Women's Biography* (1982).

MARQUE-LUISA MIRINGOFF

**Keller, Helen** (June 27, 1880–June 1, 1968), blind deaf mute remembered not only for her own extraordinary educational attainments but for her work on behalf of all handicapped persons, especially the deaf blind, was born in Tuscumbia, Alabama, to Arthur H. and Kate (Adams) Keller. Her father had been a captain in the Confederate army, and her mother was a descendant of the famous New England Adamses. Nevertheless, the family lived in genteel poverty until Arthur Keller was appointed U.S. Marshall in northern Alabama with the election of Grover Cleveland to the presidency.

Helen was born with normal hearing and sight and had learned to speak a few words before contracting a serious fever at age nineteen months, which left her deaf and blind. Her mother had read of Laura Bridgman, a blind deaf mute who had been taught to read, write, and speak by Dr. Samuel Gridley Howe.* Believing that something similar could be done for her daughter, Mrs. Keller appealed to Dr. Alexander Graham Bell,* inventor of the telephone, who had much experience in working with the deaf and a great interest in vocational training for handicapped persons. Bell referred Mrs. Keller to both Thomas Gallaudet* and Dr. Michael Anagnos, director of the Perkins Institute for the Blind in Boston. Anagnos immediately got in touch with Anne M. Sullivan, who soon was hired as a governess for Helen.

Sullivan had been abandoned by her father while she still was a child. She spent six years of her life at the Tewksbury, Massachusetts, poorhouse before attending Perkins Institute, from which she later was graduated. She suffered from seriously impaired vision throughout her life.

Anne M. Sullivan arrived at the Keller household on March 3, 1887. Her first step was to enforce discipline upon an unruly Helen, who had been overprotected and indulged because of her blindness and deafness. Two weeks after Helen learned to obey her teacher, she had a dramatic experience which opened the world of language to her. "Teacher," as Anne Sullivan was called, had been spelling words into the palm of Helen's hand. Helen continued to confuse the words M-U-G and W-A-T-E-R. When they later went for a walk and passed a pump where someone was pumping water, Teacher held Helen's hand under the spout and spelled the word W-A-T-E-R into the other hand. Instantly Helen realized the connection between the word "water" and the water flowing through her fingers. From that moment on she was anxious to know the names of all the objects in her world.

Helen and her teacher traveled to Boston the next year, where Helen attended the Perkins Institute; later, she would attend the Wright-Humanson School in New York City. During these years, Helen was also taught how to speak. In 1900, having passed the entrance exams, Helen Keller entered Radcliffe, from which she was graduated cum laude four years later. Her teacher attended classes with her and spelled the professor's lectures into her hand.

Anne Sullivan married John Macy, a socialist writer, in 1905. By 1909 Helen was calling herself a socialist and speaking out and writing in support of socialist causes. She accepted some financial support from Andrew Carnegie, but when Carnegie heard of Helen's socialist ideas he threatened to put her across his knee and spank her.

Helen Keller opposed World War I, especially American participation in it. She welcomed the Russian Revolution and wrote and spoke in support of Lenin, its architect. She abhorred Stalin's atrocities, however, and by World War II her pro-Russian statements were more muted.

She strongly supported the woman's suffrage movement and Margaret Sanger's* crusade for birth control. She opposed child labor and capital punishment. She supported the black civil rights movement long before it was a popular cause in America.

A Hollywood film made of Helen Keller's life, *Deliverance*, was a great disappointment, but Helen and her teacher did well on the lecture circuit. It was financially rewarding and brought many people into contact with her.

Anne Sullivan died October 29, 1936. She and Helen had been together for fifty years. Her place was taken by Polly Thomson from Scotland, who had joined their household as early as 1914, when Teacher's eyesight began to worsen.

Although Helen Keller had generally liked Woodrow Wilson and supported many of his policies, she found in President Franklin Roosevelt a kindred spirit. He had learned to live with his physical handicap and to succeed as she had done. Due to the support of Helen Keller, the Works Progress Administration (WPA) produced thousands of the first talking books for the blind. In addition, inclusion of Aid to the Blind in the Social Security Act of 1935 was due in part to her efforts and her personal friendship with FDR.

For many years, Helen Keller also worked for the American Foundation for the Blind. She was its most famous supporter and perhaps its greatest asset. She traveled widely across the United States and many countries of the world in support of the blind. She urged vocational training of the blind to make them self-supporting and independent. Always, however, she demonstrated a special interest in the deaf blind.

Throughout her life Helen Keller maintained a strong interest in socialism. Her espousal of left-wing causes often proved embarrassing to her friends, some of whom were persons of considerable wealth. The FBI developed a file on her various activities. There were times when her efforts on behalf of the blind were somewhat hampered because potential large donors were irritated and shocked by her political and social views. Nevertheless, in her later years Helen Keller became one of the best-known, best-loved, most respected persons in the world. She was the first woman to receive an honorary degree from Harvard University, as well as a host of other honors and awards from various organizations, universities, and nations. During her life she wrote a number of books, including her autobiography, *The Story of My Life* (1902), *Out of the Dark* (1913), *My Religion* (1927), *Midstream: My Later Life* (1929), her *Journal* (1938), and a book about Anne Sullivan entitled *Teacher* (1955). A documentary film on Helen's life, *The Unconquered*, was released in 1953, and four years later her life story was told in the first stage production of *The Miracle Worker*, written by William Gibson.

Helen continued her travels and untiring efforts on behalf of the handicapped, especially the blind, until she suffered a stroke in 1961, forcing her retirement from public life. Throughout, however, her philosophy could be summarized by her own statement, "I would rather walk with a friend in the dark than walk alone in the light." She died on June 1, 1968, at Arcan Ridge (near Westport), Connecticut.

There are three major collections of papers relating to Helen Keller. The most important is at the American Foundation for the Blind in New York City; the second is at the Perkins Institute in Watertown, Massachusetts, and the third is at the Alexander Graham Bell Association for the Deaf in Washington, D.C.

Several biographies of Helen Keller have been written, the most exhaustive of which is Joseph P. Lash's *Helen and Teacher* (1980). Other ones of merit are Van Wyck Brooks, *Helen Keller: Sketch for a Portrait* (1956); William Gibson, *The Miracle Worker: A Play for Television* (1957); and Richard Harrity and Ralph Martin, *The Three Lives of Helen Keller* (1962).

Substantial information about Helen Keller also can be found in Robert V. Bruce, *Bell: Alexander Graham Bell and the Conquest of Solitude* (1973); Thomas D. Cutsforth, *The Blind in School and Society: A Psychological Study* (1951); Selma Fraiberg, *Insights from the Blind* (1977); and Frances A. Koestler, *The Unseen Minority: A Social History of Blindness in the United States* (1976). A brief but splendid sketch of Keller appears in *The Encyclopedia Britannica* (1976), written by Merle E. Frampton.

JOHN W. LANDON

**Kelley, Florence** (September 12, 1859–February 17, 1932), social reformer and executive director of the National Consumers' League (NCL) from 1898 to 1932, was born in Philadelphia to Caroline Bartram (Bonsall) Kelley, a descendant of the early Quaker botanist, John Bartram, and William Darrah Kelley, a man of Protestant Irish descent with ancestors in America as early as 1662. A Garrisonian abolitionist in the 1850s, William Kelley served fifteen consecutive terms in the U.S. House of Representatives from 1860 to 1890, becoming known as "Pig-iron Kelley" for his advocacy of high protective tariffs for American industry, especially the iron and steel industries of Pennsylvania.

Florence Kelley thought of her career as building on her father's achievements, for he told her that the duty of his generation was to build up great industries in America so that more wealth could be produced for the whole people, while the duty of her generation would be to see that the product was distributed justly. William Kelley encouraged his daughter's social conscience at an early age by teaching her to read in a British book with woodcuts and text depicting the sufferings of laboring children. Apart from a few terms at Quaker and private schools in Philadelphia, Florence's education took place at home, where, between the ages of ten and seventeen, she systematically read through her father's extensive library.

Another important early influence on Kelley's subsequent career was the deaths in childhood and infancy of five sisters due to infections that were recognized as preventable fifty years later. Her mother's continuing melancholy for thirty years following these deaths cast a shadow over Kelley's adolescence and young adulthood, and doubtless contributed to her early commitment to a reform career on behalf of women and children.

Another lifelong influence was Kelley's great-aunt, Sarah Pugh, who lived with "Florrie's" maternal grandparents after 1864, giving her time for promoting the antislavery movement, peace, woman suffrage, the single standard of morals for men and women, and free trade. Young Florence was impressed by the ways Sarah Pugh put her conscience into action, refusing to consume goods produced by slaves, thus wearing no cotton and eating no sugar, and maintaining a regular correspondence with contemporary British liberals such as Richard Cobden, John Bright, and John Stuart Mill.

As a student at Cornell University from 1876 to 1882, Kelley continued the orientation toward social reform that had begun in her childhood. She was a founding member of the Cornell Social Science Club and its first secretary. Forced to drop out of college for two years due to poor nursing in Ithaca during a bout of diphtheria, Kelley lived for one year in Washington, D.C., where, under her father's tutelage, she wrote and published two ambitious research papers, using government reports in the Library of Congress. Their titles indicate the author's seriousness of purpose: "The Legal History of the Child Since Blackstone" and "Need Our Working Women Despair?"

Typical of many in this first generation of college-educated women, Florence Kelley did not find a way to translate her social concern into meaningful social action until nearly ten years after her graduation from college, when, in 1891, she joined Jane Addams,* Julia Lathrop,* and Ellen Gates Starr* at Hull-House in Chicago. Kelley's interval between college and a career differed from that of Addams, Lathrop, Starr, and other women reformers in the social settlement movement, however, in two basic respects. First, her postgraduate studies at the University of Zurich gave her a much more radical and systematic critique of the problems of her society than any of her colleagues, male or female, obtained elsewhere, and she experienced a lifelong conversion to socialism. Second, in 1884 she married Lazare Wischnewetzky, a Polish-Russian Jewish medical student who courted her with the writings of Marx and Engels. Between 1885 and 1887 she gave birth to three children, Nicholas, Margaret, and John, the last two in New York City, where she and her small family moved in 1886. In 1887 she oversaw the publication of her translation of Friedrich Engels' *The Condition of the Working Class in England in 1844*, which until 1958 was the only English translation of this classic work.

Abandoning translations and membership in the Socialist Labor Party as a formula for social reform, in 1888 Kelley resumed her interest in child labor and compulsory education, reading reports from state boards of education, census bureaus, and factory inspectors. By 1889 she had gained a reputation as an able critic of these reports through letters written to major urban newspapers. That year, during her first professional appearance, she was introduced by Carroll D. Wright, the nation's preeminent social statistician. While making her way in the world of public officials, Kelley also began to link arms with other women in forming organizations to promote protective labor legislation for women and children—particularly the Working Women's Society, a small group of women from both middle-class and working-class backgrounds, and the New York Consumers' League, founded in 1890, which also attracted a cross-class membership. These groups won a significant victory in 1890, when New York State passed legislation mandating the appointment of eight women factory inspectors. Significantly, in the late 1880s Kelley began writing for a female audience. For example, in 1889 she published a passionate and informative pamphlet, *Our Toiling Children*, with the Women's Temperance Publication Association of Chicago.

Kelley's life changed dramatically and her career rapidly accelerated from the apprentice to the journeyman stage of its development when she left her husband in December, 1891, due to grievous but unidentified actions on his part, and moved with her children to Chicago. Resuming her maiden name, Kelley quickly discovered Hull-House, founded two years earlier, where she was astonished by the generosity of the close friends she made there. Scholars of Jane Addams point to Kelley as the single most important influence in Addams' shift in the early 1890s from philanthropist to reformer.

Kelley's link with the social settlement movement supplied her with much more effective institutional support for her life work against the exploitation of women and children workers. For her and her colleagues the settlement provided a socially viable alternative to married family life and a historically unprecedented way of consolidating and collectivizing their skills and energies. Central to their success was the financial support of wealthy patrons, such as Mary Rozet Smith, devoted and lifelong friend of Jane Addams. After returning to New York to lead the National Consumers' League in 1899, Florence Kelley joined Lillian Wald's* Henry Street Settlement, where she lived until 1926.

Florence Kelley's reform activities in Chicago in the 1890s laid a solid foundation for her subsequent career with the National Consumers' League in New York. Her expertise and achievements had four dimensions, growing out of the four requirements for reform as she saw them: investigate, educate, legislate, enforce. As an investigator she was commissioned in 1892 by Ethelbert Stewart of the Illinois Bureau of Labor Statistics to investigate the sweating system of garment making in Chicago tenements, and by Carroll Wright, U.S. Commissioner of Labor, to undertake the Chicago portion of a five-city study of American slums. Information from the latter survey of Chicago's Nineteenth Ward became the basis for maps of unparalleled social detail, which were printed in 1895 in *Hull-House Maps and Papers*, a group effort for which Kelley arranged the publication. As an educator or publicist Kelley wrote primarily for professional audiences in the 1890s, including ten substantial articles on aspects of American reform published in German in *Archiv fur soziale Gesetzgebung und Statistik* of Berlin.

Most of Kelley's reform efforts in the 1890s were directed toward the Illinois state legislature, where in 1893 she successfully lobbied for antisweating legislation that included a landmark provision for an eight-hour day for all women workers in Illinois manufacturing. Kelley served as the state's first chief factory inspector, 1893–1897, the first and only woman in her lifetime to direct state factory law enforcement. With her talented staff of twelve, including Abraham Bisno, Alzina Stevens,* and Mary Kenney, housed in an office across the street from Hull-House, Kelley achieved significant gains for the eight-hour day for men as well as women until that provision of the legislation was declared unconstitutional by the Illinois Supreme Court in 1895. To enhance her power as a prosecutor, she completed a law degree at Northwestern University's night School in 1894, receiving credit for her earlier study at Zurich.

As secretary general of the National Consumers' League, Florence Kelley vastly expanded the scope and independence of her reform efforts in 1899. Through her ability to enlist persons of unusual character and talents, she had by 1905 helped to create sixty-four local leagues in twenty states, most of which looked to her and the national board for their reform agenda. League membership included large numbers of influential women in almost every industrial city in the United States. Where there was no League, as was the case in Birmingham, Alabama, Kelley assisted women who worked through the General Federation of Women's Clubs.

The League's first target was child labor, and in 1902 Kelley and Wald helped found the New York Child Labor Committee, following that in 1904 with the National Child Labor Committee. In the meantime Kelley produced a constant barrage of articles about child labor in professional journals such as *Charities and the Commons*, and in popular periodicals such as the *Sunday School Times*. Beginning in 1903 the League for many years maintained the nation's only reliable listing of current child labor legislation among the various states, holding up to other states the higher standards established by Massachusetts.

In her 1905 book, *Some Ethical Gains Through Legislation*, Kelley first proposed a national agency for the welfare of children, an idea finally realized in 1912 with the creation of the U.S. Children's Bureau, with Julia Lathrop as its director. In her book Kelley also pointed out that the 1905 U.S. Supreme Court decision in *Lochner v. New York* meant that labor legislation could only be justified on grounds of individual health, and it was on these grounds that her allies, Louis Brandeis and Josephine Goldmark,* succeeded in defending the constitutionality of state legislation concerning work hours for women in the 1908 landmark decision in *Muller v. Oregon*. (In 1917 the NCL successfully defended the constitutionality of hours legislation for men with analogous health arguments in *Bunting v. Oregon*.) After the passage of national wage legislation in Great Britain in 1909, Kelley devoted an increasing amount of her energy to the enactment of state minimum wage statutes, heading a movement that by 1923 had successfully lobbied for such laws in fifteen states, when in 1923 the Supreme Court declared the minimum wage statute of Washington, D.C., unconstitutional.

Expressing a lifelong interest in civil rights for black Americans, Florence Kelley was a founding member of the National Association for the Advancement of Colored People (NAACP). When he spoke at her memorial service in New York City in 1932, W. E. B. Du Bois* said that she had been an important ally. Before, during, and after World War I, Kelley joined Jane Addams, Alice Hamilton,* and other leading women reformers in a variety of peace campaigns.

Kelley believed that the high point of her career was reached in 1921 with the passage of the Sheppard-Towner Maternity and Infancy Protection Act, which for the first time allocated federal funds to states for the health and welfare of the American people. Testifying passionately on behalf of the act, Kelley entitled one of her 1920 *Survey* articles "Why Let Children Die?" and helped to organize the Women's Joint Congressional Committee, which oversaw lobbying for the act by a score of women's organizations. She continued to defend the act in 1927, when Congress failed to renew its funding.

The rising tide of conservatism during the 1920s plagued the closing decade of Kelley's career with political reversals. When right-wing publicists attacked her as a Bolshevik who was importing foreign ideas, Kelley wrote a brief autobiography that emphasized her blue Philadelphia blood, publishing it serially in *Survey*, where she had been an associate editor for many years.

By far the greatest reversal of the 1920s for Kelley was the campaign for the equal rights amendment waged by the National Woman's Party, which threatened to overturn her life's work on behalf of special legislation for women. From 1921 to 1923 Kelley devoted at least a third of her time to opposing equal rights legislation that might annul special legislation for women, such as the Sheppard-

Towner Act. In spite of these reversals, Kelley said that she remained confident that social legislation for children, women, and men would eventually become an accepted part of American political life.

Florence Kelley's historical significance goes beyond her critical role in the passage of specific laws to embrace the entire process by which social legislation is implemented—investigation justifying it, publicity and education promoting it, drafting it with attention to the judicial as well as the legislative branches of government, and enforcing it through the action of concerned citizens as well as government officials. She organized women to advance the rights and interests of children and women workers before women could vote in most states, drawing them into the process by which state and federal governments began to assume some responsibility for the health and welfare of average people.

Kelley died of cancer at Germantown (Pennsylvania) Friends Hospital.

Florence Kelley's family papers and a significant portion of her professional papers can be found in the Kelley Family Papers at Columbia University, and in the Nicholas Kelley Papers at the New York Public Library. Most of her professional papers are in the National Consumers' League Papers at the Library of Congress. Valuable correspondence between Kelley and Jane Addams can be found in the Hull-House Papers at the University of Illinois, Chicago. Other pertinent manuscript collections include the papers of the Massachusetts Consumers' League at the Schlesinger Library, Cambridge, Massachusetts.

Among Kelley's most important writings are her autobiographical articles, "My Philadelphia," *Survey* (October 1, 1926), 7–11, 50–57; "When Co-education Was Young," *Survey* (February 1, 1927), 557–561; "My Novitiate," *Survey* (April 1, 1927), 31–35; and "I Go to Work," *Survey* (June 1, 1927), 271–277. These articles have been reprinted in Kathryn Kish Sklar, ed., *Notes of Sixty Years* (1985), and in Leon Stein, ed., *Fragments of Biography* (1974). In the late 1890s she published seven articles in German in *Archiv fur soziale Gesetzgebung und Statistik* (Berlin). The most important of Kelley's voluminous writings are her books, *Some Ethical Gains Through Legislation* (1905; repr. 1969); *Modern Industry in Relation to the Family, Health, Education and Morality* (1914; repr. 1975); and *The Supreme Court and Minimum Wage Legislation* (1925). Most of her writings appeared in serial publications, especially *Charities and the Commons*, the *Survey* (where she was an associate editor), the *Annals of the American Academy of Political and Social Science*, the *Child Labor Bulletin*, *American Journal of Sociology*, *Journal of Political Economy*, *Arena*, *Independent*, *Outlook*, *Century*, and many others. Some of her major writings were published as pamphlets by the National Consumers' League, such as *The Present Status of Minimum Wage Legislation* (1913); *Wage-Earning Women in Wartime: The Textile Industry* (1919); and *Children's Compensation for Industrial Accidents: How the States Love Their Children* (1926).

For a brief study of Kelley's life see Louise Wade, "Florence Kelley," in *Notable American Women, 1607–1950: A Biographical Dictionary* (1971). For her early career before 1900 see Jane Addams, *My Friend, Julia Lathrop* (1935), chap. 7; Nicholas Kelley, "Early Days at Hull House," *Social Service Review* (December, 1954), 424–429; "Dear Mr. Engels: Unpublished Letters, 1884–1894, of Florence Kelley (-Wischnewetzky) to Friedrich Engels," *Labor History* 5 (1964); and Dorothy Rose Blumberg, *Florence Kelley: The Making of a Social Pioneer* (1966). For her work as general secretary of the National Consumer's League, see Josephine Goldmark, *Impatient Crusader: Florence Kelley's Life Story* (1953; repr. 1976); Louis L. Athey, "The Consumers' Leagues and Social Reform, 1890–1923," Ph.D. dissertation, University of Delaware, 1965; and Frances Perkins, "My Recollections of Florence Kelley," *Social Service Review* (March, 1954).

KATHRYN KISH SKLAR

**Kellogg, Arthur Piper** (March 18, 1878–July 20, 1934), editor and social reformer, was born and raised in Kalamazoo, Michigan, the eldest son of Frank Israel and Mary Foster (Underwood) Kellogg. His father administered the family lumber business until the 1890s, when it failed. Arthur and his more famous brother Paul,* best known as the team that for years edited the *Survey* and other social work publications, were as inseparable in their youth as they were during their adult years.

Arthur Kellogg married Augusta Louise Coleman on June 24, 1902. The two were divorced in 1925, and Kellogg then married Florence Loeb Fleischer, art editor for the *Survey Graphic*; he had no children by either marriage.

As Paul recalled in his obituary of Arthur, their first business venture was the "Kellogg Brothers: Chicken Dealers," a backyard enterprise of their boyhood days. Although Arthur Kellogg was the eldest of the two, both graduated from Kalamazoo High School in 1897, Arthur as class president and Paul as class historian. Following graduation, both joined the staff of the *Kalamazoo Daily Telegraph*, Arthur initially in the business office, later in the editorial department.

Arthur remained with the *Daily Telegraph* until 1902, when he resigned as city editor. During his term of employment with the Kalamazoo newspaper, he served for a year, 1900–1901, as clerk of the Michigan state legislature's Ways and Means and Railroad Committees, chaired by State Senator E. M. Dingley, the *Telegraph*'s owner. Kellogg then worked for a short time with the Dunkley-Williams Transportation Company in South Haven, Michigan, returning to newspaper work in January, 1903, as city editor of Kalamazoo's *Gazette-News*. He left that post in April, 1903, to join his brother in New York City.

Paul Kellogg had completed the course of study at the New York Charity Organization Society's Summer School of Philanthropy in 1902. Arthur completed the same program during the summer of 1903, and then joined his brother on the editorial staff of the Charity Organization Society's publication, *Charities*. Kellogg was to remain at his brother's side at *Charities*, ultimately renamed the *Survey*, until his death in 1934. He held a variety of posts with the publication: managing editor, 1908–1919; business manager, 1919–1925; and then managing editor again, 1926–1934. From 1920 he also served as treasurer for the Survey Associates, the journal's publishing company.

To write of Arthur Kellogg without describing the work of Paul Kellogg is nearly impossible. Yet writers and other commentators who have praised the work of Paul Kellogg and the *Survey*'s role—and that of its children, the *Survey Graphic* and *Survey Midmonthly*, as well—in advancing solutions to social problems often have overlooked Arthur Kellogg's contributions. Leon Whipple, *Survey Graphic* associate editor, said that Arthur was the unrecognized and anonymous force behind the *Survey* and the *Graphic*: Paul "cherished" the idea of the *Survey*, Whipple contended, but it was Arthur who gave that idea "body and breath."

As managing editor, Arthur Kellogg made sure that the publications went to press and were delivered to subscribers on time. All manuscripts for both publications—the *Survey Graphic* and the *Survey Midmonthly*—passed over his desk: Arthur was responsible for the editing, illustrations, layout, and proofreading. If the public failed to notice Arthur's work, the *Survey*'s staff did not: Lewis Hine* should be hired to photograph Arthur, quipped one staff member in 1922; the result would be yet another portrait of hard labor.

Arthur Kellogg's duties as managing editor gave him little time to exercise his writing talents. In 1927, however, he accompanied Secretary of Commerce Herbert Hoover and James L. Fieser, acting director general of the American Red Cross, through the flooded areas of the lower Mississippi River, from Vicksburg to New Orleans. The result was two major pieces: "Behind the Levees" (*Survey*, June, 1927, 277) and "Up from the Bottom Lands" (*Survey*, July, 1927, 360), and a *Survey* campaign to improve government watersheds planning. He also regularly penned the journal's "Gist" pages, editorial notes, captions, brief reviews, and the "Common Welfare" section. Kellogg died of a heart attack while asleep in his summer cottage near Katonah, New York.

Arthur's significant contribution to the *Survey* and its offshoots and his importance to his brother Paul are well described by historian Clarke A. Chambers in *Paul U. Kellogg and the Survey: Voices for Social Welfare and Social Justice* (1971). The publications' difficulties in adjusting to Arthur's early death are also described in that work.

Primary sources for studying the works and life of Arthur Kellogg are housed at the University of Minnesota's Social Welfare History Archives Center. They include the records of the Survey Associates and the papers of Paul U. Kellogg. As with the biography cited above, other printed sources focus on Paul Kellogg, secondarily mentioning Arthur.

SUSAN D. STEINWALL

**Kellogg, Paul Underwood** (September 30, 1879–November 1, 1958), editor and social reformer, was born and raised in Kalamazoo, Michigan, the youngest son of Frank Israel and Mary Foster (Underwood) Kellogg. Kellogg's father ran the family's lumber business until the early 1890s; when the company failed he left his family for Texas.

Shortly after graduating from Kalamazoo High School as class historian in 1897, Kellogg joined his older brother, Arthur Piper Kellogg,* on the *Kalamazoo Daily Telegraph*'s editorial staff. There, the brothers worked side by side until 1901, when Paul left Michigan to attend Columbia University in New York City. In 1902 he studied at the New York Charity Organization Society's Summer School of Philanthropy. Edward T. Devine* subsequently hired Kellogg as assistant editor of *Charities*, the Charity Organization Society's official publication. Arthur joined his brother at *Charities* in 1903. Together, the Kellogg brothers greatly expanded the publication's scope, merging it with the *Commons*, the settlement movement's official organ in 1905, and with the *Jewish Charity*, the voice of the United Hebrew Charities, a year later, making it into *Charities and the Commons*.

In 1909 Paul Kellogg married Marion Pearce Sherwood of Kalamazoo. The couple, who had two children, were divorced in 1934. In February, 1935, Paul married Helen Hall,* head resident of New York City's Henry Street Settlement, where he then resided.

Kellogg headed the research team that produced the first major survey of an American city, the Pittsburgh Survey. A team of scholars and Pittsburgh, Pennsylvania, community leaders gathered materials on nearly every aspect of life, publishing their findings in articles and then in a six-volume series. The study became a model for later sociological surveys and aided enormously in reform efforts to shorten the industrial work week, improve housing, and establish workers' compensation coverage.

Kellogg headed the Pittsburgh Survey research team full-time between 1907 and 1908 and then returned to his offices in New York to edit the thousands of manuscript pages the study team had generated. At the same time, he set about reshaping *Charities and the Commons* into the *Survey*. Borrowing its new name from the Pittsburgh Survey in 1909, the *Survey* was soon to become social work's "semi-official" journal and a stalwart reporter of social ills and the policies and programs designed to improve or eliminate them. In October, 1912, the Survey Associates, the journal's cooperative publishing society, was organized, thus severing ties between the publication and the New York Charity Organization Society. Also in 1912, Paul became editor-in-chief and brother Arthur assumed the managing editor's chair.

The *Survey Graphic*, published alternately with its parent, now known as the *Survey Midmonthly*, between 1921 and 1933 and then separately until 1949, was created to appeal to the general public. It lavishly used maps, charts, and illustrations to enliven its pages.

Kellogg believed, and the survey publications held, that once citizens were informed of the facts of social injustice they would be compelled to act to improve life. As a journalist, Kellogg also believed that the facts were much more forceful if they were expressed in terms of real people, something he practiced as well as preached. The *Survey*'s agenda of concerns included the major issues of urban and rural America during the first half of the twentieth century: housing, recreation, urban renewal, improvement of industrial conditions and workers' benefits, social insurance, regional planning, public health, and environmental conservation. Throughout its forty-year publishing history, the *Survey* frequently produced "special numbers" that gave the editorial staff space to explore issues in depth. These special issues covered Blacks (October 7, 1905; March, 1925), coal mining (April, 1922), Mexico (May, 1924), fascism (March, 1927), unemployment (April, 1929), juvenile delinquency (March, 1944), and other subjects.

The *Survey* employed a small staff of talented persons, including Beulah Amidon,* who wrote of industry and education, and Gertrude Springer,* who wrote a popular column under the name of "Miss Bailey" in the *Midmonthly*; these two women managed the *Graphic* and the *Midmonthly* following Arthur Kellogg's death in 1934. Although the *Survey*'s staff was small, the list of authors who wrote for it read like a who's who of early twentieth century reform; most wrote for little or no pay.

Paul Kellogg's career was consumed by the *Survey*, and the little time he spared for outside activities paralleled the publication's interest in social work and social reform. Kellogg chaired the National Conference of Charities and Correction's Committee on Occupational Standards in 1910; he was secretary to the Committee to Secure a Federal Commission on Industrial Relations, 1911–1913, and director and founder of the Foreign Policy Association. He was extremely active in the National Federation of Settlements, the American Association of Social Workers, and the National Conference on Social Welfare; participated in the defense of Sacco and Vanzetti; and was vice chair of an advisory council to President Franklin Delano Roosevelt's Committee on Economic Security, 1934–1935, which helped draft the Social Security Act.

As historian Clarke A. Chambers has pointed out, although Paul Kellogg was a superb editor, he was an ineffective administrator, and for that reason Arthur Kellogg's early death in 1934 ultimately crippled the organization. By the late 1940s, Paul was in ill health and the *Survey* was in grave financial trouble. The journal ceased publication in 1952. Kellogg died six years later in New Paltz, New York, where he and his wife Helen Hall had retired.

In addition to the numerous articles that appeared in the *Survey*, Kellogg was also author with Arthur Gleason of *British Labor and the War* (1919). Primary sources for studying his life and career are housed at the University of Minnesota's Social Welfare History Archives. Inventories to the records of the Survey Associates and the papers of Paul Kellogg are included in *DescriptiveInventories of Collections in the Social Welfare History Archives Center* (1970).

Secondary sources include Clarke Chambers' *Paul U. Kellogg and the Survey: Voices for Social Welfare and Social Justice* (1971). A brief account of the Survey Associates' history appears in *Social Service Organizations*, ed. Peter Romanofsky and Clarke Chambers (1978), 677.

The Pittsburgh Survey series includes: Elizabeth Beardsley Butler, *Women and the Trades, Pittsburgh* (1909); Crystal Eastman, *Work Accidents and the*

*Law* (1910); J. A. Fitch, *The Steel Workers* (1910); Margaret F. Byington, *Homestead: The Household of a Mill Town* (1910); Paul U. Kellogg, ed., *The Pittsburgh District Civic Frontage* (1914); and Paul U. Kellogg, ed., *Wage-earning Pittsburgh* (1914).

SUSAN D. STEINWALL

**Kellor, Frances** (October 20, 1873–January 4, 1952), social investigator and reformer who was especially active during the first two decades of the twentieth century in the efforts to improve the conditions under which black migrants (particularly women) moved from the South to northern cities, as well as in efforts to develop an organized, rational, and efficient response to the immigration of millions of Europeans, was born in Columbus, Ohio, to Daniel and Mary (Sprau) Kellor. Young Frances grew up in a middle-class family; her parents recognized the value of a good education for women and implanted a sense of service in their daughter not unlike that transmitted to children from similar circumstances who became active in the social settlement and other social reform movements of the early twentieth century.

However, due to financial difficulties arising from the death—or desertion—of her father, Kellor was able to secure only two years of a high school education (in Coldwater, Michigan) before taking a full-time job on a local newspaper. Later, however, after passing a special examination, she was admitted to Cornell University Law School, from which she graduated in 1897 with an LL.B. In 1898 Kellor continued her education, in sociology and social work, at the University of Chicago, maintaining formal affiliation with that institution for the next several years. In the summer of 1902, however, she moved to New York City to enroll in the New York Summer School of Philanthropy. Her outstanding work in that program brought her fellowships from the College Settlement Association between 1902 and 1904 for continued study.

Kellor's publications and activities reflected her recognition of the significant role environment played in the successful adjustment of migrants to their new homes. Both black migrants from the South and European immigrants were greeted by conditions that undermined successful adjustment and assimilation. She wrote continually of their dilemma and participated in the formation of committees and bureaus and in the formulation of laws and regulations that sought to improve the circumstances surrounding their reception and integration. One important result of her research was the revelation of how little information was available on unemployment and its impact upon black migrants and European immigrants alike.

To remedy that dearth of information and thus be able to advocate legal remedies, she organized with other social workers in New York City the Inter-Municipal League for Household Research. Sensing the need for a more extensive national network than the two associations in New York and Philadelphia to protect northward-bound black women from exploitation, Frances Kellor and Inter-Municipal League associates organized in 1906 the National League for the Protection of Colored Women, with the goals of providing accurate information to those coming north, protecting them during the trip, and assisting them in securing work upon their arrival. In 1911 the League became one of three agencies committed to assisting black adjustment to the urban environment to unite in the formation of the National League on Urban Conditions Among Negroes, better known as the National Urban League.

While Frances Kellor sought means to aid the transition of black Americans from the rural South to the urban North, she also was involved in assisting the adjustment of European migrants to America and that of the native-born to the new arrivals. They were a focal point of the research discussed in her publications and in the advocacy of the Inter-Municipal Bureau for Household Research. In fact, investigations of the Bureau convinced New York's Governor Charles Evans Hughes to appoint, in the fall of 1908, the New York State Immigration Commission, which Kellor served as secretary.

With Lillian Wald,* Kellor spent the following year studying the living and working conditions of New York's immigrants. There is little doubt that the environment in which Frances Kellor found them, and the apparent lack of any state or federal concern for those conditions, led to a heightened commitment by her to the process of assimilation and Americanization of the immigrant.

Convinced by the Wald and Kellor reports that New York must both strengthen legal protection of immigrants and provide continuing oversight of their reception, the Commission recommended the establishment of a permanent agency. The Governor and the legislature concurred and in October, 1910, created the Bureau of Industries and Immigration, with Frances Kellor as director, a position she held from 1910–1913.

The findings of the Immigration Commission were promoted, as well, by another organization in whose founding (December, 1909) and subsequent work Kellor played a major role, the New York branch of the North American Civic League for Immigrants. Under her influence the New York committee developed a five-point program in which the federal government had the major role for the implementation of a national domestic policy for aliens. This emphasis upon a positive role for the state in the Americanization process created tension with the parent Boston branch of the Civic League. Reflecting its dissatisfaction with the immigration restriction positions of Boston, the New York group reorganized itself early in 1914 as the Committee for Immigrants in America, with Frances Kellor as vice chairman.

Kellor's influence extended beyond New York's border to other states that were considering how to respond to the influx of immigrants. Her voice was heard in the White House by Theodore Roosevelt, and she became a firm supporter of his bid for the presidency in 1912. Roosevelt's New Nationalism, with its emphasis on an active governmental role in the regulation of the nation's economic and social spheres, coincided with her sense that organization, efficiency, and justice were needed in those areas and could be realized only by strong federal action.

During the 1912 campaign Frances Kellor directed the publicity and research department for the National Progressive Committee. Subsequently, she headed the party's Progressive National Service. While the Service sought to organize and win new adherents to the party, it planned to do that by applying the research techniques of social and political science to the writing of national platforms, promoting laws, and educating citizens to vote, all quite apart from the election of officials.

Although Kellor succeeded in establishing a number of regional and state organizations in concert with the goals of the Progressive Service, it was questionable by 1914 whether they would have any major national political party for which to work. In the meantime, her Committee for Immigrants in America attempted to become the national focal point for information about advocacy for the immigrant. Efforts to persuade the federal government to take a more positive role in the alien's adjustment went unheard until a group of wealthy members of the Committee agreed to underwrite a Division of Immigrant Education within the Bureau of Education.

The outbreak of the European war in 1914 had its impact upon the programs for immigrants for which Frances Kellor worked. While never abandoning entirely her sensitivity to their needs, in 1915 and thereafter her emphasis upon Americanization took a more nationalistic bent, with concern for divided loyalties never far behind issues of social welfare. Reflective of that trend was the decision of the Committee for Immigrants to establish the National Americanization Day Committee, with the express purpose of impressing the foreign-born with the need for loyalty to their adopted land and the natives with heightened sensitivity to the concerns of immigrants. Observance of the day on July 4, 1915, was so successful that Kellor and her colleagues dropped the word ''Day'' in the organization's title and absorbed into it all the work and staff of the Committee for Immigrants.

By 1915 Frances Kellor was emphasizing the significant role of industry in the Americanization of the immigrant. The campaign for industrial Americanization led her to the U.S. Chamber of Commerce, where she received a warm welcome from colleagues who worked with her on the National Americanization Committee. The Chamber reacted to her call for industrial Americanization by creating the Immigrant Committee, to which Kellor was appointed as assistant to the chairman. Before America's entry into the war, the industrial Americanization program focused upon the workplace as the most influential site in the Americanization process. With active U.S. involvement in the war, industrial Americanization assumed a more defensive, security posture for Kellor.

At the end of the war, the National Americanization Committee disbanded. Subsidization of the Bureau of Education's Division of Immigrant Education ended. Frances Kellor remained convinced that the most effective way to Americanize the immigrant was through industry. With the support of industrial corporations, she launched the Inter-Racial Council, with the goals of stabilizing labor conditions among immigrants and of countering the influence of Bolshevik and Industrial Workers of the World (IWW) propaganda with accurate information about American business and about opportunities in their adopted homeland. To reach the immigrants, the Council bought the American Association of Foreign Language Newspapers, which controlled almost all advertising in foreign-language newspapers, and named Frances Kellor as president of the Association.

With the demise of the Inter-Racial Council in 1921, Frances Kellor shifted her professional focus from concern with the interrelationship and adjustment of the immigrant and native-born to a search for ways to bring efficiency, order, and justice to the resolution of industrial and international problems, mainly through arbitration. In one of her last statements on the immigrant and American society, however, she called upon the alien and the native to recognize the need for both economic and spiritual assimilation of the newcomer.

Frances Kellor died in New York City on January 4, 1952.

Apparently, there is no manuscript collection of Kellor papers. Correspondence between her and other members of the social work community can be found in the following collections: Jane Addams Papers (Swarthmore College Peace Collection, Swarthmore, Pennsylvania); Sophonisba Breckinridge Papers (Library of Congress); Raymond Robins Papers (State Historical Society of Wisconsin, Madison, Wisconsin); Lillian Wald Papers (New York Public Library).

A 1971 senior thesis at Princeton University examines Kellor's professional career from 1900 to 1920 and seeks both to place and to interpret it within the context of the social welfare, political, and economic climates of the first two decades of the twentieth century. See Paul C. Marengo, "Frances Kellor: A Career Study, 1900–1920," Senior thesis, Princeton University, 1971.

Frances Kellor wrote extensively on issues related to black migration and immigration. During the first two decades of the twentieth century her articles appeared frequently in *Charities, Survey, Outlook, North American Review*, and other journals. Her most influential books on these subjects were *Out of Work: A Study of Employment Agencies, Their Treatment of the Unemployed, and Their Influence upon Homes and Business* (1904); *Out of Work: A Study of Unemployment*, (1915); and *Straight America: A Call to National Service* (1916).

Allan F. Davis, *Spearheads for Reform: The Social Settlements and the Progressive Movement, 1890–1914* (1967), an excellent study of the origins of the social settlement movement, relates it well to the social, economic, and political environment of the turn of the century and discusses Frances Kellor's role in all areas of the reform drive. Eugene Hartmann's *The Movement to Americanize the Immigrant* (1948) presents well all facets of the Americanization movement and includes extensive discussions of Kellor's strategic position in it. John Higham's *Strangers in the Land: Patterns of American Nativism, 1860–1925* (1965) provides a thorough and more critical analysis of Frances Kellor's leadership of groups responding to immigration. Finally, Gilbert Osofsky, *Harlem: The Making of a Ghetto* (1966), and Nancy J. Weiss, *The National Urban League, 1910–1940* (1974) underscore Kellor's role in providing research and organizational assistance to Blacks migrating north and in molding three groups into the one that became the National Urban League.

RALPH L. PEARSON

**Kennedy, Albert Joseph** (January 20, 1879–June 4, 1968), settlement house worker, was born in Rosenhayn, New Jersey, to Thomas and Molly (Barnhardt) Kennedy. After graduating from Marion Collegiate Institute in Marion, New York, Albert J. Kennedy earned an A.B. from the University of Rochester in 1901. Like so many of the men in the early settlement house movement, he prepared for the clergy. In 1904 he graduated from Rochester Theological Seminary. He served a year as a clergyman in Granite Falls, Minnesota (1904–1905), then attended Harvard University as a Williams Fellow (1905–1906), studied economic change in sociology as a South End House Fellow (1906–1908), and in 1907 received the Bachelor of Sacred Theology degree from Harvard Divinity School. The following year he married Edith Forbes Knowles, by whom he had three sons, Robert Woods, Fitzroy, and Edmond. While living at South End House, Kennedy was among a handful of settlement residents nationally to bring up his family in a social settlement. His first marriage ended in divorce in 1929. In 1930 Kennedy married Marjorie Patten and had a fourth son, Michael.

From 1908 to 1928 Albert J. Kennedy worked in various capacities for South End House in Boston. Beginning as director of investigations, he became associate head worker in 1914 and head worker in 1926. Throughout this period, Kennedy worked closely with, but also existed in the shadow of, South End's more famous head worker, Robert A. Woods.* Unlike some settlement leaders who were pacifists, Woods and Kennedy endorsed the United States' entry into World War I. The two men also shared a concern for the psychological impact that unemployment had on individuals, and they collaborated on various projects. Kennedy's best-known publications were done with Woods. The first, *Handbook of Settlements* (1911), was an annotated listing of 413 settlement houses that included brief descriptions of their daily educational and recreational activities along with accounts of specific settlements' efforts in the area of social action. The two men followed that book with *Young Working Girls* (1913) and *The Settlement Horizon: A National Estimate* (1922). Written at the suggestion of fellow settlement workers, *The Settlement Horizon* was a realistic account of the history, administration, and actual functioning of settlement houses. It avoided the human interest narrative characteristic of earlier settlement house books and adopted a professional as well as a national perspective. Its appearance signified a maturing of the movement. The following year, Kennedy published a five-page review of Woods' *Neighborhood in Nation Building* that strongly praised Woods' wisdom and character. When Woods died in 1925, Kennedy succeeded his mentor as head of South End House, a post he held until moving to New York City as director of University Settlement in 1928.

Among the joint projects of Woods and Kennedy was the establishment of the National Federation of Settlements in 1911. South End House provided office space, and Woods served as that organization's first executive secretary, or head, until 1922, although in *The Settlement Horizon* the two men identified themselves as "joint secretaries." By 1923 Kennedy alone was the head. He brought to the National Federation a strong interest in promoting the visual and performing arts in settlement houses. When the Great Depression arrived, the high priority Kennedy placed on the arts clashed with the growing desire of other settlement leaders for a social action emphasis. A certain stubbornness and a tendency to antagonize fellow workers also may have contributed to his replacement as the executive head of the National Federation by Lillie M. Peck* in 1934, although she had been performing those duties as Kennedy's assistant at University Settlement since 1930.

Kennedy remained head of University Settlement until he retired from that post in 1944. Although it was the first settlement house to be established in the United States, University Settlement was a relatively small operation. In 1941 its staff included only two full-time and nine part-time professionals, supplemented by volunteers and Works Progress Administration (WPA) workers. While head of University Settlement, Kennedy continued his writing, but without Robert A. Woods as a partner, his publications were quite minor. He accumulated a lot of material on settlements for another book, but never published it.

Once officially retired as head of University Settlement, Kennedy emerged as the elder statesman of the settlement movement. He gave a lot of thought to the development of settlements and was one of the few male settlement house leaders who was sensitive to women's issues and the impact that the early female domination of settlements had on shaping the movement. He also was sensitive to racial issues and in the early 1940s was among those settlement leaders who perceived the growing importance of Blacks in the settlement house movement. As a result, beginning in 1946 he carried out a major study of race relations in settlement houses for the National Federation of Settlements. In addition, he taught a social work course at the City College of New York in 1947, and his activities as a consultant increased, with studies of settlements in different cities, such as Des Moines (1950), Detroit (1951), Evansville (1952), and Sioux City (1954). Thus, through his publications with Woods, his early efforts on behalf of the National Federation of Settlements, and his later activities as a researcher, consultant, and settlement house philosopher, Kennedy played an important role in the professionalization of the settlement house movement. He died in Peekskill, New York, on June 4, 1968.

Correspondence and other items by and about Albert J. Kennedy may be found in the Albert J. Kennedy Papers, Social Welfare History Archives, University of Minnesota, and in the Papers of the University Settlement Society of New York City at the State Historical Society of Wisconsin. The latter collection is available on microfilm through interlibrary loan.

Publications by Albert J. Kennedy include "Settlement Contributions to Theory and Practice of Local Community Organization," *American Review* (May-June, 1923), 338–348; "The District as Unit for Community Organization,"*Social Forces* (March, 1927), 458–463; review of Robert A. Woods' *Neighborhood in Nation Building*, in *American Review* (November-December, 1923), 726–731; "The Saloon, Retrospect and Prospect," *Survey Graphic* (1923), 203–206, 234–240; with Kathryn Farra et al., *Social Settlements in New York City—Their Activities, Policies, and Administration* (1935); and with Robert A. Woods et al., *The Zone of Emergence*, abridged and edited by Sam B. Warner, Jr. (1962).

See also *Who Was Who in America*, vol. 6 (1976), 223.

JUDITH ANN TROLANDER

**Kerby, William Joseph** (February 20, 1870–July 27, 1936), priest, sociologist, teacher, founder of many welfare organizations and the Catholic "scientific charity" movement, editor, and author, was born in Lawler, Iowa, to Daniel P. and Ellen (Rockford) Kerby, both Irish immigrants. His father was eminent in town as a banker and a man of learning, while his mother was respected for her solicitude toward the sick and poor of the area. Both were fervent Catholics and raised their ten children as such, imparting to "Will" an attachment to religion, learning, and works of charity. After elementary school at both the public and parochial schools in Lawler, Kerby obtained his high school and college diplomas at St. Joseph's (new Loras) College in Dubuque. Discerning a call to the priesthood, he enrolled at St. Francis de Sales Seminary in Milwaukee in 1889 and was ordained for the diocese of Dubuque on December 21, 1892.

Impressed by his academic achievements, his bishop, John Hennessy, sent him in 1893 for graduate work in theology at the four-year-old Catholic University of America in Washington, D.C. Kerby would remain an intimate part of that institution until his death. The young priest was particularly influenced by the French professor of moral theology, Thomas Bouquillon, whose main theme was that, to be credible and relevant, Catholic ethics had to utilize the findings of contemporary scholarship, especially those of the social sciences. The French professor was also an advisor to the liberal wing of the American Catholic hierarchy, especially to John Ireland, the flamboyant Archbishop of St. Paul, who advocated an alliance between the ideals of American democratic progress and Catholic teaching, and thus Kerby became a disciple of this viewpoint.

When Kerby finished his studies at the university, its chancellor, James Cardinal Gibbons of Baltimore, personally requested his appointment to the faculty as a professor of sociology, and this took place in 1895. To prepare for his teaching, he spent two years in Europe, attending lectures in the social sciences at the universities of Berlin, Bonn, and Louvain. From the last he received his doctorate in social and political science, writing his dissertation on socialism in the United States. While critical of socialism, Kerby treated it openly and objectively and praised some of its tenets.

Returning to Washington in 1897, he became the first of the students from the Catholic University of America to join its faculty. Through the next four decades, by teaching, writing, and organizing, he attempted to place the Church's social welfare system on a more professional, structured foundation. A popular and effective teacher, he influenced a generation of Catholic leaders in the field of social welfare, including John A. Ryan,* John O'Grady,* and Francis J. Haas.

Undoubtedly, Kerby's major contribution to Catholic social work was his indefatigable insistence that works of charity had to be professionally organized, cognizant of the findings of the social sciences, and concerned about not only the immediate relief of the individual but the long-range reform of society. He is thus called "the founder of scientific charity" within American Catholicism. Although he admired the variety of welfare work sponsored by the Church, he felt it was hampered by its lack of coordination and professional direction. Many Church leaders—feeling that religious social work should be done quietly, concerned only with amelioration of present suffering, and suspicious of all organization—criticized him. Kerby advanced his case through his voluminous writings, editing the *St. Vincent de Paul Quarterly* from 1911 to 1916, founding the *Catholic Charities Review* in 1916, and writing *The Social Mission of Charity* in 1921. In this book he contended that Catholic social welfare was crippled by duplication of effort, lack of communication among persons involved in the apostolate, inadequate training given to volunteers, and poor record-keeping.

Kerby's organizational accomplishments personified his vision. At the 1904 World's Fair he had organized a display of many Catholic welfare agencies. Developing these contacts, he founded in 1910 the National Conference of Catholic Charities, an umbrella organization giving direction, coherence, and standards to the hundreds of member groups. He remained general secretary for ten years, and, when he resigned, urged that lay people, not clergy, provide the leadership in the Catholic social apostolate. In 1917 he worked closely with his friend John J. Burke, C.S.P., in founding the National Catholic War Council. Initially intended to coordinate the participation of American Catholic citizens in the war effort, it became the National Catholic Welfare Council (later Conference) in the postwar years, providing goals, harmony, and structure to American Catholic life. Kerby was on the executive committee of its Social Action Department, which became the most cogent voice in the advocacy of principles of social justice. Then, in 1921, working with Agnes Regan,* he founded the National Catholic School of Social Service, the first residential professional school of social work for women in the country. There he was a teacher and administrator, training women as qualified social workers.

Kerby's amiable personality animated his teaching, writing, and organization. His dream—that religious welfare work be professional, thorough, and coherently structured—is now taken for granted. He died in Washington, D.C.

Monsignor Kerby's papers are housed in the archives of the Catholic University of America, Washington, D.C. The only full-length biography of Kerby is Timothy Michael Dolan, "Prophet of a Better Hope: The Life of William Joseph Kerby," Master's thesis, The Catholic University of America, 1980. For a complete listing of Kerby's voluminous writings, consult Mary Klein's "A Bio-Bibliography of William J. Kerby," Master's thesis, The Catholic University of America, 1955. Two articles written shortly after his death succinctly present the main activities of his life: John J. Burke, "The Rt. Rev. William J. Kerby: An Appreciation," *Ecclesiastical Review* (September, 1936), 225–233; and John O'Grady, "Monsignor Kerby: In Memoriam," *Catholic Charities Review* (September, 1936), 224–247.

TIMOTHY MICHAEL DOLAN

**King, Martin Luther, Jr.** (January 18, 1929–April 4, 1968), minister and civil rights leader, was born and raised in Atlanta, Georgia, the son of Michael (Martin) Luther King, Sr., a Baptist minister, and Alberta (Williams) King. He had one sister, Christina, and one brother, A.D. (Alfred Daniel). He attended the Yonge Street and David T. Howard elementary schools and Booker T. Washington High School, completing the curriculum in three years. After graduation in 1944 at age fifteen, King was admitted to Morehouse College as a special student. In June, 1948, King graduated from Morehouse with a bachelor's degree in sociology and ordination in the Baptist ministry. He continued his education immediately by enrolling at Crozier Theological Seminary in Chester, Pennsylvania. While studying there he read deeply in the works of Reinhold Niebuhr, Mahatma Gandhi, and Richard Gregg and began to develop his theory of nonviolent protest. He served as president of the student body and graduated with highest honors in 1951, after which he enrolled for doctoral studies at Boston University. While at Boston University he also attended classes in philosophy at Harvard. His dissertation was entitled "A Comparison of the Conception of God in the Thinking of Paul Tillich and Henry Nelson Wieman." King received his Ph.D. in systematic theology from Boston University in 1955. Later in his career he received honorary degrees from Howard University, the University of Chicago, and Morehouse College.

Martin Luther King, Jr., was married to Coretta Scott on June 18, 1953. They had four children; Martin Luther III, Dexter Scott, Yolanda Denise, and Bernice Albertine.

The Dexter Avenue Baptist Church in Montgomery, Alabama, was King's first and only pulpit assignment. His duties began there in January, 1954, and it was there that his career as a civil rights leader also began. He was elected president of the Montgomery Improvement Association immediately after the Rosa Parks incident in December, 1955. The success with which his organization broke the barrier of segregation on public transportation in Montgomery catapulted King to prominence. Shortly thereafter, along with Ralph Abernathy, he founded the Southern Christian Leadership Conference in Atlanta. King was elected president and began his duties in 1960.

In his civil rights advocacy, King promoted nonviolent, passive resistance, basing his approach largely upon the teachings of Gandhi and the Fellowship of Reconciliation, an organization of liberal churchmen. King admired Booker T. Washington,* but he rejected the philosophy of W.E.B. Du Bois* because it was biased in favor of educated upper-class Blacks and left no room for the mass of the black people. It demanded equality for the so-called Talented Tenth and ignored the pitiful condition of the other 90 percent. At first, King was concerned primarily with the civil rights of Blacks in the South. Later, he expanded his concerns to include housing, working conditions, and other problems faced by Blacks throughout the nation. His great contributions were recognized very early. In 1957, following his victory in Montgomery, the National Association for the Advancement of Colored People (NAACP) awarded him the coveted Spingarn Medal.

The career of Martin Luther King, Jr., as a civil rights leader extended from 1956 to 1968. His peaceful tactics were often met with a violent response which generated worldwide sympathy and support for his movement. In October, 1960, for example, King was imprisoned in Georgia on a minor traffic violation. The nation was outraged, and the incident influenced the outcome of the presidential election. President Eisenhower and Richard Nixon refused to intervene, but John F. Kennedy publicly expressed his concern by telephoning Mrs. King on October 26. King was released soon thereafter.

From December, 1961, to August, 1962, King led the desegregation movement in Albany, Georgia. In the spring of 1963 he turned his attention to Birmingham, Alabama. His "Letter from a Birmingham Jail" and "Birmingham Manifesto" became classics of civil rights movement literature. His influence mounted and reached its high point during the summer of 1963 when, after leading the famous March on Washington, he delivered his "I Have a Dream" speech at the Lincoln Memorial. Subsequently, he was named Man of the Year by *Time* magazine (in January, 1964), and he received the Nobel Peace Prize in December, 1964.

King's efforts in Selma, Alabama, in early 1965, and his assault upon *de facto* segregation in Chicago in 1966 were not wholly successful, and he began to lose the support of the young militant leaders in such organizations as the Congress of Racial Equality and the Student Nonviolent Coordinating Committee. As a result of these developments he began to alter his approach to the problem of race in America. By 1967 he professed to believe that racism represented more than mere prejudice. It was a function of the entire economic and social structure of the nation. He therefore began to advocate what he called a reconstruction of the entire society, a revolution of values. As a part of his broadening approach he denounced the Vietnam War and set out to make himself the advocate of all of America's poor by organizing a coalition of antipoverty and antiwar supporters. His mission took him to Memphis in early 1968, where he intended to assist striking garbage collectors. There, on April 4, he died at the hands of an assassin, James Earl Ray. His birthdate, January 18, was declared a national holiday in 1984.

In addition to his numerous speeches and articles, King authored six books: *Stride Towards Freedom: The Montgomery Story* (1958), *Strength to Love* (1963), *Why We Can't Wait* (1964), *Where Do We Go from Here? Chaos or Community* (1967), *The Measure of a Man* (1968), and *Trumpet of Conscience* (1968).

The major sources on Martin Luther King, Jr., include Lerone Bennett, Jr., *What Manner of a Man: A Biography of Martin Luther King, Jr., 1929–1968* (1964); Lenwood G. Davis, *I Have a Dream: The Life and Times of Martin Luther King, Jr.* (1973); William M. Fisher, *Free at Last: A Bibliography of Martin Luther King, Jr.* (1977); C. Eric Lincoln, *Martin Luther King, Jr.: A Profile* (1969); Stephen B. Oates, *Let the Trumpet Sound: The Life of Martin Luther King* (1982); Ralph Reavis, *Martin Luther: Martin Luther King Jr. and the Black Experience* (1978); Flip Schulke, ed., *Martin Luther King, Jr.: A Documentary . . . Montgomery to Memphis* (1976).

KENNETH E. HENDRICKSON

**Kingsbury, John Adams** (August 30, 1876–August 3, 1956), social service administrator and foundation executive, was born in a rural area which was later named Horton, Kansas, the son of John T. and Anna Gibson (Adams) Kingsbury. He was proud of his mother's descent from the famous Adams family of Massachusetts. His father, after serving as a captain in the Union army during the Civil War, was a civil engineer with the Northern Pacific Railroad—mainly in the state of Washington—until 1884, when he became a county surveyor and consulting engineer. His mother, an invalid since his birth, died in 1884, leaving John and his two older sisters in the care of his father, who became a chronic alcoholic. John spent most of his childhood boarding with relatives on various farms. His education was frequently interrupted by the need to work, and he did not complete high school, in Yakima, Washington, until he was twenty-one years of age. For the next nine years he taught school in various towns in Washington and periodically attended the University of Washington. He ran for state superintendent of schools on the Socialist Party ticket in 1899. His last teaching job, between 1904 and 1906, was as principal of a high school in Seattle. At this time he met his future wife, Mabel Glass, whom he married in 1909; they had two girls and a boy.

Kingsbury came to New York in September, 1906, and though he quickly changed the direction of his career, he retained many of the characteristics he had shown in his earlier life. He was a political radical who took pride in his ancestry, a blunt veteran of manual labor who was articulate and socially adept, and a self-educated man who strove to acquire systematic knowledge and intellectual credentials.

Kingsbury came to New York City to attend Teachers College of Columbia

University—from which he received a B.S. in 1909—but at the suggestion of a professor, he soon accepted the first of several major positions in the field of social service. Between 1907 and 1911 he was assistant secretary of the New York State Charities Aid Society. From 1911 to 1914 he was general director of the New York Association for Improving the Condition of the Poor. During the administration of Mayor John Purroy Mitchel, 1914–1918, Kingsbury was Commissioner of Public Charities of the City of New York. After the United States entered World War I, he went to France, serving first with the American Red Cross and then with the YMCA Army Education Commission.

Kingsbury observed or participated in many important events in the history of social welfare in the United States during his years as an administrator of voluntary and public social service agencies. His incomplete manuscript autobiography and his correspondence contain important data about the careers of such contemporaries as Homer Folks,* Frances Perkins,* and Harry Hopkins,* and about such events as the aftermath of the Triangle Shirtwaist Co. fire, Theodore Roosevelt's 1912 campaign for the Republican presidential nomination, and the reform administration of Mayor Mitchel of New York.

He was at the height of his influence and visibility between 1921 and 1935 as chief executive officer (called secretary) of the Milbank Memorial Fund. He led the Fund in its initial years, when its studies and demonstration programs helped to expand the repertoire of public and philanthropic policies for organizing and financing medical and public health services. In his own writings, including two controversial books, he called attention to the achievements of the Soviet Union in organizing medical services and advocated compulsory health insurance as well as the reorganization of medical practice in the United States.

As both a foundation executive and an intellectual, Kingsbury was a leader of the group of reformers who considered themselves in the vanguard of health policy in the United States. He and his colleagues loathed—and in turn became anathema to—the leaders and publicists of the American Medical Association and its constituent state societies. Beginning in 1934, Kingsbury was under increasing pressure from the chairman of the board of the Milbank Fund to moderate his public criticism of the medical profession in order to reduce attacks on the Fund in the medical and general press and to avert a threatened medical boycott of the Borden Milk Company, a principal source of the Milbank family's wealth. Other aspects of his supervision of the Fund's affairs also were criticized by members of the board in 1934 and 1935. In April, 1935, Kingsbury was asked to resign from the Fund.

The remainder of Kingsbury's life was anticlimactic. After leaving the Fund, he served for several years as a consultant to the Works Progress Administrator, his former protégé, Harry Hopkins. Thereafter he lived quietly, working on his autobiography and participating in several voluntary associations, notably the Serbian Child Welfare Society, the American-Yugoslav Society, the Council on Foreign Relations, and the American Council on Soviet Relations. His activities as an officer of the latter organization earned him two appearances before the Subversive Activities Control Board in 1954 and 1955. Kingsbury died in New York City on August 3, 1956.

Kingsbury left an extraordinarily rich collection of manuscripts to the Library of Congress. The 117 boxes of his papers contain many drafts of an unpublished autobiography and correspondence with many distinguished contemporaries. Other Kingsbury manuscripts are in the papers of the Milbank Memorial Fund at the Yale Historical Medical Library.

Kingsbury published many reports and a number of magazine articles. Many of his reprints can be located in the New York Academy of Medicine, *Author Catalogue of the Library* (1969). He published two books: in collaboration with Sir Arthur Newsholme, *Red Medicine: Socialized Health in Soviet Russia* (1933); and *Health in Handcuffs* (1939).

Very little has been written about Kingbury. James Rorty, *American Medicine Mobilizes* (1939), is both a primary and a secondary source. Clyde Kiser describes aspects of Kingsbury's career as a foundation executive in *The Milbank Memorial Fund: Its Leaders and Its Work, 1905–1974* (1974).

DANIEL M. FOX

**Kingsbury, Susan Myra** (October 18, 1870–November 28, 1949), social investigator, was born in San Pablo, California, to Helen Shuler (De Lamater) and Willard Belmont Kingsbury. Her father was a physician who moved with his wife from southern Michigan to California soon after serving in the Civil War. When Kingsbury was approximately six years old, her father died. To support and educate her children, Mrs. Kingsbury became dean of women at the College of the Pacific in Stockton, California. In 1890 Susan Kingsbury received her B.A. from that college, Phi Beta Kappa. For the following two years, she taught in a small country school. In 1892, however, she taught history at the all-boy Lowell High School in San Francisco. This highly unusual situation of a young woman teaching in a school for boys required her quick wit and high regard for discipline. In 1899 she received a master's degree in history from Stanford University.

In 1900 she began further graduate work in history and economics at Columbia University. Part of her doctoral study was spent in England as a fellow of the Women's Educational Association of Boston (1903–1904). For a year, she also was an instructor in history at Vassar College. In 1905 she earned a Ph.D. in American colonial history under Professor Herbert L. Osgood at Columbia University. Her dissertation, "An Introduction to the Records of the Virginia Company of London" (1905), and the subsequent publication by the Library of Congress of the *Records of the Virginia Company of London* (four volumes, 1906–1935), edited by Kingsbury, established her reputation as a scholar.

Rather than continuing to teach history, however, Kingsbury then turned to what would be her lifelong work—pioneering social investigation and social work education. She had long shared her mother's interest in the cause of women, and in her year in England she had become acquainted with Beatrice Webb's social investigations and Seebohm Rowntree's cost-of-living studies. Thus, in 1906 Kingsbury became director of the Massachusetts Commission on Industrial and Technical Education's investigation of factory and home conditions arising from women's and children's employment in industry. From 1906 to 1915 she also was professor of economics at Simmons College and director of the Research Department of the Women's Educational and Industrial Union in Boston. During this period, building on her observations of social investigation in England, she began to develop methods of field study for work in the United States, which she applied in her studies, published by the Women's Educational and Industrial Union under the titles *Labor Laws and Their Reinforcement* (1911) and *Licensed Workers in Industrial Homework in Massachusetts* (1915).

In 1912 Kingsbury addressed the Association of Collegiate Alumnae (which later became the American Association of University Women) about the need to develop better techniques for making constructive reports on social conditions. One member of her audience was M. Carey Thomas, president of Bryn Mawr College, who had been planning a Department of Social Economy which would offer advanced scientific training in social service on a par with other graduate departments in the college. The Carola Woerishoffer* Department, named for the young Bryn Mawr graduate who had bequeathed a legacy to the college and who herself had worked to improve the lot of women workers in industry, needed a director. Legend has it that it took three years for President Thomas to convince the reluctant Kingsbury to assume the post. In any event, in 1915 Kingsbury became the director of the Carola Woerishoffer Graduate Department of Social Economy and Social Research (now the Graduate School of Social Work and Social Research of Bryn Mawr College), the first graduate department founded by an American college or university specifically for advanced training in the social services. The curriculum, designed by Kingsbury and her colleagues, involved theory, supervised field experience, and ongoing research. She outlined four fields of study: social and industrial investigation; industrial relations; social casework; and community organization. Two-thirds of the work was in social theory and statistics, and one-third was practical, including a half-year requirement of continuous residence in a social service organization. Throughout her tenure as director, Kingsbury continued to teach and to do research. She regularly taught a seminar on community life which focused on what a community normally needed in relation to such aspects as living conditions, social security, questions of health, and use of leisure time for education. Another seminar she regularly offered, on social and industrial research, taught students to see the relationship between social forces in the community, to recognize and evaluate factors conditioning or controlling social situations, and to establish facts concerning social problems through actual experience.

Kingsbury also was the first director of the Bryn Mawr Summer School for Women Workers, established in 1921, which, until it outgrew its facilities seventeen years later, used the Bryn Mawr campus to further the education of women working in industry. Like programs available to laborers in Great Britain, the Summer School offered courses in labor relations, economics, and the English language, in order to stimulate effective self-expression.

Kingsbury published a variety of studies. Among the more important ones was the "Relationship of Women to Industry," which appeared in the *Journal of the American Sociological Society* (1921) and which reported on the results of a survey of 11,000 families in Philadelphia in an effort to discover the extent to which the financial contributions of working mothers and children were necessary for the support of the family. In 1928 she and Hastings Hornell Hart* published a study which measured the ethical behavior of thirty-four representative newspapers, *Newspapers and the News*. Kingsbury also made several data-gathering trips to the Soviet Union which formed the basis for a series of studies on that country, including "Social Process in Russia," published in 1932 in the *Journal of the American Sociological Society*; it discussed the origin of the Russian Klub, something akin to the settlement house in England and the United States. With Mildred Fairchild Woodbury, her student and successor, she also wrote "Employment and Unemployment in Pre-war and Soviet Russia" and *The Factory, Family, and Women in the Soviet Union* (1935), a pioneering study of the status of women and the family in Soviet Russia.

Kingsbury formally retired in 1936. However, she remained active in a number of ways. She continued to hold the presidency of the Alfred Lake Camp for Girls in South Hope, Maine, where she spent many summers. In addition, she continued to play a leadership role in the American Sociological Society, the American Economic Association, and the American Association of Schools of Social Work, which she earlier had helped to found. Always active in the American Association of University Women, Kingsbury also served as chairman of its Committee on the Status of Women and helped to develop a national program to advance the economic and legal status of women. She died at age seventy-nine in Bryn Mawr, Pennsylvania.

There are a number of primary sources for a study of the life and work of Kingsbury. See especially Mildred Fairchild Woodbury's papers in the Archives of Bryn Mawr College, which are useful, especially for understanding Kingsbury's role in founding and administering the Summer School for Women Workers and her curricular work for the Graduate Department of Social Economy and Social Research. Also, the papers of Bryn Mawr president M. Carey Thomas describe Thomas' initial meeting with Kingsbury and her successful attempt to convince her to become director of the new department; they also shed light on the establishment of the Summer School and the subsequent history of the new department. Another useful item is Frederica de Laguna's manuscript on Kingsbury in the Sophia Smith Collection at Smith College in Northampton, Massachusetts, which is an extensive work covering aspects of her personal life and includes observations on Kingsbury written by close friends and colleagues.

Some good secondary accounts are Amey E. Watson, "Tribute to Susan M. Kingsbury," *Bryn Mawr Alumnae Bulletin* (February, 1950); and Mildred Woodbury's sketch of Kingsbury in *Notable American Women* (1971).

                                                                              TOBA SCHWABA KERSON

**Kirchwey, Freda** (September 26, 1893–January 3, 1976), editor, journalist, publisher, and reformer, was born in Lake Placid, New York, to George Washington Kirchwey, a pacifist, who taught law and criminology, and Dora (Wendell) Kirchwey, who taught English at Albany High School. On November 9, 1915, Freda Kirchwey married Evans Clark, who became the director of the Twentieth Century Fund. Two of their three children died in childhood. Brewster, born in 1916, died within his first year; Jeffrey, born in 1923, died in 1930. The second son, Michael, was born in 1919.

Freda Kirchwey traced her family of reformers to her grandfather, who fled Prussia's militarism in 1848. His son, Freda's father, believed in speaking and writing about reforms. Leaving a long, successful career as a law professor and dean of the Columbia Law School, he began teaching criminology at the New School for Social Research. During 1915–1916 he put his theories into practice by serving as the warden of Sing Sing Prison. Freda was educated at the elite Horace Mann Schools and at the family dinner table, which fed a host of her family's reformer friends.

Graduating from Horace Mann High School in 1911, she continued her education at Barnard College, where she earned a bachelor's degree with a major in history. She learned best and most by firsthand experiences, such as cutting class to join picket lines of striking shirtwaist factory women. Observing people in dire economic straits made her want to do something to better their lives. Early on she took pencil in hand to expose injustices so that they could be remedied. Her first crusade with words was directed against Barnard's sororities (then called fraternities). The secret societies discriminated against Jews specifically and were generally undemocratic. Freda Kirchwey's pieces against sororities generated enough criticism to result in their abolution on Barnard's campus. Words and actions characterized her next campaign, this time in support of woman suffrage. She sold the suffrage publication *The Woman Voter*, drove a little Sulphite car through Connecticut to speak at suffrage rallies, and reported on the struggle for woman suffrage first in the *Barnard Bear*, and after graduation, at her first job on the *Morning Telegraph* (1915–1916).

A racing news daily, the *Morning Telegraph* was an unlikely place for a reformer, but Kirchwey, already a strategist, manipulated assignments that had no connection with suffrage to bring suffrage issues before her readers. Her next position, editorial assistant for *Every Week*, Bruce Barton's weekly literary and family publication, ended with the demise of the paper in 1918. Another job on the *New York Tribune* lasted only two months when wholesale firings of everyone hired by then managing editor Ernest Gruening left her without a job.

In August, 1918, she began work on Oswald Garrison Villard's newly reorganized *Nation*. This began her lifelong career on one of the country's oldest liberal political journals. She started as a clipper for the *Nation*'s new international relations section, filing English or English translations of news from around the world. Soon she wrote editorial paragraphs about the clippings, and within a year she was promoted to editor of the international relations section. In 1922 Freda Kirchwey became the *Nation*'s managing editor.

Her career on the *Nation* included the literary editorship from 1928 to 1929. She became the executive editor of a board of four in 1933. In 1935 she negotiated Villard's sale of the journal to financier and benefactor Maurice Wertheim. Two years later, in 1937, she bought the *Nation* from Wertheim and became owner, editor, and publisher. Difficult financial times for the journal necessitated a major reorganization plan. In 1943 Kirchwey transferred ownership of the *Nation* to a new nonprofit organization, the *Nation* Associates. Remaining editor and publisher of the *Nation*, she became president of *Nation* Associates and ran both organizations until her retirement in 1955.

During a long career on the *Nation*, Freda Kirchwey developed journalistic skills to accompany a deepening commitment to a particular kind of writing: sociopolitical journalism. In the twenties many of her crusades were about domestic concerns. Often she observed social problems firsthand so that she could vividly portray bleak realities to motivate action. Using the muckraking approach of her progressive upbringing, she exposed the grimmest sides of issues to the readers to convince them to better working conditions, legalize birth control information, and liberalize college admission policies to recruit poor girls.

Writing and speaking on these and other issues, Freda Kirchwey was also able to help funnel some funds into various causes by serving on the board of the American Fund for Public Service, commonly called the Garland Fund (established by Socialist Charles Garland in 1922). She served on the board from 1924 to 1940. Garland's board of directors dispensed his considerable inheritance to radical, liberal, and labor causes. Among other projects, it aided in Sacco and Vanzetti's defense, supported the National Association for the Advancement of Colored People's campaign for a federal antilynching bill, and put up bail money for arrested labor union organizers.

Freda Kirchwey was also concerned with changing values in the twenties, and she was dubbed the *Nation*'s " 'informal morals editor.' " She selected articles for a *Nation* series entitled "New Morals for Old" and edited them into a book, *Our Changing Morality* (1924). She also began what would become a trademark over her years of editorship: she arranged forums on controversial issues. In 1925 she asked her panelists to discuss "Is Monogamy Feasible?" In 1950 she wondered about "The Atomic Era: Can It Bring Peace and Abundance?" and edited the answers into book form (1950).

The change in topics reflected Freda Kirchwey's increasing focus on international affairs. On the *Nation*, a meeting place for foreign dignitaries, she had early developed a heightened international consciousness. With the rise of fascism and the outbreak of World War II, she increasingly turned her attention to waging a "Political War" against fascism. Always an activist, during the forties and fifties she focused her considerable energy and used her access to public figures to influence public policy. Refugees from fascism were of utmost concern to her, and she worked both on her journal and in organizations such as the Emergency Committee in Aid of Political Refugees from Nazism and the International Relief Association to aid those fleeing from fascism.

Also on the board of editors for the publication *Free World*, she helped the International Free World Association. This group of exiled democratic leaders included Albert Einstein, Louis Dolivet, Gunnar Myrdal, and Count Sforza, among others. During her last decades on the *Nation* Kirchwey mostly wrote to defeat fascism by exposing its horrors. Domestically, she revealed the ill-treatment of Japanese Americans during the war. She supported the establishment of the United Nations but worked to keep Fascist Spain out of it. She supported the establishment of Israel. At home she supported civil liberties as a vehement opponent of Senator Joseph McCarthy and his ilk. Her retirement in 1955 left her without the deadlines that had made her so productive. She continued work with the Women's International League for Peace and Freedom and the Committee for a Democratic Spain. In ill health for some time, she died on January 3, 1976, in St. Petersburg, Florida.

The bulk of correspondence with and about Freda Kirchwey appears in the following collections: Houghton Library, Harvard University: Oswald Garrison Villard Papers; Schlesinger Library, Radcliffe College: Dorothy Kirchwey Brown Papers and Freda Kirchwey Papers. Additional, less extensive, sources appear in: Library of Congress: Joseph Wood Krutch Papers and Reinhold Niebuhr Papers; Princeton University: American Civil Liberties Union Papers and Louis Fischer Papers; Social Welfare History Archives: Paul Underwood Kellogg Papers; Yale University: Max Lerner Papers, Dwight Macdonald Papers, and Margaret Marshall Papers.

Freda Kirchwey wrote countless signed *Nation* articles. For her many other unsigned editorials consult annotated copies of the *Nation* in the New York Public Library. Freda Kirchwey edited *The Atomic Era—Can It Bring Peace and Abundance?* (1950) and *Our Changing Morality* (1924).

*Freda Kirchwey: A Woman of the Nation*, by Sara Alpern (forthcoming), is the only biography to date on Kirchwey. Several brief magazine articles are collected in her papers at the Schlesinger Library. A particularly good one is Oliver Warren, "Oh, Stop That Freda!" *Saturday Evening Post* (February 9, 1946), 21–22. See also *Independent Woman* (November 1, 1937), 40f; *Current Biography* (1942); and *Who's Who in America* (1942–1943). Obituary notices include *Barnard Bulletin* (January 26, 1976), 3; Carey McWilliams, "The Freda Kirchwey I Knew," *Nation* (January 17, 1976), 38; *New York Times* (January 4, 1976), 47; *Washington Post* (January 10, 1976), E6.

SARA ALPERN

**Knopf, Siegmund Adolphus** (November 27, 1857–July 15, 1940), physician and author, was born in Halle-on-the-Saale, Germany, the son of S. Adolphus and Nanina (Bock) Knopf. He came to the United States after completing his secondary education, living first in New York City and then in Los Angeles, where he taught languages and studied at the University of Southern California. In 1886 he entered Bellevue Hospital Medical College, receiving the M.D. degree in 1888. After a brief period of medical practice in Los Angeles, he went to Paris, where he studied at the Sorbonne until 1890 and at the Faculty of Medicine of the University of Paris until 1895. His French doctoral dissertation was a study of tuberculosis sanitoria. During his years in Europe he also worked for a time as an assistant to Professor Peter Dettweiler at the Falkenstein Sanitorium in Germany. Knopf settled permanently in New York City in 1896, devoting his career to the prevention and treatment of tuberculosis. He married Perle Nora Dyer of Los Angeles in 1899. She died in 1931. In 1935 he married Julia Marie Off, also of Los Angeles. He had three children by his first wife, two girls and a boy.

Knopf attracted attention as an expert on tuberculosis soon after settling in New York. In 1898 he was awarded a prize by the College of Physicians and Surgeons of Philadelphia for a treatise on pulmonary tuberculosis. A year later, he won a prize offered by the International Tuberculosis Association, meeting in Berlin, for an essay on tuberculosis as a disease of the masses and methods to combat it. This essay remained in print as a pamphlet for many years and was translated into twenty-one languages.

Knopf maintained a private medical practice while he held positions involving the care of poor patients and both public and medical education about tuberculosis. In 1904 and 1905 he served as associate director of the Clinic for Pulmonary Diseases of the New York City Health Department. From 1906 to 1922 he was a senior visiting physician to the Riverside Tuberculosis Hospital, a Health Department facility. From 1908 to 1922 he was a professor of medicine in the department of phthisiotherapy at the Post Graduate Medical School of Columbia University. He was a consultant to numerous hospitals and sanitoria for patients with tuberculosis. Knopf was one of the organizers of both the New York and the National Tuberculosis Associations. He held many offices in these organizations and was the first official historian of the antituberculosis movement.

Knopf was a prolific writer, publishing 419 articles, books, or pamphlets between 1889 and 1939. Most of his writings were about tuberculosis, but after 1910 he wrote frequently about ways to maintain health, and in the 1920s he began to advocate legalized birth control and contraception and to call attention to the problem of the impaired physician.

He was a forthright, impatient, and at times contentious person. As a part-time employee of the New York City Health Department, Knopf complained frequently about alleged administrative discourtesies. In 1926 he resigned from the New York Tuberculosis and Health Association during an acrimonious controversy about medical etiquette. In his last publication, in 1939, he angrily attacked group practice and compulsory health insurance. He was also an energetic worker, a zealous advocate, and an effective enemy of medical and philanthropic fraud.

Knopf died in New York City on July 15, 1940, after a brief illness.

A few of Knopf's letters, none of them particularly revealing, are in the Rare Book Room of the New York Academy of Medicine. More useful is a typescript "List of Writings, 1889–1939" in the Academy's library, which itemizes 419 publications by Knopf.

Most of Knopf's publications were in medical journals. Almost all of his articles advocate particular measures to prevent or treat tuberculosis or promote other health causes. Many are biographies or eulogies of contemporaries. His best-known books were *Tuberculosis as a Disease of the Masses and How to Control It* (1901), which was published in many editions in many languages, and *A History of the National Tuberculosis Association* (1922).

Knopf has had no biographers. The facts of his career are summarized in his obituary in the *New York Times*, July 16, 1940, 17:1. Also useful is Richard H. Shyrock, *National Tuberculosis Association, 1904–1954* (1957).

DANIEL M. FOX

**Kohut, Rebekah Bettelheim** (September 9, 1864–August 11, 1951), communal worker and educator, was born in Kaschau, Hungary, to Rabbi Dr. Alfred Siegfried Bettelheim and Henrietta (Wientraub) Bettelheim. Her family migrated to the United States in 1867, settling first in Philadelphia and then moving in 1869 to Richmond, Virginia. After her mother died in 1870, her father remarried and had another child by his new wife. The stepmother soon became an invalid, leaving Rebekah and her two older sisters, two younger brothers, and stepsibling to assume the care of the household.

In 1875 the family moved to San Francisco, where the seeds for her major interests were planted. As a teenager she began her social welfare career by serving on the Fruit and Flower Mission of San Francisco and becoming active in the Perry Street Kindergarten as field work for her normal school course. She then spent two years at the University of California, where she began to identify with the women's rights movement, seeing a connection between it and her status as a Jewess.

In 1885 Rebekah moved east, where she married (in 1887) Dr. Alexander Kohut, a widower twenty-two years her senior with eight children. He was an eminent rabbinic scholar, and she visualized her marriage to him as being part of a life of service. During the early years of her marriage, she spent much time translating her husband's work from the German and maintaining his correspondence.

Her adult involvement in volunteer activities was launched in the Women's Health Protective Association, campaigning against inefficient street cleaning. Soon her leadership ability in social welfare led her to organize within the Central

Synagogue, her husband's congregation, a second Sisterhood of American Jewish Women (the first belonged to a neighboring congregation). Under her guidance as president, the Sisterhood initiated settlement house activities, administering relief to neighboring families, providing lunches for poor children, and running a day nursery and kindergarten. She helped organize similar individual sisterhoods in other reform congregations throughout the United States, and helped organize their unified national affiliation. Through this affiliation the women cooperated with the United Hebrew Charities, giving them political clout within the Jewish community.

Her reputation as a speaker and as a social service innovator led to an invitation to deliver a paper at the 1893 Chicago World's Fair to the Congress of Jewish Women of America. To her regret, at the last minute she was unable to go because her husband was ill and did not wish her to leave his side. Each of the women who had attended the Congress had been charged with starting or aiding a local chapter of the National Council of Jewish Women. The New York chapter, which had existed prior to the Congress, was in trouble because of internal disagreements. Despite her husband's death in 1894 and her need to rear his eight children, Rebekah Kohut took the presidency of the New York section (1894–1898) and healed its rift.

She began to speak before many new Council of Jewish Women sections throughout the country and attended and participated in the Mothers' Congress in Washington, D.C., as a representative of Jewish women. She spoke on "Parental Reverence in the Jewish Home," the only Jewess to speak during the three-day program. Her address was distributed throughout the world, giving her recognition for the first time in non-Jewish circles. As a consequence, she was invited to appear before Christian audiences, appearing also before the Woman's Christian Temperance Union.

In 1901, shortly after the National Council of Jewish Women held its first national triennial convention in New York City, her inheritance from Alexander Kohut was lost, forcing Rebekah Kohut to devote substantial energies to obtaining an income. After a brief attempt at giving salon lectures, she went to financier-philanthropist Jacob Schiff and asked him to help her handle her investments and to help her found the Kohut School for Girls. Although successful, she gave up the school after five years because she felt that she was neglecting her younger stepchildren.

Over the years her volunteer activities expanded into employment issues beyond the Jewish community, although that remained her primary focus. In 1914, as World War I began and a depression followed, she opened the Young Women's Hebrew Association Employment Bureau. She not only provided employment assistance but also organized small shops that promoted work for unemployed individuals. Eventually she became the industrial chairman for the National League for Women's Services. She also raised funds for the international activities of the American Jewish Relief and the Joint Distribution Committee, and was active in the Federal Employment Clearinghouse. Later, as a representative of Jewish women, she received an appointment to the United War Work Campaign.

Kohut was able to combine her interests in the National Council of Jewish Women and employment when, in April, 1920, she was made chairman of the Reconstruction Committee of the National Council of Jewish Women, whose goal was to help the Jewish communities of Europe reconstruct their lives. Rebekah Kohut's contribution was to help organize local groups throughout Europe to take charge of meeting their own needs.

In May, 1923, the World Congress of Jewish Women had a meeting in Vienna, during which it created a permanent international organization with an affiliation of more than 1 million women and elected Rebekah Kohut president. She fought for recognition for women's organizations as innovators and social activists instead of as fund-raisers or figureheads. In 1931 she was appointed by Governor Franklin Roosevelt to the New York State Advisory Council on Unemployment and to the Joint Legislative Committee on Unemployment. She returned to school administration in 1934 at the Columbia Grammar School but remained active in philanthropic, governmental, religious, and women's organizations until the end of her life. She died in New York City in 1951.

Rebekah Kohut's papers are at the American Jewish Historical Society in Waltham, Massachusetts. Additional correspondence and clippings are at the American Jewish Archives, Hebrew Union College, Cincinnati, Ohio.

Kohut wrote extensively, including *My Portion: An Autobiography*(1925); *As I Know Them: Some Jews and a Few Gentiles* (1929); *His Father's House: The Story of George Alexander Kohut* (1938); and *More Yesterdays: An Autobiography 1925–1949* (1950).

The following sources have information about Kohut: D. Askowith, *Three Outstanding Women* (1941); *Notable American Women 1607–1950* (1971); J. R. Marcus, *The American Jewish Woman 1654–1980* (1981); H. J. Ribalow, *Autobiographies of American Jews 1880–1920* (1965); and J. R. Rapport, "Notable American Jewish Women: A Computer-Aided Study in Collective Biography," Rabbinic thesis, Hebrew Union College, 1984.

Obituaries appeared in the *New York Times* (August 12, 1951), the *Wilson Library Bulletin* (October, 1951), and the *American Jewish Yearbook* (1952).

                                                         ARLENE RUBIN STIFFMAN

**Kraft, Louis** (January 2, 1891–July 11, 1975), pioneer in the field of Jewish communal service and architect of the Jewish Community Center movement in America, Western Europe, and Israel, was born in Moscow, Russia, the son of tailor Abraham Kraft and Etta (Gellis) Kraft. Kraft's family immigrated to the United States when Louis was six years old. Reared in an observant Jewish home, Kraft attended the public schools of New York City. He later studied at the City College of New York, where he earned a degree in civil engineering in 1912. While yet a student at City College, Louis Kraft joined the 92nd Street

Young Men's Hebrew Association (YMHA). He was a member of the Y's Jewish Culture Society, organized by Rabbi Mordecai M. Kaplan,* who later founded the Reconstructionist movement in Judaism. Kraft remained an active Zionist all of his life. In 1909 he joined the Herzl Zion Club, together with future Zionist spokesman Abba Hillel Silver. While at City College, Kraft was president of the CCNY Zionist Society and a leader of the Inter-High School Zionist League. He also served as an officer of the Labor Zionist Organization of America (now the Labor Zionist Alliance). Louis Kraft married Isabelle Jacobson (from whom he was later divorced) on April 12, 1919, and they had three children: Stephen, Arthur, and Barbara. Kraft subsequently married Pauline Roman Jackson on July 1, 1948.

Although formally trained for work in the field of civil engineering, Kraft turned to Jewish communal service as a profession. He obtained his first full-time position in the Jewish community in 1914 when he became the executive director of the Bronx YMHA. When the Jewish Board for Welfare Work in the United States Army and Navy (later the National Jewish Welfare Board or JWB) was established in 1917 for the purpose of supervising welfare work for Jews serving in the United States armed forces during World War I, Kraft assumed the position of director of activities in military camps and communities. Throughout the war, the JWB used the local YMHAs and Jewish Community Center facilities to house programs for servicemen. At the war's end the Council of Young Men's Hebrew and Kindred Associations (YMH & KA)—the national organization linking the local YM & YWHAs—formally merged with the JWB, and in 1921 Louis Kraft was named director of Jewish Community Center Activities of the JWB.

In this new capacity, Louis Kraft supervised the development and expansion of community centers across the United States. Under his guidance, the JWB published communal studies and created a Building Bureau to offer guidance to communities seeking to establish community centers. He visited scores of communities and helped them with the design and administration of new buildings. Kraft's contributions to program development influenced hundreds of local center workers. Simultaneously, he trained JWB staff to oversee the national community center movement.

During the Great Depression of the 1930s, some Jewish community centers lost up to 40 percent of their membership and consequently were faced with foreclosure. Kraft and his staff at the JWB undertook to save these failing Jewish community centers from defaulting on their mortgages. By working with local bank officials and directing community funding campaigns, he was largely responsible for saving all but one center building from bankruptcy.

Louis Kraft became the acting executive director of JWB in 1938, and the following year he was appointed executive director. With the outbreak of fighting in Europe prior to the United States' entry into World War II, the JWB again turned its attention to supervising welfare work for Jews in the armed forces. Early in 1940, Kraft represented the JWB at a meeting which laid the groundwork for the United Service Organizations for National Defense (USO). He led the JWB into sponsorship of the USO along with the Young Men's Christian Association, the Young Women's Christian Association, the Salvation Army, the National Catholic Community Service, and the National Travelers' Aid Society. Kraft served as acting secretary of the newly formed USO (1940–1941), and he remained a member of its executive committee throughout World War II.

In 1947 Kraft stepped down from his post as executive director of the JWB to become the general secretary of the National Council of the JWB. In this capacity he supervised the reorganization of the Jewish Community Center movement in the United States, and he founded Jewish centers in other countries. When the World Federation of YMHAs and Jewish Community Centers was organized in 1947, Kraft was elected secretary, a position he retained for the remainder of his life. Under the aegis of the World Federation, Kraft traveled to Israel in 1948 and established the Jerusalem YM & YWHA. By doing so, Kraft inspired the emergence of a vast network of nondenominational, nonpolitical community centers which later developed throughout Israel.

He returned to Israel again in 1950–1951 under the State Department's Point Four Program (a United States foreign aid project set forth by President Truman to provide technological skills, knowledge, and equipment to poor nations throughout the world). During this time, Kraft undertook the reorganization of the Paul Baerwald School of Social Work (originally sponsored by the Joint Distribution Committee in France) at Hebrew University in Jerusalem.

In 1953 the Conference on Jewish Material Claims Against Germany and the Joint Distribution Committee (JDC) appointed Louis Kraft to direct the reconstruction and development of European Jewish communities. Working in the JDC headquarters, first in Paris and then in Geneva, Kraft served as a consultant to help plan the reestablishment of Jewish school facilities, synagogues, homes for the aged, summer camps, and hospitals in fourteen European countries. Calling upon his extensive background in the Jewish Community Center movement, Kraft persuaded European Jewish communal leaders that the community center could serve as a central organization catering to all segments of the Jewish community, especially the young. As a direct result of his initiative, the concept of the community center took hold in many European Jewish communities.

Louis Kraft was president of the National Conference on Jewish Communal Service, the Social Group Work Section of the National Conference of Jewish Social Work. He also served as president of the National Association of Jewish Center Workers, an organization for which he later became voluntary executive secretary from 1961 until his retirement in 1974. One year later, at age eighty-four, Kraft died at his home in New York City.

Until 1974 Kraft frequently wrote articles and book reviews for the JWB's house publication, the *JWB Circle*. His other written works include "Jews in the Armed Forces," *American Jewish Yearbook*, vols. 45–47 (1943–1946);

"Servicemen and Veterans," *American Jewish Yearbook*, vol. 48 (1946–1947); and *A Century of the Jewish Community Center Movement* (1953). He edited *Aspects of the Jewish Community Center* (1954) and *Change and Challenge: A History of Fifty Years of JWB* (1967). *The Development of the Jewish Community Center* (1967) is a collection of seventy articles and essays written by Kraft between the years 1922 and 1965, many of which are reprints of earlier publications.

Regrettably, no biography exists on Louis Kraft. The most extensive obituary is in the *JWB Circle* (October, 1975). Other helpful obituaries include Herbert Millman, "Remembering Lou Kraft," *Journal of Jewish Communal Service* (Fall, 1975), 108–111; *American Jewish Yearbook*, vol. 77 (1977), 596; *New York Times* (July 12, 1975); and *Washington Post* (July 13, 1975). See also Ira Eisenstein, "An Interview with Louis Kraft," *Reconstructionist*(January 20, 1967), 10–21; *New York Times* (May 12, 1928; November 6, 1939; April 20, 1942; October 13, 1944; June 27, 1947; June 9, 1949; June 4, 1951); *The Universal Jewish Encyclopedia*, s.v. "Kraft, Louis" (1939–1943); *The Encyclopedia Judaica*, s.v. "Kraft, Louis" and "National Jewish Welfare Board" (1972); *Who's Who in World Jewry* s.v. "Kraft, Louis" (1972). Manuscript sources include Louis Kraft Personal Papers, American Jewish Historical Society, Waltham, Massachusetts (uncatalogued); and smaller collections in the JWB Archives, New York, New York, and the American Jewish Archives, Cincinnati, Ohio. See also Minutes of the Army and Navy Committee of the JWB, American Jewish Historical Society, Waltham, Massachusetts; Jacob Billikopf Papers, American Jewish Archives, Cincinnati, Ohio.

GARY P. ZOLA

# L

**La Farge, Oliver Hazard Perry** (December 19, 1901–August 2, 1963), novelist, applied anthropologist, linguist, and American Indian rights activist, was born in New York City to an aristocratic family. His father, Christopher Grant La Farge, was an architect. His mother, Florence Bayard (Lockwood) La Farge, raised three other children and provided a family atmosphere that nurtured the arts and self-expression. The La Farges lived in New York City and spent their summers at Saunderstown on the west shore of Narragansett Bay.

Oliver La Farge had a distinguished education. He attended St. Bernard's School in New York City, which emphasized grammar and classical studies. Between 1914 and 1920 La Farge was a student at Groton, a Massachusetts preparatory school. There, he developed an interest in anthropology after reading Charles Darwin and Henry Fairfield Osborne's *Men of the Old Stone Age*.

In 1920 La Farge enrolled at Harvard University and majored in anthropology. He was drawn to this discipline because of his father's interest in Indians. La Farge also wanted to escape the confinement of the upper-class world of his family, which he believed represented only a splinter of the real American experience. While he was an undergraduate student, La Farge went on two expeditions sponsored by the Harvard Peabody Museum to study the culture of the Navajo Indians. He graduated cum laude in 1924.

La Farge remained at Harvard after receiving a Hemmenway fellowship for graduate study in anthropology, and he undertook a third field trip to Arizona. His graduate education was temporarily interrupted when he met Frans Bloom, who persuaded him to work as an assistant on a field trip to Mexico and Guatemala, in 1925, under the auspices of the Department of Middle American Research at Tulane University. This trip resulted in the discovery of three centers of Mayan culture. Two years later, La Farge returned to Guatemala, where he studied the Mayan religion of the Jacalteco Indians.

In 1928 La Farge went back to Harvard to begin research on Mayan dialects. He received an M.A. degree in 1929. La Farge married Wanden E. Mathews on September 28, 1929, and they had two children. In 1929 La Farge published

*Laughing Boy*, a novel about life on the Navajo Reservation, which won a Pulitzer Prize.

One year later, he joined the board of directors of the Eastern Association on Indian Affairs (EAIA). La Farge supported the reform program of Indian Commissioner Charles Rhoads; carried out an investigation of the economic conditions on the Jicarilla Reservation; helped raise funds to hire public health nurses for the Pueblo Indians; promoted the revival of Indian arts and crafts; and helped supervise, in 1931, an Inter-tribal Exhibition of Indian Arts in New York City.

In 1933 La Farge was elected president of the EAIA, and he changed its name to the National Association on Indian Affairs to encourage new membership. He worked closely with John Collier,* the Indian commissioner during the New Deal. Both men were attracted to the Indian's simplicity, religious intensity, and sense of human equality. They also were committed to using applied anthropology and other social sciences to better administer Indian affairs. La Farge supported Collier's efforts to establish a close working relationship between the Bureau of Ethnology at the Smithsonian Institution and the Indian Bureau. And he assisted Collier in the preparation of an executive order that required employees of the Indian Bureau to respect Indian religious freedom and culture. La Farge played an important role on the Young Committee, which formulated recommendations that led to the creation, in 1935, of an Indian Arts and Crafts Board in the Interior Department.

More important, La Farge helped formulate and secure passage of the Indian Reorganization Act of 1934, which ended land allotment and established formal tribal self-government. In 1935 and 1936 he met with the Hopi Indians to prepare a constitution that would safeguard their culture while providing a mechanism to address modern economic problems. Unfortunately, this constitution never worked properly because Hopi traditional institutions were incompatible with white concepts of democratic self-government.

La Farge remained deeply interested in the social welfare of the Navajo Indians. He urged government administrators to make Navajo chapters the unit of representation in plans to reorganize the tribal council, lobbied for the passage of the Navajo Boundary bill, and investigated the arrest and beating of Hosteen Tso, who had refused to follow government regulations and dip his sheep. In 1937 La Farge published *The Enemy Gods*, which defended the idea of cultural pluralism. In 1940 he collaborated with John Harrington, a linguist, to develop a written form of the Navajo language for use in newspapers and school textbooks.

The National Association on Indian Affairs merged with the American Indian Defense Association in 1937. La Farge became president of the new organization, the Association on American Indian Affairs (AAIA). He asked social scientists to join the board of directors in a futile effort to develop a method of scientifically administering Indian policy. La Farge made little progress because of a lack of public support and because of personal problems that led to a divorce from his first wife. On October 14, 1939, La Farge married Consuelo Otille O. C. de

Baca; they had one child. He resigned from the presidency of the AAIA in 1942 and joined the military. He served in the Army Transport Command until 1945.

La Farge moved to Santa Fe in 1946, became a member of the Laboratory of Anthropology, and wrote columns for the *New Mexican*. In 1948 he once again became president of the AAIA. He supported the Navajo-Hopi Rehabilitation bill of 1949, since members of those tribes did not come under state law, and fought for the right of Indians in Arizona and New Mexico to vote in state elections and receive Social Security benefits, and for the right of all tribes to contract with attorneys of their own choice.

During the 1950s La Farge defended the Indians against the policy of termination carried out by officials in the Eisenhower administration. He argued that House Resolution 108 and Public Law 280 would destroy the Indians' corporate tribal existence, end the trust status of their property, and lead to the unnecessary dispersal of Indian communities. He helped tribes rally support against termination, insisted that state and federal policy-makers consult with Indians, and assisted the Taos Indians in the struggle to gain control of their sacred Blue Lake. La Farge died in 1963 at Albuquerque, New Mexico, after a lengthy illness.

Oliver La Farge's literary manuscripts are located in the Oliver La Farge Papers, Humanities Research Center, University of Texas, Austin. The Association on American Indian Affairs Papers, Princeton University Library, contain valuable material concerning La Farge's career as a champion of Indian rights. The La Farge Family Collection of Papers, at the New York Historical Society, is closed to the public.

Publications by Oliver La Farge that shed light on his involvement with American Indians are *Laughing Boy* (1929); "Revolution with Reservations," *New Republic* (October, 1935), 232–234; *The Enemy Gods* (1937); *As Long as the Grass Shall Grow* (1940); *The Changing Indian* (1942); *Raw Material* (1945); "Address at the Annual Meeting of the Association on American Indian Affairs," *American Indian* 4 (1947), 6–10; "A Way Out for the Navajos," *Indian Affairs* (Summer, 1951), 14–16; *A Pictorial History of the American Indian* (1956); "The Enduring Indian," *Scientific Monthly* (February, 1960), 37–44; and "Termination of Federal Supervision: Disintegration and the American Indians," *Annals of the American Academy of Political and Social Science* (May, 1957), 41–46.

Consult the following publications for information about Oliver La Farge: Larry Burt, *Tribalism in Crisis: Federal Indian Policy, 1953–1961* (1982); Charles Byrd, "A Descriptive Bibliography of the Oliver La Farge Collection at the University of Texas, Austin," Ph.D. dissertation, University of Texas, Austin, 1974; Everett Gillis, *Oliver La Farge* (1967); D'Arcy McNickle, *Indian Man: A Life of Oliver La Farge* (1971); Donald L. Parman, *The Navajos and the New Deal* (1976); Kenneth R. Philp, *John Collier's Crusade for Indian Reform, 1920–1954* (1977); Robert Fay Schrader, *The Indian Arts and Crafts Board: An Aspect of New Deal Indian Policy* (1983); Winfield T. Scott, ed., *The Man with the*

*Calabash Pipe* (1966); Margaret Szasz, *Education and the American Indian: The Road to Self-Determination, 1928–1973* (1974); and Graham D. Taylor, *The New Deal and American Indian Tribalism: The Administration of the Indian Reorganization Act, 1934–1945* (1980).

KENNETH R. PHILP

**Lathrop, Julia Clifford** (June 29, 1858–April 15, 1932), social worker, reformer, Hull-House resident, and chief of the U.S. Children's Bureau, was born in Rockford, Illinois, to Sarah Adeline (Potter) and William L. Lathrop.

Adeline Potter was the valedictorian in the first graduating class (1854) of the Rockford Female Seminary. She was a fervent suffragist, devoted to education, and a leader among women in her community. Julia Lathrop's father, William, was a descendant of the Reverend John Lathrop, an English nonconformist who came to America in 1634. Years later, from the Genesee valley of New York, William L. Lathrop migrated to Rockford and by 1857 had established a practice of law. He supported his wife's convictions about the rights of women and became a trustee of the Rockford Female Seminary. Julia Lathrop was instructed by her father's shared experiences in politics and law. For example, her strong interest in mental health reflected early exposure to advanced thinking when her father defended a woman by a plea of emotional insanity, the first such defense in Illinois jurisprudence.

Julia Lathrop completed high school in Rockford. To correct some academic deficiencies before seeking entrance to Vassar College, she enrolled for a year in the Rockford Female Seminary and supplemented this instruction with private tutors in German and mathematics. She entered Vassar as a sophomore and graduated in 1880. In later years, when she occasionally returned to Vassar, she was regarded as a distinguished alumna.

Upon graduation she found no open door to a vocation. She returned to Rockford, served as secretary in her father's law office, invested in two local manufacturing companies, became secretary to them, and took satisfaction from a private income. She had begun to read law with her father when in the winter of 1888–1889 Jane Addams* and Ellen Starr* came to Rockford to talk about "a new Toynbee Hall." In 1890, at age thirty-two, Lathrop became a resident of Hull-House. She moved rapidly into a lasting relationship of trust with Addams. She also became a volunteer visitor for the Cook County Charities and within a ten-block area around Hull-House witnessed the suffering of people who were pushed into poverty in a cruel winter of unemployment. She saw, too, the indifference to human need and to public service. She developed lasting convictions about the importance of competent and honest public servants and effective methods of public administration.

Under an appointment by Governor John P. Altgeld, in 1893 Lathrop assumed duties as the first woman member of the State Board of Charities. The Board had general supervision of public institutions throughout the state. Serving without compensation, Lathrop journeyed all over Illinois, mostly by country wagon, sometimes by train or river boat, visiting each of the 102 county farms and poorhouses and twelve state charitable institutions. In each, she was an open-minded but authoritative inquirer in an effort to lessen the injustices the inmates suffered and to improve their level of care. It was the "spoils system" with which Julia Lathrop struggled most. She worked for a system of merit examinations for employees in the state's institutions. However, when Richard Yates was elected governor and it became clear in 1901 that public charities were to be used openly for party ends on an unprecedented scale, Lathrop resigned from the Board in protest against the politics of exploiting sick and helpless human beings in the state's institutions. Upon the election of Governor Charles Deneen, she was reappointed to the Board of 1905 and served five more years, at which time the Board was reorganized as a nonpartisan body, as Lathrop had advocated.

Lathrop became an energetic leader to improve the care of the mentally ill. She worked closely with Dr. Adolf Meyer* in the state hopital for the insane in Kankakee. Among their common interests was the retention of the hospital's research laboratory, constantly threatened by politicians. With Clifford Beers,* Lathrop was one of the founders of the National Committee for Mental Hygiene in 1909. She recognized the need to train attendants in mental hospitals and influenced Graham Taylor* (whom she had assisted in establishing the Chicago School of Civics and Philanthropy) to offer courses for them. She believed strongly in the importance of social research as a sound base for social reform and was the first director of research in the Chicago school. From time to time throughout her career, she went abroad in search of knowledge, new methods, and experiments, as she did in 1898 when she went into Belgium, France, and Germany to study methods of caring for the mentally ill. She brought back reports and ideas which she transmitted to the National Conference of Charities and Correction. (She served as president of this body in 1918, by then called the National Conference of Social Work).

Lathrop is generally credited with having been the moving force behind the creation of the first juvenile court (in Cook County in 1899), a development that spread rapidly throughout the world. She was also influential in the founding of the Chicago Juvenile Psychopathic Institute, a fully staffed children's clinic in conjunction with the juvenile court and under the direction of Dr. William Healy.*

When the U.S. Children's Bureau was established by Congress in 1912, President Taft appointed Lathrop as chief, the first woman bureau chief in the federal government. She brought to the job her own professional network, which she had built in her Hull-House years and now used as an informal but powerful constituency for the Bureau. This network included college women, club women, suffragists, philanthropists, social welfare experts, scholars, physicians, lawyers, and politicians. The broadly based social research function of the Bureau and the limited appropriations at its founding meant that Lathrop was faced at once with the task of selecting service priorities carefully. Her first selection for research was infant mortality, which she saw as an indicator of the "preventable" deaths of children, followed by studies of maternal mortality and a national campaign for birth registration. These careful investigations laid a foundation of facts that provided the impetus for passage of legislation for maternal and infant protection (the Sheppard-Towner Act) in 1921.

The work of the Bureau showed the absence of standardized norms of children's growth and development and, overall, the limits of scientific data on children. With President Wilson's backing, Lathrop and her protégée, Grace Abbott,* planned and carried out a Conference on Standards of Child Welfare (actually eight regional conferences) for the purpose of setting up irreducible minimum standards in three areas of child welfare: child labor, the health of children and mothers, and children in need of special care. The endeavor involved a wide range of people and interests in America and Europe and marked a significant step in the systematic development of standards as a basis for national child and family policy.

Julia Lathrop was a somewhat plain-looking woman with dark hair, eyes, and skin and prominent features. She was said to have a ''redolent'' voice and an impressive supply of energy. In manner, she used persuasion and even cajolery and often seemed to make her points in a circuitous way, with frequent expressions of empathy for another's point of view. She had a quick sense of humor in daily affairs and, more rare, a quality of disinterestedness in relation to the social issues she worked for. As chief of the Children's Bureau she provided strong leadership within an atmosphere of collegiality and respect. She possessed an uncommon capacity for sound judgment and readiness to make and implement decisions. She pushed for maximum efficiency in the assignment and performance of her limited staff and at the same time retained enough flexibility to permit an innovative response to new opportunities in behalf of children and families.

When Lathrop chose to retire, she strongly favored Grace Abbott as her successor. President Harding's expansion of patronage, however, posed a threat to the integrity of the Children's Bureau. With consummate political skill, Lathrop engineered backing for Grace Abbott not only from organized women but from influential men whose support was essential. Some years later a former Bureau staff member who remembered the impressive infant and maternal mortality studies that Julia Lathrop had directed asked her what she considered her major achievement during her years at the Bureau. Lathrop replied, simply, that she had kept it from becoming politicized.

Following her resignation Lathrop returned to Rockford, lived with her sister, and remained active in public affairs. Appointed by President Coolidge, she served on a commission to investigate Ellis Island. From 1925 until 1931 she gave international services as an assessor for the Advisory Child Welfare Committee of the League of Nations.

Julia Lathrop's work reflects an unflagging commitment to social justice and reform. Her interests were wide: neglected, dependent, and delinquent children; immigrants; infant and maternal health; mothers' pensions; child labor; the mentally ill; civil service reform; and more. She believed that the scientific method was the most useful tool possessed by the modern world; social research findings formed the cornerstone of her work. She paved the way for women in federal government and demonstrated an effective model of sound public administration. She died in Rockford, Illinois, at age seventy-three.

Most of Julia Lathrop's personal papers are in the Rockford College Library. The records of the Children's Bureau in the National Archives provide extensive information about Lathrop's tenure as chief of the Children's Bureau. The Grace and Edith Abbott Papers at the University of Chicago's Regenstein Library contain relevant correspondence and reports, as does the Hull-House Collection, at the University of Illinois at Chicago.

Julia Lathrop prepared annual reports as chief of the Children's Bureau from 1913 through 1921. Her articles and speeches are found in *Proceedings* of the National Conference of Charities and Correction, the *Survey*, and other journals of the day. Lathrop contributed a chapter on the founding of the juvenile court to *The Child, the Clinic and the Court*, ed. Jane Addams, C. Judson Herrick, A. L. Jacoby, et al. (1921). *The Hull-House Maps and Papers* (1895) contains her descriptions of the plight of the poor and the mentally ill as she found them during her work with the Cook County Charities.

Jane Addams' biography, *My Friend, Julia Lathrop* (1935), is a useful personal account. The relationship between Julia Lathrop and Grace Abbott is presented in Lela B. Costin's *Two Sisters for Social Justice: A Biography of Grace and Edith Abbott* (1983). Louis J. Covotsos, "Child Welfare and Social Progress: A History of the United States Children's Bureau, 1912–1935," Ph.D. dissertation, University of Chicago, 1976, casts light on Lathrop's style of administering the Children's Bureau. Ray Ginger's *Altgeld's America* (1958) addresses numerous aspects of Lathrop's work. Jacqueline K. Parker and Edward M. Carpenter provide an analysis of Lathrop's early launching of the Children's Bureau in "Julia Lathrop and the Children's Bureau: The Emergence of an Institution," *Social Service Review* (March, 1981), 60–77.

LELA B. COSTIN

**Lee, Joseph** (March 8, 1862-July 28, 1937), play movement leader and civic reformer, was born in Brookline, Massachusetts, the seventh of eight children and the fourth son of Henry and Elizabeth Perkins (Cabot) Lee.

Through family ties and his father's position as one of Boston's leading bankers, Lee was born into the city's elite social, economic, and intellectual circles. His education befitted his social station. He received his secondary education at Noble's School and then attended Harvard University, which awarded him an A.B. degree in 1883 and an A.M. and an LL.B. in 1887. He was admitted to the Massachusetts bar in 1887, but he never practiced law. In 1897 he married Margaret Copley Cabot, with whom he had four children (three daughters and a son) and who died in 1920. Ten years later, on October 14, 1930, he married his secretary, Marion Snow; they had no children.

A quirky individualist with a biting social conscience, Lee was never comfortable with his wealth. In his early adulthood he went to Russia to consult with Count Leo Tolstoy about the advisability of disposing of it. Tolstoy convinced him not to do so. Instead of then spending his fortune on luxurious living, Lee used his money and time aiding causes he believed would strengthen community life and help individuals, especially children, develop their potential.

Lee's first important achievement was the founding in 1897 of a civic reform organization, the Massachusetts Civic League. He served as its president until 1935 and was throughout his life one of its major financial supporters. One purpose of the League was to educate people about problems in their midst and possible solutions to them. To fulfill this goal, Lee established in Boston a Town Room, a kind of legislative reference library where individuals could study what various private organizations, municipalities, and states were doing to solve a wide range of governmental and social problems. The League's other purposes were to originate socially beneficial legislation and to coordinate the lobbying and publicity efforts of groups supporting those and similar bills and other good causes. Among the League's early interests were juvenile courts, political reforms such as the simplified ballot, public health, housing, and city planning. Among its early significant successes was the passage of a state law requiring medical examinations for school children.

Lee's persistent effort to get this law passed was indicative of his lifelong interest in child welfare, a field in which he became prominent as an activist and theorist in Boston, the state of Massachusetts, and the nation as a whole. In Boston, Lee contributed large sums of money to Harvard to support its graduate program in education. He was elected to the Boston School Committee in 1908 and served until 1917, and he supported the School Visitors' Association, an organization his first wife helped found. Among the problems of Boston's schools that most concerned Lee were the age at which children left school, the provision of school lunches, and the establishment of special classes and activities for slow learners and gifted and handicapped children. For adults he advocated the use of school buildings for night classes and community meetings and events.

Nationally, Lee gained fame during his lifetime and enduring significance in the history of social welfare as a leader in the play and playground movement. He first became involved in promoting playgrounds in Boston through his activities in the Massachusetts Emergency and Hygiene Association. He served on the organization's executive committee between 1891 and 1894, and on its Committee on Playgrounds. The Association had created the city's first playgrounds in 1885–1886, and it and Lee strongly influenced Mayor Josiah Quincy's efforts in 1897–1898 to provide a measure of public financial support and additional space for playgrounds. Lee's Massachusetts Civic League was the driving force behind the passage of a state law in 1907 that finally placed Boston's playgrounds under full public control.

Because of these experiences and some of his writings, Lee gained a reputation as an authority on play and playgrounds. This led to his being included in the group that founded the Playground Association of America in 1906. He served the organization as a vice president until 1910, when he was elected president. As president until his death, Lee oversaw the organization's evolution into the National Recreation Association.

The first decade of Lee's incumbency as president was a golden age for the play movement. Cities and private organizations across the nation spent millions of dollars to build playgrounds and hire play leaders. The Association was a powerful engine pushing the play movement forward, through publicity to educate the public concerning the personal and social benefits of play, and through the activities of field workers, Lee, and other leaders of the organization. In recognition of his vigorous leadership of the play movement and his Association's growing interest in adult recreation, during World War I Lee was appointed to the federal government's Commission on Training Camp Activities, and he and the Association were asked to develop recreational facilities for soldiers. To carry out this task, the War Camp Community Service was formed as an affiliate of the Association. Lee served as the Service's president, for which he later was awarded the War Department's Distinguished Service Medal. After the war he used some Service facilities left intact and local committees to launch the Community Service of Boston. This organization started constructive leisure activities for adults, especially in music and drama, and then turned those activities over to citizens who wished to continue them.

Besides his labors in the play movement, Lee was an important theoretician of play. He believed that play enabled people to develop their physical, mental, and moral capabilities to the fullest. Organized play of the kind promoted by the Association socialized children and instilled in people of all ages the values of teamwork and loyalty that made them good citizens in a democratic society. In Lee's numerous published elaborations of his ideas he made significant contributions to the study of child development. Theories of child development played an important role not only in the progress of the play movement but also in the progress of other movements, such as child labor reform and the drive to create juvenile courts. At the same time, his writings manifested notions of social control, theories concerning the characteristics of racial and ethnic groups, and antipluralistic values that reflected Lee's ardent support of immigration restriction from the 1890s, his advocacy of charitable uplift and voluntarism rather than material assistance to people with problems, and his opposition to fundamental changes in social, economic, and political institutions.

After a long and useful life, Joseph Lee died of pneumonia at his summer home in Cohasset, Massachusetts, on July 28, 1937.

There is no record of the existence of Joseph Lee's private papers. His many articles and two books are the principal sources for studying his activities and ideas. His two most important works are *Constructive and Preventive Philanthropy* (1902) and *Play in Education* (1915). Articles of importance are "The Community, Maker of Men," *Survey Graphic* (February 1, 1923), 576–579;

"American Play Tradition and Our Relation to It," *Playground* (July, 1913), 148–159; "Expensive Living, the Blight on America," *New England Magazine* (March, 1898), 53–64; "Play as an Antidote to Civilization," *Playground* (December, 1911), 110–126; "The Philanthropist's Legislative Function," *New England Magazine* (March, 1899), 51–58; and "A People's Lobbyist," *Independent* (May 23, 1907), 1203–1206.

A memorial issue of the National Recreation Association's magazine, *Recreation* (December, 1937); Theodore Geoffrey, "A Philosopher Who Works for Fun, and Why He Does It," *World's Work* (November, 1926), 57–60; and Edward N. Saveth, "Patrician Philanthropy in America: The Late Nineteenth and Early Twentieth Centuries," *Social Service Review* (March, 1980), 77–91, deal with Lee's life and ideas. K. Gerald Marsden, "Philanthropy and the Boston Playground Movement," *Social Service Review* (March, 1951), 48–58; Dominick Cavallo, *Muscles and Morals: Organized Playgrounds and Urban Reform, 1880–1920* (1981); Clarence Rainwater, *The Play Movement in the United States* (1922); Allen Sapora, "The Contributions of Joseph Lee to the Modern Recreation Movement and Related Social Movements in the United States," Ph.D. dissertation, University of Michigan, 1952; and Geoffrey Blodgett, *The Gentle Reformers: Massachusetts Democrats in the Cleveland Era* (1966), discuss Lee's role in the play movement. Barbara Miller Solomon, *Ancestors and Immigrants: A Changing New England Tradition* (1956), shows Lee's role in the movement to restrict immigration.

                                                                    STANLEY MALLACH

**Lee, Porter Raymond** (December 21, 1879–March 8, 1939), social worker and social work educator, was born in Buffalo, New York, to Ruben Porter Lee, a banker, and Jennie (Blanchard) Lee. He was the third son and the third child of five born to the Lee household. His interest in social work as a career was apparently stimulated by an undergraduate course in methods of modern philanthropy taken at Cornell University. In 1903 he graduated from Cornell and immediately enrolled in the New York School of Philanthropy, at the time the only program of formal training for social work in the United States. Lee married Ethel Hepburn Pollock of Buffalo on January 30, 1905. They had five children: Porter Raymond, James Pollock, Margaret T., Jean Hepburn, and Ruth Tenney.

After attending the six-week session at of the New York School of Philanthropy, Lee began his social work career as the assistant secretary of the Charity Organization Society (COS) of Buffalo. In later years, he was to credit the six years spent with Frederick Almy, the secretary of the Buffalo COS, as the single most important aspect of his professional education. In 1909 he assumed the position of general secretary for the Society for Organizing Charity of Philadelphia, succeeding Mary E. Richmond.* He held this position for three years and in 1912 joined the faculty of the New York School of Philanthropy. He began his career in social work education as an instructor of social casework, and five years later, in 1917, he succeeded Edward T. Devine* as director of the school. He was to continue in this position for the remainder of his professional career, covering a period of twenty-one years. The only significant time away from the position as director occurred in 1930–1931, when he was asked to serve as a member of President Hoover's Emergency Committee for Employment.

Within the field of social welfare, Lee is most remembered for his contributions to the advancement of professional education for social work practice. It was during his directorship that the New York School of Philanthropy became the New York School of Social Work and moved toward affiliation with Columbia University, which was finally achieved in 1940. The school, under his leadership, grew in size to 1,500 full- and part-time students to become the largest school of social work in the country. This growth resulted in the development of an expanded curriculum to include the fields of community organization, group work, research, and social psychiatry.

Lee's greatest contribution to social work education was the development of the "case method" of instruction. Karl de Schweinitz* credited him with being the primary creator of this technique and indicated that this approach was as much a testimony to the quality of Lee the person as to Lee the educator. This use of case discussion and case material has endured to contemporary times as a central strategy for teaching social work practice. In addition, Lee is recognized for advancing the conceptual base for casework practice. His book *Social Work: Cause and Function* (1937), which is a compilation of his major public addresses and papers, was a landmark in integrating the dual social work roles of social reformer and social technician. Another social casework classic was *Social Case Work, Generic and Specific* (1929), written by Lee and published by the American Association of Social Workers. This report, known as the Milford Conference Report, resulted from the meetings of a conference group led by Lee over a four-year period (1923 to 1927) and set down a generic theory base for the practice of social casework. This development resulted in a movement away from agency-specific training to a curriculum designed to prepare social workers for entry into a profession.

Earlier, in May, 1919, Lee invited the directors of the existing schools of social work to a meeting in his office, out of which grew the creation of the Association of Schools of Social Work. The Association was responsible for the development of accreditation standards for graduate social work education and was a forerunner of the Council on Social Work Education.

Lee also provided leadership to the social work profession in other areas. He was involved in the creation of the American Association of Social Workers, a professional body, and was to serve as president of the National Conference of Social Work in 1929. In addition, he was to keep a keen interest in social work practice and maintained close ties with the Charity Organization Society movement, serving on several executive committees for the New York COS and making significant contributions to the literature.

An enduring aspect of the career of Porter Lee is the remembrance of his warmth as a human being. His outgoing personality and genuine interest in people served him well as a classroom teacher. It was these traits which made his case discussion technique so powerful and led students and colleagues alike down the path of self-discovery, resulting in their increased productivity as professional social workers. Lee died of a heart condition at his home in Englewood, New Jersey, on March 8, 1939.

Lee devoted considerable energy to the Charity Organization Society movement, and one can find his views on this subject in the *Collected Speeches and Papers on Charity Organization* in the Whitney Young, Jr. Memorial Library of Social Work at Columbia University in New York.

He coauthored two works of some note, one with Marion Kenworthy, *Mental Hygiene and Social Work* (1929), the other with Walter Pettit, *Social Salvage* (1924).

Material regarding Lee's contributions to the social work profession may be found in the following articles: Frank Bruno, "The Growth of Training for Social Work," *The Family* (January, 1940); Joanna Colcord, "Porter Lee, Social Work Philosopher," *Survey Midmonthly* (December, 1938); Walter Pettit, "His Philosophy and Personality," *The Family* (January, 1940); and Karl de Schweinitz, "His Contribution to Case Work Teaching," *The Family*, (January, 1940). His obituary can be found in the *New York Times*, March 9, 1939. A biography is found in the *Dictionary of American Biography*, Supplement 2 (1958).

BARRY L. LOCKE

**Leiserson, William Morris** (April 15, 1883–February 12, 1957), labor economist, mediator, and New Deal official, was born in Revel, Estonia, to Mendel and Sarah L. (Snyder) Leiserson. Fleeing the anti-Semitic campaigns of Russian authorities, which apparently claimed his father's life, Leiserson, with his mother and brothers, arrived in the United States in 1890. Leiserson attended school in New York City until 1897 and worked in a clothing factory until 1904. After passing a high school equivalency examination, he enrolled at the University of Wisconsin, known at that time for its innovative social science departments and activist professors. At first an outspoken socialist and defender of radical causes, Leiserson soon became a convert to the progressivism of the economist John R. Commons.* Focusing on the role of industrial workers, Commons argued that government regulation and democratic trade unions were the prerequisites for a new capitalist equilibrium based on social harmony and justice. Like John B. Andrews* and other Commons students, Leiserson made this view the basis of his career.

On June 22, 1912, Leiserson married Emily N. Bodman, a graduate of Simmons College who had been Commons' secretary. They had seven children.

Leiserson was quickly drawn into practical affairs. In 1907–1908 he worked on two of Commons' most important projects, the Pittsburgh Survey and the *Documentary History of American Industrial Society*. In 1909, as a graduate student at Columbia, he became an investigator for the New York State Commission on Employers' Liability and Unemployment. His dissertation, "Unemployment in the State of New York" (1911), was one of the Commission's major reports. When Leiserson finished his Ph.D. work, Commons secured his appointment as deputy industrial commissioner of Wisconsin, in charge of the state's public employment offices. In 1914, again at Commons' urging, he became assistant research director of the U.S. Commission on Industrial Relations. The following year he accepted a position as professor of economics and political science at the University of Toledo, and in 1917 guided the reorganization of Ohio's public employment offices. In 1918 he left Toledo to become head of the Division of Labor Administration in the Department of Labor.

In 1919 Leiserson began the work that would absorb most of the rest of his career. He had become acquainted with Sidney Hillman of the Amalgamated Clothing Workers during World War I and with Hillman's support was appointed chairman of the Labor Adjustment Board in the men's clothing industry in Rochester, New York. After two years he moved to a similar post in New York City, and then, in 1923, to Baltimore and Chicago. By the mid 1920s, Leiserson was one of the nation's best-known arbitrators. However, his large family demanded a more settled existence, and in 1926 he accepted a professorship at Antioch College. Under President Arthur Morgan, Antioch had acquired a reputation as a distinguished but unorthodox institution, and Leiserson found it a congenial environment. He continued to take arbitration cases and wrote and lectured widely on labor topics. He organized the research that Stanley Mathewson summarized in his seminal *Restriction of Output Among Unorganized Workers* (1929) and served as chairman of the Ohio Commission on Unemployment Insurance (1931–1932).

The advent of the Roosevelt administration catapulted Leiserson into national affairs. In 1933 he moved to Washington to become secretary of the new National Labor Board, where he helped establish a system of regional labor boards. Preferring arbitration work, he left the Labor Board in 1934 to become chairman of the Petroleum Labor Policy Board and, shortly thereafter, chairman of the National Mediation Board, the body that administered railway labor legislation. Leiserson served in that capacity until 1939, when Roosevelt prevailed upon him to accept appointment to the National Labor Relations Board (NLRB).

Leiserson's years on the NLRB, 1939–1943, were the most controversial and perhaps the most important of his long career. Besides the day-to-day tasks of administering the Wagner Act, he was deeply involved in two crucial political disputes. The first, in 1939–1941, was the so-called purge of NLRB leftists. Roosevelt had appointed Leiserson to serve as a counterweight to the politically controversial board incumbents and staff. But Leiserson, who was suspicious of the Congress of Industrial Organizations (CIO) and strongly anticommunist, could do little until 1940, when his friend and ally Harry A. Millis became NLRB board chairman. Leiserson and Millis then reorganized the staff, eliminating leftists from sensitive positions. By that time a new and more complex struggle had begun as a result of the President's decision to handle wartime labor disputes through new emergency tripartite agencies. Leiserson strongly opposed this change, decrying the politicization of collective bargaining, and was happy to return to the National Mediation Board in 1943. There he almost immediately confronted similar problems. War administrators interfered in a proposed railroad wage settlement, creating great bitterness and a more costly final agreement. In protest, Leiserson resigned in early 1944.

After three years at Johns Hopkins as a visiting professor of economics, Leiserson spent the rest of his career in semi-retirement as a mediator, government advisor, and part-time teacher. His principal professional interest was the seeming decline in union democracy, the basis of his commitment to collective bargaining. He worked sporadically on a study of this problem, published posthumously as *American Trade Union Democracy* (1959). Leiserson died in Washington, D.C., on February 12, 1957.

The voluminous William M. Leiserson Papers are available at the State Historical Society of Wisconsin. Leiserson's published writings include *Adjusting Immigrant and Industry* (1924) and *American Trade Union Democracy* (1959). The best source on his life is J. Michael Eisner, *William Morris Leiserson: A Biography* (1967). James A. Gross, *The Reshaping of the National Labor Relations Board: National Labor Policy in Transition, 1937–1947* (1981), examines his controversial years at the NLRB.

DANIEL NELSON


**Lenroot, Katharine Fredrica** (March 8, 1891–February 10, 1982), longtime member of the U.S. Children's Bureau and its chief from 1934 to 1951, was born in Superior, Wisconsin, to Clara Pamela (Clough) and Irvine Luther Lenroot, a lawyer, United States Senator, and judge of the court of customs and patent appeals. Her paternal grandfather came from Sweden in 1854 and settled in Boston, and then moved to St. Croix Falls in Polk County, Wisconsin.

After attending local public schools, Katharine enrolled at the University of Wisconsin; in her junior year, while taking classes from John R. Commons,* she appeared before the Wisconsin state legislature to speak in favor of a minimum wage law. She was awarded a Bachelor of Arts degree in 1912 and became a member of Phi Beta Kappa. After passing a civil service examination in 1913, she was appointed to the Industrial Commission of Wisconsin with the task of conducting cost of living investigations in the city of Milwaukee. She resigned from that position in 1914 to become a special agent with the newly created U.S. Children's Bureau within the Department of Labor. The Children's Bureau then became her career for the rest of her working years and the outlet through which she made a mark on social welfare in America. She served as assistant director of the Social Service Division to 1921, director of the Editorial Division to 1922, assistant chief until 1934, and chief until she retired in 1951.

Grace Abbott,* who succeeded Julia Lathrop* as chief of the Children's

Bureau in 1921, experienced health difficulties in the early 1930s and had to be away from the office for extended periods of time. Abbott found in Lenroot an ideal acting chief in her absence. Lenroot was committed to the philosophy of the Children's Bureau, as outlined by the founders, and was careful and conscientious in carrying out the required administrative tasks. She wrote long and detailed letters to Grace Abbott at frequent intervals and sought direction for important decisions. On the other hand, she must have found the vagueness of her position frustrating at times. When she and Martha Eliot* desired to undertake a new study, Grace Abbott overruled them from her sickbed in Colorado. Lenroot, however, remained loyal throughout, both to the Children's Bureau and to Grace Abbott.

When Grace Abbott retired in 1934, the two leading candidates to succeed her were Martha Eliot and Katharine Lenroot. Lenroot had strong support from the American Association of Social Workers, J. Prentice Murphy* of the Children's Bureau of Philadelphia, Allen Burns* of the American Association of Community Chests and Councils, and Homer Folks* of the New York State Charities Aid Association. Frances Perkins,* the Secretary of Labor, finally chose Lenroot and recommended her to President Franklin D. Roosevelt.

Katharine Lenroot and Martha Eliot were primary resource persons to the Committee on Economic Security, the group responsible for putting together the Social Security Act. Fortified by further input from Grace Abbott, these women worked hard to get children included in the act. This was important because Congress was seemingly more concerned about retirement provisions than child welfare. Once the act was passed in 1935, the Children's Bureau became the agency responsible for providing grants to the states for the development of maternal and child health services, services for crippled children, and other child welfare measures. Katharine Lenroot, as Chief of the Children's Bureau, was the person ultimately responsible for the success of these ventures in child welfare through the vehicle of government provisions for Social Security.

Katharine Lenroot had an ongoing concern about the employment of children and was heartened by the progress evidenced by the child labor restrictions attached to the Fair Labor Standards Act in 1938. She and the Children's Bureau worked hard to keep the standards high during World War II, when there was pressure to relax them because of the war emergency. In addition, she led the way for a conference, sponsored by the Children's Bureau in 1941, to provide day care for the children of working mothers. Indeed, this concern was continued after the war, as was her interest in the problem of juvenile delinquency. One of the great landmarks of child welfare was the passage by Congress of the Emergency Maternal and Infant Care program, which was in effect from 1943 to 1947. The concern was that the pregnant wives of servicemen in the lower grades should receive proper medical care from conception through delivery. Congress passed the bill, probably to increase morale in the armed forces, but Katharine Lenroot viewed it as another step forward in the area of child welfare.

Katharine Lenroot was active in the two White House conferences held while she was Chief of the Children's Bureau. She was the executive secretary of the 1940 White House Conference on Children in a Democracy, and worked hard to keep the needs of child welfare in focus in spite of the growing world emergency. Then she served as secretary of the Midcentury White House Conference on Children and Youth, at which there was a growing interest in the problem of juvenile delinquency.

Her interests in child welfare were not parochial. She was chairperson of the United States delegation to the fifth (Cuba, 1927) and sixth (Peru, 1930) Pan American Child Congresses. Her sincerity to internationalism was evidenced by her learning of Spanish as preparation for these experiences, and her induction as president of the eighth (United States, 1942) Pan American Child Congress. At the conclusion of World War II, she attended a Montreal meeting responsible for a preliminary draft of an International Youth Charter. Furthermore, she served as a U.S. member of the United Nations International Children's Emergency Fund Executive Board and as a U.S. alternate representative to the Social Commission of the United Nations Economic and Social Council.

These international interests were balanced by her activities outside of her duties at home as Chief of the Children's Bureau. She was a member of the board of directors of the American Public Welfare Association, the American Association of Social Workers, and the National Council of Social Work. She received the *Parents' Magazine* Medal for Outstanding Service to Children in 1940, the University of Chicago Rosenberger Medal for distinguished service in social work in 1942, the Gold Medal of the National Institute of Social Sciences for distinguished service to humanity in 1947, and the 1950 *Survey* Annual Award for constructive contribution to social work. Clearly she was active and involved in the social welfare area of American life.

The recipient of several honorary degrees, she dedicated her energies mainly to child welfare. She fought unceasingly for a child labor amendment to the constitution and believed, as did her predecessors at the Children's Bureau, that the primary essential in child welfare was a decent family living standard.

She authored numerous pamphlets put out by the Children's Bureau as well as articles, mainly dealing with social welfare issues, in the leading journals. Her name and the cause of child welfare were almost synonymous, and upon her retirement in 1951 President Harry Truman spoke highly of her accomplishments in the cause of child welfare.

Active in behalf of children nationally and internationally in her retirement years, she died February 10, 1982, at the Colonial Manor Nursing Home in Milwaukee, Wisconsin.

The Lenroot Papers can be found at the Columbia University Library. Many of her writings were published by the Children's Bureau: *Mental Defectives in the District of Columbia: A Brief Description of Local Conditions and the Need for Custodial Care and Training* (1915); *Social Responsibility for the Protection of Children Handicapped by Illegitimate Birth* (1921); *Juvenile Courts at Work:*

*A Study of the Organization and Methods of Ten Courts*, with Emma O. Lundberg (1925); *The Child, the Family, and the Court: A Study of the Administration of Justice in the Field of Domestic Relations: General Findings and Recommendations*, with Bernard Flexner and Reuben Oppenheimer (1933); *Effects of Unemployment on Child Welfare with Special Reference to Dependent Children in Ohio*, with Caroline E. Legg (1933); and, with Martha M. Eliot, "Security for Children," in U.S. Committee on Economic Security, *Social Security in America* (1937), detailing the Children's Bureau recommendations for including children in the Social Security Act. *Current Biography* (1950) has a detailed article on Lenroot. An obituary appeared in the *Washington Post*, February 13, 1982.

JAMES E. JOHNSON

**Letchworth, William Pryor** (May 26, 1823–December 1, 1910), child welfare reformer, mental health advocate, and philanthropist, was born in Brownville, New York, one of eight children of Josiah and Ann (Hance) Letchworth. The Letchworth family was financially secure, and Josiah Letchworth was himself a well-known social reformer, having fought for school reform and the abolition of slavery. William went through the public schools and went to work at the age of fifteen as a clerk in a manufacturing firm. In 1848, at the age of twenty-five, he became a full partner in Pratt and Letchworth, a hardware firm in which he remained until the early 1870s. Having amassed a comfortable fortune, he retired from private business and devoted the remainder of his life to his social reform and philanthropic interests.

In 1873 Letchworth turned down what seemed to be a sure nomination for Congress to accept an appointment as a commissioner of the New York State Board of Charities. In this position he became concerned with the number of children who were being held in poorhouses. New York poorhouses were at that time commonly used as "catch-alls" for all the categories of people society did not wish to deal with. Poor people, mentally ill and retarded individuals, petty criminals, and so-called undesirables of all ages were housed in the same institution, often with little or no system of separation or classification. Letchworth worked very hard to have children transferred to institutions of their own, and eventually secured legislation making it illegal to confine "normal" children between the ages of three and sixteen in almshouses in New York State. He also was instrumental in promoting a movement to encourage adoption of such children by private families.

Letchworth became president of the State Board of Charities in 1878 and turned his attention to other problem populations—delinquents and the mentally ill. In 1880 he made an extensive tour of Europe during which he examined, in some detail, the various types of facilities and methods of treatment used in those countries to deal with the problems of delinquency and mental illness. He returned believing that, in many ways, the European systems were superior.

In several countries he had been particularly impressed by the practice of providing industrial training for delinquents in a nonrestrictive residential atmosphere. This was very much in contrast to the situation at that time in New York and much of the rest of the United States, where delinquents were incarcerated in prisonlike settings, often in the company of adult offenders. Letchworth lobbied extensively for reform of these facilities and also worked for an improved system of classification of offenders. He lived to see the establishment of several industrial training schools for youthful offenders, the beginning of reform that continues to this day.

Another area of concern to Letchworth was treatment of the mentally ill. Public institutions for the mentally ill during this time generally were wretched places—overcrowded, brutal, and unimaginably dirty. Treatment, as such, was unknown, and patients often were beaten and sometimes actually tortured for disorderly conduct. Letchworth had observed institutions in several European countries which utilized much more humane systems, which he described in a book written in 1889 entitled *The Insane in Foreign Countries*. Several of the systems with which he was impressed utilized what he called a "farm colony" system, a farming operation where the inmates lived in cottages and tended livestock or worked in the fields. Partly as a result of Letchworth's efforts, several such colonies subsequently were established in New York State. Letchworth also was instrumental in the passage of legislation establishing state control over the institutionalized mentally ill.

In the early part of the 1890s Letchworth focused his attention on treatment for epileptics. The nature of epilepsy was little known, and epileptics were viewed with fear and often denied employment and education. They often became beggars or were confined in almshouses. Letchworth was instrumental in establishing a state-run colony for epileptics, where the disease could be studied and where epileptics could find employment. In 1900 he wrote *Care and Treatment of Epileptics*, which at that time was considered one of the best works done on the subject.

Letchworth held several other important offices. In addition to serving as president of the New York State Board of Charities from 1878 to 1888, he was the first president of the National Association for the Study of Epilepsy in 1898, and the first president of the New York State Conference of Charities and Correction in 1900. He also was a prolific writer. In addition to the two books already mentioned, Letchworth wrote several others and some sixty-five papers on a variety of subjects ranging from archeology to child welfare and mental illness.

Letchworth suffered a stroke in 1902 which left him partially paralyzed for the remaining years of his life. He had acquired a beautiful estate known as Glen Iris, in upstate New York on the Genesee River, and in 1906 he deeded the land to the state of New York. The state subsequently turned the land into a state park bearing his name.

By all accounts, Letchworth was a gentle, quiet man who enjoyed nature. He was deeply concerned about his fellow man and worked tirelessly in a number of causes, leaving a legacy of reform and innovation which can be matched by few. Letchworth never married; he died at his Glen Iris estate on December 1, 1910, at the age of eighty-seven.

There are a number of good sources relating to Letchworth's life and work. Short biographical sketches are contained in *The Encyclopedia of Social Work*, 17th issue, vol. 1 (1977), 760–761; and *The Dictionary of American Biography*, vol. 6 (1936), 193–194. An excellent comprehensive biography, written in an entertaining style and containing a chronological listing of all his writings, is J. N. Larned, *The Life and Work of William Pryor Letchworth* (1912). Other biographical information can be obtained from the following sources: *The National Cyclopedia of American Biography*, vol. 15 (1967), 324–325; obituary, *New York Herald Tribune* (December 3, 1910); obituary, *New York Times* (December 3, 1910).

JIM STAFFORD

**Levin, Louis Hiram** (January 13, 1866–April 22, 1923), lawyer, journalist, educator, and social worker, was born in Charleston, South Carolina, to Harris Levin, a peddler and merchant, and Dora Amelia Levin, a descendant of the renowned medieval rabbinic scholar Yom Tov Lipmann Heller of Prague. Levin moved to Baltimore, Maryland, with his family when he was a young boy, where he was reared in an observant Jewish home and attended the public schools. He then studied at Baltimore City College for a brief time, but received a diploma from the Bryant and Stratton Business College in 1881. While working for a number of years as a bookkeeper, he began studying law in the evenings in hopes of bettering his financial situation. In 1896 he received his law degree and joined the faculty of his alma mater, Baltimore University School of Law. In that same year, Levin entered into a law partnership with his longtime friend, Benjamin H. Hartogensis. He was first brought into the circle of social activism by his marriage on June 19, 1901, to Bertha Szold of the prominent Szold family of Baltimore (daughter of Rabbi Szold and sister of Henrietta Szold), with whom he had five children: Benjamin Szold, Harriet, Sarah, Marcus Jastrow, and Eva Leah.

Even in his youth, Levin had possessed an intense interest in literature and composition. Thus, he frequently contributed essays, poems, and short stories to the local press and to the *Jewish Exponent* in Philadelphia. When the *Jewish Comment* of Baltimore was founded in 1895, Levin became a regular contributor. He eventually wrote a weekly column entitled "Our Baltimore Letter" under one of his many pseudonyms, "Label." In this column, Levin published poems, short stories, and commentaries on issues of concern to the Jewish community. He assumed the position of editor-in-chief of the *Jewish Comment* in 1899, a post he retained until 1916. Levin also wrote editorials for the Baltimore *Evening Herald* during the period that H. L. Mencken served on its staff.

Influenced in part by his activist sister-in-law, Henrietta Szold, who believed that education was the best way to bridge the cultural gap between newer Jewish immigrants arriving from Eastern Europe and the older established German Jewish community, Levin frequently advocated Jewish unity in his editorials. Owing to his suggestion, Baltimore's German Jewish charities federated into one unified organization in 1906. Levin was then asked to become the first executive secretary of the fruits of this new merger, the Federated Jewish Charities. Levin and Hartogensis dissolved their law partnership in that year so that Levin could devote maximum effort to his social welfare work. When the Eastern European Jewish Charities followed the example of the Federated Jewish Charities in 1907 and federated as the United Hebrew Charities, Levin was elected vice president. At the Fifth Biennial National Conference of Jewish Charities, held in Richmond in 1908, Louis Levin represented both the "uptown" (Federated Jewish Charities) and the "downtown" (United Hebrew Charities) federations of Baltimore.

Although many of Levin's contemporaries believed that the uptown and downtown Jewries would of necessity remain apart, Levin was outspoken in his opposition to Jewish communal bifurcation. In 1921 his commitment to communal unity was realized: the uptown federation merged with the downtown federation, forming the Associated Jewish Charities of Baltimore. Louis Levin was largely responsible for this accomplishment and became the new Federation's first executive director.

Levin's experience with the federated Jewish charities of Baltimore convinced him of the importance of training social workers for the community. In May, 1912, he printed a notice in the *Jewish Comment* that the Hebrew Benevolent Society of Baltimore would receive applications from persons desiring to train for social service. One year later, he persuaded the Baltimore Association of Jewish Women to plan a school for training Jewish social workers. In October, 1915, Levin inaugurated a series of lectures on immigration for Goucher College's philanthropy class. An acknowledged expert on the immigration experience in the United States, in 1921–1922 Levin was invited to teach a class on immigration for future social workers studying at Johns Hopkins University.

Louis Levin had received national attention earlier, in 1915, when he was selected by several Jewish welfare organizations to lead a relief mission to Palestine. Although he was known to be an early and outspoken adherent of Zionism, his expertise in the field of social welfare undoubtedly contributed to his being selected for this task. Commissioned by Secretary of State William Jennings Bryan and Secretary of the Navy Josephus Daniels, Levin sailed on the USS *Collier Vulcan* and transported nearly 1,000 tons of supplies for impoverished Jewish refugees and other inhabitants of Palestine. While in Palestine, Levin witnessed the valuable service wrought by Henrietta Szold's women's Zionist organization, Hadassah. His report of Hadassah's successful ventures in the field of nursing and medical assistance in Palestine increased worldwide interest in the organization and its work.

In 1920 Levin was elected president of the National Conference of Jewish Social Workers, an organization he had served as voluntary secretary from 1908 to 1916 (when it was known as the National Conference of Jewish Charities). Three years later, at age fifty-seven, he died in Baltimore, Maryland, after a prolonged illness.

Several of Levin's essays on Jewish communal issues are contained in a volume entitled *Little Bits of Judaism* (1907), written under the pseudonym "Amiel." Many of these essays consider topics of perennial concern to American Jewry and are still remarkably relevant. In addition to numerous articles, essays, short stories, and editorials which appeared in the *Jewish Comment* and the Baltimore *Evening Herald*, Levin authored the "Review of the Year" for the *American Jewish Yearbook* in 1907 and 1908. These articles constitute a comprehensive picture of Jewish communal activities in the United States and around the world. A selection of his short stories portraying the plight of the immigrant Jew in America appeared under the heading "Little Tragedies" in the *Forum* (September, 1914). Several of his addresses may be found in *Jewish Charities*, bulletin of the National Conference of Jewish Charities, and *Jewish Social Service*, bulletin of the National Conference of Jewish Social Service.

Alexandra Lee Levin, *Dare to Be Different* (1972), is the only complete biography; J. Vincenza Scarpaci's "Louis H. Levin of Baltimore: A Pioneer in Cultural Pluralism," *Maryland Historical Magazine* (Summer, 1982), is an excellent but narrowly conceived article. See also Alexandra Lee Levin, *The Szolds of Lombard Street* (1960); obituaries in the *New York Times*, April 24, 1923; and Harry Friedenwald, "Louis Hiram Levin," *American Jewish Historical Society Publications*, No. 29 (1925); Manuscript sources include the Louis H. and Bertha Szold Levin Papers and the Thomas and Adele Szold Seltzer Papers, in family possession; the Benjamin and Sophie Schaar Szold Papers and the Henrietta Szold Papers in the Maryland Jewish Historical Society, Baltimore, Maryland; and "Report of Louis H. Levin to State Department," National Archives, Washington, D.C., Diplomatic, Legal and Fiscal Branch. See also Israel M. Goldman, "Louis H. Levin: Master Builder of the Baltimore Jewish Community," a centennial tribute delivered at the Sabbath Services of Chizuk Amuno Congregation, Baltimore, Maryland, January 15, 1966 (mimeographed), American Jewish Archives, Cincinnati, Ohio; smaller collections of correspondence may be found in the Henrietta Szold Personal Archives, Central Zionist Archives, Jerusalem, Israel; and also in the Gotthard Deutsch Papers and the Boris D. Bogen Papers in the American Jewish Archives, Cincinnati, Ohio.

GARY P. ZOLA

**Lewisohn, Irene** (September 5, 1892–April 4, 1944), social worker and patron of the arts, was born in New York City, the fifth daughter and the youngest of ten children of Rosalie (Jacobs) and Leonard Lewisohn. Her mother was from a New York banking family; her father was a native of Hamburg, Germany, who had immigrated to America in 1865 to establish a branch of the family export business. In 1868 his interests turned to the metals industry, and he and his younger brother Adolph were business partners in the mining and processing of copper and other minerals. The brothers also contributed to various philanthropies. Her mother died in 1900, however, and her father followed in 1902, leaving ample means for their children. Irene attended the Finch School in New York and pursued her favorite subjects, theater and dance, through private study.

Among Leonard Lewisohn's philanthropic interests was Lillian Wald's* Henry Street Settlement. Alice Lewisohn, Irene's sister, had met Wald, and began to work in the settlement program. It was Alice who channeled Irene's theatrical interests into Henry Street, and the sisters' initial activities there included teaching acting and dancing, and leading clubs. They soon began to organize amateur productions: by 1907 the Henry Street gymnasium was the site of songs, dances, and pageants.

Rather than bringing drama and music to the East Side, the Lewisohn sisters aimed at eliciting art from those who came to the settlement. Using ethnic materials and costumes to evoke pride of heritage, the two drew on the traditions of all nationalities for their productions. By 1912 a Henry Street group called the Neighborhood Players was staging spoken drama for the public at Clinton Hall in the Bowery, and the following year the Lewisohn sisters produced a street pageant to celebrate the settlement's twentieth birthday.

By 1914 Irene and Alice had given the settlement an eighty-acre farm called Echo Hill to serve as a fresh-air center for children from the city, and they had expanded their dramatic work. Nearby Grand Street became the site of the Neighborhood Playhouse, which they built and gave to Henry Street to provide adequate facilities for the settlement's Festival Dancers and Neighborhood Players. Beginning with a thirty-five-cent admission charge, the Playhouse proved to be a pioneering venture in bringing theater to people and neighborhoods that otherwise might not have access to dramatic productions.

The Neighborhood Playhouse was legally part of the Henry Street complex, but it was independent as an artistic enterprise. The Lewisohn sisters began with amateur talent, and the playhouse functioned as a dramatic school as well as a theater—a unique school where new talent was developed and displayed in workshop performances. By 1920, however, the demands of more ambitious productions had led to the creation of a resident company that combined professionals and amateurs, and such stars as Ellen Terry, Yvette Guilbert, and Gertrude Kingston appeared on the Playhouse stage.

The Playhouse was recognized as a center for experimental theater. Like other early "little theaters" such as the Provincetown Players and the Washington Square Players, its productions included works by authors whose plays were not performed in the uptown theater district. The Playhouse schedule also included esoteric works that reintroduced the mysticism, folk ritual, and poetry that were disappearing from the contemporary stage. The Lewisohns produced Japanese

Noh plays, Burmese Pwé dramas, Celtic legends, medieval miracle plays, ballet, and dance. Among the most noted productions were the *Salut au Monde* (1922), which combined music, dance, pantomime, and speech; *The Little Clay Cart* (1924), a Hindu play; and *The Dybbuk* (1925), a folk play from the Yiddish theater. In 1923 an annual revue, *The Grand Street Follies*, was instituted.

The Lewisohn sisters contributed well over $500,000 to the Playhouse, as well as working as producers, discoverers of talent, and performers. Both frequently appeared on stage: Alice as an actress, and Irene in both acting and dancing roles. World tours in 1910 and again in 1922–1923 provided much of the background and detail for their Asiatic and Middle Eastern productions. Yet in the early to mid–1920s, the Neighborhood Playhouse had financial troubles, and eventually closed in May, 1927. Alice Lewisohn, who married in 1925, began to spend much of her time abroad.

Seeking new avenues for her work as well as new forms and expressions of her art, Irene Lewisohn in 1928 joined another Henry Street worker, Rita Wallach Morgenthau, to found the Neighborhood Playhouse School of the Theatre, and she planned and produced several programs that combined orchestral works with dance or pantomime during 1928–1931. In 1937 she founded the Museum of Costume Art (later the Costume Institute, which became part of the Metropolitan Museum of Art) to house and display the extensive collections that she and Alice had gathered during their travels.

Lewisohn's concern for social welfare reemerged in the late 1930s. She supported the Loyalists during the Spanish Civil War and established the Spanish Child Welfare Association as a relief service. During World War II, her activities included entertaining servicemen through organizations such as the American Theatre Group's Stage Door Canteen.

Irene Lewisohn died in New York City in April, 1944.

The Neighborhood Playhouse Papers are in the Theatre Collection, New York Public Library at Lincoln Center, and the papers of the Spanish Child Welfare Association are in the Manuscript Division, New York Public Library. Other records are held by the Neighborhood Playhouse, Inc.

Alice Lewisohn Crowley's *The Neighborhood Playhouse* (1959) provides a history of the Playhouse. Additional information can be found in Lillian Wald's *Windows on Henry Street* (1934) and in Robert L. Duffus, *Lillian Wald* (1938). For more general background, see Kenneth Macgowan, *Footlights Across America* (1920), and John Martin, *America Dancing* (1936). On the performance of *Salut au Monde*, see "The Neighborhood Playhouse, 1915–1935," *Theatre Arts Monthly* (October, 1934), 781–784.

A biographical sketch appears in *Notable American Women*, vol. 2 (1971), 400–402. Tributes to Irene Lewisohn are: Stark Young, "Miss Irene Lewisohn," *New Republic* (April 24, 1944), 561; and Mary Rehan, "A Tribute to Irene Lewisohn," *Metropolitan Museum of Art Bulletin* (June, 1945), 233–234. An obituary notice is in the *New York Times*, April 5, 1944, 19, with additional information in the April 7 and April 22 issues. Information on Leonard Lewisohn can be found in the *National Cyclopedia of American Biography*, vol. 27 (1939), 464. Alice Lewisohn Crowley's obituary was published in the *New York Times*, January 12, 1972, 46.

JANE A. ROSENBERG

**Lindeman, Eduard Christian** (May 9, 1885–April 13, 1953), educator, lecturer, philosopher, and social reformer, was born in St. Claire, Michigan, one of ten children of Fredericka Johanna (Von Piper) and Frederick Lindeman, Danish immigrants. His mother was a Danish noblewoman disowned by her family for marrying his father, a peasant and sheepherder. The family was plagued by poverty, sickness, and accidental deaths. Upon the death of his father when Lindeman was nine, and that of his mother the year after, he was raised by two older sisters.

After a series of manual jobs (shipyard riveter, salt miner, farmer, laborer), Lindeman followed his farmer-employer's advice to attend college. Although he lacked a high school diploma, he entered Michigan Agricultural College in 1906, worked his way through school, and overcame financial and language barriers to graduate with honors in 1911. A year later he married Hazel Taft, the daughter of a professor, and subsequently fathered four daughters. Major influences on him during this period included socialism and the religious perspectives of the Federal Council of Churches of Christ.

Upon graduation, Lindeman gained employment and experience in a plethora of jobs. In 1911 he became managing editor of the *Gleaner*, a Detroit-based agricultural journal, and developed a keen interest in the cooperative movement and other rural issues. His first move toward practical social work occurred in 1913 when he became assistant to the pastor of the Plymouth Congregational Church in Lansing, Michigan. There he worked with the church-sponsored boys' club. His youth work continued in his next position as state extension director for the Michigan Agricultural College. He was responsible for the state boys' and girls' clubs—the forerunners of today's 4-H clubs. During this time he was an active member of the American Recreation Association and supported programs for children and adults, including military personnel.

Lindeman's academic career took root in 1918 when he accepted an appointment as instructor in rural sociology at the YMCA's George Williams College in Chicago. While he remained there less than a year because of the college's conservatism, he did meet Jane Addams* and even took a short course at Hull-House.

In 1919 he became director of the Sociology Department at North Carolina College for Women in Greensboro. His unorthodox teaching methods and his liberal views on race relations soon led to problems with both the faculty and the local Ku Klux Klan. The controversy, including newspaper attacks on Lindeman and his family, led to his departure in 1921. However, a trip to

Denmark during this imbroglio enabled him to study adult education and cooperatives, both of which heavily influenced his later thinking.

His 1921 publication, *The Community*, which reflected his interest in community action and self-determination, attracted the attention of Mary Parker Follett.* Follett introduced him to powerful people connected with the *New Republic*, and Lindeman received financial support for freelance writing and private research from 1922 to 1924. The reciprocal relationship with Follett, who had a major interest in group process, contributed to Lindeman's significant 1924 book, *Social Discovery, An Approach to the Study of Functional Groups*. These two years were filled with extensive writing, lecturing, and the making of stimulating contacts, such as Walter Lippman, Robert MacIver, and John Dewey.

A speech at the Recreation Congress attracted the attention of faculty members at the New York School of Social Work, who then offered him a position; the peripatetic Lindeman apparently found his niche there since he remained on the faculty from 1924 to 1950. At the New York School, he played a major role in developing and establishing community organization and group work as social work methods. However, Lindeman was concerned that preoccupation with technique was detrimental to society and the young profession of social work. He stressed the relationship between technique and philosophy—the relationship between means and ends. At a time of heavy Freudian emphasis on intrapsychic factors, he placed social work in a social context and eschewed a narrow interpretation of human behavior.

The Depression years witnessed a tremendous rise in Lindeman's reputation and participation in national and state organizations. A friend of Harry Hopkins* and a frequent visitor to the White House, in 1934 Lindeman became consulting director of the Division of Recreation in the Works Progress Administration. He also became increasingly interested in planning for social services and in the relationship between freedom and planning.

His diverse interests and mounting acclaim were evidenced by his growing organizational affiliations, to wit: chairman of the National Share Croppers Fund, consultant to the National Council of Parent Education, president of the New Jersey State Conference of Social Work, chairman of the New Jersey Social Planning Commission, board member of the Council Against Intolerance, advisor to the magazine *Rural America*, member of the Advisory Committee to the White House Conference on Children in a Democracy, director of the Service for Intercultural Education, and director of the Association on American Indian Affairs. Additionally, he was a trustee of the Hudson Guild settlement house, the National Urban League, Briarcliff College, and Adelphi College.

World War II and its aftermath found Lindeman more heavily involved in international social concerns, from curriculum development at the university to consultation in Germany and instruction in India. Outside activities encompassed attention to civil liberties (especially during the McCarthy era), child labor, and race relations. Despite ill health, he maintained a strenuous workload of consulting, presenting, writing, and teaching. Former students spoke in awe of his classroom effectiveness. He was often referred to as the father of American adult education. Lindeman's democratic values and educational creativity permeated his classes.

He retired from the New York School of Social Work in 1950 but continued to lecture and remain active in organizations. His retirement saw him honored by the creation of the Eduard C. Lindeman Chair in social philosophy at the school, then the Columbia University School of Social Work, and in 1952 he was elected president of the National Conference of Social Work.

Lindeman's legacy remains a driving force in social work to this day. While he made substantial contributions to community organization, group work, international social work, rural social work, and other areas, one of his greatest accomplishments resulted from his nondogmatic, pragmatic search for knowledge and understanding. He developed an integrated, holistic, interdisciplinary perspective on human behavior and social problems at a time when social workers were dividing into warring camps along ideological, philosophical, and theoretical lines. This perspective still serves as a model to contemporary social workers, as does Lindeman's firm insistence that action be guided by values and that values must lead to action.

Eduard Lindeman died in New York City on April 13, 1953.

A wealth of detailed information on Lindeman can be found in the Eduard C. Lindeman Collection in the Butler Library Archives at Columbia University in New York. See also Lindeman's early volumes, *The Community: An Introduction to the Study of Community Leadership and Organization* (1921), and *Social Discovery: An Approach to the Study of Functional Groups* (1924), which are regarded as major contributions to the then young social work methods of community organization and social group work. *The Meaning of Adult Education* (1926) and *Leisure—A National Issue: Planning for the Leisure of a Democratic People* (1939) gave much impetus to the development of the related disciplines of adult education and recreation.

The most thorough account of Lindeman's life and times is found in Gisela Konopka, *Eduard C. Lindeman and Social Work Philosophy* (1958). This interesting and well-researched book contains an invaluable bibliography of writings by and about Lindeman. More concise accounts may be found in the *Encyclopedia of Social Work* (1965), and in the obituary in the *New York Times*, April 14, 1953, 47. Memorial articles emphasizing his varied contributions are in *The Social Welfare Forum* (1953).

JOSEPH DAVENPORT III and JUDITH A. DAVENPORT

**Lindsay, Samuel McCune** (May 10, 1869–November 11, 1959), educator and social welfare reformer, was born in Pittsburgh, Pennsylvania, the son of Daniel Slater and Ella (England) Lindsay. After attending public and private schools in Philadelphia, he entered the University of Pennsylvania and received his Ph.B. in 1889. Doing graduate work at the Wharton School, he came under the influence of the school's two leading faculty members, Edmund J. James and Simon N.

Patten. James had done his graduate work at the University of Halle under Johannes Conrad, a leading German historical economist who espoused the positive role of the state in economic and social affairs. James himself was an apostle of the necessity of state action to promote economic, social, and moral progress. His classmate at Halle, Patten, was a more original thinker who preached a gospel of abundance based upon social cooperation rather than individual competition. As a corollary, Patten called for state intervention to assure the masses a fair share of the socially produced surplus. Recognizing the younger man's potential, they sent Lindsay on to do graduate work in economics and statistics with their old mentor at Halle.

Lindsay received his Ph.D. from Halle in 1892. While there, however, he had been employed as a special agent of the Senate Finance Committee to report on wholesale prices in Europe. In 1894, when the Wharton School expanded from a two- to a four-year program, Lindsay was appointed instructor in sociology. He was promoted to assistant professor two years later. Lindsay's Ph.D. dissertation had been on the price movements of precious metals since 1850, and several of his early articles dealt with monetary questions. But the major focus of his interests lay in what was termed "practical philanthropy"—that is, the problems of industrial relations, poverty, and social welfare. In 1896 he published his pioneering *Social Aspects of Philadelphia Relief Work*; that same year he tapped W.E.B. Du Bois* to undertake what became his classic study of the city's Negro population. Lindsay arranged summer jobs for his students with public and private social service agencies to give them firsthand exposure to social problems. In 1899 he instituted at Wharton a two-year course in social work—the first such university program in the United States.

Lindsay was active in the work of the American Academy of Political and Social Science, editing from 1895 through 1900 the "Sociological Notes" department of its *Annals* and serving as first vice president (1898–1900) and president (1900–1902). From 1902 to 1904 he was on leave as Commissioner of Education for Puerto Rico. In 1904 he was named general secretary of the newly organized National Child Labor Committee (NCLC). He traveled extensively in Europe and across the United States collecting data on child labor, worked to build up a network of support for remedial legislation, and lobbied state lawmakers. Discouraged at the slow progress of state legislation, he was instrumental in converting the NCLC's board of trustees in 1906 to endorse the national child labor bill sponsored by Indiana senator Albert J. Beveridge. When the NCLC the following year backtracked from support for a national law, Lindsay stepped down as general secretary.

Meanwhile, in 1904, he had attained full professorial rank at Pennsylvania. With James' forced departure in 1895, however, Wharton's emphasis began to switch from investigation of economic and social questions to practical business education. So in 1907 Lindsay accepted appointment as professor of social legislation in the Columbia University Faculty of Political Science and director of the New York School of Philanthropy (later renamed the New York School of Social Work). Started in 1898 by the Charity Organization Society of New York, the school had a field work–centered curriculum geared to the specialized technical training of students for employment by social service agencies. Lindsay wished to introduce a more academically oriented course offering broad professional education in the problems of community welfare and social work theory. The resulting conflict with the Charity Organization Society's Committee on Philanthropic Education led to his resigning the directorship in 1912. Thereafter, his major institutional commitment was to Columbia's Academy of Political Science. Elected its president in 1910, he inaugurated a program of twice-yearly forums and quarterly (later semiannually) published *Proceedings* ''as a means of giving detailed treatment to special subjects of importance.''

At the same time, Lindsay became a central figure in the largely New York–based network of social welfare reformers. He played a leading role in the agitation that resulted in the establishment in 1912 of the U.S. Children's Bureau and of the Industrial Relations Commission to investigate labor conditions. An admirer of Theodore Roosevelt, he supported the former chief executive's Progressive Party in 1912 and was influential in obtaining the party platform's endorsement of an advanced program of labor and welfare legislation. He was one of the twenty participants in the September, 1914, meeting at the Henry Street Nurses Settlement that was the catalyst for the launching of a reform-linked peace movement. His longtime involvement with the American Association for Labor Legislation was capped by his serving as its president in 1918–1919. He was a member of the committee named by the November, 1918, Conference on Social Agencies and Reconstruction to draft plans for postwar social reconstruction. Despite his stepping down as general secretary, he remained on the NCLC's board of trustees and in 1923 became its chairman—a position that he would continue to hold until 1935.

Like most of his fellow social welfare reformers, Lindsay was optimistic about the possibilities for a new burst of reform after the end of World War I that would achieve not only such long sought after goals as the elimination of child labor, maximum hour and minimum wage legislation, and workmen's compensation laws, but a comprehensive scheme of social insurance against unemployment, sickness, and old age. But these hopes foundered in the inhospitable atmosphere of the twenties. Probably most disappointing was the failure to achieve ratification of the proposed national child labor amendment to the Constitution. Recognizing that the battle was lost, Lindsay led the NCLC to redirect its efforts to battle for improved state laws. He himself shifted the thrust of his interests from domestic issues to international relations and the problem of world peace. His last substantial public activity was as chairman of the American Committee of the International Labor Office (ILO) in its successful early 1930s campaign for official United States affiliation with the ILO.

In 1930 Lindsay stepped down from the presidency of the Academy of Political Science. Nine years later, he retired from his Columbia professorship. By then he had so far withdrawn into the background that his attitude toward the New Deal remains unclear. He spent his last years in a nursing home in Orlando, Florida, where he died on November 11, 1959.

The Samuel McCune Lindsay Papers are located in Special Collections, Columbia University Library. A complete listing of his publications through 1930 can be found in [Milton H. Thomas, ed.], *A Bibliography of the Faculty of Political Science of Columbia University 1880–1930* (1931). Only a few scattered articles appeared in subsequent years.

Biographical information on Lindsay is sparse. The major sources are the entries in W.D.P. Bliss and Rudolph M. Binder, eds., *The New Encyclopedia of Social Reform* (1908), 715, and *Who Was Who in America, Volume 3 (1951–1960)* (1960), 521, plus the obituaries in the *New York Times* (November 13, 1959), and *Political Science Quarterly* (June, 1960), 321–322. Additional sources include, re Lindsay's University of Pennsylvania years: Steven A. Sass, *The Pragmatic Imagination: A History of the Wharton School 1881–1981* (1982); Columbia years: R. Gordon Hoxie et al., *A History of the Faculty of Political Science, Columbia University* (1955); social work education: Roy Lubove, *The Professional Altruist: The Emergence of Social Work as a Career 1880–1930* (1965); activities as a social welfare reformer: Walter Trattner, *Crusade for the Children: A History of the National Child Labor Committee and Child Labor Reform in America* (1970); Allen F. Davis, "The Campaign for the Industrial Relations Commission, 1911–1913," *Mid-America* (October, 1963), 211–228, and "The Social Workers and the Progressive Party, 1912–1916," *American Historical Review* (April, 1964), 671–688; C. Roland Marchand, *The American Peace Movement and Social Reform, 1898–1918* (1972); and Clarke A. Chambers, *Seedtime of Reform: American Social Service and Social Action 1918–1933* (1963); attitude toward the New Deal: Otis L. Graham, Jr., *An Encore for Reform: The Old Progressives and the New Deal* (1967).

JOHN BRAEMAN

**Lindsey, Benjamin Barr** (November 25, 1869–March 26, 1943), pioneer juvenile court judge, social reformer, and author, was born in Jackson, Tennessee, the son of Landy Tunstall Lindsey, a former Confederate army captain and a telegraph operator by profession, and Letitia (Barr) Lindsey. The Lindseys lived on the Jackson, Tennessee, plantation of Benjamin Barr, Ben Lindsey's maternal grandfather, until Landy Tunstall Lindsey's conversion to Catholicism precipitated an irreconcilable rift in family relations. The family dispute prompted Landy Tunstall Lindsey to move to Denver, Colorado, in 1879 to direct telegraph operations for the Denver and South Park Railroad; in 1880 he was joined by his family. Benjamin Lindsey's first stay in Denver was brief. In 1881 he and his brother, Chal, were enrolled in the Elementary School Department at Notre Dame University in Indiana. The Lindsey boys matriculated at Notre Dame for two years but returned to their grandfather's plantation in Jackson, Tennessee, after their father lost his job. Under the guidance of Benjamin Barr, Benjamin Lindsey was enrolled in Southwestern Baptist University. After three years at the Baptist institution, Benjamin and Chal Lindsey joined their parents, their sister Mary, and their brother Tunstall in Denver. Tragedy struck the family in 1887 when Landy Tunstall Lindsey committed suicide. Benjamin Lindsey, as the eldest son, tried to provide for the family by taking on a variety of menial jobs. Fortuitously, one of his jobs was as an office boy to R. D. Thompson, a prominent Denver attorney. This exposure stimulated his interest in the legal system; he studied law and was admitted to the Colorado bar in 1894.

Benjamin Lindsey went into private practice with Fred Park in 1894. However, the novice attorneys soon became disenchanted with the corruption of Denver's political and judicial system and concluded that political activism was the route to reform. In 1898 Parks was elected Democratic state senator. Lindsey's backing of Charles S. Thomas for governor in 1898 changed the course of his career. As part of the political spoils system, Governor Thomas appointed Lindsey as public administrator and guardian in 1899. In 1900 Governor Thomas appointed Lindsey county judge to finish the unexpired term of Robert W. Steel, who was moving to Colorado's Supreme Court.

Judge Lindsey's judicial-humanitarian concerns soon became focused on the plight of juveniles. Although a separate judicial process had been established for juveniles in Chicago in 1899, Denver's children still were processed essentially as adults: juveniles were placed on court dockets with adults; they were detained in adult jails; they received harsh punishments. Lindsey corrected these practices by creatively manipulating existing laws, particularly Colorado's "School Law" of 1899. In Judge Lindsey's court, juvenile and adult cases were separated, and the well-being of the juvenile took precedence over legal formalities. Hearings were informal: the judge removed his black robes; the imposing judge's bench was abandoned and cases were heard in less formal settings (including the judge's chambers); adversarial questioning was replaced with fatherly discussions. "Snitching" (confessing to the act) and "ditching" (changing one's behavior) were essential ingredients to reform. Most important, the judge's disposition of the case was primarily premised on the well-being of the child and not on guilt or innocence. Lindsey's success with Denver's delinquent and dependent children led to the passage of legislation—"An Act Concerning Delinquent Children" (1903)—which legally adopted this judicial framework for Colorado.

Following the adoption of the new court model by the Colorado legislature, Judge Lindsey became the national spokesman for the proliferation of this system. Although he was a diminutive figure (historical accounts of his stature range from 4' 11'' and eighty-nine pounds to 5' 5'' and ninety-eight pounds), he was an articulate, powerful, and persuasive elocutionist and traveled across the country extolling the virtues of his judicial system. He wrote *The Problem of the Children and How the State of Colorado Cares for Them* (1904), as well as a number of articles, to assist judges in restructuring their courts. Lindsey did not, however, abandon his reformatory zeal in other areas. He initiated legislation and reforms in child labor, voter registration, the rights of women in probate matters, and a variety of other areas. He supported women's suffrage and was also a prominent muckraker. *The Beast* (1910) captured national attention by charging that Colorado's political economy was under the control of the rich and powerful. Lindsey counted Lincoln Steffens, Upton Sinclair, and President Theodore Roosevelt as personal friends. A 1914 national poll by *American Magazine* rated Judge Lindsey in eighth place (tied with Andrew Carnegie and Billy Sunday) as "the greatest living American."

Lindsey's muckraking activities and progressive stands against prohibition, nativism, censorship, and Fundamentalism created many enemies. It was, however, his denunciation of the Colorado Ku Klux Klan that proved to be politically fatal. Lindsey narrowly defeated the Klan candidate, Royal R. Graham, in the 1923 election. In 1927 the Colorado Supreme Court ruled to exclude a key Lindsey district for voting irregularities, thereby reversing the election result. On June 30, 1927, Lindsey relinquished the bench that he had created. His problems were magnified in 1929 when the Colorado Supreme Court disbarred Lindsey for violating a state law prohibiting a judge from acting as a private attorney and receiving compensation for services. Biographers have concluded that both charges were unfounded. The primary witness charging that Lindsey supporters had contaminated the 1923 election process later recanted his testimony. The Colorado Supreme Court reversed its disbarment decision and reinstated Lindsey as an attorney in good standing on November 25, 1935. The decisions of the Colorado Supreme Court did not diminish Lindsey's activism. He remained a controversial national figure by advocating sex education and legalized birth control in *The Revolt of Modern Youth* (1925) and *The Companionate Marriage* (1927). Lindsey did not wait in Colorado for vindication. He and his wife, Henrietta Brevoort, whom he had married in 1914, moved to California, where he opened a private practice. Limited financial success and the encouragement of supporters motivated him to run for a seat on the Superior Court of Los Angeles County in 1934. Lindsey won easily, and on November 6, 1934, he assumed his judicial duties. His contributions in California, however, were limited. Internal political disputes between the judges of the Superior Court resulted in the assignment of another judge to the juvenile court. Lindsey's tenure was spent hearing adult cases until he successfully lobbied for the creation of a special "Children's Court of California" in 1939. However, this was a relatively minor achievement in comparison with his past contributions—helping to transform the nation's juvenile court system and defending a variety of progressive social issues. He succumbed to a heart attack on March 26, 1943, in Los Angeles at the age of seventy-three.

Judge Lindsey's writings are fairly extensive. Five books provide an overview of his philosophy, activities, and achievements. *The Beast*, with Harvey J. O'Higgins (1910), and *The Dangerous Life*, with Rube Borough (1931), are semi-autobiographical. The sexual revolution and concomitant problems are the central topics of Lindsey and Wainwright Evans' *The Revolt of Modern Youth* (1925) and Lindsey and Evans' *The Companionate Marriage* (1927). Lindsey and O'Higgins, *The Doughboy's Reform and Other Aspects of Our Day* (1920) discusses the judge's experiences as a member of Henry Ford's ill-fated "peace ship" mission to Europe in 1915. Lindsey also wrote a number of articles and reports on the juvenile court and other social issues.

Charles Larsen's *The Good Fight: The Life and Times of Ben B. Lindsey* (1972), the source of much of the information in this entry, is a thorough biographical account; Larsen's bibliographic essay (pp. 290–295) discusses primary and secondary sources. Francis Huber, "The Progressive Career of Ben B. Lindsey, 1900–1920," Ph.D. dissertation, University of Michigan, 1963, and J. Paul Mitchell, "Progressivism in Denver: The Municipal Court Reform Movement, 1904–1916," Ph.D. dissertation, University of Michigan, 1967, fill gaps in Larsen's work. Lincoln Steffens' "Ben Lindsey, the Just Judge," in *Upbuilders* (1909; repr. 1968), provides an exhortatory evaluation of the judge's work. Reuben Borough's "The Little Judge," *Colorado Quarterly* (Spring, 1968), 371–382, describes his personal experiences with the judge. Joseph M. Hawes' *Children in Urban America: Juvenile Delinquency in Nineteenth-CenturyAmerica* (1971), 223–248, focuses on Lindsey's impact on juvenile justice.

ALEXANDER W. PISCIOTTA

**Lothrop, Alice Louise Higgins** (March 28, 1870–September 2, 1920), welfare administrator and social work educator, was born in Boston, the daughter of Albert H. and Adelaide (Addie) A. (Everson) Higgins. Her father, who descended from Richard Higgins, a founder of Eastham, Massachusetts, was a merchant. Alice Higgins, a Unitarian, was educated in private schools in Boston. She began her philanthropic work as a volunteer with the Boston Children's Aid Society. In 1898 she became a worker in training at the Associated Charities of Boston. In 1900, while she was still in training, she was called upon to become secretary for the District 16 Conference of the Associated Charities. During the summer of 1902, she supplemented her work experience with a course at the New York School of Philanthropy. She held the position of district secretary from 1900 to 1903, until she was asked to come to the central office of Associated Charities to assist Zilpha D. Smith,* the general secretary. When Zilpha Smith retired in 1903, Alice Higgins took her place as general secretary of the organization. Her rapid advancement was indicative of her excellent leadership skills and dedication to her work.

Workers were inspired by her acute mind, resourcefulness, and zeal for her work. She encouraged individual initiative and strongly supported the role of the caseworker. She used the case record to evaluate rendered services and to determine the use of other methods appropriate to meeting the needs of a changing client population. Yet, the relationship between individual adjustment and one's environment was always an underlying premise in her work. In her presentation, with Florence Windom, at the 1910 National Conference of Charities and

Correction, for example, she spoke of the necessary involvement of relatives, clergymen, and school teachers in the assessment and individualized treatment of dependent children. The child problem was always viewed first and foremost as a family problem.

Alice Higgins thus utilized a comprehensive approach to her work. Her emphasis on serving the individual was translated into addressing broader community needs. She got involved in the issues of municipal lodgings for the homeless and prevention programs for problems related to alcohol use. She was instrumental in the passage of social legislation, including mothers' aid laws and state accountability of private charitable organizations.

In 1906 she traveled to San Francisco to help organize disaster relief after the great earthquake and fire there. She used her relief work expertise again during the 1908 Chelsea, Massachusetts, fire, the 1914 Salem, Massachusetts, fire, and the 1917 Halifax explosion.

In 1905, under the leadership of Dr. Richard C. Cabot,* Massachusetts General Hospital established the first medical social work department. Although initially expressing the view that the already established social agencies (such as her Associated Charities) could handle the needs of the sick, Alice Higgins quickly became an avid and involved supporter of medical social work.

Alice Higgins, influenced by scientific philanthropy, successfully advocated the training and educating of social workers. She conducted classes for staff and volunteers at Associated Charities. In 1904 she helped establish the Boston School for Social Workers, a joint venture of Harvard University and Simmons College. She then lectured there on various topics, including widowhood, old age, and charity organization, and served as a special assistant to the school until 1920.

In addition to her roles as an administrator and an educator, Alice Higgins also served as a member of the Massachusetts Child Labor Committee, the Massachusetts Association for Relief and Control of Tuberculosis, the Massachusetts Civic League, and the Massachusetts Commission to Investigate Employment Agencies (1910–1911).

In 1913 she resigned as general secretary of Associated Charities, due to her marriage in May, 1913, to Boston businessman William H. Lothrop. She stayed involved with the organization, however, as a director. Meanwhile, she had helped to establish the American Association for Organizing Family Social Work (later the Family Service Association of America) in 1910–1911. In 1914 she became chairman of the Association and served in that capacity until her death. Deeply devoted to the work of the Association, Alice Higgins Lothrop, a few years before her death, lent it $1,000 when it was struggling financially. In 1921 the Association put the money toward establishing the Alice Higgins Lothrop Memorial Fund, which was set up for the purpose of training family social workers or for research in the family social work field.

In 1916, due to her extensive work in organizing disaster relief, she helped establish an Emergency Relief Unit of the Boston Metropolitan Chapter of the

Red Cross. In the summer of 1917 she became director of the Civilian Relief Department of the New England Division of the Red Cross, serving in that capacity for two years. Her efforts helped to develop the practice of Home Service, which was carried out during and after World War I. The Service was based on Alice Higgins Lothrop's understanding of family life, the family problems created by the war, and serving the family as a unit. With her associates, she organized an emergency training course, the Home Service Institute, for the thousands of untrained workers. The Home Service work, which continued after the war, linked social work services to the Red Cross.

Lothrop's work with the American Association for Organizing Family Social Work made her aware of the possibilities for developing social services in smaller communities. She contributed to her small-town community by serving as director of the Newton (Massachusetts) Welfare Bureau from 1915 to 1918, where she mainly helped to educate the community about the purposes of the Bureau. Alice Higgins Lothrop died at her home in Newtonville, Massachusetts, on September 2, 1920.

Alice L. Higgins Lothrop's writings are few. However, they provide a clear and insightful understanding of her approach to social work practice. See "Comparative Advantages of Municipal and C.O.S. Lodging Houses," *Proceedings of the National Conference of Charities and Correction*, vol. 31 (1904), 148–155; "Helping Widows to Bring Up Citizens," ibid., vol. 38 (1911), 140–147; and "The Responsibility of Medical Social Workers," ibid., vol. 43 (1916), 502–507.

Biographical information can be found in the *Dictionary of American Biography*, vol. 11 (1943); *Liberty's Women* (1980); and *Notable American Women 1607–1950*, vol. 2 (1971). Briefer sketches (under Higgins) are included in *Who's Who in America: 1912–1913*, vol. 7 (1912), and *Woman's Who's Who of America, 1914–1915* (1916). Several articles written by her colleagues in the *Family* (December, 1920), 1–17, recap the diversity of her career. Obituary notices appeared in the *Boston Transcript* (September 3, 1920), 10, 12; and the eulogy from Associated Charities of Boston appeared in the *Boston Transcript* (September 11, 1920), 11. The *Family* ran a brief editorial about her death (October, 1920, 14), and the Alice Higgins Lothrop Memorial Fund is described in the *Family* (January, 1921), 15.

MINDY R. WERTHEIMER

**Lovejoy, Owen Reed** (September 9, 1866–June 29, 1961), minister and child labor reformer, was born in Jamestown, Michigan, the son of Hiram Reed Lovejoy and Harriet Helen (Robinson) Lovejoy. After attending local public schools he developed an interest in the ministry and enrolled at Albion College, a Methodist school located near his hometown in southern Michigan. He received his bachelor's degree from Albion in 1891 and then entered the Methodist ministry, pastoring at several Michigan churches. In 1892 Lovejoy married Jennie Evalyn

Campbell, and two years later he received a master's degree from Albion. Lovejoy continued in the pastorate until 1904, when an Albion classmate and good friend, Homer Folks,* convinced him to leave the ministry to begin a career in social welfare. It is for his social welfare activities, especially his efforts on behalf of working children, that Owen Lovejoy is best remembered.

As with other ministers of the time, Lovejoy's shift from a church post to social welfare work did not result from a radical change of view but rather was the logical extension of his Christian social concern. Like Charles Henderson in Indiana and Michigan, Lovejoy encouraged the discussion of pressing social and economic issues in his churches, especially when he became pastor of a Congregational church in the New York City suburb of Mount Vernon. In 1902, while still at the Mount Vernon church, he had the opportunity to closely observe conditions in Pennsylvania during the famous coal strike there. That tour, which involved extended visits with ill-treated laborers and their families, profoundly affected him. Thus, in 1904, when asked by the newly created National Child Labor Committee (NCLC) to return to the Pennsylvania coal fields in order to survey the use of children as laborers, he gladly accepted the invitation. And when, at the suggestion of Homer Folks, a founder and vice chairman of the organization, he was asked to become one of its two assistant secretaries, he quickly accepted the position, one well suited to his skills as a dynamic speaker and a strenuous advocate for those issues about which he had strong convictions, especially the child labor problem and related social injustices.

As one of two paid, full-time secretaries of the organization, headed by Samuel McCune Lindsay,* Lovejoy initially was in charge of the work in the northern states. In 1907, however, when Lindsay resigned in a dispute with the board over the question of federal legislation, Lovejoy became chief executive of the organization, first on an acting and then on a permanent basis, a post he held until 1926. During this long tenure he traveled extensively, speaking everywhere for child labor reform while strengthening the NCLC and cooperating with other social reformers and organizations on related social and economic matters.

Lovejoy was a tireless and effective speaker on behalf of the child labor reform movement. In 1907, as acting secretary of the NCLC, he gave his first speech before the National Conference of Charities and Correction. That address, "Child Labor and Philanthropy," was a clear, carefully organized statement on the ill effects of child labor and called for the collection of additional information on the evil. A year later, he called for the passage of laws and regulations to eliminate the injustice, and in 1909 he joined with fellow children's advocates in support of the 1909 White House Conference on Dependent Children—and the creation of a federal Children's Bureau, which came into being three years later. And so it went, year after year. Thanks to his efforts, and those of others as well, inside and outside the NCLC, when he stepped down from that organization in 1926, conditions had improved significantly; indeed, few others had equalled his record of achievement with regard to America's exploited youngsters.

Meanwhile, Lovejoy had become and remained active in a variety of related

510

causes. In 1912, along with Paul Kellogg,* Florence Kelley,* Margaret D. Robins,* and others, Lovejoy served on, and chaired, the National Conference's Committee on Living and Labor, whose report not only attacked child labor and sweatshops but called for a living wage, an eight-hour work day, safety and health standards, and numerous other reforms, most of which were incorporated into the 1912 Progressive Party platform. In 1914 Lovejoy became concerned about the impact of the European war on the social issues he championed, and he participated in numerous round table discussions and forums on American neutrality and its response to the conflict. In 1917 he spoke to the National Conference on "The Future of American Childhood in Relation to the War," decrying the increase in child labor during the conflict. Two years later, in a speech entitled "A War Program for Peace," he urged a vast national drive for improved health and educational opportunities—the positive causes he juxtaposed against child labor. Three years later he was elected to the presidency of the National Conference, testifying to his popularity and the respect accorded him in the field of social welfare, although some Conference members objected to his progressive views, especially his support of socialist presidential candidate Eugene Debs. In his 1920 presidential address, Lovejoy spoke of the faith of a social worker, affirming his Christian commitment to social welfare and justice.

Lovejoy's commitment and energetic work on behalf of social reform continued unabated throughout the 1920s. He was involved in the creation, and served as the second president, of the American Association of Social Workers, founded in 1921. In 1922, as chairman of the National Conference's committee on industrial and economic problems, he affirmed the report on "living and labor" he had presented ten years earlier and lamented the effects of the war on social progress. A year later he talked to the Conference about the need to improve rural education, and in his last address to that body as head of the NCLC, in 1925, he debated the proposed child labor amendment to the Constitution with Senator Charles Thomas of Colorado, an opponent of the measure, which never was ratified. Meanwhile, he also was active in the National Information Bureau, the Hudson Guild settlement house, and the Survey Associates, publisher of *Survey* magazine and *Survey Graphic*, to which he frequently contributed.

Tired of the fray and a bit discouraged by the failure to ratify the child labor amendment, in 1926 Owen Lovejoy left the NCLC, or at least its headship; he would continue to serve on its board of trustees for many more years. However, in 1927 he accepted a position as secretary of the New York Children's Aid Society, where he served until 1935, when he became associate director of the American Council on Education. Through the Council he pursued his concern for the quality of life and education for young people until he retired in 1939.

Lovejoy's first wife died in 1929, and eight years later he was remarried, to Kate C. Drake, with whom he spent his retirement on a farm in Biglerville, Pennsylvania. As a minister, as a social reformer, and as a social welfare leader,

Owen Lovejoy used his skills as an organizer and speaker to spearhead the campaign against child labor and for good health and quality education for all Americans. He died on his farm on June 29, 1961, at the age of ninety-four.

There is no collection of Lovejoy papers, nor is there a full-length biography of him. The best single source of information on Lovejoy, however, is the National Child Labor Committee Papers in the Manuscript Division of the Library of Congress in Washington, D.C. Another good source is the *Proceedngs* of the National Conference of Charities and Correction and its successor organizations. Other helpful information can be found in a variety of secondary sources, including Frank Bruno's *Trend in Social Work, 1874–1956* (1957); Walter I. Trattner's *Homer Folks: Pioneer in Social Welfare* (1968) and *Crusade for the Children: A History of the National Child Labor Committee and Child Labor Reform in America* (1970); and the *Dictionary of American Biography*, Supplement 7 (1981). Also see his obituary in the *New York Times*, June 30, 1961.

GARY R. ANDERSON

**Lowell, Josephine Shaw** (December 16, 1843–October 12, 1905), charity organizer and reformer, was born in West Roxbury, Massachusetts. Lowell was the daughter of Francis George and Sarah Blake (Sturgis) Shaw. Her father was the eldest son of Robert Gould Shaw; her mother was also from a wealthy Boston mercantile family. Members of Theodore Parker's Unitarian congregation, Lowell's parents knew Margaret Fuller, Ralph Waldo Emerson, Henry David Thoreau, and other members of Boston's liberal intelligentsia and were in contact with the Fourierists at Brook Farm. Though imbued with the radical idealism of the Boston reform tradition, Lowell lived most of her life in New York. When she was three years old the family moved to Staten Island to be close to a specialist for treatment of her mother's failing eyesight. Though Lowell attended schools abroad and in New York and Boston, her real education came from her family and its social and cultural circle; from them she acquired her values of social meliorism and public service.

Lowell's life was profoundly affected by the Civil War. Her parents were both abolitionists; her older sister Anna married the abolitionist George William Curtis; her brother, Robert Gould Shaw, who died a hero's death in 1863, was colonel of the first black Union regiment. Lowell herself joined the Women's Central Association of Relief, an auxiliary of the United States Sanitary Commission, which provided aid to Union soldiers. On October 31, 1863, Lowell married Charles Russell Lowell, nephew of the poet James Russell Lowell, and moved to Virginia, where he was stationed. Less than a year later, on October 20, 1864, her husband died from wounds received in combat. Their daughter, Carlotta Russell, was born posthumously on November 30, 1864. Rather than retreating with her grief, Lowell continued her involvement in charitable activities. She joined the National Freedmen's Relief Association and became one of its most active New York fund-raisers. With Ellen Collins, a friend and fellow charity worker, she visited freedmen's schools in Virginia, where she gave advice and support to northern teachers.

As war-related activities abated, Lowell shifted her attention back to New York, where she became active in a variety of social causes. In 1872 Louisa Lee Schuyler* asked Lowell to chair the Richmond County committee of the newly formed State Charities Aid Association. In 1875 Lowell conducted a statewide investigation into pauperism in which she discovered that those responsible for overseeing aid were profiting by running boarding houses for the poor. Her report, in which she recommended that able-bodied paupers be given mandatory vocational training, drew the attention of Governor Samuel J. Tilden, who in 1876 appointed her as the first woman Commissioner of the State Board of Charities.

Lowell's efforts as Commissioner—she served on the Board for thirteen years— brought about numerous changes in state policies. Horrified by the lack of specificity in the handling of various types of dependency, Lowell sought to separate indigent from infirm, male from female, young from old, and to establish individualized institutional treatment programs. She was interested in issues relating to women, particularly mothers, whom she saw as the key to breaking the cycle of poverty. Her concern for women and her desire to prevent reproduction of children destined for dependency led to the founding, in 1885, of the first custodial asylum for feebleminded women, in Newark, New York, and, in 1886, of a model cottage-style House of Refuge for Women in Hudson, New York (later to become the State Training School for Girls). Lowell's plan for the treatment of vagrant women and girls stressed the inculcation of regular habits and domesticity. Living conditions in women's institutions were to be patterned on the home, and female inmates were given vocational training for future placement as domestic servants. Lowell worked for the protection of women prior to incarceration as well, and helped ensure the presence of female matrons in police stations. She was also interested in child welfare and, with Board president William P. Letchworth,* worked to reduce the rate of child placements in almshouses; later she was a supporter of the playground movement as well.

Lowell's experiences on the State Board of Charities caused her to focus increasingly on the problems of charity and on relief organizations themselves. One of the main architects and advocates of the new "scientific" approach to philanthropy, Lowell sought to increase cooperation and efficiency in social welfare services and was instrumental in the founding, in 1882, of the Charity Organization Society of New York, a central coordinating agency which collected information, maintained records, and evaluated applicants, who then were referred to different charitable agencies depending on individual case histories and determination of need. Despite Lowell's insistence that the society's purpose was not to dispense direct relief, the existence of large numbers of able-bodied poor in need of aid posed a continuing problem which led to the founding, in 1883, of the Central Labor Exchange, an employment service from which private individuals could purchase tickets redeemable for work performed in the Society's woodyard. Under Lowell's guidance for twenty-five years, the Charity Organization Society was a model for organizations of this type in other cities.

Through her work with the State Board of Charities and the New York Charity Organization Society, Lowell began formulating theories about the causes and effects of poverty and methods for its relief, which she set forth in her book, *Private Charity and Public Relief* (1884). Emphasizing prevention over cure, her ideas were an amalgam of environmentalist and hereditarian positions. Though clearly sympathetic to human need and suffering, she often sounded more concerned about the ill effects of relief than the ill effects of poverty. Rather than supporting the undeserving poor, her goal was rehabilitation, which was to be accomplished by education for and about work, the enforcement of orderly habits, vocational training, and moral instruction. Lowell's faith in institutionalization was coupled with a desire for increased personal contact between members of the upper and lower classes. The mechanism for this face-to-face intercourse, upon which Lowell thought real social change depended, was the friendly visitor, who offered advice on child rearing and homemaking along with assessment and recommendations for aid, and was the model for the social worker.

Lowell's interest in women and her growing concern for the problems of the working class came together in various new efforts. Disturbed by management abuse of saleswomen in New York department stores, in 1886 Lowell and some of her friends formed the Working Women's Society, which in 1890 became the Consumers' League, an activist group which used the threat of women's economic power and buyers' boycotts to demand better working conditions. Lowell was president of the League for six years and then turned it over to her protégée, Maud Nathan.* Desirous of devoting more time to labor issues, Lowell resigned from the State Board of Charities in 1889 when a Tammany-backed state government came into office. She supported the workers in the Homestead strike; published a book, *Industrial Arbitration and Conciliation*(1893), in which she dealt positively with the labor movement; and, during the depression of 1893–1894, organized an East Side relief committee, of which the young Lillian Wald* was a member. Lowell continued to fight Tammany's political influence and in 1894 established the Woman's Municipal League, a nonpartisan good government organization which became an important force for reform during the Progressive Era. Lowell also was an active member of the women's committee of the New York Civil Service Reform Association, a cause in which her brother-in-law George William Curtis was a national leader.

Josephine Shaw Lowell was a major figure in the late nineteenth century charity movement. A believer in the importance of personal character as a force for social reform, like other Mugwumps she backed Grover Cleveland in the 1884 presidential election and worked tirelessly for good government causes. Lowell symbolized the self-sacrificing, saintly lady do-gooder. She always dressed in black, and her history of family tragedy and her graceful, feminine manner lent an other-worldly aura to Lowell's personality and public image. But she was also known for her direct, practical approach to problems and her strong, unsentimental opinions on social issues. Though not a radical feminist—she was pro-suffrage but adhered to a traditional view of women's role in society— Lowell was an important mentor for the generation of younger women whose activism typified Progressive Era reform. Her home on East 30th Street, where she lived unpretentiously with her daughter, was a locus for philanthropic and political organizing as well as a center for culture and the arts. Lowell's efforts on behalf of the needy, her increasing concern with the problems of labor, and her advocacy of humanitarian social relations and efficiency in charity organizations exemplified the transition from the genteel modes of Gilded Age reform to the scientific methods of Progressive Era social welfare. Lowell died in New York City in 1905 at the age of sixty-one.

Lowell's letters have not been gathered into a single collection. The New York Historical Society holds her correspondence with Mr. and Mrs. Charles Stebbins Fairchild about the New York State Board of Charities and other subjects, as well as letters from Louisa Lee Schuyler and Angelina Post. Letters from Lowell to her cousin Elizabeth Glendower Evans and to Leonora O'Reilly are at the Schlesinger Library at Radcliffe College. There are also some of Lowell's letters in the E. W. Ordway and William Rhinelander Stewart Papers at the New York Public Library and in the Elihu Root Papers at the Library of Congress.

Lowell's reports for the New York State Board of Charities appear in its *Annual Reports*. The *Cumulative Index of the Proceedings of the National Conference of Charities and Correction* (1907) lists her articles and reports. In addition to those previously mentioned, Lowell's published writings include *One Means of Preventing Pauperism* (1879); *Reformatories for Women* (1880); "Methods of Relief for the Unemployed," *Forum* (February, 1894); *Poverty and Its Relief: The Methods Possible in the City of New York* (1895); "Reform of the Civil Service and Spoils System," paper for the Women's Auxiliary of the Civil Service Reform Association and the League for Political Education (1896); "The True Aim of Charity Organization Societies," *Forum* (June, 1896); *Rights of Capital and Labor and Industrial Conciliation* (1897); and *Consumers' Leagues* (1897). The article by Lowell on criminal reform in *The Literature of American Philanthropy* (1893), ed. Frances A. Goodale, is also worthy of note.

The most comprehensive biographical source on Lowell is William Rhinelander Stewart's *The Philanthropic Work of Josephine Shaw Lowell* (1911). Robert H. Bremner's sketch in *Notable American Women* (1971) provides an excellent synopsis of her life and work. An article by Lloyd C. Taylor, "Josephine Shaw Lowell and American Philanthropy," *New York History* (October, 1963), is also helpful. There are short discussions of Lowell in a number of secondary works, including Bremner's *American Philanthropy* (1960) and *From the Depths: The Discovery of Poverty in the United States* (1967); Estelle B. Freedman, *Their*

*Sisters' Keepers: Women's Prison Reform in America, 1830–1930* (1981); Ellen Condliffe Lagemann, *A Generation of Women: Education in the Lives of Progressive Reformers* (1979); Roy Lubove, *The Professional Altruist: The Emergence of Social Work as a Career, 1880–1930* (1965); Robert M. Mennel, *Thorns and Thistles: Juvenile Delinquents in the United States, 1825–1940* (1973); David J. Rothman, *Conscience and Convenience: The Asylum and Its Alternatives in Progressive America* (1981); Sheila M. Rothman, *Woman's Proper Place: A History of Changing Ideals and Practices, 1870 to the Present* (1978); and Steven L. Schlossman, *Love and the American Delinquent* (1977). The *New York Tribune* for October 14, 1905, carried Lowell's obituary; a special memorial issue of *Charities and the Commons* (December 2, 1905) was devoted to her.

BARBARA R. BEATTY

**Lowenstein, Solomon** (March 3, 1877–January 20, 1942), social work administrator and leader in Jewish philanthropy, was born in Philadelphia, Pennsylvania, to Levi and Diana (Newmayer) Lowenstein. When he was a child, the Lowenstein family moved to Ohio. The young Solomon received his early education in the public schools of Cleveland. His college education at the University of Cincinnati (B.A., 1898) was followed by three more years in that city at Hebrew Union College, where in 1901 he was ordained a Reform rabbi. He married Linda Berger on January 27, 1904, and had four children: Leonore, Nathan, Judith, and Rebecca.

Solomon Lowenstein's involvement in the field of social work began after his graduation from Hebrew Union College. It was not altogether unforeseeable that he should choose a career as a social welfare executive after training for the rabbinate, for Jewish philanthropic enterprises around the turn of the century could be characterized as emerging from the more traditional notions of charity as a moral and spiritual obligation. At the same time, important changes in the structure of social work delegated responsibility for human suffering and need to special agencies whose activities were under the supervision of trained personnel. This professionalization of services was endorsed by Lowenstein from the early days of his career in Cincinnati as head of that city's Jewish Settlement (in 1900) before assuming leadership of its United Jewish Charities from 1901 to 1904. Lowenstein approved of the new standards of operation, including the more scientific approach to investigating the causes of need in order to assess the adequacy of relief practices.

After his marriage in 1904, New York City became Lowenstein's home. He moved east in that year to become head of New York's United Hebrew Charities, created in 1874 to consolidate several charities under a single directorate. In 1905, however, Lowenstein resigned in order to take on the administration of the Hebrew Orphan Asylum. Functioning as superintendent for fifteen years, he was responsible for managing an institution with an average annual budget of over $400,000 and a capacity for 1,250 children. During this period, before assuming his next major post, Lowenstein also served as deputy commissioner of the American Red Cross Commission to Palestine, in 1918–1919. Beginning in 1920, and for the next twenty-two years, Lowenstein was mainly identified with the Federation for the Support of Jewish Philanthropic Societies of New York City.

In accepting the job of executive head of the Federation, Lowenstein took the helm of the largest Jewish federation in the country. It also was one of the newest federations, for New York was among the last American cities to unite its various Jewish welfare agencies in an effort to coordinate planning, community services, and fund-raising. Established in 1917, the young organization soon took on new tasks under Lowenstein's leadership (as executive director from 1920 to 1934 and executive vice president from 1935 to 1942). In numerous presentations, Lowenstein evaluated the challenges facing his organization and offered suggestions that eventually were implemented elsewhere as well. In 1925, for example, he analyzed the reasons for the incomplete success of the original Federation program to attract and represent all sectors of the Jewish community. Among other recommendations, Lowenstein's idea of recruiting and educating a group of lay leaders to join staff professionals in organizational outreach efforts anticipated a course of action that was to become commonly practiced. Another issue which Lowenstein explored in 1930 was the existence of separate and unique Jewish social work problems. While he conceded that certain areas of social work should remain nonsectarian, Lowenstein's message foreshadowed the profession's increased awareness regarding the distinctive needs and outlooks of ethnic and religious subpopulations. In general, Lowenstein helped the Federation expand beyond the plans of its original architects to provide not only better but more comprehensive services.

Lowenstein's competence in the coordination and systematization of operations was especially crucial during the Great Depression, when the magnitude of the problem of need challenged the potency of all American philanthropic institutions. Lowenstein was named chief executive of the Welfare Council Coordinating Committee of New York and helped to raise $6 million for emergency unemployment aid in New York City during the crisis. He proposed unifying the relief work of public and private agencies and later was appointed a member of New York State's Temporary Emergency Relief Administration (1934).

With the rise of Hitler in Europe, Lowenstein turned his attention to the plight of refugees from Nazism. In 1934 he led the efforts of the German Jewish Children's Aid Society to rescue 250 youngsters from Nazi Germany. In subsequent years, he assumed a leadership position in the National Refugee Service and urged the United States to demonstrate its commitment to aiding victims of Hitler's persecution by offering asylum to large numbers of European children of all backgrounds. In light of the events of World War II, Lowenstein aptly predicted new trends in Jewish social work that inevitably would focus on the balance between overseas relief and local matters. Convinced that the war refugees would have to be welcomed and integrated into the organized community, Lowenstein pressed for centralizing the work of aiding the new immigrants.

Lowenstein's commitment to scrutinizing the factors instrumental in the growth of his field made him an active participant in the professionalization of these developments. In 1922 he was elected president of the National Conference of Jewish Social Workers. In addition, Lowenstein was president of the New York State Conference of Social Work (1923), the New York City Conference of Social Work (1932–1933), and the National Conference of Social Work (1937–1938). In 1936 he served on the New York State Board of Social Welfare. Also, his service to such organizations as the American Jewish Committee, the American Jewish Joint Distribution Committee, the Hospital Council of Greater New York, and the American Friends of Hebrew University in Palestine, and his responsibilities in the Bureau of Jewish Social Research and the Graduate School for Jewish Social Work, testify to his interest in establishing professional standards for social work.

As was indicated in 1941 when, in honor of his forty years of indefatigable leadership in social welfare, he was feted by the Federation, Lowenstein not only was a leading spokesperson for organized Jewish philanthropy but was a symbol of the advancement of communal work for all throughout the nation. He died in New York City of a heart attack while on his way to a meeting on January 20, 1942.

Several important articles which Lowenstein contributed to various journals of Jewish social service organizations were reprinted in an anthology edited by Robert Morris and Michael Freund, *Trends and Issues in Jewish Social Welfare in the United States, 1899–1952* (1966). Other samples of his many writings, all of which appeared in the *Jewish Social Service Quarterly*, include "New Factors in Federation Work" (May, 1925), 1–9; "What Makes Jewish Social Work Jewish?" (December, 1930), 20–21; "Jewish Social Work in the Economic Depression" (December, 1931), 88–93; "Trends in Jewish Social Work" (September, 1936), 18–19; and "Changes in Jewish Social Work Under the Impact of Refugee Problems" (March, 1939), 313–316.

Entries on Lowenstein's life can be found in the *Biographical Encyclopedia of American Jews* (1935), the *Encyclopedia Judaica* (1971), and *Who Was Who in America* (1950). For a longer piece, see Morris D. Waldman's "Solomon Lowenstein—An Appreciation of His Life and Work," *Jewish Social Service Quarterly* (March, 1942), 275–280. An obituary appeared in the *New York Times* on January 21, 1942.

HANNAH KLIGER

**Lurie, Harry Lawrence** (February 28, 1892–June 25, 1973), social worker, researcher, educator, and administrator, was born in Goldingen, Latvia (Russia), to S. Heiz and Lina (Blumenthal) Lurie. In 1898 he and his family immigrated to the United States, settling in Buffalo, New York. Lurie was married to Bernice Stewart in 1922, and they had two children, Alison and Jennifer.

As an immigrant youth having received an education in the American public schools, Lurie had his first association with the Jewish federations in 1909 when he taught English to more recent immigrants in classes sponsored by the Jewish Federation of Buffalo. He later served at that federation as an assistant to the executive director (1913–1914) and, in his capacity as the agent of the Industrial Removal Office, helped to resettle immigrants sent to Buffalo from New York City.

From 1915 to 1920 Lurie was director of research at the Associated Jewish Charities of Detroit and, for three years, also served on the Detroit Community Fund as secretary of the budget committee. In 1920 Lurie became involved with public agencies when he served as director of relief and social services for the Detroit Department of Public Welfare. Additional work with services in the public arena during his career included serving on the Board of Public Welfare Commissioners in Illinois (1929–1930) and on the Advisory Committee of the Children's Bureau of the U.S. Department of Labor (1931–1941).

Lurie's involvement with education began in 1921, when he was a lecturer in sociology at the Merrill-Palmer School in Detroit, and then at the University of Michigan in Ann Arbor, where he was an instructor in economics (1922–1924). He earned both his A.B. (1922) and his A.M. (1923) from the University of Michigan during these years. Additional academic endeavors during his career included teaching at the Graduate School of Social Service Administration at the University of Chicago (1926–1930), the University of California (1927, 1939), and the New York School of Social Work (1931, 1955). After his retirement, Lurie authored *The Community Organization Method in Social Work Education* (1959), a project conducted under the auspices of the Council on Social Work Education, which formulated basic curricular guidelines for the teaching of community organization in schools of social work.

Following his early years in education and nonsectarian social agencies, Lurie returned to Jewish communal work in 1925 as superintendent of the Jewish Social Service Bureau in Chicago. During this period, he also was involved in surveying Jewish communal welfare agencies in Detroit, Baltimore, and Grand Rapids, Michigan.

Lurie's major professional effort began in 1930 when he became the executive director of the national Bureau of Jewish Social Research, which conducted research on the needs and services of the Jewish community throughout America. The Bureau established the National Council of Jewish Federations and Welfare Funds in 1932 and, cooperatively, the two organizations developed services to communities all over the country. In 1935 the Bureau was incorporated into the Council with Lurie as executive director, a position he held until his retirement in 1954. As the central Jewish philanthropic organization, the Council of Jewish Federations and Welfare Funds grew under Lurie's leadership from an initial organization of 15 federations to 260, raising and allocating funds of over $100 million annually for a wide range of activities, including services to families and children, vocational services, hospitals, homes for the aged, Jewish education, recreation, and community relations activities. In *A Heritage Affirmed*, published in 1961, Lurie presented a history of the Jewish federations in the United States and Canada. Lurie regarded the book, in part, as a personal document based on his active professional participation in federations for nearly fifty years.

Lurie's leadership in social welfare extended beyond his key role in the development and growth of the Council of Jewish Federations and Welfare Funds. Publishing extensively in the *Jewish Social Service Quarterly*, he advanced guidelines for service delivery in such areas as family life (including the provision of contraceptive advice), community programs for Jewish children, and Jewish social work. Additionally, Lurie analyzed not only the impact of the Depression upon the standards of national agencies but also the functions and structures of Jewish community organization and the philosophy of Jewish social work. His contributions to Jewish social welfare were recognized by his election as president of the National Conference on Jewish Social Welfare, 1945–1946.

Lurie's concern for social welfare issues included the public sector as well. He followed closely the development of public welfare in the 1930s and, early on, was an advocate for the expenditure of public funds to meet the demands for public assistance created by the Depression. He was in the vanguard of those who recognized a legitimate function for social work in the public sector and promoted the development of professional standards for public social work. Concern for unemployment relief led Lurie to serve on an unemployment committee of the American Association of Social Workers, to convene with others a Social Work Conference on Federal Action, to present a status report on the inadequacy of relief funds to a U.S. Senate committee, and to advocate federal grants-in-aid for unemployment relief. Lurie, one of the early proponents of unemployment insurance and Social Security, pointed out to the social work profession its need to address social problems.

He called for social action and an organized movement of social work activity for social legislation. Recognizing the interrelatedness of adequate relief and security and a productive economic system, Lurie, along with Mary Van Kleeck,* was critical of the New Deal as well as of the existing economic order. For its failure to call attention to the limitations of the Social Security Act, the American Association of Social Workers was criticized as well by Lurie, who favored an alignment of social work with the progressive forces in labor and politics. With Van Kleeck, he was supportive of union organization in social work. As a result of these positions, Lurie and Van Kleeck became important figures in the Rank-and-File movement, which reflected a dissenting leftward wing in social work during the Depression. In recognition of his leadership in social welfare, Lurie received the National Conference on Social Welfare's most prestigious award. His extensive writings appeared in a wide range of journals, including *Child Welfare*, the *Compass, Jewish Social Service Quarterly, Social Service Review*, and *Social Work Today*. He also was editor of the first edition of the *Encyclopedia of Social Work* (1965).

Lurie's concern for social justice and civil liberties was a moving force throughout his career. Known for his intellectual and analytical abilities, he was regarded as a humane and compassionate person who inspired and guided others as a teacher and leader. Harry Lurie died at the age of eighty-one at his summer home in Ogunquit, Maine.

The papers of Harry Lurie are at the Social Welfare History Archives, University of Minnesota, Minneapolis. Covering 1927 to 1958, the bulk of the collection spans 1930 to 1940 and consists primarily of professional correspondence.

Important publications by Lurie include "The Role of Professional Standards in Public Social Work," *Social Service Review* (December, 1929), 569–583; "The Place of Federal Aid in Unemployment Relief," *Social Service Review* (December, 1931), 523–538; "Case Work in a Changing Social Order," *Survey Midmonthly* (February, 1933), 61–64; "Organization and Support of Social Work (The Second of a Series of Articles Critically Re-evaluating the Basic Concepts of Social Work)," *Social Work Today* (May, 1937), 5–7; "Security Must Be Planned: The Place of Welfare Programs and Standards in the Democratic Order," *Social Work Today* (June, 1938), 25–27; "Financing Private Social Work," in *Social Work Year Book 1939* (1939), 148–153; "Jewish Community Organization—Functions and Structures," *Jewish Social Service Quarterly* (September, 1949), 47–57; "How Much Social Welfare Can We Afford?" *Social Service Review* (December, 1950), 469–476; "The Approach and Philosophy of Jewish Social Welfare," *Jewish Social Service Quarterly* (March, 1953), 255–263; "The Responsibilities of a Socially Oriented Profession," in *New Directions in Social Work*, ed. Cora Kasius (1954), 31–53; and "Private Philanthropy and Federated Fund Raising," *Social Service Review* (March, 1955), 64–74.

Secondary sources of information on Lurie include *Encyclopedia of Social Work*, 17th ed. (1977); Jacob Fisher, *The Response of Social Work to the Depression* (1980); *New York Times* June 27, 1973, 42(4); and *Who Was Who in America*, vol. 6 (1974–1976).

JAN L. HAGEN

# M

McCarthy, Charles (June 29, 1873–March 26, 1921), reference librarian, government official, and progressive, was the son of Irish immigrant parents, John McCarthy, an engine-tender, and Katherine O'Shea (Desmond), who ran a boarding house. McCarthy was born and raised in North Bridgewater (later Brockton), Massachusetts. From his parents he inherited a strong Roman Catholic tradition, a love for Gaelic culture, and a sympathy for the underdog. He worked at various menial jobs to support himself and to finance his schooling at Brown University. Despite early scarlet fever and a persistent cough and sore throat, he played college football and briefly coached, after graduation in 1897, at the University of Georgia. Historians J. Franklin Jameson, E. Benjamin Andrews, and Ulrich B. Phillips introduced him to archival research and led him to enter the School of Economics, Political Science and History at the University of Wisconsin in November, 1898. There he came under the influence of Frederick Jackson Turner, who supervised his doctoral dissertation on the Anti-Masonic Party, published by the American Historical Association as winner of the Justin Winsor Prize in 1902. He also became acquainted with Charles Homer Haskins, Richard T. Ely, Paul S. Reinsch, and other social scientists who were creating a golden age on the Madison campus. Upon receipt of his Ph.D. degree he married his landlady's daughter, Lucile Howard Schreiber, on September 26, 1901; they had one daughter, Katherine. His wife, a high school teacher, shared McCarthy's academic and reform interests.

Turner recommended his ambitious and promising student not for a college professorship but as chief government documents clerk at the Wisconsin capital, a new and ill-defined position occasioned by the removal from the capitol of the State Historical Society's reference resources. McCarthy's superior was Frank A. Hutchins of the Wisconsin Free Library Commission, who foresaw significant roles for libraries and the new University of Wisconsin Extension Division in the development of progressivism. He gave McCarthy a free hand to assemble reference materials for legislators, government departments, and the general public. McCarthy believed that most legislators were ill prepared to legislate for an increasingly industrialized and complex society, and that by gathering from other states and foreign countries all relevant data he would make possible a rational approach to prospective legislation. The idea was not original with McCarthy; but he contributed enormous zeal and thoroughness in the gathering of data and a strong conviction of its usefulness to the legislative process. In 1907 his Legislative Reference Bureau (now the Legislative Reference Library [LRL]) was formally reconstituted with a bill-drafting service; while McCarthy laid down the strictest rules regarding agency neutrality in drafting legislation, LRL could not avoid charges that it was itself the initiator of bills.

McCarthy's development of LRL's services coincided with and contributed to the progressive governorship of Robert M. La Follette (1901–1906), whose proposals for the direct primary, civil service, reform of corrupt practices, regulation of railroads, and tax reform reoriented Wisconsin's politics for a third of a century. McCarthy's influence on the shaping of economic, social, and political legislation grew under La Follette's successor, James O. Davidson (1906–1911), and peaked in the Francis E. McGovern administration (1911–1915); but it even survived the initial hostility of Republican stalwart Emanuel L. Philipp (1915–1921), who grudgingly conceded that McCarthy's agency meant to be technically helpful rather than to promote a particular reform plan or overall governmental growth. In the crucial years when progressive ideas flourished in Wisconsin and the nation, however, McCarthy clearly sympathized with positive use of a service state to bring about reforms and to solve problems of a rapidly changing industrial society; he was also strongly imbued with Frederick W. Taylor's principles of economy and efficiency in government. He contributed to the practice of borrowing university faculty expertise in the service of the state, and in *The Wisconsin Idea* (1912) set forth his somewhat hazy concept of what had made Wisconsin so conspicuous a laboratory for progressivism, attributing much to German models.

Beginning in 1905 McCarthy donated his services as a lecturer in the university, and in training public servants through laboratory experience. He favored the nontraditional student and worked with the Extension Division in expanding the university's outreach. While maintaining a superficial detachment from political decision-making, McCarthy in fact agreed with many of the state and national directions of progressivism and was inevitably drawn into a more active role in reform. He traveled abroad to gather data leading to 1911 legislation on vocational and continuing education for Wisconsin and investigated foreign efforts at agricultural marketing, becoming a strong advocate of farm cooperatives. He also served under Frank P. Walsh as research director for the Federal Commission on Industrial Relations in 1914–1915. Upon America's entrance into World War I he helped shape the state's draft administration and its council of defense, then became Herbert Hoover's assistant in Washington for the Food Administration, and finally joined Felix Frankfurter on the War Labor Policies Board.

Throughout his twenty years as a state official McCarthy steadfastly declined to commit himself to a political party. He won the confidence of each governor he served without being co-opted. In 1912 he immersed himself in Teddy Roosevelt's Bull Moose Party but later became disillusioned with TR. Quixotically, he ran a poor second for the Democratic nomination for senator from Wisconsin in a special 1918 election, urging strong support for the war.

McCarthy's intense efforts in Washington and abroad during the war exhausted him physically as well as mentally, and he never resumed full working capacity on his return to Madison. He died in Prescott, Arizona, where he had gone to repair his health.

The voluminous personal correspondence of McCarthy for twenty years of state and national government service is in the State Historical Society of Wisconsin (Madison). The correspondence and reference files for the first twenty years of the Legislative Reference Bureau (called Library 1907–1963) in the Wisconsin State Archives and in the Bureau, Madison, reflect McCarthy's most important work. Edward A. Fitzpatrick, *McCarthy of Wisconsin* (1944), is a sympathetic account by a personal friend from the Progressive Era, but also uses primary sources. Marion Casey, *Charles McCarthy, Librarianship and Reform* (1981), while essentially favorable, is more scholarly and detached and reflects newer interpretations of McCarthy's era as well as emphasizing his role as an information broker; its bibliography is most useful. Many memoirs, biographies, and histories of the Progressive Era reflect McCarthy's unusually broad contacts and influence. Brief sketches are in *Dictionary of American Biography*, vol. 11 (1933), *Dictionary of Wisconsin Biography* (1960), and *Dictionary of American Library Biography* (1978).

FREDERICK I. OLSON

**McCulloch, Oscar Carleton** (July 2, 1843–December 10, 1891), social gospeler and charity organization society leader, was born to Carleton G. and Harriet (Pettibone) McCulloch in Fremont, Ohio. His father was a successful merchant and druggist in Ohio and later in Wisconsin. The elder McCullochs were Calvinists who emphasized religion in rearing their son. Carleton McCulloch also taught his son the rudiments of business and the classsics. Although McCulloch eventually deviated from his parents' orthodoxy, he retained their religious zeal and commitment throughout his life.

McCulloch came to the ministry after other experiences. He served as a volunteer in the United States Christian Commission during the Civil War. He also attended the Eastman College of Business in Poughkeepsie, New York, during the war years. After graduation he took a position as a government clerk in Springfield, Illinois. In 1865 McCulloch became a wholesale drug salesman for a firm in Chicago and did very well, earning a salary of $3,500 per year. As he advanced in business, McCulloch also did mission work and lay preaching in Chicago. His continuing interest in the ministry, combined with his religious background and the evangelistic fervor of the times, led him to enter the Chicago Theological Seminary in 1867, from which he graduated in 1870.

During his career in the ministry McCulloch served two churches—the First Congregational Church of Sheboygan, Wisconsin, from 1870 to 1877, and the Plymouth Congregational Church of Indianapolis from 1877 to 1891.

McCulloch married twice. He and Agnes Buel were married on September 8, 1870; they had two sons. After her death in 1874, he married Alice Barteau, with whom he had three daughters.

McCulloch was a leader of the Social Gospel movement. Like Washington Gladden and others, McCulloch sought to reconcile Christianity with Darwinism. He embraced the liberal faith that humanity was evolving and advancing through the spread of knowledge and the application of virtue. He rejected the orthodox Calvinism of his parents and called instead for a Christianity of social action. Sin was social as well as individual. Christians must reform society. A more perfect world was evolving, but Christians must hasten its advent through personal and collective activity.

The institutional church was one of the primary vehicles for the delivery of Social Gospel theology. McCulloch's Plymouth Congregational Church of Indianapolis was typical. He developed programs to meet the spiritual and material needs of the entire community. He formed a club for young men in 1878 to provide organized recreation and education. He initiated a lecture series in 1883 to provide quality lectures by noted public figures for moderate prices. He began a vocational training school in 1884. He established a savings and loan association in 1885. All of these programs were open to the entire city of Indianapolis and helped to fill important social needs.

McCulloch also was the leader of the Indianapolis Charity Organization Society from 1879 until his death in 1891. The organization was patterned after existing groups in Buffalo, Philadelphia, and Boston, whose members were confident that poverty could be eliminated through the application of rational procedures and moral principles to relief efforts. McCulloch and others in the movement viewed poverty as a moral defect. The poor were worthy or unworthy; the former deserved private aid, and the others deserved assignments to public workhouses. The Indianapolis Charity Organization Society followed others in advocating a system of efficient investigation and surveillance of applicants; it also opened a workhouse in 1885 to accomplish its goals.

Under McCulloch's leadership, however, the Indianapolis Charity Organization Society did much more than build workhouses. It established a nurses' training school in 1879, opened a free kindergarten in 1882, brought free public baths to Indianapolis in 1885, developed a program of public housing for the poor and elderly in 1886, and by 1890 opened a summer mission for sick children. McCulloch and his organization also worked for cleaner air and water, for more parks, and for improved libraries and hospitals. Few other charitable organizations of the era could boast as many achievements.

McCulloch was active as a reformer on the state and national levels as well. He organized the Charity Organization Society of Indiana on February 6, 1880, helped to establish the Indiana Board of Children's Guardians and the Board of

State Charities, and was active in the National Conference of Charities and Correction from 1880 until his death in 1891, serving as president of the group in 1891. His work gained the attention and admiration of his peers throughout the United States.

The weaknesses of the Social Gospel and charity organization society movements were evident in McCulloch's work. Like other social reformers of his era, he embraced an arrogant moralism which sought to amalgamate immigrants into a homogeneous mass. Immigrants needed to be taught proper habits of work, dress, and behavior and to be shorn of alien political ideas—and the "unworthy" poor needed to learn proper work habits and standards of conduct. McCulloch also was a victim of the naiveté of his era, which made him confident that anything was possible—poverty could be eliminated, cities could become utopias, evil could be removed from people's hearts, and the Kingdom of God could come to earth. McCulloch and other reformers also placed too much faith in rational and scientific methods of organization.

Yet it would be injudicious to overlook all of McCulloch's achievements; in social welfare and reform he went much futher than many of his contemporaries, and he accomplished much. Furthermore, many of the problems faced by McCulloch continue to plague social reformers today, who can learn much from him. McCulloch died in Indianapolis on December 10, 1891.

The papers of Oscar Carleton McCulloch may be found in a fourteen-volume diary located at the Indiana State Library, Indiana Division, Indianapolis. The volumes contain memorabilia of Plymouth Congregational Church, the Indianapolis Charity Organization Society, and other social reform organizations, in addition to McCulloch's writings and letters. Information about McCulloch's churches may be found in the archives of the First Congregational Church of Sheboygan, Wisconsin, and in those of the First Congregational Church of Indianapolis, Indianapolis, Indiana.

McCulloch published several books and articles. A complete bibliography may be found in Genevieve C. Weeks, *Oscar Carleton McCulloch, 1843–1891, Preacher and Practitioner of Applied Christianity* (1976), which is the major secondary work on the subject.

JOHN M. DERGE

**McDowell, Mary Eliza** (November 30, 1854–October 14, 1936), social reformer, founder of University of Chicago Settlement, and Chicago Commissioner of Public Welfare, was born in Cincinnati, Ohio, the eldest of six children of Malcolm McDowell and Jane (Gordon) McDowell. Her paternal Scotch-Irish ancestors had left Virginia for Kentucky and Ohio; her father had grown up in Columbus, where he worked in machine shops before moving to Cincinnati with a railroad construction crew. There he met and in 1850 married the daughter of a shipyard owner. Malcolm McDowell served in the Union army, and his young daughter's earliest heroes were her soldier-father and President Abraham Lincoln.

In the late 1860s McDowell took his family to Chicago, where he established
an iron-rolling mill on the northwest side of the city and built a house on Webster
Avenue. The residence and rolling mill escaped the devastating 1871 fire. Though
still a teenager, Mary McDowell assisted her Methodist pastor in relief work
that winter. Following the family's move to Evanston in the early 1880s, she
met Frances Willard and worked for a time as an organizer for the Woman's
Christian Temperance Union. She also ran a Methodist Sunday class and helped
the local black women form their first club. Still uncertain about the direction
of her life, she completed the course of study at Elizabeth Harrison's National
Kindergarten College and took a job in New York City. But in 1890 she returned
to Chicago, visited Hull-House, and promptly took up residence as the kindergarten
teacher and organizer of the women's club. Her mother's illness necessitated a
return to Evanston, where she fretted about her isolation from such important
events as the Pullman strike. In the fall of 1894, as she approached her fortieth
birthday, she found her calling.

The new University of Chicago's Sociology Department and student Christian
Union wanted a social laboratory similar to Hull-House, and the district beyond
the stockyards and packinghouses had been chosen as the site. On Jane Addams'*
recommendation, they asked Mary McDowell to head what then became the
University of Chicago Settlement, a post she immediately accepted. She moved
into rented rooms near Ashland Avenue and 47th Street in November, 1894,
and promptly started a kindergarten. As others joined her in residence and
university students volunteered, the program expanded to include a day nursery,
mothers' club, classes and activities for youth, English language instruction, and
musical groups. The settlement moved to larger quarters in 1896, incorporated
in 1898, purchased land on nearby Gross Avenue, and in 1899 built a $10,000
combination auditorium and gymnasium. Six years later it constructed residence
quarters and rooms to accommodate the many settlement functions. The "Back
of the Yards" neighborhood, predominantly German and Irish in the 1890s,
attracted Bohemians, Poles, Lithuanians, and eventually Mexicans. A founding
member of the Chicago Federation of Settlements, McDowell compared
neighborhood changes and settlement program adjustments with Jane Addams,
Graham Taylor,* Harriet Vittum of Northwestern University Settlement, and
Celia Parker Woolley of Frederick Douglass Center.

McDowell was a relentless crusader for better sanitary and health conditions
Back of the Yards. She secured cleaner alleys, a public bathhouse, a local park,
a branch library, and a trained nurse who lived at the settlement and offered
advice on diet and hygiene. McDowell experimented with a "vacation school"
to keep children off the streets in summer and sold the concept to the Chicago
Board of Education. Settlement staff published studies of neighborhood children
who worked, and John C. Kennedy prepared *Wages and Family Budgets in the
Union Stockyards District* (1914). McDowell garnered the support of many civic
organizations in her long battle against open garbage dumps and a polluted stream
which sewered the packinghouses. She investigated European methods of disposal

in 1911 and used the information to educate Chicagoans. A 1913 City Waste Commission, of which she was a member, recommended reduction plants, and the city finally built them. Eliminating "Bubbly Creek" took another two decades, but she lived to see intercepting sewers and landfills obliterate that health hazard and eyesore.

Support of organized labor and better working conditions for women constituted another of McDowell's contributions to social welfare. She helped Michael Donnelly unionize packinghouse workers prior to the 1904 strike, and she encouraged the first female local. She was a founding board member of the Women's Trade Union League, president of the Illinois branch from 1904 to 1907, and a staunch ally of Margaret Dreier Robins.* McDowell proposed the federal investigation of the problems of women and child wage earners and spearheaded the lobbying which made it a reality. Then she turned to state laws regulating women's hours and wages. When new employment opportunities opened during World War I, she pressed for a Committee on Women in Industry to keep an eye on safety conditions, standards of pay, and hours of work. She testified for the Women's Trade Union League and the Young Women's Christian Association in support of the bill to establish a Women's Bureau in the Department of Labor. Mary Anderson* would later say that creation of the Bureau in 1920 was due in large part to Mary McDowell.

Long a supporter of the National Association for the Advancement of Colored People and the National Urban League, McDowell redoubled her efforts to promote interracial understanding in the aftermath of Chicago's 1919 race riot. She was especially concerned about housing and the reforms suggested by the Chicago Commission on Race Relations in its 1922 report. Thanks to the election of reform mayor William E. Dever in 1923, McDowell became Commissioner of Public Welfare. During her four-year term she revived the employment service, provided shelter and counseling for the homeless, and investigated housing conditions for low-income families. Her 1926 housing conference led to the creation of an advisory Chicago Housing Commission of which she, Edith Abbott,* and Graham Taylor were members. Much of her work, however, was wiped out by the return of Republican mayor William Thompson.

At the age of seventy-five, McDowell retired from active direction of the settlement. She began writing an autobiography but never carried it to completion, perhaps because Howard E. Wilson's study of her life's work was published in 1928, under the title *Mary McDowell, Neighbor*. Felled by a stroke in 1935, she died the following year, mourned by Back of the Yards families who considered her their champion as well as their neighbor.

The Mary McDowell Papers at the Chicago Historical Society comprise settlement house records, correspondence, speeches, and articles, as well as the incomplete typescript autobiography. Caroline M. Hill published some of the latter in *Mary McDowell and Municipal Housekeeping: A Symposium*(1938). See also Lea D. Taylor, "The Social Settlement and Civic Responsibility—The

Life Work of Mary McDowell and Graham Taylor,'' *Social Service Review* (March, 1954); and Howard E. Wilson, *Mary McDowell, Neighbor* (1928).

LOUISE C. WADE

**Mack, Julian William** (July 19, 1866–September 5, 1943), jurist and child-saver, was born in San Francisco to William Jacob Mack, a tailor, and Rebecca (Tandler) Mack. Mack's parents were of German-Jewish extraction, his father having emigrated from Altenkunstadt in Bavaria in 1856, while his maternal grandparents also had come from Bavaria. After graduating from Hughes High School in Cincinnati (where he had moved at age four) in 1884, Mack attended Harvard Law School, where he was a founding editor of the *Harvard Law Review*. Mack received his LL.B. in 1887, graduating first in his class and winning the prestigious Parker Fellowship for study abroad. He spent from 1887 to 1890 at the Universities of Berlin and Leipzig.

Upon his return to the United States, Mack settled in Chicago, where he practiced law and became involved in social welfare. He joined Julius Rosenthal's prominent law firm and eventually obtained faculty appointments, first at Northwestern University Law School (1895–1902) and then at the University of Chicago (1902–1911). Under Rosenthal's tutelage, Mack also rose in the city's social welfare circles. He became secretary of Chicago's Jewish charities in 1892, the same year he helped found the Maxwell Street Settlement. Mack had become friendly with Jane Addams,* and with her assistance he established the settlement to serve the West Side's Jewish ghetto. Mack also served as president of the National Conference of Jewish Charities (1904), and he helped establish the American Jewish Committee in 1906.

The combination of legal expertise and social prominence in the Jewish community led to political influence as well. In 1903 Mayor Carter Harrison II appointed Mack civil service commissioner. That year Mack also won election to the Cook County Circuit Court. Mack chose to become a justice of the Chicago Juvenile Court, where he presided until 1905.

Mack's short term on the juvenile court bench belies his importance in the child-saving movement. Mack was a staunch advocate of the court in his addresses to the National Conference of Charities and Correction and in his publications. He found precedent for the court in the chancery courts in England, and he defended its extensive power by citing the doctrine of *parens patriae*. To Mack the court was at its best an extension of the social service network rather than an adjudicative agency.

Mack continued to be prominent in social welfare until after World War I. He urged the calling of the first White House Conference on Dependent Children (1909), cooperated with Graham Taylor* in support of the Chicago School of Civics and Philanthropy to train social workers, served as president of the Juvenile Protection Association and of the League for the Protection of Immigrants, became president of the National Conference of Social Work, was chairman of Survey Associates, and was elected the first president of the National Organization of Young Men (YM) and Young Women's Hebrew Associations (YWHAs). In addition, during the world war he drafted the Military and Naval Insurance Act, which provided survivor's benefits, training in case of crippling injury, and a voluntary insurance plan in case of death or total disability. The bill was widely hailed as a step toward government social insurance. Mack also umpired labor disputes in war plants as a member of the National War Labor Board, and served as a member of the federal Board of Inquiry on Conscientious Objectors.

Mack held important positions on the bench but remained a spokesman for liberal causes. President William H. Taft appointed Mack to the United States Commerce Court in 1911, and in 1913 Mack was assigned to the Circuit Court of Appeals, where he remained until his retirement in 1941. He presided over controversial cases, including the prosecution of (Malcus) Marcus Garvey,* the leader of the Back to Africa movement, and the receivership of two of New York City's transit systems. Despite his position, he aligned himself with the National Lawyers' Guild in its protest against the conservatism of the American Bar Association, and he championed the cause of Sacco and Vanzetti.

Mack's other major concern was Zionism. He served as a delegate representing American Jews at the 1919 Paris Peace Conference and was elected chairman of the Committee of Jewish Delegations, which lobbied for the creation of a Jewish homeland in Palestine. Mack was the first president of the Zionist Organization of America (1918–1921) and of the American Jewish Congress (1919), and he remained involved in Zionist activities throughout his life.

Mack married twice. On March 9, 1896, he married Jessie Fox of Cincinnati, by whom he fathered a daughter, Ruth. His first wife died in 1938, and two years later he married Mrs. Cecile (Blumgart) Brunswick, the mother of his son-in-law. Mack died in New York City in 1943.

There is Julian Mack correspondence in many collections. These include the papers of Edith and Grace Abbott (University of Chicago Library); the Survey Associates records (University of Minnesota, Social Welfare History Archives); the Harry Barnard Papers, which include Barnard's unpublished manuscript on Mack's life (American Jewish Archives, Cincinnati, Ohio); the Felix Frankfurter Papers (Library of Congress, Manuscript Division); the Louis D. Brandeis Papers (University of Louisville Library); the Herbert S. Marks Papers (FDR Library, Hyde Park, New York); the Frederick Kenelm Nielson Papers (Library of Congress, Manuscript Division); the Emily Solis-Cohen Papers (American Jewish Historical Society, Waltham, Massachusetts); the Manley Ottmer Hudson Papers (Harvard Law School Library); the Samuel Stephen Wise Papers (American Jewish Historical Society, Waltham, Massachusetts); and the Arthur Huntington Gleason Papers (Library of Congress, Manuscript Division).

Mack's published work on social welfare reflects his interest in the juvenile court. See "The Juvenile Court: The Judge and the Probation Officer," National Conference of Charities and Correction *Proceedings* (1906), 123–131; "Juvenile

Courts as Part of the School System of the Country,'' National Conference of Charities and Correction *Proceedings* (1908), 369–383; "The Juvenile Court," *Harvard Law Review* (December, 1909), 104–122; "The Law and the Child," *Survey* (February, 1910), 638–643; and "The Chancery Procedure in the Juvenile Court," in Jane Addams, ed., *The Child, the Clinic and the Court* (1925), 310–319.

Secondary sources on Mack are few. The best source is the entry by Harry Barnard in *Dictionary of American Biography*, Supplement 3 (1973), 487–490. See also *The National Cyclopedia of American Biography*, vol. 32 (1945), 73–74. For his obituary, see the *New York Times*, September 6, 1943.

ERIC C. SCHNEIDER

**McKelway, Alexander J.** (October 6, 1866–April 16, 1918), social reformer and child labor leader, descended from a line of distinguished physicians, was born at his grandfather's home in Sadsburyville, Pennsylvania, the son of John Ryan and Catherine Scott (Comfort) McKelway. His parents moved to Virginia when he was a year old. Reared in Missouri, his father graduated from Princeton University (1857) and Princeton Seminary before entering the Presbyterian ministry. With the outbreak of the Civil War, he wished to join the Confederate army, but his wife, a Virginian, would not let him because it would have broken his family ties. Instead, he taught school and preached, and after the war served churches in both the North and South. Alexander's uncle, St. Clair McKelway, was editor of the Brooklyn *Eagle*.

Upon graduation from high school, Alexander McKelway taught school for a time before attending Hampden-Sydney College and Virginia's Union Theological Seminary. He later received his Doctor of Divinity degree from Davidson College. Licensed by the Roanoke Presbytery in 1890 and ordained in 1891, McKelway married Ruth Smith, daughter of Hampden-Sydney's president, Benjamin Smith, and held churches in Buffalo, Pamplin City, and Briery, Virginia. After working as an evangelist in Johnston County, North Carolina, in 1891–1892, he located in Fayetteville, North Carolina. There, serving as a home missionary and as pastor of a church, he came to know the so-called poor Whites, who were flocking to the cotton mills for meager wages.

In 1897 McKelway became editor of his denomination's most important state newspaper, the *North Carolina Presbyterian* (after 1899 the *Presbyterian Standard*). Headquartered in Charlotte, the heart of North Carolina's mill region, the newspaper was turned into a dynamic instrument of social reform by McKelway. Utilizing the *Standard*, and later his editorship of the Charlotte *News* (a local daily), he sought to awaken his readers to the faulty economic practices of the South, especially the blind acceptance of child labor. At first, McKelway opposed legislative action and argued against a reduction of working hours if lower wages were involved. Yet his belief in the basic worth of all men, at least if they were white, inevitably led him to change his views and to urge that some effective means of excluding children under twelve be universally applied.

Obtaining the full cooperation of Governor Charles B. Aycock, McKelway was a major figure in the enactment of North Carolina's 1903 law which imposed a twelve-year age limit on children working in industry and imposed a maximum sixty-six-hour week for youngsters under sixteen.

Though he made many enemies with his blunt words, McKelway made friends as well, including Edgar Gardner Murphy,* whose pamphlets had awakened him to the true plight of southern laboring children and who strongly supported his work. Murphy suggested that the executive committee of the National Child Labor Committee (NCLC) hire McKelway and then persuaded him to accept the position. Believing that the need of the children was great, McKelway left the *Standard* and *News* to accept the NCLC secretaryship in October, 1904. His wide-ranging experience would serve him and the Committee well. Having traveled throughout the South, lived in several large cotton mill towns, and worked with the North Carolina legislature, he would become a skillful and efficient lobbyist at both the state and national levels.

Along with co-workers Owen R. Lovejoy* and Samuel McCune Lindsay,* McKelway undertook scouting trips to plan for more detailed investigations. As it traveled, the trio lectured on child labor, talked with elected officials, helped draft bills, and attended legislative hearings on child labor measures. Its findings focused the NCLC's earliest attention on the anthracite mines of Pennsylvania, the widely scattered glass factories, and southern cotton mills—industries where abuses seemed most glaring.

The Committee sent McKelway south to conduct a more detailed examination of child labor conditions in the cotton mills. The first real legislative battle occurred in North Carolina in 1905, when a McKelway-drafted bill died without even reaching a vote. The same year McKelway reactivated the Georgia Child Labor Committee. He received most of the credit for a Georgia child labor statute which was notable as the first real victory for the NCLC in the South, despite the act's low standards and the lack of effective enforcement machinery.

Senator Albert J. Beveridge's effort to secure a national child labor bill split the ranks of the NCLC. The Committee's trustees at first backed the legislation. McKelway was supportive and lobbied strongly in Washington. Murphy, who opposed federal action and believed that the states should and could handle the problem, resigned from the NCLC in protest of its endorsement of the measure. McKelway prepared a memorandum answering the Committee's critics, but its trustees eventually reversed their earlier position.

While the NCLC ultimately did not support federal child legislation at this time, it did favor a federal children's bureau. In 1909 McKelway drafted a special message calling for the establishment of a children's bureau, which President Theodore Roosevelt sent to Congress. His writings also played a vital role in the NCLC's continuing fight to knock down, wherever they appeared, seemingly plausible defenses of the existing system of child labor in the South.

Staunch advocates of federal legislation continued to urge the NCLC to work for some kind of national child labor law. By 1913 McKelway was more convinced than ever that federal legislation was the only answer. The Committee now agreed and drafted its own bill. Three years of tough fighting led to the enactment, in 1916, of the Keating-Owen bill, the nation's first federal child labor law. Believing the bill to be one of unquestioned merit, McKelway lobbied for its passage. A longtime friend of Woodrow Wilson and a solid Democrat, he reminded Wilson that public opinion was now behind such a measure and that failure to sign it would cost the President a good deal of support in the coming election; Wilson agreed.

In June, 1918, however, the U.S. Supreme Court ruled that the Keating-Owen law was unconstitutional. However, Alexander McKelway, who had devoted fourteen years of his life to the abolition of child labor, was spared the shock and disappointment which the decision brought to those who had worked so hard to secure such legislation, for he had died in Washington, D.C., on April 16, 1918.

The Alexander J. McKelway Papers are located in the Library of Congress. Representative articles by McKelway, who was a prolific writer, include "The Evil of Child Labor: Why the South Should Favor a National Law," *Outlook* (February 16, 1907), 360–364; "Child Labor in the South," *Annals of the American Academy of Political and Social Science*, (January, 1910), 156–164; "Child Labor Campaigns in the South," *Survey*, (October 21, 1911), 1023–1026; "Child Labor and Poverty," *Survey* (April 12, 1913), 60–62; and "Another Emancipation Proclamation: The Federal Child Labor Law," *Review of Reviews* (October, 1916), 423–426.

For treatments of McKelway's life and career as a social reformer, see Hugh C. Bailey, *Liberalism in the New South: Southern Social Reformers and the Progressive Movement* (1969); Herbert J. Doherty, Jr., "Alexander J. McKelway: Preacher to Progressives," *Journal of Southern History* (May, 1958), 177–190; and Walter I. Trattner, *Crusade and Child Labor Reform in America* (1970). For a brief outline of his career, see *Who Was in America*, vol. 1 (1943).

L. MOODY SIMMS, JR.

**McLaughlin, James** (February 12, 1842–July 28, 1923), administrator of Indian policy and social reformer, was born in Avonmore, Ontario, to Felix and Mary (Prince) McLaughlin. While a young adult, however, he settled in Wabasha, Minnesota, where he married the eastern Sioux mixed-blood (Louise) Marie Buissant and worked as a blacksmith until 1871. Then he served for a decade in the federal Indian Field Service at Fort Totten Reservation, Dakota Territory, first as a blacksmith and overseer, then as U.S. agent. For his success among traditional Indian peoples situated beyond the edge of the non-Indian frontier, he was chosen to take over as agent at Fort Yates on Standing Rock Reservation. Religious persuasion was partly responsible for the assignment, too; Forts Totten and Yates were headquarters for the only two Sioux reserves assigned to Roman Catholics in the period 1869–1883, during which time religious organizations were charged to appoint Indian agents. And McLaughlin's apparent capacity to communicate and deal effectively with unacculturated Indians was a strong consideration. His central role was to resettle Sitting Bull and his following as they returned from the high plains of the U.S. and western Canadian exile.

McLaughlin accomplished this work effectively for some fourteen years. He dealt with Sitting Bull personally (to his death in 1890) by keeping close watch on the activities of his closest associates and by sending the Hunkpapa leader off the reservation at every opportunity. He dealt with a larger body of residents through the rigorous application of Peace Policy standards administered by a "district" system unique to his reserve. Despite thorough investigation into circumstances surrounding Sitting Bull's death, McLaughlin emerged without occupational blemish for elevation to an Indian Field Service appointment of the highest order and national influence.

As Indian inspector (under several labels) from 1895 to 1923, he possibly exerted greater influence than any other person upon the local application of federal Indian policies designed to achieve peace between the cultures and to transform Indians into productive citizens. He conducted myriad inspections of conditions at reservations, schools, and health care facilities across forty-five states as he investigated charges against numerous employees of the Indian Service. He dealt with reservation boundary disputes and tribal band relocations as well as surplus land cessions and allotment controversies. Somewhat reluctantly, McLaughlin was a leader on the highly publicized Wanamaker Expeditions. He joined Secretary of the Interior Franklin D. Lane both to write the script for, and to administer, the ceremonies of citizenship that accompanied fee simple title delivery to Indian owners of trust allotments. Many times, McLaughlin worked laboriously on tribal claims. He was the leading troubleshooter for federal policy application down to the time of its analysis through the Indian Commissioner's Industrial Surveys (1922–1926).

As an obvious champion of an acculturation policy that has fallen into some disrepute for its thoroughgoing application, McLaughlin is regarded by some historians as a questionable asset to Indians of his era. Yet as a practical administrator of integrity with the capacity to work at scenes of potential difficulty to the benefit of most participants, he must be regarded with respect as a favorable force, if not as a constructive social reformer.

James McLaughlin died in Washington, D.C., on July 28, 1923.

James McLaughlin's own work, *My Friend the Indian* (1910; rev. ed., 1970), is both an autobiography and an expression of its author's views regarding major developments in Indian-White relations across the West during his lifetime. Whatever view one holds on his life, McLaughlin's career cannot be measured accurately without recognition of the enormous influence of his Indian wife, Marie. Readers, therefore, should see her *Myths and Legends of the Sioux* (1916; repr. 1974), which contains cultural knowledge she acquired as a child and is a reminder of why McLaughlin succeeded so readily while others failed at scenes of controversy.

Louis L. Pfaller's *James McLaughlin: The Man with an Indian Heart* (1978) is the only published biography available. Even though it is far from definitive, and less than objective, it provides an adequate survey of the agent turned inspector's life that the reader should digest with critical caution. In the absence of a reliable history of Standing Rock Reservation, biographies of Sitting Bull and his people supply the most useful insights into McLaughlin's central efforts at the agency. Stanley Vestal's *Sitting Bull: Champion of the Sioux* (1932; repr. 1969), based on careful oral and documentary research and written as literary history, remains the most complete study in book form. Herbert T. Hoover's "Sitting Bull," in *American Indian Leaders* (1980), 152–174, supplies historical context for the agent's problems and activities around Fort Yates.

HERBERT T. HOOVER

**McLean, Francis Herbert** (November 14, 1869–June 9, 1945), leader in the charity organization movement and the development of family social work, was the youngest of four children born in Oakland, California, to Edward and Sarah Emeline (Maynard) McLean. His father, who was a graduate of Yale with ambitions to become a minister, was instead, first a teacher, then an insurance agent, and finally a real estate broker. He died when Francis was seventeen, but his mother, who handled the family finances astutely, lived until age ninety-four. His parents, originally from Connecticut and Congregationalists, placed great emphasis on intellect and making a contribution to society, advice heeded by all the McLean children.

Francis graduated from Los Angeles High School in 1877 and from the University of California, Berkeley, in 1892. He studied the classics and was active in debating, Democratic Party politics, and journalism. He was a member of the University Press Club, a reporter for the university newspaper, and editor of the weekly news magazine. After graduation he was employed by the *Berkeley Herald* as city editor and was a reporter for the *Oakland Morning Times*.

In 1894 he abandoned his journalism career and moved to New York City. From 1895 to 1899 he lived in the University Settlement and was active as chairman of the Sanitary Union, did comparative analyses of food prices in different socioeconomic districts, and was concerned about conditions in New York's Bowery district. During the years from 1894 to 1898, he pursued a self-directed education for the field of social work (for which there was not yet any formal schooling) by taking graduate-level courses at several institutions. Thus he took social science courses at Johns Hopkins in 1894–1895. At Columbia University in 1895–1896 he took political economy, finance, sociology, and statistics courses. And in 1897–1898 he attended the University of Pennsylvania, where he took more sociology courses as well as work in economics and public administration.

In 1898–1899 he held his first paid position in social work. He was the assistant to the general secretary of the Brooklyn Bureau of Charities. He moved to Montreal, Canada, in 1900 to assume the position of general secretary of that city's newly formed Charity Organization Society (COS). In his two years there, one of his main concerns was the lack of public outdoor (or home) relief. This was reflected in his presentation at the National Conference of Charities and Correction in 1901, "Effects upon Private Charity of the Absence of All Public Relief." From 1902 to 1905 he was supervisor of district superintendents for the Chicago Bureau of Charities. Then he returned to the East Coast to resume employment with the Brooklyn Bureau of Charities, where he was superintendent from 1905 to 1907.

Sometime between 1902 and 1907 he married Flora Benson, whom he frequently referred to as "Lady Flo." She lived until December, 1943. Little is known about her, but their life style reflects something about the couple. They did not have children; they lived in furnished apartments, moved frequently, and accumulated few possessions. Even though he was an avid reader over a wide range of subjects, he accumulated no personal library. Instead, he would talk of his ideas from his reading, and then would give the books to friends who showed interest. Some described him as shy and inarticulate, but the positive aspect of this was his ability to totally attend to the other person and then raise questions that both enlightened and stimulated the recipient to further pursuits. This quality, and his constant orientation to positive growth, made his personality memorable. He approached relationships with individuals and organizations on a long-term basis and was willing to pursue them patiently over the course of years to see that the objectives were realized. His belief in the principles of democracy was strong and was reflected directly in his practice of helping communities carry out their own ideas, rather than imposing his, or others', on them.

In 1906 McLean's employment was interrupted by the San Francisco fire. Edward T. Devine,* who headed the disaster work for the American Red Cross during this crisis, asked him to handle the Family Rehabilitation Committee of the relief effort, a post McLean accepted. He then developed there a district system and operated under a philosophy which dealt with total rehabilitation, not simply physical needs. Following his experience, he wrote "Lessons of the Relief Survey."

Although the years from 1906 to 1911 were not the most exciting ones for the charity organization movement, it was at this time that the numerous organizations were brought into formal contact with each other, and McLean's contributions along that line were numerous. Working with Mary Richmond,* he advocated the development of an organized correspondence service which would advise newly forming societies and assist others. He became associate editor of *Charities and the Commons*, the periodical of the movement, which had established what was called the Exchange Branch to facilitate the exchange of information among the various societies. During the first year, McLean received requests for service from forty-five cities. His correspondence efforts were more formalized in 1907, when the Exchange Branch became a separate project from the periodical and received its own funding from the Russell Sage Foundation.

Mary Richmond became the chair and McLean the field secretary of the field department committee. McLean advocated the need for field visits to follow up the contacts made through correspondence, and by 1909 he had visited thirty-nine cities for the purpose of organizing or reorganizing societies.

At the National Conference of Charities and Correction of June, 1909, a committee was established to begin the formation of a national organization of the societies. The Russell Sage Foundation contributed its support and funding by establishing a Charity Organization Department, beginning October 1, 1909. Mary Richmond was employed as the full-time director of the new department, with McLean and Margaret Byington as field secretaries. At the National Conference in 1910, a national organization for the societies was established on a temporary basis, to be finalized the following year. McLean was on the committee and drew up the proposed constitution for the new organization. On June 8, 1911, the National Association of Societies for Organizing Charities (later known as the Family Service Association of America) was permanently established, and the following month McLean was installed as its first general secretary.

McLean was credited with the formation of the concept of field work on which the movement built its growth. The family was considered to be the basic unit of concern to the COS movement, but the organization of adequate services required involvement with a whole community. He clearly saw this interrelationship; he had a systematic approach which included a deliberate study and diagnosis of the community comparable to a ''case'' in casework. He left the initiative with each community to develop as it wished, but he insisted that there be a paid secretary and that the Society be adequately structured as an independent organization.

His community orientation led to concern for interagency relationships and to the concept of central councils of social agencies. The first of these was formed in Pittsburgh in 1908 with his help. His 1910 report of the Exchange Branch promoted the need for this type of joint planning of social programs. He recognized the need for a separate agency to carry out this coordination role. From 1908 through the 1930s he worked to develop and strengthen various central councils across the country.

In 1910 he wrote his well-known pamphlet, *The Formation of Charity Organization Societies in Smaller Cities*; this was revised in 1932 and again in 1944. From 1910 to 1922 he was associate director—Mary Richmond was director—of the Summer Institutes which provided four weeks of intensive training for selected workers from societies across the nation. At the Institute in 1916 he presented ''Social Progress and Perturbation,'' which many considered to be his most eloquent paper.

The years from 1910 to 1925 saw the movement continue to grow. The number of member agencies increased from 62 in 1911 to 220 by 1925. In 1920 the National Association of Societies for Organizing Charities was reorganized (and renamed the American Association for Organizing Family Social Work) with David Holbrook* as executive director and McLean as field director. In 1932

McLean became a staff consultant. He retired in July, 1938, but continued to maintain an office at the Association, where he worked on a voluntary basis. He died in Wickersham Hospital in New York City on June 9, 1945.

Two major sources of information are available on McLean. One is a well-written and comprehensive biography by Ralph Ormsby, *A Man of Vision: Francis H. McLean, 1869–1945* (1969), and the other is a special edition of *The Family: Journal of Social Case Work* (March, 1946).

McLean was a prolific writer. During the years from 1895 to 1944, he produced more than 130 journal articles, reports, and pamphlets and reviewed 39 books. His best-known pamphlet was *The Formation of Charity Organization Societies in Smaller Cities*, which was published by the Russell Sage Foundation. Among the many community surveys he was engaged in, he is best known for the 1915 report, *Charities in Springfield, Illinois*. His paper "Social Progress and Perturbation," delivered as a speech in the summer of 1916 at the Charity Organization Institute, was later published as a pamphlet by the Family Welfare Association of America.

JOYCE PREWITT DAVIS

**McMain, Eleanor Laura** (March 2, 1866–May 12, 1934), social reformer and settlement worker, was born near Baton Rouge, Louisiana, the fifth of eight children of John West McMain and Jane (Walsh) McMain. Of Scotch-Irish descent and the product of a strict Presbyterian upbringing, Jacob McMain relinquished a profitable shipping and mercantile business in Philadelphia, Pennsylvania, after his first wife's death. Moving to Louisiana in 1846, he soon became the owner of a prosperous plantation near Baton Rouge and married Jane Walsh, the daughter of devout Episcopalian parents who had left Ireland for Louisiana. Jacob McMain served in the Confederate army during the Civil War. Losing his considerable fortune, he moved his family to Baton Rouge in 1871. There, they lived in genteel poverty while Jacob served as dean and secretary of Louisiana State University until his death in 1884.

Influenced by her father's intellectual curiosity and idealism, Eleanor McMain attended private girls' schools and the Episcopal church in Baton Rouge. During the mid- and late–1880s, she was a teacher and governess and then opened a private school. In the mid–1890s she moved to New Orleans with her mother. McMain entered a training class in 1899 run by the Free Kindergarten Association (sponsored by the Episcopal church) and soon became coprincipal of a diocesan kindergarten in the "Irish Channel" section of New Orleans. In 1901 she became the head resident of Kingsley House settlement, a New Orleans social center which incorporated the kindergarten and an Episcopal mission.

Spending the summer in Chicago, during which she studied at the University of Chicago and examined the settlement movement at Jane Addams'* Hull-House and Graham Taylor's* Chicago Commons, McMain returned to New Orleans and, in 1902, reorganized Kingsley House on a nonsectarian basis.

Opening the city's first vacation school, she also inaugurated a free clinic with the cooperation of Dr. Sara Tew Mayo and other physicians. An active member of the New Orleans Playground Committee, she established in 1904 the first of many playgrounds to be backed by the Committee.

Yellow fever struck New Orleans in 1905. McMain headed an education and clean-up campaign which saved the "Irish Channel" area from the worst effects of the dreaded disease. In 1906 her interests turned to a neighborhood antituberculosis league, which grew into a citywide organization under the leadership of Kate Gordon and others. McMain became vice president of a day nursery association in 1909; the same year brought the establishment of a summer retreat for Kingsley House children called Camp Onward. Other parts of the Kingsley House program included dramatics, courses for the blind, athletics, and, for a brief period (1914–1915), a "Southern School of Social Science and Public Service."

A gift from a local philanthropist led to the construction, in 1925, of a new home for Kingsley House, giving it, in Jane Addams' opinion, the best settlement facilities in the world. The center covered a city block; it included an auditorium, library, day nursery, residents' homes, clinic, trade school rooms, and other facilities. Though much of her time was taken up with administrative duties, McMain remained the friend of many. According to a writer in the *New Orleans Times-Picayune*, she had a gift for easing the harshness of institutionalism.

McMain was interested in all phases of the civic life of New Orleans. She founded and was the first president of the Woman's League. Representing a variety of the city's women's groups, this organization worked for reform on many fronts. A League-sponsored compulsory education law became a reality in 1910. About the same time, as president of the Tenement House Association, McMain publicized bad housing conditions in various parts of the city. In 1904 she became a director of Jean Margaret Gordon's Milne Home for Girls. McMain strongly backed the efforts of Gordon in 1906 and 1908 to secure changes in Louisiana's laws governing the labor of children and women. In 1921 she helped set up the New Orleans Council of Social Agencies. Six years later she served as president of the Council, which was the forerunner of the Community Chest.

An active member of the National Federation of Settlements and Neighborhood Centers, McMain served on its executive committee for six years. Under the sponsorship of this organization, she helped spread the settlement idea abroad when she spent nearly a year in Paris establishing a new settlement house, l'Accueil Franco-Americain, founded by the American wife of a French general, Mme. J. Catlin-Tauffleib. Wishing to continue her work in New Orleans, McMain refused offers to head the Chicago Commons and other settlements in the North. In 1920 she received the *Times-Picayune* loving cup for outstanding service to New Orleans; in 1932 the city named a high school in her honor. The same year found McMain confined to her bed most of the time as her health failed. She died in New Orleans in 1934, highly respected for her long career in settlement work.

Some of Eleanor McMain's papers and letters can be found at Kingsley House, New Orleans. McMain's articles, "Kingsley House, New Orleans," and "Behind the Yellow Fever in Little Palermo," appeared, respectively, in the December 5, 1903, issue of *Charities* and the November, 1905, issue of *Charities and the Commons*.

On McMain, see Isabelle Dubroca, *Good Neighbor Eleanor McMain of Kingsley House* (1955), a biography by a friend; and Bradley Buell's "Eleanor McMain: One of the Pioneers," *Survey Graphic* (January, 1931). See also the obituary of McMain in the *New Orelans Times-Picayune*, May 13, 1934; and Katherine Hardesty, "Eleanor McMain, Trail-Blazer of Southern Social Work," Master's thesis, Tulane School of Social Work, 1936.

Also of interest are "The Work of Kingsley House During the Epidemic" and "The Housing Movement in New Orleans," which appeared, respectively, in the August 19, 1905, issue of *Charities* and the February 10, 1906, issue of *Charities and the Commons*.

L. MOODY SIMMS, JR.

**Mallery, Otto Tod** (April 27, 1881–December 16, 1956), recreation and unemployment expert, was born at Willets Point (later part of Queens), New York, the son of United States Army Major Conrad Mallery and Anna Louise (Winslow) Mallery. Mallery's religious affiliation was with the Presbyterian Church. He received preparatory education at the Hill School in Pottstown, Pennsylvania, and then went on to Princeton University, where he obtained his A.B. in 1902. After postgraduate work in economics and sociology at the University of Pennsylvania and Columbia University, he began a career in 1903 as a bond broker with the firm of Paine & Wilson in Baltimore, Maryland. Finance alone did not satisfy him, however, and he soon became involved in social activities. His commitment to help his fellow men ended only with his death.

Mallery gained national prominence in two specific areas of philanthropic engagement—the advancement of recreation and the promotion of public works to combat unemployment—and it seems that, of these, the former was closest to his heart. In 1908, two years after he had planned and financed a survey of playgrounds in Chicago—the results of which were influential in starting the recreation movement in Philadelphia—he became secretary of the Philadelphia Playgrounds Association. The Association, which in 1946 became the Philadelphia Recreation Association, was one year old at that time. From 1910 to 1925 Mallery acted as its treasurer and thereafter as president until his retirement in 1948. With the help of officials from the public schools and the city's Bureau of Recreation, he fostered the development of municipal playgrounds in Philadelphia under the auspices of the Association. In 1909 he became secretary of the Philadelphia Board of Recreation, and from 1915 to 1916 he served as its president. Occasional criticism decrying the use of public funds for recreation facilities left Mallery undaunted, and at his instigation the city converted a number of its small parks into playgrounds and recreation centers. In later years his concern extended to the needs of the elderly, and he assisted in establishing Golden Age Clubs. His dedication and ability made him a recognized leader. From 1912 to 1937 he served as a director of the Playground and Recreation Association of America (National Recreation Association in 1930) and thereafter, succeeding Joseph Lee,* as president until the close of his life. Moreover, from 1950 he was chairman of the board of that association. This position enabled him to promote the creation of the International Recreation Association, which was established in Philadelphia in October, 1956. The value of his commitment was acknowledged when, in 1946, the Otto Tod Mallery Recreation Center in Germantown (Philadelphia), Pennsylvania was dedicated in his honor. In 1956 he received an official award from the city of Philadelphia which paid tribute to him as the "Father of Recreation in Philadelphia."

The other field in which Mallery achieved distinction was in the fight against unemployment through the provision of public works. An early member of the reform-minded American Association for Labor Legislation (AALL), he soon emerged as its leading expert in public works legislation. The basic idea was to "save" municipal, state, and federal construction projects during good times and undertake them in periods of economic downturn, thus using them to smooth out the business cycle. As a member of the Pennsylvania State Industrial Board from 1915 to 1923, he was instrumental in getting an emergency public works act passed in 1917, the first such legislation in the United States. His Pennsylvania experience led Mallery to involvement on the national level. After working in 1918 for the War Labor Policies Board, he was appointed chief of the federal aid and works section in the U.S. War Department under the direction of Colonel Arthur Woods, who as assistant to the Secretary of War was in charge of easing the transition to peacetime conditions. Mallery testified as a prominent witness before several congressional committees investigating the advisability of federal public works legislation. He also officially participated in President Warren Harding's Conference on Unemployment in 1921 and contributed to the work of two of the resulting committees. In 1922 he was sent as an observer to the Canadian unemployment conference in Ottawa. While these postwar endeavors produced no immediate fruits, after the onset of the Depression Mallery's and the AALL's unceasing efforts were rewarded when, in 1931, the Federal Employment Stabilization Act was passed, a milestone on the way to more effective public works legislation. The Roosevelt administration made use of Mallery's expertise by appointing him in 1937 an advisor to the U.S. delegation to the International Labor Office and reporter of the Public Works Commission in Geneva, and by employing him as a consultant to the National Resources Planning Board, 1939–1943.

Mallery was married twice, first (November 2, 1910) to Rosamond Robinson Junkin, who died in 1915, and then (October 21, 1918) to Louise Marshall. By the first marriage he had two children, Otto Tod and Rosemary, and by the second two as well, Bayard and David. Politically, he remained independent.

A sign of his broad-minded good will was his founding in 1953 of the Interdependence Council, which in 1956 issued a Declaration of Interdependence, reaffirming man's dependence on man without regard to religion, creed, color, or geographical boundaries. The latter manifesto expressed Mallery's own convictions, which he had lived up to through many decades of altruistic service. Considering his lifelong dedication to recreation, there was an ironic element in his death, as he was killed by a car which hit him while he was taking an evening stroll near his home in Philadelphia.

Mallery was not a prolific writer. Most important for his public works ideas is his essay "The Long-Range Planning of Public Works," in President's Conference on Unemployment, Committee on Unemployment and Business Cycles, *Business Cycles and Unemployment: Report and Recommendations* (1923), 231–261. He also devised plans for a lasting peace after World War II. See "Economic Union and Enduring Peace," American Academy of Political and Social Science *Annals* (July, 1941), 125–134; and the elaboration of this article in book form, *Economic Union and Durable Peace* (1943); and also *More Than Conquerors: Building Peace on Fair Trade* (1947).

An extensive study of Mallery's life has yet to be undertaken. Many of the essential facts can be gleaned from *Who Was Who in America*, vol. 3 (1960), 549, and from *The National Cyclopedia of American Biography*, vol. 44 (1962), 90–91. Two anonymous articles in *Recreation*, "Father of Philadelphia Recreation" (August, 1948), 223, and "Otto Tod Mallery" (January, 1957), 4, stress his recreational activities. The detail of Mallery's death is recorded in "Otto Tod Mallery," *Publishers Weekly* (January 28, 1957), 251.

UDO SAUTTER

**Mangold, George Benjamin** (July 7, 1876–May 11, 1962), sociologist, social work educator, and social welfare activist, was born in Waupeton, Iowa, the son of John and Mary (Datisman) Mangold. He received the A.B. degree from Cornell College (Iowa) in 1901 and attended Drew Theological Seminary from 1901 to 1902; in 1903 he received a master's degree from the University of Chicago, and in 1906 was awarded the Ph.D. from the University of Wisconsin. Mangold married Edith E. Putnam in 1905, and they had two sons and a daughter.

Following the receipt of his Ph.D. in 1906, Mangold taught for one year at Washington State University. He then moved to St. Louis as associate director of the Missouri School of Social Economy, one of the earliest schools of social work. In 1912 he became director of the school and remained in this position, seeing the school through several crises, until it finally closed in 1924. From 1924 to 1928 Mangold was social service secretary of the St. Louis Church Federation, the only time during his career he was employed outside of academia. In 1928 he became professor of sociology and social work at the University of Southern California and associate editor of the *Journal of Sociology and Social Research*. Mangold retired from teaching at USC in 1946 but remained in his editorial position until his death. From 1948 to 1952 he served as visiting professor at George Pepperdine College.

Mangold's scholarly career passed through several distinct phases. During his doctoral studies, directed by Richard T. Ely, he concentrated on labor economics. His dissertation, *The Labor Argument in the American Protective Tariff Discussion*, was published in 1908. Following this, Mangold did no further research or writing on the subject of economics, a fact that seems strange considering that his dissertation was significant enough to have merited republication in 1976 as part of a series titled The Neglected American Economists—Economics and Technology in Nineteenth Century American Thought. During his years in St. Louis, 1906–1928, Mangold did research and published extensively in the area of child welfare. In 1910 he published *Child Problems*, and in 1914 *Child Welfare*, which not only was the first text in that field but went through three editions and remained the standard work on the subject for almost thirty years. Then, in 1921, he published the results of several years of research in *Children Born Out of Wedlock*. In the interim he supervised student research at the School of Social Economy, which resulted in monographs such as *The Newsboy in St. Louis*. When he went to California, Mangold's research interests changed from child welfare to community organization. Thus, he published *Social Pathology* in 1932 and *Organization for Social Welfare* in 1934, and a series of community studies such as *Community Welfare in San Diego* (1929), *Building a Better San Jose* (1930), and *Life in Long Beach* (1939).

While Mangold's career certainly was successful, he is important more for what he represented than for what he actually accomplished. During an era when social work was developing a perspective that viewed social problems as the aggregate of individual problems, and the development of individual treatment techniques as the paramount professional goal, Mangold remained a firm adherent to the social change–social action approach. In articles and addresses dealing with the profession, Mangold made clear his belief that individual treatment activities should be relegated to the lower echelons of the profession and that the leaders should occupy their time with social legislation, research, administration, and social change. He saw little value in the study of psychology for social workers, feeling that economics and legislation were far more important fields because social problems were, at their root, economic and political in nature. He believed that the future of the profession lay in large-scale public welfare programs and agencies rather than in private counseling agencies. In these beliefs, he was, along with Grace* and Edith Abbott* and a few others, one of a small minority of social workers. Mangold acted on these beliefs through involvement in social action activities such as the mothers' pension movement and the Pure Milk Commission in St. Louis, and through active support for public welfare when he went to California.

The Missouri School of Social Economy was a reflection of Mangold's professional philosophy. Its curriculum never became dominated by courses on the techniques of individual treatment, as was the trend at most other schools.

During its last year of operation (1923–1924), only six of twenty-three courses dealt with individual pathology and treatment techniques. The other seventeen dealt with economics, social problems, legislation, and the like. By comparison, during its first year of operation (1925–1926) the Washington University program that replaced the MSSE offered thirteen courses, nine emphasizing individual pathology and treatment techniques and none dealing with economics, legislation, or social change.

While it is impossible to prove, it appears that Mangold's beliefs about the direction the profession should take resulted in his gradual exclusion from leadership of the profession. Prior to the early 1920s, Mangold, as director of one of the few professional schools of social work, was an active and well-respected force in the profession. In 1915 he was one of four respondents to Abraham Flexner's famous paper, "Is Social Work a Profession?" In 1919 he was one of the founding members of the American Association of Schools of Social Work, forerunner of the Council on Social Work Education. However, in 1924, when his school faced a financial crisis, it was abandoned by the local social work community and replaced by a new school at Washington University, now the George Warren Brown School of Social Work. The new school was directed by Frank Bruno, a far more traditional social worker. When Mangold joined the faculty of the University of Southern California, he taught courses in the School of Social Work but actually was a member of the Sociology Department. Mangold's disassociation from the social work profession appears to have become complete when, for the 1950–1951 edition of *Who's Who*, he changed his entry from "social worker" to "sociologist" and "teacher."

It is ironic that the year of Mangold's death, 1962, represents the dawn of an era during which the social work profession would rediscover the approach to social problems that Mangold never had lost. He was eighty-five when he died in Los Angeles, California.

Unfortunately, George Mangold did not deposit his personal papers in any archive prior to his death, nor did his family afterwards. There is some material related to his years at the Missouri School of Social Economy in other collections. Relating to the years that the school was affiliated with Washington University (1909–1915) there is a good deal of information in the Washington University Archives in the Hall Papers and the Houston Papers. Relating to the years the school was part of the University of Missouri (1906–1909; 1915–1924) there is some material at the University of Missouri, Western Historical Manuscript Collection, in the President's Papers.

Mangold's major publications have been cited above. In addition, he published numerous articles and book reviews in the *Sociology and Social Research* between 1929 and 1957. A very interesting article clearly describing Mangold's conception of the social work profession is "The New Profession of Social Service," in J. E. McCullock, ed., *Battling for Social Betterment* (1914).

Emory S. Bogardus published a personal eulogy titled "George B. Mangold

(1876–1962): Scholar, Teacher, Author,'' *Sociology and Social Research* 46 (1962), 475–478. This is mainly an intellectual biography of Mangold focusing on his work as a sociologist, but it touches on his social welfare activities as well. A more complete description of Mangold's activities and problems as director of the Missouri School of Social Economy is contained in Philip R. Popple, ''Community Control of Social Work Education: A Historical Example,'' *Journal of Sociology and Social Welfare* 5 (1978), 152–167.

PHILIP R. POPPLE

**Mather, Cotton** (February 10, 1663–February 13, 1728), minister and important figure in early American charity, was born in Boston, the first son of the Reverend Increase Mather and Maria (Cotton) Mather. Mather earned his bachelor's degree from Harvard College in 1678 and a master's degree from the same institution in 1681, and received an honorary doctorate of divinity from the University of Glasgow in 1710. He was married three times and fathered fifteen children—to Abigail Phillips from 1686 to 1702, with whom he had nine children; to Elizabeth Hubbard Clark from 1703 to 1713, with whom he had six children; and to Lydia Lee George from 1715 to 1728, with whom he had no children.

Ordained as a Congregational minister in 1684, Mather devoted his life to the Puritan faith, and charity was a significant albeit unrecognized part of his work. Much of Mather's reputation is based on the Salem witchcraft episode, but other aspects of his life, particularly his contributions to early American philanthropy, merit serious attention. A recent biographer described Mather as a ''deeply charitable man'' who possessed a ''keen sympathy for others' distress.'' His concern for Boston's poor, which began in his youth with his own charity fund, continued for over fifty years, and he can be termed an ''American almoner.''

On behalf of Boston's poor he spoke more sermons, wrote more tracts, and collected more funds than any person in his day in colonial New England. In an early sermon he stated, ''It would be a great Evil in us, if we could not be ready, Charitably and Liberally[,] to relieve the Necessities of the Poor.'' His foremost historical work, *Magnalia Christi Americana* (1702), had special praise for New England's charitable men. John Wilson, Boston's first minister, was described as ''Liberal . . . in Employing his Estate for the Relief of the Needy,'' and John Winthrop, the model magistrate, he pointed out, gave his last grain to feed the hungry in the seaport. Mather also praised mariners of his day for ''their Liberal *Alms*'' and urged his Boston neigbors to ''render it a . . . town of charity!''

Mather functioned as an intermediary between the rich and the poor in colonial Boston. Wealthy merchants regularly asked him to distribute their gifts to the poor, such as a ''considerable Quantity of Corn,'' a ''pretty large Summ of Money,'' and even ''Secret Charities.'' Reports of his charity work brought the poor to Mather's house for alms, clothes, food or employment; at one point nearly 100 people regularly received assistance from him. In emergency situations, such as epidemics or fires, Mather often served as the leader of local relief efforts. He collected donations for the destitute Huguenots in 1689, gathered foodstuffs to relieve the severe shortages of the 1690s, and in the measles epidemic of 1713 distributed nearly £400 collected by local churches.

Mather devoted a considerable part of his ideas on charity to the people of the Congregational Church. As minister of Boston's Second Church, he urged its wealthy members to be generous in their alms and to remember their social responsibility to the poor. They should not, he cautioned, "Screw grievously upon them, only because they are Poor and Low, and in great Necessitie." He suggested that each church establish an "EVANGELICAL TREASURY" for its poor and pointed to the splendid example of one anonymous church member who annually gave "Twenty Pounds to be scattered among the Needy." He praised the church deacons, who collected charity for the destitute, and whom he considered his brothers in Congregational benevolence.

Social institutions also attracted his attention, such as Boston's Alms House, where Mather was a frequent visitor with sermons and material aid. In addition, he worked with local officials to improve the conditions for the poor. Thus, a proposed Christian hospital and an institution for poor children also interested him, but in spite of much effort, both institutions failed to materialize. More successful was Boston's first charity school, which he sponsored in 1706; by 1713 three were in operation. He persuaded wealthy gentlemen to support them financially, but he was the sole source of funds in 1717 for a new charity school specifically for "poor Negro's, and Indians." For many years he was involved with various religious and social organizations; he helped establish about twenty of them, and he noted with pride that they collected funds for "*Charity to the Poor.*" They contributed significantly to relieve Boston's unfortunates, as did the Quarterly Charity Lecture that he instituted in 1720.

Certainly Mather's foremost legacy in this field was to early American social thought in regard to the poor. As a young minister he followed traditional religious precepts and asserted that "Alms! Alms! was the continual cry of Christianity!" He believed that "*Alms-deeds*" were an important part of Christian living, and he advised the Puritan faithful that he who "gives to the Poor, Lends to the Lord; and the Lord will Repay him." After 1700 Mather gradually added an important secular dimension—the idea of "Do Good"—to his social thought. It brought a deep humanitarian element to his theology and made him a pre-Enlightenment figure in early American philanthropy.

Several factors affected his new social thought, particularly his experience with the church poor, the growth of poverty in early eighteenth century Boston, and the ideas of European Pietists such as Dr. August Hermann Francke. Mather's most important new work, *Bonifacius . . . Essays to Do Good* (1710), provided an outline of his new social direction and was described as a "manual of practical charity." Perry Miller thought that for Cotton Mather the "whole pyramid of doing good comes to its apex in the doing of good for the poor." Mather's social work after 1710, as revealed in his diary, reflected his new commitment to aid the poor of Boston. The numerous short entries of "GOOD DEVISED" demonstrated the extent of his new efforts. He focused on Boston's widows and asked people to consider that "Poor *Widows* be among the more special objects of your Charity." Other unfortunates, particularly the elderly and the insane, also benefited from his new direction. In addition, Boston's mentally ill, scorned by many in colonial society, received help as Mather provided material aid, solaced them with compassion, and urged local magistrates to reform their treatment.

To the end of his life Mather had great concern for the poor, which exemplified the best traditions of Puritan charity and the New England Way. He was one of the few people to offer aid to the destitute Irish who immigrated to Boston after 1715, and his last great work, *The Angel of Bethesda*, was praised for its "warm charity, sympathy for human suffering, and particular care for the poor." His approach to charity remained conservative throughout his life, and his sermons supported the social gradations of his day. He advised the poor to be patient and to remember that "a *Poor Man*, may be a *Favourite* of Heaven." In essence, Cotton Mather utilized religious charity to aid the poor and to glorify God; on a secular level he developed the American creed to "Do Good" which would motivate future generations of social reformers.

Mather died in Boston on February 13, 1728.

Cotton Mather's major manuscripts are scattered among several repositories, including the Massachusetts Historical Society (Boston, Massachusetts), the Boston Public Library (Boston, Massachusetts), and the American Antiquarian Society (Worcester, Massachusetts).

His published works, which number more than 400, are available on microfilm in *Early American Imprints, 1639–1800*; readers should consult Charles Evans, ed., *American Bibliography, 1639–1820*, 14 vols. (1903–1959), for a chronological guide; for an alphabetical list of his works on microfilm, see Clifford K. Shipton and James E. Mooney, eds., *National Index of American Imprints through 1800: The Shorttitle Evans*, 2 vols. (1969). For detailed information on each Mather publication, consult Thomas James Holmes, *Cotton Mather: A Bibliography of His Works*, 3 vols. (1940).

Mather's major sermons on early American charity include *Durable Riches* (1695), *The Bostonian Ebenezer* (1698), *The Good Old Way* (1706), *Orphanotrophium* (1711), *Insanabilia* (1714), and *The Widow of Naim* (1728).

Modern editions are available for his major works, such as *Magnalia Christi Americana*, *Bonifacius*, *The Angel of Bethesda*, and his autobiography, *Paterna*. Considerable information on Mather's social work is recorded in his diaries and letters; see Worthington C. Ford, ed., *Diary of Cotton Mather*, 2 vols., in the Massachusetts Historical Society, *Collections*, Seventh Series, vols. 7 and 8 (1912); William Manierre, ed., *The Diary of Cotton Mather for the Year 1712* (1964); the *Mather Papers*, in the Massachusetts Historical Society, *Collections*, Fourth Series, 8 (1868); and Kenneth Silverman, comp., *Selected Letters of Cotton Mather* (1971).

For secondary sources on his life and social work, see Virginia Bernhard,

"Cotton Mather and the Doing of Good," *New England Quarterly* 29 (1976), 225–241; Virginia Bernhard, "Essays to Do Good: A Puritan Gospel of Wealth, 1640–1740," Ph.D. dissertation, Rice University, 1971; Christine Heyrman, "A Model of Christian Charity: The Rich and the Poor in New England, 1630– 1730," Ph.D. dissertation, Yale University, 1977; David Levin, *Cotton Mather: The Young Life of the Lord's Remembrancer, 1663–1703* (1978); Richard F. Lovelace, *The American Pietism of Cotton Mather* (1980); Robert Middlekauf, *The Mathers: Three Generations of Puritan Intellectuals, 1596–1728* (1971); Perry Miller, *The New England Mind: From Colony to Province* (1953); Kenneth Silverman, *The Life and Times of Cotton Mather* (1984); and Peter Richard Virgadamo, "Colonial Charity and the American Character: Boston, 1630–1775," Ph.D. dissertation, University of Southern California, 1982.

PETER R. VIRGADAMO

**Meyer, Adolf** (September 13, 1866–March 17, 1950), psychiatrist, teacher, and pioneer in the mental hygiene movement, was born at Niederwengingen, an agricultural village near Zurich, Switzerland, the son of a Zwinglian minister, Rudolf Meyer, and his wife, Anna (Walder) Meyer. He grew up in a liberal, tolerant family whose members mixed Swiss peasant rationalism and naturalism with their orthodox Christian beliefs. Especially important to the Meyer family was the notion of encouraging the development of well-adjusted, healthy people, to be accomplished by proper heuristic child rearing. Meyer received his formal training in Europe and studied for his medical degree with August Forel at the University of Zurich, as well as with other neurologists and somatically oriented psychiatrists in Paris, Edinburgh, and London. Meyer always believed that a part of mental health and illness was determined by biology; yet he also believed, with Thomas Huxley, that science was organized common sense, so that Meyer constantly tried to work out a holistic theory of mental health and illness which, to his peers, reflected considerable eclecticism or befuddlement, depending upon one's point of view.

He received his medical degree at Zurich in 1892. In that year he settled in the United States. After a brief fellowship at the University of Chicago, and a year in private neurological practice, he became pathologist at the new Illinois Eastern Hospital for the Insane, in Kankakee. A variety of experiences made him question somatic explanations, including his contact with John Dewey through the Illinois Child Study Association and his admiration of the writings of William James and Charles Peirce. He published or presented a series of papers in which he outlined his evolving position, which recognized mental illness as involving the destruction of physiological and psychological *functions*. Meyer also became highly critical of the Kankakee hospital, and, by extension, mental institutions, because of their dominance by administrators rather than researchers and their vulnerability to political harassment. When the opportunity came in 1895 to move to the State Lunatic Hospital in Worcester, Massachusetts, Meyer accepted, for now he could emphasize careful research and reorganize patient files not around the day of the week, but around the individual patient, which seemed more scientific to him. Affiliated with Clark University, he became very committed to dynamic psychiatry. In 1902 Meyer became director of the Pathological Institute in New York City, and on September 15 he married Mary Potter Brooks, a psychiatric social worker; they had one daughter, Julia Lathrop. At the Institute and at Cornell Medical College (1904–1909) he organized an outpatient service, New York's first mental clinic. Even before he went to Johns Hopkins in 1908 as director of the Henry Phipps Clinic and professor of psychiatry in the Medical School, Meyer was pushing his developing therapeutic views, which emphasized a revolt against pessimistic somaticism, the optimism that better habits could cure mental disease, and, in concert with his peers, a growing interest in the prevention of said disease.

Meyer's optimistic therapeutic ideas helped energize social workers and fitted well into the milieu of early twentieth century concern for the downtrodden and for humanitarian crusades. Meyer thus became an important champion of amelioration. His interest in the prevention of mental disease fitted well into the progressive mentality too, for it addressed such issues as budgetary restraint and efficiency of person as well as of institution, and yet was dedicated to the notion that there was a brighter tomorrow. In the second decade of the century, his interest in the prevention of mental disease attracted him to the small but growing mental hygiene movement. Clifford Beers,* a former mental patient, helped start the mental hygiene movement as a protest against institutional brutalization of inmates. Ironically, in the 1920s the mental hygiene movement, led by Meyer and others, and heavily supported by the Commonwealth Fund, had the long-term effect of turning professional psychiatric help away from the wretched plight of the mistreated in the crowded public asylums, which had been Beers' original objective, toward a general interest in promoting the adjustment of all Americans to society's norms. The Commonwealth Fund's programs did energize and advance the training of psychiatric social workers in the child guidance clinics and movement and elsewhere, but had markedly less success in influencing therapy or treatment in the large public institutions. This was a contribution to the development of social work, even if the consequences of scientific professionalization were both rather predictable and quite ironic.

It probably was at Johns Hopkins that Meyer exerted his greatest influence, in advocating a dynamic psychiatry to several generations of students; there he created the first teaching and research hospital combined with a medical school. Undoubtedly, he made easier the reconstruction of Freudianism by orthodox psychologists such as Robert R. Sears of Yale in the 1930s. As a mentor of therapy, he taught a broadly based humane view, which, whatever its internal inconsistencies, gave many psychiatrists and psychiatric social workers elements of a professional credo. He retired in 1941 and died at home in Baltimore in 1950.

Meyer's extensive papers are at the Alan Mason Chesney Medical Archives, Johns Hopkins University, Baltimore. Published collections of his works include E. E. Winters, ed., *The Collected Papers of Adolf Meyer* (1950–1952); Alfred Lief, ed., *The Commonsense Psychiatry of Dr. Adolf Meyer* (1948); E. E. Winters and A. M. Bowers, comp. and ed., *Psychobiology: A Science of Man* (1957). See also C. M. Campbell, comp., "Bibliography of Adolf Meyer," *Archives of Neurology and Psychiatry* 31 (1937), 724–731; S. Katzenelbogen, ed., *Contributions Dedicated to Dr. Adolf Meyer by His Colleagues, Friends, and Pupils* (1938). Obituaries appeared in *American Journal of Psychiatry* 107 (1950), 79–80; *Journal of Comparative Neurology* 92 (1950), 131–132; *New York Times*, March 18, 1950.

Other accounts of Meyer include Theodore Lidz, "Adolf Meyer and the Development of American Psychiatry," *American Journal of Psychiatry* 123 (1966), 320–332; Saul Feierstein, *Adolf Meyer: Life and Work* (1965); Gerald N. Grob, *The State and the Mentally Ill: A History of Worcester State Hospital in Massachusetts, 1830–1920* (1966); Gerald N. Grob, *Mental Illness and American Society, 1875–1940* (1983); David J. Rothman, *Conscience and Convenience: The Asylum and Its Alternatives in Progressive America* (1980); Roy Lubove, *The Professional Altruist: The Emergence of Social Work as a Career, 1880–1930* (1965); Norman Dain, *Clifford Beers: Advocate for the Insane* (1980).

HAMILTON CRAVENS

**Morgan, Thomas Jefferson** (August 17, 1839–July 13, 1902), minister, educator, and administrator of religious charities, was born in Franklin, Indiana, the son of an American Baptist minister, Lewis Morgan, and his third wife, Mary C. Causey. Lewis Morgan, a son of a slaveholder, advocated abolition of slavery as well as missions and educational work and had achieved some eminence in his region by his death in 1852. Meanwhile, young Thomas pursued his education in Franklin, earning an A.B. degree at Franklin College, of which his father had been one of the founders.

As for many of his generation, Morgan's experience in the Civil War gave form and meaning to his adult life. He served at the beginning of the war in the ranks and after a brief teaching stint returned as an officer in the 70th Indiana, under Colonel Benjamin Harrison. In 1863 he cooperated in the formation of "the sable arm" of the Union army, becoming a major of the 14th United States Colored Infantry. He was subsequently promoted to colonel and then brevetted brigadier-general before the war ended. He established a school for each of his regiments and took pride in their scholastic success as well as in their military performance. His battlefield experiences reportedly persuaded him to pursue the ministry. These wartime activities foreshadowed his career of religious and educational leadership with special attention to the incorporation of racial minorities as equals in the American republic.

Following the war, Morgan entered the Rochester Theological Seminary, graduating in 1868, and was ordained a Baptist minister in 1869. His first and only pastorate took him to Brownville, Nebraska, in 1871. The following year he began his academic career as president of the Nebraska Normal School at Peru. From 1874 to 1881 he served as professor of homiletics and church history at the Baptist Theological Seminary in Chicago, except for several months of study in Germany during 1879. Subsequently, he was principal of the Normal School at Potsdam, New York, from 1881 to 1884, and of the Rhode Island Normal School from 1884 to 1889. During those years he published two books on educational theory and practice and his *Reminiscences of Services with Colored Troops in the Army of the Cumberland, 1863–1865* (1885). His writings revealed great faith in education as a vehicle for encouraging equality and assuring the American national destiny. While he advocated a nonauthoritarian, child-centered approach to teaching, he assumed the universal applicability of his nineteenth century Protestant values.

His appointment as Commissioner of Indian Affairs by Benjamin Harrison in 1889 gave him the opportunity to apply his ideas and to create a national system of education for American Indians. He instituted a comprehensive program based on the American common school system, but with an even greater emphasis on assimilation. At each level, the schools removed the children farther geographically and, it was hoped, culturally from their parents. During his administration he gained a 70 percent increase in appropriations for Indian education and increased average attendance by one-third. His advocacy of land allotment and the extension of citizenship to Indians as well as his schooling program won the support of, and indeed was the implementation of the principles of, the Indian policy reform movement which had emerged in the late 1870s. The ethnocentrism of his reforms, however, triggered resistance from Indian tribes and from the Roman Catholic Church. True to his confidence in the public school system, Morgan advocated ending government subsidies to church-sponsored schools, Protestant and Catholic alike. Behind this apparently even-handed policy, however, lay Morgan's fear of the influence of the Roman Catholic Church as a vestige of the Old World and a source of unwanted pluralism. The Bureau of Catholic Indian Missions' intense and sustained opposition, first to his appointment and then to his policies, strengthened his suspicions. His counterattacks proved attractive to the more genteel nativist organizations such as the National League for the Protection of American Institutions. The defeat of President Harrison's bid for reelection ended Morgan's term as Commissioner, but the expansion of the school system and the termination of federal support for sectarian schools continued under his successors.

In 1893 Morgan continued his ameliorative efforts through a new vehicle, becoming corresponding secretary of the American Baptist Home Mission Society. As chief executive officer for the Society, he placed special emphasis on its support for higher education for black Americans. His faith in the fundamental equality of the races remained undaunted, and he resisted efforts to limit black educational opportunities to industrial education. At the same time, his confidence in his own authority and discomfort with cultural diversity led to criticisms of paternalism from black faculty, students, and leaders.

Nevertheless, he continued to support equal opportunity and attack racial oppression. His last public address, in 1902, was an assault on an initiative from the Commissioner of Indian Affairs to limit resources for Indian education. Regretting what he saw to be a resurgence of racism, Morgan advocated an increase in both public and private assistance for education as the best guarantee of individual opportunity and social stability. Thomas J. Morgan died in July, 1902, in Ossining, New York, after a brief illness; he was survived by his wife, Caroline Starr Morgan, whom he had married in 1870.

No collection of Morgan papers exists, but extensive Morgan correspondence may be found in the Indian Rights Association Papers, Historical Society of Pennsylvania, Philadelphia, and, for his service as Commissioner of Indian Affairs, in Record Group 75, National Archives, Washington, D.C. His editorials in the [Baptist] *Home Mission Monthly*, 1893–1902, reveal his special concern for Black and Indian education while he was with the American Baptist Home Mission Society and, because of destruction of the Society's records for that era, comprise the most complete documentation of his activity. See the *Home Mission Monthly* (August, 1902), 220–223, and ibid. (November, 1902), 292–298, for memorial sketches of his life. Morgan's ideas about education, racial minorities, and the American republic can be found in several publications, including *Reminiscences of Services with Colored Troops in the Army of the Cumberland, 1863–1865* (1885); *Studies in Pedagogy* (1888); *Indian Education* (1890); *The Present Phase of the Indian Question* (1891); *The Negro in America and the Ideal American Republic* (1898). *Roman Catholics and Indian Education* (1893) offers his view of his contest with the Bureau of Catholic Indian Missions.

Morgan remains without a biography. For analysis of his influence on reform of Indian policy, see Wilbert H. Ahern, "Assimilationist Racism: The Case of the 'Friends of the Indian,' " *Journal of Ethnic Studies* (August, 1976), 23–32; Francis Paul Prucha, "Thomas Jefferson Morgan," in *The Commissioners of Indian Affairs, 1824–1977*, ed. Robert M. Kvasnicka and Herman J. Viola (1979), 193–204; Francis Paul Prucha, *The Churches and the Indian Schools, 1888–1912* (1979), chaps. 2–3. James M. McPherson, *The Abolitionist Legacy: From Reconstruction to the NAACP* (1975), chaps. 9, 11, 12, 15, 16, tells of his role with black Americans.

WILBERT H. AHERN

**Moskowitz, Belle** (October 5, 1877–January 2, 1933), social reformer, was born in Harlem, New York, to Isidor and Esther (Freyer) Lindner, who had migrated from East Prussia to the United States in 1869. They operated a small watch repair and jewelry shop on Third Avenue near 125th Street. Belle Lindner grew up in a house behind the shop.

Belle attended public school until her teens, when she enrolled in Horace

Mann High School for Girls, an experimental school based on the ideas of John Dewey. She excelled in literary studies and public speaking. As a special student at Teachers College (Columbia University) from 1894 to 1895, she studied dramatic arts. Between 1895 and 1900 she helped out in her parents' shop and studied privately with Heinrich Conried, a prominent German director. She also may have done volunteer work in dramatics at downtown social settlements, for in 1900 one of them, the Educational Alliance, hired her. She served there in various capacities for three years, rising to the post of director of entertainments and exhibits at a salary of $1,000.

In 1903 Belle married Charles Henry Israels, an architect. They lived at first in Manhattan, moving later to a house in Yonkers. Belle bore four children, three of whom lived: Carlos, Miriam, and Josef. As a young matron, she continued to pursue reform interests through membership in voluntary associations, including the Charity Organization Society and the New York Council of Jewish Women. In this latter organization, she served on the board and guided the founding of the Lakeview Home for Wayward Girls, the first such institution for Jews in America. In 1908 Belle Israels began to focus on the recreational needs of urban working girls. She formed the Committee on Amusement and Vacation Resources of Working Girls to investigate possible links between female delinquency and the lack of decent recreational opportunities for girls. Upon finding that a high percentage of girls frequented commercial dance halls, many of which were associated with liquor, gambling, and prostitution, the Committee launched a successful dance-hall licensing campaign. This campaign was later widely imitated in cities across the country.

During her marriage, Belle Israels also served in executive capacities for the New York State Conference of Charities and Correction. In 1906 and 1907 she put together the Conference's first graphic exhibits, and in 1908 was its first woman vice president. She also worked part-time as a staff member and editorial assistant of the social work journal, *Charities and the Commons* (later the *Survey*). Early in 1911 she was a leader in the movement for factory and labor reform that arose after the Triangle Shirtwaist Company fire that killed over 140 workers, most of them girls. Then, in the fall of 1911, Charles Israels suddenly died of heart failure. As the sole support of her children, Belle had to look for full-time employment.

Her first job was as field secretary for commercial recreation for the Playground Association of America. In 1913 she took an even more challenging post. Three years earlier, lawyers, social workers, and businessmen concerned with stopping the endemic strikes in the garment industry had negotiated a "Protocol of Peace," or collective agreement between labor unions and manufacturers' associations in the cloak, suit, and skirt branch of the ladies' garment industry. Late in 1912 they had worked out a protocol for the dress and shirtwaist branch, where women predominated in the work force. Henry Moskowitz,* one of the negotiators, recommended Belle Israels as a grievance mediator for the manufacturers' side, a delicate role for one identified with labor reform. Belle was confident, however, that the manufacturers sincerely wished to improve conditions in their trade. Her job with them lasted three years. She eventually headed the manufacturers' association's Labor Department, settling thousands of grievances and working toward the adoption of scientific principles of determining piecework prices. By 1915–1916, however, the protocol system had broken down. In November, 1916, a group of antiprotocol manufacturers ousted Belle's supporters from the manufacturers' associations's hierarchy and fired her.

In November, 1914, Belle and Henry Moskowitz had married. After being fired by the manufacturers, Belle reactivated her memberships in voluntary associations, working for women's suffrage through the New York Women's City Club, for the suppression of prostitution through the Committee of Fourteen, and for war preparedness as executive secretary of the Mayor's Committee of Women on National Defense. In 1918, when Henry was out of a job, she opened a private industrial consulting firm. Later that year she decided to support Tammany Democrat Alfred E. Smith for governor. Thus began a most unusual and productive political relationship.

Belle Moskowitz first organized the women's vote for Smith, and then proposed and directed the establishment of a New York State Reconstruction Commission to study New York's problems in the postwar era. The Commission's reports on government reorganization, the housing crisis, unemployment, urban markets, public health, and education formed the basis of Smith's legislative program throughout the 1920s. During the rest of the Governor's years in office, Belle Moskowitz remained a member of his informal group of advisors. She kept up her interests in social welfare issues, but concentrated on using her public relations skills to promote the Governor and his programs. In 1924 she became publicity director for the New York State Democratic Committee, a post she held in the National Committee in 1928 when Smith ran for president.

After Smith's defeat, Belle Moskowitz continued to believe in his political future. She worked as Smith's literary consultant and, as publicity agent for the Empire State Building, hired Lewis Hine* to photograph its construction. In 1932 she directed Smith's futile attempt to regain the Democratic Party's presidential nomination, and then retired from politics. In the meantime, however, she not only had served as a major link between early twentieth century social reform and its legislative fulfillment at the state level in the 1920s, but had helped to establish traditions transferred to the federal level during the New Deal.

Belle Moskowitz died unexpectedly in New York City on January 2, 1933, from complications after a fall.

Belle Moskowitz did not save her personal papers. Her children gave a small collection of what remained at her death to Connecticut College (New London). The *Dictionary of American Biography* (1944) and *Notable American Women* (1971) contain biographical sketches. William C. Karg's "A Short Life of Mrs. Henry Moskowitz and Her Influence upon Governor Alfred E. Smith," M.A. thesis, St. Bonaventure University, 1967, was based on interviews of many individuals now dead, but is marred by innumerable errors. Further information can be gleaned from Robert A. Caro, *The Power Broker: Robert Moses and the Fall of New York* (1974), chap. 6; Paula Eldot, *Governor Alfred E. Smith: The Politician as Reformer* (1983); and Elisabeth Israels Perry, "Industrial Reform in New York City: Belle Moskowitz and the Protocol of Peace, 1913–1916," *Labor History* (Winter, 1982), 5–31. All of the major New York City newspapers published obituaries on January 3, 1933.

ELISABETH I. PERRY

**Moskowitz, Henry** (September 27, 1880–December 17, 1936), settlement house organizer, social reformer, and New York City civic leader, was born in Huesche, Rumania, one of five children of Meyer and Selma Moskowitz. His father worked at a variety of jobs as a peddler, a clerk, and a merchant. The Moskowitz family came to the United States when Henry was four years old, settling in New York City. As a boy, Henry quickly became part of the working class, first as a newsboy and then as a worker in several East Side sweatshops. Coming up through the public schools, he attended City College, paying his way by working as a school teacher. Henry graduated from City College in 1899 and went on to do graduate work in philosophy, education, and economics at Columbia University.

While studying at Columbia, he organized a settlement house on the Lower East Side of New York which came to be known as Madison House. Upon completion of his work at Columbia, Moskowitz went to Germany, where he attended the University of Erlangen. He was awarded the degree of Doctor of Philosophy from Erlangen in 1906, and returned to the United States, taking a position as instructor of history at City College. Shortly thereafter, he also became head of Madison House, where he pushed the idea that the settlement house should become involved in the community on a wide front and become an active force for social and political reform.

Early in 1909 Moskowitz attended a meeting with fellow settlement workers Mary White Ovington* and William English Walling* at which initial plans were drawn up for the organization of the National Association for the Advancement of Colored People (NAACP). He remained closely involved in subsequent planning meetings concerning basic issues for the organization, such as fund raising and membership, and remained an ardent supporter of the organization throughout his life.

Very active in politics, Moskowitz, along with a number of other social workers, became part of the reform-oriented Progressive movement, and was instrumental in the election of several progressives to city and state offices. He also was instumental in organizing the Progressive Party in New York and ran unsuccessfully for Congress on the Progressive Party ticket in 1912.

Through his activities in the Progressive Party Moskowitz became close to Belle Lindner Israels (later Belle Moskowitz*), whom he had known for a number of years. Belle Israels, herself a well-known social reformer, had recently been widowed, and she and Moskowitz were married on November 22, 1914. Belle had three children from her previous marriage, Josef, Carlos, and Miriam. The couple successfully combined their efforts in the areas of social reform and politics.

In March, 1911, a tragic fire at the Triangle Shirtwaist Company, a large New York sweatshop, killed 146 young women working in the building. An investigation revealed that the exits were very inadequate, and that many were locked. Moskowitz led a group of social reformers to the state capital at Albany to demand that action be taken to correct the dangerous working conditions which existed in many such factories. One of the men he met was Al Smith, who at that time was majority leader in the state assembly. This was the beginning of a lifelong relationship between the two men. Smith went on to become one of the most famous figures in New York State, serving as Governor for several terms and also making several unsuccessful bids for President. Moskowitz became one of his closest advisors and a personal friend. Moskowitz's wife Belle would go on to become even more influential than her husband in Smith's career, and both often accompanied Smith in his travels. Moskowitz wrote a biography of Smith in 1927, *Up from the City Streets: Alfred E. Smith*, and in 1928 organized a collection of Smith's papers and speeches which was published under the title *Progressive Democracy—Speeches and State Papers of Alfred E. Smith*.

Throughout his life Moskowitz was involved in many civic and political movements in the New York City area. He served on numerous committees and commissions through which he worked for reform in such areas as labor rights, housing, industrial safety, and regulation of dance halls and public markets. He also was responsible for the establishment of the Board of Motion Picture Censors in New York and was one of the founders of the ethics movement there.

In his later years Moskowitz became closely associated with the theater industry in New York and fought successfully against a move which, in effect, would have resulted in state regulation and censorship of the theater.

Moskowitz worked hard for many causes, but for most of his life stayed in the background. Several accounts describe him as a rather shy man lacking the political savvy which enabled his wife Belle to become much more influential than he. He was, however, highly intelligent, enthusiastic, and fiercely committed to his ideas of reform, contributing to a broad spectrum of societal concerns.

Belle Moskowitz died in 1933, and Henry Moskowitz spent his final years still heavily involved in civic affairs. He died at his home in downtown New York on December 17, 1936.

Very little biographical information is available concerning Moskowitz. Books on the settlement house movement, the life of Al Smith, and New York City in the early part of this century contain numerous references to him, but no comprehensive biographical account could be located. His obituary in the *New York Herald Tribune*, on December 18, 1936, provides a fairly good summary of his life. Other information can be gathered from biographical accounts of Belle Moskowitz. The following sources are useful: Robert A. Caro, *The Power Bro-*

*ker: Robert Moses and the Fall of New York* (1974); Allen F. Davis, *Spearheads for Reform: The Social Settlements and the Progressive Movement 1890–1914* (1967); obituary, *New York Herald Tribune*, December 18, 1936; J. Salwyn Schapiro, "Henry Moskowitz: A Social Reformer in Politics," *Outlook* (October 26, 1912), 446–449.

JIM STAFFORD

**Mulry, Thomas Maurice** (February 13, 1855–March 10, 1916), businessman, Catholic philanthropist, and welfare organizer, was born in New York City, the second of fourteen children of Thomas Mulry and Parthenia Crolius. After attending St. Joseph's parish grade school and the De La Salle Academy on Second Street, he joined his father's successful contracting business, which then became Mulry and Son in 1872. At the same time, he continued his education with night classes at Cooper Union. On October 16, 1880, he married Mary Gallagher, a Hunter College graduate and an elementary school teacher, and they had thirteen children: Parthenia, Thomas, William, Margaret, George, Joseph, Francis, Louis, Mary, Vincent, George A., James, and Anna. By 1890 he succeeded his father as head of the company, and he then expanded his interests to include banking, insurance, and real estate, becoming president of the Emigrant Industrial Savings Bank in 1906.

While people admired the shrewd business sense and financial competency which led to his prosperity, they respected more his deep Catholic faith, his amiable, virtuous personality, and his indefatigable charitable work. While only seventeen, he joined the St. Vincent de Paul Society, a lay Catholic organization dedicated to helping the poor, and became a welcome, familiar figure to the poor of Greenwich Village and the penniless immigrants landing at Castle Island. From there he became involved in dozens of welfare projects, including the Marquette League for Indian Welfare, the St. Vincent de Paul summer home for children, the St. Elizabeth Home for convalescent girls, the Catholic Home Bureau for Dependent Children, and the Ozanam Association. Most of his welfare work concerned children and stemmed from his devotion to his own family. He especially did battle against the abuses common in institutional care of children, where he succeeded in improving conditions, especially in Catholic children's institutions.

Yet Mulry's influence on Catholic welfare work did not stop there; he held strong opinions about the philosophy and nature of such work, and thus helped bring about a change in the direction of his church's social apostolate. When Mulry began his charitable career, he was frustrated by the aloofness, lack of cooperation, and hesitancy to organize which he found in those people and societies dedicated to welfare. It was almost as if they believed that the Christian virtue of humility prohibited them from the coordination, accountability, and professionalism Mulry believed the work of charity required. He felt that the social apostolate deserved the same type of structure his successful business did.

Until his death, then, he was the leading lay proponent of professionalism and organization in Catholic welfare work.

Beginning with the St. Vincent de Paul Society, he implemented his programs. He became a member of the Society's Superior Council of New York in 1885, serving as its secretary in 1887 and as president from 1905 to 1915. All this time he advocated cooperation among all the individual societies, as well as accurate record-keeping, sharing of resources, and follow-up care for cases. In 1915 he reorganized the Society in the United States on provincial lines, with a national superior council—of which he was elected the first president—coordinating national efforts. Through the pages of the *St. Vincent de Paul Quarterly*, one of the first Catholic periodicals devoted to a scientific, professional style of welfare work, he propagated his theories.

A lifelong advocate of close cooperation among all charitable groups, Catholic and non-Catholic alike, he was the first Catholic member of the New York Charity Organization Society, founded in 1882 to bring such cooperation about. Such fondness for structure in welfare work also led to his involvement with the National Conference of Charities and Correction, the New York State Board of Charities, and the National Conference of Charity. In addition, in 1909 he was one of the committee of three appointed by President Theodore Roosevelt to organize the first White House Conference on Dependent Children.

In his crusade for a more organized, professional approach to welfare work, he found an ardent ally and friend in Monsignor William J. Kerby.* Together they founded in 1910 the National Conference of Catholic Charities, the first attempt to nationally coordinate the Church's social responsibilities; he became vice president of the organization. Convinced that social workers needed academic credentials, he helped establish the Fordham University School of Social Service.

Not only was Mulry a pioneer in demanding that Catholic charities be characterized by cooperation, accountability, and professionalism, but he was one of the first to welcome government involvement in the work of welfare. Although he warned against excessive secularization of social work, he recognized that some social problems were just too widespread and severe to be competently handled by the family or the Church. In his major publication, *The Government in Charity* (1912), he encouraged the state to assist private welfare agencies.

Mulry died in New York, the city he had served so devotedly, in 1916.

The Archives of the Archdiocese of New York house some of Mulry's papers. The only biography is that by J. W. Helmes, *Thomas M. Mulry: A Volunteer's Contribution to Social Work* (1938). Helpful is the work of Daniel T. McColgan, *A Century of Charity*, 2 vols. (1951), a thorough treatment of the history of Catholic charity in the United States. To situate Mulry in local history, see Florence D. Cohalin, *A Popular History of the Archdiocese of New York* (1983).

TIMOTHY MICHAEL DOLAN

**Murphy, Edgar Gardner** (August 31, 1869–June 23, 1913), Episcopal priest, publicist, and child labor reformer, was born near Fort Smith, Arkansas, the son of Samuel W. Murphy and Janie (Gardner) Murphy. Following his birth, Edgar Gardner Murphy knew the poverty of Reconstruction, complicated by his father's desertion of the family when Edgar was only five and by his mother's tuberculosis. Told to move west for her health, his mother took young Murphy and his sister Ethel to San Antonio, Texas. There he was educated in the city's schools and confirmed at St. Mark's Episcopal Church. While still in his teens, he resolved to become a priest. In 1885, when only sixteen, he entered the freshman class at the University of the South, Sewanee, Tennessee. Much influenced by his mentor, the Reverend William Porcher DuBose, Murphy graduated from Sewanee in 1889, imbued with DuBose's spirit and zeal for learning. He then attended the General Theological Seminary in New York City but took no degree. On August 31, 1891, he married Maud King of Concord, Massachusetts; they would have two sons, DuBose and Gardner.

Ordained as a deacon (1890) and as a priest (1893) in the Protestant Episcopal Church, Murphy served with distinction for over a decade as rector of churches in San Antonio and Laredo, Texas; Chillicothe, Ohio; Kingston, New York; and Montgomery, Alabama. His perception of the faith and his desire to propagate it led him to write and publish in 1897 two books setting forth his theological views. Much of *The Larger Life* was directed at those on the periphery of Christianity who needed more knowledge and insight to grow in the faith, while *Words for the Church* provided a rationale for the polity, dogma, and worship of the Anglican churches. The erection and equipping of the Young Men's and Young Women's Christian Associations in Montgomery were due in large part to Murphy's initiative, and Andrew Carnegie's gift to the city of the first public library building in Alabama was made in response to his efforts.

While rector of St. John's in Montgomery, Murphy found that the Episcopal Church had made no attempt to reach the city's Blacks. With the aid of the Bishop of Alabama, St. John's, and the Blacks themselves, he was instrumental in founding, in 1899, the Church of the Good Shepherd for the community's black population. Murphy was also largely responsible for organizing a conference for a discussion of the race problem and conditions in the South. Meeting in Montgomery in 1900, with Hilary A. Herbert as the presiding officer and Murphy as secretary, the conference was notable for its candor and fairness. Its published proceedings aroused wide interest in both America and Europe. As a racial moderate, Murphy believed that the solution of the race problem would necessarily involve many things, among them justice, unselfishness, and truth. Furthermore, he believed that it was imperative that all southern states begin a positive policy of development and that this policy be applied to both races.

In Montgomery, Murphy became familiar for the first time with the particular problems of mill workers. His warm and sympathetic nature led him to resolve that a Christian society must do something to improve their intolerable conditions. Experiences here gave him the moral indignation necessary to launch a crusade against child labor. In 1901 Murphy helped organize and assumed the leadership of the Alabama Child Labor Committee. Investigations disclosed that a number of Alabama cotton mills were owned by northern interests; these same interests had been influential in obtaining repeal of laws enacted to protect women and children working in factories. Realizing that child labor was a national problem, Murphy became a leader in the organization in 1904 of the National Child Labor Committee, which soon became the prime molder of opinion on the child labor question. Convinced of the need for an aroused and sustained public opinion expressing itself in local rather than national legislation, he opposed the Committee, however, in its efforts to secure congressional action regulating child labor. Murphy later resigned from the Committee because of differences on this issue, but his interest in its work never subsided. Not long after his death, he was cited for having awakened the conscience of America to the existence of child labor as a shame and a curse.

As Murphy became increasingly involved with the social, racial, and industrial problems of his day, he saw the need for a broader base of support and for more effective policies of education. Though he never abandoned any of his firmly held Christian beliefs, he came to see that these beliefs required a secularized presentation in a secular age. Realizing, therefore, that his best work could be done outside the official ministry of the Protestant Episcopal Church, he withdrew from its ministry in 1903. The same year, he became executive secretary of the Southern Education Board, a position he held until 1908. In addition to editing the proceedings of several conferences on education and race relations in the South (he continued to advocate better educational opportunities for Blacks), he contributed his ideas to such periodicals as the *North American Review*, the *Outlook*, and *Century Magazine*. His *Problems of the Present South* (1904) dealt with race, child labor, and education, while *The Basis of Ascendancy* (1909) developed more fully the previous book's racial themes, especially Murphy's disgust with unfair white regimentation.

Ill health forced Murphy to give up active public work in 1908. Shortly before his death, he was discussing plans for finishing a volume of essays entitled *Issues, Southern and National*. The finest assessment of Murphy's career was given by the *Outlook* when it proclaimed him a true leader not only of southern liberalism but of national progress in education and social welfare. Murphy died in New York City on June 23, 1913.

Manuscript sources of interest to the student of Murphy include the Edgar Gardner Murphy Papers and the Southern Education Board Papers, both at the University of North Carolina, Chapel Hill, and the National Child Labor Committee Papers at the Library of Congress, Washington, D.C.

In addition to those mentioned in the text, other works by Murphy include *The Case Against Child Labor: An Argument* (1902), *The Task of the South* (1903), *The Child Labor Question in Alabama—A Plea for Immediate Action* (1907), and *The Federal Regulation of Child Labor: A Criticism of the Policy Represented in the Beveridge-Parsons Bill* (1907).

The essential study of Murphy is Hugh C. Bailey, *Edgar Gardner Murphy: Gentle Progressive* (1968). Also of interest are Hugh C. Bailey, "Edgar Gardner Murphy and the Child Labor Movement," *Alabama Review* (January, 1965), 47–59; Allen J. Going, "The Reverend Edgar Gardner Murphy: His Ideas and Influence," *Historical Magazine of the Protestant Episcopal Church* (December, 1956), 391–402; and L. Moody Simms, Jr., "Edgar Gardner Murphy and the Race Question," *Alabama Review* (July, 1968), 230–234.

L. MOODY SIMMS, JR.

**Murphy, J. Prentice** (September 12, 1881–February 3, 1936), child welfare expert, was born in Philadelphia, Pennsylvania, to John and Mary Murphy. Little is known about his parents or his early life, except that his father was a factory foreman and he was brought up in Philadelphia not far from the city's Children's Bureau, which he would serve for many years. Also, he had one sister and four brothers, and he was married to Ida Garrett, with whom he had one daughter and two sons.

Murphy attended public schools in Philadelphia and then worked at the foundry department of the Baldwin Locomotive Works for four years. He then entered the University of Pennsylvania, which he attended for three years, but from which he never received a degree. While in school he worked part-time for the Pennsylvania Society to Protect Children from Cruelty. This was the beginning of a long career dedicated to social work in general and to child welfare in particular.

In 1908 he left school to take the position of general secretary of the Children's Bureau in Philadelphia, where he concentrated on organizing the city's charitable agencies to jointly meet the needs of its destitute and dependent children. In 1911 he left Philadelphia to become general secretary of the Boston Children's Aid Society, where he remained until 1920, working for the passage of progressive child welfare legislation throughout the state of Massachusetts and doing some teaching at the Boston School of Social Work. In 1920 he returned to Philadelphia as executive head of the Children's Bureau and the Seybert Institute (established under the provisions of Henry Seybert's will to finance various child welfare activities); he remained there for the rest of his life.

At the same time, however, he did some teaching at the Pennsylvania School of Social and Health Work and, at one time or another, also lectured at the University of Pennsylvania, the University of Chicago, Iowa State University, and the University of California. He also was active in numerous aspects of child welfare organizing on the local, state, national, and sometimes even international level. In addition, he was a member of the Pennsylvania Children's Commission, 1923–1927; vice president of the Committee for Handicapped Children of the 1930 White House Conference; a member of the board of directors of the National Committee for Mental Hygiene; a member of the Federal Advisory Board on Social Security of the Pennsylvania State Welfare Commission from

1932 to 1935, and a longtime member of the Committee on Dependent Children of the U.S. Children's Bureau.

Furthermore, he was an active, working member of the National Conference of Social Work for more than twenty-five years. Among his many positions in that organization were: 1911–1925, Committee on Children; 1921–1925, chairman, Division on Children; 1934, first vice president; 1936, unanimous president-elect.

He also was one of the founding members (in 1921) of the Child Welfare League of America and served for years as a member of its board of directors. He was its president from 1932 to 1934, when he was instrumental in seeing that the League obtained the necessary financial security to ensure its continued existence.

Throughout his career, Murphy also maintained a special relationship with *Survey* magazine and its editors, Arthur* and Paul Kellogg.* Not only did he write many articles and book reviews for that important journal, but he frequently reviewed material submitted for publication and always was on the lookout for conference papers, articles, and other materials that merited publication. Of his assistance in that regard, Paul Kellogg once wrote to Murphy, "Your's has been one of the most genuine contributions we have ever had in our whole history."

Murphy is best remembered for the legislation and social action he promoted on behalf of needy children. He was active in efforts to protect against the separation of children from their parents—and in the development of good foster home, as opposed to institutional, care for those children who had no homes or who, for whatever reason, had to be taken from their own homes. But he was significant not only for those activities and for the many positions he held in connection with them. He also was important for the kind of person he was; he was admired by those who knew and worked with him for his humanity, devotion, loyalty, accessibility, good humor, and gentleness. He symbolized the ideals of all child welfare workers, and he was an inspiration to many.

J. Prentice Murphy died on February 3, 1936, at Bryn Mawr Hospital, in Pennsylvania, following a short illness with pneumonia.

Published information on Murphy is limited in detail. Brief articles include E. O. Lundberg, "Pathfinders of the Middle Years," *Social Service Review* (March, 1947); "J. Prentice Murphy," *The Family* (March, 1936); and an article in the *Bulletin of the Child Welfare League of America* (February, 1936). Other material can be obtained from the files of the Children's Bureau of Philadelphia. Also, the Social Welfare History Archives Center at the University of Minnesota in Minneapolis contains the Survey Associates records, which include personal correspondence between Murphy and Paul Kellogg (Box 99, Folder 728).

In 1935 Murphy, along with William Healy, Augusta Bronner, and Edith Baylor, authored *Reconstructing Behavior in Youth*. He was a frequent and regular contributor to *Survey* magazine, and his many articles can be found in its pages. He also was a contributor to the 1930 White House Conference volume on dependent and neglected children, and he delivered a total of eighteen papers at the meetings of the National Conference of Social Work, many of which can be found in its *Proceedings*.

JOYCE PREWITT DAVIS

**Muste, Abraham Johannes** (January 8, 1885–February 11, 1967), labor reformer and educator and internationally prominent pacifist activist and essayist on nonviolent resistance, was born in Zierikzee, Zeeland, the Netherlands, to Adriana (Jonker) and Martin Muste. Before migrating to the United States in 1891, his father had served as a coachman to a family of the provincial nobility in the Netherlands; later, he would utilize the same skills as a teamster in Grand Rapids, Michigan. In 1896 the family received American citizenship. "A.J.," as Abraham J. Muste was called by most friends and colleagues, became an ordained minister in 1909 when he graduated from the New Brunswick Seminary in New Jersey. He continued his education at Union Theological Seminary in New York City, where he received a Bachelor of Divinity degree, magna cum laude. Meanwhile, on June 21, 1909, he married Anna Huizenga. The couple had two daughters, Nancy Baker and Connie Hamilton, as well as a son, John Muste, who became prominent in his own right as a professor of English.

A. J. Muste's pacifist work was concentrated within two periods in his life— during World War I, when he was between the ages of twenty-nine and thirty-four, and during World War II, the Korean War, the Cold War, and the Vietnam War, when he was between fifty-five and eighty-one years of age. The interim twenty-one years (1919–1940) are distinguished by Muste's successful organizing of labor and the unemployed. It was the 1919 textile workers' strike in Lawrence, Massachusetts, which established Muste as the first successful cleric labor leader in the United States. His efforts not only contributed to the strikers' success at achieving their goals, but, more important, this particular strike was a landmark in the application of nonviolent resistance.

At the Lawrence strike, A. J. Muste and other promoters of nonviolent activism overruled a member of the strike committee who urged fellow workers to seize the policemen's automatic weapons. One rank and file worker, schooled in nonviolence, commented persuasively that they could not weave wool with machine guns. Later, it was discovered that the provocateur of violence was being paid by the Lawrence mill owners to disrupt the strikers' effort. Eventually, to Muste's and the workers' surprise, the mill owners gave in to the strike committee's demands. Muste observed that a postwar increase in orders for textiles partly accounted for the mill owners' unexpected readiness to negotiate an end to this strike.

Following this success, Muste became active as secretary of the Amalgamated Textile Workers of America. He left this post in 1921 to become educational director of Brookwood Labor College in Katonah, New York, a position he held until 1933. During those years as director of Brookwood, Muste participated in the 1929 textile workers' strikes in Marion and Gastonia, North Carolina. At a burial of one of the workers gunned down by the police near Marion on October 2, 1929, A. J. Muste was the only minister willing to say the last words at the open grave.

For four years after the 1929 Marion and Gastonia strikes, A. J. Muste continued with his teaching and administration at Brookwood. In March, 1933, he led a faction of nineteen students and two faculty who left Brookwood protesting that the college was too academic and out of touch with the struggles of working people.

During the year of his break with Brookwood (1933), Muste and other labor leaders were active in grass-roots organizing of the unemployed. In that year, they convened in Columbus, Ohio, to establish the National Unemployed League. Then Muste and others at the convention went directly from Columbus to Toledo to participate in the Auto-Lite strike. Unemployed Leagues were scattered throughout the nation; they agitated for raising local relief allotments, and, where possible, they prevented evictions. These organizations also marched on state capitals to make demands on local officials.

In the latter part of 1933 A. J. Muste led the formation of the American Workers Party. A goal of this party was to function as a "democratically organized revolutionary party." Muste further stated in one of his essays that the program was based on the Marxist philosophy of class struggle. In the following year (1934), the Musteites merged with the Trotskyites to form the Workers Party of the United States. During 1935 Muste was active in the General Motors Corporation strike in Michigan, and in 1936 he was active in the Goodyear Tire and Rubber strike in Ohio.

A. J. Muste remained a leader in the Workers Party until the summer of 1936, when he visited Leon Trotsky in Europe. Although maintaining his Marxist orientation, Muste publicly dissociated himself from Trotsky and violent revolution and made an abrupt return to radical Christian pacifism when he came back to the United States.

In the fall of 1936 A. J. Muste was elected to the board of the Fellowship of Reconciliation (FOR) and was appointed industrial secretary. This allowed Muste to continue to use his talents and enthusiasm for workers' struggles in the garment industry. In 1936 and 1937 he was an active participant in the hosiery workers' strike in Reading, Pennsylvania. From August, 1937, to August, 1940, he held the post of director of the Presbyterian Labor Temple on the Lower East Side of New York City. He resigned this position to become executive secretary of the Fellowship of Reconciliation, with which he continued until retirement in 1953 at age sixty-eight.

A. J. Muste will be primarily remembered as a leading American clerical advocate of nonviolent resistance who influenced younger leaders—notably Bayard Rustin and Martin Luther King, Jr.* However, some Americans of the twentieth century will remember A. J. as *Liberation* magazine's eloquent and activist Christian Marxist who did not conform to any one ideological group. It was for this ideological unconventionality and for his charisma that A. J. Muste was one of the few prominent radicals of the 1950s who was willing and able to initiate a dialogue between communists and noncommunists.

Muste and nine other noncommunists attended the Communist Party USA Convention in February, 1957. Dorothy Day* of the *Catholic Worker* and Lyle Tatum of the American Friends Service Committee accompanied Muste. This gesture of reconciliation with the communists was criticized by major personages across the political spectrum from Roger Baldwin* of the American Civil Liberties Union on the left to Senator James Eastland on the right. Moreover, in May, 1957, with support from Dave Dellinger, publisher of *Liberation*, Muste created the American Forum for Socialist Education. This was a series of conferences and debates within various cities in which both communists and noncommunists participated. A. J. Muste was one of the few radical leaders who had the qualifications and long-term respect to facilitate dialogue and build such liaisons during the Cold War of the 1950s. He died in New York City on February 11, 1967.

The major source of A. J. Muste's writings is the collection edited by Nat Hentoff, *The Essays of A. J. Muste* (1967). Muste's "Sketches for an Auto-biography," first published serially in *Liberation* (1957–1960), is included in the first 174 pages of this volume.

There are two major biographical monographs on Muste: Nat Hentoff's *Peace Agitator: The Story of A. J. Muste* (1963), and Jo Ann Robinson's *Abraham Went Out: A Biography of A. J. Muste* (1981). The latter includes a complete listing of writings by Muste as well as an exhaustive bibliography about his life. Also, there is a four-page biographical sketch in the 1965 edition of *Current Biography Yearbook*, ed. Charles Moritz.

A. J. Muste's important books, *Nonviolence in an Aggressive World* (1940) and *Not by Might* (1947) were published by Harper & Row. *Not by Might* was republished in 1971 by Garland Publishing Company with a new introduction by Jo Ann Robinson.

Other references documenting Muste's significance as an advocate of nonviolent activism are Martin Luther King, Jr.'s *Strike Toward Freedom* (1958) and his essay "Pilgrimage to Nonviolence," in *Nonviolence in America: A Documentary History*, ed. Staughton Lynd (1966). For additional commentary on Muste's leadership in antiwar activity and in nonviolent resistance, see Lawrence S. Wittner's *Rebels Against War* (1969). References reporting on Muste's role in founding Marxist political parties and in labor struggles of the period between the world wars include David McLellan's *Marxism After Marx* (1979), and *Strike!* by Jeremy Brecher (1977).

JOYCE M. KRAMER and ANTHONY E. THOMAS

# N

**Nathan, Maud** (October 20, 1862–December 15, 1946), social reformer, philanthropist, and feminist, was born in New York City, the second of four children and the first daughter, of Annie Augusta (Florance) Nathan and Robert Weeks Nathan, both from wealthy Sephardic Jewish families whose ancestors had come to America in the early eighteenth century. Robert Nathan was a member of the New York Stock Exchange until 1874, when business reverses forced him to sell his seat and move with his family to Green Bay, Wisconsin. For four years he served as general passenger agent for a small midwestern railroad.

Maud attended Mrs. Ogden Hoffman's School and the Gardiner Institute, both private schools for girls in New York City. She continued her studies in Green Bay, graduating from the local high school at the age of fourteen and a half. In 1878, shortly before her mother's death, Maud returned to New York. On April 7, 1880, she married her first cousin, Frederick Nathan, a wealthy stockbroker almost twenty years her senior. Her early married life was filled with housekeeping duties, home entertaining, visiting friends and relatives, shopping, embroidering, and other activities deemed appropriate for women of her social set. She also assumed a number of charitable responsibilities, becoming a director of the Mt. Sinai Training School for Nurses and of the Hebrew Free School Association. By 1890, however, with the support of her husband and the encouragement and guidance of social reformer Josephine Shaw Lowell,* Maud Nathan began to develop a particular interest in the welfare of working women and children. She joined the board of managers of the New York Exchange for Women's Work and helped Lowell investigate the working conditions of women employed in New York retail establishments. Out of these investigations emerged the Consumers' League, aimed at ameliorating, through consumer pressure, the working conditions of women and children in New York City department stores. Its goal was to convince consumers to patronize only those stores that appeared on the League's "White List," indicating that certain just practices, as defined by the League, were being followed. These included equal pay for equal work regardless of sex; overtime compensation; paid summer vacations; behind-the-counter seats for saleswomen; and the refusal to employ children under the age of fourteen.

From 1897 until 1917 Maud Nathan served as president of the League. She was also instrumental in the founding of the National Consumers' League in 1899, serving on its executive committee and later as a vice president; the Consumers' League of New York State in 1900, functioning as acting president until 1903; and local consumers' organizations throughout the United States. She remained active in the League for thirty-five years, speaking of its work both in America and abroad. By her own admission, she was viewed as an authority on the welfare of women and children and, as such, was invited to serve on numerous committees, including the Industrial Committee of the General Federation of Women's Clubs, of which she became chairman.

While Maud Nathan maintained that she only accepted invitations that concerned matters close to her heart, her interest in the welfare of women and children led her into many fields of activity. After the death of her only child, her eight-year-old daughter Annette, in 1895, she devoted most of her time and energy to social and civic reform. Seeking to improve city government in New York, she became a vice president of both the Women's Municipal League and the Social Reform Club. She also became chairman of the former's Committee on Ballot-Instruction Booths, aimed at teaching interested voters the correct method of casting a split ballot.

These activities, as well as her work for the Consumers' League, convinced Nathan that legislators would never take women's views seriously so long as women did not have the right to vote. Consequently, with the enthusiastic support of her husband (and against the opposition of most of her family, including her sister, Annie Nathan Meyer, founder of Barnard College), she became active in the woman's suffrage movement, serving as a delegate, and often as a speaker, at international suffrage conventions throughout the United States and Europe. Invited by Theodore Roosevelt in 1912 to become chairman of the Women's Suffrage Committee of his National Progressive Party, she also served as a vice president of the New York State Suffrage Association and the Equal Franchise Society. In 1919, with women about to receive the vote, it was she who suggested that the organization created to replace the National American Woman Suffrage Association be called the League of Women Voters.

While Maud Nathan involved herself in activities outside of Jewish philanthropy and communal service (becoming one of the first Jewish women in America to do so), she never lost her strong sense of Jewish self-identity. Indeed, she continued to be a part of the Orthodox community in which she was raised. Though she acknowledged Orthodoxy's subordination of women, she dutifully accompanied her husband to synagogue on the Sabbath and holidays and became the first president of the Sisterhood (the women's auxiliary) of Shearith Israel, the Sephardic congregation with which her family had long been affiliated. Her own religious views, however, were liberal in nature, as was evident from the sermons she preached at numerous synagogues on Judaism's universal teachings. An active member of the National Council of Jewish Women, she was once asked to run for its presidency. Though she declined, the offer itself, she later wrote, underscored her continual identification with Jewish interests, feeling, and thought.

Maud Nathan died at the age of eighty-four in her New York City apartment.

Twelve scrapbooks containing newspaper clippings and letters are at the Schlesinger Library, Radcliffe College, Cambridge, Massachusetts. For detailed descriptions of her work for the Consumers' League, see the papers of the New York Consumers' League, located at Cornell University, Ithaca, New York, as well as copies of the League's *Annual Reports*.

Nathan's own assessment of her life and work can be found in *The Story of an Epoch-Making Movement* (1926), about the Consumers' League, and her autobiography, *Once upon a Time and Today* (1933).

To date, relatively little has been written about Maud Nathan. The biographical essays by Robert Cross in *Notable American Women*, vol. 2 (1971), and by Nancy Schrom in the *Dictionary of American Biography*, Supplement 4 (1974), are brief but informative. See, too, the unsigned biographical essay in the *Universal Jewish Encyclopedia* (1942). Ellen Condliffe Lagemann's *A Generation of Women* (1979) includes a highly speculative chapter on Nathan which attempts to uncover those figures most responsible for her educational growth. Jacob Radar Marcus, in *The American Jewish Woman: A Documentary History* (1981), offers a brief but accurate description of Nathan's achievements plus an excerpt from her autobiography. Maud Nathan's obituary notice appeared in the *New York Times*, December 16, 1946. For a description of the memorial service held for her, see the *New York Times*, December 18, 1946. See, too, its December 31, 1946 edition for a list of some of the charitable and public institutions that Nathan named as beneficiaries in her will.

ELLEN M. UMANSKY

**Nestor, Agnes** (June 24, 1880–December 28, 1948), trade union leader and social reformer, was born in Grand Rapids, Michigan, the second daughter of Thomas and Anna (McEwen) Nestor. Despite a career which brought her into touch with presidents, kings, and governors, a career in which she developed a reputation as a canny and fierce negotiator for the rights of labor, Agnes Nestor, until her death, received the sobriquet "Our Little Agnes" from her hometown Chicago press.

Nestor, indeed a little woman, barely five feet tall and often in frail health, was the daughter of Irish immigrants. Her mother, Anna McEwen, had labored in upstate New York cotton mills before moving to Michigan to marry Thomas Nestor, a machinist and sometime local politician, originally from County Galway. In 1800 Anna Nestor gave birth to Agnes, the third of her four children. In 1897, thrown out of work in the depressed economy of the 1890s, Thomas

Nestor moved his family from Grand Rapids to Chicago, the city which would remain Agnes Nestor's home until her death in 1948. Agnes went to work immediately as a learner in the glove factory.

In 1898, within a year of taking work as a glove bander, Nestor, then eighteen, led a strike to protest a change in piecework rates. Improvement of wages and conditions for workers, especially women workers, and expansion of workers' education would become lifelong social reform goals for Agnes Nestor. By 1902, as president of her local, she had helped organize the International Glove Workers Union, which she served as vice president from 1903 to 1906 and again from 1915 to 1938, as secretary-treasurer from 1906 to 1913, as general president from 1913 to 1915, and as director of research and education from 1938 to 1948. Therefore, from participation in its founding convention in 1902 until her death in 1948, Nestor held a national office in the Glove Workers International. She often used that position as a soapbox from which to preach for equal wages and equal opportunities for women workers, despite the fact that she was often the only woman present in the room, seeking to convince unsympathetic male union leaders. Nestor participated as a labor advisor to the federal government during both world wars, though her efforts to gain equal pay for women war workers and to win retention of maximum hours' standards met with defeat.

Nestor maintained a parallel organizing career as an officer of the Women's Trade Union League (WTUL). The Chicago chapter of the WTUL, under Nestor's presidency from 1913 to 1948, was a vital center for the women's trade union movement. As a local official as well as a member of the WTUL executive board from 1907 until her death, Nestor tried to organize not just women glovemakers in her own union, but also women garment workers, waitresses, brewery workers, and women workers in many other trades. For decades she traveled the country, counseling, orating, and coordinating strike and negotiation strategies for the WTUL and the Glove Workers.

Among Agnes Nestor's strategies for improving the lot of women workers, protective labor legislation ranked with union membership. Advocacy of protective labor legislation was a major lifelong passion. A self-deprecating woman, Nestor seemingly encouraged her "Little Agnes" image by downplaying her skills as a legislative lobbyist and graciously sharing credit for victories in Springfield, Illinois, or Washington, D.C. Her contemporaries more accurately judged her decades of efforts in their behalf to be instrumental in the passage of eight-hour day and five-day week laws, federal minimum wage legislation, and federal infant and maternal health programs.

Battles for worker education were another major element in Nestor's career. In 1914 she served as a member of a national commission to study federal aid to vocational education and fought fellow members who sought to recommend that girls be trained in domestic science only. Nestor knew that many girls and young women needed training to be workers, not just wives. Nestor was an enthusiastic supporter of the workers' schools movement and in 1921 helped to establish the Workers' Education Bureau within the American Federation of

Labor (AFL). In her old age, she reminisced fondly about the young women who attended such workers' schools as the Summer School for Working Women at Bryn Mawr, remembering especially the ones who, like herself, had begun full-time work as teenagers but who hungered for formal schooling.

Nestor, who never married, devoted her life to the passage of a progressive's labor agenda. Wistfully, in her old age, she assessed successes and failures. She argued correctly that in her lifetime she had witnessed great improvements in conditions for working women. She warned, however, that workers, especially women workers, had to be vigilant, and worried that unions of the 1940s offered, if anything, even fewer opportunities for women leaders. Contemporaries as well as historians have challenged the efficacy of some of Nestor's solutions to problems faced by working women, arguing, for example, that even in the 1920s protective legislation hindered rather than helped female wage earners. None could doubt, though, that Agnes Nestor remained vigilant until her death in Chicago from rheumatic fever at age sixty-eight.

The major manuscript sources for the life of Agnes Nestor are the Agnes Nestor Papers, Chicago Historical Society, Chicago, Illinois; and the Papers of the National Women's Trade Union League, Library of Congress, Washington, D.C. Also useful are Nestor's autobiography, *Woman's Labor Leader: An Autobiography* (1954), and the autobiography of her close friend and colleague, Mary Anderson, *Women at Work* (1951). Evaluations of Nestor appear in Rosalyn Baxandall, Linda Gordon, and Susan Reverby, *America's Working Women* (1976); Sandra Conn, "Three Talents: Robins, Nestor, and Anderson of the Chicago Women's Trade Union League," *Chicago History* 9 (1980–1981), 234–247; and *Notable American Women* (1971).

JUDITH SEALANDER

# O

**O'Grady, John** (March 31, 1886–January 2, 1966), priest, sociologist, spokesman for Catholic charities, and social reformer, was born at Annagh Feakle, County Clare, Ireland, to Francis and Margaret (Hayes) O'Grady, poor Irish farmers. Nevertheless, they encouraged their son to become a priest and made the necessary sacrifices that allowed him to gain a formal education. First, O'Grady attended the local national school, and then at the age of thirteen he became a boarding student at a secondary school in Killaloe, some ten miles from his home. At the age of sixteen he was admitted to All Hallows College, the Dublin seminary that provided training for future missionary priests.

After his ordination in 1909, O'Grady was assigned to St. Cecilia's Cathedral in the Omaha, Nebraska, diocese. It was run by an alumnus of All Hallows, the Irish-born bishop Richard Scannell. There, in addition to his priestly duties, O'Grady also served as the assistant editor of the diocesan paper, the *True Voice*.

In 1912, with the encouragement of Bishop Scannell, O'Grady became a graduate student at the Catholic University of America. It was a momentous decision for the young cleric. At Catholic University, he began a career as an educator with a strong voice for the professionalization of Catholic charities, as an advocate of the ecumenical movement in the charities arena, and finally, as a passionate supporter of international charity.

First, though, he began the study of economics and sociology under the tutelage of Monsignor William J. Kerby.* Kerby encouraged his young, dedicated Irish student to expand his knowledge by attending summer school at the University of Chicago. There, in 1913 and again in 1914, he met Jane Addams,* Sidney Hillman, Samuel Gompers, and others active in secular social work and labor reform. These contacts stood him in good stead during the New Deal years.

Meanwhile, he received his M.A. in 1913 and his Ph.D. in 1915 from Catholic University, where he immediately became an instructor of sociology; by 1928 he was a full professor, not only there but at neighboring Trinity College as well.

Through Kerby, one of its founders, O'Grady became active in the National

Conference of Catholic Charities (NCCC) in 1912. After Kerby's resignation in 1920, O'Grady became secretary of the organization as well as editor of the *Catholic Charities Review*, the organ of the NCCC. He held both posts until 1961.

In his role as secretary and editor, O'Grady not only spoke *for* Catholics on charity matters but also *to* them. He saw his role as an educator at Catholic University as helping to supply professional leadership for the various Catholic organizations involved in charitable work as well as providing a bridge to the non-Catholics who worked on behalf of the poor. He also saw the necessity for professional training. This emphasis, however, caused some stress between himself and the lay leaders of the Society of St. Vincent de Paul. In all of these endeavors, he was an able speaker, a diligent writer, and a disciplined worker in the cause of the poor.

O'Grady did not confine his activities to Washington, D.C. While he organized the central Catholic Charities administration in the District of Columbia and remained its director from 1920 to 1938, he traveled extensively. He set up similar central organizations in Pittsburgh, New York, and Cincinnati. In 1918 he was the special investigator for the Health and Old Age Commission of Ohio. After he completed that job, he was appointed secretary of the Committee on Reconstruction, and then, after the war, of the National Catholic War Council. In this position, he turned for advice to Father John A. Ryan* who had become a faculty member at Catholic University.

Not only did he meet and work with Father Ryan, the so-called New Deal Priest, but O'Grady also met, worked with, and admired the associate director of the Association for the Improvement of the Condition of the Poor, Harry L. Hopkins,* who at the time also was director of the New York Tuberculosis Society. O'Grady had an equally sincere admiration for both Ryan and Hopkins, who later, as the head of the Federal Emergency Relief Administration during the New Deal, became a close friend of O'Grady.

O'Grady also was a scholar. He published *Directory of Catholic Charities in the United States* (1922; second edition, 1930), *Introduction to Social Work* (1928), and *The Catholic Church and the Destitute* (1929). He also published *Levi Silliman Ives* (1933), a short, scholarly biography of a Catholic convert who was a lay leader in Catholic charitable work in the Civil War era.

In 1931 O'Grady was one of the founders of the National Public Housing Conference, which met in New York City. From 1934 to 1938 he served as the first dean of the School of Social Work at Catholic University. In 1935 he was elevated to the rank of Domestic Prelate. In the academic year 1937–1938 O'Grady clashed with the more traditionally minded Bishop John Corrigan. As a result, he resigned as dean (in 1938) and severed his connection with Catholic charities in the District of Columbia.

As the spokesman for Catholic organizations, O'Grady initially opposed federal intervention in the field of charity. He preferred state and local initiatives in cooperation with local voluntary organizations. These groups, he believed, had a better grasp of the situation than a federal bureaucracy. But the Great Depression changed his mind.

The Depression increased O'Grady's role as spokesman for Catholic charities. He became, according to one observer, "a familiar and commanding figure in the committee rooms of Congress." First, he cooperated with the Hoover administration, especially Fred Croxton, head of the President's Emergency Committee for Employment. By 1931 he was lobbying for a federal public works bill. Friendly with the Roman Catholic senator from Montana, Thomas Walsh, O'Grady helped draft a positive report on the bill. His advice was succinctly put: "If you care to save the country now, spend now!" O'Grady thus accepted the new role of the federal government as protector of the poor.

During the New Deal years, both his political sense and his political contacts developed further. To all intents and purposes, he became one of the major spokesmen before the New Deal for Catholic charities. He also emphasized the role of the possible. He believed that private social agencies should be positive advocates for the poor. He emphasized the need for social change. Short-term relief in the form of welfare he found less satisfying than long-range federal work programs that would obviate the need for handouts. Thus, during the remainder of his career, he was an advocate of increased federal participation, in cooperation with private agencies, in old-age and unemployment insurance, in housing, and in national health insurance schemes. He came to oppose direct relief, however, and developed a positive horror for the old poor law system.

As a spokesman for Catholic charities, he always placed great stress on the role of voluntary agencies cooperating with the federal government to improve the conditions of the poor. He opposed direct public assistance in favor of social insurance. And as editor of the *Catholic Charities Review*, he continued his role as educator to the Roman Catholic community by alerting his readers to an increased need for federal involvement in the care of the poor. He also became a firm friend of migrant workers. In order to understand their plight, he went to South America, where he followed what one student of the subject referred to as the O'Grady method: traveling to the local scene and interviewing the people involved. Thus he came to see the problems of the migrant farmers through the eyes and words of the migrants themselves.

In January, 1947, the War Relief Services of the National Catholic Welfare Council sent him to Latin America to find settlement areas for the refugees created by World War II. He was called to the Vatican to discuss the possibilities of settlements in nations like Brazil, Argentina, Paraguay, and Chile. In mid-July, 1947, he attended the meeting of the International Refugee Organization at the recommendation of Pope Pius XII. He made his report directly to the Pope. He then toured the various European displaced person camps and became a "passionate crusader" for immigrant legislation.

In 1950 he became president of the National Council on Family Relations. In 1951 he helped organize the International Conference of Catholic Charities and served as vice president of that organization until his retirement from the social action scene. He was the Conference's representative at the United Nations and served as a consultant to UNESCO. He also served as the International Conference's representative in a number of African countries.

O'Grady's health declined after 1961, however, and on January 2, 1966, this "Lover of People," as a longtime assistant dubbed him, died in Washington, D.C.

For additional information on O'Grady see his letters and the files of the National Conference of Catholic Charities at the Archives of Catholic University of America. No biography is yet available, though I have leaned heavily on Thomas W. Tifft, "Toward a More Humane Social Policy: The Work and Influence of Monsignor John O'Grady," Ph.D. dissertation, Catholic University, 1979. O'Grady's former assistant has also provided a glowing view of O'Grady in Alice Padgett, "Monsignor John O'Grady, Lover of People," *Catholic Charities Review* (March, 1966), 5. O'Grady's thoughts can be followed on the editorial page of the *Catholic Charities Review* during the more than four decades that he served as editor.

THOMAS J. CURRAN

**O'Reilly, Leonora** (February 16, 1870–April 3, 1927), labor leader and social reformer, was born in New York City to Winifred and John O'Reilly, a garment worker and a printer, respectively. After her husband's death in 1871, and that of an infant son as well, and then the failure of a grocery store business, Winifred O'Reilly was a poverty-stricken widow—and Leonora's childhood on the East Side of New York was very difficult. Her mother worked in a factory by day and at home sewing by night. At age eleven, with just a few years of public schooling, Leonora began working in a collar factory.

She and her mother were naturally drawn to working-class politics and reform, and her later life and thought would be the product of these, including turn-of-the-century progressive feminism. By 1886 she had joined the Knights of Labor and studied Fourierist philosophy. As a result, she organized the Working Women's Society, which gained her the friendship of Josephine Shaw Lowell.* Together, she and Lowell created the New York Consumers' League in 1890. Leonora continued to meet and work with middle-class reformers such as the Rev. James O.S. Huntington and Louise S.W. Perkins. She actively associated with Positivists such as Edward King in studying sociological theory. After his death in 1922, she led his organization, the Synthetic Circle. Her reform activities continued to increase with her active support of Lillian Wald's* Henry Street Settlement and the Social Reform Club, committed to improving industrial conditions. By 1897 she was vice president of the Social Reform Club. She became a close friend of Felix Adler and other reformers.

During these years, Leonora worked ten hours a day in a shirtwaist factory, rising to forewoman. In 1897 she organized a women's local of the United

Garment Workers of America. Her friends raised money for her to "retire" in 1909 to study and pursue her reform activities.

One of her major contributions was her speaking ability. Her speeches were effective and inspirational, reflecting the marks of her working experience. By 1900 she graduated from Pratt Institute. She was active in the affairs of Asacog House, a Brooklyn settlement, and the Alliance Employment Bureau, teaching sewing to working-class girls.

From 1902 to 1909 Leonora taught at the Manhattan Trade School for Girls. She served as supervisor of the machine operating department. Firmly believing in vocational education, she felt that better-trained girls made better trade unionists. Her belief brought her into John Dewey's camp of progressive education.

Her greater organizational contribution, however, was her work in the National Women's Trade Union League (WTUL), starting in 1903. In 1905 she briefly resigned, because she feared that the organization might be too upper-class in tone and policy. Upon returning, Leonora served the organization full-time; she was elected vice president of the New York branch. With her strong speaking style, many people in and out of the organization turned to her for leadership.

She did not disappoint them. She actively took part in the New York garment workers' strike of 1909–1910. Then, as a result of the infamous Triangle Shirtwaist Company fire of 1911, she and Rose Schneiderman* conducted a significant survey of fire safety and working conditions. The International Ladies' Garment Workers' Union praised their efforts in 1912.

Having received a small lifetime annuity from her friends in 1909, Leonora O'Reilly expanded her reforming activities beyond trade unionism. She was one of the founders of the National Association for the Advancement of Colored People. A friend of Victor Berger, she supported the Socialist Party in New York. She encouraged industrial democracy by endorsing woman suffrage. She was head of the industrial committee of the New York City Woman Suffrage Party. Her health, unfortunately, began to fail, and in 1914 she withdrew from the Women's Trade Union League.

The outbreak of the Great War was the occasion for her last significant round of reforming efforts. She joined Jane Addams* and others at the International Congress of Women at The Hague in 1915. Her speech at the Congress received praise from fellow reformers and progressives. Like some progressives, she opposed America's entry into World War I and endorsed the Russian Revolution. Renewing on a limited basis her activity in the WTUL, she served as a delegate to the International Congress of Working Women at Washington in 1919. As her health problems increased, she reduced her varied activities. In 1925–1926 she taught a course on the labor movement at the New School for Social Research.

A particular form of progressive feminism shaped Leonora O'Reilly's reforming activities. Along with many of her contemporaries, she believed that women had inherent virtues that provided the major rationale for equal rights. Women were different, emotionally and culturally. Supported by fellow members of the Women's Trade Union League of New York, O'Reilly maintained that women were more gentle, moral, and sensitive than men. Women's inherent maternal nature equipped them for the special task of reforming the United States. And yet, given women's "weaker" biological nature and their childbearing abilities, she argued that the state, in the interest of societal survival, should pass protective legislation for women in the market place. The sum of Leonora O'Reilly's roles in reforming organizations and activities, therefore, pointed toward a positive conception of the state's responsibilities for effecting and directing social change and welfare. In her limited and yet significant manner, O'Reilly thus contributed to the development of the welfare state.

Yet, her chief contribution—and legacy—was her life. Leonora O'Reilly never wrote a book and published only a few articles in labor journals. She was a tall, angular woman, and her speeches and actions revealed a dedicated reformer and a noble spirit. With a plain and effective style of public speaking and a firm belief in social justice, her life was her message. She was a true daughter of American working-class culture.

In the end, though, private sorrows marked her achievements in public life. Living in a modest home with her mother, Leonora's adopted daughter had died in 1911. And although numerous friends had lived with them over the years, in the end Leonora was left alone with her invalid mother. She died from heart disease in New York City at the age of fifty-seven.

The major body of Leonora O'Reilly materials (sixteen boxes of paper) is at the Schlesinger Library at Radcliffe College in Cambridge, Massachusetts. Charles Shively's article on O'Reilly in *Notable American Women*, vol. 2 (1971), 651–653, is quite informative and includes a good bibliography. Two recently published books deal with O'Reilly: Ellen C. Lagemann, *A Generation of Women: Education in the Lives of Progressive Reformers* (1979), relates O'Reilly's life and activities to her contemporaries, such as Lillian D. Wald and Rose Schneiderman; and Nancy S. Dye provides a solid institutional history in *As Equals and as Sisters: Feminism, the Labor Movement, and the Women's Trade Union League of New York* (1980). For a different social origin of female reformers who shared the general philosophy of innatism and feminism, Karen J. Blair, *The Clubwoman as Feminist: True Womanhood Redefined, 1868–1914*(1980), is quite informative.

DONALD K. PICKENS

**Osborne, Thomas Mott** (September 23, 1859–October 20, 1926), penal reformer, was born in Auburn, New York, the son of David Munson Osborne and Eliza (Wright) Osborne. He was educated in the public schools of Auburn, at Adams Academy of Quincy, Massachusetts, and at Harvard University, where he received an A.B. in 1884. While at Harvard Osborne was active in founding the Harvard Cooperative Society. On his graduation from Harvard, Osborne returned to Auburn, where he joined his father's agricultural implements manufacturing firm, D. M. Osborne & Company. He assumed the presidency of the company in

1887 on his father's death, and directed the firm until 1903, when it was purchased by J. P. Morgan and associates for the International Harvester Trust Company. Osborne remained involved in Auburn businesses and retained interests in the Auburn Iron Works, Cayuga County Dairy Company, Columbian Rope Company, Eagle Wagon Works, and the National Bank of Auburn.

Osborne married Agnes Devens of Cambridge, Massachusetts, in 1886. The couple had four boys: David Munson II, Charles Devens, Arthur Lithgow, and Robert Klipfel. Agnes Devens died in 1896 at the age of thirty-one, a month after giving birth to her fourth child.

Osborne's political life began in 1894, when he was candidate for Lieutenant Governor of New York on the Citizens' Union ticket. During his lifetime, Osborne generally was found among the Democrats, although he did support various third-party movements and join the Republicans on occasion. In 1896 and 1900 he left the Democrats over the issue of Free Silver, although he returned to the party in 1906. He was mayor of Auburn between 1903 and 1905. In 1906 he was among the "Honor Democrats" who opposed the Democratic candidate for Governor of New York, William Randolph Hearst, and instead supported the Republican candidate, Charles Evans Hughes. Upon Hughes' election, Osborne was appointed to the Public Service Commission.

Osborne stayed with the Hughes administration for two and a half years. During his tenure on the Public Service Commission he wrote two striking opinions against the New York Central Railroad. In order to gather information about the railroad, Osborne used a hobo disguise to travel about. The use of a disguise to get an insider's view was employed by Osborne throughout his public career.

Osborne resigned from the Public Service Commission to convene the Saratoga Convention, which resulted in the creation of the Democratic League, with Osborne as its leader. Cayuga County delegates then put him forward as a gubernatorial candidate, but he failed to get the Democratic nomination in 1910.

In 1913 Osborne was appointed chairperson of the New York State Commission on Prison Reforms, under the administration of Governor William Sulzer. Osborne's interest in prison reform had begun shortly after his wife's death when he became involved in the George Junior Republic, an institution for the reform and education of delinquent boys in Freeville, New York.

Osborne's first act as chairperson of the Prison Reform Commission was to disguise himself as a prisoner and have himself incarcerated in Auburn Prison. His book recounting his experiences, *Within Prison Walls* (1913), created a public sensation. With the support of the public and the state, Osborne, along with Warden Charles Rattigan at Auburn, organized a self-governing body of convicts at the prison. The prisoners' group, the Mutual Welfare League, was intended to begin reform and rehabilitation of the prisoners within the walls of their jail. An affiliate branch on the outside was formed to help parolees.

In 1914 Osborne was appointed warden of Sing Sing, the state prison at Ossining, New York. His reforms and the Sing Sing chapter of the Mutual

Welfare League aroused resentment with the Westchester County Democratic machine, which had considered the warden's position theirs to dispense. In 1915 Osborne was indicted by the Westchester County Grand Jury on charges of perjury and neglect of duty. Judge Arthur S. Tompkins dismissed the case in mid-trial, however, without even hearing the defense. The bitterness of the trial and lack of support from Albany led Osborne to publish an open letter of resignation accusing Governor Charles Whitman of a lack of resolution and principle.

In 1917 Osborne was offered the wardenship of the U.S. Naval Prison at Portsmouth, New Hampshire, through the influence of Franklin D. Roosevelt, then Assistant Secretary of the Navy. Once again, Osborne began his duties by spending some time disguised as an imprisoned seaman. Although anticipating opposition to the reforms he planned, Osborne was supported by Franklin Roosevelt and his boss, Secretary of the Navy Josephus Daniels.

On his resignation from Portsmouth in 1920, Osborne continued his work for penal reform. He was honorary chairperson of the National Committee on Prisons, president of the New York State Prison Council, and chairperson of the National Society of Penal Information.

Thomas Osborne died in Auburn, New York, on October 20, 1926.

The Thomas Mott Osborne Papers are located in the Syracuse University Libraries, Syracuse, New York. They contain *The Osborne Family: An Inventory of Papers*, the introduction to which, written by John Janitz in 1971, is the most helpful discussion of Osborne's life and work. See also Osborne's books, *Within Prison Walls* (1913), *Society and Prisons* (1916), and *Prisons and Common Sense* (1924), all of which reflect his belief that prisons must become agents of reform and rehabilitation rather than instruments of societal revenge.

Shorter accounts of Osborne's life can be found in the *Dictionary of American Biography* (1934), the *National Cyclopedia of American Biography* (1931), and *Who Was Who in America* (1942). Readers also may wish to consult Jack M. Holl's *Juvenile Reform in the Progressive Era: William R. George and the Junior Republic Movement* (1971).

SUZANNE S. ETHERINGTON

**Ovington, Mary White** (April 11, 1865–July 15, 1951), settlement worker, civil rights leader, author, and lecturer, was born in Brooklyn Heights, New York, the daughter of a wealthy Fifth Avenue businessman, Theodore Tweedy Ovington, and his wife Louise (Ketcham) Ovington. Both parents and her maternal grandmother were ardent abolitionists. Although she had no personal contact with black Americans, she early came to regard fugitive slaves, discovered in her reading and her grandmother's stories, as heroes. As a child, she often heard Henry Ward Beecher preach and was impressed with Frederick Douglass' speaking, adding to her equalitarian attitudes.

Her education at the Brackett School and Parker Institute was followed by two years at Radcliffe College (1891–1893), where her interest in the working class was stimulated and her concern for Blacks continued. From 1896 to 1903 she was a worker at Greenpoint Settlement, run by the Pratt Institute Neighborhood Association on Twenty-third Street in New York City. At the settlement she saw firsthand the difficult life of the white working class. Discovering the even more tragic life of Blacks in the city, she left Greenpoint Settlement to become a fellow of Greenwich House and to begin what would turn out to be a four-year survey of Blacks in New York City, published in 1911 as *Half a Man*. The study covered every income level of the 60,000 black people in the city, and its goal was the establishment of a settlement house.

*Half a Man* was a sound, objective look at many areas of black life in New York City, including a history of race relations, housing conditions, the state of children in the tenements, discrimination at all levels of employment, the life of the black woman, and unequal treatment in public places. The book was based on extensive research in the 1900 census material, juvenile courts records, church visits, and countless interviews.

While working on the study, Ovington was invited by Dr. W.E.B. Du Bois* to attend the Atlanta Conference in 1904. There for the first time she saw the segregated world of southern Blacks. Later, as a reporter for the *New York Evening Post*, Ovington attended the second meeting of Du Bois' Niagara Movement at Harper's Ferry (1906). She also toured the South chronicling in articles the lives of Blacks under the Jim Crow laws. While writing *Half a Man*, Ovington lived in the newly constructed Tuskegee Apartments in New York City, model housing for Blacks which she had a hand in developing.

Ovington is best known as one of the founders and a longtime leader of the National Association for the Advancement of Colored People (NAACP). In January, 1909, William English Walling,* Dr. Henry Moskowitz,* and she organized a call for a national conference of people concerned about the lack of democracy for Blacks in America. The call for the conference went out on the centennial of Abraham Lincoln's birth, February 12, 1909. Oswald Garrison Villard drafted the statement, and sixty prominent persons added their names to it. The first conference took place in May and was followed a year later by a second one, where the NAACP was legally incorporated with Mary White Ovington as one of the original incorporators. The first days of the NAACP were later described by Ovington in her publication, *How the National Association for the Advancement of Colored People Began* (1914). Among the other founders of the organization, most of whom were white, was Du Bois, by now a close friend of Ovington and the first director of publications and research for the NAACP.

The life and work of Ovington from 1910 to her retirement in 1947 closely paralleled the growth and accomplishments of the NAACP. Her life was devoted to achieving the goals of the organization. She was involved in the antilynching campaign which documented and publicized the horrors of the all too frequent lynchings in the South, as well as in the North. Although never successful in lobbying for federal legislation, the NAACP's long campaign against lynching united Blacks around the country and shamed the nation through public coverage of the brutal events. Ovington, through the NAACP, fought the negative effects of the film, *The Birth of a Nation*, first attempting to stop its showing in cities such as Boston and then attempting to reverse the negative, discrediting picture it gave of Blacks.

During World War I, Ovington was involved in the NAACP's efforts to help black soldiers, who faced terrible situations of racism and prejudice from their fellow white soldiers and superiors, both at home and abroad. The black soldiers' plight was investigated, monitored, represented, and publicized by the NAACP. In the 1920s Ovington was a field worker and lecturer for the NAACP. She visited branches all over the country, gave lectures, and helped raise money to support the organization's legal defense work. The NAACP was assisting people throughout the United States whose rights were being violated, whether through housing segregation, false arrests, or other injustices. She raised money to hire attorneys, such as Clarence Darrow, who represented NAACP-supported clients. In 1927 Ovington published *Portraits of Color*. In this book, she presented twenty portraits of black Americans from varying walks of life whom she personally knew and had seen at work. Paul Robeson, W.E.B. Du Bois, James Weldon Johnson, and Walter White* are just a few of those sympathetically portrayed.

With the Depression years, the NAACP's and Ovington's work turned to securing equal opportunities for Blacks in government work projects. Government public works were investigated and complaints lodged, but not always with success. Also, in the 1930s she was a part of a thrilling victory to block President Hoover's Supreme Court nomination of a former governor who had supported literacy tests for voters. During World War II, work again turned to segregation and discrimination in the armed services.

Mary White Ovington retired in 1947 after thirty-eight years of work with the NAACP, including ten years as chairman of the board. During her association with that organization, it grew from three people to a huge national association with access to Congress and the White House. Called "a fighting saint" and "the mother of the New Emancipation," Mary White Ovington was indeed a selfless leader in the fight for racial equality.

Her autobiography, *The Walls Came Tumbling Down*, published in 1947, still is a much-quoted history of the work of the NAACP. In addition, Ovington wrote a novel, *The Shadow* (1920), and two children's books, *Hazel* (1913) and *Zeke* (1931), before her death in Newton Highlands, Massachusetts, on July 15, 1951.

The Mary White Ovington Papers are in the Archives of Labor History and Urban Affairs at Wayne State University in Detroit. The NAACP Papers in the Library of Congress also are important sources of information about her work with that organization. Daniel W. Cryer has written the only biography of White, "Mary Ovington White and the Rise of the NAACP," Ph.D. dissertation, University of Minnesota, 1977. Histories of the NAACP, such as Charles Flint Kellogg, *NAACP: A History of the National Association for the Advancement of Colored People, 1900–1920* (1967), B. Joyce Ross, *J. E. Spingarn and the Rise of the NAACP, 1911–1939* (1972), and Langston Hughes, *Fight for Freedom* (1962), discuss the role of Mary White Ovington. There are several articles by Ovington in the *New Review*, including ''The Status of the Negro in the United States'' (September, 1913), 744–749, and ''The War on Dogma'' (December, 1914), 691–693. Her obituary appeared in the *New York Times* on July 16, 1951.

JANET M. HOLMES

# P

**Paine, Robert Treat** (October 28, 1835–August 11, 1910), lawyer, philanthropist, and reformer, was born in Boston, the great-grandson of a signer of the Declaration of Independence and the son of Charles Cushing and Fanny Cabot (Jackson) Paine. Educated at Boston Latin School and at Harvard, from which he graduated in 1855 at the head of his class, Paine studied law for a year at Harvard Law School and then devoted two years to travel in Europe. Upon his return, he entered the law office of Richard H. Dana and Francis E. Parker in Boston. He was admitted to the Suffolk bar in 1859. Three years later he married Lydia Williams Lyman, by whom he had seven children.

Paine successfully practiced his profession for some eleven years. His family's wealth had undergone considerable attrition in preceding generations, but by judicious investments in real estate, mining, and railroad enterprises, he was able to retire in 1870 with an ample fortune.

Rich, and only thirty-five years of age, Paine might well have looked forward to a long life of leisure and travel. Instead, he chose another path, that of public service. While he tried elective politics—he served a term in the Massachusetts House of Representatives and in 1884 ran for Congress—he concentrated his energies and fortune on philanthropic causes.

Paine was deservedly famous for his part in launching the Associated Charities of Boston in 1879. This organization, of which he was for many years the president, helped to bring some order and cooperation among the charitable societies of that city.

Not satisfied with his role as a general, Paine also insisted on being a soldier in the field. To acquaint himself with the life of tenement dwellers, he became a "friendly visitor." (The motto of the Associated Charities of Boston was "Not alms but a friend.") This experience convinced him that to better the condition of the "deserving" poor, it was necessary to improve their housing. One could not expect to find the "germs" of education and refinement, he believed, amidst squalor and filth. Indeed, Paine was persuaded that a substantial part of the solution to the tenement problem lay in individual home ownership.

To further this goal, Paine, along with his brother and father-in-law, undertook a large-scale project in Roxbury, Massachusetts. Between 1886 and 1890 they supervised the building of two-story, single-family row houses. Though somewhat cramped, these houses, constructed of brick and with a full set of plumbing facilities, were safe and clean.

In a later experiment, Paine built larger, detached houses, on small lots, in the outer Tremont Street area of Boston. Most of these were sold by amortizing the mortgages (the rent going toward paying off the principal), a rather novel practice at the time.

To handle the planning and financing of these houses, Paine established the Workingmen's Building Association in 1888. Another of his organizations was the Workingmen's Loan Association, whose object was to lend money on chattel mortgages at reasonable terms. When Paine began the experiment, with $25,000 of his own money, the average rate on a chattel mortgage in Boston was as much as 2 1/2 percent—and sometimes more—a month. Paine started at 1 percent, and, satisfied with the results, organized in 1888 the Workingmen's Loan Association, with a capital of $100,000. The success of the Association contributed to the lowering of interest rates for chattel loans in the city.

Influenced by the example of workingmen's centers in England, Paine, a great traveler and an eager learner, became the financial angel, as well as the guiding spirit, of still another organization, the Wells Memorial Institute. It was his intention that this agency, a pioneer among organizations of this type in America, should serve the needs and interests of Boston's working people. The Wells Institute, set up in 1879, was first of all a club, with concerts and dances, smoking and game rooms. It was, too, a successful school in which men and women received practical, job-oriented training. Its halls became a meeting place for trade unionists. And the Institute housed a cooperative bank and an associated purchasing agency.

Paine's interest in the Institute was such that, on a regular basis, and for many years, he spent an evening or two a week participating in the discussions of various workingmen's committees. At the time of Paine's death, the Wells Memorial Institute was one of the largest workingmen's clubs in the United States and represented perhaps his single most impressive institutional legacy.

Another original philanthropic contribution was the Robert Treat Paine Fellowship founded in 1887 at Harvard University. Based on a $10,000 grant from Paine, the purpose of the fellowship was to promote the study of the ethical problems of society, as well as the efforts of legislation, governmental administration, and private philanthropy to ameliorate the lot of mankind.

No account of Paine's endeavors would be complete without mentioning the Robert Treat Paine Association, a trust of about $200,000. Established in 1890 in cooperation with his wife, the Association was intended to promote the spiritual, moral, and physical welfare of working people. Among the agencies under the control of the trust were the People's Coffee House, the Windsor Home for Aged Women, and the Working Girls' Club.

Along with his numerous philanthropic and reform interests, Paine was also a pioneer in the peace movement in this country. He was for many years president of the American Peace Society, and in 1893 presided over the World's Fair Peace Congress in Chicago. His pamphlet on the material advantages of European disarmament was translated into several languages.

Lastly, a notable aspect of Paine's life—and an aspect he himself would doubtless have emphasized—was his close relationship to the Episcopal Church. He was, in fact, one of the most prominent Episcopalian laymen in the United States; a warden of Trinity (Episcopal) Church; and a trustee of donations of the Episcopal Church. Moreover, he was a lifelong friend of Phillips Brooks, the famous Episcopal rector.

Phillips Brooks was a favorite with the upper class of Boston, and this serves to remind us of something else: Robert Treat Paine, by family, education, and religion, as well as in appearance, manners, and taste, was a patrician. But he was a patrician who was concerned about the welfare of the working class of Boston. He devoted forty years, and a private fortune, demonstrating that concern.

Having led a life of uncommon usefulness, he died at his country home in Waltham, Massachusetts, on August 11, 1910.

There is a collection of Paine Papers at the Massachusetts Historical Society. Illustrative of his ideas and interests in the field of social welfare are the following: "The Work of Volunteer Visitors of the Associated Charities Among the Poor," *Journal of Social Science* 8 (1880), 101–116; *The Empire of Charity Established by the Revolution of This Century: Its New Allies, Broader Functions and Stupendous Tasks* (1895); and *The Inspiration of Charity* (1905).

For biographical information, consult the obituaries in the *Boston Globe* (August 12, 1910); *Survey* (August 20, 1910), 717–719; and the *Boston Transcript* (August 12, 1910). An excellent examination of Paine's efforts in the housing field will be found in Sam B. Warner, Jr., *Streetcar Suburbs: The Process of Growth in Boston, 1870–1900* (1962), 101–106.

RICHARD HARMOND

**Park, Maud Wood** (January 25, 1871–May 8, 1955), suffragist and social and civic reformer, was born in Boston, the eldest child of Mary (Collins) and James Rodney Wood. After graduating at the head of her class from St. Agnes School in Albany, New York, Park taught school for eight years. She then entered Radcliffe College, graduating summa cum laude. She was secretly married while in college, to Charles Edward Park, a Boston architect, and widowed seven years later. During her marriage, Park and her husband lived in a settlement house in Boston where she became an activist on behalf of women's suffrage and municipal reform. She combined the two efforts as executive secretary for the Boston Equal Suffrage Association for Good Government. She also helped found the College Equal Suffrage League in 1904, to enlist young women in the movement.

Her activities as a suffragist and her knowledge of women's status in other countries, gained on a round-the-world tour, combined to form the content of popular lectures she gave upon her return to the United States. In 1910 (two years after another and permanently secret marriage to actor-agent Robert Hunter) she settled in Boston and resumed her work on behalf of the Massachusetts suffrage campaign and civic reform. Seven years later she moved to Washington, D.C., to help promote the federal suffrage amendment then promoted by the Congressional Union and the National American Woman Suffrage Association (NAWSA). Passage and ratification of the Nineteenth Amendment were in part a tribute to Park's skills as a congressional lobbyist.

When NAWSA was transformed into the League of Women Voters (LWV), Carrie Chapman Catt, its head, insisted that Park lead the new organization. In 1920 she was formally elected League president. While the nonpartisan LWV focused on educating the newly enfranchised voters on voting procedures and political issues at all levels, Park set forth an agenda of social reform. Protective legislation for women workers, abolition of child labor, appropriations for the Children's Bureau and the Women's Bureau in the Department of Labor, mothers' pensions, and infant health care were all goals that Park insisted be part of a significant body of League-supported legislation. To lobby for these federal measures, the LWV joined with a number of women's organizations, including the National Consumers' League, the Women's Trade Union League, and the Business and Professional Women's Federation, to form the Women's Joint Congressional Committee (WJCC). Park headed this group, which pressured Congress on social feminist measures.

The WJCC enjoyed its greatest successes during the early 1920s. It lobbied intensely for the Sheppard-Towner Maternity and Infancy Protection Act of 1921. The act was the first federal legislation to promote health care among Americans. Continued support by the WJCC helped maintain congressional appropriations for the Children's Bureau, which implemented the act until Congress let the law lapse at the end of the decade. Park led female reformers in a futile attempt to forestall this action.

With Park in the forefront, the WJCC also was instrumental in the "front door lobby" on behalf of nationality status for married women. Prior to passage of the Cable Act in 1922, an American woman who married a foreigner lost her citizenship. The act guaranteed independent citizenship for women regardless of marital status, but provisions did not make citizenship status and naturalization procedures identical with those for men. The battle for equality of nationality continued in national and international arenas after Park's retirement. Park also worked with WJCC allies to ensure that women did not experience discrimination in civil service grading. While a compromise bill finally mandated grade by skill and function, implementation perpetuated job and pay differentials based on sex.

These limited successes on behalf of the social, economic, and legal welfare of women coincided with Park's most active years with the League and the WJCC. After the mid–1920s, the thrust of social feminism diminished. The child labor amendment failed to be ratified, Sheppard-Towner expired, reformers clashed with feminists of the National Woman's Party over a proposed equal rights amendment, and women's organizations were attacked by red-baiting patriots. Simultaneously, Park suffered from physical illness and emotional disappointment following a dispute with Carrie Chapman Catt. She resigned as president of the League of Women Voters in 1924.

Although she continued to lecture and served briefly as a legislative consultant for the League, Park's work as an organizational leader and social reformer effectively ended. The mid–1920s marked a turning point in the women's movement, and the coincidental departure of Park from the scene was an additional blow. She had made social welfare concerns and political pressure on their behalf a hallmark of LWV activity, at least at the national level. State and local League branches were often more concerned with civic issues close to home and with study and education as political tools. Park's influence did not always "trickle down" to become the dominant model for LWV action.

In retirement she retained her interest in women's rights. She wrote a play, *Lucy Stone*, in the 1930s. A decade later she helped assemble the records of the Massachusetts suffrage campaign, which became the centerpiece of the Women's Rights Collection of the Schlesinger Library at Radcliffe College. She died in Reading, Massachusetts, in 1955.

Park's papers are in the Schlesinger Library and scattered throughout organizational records at the library and at the Library of Congress. Park's *Front Door Lobby* was published posthumously in 1960. *The Woman Citizen: Social Feminism in the 1920's* (1973), by J. Stanley Lemons, describes reformers' activities after suffrage. Sharon Hartment Strom wrote the biographical entry in *Notable American Women: The Modern Period* (1980).

                                                                LOIS SCHARF

**Peck, Lillie M.** (December 28, 1888–February 21, 1957), a major figure in the national and international settlement movement for three decades, was born in Gloversville, New York, one of four children of Clara (Sperling) and Adolph L. Peck, a librarian. As an undergraduate at Simmons College, she began doing volunteer work at Boston's South End House. Following her graduation in 1913, that settlement provided her with a workshop in settlement practice and philosophy for the next seventeen years. South End House had long supplied leadership in the movement to federate American settlements. With the founding of the National Federation of Settlements (NFS) in 1911, South End head worker Robert A. Woods* became the organization's first executive secretary, serving until his death in 1925. He was followed at the national post by his successor as head worker at South End House, Albert J. Kennedy.* Kennedy retained his Boston post, and Lillie Peck joined him as assistant head worker at South End House after 1928. When Kennedy moved the NFS to New York City in 1930, she became assistant secretary of the National Federation; and she succeeded him as chief executive of the national organization in 1934.

Peck was no stranger to federated settlement activity, having served from 1918 to 1924 as secretary to the Boston Social Union, a predeccessor to the Boston Settlement Council. While at South End House, she formed a lifelong friendship with yet another South End leader, Ellen W. Coolidge. Peck assisted Coolidge in founding the International Federation of Settlements (IFS) in 1921–1922. Subsequently, she spent two years in Europe, visiting various settlements and laying the groundwork for the IFS's second conference, held in Paris in 1926. The human ties engendered during these travels provided the foundation for a lifetime of involvement facilitating international communication in the settlement movement. Characterizing her contributions, Albert Kennedy noted especially ''her innate fostering impulse'' and her ''massive substructure of acquaintances,'' which both enriched and disseminated the expertise that she brought to settlement affairs.

These qualities stood Peck in good stead as executive of the NFS during the trying years of the Depression and World War II. Beginning in this period, and for the last thirty-four years of her life, she combined her national and international duties with residence at New York's Henry Street Settlement. In several of her rare published articles, she emphasized the importance of residence in the neighborhood in fulfilling the ''characteristic'' settlement function. Despite hard times, the Federation adjusted and grew as Peck crisscrossed the country, providing ''field service'' to NFS member settlements.

Meanwhile, she maintained her international relationships through conferences in 1929, 1932, and 1936, during worsening developments on the political and economic scene. The coming of war brought these connections to a temporary halt, but Peck resumed contact immediately following the cessation of hostilities. Following her retirement as NFS executive in 1947, she traveled extensively in her role of international secretary for the Federation during the last ten years of her life. In the course of her travels, she helped rebuild European settlement relationships, and she was elected president of the International Federation of Settlements from 1947 to 1952.

With aid from the prestigious Barnett Fellowship, Peck made a study of the British community centers movement in 1946–1949. During the Berlin Blockade of 1949, she also served as a consultant to the U.S. military government in reviving the German tradition of neighborhood centers. At the invitation of the Unitarian Service Committee and the Arbeiter Wohlfahrt, she returned to Germany in 1951–1952 to found a settlement house in Bremen. She then served as its first director. In 1952 she was appointed as a representative of the National Federation to UNESCO. And she organized two further IFS international conferences in 1954 and 1956. In recognition of her nurturing role in that organization for over twenty-five yeears, Peck was elected honorary president of the International Federation at this last conference. For many years following the war, she assisted the U.S. State Department in planning itineraries for foreign visitors; and throughout her career she gave orientation to hundreds of people in settlement work.

Her career exemplifies her faith that critically supportive human relationships provided a foundation for settlement functioning. The vast geographic scope of her labors was founded on a pragmatic faith in the settlement's flexibility in democratically fostering social change. Methodological flexibility and a personal emphasis were the hallmarks of her approach to settlement work throughout the world. Peck died in New York City on February 21, 1957.

Sources for the study of Lillie Peck are quite fragmentary. Significant manuscript resources may be found in a number of collections at the University of Minnesota's Social Welfare History Archives. Foremost among these are two collections of papers of the National Federation of Settlements and Neighborhood Centers. Included is a 165-page typescript report of Peck's Barnett Fellowship experience, "Toward a Sense of Community." Lesser accumulations of Peck material may be found at the same repository in the papers of Helen Hall, Albert J. Kennedy, United Neighborhood Houses, and United South End Settlements.

Peck rarely published, and then only several short articles in the *Survey* of the late 1940s and contributions to the *Social Work Yearbook*, 1943 and 1945. She is mentioned briefly in Helen Hall's memoir, *Unfinished Business* (1971), and in histories of the settlement movement by Clarke Chambers and Judith Trolander, but no full-length study has been published.

BRIAN J. MULHERN

**Perkins, Frances** (April 10, 1880–May 14, 1965), social worker, reformer, and the first woman member of a U.S. President's cabinet, was born in Boston, Massachusetts, the daughter of Fred and Susie (Bean) Perkins. After graduating from Worcester (Massachusetts) Classical High School in 1898, she enrolled in Mount Holyoke College, graduating four years later as permanent class president. An average student but a popular leader, she went into teaching for five years and then worked at Hull-House in Chicago. In 1910 she received a master's degree in political science from Columbia University, after completing an essay that dealt with malnutrition among school children.

Perkins then became secretary of the New York City Consumers' League (in 1910). From 1912 to 1917 she served in a similar capacity with the New York Committee on Safety. As a lobbyist at the state capitol she met Assemblyman Alfred E. Smith and State Senator Robert F. Wagner, whom she worked with over many years on social and labor legislation. In the same year she happened to witness the horrendous Triangle Shirtwaist Company fire in New York City in which 146 women laborers, trapped behind locked doors, died, and many others were injured. This propelled Perkins into work on a factory investigating commission which eventually led to her appointment, by then Governor Al Smith, as a member (1919–1921, 1923–1926) and as chairman (1926–1929) of the New York State Industrial Commission, which administered the state's labor legislation.

When Franklin D. Roosevelt succeeded Smith as Governor of New York in 1929, he appointed her the Industrial Commissioner, despite the advice of Smith and others that men would not work for a woman. In that position she developed her administrative skills and nationwide contacts which helped her in her subsequent responsibilities.

In 1933, when he became President of the United States, Franklin Roosevelt appointed Perkins Secretary of Labor, again despite the misgivings of many people, especially business leaders and southern politicians. As Secretary of Labor, perhaps Perkins' most significant contribution was the role she played as the chairman of President Roosevelt's Committee on Economic Security (1934–1935), charged with the responsibility of developing a social security program for the nation. As head, she influenced other members of the committee to not only carry out Roosevelt's election promise to establish state unemployment insurance programs and provide aid to the aged but to pursue a comprehensive system of social security. With her support, provision for maternal and child health, crippled children, child welfare services, vocational rehabilitation, public health, aid to dependent children, and assistance to the blind also were included in the omnibus legislation—the Social Security Act of 1935. Congress, however, would not place the Social Security system under her administrative jurisdiction; instead, a wholly new Social Security Board was created to handle the new programs. But this deliberate rebuke did not undermine her influence in the matter since she was successful in having her associate, Arthur J. Altmeyer,* appointed a member, and subsequently chairman, of the Board, and then Commissioner for Social Security (until 1953), which enabled him (and her) to exercise a long-term impact on the policy and administration of those programs.

Perkins meanwhile served as Secretary of Labor throughout Roosevelt's presidency (1933–1945); she resigned when Truman entered the White House. Truman, however, appointed her to the U.S. Civil Service Commission, on which she served for seven years (1946–1953), although she would have preferred to have been appointed to the Social Security Board. She completed her career as a visiting professor at the Cornell University School of Industrial Relations and as a lecturer at a number of other colleges and universities from 1955 to 1965.

Although by her preference she was known as Miss Perkins, she was married to Paul Wilson on September 26, 1913, at the age of thirty-three. Her husband, however, who had serious health problems, died in 1952, and she spent the remaining thirteen years of her life as a widow. Perkins was very religious, and an unpretentious, frugal, and private person. Thus, although she was responsible for much of the key social legislation of the New Deal, she did not receive during her lifetime the recognition she deserved for the monumental and long-term contributions she made to the nation's social welfare. The Department of Labor building in Washington, D.C., however, eventually was named after her (in 1980) in recognition of her many significant achievements.

Frances Perkins triumphed over several handicaps. She was not always accepted in the dominant male circles. She was criticized for using her maiden name when she was married; for being more of a social worker than a typical labor representative; for wearing strange hats; and, erroneously, for being a Russian Jewess and a communist. Although not a feminist in the current sense of the term, she was conscious of her pioneering role as a woman among male political and labor leaders. Her ability to communicate and to influence Roosevelt was the major factor in her successful accomplishments, both as a creator of new policies and programs and as a conscientious administrator. She motivated her administrative associates and colleagues by her dedication, her sincerity, and her great ability.

Frances Perkins died in New York City on May 14, 1965, at the age of eighty-five.

Frances Perkins' major papers are in the Columbia University Library in New York City, as are an extensive oral history she dictated before her death and drafts of the opening chapters of a biography she began on Alfred E. Smith. A number of other libraries, including the Franklin D. Roosevelt Library at Hyde Park, New York, also have material on Perkins; for a list of those libraries, see pages 557–559 of George Martin's *Madam Secretary: Frances Perkins* (1976), which is the most comprehensive biography of her. Perkins published several books, but her most important one is *The Roosevelt I Knew* (1946), which contains her personal reminiscences of her relationship and work with Roosevelt. Also, readers should consult the fine sketch of her in *Notable American Women: The Modern Period* (1980) and the lengthy bibliographic essay at the end of it.

WILBUR J. COHEN

**Pettit, Katherine Rhoda** (February 23, 1868–September 3, 1936), educator and helper of the rural poor, was born on a bluegrass farm near Lexington, Kentucky, the daughter of Benjamin F. Pettit, a prosperous farmer, and Clara Mason (Barbee) Pettit. She was named Katherine Rhoda, but never used the middle name that she so disliked. As a youth, she joined the Presbyterian Church. Pettit received her early schooling in Lexington and Louisville, and her later education at the Sayre Female Institute of Lexington, Kentucky. She never married.

As a child, Pettit was fascinated by the mountain folk who dwelled in the Cumberland Mountains, in eastern Kentucky. She found the maze of deep hollows and mountain streams intriguing, and was touched by the life style of the isolated families who lived in much the same manner as their Scotch-Irish ancestors 150 years earlier. A family friend, the Reverend Edward O. Guerrant, added to her fascination the sobering reality of the harsh and narrow existence that resulted from the extreme poverty endured by the mountain folk. Guerrant's influence led Pettit to the Woman's Christian Temperance Union, in which she became an active worker. She also involved herself in the State Federation of Women's Clubs in order to help with that organization's rural library service. In the summer of 1895, she toured the feud-ridden mountains of Harlan and Perry counties and saw firsthand the inadequate schoolhouses and the poverty-ridden homes. She witnessed the hard lives of the mountain women and instantly became a crusader. Her sympathies were heightened by the kind treatment she received from the residents; thus she returned the next five summers with seed and pictures to share with her new friends.

Reverend J. T. Mitchell of Hazard, Kentucky, requested that the 1899 convention of the State Federation of Women's Clubs send someone to his county to give domestic education to the women. Pettit and May Stone of Louisville agreed to hold a homemakers' ''campmeeting'' to help the women with cooking, sewing, and home nursing. The six weeks of meetings were held in a large tent on the edge of Hazard, and eventually included Bible studies, temperance readings, and classes to teach children games and songs. Similar events were held in Hindman the two following summers. Pettit kept a diary each summer which contains a wealth of information on the mountain communities.

Influenced by Jane Addams* and Ellen Gates Starr,* Pettit and Stone determined to establish a permanent settlement school in the Hindman area. The two women spent the winter of 1901–1902 traveling in the East soliciting funds. Backed by pledges from philanthropists and contributions from the State Federation of Women's Clubs, the Woman's Christian Temperance Union, and local residents, they purchased land and by August, 1902, successfully opened the Hindman Settlement School. After initial misfortunes, the school grew to 200 students by 1911. Pettit believed that vocational education was as important as academic subjects; thus courses were offered in sewing, cooking, basketry, woodworking, and various other handicrafts. The school also became an important laboratory for research in trachoma, a contagious eye disease common in the mountains.

In 1913 Pettit left the Hindman school to join Ethel de Long in establishing a similar school at Pine Mountain, Kentucky. The site of the school was Virgin Forest, and the clearing of the land took a year and a half. The closest sawmill was forty miles away, and it was not until 1915 that the school was ready for students. Pettit and de Long cast the school in the Hindman mold, but recast it to meet the local needs for assistance to one-room schoolhouses, health centers, and communication. Much of Pettit's success was due to the trust she gained from the mountain folk. A shy woman, Pettit avoided publicity, preferring to perform her services quietly. While at Pine Mountain, she became interested in folk music and contributed many of the songs that she collected to Cecil Sharp, who published them in 1907.

In 1930 Pettit resigned her position at Pine Mountain and moved to Harlan County to assist the coal miners. She advised the miners to leave the mines and return to the land. She taught them better farm techniques and how to produce handicrafts for giftshops. In 1932 the University of Kentucky awarded her the Algernon Sidney Sullivan Medal in recognition of her contributions to the state. She died on September 3, 1936, in Lexington, Kentucky.

The diaries and letters of Pettit are in the Berea College Library in Berea, Kentucky. For a brief biography written by a close friend and former classmate, see Lucy Furman, "Katherine Pettit," Kentucky State Historical Society, *Register* (November, 1937), 75–80. For contemporary sources on the settlement movement, see Robert A. Woods and Albert J. Kennedy, eds., *Handbook of Settlements* (1911); and for Kentucky, see Henderson Daingerfield, "Social Settlements and Educational Work in the Kentucky Mountains," *Journal of Social Science* (November, 1901), 176–195. David E. Whisnot, in *All That Is Native and Fine: The Politics of Culture in an American Region* (1983), devotes his first chapter to the Hindman Settlement School, while *One Man's Cravin'* (1945) is a history of the Pine Mountain School.

JOHN M. DOLLAR

**Pinckney, Merritt Willis** (December 12, 1859–June 7, 1920), lawyer, child welfare promoter, and juvenile court justice, was born in Mount Morris (Ogle County), Illinois, the son of Margaret Catherine (Hitt) and Daniel Jarvis Pinckney, who was active in religious, educational, and political affairs. For a time, Daniel Pinckney served as a Methodist minister; later he was a college professor and a member of the Illinois State Senate. Young Pinckney was educated at Rock River Seminary, from which he graduated in 1877. He then received a bachelor's degree from Knox College in Galesburg, Illinois, in 1881, and a law degree from Union College of Law in Chicago in 1883, where he was valedictorian of his class. On June 24, 1885, Pinckney married Mary Van Vechten of Cedar Rapids, Iowa; there were no children born to the couple.

Pinckney began his legal career in private practice with William H. Tutge of Chicago. In 1905 he was appointed an inheritance tax attorney for Cook County. Later that same year, Pinckney was named judge of the Circuit Court of Cook County, and then judge of the Juvenile Court of Cook County, Illinois, a position he held from September, 1908, to April, 1916. Among his many accomplishments on the bench were the institution of a merit system for the selection and promotion of juvenile probation officers, the appointment of a female assistant to hear the cases of girls brought before the court, the writing of the Funds for Parents Law in 1911, and, along with Franklin Chase Hoyt,* instituting the use of psychiatric examination in juvenile proceedings.

Of particular note was Pinckney's role in the passage and implementation of the Illinois Funds for Parents Law, sometimes known as widows' or mothers' pensions legislation. Not only did he write the law which was passed by the Illinois legislature, but he also was involved in the administration of this forerunner to the Aid to Families with Dependent Children (AFDC) program. It was out of concern for the children he saw that Judge Pinckney became the driving force for this legislation. Typical of the time, he was most concerned about the effects of poverty on families where children might be institutionalized for no other reason than the family's economic status. His work for the Funds for Parents

Law was motivated by a desire to honor motherhood, protect the children involved, and preserve the home. His belief that this type of aid would benefit all involved and be less costly to the taxpayer as well also was influential.

The work of Judge Pinckney cannot properly be assessed without acknowledging the work of other individuals who encouraged and supported the ideas and reforms of this jurist. Among them were members of the Chicago Woman's Club, including Louise de Koven Bowen* and Lucy Flower.* Also crucial to the work of Judge Pinckney were Hull-House and individuals such as Jane Addams* and Julia Lathrop,* as well as the influence and reputation of the Cook County Juvenile Court, the nation's first, and Hoyt's predecessor, Judge Julian Mack.* These persons and organizations provided much of the assistance and expertise which made possible the changes Judge Pinckney worked to bring about.

Yet, in his relatively short judicial career, Pinckney had an impact considerably greater than many who served on the bench for longer periods of time. And at least part of that was due to his personal qualities—his willingness to work tirelessly for the well-being of children, and his real sensitivity to the problems of those who came before him. Fairness, courage, and a knowledge of the juvenile mind were other qualities Judge Pinckney brought to his life and work.

Plagued by ill health through much of his career, Pinckney was forced to retire in 1915. He died in Chicago, Illinois, on June 7, 1920.

There is no extensive writing on Merritt Pinckney and his work; indeed, very little has been written about the man or his career. About the only available information, besides the brief sketch in *Who Was Who in America*, vol. 1 (1943), is in works dealing with the juvenile court and widows' pensions in the United States.

For the former, see Thomas D. Eliot, *The Juvenile Court and the Community* (1914); Bernard Flexner and Roger Baldwin, *Juvenile Courts and Probation* (1914); Herbert H. Lou, *Juvenile Courts in the United States* (1927); Robert M. Mennel, "Origins of the Juvenile Court," *Crime and Delinquency* 18 (1972), 68–78; Anthony M. Platt, *The Child Savers: The Invention of Juvenile Delinquency* (1977); and Ellen Ryerson, *The Best-Laid Plans: America's Juvenile Court Experiment* (1978).

For the latter, see Grace Abbott, *From Relief to Social Security* (1941), and "Recent Trends in Mothers' Aid," *Social Service Review* 18 (1934), 191–220; Winifred Bell, *Aid to Dependent Children* (1965); Mark Leff, "Consensus for Reform: The Mothers' Pension Movement in the Progressive Era," *Social Service Review* 47 (1973), 397–417; Roy Lubove, *The Struggle for Social Security* (1968); and Hace Sorel Tishler, *Self-Reliance and Social Security, 1870–1917* (1971).

GAYLE V. STRICKLER, JR.

**Pink, Louis Heaton** (December 4, 1882–May 18, 1955), lawyer, public housing proponent, and health insurance administrator, was born in Wausau, Wisconsin, the son of Bernhard and Evelyn (Heaton) Pink. Shortly after his birth, his mother died, and Pink was taken to live with a maternal aunt in Canton, New York, where he resided until he was seven years of age, when he was reunited with his father, by then a prominent Brooklyn attorney. After graduation from Erasmus Hall High School, he attended St. Lawrence University in upstate New York, where he met his future wife, Hazel Kelley. A year after graduating in 1905, Pink entered New York Law School and joined the University Settlement, coming under the influence of assistant head worker Dr. Charles S. Bernheimer, who guided his first inquiries into Old Law tenements, which Pink later published as a University Settlement pamphlet. Uncertain about a settlement vocation, Pink married, moved to Brooklyn, and clerked in the law office of a partner of Judge William J. Gaynor. In 1910 social work administrator Raymond V. Ingersoll pursuaded Pink to give up his fledgling law practice to become head worker of Brooklyn's United Neighborhood Guild, where he remained for three years, setting up lodging houses for homeless men and boys. Pink also was appointed to the Brooklyn Board of Education, where he tried to increase the public schools' role as neighborhood centers. Returning to legal practice, he specialized in insurance litigation and bankruptcy cases with the New York State Insurance Department.

Probably his old acquaintance from the University Settlement, Belle Moskowitz,* suggested Pink's name to Governor Alfred E. Smith for the new State Board of Housing, established in 1926 to pursue tax exemption and other incentives for philanthropic, "limited-dividend" housing projects. Pink poured himself into the work, expediting the development of fourteen projects, including the Brooklyn Garden Apartments, for which he engaged Al Smith and leading Brooklyn Democrats as stockholders. His enthusiasm for philanthropic housing was evidenced in *The New Day in Housing* (1927), Pink's able summary of American and European ventures in model tenements. With the onset of the Great Depression, however, he kept few illusions regarding the potential of philanthropic housing encouraged by tax incentives alone, and in 1931 he urged the State Board of Housing to create a separate authority to raise housing construction funds from the sale of tax-exempt bonds. He also led advocates for a municipal housing authority to undertake slum clearance and new construction; and as a charter member of the Public Housing Conference, along with Mary K. Simkhovitch* and Helen L. Alfred, he lobbied with Governor Herbert H. Lehman and set in motion the bill-drafting team that included attorney Charles Abrams.* Using the Port Authority of New York as a model, Pink sketched out an independent authority, run by an appointed board with full power to condemn property and build and operate new dwellings. With the enactment of the New York City Housing Authority in 1934, Pink was appointed to its board and helped to settle its early routine, before Governor Lehman reappointed him to the State Board of Housing. Serving as chairman of the State Board in the late 1930s, Pink helped draft provisions for the New York State Constitution of 1938, which for the first time sanctioned a broad state housing responsibility; and later he participated in the legislative struggle that funded the largest state effort in slum clearance.

Pink's work on the unpaid State Board remained almost an avocation, however, next to his service in the State Insurance Department, where beginning in 1932 he oversaw the reorganization of bankrupt title and mortgage guarantee companies. Named State Insurance Superintendent by Governor Lehman in 1935, Pink pushed for recodification of state insurance laws, sponsored a study of "industrial" insurance for the working poor, and pursued Louis D. Brandeis' old idea of low-cost savings bank life insurance. He was instrumental in changing the statutes to allow insurance companies to invest in limited-dividend housing, which encouraged Metropolitan Life to build Parkchester, the famous middle-income housing complex in the Bronx. Cooperating closely with Robert Moses, Pink also drafted an early version of the state urban redevelopment law to induce insurance companies to invest in condemned inner-city properties, which made Stuyvesant Town and the subsequent trend in urban redevelopment possible. With the defeat of Democratic gubernatorial hopes in 1942, Pink resigned his state insurance post and considered joining the United Nations relief effort overseas. He changed his mind, although he continued to support the UN, the Bretton Woods Agreement, and multilateral trade as a force for peace, as chairman of the Citizens' Conference on International Economic Union.

Instead, Pink pursued a third career in health insurance. As Insurance Superintendent, Pink had passed favorably on a plan submitted by New York City's voluntary hospitals for prepaid hospital care insurance on the basis of voluntary enrollment by subscribers. He insisted that this Associated Hospital Service of New York (AHS), better known as Blue Cross, develop a system of binding enrollment to ensure a stable source of premiums and a conservative reimbursement schedule to member hospitals to discipline them into maintaining adequate cash reserves. In 1943 Pink left state service to become president of AHS. He guided its expansion, relying on large corporate employers and their unions who had clamored for health coverage, and nearly quadrupled the membership to 4.2 million by 1949. Pink emerged as an influential opponent of the Harry S. Truman administration's proposals for federal compulsory medical insurance. Conceding a federal role in providing grants for local hospital construction and for preventive medicine, he nevertheless argued that the "local Blues," as careful watchdogs of community medical care, voluntarily coordinated by a nationwide Blue Cross Commission, could well serve the nation's health needs.

By the 1950s Pink had played a major role in laying the foundation for New York State's social welfare system, that partnership of state authority and the corporate sector that allowed social welfare provisions to expand in a regular progression from the tenure of Al Smith to that of Thomas E. Dewey. The lawyer turned insurance regulator was in a strategic position to bring together fiduciary giants like Metropolitan Life, large employers like New York Telephone, and city labor unions to build huge social welfare trust funds and philanthropic housing ventures, the actuarially sound, businesslike liberalism that was New York's hallmark for a generation. Pink was putting the finishing touches on his last middle-income housing venture, Queensview, a cooperative project for an interracial clientele, when he died at his home in New York City on May 18, 1955.

"The Reminiscences of Louis H. Pink" (1949) is in the Oral History Collection at Columbia University. There is no collection of Pink's manuscripts, but one can consult the minutes and correspondence of the State Board of Housing and the files of the State Insurance Department, Albany, New York, as well as the Herbert H. Lehman Papers and the Edith Elmer Wood Papers at Columbia University.

Pink's published works include *Old Tenements and the New Law* (1907); *The New Day in Housing* (1928); *Gaynor, the Tammany Mayor Who Swallowed the Tiger* (1931); *Freedom from Fear* (1944); and *The Story of Blue Cross* (1945). *Industrial Life Insurance* (1938) is one of many manuals and studies that Pink wrote as Insurance Superintendent. *An Economic United States of Europe—Now* (1946) is representative of Pink's pamphlets on behalf of the cause of economic multilateralism. His occasional housing articles include "Tax Exemption Plays Its Part," *American City* (May, 1928); "Queensview," ibid. (April, 1951); and, with Frederick H. Allen, "Housing Program for the City of New York," ibid. (September, 1953).

An obituary appeared in the *New York Times*, May 19, 1955.

JOEL SCHWARTZ

**Pratt, Anna Beach** (June 5, 1867–January 3, 1932), social worker, administrator, and pioneer proponent of school social work, was born in Elmira, New York, the eldest of the three children of Timothy Smith Pratt and Catherine Elizabeth (Beach) Pratt. Anna's father, who was born in New York State and claimed a New England lineage dating back to the *Mayflower*, was a dry goods merchant, and her mother, of French Huguenot descent, was born in Connecticut. Raised as a Presbyterian, Anna Pratt converted to Quakerism in her adult life; she never married, pursuing instead a lifelong career in social work.

After attending local public schools, Anna remained close to home, enrolling in Elmira College. She received a B.A. degree from Elmira in 1886, and then taught at a private girls' school and at her alma mater. In the early 1890s Pratt undertook an experiment which was to lead to her life work: she formed the Alpha Club, which was designed to provide local working girls with a healthy environment apart from their employment in Elmira's mills. Her career took a decidedly professional turn when Pratt attended the summer course offered by the New York School of Philanthropy in 1906, and subsequently she was named the head of the local Bureau of Associated Relief in Elmira. By engaging in intensive interviews with clients and maintaining an effective method of record-keeping, Pratt systematized relief efforts, and, at her prompting, in 1912 the Bureau merged with the Women's Federation to form the Elmira Federation for

Social Service. For the next several years, Pratt's efforts were influential in coordinating the activities of welfare organizations in her home town.

In 1915 Pratt made a decision which was to remove her from Elmira for the remainder of her life. She left to attend the University of Pennsylvania in Philadelphia. After receiving a master's degree in the spring of 1916, Pratt was chosen to be the executive director of the Magdalen Society of Philadelphia in the fall of the same year. The Society began to redirect its work toward educational reform, and in 1917 the superintendent of the Board of Public Education invited the Society to attempt social work from the perspective of vocational guidance. Pratt developed a junior employment department to assist students and their families in evaluating the full range of vocational opportunities before leaving school for the work force. In 1918 the Magdalen Society was renamed the White-Williams Foundation for Girls, and two years later the Foundation further broadened its interests to include boys and became the White-Williams Foundation; it retained its focus on improving the education of children.

Social work in the 1920s was heavily influenced by the steadily growing interest in psychology as a means of treating maladjusted individuals, along with the emerging professionalization of social workers through the use of casework. Under Pratt's leadership, the White-Williams Foundation worked to integrate school social work into both public and private educational institutions by creating a cadre of highly trained "visiting teachers." Through the development of visiting teachers, or school counselors, the purpose of school social work, as envisioned by Pratt, was to permit the teacher to recognize the student as an individual and to know the "whole child" in his or her home, work, school, and community environments. The Foundation received generous grants from the Commonwealth Fund and the Keith Fund, as well as monies from private and public educational institutions, to be applied toward the implementation of training programs for teachers and scholarships for deserving students. For her part, Pratt wrote extensively on the concept of the professionally trained school social worker, and she established supervisory programs in conjunction with college departments of sociology and education, welfare organizations, and schools of social work. Pratt believed that the merger of teaching and social work should involve new methods of instruction which fostered expertise while maintaining flexibility in treating individual cases. For Anna Pratt, the acceptance of the child as an individual was of paramount concern, and school social work was an innovative, modern means of confronting the often brutalizing nature of mass public education.

Pratt pushed for the acceptance of school social work through other channels as well. In 1925 she was elected president of the Philadelphia Council of Home and School Associations, and this position provided her, and the White-Williams Foundation, with the opportunity to introduce counseling to parents and to agitate for more cooperation with the schools in awarding scholarships. Pratt served in that capacity until 1929, the same year in which she was appointed to the Philadelphia Board of Education. Further involvement and national notice came in 1930 when she acted as a delegate to the White House Conference on Child Welfare.

Anna Pratt's major contribution to social work was in demonstrating that school counseling was a practical and vital means of aiding both the child and the teacher. By obtaining knowledge of the student's home and family environment, the school social worker employed the casework method to its fullest advantage. Aligned with the attempts to use scientific, objective treatment of individual students, the procedures outlined and advocated by Pratt were designed to humanize both the students and the schools.

Anna Pratt died of cancer in Philadelphia in 1932.

Manuscript materials relating to Pratt can be found at the Steele Memorial Library, Elmira, New York, and at the White-Williams Foundation. Two pamphlets published by the Foundation provide helpful accounts of Pratt's activities as director: *Five Years' Review for the Period Ending December 31, 1921* (1922), and *School Children as Social Workers See Them* (1927). The latter contains a useful chronology of the activities and publications of Pratt during her first ten years with the White-Williams Foundation.

Pratt wrote much during the 1920s on the subject of school social work; of particular importance are the following: "The Relation of the Teacher and the Social Worker," *Annals* of the American Academy of Political and Social Science (November, 1921), 90–96; "Social Work in the First Grade of a Public School," *American Journal of Sociology* (January, 1923), 436–442; "Should the Visiting Teacher Be a New Official?" *Journal of Social Forces* (March, 1923), 300–304; "Courses of Training for Visiting Teachers," *Proceedings* of the National Conference of Social Work (May, 1923), 425–428; "Training for Educational and Vocational Counselors from the Standpoint of the Field Worker," *Vocational Guidance Magazine* (April, 1927), 318–322.

To better understand Pratt and the development of social work in the 1920s, the following will provide information: Clarke A. Chambers, *Seedtime of Reform: American Social Service and Social Action, 1918–1933* (1963); Roy Lubove, *The Professional Altruist: The Emergence of Social Work as a Career, 1880–1930* (1965), and "Pratt, Anna Beach," in *Notable American Women, 1607–1950* (1971); *Woman's Who's Who of America* (1914–1915). An accurate obituary can be found in the *New York Times*, January 4, 1932.

EARL F. MULDERINK III

**Pratt, Richard Henry** (December 6, 1840–March 15, 1924), soldier turned Indian educator, was born in Rushford, New York, to Mary (Herrick) and Richard Pratt. Raised at Logansport, Indiana, in a devoutly religious Methodist family, Richard was turned out of school at age thirteen by the untimely death of his father, and thereafter he worked to support his mother's household until he enlisted in the Union army at the outset of the Civil War.

There he rose to the rank of first lieutenant before his discharge in May, 1865, and after a brief period of frustration with civilian life he reenlisted for assignment to Indian Territory, where he worked with a black regiment and commanded Indian scouts. Due to successful service among the two minority groups for seven years, in 1874 Pratt was ordered to gather up Indians around Fort Sill who had engaged in depredations during the Red River War, and to lead them into holding camps in exile at Fort Marion, Florida. On duty at this prison, his commitment to Christian principles and the needs of downtrodden peoples led him to the conclusion that any hope for his charges lay not in confinement, but in thoroughgoing cultural transformation to the ways of the mainstream society of the United States. Accordingly, with help from townspeople nearby, he supervised the education of his charges, released them as rehabilitated inmates within two years, and called for additional enrollees.

Federal officials refused to sustain the work in Florida, but in 1878 General Samuel C. Armstrong* invited Pratt to blend Indian students into an all-black student body at Hampton Institute in Virginia, and made a place for him on the teaching staff. Cabinet-level officials were so impressed by his success that when the army called him back to regular duty they arranged the opening of an all-Indian school at the abandoned army barracks in Carlisle, Pennsylvania. Following some brief preparations, he opened the doors to Carlisle Indian School in time for the 1879 fall session, enrolling eighty-two Sioux recruits and initiating a career as superintendent that lasted until he was forced into retirement. After that, he continued to work as a private champion of Indian citizenship through education until he died in 1924.

The formula for an Indian's adjustment was simple: formal education in a boarding school far removed from tribal society, coupled with "outing experience" among educated, Christian Whites who would transform the person into a citizen equal to all others in the mainstream society of America. His rigorous opposition to any degree of Indian cultural survival made him the adversary of numerous influential people who agreed with the general goal of acculturation through formal education. Missionaries, especially Roman Catholics, were incensed by his insistence that public funds which had long been funneled into their reservation contract schools to support "civilization" along with Christianization be allocated to support secular, off-reservation boarding schools. Teachers and administrators involved with a burgeoning reservation day school system were at odds with him, too, for he opposed the location of their work among students in continuous contact with Indian mores. Many reformers who were in close agreement with Pratt about most issues related to acculturation shrank from his stern refusal to acknowledge any value in the salvage of Indianness. Although most of the growing body of adversaries were in some ways supporters of Carlisle, they became incensed over the implications of Pratt's unbending determination to snuff out all aspects of Indian tradition and tribal organization. In time, they joined public officials who opposed Pratt on other grounds to force his retirement from the army on February 17, 1903, and from the Carlisle superintendency on June 30, 1904.

As much as any other person of influence in official circles governing Indian policy through the late nineteenth century, Paratt exemplified commitment to formal education leading to acculturation and citizenship, which was part of official federal policy throughout the Peace Policy Era. In light of policy change since the appointment of John Collier* to the Office of Indian Affairs in 1933, which has encouraged the retention of Indian ways despite cultural adaptation, Pratt's extreme posture is regarded with little favor. Yet, in retrospect, the positive impact of his work is acknowledged. Its merits were recognized openly by the beginning of the twentieth century through frequent reports on the accomplishments of successful "Returned Students." The constructive effects have been evidenced, too, in many families that were touched personally by Richard Henry Pratt. None better represents this than the family of Chauncey Yellow Robe, a Rosebud Sioux who went to Carlisle at age fifteen almost without knowledge of or exposure to the ways of white people. After graduation, he became truant officer at the federal Rapid City Boarding School, where he married a non-Indian nurse from Zumbro Falls, Minnesota; imposed the principles he had learned from Pratt; and raised three daughters according to his mentor's plan. The elder, Chauncina Yellow Robe White Horse, rose to eminence as a leader in the Chicago Indian community of some 27,000 enrolled in more than thirty-five tribes. For many years, her contributions to education were considerable, and shortly before she died she arranged the founding of the Chicago Indian Community Oral History Project to preserve heritage for Indians adjusted to metropolitan white culture. Rosebud Yellow Robe has earned recognition as a distinguished author of works including *The Album of the American Indian* and *Tonweya and the Eagles and Other Lakota Indian Tales*. The younger daughter, Evelyn Robe, earned baccalaureate and master's degrees in languages from Mount Holyoke College, then a Ph.D. from Northwestern University. For years, she gained wide attention in the United States because of her work on treating cancer of the larynx through speech pathology, and since her marriage to a German physician she has had similar recognition across Western Europe. Father "wouldn't let us learn to speak Lakota at all, because of General Pratt. We walked a whole mile to a little red school house" for exclusive exposure to non-Indians and their ways, Rosebud recalled recently with some regret. But she praised her father, and in turn General Pratt, for unwavering dedication to the transformation of original Americans into successful citizens of the United States.

Richard Henry Pratt died in Washington, D.C., on March 15, 1924.

Information about Carlisle Indian School abounds in every facility of the National Archives system and in almost countless books and articles about the importance of education to the implementation of the Peace Policy. The life of Pratt should be studied through these materials in broad context. The best single source remains the biography by Elaine Goodale Eastman, who served as superintendent of education for western Sioux after she had been exposed to the Carlisle superintendent's methods back east: *Pratt: The Red Man's Moses* (1935).

However, one also should see Pratt's principal writings, edited by Robert M. Utley: *Battlefield and Classroom: Four Decades with the American Indian, 1867–1904* (1964) is a substantial volume; *The Indian Industrial School, Carlisle, Pennsylvania: Its Origin, Purposes, Progress and the Difficulties Surmounted* (1908; repr. 1979) is shorter. Together, they supply detailed information on the performance of Pratt as an educator of Indian people. Readers also may wish to consult Everett Gilcreast's "Richard Henry Pratt and American Indian Policy, 1877–1906: A Study of the Assimilation Movement," Ph.D. dissertation, Yale University, 1967, an account of the central theme of the educator's work.

HERBERT T. HOOVER

**Purdy, Lawson** (September 13, 1863—August 30, 1959), pioneer in tax, zoning, and housing reform and a leader in family welfare services, was born in Hyde Park, New York, to Frances H. (Carter) and James S. Purdy, an Episcopal clergyman. After graduating from St. Paul's School in Concord, New Hampshire, in 1880, Purdy attended Trinity College in Hartford, Connecticut, from which he received a bachelor's degree in 1884. A year later he married Mary J. McCracken, with whom he had one child; shortly after her death in 1939, he married Helene S. Wexelsen. Meanwhile, in 1887 Purdy was awarded a master's degree from Trinity, and then he held a number of jobs. From 1891 to 1896 he was employed as treasurer of the New York Bank Note Company while attending New York Law School; a year later he was admitted to the bar. However, rather than pursue private law practice, he decided to devote his life to public service, primarily in his beloved adopted home, New York City.

An ardent follower of Henry George, author of *Progress and Poverty* (1879) and the "single tax" idea, Purdy achieved national prominence as a tax authority and reformer while holding a series of positions: secretary of the New York Tax Reform Association (1896–1906); president of the New York City Department of Taxes and Assessments (1906–1917); and president of the National Municipal League (1916–1919). Among his many accomplishments during these years, perhaps most important were passage in 1902 of a New York City law that required publication of the assessment rolls, and enactment, four years later, of a statute that required the separate listing of land and the total value of an assessed property, both of which he was largely responsible for. He also was deeply involved in housing reform and, along with Robert W. de Forest,* president of the New York Charity Organization Society (COS), played an instrumental role in enactment of the famous New York Tenement House Law of 1901 and was deeply involved in the drafting and passage of the city's first comprehensive zoning law, in 1916.

From 1918 to 1933 Purdy served as the executive secretary of the New York City Charity Organization Society, during which time he not only brought continued financial stability to that organization but made it a leader in the transition from the older individual approach to the new professional family social work. He also chaired that agency's Tenement House Committee, whose function was to monitor enforcement of the state statute. Later he was appointed to a state commission which, in 1929, revised the Tenement House Law into a Multiple Dwelling Law which provided for additional sanitary requirements and other safeguards in tenement buildings.

After leaving the COS in 1933 (by which time he already had laid the basis for its merger, in 1939, with the New York Association for Improving the Poor, thereby creating the Community Service Society of New York), Purdy served, on two different occasions (1933 and 1938), as chair of the New York City Emergency Work and Relief Administration. He also was controller of the Trinity (Protestant Episcopal Parish) Corporation and the first chair of the New York City Planning Association. In addition, he was treasurer of the Family Welfare Association of America and was active with the Russell Sage Foundation, the Robert Schalkenback Foundation, the National Municipal League, and the Provident Loan Association.

Lawson Purdy was an intelligent, fearless, and kind citizen, a reformer who worked for the public good rather than for personal power, wealth, or status. His contributions to the fields of housing, tax reform, and zoning were outstanding. In fact, at the time of his retirement in the early 1950s, the *New York Times* stated that he contributed more to these areas than perhaps any other single person. However, his kind heart and keen mind dealt not only with large urban problems but with the needs of troubled and economically distressed individuals as well, as his tenure with the New York Charity Organization Society attests. Although not a trained social worker, he saw the need for such service and helped bring the agency founded in the nineteenth century by Josephine Shaw Lowell* into the twentieth, especially during the ''age of professionalization''— the 1920s.

Lawson Purdy died in Port Washington, New York, on August 30, 1959.

The single best source of material on Purdy's life and career is his contribution to the Columbia University Oral History Project at Columbia University in New York City. However, Purdy also was mentioned very frequently in newspapers, and many of his writings were published, especially in the *Family*and the *National Municipal Review*. See those journals, the *Readers' Guide to Periodical Literature*, and the *Personal Name Index to the New York Times* from around 1900 until his death in 1959. An obituary appeared in the *New York Times* on September 1, 1959. By far the best secondary account is Roy Lubove's sketch of Purdy in Supplement Six to the *Dictionary of American Biography* (1980).

LARCY D. MCCARLEY

# R

Rapoport, Lydia (March 8, 1923–September 6, 1971), educator and promoter of social casework, was born in Vienna, Austria, to Samuel J. and Eugenia (Margolis) Rapoport. Samuel Rapoport was a man of unusual gifts who studied law in Vienna but whose interests seemed more in the artistic and aesthetic areas. His major talents lay in linguistics, where he was known for his proficiency in seventeen languages. Mrs. Rapoport studied to be a teacher prior to her marriage, but then devoted herself to familial duties. After her death, Rapoport remained a widower for many years before remarrying late in life. Throughout, Lydia remained a devoted daughter to him.

In 1906 Samuel Rapoport left Vienna for the United States, intending to settle in Philadelphia; however, he soon became disenchanted with the United States and returned home. In 1928, sensing a rising nationalism and anti-Semitism in Europe, he returned to America, this time settling in New York City. Four years later, his wife, son Emanuel, age fourteen, and daughter Lydia, nine years of age, joined him there.

Lydia attended New York City public schools and then graduated from Hunter College in 1943, where she was described as a brilliant student and was elected to Phi Beta Kappa. She then enrolled in an accelerated program at the Smith College School of Social Work, from which she received a master's degree the following year. After leaving Smith in 1944, Rapoport sought employment in the mental health field in Chicago, where she eventually held numerous positions. In the late 1940s, she earned a certificate in child therapy from the Institute of Psychoanalysis in the Windy City, and in 1952 she left Chicago to attend the London School of Economics on a Fulbright Fellowship. While in London, where she remained until 1954, she met the renowned Richard Titmuss and Dame Eileen Younghusband, establishing close personal relationships with both which lasted the rest of her life. During her stay in England, she also became associated with the Tavistock Clinic in London. There, her interest in mental health expanded, especially in British developments in that field, and she became recognized for her knowledge and expertise in social work training: indeed, she was invited to lecture extensively on the subject throughout England.

Upon returning to the United States in 1954, she received her first full-time faculty appointment, at the University of California, Berkeley School of Social Welfare, a position she held until her death.

In the interim, however, she continued her own studies and held several temporary and part-time teaching positions, beginning at the Harvard University School of Public Health in 1960. At Harvard's Laboratory of Community Psychiatry, she studied with many mental health specialists, including Eric Lendlemann, with whom she also developed a lifelong friendship. Out of that association came what many consider to be her major contribution—perhaps the most creative in social casework during the decade—crisis intervention and short-term treatment.

In 1963 she took another appointment, this time for a year as an educational consultant at the Paul Baerwald School of Social Work of Hebrew University in Jerusalem, at which time she gained preeminence in the international social welfare field with her works in cross-cultural projects dealing with family planning in health and welfare programs. Her work in international social welfare resulted in her being selected the first United Nations interregional family welfare and planning advisor, and in 1971 she took yet another leave from the University of California at Berkeley to go to New York to serve in that capacity.

Lydia Rapoport often was depicted as a person of deep complexity, portraying a private and public self. Music, art, and literature were a cherished part of her personal life, which she shared with few people. In her professional life, however, Rapoport appeared quietly confident and in control of herself, and, although she was not very outgoing, many people sought her out. Perhaps more important, however, were her extensive writings, which dealt with various areas of social work, including creativity in social work, crisis theory and preventive intervention, consultation, supervision and professional education, and family planning.

To commemorate Rapoport's many accomplishments in social work, a book with some of her best-known writings was published. Entitled *Creativity in Social Work: Selected Writings of Lydia Rapoport*, and edited by Sanford N. Katz (1975), the work depicted her professional development and growth as well as her contributions to social work theory and practice. Unlike some social work theorists, she made actual practice an integral part of her professional development. Her work with Gerald Caplan described the application of crisis theory in social work. Her stand on prevention and her controversial position against the use of the medical treatment model, with its emphasis on disease and causation, were depicted in these works. In the mental health field, which was Rapoport's specialization, her focus on the "life model" and "ecological approach" in helping others was indicative of her keen perception and visionary genius. Lydia Rapoport's distinguishing legacy to social work, however, was her belief in, reaffirmation of, and fight for a proper perspective of social casework in the profession. She died of acute bacterial endocarditis in New York City on September 6, 1971, at the age of forty-eight.

Lydia Rapoport's major writings can be found in Sanford N. Katz, ed., *Creativity in Social Work: Selected Writings of Lydia Rapoport* (1975), which also includes a biographical narrative, traces her professional growth and development, and gives an overview of her contribution to social work. Brief biographical sketches also may be found in *Who's Who of American Women*, 7th ed. (1972–1973), and *Notable American Women: The Modern Period* (1980). An account of her career also may be found in Ernest Greenwood, Gertrude Wilson, and Robert Apte, *Lydia Rapoport, In Memoriam* (1975). For her position and view on prevention, see the article in the *Encyclopedia of Social Work* (1971) on "Preventive Social Work," written by Milton Wittman. Obituaries appeared in the *San Francisco Chronicle*, September 8, 1971, and the *Oakland Tribune*, September 8, 1971.

CONSTANTINE G. KLEDARAS

**Raushenbush, Elizabeth Brandeis** (April 25, 1896–April 30, 1984), educator, social researcher, promoter of unemployment compensation, and protector of migratory laborers, was born in Boston, Massachusetts, to attorney and later U.S. Supreme Court Justice Louis Brandeis and Alice (Goldmark) Brandeis. Elizabeth received a B.A. from Radcliffe College in 1918 and earned an M.A. (1924) and a Ph.D. (1928) from the University of Wisconsin. As the daughter of Louis Brandeis, Elizabeth watched the development of the American welfare state from a privileged position. She learned of the attempts of the National Consumers' League and other organizations to pass minimum wage laws for women, child labor legislation, and other social welfare measures. Since she also was the niece of Pauline* and Josephine Goldmark,* she was brought even closer to the world of Florence Kelley* and other progressive advocates of such causes. As a result, Elizabeth Brandeis also would help to edit Josephine Goldmark's influential biography of Florence Kelley, *Impatient Crusader* (1953).

Meanwhile, after graduating from Radcliffe, where she exerted considerable influence over Mary Switzer* and other important reformers, E.B., as she was fondly called, obtained a series of jobs in Washington, D.C. She followed a short stint with the U.S. War Labor Policies Board (1918–1919) with a job as assistant secretary and later secretary of the District of Columbia Minimum Wage Board (1919–1923). In 1923, when the U.S. Supreme Court, in the celebrated case of *Adkins v. Children's Hospital*, ruled that minimum wages for women were unconstitutional—thus overturning Justice Brandeis' work both as a lawyer and a judge—Elizabeth was out of work.

Convinced that the states, not the federal government, would remain the center of influence in the field of social welfare, Elizabeth Brandeis traveled to Madison,

Wisconsin, with the intention of studying law. In Madison, however, she met a number of students working with John R. Commons* and decided to study labor economics, or "institutional economics," as Commons referred to it. There, she also met, and in July, 1925, married, Paul A. Raushenbush* and acquired some of his enthusiasm for the passage and administration of unemployment compensation laws.

The Raushenbushes, who had one child, a son, Walter, became an important part of the Wisconsin scene. Elizabeth taught courses in American economic history and labor legislation. When Commons and his associates published the final volume of their history of American labor, *History of Labor in the United States, 1896–1932* (1935), it included an essay on minimum wages written by Elizabeth Brandeis. The essay remains a classic source of information on the topic.

Despite this incursion into other fields of labor economics, unemployment insurance was the Raushenbushes' main concern. Their involvement in this issue led them to be known as Mr. and Mrs. Unemployment Compensation. They helped Harold M. Groves perform the research that led to the signing of the nation's first unemployment compensation law on January 28, 1932. During this time, Elizabeth was invited to prepare research and to testify before the Wisconsin state legislature. She was involved in the preliminary work on Wisconsin's unemployment compensation bill and testified before the legislature's Interim Committee on Unemployment. At the Committee's request, she drafted the unemployment compensation section of its report in 1931.

With Paul Raushenbush directing the Wisconsin Unemployment Compensation Division from 1934 to 1967, Elizabeth Brandeis Raushenbush continued to teach at the University of Wisconsin in the Department of Economics. In the years between 1928 and 1967, she advanced within the academic hierarchy from instructor to full professor.

In later years, Elizabeth developed a keen interest in the plight of the migrant worker. She served as chairperson from 1960 to 1967 on the Governor's Committee on Migratory Labor. In this capacity she fought for improved conditions for migratory workers and their families. Her commitment to migrant workers and their families enabled them to be brought under the protection of the workmen's compensation act. She also proved instrumental in establishing summer schools for the children of migrant workers.

Elizabeth published numerous articles on labor history and unemployment compensation with Harold Groves, John Commons, John Andrews,* and her husband. She and her husband also wrote *Our U.C. Story, 1930–1967*, an account of their involvement in the unemployment compensation movement in Wisconsin.

Upon her death, Jack Barbash, himself a product of the Wisconsin school of institutional economics, said, "EB lived her life according to the concerns which her inheritance, experience and character instilled in her." To use Elizabeth's own words, she engaged in research "for the purpose of using it." In this manner she bridged the gap between the early activism of her father and the National Consumers' League and the later development of state social welfare laws. She died in Madison, Wisconsin, on April 30, 1984.

The papers of Elizabeth Brandeis Raushenbush are available to researchers at the State Historical Society of Wisconsin in Madison. These may be supplemented with the papers of Paul Raushenbush, also at the State Historical Society of Wisconsin. Other sources include Paul and Elizabeth Raushenbush, *Our U.C. Story, 1930–1967* (1979). The *Milwaukee Journal*, May 1, 1984, and the *Madison State Journal*, May 1, 1984, contain excellent obituaries.

ANN-MARIE CARROLL and EDWARD D. BERKOWITZ

**Raushenbush, Paul A.** (December 5, 1898–January 17, 1980), social insurance draftsman and administrator, was born in Rochester, New York, one of five children of Walter and Pauline (Rother) Rauschenbusch. The elder Rauschenbusch, a distinguished Baptist clergyman and theologian, was a well-known "social gospeler," one who in his writings and work applied the principles of Christianity to social reform. Paul Raushenbush (who changed the spelling of his name) received a B.A. degree from Amherst College in 1920. Afterward, he traveled and studied in Germany and other nations in Europe. In 1922 he went to the University of Wisconsin, where he studied economics under John R. Commons* and taught part-time in the economics department from 1922 to 1932. He also was a part-time teacher of Greek and American civilization in the university's Experimental College from 1927 to 1932. On July 2, 1925, he married Elizabeth Brandeis (Raushenbush*), the daughter of United States Supreme Court Justice Louis D. Brandeis, with whom he had one son and who taught economics at the University of Wisconsin from 1924 to 1966.

Raushenbush's importance in the history of social welfare rests on his association with unemployment compensation legislation and its administration. Working with his wife, with Harold Groves, a member of the University of Wisconsin economics faculty and in 1931 a member of the state assembly, with Arthur Altmeyer,* secretary of the Wisconsin Industrial Commission, and with Edwin E. Witte,* chief of the Legislative Reference Library, Raushenbush was the principal author of the version of the bill that became the nation's first unemployment compensation law in 1932. In recognition of this, his leading role in campaigning for the bill, and his work as a consultant on setting up the machinery to administer the law, in 1934 Raushenbush was appointed director of the unemployment compensation department of the Wisconsin Industrial Commission. The year before, he had assumed the chairmanship of an advisory committee on unemployment compensation, composed of business and labor representatives, that for many years had dominated all decisions on statutory changes and changes in administrative rules and procedures. He held both positions until his retirement in 1967.

During the 1930s Raushenbush served as a consultant for various states that were establishing unemployment compensation programs, and he continued consulting on state programs throughout his life. He also exerted influence through lectures, articles, and testimony before Congress and state legislatures. In 1936 he was one of the organizers of the Association of State Administrators. Through its Interstate Conference of Employment Security Agencies, of which he was president in 1943, he promoted the coordination of state unemployment compensation programs.

Raushenbush also was involved in the origins of Social Security, working not only for the inclusion of unemployment compensation in the program but also for the incorporation into the bill of the fundamental ingredients of the Wisconsin law. He was a principal architect of the Wagner-Lewis unemployment insurance bill of 1934, which included a tax credit device that the authors of the Social Security Act used to induce the states to establish unemployment compensation programs. He wrote the first model unemployment compensation bills the Committee on Economic Security distributed to governors and state legislatures during the drafting of the Social Security Act. After Social Security passed, Raushenbush was invited to head the unemployment compensation division of the Social Security Board, but, feeling that his work in Wisconsin was more important, he turned down the invitation.

Raushenbush was a vigorous and effective champion of state responsibility for unemployment compensation, and for more than three decades opposed all efforts to federalize it. At the same time, however, he worked to strengthen state programs through federal action. In 1939 he helped pass an amendment to the Social Security Act that required merit selection or civil service status for workers in unemployment compensation programs. During World War II he was a leader in the fight for the creation of a temporary federal loan fund to assist financially troubled programs. This, he believed, would allow the states to meet emergencies and blunt arguments that federalization was necessary to perpetuate benefits. The loan fund was made permanent in 1954.

Raushenbush was one of a group of Wisconsin-trained social insurance experts and administrators who were instrumental in creating the modern American system of social insurance and in establishing the machinery to administer it efficiently and humanely. Unlike the better known Altmeyer and Witte, Raushenbush chose to work at the state rather than the national level, and in Wisconsin he did his most significant work, helping to build one of the nation's best unemployment compensation programs. He died in Madison, Wisconsin, on January 17, 1980.

The private papers of Paul A. Raushenbush and Elizabeth Brandeis are on deposit at the State Historical Society of Wisconsin. Among Raushenbush's numerous polemical and technical writings, "The Wisconsin Idea: Unemployment Reserves," *Annals of the American Academy of Political and Social Science* (November, 1933), 65–75, provides a lucid discussion of the fundamental principles and the original provisions of the Wisconsin law; and "Unemployment

Compensation: Federal-State Cooperation," *National Municipal Review* (September, 1943), 423–431, presents his arguments against federalizing employment security programs. A Columbia University oral history done in 1966 with Raushenbush and Elizabeth Brandeis, and Paul A. Raushenbush, "Starting Unemployment Compensation in Wisconsin," *Unemployment Insurance Review* (April-May, 1967), 17–24, are the best sources on Raushenbush's role in the history of unemployment compensation. Daniel Nelson, *Unemployment Insurance: The American Experience, 1915–1935* (1969), is an excellent study of the background and early history of unemployment compensation legislation. Arthur J. Altmeyer, *The Formative Years of Social Security* (1966), contains the federalizing views of a professional foe and personal friend of Raushenbush. Raushenbush's son, Walter Raushenbush of Madison, Wisconsin, contributed information for this biography.

STANLEY MALLACH

**Reeder, Rudolph Rex** (January 5, 1859–October 13, 1934), educator and child welfare leader, was born in Lebanon, Ohio, the last of fifteen children of George W. and Jane (Thompson) Reeder. A farming family, the Reeders moved to central Illinois while Rudolph was a boy. Rudolph Reeder was married twice, first to Mary Hewett, with whom he had five children. After her death in 1919, he married Alma C. Haskins, a prominent figure in New York child welfare.

As a young man, Reeder displayed qualities of leadership, initiative, and self-discipline that were to become hallmarks of his philosophy of child welfare and education. He graduated from Illinois State Normal University in 1883, meanwhile acting as principal of public schools in Rutland, Illinois. He taught in the Model School at Illinois State Normal, 1883–1890, then taught psychology and reading at the same university, 1890–1893. After working for four years as secretary of the Overman Wheel Company, a bicycle manufacturing firm in Chicopee Falls, Massachusetts, he returned to do graduate work at Columbia University, receiving his Ph.D. in 1900.

Although Reeder had an active and diverse career, his primary interest and accomplishments were in the field of child welfare (or life-caring, as he sometimes called it). His career falls chronologically into three major phases. From 1900 to 1920 Reeder was superintendent of the New York Orphan Asylum. During and immediately after World War I, he served with the Red Cross and Herbert Hoover's American Relief Commission in Europe. After the war, the trustees of the Marsh Foundation School in Van Wert, Ohio, hired him as the first director of that institution. Throughout his career, Reeder developed and disseminated, through activity in professional organizations and publications, his philosophy of child welfare.

When Reeder assumed the superintendency of the New York Orphan Asylum, it was a traditional, dormitory-style institution in Manhattan. Two years later the orphanage moved to Hastings on the Hudson River. There, in a rural, cottage-structured setting, Reeder developed and applied his approach to the care of dependent children. Reeder's approach to child care was holistic. He emphasized proper diet, training in work skills, respect for society and law, and participatory rather than force-fed education. On such principles, and on love as an expression of honor and affection, he believed healthy individuals and a harmonious society would develop. Active in both state and national charities and corrections organizations, he was, in 1909, one of 200 persons invited to the first White House Conference on Dependent Children.

In 1918 Reeder served with the American Red Cross in Lorraine, France. He later recalled that his greatest challenge to motivate youth as a group came while organizing successfully a clean-up campaign of the miserable sanitary conditions of the children's quarters in that war-ravaged city.

After the war, Reeder served as an official of the American Relief Commission in Serbia. He organized the hospitalization of children, directed the reconstruction of over 100 village schools, and drew up a program whereby thousands of orphans were placed in the homes of Serbian families rather than in institutions. His rationale was that home life, whenever possible, was superior to that offered by even the best institutions. In homes, the great army of war orphans would merge into all the interests and activities of the community, and would, he believed, contribute to and share in the returning prosperity of the country.

His work in Serbia completed, Reeder returned to the Unites States. The Serbian experience convinced him that a home, no matter how humble, was preferable to any orphan asylum. He proposed that American orphan asylums be converted into clearing houses to which children would be admitted for temporary care, then, whenever feasible, placed in foster homes.

Reeder's last position, however, was as director of a children's institution. In 1919 George H. Marsh, a Van Wert, Ohio, businessman, provided, through his will, 1,400 acres and several million dollars to establish a home and school for disadvantaged children. Reeder was hired as director of the institution, known as the Marsh Foundation School, on July 15, 1922, and retired on June 1, 1933.

Reeder conducted the Marsh Foundation School on the principles he had developed at Hastings-on-Hudson, and which guided his work in Europe. As reflected in his book, *Training Youth for the New Social Order* (1933), he came to emphasize group thinking as the means of social progress. His aim was to protect and nurture the individuality of the child while developing group thinking and leadership. The program at the Marsh Foundation School, he asserted, was concerned less with preparing for life than with living a life that prepares. In 1930 Reeder participated in the third White House Conference on Children and Youth, calling its Children's Charter of seventeen basic rights of the child the Magna Charta of American childhood. He died of pneumonia in 1934 at his home at Quaker Hill, a suburb of Pawling, New York.

There are on file at the Marsh Foundation a number of typed memoranda of staff meetings that provide an excellent view of Reeder's methods and style of leadership.

Reeder's two books, *How Two Hundred Children Live and Learn* (1909), and *Training Youth for the New Social Order* (1933), are indispensable for an understanding of his theory and practice regarding child care. Brief introductions to Reeder's ideas in the earlier and later periods of his career are in his articles, "Study of the Child from the Institutional Standpoint," *Proceedings*, National Conference of Charities and Correction (1907), 265–273, and "Children's Institutions: Principles," *Social Forces*, vol. 4 (1925–1926), 92–93.

An obituary of Reeder is in the *New York Times*, October 14, 1934, and one of his second wife is in the *New York Times*, July 6, 1950. Reeder's career while at Hastings-on-Hudson Orphanage may be followed by referring to the yearly *Proceedings* of the New York State Conference of Charities and Correction.

PAUL C. BOWERS, JR.

**Regan, Agnes Gertrude** (March 26, 1869–September 30, 1943), educator and organizer, was born in San Francisco, California, the third daughter and the fourth of nine children of James Regan and Mary Ann (Morrison) Regan. Her father was born in Valparaiso, Chile, son of an Irish father and an English mother. He came to California in 1849 and worked first in the gold mines. For ten years he was private secretary to Joseph S. Alemany, first Catholic archbishop of San Francisco. He also was a director of the Hibernia Bank, one of whose founders was his brother-in-law, Richard Tobin. Agnes Regan's mother was a member of an Irish family that migrated to America in 1847. Following their marriage in 1863, the Regans moved to Chile but soon returned to San Francisco. Mary Ann Regan was a charitable person who did much to help her neighbors. While James Regan was not wealthy, there was sufficient income to provide a comfortable standard of living and to enjoy the best in operas, plays, and concerts. The good taste and interest in cultural matters and the warmth and hospitality that characterized Agnes Regan were part of her early heritage. The Regans were devout Catholics, and two of their daughters became nuns.

After completing grade and high school at St. Rose Academy, Agnes Regan attended San Francisco Normal School, graduating with a life certificate in 1887. For over thirty years she served in the San Francisco school system as a teacher, principal, and, from 1914 to 1919, member of the board of education (part of the time as president). She was a member of the City Playground Commission and of the Advisory Committee of the Associated Charities. Cooperating with Hiram Johnson, then Governor of California, she helped secure passage of the state's first teachers' pension law. Her second career began in 1920 when Archbishop Edward J. Hanna appointed her to represent the archdiocese of San Francisco at the organizational meeting in Washington, D.C., of the National Council of Catholic Women (NCCW). She was elected second vice president of the board of directors and soon after received the appointment as first executive secretary of the Council, a position she held from 1920 until 1941, when ill health forced her resignation. In 1921 the Council assumed responsibility for the National Catholic School of Social Service (NCSSS), successor to a school established in World War I to train women for welfare and reconstruction work at home and abroad. Regan joined the faculty in 1922 as an instructor in community organization, became assistant director in 1925, and served as acting director from 1935 to 1937. She continued her work as executive secretary of the NCCW, dividing her time between the two organizations. There was a close connection between them since the Council, at the request of the American hierarchy had undertaken the sponsorship of the school in recognition of the need to provide, under Catholic auspices, professional education for women in the fast-developing field of social work. The Catholic University of America, which had been invited to take over the school, had refused to do so, since at the time it did not enroll women students. However, in 1923 an affiliation was arranged through which students at NCSSS could earn a master's degree from the Department of Sociology.

The programs of both the NCSSS and the National Council of Catholic Women had many novel features. A Catholic residential school offering graduate-level work and sponsored by lay women was unique. So was an organization which federated existing Catholic women's groups all the way from the parish to the national level. For Agnes Regan, the school and the Council became the vehicles through which she could give substance to her ideals for trained leadership and united action on the part of Catholic lay women. In both organizations her work was strongly influenced by such leaders as John Burke, the Paulist priest whose vision led to the establishment of the National Catholic Welfare Conference (today's United States Catholic Conference), John A. Ryan,* director of its Social Action Department and a member of the school's faculty, and William J. Kerby,* professor of sociology at the Catholic University and for several years acting director of the NCSSS. The National Council of Catholic Women served as a channel between the other departments of the National Catholic Welfare Conference and the Catholic women of the country. Information and service from the Washington office went out to local groups, helping them to develop and strengthen their programs and coordinate their efforts with those of other Catholic women. Reciprocally, through the diocesan councils of Catholic women, the departments of the National Catholic Welfare Conference were given knowledge of the needs of the Catholic laity throughout the country.

Organizing the NCCW involved not only establishing a headquarters in Washington but traveling throughout the country interpreting the new organization and its program to bishops and priests as well as to lay women. Agnes Regan acted on the conviction that Catholic women had obligations extending beyond their local interests. Through its affiliated organizations the Council provided Americanization training and aid to immigrants, supported religious vocational schools in rural areas, met the needs of working girls for housing and protective services, organized study clubs, kept its members informed about pending legislation, and established scholarships and other support for the National Catholic School of Social Service. Regan believed that one of the most important tasks of the NCCW was to keep its members well informed on federal and state legislation and to educate them to carry out their social and civic responsibilities.

She herself appeared before congressional committees to advocate or protest against pending legislation. She supported the proposed child labor amendment to the Constitution in spite of opposition to it by many Catholics, including the cardinal and archbishop of Boston. She spoke against the equal rights amendment and various birth control measures and testified in favor of federal housing legislation. The NCCW was one of the sponsors of a national conference in Washington in 1920 held to consider race problems, and Regan herself gave strong support to the education and advancement of Blacks and Hispanics. In 1928 the NCCW joined with the YWCA, the National Council of Jewish Women, and the Women's Industrial League in effective support for a change in restrictive immigration laws which were causing hardships to families. NCCW was represented at meetings of other national organizations, and Regan for many years was a member of the board of the Washington affiliate of the National Travelers' Aid Society. Under her leadership the NCCW was affiliated with the International Union of Catholic Women's Leagues and was frequently represented at the meetings of other international organizations. Her interest in international cooperation was also reflected in the NCSSS, where foreign students, particularly those from Latin American countries, were given scholarships whenever possible. The school itself became a model for the establishment of Catholic schools of social work in some of these countries.

Under the leadership of Agnes Regan, for twenty-five years the NCCW carried the increasingly heavy financial responsibility for the school of social service, a responsibility which ended in 1947 when NCSSS merged with the university's own school of social work. In the meantime, Regan's conviction of the importance of the mission of NCSSS never wavered, and her faith sustained directors, faculty, board members, and others in periods of crisis. When money was in short supply she did not accept a salary, and she willed the bulk of her modest estate to the school. When the school was threatened with suspension of its membership in the American Association of Schools of Social Work because of inadequacies in faculty and administration, Regan, acting director at the time, faced the situation, rallied substantial help from two former directors, and through their joint efforts found a new director who immediately undertook a program of reorganization that led the school into one of its most productive periods. Not herself a professional social worker, she was determined that the school should provide the best scientific knowledge and technique based on Christian philosophy. The National Council of Catholic Women she regarded as the instrument for carrying out this mission. In the early years of the NCSSS there was the expectation that some of its graduates would be prepared for positions of leadership in the Council. While a number did serve in this role, the majority found employment in the usual range of social agencies.

Agnes Regan was well qualified for the leadership she gave to both the National Council of Catholic Women and the National Catholic School of Social Service. She was a handsome, vigorous woman with social poise and a personality characterized by a vital interest in life, a balancing sense of humor, and a profoundly religious spirit. She was an able speaker and had unusual talent for organization. By the time she retired as executive secretary, there were 64 diocesan councils, 18 national organizations of lay women, and 3,500 local organizations affiliated with the NCCW. Not an outstanding classroom teacher, she served best in her relationships with students on an individual basis, and many of them sought her out for personal counseling. The fact that the school was a residential institution gave it a homelike atmosphere which Regan encouraged. Alumnae were invited to come back for visits, especially on holidays when they might be unable to be with their own families. She was a gifted correspondent, and her letters to women in the Council and to school alumnae reveal her affection and concern for the individual as well as her gentle humor and her practical wisdom.

She died on September 30, 1943, where she had lived during all her years in Washington, at the National Catholic School of Social Service.

The principal manuscript sources on Agnes Regan are in the Archives of the Mullen Library and at the National Catholic School of Social Service, both at the Catholic University of America in Washington, D.C. The texts or excerpts from her speeches and annual reports relating to the National Council of Catholic Women and the National Catholic School of Social Service were published in the *NCWC Bulletin*, the *NCWC Review*, *Catholic Action*, *NCWC Annual Reports*, and the NCWC *Monthly Message*. These publications are available in the Mullen Library.

The most informative secondary work is Loretta Lawler's *Full Circle: The Story of the National Catholic School of Social Service, 1918–1947* (1951). See also Aaron I. Abell, *American Catholicism and Social Action: A Search for Social Justice, 1865–1950* (1960); Francis L. Broderick, *Right Reverend New Dealer: John A. Ryan* (1963); *Notable American Women, 1607–1950*, vol. 3 (1971); John A. Ryan, *Eulogy—Agnes G. Regan* (n.d.); Robert Trisco, ed., *Catholicism in America, 1776–1976* (1976); *Dictionary of American Biography*, Supplement 3, 1941–1945 (1973); and *New Catholic Encyclopedia*, vol. 12 (1967).

Additional information was obtained from a niece, Mother M. Justin, and from Clara Bradley, a friend and colleague.

                                                                DOROTHY A. MOHLER

**Reynolds, Bertha Capen** (December 11, 1885–October 28, 1978), educator, author, social work practitioner, and seminal thinker in the field of social work, was born in Brockton, Massachusetts, to Mary (Capen) Reynolds, a secondary school teacher of Latin and chemistry, and Franklin Reynolds, an organ builder and tuner. Her family, whose ancestors were among the earliest settlers of the Plymouth and Massachusetts Bay Colonies, was well acquainted with hardship and loss: two siblings died before Reynolds was born, and her father died from tuberculosis when she was only two years old. She had to work hard to gain acceptance from her mother, a cold and exacting woman who nonetheless gave her a firm foundation in the values of intellectual discipline and professional achievement.

In addition, the Methodist Church in Stoughton, Massachusetts, where she was brought up, offered Reynolds a strong sense of the hope of spiritual fulfillment and purpose that was to remain with her throughout her life. Looking for the path to salvation, her mission in life was "to do good." Her religious and moral life clustered around the traditional New England ideals of self-sacrifice and self-examination. These same values provided her with a source of strength from which she was to speak out for human rights and social justice throughout her career.

In 1904, after graduating from Girls High in Boston, Reynolds entered Smith College. Four years later, at age 23, she held a B.A. degree, a Phi Beta Kappa key, and a "determination to save the world," which led her to a teaching job in the High School Department of Atlanta University, an all black school. Exposed there to the ideas of W. E. B. DuBois,* the well known militant black educator and leader, she began to understand the harsh realities of injustice and exploitation suffered by black Americans. However, she suffered what then was called "nervous prostration," and returned home. Acting on the advice of Dr. James Putnam, the notable Freudian psychiatrist, she attended and obtained a certificate from the Boston School for Social Workers at Simmons College (1912–1913).

Particularly sensitive to the dilemmas of social work and social workers because of the difficulties and demands of her religiously conditioned conscience and family life, Reynolds then secured a job as placing-out-visitor for the Boston Children's Aid Society (1914–1918). Her first monograph, *The Selection of Foster Homes for Children* (1919), based upon that experience, presaged future professional concerns for assessment as a complex transactional phenomenon: Reynolds presented a view of natural family life as a dynamic interactional social system.

Meanwhile, following eight months of intensive psychiatric training at the Smith College School for Social Work in 1918, Reynolds became a psychiatric social worker at Danvers (Massachusetts) State Hospital. But she began to challenge the "medical model" and its notion of patient cure. She believed that patients need to learn how to cope with the inner and outer tensions in their lives. When she went to work for the Massachusetts Department of Mental Hygiene Habit Clinic in 1923, Reynolds wrote a number of articles that revealed not only her interest in mobilizing environments to facilitate positive adaptations, but her respect for the client's innate potentialities and strengths.

After hearing Reynolds deliver an impressive paper on "The Mental Hygiene of Young Children" at the National Conference of Social Work in Toronto in 1924, Dr. Everett Kimball, Director of the Smith College School for Social Work, offered her the job of Associate Director, which Reynolds quickly accepted. Reynolds' educational philosophy was consistent with her practical philosophy of growth. She called for the education of "whole persons rather than disembodied intellects." Her commitment to educating the spiritual, intellectual, and social aspects of students was reflected in the popular Sunday evening discussion groups she held on the philosophical meaning of religion and life.

However, for Reynolds, as for many progressive intellectual leaders in the thirties, the Great Depression served as a catalyst in her search for radical political solutions to the plight of the poor. She found a "science of society" in Marxist ideology that complemented the "science" of person-in-environment of social work; her views of social work, in other words, became intertwined with her political views on the social order. In her bold book *Between Client and Community* (1934) she identified a fundamental conflict in the profession of social work: the social worker cannot serve people when the social service system is dependent upon the economic resources of a propertied class (whose interest is in maintaining the status quo of the socioeconomic structure). Her open support for unionization of social workers and her involvement in movements of the left created an irreconcilable rift in her relationship with Dean Kimball. Even Plan D, her attempt to develop a broadened advanced program for post-masters degree social workers, failed to bridge the gap between them.

Thus, in August, 1937, Bertha Reynolds left Smith College. For several years, her reputation as a teacher and a consultant brought her opportunities for "free-lance" work. When these slackened she continued to write searching articles for *Social Work Today*, a radical journal (1934–1942), and the masterful book *Learning and Teaching in the Practice of Social Work* (1942). Although "left wing" and union colleagues arranged for her to give lectures and seminars around the country, by the end of 1942 Reynolds essentially was unemployed. The social work profession turned away from the political arena for the solution of its problems and Reynolds was isolated from it.

An opportunity to work closely with workers in the labor movement came to her in 1943 when she was asked to be the United Seamens' Service Representative in the Personal Service Department of the National Maritime Union. This innovative program served as a prototype for social work in unions. Her book *Social Work and Social Living* (1951) and her significant article "Advance or Retreat for Private Family Service" (1948) were stimulated by her work in the National Maritime Union, in which social services were a democratically controlled function of its users.

In 1947 a series of political and ideological upheavals within the union, resulting from the onset of the Cold War and what later would be called "McCarthyism," led to the termination of the personal social service program. Unable to find other work in her field, Reynolds went into early retirement, at the age of sixty-two, returning to the family homestead in Stoughton, Massachusetts. For the next thirty years, however, she continued to maintain contact with colleagues, and to think and write about professional, philosophical, and ethical issues. She remained active with such groups as the United Office and Professional Workers of America and the Social Service Volunteers for Peace, and wrote many articles on a variety of matters. One of her most provocative papers, "From Mass to Individual," indicating the sweep and depth of her Marxist approach to social work, was delivered at the Jefferson School for Marxist Studies in 1956. Her last book, the autobiographical *An Unchartered Journey*, an important critical commentary on the history of social work from the point of view of one of its foremost pioneers, was published in 1963 through the efforts of loyal colleagues and friends.

At Stoughton, Reynolds—the woman ahead of her times, the maverick who had critically approached social work theory and practice from the radical perspective—centered her social life and found intellectual stimulation in the Methodist Church. Openly stating her Marxist views, she participated in dialogues with various ministers on the divergent and congruent ideologies of Marxism and Christianity, culminating her ideas in a series of essays, "Where Do You Get Your Ethics From?," written over a period of four years when she was in her eighties. Those essays, on the ethics of Christianity and dialectical materialism, were the final contributions to the rich heritage of creative and integrative scholarly writing Reynolds left to the profession of social work. She died in Stoughton, Massachusetts, in 1978, at the age of ninety-three.

The most comprehensive collection of primary and secondary material on Reynolds is the Bertha Capen Reynolds Collection at the Sophia Smith Women's History Archives, Smith College, Northampton, Massachusetts. This collection includes published and unpublished papers and manuscripts, records of institutes and speeches, personal correspondence, and autobiographical and biographical material. Another source of informal papers and correspondence is at The American Institute for Marxist Studies, New York. See also Reynolds' own writings, especially her books, *The Selection of Foster Homes for Children* (1919), *Learning and Teaching in the Practice of Social Work* (1965), *Social Work and Social Living* (1951), and *An Unchartered Journey* (1963).

Most recent interest in Reynolds is indicated by two dissertations, Joan Goldstein, "Bertha C. Reynolds—Gentle Radical (D.S.W. dissertation, Wurzweiler School of Social Work, 1981); and Sharon M. Freedberg, "Bertha Capen Reynolds—A Woman Struggling in Her Times" (D.S.W. dissertation, Columbia University School of Social Work, 1984). For additional information on Reynolds see L. Ann Hartman, "Casework in Crisis 1932–1941," chapters 4 and 5 (D.S.W. dissertation, Columbia University School of Social Work, 1972); and Louise Bandler, "Bertha Capen Reynolds: Social Worker of All Times," *Journal of Education for Social Work* 15 (Fall, 1979), 5–11; Carel Germain and L. Ann Hartman, "People and Ideas in the History of Social Work Practice," *Social Casework* 61 (June, 1980), 324–33; Yvonne Cullen, "An Alternative Tradition in Social Work: Bertha Capen Reynolds, 1985–1978," *Catalyst* 4 (1983), 55–73.

SHARON M. FREEDBERG and JOAN L. GOLDSTEIN

**Reynolds, James B.** (March 17, 1861–January 1, 1924), settlement house resident and social and political reformer, was born in Kiantone, New York, to Reverend William T. Reynolds, a Congregational minister, and Sarah Maria (Painter) Reynolds. Ancestors of the family emigrated from Cheshire, England, and lived in West Haven, Connecticut, from the time of the American Revolution.

Reynolds prepared for college in Connecticut schools and earned his B.A. from Yale University in 1884. At Yale he was a class deacon. Deacons were elected by students in recognition of religious zeal to lead religious services. Reynolds also worked for the Yale branch of the Young Men's Christian Association (YMCA) and served in a New Haven church mission.

For a year after graduation Reynolds toured Europe and took courses at several European universities. On his return to the United States he attended Yale Divinity School and resumed his YMCA activities. He graduated from divinity school in 1888 but was not ordained a minister. Reynolds' first position was as the representative of the College YMCA of the United States to European universities. His duties were to promote and to encourage cooperation among Protestant student associations. European student concern about urban-industrial social ills, however, convinced Reynolds of the importance of social betterment. But for the next two years he was inactive because of illness.

In 1894 prominent trustees of Columbia University–affiliated University Settlement Society recruited Reynolds to replace Stanton Coit* as director. From May 1, 1894, to January 1, 1902, Reynolds worked in a piecemeal way for social improvement on New York City's Lower East Side. He held several municipal positions, such as public school trustee. Later, he joined the reform struggle to replace the trustee system with a centralized board. He was also appointed to identify sites for several parks and afterwards joined the Outdoor Recreation League. In 1900 Governor Theodore Roosevelt appointed him to the Tenement House Commission. University Settlement also pioneered in voluntary probation work and publicized the need for equal legal protection of the poor. But most of all, the Reynolds administration transformed University Settlement in 1898 from a small-scale tenement facility into a new and expanded urban social service and social research center. The center paid some of its staff members and provided settlement fellowships to encourage college students to become involved in social work.

Of the several strands of social settlement community action, Reynolds' expertise was in the field of social investigation. He placed his faith in research, facts, and public enlightenment as vital tools to social improvement. Much of Reynolds' standing in social work circles, moreover, derived from his roles as an expert and as an advisor to political elites on public policy. Reynolds supervised University Settlement's interpretation of its predominantly Jewish district in reports which were published annually by the Settlement. Data and testimony were given to special commissions and legislative bodies such as the Tenement House Commissions of 1894 and 1900. Reynolds recognized the adverse impact of the tenement environment, but also described the urban poor as handicapped by moral and intellectual deficiencies.

Reynolds was a leader among early social workers in taking the struggle for social improvement into municipal political campaigns. He encouraged other settlement houses to help defeat corrupt political bosses who frustrated social betterment and undermined political democracy. Reynolds fought Tammany Hall on the Lower East Side with such zeal that he sometimes had to be restrained by Settlement trustees. He became a sophisticated politician on the ward level and even copied the methods of the bosses by using welfare-type measures in his appeal to lower-income voters in his district political club. Reynolds also participated in several good-government associations such as the Committee of Seventy of 1893, and helped organize the Citizens' Union of 1897.

In 1898 Reynolds began to drift away from the social settlement. To begin with, he married Florence Blanchard Dike, daughter of a wealthy New York City family. In addition, he studied law at New York University and was admitted to the bar in 1900; but he did not practice law until 1909. In the intervening years, he played a larger part in politics. Reynolds was especially effective behind the scenes and used his organizational skill to help his close friend, philanthropist Seth Low, win the New York City mayoral campaign of 1901. As Low's secretary, Reynolds was a conduit for social work projects and helped enlarge the public welfare functions of New York City government.

Reynolds also had close ties to President Theodore Roosevelt and served as an informal advisor. In addition, Roosevelt appointed him special advisor on municipal affairs in the District of Columbia. Reynolds also served on different special commissions that dealt with such matters as the consular service in Asia, labor conditions in Panama, the immigration service, and the Chicago stockyards. In the aftermath of the stockyards investigation, Reynolds helped influence public opinion in support of a legislative remedy.

During the Progressive Era Reynolds participated in several of the national-level organizations formed by social workers. Reynolds helped organize the National Playground Association of America in 1906. He also participated in the strategy sessions held in 1911 by social workers with national reputations who favored the creation of an industrial commission. Involvement in social betterment, however, was mainly from the angle of preventive reform. Reynolds helped form the National Vigilance Association and later served as counsel to that organization and to the American Social Hygiene Association. Reynolds was also among the minority of social settlement personnel who favored immigration restriction. He served as vice president of the Immigration Restriction League. Criminal justice reform was another concern. He was a member of the executive board of the National Prison Association and president of the American Institute of Criminal Law and Criminology. Reynolds died in North Haven, Connecticut, in 1924.

The James B. Reynolds Papers are included in the University Settlement Society Papers of New York, which are located at the State Historical Society of Wisconsin. The Reynolds Papers deal mainly with his municipal political activities in the 1890s. The Settlement Society Papers have internal reports and other items about Reynolds as director.

Reynolds wrote about the social settlement and social betterment in "Report of the Headworker," *University Settlement Society of New York, Annual Report* (1894–1901); "Commercial Relations of the Poor," *Yale Review* (May, 1896), 76–84; "The Settlement and Social Reform," *Proceedings of the National Conference of Charities and Correction* (1896), 138–142; and "The Need and Value of Settlement Work," *Proceedings of the First New York State Conference of Charities and Correction, 1900* (1901), 49–55. Reynolds expressed his concern for preventive measures in "The Peril of City Loneliness," *Literary Digest* (February 3, 1912), 215–216; and "Prostitution in Europe—The Failure of Licensing and the Medical Inspection," *American City* (February, 1914), 155–156.

Charles B. Stover's *James Bronson Reynolds, March 17, 1861-January 1, 1924: A Memorial* (1927) has a brief outline of Reynolds' career and reprints of some articles and addresses. A comprehensive profile of Reynolds is in the files of the Yale University Alumni Records Office.

JOHN J. CAREY

**Richmond, Mary Ellen** (August 5, 1861–September 12, 1928), social work administrator, researcher, and author, was born in Belleville, Illinois, to Henry Richmond, a carriage blacksmith, and Lavinia (Harris) Richmond, who soon returned to their home city of Baltimore. Mary's mother died of tuberculosis when she was three years old, and she was brought up by her widowed maternal grandmother, Mehitabel Harris, and two maiden aunts.

The grandmother operated a rooming house in a lower-middle-class neighborhood. Other family members, factory workers and painters, lived nearby. Spiritualism and discussion of "radical" post-Civil War issues—woman's suffrage, Negro status, compulsory education, political reform—were a part of daily life. At the age of sixteen, after six years of formal schooling, Mary graduated from the rigorously academic Baltimore Eastern Female High School.

Two years in a routine clerical job in a New York City publishing house specializing in tracts for radical and unorthodox causes were the loneliest, most frustrating period of her life. Illness forced her back to bookkeeping jobs in Baltimore, but there she also led literary and social programs at the Unitarian church.

In 1889 Mary Richmond became assistant treasurer of the Baltimore Charity Organization Society (COS), part of a reform movement to systematize and improve the practices of relief agencies. She worked closely with prominent community leaders in public relations and fund-raising. She reviewed the latest philanthropic literature with the blind president of the organization, John Glenn.*

In 1891 she became the agency executive, a position usually held by an advanced Ph.D. candidate.

As she supervised volunteer workers, she recognized that in some cases judicious financial aid contributed to the rehabilitation of needy persons. Inconsistent volunteer performance, however, made it hard to validate this departure from the traditional COS doctrine that all financial help led to pauperism. Thus she introduced training classes "for the study of charitable work in the homes of the poor." Also, while still a strong believer in volunteers, she nevertheless used an increasing number of paid workers, whom she found more effective than most volunteers in investigating and handling difficult cases.

As she sought reasons for variations in accomplishment between cases and between workers, her associations with leaders of the Johns Hopkins Medical School persuaded her that professional training was needed for treatment of the personality disorders then thought to lead to pauperism. In 1897 she advocated the establishment of a professional training school, and then she taught in it when the New York COS Summer School of Philanthropy—the first of its kind in America—was established in 1898.

Meanwhile, her practical and theoretical orientations found expression in her society's annual reports and, beginning in 1894, the *Baltimore Charities Record*. These became intellectual stimuli for COS leaders throughout the country. Organizational and administrative skills stood out in agency manuals; teaching skills were evident in *Friendly Visiting Among the Poor* (1899). She thought much about the reasons for detailed social study (investigation) and the use of personal and community resources in improving the life of individual families. Her journal articles and participation at the National Conference of Charities and Correction established her national reputation.

She left the highly organized Baltimore COS in 1900 to go to the Philadelphia Society for Organizing Charity, a disorganized confederation of autonomous, often competing "districts." By aggressive leadership she overcame deep-seated resistance to centralized agency administration. She used a training class to develop a core of new district staff leaders at the same time that she ended independent district fund-raising. She herself proved a skilled fund-raiser and program interpreter. A display of her printed materials at the National Conference led to a regular exchange of information on casework, administration, and fund-raising in the columns of *Charities*. Later, as the Field Department of *Charities and the Commons* with Richmond as editor, this stimulated experimentation and research and contributed to a growing sense of cohesiveness among the scattered COS agencies.

She also was active in artistic and other cultural activities. She also recognized and promoted measures to deal with community needs outside the scope of her agency, either through legislation (on compulsory education and child labor) or through the establishment of new agencies and services. This comprehensive view took literary form in *The Good Neighbor in the Modern City* (1907), which explained how citizens could use a well-developed and organized set of agencies to improve the community. She began to influence generations of future social work leaders by teaching short courses at the University of Pennsylvania and at the developing schools of social work in New York and Boston as well.

In 1909 she made a final move—to the Russell Sage Foundation in New York as director of the Charity Organization Department. This pioneering foundation, at that time the largest to stimulate and underwrite social innovation, still was feeling its way in program development. Richmond's Baltimore associate, John M. Glenn, was director, and was encouraged to develop the department by Robert de Forest,* executor of the Sage estate and a strong supporter of the New York COS. The Field Department came under Russell Sage's province, where it remained under Richmond's supervision. However, with special staff to expand this service for COS organizations, it was separately incorporated in 1911 as the American Association for Organizing Charity.

Richmond devoted major attention to research and teaching, testing and refining her ideas in formal and informal staff discussions with specialists from the other departments representing a variety of fields. She was specially interested in the family and in casework to deal with problem situations. With her assistant, Fred Hall, she made a series of studies of marriage and broken families. She also edited the Social Work Series, including *What Is Social Case Work?* (1922), in which she articulated the processes and rationale of casework and placed them within the wider field of social work. These studies were overshadowed, however, by her path-breaking earlier work, *Social Diagnosis* (1917). Here she presented the results of extensive field testing of methods of investigating and studying cases, listing assets and liabilities leading to a medical type of "diagnosis" on the basis of which treatment might be undertaken. There had been nothing comparable for the emerging social work profession. It immediately became, and for two decades remained, the dominant textbook in the field. She projected a study of social treatment but never brought it to conclusion.

Richmond's impact on social work practice and education went far beyond her writings. From 1910 to 1922 she conducted invitational summer institutes on various practice issues. Young, innovative workers shared in these intensive seminars and went on to become some of the most noted among the next generation of social work leaders. The basic scheme of social work education, classroom instruction in theory and methods combined with supervised field experience, was laid down by her in 1897 and then vigorously defended when challenged. From Russell Sage she directed subsidies to schools which met her criteria, and she influenced field teaching through the annual conferences she led for student supervisors and agency executives, beginning in 1915. She emphasized the case method of teaching and kept herself in touch with practice by chairing the case committee for a New York COS district used as a model in training and experimentation. Her violent opposition to any form of public relief in the client's home was reflected in the curricula of most schools.

Her forceful personality won her support in important places. Plagued with ill health from childhood, she was impatient with those who were less able to cope, as seen in her opposition to public widows' pensions. An effective fundraiser for her agencies, she fought the community chest movement. She operated from a secure position, but the opposition she had generated found expression in her devastating defeat for president of the National Conference of Social Work in 1922 by Homer Folks,* who was nominated by petition. This dulled the great satisfaction she had received when, in 1921, despite not having attended college, she had been granted an honorary degree by Smith College. Her last public appearance was at the 1927 Family Welfare Association of America meeting, where she gave the address which provided the title for her collected papers. After a long illness, she died in New York City the following year.

The Mary E. Richmond Archives of the Columbia University School of Social Work contain personal scrapbooks, correspondence, and research notes. Much material is also in the archives of the organizations where she was employed. Joanna C. Colcord and Ruth Z.S. Mann, eds., *The Long View* (1930), contains all her major papers and a complete bibliography of her publications and of those she edited, with biographical introductions to each professional period. A memorial issue of the *Family* (February, 1929) contains eulogistic descriptions by her associates.

Biographical and evaluative materials are found in Margaret Rich, "Mary E. Richmond, Social Worker," *Social Casework* (November, 1952); Muriel W. Pumphrey, "Mary Richmond and the Rise of Professional Social Work in Baltimore" (Ph.D. dissertation, Columbia University School of Social Work, 1956); *Social Casework* (May, 1973), which includes four articles evaluating the influence of Richmond's work, given in a symposium commemorating the fiftieth anniversary of *What Is Social Case Work?*; Patricia Drew, *A Longer View: The Mary E. Richmond Legacy* (1983); Peggy Pittman-Munke, "Mary Richmond, the Hidden Years: Philadelphia, 1900–1909," Ph.D. dissertation in progress, Worden School of Social Service, Our Lady of the Lake University of San Antonio.

MURIEL W. PUMPHREY

**Riis, Jacob August** (May 3, 1849–May 26, 1914), publicist and humanitarian reformer, was born in Ribe, Denmark, the third of fourteen children of Niels Edward Riis, a senior master at Ribe Latin School, and Carolina Riis, a homemaker whose hospitality ensured that the Riis home was often filled with guests.

While Jacob Riis' parents stressed the importance of education and hoped that their son would pursue a literary or professional career, Jacob did not like formal schooling. He preferred fishing in the nearby Nibs River, catching sparrows, ice skating, and other outdoor recreations. Throughout his life, Riis would remember the opportunities afforded for creative play in the desolate and open fields and sand dunes on the outskirts of his small, cold, and neighborly hometown. Jacob Riis' childhood was also filled with loss (only three of the fourteen children survived past adolescence), genteel poverty, and work as a carpenter's apprentice after school, beginning in 1865.

Jacob Riis spent the next few years in Copenhagen learning the carpentry trade; he returned to Ribe in 1868 and found no employment as a carpenter, realized that his opportunities in his homeland were limited, and decided to immigrate to the United States in 1870. From 1870 to 1877 Riis wandered through several northeastern and midwestern states looking for work. This prolonged exposure to poverty and hard work at a variety of labor, sales, and newspaper jobs prepared him well for his eventual vocations as star newspaper reporter, activist reformer, and crusading lecturer. He returned to his native Denmark in 1875 to marry his childhood sweetheart, Elisabeth Nielsen. After Jacob Riis had left Denmark, she had become engaged to marry a minor military officer, who then died; shortly thereafter, Riis returned to his hometown to ask her to become his wife. They had five children.

After Riis returned to America with his young wife, they settled in New York City. In 1877 Riis became a reporter for the *New York Tribune*; he worked up to fifteen hours a day covering stories with which other more established reporters did not want to be bothered. This arduous apprenticeship gave Riis the opportunity to become familiar with the variety of neighborhoods, ethnic groups, problems, and living conditions which constituted his adopted land's largest and most diversified metropolis. In 1890 Riis became a reporter for the *Evening Sun* and was active as a crusading reformer. He was particularly active in his crusades against slum housing and the spirit of greed which often helped to perpetuate slums. His most effective reform efforts, however, were in the field of child welfare; he was a strong advocate of city playgrounds, "fresh air" camps for poor children forced to live in tenement housing, the establishment of settlement houses, and the promotion of the public school as a meeting place for citizens of different classes who could work together to promote the common good. Riis' personal and reportorial experiences, coupled with the public's desire to understand their changing and growing metropolitan environment, prompted him to produce a book in 1890 about the life of the poor, the immigrant neighborhoods, the delinquent children, and other outcasts of society entitled *How the Other Half Lives: Studies Among the Tenements of New York*.

The values which permeated Riis' written work, speeches, and reform efforts were largely compatible with those professed by many Americans, then and now—for example, the work ethic, the importance of family in shaping human behavior, the necessity for clean and peaceful environments to promote healthy human growth and development, the value of an education which prepares its consumers for good citizenship and adequate incomes, a romantic view of rural living (as contrasted with the impersonality and roughness of urban life), the power of the human will to overcome most obstacles when given the opportunity to do so, the importance of children as makers of the nation's future, the moral imperative for citizens of different classes to voluntarily work together to help the less fortunate, and the obligation of the government to help those whose resources and powerlessness require public intervention. What distinguished Riis from most of his contemporaries was his ability to vividly communicate these values and the necessity to implement them in a variety of specific problematic situations. His genuine concern for the poor and stigmatized and his ability to formulate practical plans for combating difficult social problems combined to help him become one of the nation's most persuasive advocates for social reform.

At the time of his death, Jacob Riis was mourned by his friend of over twenty years, Theodore Roosevelt, by his friend and admirer, Jane Addams,* and by thousands of immigrants and reformers who were moved by his persuasive appeals to build a more just and democratic society. He died on May 26, 1914, at his recently purchased farm in Barre, Massachusetts.

Manuscript collections include the Jacob A. Riis Miscellaneous File and Jacob A. Riis Papers at the New York Public Library, New York, New York; the Jacob A. Riis Papers at the Russell Sage Library, City College of New York, New York; and the Jacob A. Riis Papers at the Library of Congress, Washington, D.C., Manuscript Division.

Important books by Jacob Riis include *How the Other Half Lives* (1890); *The Battle with the Slum* (1902); *Children of the Tenements* (1903); *The Making of an American* (1904); and *The Old Town* (1909).

The definitive biography is *Jacob A. Riis and the American City* (1974), by James B. Lane. Roy Lubove's *The Progressives and the Slum* (1962), chap. 3, is also quite helpful.

ROBERT M. HENDRICKSON

**Rippin, Jane Parker Deeter** (May 30, 1882–June 2, 1953), teacher, school administrator, court system reformer, women and girls' (wartime) welfare program innovator, social worker, Girl Scout executive, journalist, and researcher, was born in Harrisburg, Pennsylvania, to Jasper Newton and Sarah Emely (Mather) Deeter. The five Deeter children lived with their mother in Mechanicsburg, seeing their father on weekends since he worked in Harrisburg at the Mather family business.

While Jane was still young, her mother extricated herself from the management of her family and turned her attention and energies toward herself and her singing talents, which were considerable. Jane's mother contributed to the economic upkeep of the home through earned wages, resisted household chores, and focused primarily upon her own aspirations while continuing to be central to the family's emotions.

Jane, like her two sisters, went to public school. Her two brothers, conversely, attended private schools, reflecting their father's priorities for his daughters' and sons' education. Deeter earned her B.S. at Irving College in Mechanicsburg, Pennsylvania, in 1902 with the financial help of her sister. Following her graduation, Deeter became assistant to the principal of Mechanicsburg High School. She held this position until 1908, when she moved to Meadowbrook,

Pennsylvania, and became assistant to the superintendent of Children's Village, a foster home and orphanage. She remained there until 1910, when she relocated once again to Philadelphia to act as casework supervisor for the Society for the Prevention of Cruelty to Children. In the months after her move to Philadelphia, Deeter, along with five other women, organized the Coop, a living collective. The venture was a successful testament to cooperative/alternative living arrangements.

Deeter married James Yardley Rippin, a Philadelphia architect and one of the early members of the Coop, on October 13, 1913. Their egalitarian marriage encouraged the continuance of her autonomous career. The couple did not have any children.

Deeter Rippin received her M.A. from Irving College, her undergraduate alma mater, in 1914 after having done postgraduate work at the University of Pennsylvania in 1909–1910.

In that same year, Deeter Rippin became the chief probation officer of the Municipal Court of Philadelphia. Between 1914 and 1917, she concentrated on improving and reorganizing the probation system for five sections of the Philadelphia courts. These included domestic relations, women's court for sex offenders, miscreants, juvenile, and petty criminal for unmarried mothers. Under her, the staff increased tremendously (from 3 to 365) in order to provide better psychological evaluations of and social work services for the women who came before the court.

Inspired by her observations within the traditional court structure, Deeter Rippin helped plan and open the Women's Court Building, which provided alternative services for women offenders, including diagnostic, treatment, and employment services, plus a dormitory-like prison. In short, the center sought to redress the material and psychological needs of incarcerated women.

Due in part to the innovative nature and success of this venture, Deeter Rippin was asked to assume supervisory responsibilities for the War Department's Commission on Training Camp Activities in 1917. In charge of overseeing the activities of girls and women congregated at military bases in the Southwest, Deeter Rippin instituted alternatives to the lure of illegal and "immoral" activities (prostitution and alcoholic consumption being prime among them) for these women, through centers in nearby towns that provided more wholesome activities. Deeter Rippin assumed the helm of this commission in 1918, and during her tenure half a million dollars was raised and nearly 40,000 delinquent women received services under her extended auspices. A final task in connection with this phase of her professional life came in 1919 with the research and collection of data that addressed the causes of delinquency. This information was used years later (1941) to found the United Service Organization (USO) which was so widely utilized during World War II.

Inspired by findings from her 1919 research, Deeter Rippin next turned her social welfare activism to the Girl Scouts, a movement that sought to provide, from an early age onward, a diversion from the lures of delinquency, and desirable alternatives for the energies of young girls and women. She served as national director of the Girl Scouts from 1919 through 1930 and figured prominently in its transformation into a movement of national significance. Accomplishments and innovations attributed to her administration during these years include a fivefold increase in Scout membership (from 50,000 to 250,000), the establishment of camps and training schools, development of the *American Girl* magazine, growth of International Scouting, the annual cookie sale, feasible coordination on the local and national levels, organization of the Juliette Low World Friendship Fund to honor the American founder of Girl Scouting, and the inclusion of more community-focused activities in addition to outdoor and homemaking pursuits. (Deeter Rippin served as a member of the National Advisory Council of the Girl Scouts until her death.)

Deeter Rippin turned her myriad talents to journalism in 1931. As research director for the women's news of the Westchester (New York) County Publishers, a fifty-plus group of papers, she wrote on issues spanning the sociopolitical realm as well as garden and club news. Despite a severely debilitating stroke in 1936 which forced her to relearn speaking and writing skills, and curtailed her centrality in the publishing circuit, she maintained her journalistic efforts as well as her interest and input in community affairs until her death. A member of the Episcopal Church and the Republican Party, Jane Deeter Rippin is remembered by neighbors and colleagues as a strong individual. Noted for her physical energy and calmness in the face of adversity, she was thought a woman of considerable bravery. And yet, intermingled with admiration for her professional leadership abilities, she is also fondly recalled as an expert and gifted horticulturalist, a testimony to her diverse interests and accomplishments. Deeter Rippin died at her home in Tarrytown, New York, on June 2, 1953.

The most complete manuscript sources on Deeter Rippin are located in the Girl Scouts of the U.S.A. Archives in New York City. The collection contains personal correspondence of Deeter Rippin's and interviews with her that illuminate her family life and professional accomplishments. See the two separate articles in the *Daily News* (Tarrytown, New York) on June 3, 1953, for a solid summary of her career, and statements by her colleagues: "Mrs. Jane Deeter Rippin, Girl Scout Leader, Dies," and "Leaders Laud Mrs. Rippin for Services." Also see the editorial in the same issue entitled "A Great Woman Passes." Mary Aickin Rothschild's entry on Deeter Rippin in *Notable American Women* (1980) was the most useful secondary source and provided needed information on familial influences, Deeter's gender-conscious activism, and her social welfare innovations. Her degrees received, positions held, and organizational affiliations are enumerated in *Who Was Who in America*, vol. 3 (1960), 730.

Also see the obituary in the *New York Herald Tribune* (June 3, 1953), penned in part in advance by Deeter Rippin. Also see the "Personal Recollections" statement given by her Tarrytown, New York, neighbor, Mary Lawson, on July 7, 1984, in the possession of the Historical Society of the Tarrytowns. This piece highlights Deeter Rippin's horticultural interests, affiliation with the Ossining Women's Club, Girl Scout activities, and verbal testimonies given at her memorial service.

SUSAN E. CAYLEFF

**Robins, Margaret Dreier** (September 6, 1868–February 21, 1945), social reformer and labor leader who led the Women's Trade Union League, (WTUL) in its years of greatest success, was born and grew up in Brooklyn, New York, the oldest child of Theodor and Dorothea (Dreier) Dreier. The Dreier family had long been prominent in Bremen, Germany, and Margaret's parents used the fortune that Theodor had made there for himself to perpetuate their heritage of civic responsibility, culture, and evangelical religion.

Dreier's formal education ended with her graduation from the Brackett School in Brooklyn, but she continued private studies while taking part in the social activities common to young women of her class. Her first welfare work was through the women's auxiliary of the Brooklyn Hospital. Visiting the wards taught her about social conditions, and she made a distinct contribution to the patients' well-being when she worked out a program to improve nutrition. In 1901 she accepted an invitation to serve on the New York State Charities Aid Association's committee to visit public institutions for the insane, which gave her a chance to develop her ideas under the guidance of Homer Folks* and drew her into public speaking for reform.

Dreier found her life's work in 1903, when she agreed to serve on the legislative committee of the Women's Municipal League. Among its concerns was the mistreatment of women by employment agencies, and she advanced the cause of reform by helping Frances Kellor* investigate the problem and then by lobbying for state regulation. In 1904 she and her sister Mary Elizabeth accepted the invitation of William English Walling* and Leonora O'Reilly* to become founding members of the New York Women's Trade Union League, and she was elected president a year later.

Dreier met and married the political reformer Raymond Robins* in the spring of 1905, and they set up housekeeping in the Chicago neighborhood where he had been a settlement worker for the past four years. She was soon as prominent among local reformers as she had been in New York. In 1907 she was elected president of both the Chicago chapter and the national organization of the WTUL, and she kept these positions until 1914 and 1922, respectively. She also became active in the American Federation of Labor (AFL), serving on the industrial education committee of the national organization and on the executive board in Chicago. At the same time she joined her husband in making their apartment a gathering place for reformers.

The WTUL was the principal focus of Robins' public life, and its analysis of the needs of working women was central to her own thinking. She believed that women of her background could best help working women by enabling them to provide for their own welfare. She favored protective legislation but gave first priority to trade union organization, and she insisted that the League seek a place in the mainstream of male-dominated labor activity by conforming to AFL policy and offering collaboration. She differed from some other leaders of the League in placing even higher value on the social and cultural development that trade union activities would stimulate in working women.

The WTUL made important progress in the early years of Robins' presidency. Her firm sense of purpose and her generous and tactful manner were vital to its achievements. The national organization sent representatives into the field, supported strikes across the Northeast and Midwest, lobbied for protective legislation, educated the public about the need for these activities, and trained future trade union leaders through membership in the League and attendance at a special school founded in Chicago in 1914. The Chicago chapter was outstanding for its fostering of labor organization, its support of the Hart, Schaffner and Marx strike of 1910–1911, its large membership of working women, and its close relations with local labor leaders. On the other hand, efforts to place the national organization in the mainstream of the labor movement failed after some early progress in overcoming the AFL's lack of interest in organizing women workers. League members were suspect for their radical and feminist sympathies despite their adherence to AFL policy on union issues, and Robins would not compromise her support for protective legislation in the face of Samuel Gompers' preference for industrial action as the principal method of labor reform.

The war years were a time of promise for the WTUL because Robins and other League members were able to assume advisory positions in the government and because the establishment of the Women in Industry Service (later the Women's Bureau) in the Department of Labor made it possible to reform labor practices through government contracts. The League also shared the optimism of other reform organizations that peace would bring a strong movement toward social democracy. While retaining its interest in labor organization and increasing its stress on protective legislation, the League entered the postwar era more centrally concerned with a broad spectrum of reforms, including social insurance, public ownership of natural monopolies, and various forms of international cooperation.

Robins herself was particularly interested in fostering an international women's labor movement. She was initially successful in holding two international conferences and becoming president of the resulting International Federation of Working Women, but this proved to be of little benefit to her own constituency. Among the Federation's first actions was to become part of the International Federation of Trade Unions, which the AFL was not to join for another decade. This symbolized the fundamental differences between the American and European trade union movements, and the WTUL withdrew from the women's federation after Robins pointed the way by declining to stand for reelection.

Robins also made time for other reform activities. Soon after coming to Chicago, she helped lead the public protest against the extradition of the labor leaders charged with murdering the Governor of Idaho. She worked for women's suffrage as president of the Chicago Political Equality Association but opposed the equal rights amendment because she thought that it would jeopardize protective legislation. She was vice chairman of the National Conference of Charities and Correction in 1912, when Progressive presidential candidate Theodore Roosevelt adopted most of its industrial platform, and she campaigned for him across the Midwest and served on the party's Illinois state committee.

Robins resigned the presidency of the WTUL in 1922, and she and her husband settled permanently on their Florida estate two years later. She remained intermittently active in the WTUL, and she was appointed to the planning committee for the White House Conference on Child Health and Protection in 1929. She also became a civic leader in Florida, playing important roles in the Hernando County Red Cross and YWCA, the Florida Botanical Garden and the Tamiami Trail, and the state organizing committees for the Women's Centennial Congress and the New York World's Fair. Her last public affiliations were on behalf of the Allied war effort in 1940–1941, and she died on her Florida estate— Chinsegut, near Brooksville—in 1945.

The Margaret Dreier Robins Papers are at the University of Florida. Records of the Women's Trade Union League can be found at the Schlesinger Library, Radcliffe College, and at the Library of Congress. The principal secondary sources are Gladys Boone, *The Women's Trade Union League in Great Britain and America* (1942); Clarke A. Chambers, *Seedtime of Reform* (1963); Allen F. Davis, *Spearheads for Reform* (1967); Nancy Schrom Dye, *As Equals and as Sisters* (1980); and William L. O'Neill, *Everyone Was Brave* (1969).

SUSAN GRIGG

**Robins, Raymond** (September 17, 1873–September 26, 1954), political reformer and social evangelist who played an important role in a variety of social, religious, and political movements in the first three decades of the twentieth century, was born in Staten Island, New York, the youngest child of Charles Ephraim and Hanna M. (Crow) Robins. The household disintegrated, however, while Robins was very young, and after making the rounds of a number of relatives, he settled with his uncle in the Florida backcountry. He left that household to make his fortune, though, before he had finished high school. As he traveled across the United States, he sampled occupations ranging from citrus crop picking to mining and thus learned about social problems firsthand. He worked intermittently for populism, labor organization, and the single tax, and he came to believe that widespread reform was necessary to avert a coming social crisis in urban industrial America.

After these years of exploration, Robins decided at age twenty-one that a career in law would make him wealthy and prepare him for leadership in reform. Within two years he had passed the bar exam and received a law degree from Columbian (now George Washington) Law School. He settled in San Francisco in time to campaign there for William Jennings Bryan in 1896, and by the following spring he had begun to distinguish himself in the practice of law. This promising start was cut short, apparently by his brother's inability to settle into a career and by his own unresolved emotional engagement with a sister who had helped raise him, and he left for the Klondike gold fields with his brother in the summer of 1897. Conversations with a missionary in the first hard winter led him to discover a strong Christian faith to replace the perfunctory religious upbringing he had shrugged off as a youth, and the resulting combination of reform ideas rapidly gave direction to his wide-ranging interests and ambitions. He soon made a place for himself as a preacher and reformer in the frontier town of Nome, Alaska. Having founded a school and a hospital and made some progress against vice and corruption there, he left Alaska late in 1900 to seek out a larger field of endeavor.

Robins chose Chicago as the site of his next ventures in reform. He rapidly became a leader in the continuing efforts of the city's social reformers to influence politics and also contributed to other reform activities. In February, 1901, he became a resident of the Chicago Commons, the settlement house founded by Graham Taylor* in 1894, and thus began a connection with Chicago's Seventeenth Ward that lasted more than twenty years. In his two years at the Commons he moderated the "free-floor discussions," helped lead the Community Club of young men from the neighborhood, and edited the magazine, *Commons*, in Taylor's absence. He also became active in ward politics, joining the Municipal Voters' League to promote reform candidates for office and helping the young politician William A. Dever to become alderman. At other times he assisted labor leaders, worked with Robert Hunter* to obtain playgrounds and parks, joined Jane Addams* in defending an anarchist publisher, and campaigned on behalf of the single tax. Little more than a year after settling in Chicago, he was appointed superintendent of the new Municipal Lodging House, an experiment in providing overnight care and help with employment for homeless men. While remaining in this position, he left the Chicago Commons in 1903 to become head resident of the nearby Northwestern University Settlement, where he organized the Civic Club as the counterpart of the Community Club. Meanwhile, he became increasingly popular throughout the city and beyond as a speaker on social reform before a variety of audiences.

While speaking in New York in 1905, Robins met and married Margaret Dreier (Robins*), a leader in the newly founded Women's Trade Union League. They set up housekeeping in Chicago in a tenement midway between the Commons and the Northwestern University Settlement and remained there for two decades. Margaret became prominent in Chicago reform activities as rapidly as Raymond had done a few years before, and their apartment was a social and intellectual center for like-minded men and women.

Following his return to Chicago, Robins expanded his political activities to embrace the entire city. Besides continuing his support for Alderman Dever, he worked closely with the new mayor, Edward Dunne. He helped him in his unsuccessful struggle for municipal ownership of the street railways, accepted an appointment to serve on the Board of Education with Jane Addams, and worked with Harold Ickes and Charles Merriam to defeat a charter revision that would have strengthened the opponents of reform. He also served on a screening committee for Democratic aldermanic candidates and was beaten on the street after having singled out a reputed gangster as especially unsuited for office.

After his first decade in Chicago, Robins was increasingly preoccupied with national and international matters in which social reform was not always the primary emphasis. For several years he was active in evangelical religion, speaking on tour for Men and Religion Forward from 1911 to 1913 and for the National Christian Evangelistic Camp in 1915 and 1916. He also became more involved in party politics, first emerging as a national leader in the Progressive Party and then supporting progressive Republicans in the 1920s. He expanded his interests to include international affairs when he went to Russia with the American Red Cross mission in 1917 and came back as a persistent advocate of recognition for the Soviet government. In the early 1920s he joined the international movement to outlaw war. He also worked to make Prohibition a success, first campaigning for strict enforcement and then settling on local option as an alternative to the national experiment.

Robins had bought an estate near his boyhood home in Florida many years before, and he and Margaret settled there in semi-retirement in 1924. He continued to travel on behalf of various reforms until a fall from a tree in 1935 left him paralyzed below the waist. They both became supporters of the New Deal, and Raymond's continuing interest in social welfare led him to declare himself a socialist in 1948. He and Margaret had given the estate—Chinsegut, near Brooksville, Florida—to the federal government in 1932 as a wildlife refuge and agricultural experiment station, and it passed to public use after his death there as a widower in 1954.

The Raymond Robins Papers are in the State Historical Society of Wisconsin. The principal secondary source in Neil Salzman, "Reform and Revolution: The Life Experience of Raymond Robins," Ph.D. dissertation, Columbia University, 1976, but William Appleman Williams offers an excellent brief sketch in the *Dictionary of American Biography* (1977). Among the studies focusing on part of Robins' life, those most useful to the student of social welfare are Elizabeth Robins, *Raymond and I* (1956), on his youth, and Allen F. Davis, *Spearheads for Reform* (1967), on his years in Chicago. See also the entry on Margaret Dreier Robins for sources focusing more on her life than his.

SUSAN GRIGG

**Robinson, Virginia Pollard** (September 6, 1883–June 28, 1977), social work educator, was born to Walter Landon and Hallie E. (Thomas) Robinson in Louisville, Kentucky, where she grew up in a rather conventional Protestant home. As an outstanding high school student, she earned the valedictorian scholarship to attend the University of Chicago. However, she turned down the award in order to attend Bryn Mawr college. She stayed at the small women's college for five years, earning a master's degree in philosophy and psychology. After her education was completed she still felt uncertain as to what career she should begin. Therefore, she returned to her hometown to teach in a girls' high school. Later, Robinson felt that it was by chance, because she was disinterested in her teaching, that she decided to attend summer school at the University of Chicago in 1908, where she first met Jessie Taft.* After that summer together, Robinson and Taft began a lifelong relationship that continued for over fifty years. She and Taft adopted two children, Marth and Everett (Taft) in the 1920s.

Beyond her meeting Jessie Taft, Robinson was excited by the education she received that summer and more confused than ever about a career choice. She returned to Kentucky to teach grammar and literature to her high school students and to become involved in the College Association for Woman Suffrage, where she debated the issue of equality for women. In April, 1908, she and Taft were asked to be a part of a research project developed by Katharine Bement Davis,* superintendent of the State Reformatory for Women at Bedford Hills, New York, and the Laboratory of Social Hygiene. Robinson was hired as a sociologist in the laboratory and had the opportunity to work with psychiatrists who were doing creative work with the mentally ill in the new field of "mental hygiene." When Davis resigned to become Commissioner of Charities and Corrections in New York City, Taft and Robinson left to find new positions.

In 1915 Robinson accepted a position working with the Public Education Association in New York helping to define the purpose of home and school visitors, which later became the visiting teacher program. She found it difficult to work with the children referred to her but found it challenging to design a program for others to help the children. From there she briefly taught at Carson College for orphan girls in Flourtown, Pennsylvania. She described herself as eager to teach when asked to become associate director of the University of Pennsylvania School of Social Work in 1920, where she became a faculty member instead.

As a faculty member there, where she would remain until her retirement, Robinson began to formulate her own ideas about social work, which still was a relatively new area of study. At this point Robinson rejected many of Mary Richmond's* ideas about casework and sought a more creative, dynamic approach to people's problems. She felt that many social workers were turning to Sigmund Freud for easy answers. Otto Rank, a psychoanalyst who disagreed with Freud, lectured and became a faculty member at the Pennsylvania School during the 1920s and 1930s. His ideas reflected a more optimistic view of the individual and the individual's will as a potentially creative force to encourage change and growth. Excited by this new approach to working with people, Robinson applied and was accepted for analysis with Rank in the fall of 1927. Her analysis continued one hour a day for six weeks. She gave credit to this experience for helping her to better understand the nature of relationships, especially of self and other, professional and personal.

It was during the 1920s that Robinson decided to return to school in order to receive a doctorate. Not wanting to leave Philadelphia or the exciting work beginning at the school, she began to work on a Ph.D. in the Sociology Department at the University of Pennsylvania. Work on her degree continued for more than seven years, during what was a miserable time for her. It was frustrating to be a student again when she found it so challenging to be a teacher at the Pennsylvania School at such an important time in the history of social work.

To complete her degree, Robinson wrote a dissertation which surveyed the *Proceedings* of the National Conference of Social Work in order to document the development of social casework. Published in 1930 under the tile *A Changing Psychology in Social Casework*, it acknowledged the importance of Mary Richmond's ideas in describing unifying procedures and methods for the caseworker; however, Robinson felt that this type of social casework was merely a study of a social situation and did not detail behavior and attitudes, which were far more important. She felt that Richmond's writings led to poor casework, superficial diagnoses, and unfounded treatment, if treatment was given. Robinson called for a new era in casework, one in which the worker was a psychotherapist and the worker's primary tool was the relationship with the client.

In the 1930s Robinson turned her attention away from casework and applied her ideas to the areas of social work training and supervision. In 1934 she taught her first class on problems and methods of supervision. She found herself teaching public welfare administrators without prior training who were supervising new caseworkers. She taught them that specific knowledge was not all that was needed for the new worker. It was necessary to develop a professional self, one that was willing to learn. Robinson's first book on supervision, *Supervision in Social Case Work: A Problem in Professional Education*, appeared in 1936. She described supervision as a unique teaching process that had grown up as part of casework but which was, in fact, different. It was a constantly shifting and changing process that depended upon how much of the learner was engaged in the process. Twelve years later, she published a second text on supervision entitled *The Dynamics of Supervision under Functional Controls: A Professional Process in Social Casework* in which she brought together her ideas about supervision within the framework of functional casework.

The term "functional casework" is credited to Jessie Taft, who defined it in 1937 in the *Journal of Social Work Process*. From 1930 to 1950 two schools of thought were at odds with one another in social work. One was the diagnostic or Freudian school of thought, and the other was the functionalist or Rankian school, as represented by the Pennsylvania School of Social Work. In 1942 Robinson wrote *Training for Skill in Social Case Work*, in which she clearly described the nature of the skills needed for functional social casework. Skill was the capacity of the worker to set in motion and control a process of change with respect for the client's ability and willingness to change, given also the function of the social agency in which this process took place.

The functional school of social work, which dominated social work in the

1930s and 1940s, clearly originated in the writings of Virginia Robinson and Jessie Taft as influenced by Otto Rank. While others developed the concepts over the years, Taft and Robinson notably conceived the theory in their writings and teaching. Robinson retired from the Pennsylvania School of Social Work in 1950. She died in Dozlestown, Pennsylvania, in 1977 at the age of ninety-three.

Although Robinson left no collection of her papers and correspondence, her colleagues at the University of Pennsylvania School of Social Work put together a collection of her writings entitled *The Development of a Professional Self: Teaching and Learning in Professional Helping Processes, Selected Writings, 1930–1968* (1978). Robinson wrote an introductory chapter for the text which reviews her professional career and is quite useful.

Virginia Robinson authored a biography of her lifelong friend, Jessie Taft, which is entitled *Jessie Taft, Therapist and Social Work Educator: A Professional Biography* (1962). In addition, she wrote numerous articles and texts on the subject of supervision and the skills associated with functional casework.

JEAN K. QUAM

**Roche, Josephine Aspinwall** (December 2, 1886–July 29, 1976), promoter of federal welfare legislation and industrial deomocracy, especially for miners, was born in Neligh, Nebraska, to Ella (Aspinwall) and John R. Roche, a coal mine operator. After attending local public schools, Roche entered Vassar with a deep interest in the working conditions of miners as well as an interest in criminology and child welfare. Upon graduation in 1908, she accepted a job in Denver as a probation officer for the juvenile court. She remained in Denver for one year before deciding to study for a master's degree in sociology at Columbia University. At Columbia Roche became a close friend of Frances Perkins.* In 1910 the Russell Sage Foundation, then in its most vigorous stage of conducting inquiries on the conditions of American workers, awarded her a two-year fellowship. Completing her fellowship in 1912, Roche returned to Denver and became the city's first female police officer. After another year she became the executive secretary of the Colorado Progressive Society.

In 1915 she traveled to Europe as a special agent of the United States to the Commission for Relief in Belgium. Returning to the United States, she directed the Girls' Department of the Denver Juvenile Court. In this environment, Roche became acutely aware of the city's delinquent and impoverished children. She returned to the court in 1925 as a referee.

In 1917 Roche served on President Wilson's Committee on Public Information and directed the Foreign Language Education Service. She continued in this role until 1923, when she became director of the editorial division of the U.S. Children's Bureau in Washington, D.C.

When Roche's father died in 1927, he left her with control of his holdings in the Rocky Mountain Fuel Company. Having spent her early years aware of the working conditions in the mines, Roche proposed at the first company meeting she attended that the United Mine Workers of America (UMW) be allowed to represent the Rocky Mountain employees. This suggestion so appalled the stockholders of the company that many of them sold their shares. In time, Roche eventually acquired a majority interest in the company.

Roche proceeded to appoint top union officials to key positions: Edward Costigan, former attorney for the UMW and later a senator from Colorado, was made counsel; John Lawson, a veteran of the Ludlow coal mine massacre and former president of the Colorado State Federation of Labor, became vice president and director. Roche served as vice president. Then she announced that the company would sign a union contract with the miners. The final contract, signed in 1924, gave the miners the highest daily wage rate in Colorado and the right to arbitration.

Nine years later, Roche's unique position as a coal mine owner and ally of the labor movement made her an important figure in the development of a National Recovery Administration code for the bituminous coal industry.

In 1934 Roche ran for governor of Colorado and lost. As a consolation, President Roosevelt appointed her Assistant Secretary of the Treasury in charge of the Public Health Service. In this capacity, Roche served as Henry Morgenthau's alternate on the Committee on Economic Security and as a member of that committee's technical board. These assignments enabled Roche to participate in the creation of what in 1935 became the Social Security Act. Roche payed particular attention to the health and disability aspects of the act. When President Roosevelt decided not to pursue the passage of health insurance or disability insurance in 1935, he asked Roche to chair the Interdepartmental Committee to Coordinate Health and Welfare Activities. He asked this committee "to bring about a complete coordination of the government's activity in the health field." On February 10, 1938, the group submitted its confidential report to the President. Among other things, the report endorsed national health insurance, administered through the states, as well as the passage of temporary disability insurance. In many ways the report marked the beginning of the modern campaign to pass health insurance.

By 1937 Roche had resigned as Assistant Secretary of the Treasury and returned to the coal company. She remained interested in the work of the Interdepartmental Committee and attended the climactic National Health Conference in July, 1938. She also maintained her links to reform politics. In 1939, for example, she became president of the National Consumers' League.

In 1947 John L. Lewis, President of the UMW, asked her to be the first director of the union's welfare and retirement fund. This institution brought income security and modern health care to the unionized miners who worked in the bituminous coal fields. She accepted the position and remained director until her retirement in 1971.

In 1971 Roche was convicted of conspiracy to invest funds in accounts that did not bear interest. She was removed as a trustee along with W.A. Boyle, president of the UMW. Roche and Boyle, however, became adamant foes, and in 1972 Roche made a $1,000 political contribution, in the name of John L. Lewis and Joseph ("Jock") Yablonski, to Arnold Miller, Boyle's opponent for the UMW presidency. Miller won the election and Boyle was sent to prison for the 1969 murders of Yablonski, his wife, and his daughter.

As Arnold Miller put it, Roche "fought for coal miners and their families all of her life; first as a coal operator who believed in the principles of industrial democracy for miners; then as the first director of the U.M.W. welfare and retirement fund, which during her 24 years of service helped literally hundreds of thousands of mining families." Roche died in Bethesda, Maryland, on July 29, 1976.

The papers of Josephine A. Roche are available to researchers at the State Historical Society of Colorado Collections in Denver. Other sources include *American Women, 1935–1940* (1981); *Current Biography, 1941* (1942); *Forum* (August, 1934); *Nation* (June 13, 1934); *Newsweek* (November 24, 1934 and November 8, 1937); *Time* (November 8, 1937 and July 10, 1939). For more information on Roche's involvement with Tony Boyle, see the *New York Times* (March 19, 1970, February 8, 1971, and November 21, 1972). The *New York Times* also ran a detailed obituary of Roche on July 31, 1976.

ANNE-MARIE CARROLL

**Roosevelt, Anna Eleanor** (October 11, 1884–November 7, 1962), political and social reformer, was born in New York City, the first child of Elliot and Anna (Hall) Roosevelt. Descended on both sides from distinguished and wealthy colonial families, Eleanor Roosevelt nonetheless experienced a lonely and unhappy childhood. By the time she was ten, both her parents and a younger brother had died, leaving Eleanor and her brother Hall as the only survivors.

Roosevelt remembered herself as "a solemn child, without beauty . . . entirely lacking in spontaneous joy and mirth of youth." She felt rejected by her beautiful mother, who called her "granny." When her parents died, she went to live with her maternal grandmother, who was equally distant. The most important person of Eleanor's early childhood was her father, a charming, loving man, who provided fun and intimacy, but was unable to provide stability. His early death left an almost unbearable emotional void in Eleanor's life. It seems possible that her later activism was a compensatory attempt to gain the love, assurance, and emotional support that evaded her as a child. And yet Eleanor Roosevelt was also part of a reform milieu that characterized the first several decades of the twentieth century. She was to provide an important bridge between early Progressive ideals, the reform movements of the 1920s, and the New Deal.

Between the ages of fifteen and seventeen, Roosevelt attended Allenswood, a girls' school outside of London, where she came under the influence of her teacher, Marie Souvestre. Souvestre had a liberal mind and a passion for radical causes. She provided Eleanor with an emotional bond and touched her awakening political consciousness. Thus, when the young woman returned to New York

City, she was uninterested in the frivolous life style characteristic of her class. Instead, she joined the National Consumers' League, headed by Florence Kelley,* and, through her visits to factories and sweatshops, developed a lifelong commitment to the poor, as well as the conception of the reformer as investigator and educator. From Kelley she adopted the idea that information was half way to reform.

Roosevelt also showed her emerging social consciousness through her activities in the Junior League and at Rivington Street Settlement House. But her main concern during the first decade of the twentieth century was marriage to Franklin Delano Roosevelt and the family life that ensued. Between 1906 and 1916 she bore six children, five of whom survived: Anna, James, Elliot, Franklin, Jr., and John. Eleanor cherished her children, but these were unhappy years. Her mother-in-law dominated the household, and it seemed that "Franklin's children were more my mother-in-law's children than they were mine."

After 1910 Eleanor's social activities revolved increasingly around Franklin's political career. But America's entry into World War I in 1917 provided her with an opportunity to concentrate on issues of vital and immediate concern. She coordinated activities at Washington's Union Station canteen for soldiers on their way to training camps, took charge of Red Cross activities, supervised the knitting rooms at the Navy Department, and spoke at patriotic rallies. In addition, she became involved in a campaign to improve conditions at St. Elizabeth's Hospital for the mentally ill.

But Roosevelt's real political training and reform activity began in the 1920s, following her husband's crippling illness and her efforts to maintain his political contacts. As a member of the Women's City Club of New York and of the League of Women Voters, she learned to compile and analyze legislation. She worked with Louis Howe on the New York Women's Democratic Committee and the New York State and National Democratic Committees, where she learned the mechanisms by which to achieve reform. She developed ties with Lillian Wald* of Henry Street Settlement and Mary Simkhovitch,* head worker at Greenwich House. Settlement house work called to her attention the complexity of urban problems and the connections between poor housing, poverty, crime, and disease.

In 1922 Eleanor Roosevelt joined the Women's Trade Union League (WTUL) and worked for maximum hour and minimum wage laws for women. Rose Schneiderman,* president of the New York branch of the WTUL, became her close friend and political ally. Through her, Roosevelt formed her commitment to the rights of labor and adopted the definition of a "living wage" that included, in addition to basic material necessities, education, recreation, and emergency needs. This was the beginning of her lifelong support of fair labor standards.

By 1928 Eleanor Roosevelt had extended her role as a political wife into a vehicle for asserting her own personality and goals. She led the national women's campaign for the Democratic Party in 1928, making sure that the party appealed to independent voters, minorities, and women. After Franklin Roosevelt's election

as Governor of New York, she was instrumental in securing Frances Perkins'*
appointment as the state's industrial commissioner. Eleanor Roosevelt's
apprenticeship in the 1920s was crucial for her own development as a reformer
and for the access that reformers had to New Deal programs. During the 1930s
she would provide a channel through which reform associations and their leaders
could move into the New Deal's programs and machinery.

Eleanor Roosevelt's devotion to social welfare causes made her the center of
a female reform network that enabled her, with the help of Mary ("Molly")
Dewson,* to bring to Washington an unprecedented number of dynamic women
activists. These included Ellen Woodward,* Hilda Smith, and Florence Kerr.
Roosevelt also provided a national forum for transmitting the views and the
concerns of such women. At regular press conferences for women reporters, she
introduced women leaders to talk about their work. These sessions underlined
the importance of women's issues and created a community of women reporters
and government workers.

Although Roosevelt had initially feared that there would be no active role for
her as First Lady, she was able to use that position to turn herself into the most
influential woman of her times. She toured the country throughout the thirties,
surveying conditions in coal mines, visiting relief projects, and speaking out for
the disadvantaged. Through her syndicated newspaper column, "My Day," and
through radio programs and lectures, she communicated her deep compassion
for those who suffered. At the White House she acted as an advocate of the poor
and disenfranchised, particularly pressing the case for Blacks and youth. She
was instrumental in the formation of the National Youth Administration. Franklin
Roosevelt was able to use her activism as a means of building alliances with
groups to his left.

With the onset of World War II, Roosevelt continued her efforts for the
disadvantaged. Her work in civil defense reflected her humanitarian goals. She
was determined not to lose the New Deal during the war, and saw civil defense
as a way of preserving it. Though she increasingly devoted herself to dreams of
international cooperation, most of her energies were directed to human needs,
particularly those of Blacks, women, Jewish refugees, and wounded veterans.
In the immediate postwar years, the cause of world peace and the desire to help
the victims of war were among Roosevelt's central concerns. In moving speeches
which portrayed the suffering wrought by war, she sought to educate the United
States to its postwar responsibilities.

President Truman nominated Eleanor Roosevelt as a United States delegate
to the United Nations, where she lobbied for the creation of a document on
human rights. On December 10, 1948, the Universal Declaration of Human
Rights, basically shaped by Roosevelt, passed the General Assembly. Delegates
rose in a standing ovation to the woman who more than anyone else had come
to symbolize the cause of human rights.

Throughout the 1950s Eleanor Roosevelt maintained her public and political
status, influencing the politics of the Democratic Party and working tirelessly

for the causes of civil rights, humanitarianism, and international cooperation. Her last official position was to chair President Kennedy's Commission on the Status of Women, to which she was appointed in December, 1961. This final appointment was a reflection of her own life of political independence and personal autonomy. On the issue of women's equality, as in so many areas, Roosevelt affirmed the right of the human spirit to grow and seek fulfillment. Once opposed to suffrage, she had grown to exemplify women's aspirations for a full life in politics.

Because of Eleanor Roosevelt's life, millions of others experienced a sense of the possible. It would be difficult to place her reform thought in a particular mold because it was so flexible. She had no conscious program: she was pragmatic, adaptable, willing to experiment, and committed to social justice rather than dogmatic ideology. Most of all, she showed a tremendous capacity for growth. She adopted causes as they arose, but she was often ahead of her times. Sometimes viewed as an impractical idealist, she was, in fact, a skilled politician with a keen understanding of the subtle exercise of power and influence. Eleanor Roosevelt died at her home in New York City in November, 1962, from a rare form of tuberculosis.

The Eleanor Roosevelt Papers of the Roosevelt Library in Hyde Park, New York, contain Eleanor Roosevelt's correspondence and drafts of her writings and speeches. Other relevant collections at Hyde Park are the papers of Mary Dewson, Hilda Worthington Smith, and Lorena Hickock; the papers of the Women's Division of the Democratic National Committee; and those of Anna Roosevelt Halsted. Several manuscript collections at the Schlesinger Library, Radcliffe College, bear directly on Eleanor Roosevelt's life: see especially the papers of Mary Anderson, Mary Dewson, Mary Drier, and Ellen Woodward. Eleanor Roosevelt's correspondence with government agencies is in the files of the Federal Emergency Relief Administration, the Civil Works Administration, the Works Progress Administration, and the National Youth Administration at the National Archives.

Of Eleanor Roosevelt's own writings, the most valuable are *This I Remember* (1949); *This Is My Story* (1937); *Autobiography* (1961); and *It's up to the Women* (1933). She also wrote a syndicated column, "My Day," from December 30, 1925, to September 11, 1962, and numerous articles in the popular press. Her monthly column, "If You Ask Me," appeared in *Ladies Home Journal* from June 1941 to the spring of 1949 and in *McCall's* after 1949.

Joseph Lash's two-volume biography, *Eleanor and Franklin* (1971) and *Eleanor: The Years Alone* (1972), is valuable for an understanding of Roosevelt's personal and public life. Two biographies that partly emphasize her evolution as a reformer are Tamara Hareven, *Eleanor Roosevelt: An American Conscience* (1968) and James K. Kearney, *Anna Eleanor Roosevelt: The Evolution of a Reformer* (1968). A centennial anthology, Joan Hoff-Wilson and Marjorie Lightman, eds., *Without Precedent: The Life and Career of Eleanor Roosevelt* (1984), contains several interpretive articles bearing upon various aspects of Roosevelt's reform activities, for example, youth, civil rights, relief, and feminism. William Chafe has written a thorough biographical essay encompassing Eleanor Roosevelt's entire career which appears in *Notable American Women: The Modern Period* (1980).

WINIFRED D. WANDERSEE

**Rubinow, Isaac Max** (April 19, 1875–September 1, 1936), social insurance expert and promoter, author, and Jewish social service administrator, was born in Grodno, Russia, to Esther (Shereshewsky) and Max Simon Rubinow. After migrating to America at the age of eighteen, he attended Columbia University, where he earned a B.A. in 1895 and an M.D. in 1898. A year later he married Sophia Himowich, with whom he had three children: Laura, Raymond, and Olga.

In the course of attending to New York City's poor, Rubinow noted that the sickness he treated was as much an economic as it was a medical problem. To gather evidence to corroborate this hypothesis, he abandoned his medical practice and turned to statistics. Rubinow served during the 1900s as an economist in the departments of agriculture, commerce, and labor while working for a Ph.D. in political science at Columbia, where he investigated trends in workers' wages and purchasing power.

In 1913 Rubinow published *Social Insurance*, in which he marshalled an impressive statistical and theoretical rationale for adopting new forms of protection for the aged and the poor. For the rest of his life, Rubinow would work for better workmen's compensation laws, unemployment insurance, old-age pensions, and national health insurance programs advanced in this work. *Social Insurance* immediately became a classic in the field and was praised even two decades later by fellow invetigators, such as Abraham Epstein* and Barbara Nachtrieb Armstrong.* In 1916 Rubinow became executive secretary of the American Medical Association's Social Insurance Commission and, a year later, director of the Bureau of Social Statistics of New York City's Department of Public Charities. He also found time to lecture on social insurance at the New York School of Philanthropy and to serve as a contributing editor of the *Survey*.

After World War I, Rubinow began to devote time and energy to the second major cause of his distinguished career: the promotion of social services in the Jewish community. From 1918 to 1922 he headed the Hadassah medical unit in Palestine, supervising the modernization of hospitals and clinics in the country. Besides his advancing work on social insurance, Rubinow considered this effort his most important achievement. He was director of the Jewish Welfare Society in Philadelphia for the next five years; he was the editor of the *Jewish Social Service Quarterly* between 1925 and 1929. Rubinow served as secretary of the B'nai B'rith from 1929 until his death. In this latter capacity, he was instrumental in launching an antidefamation movement and took steps to aid German Jews.

In 1934 Rubinow published *The Quest for Security*, which, unlike most other works in the field, was designed to inform the average reader about the importance of social insurance. The book also directly appealed to federal officials to act decisively: "Surely it cannot be part of the philosophy of the New Deal that those who are left by the wayside of modern industrial civilization always remain objects of charity, whether private or public. Social insurance must therefore become—if it is not already—an essential aspect of the New Deal," he wrote. The message was heard; FDR wrote the author to express "great interest" in the suggestions about the President's probable role in enacting social security legislation. Rubinow then served as a consultant to Roosevelt's Committee on Economic Security, which drafted the Social Security Act.

Rubinow died in New York City on September 1, 1936, at the age of sixty-one.

The best biographical details on Rubinow's life appear in *Who Was Who in America*, vol. 1 (1943), 1064, and in his obituary in the *New York Times*, September 3, 1936, 21. The significance of Rubinow's ideas and efforts to promote social insurance are discussed in Roy Lubove, *The Struggle for Social Security* (1968); Daniel J. Boorstin, *The Americans: The Democratic Experience* (1974); and W. Andrew Achenbaum, *Old Age in the New Land* (1978).

W. ANDREW ACHENBAUM

**Rush, Benjamin** (January 4, 1746 [December 24, 1745 O.S.]–April 19, 1813), physician, educator, author, politician, and social reformer, was born in Byberry, Pennsylvania, the fourth of seven children, to John Rush, a gunsmith, and Susanna Hall (Harvey) (Rush) Morris. When John Rush died at age thirty-nine, he left only a small estate, and Susanna opened a grocery store and later a china shop in Philadelphia. She continued to operate these businesses even after marrying Richard Morris, a distiller. Rush strongly disliked his stepfather, but only had praise for his mother, whom he described as kind, generous, and well-educated in the common branches of female education. She was committed to seeing that her children had a strong moral and religious outlook on life. Although Benjamin shifted religious affiliations among different Protestant churches, he shared his mother's ideals on the importance of religion and moral convictions.

In 1753 or 1754 Rush entered West Nottingham Academy in Maryland and went from there to the College of New Jersey (now Princeton) in 1759, from which he obtained a B.A. in 1760. He served as apprentice to Dr. John Redman of Philadelphia (1760–1766) and then entered the University of Edinburgh, from which he was granted an M.D. in 1768. Rush returned to Philadelphia in the summer of 1769, established a medical practice, and became professor of chemistry at the College of Philadelphia (now the University of Pennsylvania). He married Julia Stockton (1759–1848) on January 11, 1776, and the couple had thirteen children, nine of whom survived to maturity.

Rush took an active part in the Revolution. He served in the Continental

Congress in 1776 and signed the Declaration of Independence. He also was surgeon general and then physician general of the Middle Department in the Continental Army from the spring of 1777 until January, 1778, when he resigned over a dispute with Dr. William Shippen, Jr., director general of hospitals for the army. Rush opposed the radical Pennsylvania Constitution of 1776 and was one of the founding members of the conservative Republican Society (1779). He supported the adoption of the federal Constitution as a member of the Pennsylvania ratifying convention. While still pursuing private practice, Rush became a member of the attending staff of the Pennsylvania Hospital in 1783. For the rest of his life, he remained on the staff of this private hospital designed to aid the sick poor, and he devoted great energy to trying to improve the treatment of the insane. His pioneering work in this field has led some to call him the father of American psychiatry. From 1789 on, he held various professorships in medicine at the University of Pennsylvania.

Rush was an inveterate social welfare reformer who, in addition to his work at the Pennsylvania Hospital and among the poor generally, pursued reform both as a prolific author and as an organizer and member of social reform organizations. Rush published his first plea for temperance in 1772 and thereafter continued that plea, most especially in his widely reprinted *An Enquiry into the Effects of Spiritous Liquors . . .* (undated, but in print by 1784). Although Rush was a slave owner until 1794, he joined the Pennsylvania Society for Promoting the Abolition of Slavery in 1787, lent his moral and financial support to the creation of the First African Church (St. Thomas') of Philadelphia (1791–1793), and served as president of the National Conference of Abolition Societies (1795). Beginning in 1788, he published essays condemning capital punishment and worked to eliminate the death penalty in Pennsylvania. A firm believer in education, especially for the poor, Rush, beginning in 1786, published various plans calling for government-funded education that should, he noted in 1787, be run by the various religious denominations of the state. Although Rush adamantly believed that women should be kept in a subordinate position, he also advocated expanding educational opportunities for females.

Rush had many poor patients, and he often assisted them gratis. He was, nevertheless, deeply bothered by what he perceived as moral weaknesses among the poor, and he supported reforms designed to aid those called "the worthy poor." He was the driving force behind the creation of the Philadelphia Dispensary (1786), which provided a wide range of free medical treatment to the poor. But to get that aid, one had to obtain recommendations from subscribers to the dispensary, and the founders of the organization openly noted that they aimed to limit assistance to those they called the virtuous poor.

In 1787 Rush also helped to found the Philadelphia Society for Alleviating the Miseries of Public Prisons. This organization, for which Rush was an attending physician, provided food, clothing, fuel, and medical aid to prisoners. The Society also worked to superintend the morals of the prisoners and to release those deemed to be proper objects. Rush evidenced his concern for education, especially for the poor, by being a founding member of the Sunday School Society (1790). The Society provided free education for the lower classes that emphasized moral training and religious ideals. In 1808 Rush helped create the Bible Society, which provided free Bibles to those who could not afford them.

As both his words and actions show, Rush was a humanitarian social welfare reformer. Yet he distrusted the poor and felt that great effort was needed to make them moral, upright, and deferential. In a March 28, 1787 essay in the *Independent Gazetteer*, he went so far as to tell his fellow Philadelphians that they should not "exhaust" their benevolence on medical institutions such as the dispensary and the Humane Society, which he helped to found in 1780. Rather, said Rush, the citizens had to fund education for the poor because "their morals are of more consequence to society than their health or lives." Thus, Rush's social welfare reform efforts also were what have come to be called "social control" efforts.

Benjamin Rush died in Philadelphia on April 19, 1813.

Rush manuscripts are held by a breathtaking number of archives and private individuals. The major collection is held by the Library Company of Philadelphia in conjunction with the Historical Society of Pennsylvania. The American Philosophical Society, of which Rush was a member, has attempted to compile a union list of Rush manuscripts.

Useful general guides to Rush manuscripts as well as listings of Rush's voluminous publications are contained in two indispensable editions of works by Rush: L. H. Butterfield, ed., *Letters of Benjamin Rush*, 2 vols. (1951), and George W. Corner, ed., *The Autobiography of Benjamin Rush: His "Travels Through Life" Together with His Commonplace Book for 1789–1813* (1948). Rush's *Essays, Literary, Moral & Philosophical* (1798) is especially relevant for his social welfare work.

Of the many secondary works on Rush, the most useful general studies are the *Dictionary of American Biography* (1935); Nathan G. Goodman, *Benjamin Rush, Patriot and Citizen* (1934); Carl Binder, *Revolutionary Doctor: Benjamin Rush, 1746–1813* (1966); David F. Hawke, *Benjamin Rush: Revolutionary Gadfly* (1971). Rush is a major figure in John H. Powell's superb *Bring Out Your Dead: The Great Plague of Yellow Fever in Philadelphia in 1793* (1949). Rush's social welfare ideals receive extensive attention in John K. Alexander, *Render Them Submissive: Responses to Poverty in Philadelphia, 1760–1800* (1980).

JOHN K. ALEXANDER

**Ryan, John Augustine** (May 25, 1869–September 16, 1945), priest, economist, theologian, teacher, writer, and social reformer, was born in Dakota County, Minnesota, to William and Mary (Luby) Ryan, Irish immigrants. The eldest of eleven children, John grew up on the family farm. After elementary school in the local public school, he attended the Christian Brothers' school in nearby St.

Paul, and then, attracted to the priesthood, entered the seminary for the archdiocese of St. Paul, to be ordained by Archbishop John Ireland on June 4, 1898.

Even as a young student John displayed a scholarly interest in economics, politics, and social studies. He read Henry George and cheered neighbor Ignatius Donnelly and other dynamic populists of the state. What impressed him most, however, was the epochal 1891 encyclical of Pope Leo XIII, *Rerum Novarum*, in which the pontiff condemned the excesses of both unrestrained capitalism and centralized socialism, insisted that every laborer had a natural right to a wage which would allow him to live in "reasonable and frugal comfort," and encouraged the state to act on behalf of economic justice. When the pope exhorted priests to become involved in the problems of the laborer and social justice, he found an ardent disciple in John Ryan.

Ryan's sensitivity to such issues attracted the attention of Archbishop Ireland, who had consistently advocated an alliance between the ideals of American democratic progress and Catholic teaching, and the young priest was thus sent to the Catholic University of America in Washington, D.C. There he earned a licentiate in moral theology in 1902, and was heavily influenced by his professor of sociology, William J. Kerby.* It was Kerby's theme that moral theology was ineffective unless applied to contemporary social situations. Returning to St. Paul Seminary in the fall of 1902 as professor of moral theology, he worked on his doctoral dissertation, *A Living Wage: Its Ethical and Economic Aspects*. Appearing as a book in 1906, the work established Ryan's reputation in progressive circles. He applied Pope Leo's standard—"reasonable and frugal comfort"— and his solution—the power of the state if necessary—to argue that every worker was entitled to a living wage for himself and his family, and that government must guarantee that minimum when employers failed to supply it voluntarily.

While continuing to teach at St. Paul, he also became active with reforming groups such as the National Consumers' League, especially pushing for minimum wage legislation. A popular lecturer and writer, he stressed that the economy was not autonomous but subordinate to morality, and that the Church should be a friend of the worker, a proponent of social reform, and a defender of human rights. He detested the attitude that saw the Church as the enemy of progress, the ally of the wealthy, and the foe of liberty, and, more than any other Catholic leader of the century, made progressive thinkers aware of the value of the Church's social teachings. He amplified his beliefs in a second book, *Distributive Justice*, published in 1916. Here he offered an analysis of the ethical obligations of all parties—labor, capital, consumer, government—to a just, harmonious industrial society. The next year he became editor of the *Catholic Charities Review*, a position he held until 1921.

Ryan's reputation outgrew St. Paul, so in 1915 he joined the faculty of the Catholic University of America, teaching both political science and moral theology. The nation's capital was the scene of his social welfare work for the next three decades. When the American Catholic bishops created the National Catholic Welfare Council (later Conference) in 1919, they chose Father Ryan to direct its social action department, which became the most cogent voice promoting principles of Catholic social justice in the country, and he held this office until his death. He had written the basic draft of the controversial "Bishops" Program for Social Reconstruction," issued on Lincoln's Birthday of that year, which gave a blessing to such "radical" proposals as minimum wage legislation, unemployment, health, and old-age insurance, and housing subsidized by the government.

Through the complacent 1920s he continued to write, teach, and lecture. American society looked to him as a Catholic spokesman on most civic issues. He upset conservative Catholic leaders such as William Cardinal O'Connell of Boston by supporting the proposed child labor amendment to the Constitution, which the prelate considered a dangerous intrusion by the government into family life. On the other hand, liberal critics attacked him for a statement made in his *The State and the Church* (1923), which implied that once in power Catholics would deny religious freedom to all non-Catholics. Ryan rejected this vociferously during the 1928 presidential campaign of Alfred Smith. Although pained at the religious bigotry of that election, he continued to work with the Federal Council of Churches and the Central Conference of American Rabbis to promote social, racial, and religious justice. In 1927 he helped organize the Catholic Association for International Peace.

The advent of the Great Depression made Ryan's theories more relevant. Because he owed his economic ideas to John A. Hobson's underconsumption theory, he bitterly criticized Herbert Hoover and welcomed the New Deal. Dubbed "the Right Reverend New Dealer," Ryan made no attempt to hide his affection for Roosevelt, and publicly lobbied for higher wages and a $5 billion public works program to increase employment and stimulate the economy. For the priest, FDR's programs came close to implementing the principles articulated by Pope Pius XI's 1931 encyclical, *Quadragesimo Anno*. Ryan never tired of quoting the pontiff's approval of unions, his hope that governments would protect the rights of the poor, and his condemnation of laissez-faire capitalism. Besides delivering the benediction at the President's inaugurations of 1937 and 1945, Ryan served as a member of the Industrial Appeals Board of the National Recovery Administration and lauded the National Labor Relations Act and the Fair Labor Standards Act as the most just and beneficial pieces of labor legislation in American history. To counter the nasty attacks upon Roosevelt made by the popular radio priest Charles E. Coughlin, during the 1936 campaign, Ryan, at great risk to his career, delivered a speech endorsing the President over national radio. His point was clear: the reforms of the New Deal were in line with Catholic social justice principles. He also vexed conservative Catholics with his support of industrial unionism.

That the Catholic Church in the United States is today considered progressive in social justice matters, an ally of unions, and a defender of civil rights is due in no small part to Monsignor Ryan. He remains the most respected and influential American Catholic social reformer. He died in Washington, D.C.

The papers of John A. Ryan are housed in the Archives of the Catholic University of America. Besides the books by him noted above, students should consult his memoirs, *Social Doctrine in Action* (1941). Francis L. Broderick's concise and perceptive biography, *Right Reverend New Dealer: John A. Ryan* (1963), is most valuable. To put Ryan in the context of American Catholic social reform, consult David J. O'Brien, *American Catholics and Social Reform* (1968).

TIMOTHY MICHAEL DOLAN

# S

**Salmon, Thomas William** (January 6, 1876–August 13, 1927), psychiatrist and leader in the mental hygiene movement during the early decades of the twentieth century, was born in Lansingburgh, New York, the son of English parents, Annie (Frost) Salmon and physician Thomas Henry Salmon. The family had only modest means since his father struggled to keep his country medical practice afloat, and Salmon himself struggled with financial troubles and illness throughout his life. Yet he was described as affable and optimistic, if sensitive and eccentric. Salmon was, above all, zealously devoted to his work on behalf of mental patients.

Salmon's family could offer him no money for college, so that after graduation from high school he taught school for a short time and saved money to attend medical school. He then went to Albany Medical College and graduated with honors in 1899. He married Helen Ashley that same year. Salmon began his career by opening his own general medical practice, but he was unable to manage the financial details of a private practice and had to close his office after two years.

Salmon's need for financial stability led him to join the New York State Health Department as a bacteriologist, and his Health Department experience brought him to the field of psychiatry and launched his distinguished career. Salmon's first Health Department position was at Willard State Hospital, and his 1901 investigation of a diphtheria epidemic was so outstanding that he was appointed bacteriologist for the New York State mental hospitals. While working at Willard State, Salmon also met William Russell, a leading psychiatrist who was then on the New York State Commission on Lunacy, and Russell invited him to attend psychiatric staff conferences and discussions.

In 1903 Salmon left Willard State and joined the U.S. Public Health Service. In 1904 he was assigned to the immigration offices at New York's Ellis Island, and was responsible for the planning and administration of psychiatric examinations to weed out the mentally ill and mentally defective from the masses of immigrants who came through the Ellis Island station. Salmon saw the psychiatric exams as a way to restrict the entrance of immigrant groups from Southern and Eastern Europe, groups which he viewed as "undesirables," but he was also outraged by the conditions for mentally ill immigrants and immediately agitated for improved facilities. His efforts were hardly welcomed by the Public Health Service bureaucracy, and he was quickly transferred to the more neutral position of assistant surgeon at the Marine Hospital in Boston.

Salmon continued his interest in mentally ill immigrants, and in 1911 was appointed chief medical examiner of the New York Board of Alienists, responsible for a study of foreign-born patients in state hospitals. This project once again revealed Salmon's blending of humanitarian concern and racist attitudes, since he claimed that there was a greater frequency of mental disorder among Southern and Eastern European immigrants, and advocated restrictive immigration legislation. His intense belief in immigration restriction placed Salmon among the more conservative members of the mental hygiene movement, which he soon joined.

In spite of the bias in his findings, Salmon achieved wide recognition for his research on immigrants, and the once obscure physician became known as a leading research-oriented psychiatrist. On the strength of his new reputation, in March, 1912, Salmon was appointed first medical director of the National Committee for Mental Hygiene (NCMH). The National Committee was founded in 1909 by reformer Clifford Beers* as the organization for a national movement aimed at improving the treatment and conditions of the mentally ill and preventing mental illness. Salmon remained medical director of the Committee until 1922, although in 1915 he was hired by the Rockefeller Foundation, which supported the Committee's work, and "loaned" to the National Committee as its medical director.

Under Salmon's leadership in the years prior to World War I, the NCMH conducted research and surveys on the incidence of mental illness, on the size of the institutionalized population and conditions in mental institutions, and on the status of existing legislation on behalf of the insane. This early research convinced many states to eliminate dual systems of state and local care of the insane in favor of total state control, and in some states new institutions were built and new methods of treatment were introduced. Salmon was convinced that the problem of mental illness could not be separated from the problem of mental deficiency, and after 1915 the Committee conducted special research on the incidence and treatment of mental deficiency. While the Committee's finding that 1.3 percent of the population was feebleminded provoked some policy-makers to advocate such extreme measures as sterilization and segregation, Salmon, together with Walter E. Fernald,* the nation's expert on mental deficiency, was horrified by such proposals and favored education and training instead.

In the spring of 1917, Salmon and the National Committee turned all of their efforts to applying the principles of psychiatry and mental hygiene to the military. Salmon's projects during the war made psychiatry indispensable to the military, and his successes attracted widespread attention at home. Salmon, who enlisted in the army and was appointed chief of psychiatry for the armed forces, instituted psychiatric examinations for the screening of military recruits. These examinations were responsible for the rejection of nearly 72,000 men because of "neuropsychiatric disorders." In addition, Salmon organized a corps of psychiatrists in the army to treat cases of war neuroses or "shell-shock" and made provisions for the rehabilitation and adjustment of soldiers and sailors afflicted with these problems once they returned home. The psychiatric treatment of war neurosis proved very effective, and all of Salmon's wartime efforts greatly enhanced the American public's perception of the effectiveness of psychiatry in diagnosing, treating, and preventing mental disorders, helping to establish a new, socially active role for the American psychiatric profession.

Salmon was awarded the Distinguished Service Medal for his accomplishments during the war, and returned to his position with the Rockefeller Foundation and the National Committee in March, 1919, although the arrangement did not last long. Salmon was impatient with his administrative duties at the NCMH and had always been insecure about his anomalous status with the Rockefeller Foundation. In addition, shortly after his return from the war, Columbia University offered him the position of dean of its medical school. He declined the deanship, but began teaching part-time at Columbia and agreed to return to the NCMH only until a successor could be found. He began working more directly with the Rockefeller Foundation, designing its mental hygiene program.

After the war the mental hygiene movement turned away from the institutionalized mentally ill and directed its energy toward remedial and educational efforts to prevent mental illness. In 1920 Salmon proposed that the Rockefeller Foundation establish its own division on mental hygiene, which would include the establishment of psychiatric clinics for children, the application of psychiatry to problems of social deviance, the training of psychiatrists, social workers, and psychiatric nurses, and the establishment of university-affiliated psychiatric hospitals. Although the Rockefeller Foundation did not take up his suggestions, Salmon's proposals anticipated many developments in the field of psychiatry during the 1920s and 1930s. At the same time, Salmon was also involved in lobbying Congress and the new Veterans Bureau to set up separate mental hospitals for veterans. These proposals were also rejected, and Salmon alienated many officials in the process.

The Rockefeller Foundation decided against establishing a separate mental hygiene division, and because of its uncertain plans in the field and disagreements between Salmon and the Foundation's new officers, Salmon resigned from the Foundation in May, 1921, and took a position as professor of psychiatry at Columbia University. In 1921, however, a proposal by Salmon to the Commonwealth Fund resulted in the creation of its Program for the Prevention of Juvenile Delinquency, and Salmon played an influential role in the establishment of this program. Commonwealth's program introduced a network of child guidance clinics which fulfilled a major goal of Salmon's original proposal to the Rockefeller

Foundation. Salmon stayed on as medical director of the NCMH until January, 1922.

After he left the National Committee, he turned to developments within the psychiatric profession. As president of the American Psychiatric Association during 1923–1924, Salmon was particularly concerned with integrating psychiatry into the general medical profession and expanding opportunities for clinical instruction in psychiatry at medical schools. He also was an active member of the Columbia faculty and was instrumental in arranging for the affiliation of the New York Psychiatric Institute with Columbia Medical Center.

In his short career, Salmon not only improved the treatment of the mentally ill, of criminals, and of children, but his efforts to deal with the immigrant question and the problems of crime and delinquency expanded the social applications of psychiatry and transformed American psychiatry into a dynamic and effective specialty. Salmon died in a sailing accident on Long Island Sound in August, 1927.

Manuscript sources on Salmon are found in the Thomas W. Salmon Collection, Archives of Psychiatry, New York Hospital-Cornell Medical Center, New York, and in the records of the National Committee on Mental Hygiene, Rockefeller Foundation Archives, Hillcrest, Pocantico Hills, North Tarrytown, New York. The only secondary accounts of Salmon's career are Earl D. Bond, *Thomas W. Salmon, Psychiatrist* (1950), and Norman Dain, *Clifford W. Beers: Advocate for the Insane* (1980). Also see *Who's Who in American Medicine* (1925) and obituaries of Salmon in the *Medical Journal and Record*, vol. 126 (1927), 317, and the *Journal of the American Medical Association*, vol. 89 (1927), 709.

MARGO HORN

**Sanborn, Franklin Benjamin** (December 15, 1831–February 24, 1917), teacher, journalist, abolitionist, social welfare reformer, and biographer, was born in Hampton Falls, New Hampshire, the fifth of seven children of Aaron and Lydia (Leavitt) Sanborn. Aaron Sanborn was a farmer and town clerk, and was a direct descendant of New Hampshire settlers of 1640. In his early youth, Franklin Sanborn was very close to Ariana Walker, who encouraged him to attend preparatory school at Phillips Exeter Academy. From 1852 to 1855 he attended Harvard College. During his second year at Harvard, Sanborn was called back to New Hampshire to Ariana's deathbed, where he married her. She died eight days later, after which he returned to college. In August, 1862, he again married, this time to his cousin Louisa Augusta Leavitt, with whom he had three sons: Thomas Parker, Victor Canning (who died after two years), and Francis Bachiler.

During his college years, Sanborn was strongly influenced by Theodore Parker and Ralph Waldo Emerson. They encouraged him to move to Concord, Massachusetts, after graduating from Harvard. In Concord he began a private school, mostly for Emerson's children. He lived in Concord for almost all his adult years and was affectionately nicknamed "the Sage of Concord."

Committed to abolition, Sanborn became secretary of the Massachusetts Free Soil Association. He also was involved in an attempt to keep Kansas a free state. As part of this enterprise, he spent the summer of 1856 touring certain key western territories and states, including Iowa and Nebraska. Sanborn's abolitionist activities resulted in his forming a close friendship with John Brown. Although there is no evidence that he was apprised of or directly involved in the Harper's Ferry raid, he was implicated in it. Refusing to testify against Brown before the United States Senate in 1860, Sanborn was arrested. To avoid further political pressure, he fled twice to Quebec, but was persuaded by friends to return to Massachusetts, where he was apprehended. The case against him ultimately was dropped by the Massachusetts Supreme Court.

During the Civil War years, attendance fell at Sanborn's Concord school, and by 1862 it was closed. During the following seven months, Sanborn became involved in another field, journalism, and edited the *Boston Commonwealth*. His interest in journalism and his friendship with Samuel Bowles, the owner of the *Springfield Republican*, led to his becoming a resident editor of that newspaper. During the two years he worked at the *Republican*, 1872–1874, Sanborn resided in Springfield, Massachusetts. In 1874 he returned to his home in Concord, where he lived for the rest of his life. In addition to his work at the *Republican*, Sanborn wrote a daily column for the *Boston American*. Much of his journalism consisted of reporting and commenting on charitable activities, on which his views were considered to be radical.

In 1863, as part of an effort to centralize various state charities, Sanborn was appointed the first secretary of the Massachusetts Board of State Charities. Determined to create a more scientific basis by which to categorize and treat the poor, especially the so-called deviant poor, he and Samuel Gridley Howe,* president of the Board, coauthored the *Second Annual Report* of the Board of State Charities (1864), known as the Howe-Sanborn Report. This document reflects Sanborn's efforts to use social science to explain the hereditarian causes of dependency and deviance. Sanborn also organized a system of inspection and reporting about various public charities to the state. The method was praised for its scientific soundness and was adopted by many other state boards.

From 1874 to 1876 Sanborn was chairman of the Board of State Charities. Then, as a result of the Massachusetts Reorganization Act of 1879, he became the state Inspector of Charities. He served in that capacity until 1888.

Sanborn's belief in scientific charity is also reflected in other activities. He was founder of the American Social Science Association, the National Prison Association, and the National Conference of Charities and Correction. He also was active in establishing new charitable organizations, such as the Clark School for the Deaf and the Massachusetts Infant Asylum, and he became an expert on the treatment of the insane. He and Samuel Gridley Howe wrote a great deal of legislation to establish a legal framework for the development of charitable institutions and the administration of public assistance. In a continuing effort to learn as much as possible about care of the poor and defective, Sanborn visited many European institutions, especially in Italy and Greece, and attempted to incorporate some of the practices he observed there into programs in Massachusetts.

In 1879 Sanborn, along with Bronson Alcott and William Torrey Harris, established the Concord School of Philosophy. Members of this school wrote many philosophic tracts, some of which were considered of critical importance to American philosophic thought. During this same period, Sanborn wrote a number of biographies of reformers, transcendentalists, and philosophers. Some of these include the lives and/or noteworthy activities of Henry David Thoreau, Samuel Gridley Howe, Bronson Alcott, William Torrey Harris, Ralph Waldo Emerson, and Nathaniel Hawthorne.

Sanborn serves as a critical link between the early nineteenth century transcendentalists and the late nineteenth century empiricists, from social idealists to social decision-makers. Initially he worked for causes such as abolition and later became convinced that empirical evidence was essential for fair decision-making in charitable activities. Sanborn decried class distinctions, considering them responsible for increasing divisiveness and disorder, and embraced social science as a means of remedying social chaos. Sanborn died while visiting his son in Westfield, New Jersey, on February 24, 1917.

Franklin B. Sanborn's autobiography, *Recollections of Seventy Years* (1909), is particularly useful. Much of the research done on Sanborn has been condensed in the *Dictionary of American Biography* (1935); many references in this dictionary pertain to discussions of Sanborn initially found in the *New England Historical and Genealogical Register* (October, 1917), and the *Proceedings of the Massachusetts Historical Society*, vol. 50 (1916–1917). Most of Sanborn's biographies are located at the Boston Public Library or the Massachusetts State House, Boston. Annual reports to the Board of State Charities are also at the Massachusetts State House. Many of Sanborn's articles which appear in the *Journal of Social Sciences* are worthy of note.

The following secondary sources include references to Sanborn's work: June Axinn and Herman Levin, *Social Welfare: A History of the American Response to Need* (1975); Robert H. Bremner, *American Philanthropy* (1960); Barbara M. Brenzel, *Daughters of the State: A Social Portrait of the First Reform School for Girls in North America, 1856–1905* (1983); Michael B. Katz, *The Irony of Early School Reform* (1968); Robert H. Mennel, *Thorns and Thistles: Juvenile Delinquents in the United States 1825–1940* (1973); Anthony M. Platt, *The Child Savers: The Invention of Delinquency* (1969); and Walter I. Trattner, *From Poor Law to Welfare State: A History of Social Welfare in America* (1974).

BARBARA M. BRENZEL

**Sanger, Margaret** (September 14, 1879–September 6, 1966), leader of the American birth control movement, was born Margaret Louise Higgins in Corning, New York, the sixth of eleven children and the third of four daughters of Anne (Purcell) and Michael Hennessey Higgins, owner of a stone monument shop.

Michael Higgins was an outspoken atheist and champion of the single-tax socialism of Henry George, and his iconoclastic ideals hurt his business in a conservative factory town. The two eldest Higgins daughters sacrificed personal ambitions to family need and worked to supplement a family income that always seemed inadequate to Margaret Higgins. She associated her mother's tubercular cough and the family's financial insecurity with her parents' high fertility. Anne Higgins died when she was forty-nine, prematurely aged, in her third daughter's view, by the endless drudgery of raising eleven children on the uncertain income of a village atheist. Michael Higgins lived past eighty. The contrast between her parents' fates was one source of Margaret Sanger's ambition to win reproductive autonomy for women.

Margaret's youth was shaped by rebellion against authority and by efforts to escape her father's household. After she refused to continue attending public school in Corning, her two older sisters paid her tuition at Claverack College, a private coeducational preparatory school in the Catskills, where she spent three happy years before taking a job teaching school. Obeying her father's summons, she returned to Corning, where her mother was dying of tuberculosis. Michael Higgins expected her to manage his household with the stoic resourcefulness of a traditional woman, but Margaret resented her father's domestic authoritarianism and escaped Corning a second time by entering nursing school.

In 1902 she left nursing to marry William Sanger, an architect. A tubercular condition led to confinement at an Adirondack sanatorium during her first pregnancy, and after the birth of a son, Stuart, in 1903. Her health eventually improved; the Sangers built a home in suburban Westchester County, New York; a second son, Grant, was born in 1908, and a daughter, Margaret (Peggy) in 1910. After the birth of her third child, Margaret Sanger became increasingly dissatisfied with her life as a housewife. The Sangers sought to thwart a growing estrangement through joint participation in radical politics, and they left their Hastings-on-Hudson home for a Manhattan apartment. She worked as a home nurse on the Lower East Side and enlisted as an organizer in the Industrial Workers of the World's (IWW) effort to enlist textile workers in the Northeast.

Sanger made important contributions to the IWW strike efforts of 1910–1913 and learned from Emma Goldman and other radical women that issues of economic justice might be joined with feminist demands for recognition of the right of women to control their bodies. Responding to the widespread desire among women of all classes for information about venereal disease, birth control, and sex education, Sanger established herself among radicals as a speaker and writer on sexual reform. She became convinced that women needed a distinctive voice representing them as an interest group in the struggle for social justice, and she took the position that sexual reform was the paramount issue for women, a cause that could not wait for the anticipated socialist revolution.

Sanger's emerging feminist consciousness was also spurred by repression of her publications. An article about syphilis for the February 9, 1913 issue of the socialist weekly the *Call* was declared unmailable by the United States Post

Office under the Comstock Act of 1873, whose sweeping provisions also banned information on contraception. Sanger's resentment over the degradation of women finally focused on the issue of access to contraceptive information. She claimed that the death of one of her clients from a self-induced abortion was the traumatic event that led her to a single-minded crusade against the prohibitions on contraceptive information. In the story of Sadie Sachs, a truck driver's wife who was scornfully refused contraceptive advice by a doctor and instructed instead to have her husband sleep on the roof, Sanger found a compelling myth. She used it to convey her outrage at the suppression of knowledge that women needed. Sanger's feeling of having been trapped by marriage, as well as her resentment of her mother's premature death, made the suffering of tenement mothers her own. Thus, in 1914, Sanger, then living apart from her husband, set out to remove the stigma of obscenity from contraception and to establish a nationwide system of advice centers where women could obtain reliable birth control information.

Sanger hoped to mobilize a mass demand for legalization of birth control through publication, beginning in March, 1914, of her militantly feminist journal, *Woman Rebel*, which the post office declared unmailable. After being indicted for violation of the postal codes, Sanger fled to Great Britain in October, 1914, leaving behind instructions for the distribution of her how-to-do-it pamphlet, *Family Limitation*, which provided the most detailed and informed discussion of contraceptive technique then available in English. During a year of exile in Europe, Sanger, under the influence of genteel British sexual reformers, began to develop a more cautious propaganda that exploited the rhetoric of social science and sought to win social elites to the cause of birth control. In the Netherlands Sanger found contraceptive advice centers staffed by midwives and learned to fit the spring-loaded vaginal diaphragm.

Returning to the United States in October, 1915, Sanger toured the country urging women to open contraceptive advice centers, and in October, 1916, her own Brownsville "clinic," staffed by Sanger and her younger sister, provided 488 Brooklyn mothers with contraceptive advice during the ten days before the police closed it. The trial and imprisonment of "the birth control sisters" helped make Sanger a national figure, and in appealing her case, she won a clarification of the New York law that forbade distribution of birth control information. In rejecting Sanger's claim that the prohibition on contraceptive information was unconstitutional because it forced women to risk death in pregnancy against their will, Judge Frederick Crane ruled that physicians might provide women with contraceptive advice if their health would be threatened by pregnancy.

Sanger interpreted the Crane decision as a mandate for doctor-staffed birth control clinics and adopted the strategy of lobbying for "doctors only" bills that removed legal prohibition on medical advice. This pragmatic concession to the self-conscious professionalism of doctors was part of a larger shift of strategy as a reformer. Gradually Sanger broke her ties with old comrades, played down her radical past, stressed eugenic arguments for birth control, and found financial support among socialites and philanthropists. Such support allowed her in 1921 to organize the American Birth Control League, the national lobbying organization which later became the Planned Parenthood Federation of America (1942). Having divorced William Sanger in 1920, she completed her social transition in 1922 by marrying millionaire J. Noah Slee, who proved a faithful funder of her cause.

By 1923 Sanger had developed the network of support that allowed her to open, and to keep open, the Birth Control Clinical Research Bureau in New York City. The first doctor-staffed birth control clinic in the United States, the Bureau provided a careful clinical record that established the safety and effectiveness of contraceptive practice, an important accomplishment during a period when medical leaders claimed that contraception was a dangerous interference with a natural process and often led to cancer or madness. The Bureau served as a teaching facility where hundreds of physicians received instruction at a time when contraceptive technique was not part of the medical school curriculum, and it provided the model for the nationwide network of over 300 birth control clinics established by Sanger and her supporters by 1938. Staffed mainly by women doctors and supported by the efforts of women volunteers, these clinics provided access to reliable contraceptive advice and were responsible for important improvements in the effectiveness of contraceptive practice.

Sanger tirelessly raised money to make up clinic budget deficits and to support legislative lobbying campaigns. She fought a series of court battles to establish the legality of the birth control clinic, and in 1936 realized her goal of reversing the Comstock Act's classification of birth control as obscenity. In *United States v. One Package*, a federal court ruled that the new clinical data forced reinterpretation of the 1873 law to permit the mailing of contraceptive materials intended for physicians. The decision made possible the 1937 resolution of the American Medical Association recognizing contraception as a legitimate medical service that should be taught in medical schools.

After the *One Package* case, Sanger played a less important role in the American birth control movement. Her brand of feminism seemed counterproductive to new leaders who hoped to gain acceptance of their cause from supporters of other voluntary health organizations. They replaced "birth control" with "family planning" in an effort to broaden the appeal of the movement and sought to observe the still existing limitations on who could receive contraceptive advice, restrictions which Sanger viewed with contempt.

After World War II and the discovery of the so-called population explosion, Sanger's vision began to command new respect, and in 1952 she played a creative role in the founding of the International Planned Parenthood Federation, which she served as first president. Despite her role in promoting the diaphragm, she had never been satisfied with it and raised large sums throughout her career for research on new methods. In 1952 she helped to realize her dream of a female-controlled physiological contraceptive when she brought the work of biologist George Pincus to the attention of her longtime financial angel, Katharine Dexter

McCormick, who subsidized the development of the birth control pill marketed in 1960.

When Margaret Sanger died of congestive heart failure in Tucson, Arizona, on September 6, 1966, her goal of reproductive autonomy for all women remained unattained, but she had done more than any other individual to spread the good news that sex could be separated from reproduction.

Over 500 boxes of personal and organizational papers are divided among the Library of Congress, the Sophia Smith Collection at Smith College, and the American Birth Control League Papers at Houghton Library, Harvard University. The Sophia Smith Collection has a microfilm of the Sanger Papers in the Library of Congress, as well as the papers of the Planned Parenthood Federation of America.

Sanger left two autobiographies, *My Fight for Birth Control* (1931) and *Margaret Sanger: An Autobiography* (1938). Her other major books are *Woman and the New Race* (1920), *The Pivot of Civilization* (1922), *Happiness in Marriage* (1926), and *Motherhood in Bondage* (1928). She published three important journals: *Woman Rebel* (1914), *Birth Control Review* (1917–1940), and *Human Fertility* (1940–1948).

For an annotated bibliography on works about Sanger, see James Reed, *From Private Vice to Public Virtue: The Birth Control Movement and American Society Since 1830* (1978). Also see Joan M. Jensen, "The Evolution of Margaret Sanger's *Family Limitation* Pamphlet, 1914–1921," *Signs* (Spring, 1981), 548–567.

JAMES REED

**Schneiderman, (Rachel) Rose** (April 6, 1882–August 11, 1979), labor organizer and social reformer, was born in Savin, Poland, to Samuel Alter Schneiderman and Deborah (Rothman) Schneiderman. Rose attended a traditional Hebrew school and later a Russian public school in Khelm, a rarity for women. In 1890 her family migrated to the United States and settled on New York's Lower East Side. Her later sensitivity to the poor was forged in her own poverty after her father died in 1892. Rose, her mother, her infant sister, and her two brothers lived on charity for three years. Poverty then forced her mother to place the three older children in an orphanage. After one year, Rose returned home, where she did the housework and child care while her mother was at work. Rose obtained her first job at age thirteen as a cash girl for approximately $2 a week, often working up to seventy hours. After three years she went to work in the men's cap industry, less prestigious work, which, however, paid a better salary.

Rose Schneiderman became involved in union work after a one-year interlude in which she lived with a socialist family in Montreal. Upon her return she organized the first female local of the Jewish Socialists United Cloth Hat and Cap Makers Union (1903). Under her leadership—she was both its secretary and its delegate to the New York Central Labor Union—it grew in membership to several hundred. In 1904 she participated in her first strike and spoke in public for the first time. Her short stature, combined with her fiery words, soon gave her a reputation as a dynamic speaker. At age twenty-two, she was the first woman ever elected a member of the General Executive Board of the Central Labor Union.

Rose Schneiderman's activities swiftly moved beyond her union participation. In 1905 she joined the National Women's Trade Union League (NWTUL), a coalition of workers and middle- and upper-class reformers which she considered the most important influence on her life. She was elected vice president in 1906. In 1908 she received a stipend which enabled her to quit her factory work and return to school, while simultaneously becoming a national part-time organizer for the League. By 1910 the League induced her to leave school by offering her a job as a full time organizer at $25 per week.

Rose Schneiderman played a key role in the successful organizing of the International Ladies' Garment Workers' Union (ILGWU). She helped bring several hundred thousand workers, a majority of them women, into the union. She organized and raised their funds and sat on the Women's Executive Board. After the Triangle Shirtwaist Company fire in 1911, Rose Schneiderman gave a major impassioned speech calling both for relief and for safety codes. During her tenure with ILGWU, she was active on settlement committees, dealt with grievances, worked as an organizer, and became head of its Speakers Bureau.

Rose Schneiderman was always intensely interested in women's issues and worked for the advancement of education for women. She was among the organizers of the Bryn Mawr Summer School for Women Workers in 1921. She also organized and purchased a clubhouse for the New York League which became both an educational and a social center for working women. For a short time she took a leave of absence as a union organizer to work for the suffrage movement. As president of the NWTUL she concentrated on promoting workers' education as well as on lobbying for protective legislation, minimum wage laws, and eight-hour days for women workers. Like other such lobbyists, she opposed the proposed equal rights amendment, as she felt that working-class women would lose their union gains—protective legislation—if they supported such an amendment.

After World War I, her union activities took on an international scope when she was elected as a delegate to the Peace Conference in Europe. She was involved in reconstruction for trade union women and was appointed a delegate to the Conference of the International Committee of Women for Permanent Peace in Zurich. She organized the first International Trade Union Women's Meeting in Washington, D.C., and made sure that one of the advisors of each of the delegates at the International Labor Conference was a woman. She suggested the formation of an international labor office to be headquartered at the League of Nations, and she established the International Congress of Working Women.

Her international League activities brought her in touch with prominent politicians and reformers. During a long friendship with Franklin and (Anna)

Eleanor Roosevelt,* she and NWTUL leader Maude Schwartz helped to shape the Roosevelts' views on labor relations and the labor movement. Under President Roosevelt's tenure, she was appointed to represent the Labor Advisory Board for the interests of working women as part of the National Recovery Administration (NRA). In that role she was sent to Puerto Rico to oversee codes for industries that employed large numbers of women and to see that wages and hours provisions were fair to the workers.

She returned to the NWTUL in 1934 (after the NRA was declared unconstitutional and the Labor Advisory Board went out of existence), where she helped found the Laundry Workers Union and the Hotel Employees Union.

Although she had resumed her League work, Rose Schneiderman continued to be politically active throughout World War II. From 1937 to 1943 she was the Secretary of the New York State Department of Labor and worked with various compensation boards. After Pearl Harbor, Rose Schneiderman actively opposed isolationists and devoted herself to the war effort, including selling bonds to union employees.

In 1943 she resigned as the Secretary of the Department of Labor due to her frustration at being too inactive, and returned to the presidency of the New York WTUL, at a time when the organization was weakening. By 1947 the National Women's Trade Union League closed its office. Rose Schneiderman retired as its president in 1949, and in 1955 the New York League closed its doors. She retired quietly to Manhattan, devoting her last years to writing her autobiography. She died in New York after five years in the Jewish Home and Hospital for the Aged.

Rose Schneiderman's papers are in the Tamiment Library, New York University. Papers concerning her union career are also in the New York State Labor Library, Department of Labor, New York City, and the Library of Congress, Washington, D.C.

She wrote several articles and an autobiography, including "A Cap-maker's Story," *Independent* (April 27, 1905); "The White Goods Workers of New York," *Life and Labor*, National WTUL Journal (May, 1913); and, with L. Goldthwaite, *All for One* (1967).

Articles and books about her include G. E. Endelman, "Solidarity Forever: Rose Schneiderman and the Women's Trade Union League," Ph.D. dissertation, University of Delaware, 1978; *Notable American Women 1607–1950*(1971); J. E. Marcus, *The American Jewish Woman 1654–1950* (1981); and J. R. Rapport, "Notable American Jewish Women: A Computer-Aided Study in Collective Biography," Rabbinic thesis, Hebrew Union College, 1984. An obituary appeared in the *New York Times*, August 12, 1972.

                                                    ARLENE RUBIN STIFFMAN

**Schulze, Oskar** (May 22, 1882–October 24, 1973), welfare administrator, social group worker, recreationist, and founder of the Golden Age Clubs, was born in Germany and raised a Christian. Schulze (who pronounced his name "Schultze," and about whom some personal information cannot be ascertained) was graduated from Teachers Training College in Dresden in 1908. He taught public school and did graduate work in social sciences and administration at the Polytechnicum in Dresden (1908–1914). During the war he was a civil administrator, stationed in Eastern and Southern Europe. As a Dresden city councilor from 1919 through 1922, Schulze placed foster children in rural communities and supervised the care of old people in two large city homes. Schulze became government representative at Annaberg in Saxony in 1924 and was Governor at Annaberg in 1924–1925, organizing a labor exhange and a vocational guidance department.

From 1926 through 1928 Schulze was chief government representative in Leipzig and in 1929 became third mayor of Leipzig, heading the Social Welfare and Legacy Department. In that position, he supervised construction of housing units for low-income workers, reorganized the city's public relief system, and administered the child welfare department. Increasingly aware of the need of the elderly for recreation, he also created old-age clubs.

When Adolph Hitler came to power in 1933, Schulze refused to become a Nazi. He quit his post and fled, escaping through Berlin, Switzerland, and Istanbul, where in 1935 and 1936 he tutored foreign children. With his second wife, Suzanne, he emigrated from Turkey in January, 1937, arriving in Cleveland in the spring. While Suzanne found a position teaching social work at the School of Applied Social Sciences at Western Reserve University, Schulze, less adept at English, languished in a series of odd jobs through 1939.

Convinced that a temporary separation from Suzanne would improve his facility with English, Schulze traveled to Chicago in January, 1940, to take a position as a temporary staff member at the Olivet Institute, a settlement house interested in recreation for old people. There, among the area's German population, Schulze found isolated, lonely, and impoverished elderly. Within five months, he had brought some thirty older persons into a viable old age club.

In the summer of 1940 Schulze returned to Cleveland, where he repeated his Chicago experiment at Alice Gannett's Goodrich House settlement. This success brought funding from the Cleveland Foundation, the Jewish Welfare Federation, and the Benjamin Rose Institute, a foundation created in 1908 to provide charitable relief for aged women. The new program of old age clubs was operated under Recreational Services for Older People (RSOP), created in 1940 under Rose Institute auspices. Schulze headed the RSOP staff of over 100 social workers and volunteers until 1948, when he left for Chicago.

During his directorship, Schulze reported on the club program to the National Conference on Social Work (1941) and traveled widely explaining the club idea. Much of his time, however, was spent in day-to-day club management. By 1950 the movement had taken root in St. Louis, Chicago, Pittsburgh, New York, and Detroit, among other cities, and the clubs had for some years been known as Golden Age Clubs. The first Golden Age Club was created in November 1955, to assist the Cleveland Housing Authority in caring for older residents.

The Golden Age Clubs functioned on two levels. They were social institutions.

Members played board games, celebrated holidays and birthdays, heard speakers from the community, and took part in discussions that were sometimes led by the energetic and charismatic Schulze. At this level, the clubs expressed Schulze's belief that the elderly needed social activities and that these activities should not, as in Germany, be left to the politicians.

The clubs also were intended to be mechanisms of social engineering. They were designed to serve as an alternative to Francis Townsend's pension movement, to counter political radicalism among the elderly, to prevent the development of an age-based politics, and to encourage responsible habits of political participation. Familiar with group work precepts, Schulze believed that these goals could be accomplished within the participatory and "democratic" atmosphere of the clubs. He was a practitioner of a form of social engineering that emphasized process rather than content. In theory, club leaders would facilitate rather than control, encouraging members to arrive at their own (it was hoped, socially conservative) conclusions. This vision of club goals and operations links Schulze to a tradition of social group work best exemplified by Grace Coyle,* the Western Reserve professor and John Dewey disciple whose theoretical work underpinned the clubs.

Schulze's latter years were spent in Chicago consulting on old age. He died in the Windy City on October 24, 1973.

The Benjamin Rose Institute, Cleveland, has a small collection of material on Schulze and the Golden Age Clubs. The collection includes some correspondence, a vita, newspaper clippings, drafts of speeches, and Schulze's account of the founding of the clubs, published as "Recreation for the Aged," *Journal of Gerontology* (October, 1949), 310–313. Among newspaper articles not included in the Rose Institute collection, see *Cleveland Plain Dealer*, April 9, 1937; March 12, 1939; July 8, 1946; and December 12, 1965. For the fullest treatment of Schulze, the clubs, and available source materials, see William Graebner, "The Golden Age Clubs," *Social Service Review* (September, 1983), 416–428. An obituary appeared in the *Chicago Tribune* on October 25, 1973.

WILLIAM GRAEBNER

**Schuyler, Louisa Lee** (October 26, 1837–October 10, 1926), pioneer in citizen action for public welfare, was born in New York City to George Lee Schuyler and Eliza (Hamilton) Schuyler. Louisa was born into a distinguished family; her father, a lawyer and engineer, was a grandson of the Revolutionary War general Philip John Schuyler, and her mother was a granddaughter of Alexander Hamilton and his wife, Elizabeth Schuyler.

Louisa, along with her brother Philip and her younger sister Georgina, spent her childhood on the spacious estate of their grandfather, James Hamilton, and in the family home in New York City. She was educated by private tutors. In her later years, as a woman of independent means, she, too, maintained an apartment in New York City and a country home upstate, and traveled to Europe frequently.

Although she was reared in an atmosphere of wealth and secure social poition—or perhaps because of it—she followed the family tradition of charitable service for the less fortunate members of the community. Her maternal great-grandmother, Elizabeth Hamilton, had served for many years as a leader of the first orphan asylum in New York State along with the founder, Joanna Bethune. During Louisa's lifetime, the entire Schuyler family was closely associated with the work of Charles Loring Brace,* the first secretary of the New York Children's Aid Society (CAS). Louisa's father was an active financial contributor to the agency when it was formed in 1853. Louisa's mother served as a volunteer teacher in the Society's industrial schools, organized to give elementary education and vocational training to poor immigrant children. At the age of twenty-three, Louisa Schuyler joined her mother as a volunteer teacher at a CAS industrial school.

Soon after Louisa began her teaching, the Civil War broke out. Dr. Henry Whitney Bellows* of the All-Souls Unitarian Church in New York City, which the Schuylers attended, became the president of the United States Sanitary Commission. A forerunner of the American Red Cross, the Sanitary Commission supplemented the work of the medical department of the Union army by sending clothing, foodstuffs, and medical supplies to the troops, finding lodgings for men on furlough, and assisting soldiers with their claims for pay. Louisa's mother, Eliza Schuyler, was one of the founders and a member of the executive committee of the Women's Central Association of Relief, which soon became the most important auxiliary of the United States Sanitary Commission.

At the invitation of the Reverend Bellows, Louisa Lee Schuyler joined in the work of the women's branch of the Sanitary Commission. She served with distinction as chairman of the Committee on Organization and Publicity of the New York branch during the four years of the war. She set up an efficient distribution service as an intermediary between the local women's groups that sent supplies to the central office and the soldiers in hospitals and army camps who finally received them. In addition, she spearheaded a pubic information campaign which stimulated the formation of a large network of additional local women's groups. Through the central office, she then supervised the work of the local committees.

When the war ended, Miss Schuyler, emotionally drained by four years of uninterrupted work, suffered a complete physical collapse. She spent the next seven years traveling abroad, resting and recuperating. For the remainder of her life she followed the same pattern. She was able to work with energy and effectiveness on projects that lasted for several years, but when the project was completed, she withdrew for an extended period of rest.

When she returned to the United States in 1871 with greatly improved health, she began to look for another activity where she could once again use the authority of her social position and her formidable executive and political skills for the public good. After consulting with the former leaders of the Sanitary Commission, Louisa Schuyler chose the reform of public charitable institutions—the almshouses, hospitals, and asylums—as a goal for organized volunteer effort. She began by inspecting the Westchester County poorhouse near her home. Appalled by the barbarous conditions she observed, in January, 1872, she organized a visiting committee of neighbors to view the neglect and abuse of the pauper inmates and to make recommendations for change.

Later that month her neighbor and friend, General James Bowen, a New York City Commissioner of Charities and Corrections, invited her to inspect the care of the sick poor at Bellevue Hospital. She convened a group of society women to her father's home in New York City. They agreed to visit the hospital and observe the facilities and the standard of care of the patients. The committee soon came to the conclusion that the biggest obstacle to adequate patient care was the incompetence of the untrained pauper women who were serving as nurses.

As a result of these preliminary institutional visits, Louisa Schuyler decided to form a permanent voluntary agency. Private citizens would visit public institutions on a regular basis, report their findings to the newly organized State Board of Charities, and, if necessary, press for legislative reforms. Accordingly, in May, 1872, Louisa Schuyler recruited a group of prominent men and women who represented a cross-section of the social, business, and government elite of New York City to serve as an independent citizen watchdog group to oversee the public charities throughout the state of New York—the New York State Charities Aid Association (SCAA). A number of young women who had been associated with Schuyler in her war work, notably Josephine Shaw Lowell* and Gertrude Stevens Rice, began to work again under her direction in the SCAA. In time the SCAA became the legally designated representative of the State Board of Charities. Like the Sanitary Commission, it operated through local committees that were closely supervised by a central office.

The Bellevue visiting committee became a branch of the SCAA. Under Schuyler's leadership, within two years the committee established the first training school for nurses in the United States, one modeled on Florence Nightingale's precepts for nurses' training. The Bellevue Hospital Training School for Nurses is credited with popularizing nursing as a respectable profession for educated American women.

Under Schuyler's guidance, the SCAA achieved outstanding legislative reforms. In 1875 it could take credit for the state law which mandated the removal of all normal children over the age of three from county almshouses. In 1890, as a result of Schuyler's effort, particularly a long campaign of education and lobbying, New York State began building special institutions for the care of the mentally ill. In 1892 she obtained legislation segregating epileptics from the mentally ill and providing special treatment for them.

In 1893 Homer Folks* was chosen to succeed Dr. John H. Finley* as executive secretary of the SCAA. Although Schuyler retained titular leadership of the agency until her death, from the time Folks joined the organization she willingly relinquished its active direction to him. The SCAA continued to expand its influence, helping to create new facilities and shape state legislation for child care, mental hygiene, and public health for many years to come.

Meanwhile, in 1907 Schuyler, in her position as trustee of the newly formed Russell Sage Foundation, became interested in developing new programs for the prevention of blindness. She created an agency which in 1915 became the National Committee for the Prevention of Blindness, an organization credited with saving the sight of thousands of children.

She continued to plan for additional programs for public service. A life of innovative and lasting achievements came to an end, however, when Louisa Lee Schuyler died in her eighty-eighth year at the country estate of J. P. Morgan at Highland Falls, New York.

Selections of Schuyler's papers may be found in the New York Historical Society, in the U.S. Sanitary Commission Papers in the New York Public Library, in the archives of the State Charities Aid Association and of the Russell Sage Foundation, in the Homer Folks Papers at the Columbia University School of Social Work, and in the Sophia Smith Collection at Smith College. For details of Schuyler's life, see the obituary and editorial, *New York Times*, October 11, 1926, as well as Louisa L. Schuyler, *Forty-Three Years Ago* (1915). See also the annual reports of the SCAA published by the National Committee for the Prevention of Blindness. Her earlier published writings appear in the *Bulletins* of the Sanitary Commission and the reports of the Women's Central Association of Relief.

There is no full-length biography of Louisa Lee Schuyler. Further details of her life can be found in the adulatory article written by a contemporary, in Francis G. Peabody, *Reminiscences of Present-Day Saints* (1927). Scattered references to her work appear in William R. Stewart, *The Philanthropic Work of Josephine Shaw Lowell* (1911). The story of the renovation of Bellevue Hospital is told by Elizabeth C. Hobson, *Recollections of a Happy Life* (1916). For a more objective and comprehensive view of both her personality and her achievements, two more recent articles are of value. See Robert D. Cross, "The Philanthropic Contributions of Louisa Lee Schuyler," *Social Service Review* (September, 1961), 290–301; and Walter I. Trattner, "Louisa Lee Schuyler and the Founding of the S.C.A.A.," *New York Historical Society Quarterly* (July, 1967), 233–248.

DOROTHY G. BECKER

**Scudder, Vida Dutton** (December 15, 1861–October 9, 1954), settlement house worker, social reformer, Christian socialist, professor of literature, and author, was born Julia Davida Scudder, in Madura, India, the daughter of David Coit Scudder, a Congregational missionary, and Harriet Louisa (Dutton) Scudder. Following her father's death by drowning in 1862, her mother returned with her infant daughter to the protection of the Dutton and Scudder families in Massachusetts. Scudder was educated at private schools in Boston, worshipped in the Congregational and then the Episcopal Church, and traveled at length in Europe with her mother and other relatives. From this privileged and protected girlhood, spent largely with adult women, Scudder emerged a painfully sensitive youth, shy and dutiful, with deep and enduring attachments to her mother, a circle of female relatives, and an expanding network of intimate women friends and companions. She was devoted to study and possessed an elevated religious sensibility along with an abiding feeling of personal isolation, of being divorced from reality.

Scudder attended Smith College, a women's school in Northampton, Massachusetts, in the early 1880s. After graduating in 1884, she left for Europe, where she began postgraduate work in literature at Oxford University. Following her return to Boston in 1885, Scudder spent two years somewhat adrift. She earned the M.A. degree in literature from Smith in 1887, meanwhile widening her knowledge of the arts and letters, history, religion, and new social thought of Tolstoy, Ruskin, the Christian socialists, and the Social Gospel. In 1887 Scudder accepted a teaching position at Wellesley College, a women's school in Wellesley, Massachusetts, where she remained, but for brief interludes, for over forty years, teaching, writing, and developing her ties within the emerging collegiate sisterhood that played a role in contemporary feminist and social welfare and reform movements.

Twenty-five years would pass, however, before Scudder and her mother moved from Boston to live in Wellesley near the college, for even as Scudder began her career in education she was also embarked upon a career in urban social work and social action. In the late 1880s, Scudder became one of the early advocates of the idea, recently imported from England by Stanton Coit,* of settling college graduates to live and work in poor urban neighborhoods. She participated in the development and opening of settlements in New York City and Philadelphia, helped to organize and direct the College Settlements Association, and in 1893 took a leave of absence from Wellesley to join Helena Dudley* in opening Denison House in the South End of Boston. During this period, Scudder became a member of the Boston Nationalist Club, participated in various Christian socialist enterprises in the city, and was active in several organizations attempting to bring the Episcopal Church into social service and social action. Scudder also worked in the labor movement in Boston, helping to organize women, speaking and writing on behalf of labor, and serving for a time as a delegate to the Boston Central Labor Union. As Scudder attempted to bring her Christian socialism and her connections into the labor movement to bear on her settlement work, she became an early and persistent opponent of the settlement house as an exemplar of social justice and an instrument of social action, one of several competing interpretations of the settlement idea then in currency. She deplored the development of institutional settlements, lamented the decline of social idealism among settlement workers more concerned with career than cause, and called upon the settlements to renounce their attachment to wealthy benefactors and join the working class in a crusade for social justice.

Friends and family were openly dismayed by Scudder's drift from a genteel social idealism through social service into social action, while Scudder found herself to be unsatisfied with her protected life of literary scholarship yet uneasy in the rough and tumble of social work and social action. Alternately, she congratulated herself for bridging the gap between Wellesley and the South End and accused herself of infirmity of purpose, of dabbling in matters that demanded commitment. As she struggled in the 1890s to bring into a common focus her religious ideals, her socialism, her practical settlement work, and her friendships with the people of privilege, Scudder began to produce in her teaching and writing a rich and penetrating exploration of some of the most vexing problems of contemporary social work and social reform. But the divisions in her life gradually grew unbearable and, in 1901, as she reached the age of forty, following a battle over a gift to Wellesley College from Rockefeller, Scudder suffered a severe breakdown that required two years of rest, travel, and study in Europe to mend.

Scudder returned from Europe to teaching at Wellesley in 1903 with her social ideals renewed by further study of economic socialism and Marxism and radical social Christianity, especially the teachings of the Italian saints, Francis of Assisi and Catherine of Siena. During the following two decades, through her membership and leadership in dozens of academic, religious, and socialist organizations (including the National Women's Trade Union League, the Episcopal Church Socialist League, the Joint Commission on Social Service of the Episcopal Church, the Socialist Party, the Intercollegiate Socialist Society, and the League for Industrial Democracy), Scudder intensified her efforts to bring her social ideals into both the academic community and the church, and her religious beliefs into socialist and reform movements. She resumed her active work in the settlements but gradually became convinced of their inherent limitations, even as they grew more offended by her socialism. She gave up active work at Denison House in 1912 and resigned from the Denison House board of directors at the end of World War I. During this period Scudder continued to ransack the literary and religious traditions of America and Europe, concentrating increasingly now on the monastic, communitarian, mystical, and ascetic traditions of the Catholic Church, bringing it all to bear in her writings on contemporary social issues.

Scudder remained active well into the 1940s, but after World War I, and especially following her retirement from Wellesley in 1928, her paramount interest was in extending her examination of the religious and spiritual foundations of her social ideals. She gained a considerable reputation as a Franciscan scholar, wrote admiringly of the contemporary revival of monasticism and the Franciscan way, and experienced a deepening personal commitment to pacifism and contemplative prayer.

Although she was a leader in the development of urban social settlements, social action in the churches, and women's higher education, Scudder's distinctive contribution to modern social work and social welfare thought grew out of her refusal or inability to concentrate her activity or confine her commitments. Both her work and her writings were marked by unremitting efforts to reconcile her religion, her socialism, her social work, and her educated tastes, resulting in a penetrating analysis of issues and an unlikely intellectual combination of Western humanism, radical Christianity, revolutionary socialisms old and new and large and small, contemplative and pacific ideals, feminism, and practical social work and reform. Although it caused her much personal anguish and probably robbed her of outstanding achievement in any one field, her greatness was in her resistance to purified loyalties, her lonely and persistent struggle to exist in the huge social, institutional, and intellectual interstices of Western industrial society.

Scudder died in Wellesley, Massachusetts, aged ninety-two.

Manuscript sources on Scudder are scattered and thin. The most useful materials are in the Sophia Smith Collection, Smith College, Northampton, Massachusetts, and in the Archives of Wellesley College, Wellesley, Massachusetts, and of the Companions of the Holy Cross, Byfield, Massachusetts.

Scudder's voluminous writings on literary and social topics include *The Life of the Spirit in Modern English Poets* (1895), *The Witness of Denial* (1895), *Social Ideals in English Letters* (1898), *Socialism and Character* (1912), *The Church and the Hour: Reflections of a Socialist Churchwoman* (1917), *The Social Teachings of the Christian Year* (1921), and *The Franciscan Adventure: A Study of the First Hundred Years of the Order of St. Francis of Assisi* (1931). Her disenchantment with the settlements is expressed in "Settlement Past and Future," in *Denison House College Settlement Report* (1900), reprinted in Lorene M. Pacey, *Readings in the Development of Settlement Work* (1950), and in her semi-autobiographical novel of ideas, *A Listener in Babel* (1903). *On Journey* (1937) is Scudder's rich autobiography, supplemented by a sequel, *My Quest for Reality* (1952). Some of her mature reflections are collected in *The Privilege of Age: Essays Secular and Spiritual* (1939).

Scudder's social work is discussed at some length in the following general works: Allen Davis, *Spearheads for Reform: The Social Settlements and the Progressive Movement, 1890–1914* (1967); Peter J. Frederick, *Knights of the Golden Rule: The Intellectual as Christian Socialist Reformer in the 1890s* (1976); Arthur Mann, *Yankee Reformer in an Urban Age* (1954); and William L. O'Neill, *Everyone Was Brave* (1969). Specifically on Scudder, the only book-length study is Theresa Corcoran, *Vida Dutton Scudder* (1982), which concentrates on her writing but contains a short life and an excellent bibliography. Corcoran is also the author of *Vida Dutton Scudder: The Progressive Years*, Ph.D. dissertation, Georgetown University, 1973; "Vida Dutton Scudder: The Impact of World War I on the Radical Woman Professor," *Anglican Theological Review* (April, 1975), 164–181; and "Vida Dutton Scudder and the Lawrence Textile Strike of 1912," *Essex Institute Historical Collections* (July, 1979), 183–195. Other articles on Scudder are Peter J. Frederick, "Vida Dutton Scudder: The Professor as Social Activist," *New England Quarterly* (September, 1970),

407–433; and Nan Bauer Maglin, "Vida to Florence: 'Comrade and Companion,' " *Frontiers* (Fall, 1979), 13–20.

THOMAS MARSHALL TODD

**Shattuck, Lemuel** (October 15, 1793–January 17, 1859), public health pioneer
and statistician, was born in Ashby, Massachusetts, the youngest of five children
of John and Betsy (Miles) Shattuck. Soon after his birth, Lemuel's family moved
to New Hampshire, where his father pursued a meager living by working a small
farm and making shoes. His early life was harsh, and he received little education,
supplementing his limited formal schooling by studying independently.

As a young man, Shattuck taught school in Albany and Detroit before moving
to Concord, Massachusetts, in 1823 to work as a merchant in partnership wth
his brother Daniel. He married Clarissa Baxter of Boston in 1825. They had five
daughters, three of whom survived him. While in Concord he wrote a detailed
history of the town. It was while preparing this work that he began to formulate
his ideas concerning the role statistical analysis could play in giving order and
meaning to facts. During the ten years he spent in Concord, Shattuck also
developed a new code of school regulations, including a system of reports set
up to provide statistical data. This system was subsequently adopted for use
throughout the state.

His work in the areas of history and statistics had established him as a well-
known scholar by the time he moved to Boston in 1835, where he opened a
publishing house. He became a member of the City Council in 1837, and four
years later he was asked to complete a statistical analysis of Boston from 1810
to 1841. His analysis revealed serious public health problems in the Boston area.
Consistent with the predominant beliefs of the times, Shattuck felt that these
problems were a consequence of immoral behavior, and that this situation could
be solved through a strict adherence to the divine laws of nature.

Shattuck initiated a city census in 1845, the results of which led him to the
conclusion that most, if not all, of the public health problems could be directly
attributed to Boston's large population of immigrants. He believed that the life
style and behavior of the immigrant population, combined with the crowded
conditions in which they lived, produced an unhealthy atmosphere which not
only affected the immigrants themselves but anyone living near them.

Shattuck also was in part responsible for establishing a standard system of
nomenclature for diseases. His earlier work in Boston had shown that different
physicians tended to label the same disease with a variety of names, resulting
in confusion and creating obvious difficulties in the collection of data. As a lay
member of the American Medical Association's committee on medical
nomenclature, he advocated a system developed by William Farr, which
subsequently was adopted by the AMA in 1846.

By that time Shattuck had retired from his private business ventures and had
devoted himself full-time to public service. As the acknowledged leader in the
field of statistics, Shattuck continued to press for statewide collection of data

related to disease and life style through the auspices of the American Statistical Association, which he had helped found.

The call for a sanitary survey was finally heeded in 1849, and Shattuck was appointed to a commission to conduct the survey. While there were two other people on the commission, all accounts agree that Shattuck conducted the investigation, and wrote the report, by himself. The result of his labors, published under the title *Report of a General Plan for the Promotion of Public and Personal Health*, is a detailed, comprehensive examination of the state of public health in Massachusetts; the report, however, also addressed future public health needs not only in the state but in the entire nation as well. The report has been repeatedly praised for its insight and foresight, which can be illustrated by listing a few of its many recommendations, among which were:

1. Immediate establishment of state and local boards of health;
2. Systematic exchange of health information;
3. Teaching the science of sanitation in medical schools; and
4. Routine collection and analysis of vital statistics.

In fact, there are few public health principles today which were not in some way anticipated by Shattuck in his report.

In spite of its insight and vision, the report had little immediate impact for several reasons. First, many of the ideas put forth in the report were simply too far ahead of their time to be taken seriously. Second, Shattuck's writing style was direct, unemotional, and uninteresting. Finally, the report was issued at a time when many other events were taking center stage in history, including the slavery controversy and the upcoming Civil war. Years later, the report was finally recognized as the important work it was, and it stands today as possibly the most remarkable of all American public health documents.

Shattuck withdrew from public life after the completion of the report, spending his final years working on several private projects, including his family's genealogy. He was described as a rather pompous, precise man, yet it was this preoccupation with precision and exactness which enabled him to make such a lasting contribution to the fields of public health and statistics. He died in Boston on January 17, 1859, at the age of sixty-five.

While there is no full-length biography of Shattuck, there are several sources which do provide valuable information on his life and career. Scattered references to the importance of his work are contained in C. L. Anderson, *Community Health* (1973), and John J. Hanlon, *Public Health–Administration and Practice* (1974). Additional insight into some of the issues with which he was most concerned can be gained from James H. Cassedy, "The Roots of American Sanitary Reform, 1843–1847: Seven Letters from John R. Griscom to Lemuel Shattuck," *Journal of the History of Medicine and Allied Sciences* (April, 1975), 136–141. Perhaps the most comprehensive account of his life and work is contained in Barbara Gutmann Rosenkrantz, *Public Health and the State—Changing*

*Views in Massachusetts, 1842–1936* (1972). Shorter biographical accounts can be found in the following sources: *Appleton's Cyclopedia of American Biography*, vol. 5 (1900), 484; *Who Was Who in America, Historical Volume, 1607–1896* (1963), 478; *Dictionary of American Biography*, vol. 9, part 1 (1936), 33–34.

JIM STAFFORD

**Simkhovitch, Mary Melinda Kingsbury** (September 8, 1867–November 15, 1951), settlement leader and social welfare and public housing advocate, was born in Chestnut Hill, Massachusetts, the first daughter of Laura and Isaac Kingsbury, a merchant prominent in Congregationalism and Republican politics. Mary grew up sheltered in Boston's suburbs, but went to Boston University, studying Latin on campus and becoming acquainted with a world of Bellamyite socialism and startling poverty in her jaunts downtown. After teaching Latin in a nearby high school for a year, she obtained a fellowship to study at the University of Berlin. Accompanied by her mother, she toured Europe and attended seminars with famous German scholars, becoming awed by the triumph of ideas, including socialism and Marxism, across Europe. At Berlin she also met and became engaged to the Russian emigré scholar Vladimir Simkhovitch before returning to the United States to enroll in history and economics courses at Columbia University.

In 1897 Mary Kingsbury entered the settlement house world, becoming head resident of the College Settlement on the Lower East Side of New York City. She was fascinated by this alien world, learned Yiddish, and frequented the immigrant theater and the Rumanian coffee houses, with their heady talk of labor agitation and socialist progress. But a year later, she left for the East Side's Friendly Aid House, run under Unitarian auspices. She soon became restive with the settlement's religious uplift and apparent detachment from the district's material needs. Her three years' experience at Friendly Aid confirmed her feelings that the settlement must remain in solidarity with the mores of its neighbors while remaining a force for social change. In the meantime, she married Vladimir and moved fully into the circle of economic and social inquiry being directed at Columbia University.

In 1902, with Vladimir's contacts at Columbia and her growing influence in social reform circles, Mary Simkhovitch gathered supporters, including Jacob Riis,* Robert Fulton Cutting,* and Felix Adler, to raise money to buy a tenement on Jones Street, which she then converted into her own settlement, Greenwich House. She was impressed by her Irish and Italian neighbors, members of the working poor struggling to hold on to the shreds of their family dignity. She vowed to make her settlement a solid place of resort for neighbors in distress, a house of warm cozy fireplaces and alcoves where all could comfortably meet. At the same time, she also leaned toward an interventionist casework that would goad the more sturdy of her charges to improve their lot—a posture that from the beginning also shaped her relations with city bureaucrats. Cajoling, flattering, sometimes arguing with local officials, Simkhovitch made Greenwich House virtually a City Hall for the district, getting the Tenement House Department to inspect local buildings, the city to provide bathhouses and parks, and the board of education to build school annexes and playgrounds. From the beginning as well, she made her settlement the locus of a powerful social inquiry using Vladimir's Columbia University colleagues to review the neighborhood research conducted by Greenwich House residents. Her activism attracted some of the era's most effective social investigators, such as architect George B. Ford and polemicist Benjamin C. Marsh, who collaborated on the Commission on Congestion of Population, and Mary White Ovington,* who resided at the settlement while researching her path-breaking articles on black life in Manhattan. Through Crystal Eastman,* Mary Simkhovitch became a patron of the New York Consumers' League's war on sweatshops; and she staunchly supported the campaign by Florence Kelley* and the Women's Trade Union League to upgrade female factory work. In addition to conducting what had become a kind of progressive salon, Simkhovitch also gave birth to two children, a son in 1902, and a daughter in 1904.

The war era seemed to make it increasingly difficult to hold on to ideals of neighborhood work. Over Vladimir's objections to wartime expansion, Mary moved the settlement into a larger building on Barrow Street and later conceded that she missed her old ties on Jones Street. As president of the National Federation of Settlements in 1917, she welcomed the war as a sober, bracing venture, but her settlement was soon overrun by war services personnel. Then, in the 1920s, the Village was invaded by chic "bohemians," whose arrival seemed to herald a new privatism and a withdrawal from civic causes. Greenwich House also found more of its initiatives superceded by the public schools, with their social centers, and the city, which had begun to routinize many of its health and tenement house services. Simkhovitch thus softened her notions about interventionist casework, and viewed her settlement as more of a place to nurture the whole individual amid the confines of modern industrial society. She expanded Greenwich House's music classes into a separate Music School and turned its pottery instruction for local boys into a renowned cottage industry. At the same time, though, understanding the new primacy of the social welfare state, Simkhovitch became the key settlement supporter behind Governor Alfred E. Smith's state housing program, where she probably first worked with her longtime collaborator, Helen L. Alfred. She and Alfred soon became the New York leaders of the American Association for Old Age Security, which Abraham Epstein* organized to press for a federal system of old-age pensions based on social insurance principles.

The Great Depression merely confirmed Mary Simkhovitch's convictions about the social welfare state and federal responsibility. Helen Alfred persuaded her to head the Public Housing Conference, which campaigned for New York municipal slum clearance and housing. The women proved adroit lobbyists and emerged in 1934 with a charter for the New York City Housing Authority, the country's first such municipal agency. Mayor Fiorello H. La Guardia appointed Simkhovitch vice chairman, where she helped establish tenant selection procedures and a management policy concerned with tenant morale and social adjustment. But even before, she and Alfred had seen the necessity of housing funds from Washington, and with their National Public Housing Conference (NPHC) buttonholed prominent New Dealers to inject provisions for public housing construction in the 1933 National Industrial Recovery Act. When this commitment faltered, the NHPC built a groundswell of local support for a full-fledged, independent, federal housing program. Mary Simkhovitch wrung personal assurances from President Franklin D. Roosevelt that he would support the Wagner-Steagall bill that established the United States Housing Authority in 1937. When the Roosevelt administration again reneged on the funding commitment during the national defense crisis, Simkhovitch headed the NHPC's struggle to obtain a new federal housing strategy for postwar America.

Mary Simkhovitch served on the New York City Housing Authority board until 1947, when she failed to gain reappointment. She remained long enough to see herself and other municipal housing pioneers superseded by a new generation of professional housing managers and her Housing Authority transformed into a huge, multiproject system that had begun to obliterate the Old Law tenement neighborhoods of the poor—and many of their neighborhood settlements. She retired as director of Greenwich House in 1946, but stayed on with her husband until her death there on November 15, 1951.

The Mary K. Simkhovitch Papers in the Schlesinger Library, Radcliffe College, contain mostly speeches and articles, but Simkhovitch's letterbooks reportedly remain at Greenwich House, still closed to researchers at this writing. These can be supplemented with the New York City Housing Authority Papers, Fiorello H. La Guardia Community College, Long Island City, New York; the Robert F. Wagner, Sr., Papers at Georgetown University; and the National Federation of Settlements and Neighborhood Centers Papers, Social Welfare History Archives, University of Minnesota, Minneapolis.

Mary Simkhovitch's published books included her charming reminiscences of Greenwich House, *Neighborhood: My Story of Greenwich House* (1938); and her last musings on social reform, *Here Is God's Plenty: Reflections on American Social Advance* (1949). Her early calls for a strenuous, efficient settlement in "The Case Work Plane," *Proceedings of the National Conference of Charities and Correction* (1909); and in "Standards and Tests of Efficiency in Settlement Work," ibid. (1911), can be contrasted with her later mellowed opinions, "The Place of Recreation in the Settlement Program," *Proceedings of the National Conference of Social Work* (1930); and "The Changing Settlement," *Better Times* (January 5, 1931). Her yearly "Statement of the Director" in Greenwich House, *Annual Reports*, 1902–1946, remains indispensable, as does her occasional exhortations to the housing troops in the National Public Housing Conference, *Public Housing Progress*, 1934–1943.

Simkhovitch's obituary was published in the *New York Times*, November 16, 1951. A fine short sketch of her life by Carroll Smith-Rosenberg appears in *Notable American Women: The Modern Period* (1980). Robert A. Woods and Albert J. Kennedy, *Handbook of Settlements* (1911), contains an important glimpse of Greenwich House and its residents' activities at the height of the Progressive Era. Allen F. Davis, *Spearheads of Reform* (1967), and Timothy L. McDonnell, *The Wagner Housing Act* (1957), contain crucial appraisals of Simkhovitch's contribution to urban liberalism.

JOEL SCHWARTZ

**Smith, Stephen** (February 19, 1823–August 26, 1922), surgeon and sanitary reformer, was born in Spafford (Onondaga County), New York, to Chloe (Benson) and Lewis Smith. Smith was descended from English families that settled in Connecticut in the seventeenth century. His father was a farmer and a member of the New York State Assembly. His mother was also of English origin. Stephen Smith attended local schools and Cortland Academy in Homer, New York. He did not begin medical studies until age twenty-three, when he attended classes in Geneva, New York (in 1847), where Elizabeth Blackwell,* the first woman to graduate from an American medical school, was a classmate. Smith also attended the medical school in Buffalo, in 1849, and in 1850 was awarded the M.D. degree from the College of Physicians and Surgeons in New York City. From 1850 until 1852 he was an intern at Bellevue Hospital.

In 1857 Smith married Lucie Culver, the daughter of a prominent Brooklyn judge who later became minister to Venezuela. They had nine children.

Smith's active career in medicine and public affairs spanned more than sixty years, including the entire second half of the nineteenth century. It was unusual not only for its length and accomplishments, but for its breadth as well. He became an attending surgeon at Bellevue in 1854 and at several other New York hospitals. In the next forty years his principal source of livelihood was medical practice. As a surgeon, he was a popular teacher, often with large private classes, and had faculty appointments at Bellevue Hospital Medical College from 1861 to 1875 and then at New York University. He was a prolific author of surgical papers and of two popular textbooks, published in 1862 and in 1879. His improvement in the operation of knee joint amputation, a common procedure in the nineteenth century, was widely acknowledged. At Bellevue, he was one of the first surgeons to use and to advocate Joseph Lister's methods of antiseptic surgery after 1867, when most American physicians were still very resistant to the idea. Smith also was one of the most supportive medical staff members for the small group of women who, under Louisa Lee Schuyler's leadership, founded the Training School for Nurses at Bellevue in 1874, an important pioneer venture.

Smith was a reformer and a publicist of causes throughout his career. He began to influence his medical colleagues as an editor. In 1853, at age thirty and only three years out of medical school, Smith became joint editor with Samuel S. Purple of the well-known *New York Medical Journal*. Four years later he became the chief editor of this quarterly, and in 1860 he began the *American Medical Times*, an influential weekly journal that was read throughout the North during the Civil War years. For the entire four-year existence of the *Medical Times*, Smith wrote weekly editorials, some about medical matters, but many touching on the concerns of social medicine, particularly public health.

Smith's public health interests moved from the call for sanitary reform to very active work in its cause when, in the summer of 1864, he organized and supervised a major sanitary survey of New York City carried out by thirty-one young physician-volunteers. Their findings were published in a large *Report* of the Citizens Association, the sponsoring organization. It was this *Report*, and the lobbying by Smith and his colleagues, that finally persuaded the state legislature in Albany to pass a landmark bill in 1866 creating an active and efficient health department for the city. For the first time, appointments were not simply based upon political favor, and the health department now had the legal power to remove sanitary nuisances. Smith served as a member of the board from 1868 to 1875.

During those years public health as a specialty of medicine, with the close cooperation of sanitary engineers, began to take shape. One indication of this emerging discipline was the need felt for a national organization. Smith and a handful of colleagues organized the American Public Health Association in 1872. His leadership role in this endeavor was acknowledged when he was elected the first president of the Association, serving for the first three years of its existence.

In 1879 President Rutherford B. Hayes appointed Smith as one of five civilian members of the newly established National Board of Health. He served on its executive committee during the entire four years of the Board's existence and wrote extensively about its work. In 1894 Grover Cleveland appointed him as one of the three American delegates to the International Sanitary Conference in Paris.

Smith's work on behalf of the public charities in New York began when he was appointed by the Governor to the New York State Board of Charities in 1881. He left the Board for the period 1882 to 1888 when he served as the State Commissioner in Lunacy. At first this appointment met with some hostility from the psychiatrists, who wondered why a surgeon should be appointed to oversee the state's mental hospitals. But his keen interest in and energetic attack on the problems faced by the overcrowded and understaffed state hospitals quickly won him new admirers. Smith initiated a training school for mental hospital attendants, the first of its kind, in Buffalo in 1884. Soon thereafter he began to urge the legislature to remove the mentally ill from county jurisdiction, where they frequently were kept in shameful almshouses. At Smith's instigation, the State Care Act, which he drafted, was finally passed in 1890. It required that mentally ill patients be sent to state hospitals, except in those counties that ran their own psychiatric facilities.

After leaving the Commissionership in Lunacy in 1888, Smith resumed his seat on the State Board of Charities. With the exception of a short term on the

New York City Board of Charities, 1897–1898, Smith continued to serve on the State Board until 1918, his ninety-fifth year. He was a faithful attendant at the Board's meetings and participated actively in the inspections and the decisions of the Board. He was president of the New York State Conference of Charities and Correction in 1912.

During his several decades of work in public health and charities, Smith continued his medical writing and, until the mid–1890s, his surgical practice and teaching. He used the presidency of the American Public Health Association and of the New York Medical Association in 1891 to exhort his medical colleagues to pay more attention to the plight of the poor and the mentally ill. He described his work in dozens of journal articles and in two books listed below.

Smith lived the last few years of his life with his daughter in Montour Falls, New York, where he died on August 26, 1922, a mere six months short of his one-hundredth birthday.

Smith published over sixty articles in medical journals between 1851 and 1917. He wrote many long reports for the various boards on which he served. His books include *Handbook of Surgical Operations* (1862); *Doctor in Medicine* (1872); a collection of some editorials from the *American Medical Times*; *Manual of the Principles and Practice of Operative Surgery* (1879; rev. and enl. 1887); *The City That Was* (1911), describing the public health campaign in New York City in the 1860s; and a description of his work as Commissioner in Lunacy and on the State Board of Charities in *Who Is Insane?* (1916).

Major biographical dictionaries, both general and medical, contain sketches of Smith. See also Gert H. Brieger, *Stephen Smith: Surgeon and Reformer*, Ph.D. dissertation, Johns Hopkins University, 1968, and "Sanitary Reform in New York City: Stephen Smith and the Passage of the Metropolitan Health Bill," *Bulletin of the History of Medicine* 40 (1966) 407–429.

GERT H. BRIEGER

**Smith, Theobald** (July 31, 1859–December 10, 1934), bacteriologist and public health reformer, was born in Albany, New York, to Teresia (Kexel) and Philipp Schmitt, a tailor. He was raised a German-speaking Catholic but abandoned his religion and Americanized his surname before entering Cornell University in 1877. Upon graduation in 1881, he returned home to study at Albany Medical College, receiving his M.D. in 1881. He then took a position in Washington with the U.S. Department of Agriculture's (USDA) Bureau of Animal Industry, where he did research and published on a wide range of medical problems, the most significant of which was Texas cattle fever. Not only did his work eliminate a serious threat to the nation's beef supply, but his elegant solution added much to the prestige of American biomedical research. Smith's identification of a tick as the vector set a precedent and contributed to the atmosphere in which a mosquito was identified as the yellow fever vector a few years later. Smith married Lilian Eggleston in 1888. The couple had two daughters and a son.

Smith left the USDA in 1895 when he was offered the opportunity to direct the laboratory of the Massachusetts Department of Health. This was an era when public health agencies and hospitals were establishing laboratories whose personnel were expected to carry out original investigations as well as routine tasks. Smith did important work there on standardization of vaccines and antitoxins, and under his leadership the laboratory became a producer of such biologics on a scale to compete with commercial firms. If Smith accomplished a single feat in Boston that could rival his work on Texas fever, it was his demonstration that the bacilli of human and bovine tuberculosis were of two distinct varieties. This proof had the immediate effect of eliminating widespread fears about the transmission of tuberculosis to humans through milk and beef, and its policy implications were gradually adopted throughout the country and the world.

In Washington, Smith had established himself as perhaps the foremost of the first generation of American bacteriologists. His position in Boston allowed him to enhance this reputation through more laboratory work and to make use of that reputation in policy-making and social cricitism. In Boston, as in Washington, Smith also had a medical school position; and as a Harvard professor as well as the personification of scientific medicine in the state bureaucracy, Smith was in a position to expound upon public health issues. A 1908 speech of his on flies was reprinted twice—despite his admitted lack of specific expertise and the mid-nineteenth century sanitarian tone of his practical advice.

Smith's career extended from shortly after the acceptance of the germ theory of disease, through the crisis of the mechanical application of bacteriological findings to public health, into the era of the social programs of "the new public health." He was not an aggressive ideologue (as, for example, was Charles V. Chapin*), but he consistently defended the intrusion of the state medical apparatus into the daily life of its citizens. He stressed that disease was a natural phenomenon and that the best that people could hope for was to control the balance between parasites and hosts. Controlling the balance, the job of state medicine, involved manipulating a number of environmental variables—including the behavior of human beings. What science offered was an aid to making rational decisions in public health policy. Smith was willing to lend the prestige of natural science to the social sciences by pointing out analogies between biological and political parasites, and by calling for exchanges of ideas between students of social and of biological pathology. He made a clear distinction between preventive public medicine and curative individual medicine. He regarded the latter as wasteful of resources in an era of scientific public health, and he looked forward to its decline, because its expense made it the medicine of the wealthy alone.

In his discussions of bovine tuberculosis and throughout his writings, Smith revealed an underlying evolutionary thought structure. He regarded it as unlikely that the same variety of germ could survive equally in the different environments of the human and bovine bodies. Whichever species had originally hosted it, as the parasite extended its range of habitats it would adapt to the new host. This notion of adaptation and evolution is basic to Darwinian theory, and much of

Smith's understanding of parasitism, disease, and social problems also reflected a fundamental Darwinism. Disease could not be completely eliminated, precisely because every measure taken against it would provoke an adaptive response by the pathogen. Smith's frequent use of an analogy between biological and social parasitism thus suggests a fatalism about societal ills. While in a public position in Massachusetts, Smith operated on the assumption that disease was both a natural condition and a social problem. For this reason, like other social problems, it could at best be ameliorated—and the most effective ameliorative measures were those developed by experts in the biomedical and social sciences.

Smith remained in Boston until 1915, spending part of 1912 in Berlin on an international faculty exchange. When he left Massachusetts, it was to head another new laboratory, the Rockefeller Institute laboratory of animal pathology in Princeton. Smith had sat on the Institute's Board of Scientific Advisors since 1901 (when he had rejected an offer to be its first director, for fear of the pressures of administrative responsibility), and he had always maintained his ties to its networks. He retired as director of the laboratory in 1929, but stayed in Princeton and continued his research and writing until shortly before his death in 1934 at the Rockefeller Institute Hospital in New York City.

Smith's letters and other personal papers are held by his family and are not readily accessible. Manuscript collections which include significant Smith material are the Simon Henry Gage Papers (Olin Research Library, Cornell University, Ithaca, New York) and the Simon Flexner Papers (American Philosophical Society Library, Philadelphia). Other repositories worth investigating include the Countway Library of Medicine, Boston; the Rockefeller Archive Center, Tarrytown, New York; and the National Library of Medicine, Bethesda, Maryland.

Smith authored almost 300 items. A complete, classified bibliography is included with Dolman's *Dictionary of Scientific Biography* entry on Smith. Smith's findings on Texas cattle fever were published as Bureau of Animal Industry Bulletin No. 1, *Investigations into the Nature, Causation and Prevention of Texas or Southern Cattle Fever* (1893). His work on bovine tuberculosis appeared as "A Comparative Study of Bovine Tubercle Bacilli and of Human Bacilli from Sputum," *Journal of Experimental Medicine* 3 (1898), 451–511. The following articles give a flavor of his approach to social issues: "Public Health Laboratories," *Boston Medical and Surgical Journal, 143 (1900), 491–493;* "The Relationship of Animal Life to Human Disease," *Public Health Reports and Papers* 31 (1905), 328–338; "Research into the Causes of Disease: Its Importance to Society," *Boston Medical and Surgical Journal* 153 (1905), 6–11; "The Housefly as an Agent in the Dissemination of Infectious Diseases," in *Fly Danger* (1920). In 1933 Smith presented the Vanuxem Foundation lectures at Princeton University. He described the published version, *Parasitism and Disease* (1934), as his only attempt at popularization. This is a good summary on the scientific and social views he held throughout his life.

The following are the most useful secondary sources on Smith: A. E. Cohen,

"Obituary: Theobald Smith, 1859–1934," *Bulletin of the New York Academy of Medicine*, 2nd ser., 11 (1935), 107–116; Claude E. Dolman. "Theobald Smith, 1859–1934: Life and Work," *New York State Journal of Medicine* 69 (1969), 2801–2816; Dolman, "Texas Cattle Fever: A Commemorative Tribute to Theobald Smith," *Clio Medica* 4 (1969), 1–31; Dolman, "Theobald Smith," in *Dictionary of Scientific Biography*, vol. 12 (1975), 480–486; Simon Henry Gage, "Theobald Smith, 1859–1934," *Cornell Veterinarian*, 25 (1935) 207–228; Earl Baldwin McKinley, "Theobald Smith," *Science* 82 (1935), 575–586; and Barbara Gutman Rosenkrantz, *Public Health and the State: Changing Views in Massachusetts, 1842–1936* (1972).

EDWARD T. MORMAN

**Smith, Zilpha Drew** (January 25, 1852?–October 12, 1926), social worker and social work educator, was born in Pembroke, Massachusetts, the second daughter and the third of six children of Judith Winsor (McLauthlin) and Silvanus Smith. Soon after her birth the family moved to East Boston, where her father, a skilled builder of sailing vessels, established a shipyard. Her parents, as descendants of *Mayflower* passengers and with a proud New England heritage, instilled the basic virtues of the Protestant ethic in their children by teaching them the value of hard work and the necessity for social service. Zilpha was raised in a family which actively supported most reform movements, such as temperance, education reform, religious tolerance, and woman suffrage. Her mother, who engaged in various types of benevolent reform, nurtured her daughter's interest in social work. At an early age, then, Zilpha learned the importance of family ties, human rights, and community service, three principles which would prepare her for a central role in the progressive age of reform.

In 1868 Smith graduated from Boston's Girls' High and Normal School. Despite her training for the teaching profession, she became a telegrapher in the Commercial Telegraph Office at Boston. Her activities, however, never strayed far from social service. Like their mother, both Zilpha and her sister Frances contributed their time as volunteers in the Co-operative Society, a local relief organization in Boston. At the same time, Smith had the opportunity to reorganize the index of the Probate Court of Suffolk County, an experience which allowed her to further develop her organizing abilities as well as the capacity to analyze a problem with methodical detail. These skills, combined with her relief work, particularly after the Boston fire of 1872, clearly provided Smith with the reputation and qualifications for her appointment in 1879 as the registrar of the newly formed Boston Associated Charities.

Under Smith's leadership, the Boston Associated Charities successfully consolidated most of Boston's relief agencies. As the director of its registration bureau, or what was called the "confidential exchange," Smith also played a pivotal role in coordinating the operation of the agency's central file. With her penchant for bureaucratic efficiency, Smith organized her department as a clearing house of information which maintained an extensive system of records on every individual served by the association. Although she did not receive the formal title of general secretary until 1886, almost seven years after her appointment, Smith's duties could more appropriately be described as those of a general administrator through her systematic management and coordination of the various agencies affiliated with Boston Associated Charities.

Like some of the other leaders of the organized charity movement at the end of the nineteenth century, Smith increasingly directed her efforts away from voluntary benevolent action toward social work as an emerging profession. One of her central concerns lay in redefining the responsibilities of the volunteer "friendly visitor," an informal form of religious and social service first developed by Josephine Shaw Lowell.* Although Smith still believed that friendly visitors could reform the individual through their moral influence, she also recognized that volunteer charity workers required some level of professional training. Favoring an approach similar to that of the settlement reformers, Smith believed that social service demanded the skills of an investigator combined with the objectivity and precision of the social scientist. Through library and field research, Smith felt the social worker would be prepared not only to reform the individual but to educate the courts, legislators, and the public at large on social reform policy. In this capacity, Smith extensively researched and compiled charity statistics for her published reports and projects, presenting her most complete study at the Paris Exposition in 1900.

Smith's leadership gained national recognition for herself and for the Boston Associated Charities. For many years she assumed a prominent role in the National Conference of Charities and Correction, and for many other organizers she was an advisor and a model administrator. Smith also established a training program for paid and volunteer workers who joined Associated Charities, and she served as a mentor for many young women who chose social work as a profession. As a pioneer in social work education, Smith formed study classes and founded the Monday Evening Club, a social work discussion group, with the assistance of Charles Birtwell* of the Boston Children's Aid Society in 1888.

After her retirement from Associated Charities in 1903, Smith formally instituted her educational program in an academic setting with the establishment of the Boston School of Social Work in 1904. Smith became the assistant director of the Boston School, which created a branch for men at Harvard University and one for women at Simmons College. The initial purpose of the program was to allow male and female students the opportunity to study social problems through "practical methods." In the one-year certificate program, Smith used actual case studies for the course work, and she recruited other prominent social workers as lecturers, including Florence Kelley* and Lillian Wald* during the first year.

Following years of social service, Smith retired in 1918, leaving behind a legacy in charity organization and social work education. Throughout her career Smith remained committed to the progressive ideal for casework investigation in all areas of reform. Ultimately, however, her most visible achievement was transforming the friendly visitor of the nineteenth century into the twentieth century professional social worker. Smith died in Boston in 1926 at the age of seventy-four.

A scrapbook and folder in the Colonel Miriam E. Perry Archives of the Simmons College School of Social Work Library contain school materials, unpublished papers, and personal writings. The Mary Richmond Papers at the New York School of Social Work include several letters by Smith.

Smith's published writings are not extensive, but the following articles, drawn from the *Proceedings* of the National Conference of Charities and Correction, are useful for understanding her professional ideas: "Volunteer Visiting: The Organization Necessary to Make It Effective" (1884), 69–72; "How to Get and Keep Visitors" (1887), 156–162; "Report of the Committee on the Organization of Charity" (1888), 120–130; "The Education of the Friendly Visitor" (1892), 445–449. In addition, Smith authored the following: "A Study of Charities Statistics," *Labor Bulletin of the Commonwealth of Massachusetts*(October, 1899), 1–20; "Friendly Visitors," *Charities* (1901); "Methods Common to Social Investigation," *Field Department Bulletin* (February, 1909), 43–50. Smith also published the following pamphlet on broken families: *Deserted Wives and Deserting Husbands: A Study of 234 Families Based on the Experience of the District Committees and Agents of the Associated Charities of Boston* (1901).

Accounts of Smith's life and work include the following: a memorial volume, *A Meeting in Memory of Zilpha D. Smith* (1926); Jeffrey R. Brackett, "Zilpha D. Smith," *Social Worker* (October, 1926), 7–8, and "Smith, Zilpha Drew," in *Encyclopedia of the Social Sciences*, vol. 14 (1934), 118–119; Roy Lubove, *The Professional Altruist: The Emergence of Social Work as a Career, 1880–1930* (1965), and "Smith, Zilpha Drew," in *Notable American Women, 1607–1950* (1971); and Margaret E. Rich, "Zilpha Drew Smith, 1852–1926," *The Family* (May, 1930), 67–79.

NANCY G. ISENBERG

**Springer, Gertrude Hill** (April 19, 1879–July 17, 1953), social worker, journalist, and editor, was the first of two daughters born to Eben and Sarah Hill, ranchers in Grant County on the western Kansas frontier. By the time she reached high school the family had moved to Lawrence, and in 1896 she enrolled at the University of Kansas. Her course work emphasized history and foreign languages, but beyond the classroom she carried editorial responsibilities on the university's weekly paper and worked for the *Lawrence Daily Journal*. With an aptitude for writing and an irreverence for social correctness, she left school with an A.B. in 1900 and struck out for prairie news posts.

In 1903 she was hired by the *Kansas City Journal*, where Louis A. Springer was city editor. Springer had been educated in the United States and Europe; his journalistic career included travel abroad for the United Press. He and Gertrude were married in the fall of 1903 and left for the East, where he had accepted an editorial position on the *New York Sun*.

Gertrude often traveled with him during the next years, and her appraisals of social conditions abroad appeared in print. When World War I engulfed Europe, she committed her energies to American Red Cross relief in Italy and supervised efforts to alleviate the needs of refugees displaced from war zone villages.

Returning to the States, she combined her social work knowledge and her ability to interpret events by working at the Bureau of Advice and Information of the New York Charity Exchange. For a time, Springer edited a magazine for the Girl Scouts and in 1921 began a nine-year stint as managing editor of *Better Times*, published by the New York Welfare Council for social workers. In the spring of 1930, the *Survey*, the nation's foremost journal in social welfare, edited by Paul Kellogg,* noted Springer's resignation from *Better Times* and complimented her work and wit. In October she brought these assets to the *Survey* (which earlier had split into two publications, the *Midmonthly* and the *Graphic*) as associate editor for social work practice.

At the magazine Gertrude Springer was increasingly responsible for production of the *Survey Midmonthly*, directed to a narrower audience of social workers than the more general *Survey Graphic*. Her previous jobs and her role as chairman of the New York Council of Social Work's committee on publicity in the 1930s provided her with familiarity with the local response to the Great Depression. Quickly her knowledge about the rest of the country expanded through field trips and annual attendance at the National Conference of Social Work, where she recorded ideas characterizing the profession and built a network of friends for exchanging information. The American Public Welfare Association, organized in 1935, put her on the payroll to attend its conferences and provide an interpretation of its affairs.

Federal public welfare was new in the 1930s; her articles documented its introduction, as social workers trained in private agencies came to welcome the New Deal's intervention, first with relief monies, then with work programs, and finally with social insurance and child welfare measures with the Social Security Act of 1935.

Springer evaluated new program goals against what she saw as the historical inadequacies of welfare. The Red Cross experience in Italy taught her how indirect the route was between policy conception and the individual recipient, and that ultimately program effectiveness depended on local leadership. Cognizant of innovations facing trained workers and of the number of inexperienced people being pulled into burgeoning bureaucracies, Springer began writing a column called "Miss Bailey Says . . . ," which continued for almost a decade and eventually made "Miss Bailey" better known than Gertrude Springer herself.

In March, 1933, "When Your Client Has a Car" appeared, in which a fictional relief supervisor—Miss Bailey—counseled a worker upset by a recipient spending money on a car rather than food; the next month Miss Bailey advised about the futility of using the relief office to try to change individuals' behavior in "Are

Relief Workers Policemen?'' The first articles referred to policies garnered from officials around the country, but increasingly Miss Bailey dominated the column with Springer's own ability to laugh at herself and to listen to others. The writing reflected changes taking place in government programs, and the supervisor continually weighed the contradictions between what the rules said and how humans behave—be they workers or clients. The first eight articles were collected in a pamphlet and sold as common sense teaching tools; more collections were demanded and produced at a profit for the *Survey*.

While Miss Bailey flourished, Springer's own life changed with her husband's deteriorating health. He left the *Sun* in 1937, and from that time until his death in 1940, she spent periods away from the magazine caring for him. Early in 1942 she resigned from the *Survey* and moved to Cape Cod, tired of urban living but also feeling unable to put her energy into another war. That summer she was asked to speak at the National Conference. Addressing a record-breakingcrowd with ''The Responsibility of the Social Worker in a Democracy,'' she encouraged social workers to use their warmth and to guard against the elitism of the private agency training as they worked cooperatively within the new public welfare system.

At the Cape she chaired the local Red Cross chapter and wrote book reviews for the *Survey*, sending them along with personal notes that expressed her pride in the magazine and her deep affection for the staff. In 1943 the American Public Welfare Association (APWA) began a journal, *Public Welfare*, and asked Springer to be a consultant and book reviewer. At the APWA's annual conference in 1952 she was presented with the W. S. Terry, Jr. Memorial Merit Award, which acknowledged her role in helping administrators better understand their experiences. As Miss Bailey she had shared simply stated wisdom and respect for social workers and their clients.

Gertrude Springer died the next year in Hyannis, Massachusetts.

Gertrude Springer's college years are documented in materials at the Kenneth Spencer Research Library, University of Kansas, Lawrence, Kansas. Her role at the *Survey* and the friendships that grew out of that appear in correspondence within the following collections: Helen Cody Baker, Paul U. Kellogg, Survey Associates, and Louis H. Towley, all located in the Social Welfare History Archives at the University of Minnesota, Minneapolis, Minnesota.

The *Graduate Magazine of the University of Kansas* (February, 1919), 151–154, and (March, 1919), 182–183, contains a detailed letter by Springer about her Red Cross experiences in Italy. A variety of her outstanding features in the *Survey* include: ''Funds for Another Bleak Winter,'' *Survey* (June 15, 1931), 302–304; ''The Fighting Spirit in Hard Times'' (Coverage of the National Conference), *Survey* (June 15, 1932), 260–271; ''The New Deal and the Old Dole,'' *Survey Graphic* (July, 1933), 347–352; ''Security Has Its Growing Pains,'' *Survey* (February, 1937), 42–43; ''Public Welfare Life Is Real and Earnest'' (Coverage of an APWA Conference), *Survey* (January, 1939), 322–327; and

"The Meeting Will Please Come to Order," *Survey* (November, 1940), 322–327. The latter is a scenario for an imaginary meeting of county commissioners dealing with relief.

Springer's career at the *Survey* is covered in Clarke A. Chambers' book *Paul U. Kellogg and the Survey: Voices for Social Welfare and Social Justice* (1971). It is touched on briefly by Frank Luther Mott in *A History of American Magazines*, vol. 4 (1957). An early interview with Springer by Agnes Thompson appears as "Among Others," *Graduate Magazine of the University of Kansas* (December, 1915), 73. See also "Gertrude Springer—Free Lance," *Survey*(May, 1942), 146; "Gertrude Springer Receives Terry Merit Award," *Public Welfare* (January, 1952), 3–4; and "Terry Award to Our Miss Bailey," *Survey*(January, 1952), 38–39.

Obituary notices appeared in the *New York Times*, July 18, 1953, 13:4; *Social Service Review* (December, 1953), 428; and *University of Kansas Alumni Magazine* (October, 1953), 38. An obituary notice for Louis A. Springer can be found in the *New York Times*, January 7, 1940, 48:2.

BEVERLY A. STADUM

**Starr, Ellen Gates** (March 19, 1859–February 10, 1940), social reformer and labor activist, was born on the family's farm near Laona, Illinois, the third child of Caleb Allen and Susan (Gates) Starr. During her youth she traveled frequently to Chicago to visit her aunt, Eliza Allen Starr, a devout Catholic convert and a prominent author and lecturer on religious art. The elder Starr was to have a profound influence on the later development of her niece, introducing Ellen to a lifelong interest in promoting the social significance of art and planting the seeds of a religious quest that would lead to Ellen's conversion to Roman Catholicism. Meanwhile, Ellen was educated in the rural school system of northern Illinois and attended the Rockford Female Seminary in 1877–1878, where she met Jane Addams,* her lifelong friend. Unable to afford the seminary's tuition beyond the first year, Ellen left Rockford to become a school teacher at nearby Mount Morris. A year later, in 1879, she moved to Chicago, where she joined the staff of the prestigious Miss Kirkland's School for Girls. During the next nine years (1879–1888), she devoted herself to teaching art appreciation and English literature, while furthering her understanding of the role of art in industrial society through reading the works of Thomas Carlyle, John Ruskin, and William Morris. During these same years she deepened her friendship with Addams as the two young women contemplated the uncertainties of their futures.

Early in 1888, Starr left Chicago for an extended tour of Europe. There she met and traveled with Addams. It was on this trip that Addams first discussed her aspiration to establish a settlement house for Chicago's immigrants. Starr was immediately enthusiastic about the idea, and upon their return to Chicago the two initiated promotional and fund-raising activities which led to the opening of Hull-House on the city's West Side in September, 1889. During the next forty years (1889–1929), Starr worked tirelessly to promote the activities of Hull-

House, being chiefly responsible for the many settlement house programs designed to morally and culturally uplift the immigrants and aid in their assimilation. Literature and art appreciation classes were established, the preservation of folk arts encouraged, and an art gallery constructed under her direction. Her interest in promoting art appreciation led her to undertake many community-wide activities during the 1890s, incuding the founding of the Chicago Public School Art Society (1894), which she served as its first president. Committed to advancing the arts and crafts among the working classes, she left Hull-House in 1897 to study bookbinding in London. Upon her return in 1898, she established a bindery at the settlement house. Although bookbinding proved ill-suited to the needs of the Hull-House clients, her efforts did spur the arts and crafts movement in America. In 1900 she helped establish the Hull-House Labor Museum as a means of preserving the traditional weaving skills of Italian immigrants.

By the turn of the century, Starr realized that the working-class poverty and subsistence-level conditions engendered by rapid industrialization required a more direct, confrontational approach than that envisioned at Hull-House. As a consequence, she became a leading advocate of unionizing activities in the first two decades of the twentieth century. Already in the 1890s, Starr had joined with Florence Kelley* to speak out against child labor, had helped to establish an ''Eight Hour'' Club to promote the eight-hour day among women laborers, and had served on a citizens' committee to raise funds for striking textile workers. In 1903 she became a charter member of the Illinois branch of the National Women's Trade Union League. In 1910, 1913, and 1915 she aided garment workers in strikes against the textile industry, and in 1914 she picketed in support of striking restaurant workers. To each of these struggles, she brought her considerable talents as an organizer, fund-raiser, and publicist for the causes of labor. Her efforts to collect money, food, and clothing for strikers, her many speeches to labor rallies, and her willingness to suffer arrest on the picket lines were acknowledged in 1915 when Sidney Hillman's Amalgamated Clothing Workers of America made her an honorary life member. This close association with the workers' struggle to achieve fair treatment and her Christian belief in the inherent dignity of labor led Starr to join the Socialist Pary in 1913. In 1915 she was elected to the party's executive committee, and the following year she ran unsuccessfully as the party's candidate for alderman.

Throughout her years as a settlement house worker and labor advocate, Starr continued her search for religious meaning. Raised a Unitarian, and a practicing Episcopalian, Starr gradually moved toward Roman Catholicism in her later life. In 1920 she formally converted to Catholicism and embarked on still another career as a writer and lecturer on Catholic art and liturgy and on her conversion experience. In 1929 she underwent spinal surgery from which she never fully recovered. Bedridden, she retired in 1930 to the Convent of the Holy Child in Suffern, New York, where she maintained an active correspondence with her many colleagues, friends, and admirers. In 1935 she became an Oblate of the Third Order of St. Benedict. She died at the convent in Suffern in 1940.

The Ellen Gates Starr (1859–1940) Papers, the Sophia Smith Collection, Women's History Archive, Smith College, are the major source of information. This extensive collection of manuscript and printed sources (indexed and available through photocopying services) includes personal and professional correspondence, biographical materials, and Starr's notebooks, lectures, and articles.

In addition to numerous articles and editorials printed in Chicago newspapers, Starr's principal published writings include "Art and Labor," in *Hull-House Maps and Papers* (1895); "Efforts to Standardize Chicago Restaurants: The Henrici Strike," *Survey* (May 23, 1914), 214–215; "The Chicago Clothing Strike," *New Review* (March, 1916), 62–64; "A Bypath into the Great Roadway," *Catholic World* (May, 1924), 177–190, and (June, 1924), 358–373; and "Two Pilgrim Experiences," *Catholic World* (September, 1930), 680–684.

Brief biographical essays appear in *Commonweal* (March 15, 1940), 444–447; *Dictionary of American Religious Biography* (1977); and *Notable American Women* (1971). Important information on Starr's life and contributions is also found in Jane Addams, *Twenty Years at Hull House* (1910); Allen F. Davis, *Spearheads for Reform* (1967); Laurel W. Glassman, "Ellen Gates Starr, the Founding of Hull House, and the Social Settlement Movement," Master's thesis, Smith College, 1971; Mary L. McCree, "The First Year of Hull House, 1889–1890, in Letters by Jane Addams and Ellen Gates Starr," *Chicago History* (Fall, 1970), 101–114; and Charlotte M. Meagner, "Ellen Gates Starr: Miracle of Service," *Ave Marie* (September 28, 1946), 391–396.

DAVID L. FERCH

**Stevens, Alzina Parsons** (May 27, 1849–June 3, 1900), social investigator, factory inspector, social settlement worker, and the first juvenile court probation officer in the United States, was the youngest of seven children born to Enoch and Louise (Page) Parsons, farmers and small manufacturers in Parsonsfield, Maine. Parsonsfield was founded by Alzina's paternal grandfather, Colonel Thomas Parsons, who commanded a Massachusettts regiment in the Continental Army during the Revolutionary War. Alzina's father was a soldier in the War of 1812 and also served in the Civil War. Following his death, the family's fortunes declined. At the age of thirteen, Alzina was forced to find employment in a cotton mill. When engaged in this work, she lost her right index finger while cleaning her loom. This injury apparently stimulated her later efforts to abolish child labor and to safeguard industrial machinery.

By 1867, at the age of eighteen, Alzina had entered the printer's trade. There is no information about her unsuccessful marriage, which occurred around this time and about which she refused to speak, although she retained her married name. Alzina Stevens moved to Chicago, where she became the first American woman to become a member of a typographical union, joining local Number 16. In 1877 she organized and became the first president of Working Woman's Union Number 1 of Chicago. Moving to Toledo, between 1882 and 1891 she was employed by the *Toledo Bee* as a proofreader, compositor, and correspondent and then ended her tenure there as editor of the newspaper. She became a labor leader in the Knights of Labor, organizing the Joan of Arc Assembly and becoming its president and a delegate to the Knights of Labor District Assembly. Elected District Master Workman, she became chief officer of District Assembly 72, representing twenty-two Toledo local assemblies of Knights. She also represented District 72 at three national conventions between 1888 and 1890. In 1890 her achievements as a women's labor leader were recognized in her nomination as director of women's work by the national convention, an honor she may have declined because of other commitments. In 1892 she represented the labor organizations of northwestern Ohio at the convention of the Populist Party. She remained a lifelong union member.

In 1892 Alzina Stevens returned to Chicago and became half-owner and coeditor, with Lester C. Hubbard, of the *Vanguard*, a weekly newspaper devoted to economic and industrial reform through political action. By the end of the next year the *Vanguard* had ceased publication, and Stevens bemoaned to colleague Henry Demarest Lloyd the loss of the only weekly "people's paper" in the city. After the devastating blow dealt the working poor and the labor movement during the Pullman strike of 1893–1894, Stevens shielded Eugene V. Debs from public scrutiny in her suburban Chicago home.

In 1893, at the age of forty-three, Alzina Stevens's life work shifted as a result of a growing interest in social legislation and its administration. Her prior experience as a worker and union organizer had given her an invaluable perspective on the conditions of industrial labor, which she now put to good use. In 1892 a study of the Chicago sweatshop system and the intensive political lobbying of many Hull-House residents, including Henry Demarest Lloyd and Clarence Darrow, led to the passage of the 1893 Workshop and Factories Act. This law stipulated a maximum eight-hour working day for women and children, prohibited the employment of children under the age of fourteen in factories, manufacturing establishments, and workshops, and created a state department of factory inspection. (In 1895 the Illinois Supreme Court struck down the eight-hour provisions of the act, greatly disappointing the reformers who had advocated it.) Alzina Stevens was appointed assistant factory inspector under chief factory inspector Florence Kelley,* along with ten other deputy inspectors in the newly created Illinois Department of Factory Inspection. In 1893 a smallpox epidemic in Chicago led to an investigation of garment manufacture in the tenement houses of the city. The report, for which Alzina Stevens was predominantly responsible, was entitled "Smallpox in the Tenements and Sweatshops of Chicago," and concluded by stressing the national interest in regulating against tenement manufacture and its associated health risks. In an 1895 publication coauthored with Florence Kelley and published in the *Hull-House Maps and Papers*, entitled "Wage-Earning Children," Stevens and Kelley documented the problems of the employment of children in the nonmanufacturing establishments which were not covered by the new law. The authors suggested that child labor could be eliminated by legislation providing for a minimum working age of sixteen, compulsory education laws, and the appointment of factory inspectors and truant officers to enforce such laws.

After the loss of her job when Governor John Peter Altgeld left office in 1897, Alzina Stevens went to live at Hull-House and continued her work on behalf of children through her advocacy of a state juvenile court law to protect dependent and delinquent children. In 1898 she traveled to Boston to study the juvenile court issue. Stevens also spoke before the Illinois legislature on behalf of the first Juvenile Court Act passed in the United States, in 1899. The new Juvenile Court Act provided separate courts and places of detention for juveniles, mandated the appointment of probation officers, and established the court's domain in cases of dependent and delinquent children. Chicago reformer Lucy Flower* raised the money to pay Stevens' salary as the nation's first probation officer in the court presided over by Judge Richard Tuthill. Stevens was the senior of six probation officers at the time of her death, a year later, when she also was secretary of the Council of Women's Trade Unions of Chicago, chairman of the Educational Committee of the Cook County League, and a member of numerous clubs, including the Hull-House Women's Club, Social Economics and Municipal Science Clubs, Union Labor League, and the Ethical Culture Society.

Alzina Stevens died from diabetes at Hull-House in 1900.

Alzina Stevens left no single collection of papers. Documents and letters relating to her work and interests can be found in the Jane Addams Memorial Collection, the Hull House Association Papers, and the Juvenile Protective Association Papers, all at the University of Illinois at Chicago, and in the Henry D. Lloyd Papers, at the State Historical Society of Wisconsin.

In addition to her factory inspection reports and *Hull House Maps and Papers* studies, Stevens also wrote "Life in a Social Settlement—Hull House, Chicago," *Self Culture* (March, 1899).

Biographical accounts of Stevens' life include obituaries in the *Chicago Tribune* and *Toledo Bee*, June 4, 1900; Francis E. Willard and Mary A. Livermore, eds., *A Woman of the Century* (1893); and Edward T. James, *Notable American Women*, vol. 3 (1971). Additional information on Stevens can be found in Jane Addams, *Twenty Years at Hull-House* (1910); John B. Andrews and W. D. P. Bliss, "History of Women in Trade Unions," in *Report on the Condition of Women and Child Wage-Earners in the United States*, Senate Doc. No. 645, 61 Cong., 2 Sess., 1911, vol. 10; Allen F. Davis and Mary Lynn McCree, eds., *Eighty Years at Hull House* (1969); and Alice Hamilton, *Exploring the Dangerous Trades* (1943).

                                                           ELIZABETH WEISZ-BUCK

**Stokes, Isaac Newton Phelps** (April 11, 1867–December 18, 1944), architect and urban reformer, was born in New York City, the son of banker and philanthropist Anson Phelps Stokes and Helen Louise (Phelps) Stokes. He was reared in an Episcopal household, and patrician traditions of public service, benevolence, and philanthropy were instilled in him throughout his childhood and adolescence. Befitting a boy of his upper-class origins, Stokes attended the Berkeley School in New York City, St. Paul's Academy in Concord, New Hampshire, and Harvard, graduating in 1891. After a short stint as a banker, undertaken at family insistence, Stokes entered Columbia University in 1893 to study architecture and economic planning. The following year he traveled to Paris and spent three years studying architecture at the École des Beaux Arts. Upon his return to the United States in 1897 he entered a partnership with John Mead Howells, and during the next two decades they designed various public buildings, including St. Paul's Chapel at Columbia University, the Baltimore Stock Exchange, and the headquarters of the American Geographical Society in New York City. Meanwhile, on August 21, 1895, Stokes had married Edith Mintum, and although the couple had no children, they adopted a daughter, Helen Bicknell.

Stokes reconciled his interest in art, design, and architecture with his concern for public service through his advocacy of better and cheaper housing for the urban poor and working classes. Conversations with Josephine Shaw Lowell,* Robert W. de Forest,* and the English reformer Samuel Barnett convinced him of the prime importance of this issue. His approach to the problem reflected his beliefs in organization, education, efficiency, and expertise exercised by an elite as essential to achieving meaningful reforms in urban housing. As early as 1896 he was drafting blueprints of model tenements for consideration by the New York Improved Housing Council. The following year Stokes and Howells submitted the winning design for the University Settlement building. In 1898 Stokes helped to establish the New York Charity Organization Society's Tenement House Committee; along with Lawrence Veiller,* Stokes prepared an exhibit on tenement housing designed to inform and educate the public on the problems and possibilities of tenement house design. The committee also sponsored a tenement house design competition in an effort to attract leading architects to suggest solutions and to offer alternative designs. The 1898 competition marked the beginning of Stokes' contribution to housing improvement. His own ideas about economic planning, architectural design, and technical expertise were perfectly suited to the exhibit-competition format.

The exhibit and the competition had their desired effect: New York Governor Theodore Roosevelt came away from the exhibit determined to remedy the situation. In 1900 the Governor established the New York State Tenement House Commission and appointed Stokes a member. In that capacity Stokes helped draft the New York Tenement House Law of 1901, which regulated the design and construction of tenement housing with an eye toward health and safety. One casualty of the legislation was the notorious "dumbbell" tenement (so called because of its shape), which was rendered illegal by the new rules. Stokes continued to campaign for designs which featured improved ventilation and light, but grew increasingly frustrated as a welter of regulations thwarted the development of new designs. The Tenement House Department took three years to approve his Dudley model tenements, convincing him that legislated solutions tended to impede innovations in design. In 1912 he resigned from the Tenement House Commission.

Stokes shifted his efforts to advocating reform through private efforts after assuming the presidency of the newly established Phelps-Stokes Fund in 1911. He shifted from the presidency in 1924 to serve as the Fund's secretary, a position he relinquished in 1937. He also chaired the housing committee of the Fund, seeking new solutions to the tenement problem through technological development, improved design, and better yet cheaper housing materials.

As head of the Phelps-Stokes Fund's housing committee, Stokes was chiefly responsible for the Fund's sponsoring housing design competitions in 1921 and 1933, as well as its publication of a two-volume study, *Slums and Housing, with Special Reference to New York City*, in 1936. Stokes' support of the competitions and his contributions to *Slums and Housing* exemplified his approach toward both housing problems and reform in general. His experience on the Tenement House Commission and his naturally conservative elitist tendencies taught him that legislative fiat in housing reform merely stifled innovative design and unduly interfered with market forces. While Stokes supported government subsidies of low-income housing, he believed that architectural competitions, judged by disinterested experts, would produce innovation while ensuring profitability. Stokes thereby fought for housing reform within the speculative market framework of urban America.

Stokes' interest in architecture also led to an interest in iconography. At first a sidelight, his hobby soon snowballed into an obsession. Between 1915 and 1928 he produced *The Iconography of Manhattan Island, 1498–1909* in six huge volumes. He also published a short history of New York City on the occasion of the 1939 World's Fair, and earlier served on the New York Art Commission (1911–1939) and as a trustee of the New York Public Library (1916–1938). During World War I he worked for the Department of Labor in the Bureau of Industrial Housing and Transportation.

Suffering from ill health in his last years, Stokes was taken to Charleston, South Carolina, where he died on December 18, 1944.

Primary sources for Stokes' life include his autobiography *Random Reflections of a Happy Life*, which he distributed privately in 1941, and his papers at the New York Historical Society. His most important writings are in Robert W. de Forest and Lawrence Veiller, comps., *The Tenement House Problem*, 2 vols. (1903), and James Ford et al., *Slums and Housing, with Special Reference to New York City*, 2 vols. (1936). See Roy Lubove, "I. N. Phelps Stokes: Tenement Architect, Economist, Planner," *Journal of the Society of Architectural Historians* (May, 1964), 75–87, for more extended treatment. Obituaries are in the *New York Historical Society Quarterly Bulletin* (January, 1945), 40–42; *New York History* (April, 1945), 263–64; and in the *New York Times* and the *New York Herald-Tribune* of December 19, 1944.

BROOKS D. SIMPSON and CHRISTOPHER BERKELEY

**Stokes, James Graham Phelps** (March 18, 1872–April 8, 1960), reformer and philanthropist, was born in New York City, the second son of Anson Phelps and Helen Louise (Phelps) Stokes. The interrelated Phelps Stokeses were leaders of New York society and derived their fortune from the Phelps-Dodge Company and subsequent railroad and real estate holdings. The family had a long history of interest in religious and philanthropic activities and had been particularly active in the American Board of Commissioners for Foreign Missions, the American Bible Society, and the American Tract Society. Anson Phelps Stokes was active in more secular organizations, such as the Reform Club of New York, which he served as president, and the Nineteenth Century Club.

James was educated at the Berkeley School in New York City and entered Yale as a member of the class of 1892 of the Sheffield Scientific School. While at Yale he was director of the Cooperative Society and a member of the executive board of the YMCA. After graduation he spent a year traveling and then entered the College of Physicians and Surgeons at Columbia with the class of 1896. In medicine he hoped to combine his religious and scientific interest to become a medical missionary. While a medical student he served as an ambulance surgeon at Roosevelt Hospital, which covered Hell's Kitchen, and from this experience he came to be interested in the environmental influences on disease. Stokes, who as a member of New York Society's 400 was spending his leisure time being entertained at the homes of the Gilded Age's wealthiest families, soon perceived that the roots of the conditions in Hell's Kitchen were intimately related to the great disparities of wealth in American society. This perception of the contrast between wealth and poverty joined a strong religious impulse in the formation of his social conscience.

Upon graduation he had to forego his desire to enter the missionary field to replace his ailing father in the family business. He combined his entry into business with a year of study of political science at Columbia. He also continued his settlement house work, which he had begun in the summer of 1895 as a member of the Committee on Site for the new University Settlement. Despite his business commitments, in the years after 1897 settlement house work became the focus of his life. He served on the board of directors of the University Settlement and immersed himself in the study of life on the Lower East Side. This commitment was interrupted only by a thirteen-month call to duty in the Spanish-American War.

When Stokes came home from the war, he plunged into reform work. As with many members of the settlement house movement, experience in the field led him to the belief that social reform was necessary to alleviate the problems of the slums. His social position allowed him to promote reform most effectively by serving on innumerable boards, including those of the Outdoor Recreational League of New York, the Prison Association of New York (he eventually became a state inspector of prisons and a delegate to the International Prison Congress of 1905), the League of Political Education, the Citizens' Union, the New York State Conference of Charities and Correction, the New York Child Labor

Committee, and Tuskeegee Institute. He also was a founder and chairman of the board of trustees (1897–1917) of Hartley House, a settlement house on West 46th Street.

After 1902 he lived at the University Settlement with such eminent fellow reformers as Ernest Poole, Robert Hunter* (who would become his brother-in-law), and William English Walling.* It was at the University Settlement that he met Rose Harriet Pastor, a former cigar worker and militant reporter for the *Jewish Daily News*, who would become his wife in the much publicized marriage of the "Millionaire and the Factory Girl."

At this time Stokes was evolving a collectivist philosophy which he called "Omnilism," one which looked "primarily to the Well-being of the Whole which Others and Self are but parts" and called for dedication to the advancement of the whole. This philosophy and his activist wife led him to politics and socialism. In 1904 he was a presidential elector on the Populist ticket, and in 1905, running on the Municipal Ownership League ticket headed by William Randolph Hearst, he was nearly elected president of the Board of Aldermen of New York City. He also was a founder of the Intercollegiate Socialist Society and would serve as its president from 1907 to 1917. Socialist Party membership came in 1906. In 1907 he renounced the concept of philanthropy in favor of the collective ownership of capital for the public welfare, and in 1908, he was elected to the National Executive Committee of the Socialist Party. In the same year he ran for the New York State Senate on the Socialist ticket. He also was one of the participants in the 1909 meeting on the status of the Negro, which led to the calling of the National Negro Congress and the founding of the National Association for the Advancement of Colored People (NAACP). In 1912 he ran for mayor of Stamford, Connecticut, on the Socialist ticket. In 1916 he helped edit *The Socialism of Today*, a source book of contemporary socialism.

James and Rose Pastor Stokes split with the majority of the Socialist Party on the issue of support for American intervention in World War I. Stokes had been a member of the New York National Guard since his graduation from Columbia and promoted the war effort, both through military service and as a founding member of the American Alliance for Labor and Democracy. Rose returned to the Socialist fold after the October Revolution and moved toward communism. Their ideological split led to a divorce in 1925.

In the years after World War I, Stokes became progressively more conservative and increasingly centered his attention on veterans and on cultural and philanthropic activities. In 1926 he married Lettice Lee Sands, a woman of his own social class. While he vigorously supported the New Deal and America's role in World War II, his later years were devoted to the study of religions. He published two books on Christianity and the religions of the East. From 1897 on, even during his most active socialist period, Stokes remained a businessman and served as president of the Nevada Company and the Nevada Central Railroad and, after 1927, as a member of the board of directors of the Phelps-Dodge Company.

Perhaps James Graham Phelps Stokes' greatest contributions were to demonstrate that great wealth did not preclude the formation of a social conscience and that the fight for social justice could take place at many levels. He exemplified part of a generation of genteel American youth who were drawn by the obvious gap between rich and poor and their religious sensibilities to the settlement houses of the great cities and were to form there a commitment to social reform and even to the complete reconstitution of the social and political system. James Graham Phelps Stokes died in New York City on April 8, 1960.

The J. G. Phelps Stokes Papers are at Columbia University. The papers for the period 1906–1917 are incomplete. Many of the papers relating to his connections to the socialist movement were destroyed by his widow prior to donation. Stokes' most important writings are contained in a pamphlet entitled *Hartley House and Its Relation to the Social Reform Movement* (1897) and in two articles published in *Wilshire's* (1903), "Ominism" and "Child Labor Versus Education."

The most detailed account of Stokes' reforming years can be found in Robert Dwight Reynolds, "The Millionaire Socialists: J. G. Phelps Stokes and His Circle of Friends," Ph.D. dissertation, University of South Carolina, 1974. See also Allen F. Davis, *Spearheads for Reform* (1967); and *Who's Who in America* (1956–1957). An obituary is in the *New York Times*, April 9, 1960.

CHIRSTINE BRENDEL SCRIABINE

**Stover, Charles B.** (July 14, 1861–April 24, 1929), settlement house leader and pioneer recreation reformer, was born to Cyrus and Anna (Bunstein) Stover in Riegelsville, Pennsylvania. Ancestors on his father's side emigrated from Rhenish Prussia during the eighteenth century. Several participated in the American Revolution.

Stover was raised in a religious home atmosphere by his Presbyterian parents. His father, the owner of a small store, died during his son's early childhood. A major influence on Charles' early life was his uncle, Reverend Henry Bunstein, a Presbyterian minister. Stover used his uncle as a model and attended the same colleges in an identical career path—Lafayette College and Union Theological Seminary. He received the B.A. from Lafayette in 1881 and attended Union Theological Seminary from 1881 to 1884. As a seminary student Stover did field work by preaching in the Dakota Territory and engaging in city mission activities in the Bowery. He resumed his religious studies in 1885–1886 as a seminary student at the University of Berlin. During his studies he experienced a crisis of religious faith and left the ministry.

Without ties to a sect, Stover was unable to find church-related work in New York City. He was familiar with the social settlement, however, because he had visited Toynbee Hall in England. In February, 1887, with a recommendation from Reverend Lyman Abbott, a leading Congregational minister, Stover met Stanton Coit* at his fledgling settlement, the Neighborhood Guild. Stover is often regarded as a cofounder of the Guild, about which he published the first article in 1889. He shared Coit's view that tenement residents had inner resources for social improvement, and that tenement dwellers would identify with their neighborhood and rehabilitate it through mutual aid. Stover expected lower-middle-class families with limited financial means to duplicate his own unselfish concern for others. Stover refused payment for his years of social service. He was not wealthy. He used several inheritances to maintain himself and help pay bills for different reform projects. The inheritances were depleted well before his death.

From August, 1887, until the Guild was reorganized as the University Settlement in 1891, Stover and others served as its directors. Stover also spent a year as head of the Cherry Street model tenements built by the Ethical Culture Society. Toynbee Hall was revisited in 1890, and the East London slum was studied. The following year Stover led a successful petition drive for a Sunday opening of the Metropolitan Museum of Modern Art. The petition drive was criticized by some as a radical tactic.

In 1891 Stover participated in the reorganization of the Guild by helping to involve philanthropist Seth Low and others in the project. Stover and a circle of intellectuals moved across the street to establish their own quasi-settlement, the Chadwick Civic Club. Except for occasional trips, the original tenement headquarters of the Club was his home until 1908. The main accomplishment of the Chadwick Civic Club was its lobbying to win public ownership of New York City's mass transit system.

Stover was also active in the Social Reform Club and the East Side Civic Club. The Social Reform Club, initiated by Felix Adler in 1894, engaged in a variety of municipal causes as well as some national social improvement ones. Stover served on several committees and participated in the effort to influence the federal government to improve the rights of seamen. The East Side Civic Club of the early 1900s, on the other hand, defeated a plan for an elevated loop on the Lower East Side.

Stover made a national reputation in social work as a champion of public recreation. In 1887 he wrote a park bill that was passed by New York City which provided for small parks and play equipment. Because the city council refused to spend funds for parks, Stover and others lobbied for about fifteen years to persuade political leaders to expand the functions of city government to include a program of parks and playgrounds. In 1890 Stover helped organize the Society for Parks and Playgrounds, which operated a few parks at its own expense. Stover and a coalition of reformers organized the Outdoor Recreation League in 1898. Stover was an expert of sorts on public and private sites suitable for recreation. He also had an immense capacity for work and helped publicize the League's major pilot project, Seward Park. Lobbying by the League influenced the city government to assume the financial expense of operating Seward Park and other playgrounds. Stover also participated in the national organization of the recreation movement by helping to form the National Playground Association of America in 1906.

From 1910 to 1914 Stover served a controversial term as Park Commissioner of Manhattan and Richmond. His accomplishments, such as the creation of a Bureau of Recreation, were marred by policy disputes, especially with the press. Stover was also handicapped by a lack of administrative skill, an attitude of omniscience, and ineptitude as a public speaker. He also suffered from periods of mental depression which often led to sudden disappearances. Following a highly publicized disappearance, Stover resigned as Park Commissioner.

Stover, now in his early fifties, was destitute. He was maintained at University Settlement through a fund established by friends. Living in near poverty, he devoted himself to the settlement's activities, especially its summer camp, and participated on the periphery of social betterment. Stover died in New York City in 1929.

The Charles B. Stover Papers are included in the University Settlement Society of New York Papers, which are located at the State Historical Society of Wisconsin. The Stover Papers are mainly writings about Stover by others. Materials on Stover's activities in support of public recreation are contained in the papers of the Outdoor Recreation League, which are also included in the University Settlement Society collection.

Stover wrote about the origins and early activities of the University Settlement Society in "The Neighborhood Guild in New York," in F. C. Montague, *Arnold Toynbee*, Johns Hopkins University Studies in Historical and Political Science, 7th Ser., no. 1 (January, 1889), 65–70; and in "The Neighborhood Guild in New York," *University Settlement Society Quarterly* (July, 1906), 19–26. He advocated public responsibility for urban recreation in "Playground Progress in Seward Park," *Charities* (May 4, 1901), 386–393; and in "Plea for a Great Ocean Park at Rockaway," *Charities* (June 4, 1904), 576–580.

James K. Paulding's *Charles B. Stover* (1938) is a sympathetic account of his life written by a close friend. A useful supplement for Stover's early career is Gregory Weinstein's *The Ardent Eighties: Reminiscences of an Interesting Decade* (1928).

JOHN J. CAREY

**Street, Elwood Vickers** (November 23, 1890–September 12, 1978), teacher, author, community organizer, and social welfare administrator, was the eldest of four boys born in Cleveland, Ohio, to Thomas Elwood and Josephine (Hanks) Street. His grandparents, on both sides of the family, came from England to New England at various times in the seventeenth and eighteenth centuries, and were among the first settlers in Ohio (at that time the Western Reserve). His father, of Quaker background, attended Western Reserve University and was a businessman, and his mother, a Congregationalist and a normal school graduate, was a housewife, musician, and a piano teacher. Both parents were gentle, kindly, romantic idealists who were unaffiliated with any church most of their lives, and the family income always was meager.

Elwood was frail at birth. However, influenced by Theodore Roosevelt and other proponents of the strenuous life, he arduously exercised and dieted throughout his life and was able to maintain an extremely high energy level from early boyhood on. He also was exceptionally well organized and ambitious and, as a result, his abilities and achievements were many and wide-ranging, from scientific experiments in his homemade laboratory through omnivorous reading in the humanities and social sciences to photography, creative writing, and a wide range of active sports. His enthusiasm particularly included history and literature, especially poetry, and, most especially, the works of Walt Whitman and Alfred Lord Tennyson, whose philosophies influenced him deeply throughout his life.

Street worked his way through Western Reserve University, from which he graduated in 1912. He was a part-time reporter and photograher for the *Cleveland Plain Dealer* where, among other things, he covered some of the news of social problems and the welfare agencies designed to meet those problems. While covering a settlement house story, he met his future wife, Augusta Jewitt, who at the time was a summer instructor on the agency playground and was an ardent suffragist and social reformer. The two were married in 1913 and eventually had four children, three girls and a boy. A hospitable and generous couple, the Streets would open their home to many of the social welfare leaders of the day and would be influenced by (and probably influence) such persons as Paul Kellogg,* Helen Hall,* Grace* and Edith Abbott,* Frank Bruno, William Hodson,* and others.

Meanwhile, Street's first job after graduating from college was as public relations director in Cleveland for the first modern Community Chest and Council in the United States (1913–1915). For years, his photograph of a small, ragged newsboy asleep in an alley was the logo (along with the question, ''Suppose Nobody Cared?'') for community chest campaigns not only in Cleveland but in many other parts of the country as well. Throughout his professional career, first as a public relations specialist and later as a community organizer and administrator, Street was dedicated to the principle of united giving for the meeting of human needs through the coordinated, planned efforts of a range of voluntary social agencies. He firmly believed in the good will of most community members (brushing off frequent evidence to the contrary) and the equal rights of all people to assistance (public as well as private) in time of need. Nonconformist in religion—variously a member of the Unitarian Church and Ethical Culture societies—he believed that social work, both public and private, was the highest expression of applied religion, an expression of humanitarian love of others, of social justice put to work in practical terms. Like his parents, he was a romantic idealist; unlike his parents, however, he believed in the importance of efficiency, competent management, and systematic planning, concepts borrowed from social engineering and business theories of the period, the 1920s.

These principles were applied in the various positions Street held: reporter and photographer for the New York-based social reform journals *Survey* and *Survey Graphic* (1915–1917); initiator and director of the Community Chest and Council of Louisville, Kentucky (1917–1921), where he also obtained a master's degree in sociology at the University of Louisville; initator and director of the Community Chest and Council of St. Louis, Missouri (1921–1927); and a similar position in Washington, D.C. (1927–1933), which he accepted only on the condition that all staff meetings, agency committees, and volunteer fund-raising efforts be racially integrated—thus becoming an early leader in the drive to desegregate the nation's capital.

Moved by the tragic consequences of the Great Depression, Street then became the director of the District of Columbia Department of Public Welfare in 1933, a position he held until 1937, when he was forced out by a Congress angered over his insistence that equal public assistance be given to black and white recipients. He then went to Richmond, Virginia, as Community Chest and Planning Council director (1937–1942), and from there to Houston, Texas, for a similar position (1942–1947), and then to Bridgeport, Connecticut, for similar work (1947–1955). Upon retirement in 1955, he was asked to teach social work at the Hartford Theological Seminary, a position he held with his wife as co-instructor until 1960, when he again retired and the couple moved to Falls Church, Virginia.

Street remained active even after this "second retirement," writing a manuscript on the history of private social work for the United Way of America. Always enthusiastic about "human organizations to meet human needs," he also remained active as a leader in many local, state, and national professional and community organizations, did part-time teaching at various colleges and universities, and continued to write a number of articles and books, adding to the impressive list of works he had authored earlier, some of which were used as classroom texts, including *Sympathy and System in Giving* (1921), *Social Work Administration* (1931), and *Public Welfare Administration* (1940).

Throughout his life, Street was fond of quoting the ancient motto, *"Non nobis solum nate"* (We are not born for ourselves alone), an old-fashioned concept that he believed in deeply and sincerely adhered to until his death in Falls Church, Virginia, in 1978.

Street was a prolific writer for professional social work journals. His articles, written primarily between 1914 and 1937, appeared in such places as *Survey*, *Social Forces*, *Social Service Review*, and the *Journal of Social Hygiene*. For specific references, see the *International Index of Periodic Literature*, especially volumes 3 through 10. Some of Street's published addresses also appear in the *Proceedings of the National Conference of Social Work* (1925, 1928). His three major books, all concerned with community organization and social work administration, are *Sympathy and System in Giving* (1921), *Social Work Administration* (1931), and *Public Welfare Administration* (1940). Street's extensive, unpublished multivolume history of organized charity from earliest recorded times through 1965 is at the Information Center of the United Way of America in Alexandria, Virginia; a microfilm copy of the work is at the Social Welfare History Archives Center at the University of Minnesota in Minneapolis. A condensed and highly popularized version of the work was published by the United Way as *People and Events, A History of the United Way* (1977).

Street's career was briefly reviewed by *Community* (February, 1956). His leadership role in racial integration in Washington, D.C., in the late 1920s and early 1930s is reviewed in Constance McLaughlin's *The Secret City* (1967), 215–216, 247. An obituary appeared in the *Washington Post*, September 17, 1978.

CATHERINE S. CHILMAN

**Swift, Linton Bishop** (?, 1888–April 11, 1946), family welfare administrator, was born in St. Paul, Minnesota, the son of George L. and Tryphena (Bishop) Swift. He graduated from the University of Minnesota and the St. Paul College of Law, and practiced law from 1910 to 1917 in St. Paul. After America's entry into World War I, Swift enlisted in the army, serving in France as a lieutenant and marrying a French woman, Marie Louise Arnoux. Appointed by President Wilson to the United States Peace Commission, he was the U.S. representative on the Commission for the Protection of Minorities in the Newly Created States. In 1920 Swift returned to St. Paul and entered social work by becoming assistant general secretary of the St. Paul United Charities.

After that, he served a brief term as general secretary of the Family Service Organization of Louisville, Kentucky, and then joined three other Minnesotans from Minneapolis and St. Paul—William Hodson,* David Holbrook,* and Walter West*—who left welfare agencies in the Twin Cities to take executive posts in welfare organizations in New York City. All moved during the 1920s. Hodson became director of the Welfare Council of New York City and later Commissioner of Public Welfare under Mayor Fiorello La Guardia. Holbrook headed the National Social Work Council (NSWC). West was executive secretary of the American Association of Social Workers. Swift directed the Family Welfare Association of America (FWAA), which had been the American Association for Organizing Family Social Work and later became the Family Service Association of America. Each Minnesotan, respectively, and the four working together as a team, guided the transition from private social work to public welfare programs during the Depression years of the 1930s.

Swift's FWAA promoted the extension of family casework in the United States and Canada by organizing local societies and giving them direction. The FWAA published the *Family* and the *News Letter* in addition to circulating influential reports, memoranda, and brochures that addressed issues pertinent to the quality of family life, including unemployment. Late in 1931, when the devastating impact of a spreading depression had surpassed the resources of private philanthropy and local public welfare programs, Linton Swift joined Holbrook, West, and Hodson in forming the Social Work Conference on Federal Action, a steering committee that functioned under the auspices of Holbrook's National Social Work Council. In November, 1931, the group went to Washington to meet with President Hoover's Committee on Unemployment Relief and several congressmen. About six weeks later, it appeared before the Senate Subcommittee on Manufactures, which was headed by Senators Robert La Follette and Edward Costigan, and testified to the necessity of federal action on unemployment relief. From that time on, the group worked for the adoption of a model program of federal assistance to the states and localities that derived from New York State's Temporary Emergency Relief Administration (TERA), a microcosm at the state level. Finally, during the spring of 1933, after the former governor of New York, Franklin D. Roosevelt, became President of the United States, the TERA model was adopted at the national level in the form of the Federal Emergency Relief Act, and the law's administration was placed in the hands of Harry Hopkins,* a New Yorker who was former admininstrator of the TERA and a member of the NCSW's steering committee.

Even though the contributions of Swift, Holbrook, West, and Hodson to federal action are difficult to separate, Linton Swift was a significant figure because he spoke on behalf of approximately 200 local agencies that dealt with millions of families beset with unemployment and poverty. He had become a spokesman for family caseworkers and the poor, and in 1934 he and Walter West served on the Advisory Committee on Public Employment and Public Assistance of the President's Committee on Economic Security, which helped to promote the legislative package that became the Social Security Act of 1935. In addition, Swift helped facilitate the change from private to pubic welfare programs by writing ''New Alignments Between Public and Private Agencies in a Community Family Welfare and Relief Program'' (1934) and ''Creed for Social Workers'' (1935), each of which appeared in booklet form as a widely distributed text.

The influence that Swift exerted on the rapid development of public social work during the Depression era never lessened his commitment to private social services. He was president of West's American Association of Social Workers from 1936 to 1938 and a member of the National Conference of Social Work, which he served as vice president in 1944–1945. In 1940 he helped organize the Social Work Vocational Bureau, an agency that placed trained personnel in nonprofit organizations. In 1946 Swift also participated in the reorganization of Holbrook's NSWC as the National Social Welfare Assembly. In the meantime, he led the integration of six national organizations in an American War-Community Services program and coordinated their activities during World War II. Most involved field services that assisted communities in ministering to the needs of servicemen's families. In addition to advancing casework methods as part of family welfare practice, Swift's new wartime organization initiated such special projects as day care for the children of women working in war industries.

Of the four former Minnesotans and longtime social work colleagues in New York, Linton Swift was the second to die when he passed away in New York City in April, 1946 (Hodson had died three years earlier).

Except for a rare portrait such as an obituary in the *New York Times* and a brief biography in *The Encyclopedia of Social Work*, Linton B. Swift has been ignored. Even basic information is hard to find because he was never listed in reference books such as *Who's Who in America*. The Social Welfare History Archives at the University of Minnesota holds papers of the Family Service Association of America, including its publications, which can be used to extrapolate Swift's role and influence. He is represented in other collections at the Archives as well, such as the National Social Welfare Asembly Papers, in which the actions of Holbrook, West, Hodson, and Swift on behalf of federal unemployment relief are shown. Swift was not a frequent author, but a few of his articles appeared in social work journals, including *Survey* and the *Social Service Review*.

WILLIAM W. BREMER

**Switzer, Mary Elizabeth** (February 16, 1900–October 16, 1971), developer of health and welfare policy at the federal level, especially vocational rehabilitation, was the oldest of three children—two daughters and a son—born in Newton Upper Falls, Massachusetts, to Margaret (Moore) and Julius F. Switzer, a manual laborer who left the family when Mary still was a young child. When Mary was eleven her mother died, and she was sent to live with two aunts and an uncle who apparently urged her to do something useful with her life. Meanwhile, she attended the local schools, graduating from high school in 1917. Thanks to a scholarship and a variety of jobs, she managed to attend Radcliffe College, from which she graduated in 1921 with a major in international relations.

She then moved to Washington, D.C., where, through the help of Elizabeth Brandeis (Raushenbush*), whom she had met at Radcliffe, she became an employee of the District of Columbia Minimum Wage Board. When the 1923 U.S. Supreme Court decision in the *Adkins v. Children's Hospital* case forced her from this job, she entered the civil service, performing a routine job clipping articles for the Secretary of the Treasury. Her liberal college friends accused her of "going to work in the heart of the present system." Working at the Treasury Department, Switzer learned of the social welfare problems of the twenties through such friends as Mary Anderson* of the Women's Bureau in the Department of Labor.

The Treasury Department included the Public Health Service. Switzer used her influence with (Anna) Eleanor Roosevelt* and with the wife of Treasury Secretary Henry Morgenthau to secure a new job as assistant to Josephine Roche,* whom President Roosevelt had appointed as an assistant secretary in charge of the Public Health Service. Starting the job in 1935, Switzer became involved in the deliberations over the content of the Social Security Act of 1935, particularly the never-passed health and disability insurance aspects of the act. Switzer also played a key role as Roche's assistant in other efforts to pass national health insurance in the thirties. She helped to supervise the National Health Survey, the nation's first federally sponsored morbidity study, in 1935 and 1936, and she completed much of the staff work for President Roosevelt's interdepartmental Committee on Health and Welfare. In 1938 Switzer arranged a national health conference that marked the beginning of a major New Deal/Fair Deal effort, ultimately unsuccessful, to pass national health insurance.

In 1939 Switzer moved with the Public Health Service to the newly created Federal Security Agency, where she became an assistant to former Governor of Indiana and future presidential aspirant Paul McNutt. Her duties included overseeing the Public Health Service, the Office of Education, and the short-lived National Youth Administration. She remained as an assistant to McNutt and his successors until 1950. During those years she served on the Procurement and Assignment Service of the War Manpower Commission and helped to allocate medical doctors to the American communities most in need of them. After the war, she became the federal government's unofficial liaison with the American Medical Association. In that capacity, she helped to create such important pieces of postwar health legislation as the National Mental Health Act of 1946 and the Hospital Survey and Construction Act of 1946. Few advocates of national health insurance enjoyed Mary Switzer's access to the leaders of organized medicine.

Her service during the war brought her into contact with prominent medical doctors, among whom were Henry Kessler and Howard Rusk. These doctors developed a new form of medical care known as rehabilitation medicine. Switzer proceeded to forge a professional alliance with Rusk that lasted for the rest of her life. Together they used their influence to advance the field of rehabilitation medicine and the vocational rehabilitation program.

In 1950 Oscar Ewing, then the Federal Security Administrator, asked Switzer to end her career as a staff assistant and to become the head of the vocational rehabilitation program. She accepted and proceeded to make the program one of the most dynamic social welfare programs within the federal government. This program, created in 1920, offered vocational guidance and training to the handicapped. It operated through the device of grants-in-aid. Switzer used her professional contacts with the rehabilitation doctors to bring a greater medical component to the state–federal vocational rehabilitation program. She developed close ties with the authorizing and appropriating committees of Congress. Her talents led to the passage of monumental new rehabilitation laws, such as the 1954 amendments to the vocational rehabilitation act. This law increased the appropriations to the program, initiated a new series of grants to the states for the extension and improvement of vocational rehabilitation, and started a program of professional training for rehabilitation counselors. As a result of her efforts, vocational rehabilitation became a major force within the federal government. In the years between 1954 an 1961, for example, expenditures increased three-fold to reach $70 million. When disability insurance became part of Social Security in 1956, Congress and the Eisenhower administration insisted that officials from the vocational rehabilitation program make the initial determination of disability; this insistence was a form of tribute to Mary Switzer and her cordial relations with the American Medical Association.

Secretary of Health, Education and Welfare John Gardner called Mary Switzer "a dynamo" and promoted her to the rank of Commissioner, in charge of the government's welfare and social service programs, in 1967. Mary Switzer hoped to imbue public assistance programs with the self-help philosophy of the vocational rehabilitation program. "People should not get something for nothing," she said, lamenting the lack of emphasis on work in the public assistance programs. Switzer spent a frustrating three years in the job, unable to make the welfare rolls go down. She retired in 1970 as the highest ranking female bureaucrat in the federal government.

From minimum wage programs to workfare, Mary Switzer participated in the development of federal welfare programs in this century. Her career illustrated the influence wielded by staff assistants over major programs and how webs of personal contacts, which she had an extraordinary ability to form and use as a means of rising through the federal bureaucracy, have accounted for the passage and implementation of social welfare laws. More specifically, Switzer managed to translate her personal intelligence and charm into congressional support for vocational rehabilitation and to make this program an important component of the modern social welfare bureaucracy. She died of cancer in Washington, D.C.

The papers of Mary Elizabeth Switzer are available to researchers at the Schlesinger Library at Radcliffe College. Martha Lentz Walker of Kent State University is preparing a book-length biography of Switzer. Other sources include Martha Derthick, *Uncontrollable Spending for Social Service Grants* (1975); Edward E. Berkowitz, "Mary Switzer: The Entrepreneur Within the Welfare State," *American Journal of Economics and Sociology* (January, 1980), 79–81; and the *New York Times*, October 17, 1971, 77:1.

                                                    EDWARD D. BERKOWITZ

# T

Taft, (Julia) Jessie (June 24, 1882–June 7, 1960), psychologist, therapist, and social work educator, was born in Dubuque, Iowa, the oldest of three daughters of Charles C. and Amanda May (Farwell) Taft. Her father owned a wholesale fruit business and had moved the family to Iowa from Vermont. Jessie excelled as a young student and attended the Unitarian Church, although her family had no religious affiliation. After receiving an A.B. degree from Drake University, she moved to Chicago for a year of study in 1905. After that she returned to Des Moines, Iowa, to teach high school mathematics, Latin, and German. In the summer of 1908 she returned to summer school at the University of Chicago, where she met Virginia Robinson,* with whom she began a lifelong personal and professional relationship, one that lasted over fifty years. She and Robinson adopted two children in 1921, a boy named Everett and a girl named Martha Scott (Taft).

Taft was offered a fellowship in philosophy at the University of Chicago, which she accepted in 1908. She interrupted her studies briefly to work with Virginia Robinson on a project developed by Katharine Bement Davis,* superintendent of the State Reformatory for Women at Bedford Hills, New York. While interviewing women committed to the Bedford reformatory, she decided that she enjoyed working with people. She returned to Chicago to complete her work, however, where she studied under George Herbert Meade. In 1913 she graduated magna cum laude with a doctor of philosophy degree in psychology and philosophy, one of only two women who received advanced degrees that year. Her dissertation was published under the title *The Woman Movement from the Point of View of Social Consciousness*.

After finishing her doctoral work, Taft was hired again by Katharine Bement Davis as assistant superintendent at the New York State Reformatory for Women. But she left that position when she became more interested in the new mental hygiene movement. Unsure of how to continue her career, she sought the advice of Mary Richmond,* who suggested that Taft needed training under a good supervisor. However, Taft felt she had more than enough education, and in 1915 she accepted a position as director of the Mental Hygiene Committee of the State Charities Aid Association in New York. In that role, she developed educational programs for mental hygiene in the state hospitals and in other institutions as well. One day a week she also worked at the Cornell Clinic of Psychopathology, the first mental hygiene clinic in New York. At the clinic, she worked to find a role for social workers, who she began to realize could perform the unique function of visiting patients in their homes. In 1918 she became a mental hygienist for the Seybert Foundation and spent most of her time testing children in sheltered care. An experience that represented a fundamental change of direction for her occurred in the summer of 1918 when she was asked to speak at the summer school of the Smith College training course for psychiatric social workers. She saw herself as part of a small group who were clarifying the relation between psychiatry and social work and defining the role of the psychiatric social worker.

In the fall of 1918 she became director of the Child Study Department of the Children's Aid Society of Pennsylvania. During this period she wrote extensively about child development and the behavior problems of children. In 1924 she first heard Otto Rank, a psychoanalyst who was beginning to challenge Freud's ideas. Deeply impressed by his speech, she entered analysis with him in the fall of 1926. She realized that while her past experience of testing children had been somewhat useful, it had not been therapeutic for the children. Her frustration with her work with children seemed more understandable during analysis. Thus, when her analysis with Rank ended, she joined a Rankian study group and opened an office in Philadelphia to begin practicing psychoanalysis. In addition, she began work on a translation from the original German of Rank's *Technique of Psychoanalysis*, in three volumes, and *Genetic Psychology, Volume 3*.

Her therapy with two children resulted in the publication in 1933 of *The Dynamics of Therapy*. Her reputation as a follower of Rank and her distinguished work in therapy with children led her to be asked to join the faculty of the Pennsylvania School of Social Work on a full-time basis in 1934. There, she initiated an advanced curriculum in which she not only interviewed the students to be admitted but also planned their placements and taught their basic coursework.

Jessie Taft has been recognized by many as the founder of what came to be known as the functional approach to social casework. In the first issue of the *Journal of Social Work Process*, published in 1937, Taft defined the functionalist point of view in an article entitled ''The Relation of Function to Process in Social Case Work.'' Function was described as the limitation within which social workers operate—the known, comparatively stable fixed point. The worker must explain the agency's functions, and the client can then react to it over a period of time. Otto Rank never fully understood function as it was used by Taft and other social workers, even though his name was often associated with the functional perspective (in contrast to Freud, who was associated with the diagnostic approach to social casework). These two schools of thought continued to develop in the 1940s and remained in conflict with one another. In 1947 the Family Service Association sponsored a committee to study the differences between the two approaches, but after two years the committee concluded that the two perspectives could not be reconciled.

Taft found many ways to encourage writing about the functional school of thought. She organized and edited the *Journal of Social Work Process*, which was a technical periodical specifically about the development of functional casework practice. Taft had long maintained an interest in child placement and family casework practice. In 1943 she organized a summer institute at the school and collected the papers presented into an edited text, *A Functional Approach to Family Casework*. She continued to support the publication of her colleagues' work in this area by editing two additional volumes, *Counseling and Protective Service as Family Casework: A Functional Approach* (1946) and *Family Casework and Counseling: A Functional Approach* (1948).

Taft continued her friendship with Otto Rank until his death in 1939. Although Rank left no will, his papers were sent to Taft by his wife for use in a biography she wanted to write about him. Taft gave him credit for her understanding of the effects of time limitations and the will of both the therapist and the client on the therapeutic process. After her retirement from the Pennsylvania School of Social Work in 1950, she devoted most of her time to work on Rank's biography. In 1958 it finally appeared under the title *Otto Rank: A Biographical Study Based on Notebooks, Letters, Collected Writings, Therapeutic Achievements and Personal Associations*. Two years later, on June 7, 1960, Jessie Taft died of a stroke at the age of seventy-seven.

The personal papers and writings of Jessie Taft have not been saved in any private collection. However, two of her early articles, "Qualifications of the Psychiatric Social Worker" (1919) and "The Relation of Psychiatry to Social Work" (1926), illustrate her ideas about psychiatric social work and can be found in her biography, written by Virginia Robinson. Perhaps Taft's best-known works were *The Dynamics of Therapy in a Controlled Relationship*(1933) and her translations of the works of Otto Rank.

The major biographical source on Taft is Virginia Robinson, ed., *Jessie Taft, Therapist and Social Work Educator: A Professional Biography* (1962), which incorporates most of Taft's writings as well as a complete bibliography of her works. Biographical pieces can be located in the *Encyclopedia of Social Work* (1977), in *Who Was Who in America* (1981), and in *Notable American Women* (1980). Her obituary appeared in *Social Service Review* in September, 1960. Some autobiographical notes about Taft's relationship with Otto Rank may be found in the foreward she wrote to *Otto Rank: A Biographical Study Based on Notebooks, Letters, Collected Writings, Therapeutic Achievements and Personal Associations* (1958).

JEAN K. QUAM

**Taylor, Graham** (May 2, 1851–September 26, 1938), minister, educator, settlement house founder, writer, and social reformer, was born in Schenectady, New York, the second son of Dutch Reformed minister William James Romeyn Taylor and Katherine (Cowenhoven) Taylor. Following his mother's death in

1852, his father married her sister, Maria Cowenhoven, who bore two more sons. Taylor grew up in Philadelphia and New Brunswick, New Jersey, attended Rutgers College Grammar School, and graduated from Rutgers College in 1870. Influenced by four generations of Taylor and Romeyn family service in the Dutch Reformed Church, he continued his education at the Theological Seminary of the Reformed Church in America at New Brunswick. In 1873, the year he was ordained, he married Leah Demarest, daughter of a seminary professor. Four children were born to the couple between 1876 and 1888: Helen, Graham Romeyn,* Lea Demarest,* and Katharine.

Taylor's first church was in the village of Hopewell, Dutchess County, New York. He soon increased attendance and added prayer meetings in outlying regions, but his attention to tenant farm families alienated some of the wealthy landowners. The struggle to apply Christian tenets in this rural parish forced him to rethink his conservative theological training and to place greater emphasis upon the interdependence of mankind. By 1880 he was ready for the call from the Fourth Congregational Church in Hartford, Connecticut, even though it meant leaving the Dutch Reformed Church.

The inner-city parish had long since lost its social distinction, and the debt-ridden church needed repair. Taylor welcomed all residents in the vicinity of the Fourth Congregational Church and with their help managed to clear the debt and renovate the church. Inspired by the Connecticut Bible Society's canvass of Hartford in 1883, Taylor persuaded the city's Congregational ministers to support a missionary program headquartered at his centrally located church. Using techniques he had observed in other cities, Taylor was so successful that he soon needed volunteers from Hartford Theological Seminary and more space for the institutional church work. Appointed professor of practical theology at the seminary in 1888, he trained students for careers in city missions, temperance societies, charity organizations, and the Young Men's Christian Association as well as churches. Taylor's "Religious Census of the City of Hartford" (1890) contained demographic and religious statistics and descriptions of the preventive agencies. He frequently reported on his work to the American Missionary Association, the Evangelical Alliance, and the National Council of Congregational Churches.

The leading Congregational training school in the Midwest, Chicago Theological Seminary, offered him a professorship in 1892 and a free hand to organize a department of christian sociology, the first of its kind in any seminary in the United States. Taylor grabbed this opportunity to extend his application of Christianity to urban-industrial society. For the next three decades he was instrumental in the seminary's fund-raising, administration, and curriculum development. A popular lecturer, Taylor reached beyond the classroom with his "Syllabus in Biblical Sociology" (1900) and his bibliography for lay readers interested in "Christian Sociology and Social Economics." During 1911 and 1912 he wrote a series of articles on social Christianity for the *Survey*, later publishing them as *Religion in Social Action* (1913).

Taylor's major commitment after 1894 was to his settlement house, Chicago Commons. Modeled after Jane Addams'* Hull-House, his experiment was launched in a spacious though dilapidated house on the near northwest side of the city. When the six Taylors moved into the building in October, 1894, they became the first family to reside in an American settlement. Within five years, Chicago Commons had twenty-five residents and a kindergarten, a day nursery, clubs and classes, a civic forum, and a branch of the Municipal Voters' League. Between 1899 and 1901 Taylor solved the space problem by acquiring land and building an L-shaped, five-story brick structure, a model for other settlements undertaking new construction. Although the Irish, German, and Scandinavian neighbors of the 1890s gradually gave way to Poles, Italians, and other southeastern European newcomers, the settlement weathered the transition. Lea Demarest Taylor worked closely with her father, and he named her head resident in 1922. Graham Taylor's standing in the emerging profession of social work earned him the presidency of the National Conference of Charities and Correction (1914) and of the National Federation of Settlements (1918).

A Chicago training school for social workers was an outgrowth of Taylor's experiences educating ministers and new settlement residents. He started it in 1903 with courses in the University of Chicago extension program. Five years later it was incorporated as the Chicago School of Civics and Philanthropy, and the Russell Sage Foundation agreed to underwrite its research department. The most active lecturers were Alexander Johnson,* Charles R. Henderson,* Julia Lathrop,* Sophonisba Breckinridge,* Edith Abbott,* and Taylor, who also was chief fund-raiser and administrator. Soaring enrollments during World War I caused the board of trustees to explore university affiliation. Breckinridge and Abbott helped steer it into the University of Chicago where, in 1920, the Chicago School of Civics and Philanthropy became the Graduate School of Social Service Administration.

Finally, Graham Taylor was an effective spokesman and publicist for settlement house objectives and Progressive Era reforms. In 1894 he, Jane Addams, and Mary McDowell* started the Chicago Federation of Settlements, a forerunner of the National Federation. In 1896 Taylor and John Palmer Gavit* launched a monthly magazine, the *Commons*. As coverage and circulation increased, Raymond Robins* and Graham Romeyn Taylor assisted with editorial duties. That journal merged with Edward T. Devine's* *Charities* in 1905 and in 1909 became the *Survey*, of which Taylor was an associate and later a contributing editor. From 1902 until shortly before his death, Taylor wrote a weekly column for the Chicago *Daily News*, in which he tackled a wide range of topics but always analyzed "current events from the settlement point of view." His autobiography, prepared in the 1920s, appeared under the apt title *Pioneering on Social Frontiers* (1930). A thematic history of the settlement, *Chicago Commons Through Forty Years* (1936), was his final publication. He died in his suburban Chicago (Highland Park) home on September 26, 1938.

In addition to the pamphlets, books, and *Daily News* columns, Taylor published over 500 articles. The voluminous Graham Taylor Papers are in the Newberry Library, Chicago, and their contents are described in *Newberry Library Bulletin* (October, 1953). See also Lea D. Taylor, "The Social Settlement and Civic Responsibility—The Life Work of Mary McDowell and Graham Taylor," *Social Service Review* (March, 1954); and Louise C. Wade, *Graham Taylor: Pioneer for Social Justice, 1851–1938* (1964). The latter has a complete bibliography of Taylor's writings.

LOUISE C. WADE


**Taylor, Graham Romeyn** (March 17, 1880–August 30, 1942), journalist and editor who specialized in social welfare topics, was born in Hopewell, New York. He was the second child and only son of Leah (Demarest) and Graham Taylor.* His father, a Dutch Reformed pastor, moved to a Congregational church in Hartford, Connecticut, soon after his birth. In 1892 the Taylors went to Chicago, where Graham Taylor became head of the department of christian sociology at Chicago Theological Seminary. When Graham Romeyn was fourteen years old, he, his three sisters, and his parents established their residence at Chicago Commons, a new settlement house on the near northwest side of the city. Following his graduation from Harvard University in 1900, he returned to Chicago to share the family's commitment to the settlement house way of life.

His strongest interest was reporting and helping edit copy for the *Commons*, a monthly magazine launched by his father and John Palmer Gavit* in 1896. After the *Commons* merged with Edward T. Devine's* *Charities* in 1905, Graham Romeyn Taylor served as chief western correspondent and reporter. With the creation of the *Survey* in 1909, he moved to New York City as a staff member. His investigations of industrial suburbs appeared first as *Survey* articles and then, in 1915, as *Satellite Cities*, a volume in the National Municipal League Series. Taylor traced the evolution of industrial suburbs from Pullman and Homestead to the younger town of Gary, Indiana, and communities outside East St. Louis, Cincinnati, and Birmingham. He looked at housing, municipal services, schools, health care, and voluntary associations, and he argued for an American version of the British Housing and Town Planning Act of 1909. An unexpurgated version of Jane Addams'* essay on George Pullman, "A Modern Lear," was included in *Satellite Cities*.

In 1916 Taylor accompanied Edward T. Devine to Russia to assist in distribution of aid to interned German and Austrian civilians; he was working in Moscow in the office of the American Consul General at the time of the Russian Revolution. In 1918 he married Florence I. Taylor (no relation), an investigator and the publication secretary of the National Child Labor Committee.

In the aftermath of Chicago's 1919 race riot, Taylor and Charles S. Johnson were appointed joint executive secretaries of the Chicago Commission on Race Relations. They directed the thorough investigation of events leading up to that violence and prepared the Commission's report, *The Negro in Chicago*, which was published in 1922.

That same year Taylor returned to New York City to become executive director of the Commonwealth Fund's task force on juvenile delinquency. Five years later he was named director of the Fund's Division of Publications. In this capacity he edited reports on health and education as well as child welfare. At the time of his death in New York City, he had completed two decades with the Commonwealth Fund, including fifteen years as director of publications.

See the bibliographic essay at the end of the entry on Graham Taylor; the single largest source of information on Graham Romeyn Taylor is the Graham Taylor Papers in the Newberry Library in Chicago. Also see the obituary in the *Survey* (September, 1942)

LOUISE C. WADE

**Taylor, Lea Demarest** (June 24, 1883–December 3, 1975), settlement house director and social activist, was born in Hartford, Connecticut, the third child and second of three daughters born to Graham Taylor* and Leah (Demarest) Taylor. Her father, a Congregational minister and professor at Hartford Theological Seminary, took the family to Chicago in 1892 when he became head of a new department of christian sociology at Chicago Theological Seminary. Two years later, Graham Taylor and his family started a settlement house on the near northwest side of the city—Chicago Commons. Lea attended public schools and Lewis Institute in Chicago and graduated from Vassar College in 1904. She then returned to Chicago, and Chicago Commons, where she helped with secretarial work and some aspects of family service and eventually assumed direction of the girls' program. During World War I she and her father ran the local draft board, registering over 12,000 men in the settlement auditorium. Resembling her mother in physical appearance, Lea had her father's temperament and intellectual orientation. Graham Taylor promoted her to asistant head resident in 1917, and upon his retirement five years later she became head resident. Her father continued to chair the board of trustees and raise funds, but direction of the Chicago Commons program was in Lea Taylor's capable hands.

During the 1920s and 1930s she watched Italian families leave the neighborhood and more Poles and some Mexicans move in. She hired Polish and Spanish-speaking staff members and shifted from structured classes to many more group activities. She also acquired a 200-acre farm camp in New Buffalo, Michigan, for summer use. With the onset of the Depression, she emerged as one of Chicago's leading social activists, rallying others to fight for more generous relief stipends and for jobs for the unemployed. As president of the Chicago Federation of Settlements (1924–1937 and 1939–1940) and of the National Federation of Settlements (1930–1934 and 1950–1952), she enlisted those organizations in the campaign. Jobs, relief, and housing were central to her work with the American Association of Social Workers (vice president, 1934, 1935), the National Conference of Social Work (member of the executive committee, 1932–1934, and vice president, 1945), the Chicago Council of Social Agencies (secretary, 1935–1941), and the advisory committee of the Cook County Bureau of Public Affairs.

During and immediately after World War II, black families moved into the region around Chicago Commons, and Lee Taylor added race relations to her agenda. She secured police protection for threatened families, offered Blacks shelter at Chicago Commons, and initiated interracial clubs and camping. She served on the board of directors of the Metropolitan Housing Council, the Chicago Recreation Commission, and the Council Against Discrimination and chaired the housing committee of the Commission on Human Relations.

The year 1954 marked the sixtieth anniversary of Chicago Commons and the fiftieth year of Lea Taylor's service at the settlement. She chose that occasion to resign as director, though she continued to raise funds, attend board meetings, and be active in numerous civic organizations. Construction of a northwest arterial highway had so disrupted the settlement neighborhood that the Chicago Commons building was sold in 1957. The settlement had already absorbed Emerson House and secured a charter as the Chicago Commons Association. New headquarters were established at Taylor House on North Wolcott, northwest of the old neighborhood. Lea Taylor lived in Highland Park, Illinois, from 1957 until 1974, when she went to a retirement home in Hightstown, New Jersey. Prior to leaving Chicago, however, she formed the Highland Park Committee on Human Relations and mediated racial conflicts on the southwest side of the city.

Although she and her father shared "a community of interests very rare in the lives of a father and daughter," as he once observed, Lea did not inherit his reportorial skills. Still, she wrote a chapter for *Chicago Commons Through Forty Years* (1936), sketches of the settlement movement for the *Social Work Year Book* in 1935 and 1937, an article on her father and Mary McDowell* for the March, 1954, *Social Service Review*, and several shorter pieces and book reviews. Fortunately, the National Federation of Settlements and Neighborhood Centers taped extensive interviews with her in 1968. She died in Hightstown, New Jersey, seven years later.

The Chicago Historical Society has a transcript of the autobiographical tapes and the Lea Demarest Taylor Papers, which contain her organizational correspondence, settlement material, and copies of her speeches and publications. The Chicago Commons Records, also in the Chicago Historical Society, have the settlement material from Lea Taylor's era and some duplicates from the Graham Taylor Papers. For an assessment of her role in the 1930s, see Judith Ann Trolander, *Settlement Houses and the Great Depression* (1975).

LOUISE C. WADE

**Terrell, Mary Church** (September 23, 1863–July 28, 1954), civil rights leader, women's rights promoter, and social welfare advocate, was born in Memphis, Tennessee, the youngest of two daughters of prosperous former slaves, Louisa (Ayres) and Robert Reed Church. Her father was a boat steward who eventually became a successful businessman and a millionaire real estate operator, and her mother was a hairdresser who eventually opened her own hairpiece shop, which catered to well-to-do Memphis white women. Meanwhile, desiring the best possible education for their daughter, Mary's parents sent her, at age six, to live with a family in Yellow Springs, Ohio. There, she attended the Model School conducted by Antioch College, and then the public schools in Yellow Springs and Oberlin, Ohio, where she finished high school in 1879. In 1884 she graduated at the top of her class from Oberlin College, where she majored in the classics and became one of America's first black women to earn a college degree; later she would receive an M.A. from Oberlin. Although her parents at first disapproved because they thought it undignified, she taught for a number of years after graduating from college, first at Wilberforce University and then at the black high school in Washington, D.C.

At her father's urging and expense, Mary Church then traveled and, for more than two years, from 1888 to 1890, lived in Europe, where she studied languages at schools in France and Germany. This gave her a command of foreign languages (primarily French, German, and Italian) which she put to good use in various speaking engagements, including the meeting of the International Council of Women in Berlin in 1904 when she electrified the assembled by addressing them first in German and then in both English and French. Meanwhile, however, when she returned from her European studies she turned down several teaching offers, including one from Oberlin, and instead (in 1891) married her longtime suitor, Robert Terrell, a teacher-lawyer and Harvard University graduate who later became a municipal court judge, the only black judge in the nation's capital. The couple settled comfortably in Washington, D.C. where they had four children, three of whom died in infancy; they later adopted a niece, Mary, who was four years older than their surviving daughter, Phyllis.

Mary Church Terrell then became a busy civic worker and a continual fighter for rights; she spent the rest of her life seeking to liberate blacks and women from their unequal status and treatment. Among the list of "firsts" she accomplished was being the first black person to serve on the District of Columbia's Board of Education. She served in that capacity for eleven years, from 1895 to 1906. Also, she was the first president of the National Association of Colored Women, which she helped organize. After serving three terms (from 1896 to 1901), she continued as honorary president for the remainder of her life.

During speaking engagements throughout the nation and the world, she focused on the issues of women's rights, racial problems, and the need for more and better social services. She was active in volunteer work during World War I, and at the end of the war she served as a delegate to the 1919 meeting of the Women's International League for Peace and Freedom in Zurich, Switzerland.

She made several additional trips abroad during her lifetime, speaking to a variety of groups, including the International Assembly of the World Fellowship of Faiths in London in 1937.

For her charitable work in a number of social service activities and her tenure as president of the Southwest Community House in Washington, D.C., Terrell received a social service citation from the Women's Centennial Congress in 1940. That same year Terrell wrote her autobiography, *A Colored Woman in a White World*, which chronicled her unusual life and her many contributions in a positive manner, but, at the same time, made clear her belief that her race and gender denied her the opportunity to contribute even more. In it, she provided a number of poignant examples of how racism and sexism affected her life.

Terrell was a prolific writer. Besides her autobiography, she wrote many articles for magazines and journals, covering such subjects as lynching in the South, difficulties in traveling accommodations encountered by Blacks, and virtual peonage in this country. For these and for her many other activities and services, Oberlin College voted her one of its "100 Famous Alumni."

One of Terrell's most publicized actions was her attempt, in 1946, to join the then all-white Washington, D.C., branch of the American Association of University Women (AAUW). Although she met the criteria for admission—she was a college graduate and a resident of the district—her application was rejected because she was black. Although eighty-three years of age, she remained a fighter; she applied, and was accepted into the national AAUW organization. The Washington chapter then was ordered to accept her membership. It refused, however, and took the case to court. After a three-year legal fight, the Washington chapter won the case when the courts declared that it had the right, under the Association's national bylaws, to exclude whomever it chose. The AAUW promptly responded by changing its bylaws to read that a college degree be the only requirement for membership. However, Terrell never was able to become a member of the organization for, rather than accept her, it seceded from the national association.

She did not stop battling for social and racial justice, however. In her late eighties, she led the drive that resulted in the 1953 Supreme Court ruling that ended segregation in public accommodations in the nation's capital—and lived to see the nation's highest court declare racial segregation everywhere unconstitutional in May, 1954.

Mary Church Terrell died at the age of ninety in Annapolis, Maryland, on July 28, 1954.

Probably the single best source of biographical material on Terrell is her autobiography, *A Colored Woman in a White World* (1940), which, however, should be used with care. There are, however, Terrell Papers in the Manuscript Division of the Library of Congress in Washington, D.C., and at the Moorland-Spingarn Research Center at Howard University in Washington, D.C.

By far the best secondary accounts of Terrell's life, however brief, are the entries on her in *Notable American Women: The Modern Period* (1980) and the

*Dictionary of American Biography*, Supplement 5 (1977). Also see Elizabeth L. Davis, ed., *Lifting as They Climb: An Historical Record of the National Association of Colored Women* (1933); August Meier, *Negro Thought in America, 1880–1915* (1963); and Edgar A. Toppin, *A Biographical History of Blacks in America Since 1528* (1969). Obituaries appeared in the *New York Times* and the *Washington Post*, July 29, 1954.

JANICE ANDREWS

**Towle, Charlotte Helen** (November 17, 1896–October 1, 1966), practitioner, teacher, consultant, and author, was born in Butte, Montana, the second of four children of Emily (Kelsey) and Herman Augustus Towle, a prosperous jeweler. Prior to her marriage Emily Towle taught school. Butte, in Charlotte Towle's growing-up years, was a copper mining town, and both of her parents maintained an interest in labor–management issues associated with mining.

In 1915, after graduation from Butte High School, Charlotte and her older sister went east to attend junior college in Virginia. The following year she transferred to Goucher College in Baltimore. She wanted to be a writer but majored in education in order to be assured of employment. An elective course in social work, which included field work at the Baltimore Prisoners' Aid Society and the American Red Cross, however, led her to a career in social work.

Following graduation from Goucher in 1919 with a B.A. degree, Towle worked as a Red Cross caseworker in Baltimore, Denver, and Thermopolis, Wyoming (1919–1921). She also was a caseworker at the United States Veterans Bureau in San Francisco (1921–1924). From 1924 to 1926 she worked at the Neuropsychiatric Hospital in Tacoma, Washington, where she became the director of psychiatric social service. Under a Commonwealth Fund Fellowship, in 1926 she studied at the New York School of Social Work. There she met Dr. Marion Kenworthy, whose teaching deeply influenced her, and who remained a lifelong friend. Towle received a certificate of completion of the psychiatric social work curriculum at the New York School. She thus possessed a foundation in psychoanalytic theory upon which she would build in the ensuing years. Now she took a position as director of the Home Finding Department of the Children's Aid Society in Philadelphia and taught part-time at the Pennsylvania School of Social Work (1927–1928). In Philadelphia she met Jessie Taft* and Virginia Robinson,* founders of the functional school of social work.

In 1928 Towle went to the Institution for Child Guidance in New York City, where she supervised students from the New York and Smith College schools for social work. From 1932 until her retirement in 1962, Charlotte Towle was a full-time faculty member at the University of Chicago's School of Social Service Administration. Edith Abbott,* dean of the school, recruited her to develop a sequence in psychiatric casework to balance the school's emphasis on social welfare policy. In 1944 she became a full professor.

At Chicago, Towle taught at both the master's and doctor's levels. Her teaching was concentrated in the casework and human growth and development sequences, but she also taught courses in the dynamics of learning and supervision. In addition to the students she taught, Charlotte Towle deeply influenced the profession of social work. Her major achievements included (1) development of a client-centered generic casework curriculum, which enabled all social workers to secure knowledge of human behavior and a variety of ways of helping; (2) establishment of a focus on the relationship between inner life and the social environment; (3) development of a human growth and behavior sequence in which content was selected and taught by social workers rather than psychiatrists; and (4) development of a theory of professional education.

Towle's philosophy and ideas were spread in several ways. She taught courses at other schools of social work, conducted workshops and institutes throughout the country, served as consultant to a variety of local and national health and welfare programs, and maintained an ongoing involvement with the American Association of Schools of Social Work.

Charlotte Towle wrote sixty-nine articles and three books. Her journal articles covered a range of social work topics. Towle's first book, *Social Case Records from Psychiatric Clinics*, was published in 1941. Her second, *Common Human Needs* (1945), resulted from a request by the Bureau of Public Assistance of the United States Social Security Board to develop a manual for public assistance workers. In *Common Human Needs*, Charlotte Towle brought knowledge of human behavior to public assistance programs. She also emphasized the right to receive public assistance. *Common Human Needs*, however, embroiled Towle in controversy. The president of the American Medical Association interpreted the use of the word "socialized" in the book to mean "socialistic." As a result of the protest he initiated, the Government Printing Office ceased publishing *Common Human Needs* and destroyed its inventory. Social workers and other protested the banning, but it was not lifted. The National Association of Social Workers (NASW) subsequently republished the book, which remains a classic. In her third book, *The Learner in Education for the Professions* (1954), Towle merged personality and learning theory and created a theory of professional education. From 1944 to 1962 she served on the editorial board of the *Social Service Review*.

In 1955 Charlotte Towle received a Senior Fulbright Award to serve as consultant to the faculty of the London School of Economics in its effort to establish a generic social work program. As she prepared to leave for England, her passport was withheld. She was asked to explain her membership in two organizations alleged to be communist fronts and her signature on a clemency petition for Julius and Ethel Rosenberg. Her own statements along with support from the university and others cleared her.

Charlotte Towle lived in the Hyde Park area, near the University of Chicago campus, with her older sister Mildred and her longtime friend, Mary Rall. Although she consistently carried a heavy workload, she was known for her generosity in helping others develop their potential. She also was described as brilliant, easy to relate to, having a sense of humor, and being a good person.

Charlotte Towle died of a stroke while on vacation in North Conway, New Hampshire, in 1966.

Charlotte Towle's papers are located in the Department of Special Collections, Joseph Regenstein Library, the University of Chicago. The collection consists of correspondence, teaching outlines, and other materials.

Helen Harris Perlman collected and edited some of Towle's most significant writings in *Helping: Charlotte Towle on Social Work and Social Casework* (1969). Lela B. Costin, in *Two Sisters for Social Justice: A Biography of Grace and Edith Abbott*, discusses Towle's relationship with Edith Abbott.

Biographical sketches can be found in the *SSA Newsletter* (Autumn/Winter, 1966–1967), *Encyclopedia of Social Work* (1977), and *Notable American Women* (1980). The *New York Times* carried an obituary on October 2, 1966.

MARY CARROLL

**Tucker, William Jewett** (July 13, 1839–September 29, 1926), liberal clergyman and Social Gospel advocate, educational innovator, and settlement house founder, was born in Griswold, Connecticut, to Henry Tucker, eldest son of William "Squire" Tucker, a pioneer manufacturer in Griswold, and Sarah White (Lester) Tucker, elder daughter of Captain Joseph Lester, also of Griswold. Henry Tucker went into business with his father and made his home in Norwich, Connecticut, with his young family until the death of his wife, when their son William was eight years of age. Thereafter, young William lived with his mother's sister and her husband, Reverend William R. Jewett, pastor of the Congregational Church in Plymouth, New Hampshire. After his father remarried and moved to Chicago, young William was informally adopted by his aunt and uncle and their name incorporated into his own, William Jewett Tucker.

W. J. Tucker married twice. His first marriage, in 1870, was to Charlotte Henry Rogers of Plymouth, New Hampshire; she was the mother of two of his daughters and died in 1882. His second wife, whom he married in 1887, was Charlotte Barrell Cheever, daughter of Dr. Henry Cheever of Worcester, Massachusetts; she was the mother of his third daughter. His wife and daughters survived him.

Meanwhile, Tucker attended Kimball Union Academy, a popular preparatory school for Dartmouth College, and then graduated from Dartmouth in 1861. After teaching for two years in Columbus, Ohio, he was drawn to service in the ministry and entered Andover Theological Seminary. In the spring of 1864, he took a leave from the seminary to join the United States Christian Commission in order to minister to Union soldiers in the Civil War.

After the war, he finished his courses at Andover and served several months in the American Home Missionary Society in Missouri and Kansas. He hoped to bring religious cooperation and religious reconstruction to this ravaged region; however, the sectarian and denominational squabbling ran so deep that he left to return to New England. After his ordination, in June, 1867, he accepted his first pastorate at the Franklin Street (Congregational) Church in Manchester, New Hampshire. He served happily there until 1875, when he accepted the pastorate of the Madison Square (Presbyterian) Church in New York. The denominational change meant little since New England Congregationalism was affiliated with that branch of Presbyterianism represented by the Madison Square Church. His was the downtown church on the east side of Madison Square; many distinguished New Yorkers were his parishioners. He deliberately preached for spiritual reawakening and visited virtually every part of the great city, in the company of policemen or others who knew each section well, in an effort to learn about the problems of its inhabitants. The social segregation of his parish from the poor in the city was, he believed, a distinct liability. His activities and fame as a preacher brought him an invitation, in 1877, to serve as president of Dartmouth College, which he refused. A few years later, he was offered the chair of homiletics of pastoral preaching at Andover Theological Seminary. His decision to accept that offer in 1880 came from his conviction that modern Christianity had to solve critical social questions, and he believed that the ministry offered the best opportunity for active intervention in the newly industrialized society. His role in training prospective ministers to change evil conditions wrought by urbanization and industrialization he saw as a new kind of mission.

The Andover Theological Seminary was the oldest and most influential school of theology in New England. A strong missionary spirit permeated Andover, even in the period when W. J. Tucker was a student. At Andover, the Reverend Dr. Tucker espoused the practical application of progressive orthodoxy, a term he used for the philosophy that social reconstruction should come through the united work of the members of society, through religious cooperation and recognition of the immanence of God in the universe. Essentially, he called for applying the teachings of Christ to society and became a leader in the emerging Social Gospel, or Social Christianity, movement in the nation. The church in the industrialized and urbanized age had to engage in social reform; this was, he insisted, progressive, not theologically revolutionary. Charity had to be replaced by the "higher philanthropy," the term Tucker coined to define the idea that social justice meant putting right the social conditions which caused social evil. To achieve his goals, he introduced two innovations during his first years at Andover: he developed a pioneer course called social economics, a venture into the field of sociological study, and he founded, with four other professors, the *Andover Review*, a religious magazine, to disseminate the ideas of a progressive orthodoxy.

The course in social economics, an intensive study of specific problems of society, such as problems of labor and tenement house evils, evoked national comment. In response to requests from other seminaries for aid in preparing similar courses, Tucker published, in the *Andover Review*, outlines, reading lists, and suggestions for field work. If prospective ministers were to lead in social reconstruction, they had to know the sources and nature of the problems and seek practical solutions; this was the purpose of the course.

Editorials, which the professors wrote for the *Andover Review*, were unique in a religious publication and became the basis for serious controversy from those who disagreed with the progressive professors. In 1886 the five professor-editors were charged with teaching doctrines contrary to the foundation principles of the seminary. A group of conservatives, called the Congregationalists, brought the suit, which was called the Andover Controversy. From 1886 to 1892 the suit was alive in various courts; in the end, the professors were vindicated. Tucker believed that, though protracted and frustrating, the outcome assured theological freedom. The life of the seminary continued without disruption during the conflict, but Andover and the professors became symbols of the new social-mindedness of the church.

In 1885 Tucker started a fellowship for the course to send a student abroad to study new forms of church work; the first traveling fellow gave a brief account of Toynbee Hall in London's East End. Intrigued by the idea of a settlement house and questioning whether the idea could be applied in the United States, Tucker sent Robert A. Woods,* an advanced student in the class, to London to investigate and report his findings. After Woods returned, Tucker decided that the settlement offered a special challenge to apply the higher philanthropy. He founded Andover House, in 1891, in the South End of Boston, with four Andover students as residents; Robert Woods was head resident. The dedication, courage, and enthusiasm of the residents and Tucker's support kept the doors of the house open during the crucial first year. Tucker even paid some of the operating expenses from his personal funds. The social settlement seemed to Tucker a significant instrument in the movement toward social unity, and Andover House (later called South End House) became a leader in the settlement house movement.

In 1893, for the third time in his life, William Jewett Tucker was invited to accept the presidency of Dartmouth College. This time he agreed to serve. He did so because he decided that the aims of Social Christianity could be furthered now by training college men to render practical service to society by offering them studies in economic justice in the college curriculum. His work at Andover seemed complete when a department of christian sociology was established and enlarged.

Tucker's presidency at Dartmouth, from 1893 to 1909, was known there as the "Great Awakening." He initiated the reconstruction of the curriculum to introduce new subject matter, such as sociology, economics, anthropology, and social sciences (history); the faculty more than doubled in size in six years early in his Dartmouth tenure. In addition, he set the college on a sound financial basis, the physical plant was expanded, fourteen dormitories were built in fourteen years, and the faculty was reorganized into departments of instruction, rather than individual chairs of instruction. An innovative new school on the graduate level for the study of economics, political science, sociology, and modern languages was founded through the beneficence of a roommate of Tucker's during his college years, Edward Tuck; the school was named in memory of his father, Amos Tuck.

Tucker continued his church activities during these years; he was the Lyman Beecher Lecturer at Yale Divinity School (1897 and 1898); he was a member of the Harvard Board of Preachers (1899–1901); in 1901 he and Washington Gladden were members of the Committee on Labor for the National Council of Congregational Churches, which moved officially toward setting up a social service program. In 1905 he was a speaker at the conference which approved the beginning of the Federal Council of Churches of Christ in America, a step toward the unity and coopertion he favored; there was at the convention also the pledge that the churches would try to influence matters affecting the social and moral condition of the people.

After a long fund-raising trip for Dartmouth, Tucker suffered a heart attack in 1907, which led to his retirement in 1909. During his retirement, he devoted himself to reading, writing, and editing.

Patrician in appearance and an example of the qualities of fortitude, compassion, and social action which he espoused, Tucker inspired respect and devotion in numerous disciples, who would carry his ideas into their own milieu. He tirelessly put forward the goal of social unity through the application of ethical principles and the extirpation of social injustice. He publicized the ideas of the Social Gospel movement, attacked laissez-faire, initiated the discipline of careful study of social conditions in his pioneer course as a preparation for practical reform, founded Andover House, and sensitized the social conscience of a generation of young people. He was among the early critics of the urban-industrial inequities and sought practical, ethical principles for reform.

He was virtually an invalid for the last six years of his life, and he died at his home in Hanover, New Hampshire, on September 29, 1926, at age eighty-seven.

The William Jewett Tucker Collection in the Dartmouth College Library, Hanover, New Hampshire, contains Tucker's speeches to classes and some correspondence during the presidency of that institution. Most of the papers were used in his autobiography and in pubished collections of his addresses to students.

Tucker was a popular and prolific writer, and his published sermons and articles are extensive; among the most significant of his works for social welfare history are the syllabi for his pioneer course in social economics, his assessment of the settlement house movement and of Andover House, and his collection of articles made during his retirement, which he considered an important summary: See respectively, "Social Economics: The Outline of an Effective Course of Study," *Andover Review* (January, 1889), 85–89, (February, 1889), 203–207, (March, 1889), 310–311, and (July, 1889), 100–103; "The Work of Andover House in Boston," in *The Poor in Great Cities: Their Problems and What Is Christianity Doing to Solve Them* (1895), 177–193; and *New Reservations of Time* (1916).

The most valuable work on Tucker is his autobiography, written to give an interpretation of the inner life of one who lived through the challenges of post– Civil War America: *My Generation: An Autobiographical Interpretation*(1919). An evaluation of his contributions to educational reform at Dartmouth, with reminiscenses about him, can be found in Robert F. Leavens and Arthur H. Lord, *Dr. Tucker's Dartmouth* (1965). For contemporary reaction to his life and career, see his obituary in the *New York Times* (September 30, 1926), 25:3. Also see the sketch of him in the *Dictionary of American Biography*, vol. 19 (1936), 41–42.

DOROTHY T. SCANLON

**Tuckerman, Joseph** (January 18, 1778–April 20, 1840), minister, social worker, and social reformer, was born in Boston, Massachusetts, to Elizabeth (Harris) and Edward Tuckerman, a successful Boston merchant. As a child, Tuckerman lived in a quiet middle-class neighborhood and attended Boston Latin School (1790–1791) and Phillips Andover Academy (1791). He matriculated at Harvard University in 1794, and after having taken his baccalaureate degree read for the ministry with the Reverend Thomas Thacker of Dedham. He returned to Harvard for an M.A. in 1801 and then became the pastor of the (Congregationalist) Church of Christ in Chelsea. He married Abigail Parkman on July 5, 1803, with whom he had three children. She died on July 28, 1807, and he then married Sara Cory on November 3, 1808; they had seven children.

Largely through the efforts of his close friend, William Ellery Channing, in 1826 Tuckerman gave up the pulpit in Chelsea to become "minister to Boston's poor" under the auspices of the American Unitarian Association. In this role, Tuckerman visited the jails and prisons of Boston, preached to the indigent, and visited them in their homes. He functioned essentially as a social worker, in other words: he found jobs for newly released convicts, aided those who were alcoholics or were accused of drunkenness, and became an early advocate of an expanded public school system. In these and other efforts, he was heavily influenced by the work and writing of Thomas Chalmers of Edinburgh, Scotland, especially Chalmers' *Christian Economy of Large Towns* (3 vols., 1821–1826). In 1829 he wrote an essay on female wages notable because it attributed poverty to social and economic conditions rather than to individual character. He was a supporter of the Boston House of Reformation and, in 1833, helped to found the Boston Asylum and Farm School, located on Thompson's Island and designed to rescue boys before they became delinquent. He also held a number of public welfare posts, including overseer of the poor, and was an active member of a number of social welfare agencies in early nineteenth century Boston, including the Boston Society for the Prevention of Pauperism. In addition, he was the author of numerous publications (cited below), of which the most accessible is *Joseph Tuckerman on the Elevation of the Poor* published in 1874, long after his death.

Tuckerman deserves to be better known in social welfare circles, for it could be argued that he was America's first notable social worker. His approach to welfare problems anticipated many late nineteenth century developments, hailed at the time as innovations, including distinguishing between poverty and pauperism, organizing various relief agencies, visiting the homes of the afflicted, and blaming poverty on social as opposed to personal causes. He rightly could be called "the father of American social work."

Tuckerman died in Havana, Cuba, on April 20, 1840.

Tuckerman wrote a great deal, including *A Letter Addressed to Hon. Harrison Gray Otis, Mayor of Boston, Respecting the House of Correction and the Common Jail in Boston* (1830); *A Letter to the Executive Committee of the Benevolent Fraternity of Churches, Respecting Their Organization for the Support of the Ministry at Large in Boston* (1834); *Christian Service to the Poor in Cities* (1839); and *Joseph Tuckerman on the Elevation of the Poor* (1874; repr. 1971).

For manuscript collections and printed sermons, see the bibliography in Daniel T. Colgan, *Joseph Tuckerman: Pioneer in American Social Work* (1940). Also see William Ellery Channing's *A Discourse on the Life and Character of the Rev. Joseph Tuckerman* (1841), and the obituary in the *Boston Transcript*, May 18, 1840.

Major secondary treatments include sketches of Tuckerman in the *Dictionary of American Biography* (1936), the *National Cyclopaedia of Biography* (1929), *Appleton's Cyclopedia of American Biography* (1889), *Who Was Who in America* (1967), and the *Dictionary of American Religious Biography* (1977). Also see Robert S. Mennel, *Thorns and Thistles* (1974), and Joseph M. Hawes, *Children in Urban Society* (1971).

JOSEPH M. HAWES

# V

**Vaile, Gertrude** (January 20, 1878–October 15, 1954), public welfare reformer and social work educator, was born in Kokomo, Indiana, in 1878, the daughter of Joel Frederick and Charlotte (White) Vaile. Her father was a well-known, prosperous lawyer in Indiana. In 1883 the family moved to Denver, where Mr. Vaile became general counsel for the Denver and Rio Grande Western Railroad. The Vaile family became very prominent socially and politically in the Denver area, as exemplified by Gertrude's older brother William who served in the U.S. House of Representatives from 1924 to 1927. Gertrude attended public shools in Denver and graduated from Vassar College, before moving to Chicago in 1909 to attend the Chicago School of Civics and Philanthropy.

While attending school in Chicago, Vaile became a resident at Chicago Commons, a settlement house founded by Graham Taylor,* under whom she studied. Shortly after completing school in 1910 she became a caseworker for United Charities in Chicago. During this time she also did some work for the Russell Sage Foundation, where she attracted the attention of Mary Richmond.* Richmond considered her a promising young social worker, and the two collaborated on several projects in later years.

In 1913 Vaile was asked by the mayor of Denver to take a position on the City Board of Charities and Correction. She accepted the position and within a year became executive director of the Board. As executive director, Vaile sought to apply the casework principles of the charity organization society movement to the field of public welfare. This idea was considered quite revolutionary at that time, and many casework experts were skeptical that it would work; the experts, however, were wrong. Vaile gradually changed the archaic county agent's office into a legitimate social service department. The first of its kind in the United States, the Denver office used casework, case conferences, and friendly visitors. Vaile also introduced the use of interagency case conferences, at which representatives of all public and private social agencies met to marshal community resources for clients. She also made extensive use of volunteers, a practice which had proved effective in her earlier work in Chicago.

As director of the Department of Social Services, Vaile was constantly under attack by political opponents. A move was undertaken in 1916 which would have made confidential material in case records subject to public disclosure. This move was designed to cripple the department by driving away clients. Vaile fought the attempt and was able to establish that the law mandated that only routine data be made public, and that social workers could be held liable if any other information was released. Nationwide expansion of public welfare services would not come until the depression years of the 1930s, but by the time Gertrude Vaile left in 1917, the Denver office had become a pioneering model of enlightened public welfare administration.

During World War I, Vaile served as director of civilian relief for the Mountain Division of the American Red Cross. Here again her casework principles proved effective. After the war she joined the field staff of the Family Service Association of America, where she was associate field director until 1923. She left this position to become executive director of the Colorado State Department of Charities and Correction.

In 1926 Vaile was elected president of the National Conference of Social Work. In her presidential address before the Conference, she spoke of the decline of the kind of crusading social work leadership which had been so evident in the days of the Progressive movement. She went on to correctly identify the emergence of a new type of leadership in the field, more concerned with day to day administration than with broad ideals and social vision. As one of the crusading reformers of earlier years, Vaile seemed ambivalent about this change. While lamenting the passing of the reform movement, she stated that the present need seemed to be for a decentralized, diffused leadership.

Vaile became associate director of the School of Social Work at the University of Minnesota in 1930, a position she would hold until her retirement in 1946. While serving in this capacity she worked to strengthen the Association of Schools of Social Work (now the Council on Social Work Education), believing that the potential of social work education could be realized only if the various schools united and worked together. At the time, Vaile was very much a single voice crying in the wilderness, but she is remembered today as a pioneer in social work education.

Throughout her life, Vaile's philosophy was that poverty was related to the economic setting, and not merely a matter of individual circumstances. She felt strongly that government should assume the responsibility for the welfare of its people, and one of her main accomplishments was to show that government could effectively and efficiently develop and maintain a rational system designed to meet human needs. Her approach was always to be simple and direct, and she contributed much to modern-day social work. Vaile withdrew from public life after her retirement in 1946 and died at her home in Denver on October 15, 1954.

Most of Gertrude Vaile's writings were published through the National Conference of Social Work. Of these, two of the most notable are "Public Administration of Charity in Denver," National Conference of Charities and Correction, *Proceedings* (1916); and "The Cost of Maintaining Good Case Work in a Public Agency," *Proceedings of the National Conference of Social Work* (1925).

Although several books dealing with the history of the National Conference of Social Work do mention various aspects of Vaile's career, no comprehensive biographical account could be located. Two books which do discuss her are Frank J. Bruno, *Trends in Social Work* (1948), and Clarke A. Chambers, *Seedtime of Reform* (1963). Other brief biographical sketches can be obtained from the following sources: *Encyclopedia of Social Work*, 17th issue, vol. (1977), 1511–1512; "Gertrude Vaile, 1878–1954," *Social Service Review* (March, 1955), 84–85; obituary, *Denver Post*, October 17, 1954; obituary, *Rocky Mountain News*, October 17, 1954; Margaret E. Rich, "Gertrude Vaile, 1878–1954," *Social Casework* (December, 1954), 449.

JIM STAFFORD

**Van Kleeck, Mary Abby** (June 26, 1883–June 8, 1972), social researcher, social reformer, and advocate of social planning, was born in Glenham, New York, the daughter of the Reverend Robert Boyd Van Kleeck, an Episcopal minister, and Eliza (Mayer) Van Kleeck, the daughter of a founder of the Baltimore and Ohio Railroad. Following her father's death in 1892, the family moved to Flushing, New York, where Van Kleeck graduated from Flushing High School in 1900. She continued her education at Smith College, receiving her A.B. in 1904.

In 1905 Van Kleeck began to pursue her concern for the industrial worker through social research. As a fellow in the College Settlement Association in New York, Van Kleeck conducted research on the overtime of working girls in New York factories, and then on child labor in the tenements of New York City (1905–1906). In 1907 these studies prompted the Alliance Employment Bureau, a philanthropic agency which found employment for girls in the trades and offices, to create a department of industrial investigations with Van Kleeck as director. Her studies expanded to pioneering investigations of women's employment and, beginning in 1908, were supported by the Russell Sage Foundation. In November, 1910, her studies became an established part of the Foundation and were particularly noteworthy in their research methods and their attention to the relationship between wages and the standard of living as well as to existing laws or proposed legislation. On the basis of these studies, it was concluded that the problems women encountered in employment were related to the industrial and social conditions which affected both men and women. To reflect this broadening scope for investigations on industrial problems, the Foundation, in 1916, established the Department of Industrial Studies with Van Kleeck as its director.

Except for a brief period during World War I (1918–1919), she served in this capacity until her retirement in 1948.

From 1914 to 1917, while continuing her work at the Russell Sage Foundation, Van Kleeck taught at the New York School of Philanthropy, offering courses on industrial conditions and industrial research. On behalf of the school and the Intercollegiate Bureau of Occupations, Van Kleeck, along with Edward T. Devine,* conducted an occupational study in 1915 on positions in private social agencies in New York. President of the Intercollegiate Bureau, Van Kleeck also was active in the National Social Workers' Exchange, which developed out of the Bureau. Additionally during these years, she served on New York Mayor John P. Mitchel's committees on unemployment.

Van Kleeck's expertise on women's employment was recognized in 1918 when she was appointed director of the women's branch of the industrial service section of the federal government's Ordnance Department. The standards she proposed for the employment of women in war industries were adopted by the War Labor Policies Board, on which she served in 1918–1919. In July, 1918, Van Kleeck was appointed director of the Department of Labor's Women in Industry Service, the forerunner of the U.S. Women's Bureau. In addition to setting guidelines for women's employment generally, Van Kleeck established the methods of investigation used by the Women's Bureau.

Upon her return to the Department of Industrial Studies at the Russell Sage Foundation in 1919, Van Kleeck began to focus the broadening scope of the department on the relationships between employers and employees in industry. The department, and Van Kleeck herself, began to examine the experiments being conducted at that time in organizing these relations. She was active particularly in researching employer-employee relations in the coal industry.

In this decade before the Great Depresion, Van Kleeck was a member of the 1921 President's Conference on Unemployment and was appointed to the Committee on Unemployment and Business Cycles. She also served as a trustee for Smith College (1922–1930), chaired the National Interracial Conference (1928), and promoted the profession of social work by taking part in the organization of the American Association of Social Workers and serving on a number of its committees.

In the 1930s Van Kleeck emerged as a severe critic of the New Deal. Criticizing the New Deal for maintaining the status quo of economic privilege and curtailment of workers' liberties, Van Kleeck advocated for comprehensive social insurance and social welfare plans and defended the right of labor to organize and to strike. Her opposition to the policies of the National Recovery Administration led her to resign, after one day, her appointment in 1933 to the Federal Advisory Council of the United States Employment Service. She viewed the New Deal policies as weakening trade unions and their right to collective bargaining while supporting industrial monopolies. By 1934, in *Miners and Management*, Van Kleeck had concluded that to prevent poverty and to raise the standard of living both the economic and political structure of the United States must be changed. She advanced a planned economy with socialization of industry and all natural resources. These ideas were expanded in her economic and political analysis of the United States in *Creative America* (1936). She envisioned a collective economy based on the principles of scientific management and political democracy.

Her analyses of the New Deal and the United States economy, as well as her support for an alignment of social work with organized labor, led Van Kleeck, along with Harry Lurie,* to become an important figure in the Rank-and-File movement, a dissenting left-leaning movement within social work during the Depression era.

Van Kleeck's growing understanding that analysis of the total economy must include a global perspective led to leadership roles internationally. Her international efforts included serving as associate director of the International Industrial Relations Institute (1928–1948), chair of the program committee for the World Social Economic Congress (1931), and president of the Second International Conference of Social Work, held in 1932 at Frankfurt-am-Main, Germany. She also served on the executive committees of Hospites, an organization which provided assistance to refugee social workers from Germany, and of the Social Workers Committee to Aid Spanish Democracy.

In the late 1930s, Van Kleeck and May L. Fledderus, director of the International Industrial Relations Institute, began to study the importance of technological changes and their impact upon employment and wages. Published in 1944 as *Technology and Livelihood*, their study reviewed modern technology with its resulting change in labor requirements and highlighted the increase in productivity without a corresponding increase in employment opportunities and security.

Van Kleeck continued her research and writings in the 1940s, exploring community organization, social and economic planning, social adjustment to atomic energy, and the abolishment of nuclear weapons. She retired from the Russell Sage Foundation in 1948 and made her home in Woodstock, New York. In that year she supported Henry A. Wallace in his presidential bid and ran unsuccessfully as a candidate of the American Labor Party for the state senate in New York. In 1953 she received a subpoena from the Senate Permanent Subcommittee on Investigations, chaired by Senator Joseph McCarthy.

Once described as a ''stormy petrel'' by the *Survey*, Mary Van Kleeck was committed to obtaining knowledge through the rigors of scientific inquiry. Her thorough analyses led to well-reasoned arguments on the need for social and economic planning. A social activist and an individual of great courage, intellect, and integrity, Van Kleeck sought a fundamental change in the economic structure of the United States to bring about a more secure economic future for all citizens. She died in 1972 in Kingston, New York.

The papers of Mary Van Kleeck are at the Sophia Smith Collection, Women's History Archives, Smith College. In addition to her publications and addresses, the collection incudes Van Kleeck's scrapbooks of editorial comments, clippings, and news releases; Congressional hearing transcripts; and research data. Additional material on her work at the Russell Sage Foundation, the activities of the United Mine Workers Union, and conditions of employed women is located at the Archives of Labor and Urban Affairs, Wayne State University. The National Archives and Records Service has material on Van Kleeck in its War Labor Policies Board and Women's Bureau holdings.

Important publications by Van Kleeck include "Working Hours of Women in Factories," *Charities and the Commons* (October, 1906), 13–21; "Child Labor in New York City Tenements," *Charities and the Commons* (January 18, 1908), 1405–1420; "Women and Children Who Make Men's Clothes," *Survey*(April 11, 1911), 65–69. Works published by the Russell Sage Foundation in New York include *Artificial Flower Makers* (1913), *Women in the Bookbinding Trade* (1913), *Working Girls in Evening Schools* (1914), and *A Seasonal Industry: A Study of the Millinery Trade* (1917). Significant presentations published in the *Proceedings of the National Conference of Social Work* (1934) are "The Common Goals of Labor and Social Work," 284–303; "The Effect of the NRA on Labor," 428–436; and "Our Illusions Regarding Government," 473–485.

Secondary sources of information include: Mary Anderson, written with Mary Winslow, *Women at Work* (1951); Jacob Fisher, *The Response of Social Work to the Depression* (1980); John M. Glenn, Lilian Brandt, and F. Emerson Andrews, *Russell Sage Foundation 1907–1946*, 2 vols. (1947); Eleanor Midman Lewis, "Mary Van Kleeck," in *Notable American Women: The Modern Period*, (1980), 707–709; *New York Times*, June 9, 1972, 41:1; and *Who Was Who in America*, vol. 5 (1969–1973).

JAN L. HAGEN

**Van Waters, Miriam** (October 4, 1887–January 17, 1974), progressive penologist and social worker, was born in Greensberg, Pennsylvania, the second of five children of Maude (Vosburg) and George Browne Van Waters, an Episcopal minister of the Social Gospel. In 1888 his work took the family to Oregon, where young Miriam took an active role in caring for her siblings and helping her father in his parsonage. During her father's pastoral absences and her mother's return visits to Pennsylvania, whe worked hard to maintain family life.

In 1904 Van Waters graduated from St. Helen's Hall, a school which her father founded, and then from the University of Oregon (1908), where she majored in philosophy. Van Waters intended to pursue a Ph.D. in social psychology at Clark University under the direction of the renowned psychologist G. Stanley Hall. However, she found that Hall's insistence on deterministic explanations of female criminality conflicted with her own emphasis on the role of environment in influencing behavior. Thus, Van Waters continued her doctoral work under Alexander Chamberlain and received her degree from Clark (1914) in anthropology. Her dissertation, "The Adolescent Girl Among Primitive Peoples," stressed the diversity of behavior among cultures and the reality and importance of female sexuality.

Van Waters' career in social work and the development of her professional goals were formulated even prior to the completion of her doctorate. In 1911, while a student at Clark, she observed the juvenile court in Boston presided over by Judge Harvey H. Baker. Here she saw firsthand the negative effects of parental and educational neglect. Two years later, Van Waters became an agent of the Boston Children's Aid Society, where she fought against the prevailing attitude that young women charged with morals violations were unredeemable. Upon graduation from Clark, Van Waters became the superintendent of the Frazer Detention Home in Portland, Oregon, but tuberculosis forced an interruption in her work until 1917, when she became superintendent of the Los Angeles county home for female juvenile delinquents.

Because of her rising reputation as a progressive penologist, she became superintendent of a new county facility at El Retiro, California, in 1919. She defined the institution as a "preventorium," symbolic of the new rehabilitative effort which Van Waters referred to as "enlightened penology." At El Retiro, Van Waters sought to create an institutional atmosphere of "trust and care" to offset the poverty and abuse of home and society. There was a system of self-government, inmates were paid wages, and a half-way program was established. And, in order to prepare the inmates for a useful return to society, Van Waters emphasized vocational and career development.

Van Waters magnified the impact of her reform work by assuming additional welfare posts and by becoming a part of the court system. In 1919 she took the California bar exam and became a referee of the juvenile court. In the early 1920s, Van Waters, financed by Chicago philanthropist Ethel Sturges Dummer,* undertook a national survey of homes for delinquent girls. The study, published in *Survey Graphic* (1922) as "Where Girls Go Right," lauded schools with genteel surroundings and condemned institutions practicing corporal punishment. In her two major publications, *Youth in Conflict* (1925) and *Parents on Probation* (1927), Van Waters placed particular blame "upon home, upon family" for inattention to childhood and adolescence. Society in general was also at fault for "modernization," or mechanized culture, and its adverse effects on children.

Van Waters' various publications and her work with social organizations gained her a national reputation. In 1928 she was commissioned by Felix Frankfurter to do a study of Massachusetts's juvenile institutions for the Harvard Law School Crime Survey. In 1930 she was appointed by President Herbert Hoover to serve on the Wickersham Commission on Law Observance and Enforcement, the first national crime survey. Her contribution, *The Child Offender in the Federal System of Justice* (1932), stressed the need to incorporate criminal justice procedures particular to juveniles within the adult-oriented court system. In 1932 the superintendency of Framingham (Massachusetts) Reformatory for Women became available, and Van Waters eagerly took the position.

By 1932 Framingham Reformatory for Women was regarded as a model for modern treatment of women. Former superintendents Ellen Cheney Johnson (1884–1899) and Jessie Hodder* (1910–1931) had stressed rehabilitative programs. Van Waters continued Hodder's policies of indenture and maternal care. Van

Waters also improved the atmosphere of the institution by building cottages for mothers and younger girls. She expanded medical and psychological facilities and established the first institutional chapter of Alcoholics Anonymous. Van Waters's emphasis on self-improvement was seen in the various activities the institution supported. Framingham had literary, drama, choral, and debating clubs and offered evenings with guest lecturers. Van Waters also increased educational and occupational opportunities off the premises as well as within the institution. Her attitude toward corrections is seen best in her insistence that the inmates be referred to as ''students.''

Van Waters also maintained her personal family role at Framingham. She never married, yet in 1932 Van Waters adopted a ten-year-old girl, Sarah Ann, who had come before her in the California courts. Also residing at Framingham were Van Waters's widowed mother, her brother Ralph, and his wife, Bertha, who filled various positions at the reformatory and helped Van Waters raise the child. Sarah Ann eventually married and had three children, but the marriage ended in divorce in 1949. Further tragedy struck when Sarah was killed in an automobile accident in 1953. Miriam Van Waters encouraged and supported her daughter throughout her childhood and troubled marriage.

Until the late 1940s, Van Waters ran the reformatory with discretionary authority, having the approval of six Governors and several Commissioners of Correction. But beginning in 1947, the rehabilitative aspects of the institution stressed by Van Waters were severely threatened. On November 10, 1947, a young inmate from Boston committed suicide. The Commissioner of Correction, Elliot McDowell, goaded by the strong Hearst press, called for an investigation and hurled charges at Van Waters of lesbianism, lax administration, and preferential treatment. A group of prominent Massachusetts citizens sympathetic to Van Waters's work, among them LaRue Brown and his wife, Dorothy Kirchway Brown, organized as the ''Friends of Framingham'' in defense of the reformatory's program as well as of Van Waters herself. Three separate investigations established that there was no foul play involved in the girl's death, but in January, 1949, the Commissioner dismissed Van Waters for maladministration. Three successive public hearings concerning the administration of Framingham were held. By 1950 Van Waters was reinstated, but her programs were severely restricted. One outcome of the hearings was to inaugurate not only equal sentences for equal crimes for male and female offenders but also a policy of equal treatment for male and female prisoners, which meant that several of the Framingham programs, such as day work, alcoholic treatment, and the mother-child program, were deemed ''privileged'' and hence were lost. Even under the restricted conditions, Van Waters remained at the reformatory until health forced her to retire in 1957, by which time she no longer was the leading figure in female corrections. However, she continued to write and lecture about the role of environmental factors in contributing to female delinquency and about the importance of education and vocational training for rehabilitation until her death in Framingham, Massachusetts, in 1974.

The Miriam Van Waters Collection is held at the Schlesinger Library, Radcliffe College, as are the papers of Jessie Hodder, Ethel Sturges Dummer, Dorothy Kirchwey Brown, and Friends of Framingham, 1948–1973. The Massachusetts State Library, Boston, has the records of the reformatory as well as those of the Department of Correction. All of the Boston newspapers covered the events of 1947–1950 and are held at the Boston Public Library as well as at the State Library.

Among Van Waters' own publications are "Where Girls Go Right," *Survey Graphic* (May 27, 1922); *Youth in Conflict* (1925); *Parents on Probation* (1927); "Adolescence," in *Encyclopedia of Social Sciences*, vol. 1 (1930); "Philosophical Trends in Modern Social Work," National Conference of Social Work, *Proceedings* (1930); "Juvenile Delinquency and Juvenile Courts," in *Encyclopedia of Social Sciences*, vol. 8 (1932); "The Specialized Treatment of the Women [*sic*] Offender in America and the Reasons for the Success of This Movement," *Bulletin of the International Penal and Penitentiary Commission* (November, 1948).

The only published biography is Burton J. Rowles, *The Lady at Box 99: The Story of Miriam Van Waters* (1962). *Notable American Women: The Modern Period* (1980) has a biographical sketch of Van Waters, 709–711. Van Waters has been the subject of two unpublished studies: Janet T. St. Goar, "Extending the Boundaries: Miriam Van Waters, Superintendent of the Massachusetts Reformatory for Women, 1932–1958," B.A. honors thesis, Harvard University, 1978; and Barbara Eggers, "Changing Directions in the Treatment of Women Offenders: The Career and Trial of Miriam Van Waters, Superintendent of the Massachusetts Reformatory for Women, 1932–1957," Master's thesis, University of New Hampshire, 1982.

For obituaries see the *New York Times*, January 18, 1974, and the *Boston Globe*, January 19, 1974.

BARBARA EGGERS

**Veiller, Lawrence Turnure** (January 7, 1872–August 30, 1959), housing reformer and social worker, was born in Elizabeth, New Jersey, the son of Philip Bayard Veiller, a broker and factory owner, and Elizabeth duPuy. Subsequent to attending several public and private schools, Veiller entered the City College of New York at the age of fourteen and received the B.A. degree four years later. In 1897 he married Amy Hall; they had no children.

Veiller's social activism sprang from his college years, when he read the criticisms of Victorian England by Thomas Carlyle and John Ruskin. Although raised as an Episcopalian, he became a secular reformer whose humanitarianism stemmed from a belief in the individual's social responsibilities. Unlike many of his contemporaries in the Progressive movement, he harbored little faith in the inherent goodness of his fellow men. Dismissing such prevailing orthodoxies as the inevitability of progress and the onmipotent force of reasoned argument, Veiller was more of a cynic and, therefore, more willing to engage in the grimy real world of politics than many of the more pristine reformers. Thus, the hard-boiled realist advanced the cause of housing reform on many fronts—as legislative draftsman, pressure group organizer, lobbyist, mobilizer of public opinion, and administration.

Veiller launched his career during the Depression of 1893, ministering to the needy of New York City through the East Side Relief Work Committee. Hired as a housing plan examiner in the city's Building Department during Mayor William L. Strong's administration (1895–1897), he gained invaluable firsthand experience in the technical aspects of the tenement problem. Flushed with the conviction that better housing was the touchstone of all social reform, he convinced the Charity Organization Society (COS) of New York City to form a new Tenement House Committee with Veiller as its secretary and executive officer. Under his guidance, the Committee spearheaded the housing reform movement in New York for the next generation.

When the state legislature ignored the COS's recommendations and passed an egregiously inadequate municipal building code in 1899, Veiller staged a nationally acclaimed tenement house exhibit to educate the public about the urgency of slum eradication. An estimated 10,000 people viewed the exhibit in New York City, after which it went on tour throughout the country and even to the 1900 Paris Exposition. Riding the crest of public indignation, Veiller parlayed the support of Governor Theodore Roosevelt into the creation of the New York State Tenement House Commission that same year. The fifteen-member body chose Veiller its secretary, and he quickly led the draconian revision of the hated 1899 law. The resultant New York State Tenement House Law of 1901 prohibited the construction of ''dumbbell'' tenements (so called because of their shape) in the undeveloped areas of Manhattan and the other boroughs of the city, mandated the inclusion of separate water closets in each apartment of future tenements, included comprehensive fire-prevention measures for intended structures, and detailed necessary changes in existing tenements as well. The law not only assured much-needed changes in New York City housing for the poor, but also catapulted its champion into national prominence as the foremost crusader against slum housing.

To implement the provisions of the 1901 law, Veiller helped form the Tenement House Department as an autonomous city agency and served as its first Deputy Commissioner. (Mayor Seth Low appointed Robert W. de Forest* Commissioner, but he ruled in name only; in fact, de Forest accepted only with the assurance that Veiller would actually do the lion's share of the work.) Both de Forest and Veiller resigned when Tammany mayor George McClellan ousted Low in 1904. In later years, with less hostile administrations ensconced in City Hall, Veiller acted as an unofficial advisor to the department in helping it interpret and enforce the housing code he had largely drafted. In 1917 Veiller severed his long-standing connections with the COS's Tenement House Committee in protest over its support of a questionable housing bill and increasingly devoted his time to the burgeoning nationwide housing reform movement. He helped found the National

Housing Association and served as its director from 1911 to 1936. At the same time he wrote several primers for housing experts on the successful drafting and implementation of tenement legislation, including *A Model Tenement House Law*; *Housing Reform: A Hand-Book for Practical Use in American Cities*; and *A Model Housing Law*.

As a nationally renowned housing authority, Veiller continued to emphasize restrictive legislation as the optimum reform strategy. His successes in New York City initially lent his ideas authority, but by the time of World War I many reformers saw restrictive legislation as limited solely to preventing unsatisfactory housing from being built. On the other hand, they adduced, "constructive" housing legislation, patterned after the European model in which government subsidized working-class housing, would best shore up the sagging housing stock in America. By the 1920s Veiller assumed a defensive posture and lashed out at the increasingly popular alternatives propounded by a new generation of housing experts: he criticized model tenements as a form of philanthropy unlikely to aid more than a handful of people and lambasted government-built or -subsidized housing as inimical to the sacrosanct laws of supply and demand. Consequently, he emerged as one of the most virulent critics of the New Deal's federal housing projects in the 1930s.

As his influence in the area of housing waned, Veiller immersed himself in other reform causes. In a related field, he helped formulate New York City's—and the nation's—first comprehensive zoning law in 1916 and prepared for the United States Department of Commerce its Standard Zoning Law of 1921. In 1928 he served as a member of Commerce Secretary Herbert Hoover's Advisory Committee on City Planning and Zoning. He also became involved in criminal law and court reform. In the 1920s, in his role as an unofficial advisor to the Baumes Crime Commission, he spoke and wrote against lenient parole standards. For over twenty years he acted as secretary for the COS Committee on Criminal Courts and assumed the presidency of the New York Citizens Crime Commission in the late thirties. He died of a heart ailment in his New York City apartment.

The most helpful items for understanding Veiller are primary sources, especially two manuscript collections: the Veiller Papers at Columbia University and the Veiller reminiscences in the Columbia University Oral History Project. In addition, see Veiller's public writings, especially "Tenement House Reform," *American Academy of Political and Social Science Annals* 15 (1900), 138–141; and, with Robert W. de Forest, *The Tenement House Problem: Including the Report of the New York State Tenement House Commission of 1900* (1903).

The most illuminating secondary source on Veiller's career is Roy Lubove, *The Progressives and the Slums: Tenement House Reform in New York City, 1890–1917* (1962). A brief obituary in the *New York Times* (September 1, 1959) adds additional information.

ROGER BILES

# W

**Wald, Lillian D.** (March 10, 1867–September 1, 1940), public health nurse, settlement house leader, and social reformer, was born in Cincinnati, Ohio, to Max D. (Alexander) Wald and Minnie (Schwarz) Wald. Her family, of Polish and German-Jewish background, came to America shortly after 1848. Eventually the Wald family moved from Cincinnati to Dayton to Rochester, New York. Lillian Wald had a happy upper-middle-class childhood with no personal experience of hardship or poverty. Her early promise was at first undirected. At age sixteen she was denied admission to Vassar because she was too young. Six year later, after an active social life, she decided to become a nurse. She enrolled in the Woman's Medical College in New York after training as a nurse.

It was during this period that she began her social service career. In 1893, a depression year, she went to New York's East Side to conduct classes in home nursing for new immigrants. Her experiences there led her to leave medical school and move to the East Side in order to provide nursing service to the poor and to contribute to their sense of citizenship.

Lillian Wald and her first partner, Mary Brewster, thus started visiting nursing and the first independent public health nursing service in America. Because public home relief had been abolished in New York, their first apartment on Jefferson Street became a neighborhood center for the multiple needs of poor families. Lillian Wald was extremely successful both at obtaining the affection and respect of the poor and at attracting services and money from the well-to-do. By 1895 she established the settlement in a permanent home at 265 Henry Street. As the programs of the Nurses' Settlement expanded into a social settlement, out of necessity Lillian Wald became increasingly involved in political action. Wald initiated many new community ideas. She found that she had to advocate better housing, cleaner streets, and the abolition of sweatshops. The Nurses' Settlement, also called the Henry Street Settlement, grew rapidly. By 1906, twenty-seven nurses were associated with the Nurses' Settlement. In 1900 she started school nursing in the United States by first loaning a Henry Street nurse to perform that role. The month-long demonstration induced the New York City

Board of Health to establish the first public school nursing program. Lillian Wald also initiated the idea of having ungraded classes for those children who needed special help.

Lillian Wald's continual interest in children and children's affairs led her to political innovation. She joined with Felix Adler, Jane Addams,* Florence Kelley,* Lee Everett Macy, and others in 1904 to form the National Child Labor Committee, whose initial goal was only to investigate the effects of child labor in order to further the welfare of children. Later they lobbied for the passage of various bills.

Although it was not until 1912, under President Taft, that the U.S. Children's Bureau was established, Lillian Wald first suggested it to President Theodore Roosevelt in 1905. She felt that if the boll weevil, which was endangering the cotton crop, excited the concern of the United States, then the United States should also be concerned about its child crop.

Meanwhile, during the depression of 1907–1908, Lillian Wald's activities spread, as she became active in the State Bureau of Industries and Immigration and took part in many labor battles. She fought against the mistreatment of strikers, worked for the inspection of fire and sanitary conditions in factories and working places, and supported the suffragist movement. She was very involved in the public outcry against and reaction to the Triangle–Shirtwaist Company fire in 1911. During this period she also put into operation the Town and Country Nursing Service of the Red Cross.

By 1913 the Henry Street Visiting Nurse's Service had over ninety-two nurses who were making 200,000 visits annually. The settlement occupied seven houses on Henry Street and two uptown branches, serving the East Side, the upper Manhattan area, and the Bronx. The combination of nursing and settlement activities made Henry Street a powerful source for community betterment and reform. Special attention was given to vocational guidance and training. The settlement sponsored a system of scholarships permitting children to stay in school until age sixteen and conducted drives to eradicate tuberculosis and poor housing, and to establish parks and playgrounds.

The growing hostilities that eventually resulted in World War I led Lillian Wald into new activities. When pacifism was still respectable she took part in the Women's Peace Parade. With Jane Addams, she was a member of the "Anti-Preparedness Committee." In 1915 the Committee changed its name to the American Union Against Militarism and grew from 15 to 6,000 members. Later this group gave birth to the League of Free Nations, the Foreign Policy Association, and the American Civil Liberties Union. Although participation became increasingly controversial as the war neared, Lillian Wald insisted on standing up for what she believed was right, disregarding the many veiled threats she received against continued funding for the Henry Street Settlement. When war did break out, however, Lillian Wald involved the Henry Street Settlement in registration for conscription, and in nursing the postwar veterans. She also became involved in fighting wartime encroachments on civil liberties and served as the head of the Committee on Home Nursing of the Council of National Defense.

Lillian Wald always responded to the needs around her. During the influenza epidemic of 1918 she directed the recruitment of volunteer nurses and coordinated the efforts of various nursing agencies. As the East Side changed, the Henry Street Settlement House Program expanded. By 1920 a neighborhood playhouse became a leading experimental theater, and the settlement's cultural activities included an incorporated music school.

During the postwar period, Lillian Wald continued to work for child welfare legislation and the promotion of candidates for public office who had sympathy with social welfare interests. She had close ties with (Anna) Eleanor Roosevelt* and numerous other future New Dealers, many of whom had been residents of the Henry Street Settlement.

During the mid–1902s her health deteriorated, forcing her to terminate her day-to-day association with Henry Street. She continued her interest in it and maintained the title of head worker until 1933, shortly after Henry Street's fortieth anniversary. In 1940 she died in Westport, Connecticut, her retirement home, after a long illness initiated by a stroke.

Lillian Wald's papers are in the New York Public Library and at Columbia University. Her correspondence with Jacob Schiff is with the Schiff Papers in the American Jewish Archives, Hebrew Union College, Cincinnati, Ohio.

She wrote articles appearing in the *American Journal of Nursing* (October, 1900 and May, 1902) and two books based on her experiences: *The House on Henry Street* (1915), and *Windows on Henry Street* (1934). She also wrote the foreword to M. Wales, *The Public Health Nurse in Action* (1941).

Biographical information may be found in R. L. Duffus, *Lillian Wald, Neighbor and Crusader* (1938); G. Fink, *Great Jewish Women: Profiles of Courageous Women from the Maccabean Period to the Present* (1978); *Notable American Women 1607–1950* (1971); J. R. Marcus, *The American Jewish Woman 1654–1980* (1981); J. R. Rapport, "Notable American Jewish Women: A Computer-Aided Study in Collective Biography," Rabbinic thesis, Hebrew Union College, Cincinnati, Ohio, 1984; Y. Waters, *Visiting Nursing in the U.S.* (1909); and the *Dictionary of American Biography*, Supplement 2 (1977).

Obituaries appeared in the *New York Times* and the *Herald Tribune* (September 2, 1940); *Social Service Review* (December, 1940); and the *American Journal of Public Health* (November, 1940).

ARLENE RUBIN STIFFMAN

**Walling, William English** (March 14, 1877–September 12, 1936), social theorist and activist on behalf of the working class and the oppressed, was born in Louisville, Kentucky, one of two children of Willoughby Walling, a physician, and Rosalind (English) Walling. His grandfather, William Hayden English, was the Democratic Party's vice presidential candidate in 1880. Walling attended private schools in the United States and abroad and received a B.S. from the University of Chicago in 1897. After a year at Harvard Law School he returned to the University of Chicago for graduate work in sociology and economics under Thorstein Veblen.

Walling's wealth allowed him to spend his adult life as a full-time activist and publicist on behalf of the working class and the oppressed. He was associated with numerous organizations and causes, often in a leadership position. Few of them engaged his interest and energies for long. He left one after another or became inactive when he felt his work was done, or he became bored, or he began to disagree with an organization's ideas or activities.

Between 1899 and 1901 he worked as a factory inspector for the state of Illinois, concentrating on child labor problems. Between 1902 and 1905 he was a resident of the University Settlement in New York City. He spent much of his time investigating and writing about labor problems and strikes and working with local members of the American Federation of Labor. In 1903 he was one of the principal founders of the National Women's Trade Union League, which sought to organize and help female workers, and in the same year he helped found the New York Child Labor Committee.

During his years at the settlement, Walling began turning toward radical ideas and activities. In 1905 he was involved in the founding of the Intercollegiate Socialist Society, and he remained active in that organization until 1917 as a writer, speaker, and member of its executive committee. Also in 1905, he went to Russia to examine the repressive social conditions that had recently erupted into revolution. On this trip he became firmly committed to revolutionary socialism. He recorded his observations on Russia in a series of articles and a 1908 book, *Russia's Message*. These and later writings established Walling as a leading authority on Russia's movement toward revolution. He became a vitriolic critic of the revolution after the Bolsheviks seized power in 1917 and then took Russia out of World War I and began to display brutally authoritarian tendencies. His virulent anti-Bolshevik writings and activities exerted some influence on America's anti-Soviet policies at the Versailles Conference and during the 1920s.

Meanwhile, in 1906 Walling had married Anna Strunsky, a Russian Jewish emigré, with whom he had four children: Rosamond English, Anna Strunsky, Georgia, and William Hayden English. In 1908 he and his wife went to Springfield, Illinois, to investigate a race riot in Abraham Lincoln's city. Their findings were the basis for a biting article, ''Race War in the North,'' for the *Independent*. Walling viewed the oppression of Negroes in the United States as similar to the oppression of Jews in Russia. His article and the initiative of Mary White Ovington* led to a series of meetings at Walling's apartment that resulted in the founding of the National Association for the Advancement of Colored People (NAACP) in 1909–1910. Walling was the chairman of the Association's first executive committee and was a sporadically active member of the organization's governing board during the rest of his life. One of his most important actions was arranging for W. E. B. Du Bois* to edit the Association's magazine, *Crisis*. His work with the Association was his most enduring achievement.

In 1910 Walling joined the Socialist Party and was active in its left wing, mainly as a publicist for revolutionary socialism and as a critic of Samuel Gompers and the American Federation of Labor. He was one of the most creative and influential socialist theorists of his time. In numerous books and articles he combined revolutionary socialism with John Dewey's pragmatism and the realities of American individualism and capitalism in championing equal opportunity for all and democratic institutions. Liberal reform, he believed, was a necessary episode in the movement toward socialism. He stated his ideas most fully in two books, *The Larger Aspects of Socialism* in 1913 and *Progressivism—And After* in 1914.

Walling left the party in 1917 because of its failure to recognize that a German victory in World War I would threaten democracy around the world and because of its opposition to American entry into the war. His disillusionment with the Socialist Party, his severe reaction against the Bolshevik Revolution, and his ardent support of America's war effort hurtled Walling toward anti-radicalism and more orthodox liberal ideas and activities. The major symbolic events in this transformation were his support in 1920 for the purging of socialists from the New York State legislature and his losing race for Congress in 1924 in Connecticut on the Democratic and Progressive Party tickets.

Walling spent most of the last fifteen years of his life working mainly as a volunteer for the American Federation of Labor. His wartime contacts with Gompers caused him to appreciate the man and the Federation, and Gompers was able to use Walling's skills as a publicist and his comprehensive knowledge of working-class movements in Europe. By the early 1920s Walling believed that the Federation was the most vital force for democracy and social progress in the United States. His most important effort for the organization was the publication in 1926 of *American Labor and American Democracy*, which celebrated the Federation's roots in American life and thought and presented the decade's most authoritative exposition of its principles and programs.

In 1935 Walling was appointed executive director of the Labor Chest of the Relief and Liberation of Workers of Europe. He died in Amsterdam, Holland, while on a trip to gather information from the anti-Nazi underground in Germany.

The William English Walling Papers are at the State Historical Society of Wisconsin and are available on microfilm. They contain copies of a large number of his published articles and some correspondence. Jack Meyer Stuart, "William English Walling: A Study in Politics and Ideas," Ph.D. dissertation, Columbia University, 1968, is a judicious biography. Frank A. Stricker, "Socialism, Feminism, and the New Morality: The Separate Freedoms of Max Eastman, William English Walling, and Floyd Dell, 1910–1930," Ph.D. dissertation, Princeton University, 1974, deals with aspects of Walling's thought. *William English*

*Walling: A Symposium* (1938) contains appreciations of the man and his work by friends and associates and a bibliography of his books and articles.

Walling was a prolific author. In addition to the works on socialism cited above, he wrote an important survey of the international left, *Socialism As It Is: A Survey of the World-wide Revolutionary Movement* (1912). Among his many other works, he was the actual author of a significant anti-Bolshevik tract: Samuel Gompers, with the collaboration of William English Walling, *Out of Their Own Mouths: A Revelation and an Indictment of Sovietism* (1921); and he authored Matthew Moll and William English Walling, *Our Next Step—A National Economic Policy* (1934), for Woll, who was a powerful leader of the American Federation of Labor.

On Walling and the National Women's Trade Union League, see Allen Davis, "The National Women's Trade Union League: Origins and Organization," *Labor History* (Winter, 1964), 3–17; and Edward T. James, ed., *Papers of the Women's Trade Union League and Its Principal Leaders: Guide to the Microfilm Edition* (1981). The latter source also locates some of Walling's correspondents. Charles Flint Kellogg's exhaustive *NAACP: A History of the National Association for the Advancement of Colored People, Vol. 1: 1909–1920* (1967) shows Walling's importance in the founding and first years of the organization. Walling's article leading to the founding of the NAACP was "Race War in the North," *Independent* (September 3, 1908), 529–534.

Walling is mentioned in numerous books and articles on socialism in the United States. Among the most informative are David A. Shannon, *The Socialist Party of America: A History* (1955); James Weinstein, *The Decline of Socialism in America, 1912–1925* (1967); Kent Kreuter and Gretchen Kreuter, *An American Dissenter: The Life of Algie Martin Simons, 1870–1950* (1969); and Paul Buhle, "Intellectuals in the Debsian Socialist Party," *Radical America*, (April, 1970), 35–58.

                                                                    STANLEY MALLACH

**Warner, Amos Griswold** (December 21, 1861–January 17, 1900), social planner and author, was born at Elkader, Iowa, the posthumous son of Amos Warner, a distinguished physician, and Esther (Carter) Warner, a woman dedicated to the alleviation of the social problems of her time. After her husband's death she moved with her four children to what was then known as the Territory of Nebraska. She settled on a homestead south of Roca, a small town some twelve miles from Lincoln. Here Warner received his common school education. In 1878 he entered the preparatory department of the University of Nebraska, where he became a well-respected student leader. He had intended to return to farm life after he graduated, but his academic goals were changed by his developing interest in contemporary problems, and their social and economic background required further education. In the summer of 1885 he therefore entered Baltimore's Johns Hopkins University as a graduate student in economics.

In 1887, when Warner's doctoral work was still incomplete, John Glenn,* a prominent philanthropist, invited him to become secretary of the Charity Organization Society (COS) of Baltimore, an important first step in what was to be a short professional career. The basic concept of the COS, newly imported from England, was that poverty reflected a flaw in the individual, only to be cured by a scientific approach with a firm character-building regime. Warner soon was to add to the COS principles his own recognition of the importance of environmental factors in individual growth, development, and behavior. In any event, he received his doctorate in 1888, and in the same year married Cora Ellen Fisher, by whom he was to have two children.

In 1889 he was invited to take charge of the Department of Economics at the University of Nebraska, apparently the first of its kind in an American university, and the course he developed was a scientific study of industrial corporations that included railways, always a subject of great interest to him. Those who knew him said that he had a "pioneering mind," and his students were encouraged to visit city halls, jails, police courts, asylums and almshouses, and similar institutions, presumably to alert them to the impact on society of the social and philosophical forces of the time. His instinct for reality kept his classes from being dull, and the relationship between prevailing economic theory and the problems of people was clear at all times.

In 1891 President Benjamin Harrison selected him to become the first superintendent of charities for the District of Columbia. This appointment arose from a mounting congressional anxiety about the number of voluntary agencies which had arisen after the Civil War to deal with the overwhelming social problems of the District. Services were competitive and uncoordinated, and each, with few exceptions, looked to Congress for financial support. Warner showed signal ability and tact in developing a workable and acceptable framework for overseeing the budgets of agencies requesting public funds, in an efficient manner that was acceptable to Congress, if not to the powerful lobbies that confronted him. He also played a role in the development by Congress of legislation providing for a Board of Children's Guardians, which was established in 1892 and which was the first public agency in the District to serve children.

Warner only held this position, a three-year appointment, until 1893, when Stanford University, which had just received a gift of the Hopkins Railway Library, invited him to join its faculty. He was still interested in railway problems and saw this as a unique opportunity to work again with the problems of corporations and to prepare courses in administration and engineering problems.

In 1894 he took time out—reportedly two months—to write the book by which he is remembered, *American Charities* (1894), which reflected a broad and thoughtful knowledge base. This was the first attempt ever made to find a scientific approach to the problems of poverty. He still took the position, basic to the COS approach, that deterioration of character was the primary cause of poverty, and blamed unwise philanthropy for part of the problem. He did, however, have some statistical base for his added convictions that less visible, but perhaps more significant, causes were to be found in society, including unemployment and illness, which apparently contributed to at least half of the cases of poverty which he studied. Friends blamed the concentrated effort put into the writing and publication of this work for his increasing health problems, which led doctors to advise him to give up teaching.

He attempted to return to teaching in 1897 but was unable to do so. There is no indication that he had come in contact during his brief welfare-orientedexperience with the new profession of social work, but he seems to have been willing to trust the future attacks on poverty to responsibly administered public services and to voluntary agencies operating under charity organization society principles.

Warner died in 1900 in Las Cruces, New Mexico.

The only detailed biographical material on Warner is an eleven-page summary of his life and work, prepared by George Elliott Howard, a former instructor and personal friend. This was published after Warner's death and appears as a biographical preface to the second and fourth editions of *American Charities*, and in the Johns Hopkins printing of the *Lay Sermons*. *The Dictionary of American Biography* (1936) reported a few details of his life, noting its resources as *Who's Who in America* (1899/1900), an article by Ross in the *Charities Review* (March, 1900), and family papers in the possession of Warner's daughter, Esther Warner Kallenberg.

The earliest evidence of his developing philosophy is in his *Notes Supplementary to the Johns Hopkins University Studies in Historical and Political Science* (1889), the outline of a course of lectures given after his Nebraska appointment. These notes, along with his *Economic Notes Regarding Luxury* (1889), *Some Experiments on Behalf of the Unemployed* (1890), and the introduction to *The Directory of Charitable and Beneficial Organizations*(1892) provide background for and perhaps even an outline of his one substantive work, *American Charities*. His *Lay Sermons* (1904), posthumously published by friends, were delivered to Stanford students in 1897 during his brief return there.

KATHLEEN M. JACKSON

**Washington, Booker T.** (April 15, 1856–November 14, 1915), educator and spokesman for black Americans (1895–1915), was born in Franklin County, Virginia, the son of Jane, a slave of James Burroughs. The identity of his father, who was white, is unknown, but his stepfather, the husband of Jane, was Washington Ferguson. One child, Amanda, was born to Jane and Ferguson. James, Booker's younger brother, was adopted. Booker T. Washington was married three times. His first wife was Fannie N. Smith of Malden, West Virginia. They were married in 1882 and she died in May, 1884. They had one child, Portia. Washington's second wife was Olivia Davidson, whom he married in 1885. They had two children, Booker T. Washington, Jr., and E. Davidson Washington. Olivia died in 1889. Washington married Margaret Murray in 1893, and she survived him. They had no children.

Born a slave, Washington moved with his mother and stepfather to Malden, West Virginia, a small town near Charleston, in 1865, right after the Civil War ended. Washington Ferguson worked in the salt mines there, where he was joined by his stepson, who from 1865 to 1871 worked in the mines and obtained a rudimentary education. In 1871 he went to work as a houseboy for Mrs. Lewis Ruffner, wife of the mine owner. Her influence was important. She taught him persistence and self-discipline.

With the help of family and friends, Washington went to Hampton Institute in Virginia in the fall of 1872. There he met and came under the influence of the principal, General Samuel C. Armstrong.* General Armstrong emphasized the utilitarian and practical aspects of education, and Washington absorbed this philosophy from him. It marked his approach to the education of black Americans throughout the remainder of his life. Booker T. Washington worked his way through Hampton, graduated with honors, and was chosen to speak at commencement.

After Washington graduated from Hampton in 1875, he returned to Malden, where he taught for three years. During this period his obsession with the importance of cleanliness and order as well as learning matured. In 1878 he went to Washington, D.C., to do graduate work at Wayland Seminary. There he found that too much emphasis was placed upon the liberal arts and not enough on the practical aspects of life. This experience brought to fruition his belief that black Americans could best be served by a practical education. His approach to the future welfare of black Americans was based squarely on this belief.

From 1879 until 1881 Washington taught at Hampton, where his performance and his diligence impressed General Armstrong. When in 1881 the state of Alabama sought a principal for its new school at Tuskeegee, Armstrong recommended Washington, and he was appointed. He spent the remainder of his life developing and administering Tuskeegee.

Washington went to Tuskeegee heavily influenced by his mother, General Armstrong, and other Whites who had been close to him during the formative years of his life and career. They had in common the virtues of integrity, individualism, humanitarianism, and loyalty to the Protestant ethic of selflessness and service, and they obviously had transmitted these to their protégé. Washington was convinced, moreover, that his people were inferior in terms of the cultural, social, and economic heritage necessary to compete with Whites, and that the only viable solution was to be found in the long term. Blacks would have to prove themselves capable citizens before they would be accepted as such by white Americans. Washington therefore emphasized industrial and agricultural education rather than liberal arts at Tuskeegee.

Tuskeegee had few assets, and Washington literally built it from the ground up. He became an adept fund-raiser, and his success among northern white philanthropists was derived in no small measure from the fact that Washington's philosophy coincided with their own views and with the prevailing Social Darwinist ideas of the age. He purchased an abandoned plantation on the outskirts of

Tuskeegee and built the campus with bricks manufactured at the site. In many respects Tuskeegee duplicated Hampton. However, at Tuskeegee the faculty and staff were always all black, whereas at Hampton many were white. The curriculum at Tuskeegee placed great emphasis on the practical aspects of life.

Beginning in 1892, annual conferences were held at Tuskeegee to teach better farming methods to rural Blacks. An agricultural experiment station was established in 1897. The influence of the institution spread far beyond Alabama. Tuskeegee graduates taught throughout the South, and several institutions modeled upon Tuskeegee were established in other states.

With the death of Frederick Douglass in 1895, Booker T. Washington became the leading spokesman for black Americans. His circle of influence was widened further in 1895 by a speech at the Cotton States and International Exposition in Atlanta in which he pronounced the famous "Atlanta Compromise." In this statement Washington proposed that Blacks and Whites could cooperate with one another in the realm of business and economics and yet remain socially separate. This pronouncement brought Washington wide acclaim but in time was met with disapproval from W. E. B. Du Bois* and other leaders of the Niagara movement and the National Association for the Advancement of Colored People (NAACP), who regarded it as an accommodation with segregation and the status of inferiority. Washington remained generally hostile to the NAACP until his death, but he supported the National Urban League generously after its founding in 1911.

In spite of growing opposition, Washington's prestige remained great until the time of his death. He controlled the flow of funds to black organizations and educational institutions. He dominated the black press through his ownership of the influential New York *Age*; and he virtually controlled black patronage in the South. Presidents McKinley, Roosevelt, and Taft made few moves concerning racial affairs without consulting Washington.

Washington worked quietly behind the scenes to support many black improvement organizations. He cooperated with the founders of the National Afro-American Council, established in 1898, and he was instrumental in the founding of the National Negro Business League in 1900. Moreover, he was an active opponent of segregation, he worked diligently to prevent blanket disfranchisement, and he spoke openly against lynching.

Throughout his life Booker T. Washington lived modestly. He was very much a child of his age, believing in the principles of paternalism and self-help. In his dealing with subordinates he was autocratic yet kindly and benevolent. In his dealings with Whites he was deferential to a fault and always strove to avoid what he called "embarrassing situations" in his social contacts. He died at Tuskeegee on November 14, 1915.

In addition to innumerable speeches and articles, Washington was the author of three books. *Up from Slavery* and *The Story of My Life and Work* are both autobiographical. *The Farthest Man Down*, written with the assistance of Robert

E. Park, discusses Washington's view that American Blacks were better off than the lower classes of Europe.

The Booker T. Washington Papers are located in the Manuscipt Division of the Library of Congress. The most important books on his life are Frederick E. Drinker, *Booker T. Washington: The Master Mind of a Child of Slavery* (1915, 1970); Louis R. Harlan, *Booker T. Washington: The Making of a Black Leader, 1856–1901* (1972); Louis R. Harlan and Raymond W. Smock, eds., *The Booker T. Washington Papers*, vol. 6, 1901–1902 (1977), vol. 8, 1904–1906 (1979), vol. 9, 1906–1908 (1980), vol. 10, 1909–1911 (1981); Louis R. Harlan, et al., eds., *The Booker T. Washington Papers*, vol. 2, 1860–1889 (1972), vol. 3, 1889–1895 (1974), vol. 4, 1895–1898 (1975), vol. 5, 1899–1900 (1976); Louis R. Harlan, *Booker T. Washington: The Wizard of Tuskeegee, 1901–1915*; Hugh Hawkins, *Booker T. Washington and His Critics*, 2nd ed. (1962); Booker T. Washington and Albon L. Holsey, *Booker T. Washington's Own Story of His Life and Work: The Original Autobiography Brought up to Date with a Complete Account of Dr. Washington's Sickness and Death* (1915); Basil Joseph Mathews, *Booker T. Washington: Educator and Interracial Interpreter* (1948); August Meier, *Negro Thought in America, 1850–1915: Racial Ideologies in the Age of Booker T. Washington* (1963).

KENNETH E. HENDRICKSON

**Wells-Barnett, Ida Bell** (April 16, 1862–March 31, 1931), teacher, crusading journalist and antilynching advocate, social worker and social activist, was born into slavery and grew up in Holly Springs, Mississippi. Her father, James Wells, a highly skilled carpenter, was the son of his white master and a slave woman named Peggy. Her mother, Elizabeth (Bolling) worked as a cook for the master of the plantation. As a child growing up in Holly Springs during Reconstruction, Ida's life was happy, relatively secure (despite witnessing the horrors of the Ku Klux Klan), and exciting until she reached age fourteen. Her father, who provided adequately for the family, was an outstanding member of the community, active in politics and civil rights for Blacks, and a trustee of the Shaw School, established by the Freedmen's Bureau, which Ida (and her mother) attended. Her life changed dramatically, however, in 1876 when her parents and a brother died of yellow fever, forcing the teenage girl to seek employment in order to support herself and her four younger siblings. She was well prepared for her new role, though, as she lengthened her skirt to disguise her age, claimed that she was eighteen, and secured a teaching position.

She taught first in Holly Springs and then in Memphis, Tennessee. It was by chance, however, that she left teaching for a career in journalism. On a train trip, railroad officials dragged her off the car on which she was traveling because she dared to sit in a space reserved for Whites. Thoroughly humiliated, she filed suit against the Chesapeake, Ohio, and Southwestern Railroad and won the case, only to see the decision overturned by the state Supreme Court. Her resolve to write and publish a detailed report of the incident in a local black church weekly,

*Living World*, launched her on a career in journalism as a crusader for racial justice. She was asked to write articles for the paper on a regular basis, which in turn brought requests from other papers all over the country to write pieces on the plight of Blacks and the indignities they were forced to suffer. She thus became a crusader who, through the written word and the spoken word as well, sought to arouse public opinion to the evils of racial injustice and the need to remedy the situation.

Meanwhile, having saved some money, she resigned from her teaching job to become the editor and co-owner of the Memphis *Free Speech*, a weekly that quickly gained a wide readership among Blacks in the area. In 1892, however, she revealed the true story behind the lynching of three Memphis Blacks whose only crime had been their successful competition with white grocers who previously had monopolized trade in a black neighborhood and then abused their customers. Although the night after her exposé appeared in print a mob of white citizens destroyed her office and printing press and threatened to lynch her if she returned to Memphis, from which she had fled, she continued her campaign for racial justice, especially for an end to the horrors of lynching.

Not only did she continue to write for various newspapers and journals, but she spoke often, at home and abroad. Eventually, however, she settled in Chicago, where she met Ferdinand Barnett, a prominent attorney, owner of the *Conservator*, the first black newspaper in Illinois, and a graduate of the college that later would become Northwestern University. Barnett was a widower with two sons, and he and Ida were married on June 17, 1895, when she was thirty-two years of age. Four children were born from this union: Charles Asked in 1896, Herman Kohlsatt in 1897, Ida B. Wells in 1901, and Alfreda M. in 1904.

Although frequently torn between her responsibilities to her husband, her children, and her career, her marriage proved to be an asset rather than a liability. Her husband supported her endeavors fully—financially, emotionally, and legally—and at times even encouraged her to take assignments she otherwise was reluctant to assume (sometimes taking a nursing infant with her). It is a tribute to the Barnetts that they practiced women's liberation long before the movement began: Ida Wells not ony pursued freely her many careers but maintained a healthy family life and retained her maiden name.

In any event, whenever she wrote and wherever she spoke she devoted copious attention to lynchings and other injustices perpetrated at that time against Blacks. It thus was almost inevitable that this passionate and humane woman would get involved in social work. Her endeavors as a social worker in Chicago brought her into direct contact with many well-known reformers and welfare agencies. Thus, for example, she became a close friend of Jane Addams,* with whom she worked jointly on many projects, including increasing the membership of the National Association of Colored Women's Clubs, protesting against the *Chicago Tribune*'s article in favor of segregated schools, promoting woman's suffrage, and helping to create the National Association for the Advancement of Colored People. She also worked with Celia Parker Woolley, who founded the Frederick

Douglass Center, a black settlement house in Chicago on whose board Ida served as vice-president.

In 1910 she established her own settlement house in the Windy City. Patterned after Hull-House, the focus of the center was on self-help, research, and social reform. Financed in part by gifts from Victor F. Lawson, by her later salary as an adult probation officer—the first Black and the first woman to hold such a position in Chicago—and by the center's job bureau, the settlement provided low-cost lodging, a library, an employment service, recreational facilities, legal assistance, and an advocacy service. It was staffed by herself and volunteers from the Negro Fellowship League, which she founded and on whose board she served. Like Hull-House, the center provided not only badly needed services for the deprived inhabitants of the community but practical experience for young people who wanted to engage in social service work.

Wells-Barnett was a fiery, militant, single-minded, outspoken, uncompromising, and fearless person with little patience for those whose views differed from her own. She was particularly impatient with those who did not share her militant views and strategies regarding the rights of Blacks. Thus she experienced several conflicts with Booker T. Washington,* Fannie Barrier Williams,* and others, which hurt operation of her settlement house. By 1920 the center, which had experienced financial problems throughout its existence, was forced to close. Loss of her job as a probation officer, increased competition for funds from the more popular Urban League, and the loss of some of her political influence all took their toll. She became distraught, as many of her goals had not been achieved, and she was unable to garner the kind of support she expected from Blacks, including some members of the Negro Fellowship League. By that time, however, Ida Wells-Barnett had left her legacy to Chicago and the nation. In 1940 she was designated by the city of Chicago as one of the most outstanding women in its history, and a public housing complex was named the Ida B. Wells Garden Homes. Later, her home on Martin Luther King Boulevard would be designated a historical landmark. In the meantime, she had died in her adopted city of Chicago in 1931.

A major source of information on Ida Wells-Barnett is her papers in the University of Chicago Library. Her autobiography, edited by her daughter, Alfreda M. Duster, *Crusade for Justice: The Autobiograpahy of Ida B. Wells* (1979), chronicles her life as a woman of boundless energy with a single-minded mission of justice for women and Afro-Americans. Wells-Barnett was a prolific writer herself, especially on the subject of lynching; some of her published works documenting facts about the horror, include "Lynch Law in All Its Phases," *Our Day* (May, 1893); *Southern Horrors* (1892); and *A Red Record* (1894). Among the several secondary sources, see Gerda Lerner's brief summary of Ida Wells-Barnett and her anti-lynching campaign in *Black Women in White America* (1972), 196–205; and Dorothy Sterling's *Black Foremothers* (1969), 62–116, which includes photographs and a rather thorough statement on Wells-Barnett based on personal interviews with her daughter Alfreda and use of the University of Chicago documents. John Hope Franklin and August Meier's *Black Leaders of the Twentieth Century* (1982), 38–62, is a critical analytical treatise on her personality, her work, and her relationship with associations in the movement for justice for Afro-Americans. Bert James Lowenberg and Ruth Bogin, eds., *Black Women in Nineteenth Century American Life* (1976), 252–262, is a presentation of excerpts from her autobiography and her publications on atrocities committed against Blacks. Bettina Aptheker, *Women's Legacy: Essays on Race, Sex, and Class in America* (1982), 60–71, pays tribute to the efforts of Wells-Barnett on behalf of the antilynching campaign. Majors A. Munroe, *Noted Negro Women: Their Triumphs and Activities* (1893), 184–194, is an original work about Ida Wells-Barnett written by a contemporary.

MILDRED I. PRATT

**West, Walter Mott** (December 24, 1889–October 6, 1960), social work administrator, was born in Faribault, Minnesota, the fifth of six children of Willis Mason and Millie Melissa (Mott) West. The career of West's grandfather, Judge Rodney Mott, exemplified much of the mid-nineteenth century movement toward the asylum; he helped to establish state schools in Minnesota for the deaf, blind, and feebleminded, and served for many years on the board of the Minnesota State Institute for Defectives.

After attending local public schools, West entered the University of Minnesota, where his father headed the department of history and from which he graduated in 1912. After a short stint reporting for the Minneapolis *Tribune*, he returned to Faribault to take over a paper his grandfather once edited, the Faribault *Republican* (1912–1915). He also got married at that time—in September, 1914— to Elloise H. Rogers, a childhood sweetheart with whom he had three daughters. (Later he would marry Helen Crosby, a Barnard graduate and an important social worker in her own right.) He then became publicity director (1916–1919) for the Minneapolis Civic Center and Commerce Association (CCA). Influenced by Frank Bruno of the Associated Charities and by Otto Davis of CCA, West moved into social service administration, first as a disaster director for the American Red Cross (Northern Division, 1919–1920), and then as assistant secretary for the Minneapolis Council of Social Agencies (1920–1922).

West's career took a decisive turn when he accepted the position of executive director of the Family Service Society (FSS) in Columbus, Ohio (1922–1926). The agency administered relief for the city from public funds. West increased the number of professional staff rapidly and supported adequate family budgets despite outside pressures for a ''spread-the-money-thin'' policy. Caseloads went down and expenditures went up. Those associated with a newly created community chest accused the FSS of unreasonable budgets and demanded that the president and the executive director resign or face expulsion from the fund. Thus was ushered in the ''Columbus Catastrophe,'' presenting a combination of issues mined for precedents by national organizations.

The American Association for Community Organization (AACO) was concerned about the relation of community chests to member agencies: the exclusion of a member agency meant its death knell. The American Association for Organizing Family Social Work (AAOFSW) was concerned about agency patterns of practice that included deficit spending (first with municipal tax monies, then with overdrafts on the community fund); the separation of relief administration from the source of funding; the adequacy of assistance; and the maintenance of professional standards of social service by such devices as the limitation of caseloads. The American Association of Social Workers (AASW) was concerned about due process protections for professional workers.

West resigned from FSS, his reputation unblemished. One of the authors of an AACO-AAOFSW investigation sponsored his move to AASW, as did William Hodson,* who participated in an AASW report, and Linton Swift,* who offered West a post as assistant secretary of AAOFSW (1926–1927). When West left Columbus, he also left a faculty position at Ohio State University. He returned to teaching briefly when invited to lead a social work seminar in Russia in 1937.

West's major contribution to social welfare was as executive secretary of AASW (1927–1942). The organization still was dominated at the top by the founding generation (Hodson, Swift, Neva Deardorff,* David Holbrook,* and Dorothy Kahn*). In the fifteen years of his tenure, the Association, formed on a selective membership basis, grew from a ''narrow kind of trade union'' to a shaper of federal relief policy during the Great Depression.

West sustained the move toward professional training requirements in 1933, while keeping an exception clause for leaders who, like himself, lacked graduate training in social work. ''We ought to think of education as the condensed method of getting qualifications into people,'' he said. Through consummate staff work, West advanced salary, personnel, and employment practice standards as well.

He viewed the Depression as a fortuitous event demanding professional response. He wrote in 1933, ''Our friends in Washington were interested in social workers because we had information bearing on the need for relief and on the measures which it was necessary to take. They could use our evidence of low relief standards to convince their colleagues . . . our material came from our experience and was more real than that of other groups.'' West organized social work testimony before Congress, and for the first time the AASW publicly endorsed a federal bill—the proposed Federal Emergency Relief Act. As the climate for the assumption of federal responsibility for relief developed, West, Swift, Hodson, and Allen Burns,* dubbed the Four Horsemen, descended on Washington with position papers mapped out in AASW special committees to press for federal action. They had turned from witnessing need, said West, to serving as specialists on technical questions of providing assistance. West believed this service by the Association greatly enhanced the legitimacy and public acceptance of social work, demonstrating its ''real usefulness and leadership in these coming social adjustments.''

A contest for control of Association policy, structures, and personnel developed as AASW chapters involved themselves in social action. West responded to the movement among the rank and file with an organizational remedy, the establishment in 1934 of the first delegate conference, with representation open to all chapters. Ironically, the delegate conferences became vehicles for enhancing regional, generational, and philosophical differences with the national organization, and with its executive secretary, whom some regarded as an obstacle to progress. West's early attention to federal relief policy at the expense of chapter relationships, the firing of a staff rival, and a controversial application of the AASW employment practices standards in an FSS dispute complicated the picture. Eventually, a new president, Wayne McMillen, brought charges against West for administrative oversights. West filed countercharges citing the president's misuse of position, procedural irregularities, and harm to the Association. In February, 1942, the national board approved a committee report exonerating the executive secretary, but asked both the president and the secretary to resign.

West went on to serve in the United Seamen's Service (1943–1946) and in China for the United Nation's Relief and Rehabilitation Administration (1946– 1948). He died in New York City in 1960.

The papers of the National Association of Social Workers, Inc., in the Social Welfare History Archives of the University of Minnesota, Minneapolis, contain minutes, memoranda, and correspondence which illuminate the origins and development of the American Association of Social Workers and West's role in that process. Included are records of Joanna Colcord's subcommittee on unemployment in the 1930s, transcripts of the delegate conferences, and a full account of the McMillen/West controversy (see, for instance, the "Report of the Special Study of Program, Policies and Operations of the AASW," submitted by the Executive Committee to the National Board, with Minority Report and Appendices, February 1942).

There are scattered references to West in the Survey Associates Papers and in the National Social Welfare Assembly Papers, Supplement No. 1 (both at Minnesota), where it is clear that David Holbrook of the National Social Work Council valued West as a contact person and an engaging personal friend. The David Adie–Allen T. Burns study of the Columbus crisis can be found among the published reports of the AAFOSW (later known as the Family Service Association of America).

Most of West's writings appear in the AASW journal, *Compass*. Significant work was also published in the *Survey*, in the *Social Work Yearbook*, and in the *Proceedings* of the National Conference of Social Work. His comments on federal relief policy were covered by the *New York Times* in 1936 and 1941.

Obituaries are in the *New York Times*, October 8, 1960 and *Social Service Review*, vol. 35 (March, 1967). A biographical sketch can be found in the *Encyclopedia of Social Work*, vol. 17, part 2 (1977).

For histories of the early social work profession, see Roy Lubove, *The Professional Altruist: The Emergence of Social Work as a Career, 1880–1930* (1971), and Leslie Hartrich Leighninger, "Development of Social Work as a Profession, 1930–1960," Ph.D dissertation, University of California, Berkeley, 1981. See also Joanna C. Colcord, "Social Work and the First Federal Relief Program," *Compass* (September, 1943), 18–23; and Clarke A. Chambers, *Seedtime of Reform: American Social Service and Social Action, 1918–1933* (1963). Peter Romanofsky, ed., *Social Service Organizations* (1977) also is helpful.

JACQUELINE K. PARKER

**White, Alfred Tredway** (May 28, 1846–January 29, 1921), housing reformer, was born in Brooklyn, New York, to Alexander Moss White, a wealthy businessman, and Elizabeth Hart (Tredway) White. White received his secondary education at the Brooklyn Collegiate and Polytechnic Institute. He then attended Rensselaer Polytechnic Institute, in Troy, New York, where he received a C.E. degree in 1865. Shortly afterward, he entered his family's importing firm, W. A. & A. M. White, in which he eventually became a partner. On May 29, 1878, he married Annie Jean Lyman, with whom he had one child, a daughter.

White's importance in the history of social welfare rests on his work in philanthropic housing, a branch of investment philanthropy. Like many of his contemporaries White believed that slum dwellings were the principal cause of an array of social problems: disease, crime, fire hazards, and the breakdown of the family. These maladies affected not just the poor but the entire social order. To protect their own interests and to bring about a measure of social justice, affluent people had a responsibility to build and promote decent housing at competitive rents for the "deserving poor."

Such philanthropic housing, or "philanthropy and 5 percent," as it sometimes was called, would lead to the general improvement of slum housing, White thought. He believed that housing for the poor must be profitable, or few philanthropists and no commercial operators would invest in it. For philanthropic housing he proposed that the return on investment, or dividend, should be strictly limited. At the same time, he insisted that philanthropically financed buildings, especially new ones, must be models of excellence in design, structural soundness, and management so that commercial operators might imitate them. By increasing the supply of housing in slum areas, by providing superior accommodations at competitive rents, and by turning a profit in the bargain, philanthropic housing would put pressure on slum landlords to stop gouging the poor and to improve the sanitary and safety standards in their buildings if they wanted to keep their occupancy rates high. The improvement of older dwellings for the poor and the construction of new and better ones, in short, would eliminate the social problems caused by slum housing.

White was particularly active in the philanthropic model tenement phase of late nineteenth and early twentieth century housing reform. He concentrated on building and trying to upgrade multifamily dwellings because they had become acute problems in his native Brooklyn and in neighboring Manhattan. His most important tangible contributions to housing reform were three widely praised limited-dividend model tenements erected in Brooklyn in 1877, 1879, and 1890. These were financed by White and a family owned organization, the Improved Dwellings Company.

In design, the buildings were an improved version of the philanthropic housing erected in London in 1863 by Sir Sydney Waterlow's Improved Industrial Dwellings Company. White's attractively ornamented tenements provided tenants with privacy, safety, comfort, open space, and abundant light and air. The maintenance and mangement of the properties far surpassed the common practices of most landlords. The healthfulness and financial and aesthetic success of White's buildings, along with his writings, made him the American prophet of philanthropic housing during the 1880s and 1890s. In 1896 he joined a group of Manhattan residents to form the City and Suburban Homes Company. Under the leadership of E. R. L. Gould,* it became the most prolific of all the English and American limited-dividend housing companies. At the end of its first twenty-five years the company held $6 million in capital and housed over 12,000 tenants in exceptionally well-designed and well-managed accommodations. Because of his importance as a theoretician and activist in philanthropic housing, White was chosen to serve on the epochal New York State Tenement House Commission of 1900.

White's ideas and activities were not original. Philanthropic housing had first appeared in England in the 1840s and in this country in Boston in 1871. Despite the efforts of White and others in building and promoting model single- and multi-family dwellings, philanthropic housing proved to be a feeble method of providing decent housing for the poor. Because few investors were willing to take a minimal rate of return on their capital, relatively few limited-dividend projects were ever built, and these did not inspire many landlords to improve the quality of existing housing for the poor. In retrospect, philanthropic housing actually had a negative effect on housing reform. Its modest successes engendered an enthusiasm for voluntary action that helped postpone the kinds of legislative and regulatory remedies needed to raise sanitary and safety conditions in new and old commercial dwellings.

White's social welfare activities, however, extended beyond his work in philanthropic housing. He was one of the principal founders, in 1878, of the Brooklyn Bureau of Charities, and he served as the organizations's president for more than two decades. He was especially proud that under his leadership the Bureau, during its early years, emphasized providing relief applicants with employment and training in woodyards, laundries, schools, and workrooms operated by the organization. This allowed the "deserving poor," those who accepted the jobs and training in place of alms, to maintain their self-respect.

Throughout his life White was interested in the social welfare of children. In 1876 he established a seaside home where slum children could spend their summers, and he served as a director of the Brooklyn Children's Aid Society and the Brooklyn Society for the Prevention of Cruelty to Children. He also was interested in social welfare enterprises in education. He made generous donations to Hampton Institute and Tuskegee Institute, both of which provided primarily manual and domestic training for Negroes, and over a period of years he donated money to Harvard University for the establishment in 1906 of the Department of Social Ethics. Courses in the Department and the faculty's research dealt with ethical and technical aspects of some of the social problems White tried to help solve.

White also was a trustee of the Russell Sage Foundation from 1909 until 1921. During his tenure he was instrumental in having the Foundation fund a Brooklyn Bureau of Charities project to train and employ blind women in a Bureau workshop or in their homes. He also was active in the discussions and activities that led to the most important planning study of the 1920s, *The Regional Plan of New York and Its Environs*. Five days before the Foundation trustees began considering funding the study, however, White drowned after falling through the ice while skating alone on a small lake in Harriman State Park in Orange County, New York.

At Columbia University there is a small collection of Alfred T. White's business records dealing with the rental and maintenance of his philanthropic housing projects. White wrote several articles and pamphlets on his housing and social welfare activities. *Improved Dwellings for the Laboring Classes: The Need, and the Way to Meet It on Strict Commercial Principles, in New York and Other Cities* (1879); *Sun-lighted Tenements: Thirty-five Years' Experience as an Owner* (1912); and "Better Homes for Workingmen," *Proceedings of the National Conference of Charities and Correction* (1885), 365–376, are White's major writings on his model tenements and the principles of philanthropic housing. In "The Story of Twenty-five Years: An Historical Sketch of the Brooklyn Bureau of Charities," *Charities* (January 2, 1904), 7–13, White records the major activities and principles of an organization he led for more than two decades.

Robert W. de Forest, "Alfred T. White, 1846–1921," *Survey* (February 5, 1921) 667, is an informative and insightful reminiscence, as is the chapter on White in Francis Greenwood Peabody's *Reminiscences of Present-Day Saints* (1927).

Of the works that deal with housing reform and White's role in it, the most important ones are Eugenie Ladner Birch and Deborah S. Gardner, "The Seven-Percent Solution: A Review of Philanthropic Housing, 1870–1910," *Journal of Urban History* (August, 1981), 403–438; Roy Lubove, *The Progressive and the Slums: Tenement House Reform in New York City, 1890–1917* (1962); Anthony Jackson, *A Place Called Home: A History of Low-cost Housing in Manhattan* (1976); James Ford et al., *Slums and Housing, with Special Reference to New York City: History, Conditions, Policy*, 2 vols. (1936); and E. R. L. Gould, *The Housing of the Working People* (1895).

STANLEY MALLACH

**White, Eartha M.** (November 8, 1876–January 18, 1974), social welfare activist and reformer, was born in Jacksonville, Florida. Soon after her birth, she was adopted by Lafayette White, an ex-slave who had served with the Union army during the Civil War, and his wife, Clara (English) White, who was the daughter of freed slaves and who worked as a domestic and as a stewardess on steamships. From grades one to eight, Eartha White attended the Stanton School in Jacksonville. Her father died in 1881 when she was five years old.

After an epidemic in 1881, Eartha White and her mother moved to New York City, where she attended Dr. Reason's School, Madam Hall's School, and Madame Thurber's National Conservatory of Music. As a performing artist, Eartha White toured with the Oriental American Opera Company within the United States and in Europe and Asia for a year, after which she returned to Florida and attended the Florida Baptist Academy from 1896 to 1898.

Eartha White began her professional career as a teacher in a dilapidated rural school for Blacks near Bayard, Florida. While there, she convinced the county to build a new two-room school for her students. An energetic woman, Eartha White developed excellent organizational skills which benefited many people and organizations. For a while, she was a clerk for the Afro-American Life Insurance Company. In 1900 she was a charter member of the National Negro Business League, which was founded in Boston by Booker T. Washington.* As a personal friend of Washington, Eartha White assisted him during his years as the first president of the League.

Eartha White's commitment to community uplift was reflected in a range of public service activities in Jacksonville. In 1900 she helped to organize and was a speaker for the Colored Citizens' Protective League. With a special interest in the elderly, she assisted in reviving the Union Benevolent Association, whose purpose was to aid elderly Civil War Veterans. She and her mother also raised funds for the Colored Old Folks Home, which was built in 1902. Concerned about the youth in her community, she organized a campaign called "Save 1,000 Boys from Juvenile Court," although this project was not successful. But in 1904 she was instrumental in organizing the Boys' Improvement Club. After convincing a friend to donate land for a park, Eartha White used her personal funds to hire recreation workers. This arrangement for recreational services for Blacks continued until 1916, when the city of Jacksonville took over the operation.

After saving $150 from her teaching salary, she opened a department store catering to Blacks in 1904. This investment prospered, thus allowing her to start a series of small businesses, such as a steam laundry, a taxi service, an employment agency, a janitorial contracting service, and a real estate business. Each of these ventures was started on a small scale. After building each one up, she would sell it for a profit. Although she inherited some property from her mother, Eartha White bought and sold real estate in Jacksonville for most of her life. Eventually, she accumulated an investment portfolio worth well over $1 million, using most of her wealth for her public services activities.

During World Wars I and II, Eartha White was very active in providing services to soldiers and their families. In Savannah, Georgia, she was the director of War Camp Community Services and the coordinator of recreation during World War I. Also during this period, she was the only woman who participated in the

Southeast War Camp Community Services Conference and the only Negro who attended a White House meeting of the Council of National Defense. She continued to help soldiers during World War II by setting up canteen services. She also donated a building for a serviceman's center, where she managed various Red Cross activities.

In 1928, as a memorial to her mother, Eartha White established the Clara White Mission, considered by many to be her most important contribution to social welfare. Similar in operations to Chicago's Hull-House, the Clara White Mission played an important role in helping Blacks adjust to the Great Depression and urban living. As a focal point of her community work, Eartha White lived at the mission with the transients and the dispossessed. In spite of the Depression, she was able to purchase a building for her mission through the support of friends. The mission was the center of relief activities for Blacks during the Depression. In addition to providing food packages and soup at the kitchen, the mission served as headquarters for the various activities of the Works Progress Administration.

Through her experiences at the mission, Eartha White was able to establish a range of other social welfare agencies, such as a maternity house, a child placement center, an orphan home, the Harriet Beecher Stowe Community Center, a tuberculosis rest home, a hospital, a lodging house for alcoholics, a home for delinquent girls, and a nursing home. The latter facility, named the Eartha M. White Nursing Home in her honor, was completed in 1967. Eartha White also had a personal commitment to black inmates at the Duval County Prison Farm. For more than fifty years, she led Sunday services at the prison for the inmates, worked to improve conditions for them, and helped to get a number of prisoners released in her custody.

Eartha White's many social welfare activities increasingly involved her in politics. As a follower of Booker T. Washington she held moderate racial views. She supported the notion that education, business success, and racial uplift were the major tools for improving the social conditions of black people and for achieving racial equality and cooperation. Active in the Republican Party during the 1920s she headed the Negro Republican Women Voters and was the only woman member of the Duval County Republican Executive Committee. Although not known as a civil rights leader who aggressively fought racial segregation, Eartha White worked with A. Phillip Randolph in 1941 to organize his threatened march on Washington as a protest against job discrimination. The march never took place, but it did have an impact in that President Franklin D. Roosevelt issued Executive Order 8802 banning employment discrimination in the federal government and defense industries. Believing in the importance of being a responsible citizen, she encouraged others to become active in improving conditions in their communities. She was committed to the Negro Women's Club movement by her involvement in Iota Phi Lambda Sorority and the state and national Association of Colored Women's Clubs.

Many of Eartha White's contributions were "firsts" for a Negro. She was

Jacksonville's first black census taker and the county's first black social worker. For her outstanding contributions to business and social welfare, she received a number of awards and citations from colleagues and organizations, including the Lane Bryant $5,000 Volunteer Award in 1970 and the Better Life Award from the American Nursing Home Association in 1971. With a strong commitment to helping people in need, and with great pride in her Afro-American heritage, she established an Afro-American Museum so that future generations would be able to learn about the black community's contributions to Jacksonville.

Through her ceaseless leadership and direction, Eartha White became one of Jacksonville's most decorated and recognized citizens. Inspired by her mother's passion for helping the poor, she remained active in providing services to the ill and needy well into her nineties. Well organized, and with a driving religious philosophy, Eartha White demonstrated how business and community organization methods and personal commitment could be used to develop social welfare services for persons in need of help. On January 18, 1974, Eartha White died of heart failure in Jacksonville, Florida.

Biographical materials, photographs, letters, and other items are in the Eartha White Collections at the Library of the University of North Florida. Documents and biographical materials are also located at the Clara White Mission, Jacksonville, Florida; the National Business League Archives, Washington, D.C.; and the Rollins College Archives, Winter Park, Florida.

Articles and information about Eartha White's career include C. Frederick Duncan, "Negro Health in Jacksonville," *Crisis* 49 (1942), 29–32; Harold Gibson, "My Most Unforgettable Character," *Reader's Digest* 105 (1974), 123–127; Ledell W. Neyland, *Twelve Black Floridians* (1970), 33–41; Daniel Shafer, "Eartha Mary Magdalene White," in *Notable American Women: The Modern Period* (1980), 726–728; Angela Taylor, "She's 94 and Still Busy," *New York Times* (December 4, 1970); and Fred Wright, "Eartha White, Florida's Rich, Black, 94-Year-Old Senior Citizen of the Year," *Floridian Magazine* (August 1, 1971). Obituaries appeared in the *Florida Times-Union*, the *Jacksonville Journal*, and the *New York Times* (January 19, 1974).

LAWRENCE E. GARY

**White, Walter Francis** (July 1, 1893–March 21, 1955), executive secretary of the National Association for the Advancement of Colored People (NAACP) and social activist, was born in Atlanta, Georgia, the sixth of seven children of George W. and Madeline (Harrison) White. His father was a postman and his mother a school teacher. Walter White grew up in an all-black urban, southern community during a period when occasional clashes with white families were commonplace. Despite the serious racial tension which existed within the community, his parents devised ways to give him and his siblings as much freedom as possible. At the age of thirteen (1906), White observed the Atlanta race riots and from this experience was encouraged to fight against riots, lynchings, and social injustices. This experience, along with the religious teachings of his family and the profound influence of his college teachers, imbued White with the belief that freedom was a precious gift rightly deserved by all human beings. Showing a marked scholastic ability at an early age, White entered and earned a B.A. degree from Atlanta University. In 1922 he married Leah Gladys Powell of Ithaca, New York. There were two children from this union: Jane and Walter Carl Darrow. That marriage ended in divorce and in 1949 White married Poppy Cannon.

While employed as an insurance agent with the Standard Life Insurance Company, Walter White received his first challenge to enter the arena of race relations. Several Atlanta politicians were seeking office on a platform that proposed that the budget of the city's black schools be cut on the grounds that Blacks did not pay taxes. White vigorously opposed the unfair proposal and solicited the aid of the National Association for the Advancement of Colored People. James Weldon Johnson, an outstanding author and diplomat as well as the executive secretary of the Association, came with a delegation from New York to Atlanta's aid. At the end of a successful campaign against the local politicians, an Atlanta office of the NAACP was established, and White became one of its dynamic leaders. In 1918, at the invitation of the NAACP, he came to New York to assume the position of assistant secretary to Johnson. He served in this capacity until 1931, when he was promoted to executive secretary.

For four decades White devoted himself to the work of the NAACP. In addition, however, he undertook many other activities. He traveled more than 400,000 miles, including two trips around the world, investigating and lecturing on racial discrimination. He made investigations of forty-one lynchings and eight race riots; because of his fair complexion and blue eyes he was able to move around the rioters undetected. One of the earliest investigations carried out by White was that of the Phillips County, Arkansas, sharecropping riots of 1919. In this situation, the NAACP carried to the Supreme Court the cases of seventy-nine men, twelve of whom were sentenced to death and sixty-seven to long-term imprisonment. Eventually, the men were freed and the Supreme Court ruled that mass trials were invalid. Also in 1919, White investigated the Chicago race riots and the lynchings in Brooks and Lowdes counties, Georgia, which included the lynching of a pregnant woman. In 1925 he uncovered the facts in a triple lynching case, when a woman and two men were lynched after one had been acquitted of a murder with which the three had been charged.

Walter White's political activities began in 1921, when he became a delegate to the Second Pan-African Congress, held in England, Belgium, and France. In 1934 President Franklin Roosevelt appointed White to the Advisory Council for the Government of the Virgin Islands, from which he resigned a year later. In 1934 he also organized a movement behind the Costigan-Wagner antilynching bill, and it was largely through his persistent effort that the bill came up for a vote in the Senate in 1935. However, it was removed from the calendar by a seven-day filibuster. White did not give up, however, and thanks to his tenacious reserve the Govagan antilynching bill was introduced in the House during the next session of Congress; it was brought to a vote and passed in 1937, only to be laid aside again in the Senate after a seven-week filibuster (1938). Later, though, White also influenced President Roosevelt's decision during World War II to issue his historic executive order on fair employment practices in the defense industry. Additionally, he helped to determine President Truman's position on civil rights during the 1948 presidential campaign. In 1945 White served as consultant to the United States delegation at the organizational meeting of the United Nations in San Francisco, and he served in the same capacity at the General Assembly meeting in Paris in 1948.

In addition to the many other positions held by White, he also was a member of the board of the New York State Training School for Boys, chairperson (1935) of the Harlem low-cost housing project, and a member of the Governor's Commission on the Constitutional Convention of New York (1938). For these and other efforts, White was the recipient of numerous awards and honors. Of particular significance was the Spingarn Medal in 1937 for his personal investigations of lynching and race riots and for his remarkable tact, skill, and persuasiveness in lobbying for a federal antilynching law. In 1939 he received an honorary degree of Doctor of Laws from Howard University in recognition of his many achievements.

Throughout his long and illustrious career, Walter White's energy and skill helped to accomplish a great deal with respect to racial harmony. His efforts to bring about a better understanding between black and white America were important factors in establishing the degree of interracial cooperation that exists in America today. He became a symbol of courage and hope for oppressed and disfranchised Blacks in America. He, however, was more than a symbol; his relentless efforts and hard work brought many concrete gains to Blacks as well as others who were deprived by laws aimed expressly at Afro-Americans. As a social activist and a believer in peace, Walter White labored dangerously, heroically, and nobly in behalf of civil, human, political, and social rights for all Americans.

In addition to performing so well the task of executive secretary of the NAACP, White also wrote six books and numerous articles. His books include two novels; the first, *The Fire and the Flint*, appeared in 1924. Following its success in the United States, it was reprinted in England, France, Germany, Russia, Norway, Denmark, and Japan. The second, *Flight*, was published in 1926 and won White a Guggenheim Award in creative writing which allowed him to spend a year in France working on a study of lynching and lynch psychology, *Rope and Faggot: A Biography of Judge Lynch*. He also wrote his autobiography, *A Man Called White* (1948); *A Rising Wind*, a report on black troops in World War II; and *How Far the Promised Land!*, an evaluation of black America's progress since the Civil War. White also was a regular contributor to several magazines and newspapers, among them the *Nation, American Mercury, Crisis, Bookman,*

*Saturday Evening Post*, the Chicago *Daily News*, and the New York *Evening Post*. He died in New York City at the age of sixty-one.

Biographical data on White can be found in his autobiography, *A Man Called White* (1948); *Current Biography: 1942* (1943); Benjamin G. Brawley, *The Negro Genius* (1956), 190–230; Mary W. Ovington, *Portraits in Color* (1955), 104; and Ben Richardson, *Great American Negroes* (1945). Also see T. G. Russ, C. Fairbanks, and E. Arata, *Black American Writers: Past and Present*, vol. 2 (1975), 760–763; *Who's Who in America* (1942–1943); *Who's Who in Colored America* (1938–1940); and the obituary in the *New York Times*, March 21, 1955.

SAYDE L. LOGAN

**White, William Alanson** (January 24, 1870–March 7, 1937), psychoanalyst, mental hospital administrator, and early proponent of an interdisciplinary approach to the understanding and treatment of the mentally ill, was born in Brooklyn, New York, the younger of two sons of Alanson White and Harriet (Hawley) White. His parents, Protestants of Anglo-Saxon derivation, grew up in New England, where young White spent his summers as a child. His father was a businessman of moderate means. Since White's brother was ten years older, young White grew up essentially an only child.

Educated in Brooklyn public schools, White entered Cornell University at fifteen, prior to completing high school, to avail himself of a scholarship which he supplemented by working. His voracious reading included the social sciences and the evolutionism of Herbert Spencer. White's interest in medicine was stimulated by his friendship with the sons of a neighboring Brooklyn surgeon. At age nineteen he entered the two-year Long Island College Hospital Medical School, from which he graduated in 1891. Following a year's internship he secured an appointment, which lasted eleven years, at the Binghamton (New York) State Hospital. There he acquired solid training in hospital administration and in psychiatry.

During this period White visited the newly established Pathological Institute in New York City, where he met and collaborated with Boris Sidis, then working with hypnosis on problems of "mental dissociation." This directed White's attention to the unconscious as well as stimulating his desire to understand better the language and behavior of mental patients. Also during this period, in 1896, White began a lifelong association with Dr. Smith Ely Jelliffe. They collaborated on two works of importance to the development of American psychiatry, editing *The Modern Treatment of Nervous and Mental Diseases* (1913) and together writing *Diseases of the Nervous System* (1915). Six new and expanded editions of the latter were published, the last in 1935. Their joint efforts also produced numerous shorter works and translations into English of foreign psychiatric works. In 1907 they founded the Nervous and Mental Disease monograph series, which continued until 1958; in 1913 they established the quarterly *Psychoanalytic Review*.

After rising to assistant superintendent at Binghamton, White applied for and secured appointment as superintendent of the Government Hospital for the Insane in Washington, D.C., renamed St. Elizabeths Hospital in 1916. At thirty-three he was the youngest superintendent ever appointed. His thirty-four-year tenure, ending with his death at age sixty-seven, remains the longest in the hospital's history.

White's career was launched about the time Emil Kraepelin's classification of mental disorders was introduced into psychiatry in 1896. White helped introduce and popularize the era of dynamic psychiatry, psychoanalysis, and social psychiatry in the United States during the first third of the twentieth century. His innovations while at the helm of St. Elizabeths are notable. Shortly after becoming administrator he abolished all mechanical restraints on patients. In 1905 he appointed the first woman physician to the hospital staff. The following year he assigned female nurses to male wards. In 1907 he established a psychological laboratory, one of the first in a mental hospital. In 1928 he opened the first beauty parlor for hospitalized women patients. His administrative innovations included inauguration of staff conferences so that every patient's clinical status might regularly be reviewed. Under his direction a generation of psychiatrists was trained at St. Elizabeths, or inspired by his leadership, including such notables as Ernest Hadley, Bernard Glueck, Nolan D. C. Lewis, Arthur Noyes, and Harry Stack Sullivan. His efforts to humanize care of the mentally ill helped transform St. Elizabeths into a mental hospital which served as a model for others in the United States. Until the establishment of the Veterans Administration in 1930 and the expansion of the U.S. Public Health Service Mental Health Division during the mid–1930s, St. Elizabeths was the dominant psychiatric facility on the federal scene.

On a European trip in 1907 White learned about psychoanalysis. White became a champion of psychoanalysis in the United States. St. Elizabeths was the first U.S. hospital to apply psychoanalytic principles in treatment of the mentally ill. His defense of psychoanalysis at the 1914 meeting of the American Psychiatric Association helped it win legitimacy in the United States.

In 1918, at the age of forty-eight, White married Lora Purman Thurston, widow of a U.S. senator, and became a stepfather to her daughter—and subsequently a grandfather. His work capacity and drive remained enormous. His administrative work was combined with extensive writing, lecturing, and organizing activities. His *Outlines of Psychiatry* (1907) underwent fourteen revisions, the last in 1936. During this period it was the fundamental textbook of psychiatry in the United States. The second edition (1909) contained the first exposition of psychoanalytic ideas to appear in an American book. His *Mental Mechanisms* (1911) was the first book about psychoanalysis authored by an American. White's total output was prodigious, including 19 books, 287 papers, 379 book reviews, and contributions to 12 other books. The range of subjects was enormous: psychiatry, psychoanalysis, forensic medicine, corrections, mental hygiene (especially of children), medical education, substance abuse, industrial medicine, eugenics and heredity, and the social sciences were dealt with.

Twice White served as president of the American Psychiatric Association (1915–1917; 1927–1929), using this office to encourage closer collaboration with the American Bar Association. In 1930 he served as president of the first International Congress on Mental Hygiene, an organization which he and Clifford W. Beers* collaborated in establishing. White lectured frequently at medical meetings before social work groups. As a speaker he was much in demand because of his capacity for synthesizing biological, psychological, and social concepts.

White's interest in forensic psychiatry involved him as an expert witness in the 1924 Loeb-Leopold case, which established new precedents for the use of psychiatry in the judicial process. White opposed capital punishment, writing in 1933 of the racial bias involved in its application. He supported the principle of the indeterminate sentence and argued for establishing a determination of guilt or innocence prior to assessing the mental competence of a criminal defendant. White also endeavored to ease commitment laws to assure earlier treatment of the mentally ill. He raised questions about informed consent in applying experimental procedures to captive groups, which indicated his prescience about issues of criminal responsibility which remain of contemporary relevance.

White was an early advocate of holistic medicine, stressing unity of the "organism-as-a-whole." He sought to integrate medicine and social science in order to understand and deal with both the individual and his social problems. Though strongly influenced by psychoanalysis, he moved from an intrapsychic orientation to the study of man in his social context. He inaugurated with Harry Stack Sullivan in 1928 the first of two colloquia on the interrelationship of psychiatry and the social sciences, thus seeking to integrate the study of personality with the study of culture.

Like his early predecessor, Benjamin Rush,* White lived during a period of great social change. Each was influenced by a great war, both devoted themselves to reform of their profession, and both were interested in social needs and social causes. Rush was a dominating figure in American medicine and psychiatry during America's first hundred years. White shared with Adolf Meyer* leadership of American psychiatry during the first half of America's second century. He died in Washington, D.C., in his sixty-eighth year.

White's correspondence, both personal and professional, is stored in the National Archives. Some of White's papers are in the St. Elizabeths Hospital Health Sciences Library, Washington, D.C.

Other books by White include *The Principles of Mental Hygiene* (1917); *The Mental Hygiene of Childhood* (1919); *Thoughts of a Psychiatrist on the War and After* (1919); *Foundations of Psychiatry* (1921); *Crimes and Criminals* (1933);

*Twentieth Century Psychiatry: Its Contribution to Man's Knowledge of Himself* (1936); and *William Alanson White: The Autobiography of a Purpose* (1938).

Essays assessing White's contributions to psychiatry, to psychoanalysis, and to mental health, and providing an overview of his extensive and voluminous correspondence are found in *William Alanson White: The Washington Years*, ed. Arcangelo R. T. D'Amore (1976). White's obituary notice in the *Psychoanalytic Review* (April, 1937) also includes a full list of his writings. White's influence is discussed in S. E. Jelliffe's article in the *Journal of Nervous and Mental Diseases* (May, 1937), and in Winifred Overholser's "An Historical Sketch of St. Elizabeths Hospital," *Centennial Papers of St. Elizabeths Hospital* (1956).

ARTHUR K. BERLINER

**Wiley, George Alvin** (February 26, 1931–August 8, 1973), civil rights and welfare rights activist, was born in Bayonne, New Jersey, one of six children of William Daniel Wiley and Olive (Thomas) Wiley. When George was three weeks old the Wiley family moved to Providence, Rhode Island, and a year later to Warwick, a small town near Providence and their ancestral home.

George spent his early years there, living in a community that had ony two other black families, both related to the Wileys. He had little contact with Blacks but had no difficulty making friends and was popular and well liked. Like other children in the community, he participated in sports and many other activities. Several racial incidents, which were embarrassing and traumatic, happened during his childhood. George tried hard to avoid such situations, and if they occurred he withdrew.

The Wiley family was very religious, hard-working, and achievement-oriented. They had a strong sense of family, and the children were admonished to "remember you are a Wiley." Everyone was expected to work hard and contribute to the well-being of the family. They belonged to a white fundamentalist religious sect, spent their Sundays in church, attended weekday evening prayer meetings, and studied the Bible faithfully.

In high school George demonstrated exceptional abilities, scoring in the very gifted range on IQ tests and making the Rhode Island Honor Society. He became interested in science, entered a statewide science fair in his senior year, and won a scholarship to Rhode Island State College which, in 1952, would become Rhode Island University.

George started college in 1949, majoring in organic chemistry. He did quite well academically, and managed to work and participate extensively in extracurricular activities at the same time. He was the first black member of his fraternity and a student leader. In later years he credited the development of his administrative and organizational skills to college experience with student organizations.

Those who knew George Wiley personally described him as outgoing, friendly, and likeable, able to work with many different types of people. He was also goal-directed, disciplined, and very determined.

After graduation from Rhode Island University in 1953, he began graduate study in organic chemistry at Cornell University. He received the Ph.D. from Cornell in 1957 and was awarded a grant for postdoctoral study in chemistry at the University of California, Los Angeles. Before leaving for California, he served a six-month tour of army duty in Petersburg, Virginia, where he became interested in civil rights, joined the local chapter of the National Association for the Advancement of Colored People (NAACP), and worked on voter registration.

Wiley left California in December, 1960, following postdoctoral study and a two-year faculty appointment to the UCLA chemistry department, to join the faculty of the chemistry department at Syracuse University in Syracuse, New York. There he met Wretha Frances Whittle, a white graduate student from Texas. They married in June, 1961, and had two children. Wiley settled down to research work, and his reputation grew as a scholar in organic chemistry.

During this period, he wrote an open letter to the university newspaper to protest racial discrimination by fraternities and sororities. Not long after this, he helped organize the Syracuse chapter of the Congress of Racial Equality (CORE). He was elected chairman and led the chapter in a series of demonstrations against discrimination. They exposed segregation in the public schools, protested employment discrimination, and attempted a boycott of businesses to force changes in the urban renewal program. The success of these efforts attracted the attention of the CORE national director, James Farmer, who offered Wiley the position of associate national director in November, 1964. He accepted, arranged a sabbatical from Syracuse, and moved his family to New York, where the organization's national headquarters was located.

Characteristically, Wiley immersed hmself completely in his new job. The associate national director functioned as chief administrator, making staff assignments, handling funds, and making day-to-day decisions. The administrative system had broken down almost completely, and he acted quickly to reorganize it. Perhaps because of his training in chemistry, which required him to be aware of and balance many different elements in a fluid, complex situation and not lose sight of the objective, he was able to stabilize the administration of CORE. During the 1965 southern campaign of CORE, Wiley traveled to the South frequently. He developed good rapport with the staff, who had been suspicious of him at first, but later became his strongest supporters.

The year 1965 was a turbulent one for CORE. Public resistence to further civil rights concessions, black disillusionment over the implementation of civil rights laws, and the failure to develop a successful strategy to attack northern discrimination caused CORE to reexamine its commitment to racial integration and nonviolent direct action. The organization struggled to find a new direction, and Wiley participated in the process. The Black Power philosophy that was becoming popular among Blacks found adherents in CORE. They argued, successfully, that the organization should abandon its interracial stance and become a black organization. This meant reducing the power and presence of Whites in CORE, particularly in leadership positions.

Wiley formulated his own ideas about directions for civil rights organizations as a result of this CORE experience. He rejected the idea of excluding white participation, maintaining that the minority status of Blacks made it essential. His idea was to concentrate on organizing the poor at the grass-roots level. He also felt that the concentration of power at the national leadership level was dangerous, because it could easily become self-serving and elitist.

When James Farmer resigned as national director in 1965, Wiley sought the job, but the board picked Floyd McKissack. Disappointed by the board's decision and disheartened by the new direction of the organization, Wiley resigned, effective January, 1966. After leaving CORE, Wiley decided to act on his ideas. He resigned from Syracuse University and moved to Washington, D.C., to devote all his energies to his plans for organizing the poor.

He accepted a position as national action coordinator with the Citizens Crusade Against Poverty, hoping to persuade the board to commit the organization to grass-roots organizing of the poor. Wiley quit when his plan was rejected and founded the Poverty-Rights Action Center (P/RAC).

This was the organizational vehicle Wiley used to realize his dream of organizing the poor. Influenced by the ideas of Richard Cloward and Frances Piven, he decided to concentrate on the welfare poor. P/RAC moved rapidly, organizing a march by welfare recipients on the Ohio state capital to pressure the state to raise welfare grants to the minimum level mandated by the state for health and decency. The same day—June 30, 1966—welfare groups coordinated by P/RAC demonstrated in twenty-five other cities to support the march. These activities led to the formation of a national coordinating committee of welfare groups and the creation of the National Welfare Rights Organization (NWRO) in August, 1967.

Wiley became NWRO executive director, responsible to a national board of recipients, but the goals and strategy of the organization reflected his ideas. The main goal was to build NWRO. The strategy used was to create as many new welfare groups as possible by providing immediate benefits for those who joined. NWRO launched a national special grants campaign, swamping the local welfare offices with recipient requests for clothing and furniture. This tactic worked, and the number of new welfare groups increased dramatically. Other issues, among them the sale of spoiled food by ghetto stores and getting credit from large department stores, became the focus of organizing drives.

Under Wiley's leadershp NWRO went to court to challenge welfare laws, testified before congressional committees, and lobbied Congress on welfare matters. The lawsuits were filed by lawyers who volunteered their services because of their interest in welfare rights and the persuasiveness of George Wiley. A dozen cases were argued and won before the Supreme Court that extended the rights of those on welfare.

Most of the NWRO top staff were recruited personally by Wiley, who used contacts made while he was with CORE. Many of the field staff also joined because of him. He often spoke on college campuses, which were the source of many of the field organizers.

Finances were another vital contribution of Wiley to NWRO. He took a personal interest in fund-raising, soliciting loans and gifts from individuals and foundations that kept the organization going.

By 1970 public opposition to NWRO and welfare rights stiffened and welfare demonstrations no longer worked. Wiley turned to a strategy of coalescing with allied groups, but the NWRO leadership opposed it. Internal conflicts between staff and NWRO leaders, racial tension among staff, and clashes over a national versus local program focus divided the organization and eventually destroyed it. Wiley no longer had the power he once had to influence NWRO. After a dispute with the board, he resigned on December 31, 1972. Two years later, NWRO ceased to exist as a national organization.

The formation of NWRO and its accomplishments under the direction of George Wiley were milestones in American social welfare history. Because of his vision and determination, a national organization of welfare recipients was created, which never had been done before and which many thought impossible. The public was made aware of a new perspective on welfare, which, for a brief time, acquired a measure of respectability never before enjoyed. The legal victories of NWRO enlarged welfare rights for current and future recipients. Finally, many recipients received tangible benefits of clothing and furniture that they were entitled to by law.

After he left NWRO, Wiley founded another organization, the Movement for Economic Justice, returning to his original goal of organizing all of the poor and not just the welfare poor. Before he could get very far with his new effort, however, he was washed overboard and drowned in a storm on Chesapeake Bay while on a boating holiday with his two children.

The personal papers of George Wiley are part of the Social Action Collection at the State Historical Society of Wisconsin in Madison, Wisconsin.

Articles by Wiley on welfare include "Why Workfare Won't Work," *New Generation* (Winter, 1970); "The Nixon Family Assistance Plan: Reform or Repression?" *Black Law Journal* (Spring, 1971); "Masking Repression as Reform," *Social Policy* (May-June, 1972).

The Nick and Mary L. Kotz biography, *A Passion for Equality—George A. Wiley and the Movement*, covers his early life and the CORE and NWRO years, and has an extensive bibliograhy. See also George Martin, "The Emergence and Development of a National Welfare Rights Organization," Ph.D. dissertation, University of Chicago, 1972; and William H. Whitaker, "The Determinants of Social Movement Success: A Study of the National Welfare Rights Organization," Ph.D. dissertation, Brandeis University, 1970. Obituaries appeared in the *New York Times* (August 10, 1973), and the *Washington Post* (August 9, 1973).

PHILIP JACKSON

**Williams, Aubrey Willis** (August 23, 1890–March 5, 1965), social worker, reformer, civil rights activist, and government official, was born in Springville, Alabama, the third child of five sons and two daughters in the family of Charles and Eva (Taylor) Williams. Grandfathers on both sides had fought in the Civil War. The Williamses were ruined economically by the war, and Charles Williams did not get over the feeling of being adrift in the world. He drank heavily and was constantly moving his family. By the time Aubrey was ten years old, they had lived in about twenty houses, and later he recalled his childhood "as one of living in many places and many houses, moving around, looking for a cheaper place to live."

The Williams family moved to Birmingham, Alabama, in the fall of 1890, while Aubrey was still an infant. The children were all forced to leave school at an early age to supplement the family income. Aubrey had only one full year of formal schooling before he began work as a delivery boy when he was about seven years old. He then worked as a cash boy in a department store. Throughout his youth, he was deeply affected by his connections with the Fifth Avenue Cumberland Presbyterian Church, where the pastor's wife encouraged him to read and write, and the assistant pastor gave his religous commitment a social dimension.

In 1911 Aubrey Williams enrolled in a Tennessee mountain school, Maryville College, financing his education through loans and odd jobs. In 1916 he transferred to the University of Cincinnati, but found it hard to settle down to his studies, with all of Europe embroiled in what he viewed as the war to preserve Western civilization. In June, 1917, he went to Europe with the YMCA and became a recreation official in YMCA headquarters in Paris. In November, 1917, he joined the French Foreign Legion, and in 1918 transferred to the American First Division, where he soon gained a commission.

When the war was over, Williams enrolled at the Sorbonne, then took a degree from the University of Bordeaux before returning to Cincinnati to complete the requirements for a degree in social work. He married and moved to Madison, Wisconsin, in 1922, as an executive director of the Wisconsin Conference of Social Work. He remained there for ten years, teaching at the University of Wisconsin as well.

In 1932, at the height of the Depression, Williams went to Chicago to work for the American Public Welfare Association. His task was to organize the distribution of relief money, loaned under the Reconstruction Finance Corporation, in the state of Mississippi. He set up a state organization for this task, and later in the year repeated the operation in Texas. His performance brought Williams to the attention of Harry Hopkins,* the newly appointed Federal Emergency Relief Administration (FERA) director. Hopkins brought Williams into the organization and into the New Deal during its first hectic days in May, 1933.

Williams became the southwestern field representative for the FERA, but within a few months Hopkins asked him to come to Washington, placing him in charge of the Division of Relations with the States. Williams brought with him a conviction that he had developed in Wisconsin and sharpened in Mississippi and Texas: that unemployment should involve work, rather than direct relief, which he described as "the demoralizing, dehumanizing dole." He became the FERA's most outspoken advocate of a completely federally financed and administered work program, in opposition to the prevailing policy of providing state organizations with grants or matching funds and allowing them wide latitude in distributing those funds.

The time was right for Williams' approach. By late 1933 it was clear that something had to be done to get the unemployed through the winter. So when Harry Hopkins proposed the creation of a massive, federally administered work program, the Civil Works Administration, it was not surprising that Aubrey Williams was selected to administer it. Within a few months he had lined up administrators and developed thousands of projects. By the time the program ended in 1934 it had employed more than 4 million people.

In January, 1934, Williams became deputy director of the Federal Emergency Relief Adminstration, where he was also placed in charge of the college work program. He became deeply concerned with the plight of unemployed young people, a concern that he shared with (Anna) Eleanor Roosevelt,* who was to become his White House lobbyist and political ally. The two of them were instrumental in the creation of the National Youth Administration (NYA), a youth work relief agency established on June 26, 1935.

Williams was made executive director of the NYA, which was a division of the new relief agency, the Works Progress Adminstration (WPA). The WPA had replaced the FERA early in 1935, and Williams was appointed deputy director of the WPA, which was headed by Hopkins. Hopkins gave him considerable freedom in managing day-to-day operations and carrying on the public relations of the agency. Williams was a controversial figure who had a reputation for "shooting from the hip." He was considered a "leftist" and a "radical" by conservative critics of the New Deal. Several times he made verbal blunders that embarrassed the Roosevelt Administration and nearly cost him his job. In addition, he became closely associated with the accelerating struggle for Negro rights.

In 1938, when Hopkins left the WPA, Williams expected to be appointed its director, but Roosevelt found it politically impossible to put him in this controversial position. Instead, Williams became head of an expanded and independent NYA, where he changed the focus from student aid and work relief to the development of skilled labor through an apprenticeship system for the purpose of national defense. By mid–1940 the conversion of the NYA to a defense-oriented agency was well under way, and by 1942 it was solely involved in the defense effort. But both Williams and the NYA had made political enemies, and in June, 1943, the agency was abolished—a victim of the all-out war effort and the conservative reaction against the New Deal.

Williams then took a position with the National Farmers' Union, but in 1945 Roosevelt nominated him to head the Rural Electrification Administration (REA).

Political infighting, conservative backlash, and Williams' own reputation led to Senate rejection of the nomination. Williams's liberal opinions on race were also a contributing factor. He had always followed a liberal race policy within the NYA and on numerous occasions had taken controversial stands on the race issue. During the Senate hearings on his nomination he defended his actions, advocated the desegregation of public facilities in the District of Columbia, and spoke in favor of federal intervention to prevent race discrimination. His refusal to compromise led to his political demise.

Aubrey Williams returned to Alabama, where he acquired the magazine *Southern Farm and Home*, which he turned into a liberal voice in the maelstrom of postwar southern change. His liberalism focused primarily on the race issue. He supported the 1954 Supreme Court decision on school desegregation—*Brown et al. v. Board of Education of Topeka, Kansas*—in *Southern Farm and Home*. He was involved in the organization of the Montgomery bus boycott; he formed and ran a company to build low-cost, decent housing for Montgomery's Blacks; he became an expert in civil rights litigation. Williams suffered for his commitment. After the bus boycott he was virtually forced out of white society in Montgomery. Late in the decade, he and his wife returned to Washington, where he died of cancer early in 1965.

The most important primary source is the Aubrey Williams Papers in the Franklin D. Roosevelt Library, Hyde Park, New York. The collection contains material on Williams's NYA work and on the post–1945 period of his life, particularly his work with the Southern Conference Educational Fund, a group established to fight segregation in education. Williams' unpublished autobiography, ''A Southern Rebel,'' is also housed in this collection. The second important source is the private collection of papers held by Williams' widow, Anita Williams. It contains a huge body of Williams' unpublished writings discussing his pre-Wisconsin days, as well as accounts of his activities in the New Deal and his relationship with the Roosevelts. The Carl and Anne Braden Collection at the State Historical Society of Wisconsin, Madison, Wisconsin, also contains a significant amount of material, especially on the post–1945 years. There are several important collections at the Hyde Park Library, including the Eleanor Roosevelt Papers, the Harry Hopkins Papers, and the Charles Taussig Papers.

Collections at the National Archives which give insights into the various New Deal agencies and Williams' role in them are the NYA records; the WPA records, especially the State Series File (610) and the General Subject Series (100); the CWA records; and the FERA records, especially Williams' field reports.

The records of the Wisconsin Welfare Council (formerly the Wisconsin Conference of Social Work) are the prime source for understanding Williams' public activities in Wisconsin; they are located at the State Historical Society in Madison. The Kenneth D. McKellar Papers at the Memphis Public Library contain material on the end of the NYA and the REA confirmation struggle.

The best secondary source is the excellent biography by John A. Salmond, *A*

*Southern Rebel: The Life and Times of Aubrey Willis Williams, 1890–1965* (1983). Also valuable is Salmond's essay, "Aubrey Williams: A Typical New Dealer?" in John Braeman et al., eds, *The New Deal: The National Level* (1975). Other secondary sources touching on aspects of Williams' career include Ernest and Betty Lindley, *A New Deal for Youth* (1938); Searle F. Charles, *Minister of Relief* (1963), on Harry Hopkins; Harvard Sitkoff, *A New Deal for Blacks* (1978); John B. Kirby, *Black Americans in the Roosevelt Era* (1980); and Morton Sosna, *In Search of the Silent South* (1977).

WINIFRED D. WANDERSEE

**Williams, Elizabeth Sprague** (August 31, 1869–August 19, 1922), settlement worker and social reformer, was born in Buffalo, New York, the second daughter and youngest of the seven children of Frank and Olive (French) Williams, both of whom were natives of Connecticut. Her mother had been a school teacher prior to her marriage, and Frank Williams enjoyed a successful business career as a civil engineer, surveyor, and owner of a coal mine. The Williams family was prosperous, and one in which Elizabeth was exposed to Unitarian religious principles.

Like her siblings, Elizabeth benefited from an excellent education, and she graduated from Smith College with a B.S. degree in 1891. While in college, she became aware of the settlement movement and, like many of her peers, Williams believed that her educational privileges and family background should lead to a career in social reform work. Following her experiences at Smith, Williams returned to Buffalo, where she established a library and taught classes for children while remaining active in her Unitarian congregations, which sponsored a local settlement. Moving to New York City in the mid–1890s, Williams elected to attend Columbia University and received an A.M. degree in 1896. She continued to take courses at Barnard College, where she was selected as a Fellow in her first year of study. Williams supplemented her academic and theoretical training with practical experience by living as a resident at the College Settlement on Rivington Street. Succeeding Mary M. Kingsbury (later Simkhovitch*), Williams became head worker at College Settlement in October, 1898, and remained in that position until 1919. She never married.

Under Williams's leadership, the College Settlement sponsored a broad array of reform activities which reflected the larger concerns of the Progressive Era. Williams herself both preached and practiced the virtues of self-control and self-government, and the College Settlement made bold efforts to establish community autonomy for many aspects of daily life. In association with other New York City settlements, the College Settlement pushed for tenement housing reform; Williams testified in 1900 before the New York State Tenement Housing Commission, which used information gathered from four residents who lived for a year in a local tenement. In addition to agitating for better sanitary conditions in the city, the College Settlement became headquarters for the East Side Recreation Society which, with the Outdoor Recreation League, led the move for playgrounds and parks. Other groups, such as the Public Education Association, worked with Williams and the College Settlement to improve the public schools. They created and maintained libraries, established a program of friendly visiting, organized night schools and kindergartens, and advocated greater educational opportunities for the immigrant population aided by the settlement house. Williams served as a member of the local school board, for she fervently believed that education provided a primary means of inculcating American values and practices. Moreover, the settlement attempted to alleviate the financial distress of neighborhood residents during depressed economic conditions, most notably during the hard times of 1900 and 1907–1908.

The College Settlement under Williams' guidance was virtually unsurpassed in its emphasis on club activity and group association as a healthy alternative to the problems of tenement life. The literary, social, and athletic clubs sponsored by the settlement were designed to instill the democratic ideals of discipline, cooperation, and self-control, along with the cardinal virtue of individual initiative. Another antidote to the squalid life of New York's Lower East Side was offered through the summer camp at Mount Ivy in Rockland County, New York, which prospered under Williams' hand and stood as her most enduring legacy. City children could escape the stifling summers and enjoy a semblance of farm life, and the camp itself embodied the ideals of community life in a natural, simple setting. Williams worked toward the organization of the Lackawanna, New York, Social Center in 1911, and she remained a director until 1915. She resigned as head worker of the College Settlement in March, 1919, and left for war-ravaged Europe to found an orphanage in Veles, Serbia. She remained there for the next two years, even learning Serbian so that she might enhance her efforts, and upon her return to the United States in 1921 Williams brought with her a Serbian orphan whom she adopted. Following her work, the Serbian government assumed the responsibility of maintaining the orphanage and rewarded Williams with a posthumous royal decoration.

Williams was respected and admired by her contemporaries, and she preferred to lead by example rather than through public declarations or published works. Under her direction the College Settlement became an outstanding model of an effective, neighborhood-centered settlement which featured club life and group activity as the core of its reform efforts. Moreover, the College Settlement merged its many programs with other settlements in New York City, and together they initiated a wide variety of municipal improvements based on an intimate knowledge of local conditions.

Elizabeth Williams died of cancer in 1922 in New York City.

The Sophia Smith Collection at Smith College contains a solid collection of papers of the College Settlements Association, including *Annual Reports* which cover Williams' tenure as head worker at the College Settlement on Rivington Street. The Vida Dutton Scudder Papers, also in the Smith Collection, have information dealing with the College Settlements Association and some correspondence.

Williams did not write extensively, but she did author several articles which centered on the College Settlement and on the summer camp at Mount Ivy. See "New York College Settlement," *Harper's Bazaar* (May 19, 1900), 152–155; "The Summer at the New York Settlement," *Commons* (October, 1903), 913–914; "A New Departure for the College Settlement," *Charities and the Commons* (October 19, 1907), 926. In addition, Williams contributed pieces to the *College Settlements Association Quarterly*, including "Settlement Problems and Methods in Rural Social Work" (September, 1915), 6–10; and "Enlisting the College Women" (April, 1917), 13–15.

For biographical information on Williams and on the College Settlement in general, see the following: "Alumnae Biographical Register Issue," *Bulletin* of Smith College (November, 1935); Allen F. Davis, *Spearheads for Reform: The Social Settlements and the Progressive Movement, 1890–1914* (1967); Roy Lubove, "Williams, Elizabeth Sprague," in *Notable American Women, 1607–1950* (1971); John P. Rousmaniere, "Cultural Hybrid in the Slums: The College Woman and the Settlement House, 1889–1914," *American Quarterly* (Spring, 1970), 45–66; Jean Fine Spahr, "Elizabeth Williams: In Memoriam," *Smith Alumnae Quarterly* (November, 1922); *Who Was Who in America*, vol. 1 (1942); Robert A. Woods and Albert J. Kennedy, *The Settlement Horizon, A National Estimate* (1922). An obituary can be found in the *Buffalo* (New York) *Express* (August 21, 1922).

EARL F. MULDERINK III

**Williams, Fannie Barrier** (February 12, 1855–March 4, 1944), public speaker and clubwoman, was one of three children born in Brockport, New York, a town near Rochester in western New York State, to Harriet (Prince) and Anthony J. Barrier. Although she was born before the Civil War, neither her parents nor her grandparents had lived in the South or had been slaves. Her mother came originally from Cherburne, New York, and her father from Philadelphia, Pennsylvania.

Unlike that of most Blacks of that era, her childhood was comfortable and secure. Anthony Barrier was a successful barber and coal merchant, and a homeowner. Fannie attended local schools and graduated from the state normal school at Brockport in the academic and classical course in 1870. For many years, the Barriers were the only black family in Brockport, but they associated freely with Whites, and Fannie could not recall experiencing prejudice or discrimination during her childhood.

Like many other educated young northern women, Fannie Barrier went south to teach black freedmen. In the South, as she remarked later, her life as a "colored person" began. There, for the first time, she encountered the realities of racial bigotry. A particularly humiliating personal experience occurred in an art class she took. To improve her artistic skills, she had importuned a white art teacher to admit her to a painting course. On the second day of class she found her seat surrounded by screens separating her from other students. Her experience, as she stated, unlike Blacks born and raised in the South, had not prepared her for such treatment. She protested, only to find that she could remain in class only under those conditions.

After teaching for several years, Fannie Barrier left the South and went north to continue her education. First she enrolled in the New England Conservatory of Music in Boston, and then in the School of Fine Arts in Washington, D.C. In Washington she met her future husband, S. Laing Williams, a University of Michigan graduate studying at Washington's Columbian Law School. They married in 1887 in Brockport and went to Chicago where he planned to start a law practice.

Fannie Williams quickly became active in Chicago community life, making social contacts and friends among Whites and Blacks. Chicago abounded with social reform movements and charitable organizations, and women were an important part of these activities. She joined the women's club movement and became a part of many charitable organizations. Blacks in Chicago, while relatively few in number, struggled with unemployment, slum housing, disease, and crime, exacerbated by discrimination and segregation. Their problems were overlooked by a public concerned with the immigrant population. Fannie Barrier Williams articulated the concerns of the growing black community and made the public aware of them.

The condition of black women was a special concern that she often spoke out on and worked to improve. In 1893 she delivered an address entitled "The Intellectual Progress of the Colored Women of the United States Since the Emancipation Proclamation" at the World's Columbian Exposition in Chicago; it described the problems black women faced and their gains since emancipation and appealed to "well-disposed" Whites to judge black women on merit rather than race. This speech, which later was published, attracted widespread public attention and started her career as a lecturer and black spokeswoman. Fannie Williams not only spoke on behalf of black women, she acted as well. She helped young black women find employment as bookkeepers, stenographers, secretaries, and other clerical workers in the business world. She constantly received requests for such assistance, and contacted businessmen, attempting to convince them to hire qualified black women.

Fannie Barrier Williams was a well-known figure in both the white and black women's club movement. Her application for admission to the all-white Chicago Women's Club became a cause célèbre, attracting national attention. Although her membership had been sponsored by several prominent club members, it sparked a debate over admitting her about which newspapers editorialized and other women's clubs debated. This controversy made Fannie Barrier Williams known nationwide. After fourteen months of deliberation, during which some members reportedly hired a private investigator to look into her past for improprieties, she finally was accepted.

She also played a key role in the black women's club movement, helping to establish clubs in Chicago and participating in the creation of a national organization. These women's clubs played an important role in the social welfare organization of the black community. They identified needs, tried to meet them, and supported the charitable work of other organizations in black communities.

Fannie Barrier Williams worked actively with the Frederick Douglass Center, the Phyllis Wheatley Home for Girls, the Abraham Lincoln Center, and Provident Hospital. In articles she published in the *Southern Workman* and *Charities*, she described the programs and goals of the Frederick Douglass Settlement. Its purpose, which she endorsed wholeheartedly, was to promote interracial contact between the ''better'' class of Blacks and Whites. The hope was that such Whites might begin to recognize class distinctions among Blacks. One of her main concerns was that Blacks were viewed as all being the same regardless of what they achieved. Of all her charitable affiliations, Williams was identified most closely with the Frederick Douglass Settlement.

Another facet of her interest in black women is evident in her attachment to the Phyllis Wheatley Home for Girls, which sought to protect unattached young girls, particularly those new to the city, by offering them a safe residential environment. This was an aspect of her involvement with Provident Hospital, whose school for nurses provided training denied to black women by white nursing schools. She helped raise the funds needed to open Provident, the first black hospital in Chicago and the site of the first successful open heart operation.

In 1921 S. Laing Williams died. After his death Fannie Williams became less active in public life. She was elected to the Chicago Public Library board in 1924, the first Black and the first woman to be so honored. When her term expired in 1926, she bowed out of public life and left Chicago, in declining health, to return to Brockport.

Fannie Barrier Williams spoke out at a time when urban black communities sorely needed leaders who could articulate to society their problems and needs. She was among the first to recognize and call public attention to the negative effects of employment discrimination and housing segregation on black community life. She was a central figure in the early attempts by Blacks to identify and provide for their own charitable needs. But she also was able to work across racial boundaries, with Whites, to bring black concerns to public attention. She fought for social justice for Blacks and to build a black charitable system to respond to black need.

Fannie Barrier Williams lived quietly in Brockport with a retired sister until her death there in March, 1944.

The writings of Fannie Barrier Williams are the best source for her racial thought. *Black Women in Nineteenth Century American Life*, edited by James Lowenberg and Ruth Bogan (1976), contains reprints of two 1893 addresses, ''The Intellectual Progress of the Colored Women of the United States Since the Emancipation Proclamation'' and ''Religious Duty to the Negro.'' ''A Northern Woman's Autobiography," *Independent* (July, 1904), describes the impact of racial discrimination in her life and on black women. "Social Bonds in the Black Belt of Chicago," *Charities* (October, 1905), depicts the problems created by segregation for black migrants to the city and the role of black organizations in improving conditions. "The Frederick Douglass Center," *Southern Workman* (June, 1906), portrays the interracial goals and programs of a black settlement house. "The Colored Woman and Her Part in Racial Regeneration," in Booker T. Washington, N. B. Wood, and Fannie Barrier Williams, *A New Negro for a New Century* (repr. 1969), traces the development of the black club movement.

Secondary sources that provide insight on the life of Williams are Elizabeth L. Davis, *Lifting as They Climb* (1933), which deals with her involvement with the black clubwomen's movement, and Allan H. Spear, *Black Chicago* (1967), which places her in the context of black elite thought at the turn of the century. For biographical sketches of Williams, see the *Dictionary of American Biography*, Supplement 3 (1973), *Notable American Women* (1971), and the *Dictionary of American Negro Biography* (1982); they all emphasize different aspects of her life and have useful bibliographies. Obituaries appeared in the *Chicago Defender* (March 11, 1944); the *New York Times* (March 8, 1944); and the *Chicago Tribune* (March 8, 1944).

PHILIP JACKSON

**Wines, Enoch Cobb** (February 17, 1806–December 10, 1879), educator, minister, and prison reformer, was born in Hanover, New Jersey, the son of William Wines, a farmer, and Eleanor (Baldwin) Wines. His early years were spent in Vermont, where he attended Middlebury College, graduating in 1827.

Wines began his career in the field of education. His first position was that of principal of the Academy of St. Albans in Vermont. He soon moved to a similar position in Washington, D.C. In 1829 Wines accepted a commission in the U.S. Navy as schoolmaster in mathematics. He served aboard the USS *Constellation* until 1831. He later published a popular book of his experiences, entitled *Two Years and a Half in the Navy* (1833).

On June 14, 1832, Enoch Wines married Emma Stansbury; they were to have seven sons. In the year of his marriage, Wines assumed the principalship of the Edgehill School in Princeton, New Jersey. Based on his experiences there, he published several essays on education, including "Hints on a System of Popular Education" (1838) and "How Shall I Govern My School?" (1838). In 1839 Wines accepted an instructorship at People's College in Philadelphia; in 1844 he founded a boarding school in Burlington, New Jersey, called the Oakland School.

Wines' interests eventually shifted from education to theology. In 1849 he became an ordained Congregational minister. His first theological work was entitled *Commentaries on the Law of the Ancient Hebrews* (1853). The book sought to denote the legal principles of Judaism and their contribution to modern civil societies and government. In the same year, Wines assumed the chair of ancient languages at Washington College in Philadelphia. From 1853 to 1859 Wines also held pastoral positions in Cornwall, Vermont; East Hampton, Long Island; and Washington, Pennsylvania.

In 1859 Wines accepted the presidency of the City University of St. Louis, Missouri. He held this position until 1861, when the university closed due to the upheavals of the Civil War.

It was at this time that Enoch Wines began the work for which he is best known. Wines came to New York and took the position of secretary of the Prison Association of New York, a private organization devoted to penal reform.

Wines' first major efforts were directed to fund-raising. Through appeals to churches and city and state governments, he substantially increased the revenues of the Association, thus permitting it to engage in a greatly expanded program of activities.

Wines also began to direct the programmatic activities of the Association. In one of his most famous endeavors, he undertook a major study of the existing prison system. With Theodore William Dwight of Columbia Law School, he inspected all of the penal institutions in the northern United States and parts of Canada. Their work resulted in the noted *Report on the Prisons and Reformatories of the United States and Canada* (1867), which was submitted to the New York State legislature. The report contained an important agenda for prison reform, including a recommendation for a nonpartisan State Board of Commissioners with a system of staggered terms designed to stabilize prison programs. During the same period, Wines worked with Franklin Benjamin Sanborn* to advocate systems of graded prisons, parole, indeterminate sentencing, and young men's reformatories.

At the national level, Wines collaborated with other leading penologists, such as Zebulon Reed Brockway* of the Elmira Reformatory, to organize a National Prison Congress. The first such congress met in 1870 in Cincinnati, Ohio. At this congress, the now famous "Declaration of Principles" was elaborated, which ushered American penology into a more progressive era. The thirty-seven principles emphasized new state responsibilities for humane treatment. It has been said of these principles that they were as appropriate for the guidance of penology a century after their adoption as they were when written, but as difficult to apply.

From this first congress also came a newly formed organization, the National Prison Association (now the American Correctional Association). Wines helped lead succeeding congresses in Baltimore in 1873, St. Louis in 1874, and New York City in 1876. He served as the organization's secretary until his last years.

Wines directed his energies toward the organization of international prison reform as well. In 1871 he was appointed by President Grant, through a joint resolution of Congress, to a special commissionership empowered to initiate an international penitentiary congress. Wines traveled throughout Europe to obtain cooperation and gather data. In July, 1872, the First International Penitentiary

Congress convened in London, with twenty-two nations represented. The Congress was successful in generating new national and international organizations and promoting guidelines for prison reform.

Wines was appointed honorary president of the Second International Congress, which met in Stockholm in 1878. He organized the information from these two international congresses, plus his own data, into a major work entitled *The State of Prisons and of Child Saving Institutions in the Civilized World*. In this work, Wines documented the historic transformations in attitude and organization of penal institutions throughout the world. The book included recommendations for international prison organization and reform, an analysis of crime and its causes, and an essay on penitentiary science.

Enoch Cobb Wines is remembered as a major contributor to the cause of national and international prison reform. His organizational work promoted the growth of associations and served as an impetus for social change. His writings are remarkable for their encyclopedic breadth and systematic detail. They are considered early contributions to the development of the social services. In a tribute to Wines, at the Third International Penitentiary Congress in Rome in 1885, the Count di Foresta said of Wines that it was to him, more than to any other individual, that the initiative for prison reformation was due, and that such work served to distinguish the latter half of the nineteenth century. Interestingly, his work was carried on into the twentieth century by his equally famous son, Frederick Howard Wines,* who similarly devoted himself to the ministry, to social services, and to prison reform.

Enoch Cobb Wines died in Cambridge, Massachusetts, in 1879.

For Wines' national organizational work, see *Transactions of the First National Congress on Penitentiary and Reformatory Discipline, Cincinnati, Ohio, October 12–18, 1870* (1871). This document includes the original "Declaration of Principles." See also the transactions of the National Prison Association, meetings in Baltimore, Maryland, 1873; St. Louis, 1874; New York, 1876.

For Wines' international work, see E. C. Wines, ed., *International Congress on the Prevention and Repression of Crime Including Penal and Reformatory Treatment* (1871), with the proceedings of a meeting held in London in 1871; it includes a statement of the object of the proposed congress and the result of negotiations with various continental governments; *International Congress on the Prevention and Repression of Crime*, Preliminary Report of the Commissioner (1872); *Report of the International Penitentiary Congress of London Held July 3–13, 1872*, appended to the second annual report of the National Prison Association of the United States with transactions of the National Reform Prison Congress, Baltimore, Maryland, January 21–24, 1873 (1873).

Wines' publications include *Two Years and a Half in the Navy*, 2 vols. (1833); *Commentaries on the Laws of the Ancient Hebrews* (1853); with Theodore Dwight, *Report on the Prisons and Reformatories of the United States and Canada Made* to the Legislature of New York (January, 1867); *The State of Prisons and of Child Saving Institutions in the Civilized World* (1880).

A rich source of biographical data on Wines' early life is "Memoirs of Rev. E. C. Wines," *American Journal of Education* 9 (1860). Obituary data can be obtained from the *New York Tribune* (December 12, 1879). An excellent analysis of Wines' place in the history of American penology is Blake McKelvy, *American Prisons* (1977); Wines' contributions to the social services are well documented in *Trends in Social Work 1874–1956*, 2nd ed., ed. Frank Bruno (1957).

Wines is cited in *Appleton's Cyclopedia of American Biography* (1900); *Dictionary of American Biography* (1936); *Encyclopedia of Social Work* (1977); and *Encyclopedia of Criminal Justice* (1983).

MARC L. MIRINGOFF

**Wines, Frederick Howard** (April 9, 1838–January 12, 1912), penologist and statistician, was born in Philadelphia, Pennsylvania, the son of Emma (Stansbury) and Enoch Cobb Wines.* The younger Wines can scarcely be understood apart from his father, who was ordained as a Congregational minister in 1849 and became secretary of the New York Prison Association in 1862. The elder Wines promoted the First International Penitentiary Congress in London and was president of the second one which met in Stockholm in 1878. He was the author of one of the earliest books in the social services, *Report on the Prisons and Reformatories of the United States and Canada* (1867), which publicized his findings from visits to prisons in the northern United States and Canada.

Frederick H. Wines graduated from Washington and Jefferson College in 1857 at the head of his class. He began preparation for the ministry at Princeton Theological Seminary, but his studies were interrupted first by poor eyesight and then by the Civil War. During the war, Wines served two years as hospital chaplain at Springfield, Missouri. He returned to Princeton at the end of the war and completed his theological education in 1865. He served four years as pastor of the First Presbyterian Church in Springfield, Illinois, where, in 1865, he married Mary Frances Harkney, with whom he had eight children. Upon creation of the Illinois State Board of Public Charities in 1869, Wines was appointed its first secretary.

The Illinois Board was one of the pioneer institutions of its kind, and Wines had the difficult task of defining state policies toward the mentally deficient and the criminal. His secretaryship of the Board covered a longer period than that of any of his counterparts throughout the country; he served continuously for thirty years until 1898, with the exception of the four years (1892–1896) of the administration of Governor John P. Altgeld, who as a reforming Democrat could not tolerate a conservative Republican in that important state position.

Frederick Wines was the author of many important state statutes, based on his experience with the institutions under his direction, including the Illinois lunacy law. The acknowledged excellence of his administrative abilities attracted nationwide attention, and his methods and procedures were adopted by many other states.

Wines was one of the principal organizers of the National Conference of Charities and Correction, which played a prominent role in the evolution of modern social work. He saw clearly that the problems which one state board had to deal with were similar to the problems of others—and that often they were more practical than theoretical. He thus worked to separate the National Conference from the American Social Science Association so that it remained a clearinghouse for state boards alone and, for good or bad, that it maintained a barrier between administrators and theorists.

In 1878 Wines was appointed an Illinois delegate to the International Penitentiary Congress in Stockholm; he took advantage of the opportunity to visit charitable institutions throughout Europe. Those visits enabled Wines to establish connections that allowed him to serve as an importer of new ideas for the rest of his life. From his observations in England, for example, Wines brought back the idea for the Kankakee State Hospital, the first institution in America to apply the detached ward, or cottage system, to the housing of the insane. By that method, he solved some of the difficult problems presented by the need for different treatment of patients according to the degree of their mental deficiency. Wines also cited English experience when he urged the elimination of chains and other types of physical restraints in the care of the insane, and in the 1880s he was among the first to support "pathological research" and hydrotherapy.

In 1886 Wines began the *International Record of Charities and Corrections*, a monthly publication which continued until it was absorbed by the *Charities Review*. While relieved from administrative authority during the administration of Governor John Altgeld, Wines found time to deliver numerous lectures on the history and philosophy of prison reform. Later, he expanded this material into a volume, *Punishment and Reformation* (1895), which remained for many years the standard treatment of the subject.

Wines early gave attention in his state reports to the statistical analysis of sociological data. As a result, during the Tenth U.S. Census he was named special consultant in the preparation of the report entitled *The Defective, Dependent, and Delinquent Classes of the Population of the United States* (1881). In 1887 Wines was appointed assistant director of the Twelfth Census and was given major responsibility for writing *The Report on Crime, Pauperism and Benevolence in the United States* (2 volumes, 1895–1896). Wines also collaborated with John Koren on *The Liquor Problem in Its Legislative Aspects* (1898), but hysteria on the matter of insobriety was so strong that the findings of the two dispassionate researchers went unheralded. Wines, whose investigations in states having prohibition laws predicted the failure of national prohibition, prudently kept silent on the matter in his many speeches on the question of alcohol.

Frederick Wines moved to Washington in 1898, but from 1902 to 1904 he served as secretary of the New Jersey State Charities Aid Association. In 1909 he was called back to Illinois to accept the post of statistician under the newly established Illinois State Board of Administration of Public Institutions. There he began the *Institution Quarterly* and maintained his active services until his death in Springfield, Illinois, on January 12, 1912.

The most helpful sources for Wines are *Appleton's Encyclopedia of American Biography*, vol. 6 (1889), 563; Frank J. Bruno, *Trends in Social Work as Reflected in the Proceedings of the National Conference of Social Work, 1874–1946* (1948); *Dictionary of American Biography*, vol. 20 (1936), 386; and the *National Cyclopedia of American Biography*, vol. 21 (1931), 123.

LARRY D. GIVENS

**Winslow, Charles-Edward Amory** (February 4, 1877–January 8, 1957), bacteriologist and public health reformer, was born in Boston, the only child of Erving Winslow, a commission merchant and author who was active in social reform, and Catherine Mary (Reignolds) Winslow, an English actress and author. Winslow was educated at the English Grammar School, Boston, and the Massachusetts Institute of Technology (B.S., 1898; M.S., 1899); he married Anne Fuller Rogers in 1907. They had one daughter.

As an educator, editor, and author of more than 600 publications, Winslow played a leading role in defining and shaping the public health profession in America. For the ten years following his graduation from MIT, he remained in the Department of Biology as a faculty member and as biologist in charge of the Sanitary Research Laboratory (1903–1910). During this period he acquired a national reputation in bacteriology and published several important works, including *Elements of Water Bacteriology* (1904), with S. C. Prescott, and *Systematic Relationships of the Coccaceae* (1908), with Anne Rogers Winslow.

In 1910 Winslow was appointed associate professor of bacteriology (1910–1914) at the College of the City of New York. At the same time he was appointed curator of public health (1910–1922) at the American Museum of Natural History, and in 1911 he became lecturer in public health and nursing at Columbia University's Teachers College. Winslow remained active in laboratory research throughout his career, later editing the *Journal of Bacteriology* and directing important studies in environmental and occupational health. However, his move to New York signaled a broadening involvement in popular health education and other newly emerging fields within the profession. In 1914 Winslow left CCNY to become director of the Division of Public Health Education in the New York State Health Department.

In 1915 Winslow was appointed the first Anna M. R. Lauder Professor of Public Health at the Yale University School of Medicine. At Yale, where he remained until his retirement from teaching in 1945, he developed a department that played an active role in public health programs in Connecticut and produced graduates who staffed many of the state and local health departments which were developing across the country.

While at Yale, Winslow emerged as one of the leading spokesmen within public health and as a proponent of expanding the profession's areas of activity. He was active in the American Public Health Association, serving as president (1926), chairing several important committees, and editing the *American Journal of Public Health* (1944–1954). He was one of the organizers of the Committee on the Costs of Medical Care (1928–1932) and served as chairman of its executive committee. At the same time, he was active in professional and voluntary organizations in the fields of child health, public health nursing, mental health, social hygiene, and international health.

In the 1920s Winslow became the first public health leader to argue that public health must include preventive medicine within its purview. This position both dramatically increased the scope of the profession and involved it in questions which had traditionally been jealously guarded by physicians in private practice. These questions included the costs, organization, and delivery of medical care. Preventive medicine and medical care were controversial issues within the public health profession, and became divisive issues nationally with the introduction of a national health program bill in Congress in 1939 and a succession of national health insurance bills in the 1940s. National health insurance, especially, polarized public opinion and generated massive opposition from organized medicine and political conservatives.

Winslow had originally believed that a national health program would develop naturally and did not commit himself to specific programs. Following the American Medical Association's rejection of the moderate recommendations for group payment and group practice of medicine contained in the final report (1932) of the Committee on the Costs of Medical Care, he gradually moved toward a stronger position on the need for removing the economic barriers to medical care. As the leading spokesman for moderates on the issue, he supported a staged, gradual implementation of national health insurance in preference to the comprehensive proposals which were then pending in Congress and which were ultimately unsuccessful.

By the time his career came to an end, Winslow had played a major role in shaping and defining public health as a profession, from its origins in sanitary engineering and bacteriology to the acceptance of medical care as an integral part of public health. He died in New Haven, Connecticut, in 1957.

The Winslow Papers are in the Department of Manuscripts and Archives, Yale University Library. Articles which describe aspects of Winslow's career include four works by Arthur J. Viseltear: *Emergence of the Medical Care Section of the American Public Health Association 1926–1948: A Chapter in the History of Medical Care in the United States* (1972); "C.-E.A. Winslow and the Early Years of Public Health at Yale, 1915–1925," *Yale Journal of Biology and Medicine* 55 (1982); "Compulsory Health Insurance and the Definition of Public Health," in *Compulsory Health Insurance: The Continuing American Debate* ed. Ronald Numbers (1982); and "Charles-Edward Amory Winslow," *Dictionary of American Biography: Supplement Six* (1980); as well as Roy M. Acheson,

"The Epidemiology of Charles-Edward Amory Winslow," *Journal of Epidemiology* 91 (1970).

R. JOSEPH ANDERSON

**Wise, Stephen Samuel** (March 17, 1874–April 19, 1949), liberal rabbi, social activist, and Jewish communal leader, was born in Budapest, Hungary, to Rabbi Aaron Wise and Sabine (de Fischer) Wise and brought to the United States as an infant. Wise, whose family had produced rabbis for seven generations, was a modernist in outlook and sought to wed his rich Jewish heritage to the concerns of secular society. An article he wrote as a teenager about Abraham Lincoln, focusing on Lincoln's role in emancipating the slaves, reflected an incipient commitment to social justice. Wise received his B.A. from Columbia University in 1892 and his Ph.D. from the same university in 1901. In 1892 he studied with the chief rabbi of Vienna, Adolf Jellinek, who ordained Wise and offered him a model of rabbinic social activism.

Following ordination, Wise returned to New York City, where he served as rabbi of Congregation B'nai Jeshurun for seven years and became known for his eloquent preachments on the social inequities of his generation. He was in the forefront of struggles for woman's suffrage, the abolition of child labor, the alleviation of slum life, and elimination of the sweatshop. Wise's ministry was governed by the conviction that religious leaders must address themselves to all realms of life—social, economic, and political. His thought and action were a synthesis of the ethical teachings of Liberal Judaism (inspired by the biblical prophets), the writings of Theodore Parker and other nineteenth century advocates of the Protestant Social Gospel, and turn-of-the-century secular progressivism. Refusal to separate religion from secular life was the hallmark of his work.

Wise's pioneering spirit led him to accept the pulpit of Congregation Beth Israel in Portland, Oregon, where during his six-year tenure he championed causes such as the passage of child labor laws and was appointed a Commissioner of Child Labor for the state of Oregon. While in Portland, he continually exerted himself to help Christians understand the basic tenets of Judaism and his own approach to the Jewish religion. Wise's involvement with the Christian community is considered a foundation of the interfaith movement in this country.

On November 14, 1900, Wise married Louise Waterman, who, while ancestrally Jewish, had been raised in the Ethical Culture Society. She shared Wise's social vision and his passion for social justice. During their Portland years (1900–1906), Louise gave birth to their two children, James Waterman and Justine Louise and also founded the Visiting Nurse Association of Portland. Later, in New York, Louise became aware of the number of Jewish orphans and undertook to find homes for them, an effort which developed into the Child Adoption Committee of the Free Synagogue. In twenty-five years nearly 2,000 children were placed in homes. The work of this committee was subsequently taken over by the New York Federation for Philanthropy.

In 1906, Wise, seeking an ampler forum than Oregon could provide, returned to New York City and ultimately established the Free Synagogue on the principles of full freedom of the pulpit, equal roles for rich and poor in the governance of the congregation, and a commitment both to addressing the needs of the whole community and to ameliorating the plight of all in need. Included in the structure of the Free Synagogue was a social service division. Wise employed his extraordinary physical strength, fortitude of spirit, and tenacity of character to work endless hours for the causes in which he believed.

His social commitments over the next four decades included his organizational vision in helping to found the National Association for the Advancement of Colored People (1909) and the American Civil Liberties Union (1920). He extended his activism to include advocacy of a minimum wage, old-age pensions, and trade unionism. Following the Triangle Shirtwaist Company fire in 1911, Wise was among those most energetic in demanding safer standards for laborers. His commitment to the cause of labor was evident again in his support for the U.S. Steel strike in 1919 and the Passaic textile strike in 1926.

He enjoyed decades of friendship with the Reverend John Haynes Holmes*; the two together provided religious leadership for a myriad of social and political causes in the first half of this century. For example, both fought the corruption of Tammany Hall and were instrumental in forcing New York City Mayor Jimmy Walker's resignation in 1932.

Wise's attachment to universal issues never diminished his interest in Jewish causes. He was an ardent Zionist and a founder as well as president of the Zionist Organization of America. He helped develop the anti-elitist American and World Jewish Congresses, served both agencies as president, and called public attention to the worsening plight of European Jewry. His allegiance to the Democratic Party and his reputation as the outstanding popular leader of American Jewry won him unusual access to both President Wilson and President Roosevelt.

Wise's desire to transmit his perception of the world, to achieve an amalgam of universal values and Jewish religio-ethnic loyalties, took institutional shape in his founding in 1922 of the Jewish Institute of Religion, a New York rabbinical seminary. The school, while essentially liberal, attempted to educate leaders from all branches of Judaism through a program that included training in social and communal service as well as more conventional Jewish studies. It merged with Hebrew Union College in 1950, a short time after Wise's vibrant life succumbed to cancer in New York City on April 19, 1949.

Students wishing to pursue further studies on Wise's life can discover correspondence by and about him and other archival sources concerning him in the Wise Papers at the American Jewish Historical Society on the Brandeis University campus in Waltham, Massachusetts, as well as in the American Jewish Archives on the Cincinnati campus of the Hebrew Union College–Jewish Institute of Religion and at the Oral History Collection of the Hebrew University in Jerusalem.

In addition to his Ph.D. dissertation, *The Improvement of the Moral Qualities* (1902), a translation of an eleventh century ethical treatise by Solomon Ibn

Gabirol, Wise's works include: *Child Versus Parent* (1922), *How to Face Life* (1924), and his autobiography, *Challenging Years* (1949). His sermons are bound in printed copies of the *Beth Israel Pulpit* (1902–1906) and the *Free Synagogue Pulpit* (1907–1949); articles written for *Opinion* are collected in *As I See It* (1944).

Two major studies describe in detail Wise's life and work: Carl H. Voss, *Rabbi and Minister* (1964), and Melvin I. Urofsky, *A Voice That Spoke for Justice* (1982).

LEE BYCEL

**Wisner, Elizabeth** (February 5, 1894–September 19, 1976), social worker and educator, was born in Delhi, Louisiana, to Edward Wisner and Mary (Rowe) Wisner. Her father was a businessman and philanthropist who established the Wisner Trust Fund, which after his death in 1915 provided, and continues to provide, funds for various public and private concerns in New Orleans.

Wisner received her A.B. in 1914 from Newcomb College. Between 1918 and 1920 she worked in the Home Service Division of the American Red Cross in New Orleans and Atlanta. In 1922 she received her M.S. from the Simmons College School of Social Work. In 1923 she returned to the American Red Cross as director of hospital social services. She remained in this position until 1926, when she entered the University of Chicago, where she studied under Sophonisba Breckinridge* and Edith Abbott.* In 1929 she was awarded the Ph.D. from Chicago.

While pursuing her doctoral degree, Wisner was appointed assistant professor in the Department of Sociology at Tulane University. In 1933 Wisner was named acting director of the newly developing School of Social Work at Tulane. For nearly five years, the administrators of Tulane scrutinized their first prospective female dean. In 1937, convinced that a woman could manage a university division, they appointed Wisner dean of the School of Social Work and W. R. Irby Professor of Public Welfare Administration. Wisner remained the dean of the School of Social Work until her retirement in 1958.

Among her professional positions were president, American Association of Medical Social Workers (1931–1932); president, American Association of Schools of Social Work (1935–1937); president, National Conference of Social Work (1943–1944); member, Senate Advisory Council on Social Security (1938–1939); and member, board of directors of the New Orleans Department of Public Welfare (1940–1976).

Wisner never married. She lived in her family home on Moss Street in New Orleans. There, alone with her companion and colleague, Florence Sytz, she "held court" for students, faculty, and social welfare luminaries. Teas and dinners with Dean Wisner were filled with stories about her Chicago mentors, her close personal friendship with Harry Hopkins,* her interest in establishing social work in the South, and her research in social welfare history.

Except for her work with the American Red Cross, Wisner spent her entire professional career in social work education at Tulane University. There she would develop and nurture interest in the issues of social work professional education, social work standards, social work in the South, and the history of social welfare.

During Wisner's tenure at Tulane, over 1,000 students received professional social work degrees. As dean, Wisner developed courses of study at the School of Social Work which influenced the generic curriculum eventually advocated by the Council on Social Work Education. This generic curriculum, emphasizing a "resume of the human life cycle," research skills, organizational analysis, and casework and group work skills, would become a model for the Council in the 1950s.

At the same time, Wisner remained a force in the development of social work standards. In the early 1950s, she worked through the American Association of Social Workers to develop a professional code of ethics. During this period, she was involved in the Association's protest against the Federal Security Administration's attempt to ban Charlotte Towle's* book, *Common Human Needs.* Along with others in the Association, she worked vigorously to defend social workers who had been arbitrarily dismissed by their agencies.

Along with her interest in developing social work professional education and standards, Wisner was active in the development of social work in the South. Throughout her two decades at Tulane, the School of Social Work was the largest among only a few schools of social work in the South. Graduates of the school were to build social welfare programs and organizations throughout the region. As "Dean of Social Work in the South," an accolade given to her shortly before her retirement, Wisner would devote her retirement years to her important book, *Social Welfare in the South* (1970), the first work of its kind, one which showed how the South's distinctive social and economic conditions shaped social welfare needs and responses in that region of the nation.

Finally, Wisner would remain interested throughout her career in the history of social welfare. This interest would be reflected in her Tulane course on the history of social welfare, her published writings, and her early involvement in the Social Welfare History Group.

Elizabeth Wisner died in New Orleans, Louisiana.

Items from Wisner's personal correspondence, manuscripts, and papers are housed in the Howard-Tilton Library of Tulane University.

Her published writings include *Public Welfare Administration in Louisiana* (1930); "Education for Social Work," *Social Work Yearbook* (1936); "War and Social Services," *Proceedings of the National Conference of Social Work* (1944); "The Uses of Historical Material in the Social Work Curriculum," *Social Service Review* (September, 1960), 265–272; "Edith Abbott's Contribution to Social Work Education," *Social Service Review* (March, 1958), 1–10; and *Social Welfare in the South from Colonial Times to World War I* (1970).

Biographical information on Wisner may be found in *Who's Who of American*

*Women*, vol. 8 (1974–1975), 1048; and in an obituary in the New Orleans *Times-Picayune* (September 21, 1976), 10.

JAMES W. TRENT

**Witte, Edwin E.** (January 4, 1887–May 20, 1960), educator, labor economist, and legislative librarian and draftsman, was born on a farm near Watertown, Wisconsin, the son of Emil and Anna (Yaeck) Witte. After graduating from Watertown High School, he entered the University of Wisconsin in 1905, where he majored in history under Professor Frederick Jackson Turner, author of the famous frontier hypothesis as the explanation for America's unique economic, political, and social development. Before leaving the University of Wisconsin in 1910 for Harvard, Turner advised Witte to study with Professor John R. Commons.* Under Commons, Witte combined his interest in economic history with a pragmatic interest in understanding and solving immediate economic and social problems. It was Commons who guided and directed Witte into his life's work. He received his Ph.D. in economics in 1927 after completing a dissertation entitled "The Role of the Courts in Labor Disputes."

During Witte's student and early professional years, Robert M. La Follette, Sr., dominated the Wisconsin political scene. La Follette and his progressive Republican colleagues were putting into effect a populist governmental philosophy for the benefit of the farmer, worker, and small businessman with an anti–big business and regulatory approach. Witte absorbed this emphasis and remained throughout his life a La Follette progressive and a New Dealer. He also absorbed the "Wisconsin Idea" of the intellectual committed to public service, which Commons and La Follette perfected and made effective to an expanding group of students, faculty members, and politicians. His entire lifetime was dedicated to state and federal public service in varying capacities and to teaching, primarily labor legislation and social policy, at the University of Wisconsin. He also served on several advisory boards, such as the important Advisory Council on Social Security in 1938, and published numerous articles.

Witte began his professional work in government as a secretary to a Wisconsin congressman in 1912–1914. He served as the secretary of the Wisconsin Industrial Commission from 1917 to 1922, and thus became expert on the administrative aspects of labor legislation. From 1922 to 1933 he was chief of Wisconsin's pioneering Legislative Reference Library, where he developed his skill in preparing research materials for legislative proposals and the technical drafting of general ideas into specific bills and laws. He worked with Felix Frankfurter and Donald Richberg in the drafting of the Norris-LaGuardia Act, which limited federal injunctions in labor disputes, an interest derived from his doctoral dissertation. He helped draft a 1931 version of the nation's first state unemployment compensation law, passed in Wisconsin in 1932. He then was selected as the acting director of the Wisconsin agency charged with putting the statute into effect; shortly thereafter, however, he was called to Washington to assume responsibilities in connection with his most important contribution to social welfare—the formulation of the nation's Social Security program, something he was well prepared to do.

In 1934 Witte was appointed executive director of President Franklin D. Roosevelt's Cabinet Committee on Economic Security. In that capacity he played a major role, along with Secretary of Labor Frances Perkins* and Arthur J. Altmeyer,* in the key decisions made in the formulation of policy that would be embodied in the Social Security Act; he supervised the research leading to the President's recommendations and the act itself in 1935. Almost single-handedly, he wrote the Cabinet Committee's report, and then testified repeatedly before congressional committees in support of the proposed legislation. To culminate this monumental research and legislative effort, Witte wrote a "memorandum" called *The Development of the Social Security Act*, which recounted the work of the Committee on Economic Security, the drafting of the Social Security Act, and its legislative history. It is an insider's account and explanation of the process of public policy formulation and accommodation which immediately became, and remains, a classic in its field.

Witte then returned to teach economics at the University of Wisconsin. During World War II, he was the regional director and a public member of the War Labor Board. He became the first president of the Industrial Relations Research Association in 1948 and then, in the last public recognition of the fading school of institutional economics, he was elected president of the prestigious American Economic Association in 1956. In a ringing defense of institutional economics in 1954, Witte had explained his approach and his objectives: "All or most of the institutional economists have been pragmatists, studying facts, not for their own sake, but to solve problems and to make this a better world to live in."

Witte was the last of the eminent pre-World War II economists who were not econometricians but rather blended social history with social policy in an effort to obtain social reform. He represented a group of dedicated and talented men and women who were influenced by populism and incrementalism. For them, legislation and social welfare were key elements in the creation of new institutions for remedying the faults of industrialization and a free market economy.

Witte was part and parcel of the Wisconsin Idea of public service in a period when the University of Wisconsin was pioneering in this field. With Commons, Selig Perlman, the La Follettes, the sociologist E. A. Ross, Altmeyer, and a number of other distinguished people, he investigated controversial social problems at first hand and emphasized the importance of utilizing well-trained people, especially university faculty members, in the making of major contributions to public policy issues.

Witte combined the values and experiences of an economist, social reformer, and historian. He believed in the diffusion of economic and political power. He often was critical of the power of the large impersonal corporation, the political influence of private insurance companies, the "control" of Wall Street brokers and bankers, and the influence of eastern universities in government. Yet he never was hostile or bitter to those who were critical of him. He was an optimist and believed in "progress." He saw social and economic institutions in a continual process of change.

Edwin Witte died in Madison, Wisconsin, on May 20, 1960, at the age of seventy-three.

Witte's papers are in the State Historical Society of Wisconsin in Madison, Wisconsin. The most comprehensive biography of Witte is Theron Schlabach's *Edwin E. Witte: Cautious Reformer* (1969). The best brief portrait was written by Merlyn S. Pitzele, "Witte's One-Man Economics," *Business Week* (November 26, 1955), 92–104. Witte's *The Development of the Social Security Act* (1962) is a classic legislative history and the authoritative account of the formulation of the 1935 law. Witte wrote only one other book, *The Government in Labor Disputes* (1932). He wrote many articles and speeches, however, some of which were collected and published posthumously in *Social Security Perspectives*, ed. Robert J. Lampman (1962).

WILBUR J. COHEN

**Woerishoffer, Emma Carola** (August, 1885–September 11, 1911), social reformer and philanthropist, was born in New York City, the younger of two daughters of Charles Frederick and Ann (Uhl) Woerishoffer. Her father, born in Germany, was a member of the New York Stock Exchange and became a prominent and wealthy Wall Street banker and broker. He died the year after Emma Carola Woerishoffer's birth, leaving her a legacy of more than $1 million. Her mother, also of direct German descent, was active in New York City charitable activities and was outspoken about her beliefs in the need for effective labor legislation and a progressive income tax, for which she received the Prussian Silver Medal of Merit for Women and Maidens (for contributions to social betterment). Emma Woerishoffer's life and views, however, were influenced not only by her parents but by her intimate involvement with her step-grandfather, Oswald Ottendorfer, who edited and managed the *New Yorker Staats-Zeitung*, a liberal German-language daily newspaper, and who was active in Democratic reform politics. Through him she was exposed to some of the great political and social leaders of her time. In the context of her family and social life, it is not surprising that Woerishoffer developed an early and keen interest in social problems and issues.

In 1903, after attending the Brearley School in New York City, she entered Bryn Mawr College, where she studied philosophy, economics, politics, psychology, and languages, intending to prepare for a career in social work. She graduated in 1907 with the B.A. degree and immediately entered several social reform activities in Manhattan. In 1908 she gave financial backing to a Congestion Exhibit at the American Museum of Natural History designed to inform New Yorkers about overcrowded housing conditions. Notable members of the Congestion Committee included Florence Kelley* and Mary Kingsbury Simkhovitch,* whom Woerishoffer continued to support in their reform efforts.

For three years she was a member of the Board of Managers of Greenwich House, a neighborhood settlement house. She also was active in the New York Association for Labor Legislation, the Consumers' League of New York City, and the women's suffrage movement.

She concentrated her major efforts, however, on advocating legislation to improve the safety and working conditions of wage earners in factories, especially the opportunities for supporting female members of the labor force to join trade unions. For example, she worked as an employee in more than a dozen different laundries with unguarded machinery in New York City and documented the conditions of the workers and their environment. She investigated suspicious employment offices by hiring herself out as an immigrant serving girl, and in 1909 she presented her findings to the Wainwright Commission, a New York State Labor Commission appointed to investigate the need for employer liability laws and workmen's compensation. She compiled a reference list on the subject of women in industry for the Women's Trade Union League. She served as treasurer and executive committee member of the New York Women's Trade Union League, and as president of its Label Shop, where only goods made under approved labor conditions were sold. When many women were jailed following the strike of thousands of women shirtwaist makers in 1909 and the courts demanded $75,000 worth of real estate as bond, Woerishoffer provided it, declaring that she would stay in court until the strike was settled. Then she contributed $10,000 to inaugurate a permanent strike fund to help meet future emergencies, shunning publicity about these activities so that much of her work remained anonymous. In addition, she became a member of the board of the Taylor Iron and Steel Company of High Bridge, New Jersey, in order to encourage its plans to organize a model industrial village.

When New York State's Labor Department created a Bureau of Industries and Immigration in 1910, she accepted a paid position as special investigator of labor conditions, but she gave generous personal financial support to supplement state appropriations for the work. Her duties included investigation of immigrant labor camps throughout New York State.

During her life she also made substantial gifts to settlement houses, hospitals, asylums, and other civic endeavors, including a refuge for the aging. Her will provided her most far-reaching gift, a bequest of $750,000 to Bryn Mawr College, which was used to finance the establishment in 1915 of the Carola Woerishoffer Graduate Department of Social Economy and Social Research, from which the first Ph.D. degree in social work and social research in the United States was awarded.

Her short life came to a tragic end when she had an automobile accident while driving her car to inspect rural migrant labor camps and small communities of alien laborers. She died from her injuries on September 11, 1911, in Cannonsville, New York, at the age of twenty-six.

The Emma Carola Woerishoffer Papers are housed in the archives of the Bryn Mawr College Library, Bryn Mawr, Pennsylvania. Among the items in the collection, "In Memoriam," a scrapbook containing obituaries and articles in English- and German-language newspapers in New York City and Philadelphia, Pennsylvania, and memorabilia about Woerishoffer as a college student, is perhaps the most useful. Another useful source is *Carola Woerishoffer, Her Life and Work*, published in 1912 by the Class of 1907 of Bryn Mawr College. It contains proceedings of a meeting held at Greenwich House in memory of Carola Woerishoffer, October 30, 1911; memorials printed in *Survey* (September 30, 1911) and in *Bryn Mawr Alumnae Quarterly* (November, 1911); editorials from the *New York Evening Post* (September 12, 1911) and the *New York Times* (September 15, 1911); minutes adopted by the Board of Directors of the Trustees of Bryn Mawr College (January 19, 1912); resolutions adopted by the Board of Managers of Greenwich House, the Women's Trade Union League, the Executive Board of the Committee on Congestion of Population, the Executive Committee of the New York Association for Labor Legislation, the Governing Board of the Consumers' League of New York City, the Directors of the Taylor Iron and Steel Company; and extracts from the *First Annual Report* of the Bureau of Industries and Immigration of the New York State Department of Labor and from the 1911–1912 Report of the Women's Trade Union League. The action of the Bryn Mawr College Board of Trustees to invest her $750,000 bequest as a permanent endowment fund is reported in the *Philadelphia Public Ledger* (October 29, 1911).

The most helpful article on Woerishoffer is the one written by Roderick W. Nash in *Notable American Women 1607–1950*, vol. 3 (1971), which contains references on her family background. Also see, however, Ida M. Tarbell, "A Noble Life: The Story of Carola Woerishoffer," *American Magazine* (July, 1912).

MARY RUTH LEWIS

**Wood, Edith Elmer** (September 24, 1871–April 29, 1945), housing reformer and author, was born in Portsmouth, New Hampshire, to Horace and Adele (Wiley) Elmer. She was the eldest of the couple's two children. Her father was an officer in the U.S. Navy, and as a result of his duties the family lived in numerous places in the United States and abroad during her childhood years. Later, however, she attended Smith College and obtained a B.L. degree in 1890. On June 24, 1893, she married Albert Norton Wood, who, like her father, was a career naval officer. The couple had four sons: Horace Elmer, who died in early childhood, Thurston Elmer, Horace Elmer II, and Albert Elmer.

Wood began her career as an author in 1890 and during the next two decades penned a number of books in the genres of romantic fiction and travel literature. Works written during this period include *Her Provincial Cousin* (1893), *Shoulder Straps and Sunbonnets* (1901), and *An Oberland Chalet* (1910). None of these works would suggest that Wood was concerned with social problems and reform, but during the first decade of the twentieth century, while stationed at a naval base in Puerto Rico, a dramatic change took place. When a servant girl employed by the family contracted tuberculosis and Wood learned that the island did not have a treatment facility, she undertook a crusade to improve the health conditions of the residents of Puerto Rico. She founded the Anti-Tuberculosis League of Puerto Rico and served as its president until 1910. When her husband was stationed in the Washington, D.C., area, Wood became further involved in the issue of public health, and during this time she became convinced of the crucial link between physical illnesses and poor housing conditions. She was involved in efforts to eliminate the black alley slums of the nation's capital and in 1913 was involved in drafting a local bill which would have permitted the issuance of low-interest loans to limited-dividend companies to engage in construction projects. The bill did not pass, though it indicated from an early date in her career that Wood would not be content with the more limited approach to the housing problem advanced most vigorously by Lawrence Veiller.*

Not wanting to remain an amateur in the area of reform, in 1917 she decided to devote her attention fully to the housing question. She entered a joint program at the New York School of Philanthropy and at Columbia University, where she earned a Ph.D. in 1919 with a dissertation (later published as a book) titled *The Housing of the Unskilled Wage Earner*. This work brought together a wide range of disparate statistical data in an effort to place the housing issue in national perspective. From this analysis, she divided the American populace into three categories and argued that only the wealthiest one-third of the nation constituted a genuine market for private-sector initiated construction. For the middle third of the nation, she argued that the government ought to intervene by providing low-interest loans, various tax abatements, and outright housing subsidies in order to stimulate increased private-sector housing production. Finally, for the poorest third of the nation Wood contended that such indirect methods to enlarge the supply of affordable housing would probably not suffice, and therefore the government ought to be prepared to become not only a direct housing producer but also an owner.

In this assessment, Wood (along with a few other housing specialists such as Carol Aronovici, Frederick Ackerman, and Robert Kohn) broke with the mainstream position, which advocated solely what she was to term "restrictive" or "negative" housing legislation. Such legislation established minimum standards for housing quality in an effort to remedy the manifest problems of slum housing. While Wood did not dispute the need for such legislation, she was aware that one of the unintended consequences of such acts was to increase the cost of housing, thereby shrinking the segment of the housing stock available to the most financially disadvantaged sector of the population. As a result, she became a vigorous spokesperson for a "constructive" approach to the housing problem, which was seen by her not as a replacement but as a complement to the "restrictive" type of housing law. She disputed Veiller's complaint that this approach would benefit only a "favored few" who would risk losing a spirit of self-reliance and autonomy.

During the following decade, she continued her study of the housing problem and began her crusading efforts as a lecturer and author. She saw the United States as lagging behind the rest of the industrial world in the area of social reform and contested the view that this country had created the highest standard of living in the world for the working class. In fact, she saw Western Europe as a model for the United States to emulate. In numerous countries the right to a quality home at an affordable price had been conceded by major political forces as a result of the political pressure brought to bear by organized labor and its allies; in contrast, public opinion in the United States was not as advanced, and the notion of an essentially noninterventionist state continued to receive widespread support across the political spectrum. Wood sought to convince the public that housing, like utilities, education, and recreational facilities, ought to be seen as a community service, and that decent housing should be deemed an essential right of citizenship. Furthermore, since housing affects the health, morals, happiness, and civic participation of citizens, it is in the interest of the commonweal to provide good housing to all.

Wood argued that at root the housing problem was economic, and if left to the private sector alone, it was insoluble. Citing the efforts of paternalistic capitalists, she often found their efforts abysmal, and at best only "make-shift" solutions. In addition, such efforts smacked of feudalism and were essentially undemocratic and un-American. Private philanthropy could play a valuable role by providing models but in itself was not adequate to the task. Given this situation, a role for the government in housing markets was a necessity, and with both the knowledge gained from the European experience and from American efforts during World War I to house defense-related workers, she urged resisting moves to return to the *status quo ante*. Though sympathetic to various local initiatives, best seen in various cooperative ventures, she viewed them as too limited in their impact and as not being sufficiently sensitive to the types of housing preferred by the public. Thus, in her comments on a municipally inspired cooperative housing project undertaken in Milwaukee, she saw its demise as due not only to the opposition of the local Chamber of Commerce but to the residents' lack of support for the idea of cooperative ownership as well. She was aware that a majority of Americans defined the single-family detached home as the housing unit of choice.

This was not a propitious time for reform, as powerful real estate and banking interests succeeded in keeping the government out of the housing ownership business. Although she found herself on the losing side of the political debates of the 1920s, she joined with others who had similar ideas to discuss and disseminate their views. Thus, for example, she was a member of the Regional Planning Association of America, along with such figures as Tracy Augur, Catherine Bauer,* Robert Bruere, and Lewis Mumford. During this period she also was the chairperson of the American Association of University Women's national commission on housing. Between 1926 and 1930, Wood was responsible for teaching courses on housing at Columbia, and she taught similar courses at Teachers College during the summer sessions as well.

With the advent of the Depression and the beginning of the New Deal, Wood and her colleagues found an audience for their belief that the government had to assume new responsibilities in the housing field. She advanced her increasingly critical position regarding the building industry in her activities with the National Public Housing Conference (where she was vice president from 1932 to 1936 and later served as director) and as an executive board member of the International Housing Association. She was employed as a consultant to the Public Works Administration's housing division and, after the passage of the U.S. Housing Act of 1937, with the United States Housing Authority.

Wood died, after a lengthy illness, of a cerebral hemorrhage in the hospital at Greystone Park, New Jersey.

The architecture library at Columbia University houses Edith Elmer Wood's personal and professional papers. In addition, the library at the Department of Housing and Urban Development in Washington, D.C., contains useful information on the legislative history of the passage of the U.S. Housing Act of 1937 and on the early years of the U.S. Housing Authority that is helpful in placing in perspective Wood's role during this period.

Among Wood's most important books on housing are *The Housing of the Unskilled Wage Earner* (1919); *Housing Progress in Western Europe* (1923); *Recent Trends in American Housing* (1931); and *Introduction to Housing Facts and Principles* (1939). Wood authored numerous articles which appeared in both scholarly publications and magazines. A few of her more important pieces include "Housing Problems in War and Peace," *Journal of the American Institute of Architects* (1918); "The Statistics of Room Congestion," *Journal of the American Statistical Association* (September, 1928); "Slums and the City Plan," *American City* (August, 1929); "The Housing Situation in the United States," in *America Can't Have Housing*, ed. Carol Aronovici (1934); and "Housing in My Time," *Shelter* (December, 1938).

Brief accounts of Wood's role in the housing reform movement can be found in Roy Lubove's *The Progressives and the Slums* (1962), Mel Scott's *American City Planning Since 1890* (1969), and Gwendolyn Wright's *Building the Dream* (1981). Additional information on housing reform during the New Deal can be obtained from Timothy McDonnell's *The Wagner Housing Act* (1957) and Harry Bredemeier's *The Federal Public Housing Movement* (1980). An obituary appeared in the *New York Times* on May 1, 1945.

PETER KIVISTO

**Woods, Robert Archey** (December 9, 1865–February 18, 1925), settlement worker, social reformer, educator, and writer-editor, was born in Pittsburgh, Pennsylvania, son of Robert and Mary (Hall) Woods. His father, an immigrant from Londonderry, Ireland, was a businessman in Pittsburgh for thirty-five years and a founder of the United Presbyterian Church in East Liberty, a rural community near Pittsburgh. His mother's parents emigrated from Belfast, Ireland. Robert

A. Woods was the fourth of five children in a staunch Scotch-Irish Presbyterian family. In 1902 he married Eleanor Howard Bush, a social worker with the Associated Charities in Boston; they had no children.

His father died when he was fifteen years of age, and the following year Robert entered Amherst College. He became an enthusiastic student of the respected professor of philosophy and psychology Charles Edward Garman. Professor Garman, a proponent of the Social Gospel and an inspirational teacher, was a friend of William James and a pioneer in teaching modern experimental psychology.

After graduating from Amherst in 1886, Woods entered Andover Theological Seminary, attracted there by the work and reputation of the Reverend Dr. William Jewett Tucker.* Woods concentrated on the pioneer course of study in sociology and economics Tucker introduced at Andover. Woods' field work for Tucker's course brought him to New York in 1888 to interview leaders of the Knights of Labor and other labor spokesmen, such as Samuel Gompers and Henry George. He wanted to study their views on the problems of labor and labor's relations to church and state. He was struck by their sense of isolation from both, and he developed a deep empathy for their problems. In the spring of 1890, Tucker asked him to go to England to investigate the social settlements there and report back in lectures to the seminary. To do so, he was given a traveling fellowship. The university settlement idea, conceived of by Arnold Toynbee and Reverend Samuel A. Barnett in order to give Oxford University men the opportunity to live and work among the poor, had resulted in the establishment of Toynbee Hall in 1885 in the East End of London. Woods resided for six months at Toynbee Hall, absorbing the ideas of Canon Barnett and studying English efforts to aid the poor. After he returned, the results of his study of English attempts to improve society were given in lectures to the students at Andover in 1891. At the insistence of Tucker, the lectures were published as *English Social Movements* (1891). That same year, Tucker decided to found the Andover House in Boston to test the idea of a settlement. The site chosen—6 Rollins Street in the South End— was a decaying, overcrowded area of lodging houses, impoverished working people, newly arrived immigrants, and small businesses. Woods was head resident of the four Andover volunteers who opened the doors of the house in January, 1892. Their aim was to work from within the area to improve social conditions through personal relationships with their neighbors and through cooperation with labor organizations and charitable groups. The settlement would serve as a neutral meeting ground for various elements within society, to promote better understanding among them, and to advance Social Christianity; their goal was social reconstruction.

From the beginning, Woods walked throughout the district, studying it and learning from its inhabitants what their needs were. Soft-spoken, genial, and earnest, he attracted confidence, trust, and respect. Large numbers of idle boys, drifting in gangs, prompted him to start a boys' club as the first venture of the house; this was followed by a young men's club, the establishment of a carpenter shop, and drawing classes. The operating funds came initially from Andover alumni contacted by Tucker. Later, Woods spent hours of his time seeking contributions—"beggary" he called it—something he loathed doing but recognized as a necessary aspect of his duties. In 1893, when Professor Tucker became president of Dartmouth, his direct association with the house ended, although he and Woods remained close lifelong friends. In fact, Woods referred to Tucker as his "spiritual father." Two years later, in 1895, the name of the house was changed to the South End House, in order to emphasize the connection with the district and avoid the implication that it was part of the seminary's activities. Woods' work would give the house a distinguished national reputation, and he remained head resident until his death in 1925.

His activity at the house and especially his *English Social Movements* had brought him to the attention of other settlement pioneers, and at an 1892 meeting (in Plymouth, Massachusetts) of leaders interested in the settlement idea, Jane Addams* characterized him as "the natural leader" of the group. Through the thoughtful analysis in his writings, speeches, and work, Woods came to be considered the philosopher of the movement—and its strategist as well.

In an address in 1893 to the International Congress of Charities, Correction, and Philanthropy (later known as the National Conference of Social Work) entitled "University Settlements as Laboratories in Social Science," he proposed the scientific method of observation and analysis for the settlement inquiry. As a sociological laboratory for practical investigation and action, the settlement had to show, he believed, substantial results in improving social conditions for the poor.

The fateful year of 1893 was both fruitful and frustrating for him. He traveled to Pittsburgh in 1893 to help his friend Reverend George Hodges establish a settlement house in his native city. Back in Boston, he worked closely with the settlement workers at Denison House, founded by college women, and gave lectures as well as support to Wells Memorial Institute, which was established to educate working men. His interviews with labor leaders in New York had opened contacts with trade union leaders in Boston, and during the depression of 1893 he brought trade unionists and businessmen together at meetings at the South End House, using the house as a bridge between these segments of society. Together, they lobbied both state and city governments to establish public works programs to employ the jobless.

His frequent appearances before various municipal groups, as he promoted the interests of his neighbors, brought him to the attention of political leaders. The third Josiah Quincy, elected as a reform mayor of Boston in 1896, asked Robert Woods to serve on the committee on public baths, which he had created. Woods became chairman of the Committee on Public Baths and Gymnasiums and served on the Committee for ten years. One of the early goals he had hoped to attain, an all-year municipal bath house, was achieved with the opening of the Dover Street Bath in the South End. The popularity of the Dover Street Bath led to the opening of others throughout the city. In addition, gymnasiums for public use were made a reality through Woods' vigorous support. He considered public baths and gymnasia necessary for public hygiene and health; most of the lodgers and many tenement dwellers had no available water; often one sink in the front hallway was the only running water for inhabitants of a dwelling.

In 1898 *The City Wilderness: A Study of the South End* was published; Robert Woods edited, supervised, and contributed to the work, which was the first social survey of an American city. It was modeled on Charles Booth's study, *Life and Labour of the People of London*, and consisted of the residents' analysis of the district. The second volume, *Americans in Process: A Study of the North and West Ends* (1902), was similar in format and also was lauded as a landmark American social survey. It went into a second edition within a month of its initial publication. The books brought him further national attention, and he lectured on the settlement idea from many platforms. Essentially, he believed that the neighborhood was the microcosm of life; society was an organism and the neighborhood its vital cell. From the cell of the organism, social reconstruction would spread through cooperative effort to the municipality, state, and nation. Ethical considerations were crucial in reform, he believed, for the historical evolution of the societal organism was part of the divine plan, and the individual could serve God by serving his fellow men. That service had to benefit his neighbors by bettering their lives; this was "practical idealism." Thus, the crucial role of the settlement was in improving the vitality and health of the neighborhood cell in order to strengthen the entire organism of urban society. In this was melded the ideal of service and the new scientific method.

Woods' emphasis on cooperative efforts to attain reform and social unity led him to promote the federated principle for settlement houses; in 1899 the South End Social Union was formed. This was a federation of ten settlement houses which Robert Woods served as president from its inception until 1908; by that time, he had widened the federation to twenty-six Boston houses and the name had been changed to the Boston Social Union. The efforts of Woods and his supporters to promote consolidation of settlement efforts on a larger scale resulted, in 1911, in the formation of the National Federation of Settlements, which Woods served as secretary from its founding until 1923, when he became its president; he served in that capacity until the end of his life.

An indefatigable worker, Woods also promoted the study of social ethics as a lecturer at both Andover Theological Seminary (1891–1895) and Episcopal Theological School in Cambridge (1896–1914). He used fees from his lectures to support the South End House during difficult times, including fellowships, when necessary, for Andover, Dartmouth, Harvard, Amherst, and Radcliffe students. The fellowships allowed students to reside at the house and to research a topic for study under the direction of the residents. The education of young ministers to be active in social reconstruction, and of young students who would take the knowledge of urban needs into many career fields, was to him an important part of the work.

The educational functions of the house—art, music, history, and drama classes—

were essential in affording uplifting opportunities for the young, but Woods' work with young adults convinced him that practical training for a vocation was necessary. The vast majority of young people in poorer districts did not go to high school, and, not having been trained for a career, they often drifted into joblessness. He thus became a champion of industrial arts education, designed to offer a trade or skill to such youngsters. In 1903 he was chairman of the Citizens Committee to Promote a State System of Industrial Education and was secretary of the State Committee to Establish Industrial Schools. He did the preliminary investigation for Wentworth Institute and saw the goals of industrial education reach fruition within a decade in Boston and throughout the state of Massachusetts.

He worked with his friend Joseph Lee,* "father of the playground movement in America," to have play areas established in tenement districts, and in 1904 the South End playground was opened; the first of many in the district. Robert Woods' interest in improving conditions in overcrowded areas also led him to initiate steps to improve the health of the people. He and the residents worked to eliminate dangerous conditions, in conjunction with the Board of Health. In 1906 a resident nurse was appointed at the South End House; the South Bay Union, a large settlement building, one of many which Woods had scattered throughout the South End to establish closer relationships with the neighbors, became the center for truly innovative public health measures. It was the call station for the district nurse and doctor from the Boston Dispensary. In 1907 the South End House nurse set up a modified milk station to help combat infant mortality; the provision of clean milk and instructions in the care and feeding of infants were part of the program. Mary Strong, the nurse, also developed, with Woods' support, in 1910, the first neighborhood prenatal care service in the nation; baby clinics were set up at the house, work that became a model of its kind throughout the nation.

From the first days of his residency, Woods had cited the "tramp evil" and "liquor evil" as detrimental to life in the South End. The former had been partially alleviated when, after the depression of 1893, the city had been persuaded by the tireless efforts of Robert Woods and others to purchase a house to offer temporary shelter to homeless drifters. The liquor problem was harder to solve, and Woods was a staunch foe of the liquor interests. He called the prevalence of saloons a "modern plague." The suffering, poverty, and wasted lives of the victims of alcohol abuse prompted him to seek some system of aid to them. He believed that they needed medical care of a specialized type, and thus sought, with others, the establishment of a hospital for humane and scientific treatment for that purpose. As a result, in 1907, the Governor made him chairman of the board of the State Hospital for Inebriates, and he served in that position until 1914, when he was appointed a member of the Licensing Board for the city of Boston. In the latter capacity, he tried to limit the number of establishments in the overcrowded tenement districts that were dispensing alcoholic beverages. He became a strong supporter of the prohibition amendment and, in 1918, was chairman of the Massachusetts Committee to Secure Ratification. Massachusetts was the first industrial state to ratify the amendment. His opposition was so strong because he believed that alcohol abuse limited individual freedom and impeded social reconstruction.

The study of the settlement house movement, on which Woods and the associate resident of the South End House, Albert J. Kennedy,* had been working for ten years, *The Settlement Horizon: A National Estimate*, was published by the Russell Sage Foundation in 1922. It was a significant assessment of the settlement idea and its accomplishments.

The contribution of Robert A. Woods to the movement for social justice was substantial. He helped shape the ideas and purposes of the settlement house movement, giving it focus, leadership, a philosophy, and a sense of mission. He eschewed "pious wishes" and sought verifiable results of the work. In merging the aims of the Social Gospel movement with the practical goals of social reconstruction based on the scientific method, he appealed to the pragmatic idealism of the progressive generation. His own example of dedicated leadership and success was a strong model.

Patient, kind, and modest, he measured progress by decades. His own deep spiritual life of self-renunciation for service to others found meaning in what he called "the work"; his pragmatic self insisted on practical results of better lives for his neighbors. Woods died unexpectedly in Boston in 1925 after a short illness.

Robert A. Woods' papers are in the Houghton Library of Harvard University in Cambridge, Massachusetts; they contain various notebooks, scrapbooks, diaries, correspondence, lecture drafts, financial records, books, and other uncatalogued material. The most valuable summary of his ideas is his *The Neighborhood in Nation-Building: The Running Comment of Thirty Years at the South End House* (1923). In conjunction with *The Settlement Horizon* it offers a synopsis of his thought and work. The *Andover House Association Yearly Reports*, 1892–1894, and *South End House Association Annual Reports*, 1895–1924, were written by Robert Woods and give his yearly assessment of accomplishments and failures. Also see *The Zone of Emergence* (1962), ed. Sam B. Warner, an unfinished study of the communities around the central city which reveals its author's attitudes on urban matters.

The most significant study of Woods' life is the biography written by his wife, *Robert A. Woods: Champion of Democracy* (1929); the work is an exposition of her husband's work and ideas and quotes extensively from his correspondence and unpublished materials in her possession. For a summary of his work by his associate, Albert J. Kennedy, see the entry on Woods in *The Dictionary of American Biography*, vol. 20 (1936), 503–504.

DOROTHY T. SCANLON

**Woodward, Ellen Sullivan** (July 11, 1887–September 23, 1971), Works Progress Administration (WPA) assistant administrator and Social Security Board (SSB) member, was born in Oxford, Mississippi, to William Van Amberg Sullivan, a

Mississippi attorney and U.S. Congressman and Senator, and Belle (Murray) Sullivan. After the death of her mother when Ellen was only seven, she developed a close relationship with her father and spent much of her girlhood with him in Washington, where she early demonstrated an interest in public affairs. Later, as the wife of Albert Young Woodward, whom she married when she was nineteen, she became an influential club woman and a prominent force in the community development of Louisville, a small, essentially rural town in central Mississippi. It is likely that the humane and egalitarian outlook and civic spirit she came to have resulted from her work with her husband, a lawyer, judge, and state legislator whose term she completed at his death in 1925. At the end of the 1926 legislative session, she became an official with the Mississippi State Board of Development (1926–1933) and worked to bring economic diversity to the state and to raise the standard of living of rural Mississippians.

Woodward's "social progressivism" was reflected in her service with a number of state charities and eleemosynary institutions. She was a member of the board of the Mississippi Children's Home Society (1928–1941), a trustee of the State Charity Hospital (1924–1929), executive secretary of the Mississippi Conference on Social Work (1929–1930), a member of the Mississippi Committee of the President's Organization on Unemployment Relief (1931), and the only woman on the new Mississippi State Board of Public Welfare (1932–1933). Concurrent service as the executive secretary of the Mississippi Research Commission brought her administrative competence, organizational ability, and humane and liberal outlook, as well as her considerable grace, charm, and political astuteness, to the attention of non-Mississippians. It was Frank Bane* of the American Public Welfare Association who suggested to Harry Hopkins* that she become the director of the women's work relief program of the Federal Emergency Relief Administration (FERA). Arriving in Washington in September, 1933, Woodward remained in various posts relating to social welfare and economic security until her retirement twenty years later.

Woodward shared the beliefs of Hopkins and her mentor, (Anna) Eleanor Roosevelt,* that work relief was far preferable to direct relief. Many of the projects she directed under the FERA and later the Works Progress Administration were administered through or sponsored by state departments of public welfare or local social work agencies. Although she had received no social work training (her college diploma was based on one year's work at San Souci in Greenville, South Carolina), she developed considerable knowledge about social casework practices and strongly advocated the education and professionalization of emergency and work relief social service personnel.

Woodward's commitment to public welfare deepened during her tenure as a member of the Social Security Board from December 31, 1938, when she succeeded Mary W. Dewson,* to July 16, 1946. Her concerns centered upon personnel matters, including the establishment of a strong merit system to thwart the exploitation of Social Security programs by state politicians. She also closely monitored appointments at the state and regional level to insure equal opportunities for employment, advancement, and pay for women within the Social Security system. She expended greater efforts, however, in publicizing the benefits of the various Social Security titles to potential grantees, particularly women and children. She spoke extensively to women's organizations, wrote numerous articles in women's professional journals and popular magazines, and made radio addresses. Working with Jane Hoey,* the director of the Bureau of Public Assistance, she sought to strengthen aid to dependent children and pointed to inequities in assistance that penalized working mothers. She also became a strong advocate of extended unemployment compensation for all workers, but especially women, and during World War II she sought to protect the Social Security rights of men and women in the armed forces. She was ahead of her time in her advocacy of the extension of coverage to farmers, domestic workers, and the self-employed. Because of her closeness to Mrs. Roosevelt, she was able to reach a large segment of the public through the First Lady's writings and appearances.

Much of Woodward's work with the Social Security Board lay in the arena of international welfare. From 1943 to 1946 she attended six meetings of the United Nations Relief and Rehabilitation Administration (UNRRA) as an advisor to the United States delegation on matters relating to emergency welfare service for women and children and the establishment of permanent programs. In 1944–1945 she was a member of the UNRRA Standing Technical Committee for Welfare. Her responsibilities in international social welfare expanded when she was named director of the Office of International Relations of the Federal Security Agency (FSA) in July, 1946, when the Social Security Board was abolished under executive reorganization. Her office became a clearing house for the international welfare activities of constituent divisions within the FSA, particularly the Social Security Administration and the Children's Bureau. As the FSA liaison officer with the United Nations and the Department of State, she attended the Lake Success organizational meeting of the United Nations Economic and Social Council (UNESCO) in 1947 as one of two women delegates. She continued to press for international humanitarianism in her work as a delegate to successive UNESCO sessions. She was an effective spokeswoman for United States support in establishing the UN Children's Fund and the UN International Fellows Program for social welfare as well as the beginning of a social welfare attaché program within the Department of State. Throughout her work with the SSB and the FSA, Woodward drew upon the technical assistance of Wilbur Cohen* in the former office and Savilla M. Simons in the latter.

Woodward was a member of a number of social welfare professional organizations, including the International Conference of Social Work, in which she served as a member of the U.S. Committee. On December 31, 1953, she retired from the Department of Health, Education and Welfare after twenty-eight years of public service. She died at age eighty-four at her Washington home.

The Woodward Papers in the Mississippi Department of Archives and History are voluminous and rich; there is a smaller collection, mostly speeches, in the

Schlesinger Library at Radcliffe College. The best official records are Record Groups 69 (WPA) and 47 (Social Security Administration) in the National Archives, Washington, D.C. There is some very useful material in the interviews within the Social Security Project of the Columbia University Oral History Collection; the author's personal interview with Dorothy Lally in Washington, D.C. (June, 1983) is very illuminating on the FSA phase of Woodward's work. Woodward wrote no books, but professional journals and popular women's magazines from 1934 to 1953 contain many articles by her describing various programs for women's relief and security. Representative writings include "Jobs for Jobless Women," *Equal Rights* (July 20, 1935); "Social Security for the Professional Woman," *Practical Home Economics* (September, 1942); and "UNRRA—Weaponof Democracy," *Independent Woman* (January, 1945). Essays about her include Martha H. Swain, "Ellen Woodward: The Gentlewoman as Federal Administrator,"*Furman Studies* (December, 1980); Swain, "The 'Forgotten Woman': Ellen S. Woodward and Women's Relief in the New Deal," *Prologue* (Winter, 1983); and Swain, "ER and Ellen Woodward: A Partnership for Women's Relief and Security," in *Without Precedent: The Life and Career of Eleanor Roosevelt* (1984). Woodward's obituary is in the *Washington Evening Star* (September 24, 1971).

MARTHA H. SWAIN

**Woodward, Samuel Bayard** (January 10, 1787–January 3, 1850), proponent of the moral treatment of the insane and leader of the movement to improve their care in mid-nineteenth century America, was born in Torrington, Connecticut, the son of Polly (Griswold) and Samuel Woodward, a physician. In 1815 he married Maria Porter of Hadley, Massachusetts. They had eleven children, eight of whom survived to adulthood. Woodward went to the district school of Torrington, and he received his medical education in his father's office. In 1809, after passing his examination, he earned his diploma from the Connecticut State Medical Society; later he received an honorary medical degree from Yale. In 1810 he established what was to be a twenty-year practice in Wethersfield, where he trained many medical students. Early in his career, Woodward was physician to the penitentiary in Wethersfield; he served as secretary of the State Medical Society and as examiner of the Yale Medical School; and he was active in the effort to establish the Hartford Retreat in 1824. Later he was medical superintendent of the Massachusetts State Lunatic Asylum at Worcester from 1832 to 1846, and he was the first president (1844) of the Association of Medical Superintendents of American Institutions for the Insane (later the American Psychiatric Association).

Woodward's interest in treating the insane was influenced by both religious and medical ideas. He was inspired by the Second Great Awakening to become involved in humanitarian work. Replacing the pessimism of strict Calvinism by a more optimistic perfectionist view of the progress of mankind, Woodward came to believe that it was one's Christian duty to improve the lives of the less fortunate. Woodward's perfectionist beliefs, moreover, led him to maintain that all persons, including convicts, alcoholics, delinquents, the sick, and the mentally ill, could be helped and even cured. Woodward was also influenced by the medical ideas of thinkers such as William Tuke, Philippe Pinel, Benjamin Rush,* George M. Burrows, and Jean E.D. Esquirol. Their development of a scientific understanding of insanity helped to erode the prevailing attitude that insanity was caused by demonic possession or sin; kindness was beginning to replace indifference or cruel treatment.

From 1827 to 1832, when Woodward was resident physician to the state penitentiary, he began to formulate ideas which led to his later optimistic belief in the cure of the insane by moral treatment administered within the institution. In the closed prison environment, he established kind, humane treatment of prisoners. He believed that once persons who had gone astray were properly educated to the correct natural laws of life, they would reform, in the case of prisoners, or be cured, in the case of insane persons.

Also related to Woodward's interest in the institutional care of the insane was his awareness of the impracticality and difficulty of treatment in private practice. In 1821 he and several other Connecticut physicians, including Eli Todd, conducted an investigation on the number and condition of insane persons in the state. Their report revealed the poor conditions under which 1,000 insane persons suffered; moreover, the authors argued that institutional care would prevent the plague of chronic mental illness. This report led to the opening of the Hartford Retreat, the third corporate hospital for the insane to be founded in the United States during the early nineteenth century.

A similar movement to establish a state institution for the insane occurred in Massachusetts, leading to the opening of the State Lunatic Asylum at Worcester in January, 1833. Woodward was appointed superintendent, and within a decade his leadership caused the Worcester hospital to be seen as a leader of all American mental institutions.

Woodward's treatment of the insane also replaced older techniques such as bleeding, blistering, and corporal punishment. Instead, under the regimen of moral treatment, patients received occupational therapy, religious exercises, amusements and games, a special diet, and an emphasis on personal cleanliness. Corporal punishment and mechanical restraint were banned. The philosophy behind this treatment was to create a healthy physical, social, and psychological environment for the patient. In certain cases, Woodward also used narcotics and stimulants, until the patient's health was brought to a level where moral treatment could be administered.

Woodward's annual reports of the hospital were widely read. They stimulated the movement for state asylum care and moral treatment all over America. In the annual reports, Woodward also advocated the use of the statistical analysis of cases, encouraging the use of increased knowledge in the care of the insane.

Although the statistics presented in Woodward's annual reports were later questioned for accuracy, and eventually the optimism of curability due to the administration of moral treatment waned, Woodward nonetheless helped to establish kind and humane treatment for the insane in America. He headed the leading hospital for the care of the insane in the 1830s and 1840s, and he organized medical superintendents in the first national society of medical men in America.

Woodward resigned from the hospital in 1846, in poor health. He retired in Northampton, Massachusetts, where he died on January 3, 1850.

Manuscript sources on Samuel B. Woodward include the Samuel B. Woodward Papers, American Antiquarian Society, Worcester, Massachusetts; Samuel B. Woodward, "Collected Writings," 3 vols., typescript, Library, Worcester State Hospital, Worcester, Massachusetts; and the Samuel B. Woodward Papers, Yale University Library, New Haven, Connecticut.

Writings by Samuel B. Woodward include *Essays on Asylums for Inebriates* (1838), and *Hints for the Young in Relation to the Health of Body and Mind* (1840). With Mark Hopkins, he wrote a pamphlet titled *Address to the People of Massachusetts on the Present Condition and Claims of the Temperance Reformation* (1846). Most informative are Worcester State Hospital, *Annual Reports*, 1833–1846, written by Woodward.

A detailed obituary can be found in George Chandler, *American Journal of Insanity* 8 (1851), 117–132. Good secondary sources include Albert Deutsch, *The Mentally Ill in America: A History of Their Care and Treatment from Colonial Times* (1937, 1939); Gerald N. Grob, *Mental Institutions in America: Social Policy to 1875* (1973); and Grob, *The State and the Mentally Ill: A History of Worcester State Hospital in Massachusetts 1830–1920* (1966).

VIRGINIA A. METAXAS QUIROGA

**Woolman, John** (October 19, 1720–October 7, 1772), Quaker minister, abolitionist, and friend of the needy and oppressed, was born in Rancocas, province of West Jersey (Burlington County, New Jersey), the eldest son of Samuel and Elizabeth (Burr) Woolman. His family, moderately prosperous farmers, maintained close contact with many of the leading Quaker families in nearby Philadelphia. Formally educated in the local Quaker school, Woolman read widely and remained committed to a program of self-education throughout his life. His Quaker heritage, with its emphasis on divine guidance, inner truth, and universal equality, instilled in the young Woolman a strong moral conscience which would dominate his life and work. He was recognized as a Quaker minister in 1743. Six years later he married Sarah Ellis. Of their two children, only Mary survived infancy.

Woolman's career as an itinerant Quaker minister established living testimony to his belief in universal moral law, a testimony recorded faithfully and eloquently in his *Journal*. One of America's great spiritual autobiographies, Woolman's *Journal* has provided inspiration to writers and reformers for over two centuries and has been issued in numerous editions. It was through his essays, however, that Woolman significantly influenced contemporary responses to slavery, poverty, and the ideals of social action. His essay, "Some Considerations on the Keeping of Negroes" (1754), and "Part II" (1762), was widely reprinted throughout Great Britain and North America. This work strongly influenced the decision of the New Jersey legislature in 1769 to impose a duty on imported slaves. Over the years, his ongoing testimony against slavery compelled his Quaker brethren to take a firm stand on the issue. The 1776 yearly meeting of the Society of Friends resolved to disown Quakers for slave keeping, setting in motion the earliest significant antislavery movement in American history.

The welfare of Blacks in bondage, however, constituted only one aspect of Woolman's overall concern for the poor and oppressed. In his 1763 essay, "A Plea for the Poor" (later published as "A Word of Remembrance and Caution to the Rich," 1793), Woolman identified an organic relationship between the attainment of wealth and the imposition of poverty. This essay, notable for its emphasis on the inalienable rights of all persons to land and the basic necessities of life, serves as Woolman's greatest contribution to the history of ideas about humanitarian social welfare.

In his "Plea," Woolman focused on the urgency of absolute and complete devotion to the relief of the laboring classes. Believing every individual responsible for reducing the distresses of the "afflicted," Woolman emphasized the moral duty of both rich and poor in working to achieve a balance of "universal love." Although his quest for moral justice lay at the heart of his plea, Woolman supported his argument with sound economic reasoning, detailing both the real and the human costs of high interest rates, primogeniture, and involuntary labor. He argued that all who labored must receive an equitable reward. Persecution and oppression, wrote Woolman, inevitably resulted from the failure to justly compensate workers for their labor.

Over the years, labor advocates, reformers, and socialists have referred to Woolman's concepts of equity, moral justice, and universal rights as outlined in his "Plea." Woolman, however, was not a socialist. He did not advocate the abolition of capitalism or private property, yet he detested luxury and all products of "unnecessary labour." Woolman's formula for social equity did not attempt to eradicate poverty or to equalize the classes. He proposed, instead, voluntary simplicity among the propertied classes who, he felt, were obligated to act with compassion and empathy toward the poor. Of the poor, Woolman demanded similar self-restraint. Only just and necessary labor, not material success, could redeem the poor from their unhappy plight.

Woolman's idealism, while predicated upon deep religious faith, was the product, as well, of a perceptive and sensitive social observer. Woolman was among the first to describe the destructive impact of slavery upon the personality development of both Blacks and Whites. Similarly, he identified a direct relationship between economic injustice and war. Often identifying himself with the laboring classes, Woolman addressed in his essays the problems of unemployment, inadequate educational opportunity, and malnourishment. In his travels (usually on foot) and in his essays, Woolman focused on the "invisible" members of society—sailors, servants, prisoners, native Americans, and aged slaves. Through his actions and his writings, Woolman offered an example of integrity and direction for those seeking a vision of social justice. His concern for the urban working class in Britain brought him to York, England, in 1772, where he died of smallpox.

Woolman composed two holographs of his *Journal*, designated as Manuscripts A and B. Manuscript A is located at the Historical Society of Pennsylvania, Philadelphia, and includes his "Plea for the Poor." Manuscript B, his final manuscript, is located at the Friends Historical Library of Swarthmore College. A longhand copy of the "Plea" is housed in the Quaker Collection, Haverford College Library. Portions of the "Plea" and other manuscripts are located in the Grubb Collection, Friends Historical Library, Dublin, Ireland, and in the Department of Records of the Philadelphia Yearly Meeting, 302 Arch St., Philadelphia.

In addition to those essays already mentioned, Woolman composed several additional tracts on social responsibility: "Considerations on Pure Wisdom and Human Policy" (1768?); "Considerations on the True Harmony of Mankind" (1770); and "Conversations on the True Harmony of Mankind" (written in 1772, not published until 1837).

Among the many competent editions of Woolman's works, two publications are especially useful: Amelia Mott Gunmere, ed., *The Journal and Essays of John Woolman* (1922); and Phillips P. Moulton, ed., *The Journal and Major Essays of John Woolman* (1971).

Secondary works which address Woolman's contributions to the history of ideas and social service include Sydney V. James, *A People Among People: Quaker Benevolence in Eighteenth-Century America* (1963); and Paul Rosenblatt, *John Woolman* (1969).

TERRI L. PREMO

**Woolsey, Abby Howland** (July 16, 1828–April 7, 1893), Civil War volunteer and hospital and nursing reformer, was born in Alexandria, Virginia, the first child of Charles William Woolsey and Jane Eliza (Newton) Woolsey. Charles W. Woolsey operated a sugar refining business in Boston. When he died on board the steamer *Lexington* in 1840, the family moved to New York City. Abby attended the Rutgers Female Institute, where she received a thorough education in mathematics, French, natural philosophy, painting, music, and writing. She later attended the Bolton Priory, a finishing school for young ladies. Formal schooling was supplemented by private lessons in languages and music. The Woolsey family was originally a member of the Market Street (Dutch Reformed) Church; however, in 1862 the family helped found the Church of the Covenant (Presbyterian). Abby was a devoted member of the church, teaching Sunday school, calling on sick members, and serving on church committees. She also attended classes taught by her cousin at the Union Theological Seminary. The Woolsey family was prominent in New York. The children were avid readers. Abby read in English, French, Italian, and German. The family members read philosophical and intellectual books and attended lectures on political and cultural topics. They closely monitored the news on the abolition of slavery and the events leading to the Civil War. When the Civil War broke out the family became involved by making bandages and supplies in their home. By the end of the war, Abby and her sisters Jane,* George Anna,* and Eliza would make valuable contributions to the care of the sick and wounded and the organization of hospitals.

In the 1850s Abby felt that she was leading a meaningless, useless life. She was not content just filling the social expectations of the family. Through her church, she became interested in the House of Industry and there taught sewing to women. Eventually, she was appointed assistant manager. With the start of the Civil War, Abby and other socially prominent women joined together and formed the Women's Central Association of Relief, which became a branch of the U.S. Sanitary Commission. During the war, Abby, unlike her sisters, stayed at home. Her war efforts consisted of monitoring the needs on the war front and gathering supplies, which were sent to George Anna and Jane and to the Sanitary Commission; securing chaplains for the Union forces; and corresponding with the family members. The Woolsey house became an information center and supply receiving depot. Abby developed a reputation for being an organizer and for donating the money needed to buy supplies.

After the war, when Jane was asked to organize the new Presbyterian Hospital, Abby accompanied her as acting clerk. Until 1876 they provided gratuitous service to the hospital. In 1872 Abby became a member of the organizing committee, gathered together by Louisa Lee Schuyler,* to start the New York State Charities Aid Association. The purpose of the Association was to promote interest in institutions of public charity and to stimulate their improvement and reform. Abby was a member of the Committee on Hospitals. After the Bellevue Hospital was visited, Abby became a member of the special committee to prepare a plan for organizing a school of nursing at Bellevue Hospital. What was needed was a better class of women as nurses. Abby drafted the plan of organization for the school. It was based on the ideas of Florence Nightingale and provided innovative ideas on the administration of the school and the staffing of the hospital. The opening of the Bellevue school on May 1, 1873, revolutionized the care of the sick in the United States. Abby was credited with making nursing an educated and honorable profession, and with opening avenues of professional and public service for women. She advocated keeping the standards and the quality of the education high and believed that schools of nursing should seek funds as educational institutions, not as charitable ones. In 1874 Abby became a member of the Board of Managers for the Bellevue Hospital Training School for Nurses.

Traveling to Europe in 1876, she observed nursing in a variety of hospitals and brought back information for the New York State Charities Aid Association.

Abby's skills at observing and expressing her ideas led to requests for her to write statements for the Association. These publications included *A Century of Nursing with Hints Toward the Organization of a Training School* (1876), *Handbook for Hospitals* (1883), *Handbook for Hospital Visitors* (1877), *Hospital Laundries* (1880), and *Lunacy Legislation in England* (1884). In 1880 she was appointed librarian for the New York State Charities Aid Association, a position she occupied for twelve years. In this role she tackled the job of organizing and cataloguing the Association's library and preparing scrapbooks to document its work. *The Catalogue of the Library of the State Charities Aid Association* (1880) was the outcome of her efforts. From 1872 until her death, Abby was an active member of the New York State Charities Aid Association, serving on the Committee on Hospitals, the Committee of Building Plans for Bellevue, and the Board of Managers, and chairing the Subcommittee on the Insane.

After 1880 she served as a companion and nurse to her sister Jane. Abby's intelligence, education, stamina, and social position, as well as the practical hospital experience she gained, enabled her to lead a productive life. She died in New York City at her home.

Manuscript collections containing information on Abby Howland Woolsey are in the Archives of the Bellevue Hospital School of Nursing, located at the Bellevue Hospital in New York City; the records of the New York State Charities Aid Association, located in New York; and the Woolsey Family Archives, which are in the family's possession (known in 1971 to be held by Caroline Woolsey Ferriday of New York).

A number of the New York State Charities Aid Association publications written by Abby Howland Woolsey are now available on microfiche in *The History of Nursing, Part I* (1982).

Little has been written about the Woolsey sisters. The most comprehensive source is Anne L. Austin, *The Woolsey Sisters of New York 1860–1900* (1971). A comprehensive synopsis of the three sisters' contributions, also written by Austin, is found in *Notable American Women 1607–1950*, vol. 3 (1971). Additional helpful sources include George Anna Woolsey Bacon and Eliza Woolsey Howland, *Letters of a Family During the War for the Union 1861–1865* (1899); Robert J. Carlisle, *An Account of Bellevue Hospital* (1893); M. Adelaide Nutting and Lavinia J. Dock, *A History of Nursing, vol. 2* (1907); and Isabel M. Steward, *The Education of Nurses* (1943).

LAURIE K. GLASS

**Woolsey, George Anna Muirson** (November 5, 1833–January 27, 1906), Civil War volunteer nurse and hospital and nursing reformer, was born in Brooklyn, New York, the fourth daughter of Charles William Woolsey and Jane Eliza (Newton) Woolsey. Charles Woolsey, who died in 1840 when the steamer *Lexington* sank, operated a sugar refining business in Boston. Jane Woolsey moved the family back to New York after her husband's death, where it eventually became one of the prominent families involved in caring for the Civil War wounded and improving hospitals and the training of nurses.

As a child, Georgy, as she was called, attended the Rutgers Female Institute, where she received a solid education in languages, the arts, writing, and natural philosophy (science). In 1850 she was sent to Mrs. Anable's Boarding School in Philadelphia. Private lessons, travel to Europe, and attendance at intellectual and cultural events in New York added to her formal schooling. In 1866 Georgy married Dr. Francis Bacon, a Yale Medical School graduate. After the Civil War, Frank Bacon became a successful surgeon and professor of surgery at Yale University. In history books, George Anna is occasionally referred to as George Anna Woolsey Bacon or Mrs. Francis Bacon.

Georgy was an early member of the Women's Central Association of Relief, and her adventuresome spirit provided the motivation needed to seek training as a nurse through the Association's program. Disguising her age, for she was considered too young, not yet being thirty, she was accepted and went to the New York Hospital for her instruction. In July, 1861, Georgy and her sister Eliza went to Washington, D.C., and began their nursing in various war camps in the area. In the next four months they would visit hospitals to inspect the conditions and confer with Dorothea Dix*; organize, cook, and nurse at the Patent Office Hospital; assist Louisa Lee Schuyler* by receiving the Women's Central Association of Relief nurses and starting them in their work; and approach President Abraham Lincoln about the need for army chaplains and welcome the chaplains that their sister Abby* had recruited. After a brief visit to New York in October, 1861, the sisters returned to the Alexandria, Virginia, area to continue their nursing and also to visit the jails where contraband slaves were held. At the jails the sisters distributed needed articles that were donated for the "prisoners."

Georgy and Eliza, along with Katharine Wormeley and Christine Kean Griffin, were invited to organize and outfit with supplies the hospital transport ship *Daniel Webster*. To these four women fell the responsibility of supervising the care of the wounded and preparing all the food for the wounded on board the ship and at the shore hospitals. During six months in 1862, Georgy and the other women served on board four additional ships, the *Ocean Queen*, the *Spaulding*, the *Knickerbocker*, and the *Commodore*.

After returning to New York in October, 1862, Katharine Wormeley requested the assistance of Georgy and her sister Jane* at the Portsmouth Grove Hospital near Newport, Rhode Island. Georgy and Jane were appointed assistant superintendents, and this was the first time that women nurses worked in a U.S. general hospital in such responsible positions. In 1863, after the battle of Gettysburg, Georgy was summoned to assist with the wounded. Accompanied by her mother, she quickly organized the care of the wounded. Georgy recorded this experience in her book, *Three Weeks at Gettysburg* (1863). In the next year Georgy helped organize four more hospitals. She accompanied Jane to the Hammond General Hospital at Point Lookout and to the Fairfax Theological Seminary Hospital, where she was in charge of nursing and diets. After the

Battle of Spotsylvania she set up the hospital at Fredericksburg at the request
of the U.S. Sanitary Commission. Her last activity for the Sanitary Commission
was the organization of the hospital at Beverly, New Jersey.

After Georgy married Frank Bacon, she moved to New Haven, Connecticut,
where she continued her work with hospitals and charitable institutions. In 1873
Georgy was active in setting up and managing the Connecticut Training School
for Nurses at the New Haven Hospital, one of the first three Nightingale model
schools opened in the United States. In 1878, at the request of the Board of
Managers, Georgy wrote *A Handbook of Nursing for Family and General Use*.
This was only the second such book published in the United States and was
widely used by other schools. The revised edition appeared in 1905. Georgy's
involvement with the Connecticut Training School included serving for thirty-
three years on the Board of Managers and serving as a member of the executive
committee, as secretary of the Board of Administration, and as chair of the
Committee on Instruction. Her husband, Frank, shared her interests; he served
on the Board of Managers for thirty-nine years and gave occasional lectures to
the students.

In 1883 Georgy was appointed to the Connecticut State Board of Charities,
whose main function was to inspect hospitals, prisons, reformatory schools,
insane asylums, and almshouses. This ten-year appointment renewed her interest
in prison conditions, and she again donated needed personal items to the prisoners.

The Bacons were always interested in the welfare of children. In 1896 Georgy
and Frank bequeathed a summer house on Long Island Sound to the Newington
Hospital for Crippled Children. Playridge, as it was named, was to be used for
the recreation of the children.

Georgy and her sister Abby were pioneers in establishing a new system of
nursing care and a new system of nursing education in the United States. A
perfectionist with organizational ability, she used the experiences gained in the
Civil War to make needed changes in the postwar years. Georgy believed that
nurses needed certain characteristics and training in order to be knowledgeable
in caring for the sick.

George Anna Woolsey Bacon died at her home in New Haven.

Primary sources of material referring to George Anna Woolsey Bacon's work
can be found in the Archives of the Connecticut Training School, located at the
Yale Medical Library in New Haven, Connecticut; and in the Woolsey Family
Archives, in the family's possession.

Although it is documented that George Anna wrote *A Handbook of Nursing
for Family and General Use* (1879), the book was published without a named
author and merely states, ''Published under the direction of the Connecticut
Training School for Nurses, State Hospital, New Haven, Connecticut.'' George
Anna was interested in preserving the family history and collaborated with her
sister Eliza Woolsey Howland in writing *Letters of a Family During the War
for the Union 1861–1865* (1899). As Mrs. Francis Bacon, George Anna discusses

the foundation of the Connecticut Training School for Nurses in *Trained Nurse and Hospital Review* (October, 1895), 187–193.

Few references exist which acknowledge George Anna's contributions or review her life. The most comprehensive is Anne L. Austin, *The Woolsey Sisters of New York 1860–1900* (1971). Austin's *History of Nursing Source Book* (1957) provides excerpts from her letters. Austin's contribution in *Notable American Women 1607–1950*, vol. 3 (1971), provides a comprehensive synopsis on all three Woolsey sisters.

M. Adelaide Nutting and Lavinia L. Dock discuss the establishment of the Connecticut Training School in *A History of Nursing*, vol. 2 (1907). Isabel M. Stewart discusses the importance of the *Handbook of Nursing* in *The Education of Nurses* (1943).

                                                                 LAURIE K. GLASS

**Woolsey, Jane Stuart** (February 7, 1830–July 9, 1891), Civil War volunteer, nursing educator, and hospital reformer, was born on the ship *Fanny* near Flushing, New York. She was the second child and daughter of Jane Eliza (Newton) Woolsey and Charles William Woolsey, who operated a sugar refining business. There were eight Woolsey children. Jane had interests similar to her sisters Abby* and George Anna.* The family lived in Boston until 1840, when Charles Woolsey died on board the *Lexington*. They then moved to New York City to be closer to the other members of the prominent Woolsey and Newton families. Jane attended the Rutgers Female Institute, where she received a solid education in mathematics, French, natural philosophy (science), painting, music, and writing. Private lessons in languages and music, and attendance at the Bolton Priory (a finishing school), provided a good cultural background. The Woolseys attended political and cultural lectures and were avid readers. Jane read in English, French, Italian, and German. In 1850, feeling stagnation in her life, Jane traveled with relatives to Arkansas. She spent the next year traveling in Europe. Jane, like Abby, was a devoted member of her Presbyterian church, the Church of the Covenant, which the family helped found in 1862. Besides teaching Sunday school and serving on committees, she attended classes taught by her cousin at the Union Theological Seminary. The Woolseys were intensely interested in the abolition of slavery and followed closely the activities leading to the Civil War.

When the war started, Jane joined other family members gathering supplies and making bandages for the Union forces. As a member of the Women's Central Association of Relief, Jane spent the years 1861 to 1865 working in hospitals set up for the sick and wounded troops. She helped organize the New England Rooms and Park Barracks Hospital and worked at the City Hospital on Broadway. In 1862, with her sister George Anna, she went to the Portsmouth Grove (government) Hospital near Newport, Rhode Island, as an assistant supervisor under Katharine Wormeley. This was the first time that women nurses were allowed in U.S. general hospitals in such a responsible capacity. Next, she and George Anna went to Hammond General Hospital at Point Lookout to help organize the nursing service. In 1864 the two sisters were appointed superintendents at the Fairfax Theological Seminary Hospital near Alexandria, Virginia. Jane remained there until the end of the war in August, 1865. Her experiences at the Fairfax Hospital are noted in *Hospital Days*, which was privately printed in 1868.

Jane's wartime acquaintances led her into her next volunteer work. From 1868 until 1872 she was a teacher in charge of girls' industries (housework and needlework) at the Hampton Normal and Agricultural Institute in Hampton, Virginia, which was founded in 1868 by Samual Chapman Armstrong* as an educational institute for Negroes. Besides teaching there, Jane made financial donations for scholarships.

Jane's return from the Hampton Institute coincided with the New York City Presbyterian churches' joint effort to sponsor a hospital. Jane was asked to serve as resident directress. Her task was to provide general supervision of the hospital, which included establishing and organizing the departments. Abby, Jane's older sister, accompanied her as an acting clerk. Since the two sisters were the only workers with hospital experience, they were credited with laying the foundation for a good nursing service. In 1872, when there were few nursing schools in the country, Abby and Jane trained women in the fundamentals of nursing. In addition to serving gratuitously as directress, Jane gave the hospital clothing, books, and linens, and made financial donations to the general and endowment funds. In 1876 she resigned from this position because of poor health. Although she was asked to join the Bellevue Hospital training staff, she declined. Jane's interest then focused on the advisory committee to the New York State Charities Aid Association, of which she was a member.

Through her work Jane discovered that nurses needed to have certain personal characteristics and to be taught their art. As an administrator she was a quick thinker able to act on her ideas. Jane was a pioneer in nursing education, hospital organization, and education for Negroes. She also had a special literary ability and often wrote articles for her causes—the Hampton Institute and Presbyterian Hospital. These articles were usually written anonymously.

Jane died in Matteawan, New York, at the home of her sister, Eliza Howland.

For original records related to the work of Jane Stuart Woolsey, see the Archives of the Presbyterian Hospital in the City of New York. The Woolsey Family Archives are maintained by the family as noted in the entry on Abby Woolsey.

Jane Woolsey's *Hospital Days* (1868) was reprinted in 1970 and is also available on microfiche in *The History of Nursing, Part I* (1982).

The family history and detailed references to their contributions can be found in Anne L. Austin, *The Woolsey Sisters of New York 1860–1900* (1971). Additional information is available in Samual Chapman Armstrong, "The Founding of the Hampton Institute," *Old South Leaflets*, No. 149 6 (1890), 521–535; George Anna Woolsey Bacon and Eliza Woolsey Howland, *Letters of a Family*

*During the War for the Union 1861–1865* (1899); David B. Delavan, *Early Days of the Presbyterian Hospital* (1926); Albert R. Lamb, *The Presbyterian Hospital and the Columbia-Presbyterian Medical Center 1868–1943* (1955); and Meta R. Pennock, *Makers of Nursing History* (1940).

                                                                    LAURIE K. GLASS


**Wright, Helen Russell** (?, 1891–August 14, 1969), social researcher and social work educator, was born in Glenwood, Iowa, to Carlton Clark Wright, a lawyer, and Lucy (Russell) Wright. Like many of the pioneering Chicago social workers and reformers, she sought a college education at one of the prestigious eastern women's schools. Thus, in 1908 she enrolled at Smith College, and four years later she received an A.B. from that institution. Like many graduates of those schools, she developed a sense of mission while there and was attracted to social reform. As a result, she went to Chicago, a hub of such action, and studied economics at the University of Chicago and "social work" under Edith Abbott* and Sophonisba Breckinridge* at the Chicago School of Civics and Philanthropy, one of the first such schools in America. At the latter institution she absorbed and made her own the school's philosophy that the emerging profession of social work should not be dedicated exclusively to the narrow concerns identified with casework, but should actively support social reform, mainly through the applied research so necessary for a solid foundation for such efforts.

Meanwhile, in 1922 Wright received a Ph.D. in economics from the University of Chicago; her dissertation was published later that year under the title, *The Political Labour Movement in Great Britain, 1880–1914*. With doctorate in hand, she received an appointment as a staff member at the Robert Brookings Graduate Institution of Economics, where she conducted research for its famous studies on the nation's capacity to produce goods and its ability—or inability—to purchase them. Then in 1928 when dean Edith Abbott of the University of Chicago's School of Social Service Administration (the former School of Civics and Philanthropy) sought to strengthen its research program, she asked Helen Wright to join the faculty. There, she continued to engage in the applied research necessary for the development of social services and successful social reform, thus continuing along the path laid out by her mentors, Breckinridge and Abbott. She published a number of articles in the *Social Service Review* and elsewhere, including one on "A Year's Expenditures of Ten Railroad Laborers," and another on "The Families of the Unemployed in Chicago." She also conducted several studies for the U.S. Children's Bureau and coauthored, with Walter Hamilton, a book entitled *The Case of Bituminous Coal* (1925).

In 1941 Wright was appointed as Edith Abbott's successor as dean of the School of Social Service Administration, a position she held until 1956. From 1950 to 1956 she also served as editor of the *Social Service Review*, and in 1952 she became the first president of the newly created Council on Social Work Education. With these responsibilities, she gave a great deal of attention to the future of social work in the post–World War II era, publishing a number of articles on that subject as well as others.

At the time of Wright's retirement from the deanship of the School of Social Service Administration in 1956, Charlotte Towle,* a long-time faculty colleague, remarked that she did not know whether it was more difficult to be a pioneer or to follow in the wake of one. Helen Wright was in the latter position—a member of the second generation of Chicago reformers and social workers who followed in the footsteps of such early twentieth-century pioneers as Edith and Grace Abbott,* Sophonisba Breckinridge, Jane Addams,* and others—and she did it extremely well. In the process, she became an important transitional figure in the emerging profession of social work, one who, often against the tide, carried on the reform (as opposed to the casework) tradition.

Upon her retirement in 1956 the Council on Social Work Education asked Wright to head a technical assistance team being sent to India to assist in the development of a school of social work there. Her experience resulted in a book entitled, *Similarities and Differences in Social Work Education As Seen in India and North America*. After her return from India, Wright lived in Pasadena, California, where she continued to conduct research and teach part-time at the University of Southern California. She died in Pasadena, California, on August 14, 1969, after a long illness.

Helen R. Wright's papers are located at the University of Chicago Library, Chicago. Perhaps her most important book not already mentioned in the text is an edited work entitled *Social Service In Wartime* (1944). Most of her publications appeared in the *Social Service Review* in the form of book reviews and articles. Her publications in the 1930s dealt largely with the problems of the Depression while her later work focused on the development of the social work profession. A representative article of her later period is, "Social Work Education Today—Some Questions." *Social Service Review* 25 1950, 74–86. The best piece about Helen Wright appears in *Social Service Review* 43 (1969), 466–467.

ANTHONY R. TRAVIS

# Y

Yarros, Rachelle Slobodinsky (May 18, 1869–March 17, 1946), pioneer in obstetrical education, sex education, and birth control, was born near Kiev, Russia, to Bernice and Joachim Slobodinsky. She was educated in Russian schools, and her affluent parents arranged tutors for her college work, because, as a woman, she could not enter a Russian university. She consistently refused, however, to dissociate herself from radical, egalitarian ideas, which first attracted her in her early teens. At eighteen, facing prospects of banishment because of her beliefs and associations, she fled to the United States.

Unwilling to accept more than passage money from parents whom she could not obey, she worked for two years in a sweatshop in Rahway, New Jersey, before permitting fellow Russian emigrés to assist her in obtaining a medical education. She entered the College of Physicians and Surgeons of Boston (later Tufts) in 1890—the first woman admitted there—and transferred the next year to the Women's Medical College of Pennsylvania, where she took her M.D. in 1893. She interned at the New England Hospital for Women and Children, alongside Alice Hamilton,* and took further work in pediatrics at the New York Infirmary for Women and Children and at Michael Reese Hospital in Chicago.

On July 18, 1894, she married Victor S. Yarros, a political exile from the Ukraine and a radical journalist associated with *Liberty*, a Boston-based journal of American philosophical anarchism. On a lecture trip to Chicago in 1891, Victor had visited the Haymarket survivors in Joliet Prison. The couple decided to settle in Chicago, the site of massive immigration, of the radical labor movement, and of Hull-House, where they lived for twenty years beginning in 1907.

With a range of languages at her command, Yarros readily established a practice on Chicago's densely populated Near West Side. Concentrating on obstetrics and gynecology, she opened a maternity dispensary modeled on the prototype created by her mentor, Anna E. Broomall, in South Philadelphia in 1888. Recognizing the general dearth of practical obstetric instruction in the medical curriculum of the 1890s, Yarros offered her teaching skill and large practice to several medical schools in the Cook County Hospital/Hull-House area. In 1898 she persuaded the dean of the College of Physicians and Surgeons of Chicago (a proprietary medical school soon to become the University of Illinois College of Medicine) to let his students learn obstetrics by assisting her in the home deliveries of patients drawn to her dispensary. Through twelve years of work in what the college called its "Department of Obstetrics in the Ghetto," she brought the most advanced antiseptic obstetric care to poor families, at the same time elevating standards of obstetric teaching and practice among her colleagues and students.

Yarros first became aware of the "ravages of syphilis" while working at the Tewksbury State Institution for the Insane during her vacations as a medical student in Massachusetts. She channeled her concern into the social hygiene movement, advocating sex education and legislation to combat venereal disease and prostitution. As first chairman of social hygiene in the General Federation of Women's Clubs, she addressed groups around the nation on minimum requirements for social hygiene programs and on the need for sex education. A founder of the American Social Hygiene Association in 1914 and of the Illinois Social Hygiene League, organized the following year, she directed social hygiene programs at the city, state, and national levels, serving as special consultant to the U.S. Public Health Service and as lecturer for the Council of National Defense during World War I. In 1926, in recognition of her leadership in this area, the University of Illinois College of Medicine created a professorship of social hygiene for her, providing one of the few regular channels in American medical education for instruction in human sexuality and contraceptive technique.

Yarros began prescribing contraceptives early in her practice, because she recognized frequent pregnancies ("involuntary motherhood") as a major cause of maternal and infant mortality and morbidity—and of poverty, degradation, and a flood of social evils, including abortion. In 1923 she persuaded a number of medically and socially prominent Chicagoans to establish the city's first birth control clinic (preceded only by Margaret Sanger's* in New York and Marie Stopes' in London). When prolonged litigation failed to overcome opposition by Chicago's Commissioner of Health and leading Roman Catholic clergy, Yarros and her co-workers circumvented licensure requirements for "clinics" by opening (in 1924) a "medical center" in the business district, where physicians dispensed contraceptive information and materials to patients who paid nominal fees. Secured against further legal harassment by popular support for this facility, Yarros oversaw the creation of two more "medical centers" in 1925 (one in a thickly populated Polish district, one in connection with the ethical cultural settlement); one in a black district in 1926; and two more in 1927 (one in a Jewish district, one among Italians and Mexicans in connection with the Health Center of Mary Crane Nursery of Hull-House). By 1930, largely because of Yarros' belief that all classes had a right to birth control information and that it must be easily accessible if those who most needed it were to use it, Chicago, with eight birth control clinics, provided more such facilities for its citizens than any other American city.

Yarros wrote only one book, *Modern Woman and Sex* (1933), reissued in 1938 as *Sex Problems in Modern Society* (in a less expensive edition, at her request). It is no less ambitious than the title suggests, reviewing, in a rich context of allusion to various social theorists, the progression of her life's work— from obstetrics and gynecology to contraception and social hygiene to sex education and the premarital, marital, and parental counseling in which she also pioneered. As partial solutions for the problems which had occupied her for over half a century, she called for earlier marriage and easier divorce; but the ultimate reform which she envisioned required nothing less radical than a redefinition of woman's place and a concomitant reevaluation of the role of human sexuality in modern society.

She died in San Diego, California, on March 17, 1946.

The only known manuscripts of Rachelle Yarros are in the collection of the Institute of Sex Education (formerly the Illinois Social Hygiene League) located in Special Collections, University Library, University of Illinois at Chicago. Her faculty records, including a holograph personnel form which she completed in 1919, are located in Special Collections, Library of the Health Sciences, University of Illinois at Chicago.

Her most highly autobiographical articles include "Medical Women of Tomorrow," *Woman's Medical Journal* 26 (1916), 146–149; "Birth Control and Its Relation to Health and Welfare," *Medical Woman's Journal* 32 (1925), 268–272; "The Experiences of a Graduate of 1893," in *Seventy-Fifth Anniversary Volume of the Woman's Medical College of Pennsylvania* (1925?), 184–190; "From Obstetrics to Social Hygiene," *Medical Woman's Journal* 33 (1926), 305–309; "Significance of Birth Control for Race Betterment," *Medical Woman's Journal* 35 (1928), 194–197; and "Women Physicians and the Problems of Women," *Medical Woman's Journal* 50 (1943), 28–30.

A photograph and a brief biographical article containing information omitted from later works appear in Council of Chicago Medical Society, *History of Medicine and Surgery and Physicians and Surgeons of Chicago* (1922), 906. There are several photographs of Victor and Rachelle and scattered references to them both (indexed) in Allen F. Davis and Mary Lynn McCree, *Eighty Years at Hull-House* (1969). Despite several errors, the most satisfactory recent account is by Christopher Lasch in *Notable American Women 1607–1950: A Biographical Dictionary*, vol. 3 (1971), 693–694. A better appreciation of her importance in the birth control movement may be gained from Carolyn Hadley Robinson, *Seventy Birth Control Clinics* (1930), 30, 39 and 47; for data about the Chicago clinics see pp. 15–17 as well as many scattered references. A set of lively personal impressions appears in Barbara Sicherman, *Alice Hamilton: A Life in Letters* (1984), 65–66 and miscellaneous references (all indexed). William F. Snow, a co-worker in the American Social Hygiene Association, composed a presentation brochure on the award to Rachelle Yarros of life membership in the Association, reprinted in the *Medical Woman's Journal* 49 (1942), 194. He also wrote an obituary, *Journal of Social Hygiene* 32 (1946), 184. The University of Illinois Board of Trustees *Report 61* (1981), 259–260, describes the history of the Rachelle S. Yarros Scholarship Fund, established by Victor in 1948 for deserving and needy medical students. Bertha Van Hoosen, an Illinois colleague, wrote two appreciations published in the *Medical Woman's Journal* 39 (1932), 310, and 38 (1931), 10–13; the second of these includes a "toast" by Dr. Charles Sumner Bacon, head of obstetrics, which is the most detailed account available of her faculty career at Illinois.

PATRICIA SPAIN WARD

**Young, Whitney Moore, Jr.** (July 31, 1921–March 11, 1971), social worker, race relations expert, and head of the National Urban League, was born in Lincoln Ridge, Kentucky, the second child and only son of Whitney M. Young, Sr., a black leader in Kentucky and president of Lincoln Institute, and Laura Ray Young, a teacher and postmistress of Lincoln Ridge. His two sisters earned Ph.D. degrees and worked as educators. A sympathetic white woman tutored him until he was nine years old, when he enrolled in a segregated elementary school in nearby Simpsonville, Kentucky. He finished high school at Lincoln Institute and then went on to Kentucky State College for Negroes and the University of Minnesota, where he earned the B.S. and M.A. degrees, respectively, in 1941 and 1947.

Young turned from a potential career in medicine to social work because of poignant racial experiences in the U.S. Army during World War II. While a graduate student he did field work with the Minneapolis Urban League and began a settled married life with his Kentucky State sweetheart, Margaret Buckner, whom he wed in 1944. In 1947 he became the industrial relations secretary of the St. Paul Urban League. After three years Young had helped to integrate the work forces of numerous local firms. In 1950, when he was twenty-nine, the Omaha Urban League appointed him its executive director. In repeats of his St. Paul successes, Young convinced several Omaha businesses to hire the first black cab drivers, stenographers, telephone operators, and architects. He also made attempts to integrate housing and served as an instructor at Creighton University, which helped to prepare him for a later administrative position at Atlanta University.

With his wife and two daughters, Young moved south to serve from 1954 to 1960 as dean of the School of Social Work of Atlanta University. Expanding and integrating the faculty and student body and revamping the curriculum were only a few of Young's numerous activities. He, with other young black professionals, organized the Atlanta Committee for Cooperative Action, which published reports on the racial realities in the city which cast doubt upon its liberal image. A fellowship from the General Education Board to Harvard University during the 1960–1961 academic year preceded his promotion to the executive directorship of the National Urban League.

For the next decade Young led the League in instituting numerous new programs to address critical social and economic needs among Blacks. These efforts included programs to aid black Vietnam War veterans, to develop black leadership in local communities, to promote skilled training for black workers, and to improve housing for urban residents. Never reluctant to propose bold initiatives to remedy racial inequities, Whitney Young developed in 1963 a Domestic Marshall Plan which recommended expenditures of $145 million over a ten-year period to rid the nation of its racial ghettoes. New Thrust, funded by several foundations, allowed the League to reorient its programs on the local level to allow for greater community initiative and input. Young attracted unprecedented financial support to the National Urban League from major corporations and such important agencies as the Ford, Rockefeller, Taconic, Alfred P. Sloan, and Field foundations.

Whitney Young drew the once conservative National Urban League into the thick of the civil rights struggles of the 1960s. The League helped with voter registration, and it helped to plan, and participated in, the massive March on Washington, D.C., in 1963. With Taconic Foundation backing, he was an organizer of the Council for United Civil Rights Leadership, which allocated funds to the Student Nonviolent Coordinating Committee (SNCC), to the Congress of Racial Equality (CORE), to the Southern Christian Leadership Conference (SCLC), and to the National Association for the Advancement of Colored People (NAACP).

No stranger to presidents, Young advised John F. Kennedy, Lyndon Johnson, and Richard Nixon on civil rights matters. His close relationship with Lyndon Johnson allowed him input into the War on Poverty, made him an observer during the Vietnam War to examine the condition of black soldiers, and allowed him to influence several executive and legislative initiatives to strengthen civil rights laws and address the problems of urban America. His effective advocacy of black concerns resulted in $28 million in federal grants to the National Urban League during the Nixon administration, thus leaving the League a legacy of financial solvency and effective leadership for Blacks and other disadvantaged Americans.

A tragic and untimely death awaited Young in Lagos, Nigeria, when, on March 11, 1971, at age forty-nine, he drowned offshore while swimming.

The principal primary sources on Young's life and career are the Whitney M. Young, Jr. Collection at Columbia University, New York City, and the Records of the National Urban League at the Library of Congress in Washington, D.C. Useful references to Young can also be found in the Rockefeller Foundation and Rockefeller Brothers Fund Records at the Rockefeller Archive Center in North Tarrytown, New York, and in the Records of the NAACP at the Library of Congress. General information about Young can be obtained from the following secondary sources: obituary notice, *New York Times* (March 12, 1971); Richard Bruner, *Whitney M. Young, Jr.* (1972); Nancy J. Weiss, "Whitney M. Young, Jr.: Committing the Power Structure to the Cause of Civil Rights," in John Hope Franklin and August Meier, *Black Leaders of the Twentieth Century* (1982). An introduction to Young's approach to race relations is contained in his books *To Be Equal* (1964), and *Beyond Racism* (1969).

DENNIS C. DICKERSON

**Youngdahl, Benjamin Emanuel** (July 12, 1897–September 18, 1970), public welfare administrator, social work educator, and lecturer, the son of first-generation immigrants, was born in Minneapolis, Minnesota, into a large Swedish Lutheran family. His parents, Elizabeth (Johnson) Youngdahl and John Carl Youngdahl, each had two children from prior, death-abbreviated marriages, and it was into this combined family that Benjamin Youngdahl was born. Providing for so large a family, which eventually totalled ten children, was no mean task. John Youngdahl operated the family's grocery store with the help of Elizabeth and the children, who procured fruits and berries from the family's vacation home west of the city and shipped the produce to the Minneapolis store.

Early on the Youngdahl parents stressed to their children the importance of industry, integrity, self-discipline, respect and humane concern for others, and above all, religious piety. The home environment was strict with heavy emphasis laid on rigorous religious observance: drinking, smoking, card-playing, and other "wayward" amusements (including sports) were equally shunned. If Youngdahl did not retain the more stringent moral precepts of his upbringing, his professional life evidenced deeply-held principles formed in these early years, especially a strong social conscience and a belief in the desirability of resolute action based on firm personal conviction.

While wordly pleasures and pursuits were frowned upon, healthy family disputation was not, nor it seems was competitive rivalry between the children. By the time Benjamin Youngdahl graduated from Minneapolis's South High School in 1916, he evinced a keen interest in public speaking, no doubt stimulated by a lively and challenging family setting.

Always encouraged by parents who believed in the value of education, Youngdahl commenced study at Gustavus Adolphus College, in St. Peter, Minnesota, in 1917, where he participated successfully in forensics and oratorical competition. Upon graduation in 1920, Youngdahl journeyed to New York City to observe living conditions there, an experience that apparently validated his growing interest in social service and heightened his sensitivity to social problems.

In 1923 Youngdahl earned a Master's degree from Columbia University, a degree he pursued after serving as a high school principal, and then, superintendent of schools in rural Marietta, Minnesota during the years 1921–1922. Youngdahl then assumed a professorship in sociology and economics at his undergraduate institution, a post he held until 1933. There he met Livia Alexandra Bjorkquist, one of his students, and the two were married in August 1925. Their marriage produced three sons, James, Kent, and Mark.

The exigencies of the Depression propelled Youngdahl into a leading role in Minnesota welfare administration as social programs were created to provide relief assistance. In 1933 he was appointed director of social service for the State

Emergency Relief Administration, and then, in 1937, director of public assistance under the State Board of Control. These were stormy years, embroiled with controversy surrounding the state's welfare program. Youngdahl became a convinced and passionate New Dealer, a firm believer in national and state responsibility for relief provision and full employment, particularly as local units of government were unable to do so adequately. This stand made Youngdahl suspect to many, even revolutionary to some, who opposed the expansion of government services during this period.

Impatient with those who maligned the new social initiatives as promoting abuse, corruption, and "chiselers," Youngdahl defended their integrity based on the individual's "right" to relief assistance rather than the largesse of charity. Central to his thinking during these years was the notion that changing historical circumstances demanded the overhaul of outmoded, moral-individualistic responses to social deprivation in a complex, modern society—an idea that would continue to profoundly shape Youngdahl's evolving social work philosophy in his later role as a social work educator. When the Minnesota welfare structure was reorganized in 1939, Youngdahl resigned. Although a likely candidate to head the state's revamped welfare system, Youngdahl was passed over for largely political reasons.

Shortly thereafter Youngdahl became an associate professor of social work at Washington University's George Warren Brown School of Social Work, in St. Louis, Missouri, where he remained until his death in 1970. Ever open to new challenges and responsibilities, Youngdahl accepted appointment as dean of the School of Social Work in 1945, taking over for the retiring Frank J. Bruno, and continuing in that position until 1962. It was as a social work educator that Youngdahl made the most decisive impact on the social work profession. During these years Youngdahl traveled and spoke widely in social work circles, exerting leadership as president of three social work bodies, the American Association of Schools of Social Work (1947–1948), the American Association of Social Workers (1951–1953), and the National Conference on Social Welfare (1955–1956).

As dean, Youngdahl worked to upgrade standards of professional training, and to develop an integrated curriculum, a core of social work education that might mitigate the centrifugal impact of specialization. Thus he always aimed to maintain a vision of a unified social work mission. Under Youngdahl's administration, the School of Social Work's enrollment doubled, a doctoral program was established, and scholarship monies were expanded. In 1947, with Youngdahl leading the way, the School of Social Work became the first division of Washington University to admit black students.

Unwilling to separate social work from social and political action, Youngdahl consistently admonished students of social work, as well as the larger social work community, to boldly move out into broader fields of application, even if doing so entailed swimming against the tide of popular opinion or accepted wisdom. He called into question the status quo tendencies of the casework method, urging more positive preventive strategies, along with collective work, to change people's social and economic circumstances, though he never completely repudiated the individual-oriented casework approach. Mindful of the dangers of bland conformism and political consensus, Youngdahl was an outspoken critic of McCarthyism, with its pressure tactics and other attempts to suppress civil rights.

Benjamin Youngdahl's speech, "Courage as a 'Method' of Social Work," first delivered in 1961, appropriately summarized and symbolized the importance of his life and work. Maintaining that detached apathy marked the greatest tragedy of the time, Youngdahl identified courage—the inner strength to act upon conviction—as the indispensable ingredient for true, effective social work. His message to social workers was clear: select a cause and stand up for it. By his own courage, Youngdahl earned a reputation as the conscience of the social work community. He died in St. Louis, Missouri, September 18, 1970.

Manuscript sources dealing with Benjamin Youngdahl's life and professional career can be located in papers of Benjamin E. Youngdahl (includes one supplement), Louis H. Towley, and the National Association of Social Workers, all on deposit at the Social Welfare History Archives, University of Minnesota, Minneapolis, Minnesota.

Youngdahl's articles and speeches can be found in numerous journals and publications. They include "Social Workers: Stand Up and Be Counted," *The Compass* (1947); "Shall We Face It?" *Social Work Journal* (1948); "Social Work as a Profession" *Social Work Year Book* (1949, repr. 1951); "The Role of Social Agencies in Social Action" *Social Work Journal* (1952); "Social Work at the Crossroads" *Social Work Journal* (1953); and "Leadership in a Graduate School of Social Work" *Proceedings, Education for Social Work* (1962), among others. Most of these, along with many of his other articles and addresses, are gathered in Youngdahl's book *Social Action and Social Work* (1966). Youngdahl's addresses at the National Conference of Social Work are transcribed in its *Proceedings*, 1937–1956.

For useful information regarding Benjamin Youngdahl's family background, Robert Esbjornson's biography of Youngdahl's brother Luther (former governor of Minnesota), *A Christian in Politics: Luther W. Youngdahl* (1955), can be consulted, especially chapter two. Youngdahl is mentioned in *Who Was Who in America*, vol. 5 (1973). An obituary notice appeared in the *St. Louis Post-Dispatch*, September 19, 1970, 9A.

                                                        RICHARD M. CHAPMAN

# Z

**Zimand, Gertrude Folks** (September 28, 1894–May 10, 1966), child welfare advocate and reformer, was born in New York City, the second of three daughters of Maud (Beard) Folks and Homer Folks.* Her mother, who taught school briefly before her marriage, was a strong champion of woman's suffrage, and her father was quite a well-known reformer. In fact, when Gertrude was nine years old, her father participated in the formation of the National Child Labor Committee (NCLC), for which Gertrude was to work much of her career. Homer Folks was secretary of the State Charities Aid Association in New York and later chairman of the NCLC. Her father was also a leader in the public health movement and the mental hygiene movement. Gertrude married Savel Zimand, a Rumanian journalist and health educator. They were married on March 8, 1926, and had two children, Harvey Folks and Rhoda Folks (Bernstein).

During her high school years Gertrude was active in the girls' debating society. Upon graduation from high school in 1911, she left on a year-long tour of Europe, which was cut short by her grandmother's illness. She then enrolled at Vassar, where she was again active in the debating society and also was founder and president of two groups, the local Intercollegiate Socialist Society and the local Suffrage Club. After her graduation from Vassar in 1916, she joined the National Child Labor Committee (NCLC) as a field investigator.

From 1917 to 1919 she took a leave from the NCLC to spend time in Europe. Although she considered herself a pacifist at the time, she used some prize money awarded to her at Vassar to travel to Europe to work with the American Committee for Devastated France. She helped to reestablish villages that had been destroyed during the war. For a short time she also served as her father's secretary while he was director of the Department of Civil Affairs of the American Red Cross in France. Unfortunately, she became ill with pneumonia and had to return home. During the next few years she worked as a social worker for one year and taught sociology at the University of Cincinnati for three years.

In 1926 she rejoined the NCLC as director of research and publicity. Only four years later, Lillian Wald* recommended Zimand as executive director of the organization but she declined the offer because she was expecting her second child at the time. But in 1932 she accepted the position of associate general secretary and ultimately became executive director of the NCLC from 1943 to 1955, when she retired. While at the NCLC she also edited the *American Child*.

With her creative imagination and deep understanding of the needs of children, her years with the NCLC were productive ones. She broadened the purpose of the Committee to include vocational guidance, work experience, compulsory school attendance, and improved opportunities for young people. She campaigned for state laws to reduce work days for fourteen- and fifteen-year-old children to eight hours and advocated a federal child labor amendment to the Constitution.

Although she was considered by many to be one of the major contributors toward the elimination of child labor, as that evil declined Zimand became increasingly concerned with "early school leavers." She conducted two field studies to understand the problem, one in 1946 on part-time school and work programs, and another in 1949 on experiences of children who left school for work. Her research was published in two volumes as *Young Workers in the United States* (1953) and *Young Workers and Their Vocational Needs* (1955).

Always interested in the needs of children, she actively participated in the Parent-Teachers Association (PTA) of the Friends' Seminary, the school her children attended from kindergarten to high school graduation. As president and vice president of the group, she sought benefits and salary increases for the teaching staff. She was a leading participant in the White House Conferences on Children and was largely responsible for transforming the National Child Labor Committee into the National Committee on Employment of Youth. In addition, she assisted in the organization and was a member of the board of trustees of the Social Welfare Information Service. She also served as its secretary for more than ten years.

Her major contributions were through her work with the NCLC, and even after her retirement in 1955 she continued to be a trustee of the organization. Once asked to sum up her philosophy of life, she responded succinctly, "Compassion and justice." After a life that exemplified these qualities, Gertrude Folks Zimand died in New York City at the age of seventy-one.

The papers of Gertrude Folks Zimand, 1915–1966, are located at the Social Welfare History Archives, University of Minnesota, Minneapolis, Minnesota. For the most part they cover her years with the National Child Labor Committee and her work with the PTA of the Friends' Seminary. The papers of her husband, Savel Zimand, 1917–1959, 1967, are also located in the Social Welfare History Archives. Savel Zimand wrote a short biography of his wife entitled *Gertrude Folks Zimand, A Tribute* (1967), which is located in his collection.

Zimand's major writings included *Children in the Theatre* (1941), *Young Workers in the United States* (1953), and *Young Workers and Their Vocational Needs* (1955). An article entitled "Child Labor and the Future" appeared in the *New Republic* on March 21, 1928.

JEAN K. QUAM

# A Brief Chronology of Significant Events in American Social Welfare History

| | |
|---|---|
| 1601 | Passage of the English Poor Law (An Act for the Relief of the Poor, 43 Elizabeth) |
| 1642 | Enactment of the Plymouth Colony's Poor Law—the first in the northern colonies |
| 1646 | Enactment of the Virginia Colony's Poor Law—the first in the southern colonies |
| 1657 | Creation of the Scots Charitable Society, America's first private charitable society |
| 1676 | Passage, in Massachusetts, of the colonies' first statute concerned with providing special care for the mentally ill |
| 1729 | Establishment of the colonies' first children's institution (for girls at the Ursuline convent in New Orleans) |
| 1751 | Establishment of the (Philadelphia) Pennsylvania Hospital |
| 1773 | Establishment of the Williamsburg, Virginia, State Hospital |
| 1790 | Creation of America's first public children's institution (in Charleston, South Carolina) |
| 1818 | Passage of the Revolutionary War Pension Act |
| 1824 | Issuance of the Yates Report (on the operation of the Poor Laws in New York State) |
| | Passage of the New York State County Poorhouse Act |
| | Creation of the (New York) House of Refuge for Juvenile Delinquents |
| 1843 | Creation of the New York Association for Improving the Condition of the Poor |
| 1853 | Creation of the New York Children's Aid Society |
| 1854 | President Franklin Pierce's veto of the so-called Dix Bill ("An Act Making a Grant of Public Lands to the Several States for the Benefit of Indigent Insane Persons") |
| 1861 | Passage, in Ohio, of the first state law mandating the removal of children from county almshouses |

| | |
|---|---|
| | Creation of the U.S. Sanitary Commission |
| 1863 | Creation of the Massachusetts Board of State Charities (or State Board of Charities) |
| 1865 | Creation of the U.S. Freedmen's Bureau (or Bureau for the Relief of Freedmen and Refugees) |
| 1866 | Creation of the first real municipal board of health (in New York City) |
| 1869 | Creation of the first state board of health (in Massachusetts) |
| 1874 | Creation of the National Conference of Charities and Correction (later known as the National Conference of Social Work and the National Conference on Social Welfare) |
| 1877 | Creation of the Buffalo Charity Organization, America's first such agency |
| 1886 | Creation of Neighborhood Guild, America's first settlement house |
| 1889 | Jane Addams opens Hull-House in Chicago |
| 1890 | Passage of the New York State Care Act |
| 1894 | Publication of Amos Warner's *American Charities* |
| 1898 | Creation (by the New York Charity Organization Society) of America's first "training school" for social workers |
| 1899 | Creation of America's first juvenile court (in Chicago) |
| 1904 | Publication of Robert Hunter's *Poverty* |
| | Creation of the National Association for the Study and Prevention of Tuberculosis (National Tuberculosis Association) |
| 1908 | Publication of Clifford Beers' *A Mind That Found Itself* |
| | Establishment of the Connecticut Society for Mental Hygiene |
| 1909 | Creation of the National Committee for Mental Hygiene (National Association for Mental Health) |
| | Creation of the Juvenile Psychopathic Institute (in Chicago) |
| | First (decennial) White House Conference on Dependent Children is held |
| | Creation of the National Association for the Advancement of Colored People (NAACP) |
| 1910 | Creation of the National Urban League |
| 1911 | Passage of America's first widows' pension (or mothers' aid) laws—in Missouri and Illinois |
| 1912 | Creation of the U.S. Children's Bureau |
| 1917 | Publication of Mary Richmond's *Social Diagnosis* |
| | Establishment of the American Red Cross' Home Service Division |
| 1920 | Creation of the Association of Training Schools of Professional Social Work (which, in 1952, became the Council on Social Work Education) |
| | Creation of the U.S. Veterans Bureau |
| 1921 | Passage of the Sheppard-Towner Act ("An Act for the Promotion of the Welfare and Hygiene of Maternity and Infancy") |

Creation of the American Association of Social Workers (which, in 1955, became the National Association of Social Workers)

1931    Passage of the New York State Unemployment Relief (or Wicks) Act

1933    Passage of the Federal Emergency Relief Act

Creation of the Civil Works Administration

1934    Establishment of President Franklin D. Roosevelt's Committee on Economic Security

1935    Passage of the Social Security Act

1941    Issuance of President Franklin D. Roosevelt's Executive Order 8802, which barred racial discrimination in the defense industries and established a Federal Fair Employment Practices Committee

1944    Passage of the Servicemen's Readjustment Act, or "G.I. Bill of Rights"

1946    Passage of the National Mental Health Act

1950    Social Security Act is amended to provide aid to the permanently and totally disabled

1953    Creation of the U.S. Department of Health, Education and Welfare

1956    Disability insurance is added to the Social Security system

1962    Publication of Michael Harrington's *The Other America: Poverty in the United States*

Passage of the Public Welfare (or "Social Service") Amendments to the Social Security Act

1964    Passage of the U.S. Civil Rights Act

Passage of the Economic Opportunity Act, launching the so-called War on Poverty

Passage of the Food Stamp Act

1965    Passage of the "Medicare" and "Medicaid" Amendments to the Social Security Act

1967    Creation of the National Welfare Rights Organization

U.S. Supreme Court's decision—*In Re Gault et al.*, 387 U.S. 1 (1967)—regarding children's rights in juvenile courts

Establishment of the Work Incentive Program (WIN)

1969    President Richard Nixon's proposed Family Assistance Plan (FAP)

1971    Passage of the Talmadge Amendments (or WIN II) to the Social Security Act

1972    Adoption of the Supplemental Security Income Program (SSI)

1977    President Jimmy Carter's proposed "Better Jobs and Income Program" (BJIP)

1982    President Ronald Reagan's call for a "New Federalism"

# A Listing of Subjects by Year of Birth

| | |
|---|---|
| 1663 | Mather, Cotton |
| 1691 | Douglass, William |
| 1706 | Franklin, Benjamin |
| 1713 | Bond, Thomas |
| 1720 | Woolman, John |
| 1746 | Rush, Benjamin |
| 1750 | Girard, Stephen |
| 1758 | Eddy, Thomas |
| 1760 | Carey, Matthew |
| 1774 | Griscom, John |
| 1778 | Tuckerman, Joseph |
| 1784 | Augustus, John |
| 1787 | Gallaudet, Thomas Hopkins |
| | Woodward, Samuel Bayard |
| 1793 | Shattuck, Lemuel |
| 1796 | Hartley, Robert Milham |
| 1798 | Brigham, Amariah |
| 1801 | Howe, Samuel Gridley |
| 1802 | Dix, Dorothea Lynde |
| 1806 | Wines, Enoch Cobb |
| 1808 | Bowditch, Henry Ingersoll |
| 1813 | Allen, Nathan |
| 1814 | Bellows, Henry Whitney |
| 1821 | Blackwell, Elizabeth |
| | Barton, Clara (Clarissa Harlowe) |
| 1822 | Hale, Edward Everett |
| | Hoyt, Charles S. |

| 1823 | Letchworth, William Pryor |
|------|--------------------------|
|      | Smith, Stephen |
| 1824 | Harris, Elisha |
| 1826 | Brace, Charles Loring |
| 1827 | Brockway, Zebulon Reed |
| 1828 | Woolsey, Abby Howland |
| 1836 | Howard, Oliver Otis |
|      | Jacobi, Abraham |
|      | Woolsey, Jane Stuart |
| 1831 | Sanborn, Franklin Benjamin |
| 1833 | Woolsey, George Anna Muirson |
| 1835 | Paine, Robert Treat |
| 1837 | Flower, Lucy Louisa |
|      | Gallaudet, Edward Miner |
|      | Gerry, Elbridge Thomas |
|      | Schuyler, Louisa Lee |
| 1838 | Billings, John Shaw |
|      | Fletcher, Alice Cunningham |
|      | Wines, Frederick Howard |
| 1839 | Armstrong, Samuel Chapman |
|      | Campbell, Helen Stuart |
|      | Morgan, Thomas Jefferson |
|      | Tucker, William Jewett |
| 1840 | Pratt, Richard Henry |
| 1842 | McLaughlin, James |
| 1843 | Lowell, Josephine Shaw |
|      | McCulloch, Oscar Carleton |
| 1845 | Barrows, Isabel Hayes Chapin |
|      | Barrows, Samuel June |
| 1846 | Brooks, John Graham |
|      | White, Alfred Tredway |
| 1847 | Bell, Alexander Graham |
|      | Bradford, Cornelia Foster |
|      | Johnson, Alexander |
| 1848 | de Forest, Robert Weeks |
|      | Henderson, Charles Richmond |
| 1849 | Riis, Jacob August |
|      | Stevens, Alzina Parsons |

1851       Hart, Hastings Hornell
           Taylor, Graham
1852       Cutting, Robert Fulton
           Smith, Zilpha Drew
1854       McDowell, Mary Eliza
1855       Holt, Luther Emmett
           Dodge, Josephine Marshall Jewell
           Mulry, Thomas Maurice
           Williams, Fannie Barrier
1856       Chapin, Charles Value
           Dodge, Grace Hoadley
           Evans, Elizabeth Glendower
           Washington, Booker T.
1857       Barrett, Katherine (Kate) Waller
           Chapin, Henry Dwight
           Coit, Stanton
           Coman, Katharine
           Cooley, Harris Reed
           Knopf, Siegmund Adolphus
1858       Dudley, Helena Stuart
           Eastman (Ohiyesa), Charles Alexander
           Glenn, John Mark
           Kander, Elizabeth (Lizzie) Black
           Lathrop, Julia Clifford
1859       Biggs, Hermann Michael
           Bowen, Louise deKoven
           Fernald, Walter Elmore
           Kehew, Mary Morton Kimball
           Kelley, Florence
           Osborne, Thomas Mott
           Pinckney, Merritt Willis
           Reeder, Rudolph Rex
           Smith, Theobald
           Starr, Ellen Gates
1860       Addams, Jane
           Birtwell, Charles
           Boardman, Mabel Thorp
           Brackett, Jeffrey Richardson

                Davis, Katharine Bement

                Gould, Elgin Ralston Lovell

1861          Ayres, Philip Wheelock

                Reynolds, James B.

                Richmond, Mary Ellen

                Scudder, Vida Dutton

                Stover, Charles B.

                Warner, Amos Griswold

1862          Commons, John Rogers

                Falconer, Martha Platt

                Lee, Joseph

                Nathan, Maud

                Wells-Barnett, Ida Bell

1863          Finley, John Huston

                Purdy, Lawson

                Terrell, Mary Church

1864          Kohut, Rebekah Bettelheim

1865          Carstens, Christian Carl

                Ovington, Mary White

                Woods, Robert Archey

1866          Barnum, Gertrude

                Breckinridge, Sophonisba

                Dummer, Ethel Sturges

                Goddard, Henry Herbert

                Levin, Louis Hiram

                Lovejoy, Owen Reed

                Mack, Julian William

                McKelway, Alexander J.

                McMain, Eleanor Laura

                Meyer, Adolf

1867          Balch, Emily Greene

                Devine, Edward Thomas

                Farrand, Livingston

                Folks, Homer

                Frankel, Lee Kaufman

                Hodder, Jessie Donaldson

                Pratt, Anna Beach

                Simkhovitch, Mary Melinda Kingsbury

Stokes, Isaach Newton Phelps
Wald, Lillian D.
1868    Cabot, Richard Clarke
Du Bois, William Edward Burghardt
Elliott, John Lovejoy
Follett, Mary Parker
Gavit, John Palmer
Pettit, Katherine Rhoda
Robins, Margaret Dreier
1869    Glenn, Mary Wilcox
Hamilton, Alice
Healy, William
Lindsay, Samuel McCune
Lindsey, Benjamin Barr
McLean, Francis Herbert
Murphy, Edgar Gardner
Regan, Agnes Gertrude
Ryan, John Augustine
Williams, Elizabeth Sprague
Yarros, Rachelle Slobodinsky
1870    Kerby, William Joseph
Kingsbury, Susan Myra
Lothrop, Alice Louisa Higgins
O'Reilly, Leonora
White, William Alanson
1871    Park, Maud Wood
Wood, Edith Elmer
1872    Alger, George William
Anderson, Mary
Bernstein, Charles
Stokes, James Graham Phelps
Veiller, Lawrence Turnure
1873    Baker, Sara Josephine
Brandt, Lilian
Kellor, Frances
McCarthy, Charles
Robins, Raymond
1874    Goldmark, Pauline Dorothea

|      |                                    |
|------|------------------------------------|
|      | Hine, Lewis Wickes                 |
|      | Hunter, Robert                     |
|      | Wise, Stephen Samuel               |
| 1875 | Barnard, Kate                      |
|      | Bethune, Mary McLeod               |
|      | Branch, Anna Hempstead             |
|      | Rubinow, Isaac Max                 |
| 1876 | Abbott, Edith                      |
|      | Beers, Clifford Whittingham        |
|      | Burns, Allen Tibbals               |
|      | Dewson, Mary (Molly) Williams      |
|      | Hoyt, Franklin Chase               |
|      | Kingsbury, John Adams              |
|      | Mangold, George Benjamin           |
|      | Salmon, Thomas William             |
|      | White, Eartha M.                   |
| 1877 | Cannon, Ida Maud                   |
|      | Goldmark, Josephine Clara          |
|      | Jarrett, Mary Cromwell             |
|      | Lowenstein, Solomon                |
|      | Moskowitz, Belle                   |
|      | Walling, William English           |
|      | Winslow, Charles-Edward Amory      |
| 1878 | Abbott, Grace                      |
|      | Burritt, Bailey Barton             |
|      | Kellogg, Arthur Piper              |
|      | Vaile, Gertrude                    |
| 1879 | Clopper, Edward Nicholas           |
|      | Davis, Michael Marks, Jr.          |
|      | Dinwiddie, Emily Wayland           |
|      | Holbrook, David Helm               |
|      | Holmes, John Haynes                |
|      | Kellogg, Paul Underwood            |
|      | Kennedy, Albert Joseph             |
|      | Lee, Porter Raymond                |
|      | Sanger, Margaret                   |
|      | Springer, Gertrude Hill            |
| 1880 | Andrews, John Bertram              |

|      | |
|------|--|
|      | Armstrong, Barbara Nachtrieb |
|      | Divine, Father |
|      | Haynes, George Edmund |
|      | Keller, Helen |
|      | Moskowitz, Henry |
|      | Nestor, Agnes |
|      | Perkins, Frances |
|      | Taylor, Graham Romeyn |
| 1881 | Bronner, Augusta Fox |
|      | Christman, Elisabeth |
|      | Eastman, Crystal |
|      | Fitch, John Andrews |
|      | Gruenberg, Sidonie Matzner |
|      | Harrison, Shelby Millard |
|      | Hope, Lugenia Burns |
|      | Kaplan, Mordecai Menachem |
|      | Mallery, Otto Tod |
|      | Murphy, J. Prentice |
| 1882 | Bookman, Clarence Monroe |
|      | Bruere, Henry |
|      | Colcord, Joanna Carver |
|      | Pink, Louis Heaton |
|      | Rippin, Jane Parker Deeter |
|      | Schneiderman, Rachel Rose |
|      | Schulze, Oskar |
|      | Taft, Julia Jessie |
| 1883 | Billikopf, Jacob |
|      | Leiserson, William Morris |
|      | Robinson, Virginia Pollard |
|      | Taylor, Lea Demarest |
|      | Van Kleeck, Mary Abby |
| 1884 | Alexander, Will W. |
|      | Baldwin, Roger Nash |
|      | Cannon, Marie Antoinette |
|      | Collier, John |
|      | Roosevelt, Anna Eleanor |
| 1885 | Bremer, Edith Terry |
|      | Cohn, Fannia Mary |

|      |                                        |
|------|----------------------------------------|
|      | Lindeman, Eduard Christian             |
|      | Muste, Abraham Johannes                |
|      | Reynolds, Bertha Capen                 |
|      | Woerishoffer, Emma Carola              |
| 1886 | O'Grady, John                          |
|      | Roche, Josephine Aspinwall             |
| 1887 | Brown, Josephine Chapin                |
|      | Deardorff, Neva Ruth                   |
|      | de Schweinitz, Karl                    |
|      | Garvey, Malcus (Marcus) Mosiah, Jr.    |
|      | Van Waters, Miriam                     |
|      | Witte, Edwin E.                        |
|      | Woodward, Ellen Sullivan               |
| 1888 | Chapin, Francis Stuart                 |
|      | Peck, Lillie M.                        |
|      | Swift, Linton Bishop                   |
| 1889 | West, Walter Mott                      |
| 1890 | Carr, Charlotte Elizabeth              |
|      | Hopkins, Harry Lloyd                   |
|      | Street, Elwood Vickers                 |
|      | Williams, Aubrey Willis                |
| 1891 | Altmeyer, Arthur Joseph                |
|      | Eliot, Martha May                      |
|      | Hodson, William                        |
|      | Kraft, Louis                           |
|      | Lenroot, Katharine Fredrica            |
|      | Wright, Helen Russell                  |
| 1892 | Coyle, Grace Longwood                  |
|      | Dinwiddie, Courtenay                   |
|      | Epstein, Abraham                       |
|      | Hall, Helen                            |
|      | Hamilton, Amy Gordon                   |
|      | Hoey, Jane M.                          |
|      | Lewisohn, Irene                        |
|      | Lurie, Harry Lawrence                  |
| 1893 | Ballard, Russell Ward                  |
|      | Bane, Frank                            |
|      | Buell, Bradley                         |

# A Listing of Subjects by Place of Birth

## THE UNITED STATES

### Alabama

| | |
|---|---|
| Dunn, Loula Friend | Grove Hill |
| Keller, Helen | Tuscumbia |
| Williams, Aubrey | Springville |

### Arkansas

| | |
|---|---|
| Haynes, George Edmund | Pine Bluff |
| Murphy, Edgar Gardner | near Fort Smith |

### California

| | |
|---|---|
| Armstrong, Barbara Nachtrieb | San Francisco |
| Kingsbury, Susan Myra | San Pablo |
| Mack, Julian William | San Francisco |
| McLean, Francis Herbert | Oakland |
| Regan, Agnes Gertrude | San Francisco |

### Connecticut

| | |
|---|---|
| Beers, Clifford Whittingham | New Haven |
| Brace, Charles Loring | Litchfield |
| Branch, Anna Hempstead | New London |
| Brockway, Zebulon Reed | Lyme |
| Dodge, Josephine Marshall Jewell | Hartford |
| Gallaudet, Edward Miner | Hartford |
| Hoyt, Charles S. | Ridgefield |
| Taylor, Lea Demarest | Hartford |
| Tucker, William Jewett | Griswold |
| Woodward, Samuel Bayard | Torrington |

**Florida**

White, Eartha M.                                          Jacksonville

**Georgia**

Collier, John                                            Atlanta
King, Martin Luther, Jr.                                 Atlanta
White, Walter Francis                                    Atlanta

**Illinois**

Addams, Jane                                             Cedarville
Alinsky, Saul David                                      Chicago
Ballard, Russell Ward                                    Donnellson
Barnum, Gertrude                                         Chester
Bowen, Louise deKoven                                    Chicago
Buell, Bradley                                           Chicago
Dummer, Ethel Sturges                                    Chicago
Elliott, John Lovejoy                                    Princeton
Finley, John Huston                                      Grand Ridge
Harrison, Shelby Millard                                 Leaf River
Lathrop, Julia Clifford                                  Rockford
Pinckney, Merritt Willis                                 Mount Morris
Richmond, Mary Ellen                                     Belleville
Starr, Ellen Gates                                       near Laona

**Indiana**

Billings, John Shaw                                      Cotton Township
Brandt, Lilian                                           Indianapolis
Deardorff, Neva Ruth                                     Hagerstown
Henderson, Charles Richmond                              Covington
Hunter, Robert                                           Terre Haute
Morgan, Thomas Jefferson                                 Franklin
Vaile, Gertrude                                          Kokomo

**Iowa**

Ayres, Philip Wheelock                                   Winterset
Devine, Edward Thomas                                    near Union
Hopkins, Harry Lloyd                                     Sioux City
Kerby, William Joseph                                    Lawler
Mangold, George Benjamin                                 Waupeton
Taft, Julia Jessie                                       Dubuque
Warner, Amos Griswold                                    Elkader
Wright, Helen Russell                                    Glenwood

## Kansas

| | |
|---|---|
| Kingsbury, John Adams | Horton |
| Springer, Gertrude Hill | Grant County |

## Kentucky

| | |
|---|---|
| Breckinridge, Sophonisba | Lexington |
| Bronner, Augusta Fox | Louisville |
| Pettit, Katherine Rhoda | near Lexington |
| Robinson, Virginia Pollard | Louisville |
| Walling, William English | Louisville |
| Young, Whitney Moore, Jr. | Lincoln Ridge |

## Louisiana

| | |
|---|---|
| McMain, Eleanor Laura | near Baton Rouge |
| Wisner, Elizabeth | Delhi |

## Maine

| | |
|---|---|
| Dix, Dorothea Lynde | Hampden |
| Fernald, Walter Elmore | Kittery |
| Goddard, Henry Herbert | Vassalboro |
| Howard, Oliver Otis | Leeds |
| Stevens, Alzina Parsons | Parsonsfield |

## Maryland

| | |
|---|---|
| Bond, Thomas | Calvert County |
| Glenn, John Mark | Baltimore |
| Glenn, Mary Wilcox | Baltimore |
| Jarrett, Mary Cromwell | Baltimore |

## Massachusetts

| | |
|---|---|
| Allen, Nathan | Princeton |
| Augustus, John | Woburn |
| Balch, Emily Greene | Jamaica Plain |
| Baldwin, Roger Nash | Wellesley |
| Barton, Clara (Clarissa Harlowe) | North Oxford |
| Bellows, Henry Whitney | Boston |
| Birtwell, Charles | Lawrence |
| Bowditch, Henry Ingersoll | Salem |
| Brackett, Jeffrey Richardson | Quincy |
| Brigham, Amariah | Marlboro |
| Burns, Allen Tibbals | Haverhill |

Cabot, Richard Clarke                        Brookline
Coyle, Grace Longwood                        North Adams
Dewson, Mary (Molly) Williams                Quincy
Du Bois, William Edward Burghardt            Great Barrington
Eastman, Crystal                             Marlborough
Eliot, Martha May                            Dorchester
Flower, Lucy Louisa                          probably Boston
Follett, Mary Parker                         Quincy
Franklin, Benjamin                           Boston
Hale, Edward Everett                         Boston
Howe, Samuel Gridley                         Boston
Kehew, Mary Morton Kimball                   Boston
Lee, Joseph                                  Brookline
Lothrop, Alice Louise Higgins                West Roxbury
Lowell, Josephine Shaw                       Boston
McCarthy, Charles                            near Bridgewater (later
                                               Brockton)

Mather, Cotton                               Boston
Paine, Robert Treat                          Boston
Park, Maud Wood                              Boston
Perkins, Frances                             Boston
Raushenbush, Elizabeth Brandeis              Boston
Reynolds, Bertha Capen                       Brockton
Shattuck, Lemuel                             Ashby
Simkhovitch, Mary Melinda Kingsbury          Chestnut Hill
Smith, Zilpha Drew                           Pembroke
Switzer, Mary Elizabeth                      Newton Upper Falls
Tuckerman, Joseph                            Boston
Winslow, Charles-Edward Amory                Boston


## Michigan

Folks, Homer                                 Hanover
Kellogg, Arthur Piper                        Kalamazoo
Kellogg, Paul Underwood                      Kalamazoo
Lindeman, Eduard Christian                   St. Claire
Lovejoy, Owen Reed                           Jamestown
Nestor, Agnes                                Grand Rapids


## Minnesota

de Schweinitz, Karl                          Northfield
Eastman (Ohiyesa) Charles Alexander          n.a.
Hodson, William                              Minneapolis
McLaughlin, James                            Wabasha
Ryan, John Augustine                         Dakota County

| | |
|---|---|
| Swift, Linton Bishop | St. Paul |
| West, Walter Mott | Faribault |
| Youngdahl, Benjamin | Minneapolis |

## Mississippi

| | |
|---|---|
| Wells-Barnett, Ida Bell | Holly Springs |
| Woodward, Ellen Sullivan | Oxford |

## Missouri

| | |
|---|---|
| Alexander, Will W. | Morrisville |
| Bruere, Henry | St. Charles |
| Dunham, Arthur | St. Louis |
| Hall, Helen | Kansas City |
| Hope, Lugenia Burns | St. Louis |

## Montana

| | |
|---|---|
| Towle, Charlotte Helen | Butte |

## Nebraska

| | |
|---|---|
| Abbott, Edith | Grand Island |
| Abbott, Grace | Grand Island |
| Barnard, Kate | Geneva |
| Dudley, Helena Stuart | Florence (?) |
| Hoey, Jane M. | Greely County |
| Roche, Josephine Aspinwall | Neligh |

## New Hampshire

| | |
|---|---|
| Brooks, John Graham | Acworth |
| Sanborn, Franklin Benjamin | Hampton Falls |
| Wood, Edith Elmer | Portsmouth |

## New Jersey

| | |
|---|---|
| Bauer, Catherine Krouse | Elizabeth |
| Farrand, Livingston | Newark |
| Griscom, John | Hancock's Bridge |
| Hamilton, Amy Gordon | Tenafly |
| Kennedy, Albert Joseph | Rosenhayn |
| Veiller, Lawrence Turnure | Elizabeth |
| Wiley, George Alvin | Bayonne |
| Wines, Enoch Cobb | Hanover |
| Woolman, John | Burlington County |

**New Mexico**

Heller, Florence Grunsfeld                                    Albuquerque


**New York**

Baker, Sara Josephine                                        Poughkeepsie
Barrows, Samuel June                                         New York
Bernstein, Charles                                           Carlisle
Biggs, Hermann Michael                                       Trumansburg
Bradford, Cornelia Foster                                    Granby
Bremer, Edith Terry                                          Hamilton
Brown, Josephine Chapin                                      Ogdensburg
Burritt, Bailey Barton                                       Monroe County
Campbell, Helen Stuart                                       Lockport
Cannon, Marie Antoinette                                     Deposit
Chapin, Francis Stuart                                       Brooklyn
Cutting, Robert Fulton                                       New York
Davis, Katharine Bement                                      Buffalo
Davis, Michael Marks, Jr.                                    New York
Day, Dorothy May                                             Brooklyn
de Forest, Robert Weeks                                      New York
Deutsch, Albert                                              New York
Dodge, Grace Hoadley                                         New York
Evans, Elizabeth Glendower                                   New Rochelle
Gavit, John Palmer                                           Albany
Gerry, Elbridge Thomas                                       New York
Goldmark, Josephine Clara                                    Brooklyn
Goldmark, Pauline Dorothea                                   Brooklyn
Hamilton, Alice                                              New York
Hathway, Marion                                              North Tonawanda
Hoffer, Joe Ralph                                            New York
Holt, Luther Emmett                                          Webster
Hoyt, Franklin Chase                                         Pelham
Kirchwey, Freda                                              Lake Placid
LaFarge, Oliver Hazard                                       New York
Lee, Porter Raymond                                          Buffalo
Letchworth, William Pryor                                    Brownville
Lewisohn, Irene                                              New York
Mallery, Otto Tod                                            Willets Point
Moskowitz, Belle                                             New York
Mulry, Thomas Maurice                                        New York
Nathan, Maud                                                 New York
O'Reilly, Leonora                                            New York
Osborne, Thomas Mott                                         Auburn
Ovington, Mary White                                         Brooklyn Heights
Peck, Lillie M.                                              Gloversville

| | |
|---|---|
| Pratt, Anna Beach | Elmira |
| Pratt, Richard Henry | Rushford |
| Purdy, Lawson | Hyde Park |
| Raushenbush, Paul A. | Rochester |
| Reynolds, James B. | Kiantone |
| Robins, Margaret Dreier | Brooklyn |
| Robins, Raymond | Staten Island |
| Roosevelt, Anna Eleanor | New York |
| Salmon, Thomas William | Lansingburgh |
| Sanger, Margaret | Corning |
| Schuyler, Louisa Lee | New York |
| Smith, Stephen | Spafford |
| Smith, Theobald | Albany |
| Stokes, Issach Newton Phelps | New York |
| Stokes, James Graham Phelps | New York |
| Taylor, Graham | New York |
| Taylor, Graham Romeyn | Hopewell |
| Van Kleeck, Mary Abby | Glenham |
| White, Alfred Tredway | Brooklyn |
| White, William Alanson | Brooklyn |
| Williams, Elizabeth Sprague | Buffalo |
| Williams, Fannie Barrier | Brockport |
| Woerishoffer, Emma Carola | New York |
| Woolsey, George Anna Muirson | Brooklyn |
| Woolsey, Jane Stuart | near Flushing |
| Zimand, Gertrude Folks | New York |

## North Dakota

| | |
|---|---|
| Amidon, Beulah Elizabeth | Fargo |

## Ohio

| | |
|---|---|
| Boardman, Mabel Thorp | Cleveland |
| Bookman, Clarence Monroe | Lancaster |
| Carr, Charlotte Elizabeth | Dayton |
| Chapin, Henry Dwight | Steubenville |
| Clopper, Edward Nicholas | Cincinnati |
| Coit, Stanton | Columbus |
| Coman, Katharine | Newark |
| Commons, John Rogers | Hollandsburg |
| Cooley, Harris Reed | Cleveland |
| Falconer, Martha Platt | Delaware |
| Hart, Hastings Hornell | Brookfield |
| Hodder, Jessie Donaldson | Cincinnati |
| Kellor, Frances | Columbus |
| McCulloch, Oscar Carleton | Fremont |

McDowell, Mary Eliza                        Cincinnati
Reeder, Rudolph Rex                         Lebanon
Street, Elwood Vickers                      Cleveland
Wald, Lillian D.                            Cincinnati


## Pennsylvania

Eddy, Thomas                                Philadelphia
Frankel, Lee Kaufman                        Philadelphia
Gallaudet, Thomas Hopkins                   Philadelphia
Hoehler, Fred Kenneth                       Shenandoah
Holmes, John Haynes                         Philadelphia
Kelley, Florence                            Philadelphia
Lindsay, Samuel McCune                      Pittsburgh
Lowenstein, Solomon                         Philadelphia
McKelway, Alexander J.                      Sadsburyville
Murphy, J. Prentice                         Philadelphia
Rippin, Jane Parker Deeter                  Harrisburg
Rush, Benjamin                              Byberry
Stover, Charles B.                          Riegelsville
Van Waters, Miriam                          Greensberg
Wines, Frederick Howard                     Philadelphia
Woods, Robert Archey                        Pittsburgh


## Rhode Island

Chapin, Charles Value                       Providence


## South Carolina

Bethune, Mary McLeod                        near Mayesville
Levin, Louis Hiram                          Charleston


## Tennessee

Lindsey, Benjamin Barr                      Jackson
Terrell, Mary Church                        Memphis


## Vermont

Alger, George William                       Burlington
Barrows, Isabel Hayes Chapin                Irasburg
Harris, Elisha                              Westminster

## Virginia

| | |
|---|---|
| Bane, Frank | Smithfield |
| Barrett, Katherine (Kate) Waller | Falmouth |
| Dinwiddie, Courtenay | Alexandria |
| Dinwiddie, Emily Wayland | Greenwood |
| Divine, Father | n.a. |
| Granger, Lester Blackwell | Newport News |
| Washington, Booker T. | Franklin County |
| Woolsey, Abby Howland | Alexandria |

## Washington

| | |
|---|---|
| Kahn, Dorothy | Seattle |

## Wisconsin

| | |
|---|---|
| Altmeyer, Arthur Joseph | De Pere |
| Andrews, John Bertram | South Wayne |
| Cannon, Ida Maud | Milwaukee |
| Fitch, John Andrews | Cumberland |
| Hine, Lewis Wickes | Oshkosh |
| Holbrook, David Helm | Lake Geneva |
| Kander, Elizabeth (Lizzie) Black | Milwaukee |
| Lenroot, Katharine Fredrica | Superior |
| Pink, Louis Heaton | Wausau |
| Witte, Edwin E. | Watertown |

## OUTSIDE THE UNITED STATES

## Austria

| | |
|---|---|
| Gruenberg, Sidonie Matzner | near Vienna |
| Rapaport, Lydia | Vienna |

## Canada

| | |
|---|---|
| Gould, Elgin Ralston Lovell | Oshawa, Ontario |

## Cuba

| | |
|---|---|
| Fletcher, Alice Cunningham | Havana |

## Denmark

| | |
|---|---|
| Riis, Jacob August | Ribe |

**England**

Blackwell, Elizabeth                                        near Bristol
Hartley, Robert Milham                                    Cockersmouth
Healy, William                                                near Beaconsfield
Johnson, Alexander                                         Ashton-under-Lyne

**Estonia**

Leiserson, William Morris                                 Revel

**France**

Girard, Stephen                                              Chartrous

**Germany**

Carstens, Christian Carl                                  Bredstedt
Christman, Elisabeth                                       probably Baden
Jacobi, Abraham                                             Hartum-in-Minden
Knopf, Siegmund Adolphus                             Halle-on-the Saale
Schulze, Oskar                                               Dresden (?)

**Hawaii**

Armstrong, Samuel Chapman                           Maui

**Hungary**

Kohut, Rebekah Bettelheim                              Kaschau
Wise, Stephen Samuel                                      Budapest

**India**

Scudder, Vida Dutton                                       Madura

**Ireland**

Carey, Mathew                                                Dublin
O'Grady, John                                                 Annagh Feakle

**Jamaica**

Garvey, Malcus (Marcus) Mosiah, Jr.                St. Ann's Bay

**Latvia**

Lurie, Harry Lawrence                        Goldingen

**Lithuania**

Kaplan, Mordecai Menachem                    Svencionys

**Netherlands**

Muste, Abraham Johannes                      Zierikzee

**Poland**

Abrams, Charles                              Vilna
Billikopf, Jacob                             Vilna
Schneiderman, Rose                           Savin

**Rumania**

Moskowitz, Henry                             Huesche

**Russia**

Cohn, Fannia Mary                            Kletzk
Epstein, Abraham                             Lunan
Kraft, Louis                                 Moscow
Rubinow, Isaac Max                           Grodno
Yarros, Rachelle Slobodinsky                 near Kiev

**Scotland**

Bell, Alexander Graham                       Edinburgh
Douglass, William                            Gifford

**South Pacific**

Colcord, Joanna Carver                       at sea?

**Sweden**

Anderson, Mary                               Linkoping

**Switzerland**

Meyer, Adolf                                 Niederwengingen

# About the Contributors

W. ANDREW ACHENBAUM is Professor of History at Carnegie-Mellon University.

WILBERT H. AHERN is Professor of History at the University of Minnesota-Morris.

KATHERINE AIKEN is a Visiting Assistant Professor of History at Lewis Clark State College.

JOHN K. ALEXANDER is Professor of History at the University of Cincinnati.

SARA ALPERN is Assistant Professor of History at Texas A & M University.

GARY R. ANDERSON is an Assistant Professor at the Hunter College School of Social Work.

R. JOSEPH ANDERSON is Director of the Research Library at the Balch Institute for Ethnic Studies.

JANICE ANDREWS is Director of the Social Work Program at Winona State University.

JOYCE ANTLER is Assistant Professor of American Studies and Coordinator of the Women's Studies Program at Brandeis University.

RALPH D. ARCARI is Director of the Lyman Maynard Stowe Library at the University of Connecticut Health Center.

BARBARA R. BEATTY is Assistant Professor of Education at Wellesley College.

DOROTHY G. BECKER is a former Associate Professor at the New York University Graduate School of Social Work.

CHRISTOPHER BERKELEY is a Doctoral Candidate at the University of Wisconsin-Madison.

EDWARD D. BERKOWITZ is Associate Professor of History and Director of the Program in History and Public Policy at George Washington University.

ARTHUR K. BERLINER is Director of the Social Work Program at Texas Christian University.

KAREL D. BICHA is Professor of History at Marquette University.

ROGER BILES is Assistant Professor of History at Oklahoma State University.

PHILIP BOOKER, Jr. is Assistant Professor of Social Work at Kentucky State University.

PAUL C. BOWERS, Jr. is Assistant Professor of History at Ohio State University.

JOHN BRAEMAN is Professor of History at the University of Nebraska-Lincoln.

WILLIAM W. BREMER is Associate Professor of History at Lawrence University.

ROBERT H. BREMNER is Professor Emeritus of History at Ohio State University.

BARBARA M. BRENZEL is Associate Professor of Education at Wellesley College.

GERT H. BRIEGER is William H. Welch Professor and Director of the Institute of the History of Medicine at the Johns Hopkins University School of Medicine.

PAMELA A. BROWN is Assistant Professor of Social Work at Mount Mercy College.

LEE BYCEL is a Rabbi and Associate Dean of the Hebrew Union College-Jewish Institute of Religion in Los Angeles.

JOHN J. CAREY is Professor of History and Sociology at Tunxis Community College (Farmington, Connecticut).

ANNE-MARIE CARROLL is a Research Associate in the Program in History and Public Policy at George Washington University.

MARY CARROLL is Associate Professor of Social Work at the University of Alaska-Anchorage.

IRL E. CARTER is Associate Professor of Social Work at the University of Minnesota-Twin Cities.

SUSAN E. CAYLEFF is an Assistant Professor at the Institute for the Medical Humanities at the University of Texas Medical Branch.

RICHARD M. CHAPMAN is a Doctoral Candidate at the University of Minnesota-Twin Cities.

CATHERINE S. CHILMAN is a Professor in the School of Social Welfare at the University of Wisconsin-Milwaukee.

CLAUDIA CLARK is a Doctoral Candidate at Rutgers University-Newark.

PRISCILLA FERGUSON CLEMENT is Associate Professor of History at the Pennsylvania State University-Delaware County Campus.

WILBUR J. COHEN is Professor of Public Affairs at the Lyndon Baines Johnson School of Public Affairs, University of Texas at Austin.

JOHN A. CONLEY is Associate Professor of Criminal Justice at the University of Wisconsin-Milwaukee.

LELA B. COSTIN is a Professor in the School of Social Work at the University of Illinois at Urbana-Champaign.

DAVID T. COURTWRIGHT is Associate Professor of History at the University of Hartford and Assistant Clinical Professor at the University of Connecticut Health Center.

FRED M. COX is Professor and Dean of the School of Social Welfare at the University of Wisconsin-Milwaukee.

HAMILTON CRAVENS is Professor of History at Iowa State University.

THOMAS J. CURRAN is Associate Professor of History at St. John's University (New York).

NORMAN DAIN is Professor of History at Rutgers University-Newark.

JOSEPH DAVENPORT, III is Director of the Office of Continuing Social Work Education at the University of Georgia, Athens.

JUDITH A. DAVENPORT is Assistant Professor and Coordinator of the Bachelor of Social Work Practicum at the University of Georgia, Athens.

JOYCE PREWITT DAVIS is Assistant Professor of Social Work at the University of Wisconsin-Superior.

BETTY G. DAWSON is Associate Professor of Social Work at Memphis State University.

DAVID L. de LORENZO is Archives Librarian at Gallaudet College.

JOHN M. DERGE is a Doctoral Candidate at the University of Massachusetts at Amherst.

DENNIS C. DICKERSON is Associate Professor of History at Rhodes College.

TIMOTHY MICHAEL DOLAN is a Priest in the Archdiocese of St. Louis.

JOHN M. DOLLAR is a Doctoral Candidate at Auburn University.

MARILYN A. DOMER is Professor of History at George Williams University (Downers Grove, Illinois).

JOHN DUFFY is Professor Emeritus of History at the University of Maryland.

MERLE T. EDWARDS-ORR is Assistant Professor and Chair of the Department of Basic and Applied Social Sciences at Trinity College of Vermont.

BARBARA EGGERS is Instructor in History at Phillips Exeter Academy.

DAVID ELLENSON is Associate Professor of Jewish Religious Thought at the Hebrew Union College-Jewish Institute of Religion in Los Angeles.

SUZANNE S. ETHERINGTON is a Doctoral Candidate at Syracuse University.

JEREMY P. FELT is Professor of History at the University of Vermont.

DAVID L. FERCH is Assistant Professor of History at Mount Mercy College.

JAMES J. FERNANDES is Associate Professor of Communication Arts at Gallaudet College.

DANIEL M. FOX is Professor of Humanities in the Medicine Health Sciences Center at the State University of New York at Stony Brook.

SHARON FREEDBERG is an Assistant Professor in the Department of Sociology and Social Work at Herbert H. Lehman College.

LAWRENCE E. GARY is Professor of Social Work and Director of the Institute for Urban Affairs and Research at Howard University.

ROBENIA B. GARY is Assistant Professor of Social Work at George Mason University.

LARRY D. GIVENS is Associate Professor of History at the University of Mississippi.

LAURIE K. GLASS is Associate Professor and Director of the Historical Gallery at the School of Nursing at the University of Wisconsin-Milwaukee.

JANET GOLDEN is Assistant Director of the Francis C. Wood Institute for the History of Medicine.

JOAN L. GOLDSTEIN is an Adjunct Professor of Social Work at the Westchester Community College (New York).

LYNN D. GORDON is Assistant Professor of Education at the University of Rochester.

PATRICIA PECK GOSSEL is a member of the Department of the History of Science at the Johns Hopkins University.

ROBERT J. GOUGH is an Adjunct Assistant Professor in the Department of History at the University of Wisconsin-Eau Claire.

WILLIAM GRAEBNER is Professor of History at the State University of New York, Fredonia.

SUSAN GRIGG is Director of the Sophia Smith Collection and College Archives at Smith College.

CHARLES GUZZETTA is a Professor at the Hunter College School of Social Work.

JAN L. HAGEN is an Associate Professor in the School of Social Welfare at the Nelson A. Rockefeller College of Public Affairs and Policy, State University of New York at Albany.

WILLIAM H. HARDIN is a Lecturer in History at Glenville State College.

RICHARD HARMOND is Associate Professor of History at St. John's University (New York).

ANN HARTMAN is a Professor in the School of Social Work at the University of Michigan.

JOSEPH M. HAWES is Professor and Chair of the Department of History at Memphis State University.

KENNETH E. HENDRICKSON, Jr. is Chair of the Department of History at Midwestern State University.

ROBERT M. HENDRICKSON is Chair of the Department of Social Work at Radford University.

J. DAVID HOEVELER, Jr. is Professor of History at the University of Wisconsin-Milwaukee.

JANET M. HOLMES is Associate Professor of Social Work at Ball State University.

DWIGHT W. HOOVER is Professor of History and Director of the Center for Middletown Studies at Ball State University.

HERBERT T. HOOVER is Professor of History at the University of South Dakota.

MARTIN HOPE is Chair of the Social Work Department at Winthrop College.

MARGO HORN is a Visiting Scholar at the Center for Research on Women, Stanford University.

GRAFTON HULL, Jr. is Professor and Chair of the Department of Social Welfare at the University of Wisconsin-Whitewater.

ELIZABETH D. HUTCHISON is Assistant Professor and Director of the Social Work Program at Elms College.

NANCY G. ISENBERG is a Doctoral Candidate at the University of Wisconsin-Madison.

KATHLEEN M. JACKSON is a retired faculty member at the Howard University School of Social Work.

PHILIP JACKSON is an Associate Professor of Social Work at the University of Cincinnati.

JAMES E. JOHNSON is Professor and Chair of the Department of History at Bethel College (St. Paul, Minnesota).

KATHLEEN W. JONES is a Doctoral Candidate at Rutgers University-New Brunswick.

MICHAEL B. KATZ is Professor of History and Education and Director of the Urban Studies Program at the University of Pennsylvania.

TOBA SCHWABER KERSON is an Associate Professor in the Graduate School of Social Work and Social Research, Bryn Mawr College.

PETER KIVISTO is an Assistant Professor of Sociology at Augustana College (Rock Island, Illinois).

CONSTANTINE G. KLEDARAS is Associate Director of Graduate Studies in the Division of Social Work at East Carolina University.

HANNAH KLIGER is an Assistant Professor of Judaic Studies at the University of Massachusetts at Amherst.

JOYCE M. KRAMER is an Associate Professor in the School of Social Development at the University of Minnesota-Duluth.

JOSEPH D. KREISLER is Associate Professor of Social Welfare at the University of Southern Maine.

JOHN W. LANDON is Associate Dean of the College of Social Work at the University of Kentucky.

JAMES LEIBY is Professor of Social Welfare at the University of California, Berkeley.

JOHN S. LEIBY is Archivist and Special Collections Coordinator in the Department of Libraries at Northern Arizona University.

MARY RUTH LEWIS is a Professor in the Graduate School of Social Work at the University of Houston-Central Campus.

ALICE A. LIEBERMAN is Assistant Professor of Social Work at the University of Southern Maine.

BARRY L. LOCKE is Assistant Professor of Social Work at West Virginia University.

SAYDE L. LOGAN is Associate Professor of Social Welfare at the University of Kansas.

ROY LUBOVE is Professor of Social Welfare and History at the University of Pittsburgh.

NANCY OESTREICH LURIE is Curator of the Anthropology Section at the Milwaukee Public Museum.

LARCY D. McCARLEY is an Assistant Professor at the Graduate School of Social Service, Fordham University.

STANLEY MALLACH is the Bibliographer of the Fromkin Memorial Collection at the Golda Meir Library, University of Wisconsin-Milwaukee.

EMILIA E. MARTINEZ-BRAWLEY is Associate Professor of Social Work at the Pennsylvania State University.

MARJORIE HINTON MAYO is Associate Professor and Director of the Social Work Program at Roosevelt University.

ROBERT M. MENNEL is Professor of History at the University of New Hampshire.

WILLIAM D. MILLER, Professor Emeritus of History at Marquette University, currently is teaching at St. Thomas University (Miami, Florida).

MARC L. MIRINGOFF is Associate Professor and Assistant Dean at the Fordham University Graduate School of Social Service.

MARQUE-LUISA MIRINGOFF is Associate Professor of Sociology at Vassar College.

RAYMOND A. MOHL is Professor and Chair of the Department of History at Florida Atlantic University.

DOROTHY A. MOHLER is Adjunct Associate Professor at the National Catholic School of Social Service, Catholic University of America.

GARY MOOERS is Chair of the Social Work Department at the University of Mississippi.

EDWARD T. MORMON is on the staff of the Van Pelt Library at the University of Pennsylvania.

EARL F. MULDERINK, III is a Doctoral Candidate at the University of Wisconsin-Madison.

BRIAN J. MULHERN is the Archivist at the Bio-Medical Library at the University of Minnesota-Twin Cities.

JOANNE CATHERINE NEHER is the Interim Director of the Social Work Program at the College of St. Scholastica (Duluth, Minnesota).

DANIEL NELSON is Professor of History at the University of Akron.

VICTORIA OLDS is Professor Emerita at the Fordham University Graduate School of Social Service.

FREDERICK I. OLSON is Professor Emeritus of History at the University of Wisconsin-Milwaukee.

JACQUELINE K. PARKER is an Assistant Professor in the Department of Human Services, University of Oregon, Eugene.

RALPH L. PEARSON is Professor of History and Dean of University College at Loyola University (Chicago, Illinois).

WILMA PEEBLES-WILKINS is an Associate Professor in the Social Work Program at North Carolina State University.

ROBERT A. PERKINS is Professor Emeritus of Social Welfare at Louisiana State University.

ELISABETH I. PERRY is Associate Professor of History at Vanderbilt University.

PAULA F. PFEFFER is Assistant Professor of History at Mundelein College.

KENNETH R. PHILP is Professor of History at the University of Texas, Arlington.

DONALD K. PICKENS is Professor of History at North Texas State University.

ALEXANDER W. PISCIOTTA is an Assistant Professor in the Department of Criminal Justice and Social Welfare at Kutztown University.

PHILIP R. POPPLE is Associate Professor and Director of the Social Work Program at Auburn University.

MILDRED I. PRATT is Professor of Social Work at Illinois State University.

TERRI L. PREMO is a Research Associate at the Institute for the Medical Humanities at the University of Texas Medical Branch.

MURIEL W. PUMPHREY is Professor Emerita of Social Work at the University of Missouri at St. Louis.

RALPH E. PUMPHREY is Professor Emeritus at the George Warren Brown School of Social Work, Washington University (St. Louis, Missouri).

JEAN K. QUAM is an Assistant Professor in the School of Social Work at the University of Minnesota-Twin Cities.

VIRGINIA A. METAXAS QUIROGA is an Assistant Professor of American Studies, State University of New York College at Old Westbury.

JAMES REED is Associate Professor of History at Rutgers University-New Brunswick.

KENNETH E. REID is a Professor of Social Work at Western Michigan University.

JANE A. ROSENBERG is a Program Associate at the Council on Library Resources, Inc., Washington, D.C.

EDWARD B. ROWE is affiliated with the Connecticut Center for Independent Historians, Wesleyan University (Middletown, Connecticut).

UDO SAUTTER is a Professor of History at the University of Windsor (Ontario, Canada).

DOROTHY T. SCANLON is Professor of History at the Massachusetts College of Art (Boston, Massachusetts).

LOIS SCHARF is Executive Director of National History Day.

MARY ELLEN SCHMIDER is Director of Continuing Education and Coordinator of Graduate Studies at Moorhead State University (Moorhead, Minnesota).

ERIC C. SCHNEIDER is Program Officer for the Delaware Humanities Forum (Wilmington, Delaware).

JOEL SCHWARTZ is Associate Professor of History at Montclair State College.

CHRISTINE BRENDEL SCRIABINE, a resident of Guilford, Connecticut, is a freelance writer and an editorial consultant.

JUDITH SEALANDER is Associate Professor of History at Wright State University.

L. MOODY SIMMS, Jr. is Professor of History at Illinois State University.

BROOKS D. SIMPSON is an Assistant Editor of the Papers of Andrew Johnson, University of Tennessee.

KATHRYN KISH SKLAR is Professor of History at the University of California, Los Angeles.

JOHN DAVID SMITH is Assistant Professor of History at North Carolina State University.

MILTON D. SPEIZMAN is a Professor at the Graduate School of Social Work and Social Research, Bryn Mawr College.

BEVERLY A. STADUM is a Doctoral Candidate at the University of Minnesota–Twin Cities.

JIM STAFFORD is an Instructor and Field Work Coordinator of Social Work at the University of Mississippi.

SUSAN D. STEINWALL is Director of the Area Research Center at the University of Wisconsin-River Falls.

ARLENE RUBIN STIFFMAN is a Research Instructor in Social Work in (Child) Psychiatry at Washington University Medical School (St. Louis, Missouri).

GAYLE V. STRICKLER, Jr. is a Psychiatric Social Worker at the Western Human Development Center in Marshall, Minnesota.

PAUL STUART is an Associate Professor of Social Work at the University of Wisconsin-Eau Claire.

MARTHA H. SWAIN is Professor of History at Texas Woman's University.

ANTHONY E. THOMAS (1936–1984) was a Research Associate at the Health Services Research Center, the University of North Carolina.

THOMAS MARSHALL TODD is Associate Director of the Research Department of the Minnesota House of Representatives.

ANTHONY R. TRAVIS is Dean of the Social Sciences Division at Grand Valley State College.

JAMES W. TRENT is Assistant Professor at the Graduate School of Social Work at the University of Southern Mississippi.

JUDITH ANN TROLANDER is Associate Professor of History at the University of Minnesota-Duluth.

ELLEN M. UMANSKY is Assistant Professor of Religion at Emory University.

JOHN V. VAN CLEVE is Professor of History at Gallaudet College.

PETER R. VIRGADAMO is Assistant Dean of the School of Urban and Regional Planning, University of Southern California.

LOUISE C. WADE is Professor of History at the University of Oregon, Eugene.

WINIFRED D. WANDERSEE is Associate Professor of History at Hartwick College.

PATRICIA SPAIN WARD is Historian at the Health Sciences Center of the University of Illinois at Chicago.

WALTER B. WEARE is Associate Professor of History at the University of Wisconsin-Milwaukee.

LYNN Y. WEINER is an Instructor of History at Roosevelt University and an History Department Associate at Northwestern University.

ROBERT P. WEISS is Assistant Professor of Sociology at the State University of New York-Plattsburgh.

ELIZABETH WEISZ-BUCK (1952–1984) was a Doctoral Candidate at the University of California, Los Angeles.

MINDY R. WERTHEIMER is an Assistant Professor in the Department of Social Work at Georgia State University.

CATHERINE J. WHITAKER is a Doctoral Candidate at the University of Michigan.

ROBERTA WOLLONS is an Assistant Professor of American Studies at Case Western Reserve University.

GARY P. ZOLA is a Rabbi and National Director of Admissions and Student Affairs at the Hebrew Union College-Jewish Institute of Religion in Cincinnati.

# Index

## About the Editor

WALTER I. TRATTNER is Professor of History at the University of Wisconsin-Milwaukee. A graduate of Williams College, Harvard University, and the University of Wisconsin-Madison (where he earned his Ph.D. in history), and a past president of the Social Welfare History Group, he has authored numerous articles in various professional journals and written or edited five books, including *Social Welfare or Social Control? Some Historical Reflections on "Regulating the Poor"* (Knoxville: University of Tennessee Press, 1983) and *From Poor Law to Welfare State: A History of Social Welfare in America* (3rd ed., rev., New York: The Free Press, 1984). In addition, with W. A. Achenbaum, he edited *Social Welfare in America: An Annotated Bibliography* (Westport, Conn.: Greenwood Press, 1983).